HANDEL'S OPERAS
1704—1726

Handel, portrait by Philippe Mercier, *c*.1730

$24.00

HANDEL'S OPERAS
1704–1726

WINTON DEAN

AND

JOHN MERRILL KNAPP

CLARENDON PRESS · OXFORD

1995

Oxford University Press, Walton Street, Oxford OX2 6DP

Oxford New York
Athens Auckland Bangkok Bombay
Calcutta Cape Town Dar es Salaam Delhi
Florence Hong Kong Istanbul Karachi
Kuala Lumpur Madras Madrid Melbourne
Mexico City Nairobi Paris Singapore
Taipei Tokyo Toronto
and associated companies in
Berlin Ibadan

Oxford is a trade mark of Oxford University Press

Published in the United States
by Oxford University Press Inc., New York

British Library Cataloguing in Publication Data
Data available

Library of Congress Cataloging in Publication Data
Dean, Winton.
Handel's operas, 1704-1726 / Winton Dean and John Merrill Knapp.
Includes bibliographical references (p.   ) and indexes.
1. Handel, George Frideric, 1685-1759. Operas.   2. Opera.
I. Knapp, J. Merrill.   II. Title.
[ML410.H13D37   1994]   782.1'092—dc20   93-45942
ISBN 0-19-816441-6 (Pbk.)

1 3 5 7 9 10 8 6 4 2

Printed in Great Britain by
Biddles Ltd.
Guildford & King's Lynn

PREFACE TO REVISED EDITION

SINCE this book went to press research on Handel's operas has proceeded apace. John Roberts has published nine volumes of Handel Sources throwing light on borrowings, and Donald Burrows extended his paper-datings of the autographs to most of the principal copies, notably in the Aylesford (Flower) and Malmesbury Collections. New early manuscript sources have been discovered for *Amadigi* and *Ottone*. Several scholars have contributed to clarifying the background to *Almira*. The Hallische Händel-Ausgabe has issued scores of two more operas (*Rinaldo* and *Flavio*) and others are nearing the exit of the pipe-line. Work with Terence Best on his forthcoming editions of *Tamerlano* and *Radamisto* has enabled me to correct a number of errors and supply additional details.

I have endeavoured to incorporate as much as possible of this information in the text without undue disturbance to the pagination; to a greater or lesser degree the modifications affect every chapter. Where that was not possible I have added notes at the end of each chapter, cued by asterisks in the margin of the text (the notes to Chapter 7 will be found at the end of Chapter 6). The Appendices have been updated to the end of 1993.

It is encouraging to note that in the last few years all but two of the operas covered in this book have been commercially recorded, the majority complete and in good style. Only *Almira* and *Silla* (not surprisingly) are missing, together with the first versions of *Il pastor fido* and *Radamisto*; there is still room for more satisfactory recordings of *Rodrigo* and *Rinaldo*, and of *Tamerlano* as Handel performed it.

My thanks are due to Dr. Jürgen Kindemann of the Deutsches Musikgeschichtliches Archiv, Kassel, for films of the *Amadigi* material in the Fürstenberg Library, and to Canon B. L. Barnby for allowing me to examine his early manuscript of *Ottone*. For valuable assistance and advice I am grateful to Terence Best, Malcolm Boyd, Donald Burrows, Anthony Hicks, Lowell Lindgren, and John Roberts.

W. D.
May 1994

PREFACE

SOMETHING needs to be said about the origins and long gestation period of this book. More than twenty years ago both authors became interested in Handel's operas. We decided to pool our efforts, and to follow the general plan adopted in my *Handel's Dramatic Oratorios and Masques* (1959): each opera would have a chapter to itself, the first half devoted to a discussion of the libretto and music, the second to more detailed matters of text and history. There would be preliminary and intermediate chapters on background, performance practice, etc. It was agreed from the start that I should write the book, incorporating the judgements and the products of the research of both authors.

This worked well for the sections on the music of the individual operas, which (except in Chapters 4, 7, 8, 11, and 22, where those sections were written by me) are in a true sense joint work. Later, after we had both been busy at different times with other commitments, it became apparent that we held different opinions about the scope of the book. Handel's operas were an untilled field. My Bloch Lectures, delivered at the University of California, Berkeley, in 1966, had been published in 1969 as *Handel and the Opera Seria*. They were intended as a preliminary survey, an assessment of Handel's intentions and achievements in the light of modern interest in the revival of his operas. Apart from Joachim Eisenschmidt's useful dissertation on Handel's theatre, which does not deal with the music, this was the only book ever published on the subject. It was not based on a comprehensive study of the manuscripts, though I had used some of them. We had been aware from the start that the early sources, including printed librettos and music as well as manuscripts, were likely to contain valuable material and unpublished music. It now transpired that they were far more extensive than had been generally supposed; new ones were being discovered, and others of cardinal importance, hitherto inaccessible, could now be reached. None of them had been fully examined, and a great many had never been looked at at all.

This convinced me that we were confronted with a scholar's paradise, a heaven-sent opportunity to study in depth a large body of music of superb quality, which was not only unexplored but in increasing demand in the modern theatre—where it was constantly misinterpreted. Our subject was not one of Tovey's interesting historical figures, but a central part of the output of one of the world's greatest creative artists. If the job was worth doing at all, it was worth doing as thoroughly as possible. Two conclusions followed. We ought to seek out and examine every discoverable manuscript and relevant source. And we ought to apply the new tools of modern musical scholarship—paper types, watermarks, rastration, the identification of copyists, and the use of all these methods for dating—which were beginning to yield copious fruit in the parallel fields of Bach, Haydn, Mozart, Beethoven, Schubert, and others, but in which Handel scholars (with one or two honourable exceptions) had shown little interest. Unless all the material were taken into account, it would not be possible to determine what was important and what could safely be left on one side. A brief inspection revealed that a vast wealth of information awaited discovery, and that it was likely to undermine traditional opinions and accepted texts, expecially of the early operas where autograph material is deficient. Chrysander's edition was a century old; the new Halle edition had, by common consent, made a precarious start and barely begun to touch the operas. If we could clarify their origins, history, and text, we should be making a massive contribution to Handel scholarship, of service to editors, performers, and public alike.

It was obvious that such an extension of the terms of reference (not that they had been strictly defined in the first place) would delay the completion of the book and require its division into two volumes. In the event, many fresh trails that presented themselves in the last few years proved highly productive, and, while J.M.K. had made notes on a good number of sources, the full examination and assessment of the material in the history and text sections, especially the manuscripts, fell to me. For the rest, I am responsible for Chapters 1, 2, and 22, nearly all of Chapter 6, and the detailed libretto summaries. J.M.K. contributed to the discussion and comparison of source librettos; in the general chapters (especially 9, 10, and 16) he supplied all the material on the librettos of the non-Handel operas and most of that on their music. The appendices, except for the first draft of Appendix D and some of the libretto locations in Appendix C, are my work.

W.D.

ACKNOWLEDGEMENTS

IN the course of working on this book over more than twenty years I have accumulated many debts, to public and private libraries and to individuals. No serious research on Handel would be possible without frequent recourse to the great public collections where so many of his manuscripts are preserved, in particular the Music Room and Department of Manuscripts at the British Library; the Fitzwilliam Museum, Cambridge; the Staats- und Universitäts-bibliothek, Hamburg; and the Henry Watson Music Library, Manchester. The librarians and staff of these institutions have been continuously helpful in many ways, including the provision of microfilms and photocopies, answering enquiries by post, and granting permission for the use of illustrations. A smaller but still substantial debt is due to the staffs of the Royal College of Music, London; the Bodleian Library, Oxford; the Rowe Library, King's College, Cambridge; Durham Cathedral Library; the National Library of Scotland; the Berlin Staatsbibliothek, Preussischer Kulturbesitz; the Öster-reichische Nationalbibliothek, Vienna; the Schönbornsche Bibliothek, Wiesentheid; the Herzog-August-Bibliothek, Wolfenbüttel; the Bibliothèque Nationale, Paris; and the Library of Congress, Washington.

I am especially grateful to Lord and Lady Malmesbury and Mr and Mrs Gerald Coke, who not only allowed me access to their valuable collections on numerous occasions over a long period, but put themselves to considerable inconvenience on my behalf and gave me much hospitality. More recently Lord Shaftesbury allowed me similar facilities. Professor Howard Mayer Brown and Herr Armin Wiegand permitted me to examine scores and librettos in their possession, either in person or on microfilm.

In the early stages of this project the members of my graduate seminar at the University of California, Berkeley, in 1965—Tharald Borgir, Oliver Ellsworth, Sarah Fuller, Charlotte Greenspan, Margaret Radin, and John Roberts—by their enthusiasm and pertinacity helped to identify and unravel many problems. More than one of them, Dr Roberts in particular, have given me valuable assistance since. Among many other colleagues and friends who have been generous with their help, Professor Bernd Baselt, Dr Nigel Fortune (whose eagle eye detected countless errors and inconsistencies in the proofs), Mr Anthony Hicks, Mr Philip Radcliffe, and Professor Reinhard Strohm deserve particular mention. Professor Strohm put at my disposal his large collection of material relating to the librettos and their sources, including many microfilms and photocopies and information about the holdings of German libraries. I am also indebted in various ways to Mr Terence Best, Dr David Bryant, Dr Donald Burrows, the late Edward Croft-Murray, Mr Brian Crosby, the late Charles Cudworth, Mr Charles Farncombe, Dr Elizabeth Gibson, Herr Otto Gossmann, the late Dr James S. Hall, Professor Ellen T. Harris, Professor Robert D. Hume, Professor David Kimbell, Professor Jens Peter Larsen, Professor Lowell Lindgren, Professor Judith Milhous, Dr Craig Monson, Dr Michel Noiray, Dr Curtis Price, Professor Manfred Rätzer, Professor Martin Ruhnke, Herr Eugen Schüepp, Professor Howard Serwer, Mr Stephen Simon, the late William C. Smith, Dr Colin Timms, Professor

Brian Trowell, and Mr Arthur D. Walker. There may be others whom I have
inadvertently omitted; if so, I offer my sincere apologies.

Finally I should like to pay a special tribute to my wife Thalia, who (with
remarkably few complaints, even when confronted with the appendices)
typed the whole book twice, and some chapters many times, and to my son
Stephen, whose assistance in correcting the proofs was invaluable and who
also compiled the index.

W.D

WHEN a book has taken many years to complete, the list of students,
colleagues, friends, and libraries, who have helped to put it together, is a long
one. To acknowledge their assistance is an exercise in memory and grateful
thanks spanning two continents and several decades. There are also graduate
seminar students who may not be specifically mentioned, but whose papers
and ideas were often very fruitful in generating discussion and further
investigation into the subject of Handel's operas, which of necessity has
embraced a good deal of theatrical and social history of the first half of the
eighteenth century in Germany, Italy, and England.

Former students at Princeton University who either copied music or
searched out and analysed sources were (alphabetically): John Bogart, Karen
Franklin, Dennis Libby, Jessie Ann Owens, Kevin Shopland, Karl Tamburr,
Michael Tusa, and James Winn. In Oxford and Hamburg, David Kimbell
and Hans Dieter Clausen, respectively, were very helpful. Faculty colleagues
and friends both in the United States and abroad who gave valuable
suggestions were: Robert Freeman, Jens Peter Larsen, Kenneth Levy, Lowell
Lindgren, Alfred Mann, the late Arthur Mendel, Harold Powers, John
Roberts, Reinhard Strohm, the late Oliver Strunk, and Percy Young. In
England, two Handelians were particularly kind and hospitable to a younger
one who was groping his way and often losing it. They were the late James S.
Hall and the late William C. Smith, who as old hands in the field, gave fine,
practical advice.

Numerous libraries, and the librarians in them, must be mentioned very
thankfully. In England, the music staff of the British Library above all, but
also of the Fitzwilliam Museum, Rowe Library, King's College, and Pendle-
bury Library, Cambridge; the National Library of Scotland; the Henry
Watson Music Library, Manchester; and the Bodleian Library, Oxford. For
the private libraries, Gerald Coke was most kind in giving access to his
remarkable collection as were Lord and Lady Malmesbury. In France, the
Bibliothèque Nationale (especially within it, the former Bibliothèque du
Conservatoire) yielded treasures. In Germany, the well-known collection in the
Staats- und Universitätsbibliothek, Hamburg was very important as were
Handeliana in the Niedersächsische Landesbibliothek, Hannover; the Berlin
Staatsbibliothek, Preussischer Kulturbesitz; the Santini collection, Münster;
Herzog-August-Bibliothek, Wolfenbüttel; and the Schönborn collection, Wie-
sentheid. In the United States, the list includes the Library of Congress,
Washington; the New York Public Library; the Boston Public Library; the
Huntington Library, San Marino, California; the Clark Library (UCLA),
Los Angeles; the Newberry Library, Chicago; the Folger Shakespeare Library,

Washington; and the University libraries of Princeton, Yale, Harvard, Berkeley, Michigan, Illinois, and Maryland.

Finally, I would like to thank my wife for her utmost patience.

J.M.K.

CONTENTS

ILLUSTRATIONS

Frontispiece. Handel, portrait by Philippe Mercier, c.1730.

Plates (*between pp. 298–299*):

1. Stage of Teatro San Giovanni Grisostomo, Venice, 1709. Engraving by A. Coronelli from *Venezia festeggiante* (1709).

2. Elevation and plan of the King's Theatre in the Haymarket after the alterations of 1707–8. Unnumbered plate from G. Dumont, *Parallele de Plans des plus belles salles de Spectacle* (1764).

3. Interior of Neues Opernhaus on the Zwinger, Dresden, during performance of Lotti's *Teofane*, September 1719. Engraving from *Recueil des dessins et gravures représentant les solemnités du mariage de Prince Frédéric Auguste ... et de Madame la Princesse Marie Josephe Archi-Duchesse d'Autriche, en 1719*.

4. Stage Scene in Lotti's *Teofane*, Dresden, September 1719.

5. Autograph of original opening of 'Ah! crudel' in *Rinaldo*, Act II.

6. Autograph sketches for *Teseo* (1712) on blank page in autograph of *Rodrigo* (1707).

7. *Teseo*, Linike copy (December 1712), showing recitative for Fedra in Act V, suppressed before performance.

8.A. Stage set for *Rinaldo*, Act III, Hamburg Theater am Gänsemarkt, November 1715. Frontispiece of printed libretto.

   B. Stage set for final scene of *Giulio Cesare*, Hamburg Theater am Gänsemarkt, November 1725. Frontispiece of printed libretto.

9. Paolo Rolli, portrait by Giovanni Battista Bellucci.

10. Libretto of *Radamisto*, April 1720, prepared for use as prompt copy.

11. Performing score of *Radamisto* (Act II), December 1720: signatures, voice part and bass written by Smith, upper parts, dynamics, and amended scoring by Handel.

12. Autograph of *Tamerlano*: discarded and alternative versions in final scene of Act II.

13. Stage of the King's Theatre in the Haymarket, c.1725. Anonymous pen and water colour drawing.

14. Smith copy of 'Alla fama' in *Ottone* (transposed), with vocal ornaments added by Handel, mostly on viola stave, ?1727.

15. Performing score of 1734 revival of *Il pastor fido* (Act III), showing hands of Smith (three top systems) and S1.

16. Thomas Lediard's design for fireworks in epilogue of Hamburg production of *Giulio Cesare*, 9 June 1727. Engraving from T. Lediard, *Eine Collection von verschiedener Vorstellungen und Illuminationen ...*, Hamburg (1729).

ABBREVIATIONS

Add MSS	Additional Manuscripts, British Library
AMZ	*Allgemeine Musik-Zeitung*
Baselt, *Verzeichnis*	*Händel-Handbuch* Band I, *Thematisch-systematisches Verzeichnis: Bühnenwerke* (Leipzig, 1978).
Best, *Twenty Overtures*	G. F. Handel, *Twenty Overtures in Authentic Keyboard Arrangements*, ed. T. Best (London and Sevenoaks, 1985–6).
BL	British Library
Burrows, 'Handlist'	'A Handlist of the Paper Characteristics of Handel's English Autographs' (typescript, 1982)
Coke Papers	Milhous and Hume, *Vice Chamberlain Coke's Theatrical Papers, 1706–1715* (Carbondale, 1982)
Exhibition Catalogue	*Handel: a Celebration of his Life and Times 1685–1759*, ed. J. Simon (London, National Portrait Gallery, 1985)
Gibson, *The Royal Academy*	E. Gibson, *The Royal Academy of Music 1719–1728: the Institution and its Directors* (New York and London, 1989)
HG	Händel-Gesellschaft edition (ed. F. Chrysander)
HHA	Hallische Händel-Ausgabe
HJb	*Händel-Jahrbuch*
HWV	*Verzeichnis der Werke Georg Friedrich Händels*
JAMS	*Journal of the American Musicological Society*
M & L	*Music and Letters*
MQ	*Musical Quarterly*
MT	*Musical Times*
NOHM	*New Oxford History of Music*
PRMA	*Proceedings of the Royal Musical Association*
RCM	Royal College of Music
RIM	*Rivista italiana di musicologia*
RM	Royal Music Collection, British Library
SIMG	*Sammelbände der Internationalen Musik-Gesellschaft*
Strohm, *Essays*	*Essays on Handel and Italian Opera* (Cambridge, 1985)
Strohm, *Italienische Oper*	*Die italienische Oper im 18. Jahrhundert* (Wilhelmshaven, 1979)

Note on the text

Unless otherwise qualified, references in the text to Chrysander, Clausen, Deutsch, Eisenschmidt, Leichtentritt, and Mainwaring are to the items cited in the Bibliography; references to Dent are to his chapter on the operas in *Handel: a Symposium*; references to Burney are to the 1935 edition of his *History*, where the operas are indexed under 'Operas, Handel'. The revised German edition of Deutsch (*Händel-Handbuch IV*), published without consultation with British and American scholars, expands the German sources and adds some other details, but omits much significant material and repeats a good many mistakes in the English edition.

Virgole are inverted commas printed in the margin of librettos, indicating passages omitted in performance.

Stage directions in libretto summaries are italicized; see also note on p. 15.

The Colman Opera Register was not compiled by Colman since the entries continue after the date of his death. The Register is reproduced in K. Sasse, 'Opera Register from 1712 to 1735 (Colman-Register)', *HJb* (1959), 199–223.

Performing scores and other manuscripts with prefix MA are in the Staats- und Universitätsbibliothek, Hamburg.

NOTE ON SOURCES

THE voluminous manuscript sources on which this study is based require a brief description. The celebrated collection of autographs in the Royal Music Collection at the British Library, the fifteen volumes of miscellaneous works and fragments, many of them autograph, in the Fitzwilliam Museum, Cambridge, and the substantial body of Handel's performing scores in the Staats- und Universitätsbibliothek, Hamburg, have long been available. They have never attracted a fraction of the attention devoted to the manuscripts of Bach, Mozart, and Beethoven, and the operas are still virgin territory. Chrysander used the autographs and performing scores (especially the latter) in preparing his edition, but did not print or mention a sizeable proportion of their contents, and was not primarily concerned with the light they throw on Handel's method of work. Although aware of the Fitzwilliam manuscripts, he did not incorporate their evidence. All three collections have yielded an enormous amount of fresh information.

They are very far from exhausting the sources, even of primary material. Many of the most important opera manuscripts are (or were until recently) in private hands; others have been gathering dust in libraries all over the world. Scarcely any have hitherto been examined or collated with the autographs or performing scores, and the existence of a considerable number was unknown. These manuscripts, briefly listed below, are of particular significance for the early period. None of the eleven operas Handel composed before 1720 is fully covered in the Royal Music and Hamburg holdings. Three operas composed in Hamburg are lost, though fragments of two of them have come to light in later transcripts. The autographs of *Almira* and *Amadigi* have vanished; of *Teseo* only a few pages remain; *Rodrigo*, *Rinaldo*, *Il pastor fido*, and *Silla* have major gaps. Only *Agrippina* and the operas from 1720 (except *Admeto*, which falls outside this volume) are more or less complete in autograph. The regular series of performing scores, mostly the work of the elder Smith, does not begin till the second version of *Radamisto* in December 1720, though it is possible that a few surviving copies of previous operas were used by Handel in the theatre.

Early copies are therefore of paramount importance for establishing the text, especially if they can be dated. Even where an autograph survives, it does not necessarily represent what Handel performed, and it scarcely ever includes music composed for revivals, of which there were a great many covering the operas in this volume. The printed librettos are likewise incomplete; for some revivals none may have been printed. Early manuscripts of complete operas and miscellaneous selections have yielded a substantial amount of unpublished and unknown music, often of high quality. Most of it can be attributed to the opera for which it was composed, and a good deal to the particular revival.

In addition to the performing scores, five large eighteenth-century collections of Handel copies survive, cited as follows:

   (i) Malmesbury: copied for Elizabeth Legh, now owned by the Earl of
                       Malmesbury (microfilm in the Hampshire Record Office,
                       Winchester);
  (ii) Flower: copied for Charles Jennens, whence it passed to the Earls of
                       Aylesford; most of it was bought by Sir Newman Flower and is
                       now in the Henry Watson Music Library, Manchester, but a
                       few volumes are in the Royal Music Collection[1] and elsewhere;
 (iii) Shaftesbury: copied for the Fourth Earl of Shaftesbury,[2] since 1987 in the
                       Gerald Coke Collection;
  (iv) Granville: copied for Bernard Granville (the operas c.1740–43), now
                       among the Egerton MSS at the British Library;
   (v) Lennard: possibly copied for Handel's publisher John Walsh the
                       younger; later owned by H. Barrett Lennard, who left it to the
                       Fitzwilliam Museum, Cambridge.

The last two are late and not of great consequence for the operas. None of the
Shaftesbury scores was copied before about 1736, but they supply a few gaps,
notably in *Rodrigo*. Flower contains volumes of widely varying date and
importance, including unperformed music copied from the autographs and a
few passages whose originals have been lost. It has interesting annotations by
Jennens, but its most remarkable feature is an almost complete collection of
vocal and instrumental parts. They were never used in performance, and it is
not known why Jennens required them, but in the absence of Handel's theatre
parts they throw much light on the practice of a copyist from Handel's circle
(generally S2) in extracting parts from a score.[3] By far the most important of
these collections is Malmesbury. Elizabeth Legh died in 1734, thereby
supplying a terminal date; she also annotated and dated a number of the
volumes, and in two instances supplied the name of the copyist. The collection
is rich in otherwise unknown music and contains the earliest complete copy of
several operas and the only complete score of the first version of *Radamisto*.[4]

   None of the music in these collections was intended for public performance.
They are library copies, and therefore contain alternative and rejected
versions often missing from the performing scores. None was available to
Chrysander. Ranking with them is the modern collection assembled by Gerald
Coke, which includes the earliest copies of *Teseo* and *Amadigi* and many other
treasures. Smaller collections and single copies of major importance are to be
found in Vienna, Berlin, Washington, Tokyo, and Oxford, as well as in the
Royal Music and Additional MSS at the British Library. Some of the
Shaftesbury, Coke, and Royal Music copies contain autograph insertions.
Other early copies, whether of whole operas or selections, are in Hamburg (in
addition to the performing scores), Wiesentheid, Munich, Durham, Cambridge, and the Royal College of Music (London). All are described in the
relevant chapters, where possible in chronological order.

   For the proper assessment of this material it is essential to study, identify,
and date the copyists. Much valuable preliminary work has been done by Jens

---

[1] Cited as Aylesford, to distinguish them from those in Manchester.
[2] The bulk of this collection disappeared from view in 1855 and was only rediscovered in 1983.
[3] See Chapter 2, p. 34.
[4] Two volumes formerly in this collection (cantatas) are now in the Bodleian Library, Oxford,
and one (harpsichord arrangements) in the Coke Collection.

Peter Larsen in his book on *Messiah*[5] and Hans Dieter Clausen in his study of
the performing scores.[6] Clausen's work however was virtually confined to the
contents of the Hamburg library, and Larsen did not have access to Flower
and was unaware of the Malmesbury, Shaftesbury, and Coke Collections and
most of the scattered copies. Since these include nearly all surviving pre-1720
scores, the copyists of that vital and obscure period have hitherto escaped
investigation. Both Larsen and Clausen misattributed to Smith the work of
the most important of them, D. Linike, who was active for several years before
Smith's arrival in England.

The symbols for copyists propounded by Larsen and Clausen are thankfully
adopted here, with a few necessary modifications:

S1–S13	the Smith circle of the 1730s and later
RM1–RM9	Royal Music Library
BM1–BM6	British Library Additional MSS
Lenn 1, 2, and	
Fitz 1	Fitzwilliam Museum
Tenb 1–3	Tenbury MSS, now in the Bodleian Library, Oxford
Hb 1, 2, and	
H1–12	Hamburg Staats- und Universitätsbibliothek

Elizabeth Legh named two copyists, Linike and Newman, and it has been
possible to establish that the younger Smith acted as a Handel copyist in his
youth (*c.*1726–8). Larsen's and Clausen's lists each contain two duplications:
RM5 and RM6 are identical, as are RM7 and RM9, H6 and H9, and H11
and H12. Larsen's Smith circle was preceded by two others, one centred round
Linike, a viola player in the Haymarket orchestra and the theatre's principal
copyist, whose work can be dated between 1712 and 1725 (mostly 1712–19),
the other round Smith during the early years of the Royal Academy (1720–5).
The first group included RM1, RM4, and at least one more; it subsequently
recruited Smith, whose earliest known copies belong to the winter of 1718–19.
The second comprised H1–H5 and several others, with a little continuing help
from RM1 and RM4; not all of them were equally prominent.[7] The earliest
S2 copy occurs in a volume dated 1720, but is probably an addition of some
five years later; S1, the next of the S series, emerged about 1728. During the
early Royal Academy years the pressure on the scriptorium was evidently so
great that work on many manuscripts was divided between three, four, or
even five hands. Copyists certainly or probably associated—for however brief
a period—with Handel's immediate circle, if they have not already acquired
symbols, have been allotted the letters of the Greek alphabet in approximate
order of their appearance. Their hands are found in the following manuscripts:

Alpha (*c.* 1717)	Malmesbury (keyboard volume)
Beta (*c.* 1717–18)	Malmesbury (keyboard volume), RM18 b 4, RM18 b 8 (both keyboard works), Bodleian MS Mus d 61 (cantatas)

[5] *Handel's Messiah, Origins, Composition, Sources* (London, 1957).
[6] *Händels Direktionspartituren ('Handexemplare')* (Hamburg, 1972).
[7] For a fuller account, see W. Dean, 'Handel's Early London Copyists', in *Bach, Handel, Scarlatti: Tercentenary Essays*, ed. P. Williams (Cambridge, 1985).

Gamma (1720–?22)   Malmesbury   (*Radamisto*),   RCM   905
                        (*Radamisto*), Malmesbury (keyboard over-
                        tures)
Delta (1720)   Fitzwilliam Mus MS 72 (*Radamisto*)
Epsilon (*c.* 1721–2)   Fitzwilliam Mus MS 54 (arias)
Zeta (*c.* 1724)   Malmesbury (*Ottone*), Add MS 31571 (arias)
Eta (*c.* 1724–5)   Malmesbury (*Giulio Cesare*), Bodleian MS Mus
                        d 220 (*Giulio Cesare*), Cardiff Central Library,
                        Mackworth Collection, MS M.C.1.34(b) (*Giulio
                        Cesare* arias), Royal Academy of Music Mus MS
                        140 (*Giulio Cesare* arias)
Theta (*c.* 1724–5)   Bodleian MS Mus d 220 (*Giulio Cesare*)
Iota (*c.* 1724–5)   Bodleian MS Mus d 220 (*Giulio Cesare*)
Kappa (*c.* 1729 or later)   RM18 c 2 (keyboard overtures)
Lambda (*c.* 1729 or later) RM18 c 2 (keyboard overtures and aria)

The hand of another unidentified copyist is found in Add MS 31562
(*Radamisto*, 1720). Several more were active in the 1730s and later.

W.D.

Additional Note

* (p. xviii) *Add* Kassel (Deutsches Musikgeschichtliches Archiv, on film),
Cardiff, and the Royal Academy of Music (London). The principal collections,
and some of the lesser ones, are discussed in detail in T. Best (ed.), *Handel
Collections and their History* (Oxford, 1993).

CHAPTER I

HANDEL AS OPERA COMPOSER

Defects of modern revivals and published scores (p. 1)—the art of opera (p. 3)—evolution of opera seria (p. 4)—Handel's approach (p. 5)—range and method of characterization (p. 7)—treatment of da capo aria (p. 9)—exit convention (p. 10)—recitative (p. 11)—duets and ensembles (p. 12)— instrumental movements and overtures (p. 12)—operation of Baroque theatre (p. 13)—effect on musical design (p. 14)—long-term organization (p. 14)—librettos and theatre poets (p. 15)— Handel's influence on librettos (p. 17)—rejection of Metastasio (p. 18)—Handel's audience (p. 19)—treatment of orchestra (p. 20)—heroic male parts and octave transposition (p. 20).

I T is the contention of this book that Handel ranks with Monteverdi, Mozart, Verdi, and Wagner among the supreme masters of opera. To many, perhaps most, readers that may appear an extravagant claim. Not so long ago it would have been laughed out of court. It is still exceptional to find Handel's operas accepted as serious works of art, whether by critics, impresarios, or the general public. We encounter them with growing frequency in the theatre, but scarcely ever in a form that releases more than a fraction of their potential impact. The most celebrated companies, whether in Britain, Germany, or the United States, have the worst record in this respect. Their attitude is consistently apologetic; instead of presenting the operas on their own terms, they shuffle them into postures considered more likely to win public acceptance, regardless of their integrity, the intentions of the composer, or the conventions of his epoch.

The earliest stage revivals, initiated by Oskar Hagen at Göttingen in 1920 and for long confined to Germany, butchered the scores unmercifully, but did return Handel to his proper medium, the theatre. At that time, when the Wagnerian backwash of late Romanticism had not subsided, it probably was necessary to temper the music to contemporary taste if it was to be heard at all. There is no such excuse today, when the Early Music movement has recovered and popularized forgotten material from several centuries, much of it by composers without a tithe of Handel's genius. Monteverdi supplies an instructive parallel. His operas have moved through an era of compromise and won universal acclaim as masterpieces in their own right, though only three of them survive. Handel left nearly forty, far more than any other composer of comparable stature. Having weathered the ministrations of Hagen, he has fallen into the hands of conductors and producers who too often betray their unfamiliarity with the composer and his art and set up a barrier of murky fog between the operas and their audience.

What are the reasons for this? The principal one is sheer ignorance. Despite his long public career and a mass of available documentation, including nearly all his autograph manuscripts, Handel is the least known of the great composers. The image of a revered and bewigged master, the creator of entertainments associated with substantial forces and more or less edifying content, still hovers at the back of popular consciousness. Until recently even his oratorios, two or three untypical works apart, were little known. His orchestral music and some of his anthems, which together amount to a fraction of his output, have won greater acceptance. Yet despite a climate increasingly favourable to research into the music of the past he has received little attention from musicologists, and his operas constitute one of the biggest blanks in the history of the last three centuries. In view of Handel's long residence in England, and the presence there of most of the source material, some of the blame must rest on the backwardness of British musicology, which took several generations to catch up with the continent; if England was never a land without music, for a long time it failed to maintain sufficient depth of soil for the cultivation of a more than provincial taste.

Although that is no longer true, we are still suffering from the after-effects. Among them must be numbered the failure to launch a complete critical edition of the works of London's greatest resident composer. Chrysander's, published during the second half of the nineteenth century, was a remarkable achievement for one man, worthy of the first great generation of German scholars. But he was operating in a foreign land, without access to numerous important sources. Even had he found them, the confines of a single life-span might have left insufficient time for their digestion. Moreover the operas must have seemed a stagnant backwater in the age of high Romanticism. The texts of many of them were a veritable tank-trap even to such a Panzer-like editor as Chrysander. The scores he published vary widely in standards of accuracy. Some are admirable, and can still be used with a minimum of adjustment. Others were crippled by the inaccessibility of essential evidence, and a few by perverse decisions and prejudice. Chrysander was so contemptuous of previous editors, who happened to be English, that in an unworthy exhibition of *odium musicologicum* he seized every opportunity to ridicule their pretensions. The abortive English Handel Society edition never reached the operas. Samuel Arnold in the late eighteenth century, attempting the first collected edition of any composer, published four, all from sound texts of early date. By deploying the heavy artillery of German scholarship against Arnold, Chrysander branded him with the stigma of amateurishness and incompetence. Yet despite imperfections to be expected of a pioneer venture into uncharted territory, at least two of Arnold's four scores are demonstrably superior to Chrysander's in faithfulness to the composer.

The failure of later scholars to follow up Chrysander was in some sense a tribute to his achievement, though an ill-judged one. Ironically, while England did nothing, his reputation remained so high in Germany that when Halle, Handel's birthplace, promoted a new edition in the 1950s it was begun as a mere supplement in the belief that little more was required. The Hallische Händel-Ausgabe (HHA) was later upgraded, and after a reconsideration of editorial principles has begun to free itself from the consequences of this uncertain start. The five operas it has produced up to the time of writing are the only full scores of any of Handel's operas to appear in the twentieth century.

Defective as the printed sources are, they cannot be held solely responsible for Handel's shaky reputation as an opera composer. The cause lies deeper, in a failure to come to terms with the operatic conditions of his day; and that in turn is founded on a blinkered view of the entire aesthetic of opera. This complex form, which aspires to a synthesis of vocal and instrumental music, drama, scene-painting, spectacle, dancing, and ritual, has been exalted as the loftiest and ridiculed as the most abysmal of human aspirations. It can be both; its very precariousness, the rarity with which it succeeds in reconciling several wilful and centrifugal arts, is part of its fascination. It is of its very nature a highly volatile compound. At different periods one or other of the components has gained a position of dominance, overreached itself, and been pushed into the background; whereupon the process begins again until a new balance is evolved. Operatic 'reform', that perennial of the history books, amounts to little more than the supplanting of one such synthesis, at its point of overreach, by another. If Gluck reformed the *opera seria*, the first Romantic generation reformed Gluck, Wagner reformed the *bel canto* opera of Rossini, and Stravinsky reformed Wagner. In the long run the reformed remains as aesthetically valid as the reformer, if it contributed a temporarily satisfying equilibrium. But two aspects of opera never change: it must be a compromise between two or more competing arts, and it must be rooted in conventions. Realism in any but a comparative sense is wholly foreign to it. This is as true of the *verismo* composers as of Mozart. People do not normally sing when making love or threatening each other with torture, and if they did they would be unlikely to enjoy the services of an orchestra. The executioner does not wait for a pair of condemned lovers to finish their duet or an ensemble of spectators to reach a satisfying cadence before performing the decisive deed that must terminate the action.

The history of opera is the history of the compromises evolved at different periods in different countries. It is not a matter of one set of conventions being superior to another, though every opera-lover has a right to his preferences. Unless his outlook is hopelessly narrow, he will adjust himself according to whether he is attending a performance of *L'incoronazione di Poppea* or *Le nozze di Figaro* or *Wozzeck*. The world of opera has many mansions, and the listener who refuses to enter one (or more) of them is shortening his experience and depriving himself of enjoyment. The essential prerequisite of course is that the composer and his collaborators should achieve the highest possible standard within the convention they are employing; and it will be found that the greatest artists expand that convention to the utmost.

The popular repertory is generally taken to stretch from Mozart to Puccini and Richard Strauss, with an extension backward to Gluck and (more recently) forward to Janáček and Britten. The great majority of operas during this period of two centuries exploit a peculiar advantage available in no other dramatic form, the vocal ensemble. If several characters in a play speak at once the result is chaos; in an opera they can express simultaneously not only their individual emotions but the conflict between them, thereby advancing the plot and, with the aid of the orchestra, adding a whole new dimension. The vocal ensemble is not indispensable; neither Wagner (*Die Meistersinger* apart) nor Janáček made much use of it in his greatest works. They relied on the alternation of solo voices and the manipulation of the orchestral continuum, whether symphonically or as a commentary, to express character, conflict, and development. This is a limitation—a deliberate one. The rarity of the vocal ensemble in serious opera before Mozart imposed an extra responsibility on the composer, and in a historical sense served to weed out the second-rate. That is why the first century and a half of the form's existence produced many interesting figures but, with the possible exception of Rameau, only two great masters (we can hardly include Purcell on the basis of one short work). Monteverdi triumphed by means of a pregnant melodic idiom and an extraordinary sensitivity to words. He needed both to impose order on a fluid form derived from the new invention of recitative. Handel was confronted with a situation that was almost the reverse.

By the end of the seventeenth century the flexible arioso style which had been the staple medium of Monteverdi and Cavalli had given way to a more formal and restrictive design. The recitative became progressively detached from the aria, the former reserved for the advancement of the plot, the latter for the release of emotion. (The distinction, though strongly marked, was not absolute; orchestrally accompanied recitative could be as emotional as any closed form, and it is not true that nothing ever happened in an *opera seria* aria.) The arias were still relatively short, and very numerous, often more than fifty to an opera; they occurred haphazard at the beginning, in the middle, and at the end of scenes. This was not a stable situation; it produced a great many minor climaxes but little sense of dramatic gradation or long-term control. The next development, the emergence of the da capo aria as the standard form and its gravitation to the end of the scene, followed by the character's exit, has been attributed to the baleful influence of the virtuoso singer and his desire for applause. That was certainly a relevant factor, but not the only one. Spectacular singing is not necessarily destructive of musical drama; many audiences at all periods have regarded it as an essential ingredient. There was a growing need to give the scene a coherent musico-dramatic shape, and the exit aria, discharging the emotion accumulated in the course of the recitative, certainly achieved this. Nor would it have exercised such an overwhelming sway if it had not satisfied the audience, including sophisticated listeners, as well as the performers.

Of course the process went too far, not for the last time in operatic history. A great singer, by extruding his personality, can all too easily distort an opera even when the balance is less heavily weighted in his favour. The influence of castratos in particular accentuated the prominence of the aria until it threatened to squeeze out everything else, like a young cuckoo ejecting from the nest the eggs and offspring of its foster-parents. By the same token arias grew longer, more elaborate, and more static; the notorious simile type, in which the character compares himself to a pilot in a storm, a river in search of the sea, a tiger defending its young, or almost anything else in the world of animal, vegetable, or mineral, can only be said to discharge emotion at a considerable distance from its source. The apparent ossification of the extended and formalized da capo aria is responsible for the received opinion that the *opera seria* of Handel's day could not possibly be a viable dramatic form. We are told that even in its own time it was regarded less as a living art than as a species of circus entertainment for a public that came to applaud the singer and perhaps the aria but took no interest in the opera as a dramatic unity. This is the point where the argument takes a false step. We have no right to assume that, because many listeners or even composers may have taken such a view, they necessarily all did so, or that the obstacles placed in the path of the musical dramatist, though formidable in the extreme, were insuperable.

It is the nature of artistic genius to bring off the seemingly impossible. We cannot know whether Handel succeeded or failed until we have put his operas to the test: which means staging them in the theatre with a full knowledge not only of what he wrote but of how he intended it to be performed and how he exploited the conventions, theatrical and musical, of his age. Except to a limited degree by companies with straitened resources no such attempt has ever been made; no one has studied in detail the intimate and subtle links between the music and the mechanical techniques of the Baroque theatre. The case has gone by default. If it is to be argued afresh, we need to know everything possible about the period, its musical and theatrical practices, and its artistic conventions.

*

Handel was not a typical composer of *opera seria*. Born in central Germany, he began his career in the cosmopolitan city of Hamburg, and all but two of his subsequent operas were composed for a country on the periphery of the main stream of the art. While German and English opera were shallow-rooted, French opera had developed into an independent form with idiosyncratic conventions; but it flourished only in France and a few Francophile German courts. Its influence on Handel, if we exclude the one-act opera-ballet *Terpsicore*, was confined to instrumental music and dances and the occasional linking of vocal and instrumental pieces by common material, all of which he had absorbed in Hamburg. Even in his two operas based on French librettos, *Teseo* and *Amadigi*, the example of the source, though it subverted the balance of scenes and the exit convention, left the substance of the music unaffected. Handel wrote almost exclusively for Italian singers in the Italian style, and his work must be assessed in terms of that tradition.

During the first half of the eighteenth century thousands of Italian operas were brought to birth. They were composed for a particular group of singers and a particular audience in a particular city. At revivals, which were rare in the theatre of first instance, these variables altered the opera in material respects and sometimes transformed it almost beyond recognition. Scores were scarcely ever printed (Handel's were exceptional in this respect; but they were aria collections for domestic use, with no recitatives and incomplete orchestration, not blueprints for complete performance). In consequence vast numbers of operas have disappeared altogether or survive as a handful of arias that cannot always be ascribed to one production or locality or even to one composer. It is often difficult to establish a definitive text, since every production is likely to have been different. This impression of casualness and discontinuity would seem to be confirmed by the notorious popularity of the pasticcio, in which existing arias from different operas and different composers were stitched together with recitative settings of an old libretto.

Except in one respect Handel's practice did not vary from that of his contemporaries. Most of his revivals, in opera and oratorio, were hurriedly mounted for a company of singers different from the original cast. Some, like those of *Tolomeo* in 1730 and *Il pastor fido* in May 1734, were in effect pasticcios, and he created others from his own works and other people's. He transferred arias from opera to opera and from one character to another in the same opera, without regard to any artistic principle. In the 1736 revival of *Alcina* he gave Morgana's brilliant 'Tornami a vagheggiar', composed for the high soprano Cecilia Young, to the heroine (sung by Strada) because in that season he had no second soprano and was forced to cast Morgana as a mezzo. One can see why he wished to retain the aria, but it makes nonsense of the characterization and the drama. (There are a few exceptions to this brusque procedure: he took great trouble over the December 1720 revival of *Radamisto*, and in 1725 rewrote the soprano part of Sesto in *Giulio Cesare* for a tenor, creating a radically different character.) But it is essential to draw a firm distinction between Handel's treatment of revivals and his approach to the composition of a new opera. Here the creative artist took over from the impresario and, as the autographs demonstrate again and again, he devoted infinite care to the finer details of characterization and dramatic structure. In an overall estimate of his work, revivals and pasticcios are best ignored; they suggest all too faithfully the stereotype that has brought the whole of *opera seria* into contempt.

If claims are to be made for Handel, can they be extended to his leading contemporaries, Scarlatti, Giovanni and Antonio Maria Bononcini, Pollarolo, Ariosti, Gasparini, Lotti, Porpora, Vivaldi, Vinci, and many more? Would their operas come to life if given an adequate hearing?[1] It is important not to exclude such a possibility, and every opportunity to test it must be welcomed. Most of these composers had conspicuous gifts. Scarlatti's quirky harmonic style and rhythmic unpredictability give his operas a highly individual flavour. Those of Giovanni Bononcini and Gasparini are rich in melodies capable of charming the ear and sometimes touching the heart. Vivaldi and Vinci, writing in the later style of the 1720s, imparted an exhilarating vitality to their fast arias that grips attention, even if it tends to monotony over a whole opera. There is a case for their revival in the theatre.

It is not hard to show that Handel possessed all these gifts and more. He was a master of every type of melody, with scarcely a rival at any period. The flexibility of his rhythmic paragraphs was exceptional even in an age that had not fully succumbed to the clamp of the four-bar phrase. He used chromatic and dissonant harmony sparingly, but with all the greater effect for confining it to moments of acute dramatic and emotional conflict. While able to draw rich sonorities from the standard forces of his day, he can ravish the ear with an extraordinary range of novel sounds and textures. In short, his musical invention was prodigious. That of course is what fuelled the movement to revive his operas. But it was not enough to make him a great opera composer. Several of his peers in other periods, notably Haydn and Schubert, have fallen at this hurdle. Two further demands must be satisfied: the creation of memorable characters who interact, develop, and grow in stature, and the fusion of the loose strands of the opera in an indissoluble musical and dramatic unity. Handel possessed both these gifts; if they existed elsewhere in his age, they have not been discovered.

Their exercise called for an all but superhuman strength, since it involved the subjugation of the most rebarbative set of conventions ever imposed on the art of opera. The story of Handel's greatest operas is the story of a giant bending unpromising material to his will and making it serve a purpose for which it was not consciously intended and which it seemed positively to exclude. Using the same language of symbolic gesture (*Affektenlehre*) as his

---

[1] The useful series of facsimile reproductions edited by H. M. Brown and E. Weimer (*Italian Opera 1640–1770*, New York and London, 1977–) has made some of them available for study.

contemporaries, often with the same connotations, he not only infused it with greater musical force and intensity; a natural genius for thinking in dramatic terms led him to treat every formal obstacle as a challenge and neglect no opportunity to throw his not inconsiderable weight into the opposite scale. While his contemporaries may have been content to give the singers their head and not concern themselves unduly with consistency or overall proportion, he contrived at once to satisfy the singers—who for the greater part of his career were the most celebrated and demanding of the age—and to ensure that the characters they presented and the dramatic conflict they enacted remained paramount.[2]

The evidence for such a claim appears in this book and its sequel, but it can be appreciated only if we approach the operas not as a string of disconnected episodes but as living wholes, and only then proceed to details in order to discover how the trick is done. Here a mountain of prejudice and misrepresentation has to be overcome. We are told that Handel's operas are so long that no modern audience would be prepared to swallow them whole. On the very few occasions when one of them has been staged in full with a proper regard to style, that has not been the audience's reaction. None of them approaches the length of Wagner's mature operas, or even some of Verdi's. This is not an argument against shortening the weaker scores, or making an occasional cut in the stronger ones. But the operation must be performed with care and understanding. What we commonly encounter is crude butchery, not the removal of tangential material but the severance of main arteries, which does indeed make the operas seem intolerably long because it destroys the connective tissue.

Given the components of *opera seria*, it was inevitable that Handel's methods of characterization and structural organization should differ radically from those of other periods. In the absence of ensembles the development and clash of character cannot be expressed through the confrontations of a Mozart, Verdi, or Puccini. Secco recitative cannot do it, since it carries a minimal emotional charge. It must be done through the aria. Yet with rare exceptions each aria is confined to a single mood or *Affekt*, or two if the B section is contrasted; and the da capo has to be taken into account. Handel tackles the problem by building up the character facet by facet in the course of the arias until he or she stands complete. Cleopatra in *Giulio Cesare* begins as a tease and a scheming minx; when she falls in love with Caesar she passes through passion, anxiety, and desolation before emerging as a mature woman. Sesto develops from a young boy into a warrior capable of avenging his father's murder. The grief-stricken widow Cornelia attains peace of mind through the exploits of her son. Caesar, the arrogant conqueror and politician, is deepened by love and the pain it brings. Villains generally have less scope, but the weak vacillating Grimoaldo in *Rodelinda* is one of Handel's subtlest portraits, and he too has become a different person by the end of the opera.

The range of Handel's characters is exceptional by any standard. Few composers have created so many persons—women even more than men—who haunt our memory as distinct individuals, governed by personal motives and

---

[2] The usual approach has been neatly put by Michael Talbot with reference to the rudimentary characterization in Vivaldi's operas: 'The prime aim [of the aria] is still to depict a situation as viewed by a character rather than a character as revealed by a situation' (*Vivaldi*, London, 1978, 197).

passions. Ostensibly they may be stiff potentates, remote classical heroes or sorceresses from the world of myth; the music melts them into human beings whose sufferings work on our susceptibilities with such intensity as to rank them with the supreme creations of dramatic art. By no means all are heroic or serious. They can be richly comic, even absurd. Thanks to the breadth of his sympathies, his gift of dramatic detachment, and his command of irony on many levels Handel can place tragic, contemptible, and frivolous characters in the same opera, and even in the same situation, without corroding the framework that holds them together. Like Mozart he views his characters in the round and presents them from several angles, enormously enriching the texture of the operas. Writing of the arias, though it is equally applicable to the characters, Donald Grout says that their 'number and variety... is so great, and the power of capturing the most subtle nuances of feeling so astounding, that one is tempted to believe there is no emotion of which humanity is capable that has not found musical expression somewhere in Handel's operas.... We are moved by the spectacle of suffering, but our compassion is mingled with admiration at suffering so nobly endured, with pride that we ourselves belong to a species capable of such heroism.'[3]

As with the characters, so with the operas themselves. While it is possible to divide them into types, and naturally they differ in quality, one of their most striking characteristics is the variety in what may be called their dramatic climate. The works in this volume alone, which covers less than half the total, illustrate ironic comedy (*Agrippina*), medieval pageantry (*Rinaldo*), erotic pastoral (*Il pastor fido*), romantic melodrama (*Amadigi*), lofty heroism (*Radamisto*), domestic tragicomedy (*Flavio*), claustrophobic tragedy (*Tamerlano*), and monuments to marital love and extramarital passion (*Rodelinda* and *Giulio Cesare*). Not only do the operas present a wide spectrum of human experience; they mix the genres boldly but with unfailing success. *Agrippina* and *Il pastor fido* carry undercurrents of tragedy; *Flavio* contains both a hilarious denouement and a death on stage; *Amadigi* and *Tamerlano* end with the sympathy on the 'wrong' side, as if Handel were pointing an accusing finger at destiny.

His means of pacing and unifying the drama are subtle and multifarious. Since many examples are discussed later, they need only be touched on here. Flexibility rather than uniformity is the significant feature. Few even of the early operas consist of a routine alternation of recitative and aria: set pieces merge into one another to create dramatic climaxes in *Il pastor fido*, *Teseo*, and *Silla*, and there are more complex structures in the Royal Academy operas. Some later works are very free in form: the operas of 1734/5 make elaborate use of chorus and ballet, *Serse* abandons the da capo in half the arias, and the little-esteemed *Giustino* contains a sequence of six movements (amounting to 286 bars) without secco recitative, of which only the last is in da capo form. The guiding principle is the urge to press on with the drama. Nor need this be arrested where the recitative–aria succession is preserved, provided the tension is not allowed to drop through pauses or a slack treatment of recitative. Abrupt switches of tonality coinciding with a fresh development of the plot, whether at set changes ('Alma del gran Pompeo' in Act I of *Giulio Cesare*) or not ('Dall'ondoso periglio' in Act III), can rivet the audience's attention and project it forward. In the major operas scenes and arias, quite apart from their

---

[3] *A Short History of Opera* (New York, 1947), 174–5.

musical expressiveness and the opportunities they afford the singers, are so juxtaposed as to develop character, advance the plot, and, whether by contrasts of word or tonality or more particularly by the use of dramatic irony, act as a joint in the articulation of the drama.[4]

One of Handel's most potent weapons is the da capo aria itself. The form is not entirely static; its two components carry an element of contrast which can be stressed to a greater or lesser degree. Contemporary writers derived its dramatic significance from the consideration that no strong passion can be sustained for long: the B section checks it, whereupon the da capo allows it to burst out with increased energy. Handel went much further than this. Dramatic impact in opera depends to a great extent on surprise, on the composer deceiving the ear (and sometimes the eye) into expecting one thing and confronting it with something quite different. A narrow convention has the advantage that, in the hands of a great artist, a comparatively minor deviation can produce a much greater effect than in an idiom where almost anything is possible. Having led the ear to expect a da capo, Handel can bring off a genuine *coup de théâtre* by delaying, withholding, or interrupting it, in a number of different ways. He does this as early as *Rodrigo* and *Agrippina*, and there are countless later examples. The interruption of the love duet in Act I of *Ariodante*[5] achieves a musical surprise on several levels, advances the plot, and establishes a new character, all in half a dozen bars, just when we have been conditioned to expect a regular da capo.

It is not necessary to sacrifice the da capo. A wide range of possibilities is opened by the manipulation of the orchestral ritornellos. In seventeenth-century opera, ritornellos were commonly used to round off an aria or a scene, or in strophic pieces to punctuate the stanzas. They varied the texture or accompanied stage business, but were too casual for structural use on a broader scale. By the turn of the century, with the da capo established, the ritornello had become a regular feature of most arias, usually serving as introduction and postlude to the A section. It could be omitted or varied; the motto phrase, enunciated first by the voice, was a popular device and sometimes became a mannerism. Another favourite gambit, especially in continuo or lightly accompanied arias, was the fully-scored and expanded ritornello at the end of the A section or after the da capo, where it made a satisfying conclusion.

Of course Handel did not invent the idea of varying the ritornello for dramatic purposes (a feature of his whole career is that he originated very little); but he showed exceptional resource in the way he managed it, and there can be little doubt that in the range of dramatic effects achieved by this means he far surpassed his contemporaries. What may be called the standard form of the aria—A section with initial, intermediate, and closing ritornellos, the first and last balanced in length and material, the intermediate a briefer point of punctuation between two tonally distinguished statements of the text; shorter B section contrasted in key or mode, generally without a ritornello of its own; exact da capo—is comparatively rare in Handel's maturity, though he exploited it in formal operas like *Radamisto*. He preferred to tease the ear by lengthening, shortening, or suppressing one or more of the ritornellos, adding

---

[4] See the analysis of the aria structure in *Alcina* in W. Dean, *Handel and the Opera Seria* (Berkeley and Los Angeles, 1969), 43–53.

[5] See ibid. 105.

new material (or developing what has just been heard) in those after either main section, or interposing ritornellos where we least expect them, for example at the start or in the middle of the B section. The most striking instances are to be found at the end of the A section and the return to the da capo. His object was not simply to adjust the balance, a common practice for example with Vivaldi, but to make a specific dramatic point. The range of expression thus achieved, if not infinite, is astonishingly wide, and Handel seldom follows exactly the same procedure twice. In extreme cases, such as 'Deggio dunque' in *Radamisto* and 'Ah mio cor!' in *Alcina*, he converts the da capo structure into a new organically developing form that disguises its ABA basis, though this remains at the back of the listener's mind as a point of reference.[6]

The exit convention can be another source of strength. The rare occasions when it is not observed—where an important character goes out during a recitative or hangs around after singing an aria—can generally be traced to clumsy adaptation of an old libretto or the inadequacy of a particular singer; they are apt to produce a faint but perceptible sense of anticlimax. Sometimes the singer of an aria is required in the following scene; in which case he leaves the stage and at once returns, or 'offers to retire'. These awkward expedients draw attention to the virtue of the convention, which much more often allowed Handel to brace the dramatic design by bringing each release of emotion to a satisfying climax. It was responsible for two master-strokes, inaccessible in any other medium, in the second acts of *Agrippina* and *Tamerlano*. It is noteworthy too how often Handel compensates for the sluggish potential of the simile aria by concentrating on it his full inventive powers, whether of melody, harmony, or orchestration.

Not all arias are in da capo form. There are a few rondos and binary ariettas, again usually evoked by the dramatic context (Act II of *Tamerlano*, Orlando's mad scene, 'Verdi prati' in *Alcina*). If we exclude *Almira*, an early work in a local tradition, and *Serse*, a deliberate reversion to seventeenth-century practice, most of the other exceptions belong to the cavatina type. Handel did not use the term, though one such piece in Act II of *Alcina* is headed *cavata*; we have preferred it to arioso, a freer lyrical movement without a central cadence and sometimes merging into accompanied recitative without a cadence at all. A cavatina is generally in effect a detached A section; some of these, such as the first vocal movement in *Rodelinda*, originally possessed a B section and da capo,[7] and Handel often used the first part of what had been a da capo aria in his source. They are found in the operas of his contemporaries, as a rule indiscriminately at different points in the scene. Handel used them for a structural purpose, based on the fact that they did not require an obligatory exit. They commonly occur at the beginning of a scene as the first element in an extended design which, after some significant action in recitative, is concluded by a full da capo aria and exit for the same character. Since the cavatina is nearly always slow and the succeeding aria fast, there is a resemblance in plan and function to the double aria of Romantic opera. It is

---

[6] For further examples, many of them involving tonal surprise as well, see ibid. 156 ff. Reinhold Kubik (*Händels Rinaldo, Geschichte, Werk, Wirkung*, Stuttgart, 1982, 118 ff.) analyses the structure of arias and ritornellos in *Rinaldo*. This is the most detailed study of any Handel opera, but fails to recognize it as in some respects untypical and immature. Kubik pays little attention to what most distinguishes Handel from his contemporaries, the treatment of character and drama.

[7] The B section, bracketed by Chrysander, was removed before performance. See p. 578.

not necessary to credit Handel with the invention of this design to see it as a personal feature of his style with an obvious dramatic potential.

The temptation to give the secco recitatives a casual glance and dismiss them as mere suspenders to the arias should be resisted. No doubt Handel wrote them rapidly; it was his practice to jot down the words only, draft the arias in outline—voice, bass, and the top line of ritornellos—then return to set the recitatives and fill out the instrumentation of the arias. This helped him to lay down the plan and tonality of the opera as it were with a single brush-stroke and, since afterthoughts were apt to occur at any stage, it allows us to look over his shoulder and observe the process by which the score reached its definitive form. The recitatives are the sinews of the opera, setting up the context of the arias, which they prepare in a variety of ways, dramatic and musical. Handel liked to use their cadential points as another means of surprise, sometimes omitting a perfect cadence and frequently launching the aria in an unpredictable key or on an unexpected chord.[8] Nor is the musical content negligible. The harmonic movement in particular can be complex and subtle. The fruits of Handel's study of the Scarlattian cantata can be seen throughout the operas, sometimes—as in Act I of *Amadigi* and Act II of *Tamerlano*—on an elaborate scale.

The orchestrally accompanied recitative was the one department in which the composer was able to throw off all formal restraint. Combining the impetus of secco recitative with the emotional intensity of the aria, it could range far and wide without any restrictions except those of character and situation. Handel's accompanied recitatives, especially those of the Royal Academy operas, in boldness, unpredictability, harmonic range, and sheer scale easily surpass those of his contemporaries and look far into the future. He explores rare tonalities—F sharp major in *Rodelinda*, G sharp minor in *Giulio Cesare* and *Lotario*, E flat minor in *Ezio*—incorporates symphonic passages (not confined to strings), changes of metre and tempo, enharmonic modulations, sustained arioso, and the most abrupt switches of mood and dynamics, and establishes a variety of links with preceding and following arias. Some of the bigger accompanied recitatives are in cyclic form, the initial bars returning to introduce the aria. It is here that he bursts right through the barriers of the *opera seria* convention. It would be difficult to find eighteenth-century parallels, whether in originality of design or dramatic potency, to the churchyard and prison scenes in *Rodelinda*, Caesar's escape from Alexandria Harbour in *Giulio Cesare*, Bajazet's suicide, and Orlando's decline into insanity. All are based on an expansion of accompanied recitative melting the formality of the adjacent aria scheme, and each reaches its goal by a different route.

Handel is careful to reserve such procedures for moments of extreme tension. To set all or most of the recitatives with orchestra would overload the texture and undermine the swift interplay of light and shade which governs the climate of *opera seria*. This is particularly important in view of the scarcity of ensembles. We may feel initial surprise that Handel made so little use of the dramatic potential in duet, trio, and quartet. It is not that he lacked the skill. The trios in *Tamerlano*, *Orlando*, *Alcina*, and *Imeneo* and the quartet in the

---

[8] The HHA score of *Serse*, which adapts every recitative cadence to end on the dominant of the aria, is a particularly crass example of the misapprehension to which Handel is still subject. For the practice of Scarlatti and other *opera seria* composers in linking recitative with aria, see D. J. Grout, *Alessandro Scarlatti: an Introduction to his Operas* (Berkeley, Los Angeles, London, 1979), 97.

second version of *Radamisto* show him as adept as Mozart; they are action pieces combining conflict with individual expression within a strict design, often da capo form itself. But *opera seria* was geared to the solo voice; audience and singers alike expected and appreciated this. Handel cut the *Radamisto* quartet after December 1720 and the *Tamerlano* trio in 1731. There are one or two duets of opposition in the later operas and occasional masterpieces of irony such as the duet at the end of Act I of *Poro* and that for the hero with the wrong woman in Act III of *Admeto*; but as a rule the participants share a common emotion. While duets supply a useful contrast in texture, their chief function is to emphasize a key moment in the drama. Many are for lovers, husband and wife (*Rodelinda*), or mother and son (*Giulio Cesare*), threatened with death or imprisonment and meeting as they believe for the last time. They tend to occur at the end of an act, where the addition of a second voice after so many arias makes for a satisfactory climax; nearly all are of superb quality.

Before 1734 Handel scarcely used a chorus in opera, and only once or twice introduced a ballet. Movements labelled *coro*, as in the first scene of *Giulio Cesare*, were sung by the available soloists. The *coro* at the end of the opera, an ensemble designed to bring down the curtain on the indispensable happy end, was a convention inherited from the seventeenth century. In Handel's early operas the *coro* is as perfunctory as it almost invariably is with Cavalli and Scarlatti. Later, characteristically impelled by dramatic considerations, he introduced refinements. In some operas—*Rodelinda* and *Giulio Cesare* for example—the happy end is a proper consequence of the plot. Elsewhere it is repulsive to every human instinct, not least those of the composer. Handel's solution in *Tamerlano*, preserving the outer decorum but subduing it to the spirit of tragedy, is a stroke of genius that derives its strength from the pull between text and music, another example of his subjugation of a restrictive convention. He brings several other operas and oratorios to a similar ironical end. From the mid-1720s, beginning with *Alessandro*, he was to develop the *coro* in the direction of the later operatic finale by linking it with preceding movements, whether aria, ensemble, ballet, full chorus, or all four, through the organic use of shared material. The earliest example, indeed the longest finale in any of the operas, is that of the unpublished April 1720 score of *Radamisto*, where an elaborate rondo incorporating three duets and two dances supplies a brilliant conclusion to one of his grandest dramas.

Instrumental movements during the course of an opera are seldom ambitious, except occasionally in orchestration (four trumpets in *Rinaldo*, four horns in *Giulio Cesare*). Their function is to illustrate stage action such as a battle or ceremonial entry. Again the examples in the early operas are something of a disappointment. The sinfonias in *Amadigi* I vii and *Rinaldo* III ii, accompanying displays of magic, are truncated French overtures, decorative rather than descriptive. Others are mere flourishes. Later Handel grew bolder. The music for Hercules's descent to Hades in *Admeto* is still a French overture, but the extraordinary chromatic harmony leaves us in no doubt about the hazardous nature of the enterprise. The seductive sinfonias of the Parnassus scene in *Giulio Cesare*, the descent of the genii in *Orlando*, and the moonrise over the garden in *Ariodante* (a stroke of poignant irony in its context) are little romantic tone-poems, not only beautiful in themselves but contributions to the drama.

The overture is never thematically related to the opera; indeed several of the early ones almost certainly originated as independent concertos, pressed into service perhaps when Handel was short of time. All are of the standard French type: sharply dotted introduction leading to a lively fugato, generally with a return to the first tempo and sometimes a repeat of the Allegro. In a few operas, such as the serious *Radamisto*, Handel stopped there. Elsewhere he appended one or two dance movements. But if the pattern is stereotyped, he developed a decidedly original method, or series of methods, of linking it with the opera. The earliest memorable instance occurs in *Giulio Cesare*, where the orthodox Minuet after the fugato is suddenly expanded by the entry first of four horns and then of the soloists in chorus acclaiming Caesar's victory. In *Scipione* the place of the dance movement is taken by a March, which accompanies the procession of the conqueror, his army, and his prisoners through a triumphal arch.

Here Handel exploits another convention to achieve a simultaneous aural and visual surprise. It was customary for the curtain to be raised after the overture and lowered at the end of the last act. We know that the Minuet of the *Arianna* overture was played with the curtain up: its lovely tune accompanied, with vivid irony, the disembarcation of the Minotaur's destined victims in the port of Knossos. Handel undoubtedly treated the overtures to *Giulio Cesare* and *Scipione*—and to a number of later operas, including *Ezio* and *Deidamia*—in a similar way: he raised the curtain not after the overture but in the middle, treating its last movement as the first of the main action and launching the opera with the acceleration of a ship gliding down the slipway. In *Scipione* he went further and bound the long first scene together by unified tonality and large-scale extension of da capo form.

It is impossible to understand the musical design of a Handel opera without a knowledge of how the Baroque theatre worked. It was celebrated for its scenic effects. Ever since the early days in Venice, opera had been a *Gesamtkunstwerk* in which music was only one (if the most important) of many constituent elements. This was not just a matter of the spectacular machines for the descent of immortals and the disturbance of the natural order by magic, whose operations are familiar from the writings of Addison and Steele about *Rinaldo*. The entire stage apparatus was different from that of the modern theatre. Every set-change—there were usually two or three in each act—was executed in full view of the audience. The Haymarket Theatre had five series of grooves on either side of the stage for sliding wings, moved manually or by machinery, which also controlled borders, ground-rows, and shutters or back-flats to close the prospect. According to the prompter W. R. Chetwood[9] 'a Machine to move the Scenes regularly all together' was common in English and French theatres. Alternatively, while a scene was being played before one group of wings and shutters, the next could be set up behind it, a deep and shallow stage being employed in turn. The most elaborate manoeuvres, such as the departure of a boat containing some of the characters in Act II of *Rinaldo*, could exploit the full depth of the stage, which with the area behind the wings used for operating machines was greater than that of the auditorium and further increased when necessary by an extra room open at the back (see Plate 2).[10]

[9] *A General History of the Stage* (London, 1749).
[10] For technical details and proportions of Vanbrugh's theatre, see R. Leacroft, *The Development of the English Playhouse* (London, 1973), 99 ff., with scale reconstruction of the interior after the alterations of 1707–8 (fig. 71).

The crucial feature of all set-changes was that they did not interrupt the music. The modern habit of dropping the house curtain during an act, or otherwise breaking it up, is fatal to this continuity. Handel wrote the changes into the music. The switches of tonality at such moments coincided with the movement of the wings and shutters, reinforcing the forward impetus of the drama. Other refinements were possible. A scene in Act I of *Teseo* ends with a secco recitative, which looks ludicrously undramatic in the score until we grasp its purpose: Arcane tells Egeo that the people are acclaiming Teseo as his rival, whereupon the wings and shutters change to show this actually happening.

The fact that the curtain remained up for the whole opera had a decisive effect on the design, sharply differentiating it from that of later periods. In Mozart and Romantic opera the act, and sometimes the intermediate scene, builds up to a climax based on an ensemble (with or without chorus), which is then closed at the decisive moment by the curtain. In *opera seria* this is only possible in the final act. The curtain can rise on a tableau and a crowded stage—Handel makes full use of this, often beginning at a climactic point that establishes the central theme of the plot, outlines the principal characters, and launches the action before the exit arias start—but the intermediate acts and scenes must end with an aria (occasionally a duet) and an exit. The typical scene, instead of constituting what the Germans call a *Steigerung* or mounting up, is the exact opposite, a tapering down as the characters go out after their arias. If this is not to produce a series of anticlimaxes, the composer must devise some compensating mechanism. Here again Handel displays the fertility of genius. He ensures that the concluding aria of a scene, and still more of an act, carries so strong an emotional charge that it substitutes an inner for an outer climax. Whereas his predecessors and contemporaries frequently ended their intermediate acts with arias for secondary figures, he swept these away during the adaptation of the librettos and gave the final say to one or other of the principal characters, concentrating on a crucial issue of the story. Almost every intermediate act in his mature operas ends with a movement in which emotional intensity is combined with the utmost care in craftsmanship and invention. These are often the weightiest movements in the score.

They are not always the most brilliant. Extrovert virtuoso arias, supplemented by obbligato instruments or otherwise enriched orchestration, such as those that end the first two acts of *Rinaldo*, Act III of *Teseo*, Act I of *Silla*, Act II of *Amadigi*, and Act II of *Scipione*, can of course create a stunning effect in the theatre. But some of Handel's most moving climaxes are achieved by means of slow arias, simple in construction and accompaniment and tragic in tone, in which the character reacts to a shattering experience and quits the scene in despair, leaving his or her emotion echoing through the minds of the audience. The hero's G minor aria in Act I of *Amadigi* and Emilia's in F sharp minor in Act II of *Flavio* are outstanding examples. The duets of agonized parting already mentioned fall into this class. Sometimes, as in the first acts of *Amadigi* and *Giustino*, Handel places such a piece after a whole string of extrovert arias in lively tempo, fuller scoring, and major tonality, which by throwing it into relief contribute to an overwhelming theatrical impact.

Such long-term organization, on many levels, is characteristic of his operas. It is not easily perceived from a reading of the score, and it falls an easy victim to the Procrustean whims of producers and conductors. That Handel thought in terms not of the aria or the scene but of the act and even the entire opera could be demonstrated in other ways, and will emerge in some of the following chapters. Here a few words may be added about tonal design. Many of the operas—not all, but including most of the outstanding ones—preserve a careful balance between tonal areas, major and minor modes, and flat and sharp keys, often associated with individual characters or *Affekte*. If this is barely perceptible to listeners without perfect pitch, it still operates at a subliminal level. It can be no accident that in *Rodelinda*, a very carefully wrought opera with the widest tonal spectrum in the whole of Handel's work, the only occasion on which a character (Rodelinda herself) returns to a key she has used before is in an aria that vibrates the central nerve both of her nature and of the drama.

It is instructive to compare Handel's work with that of an equally inventive contemporary working in a very different convention but still in the opera house. Rameau's operas are superficially more variegated, but they are made up of a multitude of small units that resist absorption into a large-scale entity. They can nearly always be cut without suffering major damage. That is seldom true of Handel's greater operas. Employing a restrictive convention that fettered his contemporaries and struck posterity as insurmountable, he naturally had failures and near-misses. Yet he created about a dozen major masterpieces capable of holding their own with those of any age, and he did this not by breaking the mould of the convention but by putting it to constructive use. On paper this may not appear to come off. In an enlightened performance it unquestionably does. It is the extreme rarity of enlightened performances that inhibits its general recognition.

No opera composer, however gifted, can construct a great opera on a ramshackle or broken-backed libretto. This applies to Handel as to everyone else. All too often his librettos are condemned, lock, stock, and barrel, as complex, obscure, and absurd. Complex they are, when read in the study; a little thought will show that this was inevitable. It would be idle to deny a fair ration of obscurity and absurdity, especially in the late operas. But the best of them, when clothed in music, are not only perfectly clear in the theatre; they show a high degree of technical skill in terms of their peculiar convention, which as we have seen required a cunning deployment of incident and climax to allow plot and characters to develop in fruitful conjunction and to ensure that the characters spin the plot rather than vice versa. Because of their importance and the neglect or contempt that has been their fate, Handel's librettos receive close attention in this book. The chapter on each opera begins with a detailed summary in which the full stage directions, often omitted by Chrysander, are supplied (in italics) from Handel's autograph or the printed text on sale in the theatre,[11] and a critical examination of the libretto's quality and the source from which it was derived.

Most operas, even in Italy, were based on refurbished librettos, and very few new ones were written for London. Certain limitations, general and local,

[11] Most directions are taken from the English version printed opposite the Italian; where none exists, as in *Almira, Rodrigo, Agrippina,* and *Silla,* or where the English version omits them, they are translated.

need to be borne in mind here. Every text had to be specially tailored to the cast who were to sing it. This depended on the size of the company (which could compel the elimination of one or more characters in an old libretto), the pitch of the voices, and their relative ability, all of which the composer and his poet had to take into account. In London there was an additional factor, the unfamiliarity of the Italian language. Although librettos were printed with an English translation for following in the theatre, audiences could not be expected to appreciate the finer points. Consequently, while the number of arias varied little from continental practice as shown in the source librettos, there was growing pressure for the shortening of recitatives. After about 1730 this threatened to make the plot impenetrable, and sometimes it succeeded.

*   All Handel's librettos were based on earlier literary or historical material; with the exception of *Agrippina* and *Rinaldo*, and possibly *Il pastor fido* and *Silla*, none was specifically written for him. The others were adaptations by theatre poets. The originals have now been identified, though in a few cases (*Muzio Scevola*, *Giulio Cesare*) some intermediate version may remain to be unearthed. Many of them had been set by several composers, and Handel's was seldom the final grappling with the material. We do not know how often he was responsible for the choice of subject; in many instances this seems likely. Reinhard Strohm in a fascinating article[12] has suggested that during his Italian years he collected printed librettos with a view to future use, and continued to do so on later excursions to the continent. Six of his operas are based on librettos written between 1703 and 1710 by Antonio Salvi, the Medici court poet whom he must have met in Florence, and two others, *Radamisto* and *Floridante*, use adaptations made in Tuscany. *Alessandro* and *Admeto* came via Hanover; *Ottone* he picked up in Dresden, where he had seen Lotti's original setting; the source librettos of *Lotario*, *Poro*, *Ezio*, *Arianna*, and *Alcina*, some of which he may have heard in the theatre, he probably acquired in Italy in 1729.

We have little evidence—and that entirely circumstantial—about his relations with the theatre poets. No correspondence survives, such as that with Jennens over *Belshazzar*, and probably none ever existed. The composer and his collaborators were resident in the same city and can have had little inducement to correspond about local adjustments, and still less to discuss aesthetic issues. The poets chiefly responsible for the London adaptations were Giacomo Rossi, Nicola Haym, and Paolo Rolli; some of the attributions are doubtful and others unknown. Rossi's methods are difficult to assess, since the models for his three early librettos, if any, remain unknown; but Handel must have been closely concerned, for all three contain aria texts taken in whole or part from works he had written in Italy. These librettos show little feeling for character or dramatic design. If Rossi resumed the collaboration after Haym's death in 1729, which is not fully established, he adapted himself, perhaps at Handel's instigation, to the methods of Haym rather than Rolli.

The approach of these two men was sharply contrasted. Rolli, who fancied himself as a poet and published some of his librettos independently as well as in the bilingual theatre versions, preserved a few lines of recitative from his models but nearly always rewrote the aria texts. It is clear from one of his epigrams, published posthumously in *Marziale in Albion* (1776), that he took a

---

[12] 'Händel und seine italienischen Operntexte', *Händel-Jahrbuch*, xxi/xxii (1975–6), 101–59; *Essays*, 34–79.

cynical view of his task, regarding it as ill-rewarded hackwork. He was a friend of Giuseppe Bononcini, for whom he perhaps took more trouble, and secretly if not openly hostile to Handel. His correspondence with Giuseppe Riva, the Modenese diplomatic representative in London, reveals him as a devious character with a propensity for obscure allusions, not absent from his librettos. In those he prepared for Handel he never failed to muddle the development of the plot and the motivation of the characters, with the result that every product of their collaboration is seriously flawed.

Haym, who has cut a poor figure with posterity, was a man of very different calibre. A cellist, composer, book-collector, and antiquarian rather than a man of letters (he left a remarkable library), he had been a member of Ottoboni's orchestra in Rome before coming to London as chamber musician to the Duke of Bedford in 1700. He played a significant part in establishing opera in London.[13] For several possible reasons—because he was himself a musician, or took a more modest attitude to his duties, or proved temperamentally more compatible—Haym's collaboration with Handel was infinitely more fruitful than Rolli's. All the masterpieces of the Royal Academy years are based on Haym's librettos, or rather on his skilful adaptation of the work of others. While his abridgement of the recitative (except in *Tamerlano*) was severe and occasionally cut the corners of the plot too fine, unlike Rolli he retained many aria texts, and so preserved much of the quality of his sources. Since Salvi, Piovene, and others were competent practitioners, Handel generally received from Haym a workmanlike text with a coherent plot and consistent characters.

What we should like to know of course is the extent to which Handel was personally responsible for the London alterations. We do have some pointers. There are several instances, for example in *Radamisto* and *Sosarme*, where his libretto borrows a text from a source with which he is known to have been acquainted; he is more likely than the poet to have suggested this. Eisenschmidt[14] was the first to point out that additional or substituted arias inserted in the London librettos, especially those by Haym, conform to a definite pattern. The majority of them have a powerful emotional content, giving direct expression to grief, longing, remorse, or some other passion. They often replace decorative or neutral pieces, vague generalizations, far-fetched similes, and mythological metaphors—the space-fillers that formed the staple fare of pasticcios. By the same token they offer enlarged opportunities for characterization. Since an instant response to concrete rather than abstract imagery is one of the most striking features of Handel's style at all periods, and in view of his profound interest in all the workings of human nature, there is a strong probability that these new texts were included at his instigation.[15]

Sometimes the autographs confirm this. The most famous and one of the most dramatically potent arias in *Rodelinda*, 'Dove sei?', occurs neither in the source libretto nor in Handel's first draft; he inserted it during one of his revisions, and modified it more than once later. It is impossible to believe that, had it been present in Haym's original text, Handel would have left it out, or that Haym would have supplied it unasked. The autographs tell us a great

---

[13] See Chapter 9.
[14] See Bibliography.
[15] It may be worth remarking that Haym's librettos for Ariosti (Bononcini apparently refused to work with him) are much less effective, perhaps because Ariosti exercised less control.

deal about Handel's struggles with his librettos; many examples are cited in the following pages. The most remarkable instance is afforded by *Tamerlano*: after composing the entire opera to one libretto, Handel incorporated large sections of another on the same subject only weeks or even days before the performance, and continued to make major alterations up to the last moment.

He was clearly more attracted by the older type of libretto, with its admission of humorous, grotesque, and supernatural elements, than by the rationalist style of the reformers Zeno and Metastasio. At least fourteen of his librettos hark back to the seventeenth century, though some were updated, and others to the first decade of the eighteenth. This was as much a matter of temperament as of generation. The strong romantic cast of Handel's imagination, conspicuous in nocturnal and sleep scenes and throughout the magic operas, must have been repelled by the stilted characters and moralizing tone of Metastasio's librettos. He set three of them, much cut down,[16] in 1728–31 when they were the fashionable pabulum of continental composers, but moved sharply away later. It is easy to see why. Metastasio, very much the professional man of letters, typified the aesthetic standards of the age, which ranked the composer beneath the poet and the note lower than the word. He attracted musicians on account of the admirable lyric poetry of his aria texts (Schubert and Rossini were still setting them a century later); but he considered his dramas capable of being staged without music, as they sometimes were, and laid them out in a form that was not only literary but slow-moving, verbose, predictable in its patterned symmetry, and infused with a strong ethical tone designed to lay down standards of conduct, based on the old Roman virtues, for his princely patrons. Above all, he manoeuvred his characters like puppets on a political chessboard, subordinating their behaviour to the laboured ramifications of the plot, with the result that for all his edifying intentions they are apt to emerge as morally contemptible.[17] This is the antithesis of Handel's approach, which in his greatest operas concentrates on some central facet of human experience—Cleopatra's eternal seductiveness, the mutual devotion of a loving couple, or a parent and child in the face of political oppression and overwhelming odds—and projects it in music of timeless spiritual grandeur.

Handel's rejection of the Metastasian ideal is the crucial factor that distinguishes him from his contemporaries and in the last resort, thanks to his inventive genius, raises him far above them. As Strohm has shown in a penetrating study,[18] the literary bias of the reform librettists was congenial to the Italian public and accepted without question by leading composers, whose first concern was not to release the emotional content of the arias, still less to use them for the development of character over the full span of the opera, but to offer a careful and accurate declamation of the texts. 'The Italian public regarded the singer more as a kind of acoustic instrument for reciting poetry, distinct from his or her role.' There could be no question here of the dissolution of drama in music. The composers became servants where they should have been masters. The prescription of a subsidiary role for music provides too damp a soil for the spontaneous combustion of great opera: the

---

[16] Eisenschmidt suggests that Handel himself may have shortened many scenes in his later librettos, since no literary skill was required. This is possible, but we have no proof.

[17] For examples see Dean, *Handel and the Opera Seria*, 56 ff.

[18] *Italienische Oper*, especially 171–211; *Essays*, 213–48.

hundreds of settings of Metastasio texts include not a single acknowledged   *
masterpiece. It was Metastasio and the composers who treated him with
excessive respect, notably his favourite Hasse, who sounded the knell of *opera
seria* later in the century.

Handel's audience varied according to the country for which he was writing.
The ungainly mixture of heroic attitudes, elaborate spectacle (including
ballet), and broad farce, characteristic of *Almira* and the contemporary work
of Keiser and Mattheson, was the preferred diet of the citizens of Hamburg.
Rodrigo, written for a theatre under court protection, conforms closely to the
mainstream convention, whereas *Agrippina* reflects the sophisticated taste of a
city with a long tradition of public opera-going. London had no such
tradition; Italian opera was still a novelty in 1710.[19] To some extent Handel
had to create his own audience. It came predominantly from the nobility, the
upper ranks of the middle class (such as the future Mrs Delany and her
family), and the numerous foreign residents. The average British citizen's
attitude is probably represented by Byrom's notorious epigram about Handel
and Bononcini and Johnson's later reference to 'an exotick and irrational
entertainment', though the wider public, then as now, enjoyed the gossip and
scandal engendered by the leading singers. Hellmuth Christian Wolff's
contention[20] that *opera seria* attracted a broad spectrum of society, and
Strohm's remark[21] that it fulfilled the functions now associated with films and
television, may be true of the continent but have no relevance to London.
Until the disastrous rivalry inspired by the Opera of the Nobility in 1733 the
Haymarket was the only theatre in the kingdom to mount Italian opera.
Inevitably it was not cheap; that alone must have restricted audiences. It is as
if the only British opera-house open today were Covent Garden, with its
economics geared to Joan Sutherland and Luciano Pavarotti.

Apart from his cosmopolitan background, though perhaps in some obscure
way connected with it, Handel possessed a peculiar and well-nigh unique
power of assimilation. As he moved through his operatic career of more than
thirty-five years he neither discarded the styles and methods fashionable in his
youth, whether acquired in Germany, Italy, or England, nor eschewed the
innovations of his juniors. He retained the first and adopted the second, not
simply making room for them alongside each other but drawing out their
essence, so that, while they remain perfectly recognizable, the result is always
his own. The contrapuntal intricacy and occasional contorted chromaticism
of his German predecessors, the lyrical melody and graceful dance measures
of Gasparini's generation, the mannered irregularities of Alessandro Scarlatti,
the new style of the 1720s with its emphasis on long melodies and a
homophonic chordal accompaniment, and the English features of false
relations, idiosyncratic word-setting, and the idyllic pastoral—all remained, in
however refined a form, essential features of his style to the end of his life. He
never abandoned the continuo aria, the ground bass, the canto fermo, or the
fugato aria at a time when his colleagues, on the continent and in England,

[19] See Chapter 9.
[20] 'Das Opernpublikum der Barockzeit', *Festschrift Hans Engel zum 70. Geburtstag* (Kassel, 1964),
442–52.
[21] *Italienische Oper* 11 f.

were approaching a rococo idiom little different from that of J. C. Bach or the young Mozart. Yet his musical personality is so strong that we are never conscious of any discrepancy.

His treatment of the orchestra was exceptionally inventive even in a period when semi-obsolete instruments persisted alongside novelties like the clarinet. Here he learned something from the Hamburg composers, especially Keiser. While his basic orchestra of strings, oboes, bassoons, and continuo, enlarged on occasion by both types of flute, horns, and trumpets, remained that of the period, he sometimes expanded it with more exotic additions. Alto flute (traversa bassa), flageolet, clarinets, harp, a whole family of recorders, and the specially invented violetta marina appear in the operas, together with the viola da gamba and instruments of the lute family (as late as 1741). *Giulio Cesare* is by far the earliest opera to use two pairs of horns of different pitch. More striking than any innovation however is Handel's extraordinarily keen ear for the texture of sound, employed both for pictorial and dramatic purposes. The nature music in a dozen operas calls into play all manner of delicate instrumental nuances, from the pointillistic echoes of 'Con rauco mormorio' (*Rodelinda*) to the haunting poetry of recorders, horns, echoes, and string pedals of 'Senza procella ancora' (*Poro*). On the other hand the muted upper strings, pizzicato basses, and doleful bassoon suspensions in 'Scherza infida' (*Ariodante*) paint an internal picture of despair and disillusion. Handel's bassoons are generally tragic or pastoral, sometimes rumbustious, never comic. He uses transverse flutes and recorders in quite different contexts; to substitute the former for the latter, even with modern strings, is a major solecism. His doublings, especially where they involve flutes or recorders, are precisely calculated and produce a blend with a quality of its own. Seven different instruments are featured in pairs in *Teseo*, and a second orchestra on stage in at least three operas, most notably in *Giulio Cesare*. Handel's scoring is always apt to the context, a point that can work negatively, for example in the claustrophobic *Tamerlano* with its sparing use of woodwind and total absence of brass instruments, at a time when they had become regular members of the band.

No discussion of the sound world of Handel's operas can overlook his treatment of the solo voice. His years in Italy and long association with the greatest exponents gave him complete control of an art that intensive specialist training had developed to a peak of sophistication, virtuosity, and expressiveness. So sensitive was he to the 'feel' of an individual voice that we can sometimes identify the singer for whom a detached aria was composed from the music alone. Perhaps only Mozart among opera composers has equalled his mastery of the voice both as an instrument and as a vehicle for characterization. The two functions of course are inseparable, and equally dependent on pitch. Here again—not that he had any choice—Handel operated within the conventions of his age. As is well known, heroic male parts in *opera seria*—and the great majority of male parts are heroic—were the inalienable prerogative of sopranos and altos. With rare exceptions tenors and basses were confined to old men, tyrants, and servants, and regarded as subsidiary in status both on and off stage (their salaries were much lower). The high voices were by no means all castratos; many male parts were written for women, and many women specialized in breeches roles. (The inverse of this, the assumption of women's parts by castratos, enforced in Rome and some other Italian cities by Papal objection to women in the theatre, fortunately does not concern us.) Handel of course made the most of such contrasts in vocal timbre as were available to him, and some of his operas cater for all four vocal pitches, but the emphasis was always on the high registers.

There is no reason to suppose that he considered this a limitation. The decisive factor for him was not sex but pitch. He regularly interchanged such roles between castratos and women, but his revivals supply no known instance of an alto part, or even an alto aria, being transposed down an octave for a bass. In the less numerous male soprano roles he did occasionally allow such a transposition in a limited range of arias, chiefly demands for vengeance. Far more often, if a soprano was not available, he preferred to write new music. There were sound reasons for such fastidiousness. Most singers of heroic parts, especially leading castratos, were renowned for expressiveness and breath-control rather than an extensive compass. This was the age not of the top C but of the exquisitely modulated *messa di voce*, on which all singing teachers laid emphasis. Senesino's voice in particular had a restricted range, and the long and taxing divisions Handel wrote for him are largely confined within the interval of a sixth. For natural male voices he used a totally different style featuring a striding coloratura based as much on leaps and arpeggios as on stepwise movement and sometimes covering up to two octaves.

It should be obvious that the two are not interchangeable, and that octave transposition subverts the characterization and the texture of the entire opera, smudging the rich palette like a coarse reproduction of a great picture. By placing the coloratura in the most awkward part of the voice, especially for baritones, it turns ardent youth into querulous or flatulent age, wheedling hypocrites into blustering buffoons, and expressions of noble defiance into gargling tirades. It sometimes takes the vocal line below the written bass, and almost invariably leaves yawning gaps in the fabric of sound. In duets where the male voice is the higher, which are not infrequent, it inverts the parts and destroys the intervallic structure. It is an oblique tribute to Handel's genius that such disfigurement has not driven his operas out of the theatre. Its abandonment even in Germany, where it was regular practice until very recently, should remove one obstacle to the emergence of the operas at their full stature.

Additional Notes

* (p. 5) An exception might be made for recent productions of *Teseo*, *Ottone*, and *Radamisto* conducted by Nicholas McGegan; but they were not mounted by a regular opera company and had only a limited number of performances.

* (p. 16) The publication of Handel's Italian librettos and their sources in twin volumes has been undertaken by Lorenzo and Giuseppina La Face Bianconi; only the first pair of volumes, dealing with the operas up to 1725, has so far appeared. Handel's pasticcios are covered, but not the Hamburg operas or Handel's subsequent revivals. The librettos for Handel's performances, including revivals but not pasticcios, are reproduced in facsimile in 13 volumes, edited by Ellen T. Harris. (See Bibliography, Appendix H.)

* (p. 19) *La clemenza di Tito* is perhaps an exception; but Mozart noted that Metastasio's text was converted into 'a true opera' by Caterino Mazzolà's alterations.

PERFORMANCE PRACTICE

OUR knowledge of performance practice in Handel's operas comes from a variety of scattered sources: general treatises and manuals, letters and personal reminiscences, and what can be deduced from scores and librettos. Although they supply a good deal of information, there are some tantalizing gaps; and much of what we do know needs careful application to a composer who was both atypical and a genius. We must read between the lines to detect any deviation from the normal.

Eighteenth-century aesthetics did not deal seriously with opera as an art. Writers of all kinds never tired of debating the relative status of poetry and music, but the standard of reference, as in all the arts, was the natural world. Music was assessed as an imitation of nature, including human nature, which it expressed according to the theory of the affections (*Affektenlehre*). No one considered the possibility that its union with drama might produce something greater than the sum of the parts; the crucial borderland remained unexplored. This is nowhere more apparent than in the writings of Burney, who left by far the fullest eighteenth-century account of Handel's operas, though he never heard any of them under the composer. He goes through each opera aria by aria, naming the singer rather than the character, and discusses the *Affekt* of each but never its position as part of a larger whole. To him the best opera is the one with the highest proportion of beautiful, inventive, and expressive arias. The theatrical aspect is ignored. Burney was not alone in this, but he was partly responsible for the lopsided view of the operas that we are concerned to refute. When contemporary writers ignored the whole for the part, and those who discussed one aspect took little account of the rest, it is doubly difficult for us to bring together in our minds two performing conventions, both long obscured by change and time. We can only discuss them separately before attempting to connect them.

The staging of Handel's operas has inspired one valuable monograph, Joachim Eisenschmidt's two-volume study (based on a Halle doctoral dissertation) *Die szenische Darstellung der Opern Händels auf der Londoner Bühne seiner Zeit* (Wolfenbüttel and Berlin, 1940–1). Eisenschmidt collected a great deal of information about the theatres of Handel's day, their size, equipment, and method of operation, administrative and technical, and about librettists, singers, and acting style. He cited the stage directions in Handel's librettos to pertinent effect, and drew some conclusions about textual changes, but did not attempt to investigate how all this was reflected in the music. (He might have followed up his work had he not been killed in Russia in 1942.) Further evidence can be found in books by theatre historians, notably Richard Southern's *Changeable Scenery* (London, 1952), and in scattered articles in *Theatre Notebook*, *Theatre Journal*, *Theatre Survey*, and *Theatre History Studies*. This too needs to be supplemented by study of the music.

The Baroque theatre employed no specialist producer or director. In opera that duty devolved on the librettist or theatre poet. Although he can never have exercised the authority of the powerful stage directors of today, we should not ignore his activities because so little evidence of them has survived. Someone must have taken care to co-ordinate exits and entrances and the movements of singers, scenery, and machines. The letters of Metastasio show him much concerned with such matters. Unable to be present at a production of *Demetrio* in Rome in 1732, he sent detailed instructions to the singer Marianna Benti Bulgarelli about stage business, properties, the depth of stage to be used for different scenes, and other matters. In 1748 he supplied even fuller particulars, including a scenic and movement plan for the whole opera, to the Dresden theatre poet Pasquini for the production of Hasse's *Demofoonte*.[1] Rehearsal time in London was very short; some of Handel's operas went on stage within a week or two of the completion of the score, and the copyists were set to work on the earlier acts before Handel had finished the last (the performing scores show many signs of last-minute alterations and adjustments). The mounting of a new opera must have been a frantic business. Handel may have owed a good deal to Haym, with his additional experience as continuo cellist and organizer of some of the earliest Italian operas in London. The librettist-producer was responsible for the printed text and its stage directions, which were not always those of his source. Great care was taken to make these librettos accurate and to update them for revivals. They served as something between a programme and a prompt copy, nearly always listing the cast and indicating cuts, and probably represent very closely what was performed, though of course they could not take account of changes due to sudden illness.

The leading Italian scenic designers and engineers had a European reputation, and many of their designs for continental opera-houses were illustrated in prints. There are also a number for the Hamburg opera, published as frontispieces to printed librettos; Eisenschmidt in his second volume reproduces seven of them, including two for Handel's *Rinaldo* (1715) and *Giulio Cesare* (1725) (see Plate 8), as well as dazzling views of the stage and auditorium at the Dresden production of the Pallavicino–Lotti *Teofane* (the source of *Ottone*) in 1719 (see Plates 3 and 4). Unfortunately we have nothing comparable for the Haymarket in London or any pictorial evidence for Handel's operas, apart from one or two caricatures. The etching by Vanderbank, possibly based on Hogarth, reputed to show Senesino, Cuzzoni, and Berenstadt in *Flavio* and reproduced in Deutsch (opposite p. 129), is now thought to represent a scene in Ariosti's *Coriolano*. The frontispiece of an anonymous pamphlet, *An Epistle from S——r S——o to S——a F——a* (March

[1] Quoted by Eisenschmidt, ii. 8–10, 25–8.
[2] For a recently discovered libretto of *Radamisto* used as a prompt copy, see p. 354 and Plate 10.

1727), has a caricature of Senesino and Faustina Bordoni in *Admeto*. The Venetian scene-painters Marco Ricci and Giovanni Antonio Pellegrini were engaged by the Haymarket before Handel's arrival. Roberto Clerici designed a spectacular palace for *Pirro e Demetrio* in 1716[3] and 'a Magnificent Transparent Scene, exceeding in Length 30 Foot than any Scene ever before seen anywhere' for a concert on 21 March 1719.[4] This was doubtless connected with his appointment as scenic artist and machinist to the Royal Academy of Music, where he was responsible for the sets of Porta's *Numitore* and possibly *Radamisto*. Giovanni Niccolò Servandoni was employed as scene-painter at the Haymarket in 1721–3,[5] Joseph Goupy and Peter Tillemans about 1724–5[6]. Goupy was credited in the printed librettos of *Admeto* and *Riccardo Primo* in 1727.

Not every opera had new scenery. It was often supplied out of stock, especially when the theatre was doing badly, and it is sometimes possible from scene-headings in librettos to identify sets from an earlier production.[7] Many of them were generalized—a royal hall, an antechamber, a pastoral prospect with cottages—and not intended to suggest a specific locality. But quite a few of Handel's operas were dignified with new designs, a privilege seldom accorded to those of his rivals. During his first London period (1711–17) the management spent much effort and money on spectacular machines and transformations; the magic operas *Rinaldo*, *Teseo*, and *Amadigi* all had new scenery, from which a great effect was expected. During the Royal Academy period (1720–8) attention was directed more to the ear than the eye; the sensational element was supplied by the singers. There were no magic operas or flown machines, but several operas—*Radamisto*, *Giulio Cesare*, *Alessandro*, *Admeto*, and *Riccardo Primo* among them—contained scenes calculated to make a striking impact. After 1730 the emphasis reverted to spectacle, though not to the same extent as twenty years earlier, as we can see by comparing the stage directions in the 1731 revival of *Rinaldo* with the original production. Several operas of this period, notably *Poro*, required machines for military operations, and new magic effects were introduced in *Orlando* and later *Alcina*. By that time Handel was working at Covent Garden, where he must have reaped benefit from the elaborate facilities developed by John Rich for his harlequinades, the immensely popular circus of the age.

An inventory of the backstage contents of Covent Garden in 1743[8] lists the scenery, costumes, properties, and stage machinery in extraordinary detail, sometimes specifying the operas to which they applied (many were for pantomimes). Back-flats, wings, borders, cloudings, transparencies, and 'pieces' include falling rocks for *Alcina*, two oxen, four furrows, and six columns to Fame's temple for *Giustino*, a ground piece, wings, 'the compass border', and a pyramid for *Atalanta*, and a whole range of special features for *Ariodante*, which though not a magic opera had one of the most splendid productions of the period. They included eight moonlight wings for Act II and a palace with staircases and a gallery for the stage orchestra, with its own wings and borders, in the last scene. The mass of machinery on and under the

---

[3] See p. 163.
[4] Michael Tilmouth in *RMA Research Chronicle*, i (1961), 105.
[5] *Exhibition Catalogue*, 215.
[6] Deutsch, 176.
[7] See p. 158.
[8] Add MS 12201, ff. 34–73.

stage—pulleys, chains, ropes, swivels, cogs, weights, scaffolds—included 'the great counterpoize to all the traps and iron hooks 487 lb', 'the counterpoize to front lamps 170 lb', and barrels for operating the cylinders that represented the heaving sea on the back stage.[9]

The Haymarket must have been similarly equipped, for it employed equally sophisticated effects, including a fountain on stage. Coloured transparencies and cut-outs were used, for example in *Admeto* when Hercules descends to hell and engages in battle with the Furies. Thomas Lediard introduced a number of refinements at the Hamburg Opera, where in the 1720s he was both scenic designer and director.[10] He specialized in what he called 'the Transparent Theatre', which evidently employed drop-curtains with cut-outs as well as genuine transparencies with magic-lantern projections. He published two vast folios with pull-outs illustrating his designs, eighteen in all, for the Hamburg Opera between 1724 and 1730, most of them pyrotechnical displays for royal occasions.[11] Some of these were also issued in England, and another illustrated the printed libretto of Lampe's *Britannia*, produced unsuccessfully at the Little Haymarket Theatre in 1732. Lediard wrote the text himself and furnished it with a long preface. His stage fireworks do not seem to have caught on in London; those that celebrated the Prince of Wales's wedding in the last scene of *Atalanta*, which would certainly be ruled out in today's Covent Garden, were the work of 'the ingenious Mr. Worman'.

All scenery was painted in elaborate perspective, especially the wings, which at the Haymarket were set square to the stage (see Plate 2). The aim of the entire production was not to create realistic illusion, which would have been impossible when the singers entered between the wings and stood near them, but to excite wonder and delight. The conception was not static but dynamic: the opening and closing of wings and shutters was designed to carry the imagination of the audience from place to place. The technique resembles that of the cinema rather than the modern theatre.

The lighting, mostly by candles but also employing oil lamps, to judge from the nightly payments specified in the Haymarket accounts of 1716–17, though primitive by modern standards, permitted a fair degree of flexibility. Footlights were in use in London by 1709, and the ramp on which they were mounted could be lowered for night scenes. The wings contained 'scene-ladders' carrying an array of tin candle-holders fitted with shields or blinds. They were operated from below the stage, and could be dipped, reducing the light without disturbance to scene-changes. When a sudden increase of light was required, as often happened in magic operas, sulphur was thrown on the candles. It would appear from the Covent Garden inventory that the chandeliers that supplied the principal stage lighting could be raised to the flies. Nocturnal scenes were popular in opera, and much care was lavished on them; there are memorable examples in Act III of *Rodelinda* ('a very dark prison') and Act II of *Floridante*, where black wings may have been employed. But the stage was never completely dark; the house lights were kept burning to allow the audience to follow the action in their librettos.

[9] Such an appliance survives in the Drottningholm Theatre today.

[10] See pp. 505–7, and *Theatre Notebook*, ii (1948), 42–57.

[11] *Eine Collection verschiedene Vorstellungen und Illuminationen ... Auf dem Hamburgischen Schau-Platze unter der Direktion, Und Von der Invention Thomas Lediard's ...* (Hamburg, 1729; greatly enlarged, 1730). In the first volume he describes himself as secretary to the British ambassador, in the second also as director of the opera-house. (See Plate 16.)

A French traveller, Pierre Jacques Fougeroux, who visited London in the spring and early summer of 1728 and saw three Handel operas at the King's Theatre,[12] was not at all impressed by their visual aspect and thought they ought to have been billed as concerts in costume. This needs to be received with caution. The Royal Academy was on its last legs and in no position to spend much on scenery; the two new operas, *Siroe* and *Tolomeo*, were given with old sets, and the one spectacular scene in *Admeto*, a revival, may have been cut down (or ignored by Fougeroux as an exception). Although a keen observer, Fougeroux was no musician; he had never heard of Handel and spelt his name phonetically 'Indel'. He was accustomed to the exceptionally lavish productions at the Paris Opéra with their numerous machines, choruses, ballets, and army of supers, none of which he would have encountered at the King's Theatre in 1728. He supplies us with one detail of Haymarket practice, that a little bell was rung, for the benefit of the stage staff, at scene changes.

The performances might have struck us as stereotyped and unnatural, but certainly not as concerts in costume. Singers were frequently accused of exaggeration in their acting. The style was related to that of spoken tragedy, which involved a whole repertory of conventional movements and gestures in the use of head, body, and limbs.[13] In solo scenes the actor, and no doubt the singer, would advance to the apron and address the audience. If necessary a scene-change could begin behind him, a practice for which there is some evidence on the continent, though it is unlikely that much stage business was permitted while a major character was singing. The action was arrested, but the drama continued in the music. In scenes involving several characters there is no reason to suppose that the singer ignored his colleagues to any greater extent than in opera today. *Opera seria* contains many arias where a singer addresses two others in turn, whether phrase by phrase or in alternate sections. This involved movement and gesture—acting in the full sense of the term. Often the gestures were written into the music: detached exclamations like 'Empio!', 'Barbaro!', and so on positively demand physical action.

In whatever they did on stage singers were expected to express the passion or *Affekt* appropriate to their arias, to recreate it in theatrical, not realistic terms and if possible raise it to a higher degree. Some of their movements had a prescribed association. This is often only what one would expect: turning the back signified contempt, leaning on a table, dejection. In ceremonial or judgement scenes monarchs sat on thrones, which were carried in by supers or revealed by the withdrawal of shutters. An abrupt rise to a standing posture indicated anger or excitement, though during arias, his own or those of others, the monarch apparently stood to form part of the tableau. According to Metastasio the stage position of the characters was hierarchic, the highest in rank placed stage right; he emphasizes that status derives from the rank of the character, not the singer. The modern idea of the leading actor moving to stage centre or upstaging his colleagues may be a corruption of this.

Although the acting was formal and stylized, in one respect it was less remote from the audience than we might expect. Nearly all *opera seria*

[12] See W. Dean, 'A French Traveller's View of Handel's Operas', M & L lv (1974), 172–8; reprinted in *Essays on Opera* (Oxford, 1990).

[13] A series of articles by Dene Barnett in *Theatre Research International* (May 1977, ff.), 'The Performance Practice of Acting: the Eighteenth Century', is relevant to opera as well as spoken drama.

characters were of royal or exalted rank, and they were expected to comport themselves with suitable dignity, recognized as such by their real-life counterparts in the boxes. This is implicit in Metastasio's whole approach to the libretto. Opera originated in Italian courts, and although public theatres in seventeenth-century Venice introduced a more bourgeois milieu Handel's London audience was predominantly aristocratic. Comic sub-plots with servants making fun of their masters, a staple ingredient throughout the seventeenth century and surviving later in Italy (they were eventually hived off into the intermezzos), were early eliminated in London; *Serse* is Handel's only opera of this type. The singers did not share the low social repute of straight actors and actresses. They received princely salaries and moved in aristocratic, even royal, circles. George I stood godfather to Durastanti's daughter in March 1721. Anastasia Robinson was the darling of the aristocracy and married into the peerage. Outside the opera-house leading singers were often employed to entertain the nobility at private parties, and in the off-season were to be found at fashionable spas like Bath, Bristol, and Tunbridge Wells.

Stage costumes were also related to contemporary life. Here however there was a discrepancy between the sexes. The women wore hooped dresses very like those on view in ballrooms. It is on record that Cuzzoni's brown dress in *Rodelinda*, despite her lack of physical appeal, set a fashion among the young. Male costumes were more stylized, borrowing a number of features from classical Roman attire: breastplates, greaves, short tasselled tunics, long cloaks, and helmets with towering plumes. Portraits of leading castratos show them with a kind of posterior skirt or train, perhaps for domestic scenes. They wore short wigs and carried swords—as did the men in the audience, who were known on occasion to bring them into play in scuffles in the theatre. Oriental potentates were distinguished by turbans, richer brocades, fur-trimmed cloaks, and curved scimitars.

It is not clear to what extent, if at all, singers provided their own costumes. The accounts for the King's Theatre in 1716–17[14] include payments for wigs, gloves, and stockings, chiefly for the castratos, and stays for the ladies, as well as feathers and occasional small wardrobe bills, but more substantial garments are not mentioned. A notice in *The Daily Courant* on 13 and 14 February 1722 invited applications 'to undertake the furnishing and providing of Cloths for the Operas against next Winter'.[15] In 1727 Owen Swiney tried repeatedly to persuade the directors to engage the Valeriani brothers, whom he described as 'the Two greatest Men in their profession', as scene-painters and costume-designers. At £600 a year he was sure they would save the Academy money.[16] The idea was apparently to have the clothes made in Italy. The Academy did not take it up.

Supers appeared regularly in the operas; the 1716–17 accounts record payments to them for every performance, though the sums were trifling. Women of rank were attended by child pages who managed their trains. Male attendants escorted princes, guarded prisoners (characters under arrest often go off accompanied by 'some of the guards'), and took part in processions and battle scenes.[17] These were often quite elaborate, and more realistic than the

---

[14] See p. 164.   [15] Gibson, *The Royal Academy*, 161.
[16] Ibid, 257–8, 375.
[17] For their activities in *Radamisto*, see p. 354.

movements of principals. They made a great deal of noise (superimposed on the trumpet-and-drum sinfonias) and were reported to be audible as far afield as Charing Cross. Magic operas required much activity from the supers (furies, spirits, genii, etc.) and sometimes the principals too, as well as the scenery and machines, whether flown or manoeuvred on the back stage, where a large space was kept clear for them at the Haymarket. In *Rinaldo*, *Silla*, and *Giustino* boats set sail with singing characters on board; in *Rinaldo* mermaids (in traps) danced up and down in the sea. Disembarcation from ships (*Scipione*, *Poro*, *Arianna*, *Deidamia*) and the crossing of bridges by military forces (*Giulio Cesare*, *Poro*) took place on the back stage behind the wings and may have begun in the added room that increased the depth of the stage to more than twice that of the auditorium (see Plate 2). In some continental opera-houses, though so far as we know not in London, a kind of stage sergeant-major was employed to organize battles and tattoos.

Discussion of the musical performance must focus first on the singers. Almost throughout his operatic career, and particularly in the London operas covered by this volume, Handel had at his disposal the greatest singers in Europe at a time when the art had reached one of its peaks. We cannot recover their voices, but we do know the technical aspects on which teachers laid most stress and which are repeatedly evoked by the music of Handel and his contemporaries. Apart from a few sepulchral basses like Carli and Montagnana, it was not an age that cultivated extremes of compass, as did that of Mozart or Bellini. The top C—at least as written—was rare, though pitch was lower than today. Except in *Almira*, where Hamburg pitch must have been even lower, Handel wrote a top C for only three singers, and then with extreme rarity: the sopranos Elisabetta Pilotti-Schiavonetti (once in *Rinaldo*) and Anna Strada (once in *Partenope*) and the exceptionally high castrato Gioacchino Conti (one aria each in *Atalanta* and *Arminio*). Carestini had the widest compass of his castratos (two octaves). The contraltos all had a moderate range, and he never took a tenor above a'. Most of his basses, notably Boschi, would be classed as baritones today. The extreme notes, if they occurred at all, were seldom used.

The whole art of singing lay in brilliant and flexible divisions, breath control, *messa di voce*, and the choice of tasteful graces and ornaments. The quality most admired was expressiveness. None of this is beyond a properly trained modern singer, provided he or she masters the (unwritten) graces and ornaments. Not only were they considered an essential component of the style; without them the music sounds bare, flat, and tedious, especially in da capo repeats. The Deutsche Grammophon recording of *Giulio Cesare* under Karl Richter, sung complete with no decoration whatever, is a deadly illustration of this. The requirement is now widely recognized; but the pendulum has recently swung to the other extreme. Conductors and singers, aware that such matters were left to the taste of the individual, have assumed a comprehensive licence to do whatever they please, recomposing the vocal line in da capo sections, interpolating long and grotesquely elaborate cadenzas, and sometimes defacing the A sections so that the melody is never heard as written. There were undoubtedly tasteless singers in Handel's time, but it is unlikely that they indulged in the mannerisms of Gluck, Mozart, Rossini, Donizetti, and Bellini, a not uncommon occurrence today.

There are several guides to contemporary practice. One of the most useful is Pier Francesco Tosi's *Opinioni de' cantori antichi e moderni*, published in 1723 and translated into English by J. E. Galliard (as *Observations on the Florid Song*) in 1742 and into German by J. F. Agricola in 1757, each with additional notes and examples. It should however be borne in mind that Tosi, a castrato, was writing in his old age as a *laudator temporis acti* (he was born in 1654) and to some extent reflecting a practice that was already obsolescent. Another relevant manual is J. A. Hiller's *Anweisung zum musikalisch-zierlichen Gesange*, which though published as late as 1780 largely illustrates Baroque principles. Many writers between these dates, for example Quantz and C. P. E. Bach, also throw light on the matter.[18]

On all major points they are in complete agreement. The purpose of decoration was to increase the expressiveness of the aria, in strict accordance with the *Affekt*, while allowing the singer to demonstrate his technical skill and his taste. To alter or obscure the substance of the original, especially by the substitution of a new vocal line, is to defeat the whole object of the exercise. It is not decoration but ham-fisted smudging. Hiller says that the A section should be sung as written, and Quantz agrees: 'Variations are only to be introduced after the simple Air has been heard first, otherwise it will be impossible for the Hearer to distinguish the latter from the former; nor does an Air, compos'd in a pleasing and graceful Stile, require any such additions.' At first glance Tosi appears to allow a little more licence. He states that A sections 'require nothing but the simplest Ornaments, of a good Taste and few, that the Composition may remain simple, plain, and pure; in the second [the B section] they expect, that to this Purity some artful Graces be added, by which the Judicious may hear, that the Ability of the Singer is greater; and, in repeating the Air, he that does not vary it for the better, is no great Master'. This is presented from the singer's point of view rather than the composer's; we may question any singer's ability to vary Handel's music for the better. His A sections seldom require any alteration beyond the regulation cadential trill; the habit of filling in thirds and inserting appoggiaturas in the manner of the later eighteenth century merely weakens the line. The appoggiatura, a permissible ornament in the da capo, is obligatory only in recitative.

Although by their very nature vocal ornaments were seldom written down—they were treated as spontaneous improvisation and no doubt varied from performance to performance—a number of examples survive, including autograph additions by Handel to his own arias. A volume in the Bodleian Library contains early copies of five soprano arias from *Ottone*, transposed down for mezzo or alto. Handel added decoration to both sections of two of them and part of two more. They must have been intended for an English singer (an Italian would not have required them), and they were presumably never sung, since Handel never finished the job.[19] An aria in Handel's autograph from *Amadigi*, in the Fitzwilliam Museum, has a nicely decorated vocal line, though this is partly a recomposition.[20] These manuscripts are of prime import-

---

[18] See the article 'Improvisation' in *The New Grove*, from which many of the quotations here are taken.

[19] They are published by the Oxford University Press in *Three Ornamented Arias*, ed. W. Dean (London, 1976). See also pp. 447–9 and Ex. 52.

[20] See W. Dean, 'Vocal embellishment in a Handel aria' in *Essays on Opera* (paperback edition, 1993); also p. 289.

ance; they tell us much not only about Baroque practice but about Handel's own taste. Although the ornaments are sometimes very elaborate, especially in the slow *Ottone* aria 'Affanni del pensier', they never obliterate the original line; for all Handel's congenital urge to recompose when returning to old material, they remain ornaments. They retain the original compass almost throughout, raising it by no more than a tone, and that at a single climactic point in each aria. They often fill up rests, but leave a substantial section of the aria unembellished and are more sparing in B sections. They show an addiction to triplet decoration apparent in Handel's variation technique and his occasional modified repeat of a melody later in an aria. As we might expect, they are highly expressive, intensifying the emotion implicit in the *Affekt*, sometimes by means of bold harmonic clashes such as only the composer himself would be likely to venture on.

An aria by Giuseppe Vignati in a manuscript in the Library of Congress, with ornaments sung by Faustina Bordoni at a Milan performance in 1720, illustrates exactly the same points, including the extension of the compass by a tone at a single climax, except that the ornaments—and the aria—are less expressive.[21] Much other evidence points in the same direction. A few Handel arias exist in harpsichord arrangements with the words written or cued between the staves, leaving some doubt whether the ornaments were intended for voice or keyboard; they fit either equally well. One of these, from *Floridante*, is in Handel's autograph; another, from *Radamisto*, was copied by S2 for Jennens and is probably authentic. Three more, two from *Muzio Scevola* and one from *Radamisto*, all in transposed keys, exist in identical early copies in the Coke and Malmesbury Collections; one of them is certainly Handel's own work. A number of other arias in the same two collections and Lennard have inserted ornaments not by Handel but dating from his time or a little later. They are simpler, less ambitious, and more predictable, but after the same manner. None of these versions bears even a remote resemblance to the wild excursions above the stave and into alien styles heard for example in some recent productions.[22] There is not the slightest doubt which models should be followed in modern performances.

Cadenzas are another trap. Quantz says that all cadenzas for wind instruments, which include the voice, should be short enough to be taken in one breath. Singers did not always observe this, but there can be no justification in vocal cadenzas for the sort of excursion that provoked Handel's celebrated cry 'Welcome home, Mr Dubourg!' C. P. E. Bach protested that 'it is this embellishing alone, especially if it is coupled with a long and sometimes bizarrely ornamented cadenza, that often squeezes the bravos out of most listeners'. When a composer desired or permitted a cadenza he wrote a fermata. This could happen at the main cadence in either section of the aria and sometimes in both, but is by no means invariable in Handel. Where the A section has a fermata (or an Adagio) it should almost certainly be ignored until the da capo. Otherwise the flow of the aria is broken into sections in a manner on which Tosi animadverted with pointed irony. 'Generally speaking,

---

[21] See G. J. Buelow, 'A Lesson in Operatic Performance by Madame Faustina Bordoni', in *A Musical Offering, Essays in Honor of Martin Bernstein*, ed. E. H. Clinkscale and C. Brook (New York, 1977), 79–96.

[22] The first modern revival of a Handel opera by a major British company, *Giulio Cesare* at the London Coliseum in 1979, was an extreme example.

the Study of the Singers of the Present Times consists in terminating the Cadence of the first Part with an overflowing of Passages and Divisions at Pleasure, and the Orchestre waits; in that of the second the Dose is encreased, and the Orchestre grows tired; but on the last Cadence, the Throat is set a going, like a Weather-cock in a Whirlwind, and the Orchestre yawns.' So does the audience. Handel's autograph decorations contain only one slight cadential ornament, a bar long; Faustina's decorations to the Vignati aria include cadenzas to each part, with an alternative in the B section. All are short and easily manageable in a single breath.

Contemporary authorities agree in enjoining a cautious approach to embellishment, lest the *Affekt* or the principles of harmony be endangered or the intentions of the composer obscured. Too little is better than too much. In Quantz's opinion 'those [ornaments] that consist in a continual series of swift Notes or quick Passages, though ever so much admired by some, in general are not so pleasing as those of the more simple kind, the latter being more capable of touching the Heart', and he urges inexperienced performers in particular 'to prefer the Invention of the Composer to their own'.

One of the most important features of *opera seria* performance practice is the treatment of simple or secco recitative. The matter was for long bedevilled by later deviations, on the one hand the delayed cadence introduced in the second half of the eighteenth century, on the other the ponderous delivery of the Victorian oratorio, often accompanied by the organ. These malpractices were taken over when the operas were first revived. Although the historical evidence is perfectly clear, musicological excavation has only recently uncovered it.

Though conventionally notated in 4/4 bars, secco recitative was never sung in strict time; indeed it was not sung at all in the sense applicable to arias. It was defined as a form of musical speech and delivered *parlando*, not with the full voice. This had the advantage of making the words clear. The tempo was generally rapid, always fluid and flexible, varying in pace with the sense of the text. The singer took the lead here; it was for the continuo player to follow, slipping in his chords where he could and holding himself ready to react instantly to any change of pace. The habit of giving the notes their written value and emphasizing the first beat of the bar derived from nineteenth-century performances of oratorio in England and Germany (misconceived in Handel, most of whose oratorios are theatrical, not sacred); but it had evidently crept in, presumably from the church, as early as Tosi's time. He protested that 'it is insufferable to be any longer tormented in the Theatre with Recitatives, sung in the Stile of a Choir of Capuchin Friars'. Secco recitatives were never conducted, though that objectionable practice is not unknown today.

It was not the continuo harpsichordist's business to indulge in fantasies or extraneous flourishes, least of all after an aria; the next singer should attack his recitative at once. Broken chords and arpeggios were permitted—they could help the singer to find his note—but should be as short as possible, and excluded altogether in fast passages. The primary task of both player and singer was to press on with the action, and the latter had to be left free, or if necessary encouraged, to act with the voice. None of this was affected by the presence of a string bass player, generally a cello, who sat beside the harpsichord and read from the same music. It would not be difficult to synchronize his notes, which were cut off short, not held for their written length. Fougeroux, our only contemporary witness, says that the recitatives in the operas were accompanied by two harpsichords, presumably one for each speaker in a duologue, a cello, and an archlute. There is no evidence that Handel used a double bass in recitative. Fougeroux particularly mentions the detached treatment of the chords, which he found disagreeable, as one might expect from an ear accustomed to the slower, more measured tread of French recitative.

The vocal appoggiatura was obligatory at recitative cadences, which in Italian nearly always ended with a disyllable. Although this is now recognized, the full function of the appoggiatura in recitative is less appreciated. Its purpose was expressive, to articulate the sense of the verbal phrases, and it was by no means confined to cadences. A judicious admixture of appoggiaturas can bring long sections of recitative to life, especially when different forms are used, approaching the principal note from below or above and sometimes by a leap. They can be introduced at any point of punctuation, indicated by a short rest in the music, and sometimes when a note is repeated in the middle of a phrase. Telemann gives an example, with twelve appoggiaturas in nine bars, in the preface to *Der harmonische Gottesdienst*.[23] In free declamation they served to hold the recitative together by imposing a rhythmic pattern dependent on the sense of the words. Appoggiaturas were seldom written by the composer (there are a few exceptions in Handel), presumably because they often implied a harmonic clash that flouted strict rules but was allowed—even encouraged—in practice.

This applies particularly to cadences. Until the middle years of the century, when Handel's career was over, the cadential chords in theatre music were played as written, the dominant coinciding with the last accentuated syllable of the voice part, which carried the appoggiatura. Quantz and Hiller emphasize that this applied to accompanied recitatives as well. It probably held good in the chamber cantata and sometimes in oratorio, but not in church music where the continuo was played on the organ. When composers wanted a delayed cadence, for some special emphasis, they placed a rest before the dominant chord; there are examples in Telemann and a few in Handel. The elision of cadences where the written voice part fell by a third of course produced no clash with the appoggiatura. Theorists writing before 1750, all practical musicians—Tosi, Heinichen, Mattheson, Fux, Telemann, Quantz—leave no doubt that in cadences where the voice dropped by a fourth the clash between tonic and dominant harmony produced by the appoggiatura was perfectly acceptable. Heinichen found the foreshortened cadence illogical but called it a licence sanctioned by long use in the theatre. Fux, giving only shortened examples, declared that the object of recitative was less to satisfy the strict rules of harmony than to express the emotions. Dissonant appoggiaturas were a feature of Baroque performance. They sound far less harsh on contemporary than on modern instruments, and are barely perceptible when the chords are played lightly on the harpsichord. A good continuo player no doubt varied his approach, and could if he wished avoid the clash by playing a quick 4–3 progression on the dominant chord. Later in the century,

---

[23] Quoted in the article cited in the next note, pp. 393–4.

when the fortepiano and pianoforte began to replace the harpsichord, objection was taken to the discord. C. P. E. Bach and Marpurg complained in the 1760s that even very great composers of the previous generation offended against the rules of harmony by sounding dominant under tonic; and in the age of Mozart and Haydn the delayed cadence became the rule.

Perhaps no single aspect of performance practice has such a decisive effect, especially in a composer like Handel whose operas are fully articulated dramas. The delayed cadence introduces repeated stops and starts; the recitative, and with it the opera, proceeds with the spasmodic jerks of city traffic in the rush hour. Correct performance releases the natural momentum of the opera, so that tension is carried forward into the next movement, whether it is an aria or another recitative. One of the most hampering obstacles of the convention is dissolved. In a complete opera the saving of time can be enormous: the difference between the 1977 Birmingham production of *Giulio Cesare*, the first uncut stage revival of the 1724 score, and the Deutsche Grammophon recording of the same opera, admittedly a heavy and unstylish performance, was a full half-hour. The relative saving is even greater, for the whole balance between recitative and aria is transformed and the component parts assume a new and much more dynamic pattern. An additional advantage is a reduction in the demand for disfiguring cuts.[24]

The Haymarket orchestra, especially during the Royal Academy period, was famous throughout Europe. Uffenbach gave it high praise in 1710, when he heard *L'Idaspe fedele* conducted by Pepusch; most of the players, according to him, were German or French.[25] Quantz, who heard *Admeto* in 1727, said that 'the orchestra consisted for the greater part of Germans, several Italians, and a few Englishmen. Castrucci, an Italian violinist, was the leader. All together, under Handel's conducting, made an extremely good effect.'[26] Fougeroux a year later, despite his preference for the French style, paid enthusiastic tribute to the brilliance of the violins, led by the Castrucci brothers, and the 'grand fracas' made by the whole band. In addition to the continuo instruments mentioned above, he listed 24 violins, three cellos, two double basses, three bassoons, and occasional flutes and trumpets; later he mentioned horns. He says nothing of violas or oboes, which were certainly present, doubtless including the former among the violins; flutes would have doubled oboes, and horns trumpets[27]. In size and composition this orchestra does not differ greatly from that projected for the first two Royal Academy seasons;[28] it is a little larger than that of 1708–11.[29] Throughout the period it contained the best

[24] For a full discussion of this question, with citations from contemporary writers and musical examples, see W. Dean, 'The Performance of Recitative in Late Baroque Opera', *M & L* lviii (1977), 389–402; reprinted with corrections in *Essays on Opera*.

[25] *London in 1710 . . .*, ed. W. H. Quarrell and M. Mare (London, 1934), 17–18.

[26] Quoted in Deutsch, 754.

[27] Sir John Clerk of Penicuik, after attending the last night of *Orlando* on 5 May 1733, listed a very similar orchestra in his diary: 'above 24 violins' (presumably including violas), four cellos, '2 large basse violins each about 7 foot in length at least with strings proportionable that cou'd not be less than a ¼ of an inch diameter', two oboes, four bassoons, a theorbo, and two harpsichords. He did not mention horns. The violins 'made a terrible noise & often drown'd the voices', but Clerk singled out the Castrucci brothers 'who play'd with great dexterity'—perhaps in *Orlando*'s sleep aria, where they had solos on the violetta marina. (*Exhibition Catalogue*, 145.)

[28] See p. 303.

[29] See p. 154.

players in London, several of them serving over many years. Among them at different times, in addition to the Castrucci brothers, were Banister, Corbett, Rogier, and J. H. Roman (violins), Pepusch and William Babell (violin and harpsichord), Haym, Paisible, and Amadei (cello), Weidemann (flute), Galliard, John Loeillet, and John Festing (oboe), Kytch (oboe and bassoon), Chaboud and Babell senior (bassoon), Dieupart (harpsichord), J. B. Grano (trumpet and flute), and Saggione (double bass).

One remark of Fougeroux's, though inaccurate, is revealing. He found the orchestra strong in attack but etiolated in texture, and complained that there were no middle parts except as supplied by the continuo instruments. He had the five-part texture of French orchestras[30] at the back of his mind, but his failure to notice the comparatively unobtrusive presence of violas (or even second violins?) in Handel's ritornellos points to a general characteristic of Italian opera orchestras. Handel's practice certainly favoured a strong treble and bass line at the expense of inner parts; at no time, so far as we know, did the Haymarket orchestra contain more than two violas, whereas cellos, bassoons, and double basses together numbered about ten. Of course they did not all play continuously. The alternation of solo, concertino, and ripieno groups characteristic of the concerto grosso was fully established in the opera house and sometimes specified in detail in the scores. Handel's bass lines are full of *con* and *senza* markings, omitting the double basses, bassoons, and sometimes the harpsichord (especially in siciliano arias where four-part strings complete the harmony). When the autographs are missing or not specific, early copies often supply valuable details absent from the printed scores, notably in *Teseo* and *Amadigi*. The governing principle, as so often in Baroque practice, was flexibility.

This emphasis on a strong treble line affected the treatment of the oboes. When Handel wrote *Tutti* above or against the top instrumental line he generally intended all the oboes to double the first violins, even when the second violins have a part below.[31] (There are some exceptions and doubtful cases; he used the same two staves to accommodate oboes and violins, switching the instruments from one to another and modifying the direction at the head of the movement.) From 1726 he frequently and specifically marked the top line for all oboes and first violins, or even for all oboes and first and second violins, leaving only the thirds on the second part.[32] There is no reason to suppose that this did not hold good earlier, especially as S2 in extracting the Flower parts, with few exceptions (notably *coro* movements), interpreted *Tutti* in the above sense, supplying two identical oboe parts. Sometimes the score he was using gave no guidance, and he had to guess, not always correctly. But he was a member of the Smith circle for more than twenty years, and possibly a player in Handel's orchestra, and must have been aware of Handel's practice.

As we know from the scores, including the performing copies, as well as from Fougeroux, Handel used two harpsichords in the operas, playing one of them himself. The archlute or theorbo, specified in some operas (including the

---

[30] By the 1720s this was being superseded by a four-part texture with two violas.

[31] This is regularly misinterpreted in HG, where the second oboe is almost automatically instructed to double the second violin.

[32] Several Haymarket orchestra rosters list the violins in three groups: see *Coke Papers*, 151, 158, and J. Milhous and R. D. Hume, 'New Light on Handel and the Royal Academy of Music in 1720', *Theatre Journal*, xxxv (1983), 159–60.

last, *Deidamia*) but not in the three heard by Fougeroux, was probably a regular member of the continuo group; and no doubt the viola da gamba and harp were not confined to the few contexts in which they are named. The organ of course would be wholly out of place; its only mention in any of the operatic works occurs in the 1734 opera–ballet *Terpsicore*, where it doubles the recorders and theorbo *doucement* in one movement. This was a work in the French style, where the organ was not unknown, produced at Covent Garden when Handel was beginning to introduce organ concertos in the intervals of oratorios.

This is not the place for a full discussion of Baroque performance practice; the evidence, sometimes contradictory, is set out in Robert Donington's two books[33] and articles in *The New Grove*. Nevertheless one or two points require notice. Baroque practice was essentially flexible, but not to the extent of overriding well-known differences between French and Italian taste, especially in overdotting and *notes inégales*. Some Handel conductors seem so seized with the doctrine of the unequal quaver that they dot everything in sight. This may work with Rameau; it can produce grotesque results in Handel. As already remarked, the French style in his operas is confined to overtures and instrumental movements, especially dances. The vocal movements are Italian, and require a more lyrical and less jerky approach.

Inconsistency in rhythmic notation is a problem with Handel, as with other composers of his age. What is to be done when he writes the same phrase sometimes with a dot and sometimes without? Various solutions have been offered: that the dotted version should take priority on the ground that Handel was too careless or in too much of a hurry to bother with all the dots, and that everything should be played exactly as written (a policy presumably confined to works of which the autograph has survived). Neither course is satisfactory, and the second can produce unmusical results, for example when parts moving conjunctly or even in unison are rhythmically inconsistent, or when dotted quavers in one voice coincide with triplets in another.[34] Here the note after the dot must surely be synchronized with the last of the triplet. It does not follow that dotted rhythms elsewhere in the same piece should be interpreted in the same way; in 'Sì, spietata' in Act II of *Giulio Cesare* Handel leaves no doubt about the angular rhythm of the ritornello. He may have been careless on occasion, but it is likely that he wished to preserve a certain flexibility and left the final decision to the performers, who would either follow some unwritten but well-understood prescription or apply their own standards of taste. There is evidence that Baroque practice, which took an empirical view of such matters, deliberately left the options open. One answer might be to follow a course between the two extremes and make the quavers unequal but less so than a dot would imply today. Dots were as elastic as many other symbols. Nor need every statement be identical; but to draw a sharp

---

[33] *The Interpretation of Early Music* (London, 1963) and *A Performer's Guide to Baroque Music* (London, 1973). Many details are still controversial, but the arguments advanced in recent books and articles by Frederick Neumann, notably *Ornamentation in Baroque and Post-Baroque Music* (Princeton, 1978), have not won general acceptance.

[34] The first page of the overture to *Judas Maccabaeus*, played as written in Chrysander's edition, would emerge as a series of unmannerly smudges.

distinction, for example in the three-quaver descending figure in 'I know that my Redeemer liveth', is likely to be wrong, since it contradicts the *Affekt* of the air and brings the listener up with a jerk.

It may be possible to learn something from Handel's harpsichord arrangements of his overtures, though the change of medium can affect the issue. Terence Best[35] has recently shown that the numerous keyboard versions of the overtures existing in print (Walsh published sixty-six of them) and in manuscript copies fall into at least three groups: literal transcriptions from the score, more or less clumsy adaptations, and arrangements that can be confidently attributed to Handel himself, since they not only add ornaments characteristic of his keyboard style but alter the substance of the music. An element of recomposition is involved. Twenty authentic examples have been identified, all but two (*Esther* and *Semele*) from the operas; five, one incomplete, survive in autograph. Some of them can be traced through several stages in copies written by members of the Linike and Smith circles. They confirm what has been described, with alliterative convenience, as the Dolmetsch–Dart–Donington view of overdotting: whereas in the *Alessandro* autograph Handel wrote ♩. ♪, the keyboard arrangement usually has ♩. ♪. On the other hand they show him on occasion distinguishing in autographs between dotted and undotted pairs of quavers in the same bar, removing a dot from one pair but not the other, and also how he interpreted certain ornaments, for example in bar 37 of the *Semele* overture, where the first violins have a semiquaver appoggiatura in the score but written-out crotchets in the harpsichord version.

Both autographs and copies, including performing scores, vary widely in the amount of dynamic detail they supply, as well as in solo—tutti marks and other orchestral contrasts. On occasion Handel could be very specific: both the voice and the instrumental parts of 'Un disprezzato affetto' in Act III of *Ottone* are liberally sprinkled with dynamics, not all of them in HG. The absence of dynamics does not necessarily imply carelessness; certain procedures were accepted as standard. Initial ritornellos very rarely have any dynamic mark; unless stated to the contrary, they were assumed to be *forte*. When the voice entered, copyists regularly marked the instrumental parts *piano*, changing to *forte* when it stopped. B sections, though generally more lightly scored, often only with a bass, acquired a *piano* almost as a matter of course. This may simply be a short-hand indication of when the orchestra is playing alone and when it is not. The alternation of *forte* and *piano* does not imply anything in the nature of terraced dynamics, an outmoded idea responsible in the past for many tedious performances of works like the Brandenburg Concertos. There were plenty of gradations. Although Handel did not use hairpins or the terms *crescendo* and *diminuendo*, he sometimes indicated their effect: for example *p—più forte—f* three times in the first five bars of 'Cor di padre' (*Tamerlano*, Act III) and *f—p—pp* in echoes of the same phrase in bars 9–11 of 'Vieni, torna' (*Teseo*, Act III). Both of these are in opening ritornellos, and the second is not in HG. There are many contexts where performers would have supplied such refinements.

[35] 'Handel's Overtures for Keyboard', *MT* cxxvi (1985), 88–90; and see his edition, *Twenty Overtures in Authentic Keyboard Arrangements*, 3 vols (London and Sevenoaks, 1985–6).

Modern performances should take into account all we know about Handel's practice, and the motivation behind it, both in stage production and musical realization. That does not mean slavish or pedantic imitation. In some respects the emphasis has changed. Contemporary references have lost their force; today's audience is seldom equivalent in rank to the characters on stage, and does not carry swords. The appearance of men in quasi-Roman costume and women in modern fashions would undermine the deliberate artificiality of opera. The use of the costumes of Handel's day, as in Alan Kitching's Abingdon productions, is consistent with the music—which, as Eisenschmidt remarks, is perfectly timeless because perfectly in tune with its time—though to some eyes it may suggest another kind of fancy dress. We need not be too stringent about banning the use of classical costumes, or those of any other period such as the Italian Renaissance, provided they strike the eye as consistent.

The modern theatre does not depend on grooved wings for scenery or cumbersome devices for moving machines. It can make the same points more easily by other means, including revolves and sophisticated lighting effects. There is no duty to keep the curtain raised during act intervals, when the Haymarket stage was left bare or sometimes used for entr'acte ballets. These are mentioned in connection with early performances of *Rinaldo* and other operas, and Handel wrote his own for the first production of *Radamisto*, though he soon abandoned them. It is however essential for the producer to understand the reasons for Baroque practice; he must not break the continuity of the music or distract the audience's attention from it, whether by lowering the curtain during an act or introducing irrelevant business into ritornellos (or anywhere else), in the belief that it is insufficient to hold attention. That would be to betray the composer. Most problems could be solved without difficulty if managements, conductors, and producers showed themselves less unwilling to collaborate with musicologists.

The use of Baroque instruments, original or reproductions, is now so general, and their characteristics so much better understood and exploited than they were only a few years ago, that they are to be preferred wherever possible, especially in small or medium-sized theatres. Modern instruments need not be banished into outer darkness; a good performance by a modern orchestra is preferable to a swooning or scratchy one by a less than proficient Baroque group. The one respect in which strict authenticity is out of the question, the employment of castratos, is as we have seen largely a red herring. Some listeners have an in-built resistance to countertenors, though their recent increase in numbers and improvement in technique may in time overcome this. In any event they should not aim at replacing women; travesti roles, besides adding variety, were a conspicuous and popular feature of the Baroque stage.

Additional Note

* (p. 27) They may have been paid for from a separate account. Documents connected with the Hill-Collier lawsuit in 1711 (see p. 154) include substantial mercers' bills for materials evidently intended for making costumes.

CHAPTER 3

THE GERMAN BACKGROUND: OPERA
IN HAMBURG

HANDEL's three years in Hamburg, approximately from spring or summer 1703 to summer 1706, are patchily documented: apart from the controversy inspired by the production of *Almira*, almost all our information comes from Mattheson and Mainwaring, the one a not unprejudiced witness, the other writing from hearsay long after the event. Mainwaring's celebrated remark that 'it was resolved to send him thither on his own bottom, and chiefly with a view to improvement' follows a specific reference to the high reputation of the Hamburg Opera. There can be little doubt that the young man's sights were already focused on the theatre. Although the authorities are silent on the matter, it is likely that in his Halle days he had visited the neighbouring cities of Weissenfels and Leipzig. Mainwaring mentions a family visit to Weissenfels during Handel's childhood, and says that in 1698 he went to Berlin, where he met Giovanni Bononcini and Ariosti. Unless there was more than one visit this date is impossible, since Bononcini was not in Berlin until 1702; if Handel was there during that summer he might have heard Bononcini's *Polifemo*. Weissenfels had a flourishing court opera under the direction (1680–1725) of Johann Philipp Krieger, composer of eighteen German operas, and was often visited by Reinhard Keiser for the production of his stage works. The Leipzig Opera, founded by N. A. Strungk in 1693, was directed from 1702 to 1705 by Telemann, whose friendship with Handel is known to date from the Halle period.

The part played by Keiser in Handel's early career has been interpreted in conflicting senses. In view of the fact that he was the director of the Hamburg Opera throughout Handel's residence there it must, for better or worse, have been significant.[1] Two influential and articulate writers have been at pains to play it down. Mattheson claimed to have taught Handel how to compose for the theatre;[2] but he was subsequently on bad terms with Keiser (though an admirer of his work), and naturally inclined to stake his own claim as high as possible at a time when Handel was the most famous living composer. A century later Chrysander was even more concerned to blacken Keiser's reputation, for a different reason: he could not allow any other composer to detract from the perfection of his hero. The task of rehabilitating Keiser was

[1] See pp. 43–5 and 71 below.
[2] *Grundlage einer Ehren-Pforte* (Hamburg, 1740).

begun by Hellmuth Christian Wolff and Klaus Zelm in their books on the Hamburg Opera, cited below, and clinched in an important article by Bernd Baselt.[3] It is overwhelmingly probable that Keiser acted as Handel's sponsor and protector, at least for a time, and he may have been instrumental in inviting him to Hamburg. Of only three new operas other than Keiser's staged there in 1703–6 two were by Handel.

Hamburg was the natural destination for a young German composer with theatrical ambitions. The Hamburg Opera was one of the most remarkable artistic phenomena of the age. A free city, not subject to the jurisdiction or restraints of a court, it had escaped the devastation of the Thirty Years War and grown into the most important trading centre in Germany, second in size only to Vienna, with about 60,000 inhabitants in 1680. Its position as a centre for commerce and diplomacy attracted many foreign residents, chiefly English and Dutch, and laid it open to cultural influences from the whole of Europe, including France and Italy with their contrasted musical and operatic traditions. Companies of English actors visited it frequently, bringing the works of Shakespeare among others. It nourished a number of German intellectual societies founded to promote native interests, and a vigorous school of Lutheran theologians. These competing ideals and activities made it something of a cultural supermarket. The establishment of a public opera-house, the first outside Italy, was almost a predictable consequence.

The immediate impulse seems to have come from Christian Albrecht, the exiled Duke of Schleswig-Gottorf (1641–94), who moved to Hamburg in 1675 with his Kapellmeister Johann Theile and enlisted the support of prominent local worthies, among them the jurist Gerhard Schott and the organist J. A. Reincken. As might be expected, they encountered considerable opposition from the clergy and cathedral authorities, a situation paralleled later when Handel introduced his oratorios in London. But they must have commanded wide support, for they obtained the Town Council's consent for the construction of a purpose-built opera-house, the Theater am Gänsemarkt, opened in January 1678 with Theile's biblical opera *Der erschaffene, gefallene und auffgerichtete Mensch*, or *Adam und Eva*. They evidently believed in going back to first principles.

The history of the Hamburg Opera has been the subject of much scholarly research in Germany.[4] From the start it was enlivened and envenomed by a maelstrom of controversy, pursued in pamphlets, broadsheets, sermons, and prefaces to librettos, by different methods of management (at first largely controlled by Schott and his family), and by financial crises, which persisted on and off throughout the sixty years of its existence. There is no need to go into details here, but this background explains a good deal that is peculiar about the resultant art form, and helps to account for the eventual decline of

---

[3] 'Händel auf dem Wege nach Italien', in *G. F. Händel und seine italienischen Zeitgenossen*, ed. W. Siegmund-Schultze (Halle, 1979), 10–21.

[4] See in particular F. Chrysander, 'Matthesons Verzeichniss Hamburgischer Opern...', *AMZ* (1877); W. Schulze, *Die Quellen der Hamburger Oper (1678–1738)* (Hamburg/Oldenburg, 1938); H. C. Wolff, *Die Barockoper in Hamburg 1678–1738*, 2 vols. (Wolfenbüttel, 1957); K. Zelm, *Die Opern Reinhard Keisers* (Munich/Salzburg, 1975); H. J. Marx, 'Die Geschichte der Hamburger Barockoper: ein Forschung Bericht', *Hamburger Jahrbuch für Musikwissenschaft*, iii (1978), 7–34; K. Zelm, 'Die Sänger der Hamburger Gänsemarkt-Oper', ibid., 35–73; S. Stompor, 'Die deutschen Aufführungen von Opern Händels in der ersten Hälfte des 18. Jahrhunderts', *HJb* (1978), 31–89.

the undertaking and its collapse in 1738. The theatre, after some years of darkness, was demolished in 1765.

It must have been an imposing structure. From a visit in 1687 by the Swedish architect Nicodemus Tessin and from other sources we know a good deal about the layout and dimensions of the interior.[5] Like Vanbrugh's theatre in the Haymarket it possessed a stage of great depth, surpassing that of contemporary opera-houses in Dresden (1667), Wolfenbüttel (1688), Brunswick (1689), and Darmstadt (1711), and was one of the most elaborately equipped of its age, with ample space for machinery and every technical facility. The capacity of the auditorium, with pit, four rows of boxes (each holding from nine to twelve persons), and gallery, is said to have been about 2,000, though this may be an exaggeration. The designer was Girolamo Sartorio, a specialist in theatre construction and from 1667 to 1685 principal architect to the ducal court of Hanover. His model was almost certainly the Teatro di SS Giovanni e Paolo in Venice, whose dimensions were almost identical.[6] The Venetian link was reinforced by the most distinguished of the early scenic designers, Oswald Harms (1643–1708), who had worked in Venice and held sway at Hamburg from 1695 to 1705. Some of his sketches for scenery are preserved in the Herzog-Anton-Ulrich Museum in Brunswick.[7] There were generally two performances a week, sometimes three; an average of about ninety a year, allowing for close seasons. They began in the late afternoon and were enormously long, lasting from four to six hours.

The audience, unlike Handel's in London, was cosmopolitan in the extreme, drawn from all ranks of German society and many visitors. Princes, aristocrats, solid bourgeois, and groundlings all had to be accommodated, both physically (in different parts of the theatre) and in taste. As in Venice, the boxes were rented on a yearly basis by city officials, diplomats, foreign merchants, and others. The divergent demands of the audience often clashed with the aesthetic aims and personal ambitions of individual directors, the financial interests of the owners and managers, and the moral preoccupations of the clergy. The bone of contention was seldom the music. The librettists had literary pretensions and demanded to be judged by the same standards as contemporary playwrights and poets. Their verbose prefaces, in addition to oblique attacks on their rivals, appealed both to history and to literary precedent, classical, French, and occasionally English, and contained allusions to local society. Postel's pretentious introduction to *Janus* (Keiser, 1699) employed five languages—Latin, Greek, French, Italian, and Spanish—as well as German to elucidate the story. The equally vast preface to *Hercules mit der schönen Hebe*, set by Keiser in the same year, adds English as well.

The librettos exhibited an extraordinary variety of subject and approach.[8] The biblical–allegorical operas of the early years,[9] perhaps a concession to the clergy (who however complained of their adulteration by amorous and other

---

[5] See Marx, op. cit., and H. C. Wolff, 'Rekonstruktion der alten Hamburger Opernbühne', *Kongress Bericht: Gesellschaft für Musikforschung* (Hamburg, 1956), 235–9.

[6] See plan in Sir John Soane's Museum, reproduced by Marx, op. cit. 16.

[7] For reproductions see H. C. Wolff (ed.), *Musikgeschichte in Bildern* (Leipzig, n.d.), 70–5.

[8] Some have been reprinted by R. Meyer in *Die Hamburger Opern: eine Sammlung von Texten der Hamburger Oper aus der Zeit 1678–1730*, 3 vols. (Munich, 1979).

[9] The Prologue to Theile's *Adam und Eva*, like that of Salieri's *Tarare* a century later, is set in limbo and features Earth, Air, Fire, and Water. The indispensable comic element was supplied by the Devil. No music survives.

secular elements), though they never disappeared completely—witness Keiser's *Salomon* (1703) and *Nebucadnezar* (1704), Graupner's *Simson* (1709), and Telemann's *Belsazar* (1723)—were soon joined and outnumbered by mythological, medieval epic, historical, pastoral, and contemporary plebeian themes. Of these the pastoral, after a good run in the 1690s associated with the short-lived Brunswick librettist F. C. Bressand (*c*.1670–99),[10] was the least prominent. Stories taken from Roman history under the influence of the Venetian theatre—*Porsenna, Claudius, Cleopatra, Nero, Lucretia, Octavia*—were popular in the first years of the century. Others were based on more recent events: Franck's *Cara Mustapha* (1686) on the siege of Vienna by the Turks, Keiser's *Masagniello furioso* (1706), and Mattheson's *Boris Goudenow* (1710, not produced) on seventeenth-century subjects familiar to us from much later operas. The taste for lavish spectacle (fireworks were a Hamburg speciality) was universal; there was also a demand, presumably from the groundlings, for contemporary realism in the form of satirical comedies and farces in Low German or Dutch dialect—low in more senses than one.

It was characteristic of the Hamburg Opera, even more than of its Venetian antecedents, that these elements were constantly combined, or thrown together haphazard, in the same librettos. This urge to squeeze in everything, and to give each member of the large casts plenty to do, accounts for the exorbitant length of the Hamburg operas, which can contain up to seventy or more arias and ensembles in addition to scenes of pageantry and the increasingly popular ballets introduced from France. The fatal flaw was not so much the actual length as the absence of any serious attempt at artistic synthesis, whether in the interests of drama or music. The typical product is a weird jumble of comical–tragical–historical–pastoral with at least two serious and one farcical sub-plot, spectacular episodes dragged in without reason, and a casual attitude to structure. Individual scenes could contain almost any number of arias; there was little attempt to ease the task of the composer by imposing a coherent shape, whether on a broad or narrow scale, or controlling entrances and exits. The appearance of macaronic texts when immediate Italian influence grew stronger after the turn of the century (Keiser's *Der verführte Claudius* of 1703 is the earliest example) added one more ingredient to the stew.

A few authors, notably C. F. Hunold (Menantes) (1681–1721) and Barthold Feind (1678–1721) did try to counteract the descent into wholesale banality. Hunold in *Theatralische, galante und geistliche Gedichte* (1706) saluted opera as the apex of theatrical poetry; his *Nebucadnezar* is a serious and comparatively straightforward treatment of the story in the Book of Daniel, though like the Italians he introduced much fiction in the way of love intrigues to make it more palatable. Feind, perhaps the ablest of these men and the librettist of some of Keiser's and Graupner's most successful operas, discussed the problems in a tightly argued preface to *Deutsche Gedichte* (1708).[11] He professed to regard opera as a genre with its own rules, pointed to Shakespeare and Racine as his models (while opposing French conventions), stressed the

[10] He was much under French influence, translated Racine and Corneille, and wrote most of his librettos in Alexandrines.

[11] See D. M. Hsu, 'Barthold Feind's "Gedancken von der Oper": an Early Eighteenth Century View of Drama and Music', *Festival Essays for Pauline Alderman* (Provo, Utah, 1976), 127–34; also G. Flaherty, *Opera in the Development of German Critical Thought* (Princeton, 1978), 53–65.

importance of individual characterization, and in *Masagniello* claimed to have added fiction but not distorted historical truth. This libretto is interesting for its implied attack on the municipal and religious authorities of his own city; his preface to *Lucretia* (Keiser, 1705), besides citing ancient authorities, makes explicit political comparisons between the Rome of Tarquin and the free republic of Hamburg. Even so, neither Hunold nor Feind was able to achieve much in the way of reform. The other poets of the period—Postel, Hinsch, Feustking, König—made no such lofty professions. Hinsch demanded freedom to treat his subjects as he wished, and declared in the preface to *Claudius* that 'opera provided a pleasurable poetic experience, precisely because it titillated the senses of its audience without attempting to address their reason or understanding.'[12] That was the prevailing spirit of the Hamburg Opera. Needless to say, there was no attempt to match the still tentative reforms of Zeno. In adapting the latter's *Lucio Vero* (Venice, 1700) as *Berenice* (Hamburg, 1702) Hinsch loosened the drama in favour of an even distribution of arias among the characters regardless of their importance, the almost invariable fate of Handel's operas in Hamburg later. Like Hunold, he took particular exception to the unities of place and time enjoined by French tragedy, a typically literary criterion. As in Italy, not least in Metastasio's time, the librettist tended to dominate the composer, who was expected to conform in turn to each *Affekt* indicated by the text. Musical drama in a broader sense was a secondary consideration, if indeed it occurred to anyone at all. Keiser, the strongest of the Hamburg composers, could not achieve it; much less could the nineteen-year-old Handel.

From its early years the Hamburg Opera had links with other German centres, notably Ansbach, Brunswick-Wolfenbüttel, and Hanover, and—less directly—with Venice and Paris. Of the musical directors and leading composers who succeeded Theile—N. A. Strungk (1678–82), J. W. Franck (1679–86), J. P. Förtsch (1684–90), J. G. Conradi (1690–4), and J. S. Kusser (1694–7)—Franck had studied in Italy and is thought to have brought operatic scores by Monteverdi, Cavalli, and P. A. Ziani to Ansbach, while Conradi and Kusser had French associations. Although (with one exception) only fragments remain of their Hamburg operas, and the foundation of the German style was the simple strophic song and dance, the widely diffused Italian and French influences soon made themselves felt. Franck, Conradi, and Kusser had worked at Ansbach, which became a centre for the production of Lully's operas, and Theile, Kusser, and Keiser at Brunswick-Wolfenbüttel, where Italian influence was strong; as it was also at Hanover. Antonio Sartorio as Kapellmeister had introduced Italian opera there about 1672, and for ten years (1688–98) Agostino Steffani directed a magnificent new operahouse; of the eight or nine works he composed for it at least six were soon (1695–9) revived at Hamburg.

Wolff prints extracts from these early Hamburg operas,[13] which show the style developing fairly rapidly from the simple ditties of Theile's *Orontes* (1678), via an infusion of Italianate lyricism with quasi-ostinato basses in

---

[12] Quoted by Flaherty, ibid. 44.
[13] *Die Barockoper in Hamburg*, ii; some also, with modern realization, in K. G. Fellerer (ed.), *Anthology of Music: The Opera*, i (Cologne, 1971).

Strungk's *Esther* (1680),[14] to more specifically Italian procedures—da capo arias, sequential vocal melodies, echoes between voice and strings—in the operas of Franck, who in *Aeneas* (1680) is credited with the first German aria with trumpet obbligato. Most historians attribute the French influence to Kusser, who had studied for six years with Lully in Paris before moving to Ansbach, where he introduced the French style of violin-playing. His only Hamburg opera for which any music survives, the pastoral *Erindo* (1694, libretto by Bressand), was probably modelled on Lully's *Acis et Galatée*, which he directed at Hamburg (in German) in the following year. He also put on Italian operas by Pallavicino and Steffani, and is reputed to have broadened Hamburg taste and improved the standard of performance. The *Erindo* music shows both Italian and French influence, including syncopated dance rhythms of a type often imitated by Keiser, and a characteristic Hamburg interest in the orchestra, with obbligatos for flute, two recorders, two bassoons, and colascione (colachono or calichon, a kind of lute) among other instruments. Kusser however was not the first to import the latest French style to Hamburg. Indeed *Acis et Galatée* had been produced there in French as early as December 1689—the first opera sung in a foreign language—possibly by Conradi. The identification by George Buelow of the earliest surviving complete Hamburg opera, Conradi's *Die schöne und getreue Ariadne* (1691, previously ascribed to Keiser in 1722), has clarified the picture.[15] This score reflects the overwhelming influence of Lully in plan and detail: the pompous opening of the overture in dotted rhythm, a Chaconne in Act II with nineteen variations on a ten-bar bass, a long final Passacaille [*sic*] on a descending tetrachord, and at least three substantial sequences combining French dances with solo and choral strophes on the same music. *Ariadne* was followed by a production of *Achille et Polyxène* (Lully's last opera, finished by Colasse) in 1692.

These cosmopolitan influences were inherited by the most gifted of the Hamburg opera composers, Reinhard Keiser, who had worked under Kusser at Brunswick, wrote his first Hamburg opera (*Mahumet II*) in 1696, and directed the company from 1703 to 1707. He was immensely prolific, producing an average of at least three new operas a year in addition to revivals, and is said to have composed over a hundred in all. Of those staged in 1703–6 he was responsible for eleven, at least two of them after Handel had left. The only others, apart from possible revivals of one work each by Schieferdecker and Grünewald (now lost), were Mattheson's *Cleopatra* (1704) and Handel's two operas of 1705. Handel was a member of the Gänsemarkt orchestra, as a ripieno second violin, and must have played in most if not all of the operas given while he was there. No doubt he had access to earlier scores, including Mattheson's *Porsenna*[16] and some of the innumerable operas produced by Keiser in 1696–1702. Many of these are lost and others unpublished and unavailable. Those that survive in full are *Ulysses* (1696, a double opera revived in 1702), *Adonis* (1697), *Janus* (1699), *La forza della virtù* (1700), *Pomona* (1702), *Claudius* (1703), *Nebucadnezar* (1704), *Octavia* (August 1705), *Masagniello furioso* (June 1706), and eight more dating from after Handel's departure. Modern printed editions exist of *Octavia*, *Masagniello* (a corrupt text, but

---

[14] See Haman's aria 'In eyfriger Hitze', also in *NOHM* v, 305–6.

[15] G. J. Buelow, 'Die schöne und getreue Ariadne (Hamburg 1691): a Lost Opera by J. G. Conradi Rediscovered', *Acta Musicologica*, xliv (1972), 108–21.

[16] See p. 133.

*   it was staged accurately at Sheffield in November 1973), *Croesus* (1710), *Tomyris* (1717), and the comedy *Jodelet*, as well as Mattheson's *Cleopatra*.[17]

Keiser's principal strength lay in his ability to seize a dramatic situation and express it in music of sometimes startling vividness and originality, and in his remarkable feeling for the orchestra. Whether because he always worked in a hurry or because he was defeated by the ragbag librettos, he was less successful in imposing any overall design or in assimilating the influences he inherited; German, French, and Italian elements persist alongside each other without merging. He came nearest to success in *Tomyris*, perhaps his masterpiece, an opera unencumbered by sub-plots and comic diversions; the influence of Zeno's reforms was beginning to filter through. While the kaleidoscopic interplay of moods and the rapid pace of the action arrest attention in Keiser's operas, his characters seldom emerge as fully realized creations. His melodic ideas, which include an element from popular song, are often initially striking but rarely developed to their maximum potential; Handel sometimes remedied this in his borrowings from *Octavia*.[18] Keiser is at his best in supernatural or dream scenes and in incidents of high dramatic tension, where he links accompanied recitative (employed much more freely than by his predecessors), arioso, and aria in a manner later exploited by the mature Handel. Notable examples in *Octavia* are the scenes in which the deserted empress resigns herself to death (II xv–xvi) and Nero is haunted by the ghosts of his former victims (III viii), where a wide-leaping phrase of despair occurs at intervals in three accompanied recitatives. J. A. Westrup, quoting this in *The New Oxford History of Music* (v. 312), found it not unworthy of Bach's *St. Matthew Passion*. Several episodes in *Masagniello* may have left their mark on Handel and must have impressed him: the idyllic opening with three recorders, interrupted by distant gunfire; the Act II revolution in concentrated recitative (a revolutionary slogan is repeated in several scenes); the beautiful farewell duet for a pair of lovers in chains at the end of Act II; a sleep sinfonia with recorders and muted strings, headed *Le Sommeil*; and the astonishing mad scene in which Masagniello's mind wanders back to his days as a fisherman (barcarolle rhythm), just before his assassination by his own

*   men—in the middle of a bar and an alien key. There is a hint of Bajazet here.

Keiser's arias are of several types: binary ariettas in dance rhythms, simple strophic songs, chiefly for comic characters, Italianate da capo pieces (increasingly prominent in later operas), and single-chamber cavatinas or ariosos, sometimes very brief, sometimes more developed. Accompaniments confined to continuo are less common than in other Hamburg composers, though many arias have a single unison or obbligato upper part. The texture may be homophonic, especially when richly scored, or contrapuntal. Coloratura, when present, is generally confined to sudden extended flourishes and is apt to break the pattern instead of growing out of and supporting it. Keiser was obsessed with the *Affekt* of individual words at the expense of form; there is little of the balance achieved by the better Italians or by Handel later. Many

---

[17] See B. Deane, 'Reinhard Keiser: an Interim Assessment', *Soundings*, iv (1974), 30–41. *Tomyris* has since been edited by Zelm (Munich, 1975), *Cleopatra* by Buelow (Mainz, 1975).

[18] See W. Dean, 'Handel and Keiser: Further Borrowings', *Current Musicology*, ix (1969), 73 ff., and for a fuller account, embracing nearly all the operas listed above, J. H. Roberts, 'Handel's Borrowings from Keiser', *Göttinger Händel-Beiträge* II (1986), 51–76; also Appendix D. *Octavia* was published as a supplementary volume to HG (ed. M. Seiffert, 1902).

da capo arias do not modulate in the A section and lack an internal ritornello. Keiser, at least in earlier years, was not at ease with the form; his B sections are perfunctory, modulating with little sense of direction and scuttling back to a suitable cadence just in time or even failing to reach it. That of the A minor duet 'Kann dich mein Arm umschliessen' (*Octavia* I ii) ends abruptly in G major; that of 'Die Edelmuth pranget' (II vi) in C major approaches A minor but diverges inconsequently at the last minute into E minor; there are many other awkward transitions. The effect of breathlessness is increased by the close accumulation of cadences and heavy use of sequence at intervals of two bars, one bar or even half a bar ('Du kannst hoffen', *Octavia* I ix). Nevertheless, if Keiser seldom allowed his muse to expand, if his ritornello designs lack flexibility and his procedures are often cramped, the occasional irregularity of phrase-lengths and unexpectedness of detail can be refreshing—for example the turn to the minor at the last appearance only of the word 'Pein' in 'Bei dem Zunder' (*Octavia* II ii) and the end of 'Solo con te' (III ii) with the first word repeated twice without any accompaniment. Everything seems to be motivated by the stress laid on the exact reproduction of an *Affekt*. This extends to the recitatives, which fall between the measured gait of the French and the rapid *parlando* of the Italian without quite achieving a balance or a specifically German idiom.

Orchestral enterprise was a feature of the Hamburg school.[19] Franck and Strungk introduced Lully's five-part string texture; the French spellings *Hautbois* and *Basson* were in use by the 1680s, adopted by Keiser, and retained by Handel throughout his London career. The French overture with its ceremonial dotted introduction and fugued Allegro, sometimes varied by contrasted episodes for two oboes and bassoon, soon became the rule. All Steffani's Hanover operas have French overtures. He also used obbligatos freely; elaborate examples for oboe and cello occur in *I trionfi del fato* (1699 in Hamburg). Keiser went much further. He liked to use groups of woodwind in consort and to mix his colours in all manner of surprising ways, generally to paint a specific mood. His aria accompaniments are far more varied, both in choice of instruments and internal contrast, than those of contemporary Italian and French operas. Horns appear twice in *Octavia*, much earlier than elsewhere; two soprano arias are accompanied by two bassoons and one, an expression of jealousy, by five. Later he used five recorders with harp and solo violone (*Orpheus*, 1709), muted trumpets with oboes and drums (the scene before Pompey's tomb in *Julius Caesar*, 1710), three chalumeaux (*Croesus*, 1710), and solo flute and double bass, two cellos, and very spare continuo for bassoon and harpsichord (*Tomyris*). His treatment of the violas, often in virtuoso passages and without violins, to create a sombre atmosphere, was exceptional for the period. Like Handel later he resorted to pizzicato (first in *Adonis*, 1697) and mutes (to oboes and trumpets as well as strings) for special effects, and was fond of rich crossing string parts. He often lightened the texture by silencing the harpsichord. Almost every current instrument, however recondite (except trombone and organ), appears in his scores, often in a solo capacity. The Hamburg players must have been technically accomplished; part books suggest that many of them played several instru-

---

[19] See A. McCredie, *Instrumentarium and Instrumentation in the North German Baroque Opera* (Hamburg, 1964); also W. Kleefeld, 'Das Orchester der Hamburger Opern, 1678–1738', *SIMG* i (1899–1900), 219–89.

ments. The size of the opera orchestra is not known before the 1730s, when it approximated to that of the Haymarket in the early years of the century[20] and was likewise weak in the middle register; but the number of different instruments found in the Hamburg scores was considerably larger.[21] Under Telemann in the 1730s the scoring became more standardized.

Little is known about the singers before 1720. Casts were named in librettos, a practice apparently introduced from Brunswick, only between 1722 and 1733. In the early years, according to Zelm, many of them were local amateurs who doubled in other jobs and also sang in churches; they depended on men like Kusser and Mattheson (himself an operatic tenor) for coaching and instruction. By the turn of the century some at least, to judge from the music, must have been professionals of considerable attainment. Mattheson mentions a certain Conradin (Mainwaring calls her Conratini) as the leading soprano at this time. If she sang parts like Cleopatra, Handel's Almira or Edilia, and Keiser's Tomyris, she commanded a flexible technique and a huge compass (a to d''' in *Tomyris*, exactly the compass Mattheson gives for Conradin[22]). Italian castratos (Valentino Urbani, Campioli) made occasional Hamburg appearances, but most of the singers were German. In native operas male parts were taken by tenors and basses. When from about 1718 the number of imported Italian operas greatly increased, including Handel's London works, the heroic male roles were occasionally sung by a woman or a castrato but more often rewritten or transposed down an octave, with the usual grotesque results.[23]

There can be no doubt that Keiser was Handel's principal—if not his only—model in *Almira*, which (in varying degree) reflects a substantial number of the characteristics noted above. Claims have been made for Mattheson,[24] who was four years older than Handel and seven years younger than Keiser, and whose first opera was staged in 1699. In view of the fact that Handel must have been composing *Almira* while playing in the orchestra of *Cleopatra*[25] we might expect to find traces of influence, if not direct echoes. In fact there are virtually none (though Handel was to borrow from *Cleopatra* in Italy). Such features as they have in common—French dance measures, linking of forms in climactic scenes such as the impressive apparition of Nemesis and Cleopatra's suicide, strong generative bass figures and the like—are characteristic of the Hamburg school as a whole, and Mattheson probably picked them up from Keiser, who was certainly the stronger personality. His music is much blander than either Keiser's or Handel's, marked—as theirs as a rule is not—by symmetrical stepwise melodies, regular phrase structure, more conservative harmony, much less enterprise in orchestration (*Cleopatra* has a far higher proportion of continuo arias), and little coloratura or ornament in the voice parts. Mattheson's fast arias are as sequential and short-breathed as Keiser's, with a weaker rhythmic drive; all the best music, some of it genuinely beautiful, occurs in the slow pieces. A surprising number of these are in

[20] See p. 154.

[21] See Marx, 'Die Geschichte der Hamburger Barockoper', 24.

[22] Notes to his translation (1761) of Mainwaring's life of Handel.

[23] See p. 21.

[24] By Wolff (*Die Barockoper in Hamburg*, i. 289) and Buelow, 'An Evaluation of Johann Mattheson's Opera, *Cleopatra* (Hamburg, 1704)', *Studies in Eighteenth-Century Music*, 92–107.

[25] According to Mattheson the famous quarrel, resulting in a duel (see p. 64), took place at a performance of *Cleopatra* on 5 December 1704, a month before the production of *Almira*.

siciliano rhythm, which Handel conspicuously avoids in *Almira*; the seeds of the wonderful sicilianos of the London operas were sown in Italy. Although *Cleopatra* shows no more feeling for dramatic structure than any other Hamburg opera (the first two acts end with trivial movements for minor characters), each act has a definite tonal plan, and the whole score employs the esoteric scheme of key associations that Mattheson was to publicize in *Das neu-eröffnete Orchestre* (1713). It also fulfils his later recommendation, in *Der vollkommene Capellmeister* (1739), that melody should be simple, natural, unencumbered with learned devices, and nearer to the French than the Italian style. Except in the intermittent use of a tonal plan for acts and sometimes whole operas, Handel was to pursue a very different course. His key associations diverge widely from Mattheson's. The score of *Cleopatra* offers little support for its author's subsequent claim to have instructed Handel in melodic and dramatic style.[26]

Additional Notes

* (p. 44) Facsimiles (scores and librettos) of *Adonis*, *Janus*, *La forza della virtù*, *Claudius*, and *Nebucadnezar* are included in *Handel Sources: Materials for the Study of Handel's Borrowings*, ed. J. H. Roberts (New York, 1986), vols. i-iii.

* (p. 44) There is no proof that Handel knew *Masagniello*. The fact that he is not known to have borrowed from it may indicate that he left for Italy before its production in June 1706.

---

[26] For further comment see J. M. Knapp, 'Mattheson and Handel, their musical relations in Hamburg', *New Mattheson Studies*, ed. G. J. Buelow and H. J. Marx (Cambridge, 1983), 307–26, and W. Dean, review of Buelow's edition of the score, *M & L* lvii (1976), 212–14.

CHAPTER 4

ALMIRA, KÖNIGIN VON CASTILIEN

THE Argument in the 1704 libretto explains the background to the plot.

Alfonso King of Castile sent Consalvo on a mission to Sicily, whither he travelled in company with his wife Almira. A son, Floraldo, was born to them there. On the return journey to Castile Consalvo's ship was wrecked; he himself was saved, though not before he had passed through mortal danger. Almira perished, and Floraldo was also regarded as lost, since no trace of him could be found. In fact Floraldo was rescued by a fisherman who, finding him afloat in his cradle, brought him up under the name of Fernando. When fully grown he found his way to Castile, unaware of his origin or rank. Here Consalvo out of natural kindliness received him into his household, not realizing his identity. The young man was given everything that could contribute to his happiness. Eventually Consalvo brought him to court together with Osman, his son by an earlier marriage, and here he won the esteem of the Crown Princess Almira. In the meantime the King died, leaving to Consalvo the government of his kingdom and placing Almira in his care with the specific direction that when she attained her twentieth year she was to receive the royal authority at Consalvo's hands and marry one of his sons, since his family was of royal blood.

Act I begins with Consalvo's fulfilment of this charge. *The scene is a stately amphitheatre in the capital Valladolid with a platform splendidly adorned for the Queen's public coronation; trumpeters and military drummers fill the balconies on either side. Almira is escorted by Consalvo, Osman and Fernando carrying the royal insignia, attended by the whole court, bodyguard, soldiers and people.* Consalvo, kneeling at her feet, blesses the crown and sceptre. *Trumpets and drums sound a Rejouissance, and as guns fire a salute Almira is crowned with the customary ceremony. The people acclaim her, after which the Spanish ladies and gentlemen dance.* Almira appoints Osman commander-in-chief, Consalvo chief counsellor, and Fernando 'Secretarius'. Consalvo gives her a document containing Alfonso's last wish, that she marry one of Consalvo's family. She is much distressed, since she loves Fernando. The set changes to the palace garden *with statues, trees scattered throughout and a magnificent fountain.* Edilia, a royal princess, appeals to flowers and trees to favour her love for Osman. When he enters, his equivocal behaviour infuriates her; *he draws back,* and when she asks him to swear a formal oath of devotion he says he will do so at a more convenient time. She threatens him with the fury of a woman scorned. He believes her pride and violence will abate when she discovers he is after the crown. It is now Fernando's turn to invoke the assistance of nature. Too timid to approach Almira, he decides to entrust his declaration of love to the bark of a tree. Almira watches as he begins to write, ICH LIEBE DI[E ICH NICHT DARF NENNEN] ('I love her whom I dare not name'). But he *stops carving* after the first ten letters, which she misinterprets as ICH LIEB EDI[LIA]. She denounces him furiously as a traitor, and when he *goes out sorrowfully* abandons herself to the tortures of jealousy.

Consalvo, learning from Edilia that a knight has been false to his oath, swears that he shall be punished even if he is his own son. Though bitterly distressed to hear that it is indeed Osman, and seeing his hopes of the crown blighted, he acknowledges his promise. The set changes to *a beautifully illuminated hall in the palace, with staircases and galleries, in which a ball and 'Assemblée' are to take place. A band of oboes in the gallery for the dancing.* Fernando's servant Tabarco *with dice and cards and other court attendants make preparations for the party.* He complains that since the Queen has ordered an Assemblée he has to get all this rubbish ready; but the best pastime at court is a young woman. He derides the fashionable courtier's life in a satirical song. Fernando, determined that his love shall withstand the blows of fate, overhears Osman's decision to abandon his former love for the pursuit of Almira and the throne. Edilia is resolved not to upset herself over Osman, and the pair renounce their old ties in a duet. Consalvo and the court enter, including Bellante Princess of Arando; *the ladies and the rest of the nobility, who form parties at the gaming tables; the royal pages and footmen and other servants.* Edilia makes Osman jealous by choosing Fernando as her partner. Osman approaches Bellante, who replies that her mouth must say no but her heart says yes, and tells him not to come too near. Osman, uncertain what to make of this, refuses Tabarco's jocular invitation to a game and *plays with Consalvo.* Tabarco *sits on the ground and plays dice* with himself. *The chairs and gaming tables are removed, and the ball begins. Fernando after dancing with Edilia engages her in conversation.* Edilia, thinking Almira wants to join Osman, goes out. Bellante tells Osman, who has once more abandoned himself to jealousy, that he would please her if he learned to control himself, and they depart together. Consalvo follows, foreseeing disaster to Castile. Almira, left alone, damns Fernando's ingratitude.

Act II. In *the Queen's splendid audience chamber with an ornamented throne* Fernando announces the arrival of an ambassador from Mauritania. Almira *sits on the throne.*[1] *Raymondo, accompanied by a number of Mauritanian nobles bearing letters of credence and a considerable retinue, is introduced by Consalvo. The notables of the realm and the entire royal household stand round the throne.* Raymondo, who is in fact the King of Mauritania in disguise, congratulates Almira on her accession and presents the letters of credence. She replies with a gracious speech, and all depart except Consalvo, Bellante, and Tabarco *(aside).* Bellante complains that love has proved an illusion. Consalvo makes gallant advances, and when she accuses him of toying with her youth addresses her directly in a love song. She leaves in displeasure. Tabarco is amused to note that she loves the son but is loved by the father: old men in love are always a comic spectacle. The set changes to *Fernando's room with tapestry hangings.* He orders Tabarco to admit no one and tries to concentrate on state business, but his mind strays to Almira. He *sits at a writing desk* and begins a letter to her, interrupted by repeated knocking on the door. Eventually he tells Tabarco to open it and *rises from his writing-table, leaving what he has written.* Osman enters with a request for help: he loves Almira, and begs Fernando to put in a word for him. Embarrassed, Fernando says he will do his best. As Almira approaches Osman *hides behind a tapestry,*[2] and Fernando *tries to conceal what he has written.* Almira insists on reading it and discovers it to be a declaration of love, which she assumes is addressed to Edilia. Misunderstanding her, he offers to quench the flames of

---

[1] Chrysander omits this direction.
[2] As note 1.

love if she finds them distasteful. Instead of seeking an explanation she consults him about marriage into Consalvo's family and asks if she should love Osman. Trapped, he says no mortal is worthy of her hand, while Osman (aside) curses him as a traitor to friendship. Consalvo asks Almira to sanction a marriage, but the mere mention of Edilia's name sends her into an aria of refusal. Osman *comes out of hiding and leaves.* Consalvo remarks that Osman must keep his promise to Edilia and determines to quell his pride. In *a courtyard with various buildings and doors in the walls, leading from the Queen's apartments to other rooms,* Raymondo expresses the hope of being accepted as Almira's consort; that was why he came in disguise. She can bear the prospect of concealing her love for Fernando no longer. Seeing Osman coming, she hides. Osman meets Fernando, challenges him to fight (without telling him what his offence is) and demands his sword, which he surrenders. *Osman measures it*[3] against his own and finds them alike. Almira *snatches the weapon and goes out* unrecognized. Osman taunts Fernando with sheltering under the protection of a woman; his vengeance is merely postponed. In *the Queen's antechamber* Almira, overjoyed at having saved Fernando's life, *lays the sword*[4] *on the table,* envying it for living where she wishes to be, at his side. She tells Consalvo that Raymondo has explained his status and motives, and they go off discussing court business. Edilia, finding the sword, assumes it is Osman's and that he means to face the Queen armed. Osman jumps to the conclusion that it was Edilia who stole the sword. In an outburst of mutual recrimination he accuses her of toying with Fernando while she taunts him with pursuing Almira. Tabarco comes in with *a wallet containing sundry petitions, commissions, sealed letters, etc.* which he has been ordered to deliver. He *falls* and drops them, *peeps into some letters,* finds they are all about love, and reads one out, recognizing a woman's hand. He runs off to complete his errands with ironical comments on the behaviour of his social superiors.

Act III begins with an elaborate and spectacular pageant set in *a colonnade with galleries, Almira and Raymondo sitting as spectators on one side, Edilia and Bellante on the other; the bodyguard and household are ranged below.* Three processions enter, each representing one of the continents: first Fernando (Europe) *in Roman habit in a gilded horse-drawn carriage, carrying crown, orb, sceptre and princely helmet, preceded by a band of oboes;* then Osman (Africa) *in Moorish dress under a handsome canopy borne by twelve Moors, preceded by trumpets and kettle-drums;* then Consalvo (Asia) *in oriental costume, pulled by lions and carrying quivers, arrows and arquebuses, preceded by cymbals, drums and fifes.* Each has a train of attendants representing the different nations. Each sings an aria, followed by a dance for the attendants. Almira gives the prize to Europe (Raymondo takes this as a pointer to her love); Edilia and Bellante vote for Africa. A fourth procession appears, led by Tabarco *on horseback in a ridiculous costume representing Folly, with a hurdy-gurdy and bagpipes and a train of harlequins and comedians;* he claims most of the human race as his subjects. Edilia sings a heart-broken aria. Raymondo tries to comfort her and invites her to favour him; she returns a doubtful answer. Bellante is also torn by unhappy love, since Osman prefers to seek the throne, and she detests Consalvo. She again repulses the latter, who shortly returns and orders Fernando to prison; he *surrenders his sword* and after bitter reflections about

---

[3] As note 1.

[4] The stage direction calls it Osman's sword; it is of course Fernando's, which he gave to Osman—unless Osman interchanged them.

court favour *is led away by the guard*.[5] Consalvo explains to Almira that Fernando's guilty passion for Edilia has profaned the palace. Racked by jealousy, she vows to separate Fernando from his love. In *part of the palace garden, with summer-houses and in the distance Almira's 'maison de plaisance'*, Raymondo affirms his devotion to Edilia in an aria which she overhears and echoes at the end. She accepts him and they go out. Almira is now determined to cut her faithless lover to pieces whatever becomes of the Kingdom of Castile. When Osman begins his wooing with flowery compliments she abruptly cuts him short. Tabarco *hands her a letter* from Fernando in prison. *She tears it open* and finds a cluster of rubies bearing her name ('Almira's Property'). This convinces her of his innocence, but she decides to dissemble and sends back Tabarco with a message that he must die before sunset. Osman *intercepts Edilia, who tries to give him the slip* and then compares his repentance with crocodile's tears. Raymondo adds his scorn. The set changes to *a subterranean prison*, where Fernando, secure in the laurels of innocence, is ready for death. Tabarco brings Almira's message, and asks where Fernando's money is, since he hopes to inherit it. Fernando wishes she could hear him say 'Fernando stirbet dein'; as long as he draws breath he will love her. She overhears this, savours it, and at last *coming forward*, interrupts him, and *releases his fetters*. All is explained, and they sing a love duet. The last scene takes place in *a magnificent hall*. Bellante complains that Osman's heart is harder than a diamond. He replies that on the contrary he loves her, and they fall into each other's arms. Almira tells Consalvo of her reconciliation and Fernando's gift of rubies. Consalvo, much agitated, asks him where he got it. When Fernando explains that it was round his neck when he was picked up by a fisherman, Consalvo greets him as his long-lost son Floraldo. His wife's name was Almira, the jewel was his bridal gift to her, and she hung it round Floraldo's neck. Fernando and Osman *embrace* as brothers. Amid general rejoicing—with Tabarco *on his horse*—Almira fulfils her father's last wish and accepts Consalvo's son as her King and consort.

This libretto has a convoluted history, which has understandably confused all who have tried to sort it out. Its source, which appears to have no basis outside fiction, is Giulio Pancieri's *L'Almira*, set by Giuseppe Boniventi for Venice in 1691. At least five operas deriving from Pancieri appeared in Germany during the years 1703–6:[6]

(i) *Almira*: librettist unknown, composer Ruggiero Fedeli; produced Brunswick 1703. Printed libretto extant;[7] manuscript score in Bibliothek der Hansestadt Lübeck (Mus K 86).

(ii) [*Almira*]: librettist F. C. Feustking based on (i), composer Reinhard Keiser (*c*.1703–4); not produced. Music partly published in Keiser's *Componimenti musicali* (Hamburg, June 1706).

(iii) *Almira Königin von Castilien*: librettist unknown (?Feustking) based on

---

[5] Omitted by Chrysander.
[6] There were others later: one at Leipzig in 1710, and *Almire und Fernando* by Johann Philipp Käfer at Durlach in 1717. See S. Stompor, 'Die deutschen Aufführungen von Opern Händels in der ersten Hälfte des 18. Jahrhunderts', *HJb* (1978), 42.
[7] In the Herzog-August-Bibliothek, Wolfenbüttel.

(ii), composer Keiser, probably incorporating music from (i) and (ii); produced Weissenfels July 1704. Printed libretto extant;[8] score lost.

(iv) *Der in Krohnen erlangte Glücks-Wechsel, oder: Almira, Königin von Castilien*: librettist Feustking, probably identical with (ii), music Handel; produced Hamburg 8 January 1705.

(v) *Der durchlauchtige Secretarius, oder Almira, Königin in Castilien*: librettist Barthold Feind, based on (i), (iii), and (iv), composer Keiser; produced Hamburg 1706 (after July). Printed libretto extant,[9] music lost.

Klaus Zelm[10] and other scholars have assumed that (ii) and (iii) are identical, and that Keiser's first setting was that produced at Weissenfels. Reinhard Strohm[11] concluded that Handel's libretto drew on the Weissenfels text, with which it has a good deal in common, especially in the recitatives. Neither view is tenable; on the evidence of Keiser and Feind, Handel's libretto and its first setting (by Keiser) antedated the Weissenfels opera. The 1706 *Componimenti musicali* includes Keiser's preface and a poem by Feind lauding Keiser to the skies and alluding to his success with *Almira* at Weissenfels. Keiser says that he had prepared two acts for the press before his journey to Weissenfels, and identifies this music with that printed in the *Componimenti*, consisting of the arias (with four recitatives) of the first two acts. They cannot be identical with the Weissenfels score, since many movements have quite different texts. Nor, as H. C. Wolff implies,[12] can they reflect Keiser's 1706 setting, where again many of the texts are different. They do however agree in all respects with the libretto set by Handel. Keiser's preface also promises publication of his third act, together with two arias by Fedeli ('Chi più mi piace' and 'Ingrato spietato') to please the singer who had learned them. (See also first note on p. 68.) This volume never appeared.

The only conclusion that fits the evidence is that Keiser made three versions of *Almira* within little more than two years, and published much of the first shortly before the production of the third. Since two of them are lost, we cannot say how much music occurred in more than one, though the wide discrepancy of the aria texts must have imposed limits. It is likely, in view of Keiser's intention to publish two of Fedeli's arias, that the Weissenfels *Almira* was in some degree a Keiser–Fedeli pasticcio. This is confirmed by a manuscript note on the libretto in Wolfenbüttel that the music was by both composers.

A possible reconstruction of the course of events is as follows. The production of Fedeli's opera at Brunswick brought the subject to Keiser's attention, and he commissioned a libretto from Feustking, Mattheson's collaborator in *Cleopatra* (1704). According to his own account,[13] Feustking wished to make a straight translation of the Brunswick libretto, but Keiser insisted on changes in the plot; Feustking mentions the introduction of a new character (Bellante) and the upgrading of Raymondo to royal rank, and complains that he was allowed only three weeks to do the job. Keiser then set the libretto, intending to produce it at Hamburg. He also prepared the first

---

[8] As note 7.

[9] In Washington, Library of Congress, and elsewhere.

[10] *Die Opern Reinhard Keisers*, 126.

[11] *HJb* (1975), 106; *Essays*, 38.

[12] *Die Barockoper in Hamburg*, i. 243.

[13] Quoted by Chrysander, i. 110.

two acts for publication to coincide with the first night, 'after the example of the French . . . to spare students the trouble of copying'. This would have been an innovation at Hamburg. At this point 'certain circumstances' imposed a delay. Keiser is referring to the publication, but it seems likely that a summons to Weissenfels caused him not only to break this off but to recast the whole opera.

The Weissenfels *Almira*, as the libretto makes clear, was a court piece designed for a very special occasion; it was produced at the Neu-Augustusburg palace in honour of a visit from the Elector Palatine Johann Wilhelm. An entertainment prepared for the burghers of Hamburg would not be suitable for a person of such consequence. Someone—possibly Feustking again—was therefore deputed to enlarge it, not only appending a long, fulsome, and irrelevant Epilogue in honour of the Elector but expanding the resources used throughout the opera, especially on the spectacular side. Keiser then gave   *
Feustking's original libretto to his protégé Handel. Two years later he decided to bring out the two acts of his first setting that were already printed, together with substantial extracts from his 1705 opera *Octavia*. In the same year (1706) he introduced six of his *Almira* arias into another opera, *La fedeltà coronata*, as he explained in his preface to the libretto.[14] These all had Italian words and were evidently from his Weissenfels setting; all are in that libretto, though three of them are in Handel's as well (Keiser may have set them for his first version and transferred them to his second). They too appeared in the *Componimenti*. Finally, still in 1706, Keiser made a fresh setting of the whole opera after Feustking's text had been remodelled by Feind, naturally omitting the arias used in *La fedeltà coronata*.

Although only Keiser's first setting is strictly relevant to Handel's (the music as well as the libretto) it may be convenient to straighten the record on the others. Apart from the Epilogue, the Weissenfels libretto contains six duets, eight choruses, and thirteen changes of set, six of them in Act III (the other operas have three in each act). There are five Entrées for dancers—six if we count the Grand Ballet after the Epilogue. The first two, with the paraphernalia for the coronation and ballroom scenes, are the same as in Handel's opera. Act III begins with a highly anachronistic scene before the temple of Venus, in which the High Priestess foretells the future of each character by divination from the entrails of white pigeons offered in sacrifice. This episode contains three substantial choruses and ends with a dance of 'Ericinischen Jungfrauen'. The reconciliation between Edilia and Osman is followed by a ballet of gardeners of both sexes, and there is a superfluous final scene (before the Epilogue) in a street in Valladolid, beginning with a dance of athletes. Moors haul Almira and Fernando in a gilded carriage through a triumphal arch, followed by the other characters and the whole court. This libretto includes Bellante but omits Raymondo. Consalvo is ultimately paired with Bellante, and Osman with Edilia, as the result of two startling changes of heart for which the Priestess of Venus is presumably responsible. Tabarco is less satirical about court life (perhaps this was tactful); he ends Act II with an imaginary conversation with his girl-friend, singing both parts himself, a device used in Telemann's *Pimpinone* and elsewhere.

Feind's 1706 libretto for Keiser omits the extra Weissenfels ceremonial but draws on all three earlier texts. It is closest to Handel's, differing in little more

[14] The arias are listed in Zelm, *Die Opern Reinhard Keisers*, 128 n. 1.

than the choice of arias. Feind cut or replaced nineteen arias (six with Italian words), two duets, and two choruses; he introduced nine Italian arias (all from the Brunswick libretto) and five German pieces, two arias, two duets, and a chorus in the first scene. Three of these, including the chorus, come from Weissenfels; the other two were presumably Feind's own. The macaronic libretto—the recitatives sung in German, almost a third of the arias in Italian—was as we have seen a recent innovation, introduced to Hamburg by Keiser in *Der verführte Claudius* (1703). Fedeli's *Almira* at Brunswick was sung throughout in Italian; the published libretto has a German prose translation. Handel's libretto contains 15 Italian arias out of 53, Weissenfels 17 out of 51, Keiser (1706) 18 out of 46. Nine are common to all three. All except one ('Quel labbro di coral', imported by Feustking perhaps from another Italian opera) originated in the Brunswick libretto.

Friedrich Christian Feustking (*c*.1678–1739) was a theological student who in 1701 had been sentenced to ten years' expulsion from Wittenberg University for lampooning one of his professors.[15] He spent the years 1702–5 in Hamburg, writing on archaeology and the visual arts as well as poetry and librettos, before obtaining a clerical living near Schleswig. He seems to have been a turbulent priest. Apart from his exploits at Wittenberg he engaged in an acrimonious literary controversy with Feind and Hunold, partly about the libretto of *Almira*, and was rejected at the altar by a woman whom he had avidly pursued. His libretto for *Cleopatra* was notorious for the obscenity of its comic scenes. In 1719 however he had a *Dissertatio theologica* printed in Wittenberg.[16]

If Feustking's complaint that Keiser forced him to complicate the plot when he wished simply to translate the Brunswick libretto is substantially true, the librettist deserves some sympathy. Fedeli's collaborator scarcely altered Pancieri's text (he changed 'Regni Almira' in I ii from a duet for Osmano and Raimondo to a chorus, added two arias for Consalvo and one for Osmano in Act III, and substituted a love duet for Almira's closing aria, which he placed earlier in the act). Consalvo has two elder sons, Osmano and Raimondo, both aspiring to Almira's hand. Since Osmano is publicly betrothed to Edilia and has enjoyed her favours, Raimondo thinks he has a clear run with Almira. It is he (with much more point), not Fernando, who overhears the angry parting of Osmano and Edilia in Act I. The brothers then quarrel over a game of chess, in which Pancieri plays on the double meaning of the word 'Queen', and are separated by Almira. This makes a far stronger impact than Osman's jealousy of the mistress he has just discarded and the intrusion of Bellante. In Act II both elder brothers overhear the scene between Almira and Fernando, which though complex is free from the absurdities of Feustking's version. Raimondo hopes Osmano will kill Fernando when he discovers Almira's love for him, thus promoting his own suit above that of a murderer. Almira's seizure of the sword is more credible, since the scene takes place in Fernando's room and she

---

[15] Collision with authority seems to have been an occupational hazard for Hamburg librettists. Hunold was forced to flee to Halle after satirizing the scandalous behaviour of singers (including Conradin) and other persons connected with the opera in a novel of 1706. Feind was hanged in effigy in 1707 and for a time banned from the city by the Senate.

[16] See Stompor, 'Die deutschen Aufführungen', 33 ff, and Chrysander, i. 105 ff.

has disguised herself to escape recognition. Act II ends with a quarrelling duet between Edilia and Osmano; the scene in which Tabarco carries the letters comes earlier. In Act III Edilia and Osmano are reconciled after she has tried to kill herself. Raimondo is convinced that Almira and the throne are now his for the asking, and only gives up at the very end when Consalvo identifies Fernando as his son. He remains unmatched, and there is no love interest for Consalvo. Neither Pancieri nor the Brunswick libretto has any choruses outside the coronation scene, and both confine the ballet, as usual in Italian operas, to entr'actes where it is wholly detached from the plot. Act I ends with an umbrella dance ('otto Mori con ombrelli, e ventagli'), Act II with a dance for eight Spaniards.

  Whatever we may think of the point of arboreal orthography that triggers off the first misunderstanding ('AMO, E DIRLO NON SO' in Italian), this libretto is reasonably clear in motivation and construction. In adapting it Feustking made use of the German translation in the Brunswick libretto, and in some arias—'Leset, ihr funkelden Augen', 'Liebliche Wälder', 'Wer umb Geld'— kept close to the original. To conform with Hamburg taste he increased the ration of spectacle and integrated the ballet in the plot, on the whole very successfully. The elaborate detail of the coronation and ballroom scenes, with their stage orchestras, is his, and so is the tableau of the continents at the start of Act III, where song and dance are happily combined. The popularity of French ideas at Hamburg is evident here, as also in the frequency of French words in the recitative and stage directions and the satirical edge that Feustking gives to Tabarco; originally a typical Venetian servant, he has become the vehicle for pungent comment on the Frenchified conventions of contemporary German courts. Hamburg was very conscious of being a free city.

  A less happy innovation was the prison scene, a device that seldom fails in opera, but so gratuitously introduced that it devalues the whole denouement. There is no reason why Almira, immediately after discovering Fernando's innocence, should send Tabarco with a message that he must die. But the most lamentable features of the libretto spring from the decision to introduce Bellante. This led Feustking to reshuffle the plot, tying extra knots in the intrigue and redistributing the couples at the end. The characters leap to idiotic conclusions, plunge into action without the most elementary fore-thought or explanation, and behave with the mindless inconsequence of a flock of beheaded chickens. This was by no means unique in opera of the period; but Feustking produced a particularly crass specimen. The few strong situations are confined to the relationship between Almira and Fernando, which he left undisturbed. Raymondo, losing his status in Consalvo's family, becomes visiting royalty in disguise and abruptly switches his affections to Edilia when Almira awards the prize to Europe (Fernando) in III iii. The blurring of the relationship between Edilia and Osman weakens the motivation of both. Bellante, subjected to the unwelcome attentions of Consalvo, accepts Osman, who happens to be conveniently free. Worst of all is the demotion of Consalvo from a wise counsellor into the fun figure, ridiculed by Tabarco, of a lascivious elder. In Act III he emerges as a grotesque hypocrite by making further passes at Bellante just before sending Fernando to prison for what he takes to be a guilty passion for Edilia. Feustking's German is swollen with windy rhetoric, strained metaphors and grotesque conceits, and

he is apt to place arias where they clog instead of forwarding the action, as
when at a critical moment they have to be sung aside (Almira's 'Vollkommene
Hände' in I vi) or behind the scenes (Osman's 'Scepter und Kron' in II vii),
though the latter has a precedent in Pancieri. The lax treatment of exits, with
characters hanging about after full arias or dashing off in the middle of
recitatives, points up the virtues of a convention that had not yet penetrated to
Hamburg.

It would be too much to expect an inexperienced composer of nineteen to
reduce this gallimaufry to order; the mature Handel might have been
defeated in the unlikely event of his accepting such a task. In the conditions
obtaining at Hamburg the problem was perhaps insoluble. The confusion of
genres—two languages, three national styles, elaborate ballet sequences,
abrupt shifts between near-tragedy and satirical comedy—and the absence of
any serious attempt to integrate them are not in themselves indications of
Handel's immaturity; they were characteristic of the whole Hamburg school.
What is significant is that all these elements occur in Handel's later work (even
the mixed languages in some oratorio performances of the 1730s), with the
important difference that in the course of time he contrived to subject them to
an overriding conception of the opera as an artistic entity. The decisive factor
was his development of the aria as an all-purpose structural unit of the utmost
flexibility and a means of conveying the finest nuances of character. This he
learned in Italy; the lump he was later to leaven remains scarcely permeable in
Almira. If we consider his whole career as a progressive assimilation of
centrifugal influences, the need for this—and the first impulse towards it—was
perhaps not the least important of the lessons he learned in Hamburg.

Since the Hamburg style was so heterogeneous, it is difficult—and not very
profitable—to trace every constituent to its historical source. Natalia Seifas[17]
has adduced parallels with Lully, the German orchestral suite of the seventeenth century, Zachow's cantatas, and the operas of Steffani, as well as the
new expressive manner of Keiser and Mattheson. Certainly the arias exhibit a
bewildering mixture of styles—French binary dance movements, half-fledged
Italian toccatas, German ariosos redolent of Passion music, and derivations
from the chamber cantata, sacred or secular, which may owe something to
Zachow. But it is likely that all this was filtered through Keiser, who was not
only the most successful opera composer in Germany and very much in the
ascendant at Hamburg but also a great eclectic, in this respect strikingly
similar in temperament to Handel.

We can single out several types of aria for which Handel found a ready
model in Keiser. This must be distinguished from borrowing, the result of a
conscious decision unconnected with stylistic influence. Handel's borrowings
from *Octavia* in Italy and later are nearly all incipits. He used them as a starter
to his imagination in ritornellos and launched into fresh territory at the entry
of the voice. No one could have pointed to Keiser had the score of *Octavia* not
happened to survive.

1. The continuo aria in which the bass anticipates the vocal line and
continues throughout as a free ostinato, sometimes with canonic writing: 'So

[17] 'Die Concerti Grossi op. 6 und ihr Stellung in Händels Gesamtwerk', *HJb* (1980), 19–21.

ben che regnante' (I ii), 'Alter schadt der Thorheit nicht' (II iii). Compare *La forza della virtù*, 'Wenn schoner Jugend' (I xi).

2. The big fully accompanied C major aria, generally for soprano, with mainly triadic vocal line, leaps to high notes, and brilliant taxing divisions: 'Proverai' (I iv), 'Kochet ihr Adern' (III x). Compare *La forza della virtù*, 'Mich berufft' (in D with trumpet in C), *Janus*, 'Lachen auff Rosen' (II xi), *Octavia*, 'La Roma trionfante' (I iii, with horns), 'Es streiten mit reizende Blüthe' (II iii), and 'Die Eifersucht bläset' (II x, again with horns). Keiser evidently associated this type with outbursts of anger or triumph.

3. Arias based on a short but arresting rhythmic figure—generally a quaver or semiquaver group interspersed with sudden smaller or longer note values—that persists like an ostinato in the bass or upper instruments or both: 'Ach wiltu die Herzen' (I ii), 'Schöne Flammen' (II vi), 'Svenerò' (II x), 'Edilia, du bleibest mein' (III ix). Compare *Octavia*, 'Atlas stützt den blauen Bogen' (I i), 'Non mi negate' (I v), 'Ziehet Titan aus der See' (II x), 'Wer mit Vorsatz hat gefehlet' (III ix), and several examples in *La forza della virtù*, *Masagniello*, and *Croesus* ('Erweckt in meinem Herzen' in I v, 'Schmeik ein Kleinod' in III viii). This type still haunted Handel's early London operas, for example Act I of *Amadigi*.

4. Arias with a continuous or nearly continuous running figure that operates in much the same way: 'Du irrst dich, mein Licht', 'Zürne was hin' (both I iv), 'Blinder Schütz' (III vi). Compare *Octavia*, 'Du kannst hoffen' (I ix), 'Vaghi lumi' (II ii); also *Cleopatra*, 'Ruhe sanfft' (III vii).

5. Arias in French dance measures, sometimes syncopated, whether slow (sarabandes) or fast pieces in bounding compound metres (6/8, 9/8, 12/8), always a favourite with Keiser. His operas, like Handel's, abound in vocal gavottes, rigaudons, minuets, and gigues. There are numerous examples in *La forza della virtù*, *Octavia*, *Masagniello*, and later; in *Tomyris* only five out of twenty-nine arias are in common time, and Keiser uses such unusual signatures as 1/2 and 8/16 as well as irregularly alternating 3/8 and 2/4 (if he knew 'Bel piacere' in *Agrippina*, this may be a case of reversed influence). Mattheson in *Henrico IV* worked 4/8 against 6/8. Handel broadened his style later, and dance arias were a feature of the whole period, but the flexibility of his rhythms may owe something to Hamburg.

6. Arias accompanied by solo oboe and bass only, a texture seldom if ever used by Handel in London: 'Chi più mi piace' (I iii), 'Gönne nach den Thränengüssen' (III v). Compare *Octavia*, 'Geliebte Augen!' (I iv), 'So manchesmal' (III vi). In a related type an initial signal-like solo alternates with *tutti* passages: 'L'alma mia' (*Agrippina*, I vi). Compare *Octavia*, 'Ein edles Gemüthe' (II xiv). This has a precedent in Steffani (*Henrico Leone*, I i, 'Tra le braccie').

7. Similar treatment of darkness and prison scenes. Fernando's 'Der kann im Blitz' (III xiv, F minor) is very close to Agrippina's C minor 'Grauser Finsterniss' (*Janus*, II xi) in instrumental layout, descending quasi chromaticism, and general mood.

In his book on the Hamburg Opera[18] Wolff included a detailed comparison, with quotations, between a number of scenes in Handel's *Almira* and Keiser's settings of the same words in the *Componimenti*, without appreciating

---

[18] *Die Barockoper in Hamburg*, i. 243–8, ii. 72–83.

that the latter are the earlier. He unwittingly demonstrates that Handel not only knew Keiser's settings but sometimes used them, consciously or not, as a model for his own. Among many parallels—they scarcely qualify as borrowings, and not all are noted by Wolff—are the initial vocal melodies of 'Ach wiltu die Hertzen' (Handel changed the mode to minor) and 'So ben che regnante' (improved by a canonic treatment of the bass), the B section of 'Chi più mi piace', the almost identical second phrase ('schattige Felder') of 'Liebliche Wälder', and the imitative treatment of the voices in the duet 'Ich will gar von nichtes wissen'. In each case Handel's music echoes Keiser's, if sometimes at a distance. Handel's setting of 'Ob dein Mund' seems to have been suggested by Keiser's treatment of the previous aria ('Svenerò'). Both settings of 'Sanerà' have some connection with the melodic contour of the preceding recitatives.

These resemblances are less important than the differences. There are already signs of that urge to expand a movement to its full musical capacity that was to become characteristic of Handel's maturity. Where Keiser allows nine bars to the A section of 'Schönste Rosen', Handel requires three times as many and writes a substantial B section as well—and the tempo is Adagio throughout. The abruptly foreshortened da capo—a device employed on occasion by Keiser—may have been inspired by a sense that the proportions were getting out of hand. There is also a tendency towards expressing a generalized mood rather than highlighting detail. As Wolff points out, Keiser illustrates the *Affekt* of 'Geloso tormento' by vocal melisma (as Monteverdi or Cavalli might have done). Handel diffuses it throughout the aria in an oboe obbligato. His setting of 'Liebliche Wälder' is a sustained mood-picture with long ritornellos; Keiser contents himself with a brief murmuring figure over a pedal. It is inconceivable that a later Handel opera could contain anything approaching the 53 arias of *Almira*, not to mention the three duets, three choruses, and three ballet suites.

The score is very uneven in style, quality, and technique, with abundant promise but intermittent fulfilment. That his ideas seldom yield their full potential Handel implicitly acknowledged when he refined and expanded many of them—and Keiser's as well—in later works, chiefly in Italy but also in London operas and even oratorios. His one surviving Hamburg opera provides conclusive evidence of his wisdom in abandoning provincial Germany for the living sources of the art. For it is weakest in those very respects in which his mature operas are unrivalled. Both the vocal writing and the aria design are for the most part primitive. Still more startling, to anyone familiar with his later style, is the gauche and constricted melodic idiom. The lyrical ideas are nearly all of short span and instrumentally conceived, even when given to the voice, which is treated as an instrument that happens to have the words. The coloratura, though sometimes brilliant to a fault, is applied rather than intrinsic, and ungrateful to the singer both in layout and compass; Almira and Edilia are several times required to begin a phrase on a top C.[19] As Dent remarks,[20] the voice part of 'Kochet ihr Adern' is much more apt for the violin. Handel was a violinist, but the dominant influence here was

---

[19] The tessitura of arias like 'Proverai' and 'Kochet ihr Adern' is so extreme as to suggest that the Hamburg opera used an exceptionally low pitch. The occasions on which Handel after *Almira* gave a soprano a top C can be counted on the fingers of one hand.

[20] *Handel: a Symposium*, 17–18.

undoubtedly Keiser, whose vocal music (see the arias listed under type 2 above) has the same overwhelmingly instrumental flavour. Mattheson, a singer, treated the voice more idiomatically in *Cleopatra*.

Handel's inexperience is revealed by the lack of flexibility and balance, formal, tonal, and textural, that allows the energy of the music and the many flashes of imagination so often to run to waste. Some arias are too slight to make their mark, or stumble from cadence to cadence without taking wing. Sometimes the A section does not modulate at all, whereas the B section meanders aimlessly in several directions. In 'Zweier Augen Majestät' and 'Werthe Schrift' B is longer than A, which runs aground almost before it has left harbour. All too often the vocal and instrumental elements fail to fuse or penetrate each other.[21] Handel has scarcely begun to control the internal balance of an aria by varying the length and weight of the ritornellos. While da capo form predominates, some arias repeat only the opening ritornello or, as in 'Schönste Rosen', a mere fragment of the A section. The proportion of cavatinas is high, but they occur haphazard without relation to exits, not as functional units in a carefully planned organization. The recitatives, apart from the few accompanied sections where the adventurousness of later practice is fitfully glimpsed, are for the most part stiff and angular, and sometimes take the voices so high as to inhibit a *parlando* delivery. The occasional use of coloratura on key words (Consalvo's 'donnernden' in I i, Almira's 'lebet' in III xviii) is another reflection of Keiser's practice.

The instrumental point of departure is conspicuous in the numerous arias for voice and continuo (type 3 above) where the latter develops a busy rhythmic motive in a manner half-way between an ostinato and a ground bass. The initial figures of 'Schöne Flammen' (*a*) and 'Svenerò' (*b*) are striking in themselves and effective agents in generating thrust and tension, but they defeat their own purpose by smothering the vocal line, which is elbowed into second place. Later Handel was to accommodate these self-willed and functional basses while allowing full scope for the voice. There are already signs, for example in Edilia's 'Quillt, ihr überhäuften Zähren', of a fruitful interaction between two parts that never share the same material. More often the German contrapuntist exhibits his wares without harnessing them to a dramatic and expressive purpose.

Ex. 1
(*a*)

(*b*)

---

[21] These aspects are ably analysed by David Kimbell in his dissertation 'A Critical Study of Handel's Early Operas' (University of Oxford, 1968).

One type of aria in which future glories are already presaged is the dreamy pastoral, the appeal for sympathy to the sights and sounds of nature. Edilia's 'Schönste Rosen' and Fernando's 'Liebliche Wälder' in the Act I garden scene have greater lyrical freedom and a stronger forward thrust than most of the score. The use of two recorders with a four-part string texture, though conventional for nature pieces, supplies more than a hint of that haunting sensuousness that was soon to make Handel irresistible in this mood. Fernando's aria is contrasted with Edilia's but also echoes it, for example in the rising sixth of the voice's second phrase. Most of the other extended arias are demands for vengeance and similar expressions of outrage. Handel reserves the concerto grosso style, still clumsily managed, for situations of this sort. Based on furious scales and arpeggios, with little harmonic interest but a great deal of rhythmic stamping, they have a crude animal impact. They are however somewhat devalued by conformity to a pattern; little distinction of character is perceptible between Almira's 'Vedrai, s'a tuo dispetto' and 'Kochet ihr Adern', Fernando's 'Ob dein Mund', and Edilia's 'Proverai' and 'Der Himmel wird strafen'. All are fully-scored pieces in major keys with the voice doing its best to beat the instruments at their own game.

Handel employs the traditional methods of varying the dramatic pace, though not with any high degree of imagination or with the vivid impact sometimes achieved by Keiser in *Masagniello*. Several arias begin without ritornello or with the ritornello delayed till after the voice's first phrase. Almira's 'Nò, nò, non voglio' (II vii) cuts off the previous recitative without a cadence. Two arias in Act III are interrupted by another character: Raymondo's 'Edilia, du bleibest mein' (III ix) continues in secco when Edilia answers the last phrase off-stage; he takes her first 'Ja, ja!' for an echo, whereupon she enters and repeats it in acknowledgement. 'Fernando stirbet dein' (III xv) is twice punctuated by recitative from the concealed Almira and finally broken off on the dominant when she comes forward and addresses Fernando. In two arias, 'Schönste Rosen' and 'Lass das Schicksal', the B section introduces a sharp metrical contrast as well as a new tonality. None of these points is original, but they are worth noting as the precedents for many supreme strokes in later operas.

A prominent structural detail, Italian in origin, is the frequent appearance of an extended and orchestrally elaborated ritornello, generally in binary form, after the da capo or at the end of a cavatina. This is often the most striking feature of the movement. It seems to have had a functional as well as an expressive purpose, to provide music for an exit and perhaps a change of set. Ten arias and two duets in *Almira* end in this manner. Three are solos for Tabarco, probably rounded off with a dance or other comic business. Six (two in each act) precede a change of set, and all the others except Bellante's 'Ich brenne zwar' lead to an important exit. Handel underlines the pause in the action. In the London operas, possibly because the stage machinery was more expeditiously managed, he preferred to go straight on, marking a change of scene or a fresh dramatic emphasis by a switch in tonality. The expanded ritornello after Osman's 'Scepter und Kron' (II vii), in which oboes and violas are added to the orchestra, is separated from the aria by secco dialogue. That after Tabarco's 'Schürzchen mit dem Falbala' occurs twice, at the end of the aria and again, after a short recitative, as a coda to the second act.[22] Handel's

---

[22] He was to use this idea for an explicit dramatic purpose in Theseus's aria describing his victory over the Minotaur in *Arianna*.

intention on both occasions was evidently to avoid the anticlimax of ending a scene with recitative. The most remarkable of these ritornellos is the enormous appendage (88 bars with repeats) after the duet 'Spielet, ihr blitzenden Augen' (III xv), which is totally distinct from the 36-bar duet in mood, metre, and material. It may denote a release of emotional energy as Almira and Fernando at last achieve their reconciliation.

The most prophetic feature of the score is the alacrity with which the nineteen-year-old Handel, again learning from Keiser, seizes his chance when one of the characters is found in a situation that permits the expression of deep feeling. The quickening of the pulse is immediate. The climaxes of the action—Almira's jealousy and desperation in I vi and II ix, the prison scene in III xv—inspire the strongest music, whereas the weakest occurs when the plot is at its most irrelevant or absurd. Although none of the characters is a portrait in the round, more than one is lit by intermittent flashes. Almira herself is the most favoured; as in so many later operas, the unhappy victim of passion evokes Handel's sympathy and wins our respect for her sufferings, if not for her intelligence. Pancieri placed her firmly in the centre of the picture by making her end all three scenes where the set changes in Act I (as well as the opera itself) with a solo aria. Feustking preserved this pattern in Act I, including the Italian words, though the music of the third aria is unfortunately lost. Her entire part until the middle of Act III is in minor keys (the lost 'Ingrato spietato' was almost certainly in G minor), as befits a woman distracted by violent emotion. In 'Geloso tormento' Handel succeeds in dramatizing this conflict with power and eloquence. The contrasted dynamics of the ritornello, a dialogue for solo oboe and strings with alternate *piano* and *forte* bars, establish a tension that is not permitted to relax. Almira's *scena* in II ix is equally impressive. The accompanied recitative 'Ich kann nicht mehr' anticipates a brilliant stroke of later years by bringing back the initial phrase before leading into the aria, 'Move i passi'.[23] In this substantial piece, presently adapted for *Agrippina*, Handel is flexing his wings; though a little stiff (the unremitting crotchet motion admits not a single rest in the instrumental parts), they are already capable of sustained flight. The music expresses Almira's anguish with unmistakable force. Her part in Act III is more conventional, though the accompanied recitative 'Treuloser Mensch' with its top C on the word 'Mord' strikes home. The best moments in her two display arias, the sudden pause on a diminished seventh ('crudele') in 'Vedrai, s'a tuo dispetto' and the repeated unison low G for violins and violas on the word 'Rache' in 'Kochet ihr Adern' are little more than an effective use of cliché. The duet with Fernando is disappointingly trivial and quite dwarfed by the enormous final ritornello.

The best of Fernando's music, apart from 'Liebliche Wälder', where the neat imitations between recorder, violin, and voice produce a pleasantly rich texture, occurs in the prison scene (III iv). The dramatic gestures of 'Der kann im Blitz', traditionally associated with thunder and lightning, make their point. The B flat minor accompanied recitative 'Verhängnis wiltu denn' begins impressively but allows the tension to evaporate by falling into too regular cadences, a fault Handel was not slow to correct. In the interrupted aria 'Fernando stirbet dein' he shows a nice sense of dramatic

---

[23] Compare 'Chi vide mai' in *Tamerlano* and 'O sventurati affetti' in *Scipione*.

proportion.[24] The simple syllabic setting, by no means without eloquence, is the ancestor of such sublime moments as Melissa's dying arioso in *Amadigi* and 'Stille amare' in *Tolomeo*. The second tenor, Osman, is less well endowed. His tendency to fall into gigue rhythm, for instance in 'Du irrst dich' and 'Ich will euch verdammen', may be an attempt on Handel's part to suggest his flighty nature (he trifles with the affections of all three sopranos). By far the best of his eight arias is his appeal to Fernando in II v, 'Sprich vor mir ein süsses Wort', attractively and unusually scored for two recorders, solo viola, and bass with the first recorder pleading Osman's cause by echoing the voice. His duet with Edilia in I x, one of Feustking's happier modifications (he found the model in the last scene of Brunswick's Act II, taken over without change from Pancieri), is a spirited action piece with a nice touch of malice; the treatment of the voices alternately in imitation and in tenths reflects the mixture of unanimity and defiance in their relationship. Osman's duet with Bellante is as feeble as the turn of the plot that brings them together.

Edilia is the most promising of the other characters. 'Schönste Rosen' is a fluent and graceful Adagio with a feeling for continuity, colour, and contrast. The change in the middle, not only in key and metre but in scoring (6/8 with two recorders, two solo violins, and a very light bass, after 4/4 with four-part strings), while scarcely demanded by the words, is a delightful surprise,though the abbreviated return, in which the oboes appear for the first time, is not convincing. The 6/8 section has some interesting experiments in texture and balance, with the voice acting as bass to the recorders in phrases of irregular length (five and six bars). In the A section of 'Proverai' the voice ends with what can only be described as an indignant squeal; the idea is perhaps more arresting than its execution, but the aria has spirit. 'Più non vuò' uses the same instrumental motive in both sections and develops it resourcefully in the extended four-part ritornello after the da capo. Edilia fades out in the later acts, but 'Quillt, ihr überhäuften Zähren' has moments of harmonic power, especially when the dotted ostinato temporarily breaks down.

Bellante's music contains little of note except a characteristic twinge of chromaticism on the word 'dolore' in the B section of 'Chi sà, mia speme'. Raymondo's arias are mostly short and undeveloped. 'Mi dà speranza al core' is interesting for its profusion of ideas, all of which yielded richer returns in later contexts. Consalvo gets the opera under way with an appropriately festive aria, on which Handel often drew later, but his part is otherwise negligible. It consists almost entirely of cavatinas, the best of which, 'Unartige schöne', begins with a palpable echo of the dance of 'Charlatans'. This is presumably an accident, but a not inappropriate one.

Tabarco's scenes, if not particularly distinguished, have the merit of consistency. Apart from Elviro in *Serse* he is the only character in a Handel opera who belongs entirely to the comic tradition. As we have seen, this was endemic at Hamburg. Wolff and others connect Tabarco with the fool in English drama, but Pancieri's libretto leaves no doubt that his immediate ancestors are the ribald servants of Venetian opera[25] who were later hived off

---

[24] This scene was changed for the worse in the Weissenfels libretto, where Fernando has substantial aria texts in place of Handel's first two arioso sections and four lines of recitative in place of the third (HG 108). Was Handel responsible for Feustking's original plan, which he often followed later?

[25] Both strains derive ultimately from the *commedia dell'arte*.

into the intermezzo, played between the acts. The placing of his burlesque scene at the end of the second act[26] marks a step in this direction, no doubt imitated in Hamburg from Italian models; Act II of Keiser's *Octavia* likewise ends with a comic scene and a dance. All Tabarco's five solos are in simple dance rhythms, and all except 'Habbiate pazienza' (which alone has a da capo) are in fact followed by a dance; there can be little question that the extended binary ritornellos, as long as or longer than the arias they conclude, were intended for this purpose. In 'Am Hofe zu heissen galant' he makes fun of French dance steps in words and music, and doubtless in gesture. Handel reveals his immaturity here by nearly failing to reach the dominant in time at the double bar of the ritornello. 'Alter schadt der Thorheit nicht' (II iii) was later used with striking improvements for 'Haste thee, nymph' in *L'Allegro*.

Apart from the overture, which steps out with spacious grandeur but loses its impetus in a cramped Allegro, the only purely instrumental movements are the eleven dances, grouped in three scenes. All are in the French style with French titles; eight are in G minor, the others no more remote than B flat, D minor, and F. There is no attempt at local colour; the Rigaudon for the Africans in III ii is as ceremoniously north European as could be imagined. The quality is respectable rather than inspired, though the Courante has attractive cross-rhythms (3/2 against 6/4) and the Minuet is charming. The melodies of both Sarabandes were to achieve greater distinction, and one of them immortal fame, as arias in London operas: that in Act I as 'Pena tiranna' in *Amadigi*, that in Act III as 'Lascia ch'io pianga' in *Rinaldo*.

The tonality leans heavily towards flat keys and the minor mode, and is not well balanced: including the dances there are thirty-nine movements in B flat, G minor, and D minor, but only one in A major and none in E major or any sharp minor key except E minor. Yet there is evidence of a plan. The opera begins and ends in solid B flat, and Handel regularly associates this key (described by Mattheson, in Buelow's translation, as 'very diverting and magnificent' and also 'dainty') and its relative minor with the court and ceremonial scenes, including the ballet and even the aria ('Was ist des Hofes Gunst?') in which Fernando pours out his bitterness about court favour. After the long opening sequence entirely in flat keys (with the inevitable exception of the brief *coro* with trumpets) the change to G major for Edilia's aria in the garden is singularly happy. Apart from Edilia's lament in III v, F minor is reserved for the prison scene, where Fernando has two arias in this key separated by an accompanied recitative in B flat minor. Later prison scenes, notably that in *Rodelinda*, are associated with the same keys. Two or three arias, for example 'Svenerò' and 'Unartige Schöne', follow a recitative in an inconsequent progression. This may be due to immaturity or to defects in the single manuscript source.

The scoring, though much of it is routine, has points of interest. The composition of the orchestra is regular by Hamburg standards: three trumpets and drums in the coronation scene, two treble recorders (in the three arias already mentioned), oboes, bassoons, strings, and continuo. Three arias feature a solo oboe; one has unison violas without violins, another a solo violin, solo cello, and bass. Almira's 'Move i passi' has a rich five-part accompani-

[26] The corresponding scene in Brunswick and Pancieri occurs earlier, immediately before Almira's 'Move i passi'. In Weissenfels Tabarco ends the act, but with a different aria expressing quite different sentiments.

ment for three violins, viola, and bass, to which the voice adds a sixth independent part. This sort of texture was to produce marvellous results later.[27] In Almira's aria Handel writes the third violin part in the alto clef and the viola in the tenor, possibly for the tenor violin. According to Seifas[28] the low unison string tremolando in the B section of 'Der Himmel wird strafen', with the violins exploiting their G strings, was a completely new expressive resource in Germany. It became a regular feature of Handel's style.

A large number of instruments are mentioned in the stage directions, trumpets and drums for the coronation scene, oboes for the ball at the end of Act I, and four different groups for the Act III pageant, including a Turkish band of wind and percussion and the hurdy-gurdy and bagpipes attending Tabarco. It is clear that in Act I at least Handel had part of his orchestra on the stage. Of the eight arias and dances in the pageant scene all but one are scored for a *tutti* treble line and bass; the instruments named—or some of them—no doubt played here. This is the one Handel opera in which the introduction of cymbals and bagpipes could be historically defended. Zuffoli (a rustic instrument, possibly panpipes), triangle, and cymbals are mentioned by Kleefeld as in use at Hamburg.

History and Text

Handel must have composed the music towards the end of 1704. Chrysander conjectured that Keiser, as director, intended to mount the opera in November, before the Advent intermission, and that he put it into rehearsal. Later, in his 'Geschichte der Hamburger Oper unter der Direktion von Reinhard Keiser (1703 bis 1706)',[29] he developed the theory that the delay was caused by the growing estrangement between Handel and Mattheson, which culminated in a duel after a performance of the latter's *Cleopatra* on 5 December. There is no evidence for any of this; the fact that the libretto is dated 1704 proves nothing, since the date may be Old Style. Mattheson's statement[30] that *Almira* was rehearsed on 30 December, the day of his reconciliation with Handel, need not be doubted. The first performance took place at the Theater am Gänsemarkt on 8 January 1705. The cast is not recorded, but Mattheson presumably sang Fernando (he says that in *Almira* and *Nero* he 'played the chief parts amid general applause' and then retired from the stage), and the Almira was probably Conradin. Stompor suggested[31] that Osman may have been sung by Johann Konrad Dreyer, Consalvo by Gottfried Grünewald, Tabarco by Christoph Rauch, and Edilia and Bellante by Schober, Rischmüller, or Barbara Keiser. Little is known of these singers, apart from Grünewald, who was a composer and dulcimer player. *Almira* is the only Handel opera without a castrato part; the voices are three sopranos, three tenors (Fernando, Osman, and Tabarco), and two basses (Consalvo and Raymondo).

* The opera was an immediate success,[32] running for about twenty nights, a

---

[27] See for example 'Vedrò frà poco' in *Admeto*.

[28] 'Die Concerti Grossi op. 6', 21.

[29] *AMZ* xv (1880), 17–25, 33–41, 49–55, 65–72, 81–8.

[30] *Grundlage einer Ehren-Pforte* (1740); Deutsch, 503.

[31] 'Die deutschen Aufführungen', 41.

[32] There is no evidence that Bach heard it or knew the score. The resemblances detected by P. Robinson ('Bach's Indebtedness to Handel's *Almira*', *MT* xlviii (1907), 309) are commonplaces of the North German style.

circumstance that no doubt induced Keiser to offer Handel an immediate second chance with *Nero*. The following months saw an outburst of abusive pamphleteering between Feustking on the one hand and Feind and Hunold on the other, which, as noted above, gives us a little information on the opera's background.[33] To what degree—if at all—this personal and literary cantankerousness extended to the composers is unknown; it may or may not be significant that within six months Keiser set a libretto by Feind with Nero as a central figure (*Octavia*, 5 August 1705) and followed it a year later with his own new version of *Almira*. It was for this opera, not Handel's (as Mattheson stated in *Der musicalische Patriot* of 1728), that Keiser wrote an epilogue entitled *Der Genius von Europa*.

Almira was revived at Hamburg on 7 February 1732, with alterations by Telemann; the diary of Wilhelm Willers[34] mentions only two performances. The single surviving manuscript of the score was evidently adapted for this revival. With its aid and that of the libretto it is possible to establish the changes, which are interesting. All the dances were cut, together with five arias, one chorus, and two recitatives. Telemann rewrote three arias wholly or in part, using the original words, and replaced three others with new pieces in Italian, almost certainly not his own. Some of the cuts—Osman's 'Zürne was hin', Almira's 'Ingrato spietato' and 'Sanerà la piaga', Consalvo's 'Unartige Schöne', Bellante's 'Ich brenne zwar', the chorus 'Hoffe nur der rechten Zeit' (III xvii), and the recitatives 'Und will dein Herz' (III vi, HG 87) and 'Geh, Unvorsichtiger' (III vii, HG 90)—may have been imposed for dramatic reasons, though this can hardly apply to 'Ingrato spietato'. Its omission not only brought Act I to an end with a secco recitative (as in the Weissenfels libretto) but deprived us of the music, which, like most of 'Hoffe nur', was torn out of the manuscript. If anything was substituted, there is no sign of it in the libretto or the score. Of the six replaced arias, one ('Vollkommene Hände') is the least effective in Almira's part; the other five comprise all Edilia's solo music except the duet 'Ich will gar von nichtes wissen'. Telemann supplied a new setting, still in F minor, of 'Quillt, ihr überhäuften Zähren', simpler vocal lines with a lower tessitura for 'Schönste Rosen' and 'Der Himmel wird strafen', retaining Handel's instrumental parts, and a new overture. It is clear that Edilia was a less accomplished singer than in 1705, and a mezzo-soprano rather than a soprano; Telemann does not take her above G. The inserted Italian arias were 'Se lento ancora un fulmine' for 'Proverai' in I iv, 'Timido pellegrin'—possibly the aria from Giay's *Publio Cornelio Scipione* (Turin, 1726), also used in Handel's London pasticcio *Ormisda* of 1730—for 'Vollkommene Hände' in I vi, and 'Suol così la navicella' for 'Più non vuò' in I vii. Also cut were the long final ritornellos of 'Chi più mi piace', 'Am Hofe zu heissen galant', the duet 'Ich will gar von nichtes', 'Alter schadt', 'Scepter und Kron', 'Ob dein Mund', and 'Vedrai, s'a tuo dispetto', leaving only two such appendages in the score (at the end of Act II and after the duet 'Spielet, ihr blitzenden Augen'). This may reflect a different technique in scene-changing.

Almira was the only Handel opera performed during the nineteenth century, in a version by J. N. Fuchs so decimated that it formed part of a triple bill. It was placed between Keiser's *Venus und Adonis* and Gluck's *Le Cadi dupé* at

---

[33] The unedifying details are related in Chrysander's biography, i. 105–11, 126–7. Hunold wrote a parody of 'Almira regiere', the first aria in *Almira*.

[34] In P. A. Merbach, *Das Repertoire der Hamburger Oper von 1718 bis 1750* (Leipzig, 1924).

the Hamburg Stadt Theater on 14 January 1878, the first night of 'a historic week of opera'[35] to celebrate the bicentenary of the Hamburg Opera. The same company repeated it at Leipzig on 25 June 1879 and 23 February 1885, the bicentenary of Handel's birth. The enthusiasm generated by the Leipzig performance moved the *Musical Times* to declare with unconscious irony: 'The successful revival of this work in our days is the more noteworthy as testifying to the vitality possessed by a species of music generally regarded as obsolete. Considering the unique popularity which the works of what may be called Handel's third period, viz., his oratorios, enjoy in this country, it is surprising that no attempt is being made at a similar revival of one or other of the numerous operas written by him during the earlier part of his career in England'.[36] It was thirty-five years before a Handel opera was heard again, and forty-five before one was staged in England. *Almira* was revived at Leipzig for Handel's tercentenary, 23 February 1985.

Librettos

1704 Hamburg. 'Der in Krohnen erlangte Glücks-Wechsel oder: Almira, Königin von Castilien, In einem Singspiel auf dem grossen Hamburgischen Schauplatz vorgestellet im Jahr 1704. Gedruckt bey Friedrich Conrad Greflingern.' As in most Hamburg librettos of this period the librettist, composer, and singers are not named. The characters are fully described and the dances and scene settings listed before the text as well as within it. The Argument, much of it a direct translation of Pancieri's, has been quoted above. The text of 'Habbiate pazienza' and 'Spielet, ihr blitzenden Augen' differs slightly from the score; the former was copied from either the Brunswick or the Weissenfels libretto, both of which contain a line omitted by Handel. German translations are supplied for the fifteen Italian arias. There are three issues of the libretto, all dated 1704, the second and third inscribed 'gedruckt im obgemelten Jahr' and 'gedruckt im selben Jahr' respectively. Chrysander thought this was due to great public interest aroused by the rehearsals, of which we know nothing. More probably the successful run in January and February increased the demand. It is possible, as suggested by B. Baselt, that the first issue was prepared for Keiser's abortive setting; a page with a *Vorwort* was removed from the only known copy, as shown by a cue *Vor-* on the preceding verso. In later issues the page carried the plot summary in a wider setting. Chrysander printed the words of 'Ingrato spietato' and the chorus 'Hoffe nur der rechten Zeit' from this libretto.

1732 Hamburg. 'Gedruckt bey Philip Ludwig Stromer.' 'Krohnen' in the title is spelt 'Cronen'. Evidently based on 1704, with the following changes. All references to the ballet and the instruments that appeared on stage in connection with it are removed. This affects the scene headings in I viii and III i–iv and a few other directions (HG 4 and 41). The exotic instruments in the masque disappear, but the trumpets and drums for the coronation remain. The eight pieces listed above as cut are omitted, and the three Italian substitute arias inserted. The arias rewritten on the same words and the cut ritornellos are not of course shown.

---

[35] *MT* xix (1878), 96.
[36] *MT* xx (1879), 437.

Copies and Editions

The autograph does not survive. In his biography Chrysander claimed that
the only manuscript (Berlin Staatsbibliothek Mus MS 9050) was the original
used in 1705, written out by Mattheson from Handel's sketches and corrected
by the composer. In his edition of the score he referred to it as 'a single very
incorrect copy . . . from which the later Hamburg performances under
Telemann were directed'. The latter is nearer the truth. The manuscript, in a
clear copyist's hand identified by Schulze[37] as Hamburg copyist B, certainly
represents the 1705 score as adapted for Telemann's 1732 revival. The text
differs from that already described in one important respect only: the dances
(except the Sarabande in I i) and the stage directions relating to them are not
cancelled. The other cuts, including the final ritornellos, are all indicated. The
manuscript does not contain the three substitute arias in Act I, though there
are signs for their insertion; Telemann's other amendments to Edilia's part
appear on three pages bound in Act III in the middle of Handel's (cancelled)
setting of 'Quillt, ihr überhäuften Zähren'. They are in Telemann's autograph. The simplified voice parts of 'Schönste Rosen' and 'Der Himmel wird
strafen' have been cancelled by a single stroke. The nine missing bars in the
bass of 'Ich brenne zwar' (supplied by Chrysander) were evidently an
oversight, not corrected because the aria was cut. The fragment of chorus on
HG 116 only survives because the following recitative begins on the same
page. A second overture in a different hand has been inserted at the beginning
(though Handel's is not cancelled). It is in two movements, G minor, a slow
introduction leading to a long fugato in triple time. The manuscript has a
number of corrections and annotations, none written by Handel.

A mid-nineteenth-century copy of extracts by Rophino Lacy (Add MS
31555) contains twenty-six items from *Almira*—four Italian and thirteen
German arias, one German duet, seven dances, and one detached ritornello—
in haphazard order. It has no important variants, but was probably not
copied from Berlin MS 9050. While Lacy did some light editing and
correction of errors, he is unlikely to have added the numerous minor
variants—dynamics, orchestral details, marks of emphasis, and slurs. 'Liebliche Wälder' is marked *dolce*. The Italian arias have their words; against the
German pieces Lacy merely noted 'German words', possibly because he could
not read old German script. His source was perhaps an aria collection in
Hamburg (Mus MS ND VI 81g. Theil XI) destroyed in the last war.

Chrysander's edition (1873), the only full score, is based on the Berlin
manuscript (without Telemann's emendations) and the libretto, but omits a
number of stage directions that appear in both editions of the latter. There are
also a few mistakes; for example Raymondo's recitative 'Entschliesse dich'
(HG 84) is given to Consalvo.

A vocal score of J. N. Fuchs's 1878 arrangement was published in that year
by Kistner. Described as a *Singspiel* (though it has recitatives, not spoken
dialogue), it reduces each act to diminutive proportions, sometimes changing
and reordering the text, and cuts out Edilia, Bellante, and Raymondo
altogether. Only nine of the opera's fifty-three arias survive (three of them
transferred to different characters), together with the overture, three dances

---

[37] *Die Quellen der Hamburger Oper*, 60, 85.

(HG 6–7 and 77), the duet for Almira and Fernando, and two choruses, one of them ('Viva Almira') sung twice. Consalvo has the same number of arias as Fernando (three); Almira has only two (both filched from Edilia), though her accompanied recitative before 'Move i passi' is called an aria; Tabarco is left with none. Fuchs's claim of 'all rights' in this version, without acknowledging that it was based on Chrysander's edition, drew a sarcastic comment from the latter.[38] Liszt made a piano arrangement of the Act I Sarabande and Chaconne.

Additional Notes

* (p. 53) John Roberts (*HJb* (1990), 63 ff.) suggests that Keiser may have been forced by the 'certain circumstances', which Mainwaring interprets as the need to escape his creditors, to absent himself from Hamburg for about a year from mid-1704, and that Drüsicke may have given Handel the *Almira* libretto. According to Dorothea Schröder (ibid., 147 ff.) elaborate scenery (probably by Harms) and costumes, as well as a printed libretto, had been prepared for Keiser's opera, planned for Hamburg in the autumn; it was therefore necessary to find another composer quickly. Schröder and Werner Braun (ibid., 139 ff.) both suggest that Keiser never finished his first setting. This is improbable, since in his *Vorwort* to the first issue of the 1704 *Almira* libretto he mentions *three* Fedeli arias that he refrained from setting, the third of them, 'Vedrai s'a tuo dispetto', in Act III Scene viii.

* (p. 64) Schröder, quoting Mattheson's *Der musikalischer Patriot* (1728), says that the average receipts per performance rose by 80%, from 147 to 268 marks. Between 1695 and February 1705 the average was 174 marks.

* (p. 65) Roberts argues that in *Octavia*, a more elaborate and sumptuously orchestrated score than its predecessors, Keiser deliberately sought to outgun *Nero*, and that he succeeded. Citations from poems by Feind and Hunold support this.

* (p. 65) It is not clear how many. The libretto omits them altogether. In the only score the Sarabande in the first scene is crossed out, and the four-movement suite in I xi carries the note 'Die Menuet und Rondeau wird getanzt'.

* (p. 65) It is possible, however, as suggested by Braun, that Handel never set 'Ingrato spietato' but (like Keiser in his first version) borrowed Fedeli's setting, which is in the right key.

* (p. 67) The only autograph material linked with *Almira* is a curiosity: a slightly modified version of 'Der Mund spricht zwar', written in the 1740's in someone's manuscript collection, now in the Bibliotheca Bodmeriana, Geneva. It was published in G. F. Handel: *Songs and Cantatas for soprano and continuo*, ed. D. Burrows (Oxford, 1988). See Burrows, 'Four New Handel Songs', *MT*, cxxviii (1987), 199.

* (p. 67) This has hitherto been attributed to Telemann's revival, but Tim Crawford ('Lord Danby's lute book . . .', *Göttinger Händel-Beiträge* II (1986), 32 ff.) has proved that it is by Handel; a lute arrangement in Lord Danby's manuscript (*c.* 1710) carries his name. Its authenticity is supported by the later use of the material in the Chandos Anthem 'The Lord is my light' and *The Triumph of Time and Truth*. The manuscript also contains arrangements of the aria 'No, no, non voglio' (HG 55), the Gigue in Act III (HG 82), and the ritornello after the duet 'Spielet, ihr blitzenden Augen' (HG 111).

---

[38] *AMZ* xv (1890), 109 n.

CHAPTER 5

THE LOST HAMBURG OPERAS

HANDEL's second opera followed hard on the heels of his first. *Die durch Blut und Mord erlangete Liebe, oder: Nero* was produced at the Gänsemarkt Theatre on 25 February 1705, less than two months after *Almira*, and according to Mattheson ran for three nights. It was interrupted by Lent and a closure of the theatre, and has not been heard since. Nor has a note of the music survived, though a manuscript score from the library of the Hamburg organist J. C. Westphal is reported to have been sold in 1830. However the libretto,[1] again by Feustking, merits attention, not least because it shares several characters with Keiser's next opera *Octavia*, produced on 5 August the same year, and with Handel's own *Agrippina*. The text is entirely in German; Feustking's preface says nothing about an Italian model, and he may have confined his sources to Tacitus, Suetonius, and other ancient writers, about whom he has a good deal to say, with complaints of the difficulty in reconciling their accounts.

The framework of the plot is that of Monteverdi's *L'incoronazione di Poppea*: Nero's love for Poppea, the opposition of Seneca, who yearns for the good old days of Augustus and vainly urges Nero to return to his wife Octavia, the sentencing of the latter to exile, and the coronation of her supplanter. Had Feustking kept this reasonably clear, he might have produced an excellent drama; but he throws in sub-plots and extra characters galore and every stock device known to the operatic repertory—disguise, attempted suicide and matricide, temporary insanity, a misinterpreted portrait, slumber on stage, intrigues by the queen mother, a comic servant mocking his social superiors, the burning of Rome, a play within a play (Nero in his capacity as author), and much else. The principal and rather tiresome sub-plot involves Tiridates, crown prince of Armenia, who is betrothed to the Median princess Cassandra but in love with Poppea. Cassandra follows Tiridates to Rome disguised as a man and unrecognized until the middle of Act III; she carries his portrait, which is passed from hand to hand, generating suspicion as it goes. In addition we have Nero's catamite Anicetus ('Mignon oder Liebling'), who falls in love with Octavia; Claudius's freedman Glaptus, who like Tabarco in *Almira* offers a comic commentary in the approved Hamburg style and ends the first two acts with antimasques; and the ceaselessly conspiratorial Agrippina, who is narrowly missed by a piece of masonry dislodged from a palace at her son's instigation and ends up in prison. There are five ballets, of warriors, priests, harlequins and buffoons, incendiaries, and knights and ladies. Otho does not appear, which is just as well; Nero has sent him to Portugal to get him out of the way.

[1] Reproduced from the original edition in *HJb* (1977), 71–133.

The opera begins with the funeral and deification of Claudius, poisoned by Nero, and then sets up a whole network of misunderstandings. Everyone overhears everyone else and misinterprets his or her motives. The portrait of Tiridates plays a conspicuous part; Cassandra gives it to Poppea (without telling her who it is) to identify her betrayer; Poppea shows it to Tiridates, who is forced to admit a remarkable likeness; Nero finds it in Poppea's hands and takes it for one of her lovers. Having overheard Octavia accuse him of murdering her father (Claudius) and brother in order to obtain the throne, Nero decides to get rid of her, and for good measure orders off Agrippina and Anicetus as well. Act I ends with a harlequinade led by Glaptus. In Act II we find Octavia fishing, a harmless and sensible hobby often indulged in by misused heroines in Baroque opera. After Agrippina has escaped murder by masonry and vainly attempted to bribe Seneca into disposing of Nero—she offers what one might expect; his refusal deprives us of some middle-aged love-making—Anicetus escorts Octavia back to court. Nero makes her surprisingly welcome, and, on Seneca's advice, accepts Agrippina as well when she promises to be good. He plans to entertain the Romans with a play of his own composition about the Judgement of Paris; Seneca sees this as a lamentable lapse of standards. Cassandra puts out a report of her own death, whereupon Tiridates falls on his sword but apparently misses it and goes out of his mind. Seneca leads him away; Glaptus sings a mocking aria about the various schools of philosophy.

Act III begins with Nero's play, in which he represents Paris, and Poppea, Octavia, and Agrippina the three goddesses Venus, Juno, and Pallas. Presumably they were sung by the same singers. Anicetus· points the analogy and Glaptus supplies a comic commentary. Tiridates, still out of his wits, mistakes Glaptus for Cassandra and falls asleep under a tree. Nero gives Poppea an apple as symbol of his love, and on her insistence promises to put Octavia permanently out of the way. Tiridates begins to sing in his sleep, but is cured by the sight of Cassandra in her own clothes. The city bursts into flames. Anicetus warns Octavia that Agrippina is again up to mischief and pleads his own love, but is summarily dismissed. Nero sends Octavia into exile, orders the arrest of Agrippina on a report that she has accused him of starting the fire, and initiates the double coronation: himself and Poppea, and the reconciled Tiridates and Cassandra.

The least hackneyed features of this libretto are the Judgement of Paris scene,[2] suggested perhaps by the corresponding pageant in Act III of *Almira*, the large number of ensembles (twenty, including eleven duets, against fifty-seven arias), and the bitter-sweet finale with the triumph of the adulterous pair; Feustking can scarcely have known that he was following Monteverdi's opera. It seems to have been this moral laxity that evoked Chrysander's condemnation of the libretto as among the worst of three hundred Hamburg opera texts he had examined.[3] It is much more open to objection for ramshackle construction and the prominence given to tangential characters such as Anicetus and Glaptus, who have more arias than Seneca or Agrippina. Feind and Hunold damned it on literary grounds, the latter reporting complaints that 'there is no spirit in the verse, and one feels vexation in setting

---

[2] Wolff (*Die Barockoper in Hamburg*, 250) calls it Shakespearian and says it was influenced by the English théatre.

[3] i. 127.

such stuff to music'.[4] He may have been reflecting Handel's opinion. Mattheson on the other hand called it a model tragedy ('ein Muster einer tragischen Oper'),[5] but may have been prejudiced by the fact that it gave him his last stage part as Nero. Feustking has found more recent apologists in Wolff[6] and Stephan Stompor,[7] who both thought his work offered many opportunities for dramatic expression. What Handel made of it we can only guess; it would be surprising if at this stage of his career he was able to impart the magic touch that was later to transmute so much literary dross into gold. On the whole Chrysander's severe verdict seems justified, though for quite other reasons than those he gives.

It has been suggested that Keiser hastily produced *Octavia* in order to spike his young rival's guns, and on the other hand[8] that he furthered Handel's career by offering him a subject he had marked down for himself. There is little concrete evidence to support either theory; almost all we know, from Feind's preface, is that *Octavia* was planned in Weissenfels before the production of *Nero*. What is indisputable is that there is no real parallel between the librettos. Feind deploys some of the same characters—Nero, Seneca, and Tiridates as well as Octavia—and there is an inevitable similarity in their postures, but the central intrigue is quite different. Agrippina, Otho, and above all Poppea are conspicuous by their absence. Octavia is very much the central figure. Nero falls in love with Tiridates's betrothed Ormoena and orders Octavia to kill herself so that he can marry her. This provokes an unsuccessful rebellion led by Piso. Octavia, primed by Seneca, poses as a ghost when Nero is asleep and causes his better nature to reassert itself,[9] with the result that the rebels are pardoned, three pairs of lovers reconciled, and all ends in sweetness and light, a conclusion much closer to traditional *opera seria*.

Feind handles his story far more skilfully than Feustking and seldom topples into the ridiculous. The sub-plots are better balanced, and there is no danger of the minor characters confusing the main drift or usurping the supremacy of Octavia and Nero. The score contains 48 arias divided between twelve characters, two duets, and five choruses; 25 of the arias are for Octavia, Nero, or Ormoena, and the accompanied recitative, of which there is a great deal in Act III, is confined to the two central figures. The comic servant Davus is kept in his place with a single aria. He is released in II xvii, where he comments on memorial inscriptions in a cemetery, the act ending with a dance of grave-diggers chased away by ghosts, and in III iii, where he makes fun of Seneca's learning in a recitative full of Latin quotations. In the middle of Act II Nero and his entire court go fishing, and achieve a remarkably mixed bag: Ormoena catches an eel, Octavia a lamprey, Livia a wrasse (scarus), Davus five young frogs, and Tiridates two snails. The scene ends with a violent thunderstorm. Feind also includes a playhouse scene, featuring the goddess Flora, a ballet of winds and cupids, and a stage orchestra, which is interrupted by Piso's conspiracy. The libretto contains twelve Italian arias, possibly from G. C. Corradi's *Nerone*, set by Pallavicino in 1679 and adapted for an opera by

---

[4] See Chrysander, ibid.

[5] *Der vollkommene Capellmeister* (1739), 219.

[6] op. cit. 250.

[7] *HJb* (1978), 44.

[8] Baselt, 'Händel auf dem Wege nach Italien'.

[9] Feind's preface contains a psychological analysis of Nero's character, which he defines as 'Sanguineo-Melancholicus'. We can perhaps translate this as 'manic-depressive'.

Strungk at Leipzig in 1693. Handel borrowed ideas from Keiser's score in Italy, as is well known, and in London operas as late as *Floridante, Orlando*, and *Ariodante*.[10] No doubt he also drew on his own *Nero*, perhaps in *Agrippina*; but that we shall never know.

After the failure of *Nero* Handel withdrew from the theatre, at least as composer, and during the eighteen months before his departure for Italy apparently lived by giving private lessons. Nothing is known about the reception of *Octavia*. The Hamburg Opera was undergoing one of its not infrequent crises, marked by financial insecurity, personal and political quarrels, vigorous pamphleteering, and a decline in public interest. In the spring of 1707 the Keiser–Drüsicke management collapsed and surrendered the lease to Johann Heinrich Sauerbrey. By this time Handel was in Italy; but he had left behind an opera so substantial that when it was staged in January 1708 it had to be divided into two three-act works performed on different evenings, *Der beglückte Florindo* and *Die verwandelte Daphne*[11]. That at least is the explanation given by the librettist, Heinrich Hinsch, in the preface to *Florindo*, and generally accepted. But it seems improbable that Hinsch, a lawyer and experienced librettist a generation older than Handel,[12] would have expected to get away with an opera containing nearly 100 musical numbers, even in Hamburg. It is much more likely, as Stompor suggests,[13] that the work was conceived from the start as a double opera, a not uncommon scheme in Hamburg and Brunswick at that time. *Daphne* was produced in January with an intermezzo in *platt-deutsch* dialect, *Die lustige Hochzeit, und dabey angestellte Bauren-Masquerade*, to which Sauerbrey wrote a preface. The commission must have come from Keiser or Drüsicke in 1705 or 1706. The composer of course had no control over the production, which may have been directed by Graupner.

Both operas contain a number of arias and ensembles in Italian, which suggests an Italian source libretto, though none has been identified. The various elements in the story had been the subject of innumerable operas and other entertainments. The characters are all nymphs, shepherds, and gods, the latter represented by Phoebus, Cupid, Vulcan, and two water divinities, Pineus and Enipheus, the respective fathers of the betrothed pair Florindo and Daphne. The agent of mischief, as so often, is Cupid with his magic arrows. Only a few of the intricate ramifications for which he is responsible can be mentioned here.

Florindo opens with a prolonged ceremony in honour of Phoebus's victory over Python. Cupid, annoyed that another's prowess in archery should be praised above his own, and mocked by Phoebus to boot, wings the sun god with a drugged arrow so that he falls in love with Daphne. The other characters, neatly differentiated, enlarge on their own amorous predicaments. Alfirena, daughter of another water god (who fortunately does not appear), secretly loves Florindo, and so does the more forward Lycoris. Damon is miserably in love with Lycoris. His friend Tyrsis, a noble Arcadian shepherd happy to be untouched by love, tries vainly to reason with Damon. Galathea, an elderly nymph and Daphne's confidante, feels that her time is slipping by.

---

[10] See p. 44 n. 18.

[11] Both librettos have been reproduced in *HJb, Florindo* in xxx (1984), 23–73, *Daphne* in xxxi (1985), 18–57, and by Harris.

[12] He had been writing librettos since 1683; *Florindo* and *Daphne* were his last. He died in 1712.

[13] *HJb* (1978), 55.

Act II finds river gods and naiads sporting in the water. Daphne and Florindo receive permission to marry. Galathea, making advances to Tyrsis, is rebuffed because of her age. Cupid hopes that Phoebus will make a fool of himself over Daphne, but fears she may come round in the end. Phoebus begins to press his suit; Daphne, though attracted by the material benefits offered, feels she cannot abandon Florindo, a decision criticized by Galathea as a failure to make proper use of her opportunities. Tyrsis finds Damon in a deserted spot treasuring an old shoe, once the property of Lycoris, and delivers another tirade against love. In Act III Cupid prevails on Vulcan to forge a leaden arrow that will cause Daphne to hate Phoebus. After a repeat scene for Galathea and Tyrsis the disconsolate Alfirena longs to die, but refuses to join Lycoris in a conspiracy against Daphne. Lycoris, unwilling to give up hope, goes to sleep. Tyrsis, acting as intermediary for Damon, obtains a not wholly discouraging reply from Lycoris, provided Damon remains faithful. Another ceremony in honour of Phoebus ends the opera.

Daphne begins with wedding celebrations for Florindo and Daphne, interrupted by Cupid, who wounds Daphne with Vulcan's arrow. She promptly renounces love and breaks up the service. Lycoris is delighted, hoping to catch Florindo on the rebound. Daphne rejects Phoebus too and resolves to take up hunting with Diana. Lycoris assures Phoebus that this is merely a device to encourage his pursuit. Damon sees Lycoris with Phoebus and is madly jealous; Tyrsis hopes this will cure him. Florindo, searching for Daphne, goes to sleep. Alfirena seizes her chance and writes him a love note; he wakes up and finds it but does not know to whom it refers. Cupid promises Florindo that he will be twice as happy as before, a statement that Alfirena takes as referring to herself. In Act II Florindo pleads with Daphne, who is distressed by his threats to die in the fires of hell. They go off with others to attend a service in the temple of Pan. Cupid, concluding that his arrow has failed to work, calls up the Furies to separate them. Lycoris tells Damon that he has no cause to be jealous of Phoebus, but that Daphne really loves Damon, a pronouncement that the eavesdropping Alfirena finds incredible. Alfirena and Florindo pray to Phoebus for aid. Phoebus tries to interest Florindo in Alfirena; while recognizing her love he cannot return it. Lycoris seeks to wean Florindo from Daphne by claiming that she has been unfaithful. Lycoris finds Daphne in acute misery, says she too wants to renounce love, and pretends to faint. Daphne puts her cloak round her and leaves. Lycoris takes the cloak and disguises herself to fool Florindo.

In Act III Lycoris, wearing Daphne's cloak, finds Damon moping in a thick wood and declares her love. Damon and Florindo, who has overheard, both take her for Daphne. Lycoris slips out, returns as herself, and fans Florindo's rage. Meanwhile Phoebus has abducted Daphne, but she remains obdurate: he can have her body, never her soul. He begins to think she is privy to Cupid's trickery and threatens her with the torments of Hades. When the others arrive, Phoebus excuses himself by claiming that Daphne at first declared her love for him. Damon says the same, and Florindo accuses Daphne of being false all round. She prays to her father to prove her innocence, as a sign of which, to general astonishment, she is changed into a laurel. Lycoris's guilt is discovered and confessed. Cupid lays the blame on Phoebus's pride. The latter too confesses, and Cupid gives him the laurel as his special tree. Florindo receives Alfirena as a consolation prize; Lycoris accepts Damon.

More than one tradition is combined here. The interlocking personal relationships are a commonplace of Baroque opera, transplanted to Hamburg from Italy, especially Venice. The pastoral milieu and its inhabitants are also basically Italian; their most celebrated forebear was Guarini's *Il pastor fido*, on which Handel was to draw later. We recognize some of the incidents, such as the deceiving message left beside a sleeping lover. The Apollo–Daphne story, another future inspiration for Handel, derives from Ovid's *Metamorphoses* but had long been assimilated. Hinsch, and presumably Handel, humanized the mythological characters in the same way as the authors of *Acis and Galatea*, with which the denouement has much in common. The gods have power, which they constantly misuse, but are as susceptible as everyone else to the lure of sex. Their double standards (the mortals pray to them, even though they are rivals) can be not only tolerable but artistically productive in a musical setting, as we know from *Semele*. Another important element in *Florindo* and *Daphne* is not of Italian origin: the elaborate and spectacular ceremonial scenes, with provision for solos, ensembles, choruses, and dances evidently designed to secure a high degree of musical integration. Each opera begins with a striking example: the first scene of *Florindo* is unusually sustained, that of *Daphne* builds up to a strong *coup de théâtre* when Daphne interrupts the wedding (again reminding us of *Semele*). This is a direct legacy of French *tragédie-lyrique*, which, as noted in Chapter 3, had been a lasting influence in Hamburg for many years, not only on operas with pastoral themes (though they were particularly suited to it) but on the whole repertory. Mattheson employed it in the finale of *Cleopatra*, as did Handel with increasing resource in many London operas. Ellen Harris's contention[14] that these mixed ceremonial scenes were peculiar to pastoral subjects, and that they inaugurated a specifically German operatic form, rests on foundations of sand.

Not quite all the music is lost. Three groups of fragments associated with *Florindo* and *Daphne* have recently been identified. David Kimbell[15] first drew attention to a manuscript in the Flower Collection at Manchester, MS 130 Hd4, v. 11, which though largely concerned with *Agrippina* contains at the end a 'chorus' and three arias ascribed to *Florindo*. Bernd Baselt subsequently showed[16] that two groups of movements, mostly dances, in RM 18 b 8, an Aylesford volume copied at different periods, also belong to *Florindo* and *Daphne*. He devoted an important later article[17] to a full discussion of all three groups.

Although the Manchester pieces are in full score, the voice parts and text are unfortunately missing, either because the copyist (the younger Smith, *c.*1728) was interrupted before he could add them or because he did not have access to them. For the three arias he supplied a soprano clef and left a blank stave. In the 'chorus' (no tempo, D major) the voices apparently doubled the instrumental parts (two violins, viola, and bass), which are then repeated in slightly varied form as an orchestral Minuet. Baselt linked the music with the chorus 'Streue, O Braütigam, grünende Nüsse' (*Daphne* I i). The melody also exists as a keyboard Minuet, copied by Smith junior in RM 18 b 8, f. 79ᵛ, and

[14] *Handel and the Pastoral Tradition* (London, 1980), *passim*.
[15] 'A Critical Study'.
[16] 'Händel auf dem Wege nach Italien'.
[17] 'Wiederentdeckung von Fragmenten aus Händels verschollenen Hamburger Opern', *HJb* (1983), 7–24.

published by Barclay Squire and Fuller Maitland in 1928 as no 57 of the Aylesford Pieces.[18] The arias are an Andante in E minor, 4/4, for strings in four parts, a Larghetto in D minor, 12/8, for unison violins and bass, and a movement without tempo in A minor, 4/4, for three-part strings, the second violin doubling the viola. Kimbell tentatively associated the first two with 'Mie speranze, andate' (*Florindo* I xi) and 'Mostrati più crudele' (*Daphne* III ii).[19] The third aria (the first in the manuscript) has only a patterned accompaniment without ritornellos or any hint where the voice could enter. It is in some ways the most interesting, with a texture like a Bach prelude and a distinct resemblance to the accompaniments of 'Empio fato' in *Rodrigo* and 'Deh serbate' in *Teseo*.

Ex. 2

The 12/8 Larghetto, which also has parallels from the same period—'Wer umb Gelt und Hoheit willen' in Act I of *Almira* and 'Con voi mi lagnerò' in the continuo cantata 'Se per fatal destino' (HWV 159)—is the earliest surviving Handel siciliano.

The first group in RM 18 b 8 (ff. 62–9, again in the hand of Smith junior) consists of the following, evidently copied all at the same time: 'coro' in B flat, 6/8; untitled movement in B flat, 4/4; Allemande in G minor, ¢ ; Rigadon in D

---

[18] *Pieces for the Harpsichord* (London, 1928), ii. 53.

[19] His suggestion for the chorus differs from Baselt's. All four pieces are in the appendix of his dissertation, their incipits in Baselt, *Verzeichnis*, i. 64.

minor, ¢ ; Allemande in G major, ¢ ; Bourrée in G minor, ¢ ; untitled movement in G minor, 3/4; Allemande in G major, ¢ . The first three are for four-part strings, the Rigadon and Bourrée for two oboes and bassoon, the second Allemande for four unnamed parts, the seventh movement for *Tutti* in four parts (second section for violins without oboes), and the third Allemande for *Tutti Oboei e Violini* in four parts. The 'coro' is in da capo form, the others in rudimentary binary form with repeats, both sections generally ending in the tonic. The first two movements fit the choruses 'Amor, deine Tücke stiften' and 'Dispensa il dio d'amor' in *Daphne* III vii and viii. The latter is the last vocal movement in the opera, though a ballet may have followed, as in this manuscript. Baselt classes the pieces as two suites of four movements each, HWV 352 and 353, perhaps arranged by Handel in Italy. This would imply that the first (B flat) suite ended in D minor, which seems unlikely unless one or other of the choruses was repeated at the end. It seems better to regard them as a single suite.

The second group (ff. 75–6, ? early S1), catalogued as HWV 354, contains four movements for four-part strings: Minuet in B flat, 'coro' on the same music fitting the words of the chorus 'Ihr mutigen Hörner, verdoppelt den Schall' (*Florindo* I i), Minuet da capo, Sarabande in F major, 3/2, and Gavotte in G minor, 4/4. Again the dances are binary with repeats, the first half of the Minuet ending in the tonic, those of the Sarabande and Gavotte in the dominant.

There are other connections, in addition to those already mentioned, with music of Handel's early years. The 'coro' that begins HWV 352–3 supplied material for two Italian works, the first four bars reappearing in the aria 'Ardo ben mà non ardisco' in the continuo cantata 'Qual sento io non conosciuto' (HWV 149) and bars 5–8 in the second movement of the overture ('Sonata') to the instrumental cantata 'Amarilli vezzosa' (HWV 82, before August 1708), both still unpublished. This splitting of a melody to create two new ones, a process comparable to a bisected worm growing a new head or tail, is characteristic of Handel; compare the strange history of 'Dopo l'orride procelle' in *Radamisto*. The fourth movement (Rigadon) had been used in a simpler two-part version for the dance of Africans in *Almira* (III ii, HG 80). The fifth (Allemande) recurs as a Rigadon in the unpublished ballet after Act I of *Radamisto* in April 1720. The Bourrée typically uses the same material in the minor mode, and the third Allemande is related to it.

The second group (HWV 354) has links with an early overture in B flat (HWV 336, published by Walsh in parts and keyboard arrangement in 1758, edited by Terence Best in HHA IV/15). An inaccurate keyboard version of this, copied by Beta about 1717–18 (RM 18 b 8, ff. 1–4), concludes with the Sarabande, Gavotte, and Minuet from the *Florindo* group in the same keys.[20] The overture shares material with at least three Roman works, including the D major overture to *Il trionfo del Tempo*. Anthony Hicks plausibly suggested[21] that the B flat was the oratorio's original overture to whose French style Corelli, in a well-known anecdote recorded by Mainwaring, took exception. Equally possible is Baselt's conjecture that in its longer form, copied by Beta as reduced for keyboard, it may have been the overture to *Florindo*. He also throws out the attractive suggestion that the Harpsichord Suite or Overture in

[20] Squire and Fuller Maitland published the pieces with added inner parts, op. cit. i. 51–2.
[21] 'Handel's Early Musical Development', *PRMA* ciii (1976/7), 87.

G minor (HWV 453) could be an arrangement of the overture to *Nero* or *Daphne*. Lord Danby's lute book (*c.* 1710) contains arrangements of the first Allemande in the first *Florindo-Daphne* group (HWV 352 no. 3) and the Gavotte in the second group (HWV 354 no. 4) as well as an unknown overture and a number of other pieces ascribed to Handel. Possibly they too belong to *Florindo* or *Daphne* (see Crawford, op. cit.).

Whether or not these conjectures are well founded, there is no doubt that the *Florindo–Daphne* music, if it can convey little of the flavour of the operas, adds to our small stock of evidence about Handel's style before the journey to Italy. Its primitive treatment of form, occasional German stiffness, and palpable French influence, tell much the same story as *Almira* and the early harpsichord pieces identified from stylistic evidence by Terence Best.[22] The dances in particular have plenty of melodic and rhythmic vitality. The finest is the Sarabande, which belongs to the same family as the ancestor in *Almira* of 'Lascia ch'io pianga'.

---

[22] 'Handel's Harpsichord Music: a Checklist', *Music in Eighteenth-Century England*, ed. C. Hogwood and R. Luckett (Cambridge, 1983), 171–87. A key feature for dating is the '*Almira* cadence', which is very common in works of the Hamburg period but almost disappears after 1707.

CHAPTER 6

THE ITALIAN BACKGROUND, 1706–1709

I T would be difficult to overestimate the importance for the development of Handel's style of the three and a half years he spent in Italy. He had of course some contact with Italian music in Hamburg—Mainwaring's account of his arguments with Prince Ferdinando de' Medici indicates that he did not think much of it—but life among Italian musicians was a different matter. The vast gap between *Almira* and the lesser works and fragments, mostly instrumental, surviving from the Hamburg period on the one hand and *Agrippina* and *Rinaldo* on the other tells its own story. His progress during the intervening years has scarcely been studied,[1] and there has been little attempt to identify the specific influences that governed it, a notoriously tricky task at the best of times, and complicated here by the lack of documentation as to what music— and in particular what operas—he heard. Moreover he had scarcely begun the systematic dating of his autographs.

Even his whereabouts in the peninsula during the greater part of these critical years was for long a matter of guesswork. The researches of Ursula Kirkendale,[2] Reinhard Strohm,[3] Hans Joachim Marx[4], and other scholars have established a basic pattern, filled in many of the gaps, and suggested some likely answers to the questions that remain. Nearly sixty of the works Handel composed in Italy, including cantatas and motets, have been anchored to a date and place, though the dates are sometimes those when the music was copied rather than of composition or first performance; and we know when and where his first Italian opera was staged. It is clear that he composed a great deal during the first year, and that a high proportion of the cantatas were written for Marchese Ruspoli in Rome. So far no cantatas can be conclusively assigned to Florence, though it is more than likely that some were written for the Medici court and others for Naples and perhaps Venice.[5]

[1] For a valuable though brief introductory account see A. Hicks, 'Handel's Early Musical Development'.

[2] 'The Ruspoli Documents on Handel', *JAMS* xx (1967), 222–73.

[3] 'Händel in Italia: nuovi contributi', *RIM*, ix (1974), 152–74.

[4] 'Händel in Rom—seine Beziehung zu Benedetto Card. Pamphilj', *HJb* (1983), 107–18. This supplements the documentation in Lina Montalto's 1955 biography of Pamphili.

[5] Evidence cited by K. Watanabe, 'The Paper used by Handel and his Copyists during the Time of 1706–1710', *Journal of the Japanese Musicological Society*, xxvii (1981), 129–71, suggests that six cantatas were written in Naples. Some cantatas on North Italian paper may have been

A comprehensive study of Handel's development within the Italian period is beyond the scope of this book.

It may be helpful to summarize what we know of his itinerary; the months must be regarded as approximate.

1706   autumn (? to end of year): Florence.
1707   January–October: Rome and neighbourhood, employed by Pamphili (January–May), then by Ruspoli.
            October–December: Florence.
            December–February 1708: ? Venice.
1708   February–April: Rome (Ruspoli).
            May–July: Naples.
            July–September: Rome (Ruspoli).
            September–?December: probably Florence.
1709   ?January–March: Rome.
            March–November: ?Florence and Siena.
            November–February 1710: Venice.

The first Venice visit (carnival 1707/8) is a likely conjecture by Strohm, based partly on the fact that the meeting and friendly rivalry with Domenico Scarlatti there, described at some length by Mainwaring, could not have occurred two years later, when Scarlatti was back in Rome. Nor could an encounter with the Earl of Manchester, special envoy in Venice from summer 1707 to October 1708, who according to Mainwaring invited Handel to London. It is possible that Handel paid more than two visits to Venice, the natural goal for a composer interested in the theatre; and he may have travelled to some other centre during the summer of 1709. According to Mainwaring, whose information is generally sound though confused in chronology, 'it was his resolution to visit every part of Italy, which was any way famous for its musical performances'. What is certain is that he spent more time in Rome and Florence, in the service of Ruspoli (and other Roman patrons) and Ferdinando de' Medici, than anywhere else.

There are three ways in which Handel could have imbibed the influence of Italian music: by hearing it in performance (operas in the theatre, cantatas, serenatas, and oratorios in princely palaces or private houses, sacred music in churches), by studying scores in manuscript copies, the normal method of circulation at a time when little music—especially vocal music—was printed, and by personal contact with other musicians. No doubt he availed himself of all three. We have no way of knowing what scores he studied, apart from the existence of a manuscript of Steffani's duets bearing his signature and the date 'Roma 1706' (almost certainly Old Style, that is before 25 March 1707).[6] It is possible to identify certain operas that he might have heard in the theatre. In this connection the most striking fact is that none at all were produced in Rome during the many months he spent there; this may help to account for the low ratio of operas to other compositions in his Italian output. Although Roman operas had been numerous and popular between 1690 and 1697, and were to become so again after 1709, various circumstances imposed a total vacuum in between, apart from a few performances in private buildings, none

composed for Florence or Venice, but the arguments of E. T. Harris, 'Händel in Florenz', *HJb* (1981), 41–61, are vitiated by a constant blurring of the line between conjecture and fact.
[6] In the British Library; see C. Timms, 'Handel and Steffani', *MT* cxiv (1973), 374.

of them during Handel's residence.[7] The hostility of two successive Popes, one of whom had engineered the destruction of the Tordinona Theatre in August 1697, the War of the Spanish Succession from 1701, earthquakes in 1703, clerical bans in 1704–8, and Papal preparations for battle against the Austrians in 1709, conspired to banish opera from the stage and confine all secular music-making to private buildings. The war also disturbed Naples while Handel was there, though operas by Benedetto Ricci (*L'Ateone*, 8 May) and Francesco Mancini (*Turno Aricino*) were staged during 1708.

The position in Florence was more secure. If Handel was present during all four autumn seasons, which is very probable, he could have heard eight operas in addition to his own *Rodrigo*, four of them in Ferdinando's private theatre at Pratolino and four at the Cocomero.[8] Four were by Giacomo Antonio Perti, one (*Il gran Tamerlano*) by Alessandro Scarlatti, one by Orlandini and Rocco Ceruti, one (*Radamisto*) by Nicola Fago, brother-in-law of the castrato Nicolini, and one anonymous. By an unhappy chance the only surviving score from this group is Perti's *Il Nerone fatto Cesare*, an old Venetian opera of 1693 revived at the Cocomero in 1708. The loss of *Il gran Tamerlano* is particularly regrettable, since quite apart from its authorship and subject it could have been the first opera Handel heard in Italy, in September 1706 with Vittoria Tarquini as Asteria.[9] It is of more than passing interest that he subsequently set three of the Perti librettos—*Dionisio rè di Portogallo* (*Sosarme*), *Ginevra principessa di Scozia* (*Ariodante*), and *Berenice regina di Egitto*—as well as that of the next (and last) Pratolino opera, Perti's *Rodelinda* (7 September 1710), and treated the subjects of the other three named above. Six of these operas, including all four set by Handel and *Il gran Tamerlano*, had librettos by Antonio Salvi, a doctor resident at the Florentine court, whom Handel must have met frequently. His texts were to become the source of more Handel operas than those of any other author.

The principal operatic centre in Italy, as it had been for seventy years, was Venice, where Handel could have appraised all the latest developments. Four public opera-houses gave regular seasons, and two others were open occasionally. Far more operas were given there than anywhere else—more than forty during the three years 1707–9. They are listed by Taddeo Wiel,[10] but the time of year is not always known and occasional confusion arises from different methods of dating; an opera given during the 1709 carnival season could be dated 1708 in the printed libretto and performed at any time from late December 1708 to Lent 1709. The above total includes eight operas by Francesco Gasparini (one in collaboration with Antonio Lotti), five others by Lotti, three by Tomaso Albinoni, and two each by Antonio Caldara and Alessandro Scarlatti. The two by Scarlatti were *Il trionfo della libertà* and *Mitridate Eupatore*, both produced early in 1707. There is no doubt that Handel knew the latter, whether or not he heard it in the theatre. Another of Strohm's reasons for postulating a visit to Venice in 1707/8 is the production then of Caldara's *Partenope*. Handel used this version of Stampiglia's repeat-

---

[7] For a well documented account see L. Lindgren, 'Il dramma musicale a Roma durante la carriera di Alessandro Scarlatti (1660–1725),' *Le muse galanti, la musica a Roma nel Settecento*, ed. B. Cagli (Rome, 1985), 35–57.

[8] R. L. and N. W. Weaver, *A Chronology of Music in the Florentine Theater 1590–1750* (Detroit, 1978).

[9] See below, p. 109.

[10] *I teatri musicali veneziani del Settecento* (Venice, 1897; repr. fac. Leipzig, 1979).

edly altered libretto for his own opera in 1730; it is also the source of two lines in his cantata 'Nell'africane selve' (HWV 136), almost certainly composed (? at Naples in 1708) for the sepulchral bass Antonio Francesco Carli, who sang in Caldara's opera and many others, including *Agrippina*, at Venice during these years. Handel may likewise have heard a substantial number of singers later engaged, by him or others, for London. They included, in addition to Durastanti, Croce, Pellegrini, and the two Boschis (who were in the cast of *Agrippina*), the castratos Nicolini, Senesino, Pacini, Berselli, and Bernacchi, the tenor Francesco Borosini, and the contralto Diana Vico.

Among the leading musicians with whom Handel was in contact at Rome were Corelli, Alessandro and later Domenico Scarlatti, Bernardo Pasquini, Caldara and (probably in 1708/9) Agostino Steffani, all of them except Corelli opera composers. His colleagues in Ruspoli's household included Durastanti, for whom many of his soprano cantatas were written, the violinist Pietro Castrucci and his father Domenico, and (for occasional performances) the cellist Filippo Amadei, each of whom followed him to London. Other Roman patrons, connected with Ruspoli by friendship and perhaps a degree of rivalry, were the three cardinals Ottoboni, Pamphili, and Colonna. They too from time to time employed Handel as composer or performer or both. With the opera-houses closed these activities were confined to cantatas, serenatas, and oratorios performed in one or other of the princely palaces. Musically this was a distinction without a difference. The style of the cantatas, not only the longer ones with two or more characters and orchestral accompaniment but the continuo cantatas as well, was virtually indistinguishable from that of contemporary opera—Handel often used the same arias with little or no change in both—and this is equally true of oratorio. It requires no great stretch of imagination to see him consciously using the cantata as a training ground for dramatic expression. Moreover Ruspoli's spectacular production of the oratorio *La Resurrezione* at the Bonelli palace on Easter Sunday (8 April) 1708 came very close to a fully staged performance. This was not, as some writers have maintained,[11] a contradiction in terms; Ottoboni had staged an oratorio, *Il martirio di Sant'Eustachio*, with action and dancing at the Cancelleria during Lent 1690,[12] and other instances are known.

Handel's relations with the two Scarlattis were particularly close. Alessandro lived in Rome from 1703 to late 1708, overlapping with Handel by more than a year in all and, as Kirkendale notes,[13] often appearing with him at the same court. Their principal patrons, Ottoboni and Ruspoli, were close friends, and each composer worked for both as well as for Pamphili and Colonna. Handel is unlikely to have missed performances of Scarlatti's oratorios *Il giardino di rose* (Ruspoli, 24 April 1707; repeated 26 February 1708), *Il martirio di Santa Cecilia* (Ottoboni, early March 1708), and *La Santissima Annunziata* (Ruspoli, 25 March 1708), and also of Caldara's new *Il martirio di Santa Caterina* (Ottoboni, Lent 1708). There was an even closer link with Scarlatti's Passion oratorio, whose production for Ottoboni at the Cancelleria on 4 April

---

[11] For example Kirkendale, 'The Ruspoli Documents', 235 n. 44, and H. E. Smither, *A History of the Oratorio* (Chapel Hill, 1977), *passim*.

[12] W. C. Holmes, *La Statira, the Textual Sources with a Documentary Postscript* (New York, 1983), 84–5.

[13] 'The Ruspoli Documents', 238.

1708 was clearly planned as the first part of a sequence completed by *La Resurrezione* four days later.[14] It was not only at Rome that the two composers shared patrons. Scarlatti composed operas for Ferdinando de' Medici's theatre at Pratolino in five successive years (1702–6),[15] and may have met Handel for the first time on the last occasion if he directed the performance. Cardinal Vincenzo Grimani, Viceroy of Naples from 1708, had almost certainly met Handel at his friend Pamphili's in Rome; he was responsible for

* Handel's visit to Naples, which he could not have undertaken without a special passport,[16] and for inviting Scarlatti back to that city at the end of the year. Strohm[17] plausibly suggests that Handel received the commission for *Aci, Galatea e Polifemo* through Grimani, who went on to commission *Agrippina* (on his own libretto) and ensured its production at the San Giovanni Grisostomo Theatre in Venice, which was owned by his family. It is possible that he performed a similar service for Scarlatti's two operas at the same theatre in 1707.[18]

While Venetian opera of the seventeenth century has been investigated by H. C. Wolff[19] and the Italian opera aria of 1720–30 by Strohm,[20] there is no comprehensive or synoptic account of the period in between, though information can be gleaned from studies of individual works and composers. Operatic developments during these years can be traced through the surviving works of Carlo Francesco Pollarolo and Alessandro Scarlatti, both of whom had long and immensely prolific careers in the theatre, the former from 1685 to 1722, the latter from 1679 to 1721.[21] Unfortunately the two Garland series of facsimiles of Italian operas between 1640 and 1770 edited by Howard Mayer Brown and Eric Weimer[22] include none whose first production falls within the period of Handel's residence. The great majority of the operas he is likely to have heard, including the Venetian works of Gasparini, Lotti, Albinoni, and Caldara, are lost or survive only in fragmentary (and unpublished) aria collections.[23]

By the time of his arrival in the autumn of 1706 the *opera seria* was well on the way to standardization. The division between aria and recitative was firmly established, the former accompanied almost throughout by continuo and only on rare occasions and for special effects by the full string band. The

[14] Kirkendale, loc. cit.

[15] Their interesting correspondence on the subject is printed by M. Fabbri, *Alessandro Scarlatti e il Principe Ferdinando de' Medici* (Florence, 1961). Ferdinando constantly urged Scarlatti to write less learned music.

[16] Marx, 'Händel in Rom', 112.

[17] 'Händel in Italia', 169.

[18] Lindgren, 'Il dramma musicale', suggests that this was arranged through Ottoboni.

[19] *Die venezianische Oper in der zweiten Hälfte des 17. Jahrhunderts* (Berlin, 1937; repr. Bologna, 1974).

[20] *Italienische Opernarien des frühen Settecento (1720–1730)*, 2 vols. (Cologne, 1976).

[21] For Pollarolo see O. Termini, 'Carlo Francesco Pollarolo: Follower or Leader in Venetian Opera?', *Studi Musicali*, viii (1979), 223–71, and her article in *The New Grove*; for Scarlatti, D. J. Grout, *Alessandro Scarlatti: an Introduction to his Operas* (Berkeley, Los Angeles, London, 1979). Dent's pioneer study, *Alessandro Scarlatti: his Life and Work* (London, 1905; repr. 1960) is still of value.

[22] New York and London, 1977 ff.

[23] See R. Strohm, 'Manoscritti di opere rappresentate a Venezia 1701–1740', *Informazioni e studi vivaldiani*, iii (1982), 45–51.

burgeoning ariosos and little melismatic flourishes of the old recitative had virtually disappeared. The vast majority of arias were in da capo form, though an exit did not invariably follow. Continuo arias were increasingly outnumbered by those with upper instrumental accompaniment, a process that had accelerated during the 1690s. Variety was obtained by the use of different instrumental groups—unison violins, strings in two, three, or four parts, occasionally woodwind or trumpets—and by the very effective device (often used by Handel and never wholly abandoned by him) of crowning a continuo aria with a fully-scored ritornello after the A section or the da capo. The enlargement of the orchestra and the adoption of the concerto grosso principle in arias, including on occasion pit and stage orchestras and instruments behind the scenes, are characteristic of Pollarolo, who is credited with introducing the oboe into the opera orchestra. Duets and ensembles were increasingly rare, apart from the statutory final *coro*, which showed an obstinate reluctance to develop. This was associated with an increase in virtuoso vocal writing and in the length of arias, though the majority were still concise by the standards of the 1720s.

With the important exception of Alessandro Scarlatti, considered below, the older generation of composers born up to about 1660 can have had little to teach Handel, though Pasquini, Pollarolo, and Perti were still active and he must have been acquainted with their music. As we have seen, Perti—one of those long-lived composers who spanned the ages, dying at ninety-five just three years before Handel—was writing for the Medici court in 1707–10;[24] but his surviving operas date from 1685–93 and look back to Cesti and Legrenzi. Of greater consequence were the large group some ten to fifteen years senior to Handel who were then at the height of their powers: Gasparini, Lotti, Caldara, and Albinoni in Venice, Mancini in Naples, Orlandini, a Florentine who wrote operas for many cities, including one for Pratolino in 1708, and the Bononcini brothers, Giovanni and Antonio Maria. They were all copious opera composers, and Gasparini, Lotti, and Mancini were influential teachers. Vivaldi belongs chronologically to this group, and Handel could have met him in Venice; but he was a late starter in the theatre, producing his first opera in 1713. He and Orlandini were among the first to anticipate the more homophonic style of the 1720s associated with the Neapolitan school of Vinci and Leo; this however was after Handel left Italy. Both Bononcini brothers were in Vienna throughout the first decade of the century, but Giovanni's *Il trionfo di Camilla* (Naples, 1696) had made him famous throughout Europe,[25] and Handel may have heard one of its many revivals or seen a score; he could not have avoided it in London.

Dent proposed Giovanni Bononcini as 'the real originator of what is commonly described as the "Handelian style"',[26] by which he presumably meant the lively manner of his more extrovert music. Certainly *Camilla* shows

---

[24] Perti's opinion of Handel supposedly recorded in the diary of one Francesco Maria Mannucci, 'The young Saxon will perhaps be the greatest of all, when he stops following others in order to compose more quickly' (M. Fabbri, 'Nuova luce sull'attività fiorentina di Giacomo Antonio Perti, Bartolomeo Cristofori e Giorgio F. Haendel', *Chigiana*, xxi (1964)), has been shown to be a modern fiction. See J. Riepe, C. Vitali, and A. Furnari, '*Il Pianto di Maria* (HWV 234): Rezeption, Überlieferung und musikwissenschaftliche Fiktion', *Göttinger Händel-Beiträge* V (1993), 270–307.

[25] See L. Lindgren, 'I trionfi di Camilla', *Studi musicali*, vii (1977), 79–161.

[26] *Alessandro Scarlatti*, 200.

a more advanced technique than for example Pollarolo at this period,[27] with some expansion of the aria, more enterprising treatment of ritornellos and combination of motivic material, virtuoso passages for violins, and a few striking accompanied recitatives, especially in Camilla's mad scene at the start of Act II. Ten years later many composers had adopted these practices, and it is almost impossible to assign priorities or pin down influences. We can be confident that Handel studied all these composers, but not what precisely he picked up from any of them. Parallels can be found between his music and that of Gasparini and Lotti in particular, but they could all derive from a common stock. It is easier to spot differences. The music of these men, judged largely by their arias in the absence of complete scores of early operas,[28] however high it may rise on occasion, seldom maintains a consistent level. It falls into harmonic, rhythmic, or sequential formulae far more often than the best of Handel even in these early years. If an initial idea strikes us as original, its development is often disappointing. The responses seem automatic, the consequences predictable, though this is less true of Gasparini, perhaps the most gifted of the group, than of the others. The music as a whole lacks that quality of surprise that is the prerogative of genius as opposed to talent.

What Handel undoubtedly learned from contact with Italians, singers as well as composers, was less tangible but in the last resort more crucial: fluency in the treatment of Italian verse, accurate declamation and flexible harmonic rhythm in recitative, increasing experience in writing for the voice and drawing the necessary distinction between vocal and instrumental material, and above all the release of that wonderful melodic gift, so constricted in *Almira*, still partly chained in *Rodrigo* and the early cantatas, but boundlessly inventive for the rest of his life. Albinoni, a notable melodist, may have been of assistance here, but the power must always have been latent.

Italy of course did not turn Handel into an Italian composer. There was never any question of his abjuring his German roots, as Chelleri (Keller), Hasse, and to some extent Gluck were to do. His music retained an intellectual force, a resourceful and varied treatment of the orchestra, a sense of harmonic adventure, and a contrapuntal density and intricacy found in no contemporary Italian except Alessandro Scarlatti. Not that the Italians had yet demoted counterpoint in the aria. There could still be a lively pull, even in continuo arias, between vocal line and bass, and contrapuntal or quasi-fugal ritornellos remained in favour. Gasparini, influenced perhaps by his friend Scarlatti, packed plenty of learned detail into *Bajazet*. But a growing tendency to lighten the texture and diminish dependence on the continuo—perhaps an early step towards the pre-classical style—became apparent, especially among the Venetians. Albinoni, Lotti, and Gasparini all liked to suppress it while the voice was singing, and sometimes throughout the B section or even the whole aria, either doubling the voice with the violins (occasionally in thirds) or leaving the bass to the violas or second violins. Handel from time to time

---

[27] See R. Strohm, *Italienische Oper*, 30–62.

[28] Facsimile scores of Lotti's *Alessandro Severo* (1716) and Gasparini's *Bajazet* (1719) are available in the Garland series. *Bajazet* has also been edited by M. Ruhnke (Munich, 1981). The *Atti* of the first International Gasparini Congress held at Comaiore in 1978 (Florence, 1982) contain short studies of Gasparini's early Roman dramatic works (1689–99) by Lindgren and of his late operas and their use by Handel in *Giustino* and *Faramondo* by Strohm (*Essays*, 80–92).

availed himself of this resource with conspicuous success,[29] but it remained one weapon in a well-stocked armoury. Not till the mid-1720s did he begin to echo the more homophonic style as it had developed in Italy, and then without abandoning a single one of the procedures he had mastered earlier. Italian experience polished and refined the roughness of his native idiom without sapping its strength; indeed the new lyrical freedom and flexibility notably increased it.

Something should be said about the reform of the opera libretto associated with Zeno and later Metastasio. Historians link this with the Arcadian Academy in Rome, founded by G. M. Crescimbeni and others in 1690. It was not so much a consciously directed movement, at least in the early stages, as a gradual aggregation of taste. It did not proceed at a uniform pace—there were repeated throwbacks—nor was it confined to Rome; academies were started in several cities, one of them by Zeno at Venice in 1691 (it became a branch of Arcadia in 1698). There seems to have been a widespread literary reaction against the extravagance of seventeenth-century opera, especially in Venice, with its bizarre mixture of the earthy and the supernatural, the excessive number of characters, and the fantastic complexity and improbability of the plots. Zeno in his first libretto, *Gl'inganni felici*,[30] set by Pollarolo in 1695, reverted to a quasi-pastoral background in classical Greece (Arcadia in fact) with no marvels or comic 'relief'. The dramatic context, used by Metastasio later, is the Olympic Games. Love and disguise are still prominent, but the emphasis is on straightforward human emotion. There are no grand heroic gestures, though Zeno's dramas after 1700 are almost all heroic. His motives were literary; he knew little of music, and probably did not regard himself as a reformer of opera. He withdrew his aria texts more and more from the action, which was transacted in recitatives of increasing length and elaboration. Like Metastasio, Zeno contemplated production of his librettos as spoken plays, omitting the arias—scarcely an encouraging prescription for musical drama.

Plots drawn from classical history, especially Roman history, became increasingly popular, and political themes with a moral flavour were grafted on to the purely erotic motivation of the older dramas. Not that it was possible or desirable to exclude fiction altogether. The historian Ludovico Muratori, regarded as an arbiter of taste, wrote to Zeno: 'Well-known names, as Aristotle says, render wonderful events more credible. The poet has a certain licence to invent; but he must not contradict established opinions familiar to us from history ... Existing opinions must not be warped; it is in the silent gaps of history that the fictitious may be built up.'[31] Hence the little notes appended to the Argument of so many librettos, drawing attention to what is historical and what the poet defends as convincing invention—the sort of thing that might have happened. The fact that this verisimilitude produced

---

[29] Witness 'Con saggio tuo' in *Agrippina* I i, 'Ch'io lasci mai d'amare' in *Amadigi* II ix, and the irresistible unison arias in *Agrippina* and *Rinaldo*. It occurs in Scarlatti's middle-period operas, for example *Mitridate Eupatore* ('Chi far gode', V i) and *La principessa fedele* ('Di ch'è l'ombra mia tradita', I xii).
[30] See Strohm's account in *Italienische Oper*, 30 ff, and for the general reform R. S. Freeman, *Opera without Drama: Currents of Change in Italian Opera 1675–1725* (Ann Arbor, 1981).
[31] *Epistolario di L. A. Muratori*, ed. M. Campori (Modena, 1901–12), ii. 516.

almost identical results in a wide variety of contexts and periods was not regarded as an obstacle.

A popular source for Italian librettos from the first decade of the century was the French classical tragedy of Corneille, Racine, and their contemporaries. This offered a serious theme drawn from history or mythology (which when purged of the miraculous could be treated as history) and a suitably elevated tone, though that did not often survive unimpaired when translated into terms of an Italian libretto. Antonio Salvi took many of his plots from French tragedy, and so did Agostino Piovene; from them they passed into some of Handel's operas, but it is a mistake to assume that Handel took over the stiff concepts of honour and propriety invoked by the French dramatists. One author who went further than most in imitating French models was Girolamo Frigimelica-Roberti, an architect and librarian and for many years a member of a Paduan academy. His librettos are all in five acts, often with choruses and ballets (another French feature). Handel set none of them, but one of the Italian operas that directly influenced him was Alessandro Scarlatti's *Mitridate Eupatore*, based on a remarkable libretto by Frigimelica-Roberti. Other writers belonging loosely to the same movement were Pietro Pariati, who took to the theatre in middle age after a spell in prison and sometimes collaborated with Zeno, and Silvio Stampiglia, an original Arcadian. Although Stampiglia turned to history for his subjects, he was far from abjuring comedy—the result perhaps of his links with Naples, where he wrote his first five original librettos in 1696–1702. He even increased its prominence; but he took trouble over his plots and contrived to engage the comic characters more fully than usual in the main action, for example in *Camilla* and *La caduta de' Decemviri* (A. Scarlatti, 1697). He also evinced a delight worthy of Da Ponte in exuberant intrigue.

The movement towards a limited rationalism must have been clearly perceptible during Handel's Italian years. Francesco Silvani's 1699 libretto for *Rodrigo*, adapted but not radically altered, probably by Salvi, may reflect it in that it is based on history and excludes comedy and an unrelated sub-plot. But that of *Agrippina* was a reversion towards the seventeenth century, and the three major operas of the first London period are full of romanticism, magic, and myth. (It is worth noting, however, that two of them were derived from France—the *tragédie-lyrique*, not the classical drama.) Only during the Royal Academy period, when he came closest to the mainstream of *opera seria*, was Handel predominantly concerned with the heroic libretto, and then seldom with its latest manifestions; four of the sources dated back to the seventeenth century. Although he set three up-to-date Metastasio librettos in 1728–31, he generally preferred earlier models. His only dealings with Pariati and Zeno (in *Arianna in Creta* and *Faramondo*) came as late as 1734 and 1738. His three Stampiglia operas (*Partenope*, the modified *Serse*, and *Imeneo*) are late and light in tone. It seems safe to conclude that he felt out of sympathy with the increasing rationalism and literary bias of the reform libretto, which for a composer of his romantic imagination and strong feeling for personalized as opposed to political or ethical conflict is scarcely surprising.

The one Italian composer who demonstrably influenced Handel, perhaps more than anyone else except Keiser, was Alessandro Scarlatti. This too is not surprising: twenty-five years older, Scarlatti was the most original and inventive opera composer of his age, and one with whom Handel was for some time in daily contact. Even a partial examination of his operas and cantatas, of which a limited number are available in print, shows that both left their mark. Comparison of the half dozen instances where both composers set the same cantata text,[32] even when they can be dated, proves little except that two men of different generations not unnaturally took a different approach; indeed if Handel knew an earlier Scarlatti setting, he may well have done this deliberately. As Mayo points out, Scarlatti's method is the more old-fashioned, with greater use of arioso in recitative and the motto in arias. In these particular cantatas Handel's harmony is perhaps less striking than Scarlatti's, but there are plenty of examples elsewhere of that contorted and restless chromaticism, especially but not exclusively in recitative, which Heinichen and other eighteenth-century writers considered extravagant and unnatural: for example the second recitative of 'Lungi n'andò Fileno' (HWV 128) and the first arias of 'Ne' tuoi lumi, O bella Clori' (HWV 133) and 'Stelle, perfide stelle' (HWV 168).

More significant for our present purposes are Scarlatti's operas. Since his theatrical career lasted from six years before Handel's birth to the second season of the Royal Academy in London (1721), they naturally show a great range of stylistic development. Of nearly forty that survive in full score only seven or eight are available in good modern editions,[33] but these fortunately include examples from all periods. Scarlatti's first opera *Gli equivoci nel sembiante* (1679) belongs to the world of Cesti and Stradella, and *La Statira* (1690) falls awkwardly between two stools or schools. The latest and most mature works on the other hand, such as *Tigrane, Marco Attilio Regolo*, and *Griselda*, were composed after Handel left Italy. It is the operas of the intermediate years, approximately from 1694 to 1707, that are relevant to this study. Handel may not have seen more than two or three of them in the theatre, but he must have had ample opportunity to examine scores.

One of the most notable points of contact is the slow siciliano-type aria in 12/8 time employed at moments of high emotional tension, especially laments and exclamations of despair by bereft or abandoned lovers. This of course was not the only use of the siciliano; pastoral movements in major keys are quite distinct, and many of Scarlatti's arias in this favourite metre, left without a tempo mark, are closer to gigues. The tragic or pathetic pieces are virtually confined to the minor mode with strong chromatic inflections, diminished intervals, notably the flattened supertonic (harmonized as the Neapolitan sixth), and frequent vacillation between the major and minor third; many have yearning suspensions and chromatically rising or descending passages (inspired by the text) in the bass, and sometimes in other parts as well. In early examples by both composers the accompaniment is for continuo only, perhaps

---

[32] J. S. M. Mayo, 'Zum Vergleich des Wort-Ton Verhältnisses in den Kantaten von Georg Friedrich Händel und Alessandro Scarlatti', *G. F. Händel und seine italienischen Zeitgenossen*, ed. W. Siegmund-Schultze (Halle, 1979), 31–44; and E. T. Harris, 'The Italian in Handel', *JAMS* xxxiii (1980), 468–500. The latter paper proclaims its intention 'to call into question the concept of a strong Italian influence on Handel's vocal music'. See also R. Strohm, 'Alessandro Scarlatti und das Settecento', *Colloquium A. Scarlatti, Würzburg 1975*, ed. W. Osthoff (Tutzing, 1979), 160; *Essays*, 15–33.

[33] In the Harvard series under the general editorship of D. J. Grout, still in progress. Others are partly or inadequately published.

with a final full ritornello; later a four-part string texture, intricately contrapuntal with much crossing of parts and the harpsichord sometimes silenced while the voice is singing, becomes characteristic. Scarlatti seems to have been the originator of this type of aria, which has been linked with Sicilian folk music; he was certainly famous for it, and it was probably from him that other composers adopted it—Giovanni Bononcini for example in his *Polifemo* of 1702 and Mancini in *Gl'amanti generosi* (Naples, 1705), the opera that reached London as *Idaspe fedele*. It begins to appear in Scarlatti's operas, so far as we can tell at present, in the 1690s (*Pirro e Demetrio*, 1694). There is a particularly striking specimen the following year in *Massimo Puppieno* ('Ardo sospiro', III ii) and three in Act I of *La caduta de' Decemviri* (1697), an opera that enjoyed wide popularity. According to Grout[34] they are rarer in 1700–2 (one in each of three operas); but they are again prominent in *La principessa fedele* (February 1710)—just too late to influence Handel, unless Scarlatti showed him the score in advance, but by then the connection had been established.

As noted in Chapter 3, such arias are conspicuously absent from Handel's Hamburg works, though Mattheson and Keiser used the siciliano in a less intense form. There are about half a dozen examples in Handel's continuo cantatas, some as early as spring 1707, one, likewise with continuo, in *Rodrigo* II ii, three or four in the instrumental cantatas, and as many in *Agrippina*. Those in the 1707 cantatas *Armida abbandonata* (HWV 105) and *Clori, Tirsi e Fileno* (HWV 96, incomplete in HG) are particularly Scarlattian, though the second exceptionally is in a major key. The type, with all its distinguishing characteristics and four-part string accompaniment, is a prominent and lasting feature of the London operas, especially during the Royal Academy period, and is found in the oratorios; significantly it is very rare in instrumental works, which lack the dramatic association. These emotionally charged sicilianos not only stand out from their surroundings in score after score; the resemblance to Scarlatti becomes if anything more striking with the passage of time. This was a profound and lasting influence.

Of course there are differences, notably in scale and harmonic rhythm. Scarlatti's is much faster, sometimes abrupt to the point of incoherence, Handel's broader and more spacious. Yet the procedures are basically similar. The B section of the E minor aria 'Quando poi vedrai lo strale' in *La principessa fedele* (I xvii) begins, as one might expect, in the relative major, moves to G minor with a rising chromatic scale figure in the bass (at the word 'crudeltà'), then unexpectedly back to E minor, and ends in B minor, all within nine bars (Ex. 3).[35] It is condensed, even cramped; the major key is abandoned after only half a bar. Handel often evokes a mood of restlessness and anxiety by similar means—the switch to the parallel minor after attaining the relative major (or vice versa) is particularly characteristic—but in his mature works always on a more ample scale.

Another aria for the same character, the heroine Cunegonda, in the same act ('Ti, sospiro, ti cerco', I xi), this time in F minor, is astonishingly like Teofane's 'Affanni del pensier' in *Ottone* in texture, harmony, and rhythm as well as key. Both of Cunegonda's arias and Teofane's are based on variants

[34] *Alessandro Scarlatti*, 59.
[35] Grout (121–3) prints the complete aria.

Ex. 3

(. . . for to uncover a mortal wound and not to heal it, is cruelty.)

and extensions of the rhythm ♪ | ♩ ♪ ♩.♩♩ ♩, found in many arias of
this type. The model—or at least an antecedent—may have been 'Se tu della
mia morte' in *La caduta de' Decemviri* (III xiii). This is a continuo aria until the
ritornello after the da capo, where the four-part accompaniment beautifully
extends and develops the material. The idea of course was standard, but the
contrapuntal texture with crossing strings, suspensions, and the climactic top
note in the penultimate bar anticipates a favourite device of Handel's.

Ex. 4

The most Handelian of all Scarlatti's operas—Dent considered it perhaps
the finest[36]—is *Mitridate Eupatore*, produced at Venice early in 1707. J. A.
Westrup[37] and H. C. Wolff[38] both stress the parallels with Handel. They are
indeed striking. The opera is exceptional in Scarlatti's output and in the whole
period. Frigimelica-Roberti's libretto, modelled on the Electra story as treated
by the Greek tragedians, firmly excludes not only comedy and the matrimo-
nial happy end but any love interest whatever. It may have been this that
displeased the Venetian public and gave Scarlatti one of the few total failures
of his career. The generative emotions are the mutual love of brother and

[36] *Alessandro Scarlatti*, 108.
[37] 'Alessandro Scarlatti's *Il Mitridate Eupatore* (1707)', *New Looks at Italian Opera*, ed. W. W.
Austin (Ithaca, 1968).
[38] *NOHM* v. 59–61.

sister and their desire for vengeance on the mother and her paramour who have murdered their father, an objective achieved by the killing of both on stage. The concept of magnanimity almost universal at this period is missing altogether. Scarlatti clearly sought to match the grandeur of the theme, making extensive use of orchestral sinfonias, accompanied recitatives, and obbligato instruments (only three arias and one duet are confined to continuo, and they end with orchestral ritornellos) and giving much of the score a spaciousness and a depth of characterization beyond that of his earlier operas.[39] It is difficult to disagree with Westrup and Wolff that Laodice's lament over the urn supposed to contain her brother's ashes, 'Cara tomba' in IV ii, was the model for Rinaldo's 'Cara sposa' (Ex. 5, p. 92). The expressive layout of the ritornello based on descending arpeggios for each instrument in turn, the entry of the voice before the completion of the cadence, the light treatment of the bass in comparison with the richness of the other parts (including two independent cellos, used also in *Agrippina*), the treatment of suspensions, the extensions of the vocal line (unusual for Scarlatti) in phrases of varying length and shape[40] over an accompaniment of repeated string chords—all remind us of Handel's aria. Other movements too are prophetic; Mitridate's prayer 'Patrii Numi' (II i) with its measured tread of string chords in paired quavers, the instruments entering quasi-fugally from the bass up (without harpsichord) while the voice breaks into the ritornello with a melody in different note values (Wolff cites 'Voi che udite' in *Agrippina*, in a minor key, but there are many similar movements in Handel's London operas); Farnace's tenor accompanied recitative and aria 'Ciò che al regno' (III ii) with its reiterated semiquaver figure and lively interplay between voice and violins;[41] and the solemn march that accompanies the arrival of the urn on board ship at the beginning of Act IV. Here Scarlatti deploys two orchestras of strings, trumpets, and drums, one on stage, the other (with the trumpets muted) in the pit. Dent[42] suggests that Handel remembered this at the opening of *Saul*; we might add that of *Deidamia*, which likewise features a stage band on shipboard. Nor are the characteristic sicilianos lacking; Laodice has a beautiful one in B minor ('Fra i perigli') in Act I and another in Act IV.

Perhaps the most subtle, though elusive, link between Handel and Scarlatti derives from a certain parallelism in their approach to composition. As Grout remarks,[43] the principal musical motive of a Scarlatti aria 'always gives the impression of having sprung at once and irresistibly out of the specific sense, feelings, and images of the text'. This spontaneity is partly responsible for the irregularity of his phrase-lengths and the unpredictability of his procedures whether in melody, rhythm, harmony, or modulation; when an idea occurs to him he makes a dart at it, sometimes upsetting the balance of the aria in the

---

[39] The only printed edition, arranged—or rather disarranged—by Giuseppe Piccioli (Milan, 1953), distorts the opera almost beyond recognition. The score is discussed and quoted by C. R. Morey, 'The Late Operas of Alessandro Scarlatti' (dissertation, Indiana University, 1965).

[40] Wolff quotes the first 17 bars of the voice part in *NOHM* v. 61.

[41] A number of similar parallels could be adduced: Marcello's brilliant entrance aria in Act I of *Eraclea* (1700), with trumpets, oboes, strings, and much coloratura and triplet figuration, resembles Esilena's florid 'Per dar pregio' at the end of Act I of *Rodrigo*. This however may have been a standard type.

[42] *Alessandro Scarlatti*, 109.

[43] *Alessandro Scarlatti*, 103.

Ex.5

(Dear tomb of my beloved)

process. His propensity to do the unexpected thing—for example to plunge briefly into a remote key or to insert a phrase or two in the parallel major or minor, especially towards the end of a section—is one of the features that preserve the freshness of his music. Handel's response to Italian texts was less acute, and his sense of form generally maintained the balance of his arias, but he too had a gift for the unexpected, connected perhaps with his improvisatory approach to composition. Irregular phrase-lengths, unsymmetrical paragraphs, last-minute rhythmic extensions, and unorthodox twists of melody or tonality are among the constant delights of his arias. His key associations are much closer to Scarlatti's as listed by Grout in *The New Grove* (xvi. 555) than to Mattheson's. As opera composers Scarlatti and Handel are each atypical, standing at an angle to the standard practice of their age.[44] Both had their failures, Scarlatti sometimes lapsing into incoherence, Handel into empty gesticulation; but an urge to transcend routine lies at the heart of their best work. While many of the composers he encountered in Italy could—and doubtless did—instruct Handel in the tricks and techniques of the *opera seria* trade, only Scarlatti commanded the extra ration of genius capable of stretching his imagination and inspiring him to explore uncharted territory.

Finally, as a measure of light relief, it may be interesting to quote one of the few extant descriptions of the opera in Venice during Handel's Italian years. The writer is a French traveller, M. de Blainville; his account is dated 3 March 1707.[45] He takes the usual literary–moral view of opera as far inferior to tragedy, which he fears will be ruined by these 'magnificent Fooleries' and 'pompous Trifles'. Although as a Frenchman he finds the machines pitiful, the poets inferior, the librettos absurd, and the representation of Roman heroes by castratos ('in general miserable Actors as to Gesture') 'monstrously incongruous', he has high praise for the orchestras, the women singers, and the rich costumes. 'If their Theatres are ill-lighted, they are nevertheless grand and magnificent; and if their Ballets are paltry, their Decorations are splendid and well diversified.'

I shall observe farther, that there are acted in that City [Venice] five or six different Operas all at once: So much are its Inhabitants captivated with the Charms of Music! The Theatres belong to some of the Nobility, who raise a considerable Revenue from the Boxes which they let out, either for the whole Carnaval, or only for a Day. The Ladies of Quality frequent those Entertainments every Night, especially towards the End of the Carnaval. There they make (for they are allowed to use them at that Time) their appearance all sparkling with Jewels; and the Brightness of the lighted Tapers which they have in their Boxes, set them off to all Advantage in the Eyes of their Gallants, whom they give to understand, by certain Signs, that they are pleased with their Assiduity, or dissatisfied with their Coldness.

There is something very diverting to hear the noisy Clamours which the Gondoliers

[44] Scarlatti is sometimes erroneously described as the founder of a Neapolitan school. In his own day he was often classed as a Roman composer. Mattheson in *Das neu-eröffnete Orchestre* (Hamburg, 1713), 203–4, drew a distinction between the light Venetian style with its love of simple melody and the gravity of the Roman with its more solid harmonic emphasis. The idea of a Neapolitan school led by Vinci, Leo, Hasse, etc. seems to have originated with Burney; he does not include Scarlatti.

[45] *Travels through Holland, Germany, Switzerland, and other Parts of Europe; but especially Italy*, trans. George Turnbull and William Guthrie (London, 1743), i. 560–4.

or Watermen raise, when an excellent Voïce has made an End of some moving Air.
These Fellows, who are, as I have said before, in great Numbers, may always enter
Gratis, and scarce do any Thing else at the Operas than applauding the actors. Nothing
is more entertaining than the Vows and Prayers which they put up in Favour of him or
her who has been singing; and the Burden of all commonly is: *Blessed be thou; blessed be
the Father who begat thee!* Nor are they the only People who make such a Bustle in giving
their Applauses. You often see several of the Nobles bending forward at once half out
of their Boxes; and you hear them crying out aloud, especially when it is a Woman,
Cara, cara, adding to their Enthusiasm *that they are going to throw themselves down headlong
thro' Excess of Pleasure.*

Amidst these Acclamations, others toss into the Boxes or Pit Sonnets, or other Verses,
composed in Honour of the excellent Singer, whom they always call *divine incomparable
Beauty*, tho' she be often ugly in the highest Degree. Nevertheless, ugly as she is, the
Charms of her Voice induces [*sic*] many of the Nobles to make it a Point of Honour to
get her into their Possession, and the strife is who shall carry her by Presents of the
greater Value...

The young Nobles frequent Comedy... Another of their fine Diversions is to spit
upon those in the Pit, and to let fly among them ends of lighted Candles, rotten
Oranges, and other like Things, who they chiefly sling at those who are somewhat
genteelly dressed. Those Gentlemen may commit all these Abuses with Impunity,
because the Comedy and the Opera are priviledged Places, where the least Violence is
a Kind of State-crime; not to mention, that there is always at the Door a Set of
Ruffians armed and masked, whom they constantly keep in their Pay, to protect them
in Case of Necessity...

To conclude, most People go in Mask to the Comedy and Opera, that they be there
with more Freedom, but all Things are managed at the Opera with much more
Decorum than at the Comedy: On the one Hand, because the *Venetians* are generally in
Love with Music, even to Distraction; and on the other, because it is frequented by the
more polite and sober Sort of People.

Additional Notes (Chapters 6 and 7)

* (p. 82) For further information about the oratorios Handel could have heard
in Rome, and for his visit to Naples, see the essays by L. Bianchi and A. Furnari
in *Händel e gli Scarlatti a Roma*, ed. N. Pirrotta and A. Ziino (Florence, 1987).

* (p. 99) John Roberts has drawn attention to another likely change in a note
to the facsimile edition of a Vienna manuscript (*c.* 1710) of C. F. Pollarolo's *Il
Faramondo* (*Drammaturgia musicale veneta*, v. 9 [Milan, 1987]). This score contains a
version of 'Per dar pregio all' amor mio' with altered text ('Per dar pace a questo
core'), lower tessitura, and simplified orchestration. In Handel's autograph the
aria was partly written by the copyist Angelini (see p. 111), who introduced a
major error that could only have been corrected by Handel himself. The ritornello after the A section should be identical with that at the start, ending on the
first beat of the bar instead of the third and doing away with the superfluous
tonic chord at the start of the B section. Roberts suggests that the correction,
adopted in the Vienna manuscript, was made in the Florence performing score,
and that the lower tessitura may have been written then for the singer, Anna
Maria Cecchi Torri, who had been on the boards since 1684 and whose voice
perhaps showed signs of wear.

* (p. 111) At the first revival, at Innsbruck in 1984, Alan Curtis replaced the
missing duet with the duet for Clizia and Arcane 'Addio, mio caro bene' in
Teseo.

CHAPTER 7

VINCER SE STESSO È LA MAGGIOR VITTORIA
(RODRIGO)

Two recent discoveries have clarified the text and early history of the opera, previously known only as a torso. In 1974 Reinhard Strohm[1] established the correct title from the printed libretto; it is so cumbersome that for convenience we retain Mainwaring's form, which may derive from Handel's circle. In 1983 the complete Act III came to light in a long-lost copy,[2] leaving only one gap at the beginning of Act I. This is indicated by the bracketed passage in the summary.

The action takes place in and near Seville in the early eighth century. [In the *palace garden* Rodrigo, King of Castile, *sits reading a letter*, which announces the victory of his general Giuliano over Evanco,[3] King of Aragon. Florinda, Giuliano's sister, loads Rodrigo with reproaches for seducing her and getting her with child. She demands that he fulfil his promise to marry her and send his barren queen Esilena back to her father. Rodrigo tells her to drop her anger and think of the pleasure she derived from their love: 'the king has a different law from his people'.] She looks forward to enlisting Giuliano's help in her vengeance.[4] The set changes to the *royal court-room with a throne*. Esilena tells Rodrigo's minister Fernando that the king's affections are engaged elsewhere, and when Rodrigo enters she urges him to win a further triumph over his mad rage. He warns her against jealousy. They *mount the throne as Giuliano enters with part of the victorious army, Evanco in chains, and the head of Sisibuto* (Evanco's brother) *on a pole*. The two kings indulge in a slanging match. Rodrigo thinks of putting Evanco to death, but decides to keep him a prisoner and hands him over to Giuliano, who is thanked by Esilena for his services to the throne. Having done his duty by Rodrigo, he offers Evanco his friendship as a chivalrous foe, and *is about to leave when Florinda arrives and detains him*. He greets his sister, who to his astonishment denies her right to that name: Rodrigo has seduced her and got her with child. She begs Giuliano to avenge the family honour by killing her. He replies that her repentance has wiped out the sin: he will take vengeance on Rodrigo and restore Evanco as the legitimate king. Florinda looks forward to her name being cleared by the destruction of the kingdom. Rodrigo in *his closet* is haunted by forebodings of death. Fernando interrupts and summons him to arms: Giuliano has freed

---

[1] 'Händel in Italia', 156–60.

[2] See W. Dean and A. Hicks, 'The Handel Collection of the Earl of Shaftesbury', *Early Music*, forthcoming.

[3] This is the spelling of the libretto and Handel's autograph; it is not clear why Chrysander altered it to Evaneo, which does not scan.

[4] The opening recitative and aria ('Pugneran con noi le stelle') in HG belong to Florinda, not Rodrigo.

Evanco and is in open rebellion. Rodrigo dispatches Fernando to collect his forces and tells Esilena of his affair with Florinda. She offers to surrender the throne to Florinda, that the kingdom may be spared bloodshed and gain an heir. He will not hear of this, but allows her to visit her rival with an offer of peace. Esilena hopes to set an example for all Spanish marriages; to show the quality of her love she will give up her husband but not her constancy.

Act II opens in *a military camp with a royal pavilion.* Giuliano promises to make Evanco King of Castile as well as Aragon if he will agree to marry Florinda. A soldier brings a letter from Fernando offering his help against the tyrant if Giuliano will meet him at a secret rendezvous. Despite Florinda's warning of treachery he agrees. Evanco pays court to Florinda, whom he has long loved in vain; she asks him to wait on her vengeance. Esilena enters and in a long speech offers Florinda Rodrigo's bed and throne; she herself will cut off her hair, take the rank of a servant, and if necessary wander in exile and poverty in order to bring the country peace. Florinda refuses the offer as a poor sop to her revenge and demands Rodrigo's heart torn from his breast. Esilena bitterly reproaches her and departs to give her last kisses to her husband. Florinda banishes all tender thoughts and fills her heart with hatred for Rodrigo.[5] In *a hall at night* Rodrigo faces his destiny with courage. Esilena reports the failure of her mission, but tries to encourage him with hopes of a more favourable future.[6] Fernando enters *with Giuliano in chains.* Rodrigo at once condemns him to death, but Esilena and Fernando fear that his execution may fan the rebels' anger. Rodrigo accordingly dispatches Fernando with a message: Evanco must return to captivity if he wishes to be pardoned, and Florinda can buy the life of her brother by leaving the kingdom. Rodrigo and Esilena feel their love rekindled. In *a military camp beneath the city wall with a gate into the city* Florinda, echoed by Evanco, urges her forces to the assault. *The gate opens, revealing Fernando and Giuliano surrounded by soldiers poised to kill him* (Giuliano). Fernando delivers Rodrigo's terms; Giuliano urges Florinda and Evanco to go ahead and avenge his death on Rodrigo. Florinda hesitates, but Evanco *seizes a bow and discharges an arrow, which strikes down Fernando. The defences collapse, and Evanco enters the city with his troops.* Florinda rejoices in the prospect of a bloody revenge.

Act III opens in *a temple* (of Jupiter).[7] Rodrigo, faced with death, reproaches the barbarous gods and resolves to make their shrine his funeral ·pyre. Esilena urges him to abjure such sacrilege and fight to the last with honour and hope. He yields, *places his sceptre and crown at the foot of* [Jupiter's] *statue,*[8] and prepares to devote his last breath to Esilena. She offers herself to the gods as a victim in his place. The set changes to *a courtyard.* Giuliano enters victorious, sword in hand; the palace is on fire, and it remains only to punish the tyrant. Rodrigo arrives, *hotly pursued by Evanco's soldiers* but still breathing defiance. Giuliano and Evanco raise their swords to kill him; Florinda claims that privilege for herself. She is about to strike when Esilena enters *with Florinda's child in her arms.* She appeals to Florinda to remember whose son he is,

[5] In Handel's autograph she takes a gentler line, contrasting her anger with Esilena's pity and dispersing the ashes of her love for Rodrigo.

[6] In the autograph version she proclaims that fate cannot break her devotion, even beyond the grave.

[7] Such anachronisms were required by the ecclesiastical censorship.

[8] This direction is in the Shaftesbury copy and the Venice but not the Florence libretto; see below.

tells Rodrigo to kiss him, and bids the child seek his mother. She then challenges Florinda to kill the son as well as the father. Florinda's anger fades and she offers Rodrigo his life. Evanco and Giuliano ask what is to become of their vengeance, but abandon it when Esilena suggests they imitate Florinda's magnanimity. Rodrigo invites Esilena to punish his infidelity; she prefers to pardon him in return for part of his heart, and they renew their faith in a duet. In *the palace throne-room* Florinda, who has offered Evanco some hope if he will abandon his claims on Rodrigo, at last agrees to marry him. Rodrigo restores Evanco to the throne of Aragon with Florinda as his consort and appoints his son by Florinda heir to Castile, with Giuliano as his guardian. He himself and Esilena will retire to a humble dwelling. Esilena points the moral in the title ('To conquer oneself is the greater victory') and leads the company in an appeal to Venus.

Rodrigo (Roderick), the last King of the Visigoths in Spain, whose disastrous reign led to the long Moorish occupation, was the subject of numerous Italian operas towards the close of the seventeenth century,[9] and later of an epic poem by Southey. He usurped the throne in 710, murdering the rightful king Witica (Vitizza), and was drowned the following year after a battle with the Moors, who according to legend had been called in by Count Julian of Ceuta to avenge Rodrigo's seduction of his daughter Florinda. Julian had also enlisted the support of Vitizza's sons Sisibuto and Evanco. This is explained in the librettist's Argomento, which details his deviations from history, chiefly designed to make Rodrigo a tolerable hero fit for redemption by Esilena's selfless love. Thus he is the rightful king of Castile and the usurper only of Aragon. The child is fictitious, and so is Evanco's love for Florinda. Giuliano becomes the latter's brother, not her father, and does not turn on Rodrigo until he learns of her dishonour after his defeat of Vitizza's sons.

The source libretto was *Il duello d'amore e di vendetta* by Francesco Silvani, set by M. A. Ziani and produced at Venice in the carnival season of 1699–1700, when the famous castrato Nicolini sang the part of Rodrigo.[10] Silvani, a prolific librettist who collaborated with nearly all the leading opera composers of the day and was particularly successful with Gasparini, was addicted to abstract and sesquipedalian titles.[11] It is not known who adapted this libretto for Florence; Strohm suggested the Florentine court poet Antonio Salvi, Baselt[12] one of the cantata poets with whom Handel worked in Rome during most of 1707, on the ground that one aria text ('Il dolce foco mio') comes from the cantata 'Allor ch'io dissi' (HWV 80)—but Handel himself could have appropriated this. Apart from the suppression of one character, Rodrigo's

[9] Rome 1677 and 1694, Milan 1684, Bologna 1686, Mantua 1686, Verona 1687, Naples 1687 and 1702, Florence 1692, Parma 1695, Ferrara 1696, Palermo 1703. Some of these were doubtless revivals. The composers included Gasparini (1694) and Bassani (1696). Keiser's *Desiderius* (1709) is partly based on the same story.

[10] In later productions Margherita Durastanti sang Giuliano (Mantua, 1701) and Esilena (Naples, 1715), on the latter occasion—when the music was a pasticcio—with Senesino as Rodrigo.

[11] His libretto of *Il duello* was subsequently set under different titles by G. M. Buini (*Gli sdegni cangiati in amore*, Venice, 1725) and Galuppi (*L'odio placato*, Venice, 1729).

[12] *Verzeichnis*, i. 75 n. 3.

sister Climene, who is in love with Giuliano, there are few changes of substance.[13]

The position is however complicated by the fact that we do not possess Handel's score as it was performed. He composed it in Rome, setting an earlier version of the text somewhere between Silvani's libretto and that printed for the Florence production. It is clear from the latter that a number of major changes were made between Handel's arrival and the performance. The new material, not inconsiderable in bulk, must have been entered directly into the performing score, now lost. The autograph is very incomplete, but the missing portions certainly contained three pieces, two arias and the *coro*, included in the performance; two of them survive in copies. In III ii Handel set or planned a duet for Rodrigo and Esilena which is mentioned in the autograph without music; and there is little doubt that the aria 'Così m'alletti' in III vii was intended not for Evanco but for Florinda, as in both the Venice and Florence librettos.[14]

Taking all this into account, we can tabulate the facts as shown in Table 1.

TABLE 1

	Ziani 1699/1700		Handel as first set		Handel as performed	
Rodrigo	7 arias	2 duets	7 arias	2 duets	8 arias	1 duet
Esilena	7 arias	2 duets	8 arias	2 duets	7 arias	1 duet
Florinda	9 arias		6 arias		6 arias	
Evanco	3 arias		5 arias		5 arias	
Giuliano	2 arias		6 arias		7 arias	
Fernando	2 arias		2 arias		2 arias	
Climene	6 arias					
	36 arias	2 duets	34 arias	2 duets	35 arias	1 duet
	coro		*coro*		*coro*	

It will be seen that although Climene and her six arias disappear fr·· Handel's libretto, there is little difference in the number of movemen.. Evanco's part is expanded, Florinda's contracted; the most striking change however is the increase of Giuliano's ration from two to six and later seven arias, undoubtedly because the tenor Guicciardi was a fine singer.[15] His music, and Esilena's, requires an accomplished technique.

Of the 37 vocal movements other than recitative in Handel's score as first composed, at least 24, probably 25, and possibly 26[16] took their texts from the Venice libretto; a few were slightly modified, one of them ('Heroica fortezza') developed from a recitative in *virgole*. Of the eleven new pieces, six were inserted arias (four for Giuliano). Two took the place of Silvani's love duet in

[13] Two editions of Silvani's libretto were published in the same season. The second omits Climene, but Handel's libretto is closer to the first (Strohm, 'Händel in Italia').

[14] Handel wrote no character's name against the aria, and Chrysander attributed it to the singer of the previous recitative, thus giving Evanco two arias in this scene and leaving Florinda with none, though she is its central figure. Both are sopranos.

[15] In 1719 Handel tried to engage him for London: see p. 301.

[16] Handel almost certainly set Rodrigo's aria in the first scene, 'Occhi neri'. The missing duet in III ii could have been taken from that in Silvani's II x.

Act II. Only three were straight substitutions: 'Sommi Dei' in I ix (this scene was rewritten), 'Per dar pregio' at the end of Act I, a bravura piece instead of an appeal to the god of love, and 'Empio fato' in II vi, ousting some rather forced imagery about defying Cerberus and the fates.

The late changes involved the suppression of six arias and the duet in III ii (if it was ever written) and the insertion of seven new arias, not all in the same places. Two entrance arias, Esilena's 'Nasce il sol' and Giuliano's 'Dell'Iberia', disappeared, but Giuliano gained two others, 'Con voci care in petto' in a new scene after I vi and 'Quanto belle, quanto care' at the start of Act II. 'Heroica fortezza', 'Fredde ceneri', 'Empio fato', and 'Lucide stelle' gave place to different arias for the same characters, and the duet to Silvani's original aria for Rodrigo in this scene (III ii). We can only guess at the reasons—possibly * the preference or capacity of the singers ('Heroica fortezza' goes a third lower than the rest of Evanco's part)—and since only one of the replacement arias survives we cannot judge the effect. The account in this chapter necessarily follows the autograph, together with the two unpublished pieces. While the plot is scarcely disturbed and most of the suppressed arias are no great loss, the removal of 'Fredde ceneri' and 'Empio fato', in favour of a more concentrated expression of Florinda's hatred and a tender song of love and hope, arguably weakens the characterization and certainly sets aside music of fine quality. One feature of the changes between 1700 and 1707 is the shifting of emphasis from entrance or mid-scene arias where the singer remains on stage towards exit arias at the end of scenes. Where Silvani has five entrance arias and six or seven others not followed by an exit (apart from two in the penultimate scene, where the singers naturally remain for the *coro*), Handel in his final version reduced the number to two and three respectively, and ends two scenes (I vii and ix–x in the libretto) with dramatic interruptions not in Silvani. This was an increasing trend in *opera seria*; we cannot be sure that Handel was personally responsible for furthering it here. He had not yet developed the cavatina as an entrance aria, a favourite procedure of his maturity.

Ziani's libretto has the usual extraneous ballet movements between the acts. These are not mentioned in Handel's. He and his librettist reduced the scenic spectacle, presumably to fit the resources of the theatre. The assault on the city at the end of Act II is more elaborate in the Venice libretto, where Evanco and his troops and even Florinda scale the wall with the aid of ladders. Ziani seems to have ended this act with an instrumental battle; Florinda's 'Alle glorie' is one of the more important Florentine insertions. Another scene treated differently in Venice is I ix, which begins with a sleep aria for Rodrigo, after which he is threatened in recitative by Vitizza's ghost but dismisses the visitation as a dream. This might have been effective as a warning of retribution—Handel was to make much of similar scenes in *Silla*, *Arianna*, and *Giustino*—but the librettist did not follow it up.

Handel's full libretto considerably modifies the impression left by the fragmentary printed score. The extra scenes at the beginning of the first and third acts are important for the delineation of Rodrigo; he becomes, if not more sympathetic, at least more credible. In Act I, feeling free to repudiate Florinda now that Giuliano's victory has secured the kingdom, he exasperates her beyond endurance by his callousness. This makes a stronger motive for her implacable resentment than a seduction several years earlier. One feels that he loves Esilena while only toying with Florinda, an impression confirmed at the start of Act III, where his wife's influence brings about a complete change in his behaviour.

The plot has the blood-and-thunder immediacy of a Wild West film. The characters traverse the extremes of heroism and villainy, inspired by lust, devotion, self-sacrifice, ambition, or vengeance. There are few finer shades, but the motivation is consistent and the language clear. In these respects, and in the exclusion of sub-plots and comic and supernatural episodes, the libretto comes closer to Metastasio than most of its fellows in the first decade of the century. But while the style and general plan are well above average, the detailed layout is ill-contrived for musical development. Many of the arias are generalized statements loosely tied to their contexts. On the other hand promising aria situations are repeatedly ignored, for example in I ix, where the emphasis falls not on Esilena's heroic offer but on Rodrigo's undramatic acceptance; II i, a scene full of strong incident, concluded by an aria of abstract moralizing for Giuliano; and III v–vii, the climax of the plot, where Esilena produces the child. The handling of this is particularly inept. The dramatic gestures, appeals, and changes of mind evoke nothing but pages of recitative, whereupon the resolution of the conflict is followed by a string of five arias and a duet, all more or less otiose. Handel or his collaborator cut a tender aria for Florinda when she yields to Esilena's pleading; but its inclusion, while perhaps improving the balance, would scarcely have removed the fault.

The score is very uneven in style and dramatic application, with numerous signs of immaturity. Handel had not yet found a satisfactory balance, either within the aria or over the course of a scene or act. The arias vary widely in length, weight, technical demands, and degree of sophistication, but by no means always in conformity with their content. In a sense perhaps Handel took his task too lightly. He lifted several arias with little change from instrumental cantatas composed earlier in 1707 for Prince Ruspoli in Rome, and all are conspicuous misfits. Rodrigo's 'Dolce amor' and Esilena's 'Si che lieta' in the Act II love scene, both from 'Tu fedel?' (HMV 171), are charming but far too light-boned and diversionary for so central an episode as the reconciliation of the estranged king and queen. Equally ineffective dramatically are the pair of arias at the end of II vii: 'Allor che sorge' is transcribed literally (except for the words) from 'Un sospiretto' in 'Cor fedele' (HWV 96), and 'Il dolce foco mio' derives in part from 'Lascia omai' in 'Da quel giorno' (HWV 99).[17] The former comes strangely from the mouth of the bellicose Giuliano. Still more out of place is Esilena's 'Per dar pregio' at the end of Act I; the music fits neither the text nor the character. It too was lifted from HWV 99; apart from the new B section Handel did not bother to write out most of it in the autograph. No antecedent has been found for 'Così m'alletti' in III vii, but this simple ditty strikes an incongruous note at the climax of the opera's great confrontation scene. Twice Handel precedes a set-change with a piece lacking in conclusive weight, the binary arietta 'Si che lieta' in II x (despite the repetition of the entire piece by the orchestra as a final ritornello) and a

---

[17] It would not be surprising if a closer antecedent were to turn up. The words were taken from a different cantata.

one-section cavatina in I viii, a common enough procedure in earlier opera
but out of place in a work with heroic pretensions.

Whereas the slow arias, though sometimes insufficiently developed, are full
of promising ideas, many of the virtuoso pieces are conventional; when
Handel tries to enlarge the scale he tends to become feeble and empty,
especially in Act I. One or two of these movements show a painful reluctance
to modulate, or, if they do, to achieve a proper tonal equilibrium. The
modulation to the dominant during the A section is more common than in
Almira, but there are few signs of that subdominant ballast towards the end
that becomes such a happy feature later, and fewer still of the equipoise
between form, idea, and context so prominent in most of the London operas.
Handel is alert to the dramatic significance of ritornellos, often omitting,
postponing, or extending them, but not yet adept at their structural control.
In some pieces ('Prendi l'alma', 'Lucide stelle') they seem stunted, in others
('O morte, vendetta', 'Allor che sorge') disproportionately long. Kimbell[18]
makes the interesting observation that the frequency with which final
ritornellos overlap or support vocal cadences rules out the improvisation of
elaborate cadenzas.

Nevertheless the increase in fluency since *Almira* is unmistakable. By this
time Handel had composed at least nine instrumental cantatas, the oratorio *Il
trionfo del Tempo*, and all his Latin church music except 'Silete venti'. Italian
warmth is beginning to thaw out German stiffness, especially where his
imagination is fired by the sufferings of the characters, as in much of Act II.
Several of the dance songs show an advance in melodic expressiveness and
rhythmic freedom, with a characteristic irregularity of phrase-length. This
needs emphasis in view of Dent's baffling statement[19] that 'the songs are
mostly taken from *Almira*'. They are not. Four arias in Act I and the overture's
introduction use motives from the earlier opera, but unlike most of the cantata
borrowings they are comprehensively reworked,[20] and one, 'Sommi Dei', is
gilded with genius. This is an early illustration of Handel's capacity to learn,
which increased as his career lengthened. As we shall see, many of the best
ideas in *Rodrigo* were put to more profitable use in their turn, chiefly in later
operas but also in *Messiah* and *Susanna*.

Esilena is by far the most successful character, no doubt because her
misfortunes stirred Handel's sympathy. It is a peculiarity of his early work,
not only the operas but the many quasi-dramatic cantatas, that the women are
much more vividly realized than the men. We think at once of Lucrezia,
Armida, Agrippina, and Dafne in the cantatas, Almira, Esilena, Poppea, and
Agrippina in the operas. None of the male characters, except Ottone in
Agrippina, has the same power to grip attention; perhaps not till *Radamisto* did
Handel find an equivalent touch with heroes. The fact that a high proportion
of cantata texts were concerned with the sufferings of women may have
contributed to this. Esilena has something in common with Polissena (who was
later to annex one of her arias); each is married to a brutal and licentious
soldier, and each in the face of intolerable provocation preserves a gentle
submissiveness that strains credit when we read the libretto but becomes
touchingly human and convincing in Handel's music. This type of character,

[18] 'A Critical Study'.
[19] *Symposium*, 20.
[20] The treatment of material from Keiser's *Octavia* in 'Dell'Iberia' is of the same kind.

as Metastasio's librettos make all too clear, rings truer in a woman than a man.

Esilena's eight arias are uneven in quality. In the first, 'Nasce il sol', inexperience betrays Handel into a bad miscalculation. She complains that though the sun and the breezes are full of joy they can bring her no consolation. Handel paints the moods of the weather ('ride', 'scherza'), not those of the singer, and sets the piece most unsuitably as a gigue in F major. The fact that eight of the first nine arias in the surviving score either carry the mark *Allegro* or imply it makes this all the less easy to justify. The B section has some rough edges, such as a casual bass F sharp against F and G natural in the voice, characteristic of Handel's early style; later he would have avoided them or given them greater prominence to stress a significant word. Nor would he have used full da capo form for an entrance aria. 'In mano al mio sposo' has a pleasantly enlarged ritornello after the A section, developing a cadence figure that occurs first in the voice part and was to haunt Handel all his life (Ex. 6).

Ex. 6

It appears in the *coro* at the end of the first part of *La Resurrezione* and with sublime effect in 'Where'er you walk'. 'Per dar pregio' allows the singer to show off her coloratura in competition with a solo violin and cello, but at disastrous cost to dramatic consistency; the interminable divisions strike a note of inanity, if not of self-parody.

Esilena rises to her full stature in the big Act II scene with Florinda, where she offers to surrender her husband and happiness to her rival if this will bring the country peace. The little aria 'Egli è tuo' is a stroke of inspired simplicity. After the long recitative we expect a more flamboyant gesture; by suppressing the ritornello and bringing the voice in very gently with the emotionally charged phrase later to become famous in 'Comfort ye', Handel paints Esilena's sincerity and goodness in indelible colours (Ex. 7).

Ex. 7

(He is yours!)

This is an early use of a motive,[21] always associated with consolation or self-sacrifice, that recurs in *Flavio* ('Parto, sì') and other operas as well as *Messiah*. The harmonic shift, E flat after a recitative cadence in G minor, is not found elsewhere in *Rodrigo* but was to become a favourite gambit later. The next aria, 'Parto, crudel', is also Esilena's and rounds off the scene with an exit in one of Handel's earliest examples of cavatina–cabaletta design, though 'Egli è tuo' is a miniature da capo aria. The material is nothing out of the ordinary, but the contrasts of *Presto* and *Adagio* ('ultimi baci') make a strong dramatic point. 'Empio fato' is the greatest tragic aria Handel had yet composed, a fully mature piece of superb imaginative power. The arpeggiated string writing of the A section, split between unison violins and bass, suggests a Bach prelude or even Mozart rather than any procedure typical of Handel.[22] The vocal line expresses the singer's anguish by avoiding a full cadence even at the logical middle point. The final ritornello, instead of recapitulating the start, develops ideas introduced by the voice, a foretaste of the London operas. The B section, borrowed from 'Urne voi' in *Il trionfo del Tempo*, brings a marvellous change to a dark five-part texture of slow quaver chords, the three violin parts all lying very low and constantly crossing. As Esilena imagines her spirit following Rodrigo beyond the grave, the music sets out on bold harmonic adventures through distant keys. There are links here with many later works: 'Voi che udite' in *Agrippina* (partly on the same material), the B section of 'Già lo stringo' in *Orlando*, and two of Cleopatra's greatest arias in *Giulio Cesare*. The resemblance to 'Se pietà' is one of mood rather than detail, but a striking phrase in 'Piangerò la sorte mia' is anticipated in *Rodrigo* in a different metre.

Ex. 8

Esilena

(sem-pre in-tor-no al tuo sem-bian-te tut-ta fè mi vol-ge-rò)

([As a wandering ghost] I shall always, utterly faithful, turn towards your face)

Cleopatra

(si cru-de-le e tan-to ri-a, pian-ge-rò la sor-te mi-a, si cru-de-le)

(I shall bewail my fate, so cruel and so harsh)

The same figure occurs in the first aria of the continuo cantata 'Ah! che pur troppo è vero' (HWV 77) and Mirtillo's 'Fato crudo'[23] in *Il pastor fido*; it is one of many such fingerprints to be found throughout Handel's work. Although

---

[21] The first two bars had appeared in 'Care luci' in the continuo cantata 'Aure soavi e liete' (HWV 84), copied in May 1707.

[22] There are however a few other early examples, including 'Deh serbate' in *Teseo* and the aria from *Florindo* quoted in Chapter 5 (Ex. 2, p. 75).

[23] This aria has other links with *Rodrigo*, both verbal (the idea of fate) and musical; it is based on the same ritornello as 'Sommi Dei'—which originated in *Almira*.

marking the bass of the second half *senza cembali* Handel figured it in several places, presumably as an aid to memory when filling up the parts.

'Perchè viva' in Act III is another beautiful slow aria, characteristic of Handel's early style, with some eloquent harmonic detail. In the ritornello after the da capo the full string band takes over from the continuo and indulges in a delicious development of the original bass with canons, suspensions, and an interrupted cadence (the melodic line dropping suddenly from the tonic to a dominant seventh) that occurs so often in this opera as almost to become an obsession.

Ex. 9

Esilena addresses the child in a beautiful E major accompanied recitative, and originally had two duets with Rodrigo. As noted above, Handel may have set Silvani's Act II duet, 'Più chiare e luminose', at the end of III ii, where the words would fit particularly well. In the event Rodrigo sang a valedictory love song here. 'Prendi l'alma', while on a more extended scale than the duets in *Almira*, suffers from underdeveloped ritornellos and an excess of facile ornament; Handel had not yet acquired the gift of spaciousness without triviality. Esilena has a florid solo part in the *coro*, an unpublished movement in gavotte rhythm later reworked for the finale of *Rinaldo*.

Florinda, though not drawn with particular subtlety, makes an effective foil as *seconda donna*. She has the single-mindedness of Lady Macbeth without the sleep-walking scene. Her first aria, 'Pugneran con noi le stelle', based on 'Ob dein Mund' in *Almira*, is full of vigorous scale and fanfare figures but suffers from being tied to the apron-strings of the tonic, C major; the substantial A section contains not a single accidental. If this was an attempt to suggest Florinda's implacable resolution it scarcely succeeds. In 'O morte, vendetta' Handel misses a trick by giving her a cavatina where the context—the end of a set on a forceful climax—demands a big aria. The vocal part is too short; the long final ritornello (28 bars after eight at the beginning) was presumably designed, like similar passages in *Almira*, to cover the change of scene, but it merely unbalances the design. 'Fredde ceneri d'amor' is the best of Florinda's arias. She tries to banish her love for Rodrigo; the music conveys an unmistakable tinge of regret, as if her deeper feelings belie her. Here again Handel throws his spear into the future; ambiguous cross-currents of this kind are a masterly feature of his mature operas. The urgency of the A section bespeaks his native Germany. The scoring is interesting: the bass line is entrusted to the viola without continuo in A and silent altogether in B, where the voice and upper parts (violins and recorders) are in unison throughout. At the end of Act II we meet the tigress in full cry. 'Alle glorie, alle palme' is a typical B flat vengeance aria of a type familiar in later operas and oratorios. The clattering accompaniment may have been meant to suggest the assault on the city as well as the emotions of the singer. The instrumental solo with which she disports herself in thirds, like that in 'Pugneran', is oddly marked as an alternative for oboe or violin, as if Handel were unsure of the capacity of his players.[24] Florinda fades out in Act III. 'Così m'alletti' has the archaic flavour of a survival from the seventeenth century; the love song 'Begl'occhi del mio ben' is pleasant but characterless.

Rodrigo makes an unattractive hero, but he is less repulsive than that other cuckolding tyrant Silla. His single virtue is courage; only when confronted with disaster does he spring spasmodically to life. His lost aria in the first scene, an expression of shameless cynicism, might have done something to establish him. 'Ti lascio' tells us little, but 'Sommi Dei' in the closet scene is the finest movement in Act I and offers the earliest example of a technique Handel was to make peculiarly his own, the dramatic interruption exploiting the regularity of the da capo convention. The sombre opening admirably hits off Rodrigo's mood, that of Henry IV's 'Uneasy lies the head that wears a crown', aided by a long series of interrupted cadences. The despondent monarch drags himself to the end of the A section and has just embarked on B, which threatens to intensify the restlessness, when Fernando bursts in with a summons to arms, the scene continuing in secco recitative (Ex. 10, p. 106). It is not a far cry to the sudden discharge of Saul's javelin at the corresponding point in 'A serpent in my bosom warm'd'. The next aria, 'Vanne in campo', might be taken as the cabaletta to this cavatina (it is in the relative major), except that the long intervening recitative has broken the thread, and there is more potential drama in Esilena's offer to visit the outraged Florinda, which is not dignified with an aria, than in Rodrigo's consenting reply.

'Siet'assai superbe', which begins the nocturnal second set of Act II, is chiefly memorable as the first sketch for Agrippina's 'Pensieri, voi mi tormentate'. The music does not lack atmosphere, but it is difficult to avoid comparison with the far grander later context. 'Dolce amor' too, already a

---

[24] In the autograph of both arias he first wrote the solos for oboe, then added the violin as alternative. He was composing in Rome for Florentine players whom he may never have heard.

Ex. 10

(Great Gods! if I have offended you, let my enjoyment not become the object of cruel suffering. But compassionate or cruel . . . Rodrigo, to arms!)

borrowing, was to find lasting fame and subtler treatment in *Agrippina* ('Ingannata') and *Il pastor fido* ('Di goder'). The exquisite tune is out of place in the mouth of this graceless tyrant. Rodrigo's aria in the first scene of Act III, 'Quà rivolga gli orribili acciari', begins defiantly without ritornello and is darkened by Neapolitan and minor colouring before cadences, but its principal interest is again the appearance of motives familiar in later operas, the first phrase in *Rinaldo* ('Vo' far guerra'), its consequent in *Agrippina* ('Coronato il crin') and elsewhere. Here they are interlocked (Ex. 11). The tessitura of Rodrigo's music is markedly lower in the duet 'Prendi l'alma' than in his arias, as if Handel found some difficulty in balancing two equal voices.

The second soprano monarch, Evanco (composed for a woman), has a slightly higher but less taxing part than Rodrigo. Most of it is rather flavourless; Handel, while increasing his ration from three arias to five, seems

Ex. 11

([Let the mad fury of the villains] direct the horrible swords here)

to have formed no clear conception of his character. The short siciliano 'Prestami un solo dardo' must be among the earliest Handel arias to show the fertilizing influence of Alessandro Scarlatti, both in rhythm and harmonic astringency. It stands right out of its context, like many later pieces of similar cut, and is by far the best of Evanco's arias. He has a vigorous D major battle piece ('Sù! all'armi') towards the end of Act II; but Handel wrote many better arias of this type, one of them in the next scene. Neither of his Act III arias is of consequence as drama or music. 'Lucide stelle' is the one piece rejected in Florence whose replacement survives (the rest of course may lie concealed in other works). The melody of 'Io son vostro, luci belle', another light aria, is familiar; it appears, in a different key each time, in the fragmentary Charles VI cantata (HWV 119) ('Col valor d'un braccio forte'), the continuo cantata 'Fra pensieri quel pensiero' (HWV 115), *Il pastor fido* ('Secondaste al fine'), and *Tamerlano* (first setting of 'Cerco in vano'), and was modified for Juno's 'Above measure' in *Semele*. Apart from the absence of ritornellos 'Io son vostro, luci belle' is almost identical with 'Col valor' and 'Secondaste al fine'.

Handel fobbed off Fernando with two very dull arias whose compass never exceeds the octave above middle C; he was evidently an alto castrato of the third rank. Giuliano, a hare-brained military tenor, was better served. This is indeed Handel's most ambitious tenor part before those he wrote for Borosini in *Tamerlano* and *Rodelinda*, containing six (later seven) arias and requiring considerable flexibility. All the arias were laid under contribution later, three of them with the words more or less intact.[25] Three are fiery extrovert pieces replete with the fanfares, repeated notes, and scale figures demanded on such occasions; *Rodrigo* strikes this mood too often. Much the best of them is 'Stragi, morti', which we shall meet with improvements and a richer orchestration in its later context. 'Là ti sfido' is a bouncy gigue, 'Allor che sorge' a slight dance tune that accords as ill with Giuliano's character as 'Dolce amor' with Rodrigo's. 'Frà le spine' represents an early grappling with an idea that turns up constantly later. The German, Bach-like aspect of Handel's personality

---

[25] 'Stragi, morti' in *Radamisto*, 'Spirti fieri' in a revival of *Admeto*, 'Allor che sorge' in *Il pastor fido*.

emerges in the convoluted texture, often canonic and chromatic, of the ritornellos, which lie awkwardly alongside the chamber cantata style of the vocal sections. The aria expresses Giuliano's sense of the danger besetting the path of glory, but the illustration of this moral idea can hardly be said to illuminate his character, which is never quite focused.

There are no purely orchestral movements except the overture, which diverges from Handel's usual plan in the operas. It was probably not composed for *Rodrigo* and may never have belonged to it. On internal evidence the music could date back to the Hamburg years. Like the 1712 overture to *Il pastor fido* it looks like an independent composition of the same type as the Bach orchestral suites.[26] The opening follows the pattern of the French overture; the ten-bar Lentement leading to the repeat of the 6/8 fugue has a prophetic spaciousness and grandeur. Eight dances follow, all but the final Passacaille in binary form. They have attractive tunes and beautiful melodic extensions in the B sections; the Sarabande, the best of the set, is outstanding in this respect. The Bourrée is based on the same theme as the last aria in *Agrippina*, and the second Minuet is almost identical with the *coro* of that opera,[27] which ends with a note *Segue li Balli*. It is possible that what we know as the *Rodrigo* overture served as the ballet music for *Agrippina* before being put to other purposes. In the ballets at the end of his later operas Handel invariably sought a measure of integration by treating at least one movement both vocally and as an instrumental dance.[28] The long Passacaille in the concerto style with a brilliantly ornamented solo violin part, for which at bar 15 Handel no doubt improvised an equally spectacular harpsichord accompaniment, is very much in the manner of the French ballet finale. Moreover the fact that he wrote *Il Fine* with great emphasis at the end suggests that this was either an independent composition or the close of a large work, not a mere overture.

The scoring is a good deal closer than *Almira* to Handel's practice in London, which of course is basically Italian. There are few deviations from the standard, but a number of felicitous touches. Elaborate solos for violin are common, and also for oboe and cello. The brilliant obbligato in 'Per dar pregio', which unusually for Handel takes the violin up to f#‴, may have been written (in the cantata) for Corelli. Recorders appear twice. The theatre for which Handel wrote possessed no brass. Several of the military arias seem to demand trumpets and drums, notably 'Dell'Iberia'[29] and 'Stragi, morti'; yet when 'con bellici carmi grida la tromba' an oboe takes up the cue. A tonal design is perceptible; if the overture is correct, the opera begins and ends in B flat, and this key and its relative minor are prominent in all three acts, especially in the music of Rodrigo himself, who is all but confined to flat keys. The tempo distribution is more lop-sided. Handel does not always supply tempo marks, but in Act I every aria except two (one of them incomplete) is fast, whereas six of the first seven in Act II are slow.

[26] Several other London overtures were not composed for the operas to which they became attached: see pp. 239, 268, and 430.

[27] Based on the *coro* of Mattheson's *Cleopatra*, also used as an orchestral Minuet.

[28] This happens in *Amadigi, Radamisto, Ariodante, Alcina*, and revivals of *Arianna* and *Il pastor fido*, though not all the scores have been correctly printed.

[29] E. H. Tarr and T. Walker ('Die Verwendung der Trompete in der italienischen Oper des 17. Jahrhunderts' in *Hamburger Jahrbuch für Musikwissenschaft*, iii (1978), 160) cite this B flat aria as a characteristic use of that key for strings imitating trumpet motives.

History and Text

The mutilation of the autograph has deprived us of the date of composition. It has been plausibly suggested that Ferdinando de' Medici gave Handel the commission on his arrival in Florence from Germany in autumn 1706,[30] or even in Hamburg.[31] Handel composed the opera (apart from the overture) in Rome during the summer of 1707. It was produced in Florence in the autumn, probably in late November or early December at the Cocomero Theatre. Streatfeild, followed by Strohm, suggested that the performance was in private at the Pitti Palace, but R. L. and N. W. Weaver[32] have established that the singers, with one exception, were identical with those who took part in the first opera of the Cocomero's carnival season in late December. The cast was:

RODRIGO:	Stefano Frilli (soprano castrato)
ESILENA:	Anna Maria Cecchi Torri (soprano)
FLORINDA:	Aurelia Marcello (soprano)
GIULIANO:	Francesco Guicciardi (tenor)
EVANCO:	Caterina Azzolini (soprano)
FERNANDO:	Giuseppe Perini (alto castrato)

Of these artists, none of whom sang again under Handel, Cecchi Torri, Marcello, and Azzolini were in the service of the Duke of Mantua but had moved to Florence when Mantua was involved in the War of the Spanish Succession. Marcello later joined the service of Princess Violante of Bavaria, Ferdinando de' Medici's wife. Guicciardi's patron was the Duke of Modena, Frilli's the Elector of Bavaria. Frilli had sung in Pistocchi's *Narciso* at Ansbach in 1697 and died in August 1744 at the age of eighty. Their known activity in Florence was confined to the first decade of the century, apart from Marcello, who was still singing there in 1716.

According to Mainwaring, the only early writer to mention the opera, Handel 'was presented with 100 sequins, and a service of plate. This may serve for a sufficient testimony of its favourable reception.' Mainwaring's anecdote about a love affair between Handel and the prima donna, one Vittoria, 'who was much admired both as an actress, and a Singer', and apparently the mistress of the Grand Duke, and who pursued Handel's acquaintance later in Venice, has been dismissed as scandal, especially as Vittoria Tarquini[33] did not sing in *Rodrigo*. But she was in Perti's *Dionisio rè di Portogallo* at Pratolino in September 1707 as well as Scarlatti's *Il gran Tamerlano* the previous year, and an almost contemporary account suggests that the story had some substance. On 14 June 1710 the Electress Sophia of Hanover, in a letter to the Crown Princess Sophia Dorothea of Prussia, mentioned Handel's engagement as Kapellmeister to the Hanoverian Court, adding that 'he plays the harpsichord marvellously, to the delight of the Electoral Prince and Princess. He is a fine-looking man, and rumour has it that he was the lover of Victoria.'[34]

[30] Strohm, 'Händel in Italia', 158.

[31] Baselt, *Verzeichnis*, i. 75.

[32] *A Chronology of Music in the Florentine Theater 1590–1750*, 210.

[33] Not, as Chrysander supposed, Vittoria Tesi, who was a contralto and not born till 1700.

[34] G. Schnath (ed.), *Briefwechsel der Kurfürstin Sophie von Hannover mit dem Preussischen Königshause* (Berlin and Leipzig, 1927), 189; first quoted by A. Hicks, 'Handel's Early Musical Development', 83. Mainwaring's information, which came from the younger Smith and therefore indirectly from Handel, though vague in chronology, has often proved to have a substratum of fact.

Handel used the suppressed aria 'Lucide stelle' with new words ('Sento nell'alma un tenero amor') in his London pasticcio *Oreste* (Covent Garden, 18 December 1734). *Rodrigo* had to wait until 1984 for a revival.[35] Recent research has made this a more feasible project than Chrysander's score might suggest; only some recitative and an aria in Act I and perhaps an aria in Act III are required to complete it. Anthony Hicks[36] offered the ingenious suggestion that the music of 'Occhi neri' may have been adapted by the younger Smith for 'Charming Beauty' in the 1758 revival of *The Triumph of Time and Truth* (unquestionably based on an unidentified early piece), and that 'Vibri pure', the substitute for 'Heroica fortezza' in I vi, could likewise survive in 'Great in wisdom', an addition to *Judas Maccabaeus* of the same year.

By an odd chance the *Rodrigo* overture was the first music by Handel heard in the London theatre, anonymously and doubtless without his knowledge, in January 1710, when it was played as incidental music at a revival of Ben Jonson's play *The Alchemist* at the Queen's Theatre.

Autograph

The autograph (RM 20 c 5), on Roman paper apart from the overture, is hastily and untidily written, but with comparatively few alterations and cancellations. It is clear from Handel's foliation that one gathering of four leaves is missing at the start of Act I, another at the start of Act III, and probably one at the end of the opera. They were not all lost at the same time; the copies prove that the first gathering disappeared before or during the 1730s, the rest later. We know from the libretto that the missing pieces, apart from recitative, are two arias for Rodrigo, 'Occhi neri, voi non siete' in I i and 'Quà rivolga gli orribili acciari' in III i, and the *coro* 'L'amorosa dea di Gnido', of which only the first is lost. The gathering that carries most of the recitative of II viii (ff. 73–4) is two leaves short. Handel appears to have removed something at an early stage—conceivably a setting of the duet 'Più chiare e luminose' in the next scene of the 1700 libretto—and written out the recitative again from the middle of bar 9; he used enormous characters, as if filling a gap, spreading a single bar over two lines on the verso of f. 74. Moreover, f. 73 bears the cancelled heading *Partenza Cantata di G. F. Hendel*, evidently prepared for 'Stelle, perfide stelle' (HWV 168). This has no connection with the opera, but must date from the same period, not May 1708 as suggested by Deutsch.[37] Its crabbed and chromatic first aria suggests that it was among the earliest Italian works.

Folio 104 is an insertion with a second setting of the recitative 'Bella Florinda'—'palme appese' (HG 94). The original, not in HG, differs chiefly in its clumsy word-setting. There are several other places where Handel adjusted the line and emphasis of the recitative. It runs so easily in its printed form that Dent wondered 'whether Handel, at that date, was capable of composing it himself'.[38] The modifications in the autograph may reflect some native assistance. The overture is not included in the foliation and is written on quite

---

[35] The recently discovered recitatives were first sung in the London production of July 1985.
[36] 'The late additions to Handel's oratorios and the role of the younger Smith', *Music in Eighteenth-Century England*, 120–6.
[37] p. 25.
[38] *Symposium*, 20.

different paper, the same as that used for the 'Sonata a 5' for solo violin and strings in B flat (RM 20 g 14, ff. 11–21), which probably dates from spring 1707.[39] It is headed, in different ink, *Overture* (space) *di G. F. Hendel*, without the name of the opera. The spelling suggests that Handel added these words in England. He wrote the first five dances (HG 3–5) in the order Gigue, Matelot, Sarabande, Bourré, Menuet, and renumbered them. He began the Matelot on the first beat of the bar and subsequently turned the rhythm inside out.

Much of the aria 'Per dar pregio' (ff. 43–8) was written by the Roman copyist Antonio Giuseppe Angelini, who copied most of the cantatas composed for Ruspoli.[40] He must have worked closely with Handel, for the two hands alternate throughout the aria, which is an integral part of the manuscript, not an insertion. Handel wrote the clefs at the start and for the top brace of f. 45ʳ, the text and voice part, the whole B section, and some of the instrumental parts and dynamics. Angelini supplied the rest, including the solo violin part and most of the clefs, from the cantata *Il delirio amoroso*, copied for Ruspoli on 14 May 1707.

The note at the top of HG 49 and the indicated cut are in the autograph. After the recitative on HG 55 Handel wrote the first twelve bars of 'Fredde ceneri', then crossed them out and proceeded with 'Parto, crudel' and the recitative of II iv. III ii ends with the words *NB Segue il Duetto*, as in HG, but the manuscript continues without interruption, as if the duet were already in existence. The fully-scored ritornello at the end of 'Perchè viva' (HG 80) was an afterthought. 'Dell'Iberia' and 'Begl'occhi' were composed in 3/8. In changing this to 6/8 Handel left a 9/8 bar in the middle of 'Dell'Iberia' (HG 21, second line); this is straightened out in the copies, where the final ritornello (HG 22, first bar) begins after the vocal cadence. The original tempo of 'Sommi Dei' was *Largo*; the substituted *Adagio* is presumably slower. Many tempo marks are later additions in paler ink.

Handel used the last page of Act I (f. 48ᵛ) to note down preliminary ideas for *Teseo*, composed late in 1712.[41] (See Plate 6.)

The Fitzwilliam Museum has an incomplete autograph[42] of a different version of 'Frà le spine' (*Andante*, C minor, for tenor voice, unison violins, and bass), breaking off at the equivalent of bar 34. Handel was apparently copying and recomposing as he did so; there are a number of differences from the setting in *Rodrigo*, including a cut of four bars in the ritornello after the voice's first phrase. The writing, as Mann remarked,[43] is much later in date, and the paper is Da (*c*.1731–2); Handel may have intended the aria for the 1731 revival of *Admeto*, when he had similar recourse to 'Spirti fieri'.

Libretto

'Vincer se stesso è la maggior vittoria Drama per musica Rappresentato in Firenze nell'autunno Dell'Anno 1707 sotto la protezzione del Serenissimo

---

[39] Hicks, 'Handel's Early Musical Development', 86–7. The paper, with a watermark of three crescents, was used all over Italy and cannot itself establish the date.

[40] Kirkendale, 'The Ruspoli Documents'. A page copied by Angelini is reproduced in *HJb* (1960), opposite p. 128.

[41] See p. 251.

[42] Mus MS 256, pp. 1–2.

[43] *Catalogue*, 170.

Principe di Toscana . . . Vincenzio Vangelisti.' 52 pp. The cast are named, but not the librettist or composer. The Argomento is taken directly from Silvani, omitting the reference to Climene. The relationship of the text to Silvani's libretto and Handel's autograph has already been described. Most of the lines in *virgole* in 1700 are omitted, but a few were set. Before he received the amended libretto Handel had set some 84 lines of Silvani's recitative in eight scenes (I viii, II iii and vii, III i, ii, iii, v, and *ult*.) which are in the autograph or the Shaftesbury copy but were not printed and presumably not performed. The inserted arias whose music has not survived are 'Vibri pure iniqua sorte' (for 'Heroica fortezza'), 'Con voci care in petto' (Giuliano, in a new scene after I vi), 'Quanto belle, quanto care' (Giuliano, II i), 'Vanne pur tenero affetto' (for 'Fredde ceneri'), 'Ti conforta O caro' (for 'Empio fato'), and 'Sposa diletta, io parto' (Rodrigo, for the duet in III ii). In Silvani's libretto 'Sù! all'armi' is sung by Florinda; it was transferred to Evanco, and an aria for the latter cut.

Copies and Editions

The only known copies are the Shaftesbury, Flower, and Lennard scores and the Flower parts. All derive from the autograph, not the performing score, since they contain none of the substitutions, and were written many years later in England. None contains the overture, the first scene of Act I, the passage bracketed by Chrysander in 'Frà le spine', or the ritornello after 'Si che lieta'. Shaftesbury (S1, *c*.1736) is the earliest, fullest, and most important. It begins abruptly with the aria 'Pugneran con noi le stelle', but the rest of the opera is complete except that in III ii, where Handel wrote *Segue il Duetto*, S1 assumed that the reference was to 'Prendi l'alma' (III vi) and transferred that piece to the earlier context. This was obviously an error, since the key does not fit. His source was the autograph or a near copy of it. There are a few extra tempo and dynamic marks. 'Parto, crudel' (II iii) is *Presto*, 'Alle glorie' (II xii) and 'Spirti fieri' (III iv) *Allegro*. The first two have *Tutti* on the top instrumental line. The solos in 'Pugneran' and 'Alle glorie' are for 'Oboe *e* Viol', doubtless a misreading of the autograph's *o*. Chrysander made the same mistake in 'Per dar pregio', bars 13 and 17, second staves.

Act III begins with three pages of secco recitative (25 bars), Rodrigo's aria 'Quà rivolga', four more pages of secco (49 bars), and the complete accompanied recitative on HG 78, where the first $1\frac{1}{2}$ bars are wanting. It begins 'Eccelso Giove al di cui soglio affissi'. This is not an example of realized continuo, as Chrysander supposed,[44] but a perfectly regular accompanied recitative with string parts. 'Lucide stelle' (HG 96) is followed by *Scena ultima*, seven pages of secco (82 bars), and the *coro* 'L'amorosa dea di Gnido'.

Flower and Lennard lack secco recitatives, characters' names, and act divisions. They include only the A section of 'Sommi Dei', omitting the bar and a half interrupted by recitative; but 'Quà rivolga', the complete 'Eccelso Giove', and the *coro* are present. Flower (S1), without title, is the earlier (*c*. 1741–4). It includes some of Handel's dynamic and instrumental specifications in the opening scenes but becomes spasmodic in this respect later. The basses are fully figured as far as 'Dopo i nembi' (II viii); after that only one aria, 'Sù! all'armi', is figured, though half a dozen detached figures appear in Act III, mostly agreeing with the autograph. The Lennard copy (Lenn 2), an oblong folio volume also containing *Silla*, is quite different from the other manuscripts in this collection in contents, layout, and writing. It bears the title *Roderigo Opera di Signor Handel Representata at* [sic] *Teatro Reale*. This looks like a guess; had the scribe known the name of the theatre, he would surely have mentioned it. The score (late eighteenth century) may have been copied from Flower, but the bass figuring goes only to the end of the A section of the fifth aria, 'Ti lascio'. A later hand has added in pencil many dynamics, slurs, names of instruments and characters, and a few notes. Nearly all reflect the autograph; there are none on the two pieces missing there, and no other source is possible for the comment that a duet is missing in III ii.

The Flower parts (S2, mid-1740s)—a complete set, violins 1 and 2, oboes 1 and 2 incorporating recorders, viola, cello + bassoon (the latter never mentioned), and cembalo—also bear the title *Roderigo*. They were obviously extracted from the Flower score, reproducing its mistakes and, where it omits Handel's specific instructions, often supplying them wrongly. S2 was not in his best form, making a peculiar hash of the oboe parts. They play in eleven pieces (two unpublished), including three marked for strings only in the autograph, but not in seven movements where Handel mentions them. Several times they continue to play in bars marked for violins in the autograph, yet in 'Stragi morti' and 'Per dar pregio' they are excluded from the opening ritornellos, where they should certainly play. A number of violin and other solos, including all those in 'Dolce amor', are treated as *tutti*. In these respects S2 received no guidance from S1's score; but his omission of the two cello solos in 'Per dar pregio' must have been deliberate, for they are in the score and the cembalo part. The figuring in the latter stops at the same point as in the score. In all the continuo arias the cello is silenced.

An interesting manuscript in the Minoritenkonvent in Vienna (Hs XIV 743) contains a group of Handel's keyboard pieces followed (ff. 38–42) by three arias from *Rodrigo*, not attributed to the opera: 'Io son vostro, O luci belle' (the only known survivor of the seven additions in the Florence libretto), 'Così m'alletti', and 'Allor che sorge' for soprano in A minor. A collection of arias in the Schönborn Library at Wiesentheid (SB 5) has a copy of 'Pugneran con noi le stelle' for tenor in B flat. These are both early manuscripts probably dating from Handel's years in Italy.

Smith lists Walsh's publication (1717) of 'Allor che sorge' under *Rodrigo*, but this belongs rather to *Il pastor fido*. Early in 1710 Walsh advertised 'A New Set of Tunes Compos'd by an Italian Master in the Play call'd the Alchimist'. The music appeared in July in four parts (two violins, viola, and continuo) and consists of an overture and eight dances. It includes all the movements printed as the *Rodrigo* overture except the Passacaille, but in a different order, with one extra piece, a Prelude. This arrangement survives in a single printed copy in the Gerald Coke Collection and one manuscript (Add MS 31576). In connection with a later revival of the play (1731/2) Walsh issued an edition for two violins and bass as *The Tunes for the Alchimist*. This too survives in one manuscript, in the Flower Collection, but with a blank stave for the viola.[45] Arnold printed the three-part version (*c*.1790).

Chrysander's score of the opera (1873), the only printed edition, follows the autograph. He accidentally omitted the last bar of the opening ritornello of 'Allor che sorge', consisting of a dotted crotchet B; it is in the autograph and all copies.

[45] See C. A. Price, 'Handel and The Alchemist', *MT* cxvi (1975), 787.

CHAPTER 8

AGRIPPINA

THE background to the plot is explained in the Argument of the printed libretto.

Agrippina, the daughter of Augustus's nephew Germanicus, was the wife of Domitius Enobarbus, by whom she had a son called Domitius Nero. After her second marriage to the Emperor Claudius all her energies were bent on securing the throne for her son Nero; when an astrologer told her that her son would gain the empire but kill his mother, she replied: 'Let him kill me provided he becomes emperor.'[1] This woman of great talent, eager to reign and as ambitious as she was powerful, so worked on her husband Claudius that she obliged him to give Nero the rank of Caesar. She owed her success to the spiritual weakness of Claudius, who was totally given over to luxury, off his guard and in love, and above all had won the glory of conquering Britain for Rome. Otho was the husband of Poppea, an ambitious and vain woman also loved by Nero, who later took her from Otho and married her. Claudius put boundless trust in his freedmen, especially Pallas and Narcissus, who were also used by Agrippina.

Act I opens in *Agrippina's closet*.[2] She tells Nerone that the time is ripe for him to assume the throne, and shows him a letter announcing that Claudio has been drowned at sea. She advises him to lose no time in wooing the people with promises and bribes; he willingly agrees. Aware that Narciso and Pallante secretly desire her love, she summons Pallante and *seats herself in a melancholy posture*. Pretending to be distracted by love for him, she induces him to declare his devotion. She tells him that Claudio is dead and no one else knows; if he will go to the Capitol and stir up the people to proclaim Nerone emperor, she will accept him as her consort. He is delighted. She then follows the same tactics with Narciso, with the same result, and looks forward to enjoying the fruits of her cunning. The set changes to the *Square of the Capitol with a throne*. Nerone, *surrounded by the populace to whom he is distributing money*, remarks what a pleasure it is to help the needy. Pallante and Narciso sing his praises. Agrippina enters, *followed by the people; she sits on the throne*, announces the death of Claudio, asks the people to choose a successor, and *descends from the throne*. Without waiting for them, she, Pallante, and Narciso in a quartet proclaim Nerone, who accepts. *He and Agrippina mount the throne. Trumpets are heard*, and Claudio's servant Lesbo brings news that the Emperor has landed at Anzio, having been rescued by Ottone. Amid general consternation *Nerone and Agrippina vacate the throne*; assuring him that he will get it in the end, she avows her joy that Claudio is safe. Lesbo announces the arrival of Ottone, whom the four conspirators (*aside*) blame as the cause of their misfortunes, and goes off to Poppea to make an assignation for Claudio. Ottone explains how he saved Claudio, who promised him the succession as reward. He asks to speak to

---

[1] The quotation is from Tacitus, *Annals*, xiv. 9.

[2] This and other directions, omitted by Chrysander, are in the libretto, the autograph, or both.

Agrippina alone and tells her he loves Poppea more than the throne (he is not yet married to her). She wins his confidence by agreeing to further his suit—but for her own purposes, for she is aware of Claudio's attachment to Poppea. Ottone rejoices that the same day has promised him the throne and his love. The set changes to *Poppea's room*, where she is adorning herself with pearls and flowers *in front of her mirror*. Ottone, Claudio, and Nerone have all declared their love, but none of them knows when she is telling the truth. Lesbo informs her that Claudio will visit her this very night, and she pretends that all her thoughts have been about him; she will welcome him—as her sovereign, of course, not her lover. Agrippina, who has overheard this, slips away delighted that fate is playing into her hands. Poppea wonders why Ottone is not coming rather than Claudio. Agrippina returns and asks if she loves Ottone. Terrified that Claudio may appear at any moment, Poppea admits it. Agrippina replies that Ottone has agreed to yield her to Claudio in return for the succession: if she wants revenge, let her make Claudio jealous by saying that Ottone has forbidden her to see him, then let her promise Claudio everything, but withhold it until he agrees to remove the cause of her unhappiness. Poppea falls into the trap. Agrippina promises to save her from Claudio's importunities and goes off rejoicing. Poppea, horrified at Ottone's faithlessness, decides not to tolerate his contempt. Claudio enters with a love song. She receives him coldly and follows Agrippina's plan, with embroideries of her own, repeatedly *looking off-stage* for Agrippina. Claudio declares that Ottone shall not be Emperor and begins to press his advances. As he embraces her Lesbo, who has been on guard, *runs in* and announces Agrippina: there is no time to lock the doors. In a short trio Poppea and Lesbo persuade Claudio to go, while he asks when he can enjoy her favours. Agrippina, who has heard everything, and Poppea embrace, delighted at the success of their scheme. Agrippina assures her of her devotion, and Poppea looks forward to punishing Ottone for putting his ambition above her love.

Act II opens in *a street next to the imperial palace, decorated for Claudio's triumph.* Pallante and Narciso, finding they have been hoodwinked, agree to join forces. Ottone enters, looking forward to his coronation, and the freedmen pay him compliments. *Agrippina, Poppea, Nerone, and attendants come down from the palace.* In a dialogue full of asides Agrippina tells Ottone she gave Poppea his message, and Poppea that it was a request for forgiveness. Before her lies can be exposed Claudio enters *in a triumphal machine*, and all greet him in chorus. *Descending from the machine*, he boasts of his conquest of Britain and the sea: the whole world bows to his throne. Agrippina greets him with a great show of devotion, and the others pay obsequious respect. He welcomes them (with a whispered assurance of his love to Poppea), but when Ottone asks for his promised reward he denounces him as a traitor. Thunderstruck, Ottone appeals in turn to Agrippina, Poppea, and Nerone. Each rejects him in a brief aria and goes out, followed by Narciso, Pallante, and Lesbo: Caesar's enemy is also theirs. He reproaches Claudio, his friends, the gods, and most of all Poppea for their unjust accusations, and calls on the listeners to pity his grief.[3] In *a garden* Poppea wishes Ottone were innocent so that she could forgive him. Seeing him approach, thoughtful and sad, *she sits by a fountain and feigns sleep*, hoping to find out how he excuses himself and whether he feels remorse. He begins to address the fountain, sees her apparently asleep, and bids her rest in

---

[3] The libretto (but not Chrysander) makes it clear that he is addressing the audience.

peace. *Pretending to dream,* she calls out several times 'Ottone traditore!' He hides when she *appears to wake up* and, *seemingly speaking to herself,* asks how he can deny that he surrendered her to Claudio in return for the throne. He throws himself at her feet and, *preventing her departure,* gives her his sword to stab him if she still thinks him guilty. *She takes it and turns the point towards him.* When she hesitates between believing him or Agrippina, he denounces the latter with such vigour that Poppea silences him. Let him come to her house when it is safe, and if he is innocent she will pity him. *She gives him back his sword.* He goes demanding justice, not pity. Poppea now understands the motive for Agrippina's lies and resolves to have vengeance: she can be deceived once, but never again. When Lesbo requests an assignation for Claudio at her house she accepts in the hope that it may further her design. Nerone now appears; she decides to play him up for her own ends and invites him too. Meanwhile[4] Agrippina is tortured by her own thoughts. She has trusted Narciso and Pallante too far, fears Ottone's merit and Poppea's courage, and plans further mischief. She promises Pallante her love if he will dispose of Narciso and Ottone; with a remark about her tigerish heart he gives an equivocal promise to keep faith. A similar scene is at once enacted with Narciso. When Claudio enters, full of hypocritical affection, she pretends to fear for his safety and advises him to frustrate Ottone's hopes by declaring Nerone his successor. Before he goes to meet Poppea she makes him swear to publish the announcement the same day. She gaily compares herself to a steersman crowding on sail as he makes for harbour.

Act III opens in *Poppea's room, with a doorway in front and two others at the side.* Assuring Ottone of her love, she tells him to hide and contain his jealousy, whatever he hears. He promises to suffer in silence and *hides in one of the doorways behind a curtain* just as Nerone enters, ardent and out of breath. Poppea says she loves him (to Ottone's secret agony) but tells him he is late: Agrippina is coming (*she looks off-stage*), and he must hide till she has gone. *He hides in a doorway behind a curtain, opposite that where Ottone is standing.* Next come Claudio and Lesbo. Poppea chides the Emperor for not really loving her. When he points to all he has done for her, mentioning the punishment of Ottone, she *pretends to weep* and says it was not Ottone who imposed on her but Nerone. Claudio is incredulous but promises revenge if she can prove her statement. She *leads him to the doorway in front, goes to Nerone's doorway and draws the curtain.* Thinking Claudio has gone, Nerone emerges and is denounced by the angry Emperor, to the delight of Poppea and Ottone. He departs, relying on Agrippina to avenge him. Poppea now asks Claudio to protect her against Agrippina: not till his consort's rage is assuaged shall he enjoy her love. Claudio points out that he alone rules Rome and goes. Poppea, *watching to make sure Claudio has gone, draws the curtain concealing Ottone.* She makes him promise that he loves her more than anyone or anything, including the throne, and rejoices in the happiness of mutual devotion. The set changes to *a hall in the palace.* Nerone asks for Agrippina's help against the wrath of Claudio. She rebukes him for spoiling her plans through his rash love and tells him to abandon Poppea: only the throne is worthy of him. He renounces all base desires. Pallante and Narciso inform Claudio of Agrippina's double-dealing and confess their own misdemeanours. Claudio is more puzzled than ever as to

---

[4] A change of set seems to be required before II xiii (HG 94), but none is indicated in the libretto or the autograph.

who is telling the truth; but their words corroborate Poppea, and he offers them his protection. When Agrippina renews her pleas on Nerone's behalf, Claudio accuses her of usurping his power. She admits it, but says it was for the safety of the city and the throne: did not Nerone step down when Claudio was found to be safe? She calls on Pallante and Narciso to witness the truth of her account, and they shamefacedly confirm it. Claudio is forced to admit her good faith; but she is not so sure of his, and taxes him with taking his cue from Poppea. When she says Ottone loves Poppea, he lays the blame on Nerone and sends for all three. Agrippina is confident of turning the tables. Claudio hopes to sort out the tangle and live in peace. Then, she replies, let him trust her faithful love. When Poppea, Nerone, and Ottone arrive, Claudio accuses Nerone of hiding in Poppea's room. He cannot deny it. But Claudio causes general consternation by ordering Nerone to marry Poppea and proclaiming Ottone his successor. Ottone refuses the throne: the loss of Poppea would be tantamount to death. Agrippina asks who loves Poppea now. Claudio finally satisfies everyone by reversing the male roles, invokes Juno to bless the marriage of Ottone and Poppea, and adds (aside) that he will be relieved to get rid of the minx. All rejoice at the double triumph of love and empire. The opera ends with the ceremonial *descent of Juno and her train*, who dance a ballet.

This is one of the very few Handel librettos that did not, so far as is known, serve another composer first. It is also one of the best. The author, Cardinal Vincenzo Grimani, was an eminent diplomat who espoused the Habsburg cause against France and Spain (supported by Pope Clement XI) in the War of the Spanish Succession. Exiled from Venice since 1690, he had been the Imperial Ambassador to the Vatican till his appointment on 1 July 1708 as Viceroy of Naples (he was instrumental in bringing Alessandro Scarlatti back to the city at the end of the year). Strohm[5] sees *Agrippina* as a satire on the Papal court and the Pope himself in the person of Claudio ('Io di Roma il Giove sono'), and suggests that Grimani may have grafted this element on to an earlier libretto, perhaps of his own. It is true that the *Agrippina* libretto with its multiplicity of characters and scenes and its frivolous treatment of historical characters has more in common with seventeenth-century taste than with that of contemporary Venetian authors like Zeno and Pariati, Silvani and Frigimelica-Roberti; but there is no conclusive evidence for an earlier libretto.[6] Any local references are probably now beyond recovery.

Grimani's sources were books xii–xiv of Tacitus's *Annals* and Suetonius's life of Claudius. All the characters except Lesbo are historical, and so is their general relationship, though the chronology is reshuffled: Claudius invaded Britain in AD 43,[7] married Agrippina in 49, and adopted Nero as his successor in 50, when the latter was twelve and Otho eighteen. Poppea did not come on the scene till later. While the details of the plot are fictitious, there is ample historical warrant for the character and motives of Agrippina, Claudius,

---

[5] 'Händel in Italia'.

[6] Grimani had however written at least three on other subjects between 1686 and 1699.

[7] However the Roman triumph at which the captive British chieftain Caractacus appeared (cf. Act II Scene 1 of the opera) took place in 50. The rumour of Claudius's death in Act I is based on a conflation of two episodes related by Suetonius, a reported ambush on the road to Ostia and a narrow escape from storms on his voyage to Britain.

Nero, and Poppea as presented by Grimani. Narcissus and Pallas were notorious among the Emperor's favourites. Pallas took the initiative in urging the adoption of Nero and subsequently became Agrippina's lover; he was the brother of Felix, procurator of Judea, who figures in the Acts of the Apostles. The Venetian audience would be familiar with the subsequent fate of the characters: Claudius was poisoned and Narcissus driven to suicide by Agrippina; Pallas and Poppea (as well as Agrippina) fell victims to Nero; the latter and Otho in turn married Poppea, both obtained the imperial throne, and both died by suicide.

There is no compelling reason why this story should be turned into the violent and melodramatic tragedy we might expect in the Romantic age.[8] *Agrippina* belongs to a class of libretto that, until the recent recognition of Monteverdi and Cavalli, was commonly dismissed as absurd or contemptible. It is nothing of the sort. It is an anti-heroic comedy of a type popular throughout the seventeenth century in Italy, especially Venice; Monteverdi's *L'incoronazione di Poppea* treats several of the same characters in a similar spirit. The plot, though complex, is perfectly clear in the theatre; the characters are more convincing on the human level than any of Metastasio's; the language is straightforward and free from involved conceits. The reverend librettist shows a mastery of the intricacies of intrigue which, whether or not it was acquired in the course of his profession, is admirably suited to the opera-house. His dramatic timing is unusually acute; nearly all the arias reveal character and advance the action in the same breath, so that the plot develops smoothly instead of lapsing into the jerky stop-go typical of so many *opera seria* librettos. Nor is there a spate of unmotivated coming and going: many episodes revolve round a single character who remains on stage throughout and controls or unifies the action, for example Agrippina at the start of the opera, Poppea in the third set of Act I and the first of Act III, Ottone in the first set of Act II.

The equivocal tone is more apparent than real. It is true that all the characters save Ottone are morally contemptible. Claudio is a pompous ass with a knack of finding himself in undignified situations, Agrippina an unscrupulous schemer, Nerone a self-indulgent hypocrite, the freedmen craven and lascivious, Lesbo a pander, Poppea a liar and a flirt. (Dent[9] is wrong in suggesting that we never know when she is telling the truth; this is part of her act—we know, but the other characters do not.) Since the libretto is a satire on a profligate society, whether or not it carried local as well as general implications, there is no ground for offence. We are not asked to applaud the motives of the actors, but to smile at their absurdity and to enjoy their delight in intrigue for its own sake, an element that permeates Italian opera of all periods and was to become the staple diet of *opera buffa*. Nor are they wholly without redeeming qualities. Agrippina is single-minded in her ambitions on her son's behalf, not her own. Poppea has the virtue of courage, and her love for Ottone is genuine, even if we cannot suppose her likely to remain faithful to him. Above all, there is Ottone, who saves the Emperor's life and whose willingness to sacrifice worldly ambition for love throws the

---

[8] Operas dealing with this period of Roman history were not uncommon at the time: for example Porpora's *Agrippina* (Naples, 1708), Vivaldi's pasticcio *Nerone fatto Cesare* (Venice, 1715), and Orlandini's *Nerone* (Venice, 1721), not to mention the Hamburg operas of Handel and Keiser (*Octavia*).

[9] *Symposium*, 21.

motives of the others into relief. The ironic detachment displayed by the Cardinal should not be mistaken for cynicism. If it has a parallel in English literature, it is the contemporary Restoration comedy of Wycherley and Congreve, with which it shares a profusion of barbed asides.

This amused comprehension of the foibles of humanity is marvellously conveyed by Handel's music, which adds the serious undertones appropriate to any strong emotion, however reprobate the character. *Agrippina* is the first of several masterpieces in this vein, which may be said to embrace a comic vision without abandoning a grip on passion and even tragedy. Although the situations are for the most part richly humorous, and the tone of the dialogue light and bantering, the arias express genuine feeling. Like Mozart in his Da Ponte operas, Handel does not laugh at his characters; he feels with them. They are human beings with a capacity for suffering that removes them from the shrivelled world of caricature. Such an opera relies in performance on style and timing. Some scenes, especially the two in Poppea's room, are close to the *buffo* imbroglios of Rossini and Donizetti; but they need to be played for a smile, not a belly-laugh. Everything hangs on the distinction between farce, dependent on situation alone, and comedy, arising from character.

The musical invention of *Agrippina* is unfailingly rich and varied, in melody, harmony, and rhythm alike. Four years in the artistic climate of Italy have melted what remained of the German stiffness (a faint trace survives in Nerone's 'Coll'ardor') and fused the diverse influences in a plastic idiom that was to be refined and extended but not essentially altered in London. The most potent factor was undoubtedly the experience gained in the composition of nearly a hundred cantatas, serenatas, and similar works, in which Handel wrestled with and subdued the Italian style and language. An overwhelming proportion of the material of *Agrippina* had made its first appearance earlier[10] and was now refashioned, nearly always with striking improvements. Two notable advances are the liberation of the voice from instrumental procedures, to which it is still sometimes subjected in *Rodrigo*, and the more flexible treatment of ritornellos. These no longer stand like sentries on guard over the excursions of the voice, but help to generate the conflict and penetrate the texture of the arias; the treatment of the short figure ending with a trill in 'Coronato il crin' is a happy example. By adjusting their length when they return after the A section or da capo, Handel extends his control over the proportions of the movement and enlarges and softens its outlines. 'L'alma mia' with ritornellos of seven, five, and two bars, 'Come nube che fugge' (23 bars at the start, seven after the A section) and 'La mia sorte fortunata' where Pallante expresses his excitement at Agrippina's offer by joining in the ritornello's first four bars and repeating them after the orchestra has completed the eleven-bar paragraph (this section is skipped in the da capo) illustrate this in different ways. The aria's two main components find a happier balance, the B section shorter and lighter but harmonically more adventurous. Voice and instruments, whether or not they share the same material, enjoy an equal relationship in which neither cramps the movement

---

[10] At least forty of the vocal movements, including unpublished pieces, draw on previous works of Handel, and a number are indebted to Keiser and Mattheson as well: see Appendix D. Only five arias ('Con saggio', 'Ti vo' giusta', 'Quando invita', 'Basta che sol', and 'Bel piacere') and the trio in Act I appear to lack such genealogical forebears. It would be interesting to know if any of the music went back to the lost *Nero*, which had many of the same characters (but no Italian arias).

or usurps the freedom of the other. This is particularly evident in the continuo arias, where the voice is no longer shackled to the bass. The result is an easy relaxed style, ripe for the expression of a wide range of emotion.

It is the characterization that gives the opera its lasting vitality. Though neither as fully nor as subtly drawn as many of Handel's later creations, the figures move with a clear-cut assurance that seizes and holds attention. Agrippina, as is fitting, dominates the opera, especially the first two acts, where her constant scheming initiates most of the action. Her first aria, 'L'alma mia', whose catchy melody (not his own[11]) was a favourite with Handel at all periods of his life, is brim-full of confidence: she is sure of the rewards of her cunning, and the extrovert C major of the first part never ventures beyond the dominant. But there is menace in 'Tu ben degno', where (aside) she vents her baffled rage on hearing that Ottone has stolen a march on Nerone. The angular sevenths in the bass hint at passion and violence, and the expansion of the accompaniment from cello obligato to an extended three-part string ritornello after the A section, with a sinuous chromatic line on the violins, is a vivid touch.[12] Her two remaining arias in Act I show her again at ease. 'Hò un non sò che' was lifted from *La Resurrezione*, where it had been sung by the same singer, Durastanti, in the part of Mary Magdalene looking forward to the resurrection; its irresistible melody seems out of place in the mouth of Agrippina. Nor does 'Non hò cor', with a brilliant concerto grosso accompaniment and four solo instruments, tell us much about the Empress's character, though its repetitions and smooth melismas may be intended to suggest the slipperiness beneath the deceptive façade.

She emerges in all her formidable power in the *scena* 'Pensieri, voi mi tormentate' towards the end of Act II, which reveals for the first time the strength and novelty of Handel's dramatic genius. The fourteen-bar ritornello for violins and bass in octaves contains almost as many rests as notes; by means of wide contrasts in rhythm, note values, and dynamics (*pianissimo* to *fortissimo* on the final emphatic Gs) it paints an astonishing picture of mingled stealth, anxiety, guilt, and resolution (Ex. 12).[13] The voice enters with a new phrase and develops a long irregular winding melody, attended by echoes and variations from a solo oboe and punctuated from time to time by the violin figures of the ritornello. In the B section Agrippina invokes heaven's assistance. It is a brisk demand rather than a prayer, as the change in time (4/4), rhythm (even bass quavers), scoring (four parts), key (relative major), and tempo (faster, though this is implied, not stated) makes abundantly clear. After this the da capo strikes home with decisive force. But the most imaginative stroke is yet to come—a second return in condensed form, like a bad dream, after a recitative in which Agrippina recognizes Ottone's virtue and Poppea's courage.

Once her mind is made up, and she has given orders for three murders, her anxieties disappear; she is nothing if not resilient. She ends the act with the exuberant simile aria 'Ogni vento', whose seductive rhythm, anticipating the lilt of the Viennese waltz, and fascinatingly irregular phrase-lengths must

[11] See Chrysander, i. 197 ff.

[12] The sevenths, but not the ritornello, are in the cantata aria on which this is based, 'Da che perso' in HWV 77.

[13] It is instructive to compare the much more primitive form of this ritornello in *Rodrigo* ('Siet'assai superbe') and the cantata 'Arresta il passo' ('Fermati! non fuggir').

Ex. 12

have set every foot in Venice tapping. The key, G major, is an apt choice after
the G minor of 'Pensieri' (Ex. 13).

Ex. 13

In Act III Agrippina has lost the initiative, though she can still turn some of
the tables. Her only aria, 'Se vuoi pace', is a sycophantic but successful appeal
for Claudio's confidence. The music has an insinuating rhythm, half-way
between a sarabande and a minuet, and a melody that would melt sterner
stuff than Claudio. The form is nicely judged. The one ritornello, sixteen bars
long, comes at the end of the A section, which consists of two eight-bar strains,
both repeated; the B section uses similar material, happily extended to a
paragraph of twelve bars. When Handel drew on this material nearly fifty

years later, he retained the association of flattery and deceit; it became the air 'Wise men flattering may deceive you' in the 1758 revival of *Belshazzar*.

Poppea is the first of Handel's sex-kittens, a deliciously drawn portrait of a girl who lives for sensual pleasure. She is never concerned with any other subject, and not disposed to make a tragedy of that. Her nine arias[14] are nearly all marked by gay tripping rhythms, and as light in accompaniment as they are in tone. Her essential frivolity appears at once in 'Vaghe perle' as she warbles into her mirror, introduced by the triplet figure that Handel bestowed on Galatea in both his settings of the myth[15] (he found it in Keiser's *Octavia*). 'È un foco' expresses her amorous excitement in a stammering variation of gigue rhythm tinged with Neapolitan harmony. Whether she is looking forward to punishing Ottone for putting ambition before love ('Se giunge') or resolving not to be deceived a second time by Agrippina's lies (the exquisite 'Ingannata') or playing up Nerone ('Col peso', another gigue), her music is good-tempered, melodious, and seductive. She is in every way worthy to stand beside Monteverdi's heroine. Perhaps the most individual of her arias is the last, 'Bel piacere', whose irregular combination of 3/8 and 2/4 rhythm (with a 3/4 hemiola bar in the B section) teases the ear and haunts the memory.[16] The melody, like that of Agrippina's 'Hò un non sò che', is strong enough to stand on its own, without any accompaniment except in the ritornellos.

Ex. 14

(It is a delightful pleasure to enjoy faithful love! This makes the heart content.)

Nerone (a soprano part) is shown as a young boy, not the monster of cruelty he was later to become; but he is already well schooled in following his mother's evil ways. Although less dramatically focused than the other characters, he has some fine music, including two sicilianos in minor keys, the second of which, 'Quando invita' in Act II, is very Scarlattian, with a beautifully shaped melody and rich string accompaniment. The combination of lilting rhythm with chromatic or quickly changing harmony (for instance the oscillation between major and minor in the B section of 'Con saggio') hints

[14] Only seven were performed; see below.
[15] 'S'agita in mezz'onde' and 'Hush, ye pretty warbling choir'.
[16] It is based on 'Un leggiadro giovinetto' in *Il trionfo del Tempo*, which has the same outline but none of the rhythmic flexibility.

at his sensual epicene nature, which peeps out again in the suspensions of the B section of 'Come nube che fugge', giving a subtle lie to this renunciation of the lusts of the flesh. His cavatina in the first Capitol scene, 'Qual piacer', though very impressive, seems ill-suited to the words; it was adapted, perhaps in a hurry, from the cantata 'Ah! crudel' (HWV 78). Both his Act III arias are lively with a multiplicity of semiquavers and the full concerto grosso treatment; the second, 'Come nube che fugge', is a brilliant bravura piece calculated to exercise six instrumental soloists as well as the singer. The design with its huge initial ritornello anticipates the double-exposition plan familiar in Mozart's piano concertos.

Ottone is a more memorable figure. The part was written for a contralto with strong low notes but limited compass and is entirely in flat keys, with a pronounced tendency towards the minor mode. 'Lusinghiera mia speranza' strikes the deepest note heard in the first act. Although he is ostensibly rejoicing at the success of his hopes, the music with its D minor tonality, frequent chromaticism, and interrupted cadences seems to anticipate the woes to come. The four-part string accompaniment is concentrated and powerful, the rhythms intricate in their thrusting contrapuntal energy. Handel may have wished to establish Ottone at once as a foil to the rest of the cast. He makes a similarly unexpected point in Act II by giving Ottone's anticipation of the throne ('Coronato il crin') a reflective rather than a jubilant tone, thus inviting the ironical participation of the audience. This type of emotional cross-current, words pulling against music, was to become one of the most distinctive features of Handel's dramatic style in opera and oratorio. Ottone's *scena* at the end of this episode, after all the others have turned their backs on him, is the peak of the opera. The accompanied recitative 'Otton, qual portentoso' (the only one in the score) begins strikingly with a diminished seventh over a tonic pedal, the violins divided into three parts for the occasion. Both the voice and the string parts are passionate and declamatory (the violins drop suddenly to a unison bottom G on the word 'ingiusti') in a manner that foreshadows the great recitatives of the London operas. The aria, 'Voi che udite', an appeal for sympathy addressed directly to the audience, is still finer.[17] The superb opening with its clashing suspensions, doleful oboe, and delayed entry of the bass is recognizable at once as the work of a master dramatist. There can be few more penetrating evocations of utter misery and despair (Ex. 15, p. 124).

Both Ottone's arias in the garden scene are admirable. 'Vaghe fonti', prettily scored with muted violins, pizzicato basses, and two recorders, suggesting the cool trickle of water, shows Handel's perennial mastery of texture: the ritornello melody is Keiser's, and there is not an accidental throughout, yet it is perfect in its context. 'Ti vo' giusta' is something more. Ottone demands justice, not pity, and his passionate nature emerges in the chromaticism that is so much more poignant in a major key. There is a hint of 'He was despised', in the same key of E flat. Ottone's music in Act III is less individual, though 'Pur ch'io ti stringa' pays another graceful tribute to Scarlatti and the siciliano.

---

[17] As H. C. Wolff suggests (*NOHM* v. 59–61), it may owe its initial impulse to the hero's prayer 'Patrii Numi' in A. Scarlatti's *Mitridate Eupatore* (see p. 91); but Scarlatti's aria is in a major key and lacks the harmonic intensity of Handel's. Handel may also have taken a hint from Nero's accompanied recitative 'Mein Auge starrt' in Keiser's *Octavia* (III viii).

Ex. 15

(You who hear my lament pity my grief)

The four remaining characters are predominantly comic. The servant
Lesbo is restricted to a single short arietta. The two freedmen are dramatically
parallel but differentiated by vocal pitch, the bass Pallante passionate and
inclined to bluster, the alto Narciso plaintive and accompanied by soft
recorders. Their music is agreeable, and Narciso's 'Volo pronto' rather more,
but it is not personal to them, and most of it turns up in other contexts earlier
and later. The regularity with which they appear one after the other, to be
brought sharply to heel by Agrippina, is delightfully comic. Claudio is an
imperial Polyphemus, vain, touchy, and amorous. Handel wrote the part for a
sepulchral bass with a compass of two octaves and a third from the C below
the bass stave,[18] and made the most of the opportunities for grotesque
characterization by filling his arias with giant strides and huge leaps. The
results are particularly happy in 'Basta che sol', where he hypocritically
assures Agrippina of his devotion, and 'Io di Roma', a pompous assertion of
his own omnipotence. 'Cade il mondo', another piece of complacent self-
congratulation, was adapted from one of Lucifer's arias in *La Resurrezione*;
Handel emphasizes the Emperor's pretensions by making the first phrase of six
notes span two whole octaves instead of one. The ritornello of this aria in both
contexts has a sequence used by Bach to a very different end in the *St. Matthew
Passion*.[19] Yet Claudio is not a mere buffoon: he can feel and suffer. The little
love song 'Vieni, O cara', a cavatina without ritornellos marked *sempre piano*
and his only incursion into a major key, is one of the gems of the score.

As important as Handel's growing strength in characterization is the
increase in his mastery of the design of *opera seria* and the opportunities it
allows for varying and building up tension. In this respect *Agrippina* surpasses
not only *Almira* and *Rodrigo* but several of the early London operas, including
Rinaldo. To some extent Handel is exploiting the Venetian tradition, whose
flexibility offered ample openings to composers able to profit from them. The
arias are shorter, less formal, and more numerous than in London (there are
41 in *Agrippina* as printed, 38 as performed, including cavatinas—more than in
any Handel opera except *Almira*). Many of them carry less individual weight,
and ten full arias in the printed score, five of them at the singer's entrance, are
not followed by an exit. *Agrippina* occupies an intermediate position here. In
the first two sets all the arias are exit arias; the second begins with two
cavatinas and a short quartet, but this again accords with the later manner,
where the exit depended on the da capo. In the third set however Poppea has
three full arias, and Claudio one, which are not followed by an exit; Poppea in
fact remains on stage throughout. All three sets in Act II begin with arias of
this type, and there is one ('Se vuoi pace') in Act III. When the arias grew
fewer in number but increased in weight, the exit aria became the almost
universal unit, the cavatina remaining as a useful variant at the beginning of a
set.[20] The performance changes made in *Agrippina* show this process in the
course of development. Of the five da capo entrance arias, 'Fà quanto vuoi'
and 'Bella pur' were omitted and 'Pensieri' much modified. The other two,
'Vaghe perle' and 'Pur ritorno', would certainly have become cavatinas in a

---

[18] This note is required in 'Cade il mondo', which Chrysander printed a tone too high.
[19] In the bass aria 'Gerne will ich mich bequemen'. Handel returned to the idea with even more
memorable effect in *Tamerlano* ('A suoi piedi', see p. 540 and Ex. 62(b)).
[20] For a discussion of these structural points, see pp. 4 and 10.

later opera, and are perhaps best reduced to their A sections in modern revivals.

The quartet and trio in Act I are also survivals from the older Venetian opera rather than anticipations of the later ensemble. Though highly effective in themselves and as a variation in the vocal texture, they are very short (eighteen and twelve bars respectively) and musically undeveloped; in neither of them are all the voices heard at once. The trio, in which Poppea and Lesbo hurry the protesting Claudio out of Poppea's room at the approach of Agrippina, presents a perfect *buffo* situation that would have kept Cimarosa or Rossini in play for a considerable time. The quartet is another action piece, but of a more subtle nature. Pallante, Narciso, and Agrippina by prearrangement proclaim Nerone Emperor, accompanied by a chuckling unison figure that appears at ever less regular intervals. At the end, in a four-bar solo, Nerone is graciously pleased to accept the honour. There are three neat touches here. The quartet is in A minor, but Handel ends in C major, emphasizing the advance from the offer to its acceptance by a happy use of progressive tonality. He omits the final couplet in the libretto, which is a repeat of Agrippina's words after Nerone's reply. And he follows the cadence at once with a D major trumpet fanfare[21] proclaiming the unexpected safe return of the true Emperor.

More interesting from the structural point of view is Handel's treatment of two episodes in Act II. The first set has a central climax in the *coro* where all the characters, accompanied by trumpets and drums, hail Claudio's public triumph after his conquest of Britain. Ottone's rejection follows, ending with his great accompanied recitative and aria. Here Grimani and Handel employ the exit aria to fruitful purpose. When after Claudio's departure Ottone appeals in turn to Agrippina, Poppea, and Nerone in a single line of recitative, each spurns him in a short aria without initial ritornello, in a different key and rhythm, and goes out. The first two arias have extended and more fully scored ritornellos after the da capo[22] to get the singer off-stage (Nerone's[23] already has an eight-bar ritornello after the A section). Narciso, Pallante, and Lesbo follow (in recitative), leaving Ottone to pour out his woe. Thus the scene has two climaxes, one external in Claudio's triumph, the other emotional in Ottone's outburst of grief. While the ironical dialogue in the early part of the scene builds up to the former, the latter is approached by a structural *diminuendo*—a series of exit arias—which at the same time throws the main emphasis on the character to whom they are addressed and who is left alone. This dramatic counterpoint, strengthened by the contrast between the hypocrisy of the salutation to the Emperor and the bitter poignancy of Ottone's grief, depends on the acceptance of the exit aria convention. Whether the design was original it is impossible to say; it is very effective, and important as the ancestor of the similar but more powerful scene at the end of Act II of *Tamerlano*,[24] one of the supreme achievements in eighteenth-century opera.

[21] Indicated by a stage direction (*si sente suono di Trombe*) and a D major chord in recitative.

[22] That of Agrippina's 'Nulla sperar' contains what sounds like an ironical echo of 'Coronato il crin', but this could be accidental.

[23] In the weaker alternative setting, which is not in the autograph but was preferred in performance, an initial ritornello spoils the symmetry and slackens the impact. The scoring however is deft, with the second violins supplying the bass for most of the A section.

[24] Derived from Piovene's *Tamerlano* libretto (Venice, 1711); Piovene may have picked up the idea from Grimani, but no one could have foreseen the coincidence by which it was handed back to Handel. See pp. 522–3.

The scene for Poppea and Ottone in the garden shows Handel using the expectations raised by the formality of da capo design to create and prolong tension. This too is a harbinger of things to come, for example the garden scenes in *Scipione* (Act I), *Alessandro* (Act II), and *Tolomeo* (Act II). Ottone addresses the fountain in the F major arioso 'Vaghe fonti', but breaks off into recitative when he sees Poppea apparently asleep. He bids her rest in peace; this is the B section of his aria, in the orthodox key of D minor. Twice she interrupts (pretending to be asleep) and he resumes, reaching a cadence in A minor, after which we expect a da capo. But she interrupts once more and rises, whereupon he hides. The da capo never comes; the scene continues in recitative, and he eventually makes his exit after the continuo aria 'Ti vo' giusta', which again has an amplified ritornello for full string band after the da capo.

These reinforced codas, after either the A section or the da capo, are frequent in Handel's early years; six of the eleven continuo arias in *Agrippina* (as well as the trio) have them,[25] and the effect is always happy, thanks to the overthrow of expectation and the fact that the material is extended and harmonically amplified. The scoring of *Agrippina* is light by the standard of the London operas, but there are moments of splendour when Handel applies the full concerto grosso treatment, involving solo parts for two oboes, two violins, two cellos, and double bass. *Solo* and *tutti* sections (and *piano* and *forte* indications) are noted in rather more detail than in London, where Handel had an orchestra under his personal control. On the other hand, outside the overture, there are only two tempo marks in the whole score; this matter was evidently left to be determined in rehearsal. The first oboe has a number of grateful opportunities. Trumpets and drums are used in the triumph scene (and the flourish after the quartet), recorders in three arias.[26] There is some energetic and sonorous string writing in the overture (three violin parts) and in several of the arias, notably 'Lusinghiera' and 'Come nube che fugge'; Dent commented on a rugged quality not found in Scarlatti. But the two most haunting tunes in the opera, 'Hò un non sò che' and 'Bel piacere', are artfully left unadorned, the violins doubling the voice throughout at the unison. Except for a few special effects, chiefly in Claudio's arias, Handel exploits the full compass of the voices less consistently than in the London operas. The fireworks in the first version of 'Se giunge', where Poppea disports herself in thirds with a solo oboe for 23 bars, twelve of which are devoted to an endurance test on a single note, are not very successful, and were not used in performance.

The balance and sequence of keys seems less carefully calculated than later, but (as in *Almira*) there is some evidence of long-range tonal planning. It can scarcely be an accident that whereas Poppea's first six arias, except one in the neutral A minor, are all in flat keys, as soon as she breaks away from Agrippina's domination and takes control of her own destiny (in 'Ingannata') she moves into sharp keys and stays there for the rest of the opera. Act I has two consecutive movements in G major, but the more blatant juxtaposition of two D minor arias in common time towards the end of Act II arose fortuitously from the suppression of an intermediate cavatina for Claudio. There is a strong emphasis on flat keys, especially F and B flat and their

[25] So have two of the cancelled pieces in the autograph. On the other hand the delicious two-part coda appended to 'Hò un non sò che' in *La Resurrezione* was not retained in *Agrippina*.
[26] Including 'Vaghe perle', where Chrysander omits them.

relative minors; no fewer than eighteen movements (nineteen if a cancelled duet is included) are in flat minor keys. The arias generally follow recitative cadences in dominant or relative keys, though on six occasions Handel uses the mediant minor, which was to become the favourite progression of his maturity. There are signs that he had not yet adopted a settled policy here. Two arias follow the subdominant (once minor), one ('Pur ritorno') the supertonic minor, a progression favoured by Vivaldi. If the copies are to be trusted, the B flat setting of 'Sotto il lauro' followed A, 'Quando invita' (E minor) followed D, and 'Pur ch'io ti stringa' (G minor) followed F. But these are all places where changes were introduced, and there may have been adjustments. The one cadence in HG that is certainly wrong is the C major before 'Se vuoi pace' (E major). Chrysander, following Arnold, confused two versions: Handel altered a C sharp minor cadence to C major when he transposed the aria from E to F.

History and Text

The autograph of *Agrippina* bears no date. According to Mainwaring Handel composed it after his arrival in Venice, where he was spotted by Domenico Scarlatti playing the harpsichord at a masked ball and 'strongly importuned to compose an Opera. But there was so little prospect of either honour or advantage from such an undertaking, that he was very unwilling to engage in it... At last, however, he consented, and in three weeks he finished his *Agrippina*.' We now know that Handel cannot have reached Venice before mid-November 1709. There was no time for an opera to be commissioned, and the libretto and music written, between then and the end of the year, especially as Grimani was in Naples. However Strohm has shown good reasons for believing that Mainwaring conflated two visits to Venice, the first in the carnival season of 1707–8 immediately after the production of *Rodrigo*.[27]

Handel could scarcely have avoided meeting Grimani in Rome in 1707 or early 1708. Strohm suggests that he received the commission for *Agrippina*, and perhaps the libretto, during this period, and that Grimani may have obtained for him the commission to compose a serenata for the wedding of the pro-Habsburg Duke of Alvito (*Aci, Galatea e Polifemo*, performed at Naples in mid-July 1708, probably with Carli as Polifemo). There was certainly no time for operatic collaboration during Grimani's first busy weeks in Naples, after which he seems to have had no contact with Handel. The opera had doubtless been planned by then, but although many writers, including Chrysander, Lang, Kimbell, Strohm, and Baselt, place the composition of the music in 1708, there is nothing to contradict Mainwaring's statement that it was written in a hurry shortly before the production, Handel's usual practice. The maturity of the score suggests a late rather than an early date in the Italian period. Moreover the autograph is on Venetian paper.

The date of the first performance, 26 December 1709, has recently been confirmed by a manuscript newsletter. Confusion arose because copies of arias bearing the name of the theatre in the Wiesentheid and Coke Collections refer to *Agrippina* as the second opera; but this refers to the whole winter season, not

---

[27] See p. 79.

the carnival season, which traditionally opened on 26 December. The theatre was the San Giovanni Grisostomo, owned by the Grimani family (Plate 1); no doubt the Cardinal exercised his influence. The cast was:

AGRIPPINA:	Margherita Durastanti (soprano)
POPPEA:	Diamante Maria Scarabelli (soprano)
NERONE:	Valeriano Pellegrini (soprano castrato)
OTTONE:	Francesca Vanini-Boschi (contralto)
CLAUDIO:	Antonio Francesco Carli (bass)
NARCISO:	Giuliano Albertini (alto castrato)
PALLANTE:	Giuseppe Maria Boschi (bass)
LESBO:	Nicola Pasini (bass)

The singer of the alto part of Giunone is unknown. One of the early copies lists Elena Croce in the title role; she probably replaced Durastanti at some performances.

Agrippina was a sensational success. Mainwaring says it 'was performed twenty-seven nights successively; and in a theatre which had been shut up for a long time,[28] notwithstanding there were two other opera-houses open ... The audience was so enchanted with this performance, that a stranger who should have seen the manner in which they were affected, would have imagined they had all been distracted. The theatre, at almost every pause, resounded with shouts and exclamations of *viva il caro Sassone!* and other expressions of approbation too extravagant to be mentioned. They were thunderstruck with the grandeur and sublimity of his style: for never had they known till then all the powers of harmony and modulation so closely arrayed, and so forcibly combined.'

As with *Rodrigo*, the version performed does not correspond to the autograph or HG, though the differences from the autograph are less radical. They must have been entered in the lost performing score, from which all surviving copies and the Arnold edition ultimately derive. According to the printed libretto 'Fà quanto vuoi' was omitted and 'Bella pur' replaced by an aria with similar meaning, 'Spera alma mia'. The consensus of the copies indicates that this aria too was cut (it does not survive), together with 'Basta che sol' and the final ballet, and that 'Se giunge' and 'Sotto il lauro' were sung in Chrysander's B versions. Either before the first performance or early in the run the return of 'Pensieri' during Agrippina's following recitative was suppressed and the condensed form used in place of the da capo; the full version appears in none of the copies. These show a considerable number of musical divergences from the text of the autograph, listed below under *Copies and Editions*. At least one aria was added during the run: a brilliant virtuoso piece, 'Per punir che m'hà ingannata' appears in four copies as a replacement for 'Ingannata' in II viii. This is based, like 'Per dar pregio' in *Rodrigo*, on 'Un pensiero' in HWV 99 with the solo violin replaced by an obbligato harpsichord and gaps left for improvisation, as in 'Vo' far guerra' in *Rinaldo*; in the B section the voice is accompanied by unison violins only, to which it mostly provides the bass. The aria may have been introduced as a show piece for Scarabelli, or perhaps to emphasize Poppea's changed resolution at this point, which the gentle but more distinguished 'Ingannata' hardly does. It is in G major, which would

---

[28] This seems to be a mistake. Wiel (*I teatri musicali veneziani*) lists operas performed there in 1708 and 1709.

bring Poppea's last three arias into the same key. Other possible cuts during the run, indicated by omissions in some copies, are the Prelude for strings in II iii, the B section and da capo of 'Ti vo' giusta', and 'V'accendano'; Giunone may have been dropped altogether. 'Se vuoi pace' was apparently sung in F major by Durastanti but restored to the original E major for Croce.

Handel never performed *Agrippina* in England, but at least seven items from the score were heard at the Queen's Theatre in 1710–12. The first was 'Hò un non sò che', sung by Francesca Vanini-Boschi (presumably transposed) in a revival of Scarlatti's *Pirro e Demetrio* on 6 December 1710 soon after Handel's arrival. It was evidently popular, for Jane Barbier repeated it in *Arminio* and *Ernelinda* in May and June 1714. Boschi sang 'La mia sorte sfortunata' [*sic*] with the sense reversed in the title role of *Etearco* (10 January 1711). Handel himself introduced 'Bel piacere' and 'Basta che sol' into *Rinaldo* in February. *Antioco* (12 December 1711) borrowed the *Agrippina* overture[29] and 'Pensieri', sung by Elisabetta Pilotti-Schiavonetti in its shortened form with an extra five-bar cut. Two months later (27 February 1712) 'Tu ben degno' appeared with modified text ('Tu indegno sei dell'allor') in Act III of *Ambleto*, where Pilotti as Gerilda (= Gertrude) railed against Fengone (= Claudius) for renouncing her in favour of Veremonda (= Ophelia). All these pieces were printed by Walsh; it is possible that other items from *Agrippina* found their way into some of the many pasticcios of this period from which nothing was published. 'Col raggio placido' was almost certainly sung in one of the revivals of *Idaspe* (see p. 166).[30]

Agrippina enjoyed a fair measure of success on the continent; there were productions at Naples on 15 February 1713 with additional music by Francesco Mancini, at Hamburg on 3 November 1718 (NS) on the occasion of the reopening of the theatre under the new management of J. G. Gumprecht, and at Vienna in 1719, in the large Imperial ballroom on the Tummelplatz. This last was a pasticcio also containing music by Fiorè and Caldara.[31] The Hamburg production, unusual at that city in being sung wholly in Italian, remained in the repertory till November 1722 and was heard at least 29 times (once at Altona), though according to Wilhelm Willers only ten people were present on 10 January 1719. On 19 November 1718 Willers noted that 'Gauffin has discourteously run away and threatened not to sing again, however he did sing in *Agrippina* and forthwith had his luggage removed'. This was apparently Pietro Gauzzini, who sang at Wolfenbüttel in 1716. Zelm[32] mentions two later performances, on 6 September and 5 October 1724, when the Italian soprano Dominichina Pollone sang Poppea. 'Col raggio' was one of a number of Italian arias translated into French and sung at the financier Pierre Crozat's Concert Italien in Paris in 1724.[33] Handel of course had no control over any of these performances; but he introduced 'Pensieri' into his pasticcio *Oreste* produced at Covent Garden on 18 December 1734. Modern German revivals have been fairly frequent since 1943, when Halle led the way. The first production in England was at the Unicorn Theatre, Abingdon, in 1963. *Agrippina* has since become increasingly popular in several countries.

[29] M. Ruhnke printed this as a suggested overture to Gasparini's *Bajazet* (Munich, 1981) without recognizing the source.

[30] See Chapter 10 for the operas mentioned in this paragraph.

[31] Deutsch's statement (98) that the score of this version is in the Nationalbibliothek, Vienna, is incorrect.

[32] *Hamburger Jahrbuch für Musikwissenschaft*, iii (1978), 64.

[33] L. Lindgren, 'Parisian Patronage of Performers from the Royal Academy of Musick', *M & L* lviii (1977), 19–20.

Autograph

Handel's foliation of the autograph (RM 20 a 3), each act beginning a new series (that of Act III stops before 'Come nube che fugge', HG 123), permits certain conclusions about the course of the composition.[34] In addition to changes for performance, which do not appear in the autograph, Handel made others at several earlier stages: during the original composition before he foliated the manuscript, during the filling-up process when he set the recitatives, and after foliation. In the first draft Nerone had a different aria in the opening scene, 'Sarà qual vuoi accenni' (3/4, E minor), with continuo accompaniment except for a ten-bar string ritornello in four parts after the da capo. This must have disappeared early, since Handel used the same material for another suppressed aria in III ix (it had already appeared in a different key as 'Se la bellezza' in *Il trionfo del Tempo*). The replacement, 'Con saggio', appears at the end of the autograph (ff. 120–1) in smaller neater writing; the closing words of the previous recitative were altered at the same time. Of the alternative voice parts in the B section the higher is the original; the lower, which appears in no copies, was added hastily in different ink on a separate stave, perhaps at the same time as the recitatives. Other early insertions were Poppea's 'È un foco',[35] originally in 6/8 (HG 40), the *coro* 'Di timpani e trombe' in II iii, followed by something subsequently removed—possibly a sinfonia or dances—on Handel's missing ff. 7–9, Nerone's short recitative in II xii (HG 92), and probably the recitatives on HG 83, where Handel's alteration of the scene number from 8 to 7 suggests that something had been replaced.

The opening of Act III underwent a good deal of reworking. The original scheme included neither 'Tacerò' nor 'Coll'ardor': Ottone and Nerone both hid without singing an aria. This explains the appearance of the stage directions (*si nasconde in una porta*, etc.) before the arias. Handel did not bother to change this nonsensical arrangement, and Chrysander reproduced it; the libretto correctly places the directions after the arias. Something was torn out here—possibly an aria for Poppea where 'Tacerò' now stands—for Handel's f. 3 is missing. 'Tacerò' is on an inserted leaf, but Handel wrote 'Coll'ardor' and Ottone's previous recitative on a page prepared for Poppea's recitative 'Amico ciel' (HG 113) and continued with the latter on the verso. 'Bel piacere' was composed to different words ('Chi ben ama/E sol brama/Di goder/Ama sol il suo piacer./Quella face/Cui non piace/Mai dolor/Non è mai d'un vero amor') for a different context, probably the end of III v (HG 113). It was shifted to Scene x, and the introductory recitative on HG 121 inserted, when Handel added the foliation; he had to renumber his ff. 9–18, which became 7–16. Claudio's last lines in the opera, 'Dell'augusto mio genio' (HG 136), were written out for Giunone (in the soprano clef—Handel did not yet know the singer) after the *coro*, but not set to music. Handel squeezed in the bass setting on the bottom of f. 116 at the filling up stage, and probably wrote Giunone's recitative and aria at the same time.

Three more complete pieces were suppressed after foliation, one of them

---

[34] Act II bears traces of an earlier foliation by gatherings at the top left corner (2 on Handel's f. 14, 3 on f. 28, 4 on f. 32), but they are too fragmentary to establish any conclusions.

[35] There is a muddle in bar 9, where the voice part in the autograph has an impossible number of rests. It seems likely that the first 'non si sà' was intended to come one beat earlier than in HG 41, coinciding with the violins as in bars 10–11; but the copies and Arnold agree with HG.

after undergoing substantial revision. Towards the end of Act II Claudio had a cavatina 'Vagheggiar de tuoi bei lumi' (3/4, F major, continuo only) with ungainly leaps in the voice part to suggest his clumsy wooing; this was replaced by the recitative at the bottom of HG 100 ($3\frac{1}{2}$ bars), which is not in the autograph, though the cavatina is cancelled. There were important changes in III ix and x (HG 119–22). As first composed, Scene ix ended with an aria for Poppea, 'Esci, O mia vita' (3/4, E minor, continuo only). The music is almost identical with 'Sarà qual vuoi accenni' without the final ritornello. Scene x ended with a duet for Poppea and Ottone in 3/8 time, 'Nò, nò, ch'io non apprezzo', which followed the recitative at the bottom of HG 119. The duet ended out of its key: the sixteen-bar melody was sung first by Ottone in D minor, then by Poppea in G minor (both with continuo only), then by both, partly in canon, with strings in G minor, ending with a full sixteen-bar ritornello in the same key. Handel cancelled most of this, leaving only Ottone's strophe, which he equipped with a new D minor string ritornello. This is not crossed out, but he was still dissatisfied; he later replaced it with the G minor aria 'Pur ch'io ti stringa', which is not in the main autograph. None of the suppressed pieces is of more than moderate quality.

Other changes after foliation were the substitution of the shorter B setting of 'Se giunge' at the end of Act I (both settings are in the autograph, the first conceived in 6/8) and the cancellation of eight bars of recitative on HG 113 and twelve for Agrippina on HG 127; hitherto she had remained on stage throughout Nerone's 'Come nube che fugge'. Handel marked three arias for transposition. 'Coronato il crin', composed in F, was put down to E flat when the recitatives were composed (cadence in G minor), but later restored to F and the cadence altered to A minor. 'Cade il mondo' was transposed from D minor down to C minor and 'Se vuoi pace' from E up to F. In ignoring these two instructions Chrysander falsified the text, and in 'Se vuoi pace' produced an impossible progression. There were many changes to the words and music of the recitatives as well as a number of cuts, before and after the completion of the music. 'Vaghe perle' lost a total of eighteen bars and 'Col peso' (first notated in 3/8) eleven. The numbering of the scenes towards the end of Act II is confused, both in the autograph (which has no Scene xvii) and in HG (where xviii and xix are numbered xvii and xviii, and xix is omitted); but nothing is missing. The libretto, where Handel's and Chrysander's Scene xx appears as xix, gives a consecutive sequence.

The autograph is defective at the start, lacking the overture and the recitatives of the first scene as far as Agrippina's words 'a' poveri dispensa l'or' (HG 8). Since only three leaves of Handel's foliation are missing, it seems unlikely that this included the overture. (Its introduction was adapted from that of the sacred cantata 'Donna che in ciel', probably dating from early 1707.[36]) The manuscript ends with the words *Segue li balli*. If there was a date, it would have followed the dances, but Handel may have taken (or intended to take) these from an earlier source, possibly what we know as the overture to *Rodrigo*, two movements of which are based on the same themes as the *coro* and Giunone's aria.[37]

The autograph of 'Pur ch'io ti stringa' appears in a separate volume of miscellaneous fragments (RM 20 d 2) and like other movements was revised

---

[36] Published by Arno Volk Verlag, Cologne (ed. R. Ewerhart) in 1959.
[37] See p. 108.

later for performance; it is half a bar longer than the version in HG and shows many small variants in all three parts. Chrysander never found it, with the result that he printed the improved version from Arnold, taking over one error and making one incorrect emendation (the last quaver of bar 4 should have G in the violins, B♭ in the bass; the fifth note in the bass of bar 19, F♮ in Arnold, should be F♯, not G). There is no sign in the autograph of Chrysander's B setting of 'Sotto il lauro', which he took from Arnold. Mattheson stated in his periodical *Critica Musica* (July 1722) that this was borrowed 'almost note for note' and in the same key from an aria ('Diese Wangen will ich küssen') in his opera *Porsenna*, which Handel accompanied under his direction at Hamburg, and that Handel used the melody again in 'A chi vive di speranza' in *Muzio Scevola*. The subject seems to have rankled with him, for he returned to it in *Grundlage einer Ehren-Pforte* (1740), remarking that when *Agrippina* was performed in Hamburg in 1718 'people imagined, not unreasonably, that they could perceive in it various imitations from *Porsenna* etc., quite similar to the originals'. Handel certainly borrowed Mattheson's melody, though he treated it very differently in *Muzio Scevola* (the second of two settings of this aria). In *Der vollkommene Capellmeister* (1739) Mattheson quoted a fugal entry from his overture to *Cleopatra* similar to that in the *Agrippina* overture. His implied claim received short shrift from Chrysander.[38] The overture to *Cleopatra* is lost, and the score of *Porsenna* was reputedly destroyed in the last war. Handel cannot have played in the latter, which was produced before he reached Hamburg.

The A section of 'Volo pronto' (HG 18) has a set of words in English, 'Pleasure's gentle zephyrs playing', added in faint pencil. It was sung thus in the 1758 revival of *The Triumph of Time and Truth* in the last year of Handel's life. The writing, much worn and rubbed, has been wrongly attributed to Handel;[39] it is probably the younger Smith's. The matter is of some moment in view of the debate about Handel's blindness.

An autograph aria in the Fitzwilliam Museum (Mus MS 262, pp. 1–5) appears on first glance to be a variant of 'Coll'ardor'. The principal idea, used in several other works of the Italian period, including *Il trionfo del Tempo* and the cantata *Apollo e Dafne*, is similar, but key, scoring, words ('Col valor del vostro brando'), and much of the musical detail are different. This version, which is on Ca paper (1711), was almost certainly intended for *Rinaldo*.

Librettos

1709 Venice. 'Drama Per Musica. Da Rappresentarsi nel Famosissimo Teatro Grimani di S. Gio: Grisostomo... Appresso Marino Rossetti in Merceria, all'Insegna della Pace.' 60 pp. Text of course in Italian only. Neither the librettist nor the composer is named. No change of set is indicated before 'Pensieri' (II xiii), though the context seems to demand a move to the palace. The explanation may lie in the list of ballets at the beginning: 'Di Tedeschi, Di Giardinieri, Di Cavalieri e Dame'. These presumably occurred at the end of the acts, and the music may not have been by Handel. Gardeners would be more apt if the garden scene were retained till the end of Act II. The 'Cavalieri e Dame' could be Juno's attendants, who are directed to descend

[38] i. 191 ff.
[39] By Squire (*Catalogue of the King's Music Library*, p. 3) and A. Hyatt King (*Handel and his Autographs*, London, 1967, Plate x).

with the goddess before the Act III *coro*. The Germans are less easy to account for unless they represented a gladiatorial show.

The principal differences from the autograph and HG are the omission of Poppea's 'Fà quanto vuoi' (I xix), the substitution of 'Spera alma mia' for 'Belle pur' (II vi), and different texts for the B sections of 'Pensieri' (II xiii) and 'Spererò' (II xvi). In the former the explicit appeal for Heaven's assistance in obtaining the throne for Nerone is replaced by the weaker and more anodyne 'Numi eterni ch'il Ciel reggete/I miei voti raccogliete,/La mia speme secondate'. In 'Spererò' Narciso is more ardent, emphasizing his constancy rather than the justice of his cause and addressing Agrippina not as 'donna augusta' but as 'mia speranza'. Handel strengthened the impact of the ensemble 'Di timpani e trombe' (II iii); the libretto gives the first four lines to Narciso and Pallante together, the fifth to Narciso, and only the last ('Viva Claudio trionfante') as a *coro*. Many smaller verbal changes—for example 'Tutto è tormento' instead of 'È rio tormento' in the last line of 'Pur ch'io ti stringa'—may reflect an urge to make the dramatic expression more vivid. Poppea and Ottone are spelt Popea and Otone throughout. No singer is named for Giunone. At least twenty copies of the libretto are known, and they evidently embrace more than one edition. Only the first has the repeat of 'Pensieri' during the following recitative. Deutsch's statement that Boschi is listed as 'pittore di scena' is not supported by any copies we have seen.

1713 Naples. 'Drama per musica da rappresentarsi nel Teatro di S. Bartolomeo nel presente carnevale dell'anno 1713 . . . ad istanza di Francesco Ricciardo.' 71 pp. Dedicated by the impresario Andrea del Pò to the Vicereine Camilla Barbarini Borromeo, with the date of the first performance (15 February). A note to the reader names 'Sig Giorgio Enrico [*sic*] Hendel detto il Sassone' as the original composer; but parts of the drama have been altered and comic scenes added, all the new music supplied by Francesco Mancini, vice-master of the Royal Chapel. None of the cast ever sang under Handel. Lesbo's part is much expanded and he receives a comic counterpart in Poppea's servant Zaffira. In accordance with usual Neapolitan practice they have long interpolated scenes at the end of Act II and in the latter part of Act III, where Lesbo disguises himself as a woman. Otherwise the plot is little altered, though there are a number of cuts and changed aria texts. Juno is omitted. Mancini contributed eleven new arias in addition to the intermezzos.

1718 Hamburg. 'Gedruckt bey Caspar Jakhel Buchdrucker auf dem Doms-Kirchhoff.' Bilingual throughout, including Grimani's *Argomento*. No artists are named. About 100 lines of recitative are cut, mostly in Act I, as are 'Fà quanto vuoi', 'Basta che sol', 'V'accendano', and the last two lines of 'Di timpani e trombe'; Poppea has no aria in II vi; her aria in II viii is 'Per punir', not 'Ingannata'. The basic text seems to have been a copy of the Venice libretto; 'Pensieri' and 'Spererò' follow that version, which is not in any score. The 'Pensieri' scene is specifically laid in Agrippina's closet. There are three replacement arias in Act III, 'Mio caro amato bene' (Nerone) for 'Coll'ardor', 'Sì, sì, t'amo, O caro' (Poppea) for 'Bel piacere', and 'Mora Poppea, affetti miei' (Nerone) for 'Come nube che fugge'. The second was presumably Agilea's aria from *Teseo*, never given in Hamburg; the other two are unidentified.

Copies and Editions

All the surviving copies, whether complete scores or aria collections, as well as Arnold's edition, reflect a textual tradition differing in many particulars from the autograph and HG. It can derive only from the lost performing score. The divergences from Chrysander's text (based on Arnold and the autograph) fall into two groups: variants that Chrysander found in Arnold and rejected but which are confirmed by the manuscripts, and mistakes or bowdlerizations introduced by Arnold and retained by Chrysander against the authority of the autograph. The latter are listed separately below, the former here. 'Fà quanto vuoi', 'Bella pur', and 'Basta che sol' are omitted, and there is no sign of a final ballet. The recorders play with the violins in octaves throughout the A section of 'Volo pronto'. 'L'alma mia' has a full G major chord for all the strings on the first beat of bar 25. 'Allegrezza' is a tone lower in C major with the voice part much simplified and nearly all its semiquavers removed (Pasini must have been an inept singer); there are minor discrepancies, probably accidental, among the copies. 'Lusinghiera' is shortened by the removal of the tautological bar 17 (18 in some copies) and the contraction of the B section to either thirteen or nine bars with the chromaticism toned down.[40] 'È un foco' begins with two additional crotchet beats in the bass (G and D). 'Pur ritorno' lacks bars 8–15. The violin and voice parts are differently distributed in bars 14 and 15 of 'Coronato il crin'. The first eight bars of the 4/4 section of 'Di timpani e trombe' are reduced to five, eliminating the antiphonal treatment of upper and lower voices. 'Cade il mondo' is in C minor. 'Sotto il lauro' (B setting) is introduced by a different recitative for Ottone ending in A. 'Voi che udite' is one bar shorter (bars 12 and 13 are elided), and shows other minor changes. 'Ingannata' has a continuo accompaniment throughout, except for a seven-bar ritornello after the A section. 'Quando invita' is introduced by a different recitative, ending in D. 'Pensieri' is considerably shortened, the A section from 49 bars to 40 (involving the removal of all violin semiquavers after bar 8); the da capo is replaced by a variant of the repeat at the bottom of HG 96 (which does not occur at that point), the first three bars for voice and oboe preceding the octave Gs and the cadence (bars 13–15) lengthened by one bar, again removing the semiquavers. Bar 56 of 'Come nube che fugge' is expanded to six bars, giving the voice a *mezza voce* held C between flourishes at the cadence.

These changes, with the possible exception of the recitative cadences, undoubtedly carry Handel's authority. They may have been due to the exigencies of stage performance or the singers. Many are clear improvements, though we may regret the truncation of 'Lusinghiera' and 'Pensieri'.

Three complete copies are very early and probably date from 1710. Mus MS 19160 in the Nationalbibliothek, Vienna, may have been a gift from Cardinal Grimani to the future Habsburg Emperor Charles VI.[41] It is very clearly written, and exceptionally lists the cast, with Elena Croce as Agrippina. The manuscript contains no stage directions. Its most striking feature is the inclusion (possibly an insertion, though in the same hand) of 'Per punir' as an alternative to 'Ingannata'. It ends with the *coro*, omitting Giunone's recitative and aria. The B section of 'Lusinghiera' runs to only nine bars. The top instrumental part of the quartet in I ix is marked *Violini*, that of the

---

[40] This section gave Handel much trouble; it is heavily corrected in the autograph.

[41] Strohm, *HJb* (1975), 108; *Essays*, 40.

Prelude in II iii *Unissoni tutti*, that of 'Col raggio' *Uniss.* The scene heading for II iv correctly precedes 'Di timpani e trombe'. The last word of the text in 'Bel piacere' is 'ardor', not 'cor'.[42] 'Se vuoi pace' is in E major after a cadence in C major; but the aria is a re-transposition back to the original key, presumably for Croce, and the recitative would certainly have been modified accordingly.

A second score in the same Vienna library, SA 68 B 26, is in its original form an almost exact copy of Mus MS 19160, without the names of the cast. The work was shared between three copyists. It contains very few dynamics and instrumental indications, in many movements none at all, and no tempo marks. A different (contemporary) hand has collated the verbal text with that of the printed libretto, sometimes altering the music copyist's words and sometimes adding the libretto reading underneath. This mostly affects recitative, but in the B section of 'Se giunge' 'o segue l'amore' is changed to the libretto's 'o lieve e l'amore' (Handel's autograph 'e segue l'umor' makes no sense). The same hand has added a few stage directions in I ii–iv, ix, and xxi, and III vi, but many more are not included. There are also one or two musical changes. 'La mia sorte fortunata' has been converted into a full da capo aria by the cancellation of the dal segno ritornello, and recitative cadences modified to give more forward movement at the bottom of HG 74 and 102.

Add MS 16023, another early Italian manuscript, on paper with a watermark very similar to that of the autograph, gives a slightly different text. It omits the Prelude in II iii and 'Per punir' and reduces 'Ti vo' giusta' to its A section, but includes Giunone's recitative and aria. 'L'alma mia' has a full da capo, the B section of 'Lusinghiera' has thirteen bars. The top line of 'Hò un non sò che' is *Unisoni*, as in no other source; but the autograph's *Violini unis. tutti ma piano*, omitted by Chrysander, is surely right. The basses in 'Vaghe fonti' are not marked pizzicato (the violins are muted only in the autograph). 'Se vuoi pace' is in F major after a C major cadence. Fitzwilliam Mus MS 73, signed and dated 1767 by Lord Fitzwilliam, was probably copied about that time, perhaps from Add MS 16023, with which it is almost identical.

Two groups of arias—24 in the Coke Collection and six in the Schönborn Library at Wiesentheid (SB 5), the latter with parts as well—carry on each piece the name of the theatre and a note that this was the second opera of the season; they undoubtedly date from early 1710. Both groups, except where noted, follow the other copies, not the autograph or HG. The Wiesentheid arias, dispatched from Italy by the Schönborn agent Franz Harneck, are 'Volo pronto', 'È un foco', 'Hò un non sò che', 'Se giunge' (B setting), 'Coronato il crin', and the unpublished 'Per punir' (the unison violins accompanying the B section are pizzicato). Two of the Coke arias are fragmentary, and 'Nulla sperar', 'Tuo ben è 'l trono', 'Ti vo' giusta' and 'Spererò' lack their fully-scored ritornellos. 'Lusinghiera' has the thirteen-bar B section. 'Io di Roma' is in a different hand from the rest, and has a full da capo instead of a dal segno, but this is probably a slip.

A second group in the Coke Collection, also of Italian provenance, evidently reflects the Naples production of 1713. The same volume contains arias from Feo's *L'amor tirannico* on the *Radamisto* story, produced at Naples a month earlier in the same season, as well as a number of anonymous pieces, including 'Il Tricerbero' from *Rinaldo*. The ten *Agrippina* arias are each headed

---

[42] 'Ardor' may be correct. The autograph has 'cor', but that word already occurs in the rhyme scheme.

'del Sig' Giorgio Enrico Hendel detto il Sassone', as in the Naples libretto. The three from Poppea's part are for alto: 'È un foco' in D minor (*Larghetto*), 'Se giunge' in the B version in F (*Allegro*), 'Bel piacere' in D with 'ardor' in the B section. 'Volvo pronto', 'Hò un non sò che', and 'Se vuoi pace' (in F) are *Allegro*, 'Voi che udite' *Largo*, 'Pur ch'io ti stringa' *Andante*. 'Ti vo' giusta' is up a tone in F without its final ritornello. The B section of 'Lusinghiera' has thirteen bars, as in Add MS 16023. Otherwise the text agrees with the Vienna copies, except that the B section of 'Se giunge' has the words of the Venice libretto.

The Flower score, also a miscellany in haphazard order, is curious in several respects. It contains the overture and 31 arias but no recitatives or ensembles, and involves three copyists working at two widely separated periods (a fourth at the end of the volume added the *Florindo* excerpts[43]). The overture and first sixteen arias are in S2's late hand on paper (Ch) of the mid-1740s. 'Lusinghiera' has the thirteen-bar B section. 'Se vuoi pace' is in E major, 'Volo pronto' in B flat for soprano with a lighter accompaniment (no recorders or thirds). 'Qual piacer' is marked *Largo* by Jennens. The remaining arias were copied much earlier, by H3 and Smith in alternation, on two B-type papers with slightly different watermarks. That they were working together is clear from the fact that Smith took over from H3 towards the end of 'Ti vo' giusta', copying the last six bars on the same page. This section probably dates from the winter of 1721/2, when Smith and H3 were associated in the Malmesbury score of *Floridante* (dated December 1721) and a collection of arias from the composite *Muzio Scevola* in Fitzwilliam MS 54. The first aria of this group, 'L'alma mia' (without tempo), is headed *Aria del Agrippina e Nerone del Sig' Handel*, the last three words in a hand very like the composer's. 'Per punir' is included, but not 'Ingannata'. 'Vaghe fonti' is in F *minor*. 'Nulla sperar', complete in the S2 group, makes a second appearance without its four-part ritornello. This is also missing in 'Ti vo' giusta' and 'Tuo ben è 'l trono'. 'Io di Roma' was copied as a da capo aria; Jennens altered it to dal segno but placed the sign five bars too late. In several respects this group suggests a source close to the Coke 1710 arias. The pieces missing from the manuscript (apart from the three cut) are 'La mia sorte', 'Allegrezza', 'Hò un non sò che', 'Se giunge', 'Coronato il crin', 'Bel piacere', and 'Come nube che fugge'. Much of the score is fully figured (some of it perhaps by Jennens), but twelve arias have no figures at all, and one ('Spererò') only a few. It would seem that Handel no longer had a score of *Agrippina* in his possession, apart from the autograph, which may have been ignored because it was outdated. The Shaftesbury score (S2) was almost certainly copied from Flower, with which it shares the same peculiarities and mistakes.

The Flower parts (S2, mid-1740s)—violins 1 and 2, oboes 1 and 2 (including *flauti* in 'Vaghe fonti'), viola, cello + bassoon, organo—follow the order and text of the Flower score, from which they were perhaps copied, but cover only nineteen arias chosen indiscriminately from all sections of the manuscript. The figured continuo part, though headed *Organo*, is clearly for harpsichord; the cembalo solos in 'Per punir' are so marked. Solo and *tutti* passages are seldom distinguished, though some are indicated in 'Non hò cor'. The scoring sometimes differs from HG and on several occasions, especially in the oboe parts, is demonstrably wrong. There are no violas in 'Qual piacer'. Both oboes double the first violins in 'Vieni, O cara' and the ritornellos of 'Io di Roma',

[43] See p. 74.

but are silent in 'Lusinghiera' and 'V'accendano'. Both play in unison in 'L'alma mia', 'Voi che udite', and 'Pensieri'. The cello–bassoon part is marked *senza bassone* in 'Qual piacer' and *tutti* in 'Lusinghiera' but not otherwise distinguished.

RM 19 d 12 (ff. 1–17) contains a very early Smith copy (*c.*1719) of the first five scenes of Act I without the overture, breaking off abruptly after bar 50 of 'Volo pronto'. Part of 'La mia sorte' has a soprano clef for the voice. There are copies of 'Col raggio', which seems to have been popular, in Tenbury 884 (early Smith, *c.*1719) and Berlin Staatsbibliothek Mus MS 30345; both have minor variants. According to H. C. Wolff[44] a collection of arias from Albinoni's *Astarto* at Schwerin (MS Mus 4721) includes copies of 'L'alma mia' and 'Non hò cor'. An unplayable transcription of the overture for harpsichord appears in three early copies, two in the Malmesbury Collection (RM1 and Linike, *c.*1718; Smith, *c.*1733), and one in the Coke Wesley MS (Smith, *c.*1721). RM1, who must have been an Englishman, tortured the title into *Argripini ed Nerone*. Another version, playable but harmonically incorrect, is in New York Public Library Mus Res MN* (copyist unknown).

Walsh published the overture in parts in April 1727, but no keyboard arrangement and no edition of the songs, apart from 'Hò un non sò che', which appeared separately and in collections with at least five different sets of English words between 1711 and 1731. The first score was Arnold's (*c.*1795), based on the Walsh parts of the overture and a manuscript very close to Vienna Mus MS 19160, not on the autograph. It contains no stage directions, and the scene numbering is erratic. Arnold added bass figuring and some instrumental details. Chrysander's comprehensive damnation of this edition as 'so defaced by omissions, extensions and mistakes as to be barely recognisable' is unfortunate, to say the least. Although there are plenty of wrong notes and verbal errors due to misreading the Italian text, the omissions and extensions, which are found in the copies, must reflect Handel's performing score. Arnold included a facsimile of part of 'Bel piacere', described as 'An exact Copy of the hand writing of G. F. HANDEL from the Opera of Agrippina in the possession of the EDITOR'—presumably that from which he printed his edition. The writing bears no resemblance to Handel's, but is Italian from the early years of the century, thus confirming the authenticity of the manuscript.

Chrysander's edition (1874) contrives on numerous occasions to sweep Arnold aside where he is correct and to follow him where he is corrupt or playing the part of Bowdler. The recorders should double the violins in octaves throughout the A section of 'Volo pronto' (clearly the intention of the compressed autograph as well as the reading of all copies). In bars 11 and 12 of 'Vieni, O cara' the first violins should play D, B♭, A, not F, G, F. Claudio's words in bar 4 of the trio are 'I frutti del tuo amor' (Chrysander's 'sensi' is apparently an emendation of Arnold's misreading 'scuti'). The violins' second note in bar 5 of 'Coronato il crin' is G, not F, the voice's first note in bar 4 of 'Nulla sperar' A, not D. In 'Voi dormite' (B section of 'Vaghe fonti', HG 85) 'pace' in bar 15 is set to two Gs, 'perch'io' in bar 26 to two As. In bar 13 of the shortened 'Pensieri' (HG 96) the second note of the voice is G, not F. The voice's first note in bar 34 of 'Sprererò' is F♯ (E in Arnold, F♮ in HG). Chrysander also took over a number of Arnold's verbal errors in the recitative:

<hr>

[44] 'Neue Quellen zu den Opern des Tommaso Albinoni', *Studi musicali*, viii (1979), 273–89.

'necessità di fato' (for 'stato') in I vi (HG 20), 'Pur al fin si riandò' (for 'se n'andò') at the end of I xxii (HG 52), 'infido, se tradirai?' (for 'e chi dirai?') in II vii (7 bars from end of HG 85), and 'Oh Ottone' (for 'Ora Ottone') at the start of III x (HG 119). The autograph, which Arnold probably did not see, is clear on all these points. A number of instrumental indications, notably in 'Vaghe perle' (*Violin. e flaut.*) and 'Hò un non sò che' (*Violini unis. tutti ma piano*), and stage directions have fallen by the wayside: I xiv should be headed *Stanza di Poppea*, I xxii *Lesbo correndo*. As in other operas, Chrysander misrepresented Handel's *Tutti* on the top instrumental line, for example in 'Non hò cor', 'Ogni vento', and 'Bel piacere', where, unless specifically directed otherwise, both oboes should double the first violins.

In 1950 Bärenreiter issued a vocal score of *Agrippina* edited by Hellmuth Christian Wolff. This is a practical edition intended for performances in German (the recitatives are altered to fit the translation) and was used for the Halle (1943) and subsequent revivals in Germany. Its most conspicuous feature is the copious ornamentation, especially in the voice parts; this is generally stylish but much too elaborate, even cavatinas being heavily encrusted. A few arias are cut, and some superfluous movements imported from other works. The preface rightly emphasizes the satirical content of the opera and the need for free and rapid handling of the recitative. Narciso's part remains at the correct pitch, but Nerone and Ottone are put down an octave for tenor and baritone respectively, destroying the balance of the score, undermining the characterization, and producing the absurdity of a woman's part printed in the bass clef. The attempt to adjust the balance by lowering the oboe part in 'Voi che udite' for English horn only makes things worse. Wolff's discussion of Baroque performance practice in his thirty-six page pamphlet *Agrippina, eine italienische Jugendoper von Georg Friedrich Händel* (Wolfenbüttel and Berlin, 1943) was however in advance of its time and contains many pertinent observations. He mentions the two Vienna scores, but had evidently not examined them.

Additional Notes

* (p. 128) See H. S. Saunders Jr., 'Handel's *Agrippina*: The Venetian Perspective', *Göttinger Händel-Beiträge* III (1987), 87 ff.
* (p. 130) Groups of arias began to circulate almost at once. In addition to those at Wiesentheid and in the Coke Collection (see p. 136) Pellegrini, who sang Nerone, sent some to Johann Wilhelm, Elector Palatine, in 1710 (Alfred Einstein in *SIMG* 1907/8, 409, cited by Lindgren in 'Venice, Vivaldi, Vico and Opera in London, 1705–17', *Nuovi Studi Vivaldiani*, 1988, 633 ff.).

CHAPTER 9

THE ENGLISH BACKGROUND: ITALIAN OPERA IN LONDON, 1705–1710

London an operatic backwater (p. 140) — English semiopera (p. 141) — Vanbrugh's new theatre (p. 142) — Camilla (p. 143) — arrival of Valentini, first castrato in London opera (p. 144) — failure of Vanbrugh's enterprise(p. 145) — arrival of Nicolini (p. 146) — macaronic operas and locally assembled pasticcios (p. 146) — eclipse of English party (p. 147) — fragmentary publication of music (p. 148) — assessment of aria collections (p. 148).

It would be difficult to overstate the contrast between the circumstances under which Handel travelled to London in the late autumn of 1710 and those attending his arrival in Italy four years earlier, or between the musical climates of the two countries. He went to Italy to learn his trade and broaden his style; he was invited to London to demonstrate his prowess. On leaving Hamburg for the south he entered a country that had witnessed the birth of opera a century before and nourished it as the pre-eminent branch of secular music ever since; he was approaching the centre of a culture from its outskirts. In returning north he was leaving the fountain for the barren outer deserts which it was hoped, no doubt by himself as well as others, that he would plough and fertilize.

As we have seen, he had learned a great deal in Italy about every aspect of his art, especially its lyrical and dramatic functions. Leaving aside the fact that by 1710 his style had reached its first maturity, there was little that London could teach him, and nothing at all about the commodity with which he was charged, Italian opera. In due course he was to acquire something from English music, as he did from that of every community with which he came in contact, but the influence was virtually confined to his settings of English words. His debt to Purcell is apparent in the early choral works, the *Ode for Queen Anne's Birthday* and the Utrecht *Jubilate* and *Te Deum*, and, thanks to his remarkable capacity for absorbing and digesting everything he heard, even from his juniors, an English element became endemic in his style and increasingly recognizable in some of the late oratorios and odes. It can scarcely be glimpsed in the operas, directed towards a cosmopolitan taste in a foreign language, and therefore does not concern us in this book.

The London musical background, particularly the operatic background, is however important for an understanding of Handel's career and achievement. It was this climate that saw the birth of *Rinaldo* and determined the future course of his life. The tangled story of the introduction of Italian opera to London has attracted many authors and baffled many readers, but still awaits definitive treatment. Errors and misunderstandings abound, and have won acceptance by repetition, while some aspects, notably the vital part played by John Vanbrugh, have never received their due. The discovery of fresh material and the re-sifting of old have helped to clarify obscure points, though a number remain.[1]

The trouble arises not from a lack of documentation but from an excess of it in some areas and its patchy distribution in others. As in all operatic revolutions the story has its political, social, and financial as well as its literary and musical facets. The articulate exuberance of English literary life, not least in the theatre, the birth of newspapers and periodicals, and the survival of papers from the Vice Chamberlain's office have left a mass of written material. The landscape is littered with plays, pamphlets, letters, lists, complaints, proposals, ordinances, bills (often unpaid), financial estimates, prologues, and epilogues, which admit a wide variety of interpretation and sometimes threaten to cancel each other out. The music has been forced into the background. Librettos abound, but scores are almost unknown. Printed collections of arias are incomplete and more or less fragmentary, and sometimes anonymous. This reflects the priorities of an age concerned more with spectacle and singing than musical drama, which saw no artistic inconsistency in a pasticcio assembled locally from the work of half a dozen composers in another country. It is not surprising that scholars have concentrated on the social, literary, and aesthetic issues, especially as the music, in so far as it can be judged at all, is often poor in quality and without artistic progeny of any kind. Moreover the non-musical elements are interesting and important in their own right.

Italian music other than opera had been familiar in London well before the end of the seventeenth century, and a number of Italian artists had visited the country. The castrato Siface created a sensation in 1687; an anonymous 'Italian Lady'—who was almost certainly not Margherita de l'Epine—sang at concerts in 1693. Margherita did arrive in 1703, and with other singers and instrumentalists performed Italian music between the acts of plays; in that year she introduced a song from Giovanni Bononcini's *Camilla* (1696), and Walsh published it. In view of this, the presence in London of many musicians as refugees from the continent, and the increasing popularity among the English nobility and gentry of the Grand Tour, in which Italy and its artistic traditions were a major attraction, the planting of the operatic seed was inevitable. That the wheat was mixed with tares, and the germ inadequately cultivated, was also to be expected.

At the start of 1705 the staple fare of the English theatre was, as it had been for many years, the spoken play, with music as an adjunct in the intervals and sometimes during the action. The English semiopera,[2] a play with masques and sustained stretches of music but still basically a play, was not extinct; yet except in the hands of a genius like Purcell, who had died prematurely ten years before, it possessed little life or propensity for growth. Since the principal characters did not sing, and consequently the music, even in Purcell, scarcely ever advanced the plot or motivated a dramatic event, it could never be more than an artistic mule. Indeed, though Purcell's semioperas were still in the repertory, no new specimen had been produced since 1701. Nevertheless

---

[1] A most important source containing new documents and valuable interpretation is *Vice Chamberlain Coke's Theatrical Papers, 1706–1715*, ed. J. Milhous and R. D. Hume (Carbondale, 1982) (*Coke Papers*). The best short account is by C. A. Price, 'The Critical Decade for English Music Drama, 1700–1710', *Harvard Library Bulletin*, xxvi (1978), 38–76.

[2] Roger North's term, less ambiguous than 'dramatic opera'.

the form had many supporters, especially among men of letters and actors, who saw their livelihood threatened and their aesthetic values disturbed by the upstart race of musicians. It was a cardinal principle of aesthetics, not only then but for much of the eighteenth century, that when verse was set to music the poet was the master. The musician had his place, but decorum required that he be kept firmly in it.

London had two major theatres, Drury Lane, managed by Christopher Rich, a shrewd man of business notorious for stinginess towards his employees, and Lincoln's Inn Fields under the leading actor Thomas Betterton. This situation was about to change with the opening in April 1705 of the Queen's Theatre in the Haymarket, built by Vanbrugh as a private venture with the aid of subscriptions from his friends. Betterton's company at once moved there, but Vanbrugh, whose correspondence reveals him as an enthusiastic opera-lover, almost certainly hoped to establish the new art in his theatre, which was designed for the sung rather than the spoken word.[3] He was beaten to the post by Rich, who on 16 January 1705 put on *Arsinoe Queen of Cyprus*,[4] 'An Opera After the Italian manner, All sung, being set to Musick by Master Clayton'. A distinguished painter, James Thornhill, designed the scenery.[5] It was given in English by an all-English cast, the hero sung by the countertenor Francis Hughes, and was an instant success, enjoying 35 performances in just over two years. Thomas Clayton had recently been in Italy, and the music was probably a pasticcio—rather more than half the printed songs were attributed to him—but there was no doubt about his intention, announced in the preface to the libretto: 'The Design of this Entertainment being to introduce the *Italian* manner of Musick on the *English* Stage, which has not been before attempted'. Curtis Price makes the important point that *Arsinoe* did not fill a programme but, like all its successors before *Camilla*, was appended as a tailpiece to an English play. Rich was feeling his way. Nevertheless the novelty caught on (the real novelty was the recitative, which has not survived), despite heavy bombardment from the admirers of English semiopera. Their motives were no doubt not altruistic, but they could point to the undeniable poverty of the music. It was this that drew the fire of the anonymous author of *A Critical Discourse upon Operas and Musick in England* (1709), who was an opponent not of opera in the Italian style but of the debased form in which it was introduced to England.[6] This did not worry the public, whose appetite had no doubt been whetted by travellers' tales.

[3] This was a sore point with Colley Cibber, who in his *Apology* (1740) complained that the acoustic made actors' voices sound 'like the Gabbling of so many People in the lofty Isles in a Cathedral', though 'the Tone of a Trumpet, or the Swell of an Eunoch's holding note, 'tis true, might be sweetn'd by it'.

[4] According to Milhous and Hume it was prepared or commissioned by Vanbrugh but stolen by Rich.

[5] Two of his sketches for *Arsinoe* are reproduced by P. Hope-Wallace, *A Pictorial History of Opera* (London, 1959), no. 15, and H. C. Wolff, *Oper: Szene und Darstellung von 1600 bis 1900* (Leipzig, 1968, plate 107).

[6] Lindgren, 'Parisian Patronage of Performers', n. 13, identified him with Handel's future collaborator Nicola Haym on the basis of an attribution to 'Seignior H— or some Creature of his' in Charles Gildon's life of Betterton (1710). This seems improbable. Haym was associated with Clayton and Charles Dieupart in the promotion of *Arsinoe*, as they claimed in their joint letters to *The Spectator* of 26 Dec. 1711 and 18 Jan. 1712 (see Deutsch, 46–8). They were indignant about their later exclusion from London opera: 'As we were the Persons who introduced Operas, we think it a groundless Imputation that we should set up against the Opera it self'.

Vanbrugh opened his theatre on 9 April with *Gli amori d'Ergasto*, a short pastoral opera by Jakob Greber, which on the testimony of the libretto and Congreve's epilogue ('In sweet Italian strains our Shepherds sing') was sung wholly in Italian, 'by a new set of Singers, arriv'd from Italy'. They are not named in the libretto, and no one has succeeded in identifying them. They were probably not imported but recruited locally, and doubtless included Margherita de l'Epine, who was Greber's mistress, and perhaps her sister Maria Gallia and Joanna Maria Lindelheim, known as the Baroness. The opera was a complete failure, running for only five performances. It may have been weak in spectacle because Vanbrugh's theatre was not yet fully equipped.

In the following season, while Rich continued to make hay with *Arsinoe* at Drury Lane, Vanbrugh introduced *The British Enchanters* by Eccles and Corbett (21 February 1706), a semiopera on the Amadis story—the first for five years and almost the last—followed on 7 March by *The Temple of Love*, 'A Pastoral Opera English'd from the Italian' by Giuseppe Saggione (Fedeli), Maria Gallia's husband, and on 5 April by *The Wonders in the Sun*, 'a Comical Opera' consisting of ballads put together by Thomas Durfey. The first was moderately successful (twelve performances), the other two abject failures (two and five performances). By this time Rich had gone further ahead with *Camilla* (Drury Lane, 30 March), an arrangement by Haym of Giovanni Bononcini's Naples opera of 1696, for which he obtained an advance subscription of 1,400 guineas.[7] This was the first full-length all-sung opera; Owen Swiney, who had a hand in adapting or translating the libretto, described it in his dedication as 'design'd to introduce a foreign Composition that may serve at present to give us a Taste of the *Italian* Musick, and in Time prove a Foil to the *English*'. Thanks to the superior quality of the music it soon eclipsed *Arsinoe* and was to become the most successful all-sung opera in England, not only of its period but of the entire century, attaining 111 performances by 1728. It was first given entirely in English, with new recitatives by Haym and doggerel verse dubbed on the arias; after the arrival of the castratos the performance became bilingual before reverting to English in 1716. It is significant that Haym was unusually faithful to his source (54 of the 56 arias were by Bononcini, all but one from the original Naples version[8]), and that this was the only opera of the period to win the approval of the author of *A Critical Discourse*.   *

By the summer of 1706 the theatres had been plunged into such a whirlpool of faction and controversy by rivalry between the managements, the rapacity of Rich, disputes between actors and singers over precedence, pay and benefits (two leading ladies postponed a revival of *Camilla* in November 1707 by refusing to sing), and devious manoeuvres of every description, as to provoke repeated interventions from the Lord Chamberlain. Price has done much to disentangle the motives for these upheavals. The basic trouble seems to have been that both companies endeavoured to cash in on the new operas while continuing to play traditional drama, and there were not enough resources to maintain two sets of singers and actors. In September 1706 an order from the Lord Chamberlain confined opera to Drury Lane, while

---

[7] For the subscription system see p. 152.
[8] Documentary information about Bononcini in this chapter and later is taken from L. Lindgren, *A Bibliographic Scrutiny* (Ann Arbor, 1974).

Vanbrugh leased the Haymarket to Swiney for spoken plays. The ensuing season saw two operas at Drury Lane: Clayton's *Rosamond* (libretto by Addison) on 4 March, a notorious failure taken off after three nights, and *Thomyris Queen of Scythia*, a pasticcio assembled by Heidegger and Pepusch with English words dubbed by P. A. Motteux, on 1 April. This was largely modelled on *Camilla*, and threatened to repeat its success (43 performances by 1729); Rich again obtained a substantial subscription, this time of 1,200 guineas. It was sung in English, except that the part of the hero was shared between Hughes and Valentini (Valentino Urbani), the first castrato to appear on the London stage, who used his native tongue.

There is some doubt about the date and the circumstances of Valentini's arrival. He is usually considered to have made his début (in *Camilla*) on 8 March, but may have appeared as early as December 1706. Mrs Manley's preface to her play *Almyna*, performed three times only (16–18 December), complained that it was put on 'at so ill-fated a Time, viz. The immediate Week before Christmas between Devotion and *Camilla* (the Eunuch having then never Sung but once)'. Valentini may have been engaged by Rich through Haym, who among other things acted as a musical agent, but it is more than likely that some members of the nobility were active behind the scenes. They tried for a larger fish than a castrato. Early in 1707 Lord Halifax, a former Lord Treasurer and a great patron of the arts, acting through the Earl of Manchester, British ambassador in Vienna, sent an invitation to Bononcini, then at the height of his fame as court composer to the Emperor Joseph I. Bononcini preferred not to leave a powerful patron. No doubt he was to recall the invitation later. Meanwhile he sent scores, which were to form the basis of more than one London pasticcio.

The separation of the dramatic and operatic repertories was a logical step. It ensured the survival of straight drama and Italianate opera, but at the cost of knocking out both the precarious semiopera and a more tender growth, native English opera after the Italian manner. *Rosamond* was a poor representative of this; a much finer work, *Semele* by Congreve and Eccles, was ready by January 1707. Although Congreve had been associated with Vanbrugh at the Queen's Theatre (he withdrew at the end of 1705), the Lord Chamberlain's decree required its transference to Drury Lane, where it was presumably destined for performance in the spring. Either the failure of *Rosamond* or the success of *Thomyris*—or perhaps a combination of both—squeezed it out, with the result that the period's one English opera of genuine quality had to wait two and a half centuries for its first performance.

On the last day of 1707, at the direct instigation of Vanbrugh, the Lord Chamberlain again stirred the broth, transferring the actors to Drury Lane and the musicians (together with *Camilla* and *Thomyris*) to the Haymarket, which thus became London's first opera-house, a role it was to retain for nearly a century. The arrangement took effect from 13 January 1708. Vanbrugh's personal management, with Swiney as his deputy, lasted less than five months and was a financial disaster, but its influence on the future of opera in London was crucial. Since he worked closely with Coke, this short season is well documented in the Vice Chamberlain's papers, more so indeed than any other. They reveal his artistic plans, his estimates of expenses, and his difficulties. Many of these were due to Rich, who when he discovered what was afoot refused to honour outstanding bills. His high-handed behaviour—

Swiney, formerly his manager at Drury Lane, called him 'as tyrannycall as Lewis Le Grand'[9]—had already in November driven some of his singers to mutiny. He now left Vanbrugh with commitments he felt bound to respect; one of them was the engagement, through Haym, of the alto castrato Giuseppe Cassani, who proved a total disaster. For a salary of £437.10s.od. including expenses (more than four times the average pay of a leading actor), plus a bottle of wine a day and an unspecified gift to be chosen by two noblemen (one hopes he never received it), he sang twice only in *Camilla* in February 1708, was 'hissed so severely that he does not intend to act any more' (Addison to Manchester, 24 Feb.[10]), and at the end of the season left massive debts behind him.[11]

It is difficult not to conclude that Vanbrugh was very unlucky. On 27 July 1708, after abandoning the enterprise, he gave Manchester several reasons for his failure: the season was half over when he opened; the Lord Chamberlain, expecting great profits after the experience of *Camilla* and *Thomyris*, 'Oblig'd us to Extravagant Allowances'; the town, in the same belief, refused to support a subscription; and though the pit and boxes were reasonably full, the gallery stayed at home. The prospect of rich pickings led local singers to make exorbitant demands: Catherine Tofts asked twenty guineas a night (nearly three times as much as Valentini), the secondary soprano Maria Gallia 700 guineas for the season. Twenty-three orchestral players applied for nearly three times the usual fees. Vanbrugh appealed to Coke 'to make our musitians both accept reasonable sallarys and be carefull in their Business',[12] but even after beating them down he found himself heavily out of pocket, to the tune of £606 by 8 March and £1,146 by 7 April. He had planned to mount two new operas, also part of his inheritance from Rich: *Love's Triumph* (arranged by Valentini from a pastoral produced for Ottoboni at Rome in 1705, with text by Motteux and recitatives by Dieupart) and *Pirro e Demetrio* (Haym, based on Alessandro Scarlatti's opera of 1694, text arranged and translated by Swiney). Only the first materialized, on 26 February; after a successful first night it lost support and died after eight performances. Vanbrugh had budgeted for 64 performances; early in May, after giving 28 (one more followed later), he threw up the sponge, leasing the theatre and all its stock to Swiney.[13]

He had made several attempts to escape from his impasse, among them a proposal of partnership with three senior musicians (Dieupart, Haym, and Pepusch) and three singers. On 21 February he petitioned the Queen through Marlborough and the Lord Chamberlain for £1,000 to bring over from Italy 'one man and one woman Singers of the first Rate, with one of the best masters for the direction and Government of the Orchestra', naming the great castrato Nicolini, Signora Santini,[14] and the composer Luigi Mancia.   *
Queen Anne, unlike George I twelve years later, was not interested. Three days later Vanbrugh urged Manchester 'to give your Self the trouble of

[9] Letter to Colley Cibber, 5 Oct. 1706 (*Coke Papers*, 11).

[10] Duke of Manchester, *Court & Society from Elizabeth to Anne*... (London, 1864) ii. 291.

[11] Tabulated by Haym in a letter referring euphemistically to Cassani as 'questo Virtuoso infortunato' (*Coke Papers*, 14–15).

[12] Ibid. 74.

[13] For fourteen years, according to Vanbrugh's later statement which wrongly dates the transaction 1707 (*Coke Papers*, 233). Swiney, by then bankrupt and living abroad, resigned the lease on 10 May 1714: K. Downes, *Vanbrugh* (London, 1977), 180.

[14] Perhaps the soprano Santa Stella, who married the composer Antonio Lotti.

making the Agreement', offering £1,000 on his own account. Mancia proved too expensive; on 16 March Vanbrugh suggested 'some Young Agreeable Person of a Woman, who not yet in great Vogue, yet promis'd fair to grow to it, who wou'd come for an Allowance of 80 or 100 pounds a Year, it might be of great Service to bring downe the Pride & Charge of Our Present Singing Ladys,[15] who Cost the House four hundred pounds a Year apiece'. He had heard of one Redjana at Leghorn,[16] and two months later (11 May, after his retirement) reverted to the idea if 'a Young, improving Woman cou'd be found that had a good Person and Action, and that might be esteem'd as good a Singer as Margarita'. He claimed support among the nobility, and was confident of 'bringing the Queen into a Scheme' if the top voices were obtainable. In his letter of 27 July, after trying to account for his failure, he could still add: 'And yet I don't doubt but Operas will Settle and thrive in London'.

Vanbrugh's confidence did not benefit his pocket, but it brought results: Nicolini arrived with Manchester in the late autumn. Whereas Vanbrugh had inherited the useless Cassani from Rich, he bequeathed the greatest singer of the age to Swiney. From that time, though the opera was never profitable (London had yet to learn that without a subsidy it can never survive for long), the taste was formed and the train laid that was to lead directly to Handel's engagement.

The bewildering changes of management in the next few seasons have required tabular statements for their elucidation.[17] Swiney, William Collier (a Tory MP), and Aaron Hill became involved in a kind of musical chairs, with the Lord Chamberlain pulling strings in the background. Swiney as Vanbrugh's lessee managed the Haymarket in 1708/9 and 1709/10, during the latter season with a trio of actor-managers; this recombination of the genres produced constant friction and was promptly abandoned. At Drury Lane the obstreperous Rich was finally silenced by the Lord Chamberlain in June 1709. Collier with Hill as manager controlled the theatre in the following season till it was closed by a riot, in which Hill was ejected, in June 1710. In November that year the Lord Chamberlain switched Collier and Hill to the Haymarket, and Swiney (who had quarrelled with Nicolini) and the three actor-managers to Drury Lane. Opera remained the prerogative of the Haymarket throughout. Later convulsions are mentioned in the next chapter.

All the operas between *Rosamond* and *Rinaldo* were pasticcios processed locally from Italian materials (Rich called *Thomyris* 'this Medley Opera'). *Love's Triumph, Pirro e Demetrio*, with which Swiney launched his new season and Nicolini's London career on 14 December 1708, and *Clotilda* (2 March 1709, assembled by Heidegger from music by many composers) were sung macaronically in a mixture of English and Italian. The remainder, except for detached entr'actes in *Almahide*, were wholly in Italian: *Almahide* (10 January 1710, Haym based on Bononcini and Ariosti), *L'Idaspe fedele* (23 March 1710, Nicolini based on Mancini, whose music he had brought from Naples), and *Etearco* (10 January 1711, Haym based on Bononcini). Three of these made little mark, but *Pirro e Demetrio* had 59 performances by 1717, *Almahide* 25 by 1712, and *L'Idaspe fedele* 46 by 1716. They owed much of their success to

---

[15] Catherine Tofts and Margherita de L'Epine.
[16] Perhaps Giovanna Albertini detta la Reggiana, who sang at Venice in 1708–9 and 1712.
[17] See *Coke Papers*, xix–xx, and Price, 'The Critical Decade'.

Nicolini, and something no doubt to the Venetian scene designers Marco Ricci and G. A. Pellegrini engaged by Vanbrugh. With one exception, noted in the next chapter, all subsequent operas at the Haymarket were in Italian.

Much of the music for *Almahide*, as Heidegger's preface to the libretto makes clear, was provided by Count Gallas, Viennese ambassador in London and a friend and later patron of Bononcini. Haym similarly indicated that he received *Etearco* from Halifax,[18] who 'encouraged [him] to prepare it for the *English* Stage'. Haym added that 'it is by the Assistance of such generous Patrons, that the *English* Theatre is arriv'd at its present Grandeur, and that it will shortly be in a condition to out-rival even those of Venice; especially if we, who are concern'd, resolve to second the great Abilities and Intentions of that ingenious Person, who has at present the Direction of the Operas'. The last clause refers to Aaron Hill, for a short time an important figure in the London operatic world,[19] and by implication to *Rinaldo*.

The English party had lost the battle long before 1711, though abetted by the clever journalism of Steele and Addison they continued to snipe at the Italians.[20] They had obvious targets in macaronic performance and the public's increasing interest in the singers, especially the castratos, at the expense of music and drama. Other motives were involved, including xenophobia and hatred of Popery. English semiopera found a disgruntled champion in the critic John Dennis, whose muddled aesthetics are apparent in the first sentence of his preface to *An Essay on the Opera after the Italian Manner...* (1706): 'This small Treatise is only levell'd against those Operas which are entirely Musical, for those which are Dramatical may be partly defended by the Examples of the Antients'. He complained that 'Sense upon the Stage seems to have given place to Sound', and—using the same word with an almost opposite meaning—that 'Audiences have become more capable of a Pleasure of Sense than of a Delight of Reason'. He found Italian opera at the same time 'soft and effeminate' and 'Barbarous and Gothick'. In *An Essay upon Public Spirit* (1711) Dennis opined that 'A Musical Voice is natural only to some Species of Birds, but always accidental to Men: for which reason a Cock-Nightingale sings better than *Nicolini*, nay or than *Siface* himself'. He was merely carrying to absurd lengths the Philistine fallacy behind most eighteenth-century music criticism, that the word is morally superior to the note.

Heidegger answered one batch of critics, though perhaps not as they would have wished, in a notice 'To the Reader' in the libretto of *Almahide*:

Several People of Quality, and Encouragers of the Opera's, having found fault with the Absurdity of those Scenes, where the Answers are made in *English*, to those that sing in *Italian*, and in *Italian* to those that recite in *English*, and it being impossible to have

[18] Halifax owned a score of *Camilla* with his bookplate dated 1702, now in the British Library. Lindgren points out (*A Bibliographic Scrutiny*, 232) that every London opera from *Thomyris* to *Antioco* (12 Dec. 1711), except of course *Rinaldo*, contained one or more arias by Bononcini.

[19] Thirteen days older than Handel, Hill had returned in 1703 from an extensive tour of the Middle East and embarked on an adventurous career by no means confined to music and letters. He enjoyed the double advantage of the Earl of Peterborough's protection and a rich wife. See Dorothy Brewster, *Aaron Hill, Poet, Dramatist, Projector* (New York, 1913).

[20] Addison came to accept the justification for recitative. 'However this *Italian* Method of acting in *Recitativo* might appear at first hearing, I cannot but think it much more just than that which prevailed in our *English* Opera before this Innovation: The Transition from an Air to Recitative Musick being more natural, than the passing from a Song to plain and ordinary Speaking, which was the common Method in *Purcell*'s Operas' (*Spectator*, 3 Apr. 1711).

the whole Opera perform'd in *English*, because the chief Actors would not be able to perform their parts in our language: I hope I shall be pardoned, if I have made all the Parts in *Italian*.

Heidegger tried to appease the natives by interposing a comic *Intermede* in English between the acts, a survival (as on the continent) of the comic sub-plots that had been a feature of early opera.[21] The castratos of course offered an easy target, especially to those with prurient minds, but they soon soared out of range. Two, sometimes three, sang from the beginning of the 1708 season. When unavailable they were replaced by women: Jane Barbier made her début as Valentini's substitute in *Almahide* on 10 November 1711.

The pasticcio form, to us an obvious weakness, met with little criticism except from the author of *A Critical Discourse*, who railed against 'Swiss Operas', meaning those promoted by Heidegger. 'Operas patched up out of the Compositions of several different Masters are not likely to succeed, unless they are prepared by some Person that is capable of making an Opera himself.' He added some practical and pertinent recommendations: the composer, if not personally responsible for all the music, should be able to reconcile 'different Styles so artfully as to make 'em pass for one'; should learn the capabilities of his performers and write music suitable to the talents of each; should avoid a servile imitation of Italian compositions, 'since an Opera with no more than ten or twelve good Airs in it will pass in *Italy*, whereas here in *England* five or six bad ones are sufficient to damn the whole Composition'; and should pay as much attention to the instrumental parts as to the melody. 'The Airs ought to be studied without being stiff, melancholy without being heavy, and lively without being trivial: there ought to be something new and uncommon, sweet and entertaining in every part.' This could be a prescription for *Rinaldo*. The opinions expressed here and elsewhere suggest that the anonymous author may have been Aaron Hill.

It is difficult to assess the music of the first London operas owing to the fragmentary nature of the surviving material, and the absence of full scores makes it impossible to judge them as works of art, if a pasticcio can qualify for that rank. There is the added disadvantage that it is not always possible to identify the composer. For the earlier works in particular the arias were printed in mutilated form, generally voice and bass, with truncated or missing ritornellos, no inner parts, and minimal figuring. Even at that period an opera did not live by tunes alone. By universal consent Clayton's contributions are beneath contempt; no one is likely to dispute the verdict on *Arsinoe* in *A Critical Discourse*: 'There is nothing in it but a few Sketches of antiquated *Italian* Airs, so mangled and sophisticated, that . . . it ought to be called the Hospital of the old Decrepid *Italian* Opera's.' Saggione's arias for *The Temple of Love* are an improvement, especially the first in the Walsh print, 'Charming Roses'. A bird song for Maria Gallia was printed with an obbligato recorder part played by Paisible. Standards rose with the introduction of music by more respectable composers, though it was often unrepresentative of their latest work. *Camilla* is the only opera of the period for which a London score exists (RCM 779); it shows that Haym, for the benefit of his English audience, moved away from secco recitative towards arioso with a more active bass. It is also the only opera for which *A Critical Discourse* had a good word ('the Musick admirable, and

---

[21] *Love's Triumph* was the last London opera to introduce comic characters in the main action.

Perform'd in a more regular Method than any of the former'). Bononcini appears as a graceful melodist, apt in declamation but addicted to stereotyped harmonic patterns and automatic sequences and repetitions. This forces home the catchiness of his best tunes while emphasizing their rhythmic squareness, as in 'Fair Dorinda'.

Ex. 16

Above all, the music lacks dramatic vigour, paying more attention to smoothness and regularity than to the expression of emotion or character. The B sections of the arias are often more interesting than the first part, and not so much contrasted as developed from the same material. Bononcini had a light touch for comic episodes, and there is an effective scene for the heroine at the start of Act II building up through accompanied recitative to a revenge aria. In *Thomyris*, *A Critical Discourse* found 'fifteen or sixteen Airs that were really good . . the Remnant an insipid Miscellany'. The liveliest songs are for the two comic characters. The third act of *Love's Triumph*, attributed to Bononcini, is superior to the first two, with some pretty pastoral ditties.

The publication of the songs in *Pirro e Demetrio* was less exiguous than usual, and distinguished Haym's from Scarlatti's. The former are correct but dull, though as a cellist he provided them with contrapuntally active basses. Scarlatti's, as we should expect, are much less regular than the others, with capricious twists in the melodies and a good deal of dissonance. Sicilianos and fast 3/8 pieces with frequent changes of tempo in either section are common. Act II ends with an excellent arioso ('Veder parmi un'ombra nera') and duet ('Un contento nel mio core'). *Clotilda* too is full of sicilianos, sometimes ill-adapted to their context; it seems to have been a multifarious as well as a hastily compiled pasticcio, with arias in the last two acts ascribed in a libretto at Bologna to eight different composers. Isabella (Catherine Tofts) has an amusing ironical aria proclaiming that 'Honour is a Virgin's Treasure which unlawful Love destroys' but clearly not meaning a word of it. *Almahide* introduced music from the recent Vienna operas of Bononcini and Ariosti and a Bononcini overture in almost Handelian style ending with a binary Gigue. The arias for castratos and leading ladies alike are more elaborate in coloratura but still weak in dramatic profile. Nearly all are in da capo form, the slow ones superior to the fast. Act I ends with a successful double-*Affekt* aria, 'A me tu nieghi amor', an alternation between *Adagio* and *Presto* with solo oboe acting like a trumpet, in which Celinda (Isabella Girardeau) declares her love and vows vengeance. Even when the music is attractive in itself it seems to exist outside the plot. Burney found it mechanical, 'neither dramatic, passionate, pathetic, nor graceful. If, indeed, the words imply sorrow, it is *slow*; and in a chearful scene, it is *quick*; but there is little enthusiasm and no elegance.'

The songs in *Idaspe*, mostly by Mancini, are a pleasant surprise, with a feeling for contrast and mood that contrives to bring the characters to at least momentary life. There is a striking scene at the start of Act II, where the heroine Berenice (L'Epine) longs for sleep to soothe her misery. Her cavatina 'Selve ombrose' has a descending chromatic bass like a lament, a continuously moving ostinato in quavers on the strings, and even crotchets for the voice. The aria 'Vieni, O sonno' is a G minor Largo in which a rocking semiquaver figure on the strings paints her objective. The famous lion episode in Act III, however ridiculous it appeared to Addison, is not negligible as music, especially the brief farewell for the lovers before the hero strangles the lion. Uffenbach heard this opera on 10 June 1710 and paid tribute to Nicolini, L'Epine, and the orchestra, consisting mostly of Frenchmen and Germans under Pepusch. *Etearco* exceptionally used Bononcini's recitatives. The arias once more illustrate his gift for catchy tunes, which in the absence of harmonic and rhythmic variety he often runs to death.

One or two significant facts emerge from this brief survey of Italian opera in London before *Rinaldo*. While the better singers found an enthusiastic audience, the more sophisticated listeners were critical of the music. The most successful opera, *Camilla*, was the most faithful to the original score. Although attempts had been made to import a leading continental composer, all the operas were local adaptations of foreign material, chiefly from Venice, Vienna, or Naples. However skilfully this had been done, they were no longer under the control of their authors. Above all, no composer, whether of major or minor stature, had yet composed an Italian opera specifically for the London stage.

Additional Notes

* (p. 143) A shortened version of Haym's arrangement, the only surviving score with English words, is published in the series *Music for London Entertainment 1660-1800* (London, 1990), edited by Lowell Lindgren. According to Lindgren's Introduction Haym retained 51 of Bononcini's set pieces, cut three, and substituted three of his own.

* (p. 144) According to a letter of William Clelland dated 6 December 1705 in the Scottish Record Office (quoted by Calhoun Winton at the Maryland Handel Festival, 12 November 1989) *Semele* had already been composed.

* (p. 145) Vanbrugh called him 'Manchini', confusing him with the Neopolitan Francesco Mancini.

* (p. 147) They came over with Manchester in autumn 1708 and designed scenery for *Clotilda* (used again for revivals of *Pirro e Demetrio* and *Camilla*) and *L'Idaspe fedele*.

THE FIRST LONDON PERIOD, 1711–1717

ON leaving Italy early in 1710 Handel travelled north by way of Innsbruck to Hanover. There was keen competition for his services. He had recommendations to the Elector of Hanover from his younger brother Prince Ernst and his Master of the Horse, Baron Kielmansegg, and from Ferdinando de' Medici in Florence to his brother-in-law the Elector Palatine at Düsseldorf, and (according to Mainwaring) an invitation to London from the Earl of Manchester. His intention was apparently to make for Düsseldorf and compose an opera for the Elector Palatine's court,[1] but the future King George I got in his bid first, offering such easy terms that Handel could hardly refuse. In Mainwaring's words 'he had leave to be absent for a twelve-month or more, if he chose it; and to go whithersoever he pleased'. He was appointed Kapellmeister to the Elector of Hanover on 16 June. He undoubtedly had the support of the influential diplomat and composer Agostino Steffani, whom he had met in Italy and who was or had been employed by both Electors; but Handel's reputation and personal qualities were such that he may hardly have needed it.[2] After visiting his family at Halle and paying a courtesy visit to Düsseldorf he arrived in London towards the end of 1710. There can be little doubt that the English nobility had already obtained for him a commission to compose an opera for the Queen's Theatre.

During Handel's first years in London the opera season generally ran from November to June, though this was by no means regular. At first there were two performances a week; in 1710 the Lord Chamberlain ordered Drury Lane not to act on Wednesdays, in order to help the opera, but both theatres played on Saturdays. The mid-week day was soon changed to Tuesday and varied in later seasons, being dropped altogether when business was poor. Very occasionally, for example during the visit of Prince Eugene of Savoy early in

[1] G. Schnath, *Briefwechsel der Kurfürstin von Hannover mit dem Preussischen Königshause* (Berlin and Leipzig, 1927), 187 (letter of 4 June 1710).

[2] Ibid. 189 (letter of 14 June). It would be interesting to know if Steffani showed him the score of his latest opera *Tassilone* (produced at Düsseldorf in January 1709), a work of considerable power and orchestral elaboration. Steffani had been Kapellmeister at Hanover, chiefly concerned with the court opera, from 1688 to 1696. He was there in June 1710 in his diplomatic capacity. (D. Burrows, 'Handel and Hanover', *Bach, Handel, Scarlatti: Tercentenary Essays* (Cambridge, 1985), 38.)

1712, the opera played three times a week. Performances usually began at 6 p.m. in winter and 7 p.m. in summer, or later if the opera was short. In hot weather the air could become so stifling as to require postponement or cancellation; this happened in June 1715 (King's and Drury Lane) and June 1717, when a Lincoln's Inn Fields performance of *Camilla* was put off. The Haymarket management did their best to keep the theatre cool. The advertisement for *Clotilda* on 16 May 1711 announced that 'by reason of the Hot Weather, the Waterfall will play the best part of the Opera'. This had begun as a stage attraction; subsequent announcements refer to it as 'The Water Scene', and it was presumably the 'New Cascade after the Italian Manner' first advertised for *Pirro e Demetrio* on 16 December 1710, when the audience can scarcely have been in need of refrigeration. Hot weather brought the waterfall into play on a number of later occasions, for example in *Antioco* on 28 May and 14 June 1712.

As one would expect from operatic history, the finances were always precarious. Queen Anne preferred playing cards to attending the opera, and although the Hanoverians showed more interest there was no subsidy before the foundation of the Royal Academy. Members of the nobility may have offered some private subvention. To ensure a reasonable return the management whenever possible operated a subscription system, especially for new productions. On the usual arrangement each subscriber paid ten guineas, which entitled him to three tickets for each of six performances, the number of tickets in the pit and boxes being limited generally to 400.[3] This was for the subscribers' comfort; the pit was equipped only with unnumbered benches, and more persons could be squeezed in for a popular opera on an ordinary night. The total capacity of the theatre is difficult to estimate. Emmett L. Avery[4] gives a figure of 900, excluding the footmen in the upper gallery (whose duty it had been to keep places downstairs for their employers); this is not very different from Judith Milhous's estimate.[5] A document of December 1710 notes: 'Opera/ye Pitt with rails should hold 268 of which within ye Rails 51'.[6] Privileged spectators liked to stand on the stage itself, a practice condemned by the Lord Chamberlain on 13 November 1711 and several times deprecated by the management on the ground that they obstructed the machinery and ran the risk of personal injury.

Prices of admission, naturally higher than at Drury Lane or Lincoln's Inn Fields, varied from night to night. Normal charges, 'ye usual Opera Prices' of the Colman Opera Register, were: boxes 8*s.*, pit 5*s.*, first gallery 2*s.* 6*d.*, upper gallery 1*s.* 6*d.*, stage boxes 10*s.* 6*d.* For benefits and other special occasions pit and boxes were put together, and sometimes two benches in the pit railed in; they were then charged at 10*s.* 6*d.*, with stage boxes raised to 15*s.* , first gallery to 4*s.* or 5*s.* and upper gallery to 2*s.* These were also the rates for subscription nights, apart from the accommodation for subscribers. Benefit performances had originated in the straight theatre not as a bonus but as a means for recovering arrears of salary. The practice was for the management to retain

---

[3] Presumably in addition to the thirty shareholders who had paid Vanbrugh 100 guineas towards the building of the theatre. This guaranteed them free admission.

[4] *The London Stage*, ii (1700–29), xxix.

[5] 'The Capacity of Vanbrugh's Theatre in the Haymarket', *Theatre History Studies*, iv (1984), 38–46. She suggests a variable total from 750 (comfortable) to 940 (crowded).

[6] *Coke Papers*, 161. The same document gives incomplete audience figures for *Idaspe* on 22 November and *Pirro e Demetrio* on 9 December. For the significance of the rails see below.

enough of the takings to cover the cost of opening the theatre.[7] Avery estimates this at £40 for plays and £53–9 for operas; but the 1716/17 accounts, quoted below, show that some singers were charged as much as £130. A popular singer received handsome extra gifts from his (or her) admirers among the nobility. If the theatre was empty the beneficiary could make a loss, which he had to reimburse; Berenstadt complained to Zamboni that his 1717 benefit brought him no profit, though he wrote later in the year that he would be happy to return if offered a salary of £250 and a free benefit.[8] By regulation of the Lord Chamberlain the benefit season began in March, usually after the subscriptions. At the Haymarket there were at least five such nights a season, and in 1716/17 as many as eight.[9] Each leading singer enjoyed a benefit (the Boschis shared one in 1711); sometimes one was awarded to the orchestra and the box-keepers.[10] Handel had a benefit on 16 May 1713; this was in unusual circumstances after the absconding Swiney had been replaced by a collective management. He received £73. 10s. 11d., approximately the same as the principal singers, though the unfortunate Mrs Barbier had to be content with £15. The singers had already become involved in political faction. Lady Hervey told her husband in a letter of 26 April 1711 that for *Rinaldo* on the previous (ordinary) night the theatre 'was as full as ever I saw it at a subscription, but that was by way of party, in order to get it empty on Saturday'. Saturday's performance was a benefit for Elisabetta Pilotti-Schiavonetti, who was in the service of the Dowager Electress Sophia of Hanover. On the corresponding occasion a year later (5 April 1712) Lady Hervey was careful to attend 'because poor Pilota has great faction against her'.

Singers of course were the most expensive commodity on the Haymarket's books, especially after Nicolini's arrival. The most detailed of Vanbrugh's estimates in January 1708[11] gives a total budget of £7,320, of which £2,400 was for singers, £1,030 for the orchestra, £800 for '8 Dancers & their Cloaths', and £1,275 for '2 New Operas Cloaths & scenes'. Valentini's contract (15 January) was for 400 guineas plus another 100 for arranging the score of *Love's Triumph*. In April 1709 Swiney made a three-year agreement with Nicolini giving him an annual salary of 800 guineas plus 150 for each new opera he arranged. In 1710/11, the season of *Rinaldo*, singers' salaries amounted to £3,097. 10s. 0d., of which £860 went to Nicolini, £537. 10s. 0d. to Valentini, £700 to Francesca and Giuseppe Boschi, £500 to Pilotti and her husband (a cellist in the orchestra), and £300 to Isabella Girardeau. In 1712/13, without Nicolini, the total fell to £2,482, Pellegrini receiving £645, Valentini and Pilotti the same as before, L'Epine £400, Barbier £300, and Manina £100.[12] Handel received £430, presumably for his two operas that season. In October 1714 Heidegger agreed to pay Anastasia Robinson £500

---

[7] In several financial statements of this period the yield from a benefit is apparently included in a singer's salary. This may have been some special arrangement when the coffers were empty.

[8] Lindgren, 'La carriera di Gaetano Berenstadt, contralto evirato (*ca.* 1690–1735)', *RIM* xix (1984), 45–112.

[9] Heidegger's was not advertised; see p. 164.

[10] Receipts in connection with opera benefits *c.*1717, signed by Diana Vico, Anastasia Robinson, Nicolini, and others, are in the Hanover archives. That for the orchestra's benefit in June 1717 is signed by the violinist Francis Dahuron. (Burrows, 'Handel and Hanover', 46, n.38.)

[11] *Coke Papers*, 77.

[12] Ibid. 199 f. These figures include money still owing; one assumes they received it in the end.

for the season plus a benefit. This was remarkably high for a young singer in her second operatic season, but Anastasia was the darling of the aristocracy.[13] Heidegger even promised that 'in case I should be a gainer by the Operas I oblidge me self to make her a present of a gold Watch'.[14] It is doubtful if she got it.

The composition of the orchestra varied slightly from season to season. It generally numbered between twenty-five and thirty, with an average strength of ten violins (divided equally between firsts and seconds, but two were sometimes listed as *ripieni*), two violas, five or six cellos or bass viols, one double-bass, two oboes, three (sometimes four) bassoons, one trumpet, and two harpsichords, one of whom alternated with one of the cellists. A direction in December 1710 noted: 'Heyam [Haym] & Pilotti to play every night and to take their places att ye Harpischord by Turns'.[15] Their pay varied between 8s. and 35s. a night, the highest going to the harpsichord and first cello (generally Dieupart and Haym, sometimes Pepusch), followed by the double-bass, Saggione.[16] Significant points here, confirmed repeatedly by the evidence of Handel's scores, are the weakness of the middle parts (the violas were not only heavily outnumbered but received the lowest fee, which may explain why more than one of them took on the job of copyist[17]) and the great strength of the bass department. There were always more bassoons than oboes; the latter doubled on recorders and flutes as required. Extra trumpets must have been imported for *Rinaldo*. In 1716/17 the timpanist was an extra, hired for 5s. a night, perhaps from the army; this may have been regular practice.

In November 1710 Swiney, with Vanbrugh's consent, sublet the Haymarket to Collier, who delegated the management to Aaron Hill at a rental later estimated by Colley Cibber at £600 per annum. Swiney moved to Drury Lane with the three actor-managers, who presently got rid of him, though not before he had gone to court for a settlement. On or about 3 March 1711, only a few days after the production of *Rinaldo*, Collier, who seems to have been a restless, unreliable, and envious character,[18] entered the theatre by force and turned Hill out. Early in July Hill brought a legal action against Collier for allegedly appropriating £500 of the subscription money (which amounted to £3000 for *Etearco* and *Rinaldo* and should according to Hill have been used to pay artists and tradesmen), seizing the scenery and costumes, and making himself 'sole Master and director of the Theatre Royall'. The tradesmen then sued Hill. The case seems to have been settled out of court, but the trouble continued.[19] On 17 April 1712 the Lord Chamberlain issued a series of regulations, switching Collier to Drury Lane and Swiney back to the Haymarket, with special provisions to assist the

---

[13] Her position was unusual in several respects. Although she appeared frequently with the Italian company at the Haymarket, she never sang in English operas or masques.

[14] Ibid. 228.

[15] Ibid. 160.

[16] These figures are taken from several lists in the *Coke Papers* and one in Allardyce Nicoll, *A History of English Drama* (Cambridge, 1955), ii. 278–9. None of them refers to a season later than 1710/11. Haym and Dieupart had been excluded by December 1711, as they complained in the letters to *The Spectator* cited above (p. 142, n. 6). Haym was back in 1716/17.

[17] For Linike see p. xix. W. Armstrong copied a score of *Camilla* for the Duke of Bedford, for which he received £9. 9s. 5d. on 13 July 1708 (Lindgren, *A Bibliographic Scrutiny*, 717). Collier paid Linike £26 for the score and parts of *Rinaldo* (*Coke Papers*, 176; Deutsch, 40); he earned only 8s. or 10s. a night at the viola desk.

[18] Brewster, *Aaron Hill*.

[19] Hume and Milhous, 'The Haymarket Opera in 1711', *Early Music* xvii (1989), 523–37.

opera. Hill's place was taken by Heidegger, who had been connected with the opera as early as 1707,[20] perhaps as assistant manager.

From the artistic point of view the 1710/11 season was an undoubted success, thanks partly to *Rinaldo* but also to the strong roster of singers, including three castratos, two foreign sopranos, and Boschi and his wife, and to the enthusiasm of the young Aaron Hill, who was praised in *The British Apollo* of 4 December for his plan to beautify the Haymarket and make Great Britain 'Mistriss of the most Illustrious Theater in Europe'; the stage had already been considerably extended and new decorations were in hand.[21] *Etearco* and *Rinaldo* were given by subscription, and on at least two ordinary nights (20 March and 7 April) there were 'Two Benches in the Pit Rail'd in, at the Price of the Boxes', yielding a better return. Milhous and Hume take the survival of so many box-office reports for this season as evidence that the opera was 'foundering financially'.[22] At first it did not do too badly. Whereas in Vanbrugh's spring 1708 season the average receipts for twenty-three nights had been £127 against expenses of £177,[23] twelve of the first thirteen performances in 1710/11 brought in an average of £143, varying between £173 on the first night and £114 on the twelfth. These were all revivals at ordinary prices; new productions, especially *Rinaldo*,[24] must have taken appreciably more. There was a sharp decline towards the end of the season, after the subscriptions were over: at the performances between 17 March and 2 May the average fell to barely £104, with £166 for the best night and £57 for the worst (*Idaspe* on 7 April).

At the end of the season Handel returned to his duties at Hanover. He was on the continent from June 1711 to the late autumn of 1712, and again during the second half of 1716. Nothing is known of his activities between July 1713 and autumn 1714. He may have been living quietly at Burlington House; Mainwaring says he was in England, having outstayed his leave and exposed himself to retribution on the accession of his Elector as George I, a possibility he must have known was on the cards. He had missed the 1712 revival of *Rinaldo*, but it is curious that there was no attempt to repeat it in 1713/14, especially if he was in London; it was by far the most popular opera during the seven seasons covered by this chapter (see Table 2). Of the three operas he composed for the Queen's Theatre in this period, two appeared in 1712/13 and the third (*Amadigi*) very late in 1714/15, inspired perhaps by the return of Nicolini after an absence of nearly three years. There was no resident composer before 1720; the theatre preferred to rely almost exclusively on doctored imports and pasticcios, with the inevitable consequence that the librettos became progressively distorted and often ridiculous.

The 1711/12 season at first went reasonably well. Valentini and the Boschis had left and Nicolini arrived late; local and little-known singers were

---

[20] *Coke Papers*, 34 ff.

[21] Tilmouth, *RMA Research Chronicle* i (1961), 76.

[22] *Coke Papers*, 148, and, for the figures, 160–6 and 172–3. *The London Stage* (ii. 236 ff.) gives the first series less accurately and does not include the second.

[23] *Coke Papers*, 98. *The London Stage* (ii. lx) miscalculates the receipts.

[24] The gallery receipts for the fourth, fifth, and sixth nights (see p. 181) indicate a large attendance, estimated by Milhous and Hume at between 180 and 260 persons.

TABLE 2. Opera Performances at Queen's (King's) Theatre 1710–1717

	1710/11	1711/12	1712/13	1713/14	1714/15	1715/16	1716/17	Total
Idaspe (Mancini & others/Nicolini)	16	12			7	1		36
Pirro e Demetrio (Scarlatti & others/Haym)	9					10	2	21
Etearco (Bononcini/Haym)	7							7
Rinaldo (Handel)	15	9	2		11		10	47
Almahide (Bononcini, Ariosti & others/? Haym)	4	7						11
Clotilda (pasticcio/Heidegger)	3							3
Antioco (Gasparini & others/? Nicolini)		17						17
Ambleto (Gasparini & others/Nicolini)		7						7
Ercole (pasticcio/? Nicolini)		5						5
Calypso and Telemachus (Galliard)		5						5
Il pastor fido (Handel)			7					7
Dorinda (Pollarolo & others/Haym)			8 (? 10)	3				11 (? 13)
Teseo (Handel)			13					13
Emelinda (Gasparini & others/anon)			10	7	5			22
Creso (G. Polani & others/Haym)				12				12
Aminio (M. A. Ziani & others/anon)				9	6			15
Lucio Vero (Albinoni & others/Haym)					7	3		10
Amadigi (Handel)					6	6	5	17
Clearte (Scarlatti & others/Nicolini)						9	5	14
Venceslao (Mancini & others/Nicolini and/or Haym)							3	3
Tito Manlio (Ariosti, ? pasticcio)							7	7
Total	54	62	40 (? 42)	31	42	29	32	290 (? 292)

prominent, but in March a new castrato appeared in Benedetto Baldassari. While *Almahide*, *Idaspe*, and *Rinaldo* remained popular, of the four new productions only the first, *Antioco* (12 December), a pasticcio containing arias from three Gasparini operas (*Il più fedele frà i vassalli*, *La fede tradita e vendicata*, and *Antioco*) and one by Bononcini, attracted the public. This and the next opera, *Ambleto* (27 February), both given by subscription, had been brought by Nicolini from Venice, where they were staged in 1705. His part in each contained nearly a third of the arias, and he was certainly responsible for the arrangement; he signed the dedication of *Ambleto*. Heidegger justified his 'Presumption' in dedicating *Antioco* to the Countess of Burlington by pointing to 'the great success this Opera has found in *Italy*'. Both scores, like *Etearco*, were seasoned with arias from *Agrippina*, obtained presumably with Handel's consent (they were not imported by the original singers), and *Antioco* borrowed its overture. A striking feature of this opera was the incorporation in Act II of *Agrippina*'s great *scena* 'Pensieri, voi mi tormentate' sung by Elisabetta Pilotti-Schiavonetti as the heroine Arsinoe, who throughout much of the action pretends to be mad. It was followed by a big double-*Affekt* aria in which she alternately denounces a tyrant and declares her love for Antioco. Although Jane Barbier played one of the male parts, when Baldassari arrived he replaced the second woman (L'Epine).[25] Castratos often sang female roles in Italy, especially in Rome, but this appears to have been the only instance in London.

Ambleto was derived not from Shakespeare but from his source, Saxo Grammaticus. While Hamlet feigns madness and stabs an intruder through the arras, and the usurping King is dispatched by the Polonius figure, there is no incest theme and no ghost, and the heroine, who commands an army and is pursued by most of the male characters, bears little detectable resemblance to Ophelia. The last scene takes place in 'Vineyards consecrated to Bacchus' with Hamlet dressed as the god (part of his act) and much play with poisoned and drugged potions. An extra Danish princess, Ildegarde, ensures that the amorous complications expected in *opera seria* are more than fulfilled. The music, printed by Walsh, does not name the composer; Burney thought it a pasticcio. Technically he was correct, but the Venice libretto makes it possible to disentangle the sources. Of the 42 pieces in the Walsh score 22 come from the Venice *Ambleto* and at least two more are probably Gasparini's since they appeared later in his *Vincislao* (Rome, 1716).[26] The London libretto has a few extra arias, at least one of them from 1705. Nicolini's insertions include the most beautiful movement in the opera, a tender siciliano ('Parto bel'idol mio') for Ildegarde early in Act II, where she is blatantly insincere. A lax feeling for character and unsuitability of the music to the emotions it is supposed to convey are equally characteristic of Gasparini's share. Valdemaro (= Fortinbras) abandons war for peace in a brilliant martial aria with flaring trumpet ('Tromba in campo e spada in guerra'). Hamlet, overhearing the evil plans of Fengone (= Claudius), warbles gracefully about a bee and a serpent in terms that would do nicely for nightingales. The aria in which, having stabbed an

*

---

[25] Unless the press announcement was wrong in naming the character.
[26] Information from Professor Martin Ruhnke. *Ambleto* was staged at Florence in December 1706 (with two comic characters, including Hamlet's nurse, and ten new arias, none used in London) and Verona the following year (in the Venice version). At Rome in 1715 it was sung by ten castratos.

intruder through the arras, he reproaches his mother and swears to avenge his father falls a long way below the situation. His first aria in Act II is an exception; the voice begins quite alone, and the abrupt alternations of mood and tempo do carry a hint of insanity (real or pretended).

The score is full of catchy tunes based on dance rhythms, with many sicilianos and jolly gigues and occasional touches of expressive Neapolitan harmony. Gasparini's phrase-lengths are less regular and his sequences less mechanical than Bononcini's. The slow arias in particular show a charming lyrical gift; the coloratura vengeance pieces are empty and conventional. Handel certainly knew the opera; apart from several anticipations of his later work, including 'He shall feed his flock', 'Every valley', and 'Già lo stringo' in *Orlando*, which could be coincidental, it was the source of about ten palpable borrowings, mostly in *Alexander Balus*, but also in *Arminio*, *Deidamia*, and *Jephtha*.[27]

Ambleto was succeeded by *Ercole* (3 May), a pasticcio of local manufacture executed in a great hurry. Swiney had now returned, and the tradesmen were again in arrears. Rossi obviously designed the libretto to exploit resources already in stock. Hercules has a fight with a lion, and we recognize many effects borrowed from *Rinaldo*: an enchanted palace (Alcina's, though she plays no part in the plot) which turns into 'a dark Desart' when Hercules disperses 'innumerable Spirits', a descending chariot drawn by two fire-spitting dragons for the abduction of Hippolyta, a 'Tempestuous Sea' with the palace 'at a distance upon a Rock', and much else. The opera was unusually short (it began at 7.30) and contained only four characters, sung by two women and two castratos, a precedent for the high-voice texture of *Amadigi*. It disappeared after five performances.

The last opera of the season (17 May), *Calypso and Telemachus* by Galliard and John Hughes, was unique: apart from *Rosamond* the only full-length English opera in the Italian style (that is with recitatives, though they do not survive) to reach the stage before 1730. The singers were all local, Jane Barbier and Mrs Pearson playing male parts and Leveridge the only low voice. Nicolini and Baldassari were still in London, but presumably could not manage the language, though Nicolini is said to have supported the opera. The circumstances in which the Queen's staged it are obscure. According to William Duncombe's preface to Hughes's poems (1735) and Johnson's life of Hughes it was sabotaged by the pro-Italian party, including the Lord Chamberlain, who had an Italian wife. Johnson, evidently relying on Duncombe (Hughes's brother-in-law and therefore not unprejudiced), accused the Italians of obtaining 'an obstruction of the profits'. There is no contemporary evidence for this. Duncombe says that the Lord Chamberlain was induced 'to take off the Subscription for it, and to open the House at the lowest Prices, or not at all'. Since the nobility were unlikely to subscribe, this seems a sensible precaution; admission was at the usual prices, with 'Benches in the Pit rail'd in at the price of the Boxes'. Moreover the authors were allowed a benefit. Hughes's libretto, and in particular his modest and sensible preface,[28] possess more distinction than Galliard's music, which is solid, worthy, and quite dull enough to account for its failure to capture the town.

[27] Roberts, *Handel Sources*, iv.
[28] See J. M. Knapp, 'A Forgotten Chapter in English Eighteenth-Century Opera', *M & L* xlii (1961), 4–16, where it is quoted in full.

Hughes's work inspired one of Johnson's most famous pronouncements, the definition of Italian opera as 'an exotick and irrational entertainment, which has always been combated, and always has prevailed'. *Calypso and Telemachus* might have provoked another: 'It is not done well, but you are surprised to find it done at all.'

The gradient of the opera's decline now grew rapidly steeper. Although no figures are available before 1716/17, reports of thin houses, the drop in the number of performances, the increasingly frequent advertisement of new songs and other inducements, the failure of publishers to print the usual songs, and even the temporary revival (in modest form) of competition from English works in other theatres, all point in the same direction. Of the eleven new productions during the five seasons 1712–17, including three by Handel, Walsh printed songs from only two, *Creso* and *Arminio*. Whereas the theatre had given 54 performances in 1710/11 and 62 in 1711/12 (these included extra nights for the visit of Prince Eugene), the total for the next five years fell to between 42 and 29 (see Table 2). The opening of the 1713/14 season was delayed till 9 January, that of 1715/16 till 1 February; we do not know why.

Although according to the Colman Opera Register the stage and scenery had been 'altered & emended during ye vacant Season' (summer 1712), calamity followed. After two concert performances (12 and 15 November) of *The Triumph of Love*, 'a choice Collection of Musick composed by [several of] the most celebrated Italian Masters' (five were named), Handel's *Il pastor fido* and a similar pastoral, *Dorinda* (10 December), compounded by Haym largely from Pollarolo's *La fede riconosciuta* of 1707 and economically produced with the same sets, drew poor audiences. Swiney had been unable to raise a subscription for either opera, and he failed again with *Teseo*. When the promise of magnificent new scenery had filled the theatre for two nights, he absconded with the takings to Italy, leaving Heidegger to pick up the pieces and pay the bills (see p. 249). Heidegger and the singers formed a collective management, which struggled on until 1717.

One reason for the poor houses was an undistinguished company of singers; Valeriano Pellegrini was no substitute for Nicolini, and the others, apart from Valentini and Pilotti, were all local. The arrival of two minor Italians in March brought no improvement. The management had to apologize for the performance of *Teseo* on 21 January, and another, on 15 April, was postponed because 'they could not get Company sufficient'. They did manage, with difficulty, to raise a subscription for the next pasticcio, *Ernelinda* (26 February), based on Gasparini's *La fede tradita e vendicata* (Naples 1704) with additional arias by Bononcini, Mancini, Orlandini, and others. But *Dorinda* had to be padded out with a serenata by Albinoni on 21 March and a makeshift new act or 'Entertainment of the choicest Songs out of several Operas' on 25 April; *Ernelinda* had 'an Addition of several new Songs' on 2 May, as did *Teseo* a fortnight later. The exceptional success of Addison's tragedy *Cato* at Drury Lane provided unwanted competition for a month from the middle of April. We learn from an announcement in *The Guardian* of 5 August 1713,[29] that during the winter the operas had been rehearsed at the Great Room in St. Alban's Street. It was at the end of this season (2 June) that Handel's *Silla* had its solitary production.

Heidegger's dedication of *Ernelinda* to Viscount Lonsdale referred to the

[29] Tilmouth, *RMA Research Chronicle*, 86.

company's misfortunes. 'It would be a generous Condescension in *Your Lordship* to take this Opera under Your Protection, at a *Time*, when we labour under so many unhappy Circumstances . . . By these means we may retrieve the Reputation of our Affairs, and in a short time Rival the Stage of Italy.' *Ernelinda* was one of the more successful pasticcios, with 22 performances in three seasons, but it had repeatedly to be bolstered with new music. The first cast included two travesti roles (L'Epine and Barbier) as well as two castratos. The libretto is a complex Scandinavian intrigue with the heroine again feigning madness. The music was not published, but a manuscript in the Library of Congress, chiefly of items from *Amadigi*, contains eight arias, two of which could be by Handel.[30]

The 1713/14 season saw only four productions, all pasticcios and two of them revivals; there was no sign of Handel or his work. Valentini was the sole castrato, Caterina Galerati—who played male roles and took precedence over Valentini—the only new Italian singer. Anastasia Robinson, who had appeared at concerts in the theatre the previous June, made her operatic début in the first new pasticcio *Creso* (27 January), arranged by Haym from operas by Polani and others unidentified. The second was *Arminio* (4 May), with music by several Venetian composers and a scene from *Camilla*. Heidegger dedicated it to Countess Godolphin, daughter and heiress of the Duke of Marlborough, and obtained a subscription on the usual terms. A number of substitute arias were introduced on 1 and 29 May. *Ernelinda*, revived on 3 April with 'above half the Songs . . . New', received further additions on 24 April (to the mad scene, sung by Anastasia Robinson) and on 23 June. The last was an extra performance mounted at the request of the Duchess of Shrewsbury, the Lord Chamberlain's Italian wife. Another attraction was 'the famous Veracini, lately arriv'd from Italy', who played the violin on more than one night. The printed music from the two new pasticcios is mostly dull, though L'Epine had two good arias in *Arminio*, 'Deh consola questo pianto' with syncopated and irregular phrases and a surprising amount of variety in the vocal line, and 'Quanto empietà', and Galerati (Arminio) a striking piece combining a G minor lament with a *Presto* demand for vengeance. In all the operas Anastasia Robinson as well as Galerati had larger parts than Valentini.

The accession of George I gave the opera a slight boost in the 1714/15 season, which began early on 24 October, four days after the coronation, and was much patronized by the new Royal Family, perhaps because they found it easier to follow than English spoken drama. Many performances were specially commanded by 'His Royal Highness', the Prince of Wales. On the first night, which began an hour earlier than usual at 5 p.m., the audience was requested not to call for encores, which had evidently become a habit and made the operas 'too tedious'. Several new singers appeared during the season, including the castrato Filippo Balatri, whose principal claim to fame seems to have been an autobiography in verse,[31] but apart from the contralto Diana Vico, a specialist in travesti roles, they made little mark. Colman called Balatri 'a bad Singer' and Signora Stradiotti 'a very bad Singer', and remarked that at the early performances 'Mrs Robinson's not Singing was by many much

---

[30] See pp. 292–3.

[31] See Angus Heriot, *The Castrati in Opera* (London, 1956), 200 ff. Balatri (1676–1756) paid a visit to Moscow and died a monk in Bavaria. Heriot wrongly states that his operatic début was at Munich in 1724.

regretted'. Heidegger hastened to engage her on the favourable terms quoted above,[32] and she appeared in *Arminio* on 11 December, but retired through illness after the first performance of *Amadigi* in May.

Balatri soon left, and until Nicolini's return in May the company had no castrato, the leading male roles being taken by women; there were three in the *Ernelinda* revival on 16 November, two and a bass (Angelo Zannoni) in the new pasticcio *Lucio Vero* (Haym, from Albinoni and others), first performed on 26 February. Heidegger dedicated the libretto to the Princess of Wales, the future Queen Caroline, in the hope that her 'exquisite and most refin'd Taste' would bring to the science of music 'better Days, than the *British* Climate has of late afforded her'. The plot is full of the usual melodramatic tergiversations and includes the dispatch of yet another lion. It had 'several Alterations' as early as the second performance and 'several Songs alter'd' on 23 April. At the performance of *Ernelinda* on 4 December 'there will be seen (for once only) all the New Scenes design'd for a New Opera', while for *Arminio* on 26 March 'twelve Songs will be alter'd, And several new Scenes not seen yet, (design'd for a New Opera) will be shown'. The new opera was undoubtedly *Amadigi*, whose attractions were thus pre-empted. Heidegger obtained a subscription for four nights of *Lucio Vero* and six of *Amadigi*.[33] On 7 May *Idaspe* was revived for Nicolini, who filled the theatre. Some nights during the winter—though not Anastasia Robinson's benefit on 9 April—had been poorly attended; performances in January had dropped to one a week. After a closure in mid-June on account of intense heat the season continued intermittently into July, and there was even a performance of *Idaspe* (with the *Amadigi* scenery and costumes) by royal command on 27 August.

This season saw two new enterprises, the opening of John Rich's rebuilt theatre in Lincoln's Inn Fields (planned by his father) on 18 December 1714 and an attempt by Cibber and Pepusch at Drury Lane to regain a little ground for English opera. On 12 March 1715 they put on *Venus and Adonis*, 'a New Musical Masque . . . in two several Interludes, compos'd after the Italian manner and perform'd all in English', with Margherita de L'Epine (Pepusch's future wife) and Jane Barbier in the principal roles and Blackly, one of the singers named in the autograph of Handel's *Acis and Galatea*, as Mars. All who bought tickets in the pit and boxes were offered a free libretto. Cibber's preface described the piece as 'an Attempt to give the Town a little good Musick in a Language they understand . . . We are so far from establishing Theatrical Musick in England, that the very Exhibition or Silence of it seems entirely to depend on the Arrival or Absence of some Eminent Foreign Performer . . . It is therefore hop'd, that this Undertaking, if encourag'd, may in time reconcile Musick to the English Tongue, [and that it] will want nothing of the Italian, but the Language.' This was however a very small mouse to set against the Italian lion. The interludes, like the continental intermezzos, were given between the acts of various plays; but although *Venus*

---

[32] According to a document in the Public Record Office (*Coke Papers*, 229) this agreement had been made verbally in the presence of the Duchess of Shrewsbury on 13 July. It may not have been implemented earlier because Nicolini had not returned (one of Anastasia's conditions) and Heidegger had not expected to open till the New Year.

[33] A curious document in the *Coke Papers*, 'Heidegger's account of subscription money' (ibid. 237) appears to confuse the two subscriptions. It records two payments to Handel and Galerati. Long and Potter, unidentified by the editors, were probably agents for singers.

and Adonis was performed eleven times in this season, thirteen times in the next, and again later, it was often shortened to a single interlude. Lincoln's Inn Fields likewise tried musical afterpieces: *Bacchus and Cupid* (Purcell's masque from *Timon of Athens*) on 24 March and a masque by William Turner, *Alexander the Great*, for Leveridge's benefit on 26 April. Both were failures, the first having two performances, the second one. There was still an audience for Purcell, as Drury Lane demonstrated with revivals of *The Indian Queen* and *Bonduca* in July and August.

The 1715/16 season at the King's Theatre, though not elsewhere, was delayed by the Jacobite rebellion, 'ye King & Court not liking to go into Such Crowds these troublesome times' (Colman). This left the other theatres an opening, and both had many bites at the cherry. Their approach was again cautious; they did not venture beyond short masques or pastorals 'compos'd to Musick after the Italian manner, and perform'd all in English'. Drury Lane, after reviving *Venus and Adonis*, put on *Myrtillo* (Cibber–Pepusch, 5 November, eleven performances), *Apollo and Daphne* (Hughes–Pepusch, 12 January, five performances), and *The Death of Dido* (Booth–Pepusch, 17 April, four performances); L'Epine and Barbier sang the chief parts. Lincoln's Inn Fields, where Leveridge seems to have been in charge of the music, revived several plays with Purcell's incidental music and achieved a major success with *The Prophetess (Dioclesian)*, which had a long and profitable run from 3 December and was revived in the next two seasons. This was less a challenge to the Italians than a prolongation of semiopera. The masques at Lincoln's Inn Fields were a revival of the fifteen-year-old Motteux–Eccles *Acis and Galatea* (22 November, six performances), *Presumptuous Love* (William Taverner–Turner, 10 March, three performances), and *Pyramus and Thisbe*, 'a Comic Masque, compos'd in the high Style of Italy' by Leveridge, which had a single performance on 11 April. Leveridge anticipated Benjamin Britten in turning the mechanicals' masque in *A Midsummer Night's Dream* into a parody of Italian opera, and Sheridan (*The Critic*) in having the supposed composer Mr Semibreve comment on the performance with his friends Crotchet and Gamut. He naturally made the most of the lion, but let things down by his additions to—and even corrections of—Shakespeare's text. *Presumptuous Love*, 'a Dramatic Masque', deals with the story of Ixion, who is bound to a wheel by Jupiter for lusting after Juno. The unsigned preface paid tribute to 'Mr *William Turner*, who hath a happy Genius in Naturalizing Italian Musick into a true English Manner, without losing the Spirit and Force of the Original in the Imitation, or the Masterly Touches of the Art in the Composition'. The evidence for this robust claim does not survive. The Lincoln's Inn Fields company were actors rather than singers, and their masques, for which very little music remains, inclined more to coarse farce than those at Drury Lane.

The King's Theatre opened at last on 1 February 1716 with a revival of *Lucio Vero*, 'in which above 20 Songs are chang'd' and two new singers appeared: Elena Croce Viviani, who had sung in some Venice performances of *Agrippina*, and a mysterious Giorgio Giacomo Berwillibald (or Bessiwillibald). A more distinguished artist, the castrato Antonio Bernacchi, joined the company a month later. The single new production, and the only work to qualify for a subscription, was *Clearte* (18 April), a pasticcio adapted by Nicolini from Scarlatti's 1709 Naples opera *L'amor volubile e tiranno*. His dedication of the libretto to the 'Ladies of Great Britain' alludes again to the precarious state of the company: 'I shall not presume to think of the Reason why Musick has of late lain under some Hardships, it shall suffice for me that even now I have met with a Regard superiour to my Merit.' The plot is another Scandinavian intrigue, of more than usual absurdity, with resemblances to the source libretto of *Floridante*. It offers all the statutory ingredients: princes and princesses hurled at intervals into chains, an execution foiled by a Moor with a huge sword, the King of Norway's son disguised as the Moor (carrying his own clothes on a dish), the King of Sweden's daughter masquerading as a shepherdess, a cup of poison knocked to the ground before it can be consumed, and the heroine (played by Anastasia Robinson) enjoying the pastoral life equipped with a 'Fishing Tackle'. *Pirro e Demetrio* was revived   * for the first time in five seasons, with 'New Scenes', on 10 March, a 'Famous Scene of *Thomyris*' sung by Nicolini on 2 May, 'Magnificent New Scenes, Particularly one in Perspective of a Royal Palace, which exeeds any that has been seen in England, containing One Thousand Yards of Painting by Sig Roberto Clerici, and not to be seen again this Year' on 15 May, 'an Addition of Musick . . . compos'd by Mr Peter Sandoni' (Cuzzoni's future husband) on 26 May, and 'an Addition of a New Scene perform'd by Bernacchi' on 2 June. Clerici was to receive an official appointment from the Royal Academy. Most of these were benefit performances (two were advertised for Elena Croce, but this may be a mistake). New instrumental music was twice added to *Amadigi* (see pp. 287–8).

After the next season the opera finally collapsed, despite the presence of three leading castratos, Nicolini, Bernacchi, and Berenstadt. It opened on 8 December 1716 with the first of four revivals, of which *Rinaldo* was the most successful, playing chiefly on Saturdays—and not all of them. The advertisement for *Pirro e Demetrio* on 2 March announced ominously that Maria Grasetti, a new and obscure singer, 'will Sing only Part of the Recitativo, without Songs, to shorten the Opera', which would be given without scenery, 'the Stage being in the same Magnificent Form as it was in the Ball'. Heidegger had launched his ridottos in an effort to keep the finances afloat. On 30 March *Clearte* was advertised with 'Two New Scenes'. One of them, not so new, was Clerici's of the year before, 'the other a Room adorn'd with Tapestry, representing the famous Battles of Alexander by Mons le Brun; both (in their kind) exceeding any Scenes that has been seen in England'. There were two new productions. *Venceslao* (14 March) ran a mere three nights; *Tito Manlio* (4 April) with a subscription, 'New Scenes and all New Cloaths' and seven performances, did a little better. Neither libretto has a preface or dedication. *Tito Manlio* was the last opera heard, after an interval of nearly a month, on 29 June 1717. Colman's Register did not bother to include this season.

Venceslao was based on Zeno's 1703 Venice libretto as revised for Naples in 1714; Nicolini had sung the same part in both settings, by Pollarolo and Mancini, and no doubt introduced music from one or both. The long and complex plot is set for a change in Poland, and the behaviour of the characters has a sublime inconsequence. Of two Polish brothers desiring the same woman (Erenice, a descendant of ancient Polish kings), the one with lascivious and dishonourable intentions kills the other and promptly changes into a model of penitence and humility. But he marries the Queen of Lithuania, whom he has previously disarmed in a duel when she was disguised as a man; and Erenice, deprived of both brothers but urged to accept a trusty general, is left like Donna

Anna asking for time to make up her mind. *Tito Manlio* deals with a well-known incident in early Roman history, in which a consul had his son executed for disobeying orders and killing the enemy leader. In the libretto Manlio merely disarms Geminio but is nevertheless condemned, whereupon his betrothed Servilia goes mad and throws herself into the Tiber. She is rescued by none other than Geminio and restored to her senses in time for both to intercede successfully with the consul.

Tito Manlio is unique among London operas of this period (other than Handel's) in that a score survives (Add MS 16156). Neither this nor the libretto names a composer, but another copy, formerly in the Aylesford Collection and sold in 1972, attributes the music to Attilio Ariosti. Lindgren[34] accepts this. It is impossible to compare the two scores, since the ex-Aylesford copy is not available. Add MS 16156 almost certainly represents the 1717 opera, but it looks like a pasticcio, perhaps not finally assembled (the libretto, written by Matteo Noris for C. F. Pollarolo in 1696, was set by several other composers, including Vivaldi in 1719). Some recitative is missing. Two characters change pitch and clef, one of them more than once, and design and key system are both irregular. Act I contains three consecutive duets and ends with two arias for secondary characters in the same key. In Act II Servilia has four long arias in succession; although the first announces her departure ('Parto, Signor, volando'), she does not even leave the stage after the fourth. An unusual feature, as Lindgren points out, is the exceptional quantity of accompanied recitative, especially in Act II. Some of the music is memorable and attractive, but it hardly seems consistent in style.

Heidegger's cash book for this season survives.[35] Besides confirming the unprofitable results,[36] it throws an instructive and entertaining light on the running of the opera-house. Although the figures record each night's receipts and disbursements, neither side of the account gives a total picture. There is no mention of singers' salaries or payments to composers or arrangers of the music, and no note of receipts from subscribers or the Royal Family. Moreover the outgoings list not what was due but what was paid out each night; small bills were lumped together and carried forward, and other payments, for example to the orchestra, were often in arrears.

Prices of admission varied considerably: the highest rate, for the opening performance (*Clearte*), the six subscription nights (*Tito Manlio*), and the eight benefits (except that for the box-keepers), agrees with that given on page 152 (pit and front boxes 10s. 6d., stage boxes 15s.); but there were two rates for other nights, front boxes 8s., pit 5s. or 8s., stage boxes 7s. 6d. or 10s. 6d. The gallery was always 2s. 6d., except on the orchestra's benefit night when it rose to 3s.; presumably the musicians' friends were expected to patronize the upstairs seats. Benefit receipts are not listed. The beneficiaries controlled the ticket sales, but Pilotti, Bernacchi, and Berenstadt had to pay £130 towards expenses, and the orchestra and box-keepers £67; Heidegger, Nicolini, and Anastasia Robinson were free from encumbrance, the last two no doubt as

---

[34] 'Ariosti's London Years, 1716–29', *M & L* lxii (1981), 331–51.

[35] Mildmay MSS at the Essex (formerly Hampshire) Record Office. It is analysed in part by Sybil Rosenfeld, 'An Opera House Account Book', *Theatre Notebook*, xvi (1962), 83–8, and by Milhous, 'Opera Finances in London, 1674–1738', *JAMS* xxxvii (1984), 567–92.

[36] By Milhous's calculation the nightly loss was at least £30 and possibly more than twice as much.

specified in their contracts. The house was never full; the maximum attendance in the gallery was 187, in the pit and boxes 318, not on the same occasion. On at least nine of the seventeen ordinary nights (both price ranges) the receipts fell below £100, and for two performances of *Clearte* they were down to £43 and £32. No particulars are given for one *Rinaldo* night (another is wrongly dated); the relevant page may have been lost or the performance cancelled.

The wages of the orchestra varied between £17. 18s. 6d. and £23 16s. 3d. a night, averaging just under £20; but this does not include the timpanist or additional payments to Castrucci (the leader, £43), Haym (continuo cellist, £28), and occasionally other musicians. *Clearte* required extra performers on stage, involving small sums 'For Dressing the Stage Musick'. Frequent and substantial amounts were paid to copyists, chiefly Linike but also Smith (probably another viola player) and Davies. The bill for copying *Tito Manlio* came to £8. 12s. 0d. There is an entry on 25 May for 'Translating Operas etc.'. Some of the singers enjoyed special perquisites, especially Nicolini, who seems to have consumed an inordinate amount of coffee. He was equipped with 'a Perriwig', gloves, and stockings; Berenstadt too received stockings on the house, and 'Stayes' were bought for Pilotti (twice), Grasetti, and Anastasia Robinson. There were nightly payments to 'Supernumeraries and Pages', but only one, £16. 2s. 6d. on 30 March, to the 'Dancing Women'. Wardrobe and properties included 'a Scymeter and Dagger' and 'Chaines and Collars'. Scene-painting for *Venceslao* and *Tito Manlio* cost more than £50 in March. A Mr Potter received a regular fee 'For the Scenes'—their hire, operation or both—and other backstage staff included a barber, glover, and carpenters, who on 26 January were given 10s. 'to Drink'.

Principal front-of-house costs were house rent to Vanbrugh (£12. 10s. 6d. a night[37]), wax and tallow chandlers, ticket and bill printers and posters (Heidegger advertised heavily), glazier, locksmith, 'Tin Man', 'Oylman', and other tradesmen; also a sergeant and sixteen guards to keep order, and yeomen and footmen when the King or Prince of Wales was present. A rent bill for 'Mrs Robinson's Room' confirms her favoured treatment. Among a very mixed bag of incidentals were small sums for cleaning the yard, candlesticks, snuffers, librettos for the Prince of Wales (and others), 'a Porter', an account book, '3 Quiers of Paper' (several times), and 'Inck' (eightpence).

Late in 1716 Pepusch and his musicians had moved from Drury Lane to Lincoln's Inn Fields, where, after the resident company had revived *Pyramus and Thisbe* (nine performances) in October and *Dioclesian* (ten performances) in November, they were at last bold enough to mount three full-length operas in English. All three were revivals, and two of them, *Camilla* and *Thomyris*, were among the works that had established the Italian form in London and had now ironically undergone naturalization—though Pepusch seems to have contributed one or two new songs. *Camilla* (2 January 1717) was a direct

[37] Vanbrugh let the theatre to Heidegger for £400 a year, the equivalent of 32 opera nights, from Michaelmas 1716. When the theatre closed Heidegger continued to pay the rent until Michaelmas 1720. Vanbrugh sold the building to his brother Charles in December 1720, shortly afterwards disposing of the scenery and properties to the managers of Drury Lane. See Downes, *Vanbrugh*, which prints Vanbrugh's accounts (1715–26) in full.

challenge to the Haymarket and in particular to *Rinaldo*; five performances in January were announced for the same evenings, though the last was cancelled. The old English translation of 1706 had been tidied up, and the infelicities of language ridiculed by Steele in *The Tatler* (26 May 1709) and Addison in *The Spectator* (21 March 1711) expunged.[38] For the first five nights (there were thirteen performances in all) *Camilla* did excellent business, the receipts, based on much cheaper prices, surpassing those of the King's Theatre. The principal singers were L'Epine and Barbier in travesti roles, Maria Manina (now Mrs Fletcher) as Camilla, and Leveridge in his original part of Linco. The reception no doubt inspired the revivals of *Calypso and Telemachus* (27 February) and *Thomyris* (9 May) with the same artists, but they achieved only three and two performances respectively.

The collapse of the Italian opera might have been expected to put new life into this enterprise. That it proved a false dawn must be attributed, at least in part, to the lack of adequate composers. The lasting vitality of Purcell's theatre music supports this. In 1717–19 Drury Lane kept *Dioclesian* and *Bonduca* in the repertory but mounted nothing else of musical consequence. Lincoln's Inn Fields, where Galliard replaced Pepusch and L'Epine dropped out for one season (possibly at the time of her marriage), continued spasmodically with short masques and similar pieces: *Pan and Syrinx*, 'a new Opera of one Act' on a variant of the Apollo–Daphne myth (Theobald–Galliard), had twelve performances from 14 January 1718 and two more the following season. *The Lady's Triumph*, 'a new Comic-Dramatic Opera' with new costumes and 'Machines after the Venetian Manner' (Theobald–Galliard, nine performances from 22 March) was, as the subtitle suggests, a reversion. Nor was most of it new; the main text was an old piece of crude cuckoldry by Elkanah Settle, with a masque, *Decius and Paulina*, in Act V. Rich, a famous Harlequin, was more interested in buffoonery and dancing and soon debased the masque into a harlequinade. *Amadis; or, The Loves of Harlequin and Colombine*, 'a new Dramatick Opera in Dancing in Serious and Grotesque Characters'—no doubt a parody of *Amadigi*—had thirteen performances in 1717/18 and six the following season. The subtitle indicates its level.

The 1718/19 season, with L'Epine back in action, saw revivals of *Venus and Adonis* (eleven times), *Thomyris* (ten times), and *Camilla* (four times). The only novelties were *The Passion of Sappho*, which did not survive its first performance on 15 November, perhaps because the music was by Clayton, and *Circe* (11 April, six performances), an old play or semiopera (1677) with some new music by Galliard. *Harlequin Hydaspes*, a 'Mock-Opera' by Rich performed once on 27 May 1719, is a skit on *Idaspe* with the characters given *commedia dell'arte* names. The libretto includes a number of opera arias, among them 'Torni la gioja in sen' (*Amadigi*), presumably the additional aria in the HHA appendix, 'Col raggio placido' (*Agrippina*, but attributed to *Idaspe*, in which it had probably been sung), and 'Vivi, O cara, e ti consola'. Though ascribed to *Rinaldo*, this was an addition to *Idaspe*; it is not related to arias with similar texts in *Rinaldo* and *Pirro e Demetrio*, and is not by Handel.

If the masques of 1715–17 achieved nothing towards supplanting Italian opera, they did have one important progeny. Handel's *Acis and Galatea*, composed in the spring of 1718 for Cannons, where he took employment when the opera closed in 1717, was directly modelled on them, both in text and music.[39]

[38] L. Lindgren, '*Camilla* and *The Beggar's Opera*', *Philological Quarterly*, lxix (1980), 53.
[39] See W. Dean, *Handel's Dramatic Oratorios and Masques*, 155–9.

Pepusch's *Venus and Adonis* and *Apollo and Daphne* were particularly influential; one aria with *flagelletto* obbligato in the former almost certainly suggested 'Hush, ye pretty warbling choir'. Pepusch's music, here at least, does not deserve the contemptuous dismissal it received from Burney. Galliard too, though generally dry, achieved occasional flashes of imagination. Roger Fiske quotes a fine bass air, unusually scored with solo viola and three recorders, from *Pan and Syrinx*, and an attractive melody with a perceptibly English flavour from *Apollo and Daphne*.[40] Had *Acis and Galatea* been written for the London theatre rather than a nobleman's private entertainment, subsequent events might have taken a different course.

Additional Notes

* (p. 157) John Roberts (*Handel Sources*, iv) identifies 26 pieces from Gasparini's *Ambleto* (two of them not in the Walsh score), seven from the libretto of Pollarolo's *Vincislao* (Venice, 1703), and one from that of Caldara's *Partenope* (Venice, 1708).
* (p. 163) For this revival Handel wrote three arias for Bernacchi: see pp. 184–5.
* (p. 164) One aria, 'Nò, non piangete', sung by Nicolini in Act I, is by Handel, if Walsh's ascription to *Teseo* is correct; see p. 249.

---

[40] *English Theatre Music in the Eighteenth Century* (London, 1973), 60–1, 58.

CHAPTER II

RINALDO

THE plot is summarized thus in the Argument prefixed to the 1711 libretto:[1]

Godfrey, General of the Christian Forces in the Expedition against the Saracens, to engage the Assistance of Rinaldo a famous Hero of those Times; promises to give him his Daughter Almirena, when the City shou'd fall into his Hands. The Christians with Rinaldo at their Head, conquer Palestine, and besiege its King Argantes in That City. Armida an Amazonian Enchantress, in Love with and belov'd by Argantes, contrives by Magick, to entrap Rinaldo in an Enchanted Castle, whence, after much Difficulty, being deliver'd by Godfrey, he returns to the Army, takes Jerusalem, converts Argantes and Armida to the Christian Faith, and Marries Almirena, according to the Promise of her Father Godfrey.

Godfrey (Goffredo) is Godefroid de Bouillon, leader of the First Crusade (1096–9); Rinaldo is described in the list of characters as 'of the House of Este', Armida as 'a Queen of the Amazons' in the English text but 'Regina di Damasco' in the Italian.

Act I. *The City of Jerusalem besieg'd, a Prospect of the Walls, and a Gate on the plainest side of the Town. Part of the Christian Camp on the right side of the Stage.* Goffredo is sitting on a throne in front of a stately pavilion[2] with his brother Eustazio, Almirena, and Rinaldo, surrounded by guards. He looks forward to victory. Rinaldo reminds him of his promise, and when Almirena urges action complains of the anguish of delayed love. *A Trumpet Sounds, and the City Gate being thrown open, discovers a Herald, attended by two Guards, who advances towards* Goffredo and asks for a conference on behalf of Argante. On Goffredo assenting, Argante emerges *from the City, drawn through the Gate in a Triumphal Chariot, the Horses white and led in by arm'd Blackamoors.*[3] *He comes forward attended by a great Number of Horse and Foot Guards, and descending from his Chariot addresses himself to Godfrey, who advances to meet him.* He asks Goffredo for a three days' truce, which Goffredo, though not impressed by Argante's disdainful manner, grants for reasons of humanity. All depart except Argante, who hopes his mistress and ally Armida, now seeking means to save his country, will bring him comfort. *Armida in the Air, in a Chariot drawn by two huge Dragons, out of whose Mouths issue Fire and Smoke.* She summons the furies to attend her. *The Chariot being descended, the Dragons rush forward, and draw her towards Argantes, who advances*

---

[1] As usual in London the libretto is bilingual. The stage directions are quoted from the English version, which does not always exactly correspond to the Italian.

[2] This detail comes from Handel's autograph, not the libretto. Chrysander attaches it to the 1731 version: but nearly all his stage directions for that are incorrect.

[3] The blackamoors and the colour of the horses are mentioned only in the English version of the libretto, which may reflect Hill's original draft. This part of the autograph is missing. The direction in Chrysander's 1731 score specifies six horses; but this comes from RM 19 d 5 and belongs to a much earlier version. According to Steele's account there were no horses at all.

to meet her. She tells him the result of her incantations: if Rinaldo can be detached from the European camp, Asia may smile again. Argante proposes to use force, but agrees to leave it to her subtler art. The scene changes to *a delightful Grove in which the Birds are heard to sing, and seen flying up and down among the Trees.*[4] After a love scene for Almirena and Rinaldo culminating in a duet, *Armida enters and seizing forcibly on Almirena's Hand,*[5] *is leading her away.* Rinaldo rushes to defend her. *They have drawn their Swords, and are making at each other; when a black Cloud descends, all fill'd with dreadful Monsters spitting Fire and Smoke on every side. The Cloud covers Almirena and Armida, and carries 'em up swiftly into the Air, leaving in their Place, two frightful Furies, who having grinn'd and mock'd Rinaldo, sink down, and disappear . . . Godfrey, Eustatio, etc. enter to Rinaldo, who stands immoveable, with his Eyes fix'd on the Ground.* He describes what has happened; perhaps Pluto has mistaken Almirena for Proserpine. Eustazio reassures them: he knows a hermit who 'by his magick Skill, Can read the starry Characters of Heav'n'. Let them consult him, and virtue will triumph. Rinaldo, left alone, invokes winds and tempests to second his revenge.

Act II. *A Prospect of a Calm and Sunshiny Sea,*[6] *with a Boat at Anchor close upon the Shore; at the Helm of the Boat sits a Spirit, in the Shape of a lovely Woman. Two Mermaids are seen Dancing up and down in the Water.* At first Eustazio is alone. Rinaldo and Goffredo enter hastily and grumble about the length of the journey, but Eustazio says they are nearly there. *While they are crossing to pursue their Journey, the Woman in the Boat invites ﹍Rinaldo to enter,* telling him that Almirena, confined on a 'solitary Isle', has sent her. *While they remain Confounded at this unexpected summons, the Mermaids Sing and Dance in the water,* inviting lovers to pluck the sweets while they can. *Rinaldo stands a while suspended within his Thoughts; at last resolves violently to enter the Boat; but is held by Godfrey and Eustatio.* After a short argument *he thinks again, and the Woman renewing her Invitation, he once more attempts an Entrance, but is again with-held by his Companions.* Rejecting their appeals, he vows to subdue Cerberus and repeat the chastisement administered by Hercules. *He breaks violently from their Hold, and enters the Boat; which immediately steers out into the open Sea, and Sails out of Sight. Then the Mermaids leave Singing*[7] *and disappear. Godfrey and Eustatio, seem confounded at the Accident,* which Goffredo attributes to the powers of hell. The set changes to *a Delightful Garden in the Enchanted Palace of Armida.* Almirena complains of Armida's cruelty.[8] Argante, struck by her beauty, makes advances. She begs him to leave her to her tears, and when he renews the pressure says he can prove his love by setting her free. He points out that this would call down Armida's vengeance on them both, but promises to break the spell. When they have gone, Armida rejoices at Rinaldo's capture. Two spirits lead him in. His proud defiance provokes her into offering him her love, which he scornfully refuses. After an angry duet, *Armida changes her self into the Likeness of Almirena, and follows Rinaldo, weeping.* She accuses him of diverting himself with another mistress, and he takes her in his arms. *While they Embrace, Armida reassumes her proper Shape, and Rinaldo amaz'd, starts back in a sudden Confusion.* At his

[4] The Italian text specifies fountains, avenues, and aviaries.

[5] Apparently a mistranslation: in the Italian she snatches her from Rinaldo's hands.

[6] The Italian version has *Gran mare placido, in cui riflette un bellissimo Iri.*

[7] According to the Italian direction, and Handel's autograph, they resume their singing and dancing as Rinaldo enters the boat. When this is out of sight, *le Sirene si profondano in mare* (autograph), *si sommergono nel Mare* (libretto). Chrysander omits most of this long direction.

[8] Handel's autograph, but not the libretto, has *Almirena piange* at the end of her first speech.

exclamation of horror *Armida again takes the Shape of Almirena.* Rinaldo *is running to her Arms but stops suddenly,* suspecting a trick, and goes out with an aria of rage and doubt. Armida is torn between love and the desire to avenge her slighted pride. When Argante enters, she once more assumes the form of Almirena,[9] meaning only to cover her confusion and trap Rinaldo if he returns. But Argante begins to make love to her, promising to free her 'from the ignoble Bondage of Armida'. She first views him with scorn, then *more disdainfully than before,* then *starts, and appears surpriz'd,* and at last *takes her own Shape, and flyes on him with great Fury.* He is painfully embarrassed, but when she refuses to forgive him he disowns her, admits he loves Almirena, and tells Armida to withdraw her aid and be damned: he can defend his throne without devils. He *goes off enrag'd,* leaving her to utter a furious declaration of war.

Act III. *A dreadful Prospect of a Mountain, horridly steep, and rising from the Front of the Stage, to the utmost Height of the most backward Part of the Theatre; Rocks, and Caves, and Waterfalls, are seen upon the Ascent, and on the Top appear the blazing Battlements of the Enchanted Palace, Guarded by a great Number of Spirits, of various Forms and Aspects; In the midst of the Wall is seen a Gate, with several Arches supported by Pillars of Chrystal, Azure, Emeralds, and all sorts of precious Stones. At the Foot of the Mountain is discover'd the Magicians Cave. Enter Godfrey, Eustatio, and their Soldiers, gazing on the dreadful Appearance of the Mountain . . . Eustatio calls at the Cell's Mouth . . . The Magician appears at the Mouth of the Cave.* He tells them that Rinaldo and Almirena are prisoners in the palace, but divine force equal to that of hell will be necessary to rescue them. Without hesitation Goffredo and Eustazio *with drawn Swords, and follow'd by their Soldiers, ascend the Mountain, regardless of the Magician who calls after them . . . Godfrey, Eustatio and the Soldiers, having climb'd half way up the Mountain, are stopp'd by a Row of ugly Spirits, who start up before 'em; The Soldiers, frighted, endeavour to run back, but are cut off in their Way by another Troop, who start up below 'em. In the midst of their Confusion, the Mountain opens and swallows 'em up, with Thunder, Lightning, and amazing Noises. Godfrey, Eustatio, and the Soldiers who escape return in great Confusion to the Magician's Cave.* He gives them 'fatal Wands' that no witchcraft can withstand. *They reascend the Mountain, while the Magician stands at his Cave Door, and sings, to encourage 'em. The Spirits, as before, present themselves in Opposition, but upon the Touch of the Wands, vanish upward and downward, with terrible Noises and Confusion. They gain the Summit of the Hill and entring the Enchanted Arches, strike the Gate with their Wands; when immediatly the Palace, the Spirits, and the whole Mountain vanish away, and Godfrey and Eustatio are discover'd hanging on the sides of a vast Rock in the middle of the Sea; with much Difficulty they reach the Top, and descend on the other side . . .* As soon as the Magician sees the Enchantment ended, he goes into his Cave with a pious couplet. The set changes to *the Enchanted Garden.* Armida, *holding a Dagger at Almirena's Breast,* rejects Rinaldo's desperate pleas. She *lifts her Arm to Stab Almirena, and Rinaldo draws his Sword and is striking at her, when two Spirits rise to her Assistance, and seize upon him.* Goffredo and Eustazio rush in, and Armida invokes the furies. *A dreadful Host of Spirits rise and fill the Stage, but Godfrey and Eustatio putting out their Wands, the whole Prospect of the Garden vanishes in a moment; leaving in its Place the View of a wild and open Country, with the City of Jerusalem on that side which is built upon Rocks. A Highway is discover'd from the City Gate, which leads in several Turns and Windings down the Mountain. Godfrey, Eustatio, and Rinaldo run to embrace, and in the*

---

[9] Chrysander omits a stage direction at the start of II ix (HG 76). References are to his second (1894) edition, unless stated otherwise.

mean while Armida again attempts to Stab Almirena . . . Rinaldo draws his Sword to wound Armida, who vanishes under the Stroke. All are rejoicing when Goffredo reminds them that they still have an earthly foe to conquer and orders the assault on Jerusalem to begin at sunrise. After their departure Argante appears *at the Hills Foot, follow'd by three Generals.* He is confident of victory. Armida joins him, and they resume their quarrel; but he soon begs her pardon, she admits she was partly to blame, and *they embrace* and turn their minds to the battle.[10] *The Pagan Trumpets sound a March, and the Army is seen to pass the Gate, and in military Order descend the Mountain, at whose Foot they pay the usual Compliments of War, as they pass by, to Argantes and Armida.* The pair look forward to victory followed by love and go out. The Christians return. Eustazio announces the approach of the pagan host; Goffredo orders him to guard their tents and protect Almirena. *The Christian Trumpets sound, and the Army in military Pomp and Order,*[11] *marches over the Stage, saluting their General as they pass.* Rinaldo prepares to storm the battlements from the east 'by an oblique Path, unseen, unfear'd', while Goffredo attacks in the open plain. Argante *marching in his Troops, and ranging them in Order of Battel,* encourages them with a harangue; Goffredo with the Christian army does the same. *The Armies attack each other and form a regular Battle, which hangs in Balance, till Rinaldo having Storm'd the City, descends the Mountain with his Squadron, and assaults the Pagans in the Rear, who immediately fly, and are pursued by Rinaldo.* He returns with Argante in chains. Eustazio brings in Armida, who has been captured while attacking the Christian tents. Rinaldo and Almirena embrace to general applause. Armida suddenly decides that heaven may mean to save her, and *breaks her enchanted Wand.* She and Argante profess the Christian faith and are set free by Goffredo.

Rinaldo was the first Italian opera composed specifically for London, and the libretto was new in the sense that it had not been set by another composer. Its authorship is a little involved. Aaron Hill, the ambitious young director of the Haymarket Theatre, who had been quick to appreciate Handel as a business proposition, had bold plans for establishing opera in England—and indeed in English.[12] In his Dedication of the *Rinaldo* libretto to Queen Anne he proclaims his 'Endeavour, to see the *English* Opera more splendid than her Mother, the Italian', and enlarges on this in a Preface. He criticizes the Italian operas hitherto heard in London on two counts:

First, That they had been compos'd for Tastes and Voices, different from those who were to sing and hear them on the *English* Stage; And *Secondly,* That wanting the Machines and Decorations, which bestow so great a Beauty on their Appearance, they have been heard and seen to very considerable Disadvantage.

At once to remedy both these Misfortunes, I resolv'd to frame some Dramma, that, by different Incidents and Passions, might afford the Musick Scope to vary and display its Excellence, and fill the Eye with more delightful Prospects, so at once to give two Senses equal Pleasure.

I could not chuse a finer Subject than the celebrated Story of *Rinaldo* and *Armida,*

---

[10] Handel's autograph (but not the libretto) has several unpublished directions in the recitative of Scene vi (HG 91–2): *un poco sospeso* for Argante at bar 15, *freddamente* for Armida at bar 18 and again at bar 22, *rissolutamente* at bar 24.

[11] On foot and on horseback in the Italian text and Handel's autograph.

[12] See his celebrated letter to Handel of 5 Dec. 1732 (Deutsch, 299).

which has furnish'd Opera's for every Stage and Tongue in *Europe*. I have, however, us'd a Poet's Privilege, and vary'd from the Scheme of Tasso, as was necessary for the better forming a Theatrical Representation.

It was a very particular Happiness, that I met with a Gentleman so excellently qualify'd as Signor *Rossi*, to fill up the Model I had drawn, with Words so sounding and so rich in Sense, that if my Translation is in many Places to deviate, 'tis for want of Power to reach the Force of his Original.

Hill was in effect the only begetter. He chose the story, laid out the plot, and, when Rossi had versified it, translated the result.[13] His 'Poet's Privilege' took him a long way from the narrative and the spirit of Tasso's *Gerusalemme liberata*, though many details of the libretto have their origin in the epic. Hill multiplied the love interest by inventing the affair between Armida and Argante and the entire character of Almirena, but gravely weakened the relationship between Rinaldo and Armida, comparable in its stormy and devouring passions with that of Ruggiero and Alcina in Ariosto's *Orlando furioso*. The presence of a virtuous heroine saps the vitality of the hero. Argante, a compound of Tasso's proud Circassian and Aladino King of Jerusalem, is reduced to an amorous weathercock. Hill was responsible for the absurd conversion to Christianity, no doubt a concession to English taste. In Tasso Argante is killed by Tancredi before the final Christian onslaught, and Armida, still in love with Rinaldo, is reconciled with him. There is only a discreet hint that she might one day change her religion.

The task of the theatre poet Giacomo Rossi was a menial one, as his apologetic but flowery address to the reader, which follows Hill's Preface in the 1711 libretto, makes abundantly clear. He excuses his 'hasty work', 'the delivery of but a few evenings', on the ground that 'Mr *Hendel*, the *Orpheus* of our century, while composing the music, scarcely gave me the time to write, and to my great wonder I saw an entire Opera put to music by that surprising genius, with the greatest degree of perfection, in only two weeks'. The suggestion that Handel outran his librettist masks the fact that Rossi had to make room for movements of which words and music had been composed in Italy. Three arias ('Sibillar gli angui', 'Basta che sol', 'Bel piacere') and two duets ('Scherzano', 'Fermati') were taken over with a few retouches, and the
* Mermaids' song, 'Il vostro maggio', with new words dubbed on the music.

It is scarcely surprising that the results are clumsy. Some of the insertions are almost ludicrously inappropriate; 'Sibillar gli angui', the Cyclops's outburst about Alecto's snakes and barking Scylla in *Aci, Galatea e Polifemo*, as Streatfeild remarks, is a singular utterance in the mouth of a Saracen chief opening negotiations for a truce. Poppea's 'Bel piacere' comes no better from Almirena just before the battle, and Eustazio's arias, dragged in to give a superfluous character something to sing, never fail to hold up the action. This is often halting and ill-motivated. The initial arias of Almirena and Rinaldo are inappropriate in a warlike scene, and 'Combatti da forte' is too strong-willed for the gentle Almirena; Handel would have done better to reserve her for 'Augelletti'. Armida in turn wastes her sensational first entry on her lover and then kidnaps Almirena instead of Rinaldo, whom she scarcely meets till

[13] The English and Italian texts were reprinted in his posthumous *Dramatic Works* (1760), i. 71–143. In 1710 he announced that he had attempted a translation of Tasso's 'Godfrey of Bulloign, and shall very suddenly publish a specimen' (Deutsch, 33). The libretto may have been a by-product of this enterprise. He did not use Silvani's *Armida al campo* (Venice, 1707).

the second act. The dissociation of arias from exits may owe something to Hill's desire to relax or vary the form; but it tends rather to emphasize the value of the convention.

Hill went out of his way to exploit to the utmost the spectacular opportunities afforded by the stage machinery, though he did not always bother to integrate them with the plot; his aim seems to have been to combine the virtuosity of Italian singing with the scenic extravagance of the seventeenth-century English masque.[14] In this he won the suffrage of the public, to the unconcealed alarm of unsuccessful rivals like Addison and Steele. The stage directions quoted above give some idea what effects were most popular and how they were produced. They were of two kinds, military pageantry and magic. Both demanded a large number of supers; the magic scenes employed aerial machines, rapid changes of scenery, dancing, smoke operators, lighting changes, and perhaps transparencies. The initial stage direction in Act III suggests that the mountaineering exploits may have involved the full depth of the theatre, including the room behind the backcloth.[15] This area was perhaps also used for Rinaldo's departure by boat in Act II. Handel's autograph and the early copies indicate clearly that when Armida assumed the shape of Almirena the singers changed places and Almirena sang the 'disguised' recitatives.

Hill was not afraid to mix his mythological metaphors. The Dramatis Personae in the libretto, besides naming Armida as Queen of the Amazons, include 'Mermaids, Spirits, Furies, Officers, Guards, and Attendants'. The text draws its imagery without discrimination from classical, Christian, and fairy-tale sources; the 'Christian Magician' has a foot in two or three worlds. No doubt a magic opera, even when built round a historical event of the eleventh century, enjoys the licence of the traditional pantomime. Moreover an explicit Christian imagery would probably have been forbidden on the stage. It is the abrupt abandonment of fantasy that makes the conversion of Argante and Armida not only dramatically absurd but faintly distasteful. A further charge against the libretto is its affected language and weak characterization. There is little life in these lay figures, with the exception of Armida, and she fades out after Act II.

Handel's music is full of striking invention. Since it is to some extent an anthology culled from the best works of his Italian period, this is not surprising. Reinhold Kubik in his Erlangen dissertation[16] is inclined to doubt Rossi's statement that Handel composed the score in a fortnight on the grounds that he could have reached London as early as September (for which there is no contemporary evidence) and none of the borrowings is literally exact. But it is difficult to see why he lifted texts from old Italian works unless he was in a hurry. It would be second nature to a composer of his improvisatory bent to modify and improve the earlier settings in detail as he wrote them out, a much quicker process than composing from scratch. This does not apply to all the *Rinaldo* borrowings, which cover the overture, *coro*,

---

[14] Some French influence is also possible; but nothing suggests that Hill knew Quinault's *Armide*, set by Lully and later by Gluck.

[15] See p. 28 and Plate 2.

[16] *Händels Rinaldo, Geschichte, Werk, Wirkung.*

and two-thirds of the arias. Some of them involved a good deal of rethinking and recomposition in the manner of *Agrippina*.[17] But owing to the weak libretto, and perhaps to the fact that Handel was essaying a new type of opera in unfamiliar surroundings and was still comparatively inexperienced in the theatre, *Rinaldo* for all its manifold riches is neither a consistently articulated work of art nor a dramatic masterpiece. The design produces little cumulative tension. Act I in particular is slow and halting. Act II is the strongest of the three, thanks to the dramatic force generated by Armida, and in Act III so much is going on that there is little danger of monotony. The exuberance and variety of the scoring, the vitality of the rhythms, and the presence of three duets and half a dozen symphonies go far to compensate for weakness of construction and characterization.

Moreover, it is unfair to judge the music without reference to the spectacle it was intended to accompany. Here Handel scored with one barrel but missed with the other. The scenes of war and pageantry are brilliantly successful. He is much more at a loss with the magic. Most of the transformations take place in secco recitative; there is nothing in the music to suggest the fabulous events described in the stage directions. The sinfonia for the assault on the mountain in Act III is a good stately piece, with an effective aposiopesis towards the end of the Allegro, but it is not particularly apt to the situation, and the rescue that follows is distinctly flat. Not till *Admeto* and *Orlando* did Handel find a convincing musical equivalent for the supernatural. But if *Rinaldo* is an open-air score, wanting in mystery and the powers of darkness, it retains (in Burney's apt phrase) 'something so peculiarly compact and forcible in the style' that it cannot be dismissed as a failure.

Armida alone lives up to the standard of characterization Handel set himself in *Agrippina*. The first of four great sorceresses in his operas, she is a glittering rather than a seductive figure and lacks the subtlety of her successors, but despite limited opportunities she towers above the other characters of *Rinaldo*. All her music has passion and energy. The cavatina 'Furie terribili', a splendid entrance, is a welcome burst of flame after the sedate opening scene. 'Molto voglio', based on the favourite theme of Agrippina's first aria and similarly scored with a solo oboe in the lead, has a higher tessitura than the rest of the part; one phrase is even launched from the diving-board of a top C. A singer who can hit this cleanly is sure of making a mark. But it is in Act II that Armida reveals her full stature, in the accompanied recitative and aria after her rejection by Rinaldo. The situation resembles that at the corresponding point in *Alcina*. 'Ah! crudel' is scarcely less profound than 'Ah! mio cor' as a revelation of the anguish in the sorceress's heart, torn between involuntary love and anger, and makes its point by similar means, a masterly manipulation of ritornello design. The remarkable opening for solo oboe, bassoon, and double bass (an afterthought; the aria originally began at the fifth bar) is heard once only (Ex. 17). A fresh ritornello of concentrated eloquence, developing earlier material and representing the climax of Armida's torment, crowns the A section; the Presto B section foreshortens the da capo by plunging abruptly from a furious D minor to the first phrase of the voice with its desolate diminished-seventh drop, now deprived of all accompaniment, before resuming the G minor lament. The

---

[17] They are examined in detail by Kubik, ibid. 70–113.

Ex. 17

Ex. 17 (cont.)

Ah!_____ cru - del

scoring, in eight parts (independent oboes, bassoons, and cellos, and threefold violins low in the compass) with only occasional doubling, is much richer than in Alcina's aria, the three-note wailing figures echoed in different registers and orchestral colours with haunting effect. Handel borrowed the opening of the melody and the first line of text from the instrumental cantata HWV 78 (*c.*1707), but transformed the continuation.

A little later Armida ends the act with the brilliant vengeance aria, 'Vo' far guerra', one of the earliest examples of Handel's characteristic use of what later came to be known as cavatina–cabaletta design. It is tonally linked with 'Ah! crudel' (in the tonic major), and it discharges the accumulated emotion after the dramatic balance has been altered in an intervening recitative. Although the material, based on an unpublished aria in *Rodrigo*, does not look memorable, the impact in the theatre is electrifying, thanks partly to the rhythms (with sudden bursts of triplet figuration) and partly again to the scoring. Handel's own harpsichord cadenzas, printed in Walsh's second edition and Chrysander's appendix (HG 117), are splendidly effective; so in the B section is the treatment of the strings in pizzicato octaves, a rare occurrence in Handel. Unfortunately Armida has nothing in Act III except the duet 'Al trionfo' with Argante, a spirited piece with a beautiful B section in triple time. Although this carries no tempo mark, it must be much slower than the Allegro. This is one of half a dozen da capo movements in *Rinaldo* where the sections are sharply contrasted, a stock gambit that Handel exploited with unfailing skill. It is also his last operatic duet with a bass for nearly thirty years; the only other example is in *Imeneo*.

Armida's paramour Argante is a disappointingly composite figure, borrowing one aria from Polifemo and another from Claudio in *Agrippina*. Burney described 'Sibillar gli angui' as 'a rough defiance, fit for a Pagan and a base voice'; so it is, but the pagan was a one-eyed giant. Argante's only new aria, 'Vieni, O cara' in Act I (which has no connection with Claudio's beginning with the same words), is more interesting. The gigue rhythm in a minor key, allied with the predominantly octave accompaniment, gives it a half wheedling, half sinister tone. Handel seems to have seen Argante as a humorous grotesque, a Saracen Polyphemus. But one new aria and a duet are scarcely enough to create a new and important character.

Rinaldo and Almirena are a conventional pair of lovers, though each is endowed with some lovely music. Rinaldo has by far the largest part—eight arias and a duet with each prima donna. Both duets are borrowed from cantatas; that with Armida in Act II is a lively action piece. The music Handel wrote for Nicolini, in *Amadigi* as well as *Rinaldo*, is always showy and effective, sometimes a little anonymous. By far the finest of his arias in *Rinaldo* is the justly famous 'Cara sposa', where Handel as usual rose to the challenge of his hero in distress and struck the note of high tragedy. As in Radamisto's 'Ombra cara', which it resembles in mood, the imploring accents of the voice are set against an intricately woven string accompaniment of great emotional intensity, with the parts constantly crossing. Among many happy details are the unobtrusive entry of the voice with a sustained note in the middle of a phrase, the late appearance of the bass in bar 24 at the end of the first vocal paragraph, the inversion of the viola's chromatic scale figure (bars 4–7) in the bass towards the end of the A section, the first violins' two-octave leap to a *forte* top D in bar 39, and the consolatory tenderness of the passage in the relative major. The quick B section,[18] a mere ten bars, is just long enough to establish a contrast before the da capo. Burney called this 'by many degrees the most pathetic song, and with the richest accompaniment, which had been then heard in England'. The richness applies to the counterpoint, not the scoring, which is for strings alone. Like 'Ah! crudel', 'Cara sposa' is a signal example of Handel's confidence and flexibility in the treatment of aria form. The brief but pungent intermediate ritornello, founded on the viola's chromatic scale figure, comes early in the A section and introduces a beautifully worked paragraph of exceptional length, extended by varied sequences, pedals, suspensions, and all manner of harmonic and contrapuntal resource, again culminating in a fresh final ritornello. The voice's first phrase, though repeatedly hinted at, returns only with the da capo. The entire A section of 80 slow bars is one continuous developing organism.

Rinaldo's next aria, 'Cor ingrato', on a similar but more concise plan with the Presto B section proportionately much longer, has a touching simplicity. The music leads smoothly out of the recitative, but the dramatic transition is clumsy, since it breaks up Rinaldo's account of the kidnapping. 'Venti, turbini' features a solo violin and bassoon in a vigorous concerto grosso accompaniment and makes a satisfactory close to the act, at the same time rounding off the portrait of the hero as lover and man of action. The end of the first vocal phrase later passed into *Messiah* ('For unto us') via *Tamerlano* ('Dal crudel').[19] Here Handel exploited the other side of Nicolini's technique;

---

[18] The autograph marking is *Presto*, not *Allegro*.
[19] There are likewise faint foretastes of *Semele* ('Ogni indugio', 'Sulla ruota'), *Judas Maccabaeus* ('Sibillar gli angui'), *Joshua* ('Molto voglio'), *Samson* ('Augelletti'), and other late works.

though the compass is only a ninth, the aria demands the utmost flexibility and control.

Rinaldo's music in the later acts might strike deeper if he showed the slightest sign of yielding to Armida's temptations. Hill's suppression of his spiritual struggle, present in Tasso, was a major blunder; the contrast with Ruggiero and Alcina needs no emphasis. 'Il Tricerbero umiliato' is a unison aria with a catchy tune that predictably became a popular hit, especially after it had acquired Bacchanalian associations from a new English text, 'Let the waiter bring clean glasses'. It is not clear why Rinaldo should threaten Cerberus, unless Handel took the aria from a lost cantata. 'Or la tromba' is another unfailingly effective piece, thanks to the brilliant orchestration, with four trumpets and drums as well as strings and oboes. It is the only aria Handel wrote for this combination, and it illustrates his marvellous sense of texture. The melodic and harmonic basis is rudimentary—the long A section never ventures beyond the dominant—yet it is extraordinarily exciting in performance, especially when the voice exchanges fanfares with the first trumpet, provided it is sung at the correct pitch.

The first Almirena, Isabella Girardeau, seems to have been a singer of modest gifts. Four arias is a small ration for a heroine, and three of them call for purity of tone rather than agility. The liveliest is the first, 'Combatti da forte', full of trills, flourishes, and strutting rhythms, but the display is chiefly in the orchestra, which reinforces much of the vocal line. The music is not quite in character, suggesting a resolute temperament that Almirena scarcely displays later. It is based on 'Fu scherzo' in the instrumental cantata 'Arresta il passo' (HWV 83) with a characteristic reshuffling of old ideas into a new pattern: compare the manner in which 'Tu la mia stella' in *Giulio Cesare* reached its final form (p. 511). 'Augelletti' is pretty, again largely a result of the scoring (strings and three recorders, with a sopranino or flageolet carolling away like a lark), but Handel wrote better arias of this type. 'Bel piacere', though nothing can dim its fascination, is less happily placed than in *Agrippina*. Only the incomparable 'Lascia ch'io pianga' gets inside the character; it would be impossible to guess that the melody began as a dance for Asiatics in *Almira*. As in its distant relative 'Verdi prati', Handel obtains an intensely emotional effect from a simple tune and accompaniment in a major key with a minimum of accidentals. This perfection is scarcely susceptible of analysis,[20] but one tiny detail is worth remark, the alteration of the third note of the melody when it returns in bar 15. This was an afterthought; Handel originally wrote A, as in the first bar.

Goffredo and Eustazio are heavily over-endowed, with five arias apiece. Neither shines as a character, but their music is charming and polished, and in two instances—Eustazio's 'Siam prossimi' and Goffredo's 'Sorge nel petto'— strikingly beautiful. 'Siam prossimi' evokes Purcell,[21] or perhaps (as Burney puts it) 'the favourite style of Carissimi'. The Magician's jaunty aria has another prehensile tune (adapted from a continuo cantata) that comes well enough from this specimen of complacent Christianity. Far finer is the haunting song of the Mermaids. The melody, veering seductively between minor and major tonality, conveys the timeless temptation of the Sirens with a

---

[20] See however Kubik's illuminating discussion (*Händels Rinaldo*, 85–90) of the aria's relationship to its forebears, two in *Almira*, one in *Il trionfo del Tempo*.

[21] Dent (24) makes the same point about the Pagan March in Act III.

nostalgia very characteristic of Handel. (Mozart achieves a not dissimilar effect by much the same means in Pedrillo's Romanze 'Im Mohrenland' in *Die Entführung*.) There is something deliciously unexpected and insinuating about the six- and seven-bar phrases:

Ex. 18

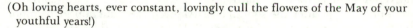

(Oh loving hearts, ever constant, lovingly cull the flowers of the May of your youthful years!)

This is the most successful of the transplanted pieces; taken from the cantata 'Arresta il passo', where it is in 12/8 time, the lament of an unhappy lover contrasting his useless tears with a stream reaching contentment in the sea, it fits the new context even better than the old.[22] The association with water may have suggested the borrowing. Handel's marking *Vivace* must (as elsewhere) refer to mood rather than tempo. A fast speed makes nonsense of the music. This is confirmed by the *Larghetto* of the Granville copy.[23]

The scoring of *Rinaldo* is calculated to make the maximum impact in the theatre; no Italian opera hitherto heard in London had employed so majestic an orchestra. Although Handel paints on a broad canvas, he deploys his forces shrewdly. The trumpets and drums, after Argante's first aria, are not released till the Christian March in the middle of Act III, where the sudden entry in the ninth bar not of two trumpets but of four[24] produces an effect of splendour and exhilaration that time has not dimmed. They dominate the closing scene. There are no transverse flutes or horns, but as well as the consort of recorders in 'Augelletti' several arias have a very full accompaniment, notably 'Venti, turbini' and 'Ah! crudel', where the concertino group includes

[22] The librettists also deserve credit for their conflation of two episodes in Tasso, the siren's song in Canto xiv ('O giovanetti, mentre aprile e maggio') and the scene in Canto xv where Ubaldo and the Danish Knight search for Rinaldo in a small boat steered by a 'fatal donzella'.

[23] For a parallel instance in *Amadigi*, see p. 294. Charles Cudworth ('The Meaning of "Vivace" in Eighteenth-Century England', *Fontes artis musicae*, xii (1965), 194–5) cites evidence that *Vivace* ranked in speed between *Andante* and *Allegretto*. When Handel used the *Vivace* first movement of the B flat oboe concerto (HWV 302a) to open the Chandos Anthem 'O come, let us sing unto the Lord', he marked it *Andante*.

[24] Argante's aria originally had three trumpet parts (one more than in *Aci, Galatea e Polifemo*); Handel may have taken out the third in order to strengthen the later impact.

solo oboe, bassoon, violin, cello, and double bass, and 'Sibillar gli angui' and the duet 'Al trionfo del nostro furore', where the instruments are used more in the mass. As in other operas of this period, Handel gives a good deal of freedom to the oboes and often contrasts them with the violins in ritornellos. The 1711 scoring of the overture—a characteristic mixture of French and Italian styles, with a beautiful little modulating Adagio between the fugato and the bouncy Gigue—remains unpublished. The autograph shows interesting changes: the solos at bar 28, originally for violin and cello, were changed by Handel to recorder (*flauto*) and bassoon; those at bar 37 were for violin and bassoon (originally cello), and at bar 43 for oboe and bassoon. If some of the accompaniments are exceptionally weighty, others display a chamber delicacy. There are two unison arias and five with continuo accompaniment, of which one has a three-part ritornello after the A section and another ('Andate, O forti') in the subsequent recitative, where it neatly rounds off the scene. If the Flower parts are accurate, Handel even silenced the cello in 'Sulla ruota' and 'Andate, O forti', except during the ritornellos, leaving the bass to the harpsichord.

'Sulla ruota' precedes the massively scored 'Sibillar gli angui', and Handel underlines the contrast with Argante's spectacular entry by an unusual juxtaposition of keys, D major following F major without intervening recitative. A similar dramatic motivation places Rinaldo's 'Cara sposa' (E minor) immediately after the sinfonia for Almirena's abduction in A minor, the subdominant minor; the earliest copy (RM 19 d 5) has the significant note *Segue subito l'Aria* here. There are many signs that Handel planned a careful scheme of tonality in *Rinaldo*, perhaps to compensate for the opera's centrifugal tendencies. The overture and first set hold to F and related flat keys till the climate changes at the entry of the heathen Argante. The second (the grove) begins and ends in G, with the weightiest aria ('Cara sposa') in the relative minor. Act II begins in E minor and ends in G, and the entire first set (the enticement of Rinaldo) is in minor keys. The earlier part of the magic garden scene is in closely connected flat keys until Rinaldo's 'Abbruggio, avvampo' pulls it sharply into G, which acts as a firm tonic till the end of the act. Act III begins and ends in B flat, and veers between that key and D (obligatory for the trumpets); it keeps remarkably strictly to this plan, with five pieces in each key and the other three closely related to one or the other (E flat, F, A). At the climax Handel associates the Saracens with B flat (March and duet 'Al trionfo'), the Christians with D (March, 'Or la tromba', 'Solo dal brando', and Battle). The entire act is in major keys; apart from the first set of Act II *Rinaldo* is an overwhelmingly 'major' opera.

History and Text

Rossi, echoed by Mainwaring, is the only authority for the statement that Handel composed the music in a fortnight; there are no dates in the autograph, whose final pages are missing. Hill supplied some advance publicity. A poem in *The British Apollo* (18 December 1710) hinted at scenic marvels, and the libretto was advertised from 13 February 1711, eleven days before the first performance at the Queen's Theatre on 24 February. The cast was:

RINALDO:	Nicolo Grimaldi, called Nicolini (alto castrato)
GOFFREDO:	Francesca Vanini-Boschi (contralto)
EUSTAZIO:	Valentino Urbani, called Valentini (alto castrato)
ALMIRENA:	Isabella Girardeau (soprano)
ARMIDA:	Elisabetta Pilotti-Schiavonetti (soprano)
ARGANTE:	Giuseppe Maria Boschi (bass)
CHRISTIAN MAGICIAN:	Giuseppe Cassani (alto castrato)
HERALD:	Lawrence (tenor)

It is not known who played the Lady in Act II; she may have sung 'Il vostro maggio' while the Mermaids danced, though the aria is attributed to *Sirene* in the plural.

The score performed in 1711 differed from that printed by Chrysander in several respects, apart from the scoring of the overture and 'Sibillar gli angui'. 'Lascia ch'io pianga' came earlier in II iv, after the cadence 'd'un amoroso affetto' (HG 60, sixth system), and the recitative on HG 61 (second system), with differences in text and music, led via a cadence in A to 'Basta che sol'. Most of the B section of 'Sorge nel petto' had a different bass. 'Solo dal brando' was probably cut; it is the one aria omitted by Walsh and occurs only in the autograph. The Sirens' song, or part of it, may have been repeated after 'Il Tricerbero umiliato', and it is possible that the *coro* was sung to the words in the libretto, which require a different rhythm. Although Eustazio's 'Scorta rea' is not in the libretto, its inclusion in Walsh's first edition of the score shows that it was added very soon, perhaps for Valentini's benefit on 11 April. The insertion entailed changes to the recitative.

The opera was an immediate success with the public, particular praise being bestowed on Nicolini and Handel himself, whose playing on the harpsichord, according to Mainwaring, 'was thought as extraordinary as his Music'. There were fifteen performances before the season ended, the tenth (11 April) for the benefit of Valentini, the twelfth (5 May) for the Boschis, the last (2 June) for the box-keepers. Valentini was specifically advertised as appearing in the twelfth, which suggests that he may have missed the eleventh. Of the latter (25 April) Lady Hervey wrote that the theatre 'was as full as ever I saw it at a subscription, but that was by way of party, in order to get it empty on Saturday'.[25] The thirteenth performance (9 May) was announced as the last, but popular demand required two more. On 20 and 24 March there was 'Dancing by Monsieur du Breil and Mademoiselle le Fevre just arriv'd from Bruxelles'. They performed as an additional attraction between acts; the Mermaids presumably came from the resident ballet. The advertisement for the performance of 26 May added that 'by reason of the Hot Weather, the Waterfall will play the best part of the Opera'. Waterfalls are mentioned in the directions for the first scene of Act III but would be equally appropriate at the start of Act II; the theatre had provision for stage fountains, which were used in *Amadigi* and other operas. The first six nights were by subscription (pit and boxes); on the last three of them (6, 10, and 13 March) the gallery took receipts of £18. 9s. 9d., £27. 2s. 6d., and £18. 9s. 3d. respectively. These figures, wrongly dated in Deutsch (p. 39) and *The London Stage*, suggest a large attendance of 180–260 people.[26] The statement, accepted by Loewenberg and

[25] A reference to Pilotti's benefit: see p. 153.
[26] *Coke Papers*, 176.

Deutsch, that *Rinaldo* was performed in Dublin with Nicolini in early April is not true.[27]

The success of *Rinaldo* was not at all to the taste of Addison and Steele, who in their new periodical *The Spectator* did their best to ridicule the whole enterprise. They were not disinterested; Steele was a patentee of Drury Lane and owned a concert room in York Buildings,[28] and stood to lose business in both capacities, while Addison's *amour propre* had not recovered from the disastrous failure of his English opera *Rosamond* (with music by Clayton) four years earlier. His remarks on recitative in different languages and Lully's reconciliation of Italian methods with French taste[29] show that he was not unfamiliar with the aesthetic problems of opera, but like many of his English contemporaries he was hostile to the Italian language and the employment of castratos, and the opportunity to attack *Rinaldo* was too good to miss. In no. 5 of *The Spectator* (6 March 1711), beginning from the premise than an opera's 'only Design is to gratifie the Senses, and keep up an indolent Attention in the Audience', he made fun of the production before he had seen it. Some of this was fair game. The release of sparrows on the stage during 'Augelletti' he condemned as an improper mixture of realism with illusion; he feared they would take up residence in the theatre, 'besides the Inconveniences which the Heads of the Audience may sometimes suffer from them'. His statement that 'the Musick proceeded from a Consort of Flageletts and Birdcalls which was planted behind the Scenes' cannot be accepted as evidence of a stage orchestra (though this would not have been impossible), since he had done no more than buy a libretto and make 'a nearer Enquiry'). He lumped the 'Tinsel of Tasso' with the 'tedious Circumlocutions' of Rossi's preface and the confused mythology of the libretto, and said nothing about the music or how it was received. Indeed his confession, in no. 18, that, 'if [music] would take the entire Possession of our Ears, if it would make us incapable of hearing Sense, if it would exclude Arts that have a much greater Tendency to the Refinement of Human Nature', he would banish it like Plato from his Republic, puts him out of court as a critic of opera.

Steele, who saw *Rinaldo* and discussed it in no. 14 (16 March), was no more perceptive. He compared it unfavourably with the Punch and Judy shows presented by one Powell at a tavern in Covent Garden. In his opinion 'the Undertakers of the *Hay-Market*, having raised too great an Expectation in their printed Opera, very much disappoint their Audience on the Stage'. The instances he gives are all concerned with matters of production. Argante made his first entry on foot 'instead of being drawn in a triumphant Chariot by White Horses'. There was 'but a very short Allowance of Thunder and Lightning', and the boy who produced the fire and smoke from the dragons'

[27] It is mentioned in J. T. Gilbert's *A History of the City of Dublin*, 3 vols. (Dublin, 1854–9) and much elaborated by W. H. Grattan Flood, *A History of Irish Music* (Dublin, 1905), 266–7, and *Introductory Sketch of Irish Musical History* (London, 1921), 33. Nicolini did visit Dublin, probably in July, but there is no contemporary reference to Handel or any opera there. See T. J. Walsh, *Opera in Dublin 1705–1797* (Dublin, 1973), 9 ff.

[28] The letters from Clayton, Haym, and Dieupart published in *The Spectator* on 26 Dec. 1711 and 18 Jan. 1712 indicate that the success of *Rinaldo* had interfered with their plans for 'exhibiting Entertainments of Musick in York-Buildings'. They were particularly sore because of their part in introducing Italian opera to London; they had been beaten at their own game.

[29] *Spectator*, no. 29 (3 Apr. 1711). The full flavour of Addison's and Steele's criticism can only be obtained if the various essays on Italian opera in *The Spectator* (nos. 5, 13, 14, 18, 22, 29, 31, 42, and 44) are read in their entirety.

mouths failed to keep his head down and to hide his candle. The sparrows and chaffinches 'either get into the Galleries or put out the Candles'. Something went wrong with the changing of the 'Side-Scenes' (wings), so that 'we were presented with a Prospect of the Ocean in the midst of a delightful Grove; and . . . I was not a little astonished to see a well-dressed young Fellow, in a full bottom'd Wigg, appear in the midst of the Sea, and without any visible Concern taking Snuff'.[30] Burney was not far wrong in ascribing 'some part of the Spectator's severity to want of skill in the art of Music; some to peevishness; and the rest to national prejudice, and the spirit of party in favour of our domestic theatre'. The pronouncements of Addison and Steele are however of value, not only as amusing journalism but for what they tell us about the staging of the opera.

Rinaldo, thanks to its sensational qualities and the fact of primogeniture, had 53 performances in London during Handel's life, more than any of his other operas. It was revived in five seasons, 1712, 1713, 1714–15, 1717, and 1731, in the course of which all the principal male parts, including Argante, were at different times sung by castratos and by women. Information is scanty about the first three revivals owing to the absence of librettos. Handel was in Hanover during the 1712 season, when *Rinaldo* was performed nine times (first on 23 January, when 'by her Majesty's Command no Persons are to be admitted behind the Scenes', no doubt to prevent interference with the machinery). In 1713 the opera was announced for 24 March but not revived till 6 May, and then only for two performances; the second, for Jane Barbier's benefit, brought her no more than £15. The advertisements mentioned 'all the proper Scenes and Machines', as they did next year, when the first of eleven performances took place on 30 December 1714. The author of the Colman Opera Register observed that there was no dancing; he mentioned a full house, with the Royal Family, on 15 January, but a very thin one on the 29th. This revival was much patronized by the Royal Family: Handel's employer George I had recently succeeded Queen Anne. For the last performance of the season (25 June 1715) Nicolini returned and took a benefit; the management announced dancing and 'New Scenes and Cloaths, particularly the Scene with the Fountains'. A satirical notice in *The Weekly Packet* the same day observed that 'Signior Nicolini's Quail-Pipe continues to lug the Nobility and Gentry by the Ears, who have gone very far on his last Benefit-Night, towards equipping him for another Purchase at Venice, he having already built a stately Edifice there, near the Rialto, upon which is Written in Characters of Gold, VILLA BRITANNICA, as a Testimony that Scaliger's Saying, that we are Hospitibus Feri, is a downright Untruth, and falsely imputed to our Nation'.

The casts of these revivals, apart from the Magician and the Herald, are recorded in the newspapers. Pilotti continued as Armida in all three seasons. Rinaldo was sung by Nicolini in 1712, Jane Barbier (contralto) in 1713, and Diana Vico (contralto) in 1714–15, except for Nicolini's benefit on the last night; Goffredo by Margherita de L'Epine (soprano) in 1712 and 1713 and Caterina Galerati (soprano) in 1714–15; Eustazio by Barbier in 1712, Valentini in 1713, and probably cut in 1714–15; Almirena by Signora Manina (soprano) in 1712 and 1713 and Anastasia Robinson (soprano) in 1714–15; Argante by Salomon Bendler ('newly arrived') in 1712, Richard Leveridge in

---

[30] He may have been one of the stage spectators who were expressly forbidden later.

1713, and Angelo Zannoni ('lately arriv'd from Italy') in 1714–15. These last three singers were all basses.

Although only one transposition was required, Goffredo changing from contralto to soprano in 1712, it is likely that both text and music underwent a fair amount of alteration during these years. Documentation is difficult owing to the absence of early scores as well as librettos, but about a dozen arias not in HG, all but one of them still unpublished, are either ascribed to *Rinaldo* in manuscript sources or can be assigned to it on internal evidence. Four, probably five, belong to the 1717 revival described below. Two more, 'La crudele lontananza' and 'Minacciami, non hò timor', are ascribed elsewhere to *Teseo* and *Amadigi* respectively and mentioned under those operas, though they may of course have been sung in *Rinaldo* as well. A soprano setting of 'Sorge nel petto' (G major, 3/8) was presumably composed for L'Epine or Galerati. It is much lighter in mood than the alto version; four bars from its final ritornello eventually came to rest in the Minuet of the overture to *Samson*. During this period Handel added a B section to 'Augelletti' which survives in at least three sources. It makes a da capo aria of immense length and is by no means an improvement. Three alto arias on the other hand show Handel at the height of his powers. 'Sà perchè pena il cor' (E minor) is a magnificent tragic aria for a tormented lover (? Armida), with prominent ninths in the vocal line and a striking enharmonic progression at the very outset of the B section:

Ex. 19

(You could not ease my grief, even if it were still caused by you)

'Con lagrime si belle' (F major) and 'Spera chi sà perchè la sorte' (B flat major) are full of expressive counterpoint, the former with an oboe line largely independent of the violins.

This is perhaps the place to mention four more floating arias from this period. Two are alto love songs attractively tinged with the tone of recorders. 'Nò, non così severe' (D major) makes happy play with pedals. 'Vieni, O cara, e lieta in petto' (F major 3/8), rich in hemiola effects, is an elaborated version of material used in several other works, including *Rodrigo* and *Teseo* ('Più non cerca libertà'). 'Sento prima le procelle', a fiery coloratura piece also for alto in D major, was used in shortened and simplified form in the 1731 revival of *Admeto*. These three arias are now known to have been written for the castrato Antonio Bernacchi as Demetrio in the 1716 revival of *Pirro e Demetrio* (libretto in the Folger Shakespeare Library, Washington). There is an early copy of 'Vieni, O cara, e lieta in petto' in the hand of H6 in the Mackworth Collection, Cardiff Central Library. All the arias so far mentioned in these two paragraphs (except the B section of 'Augelletti') occur among a group of twenty copied by Smith in Tenbury 884 (*c.* 1719). Nineteen of them reappear in a later copy (S4) in the Shaftesbury Collection; one (from *Agrippina*) is replaced by an otherwise unknown aria, 'Lusinga questo cor' (G major), with five-part accompaniment including an independent oboe.

In the 1717 revival (5 January, 10 performances) Nicolini, Pilotti, and Anastasia Robinson retained their parts, and Eustazio was cut; Goffredo was sung by Antonio Bernacchi, Argante by Gaetano Berenstadt, both alto castratos new to London. All the principal parts were thus taken by high voices, as in *Teseo*, *Silla*, and *Amadigi*. 'All the original Scenes and Machines belonging to this Opera' were again advertised in an attempt to draw the public, though the modified stage directions in the libretto suggest that the spectacle was abridged. Burney's remarks on this revival throw light on eighteenth-century taste. He says it was 'cast in a stronger manner than heretofore . . . This familiar opera, though six years old, an age more than sufficient to render the generality of musical dramas superannuated, was performed no less than ten times'. Receipts varied from £130. 9*s.* 9*d.* on the first night to £66. 13*s.* 3*d.* on 9 March.[31] The performances on 2 and 18 May were for the benefit of Pilotti and Berenstadt respectively. On 5 June, the last night (for the benefit of the box-keepers), an added attraction was 'Entertainments of Dancing by Mons. Salle, and Mademoiselle Salle his Sister, the two Children, who never perform'd on this Stage before'. Marie Sallé was to make a sensational reappearance in Handel's operas during the season of 1734/5.

There were considerable changes in the score, the most important occasioned by the fact that Argante was an alto. His original arias all disappeared except 'Vieni, O cara', which was transposed up an octave with modifications to the vocal line in bars 16–22 to keep it within Berenstadt's compass. 'Sibillar gli angui' and 'Basta che sol' were replaced by new arias, 'Sorte, amor vuol che quest'alma' and 'Ogni tua bella stilla'. The former is conventional and rather empty, though no more out of place that 'Sibillar'; the latter, an appealing love song, is if anything an improvement. After his address to his generals in III v Argante had an extra aria, 'Pregio è sol d'un alma forte', a substantial show-piece with lengthy divisions calculated to put the new singer through his paces. The duet 'Al trionfo' was retained, Argante presumably singing his part an octave higher with some necessary adjustment. He emerges as more feline and less of a blusterer than in the 1711 score. It seems likely that another additional alto aria, 'Splenda lieta al tuo disegno', was written for Berenstadt in this revival, perhaps during the run. The words are not in the libretto, but a reference to Armida by name identifies the opera, and the context suggests that Argante is addressing Armida in her disguise as Almirena just before she resumes her own shape (II x, HG 77). The music, despite the

---

[31] The theatre accounts (see pp. 164–5) include two sets of figures for 5 Jan. but none for the 12th or 19th. The figures are probably incomplete, though it is possible that one of these performances was cancelled.

presence of recorders doubling the violins, is bare in texture and not of great interest.

The suppression of Eustazio strengthens rather than weakens the opera. The essential lines in his recitative, concerning the search for the Magician, were transferred to Goffredo together with one of his arias ('Di Sion'); the rest was cut, as were Goffredo's 'Sorge nel petto' and the Magician's aria. Almirena gained two arias, 'Vieni, O caro, che senza il suo core' (with a new introductory recitative) after Argante's 'Ogni tua bella stilla' in II iv and 'Sì t'amo, O caro' shortly before the *coro* in III xiii. The latter, from *Teseo*, is of only moderate quality, but 'Vieni, O caro' is the finest of the new pieces. Although it holds up the action and makes the third aria in one scene, it expresses Almirena's continuing love for Rinaldo with a touching eloquence. The single bar of common time at the entry of the voice, after a long 3/8 ritornello that never anticipates the vocal line, is an early example of a stroke Handel often used with happy effect (Ex. 20). The low tessitura and restricted compass of the vocal line (it never goes above D), together with the similarity in the words and the identical key, suggest that Handel wrote it in the first place for Berenstadt as a replacement for 'Vieni, O cara' in I iv, just as he replaced Argante's other arias, and then for some reason gave it to Almirena, resorting to a makeshift alteration of the bass 'Vieni' for Berenstadt. The alto 'Vieni, O cara, e lieta in petto' mentioned above may also have played a part in these transactions; it likewise remains within Berenstadt's narrow compass.

Handel's last revival, on 6 April 1731, 'With New Scenes and Cloaths', after the theatre had been temporarily closed owing to 'Great Preparations being required to bring this Opera on the Stage', involved a much more drastic revision of the score. The cast was:

RINALDO:	Senesino (alto castrato)
GOFFREDO:	Annibale Pio Fabri (tenor)
ALMIRENA:	Anna Strada (soprano)
ARMIDA:	Antonia Merighi (contralto)
ARGANTE:	Francesca Bertolli (contralto)
MAGICIAN:	Giovanni Giuseppe Commano (bass)

The Herald was a bass, probably doubled by Commano. Eustazio was again cut. Here four parts—Goffredo, Armida, the Magician, and the Herald—changed voice; Argante, though again an alto, sang none of the music composed or adapted for Berenstadt in 1717; most of Rinaldo's part had to be transposed down for Senesino; even Almirena's music was extensively rewritten. Indeed the only pieces that remained unchanged from 1711 were 'Sulla ruota' (transferred to a different character), the sinfonia for the abduction of Almirena, 'Il vostro maggio' (sung by the Lady in the boat), 'Lascia ch'io pianga', 'È un incendio', and possibly 'Bel piacere' and the *coro*. This was the most radical of all Handel's operatic revisions, with the possible exception of *Il pastor fido* in 1734, affecting important details of the plot as well as almost every musical number. One motive was perhaps to lighten the load of the singers, who in the season of 1730/1 had to learn six new operas; five of the imported arias had been sung by the same artists in earlier works (four in *Lotario*, one in *Giulio Cesare*). Practical reasons of stagecraft also played a part. It is clear that the machines and the army of supers employed in 1711 were no longer

Ex. 20

(Come, O dear one, because without its heart [this breast can no longer live])

available. The pyrotechnical dragons and black clouds disappeared, along with Goffredo's pavilion and Argante's cavalry escort in Act I, the sparrows and fountains, the mermaids, and the military pageantry (both Marches and the Battle were cut). The assault on the mountain in Act III was further simplified. As some compensation Rinaldo had an energetic tussle with a magic grove, involving much timber-felling, for which the librettist (probably Rossi again) went back to Tasso (Canto xviii, 17–39); but the spectacular element must have seemed tame to those who remembered the original production.

The principal changes in the plot occur in the last two acts.[32] Instead of assuming the likeness of Almirena, Armida *places herself upon a little Bank, behind a Vase of Flowers, and as Rinaldo is going, a Voice resembling Almirena's, invites him to embrace her.* Presently *Rinaldo hastens to the Place whence the Voice comes, and thinking to embrace Almirena, discovers Armida.* This may have made the episode easier to stage (the voice was that of the Siren in the wings); but in the next scene it involves recourse to the time-honoured and artificial device of Armida overhearing Argante paying compliments to Almirena's portrait. At the point where she resumes her own shape for the last time she *rushes out furiously, and snatches Almirena's Picture out of his Hands.* After their quarrel and her exit (with a different aria) Almirena returns, addresses the first half of Armida's 'Ah! crudel' to Argante and, when he has gone, decides to wheedle her way to freedom by pretending to love him, since gentle words and looks are the woman's weapon.

Act III is completely transformed—for the worse, except in one respect. After the assault on the mountain the second set (now *A little Grove of Palm and Cypress Trees in the Garden of Armida*) begins with a condensed and perfunctory version of the quarrel and reconciliation between Armida and Argante from the original III vi, without the Pagan March or the duet. Armida goes to seek aid from Acheron, while Argante sings Eustazio's aria 'Di Sion' with different words looking forward to his own triumph. Armida's attempt to murder Almirena follows; when she summons the furies Goffredo *with his Wand touches the Grove of Palm Trees which disappears, and the inchanted Grove of Armida is seen. She betakes her self to Flight, and Godfrey, Rinaldo and Almirena embrace each other.* Almirena and Goffredo, looking forward to revenge against the pagan pair, calmly appropriate their duet 'Al trionfo', with slight changes to words and music. Rinaldo is left *viewing at a Distance the inchanted Grove* in an accompanied recitative, 'Orrori menzogneri', which is punctuated with complex stage directions: *Offers to enter the Grove, when a sudden Flame from the Earth flashes before him, and prevents his Entrance; at which he retires a little, and then appears with an Air of Resolution . . . Draws his Sword, and boldly rushes thro' the Flame, which immediately disappears, and he retires into the Midst of the Wood . . . Hews down several Trees, and then the Spirits fly thro' the Air; after which, a new Plantation rises out of the Earth . . . Destroys the new Plants, and other Spirits disperse themselves into the Air; at which the Inchantment ends, and he leaves the Grove, the Ruins of which no more appear.* After a thankful aria from Rinaldo we see *Argantes in Flight with his drawn Sword, and Armida precipitately following him.* She rails against the powers of hell for abandoning her and offers Argante her heart, hand, and a kingdom in compensation for the one he has lost (we are not told how). *Armida and Argantes are convey'd away in a Chariot drawn by Dragons*; there is no last-minute conversion. The final scene takes place in *a royal Hall with a Throne and Crown*; Jerusalem is not mentioned. In the presence of *Generals of the Army, Populace and Soldiers* Goffredo *ascends the Throne at the Sound of military Instruments*, ascribes the merit to his 'glorious Partners', *places the Crown on his Head and then descends*, before bestowing Almirena on Rinaldo.

The musical changes are best discussed under each character in turn. Of

---

[32] Chrysander's 1731 score is in places incomprehensible because its stage directions were nearly all taken from an earlier version. Those of the 1731 libretto, which he did not use, are very different. Only the most important are quoted here. The 'etc' in bar 6 of HG 202 covers a multitude of events.

Rinaldo's eight arias, 'Ogni indugio' and 'È un incendio' kept their original pitch; 'Or la tromba' was cut; the remaining five, together with the duet 'Scherzano' and a rather vacuous aria from *Lotario*, 'Vedrò più liete' (composed for Bernacchi), were transposed down a tone; the duet 'Fermati' was put down a minor third (originally a fourth), probably as much for Armida's convenience as Rinaldo's. The accompanied recitative 'Orrori menzogneri', a striking piece 50 bars long in Handel's most elaborate style, with abrupt changes of mood and two substantial ritornellos in a contrasted triple time (for the tree-felling episodes), is the only new music composed for the 1731 version, apart from secco recitatives and (possibly) the brief sinfonia at the beginning of the last scene.

Goffredo, now a tenor, retained two of his arias, 'Sovra balze' and 'Mio cor', with the voice part transposed down a sixth and the orchestra up a third (though 'Mio cor' was originally a tone lower, in A minor). He annexed the A section of Eustazio's 'Siam prossimi' with the voice part put down a fifth, and in place of 'Nò, nò, che quest'alma' received 'D'instabile fortuna' from *Lotario*, which Fabri had sung the previous season in the part of the tyrant Berengario. He lost both his arias in Act III, but shared the modified version of the duet 'Al trionfo' with Almirena.

The latter retained 'Lascia ch'io pianga' and 'Augelletti' (with seven bars lopped from its final ritornello), and gained two arias that Strada had sung in earlier operas, 'Quel cor che mi donasti' from *Lotario* in place of 'Combatti' and 'Parolette, vezzi e sguardi' at the end of Act II. Chrysander is wrong in calling this a new composition; it had been sung at Strada's benefit during the 1730 run of *Giulio Cesare* (21 March), and the words were modified for *Rinaldo*.[33] The virtuous Almirena thus delivered in rapid succession the first half of Armida's 'Ah! crudel' and a characteristically capricious aria composed for Cleopatra. In the final scene the libretto gives her 'Bel piacere', but this was replaced by 'Sì, caro' from *Admeto*, perhaps before performance; while both were copied in the Hamburg performing scores, Walsh printed 'Sì, caro' among the 'Additional Songs' a fortnight later.

Armida was even more scurvily treated than Almirena. Her two accompanied recitatives and 'Furie terribili' were modified or transposed for alto, but she lost her remaining three arias and the duet with Argante. In their place she gained a scratch collection of three others, of which the most effective is Almirena's 'Combatti', rewritten a fourth lower with the orchestra reinforced by two horns, in place of 'Molto voglio'. The others are 'Arma lo sguardo' from *Lotario*, already in Merighi's repertory, a fine piece but out of place here (Chrysander ascribes it wrongly to Argante, altering the genders in the B section) and 'Fatto è Giove', a transposed version of a Bernacchi aria in *Partenope* that makes even less sense in Act III.

Nothing remained of Argante's original part. He had no entrance aria, though the ritornello of 'Sibillar gli angui' with a single trumpet part was retained to get him on stage. Of his three arias, 'Sulla ruota' and 'Di Sion' were resurrected from the defunct part of Eustazio and placed in I v and III ii (now iii) respectively. The third was another borrowing from *Lotario* familiar to the singer, 'Per salvarti, idolo mio', which came in for 'Basta che sol'. The Magician is perhaps the only alto part in Handel's operas that he ever gave to a bass in a revival; his aria (now doubled by violins at the octave and with the final ritornello shortened) was transposed not by an octave but by a sixth.

There were slight changes in the overture, including the omission of the fugue's repeat. The sinfonia for the assault on the mountain was divided, the opening Largo and Allegro (without a repeat) being played at the beginning of the act, and the Allegro alone, with a modified first bar, during the second scene (HG 190); the concluding Largo was cut. A number of tempo marks differ from those of the autograph, but most of them had been changed earlier before RM 19 d 5 was copied. 'Siam prossimi' however was speeded up from *Largo* to *Andante*. The four trumpets were reduced to one, which played only in two short symphonies.

The 1731 version of *Rinaldo* is a striking illustration[34] of the seeming vandalism with which Handel could treat his works in revival. What there was of characterization and dramatic continuity in the 1711 score he destroyed. All the principal persons except Rinaldo are given music that is not merely irrelevant but at variance with the character as drawn in the libretto. Almirena and Armida exchange some of their most individual utterances, and the former for one scene becomes a calculating minx after the manner of Poppea or Cleopatra. Apart from the more convincing manner in which Armida and Argante are disposed of, there is little to admire except Rinaldo's new accompanied recitative and the richer scoring of 'Combatti', though Kubik[35] rightly points to improvements in the secco recitative, where better declamation, more flexible and livelier rhythms, quicker changes of harmony, and increased chromaticism reflect Handel's finer dramatic control acquired over twenty years. It is pointless to charge him with artistic irresponsibility when he was in effect creating that familiar grotesque of Baroque opera, a pasticcio.

Surprisingly few excerpts from *Rinaldo* seem to have been performed at concerts. Drury Lane copyists' bills from one Luke Pippard in 1716[36] mention 'Or la tromba', 'Molto voglio', and 'Sibillar'. Jane Barbier sang 'Or la tromba' ('with the Trumpet') at Lincoln's Inn Fields on 28 March 1726 and at the Crow Street Music Hall, Dublin, on 4 December 1731. Mrs Turner Robinson and Clarke sang the duet 'Al trionfo' at the former's Drury Lane benefit on 26 March 1729. The Christian March became a popular favourite after its inclusion in *The Beggar's Opera*, set to the words 'Let us take the road', in 1728.

Rinaldo reached the Hamburg stage on 27 November 1715 in a version by Barthold Feïnd, his last work for the theatre. He translated the recitatives and most of the set pieces, but left eight arias, the first two duets and the *coro* in Italian. There were revivals in 1720 (29 August) and 1721 (five performances in each year) and a new production on 27 May 1723 with costly decorations ('schmackhaft gemacht'), the particular attraction being a garden with a fountain of living water in the 'Augelletti' scene. According to Willers it was performed eleven times in that year, twice in 1724 (the bass Bahn sang Argante in December of that year[37]), and once each in 1727 and 1730. 'Augelletti' found its way into Keiser's *Artemisia* (Hamburg, 1715) and a pasticcio *Orlando furioso*

---

[34] There are many others, both in the operas and the oratorios.
[35] *Händels Rinaldo*, 161–5.
[36] BL Egerton MS 2159.
[37] K. Zelm in *Hamburger Jahrbuch für Musikwissenschaft*, iii (1978), 45.

(Brunswick, 1732). On 1 October 1718 Leonardo Leo conducted a much altered version, in effect a pasticcio, at the Royal Palace in Naples in honour of the birthday of the Emperor Charles VI. Leo contributed an allegorical prologue, comic scenes, and three arias, and much of the rest was not by Handel. Nicolini sang his original role; the Almirena was the contralto Anna Dotti, later a member of Handel's company in London.

The first modern revival was a single shortened performance in Czech at the Prague Conservatorium in 1923;[38] the first in England at the Century Theatre, London, in 1933, by pupils of the Hammersmith Day Continuation School;[39] the first in Germany at Halle in 1954; the first in the United States at Houston (in a corrupt version) in 1975. Revivals since then have been fairly frequent. A good recording is still needed.

Autograph

The surviving portions of the 1711 autograph are divided between the Royal Music Library (RM 20 c 3) and the Fitzwilliam Museum (Mus MS 254), the former containing 53 leaves (three of them insertions), the latter 35 (also three insertions). Together they comprise three-quarters of the score; about 30 leaves are missing. Since most of Handel's foliation (by gatherings, each act beginning a new series) has been preserved, it is possible to make deductions about the original state of the manuscript. There are seven gaps:

Bar 27 of 'Ogni indugio' to bar 53 of 'Sibillar' (HG 11–16; 1 gathering).
Bar 15 of 'Cor ingrato' to end of recit. 'Di speranza' (HG 42–6; 1 gathering).
Bar 42 of 'Venti, turbini' to end of 'Il vostro maggio' (HG 49–53; ?2 leaves + 1 gathering).
Bar 30 of 'Fermati' to end of recit. 'Crudel, tu ch'involasti' (HG 66–7; 1 leaf).
Bars 4–16 of 'Dunque i lacci' (HG 70–71; 1 leaf).
Second half of bar 18 of recit. 'Adorata Almirena' to bar 21 of 'Andate, O forti' (HG 77–85; probably 2 gatherings).
Bar 11 of Battaglia to end of opera (HG 110–15, except 'Solo dal brando'; approximately 6 leaves).

The ends of all three acts are missing, together with the opening of the second and third. It is clear that the losses are due to accident, not to the deliberate removal of material, although each of the first three gaps includes one of Eustazio's arias. Generally a complete gathering, or an incomplete one at the end of an act, has dropped out. The fourth and fifth gaps are due to the loss of the outer double leaf of the fifth gathering of Act II. The pieces totally lost are the arias 'Sulla ruota', 'Col valor', 'Siam prossimi', 'Il vostro maggio', 'Vo' far guerra', and 'Sorge nel petto', the sinfonia in III ii, and the *coro*.

The insertions are RM 20 c 3, ff. 21–2 (revision of part of 'Augelletti' after Handel decided to rearrange the text) and 53 ('Solo dal brando', on different paper, cued to follow the recitative on HG 109; Chrysander printed it in the wrong place); Mus MS 254, pp. 21–4 ('Scorta rea' with the last three bars of

---

[38] Information from Professor Manfred Rätzer, Halle.
[39] W. C. Smith, *A Handelian's Notebook* (London, 1965), 104.

the previous recitative reset; p. 24 is blank) and 47–8 (new opening of 'Ah crudel'; p. 48 is blank). Handel cued in 'Sorge nel petto' on p. 60, but the aria itself is missing.

The text shows many variants from the score printed by Chrysander, even in its second version after he had discovered the Fitzwilliam fragments. The *Overture* [*sic*], without the title of the opera and on different paper from the rest, may not have been bound with RM 20 c 3 when Chrysander saw it. There are other divergences apart from those of orchestration already mentioned. The bass is fully figured throughout. The introduction has no tempo mark; the 3/4 movement is *Staccato forte* at the start and *Adagio* only at the cadence; the 12/8, in which the second violins are directed to double the viola, is headed simply *Gigue*. Many arias likewise lack tempo marks, but 'Nò, nò, che quest'alma', 'Molto voglio', and the B section of 'Cara sposa' are *Presto*, not *Allegro*, 'Ah crudel' *Adagio*, not *Largo*, in each case agreeing with Walsh. Most of Chrysander's tempos, and his score of the overture, came from RM 19 d 5.

The third trumpet part in 'Sibillar', which survives in Walsh's *Symphonys*, is incomplete in the autograph, since most of the opening ritornello is missing and Handel did not bother to write it out after the A section. The part is notated in the soprano clef. The string accompaniment to Armida's recitative 'Se dal campo' (HG 28) was an afterthought added in the margin, with the chords held throughout the fourth and fifth bars. 'Augelletti' gave Handel a good deal of trouble. An earlier setting in 3/8 time, on the theme of the aria 'Qui l'augel' in *Aci, Galatea e Polifemo*, was abandoned after thirteen bars of ritornello. This was in four parts, with the top stave marked *Flageolett*, as in the eventual version (Chrysander mentions this, but prefers the *Flauto piccolo* of RM 19 d 5). The text of the latter began originally with the second line, 'Zeffiretti, che spirate'. The sinfonia for Almirena's abduction (HG 38) is headed *Prelude* and marked *Da Capo* at the end.

Eustazio's recitative on HG 56, altered for the insertion of 'Scorta rea', originally ran straight on to 'Ciò fù indegna' (HG 57), whose first bar had shorter note values; in his 1874 score Chrysander printed it thus (without a cadence) from RM 19 d 5, where it makes little sense, since 'Scorta rea' follows. The autograph has the libretto arrangement of II iv, with 'Lascia ch'io pianga' much earlier in the recitative. The latter continues, after 'e d'infernal furore' (top of HG 61):

> Alm.   Dunque lasciami piangere.
> Arg.   Ti consolati O mia vita
>   Che l'indegno tuo lascio
>   Io vo pur frangere.

'Basta che sol' follows; the recitative on HG 62, substituted when the aria was moved back, is not in the autograph. Scene v begins, as in the libretto, with Armida's recitative 'Cingetemi' (HG 63), Scene vi at Rinaldo's entry two lines below; Chrysander, following RM 19 d 5, has no Scene v. As first composed, 'Ah! crudel' began with a slightly different version of bar 5; there is no bassoon part, but the cello stave is marked *Violoncelli di S. Francesco e Keutch* (see Plate 5). The inserted page, five bars with the expanded opening and three instrumental solos, has a part for *Mr Keutcsh* [*sic*] at the bottom. Although no instrument is named and the autograph is ambiguous, Chrysander was undoubtedly right in giving it to the bassoon, which has it in Walsh and RM

19 d 5. The player was J. C. Kytch, better known as an oboist. Francesco, identified by Chrysander with Francesco Ernesto Alliviero of the Hanover court orchestra, was François Goodsense, a Huguenot refugee generally known as Signor Francisco. In the stage directions of Scene x (HG 76) Handel changed the disguised Armida's name to Almirena, indicating clearly that the latter was to play the part.

The insertion of 'Sorge nel petto' again involved changes to the recitative. In place of that on HG 88 the autograph has a three-bar setting of the words 'Affretto il corso Mi stimolan l'amor, gloria e rimorso', followed by the direction *Goffredo ed Eustazio sene vanno* and 'È un incendio'. The last five bars before the B flat March were rewritten; the original cadence was in A, as if Handel intended a march in D. The March is that in HG Appendix II (116), which may in fact have been performed (Walsh printed neither version). Chrysander states wrongly that it was replaced by the Christian March (HG 101). In each of these contexts Handel wrote *March*, not *Marcia*. In 'Al trionfo' Argante's first two notes in bar 7 are D and F, and his last note in bar 10 is E flat. The bass of 'Di Sion' has the large notes only (HG 100). The D major March has cancelled repeat signs at the end. 'Solo dal brando' is cued in before the stage direction describing the battle (HG 109).

In three important contexts, finding mistakes in RM 19 d 5, Chrysander failed to amend them from the autograph. In bar 21 of 'Ogni indugio' (HG 11) he supplied the correct bass from the 1731 performing score but printed it in smaller type than the error (there was no need to repeat the aria on HG 129). In bars 68–9 of 'Sibillar' and bars 15–16 of 'Lascia ch'io pianga' the viola part in RM 19 d 5 was miscopied; Chrysander regularized the harmony but ignored the better readings of the autograph, which are:

Ex. 21

(Let me bewail . . .)

The last four leaves of RM 20 c 3 pertain to revivals. The recto of f. 54 has bars 14–23 of 'Vieni, O cara' with the voice part altered for alto in 1717 (the rest of the aria was simply raised an octave), followed by a two-bar fragment for alto voice and bass. This is a puzzle: the music comes from the unpublished B section of 'Augelletti', a soprano aria in a different key. Did Handel, in 1717 or later, consider a contralto Almirena? The next three pages have 'Parolette' with the original *Giulio Cesare* words in the B section; the last bass note in bar 3 is E, not G sharp. The dal segno bars were added for *Rinaldo*. The autographs of two of the arias composed for Berenstadt in 1717, 'Sorte, amor' and 'Ogni tua bella stilla', are in RM 20 f 11; each contains a substantial cancelled passage. Those of 'Con lagrime si belle' and 'Spera chi sà', both incomplete, are in Fitzwilliam MS 262 and RM 20 f 11 respectively. Both break off just before the end of the A section, 'Con lagrime si belle' after bar 57, 'Spera chi sà' half-way through bar 49. The aria 'Col valor del vostro brando' (Fitzwilliam MS 262, pp. 1–5), expanded and elaborated from 'Coll'ardor' in *Agrippina* with fuller orchestration and brilliant soprano coloratura, was almost certainly intended for *Rinaldo*; it is on the same paper (Ca) as most of the autograph. At the end of Fitzwilliam MS 254 (p. 71) is a simplified harpsichord arrangement of 'Molto voglio' in Handel's autograph, printed in Chrysander's Appendix I (HG 116).

Librettos

1711 London. 'An Opera. As it is Perform'd at the Queens Theatre in London . . . Printed by Tho. Howlatt, Printer to the House, and are to be sold at Price's Coffee-house, by the Theatre in the Hay-Market.' 63 pp. Hill's Dedication to Queen Anne, his Preface, and the Argument are in English, Rossi's address to the reader in Italian. These documents, quoted above, are more elaborate than usual, as befits a new venture. The Dedication, as if to forestall the cool reception of a foreign product, claims proudly that 'This Opera is a native of your Majesty's Dominions, and was consequently born your Subject'. Both Hill and Rossi pay ample tribute to Handel, whose name appears (for the first time in England) as 'Signor Georgio Frederico Hendel, Maestro di Capella di S.A.E. [Sua Altezza Elettorale] d'Hanover'. While Hill offers gracious compliments to Rossi, the latter ignores Hill.

The text of the libretto differs in a number of details from that printed by Chrysander. Some of these are insignificant (a few lines of recitative for Rinaldo in I i and Eustazio in I viii were never set); but at most of the points noted above the libretto agrees with the autograph and probably corresponds to the 1711 performances. 'Solo dal brando' however follows the battle. Some stage directions are omitted by Chrysander. Eustazio's 'Scorta rea' (II iii) is absent. The most puzzling variant concerns the words of the *coro*, which run: 'Fosco velo a nobil'alma / Cieco affetto è sol quà giù. / Squarci pur l'indegna salma / Chi vuol giungere la sù'. Although no setting of this text survives, there are indications that the words in the score ('Vinto è sol' etc.) were not those to which the music was first sung (see below, p. 197).

1715 Hamburg (F. C. Greflinger). 'Musicalisches Schauspiel Auf dem grossen Hamburgischen Theatro Im Monath November 1715.' Librettist, translator, and singers are not named. Barthold Feind's anonymous preface claims that he 'followed *metre* and meaning exactly according to the music of Capellmeister Hendel, almost slavishly where necessary, so that no single note of this admirable man might be lost'. But he complains of lack of time (only five days) and apologizes for leaving eleven pieces in Italian. These are the arias 'Nò, nò, che quest'alma', 'Furie terribili', 'Molto voglio', 'Augelletti', 'Basta che sol', 'Vo' far guerra', 'Andate, O forti', and 'Bel piacere', the duets 'Scherzano' and 'Fermati', and the *coro*. Elsewhere the translation does fit the music (exceptionally for Hamburg, where most German versions were prose paraphrases), though it is not particularly close. The text is the complete 1711 version, including 'Scorta rea' and 'Solo dal brando', with 'Lascia ch'io pianga' in its original position and the *coro* 'Fosco velo' (not 'Vinto è sol'). The source was a copy of the London libretto, and repeats its mistake of beginning 'Vo' far guerra' with the second line; probably none of the Hamburg librettos corresponds to what was actually sung. There are many extra stage directions, and each act is furnished with a ballet: of 'höllischen Ungeheuren' starting from the earth (? through traps) at the end of Act I, 'Geistern im Gestalt der Amouretten' at the end of Act II, and 'Poltergeistern' in III ii. The locale for III iii is not Armida's garden but 'Ein gezaubertes Seulenwerck mit Arcs und Portiquen und allerhand Larven', evidently the set illustrated in the frontispiece to the libretto (Plate 8a).[40] Argante's chariot is drawn by lions. Naiads and Tritons disport themselves in II iii and sing 'Il vostro maggio'; the lady is a spectre (Gespenst). After 'Basta che sol' Argante and Almirena walk in a garden containing all manner of people changed into animals, a standard appurtenance of the classical and operatic sorceress. It is not clear if any extra music was required. Feind promised that if the venture was a success 'all other operas of the incomparable composer will follow this one'. He never again translated a Handel libretto; in 1721 he was killed by falling downstairs.

1717 London. 'As it is Perform'd at the Theatre in the Hay-Market... Printed for J. Tonson, at Shakespeare's Head over-against Kathcrine-street, in the Strand.' 63 pp. The principal changes are listed above. Eustazio's part disappears, except for a few lines of recitative and one aria ('Di Sion'), which are transferred to Goffredo. The latter also loses a little recitative, as well as the arias 'Sorge nel petto' and 'Solo dal brando'. He does not appear in III vii (misprinted viii in HG 99). Argante has three inserted arias (two of them replacements), Almirena two. The Magician's aria is cut. The scenes in Act II are partly renumbered. Some of the more elaborate stage directions in I i, iii, and vii, II iii, and III i, ii, and iv are abridged, removing (among other things) the view of the Christian camp, Argante's spectacular entry in a chariot, many details of Goffredo's assault on the mountain, including its disappearance and replacement by a seascape, and the panorama of the city of Jerusalem. Berenstadt's name appears as Bernstat. This libretto was evidently set up from an amended copy of the 1711 edition. It reproduces all the prefatory matter, including the Dedication (although Queen Anne was now dead), as well as a number of mistakes. 'Lascia ch'io pianga' is placed as in 1711, and the words of the *coro* are unchanged.

1718 Naples (Michele-Luigi Muzio). This *mélange* reflects Neapolitan taste as well as the need to flatter the Emperor. The first two acts end with a duet and a quartet respectively, followed by a long comic scene for Lesbina and Nesso,

[40] Reproduced by Eisenschmidt, ii. 49.

servants of Armida and Almirena, who are also prominent in Act III. The plot is brought much closer to the conventional *opera seria* intrigue of love and jealousy. The motive power for Argante's chariot is supplied by a brace of sphinxes. Only eleven of Handel's texts survive, eight of them in Act I. Armida and Argante are defiant to the last. Nicolini retained four of his London arias and his two duets, annexed one of Goffredo's arias ('Mio cor', shifted to Act I), and seems to have stolen Almirena's best tune: one of his Act III arias begins 'Lascia ch'io resta Con la mia pace'. Most of the surviving Handel arias were obvious favourites, including 'Furie terribili', 'Augelletti', 'Cara sposa', 'Il vostro maggio', and 'Or la tromba'. Leo contributed only three serious pieces; he or Nicolini collected nearly twenty from elsewhere.

1723 Hamburg (Caspar Jakhel). 'In einem Singe-Spiele Auf dem Hamburgischen Schau-Platze Im Jahr 1723 vorgestellet.' Set up from an amended copy of the 1715 libretto. This is again the complete 1711 text with its anomalies, in Feind's translation but without his preface. All the set pieces, including the accompanied recitative 'Dunque i lacci', are now bilingual except 'Vieni, O cara', 'Scorta rea', and 'Sorge nel petto', which are in German only. The ballets include in III iii 'Eine extraordinaire Entrée von zehen Personen in differenten Grotesque Habiten, welche alle aus der Leib eines bezauberten Pagods hervor kommen'. A few bars later (iv) the whole colonnade disappears and is changed into a wood. Only after 'È un incendio' (v) does the theatre open to reveal part of the city of Jerusalem. The magician becomes an astrologer (Sternseher).

1727 Hamburg. A reprint of the 1723 libretto except for date and imprint ('Gedruckt mit Stromerschen Schrifften').

1731 London. 'Revised, with many Additions, by the Author, and newly done into English by Mr Humphreys . . . Printed for Tho. Wood in Little-Britain, and are to be sold at the King's Theatre in the Hay-Market.' 53 pp. The 'Author' is presumably Rossi. Samuel Humphreys translated a number of librettos at this period, and supplied Handel with the words of *Deborah* and *Athalia* and the 1732 additions to *Esther*. The prefatory matter is omitted, except for the Argument, which is altered at the end to accord with the reconstructed last act. Goffredo's capture of Jerusalem is mentioned, though the text only implies it; *Armida and Argantes retreat in Dispair*. Armida is no longer an Amazon but Queen of Damascus in both languages. 'Il vostro maggio' is sung by the Lady, 'Arma lo sguardo' by Armida (with male epithets of abuse in the B section); 'Bel piacere', not 'Sì, caro', appears in the last scene; the *coro* is 'Vinto è sol'. 'Lascia ch'io pianga' now follows Almirena's recitative 'Dunque lasciami piangere'. Argante, as in 1717, makes his first entrance on foot. The birds and mermaids are suppressed, and the dragons confined (without smoking) to Armida's first and last appearances. The descending black cloud in the abduction scene is replaced by a rock rising from the ground. In II vi (now iv) *Armida waves her Wand, and Part of the Garden disappears* before the spirits bring in Rinaldo. The mountain in Act III is not defended by rocks, waterfalls, and precious stones, nor is the assault accompanied by 'Thunder, Lightning and amazing Noises'. The Magician, not Goffredo, touches it with his wand, and it changes simply to *a troubled Ocean*. This, and the subsequent disappearance of the palm and cypress grove, could be accomplished by the withdrawal of a pair of backflats. The tableau in the last scene must have been revealed by a similar manoeuvre. There are a few new lines of recitative, and some of those cut in 1717 are restored.

Copies and Editions

There is no performing score for any production before 1731, nor is any complete manuscript of the 1711 version known to survive, a remarkable fact in view of the opera's exceptional popularity. The only copy from before the 1720s, by which time *Rinaldo* had received 47 performances in London, is RM 19 d 5, generally ascribed to Smith but written by Linike. It can hardly be the theatre copy made by 'Mr Lunican' mentioned in Heidegger's note of 5 May 1711.[41] Although one of the three types of paper on which it is written (Ca) occurs in the autograph, Linike's writing and clefs suggest a date around 1716. He seems to have compiled it from a source containing two or more layers of alterations, perhaps a lost performing score (certainly not the autograph). Only some such explanation will account for its inconsistencies. Although 'Or la tromba' and the Battaglia are present in full, the Christian March in the same scene is in simple binary form with repeats, lacking trumpets and drums and the direction for the sounding of military instruments. It is inconceivable that Handel would have included these instruments in two movements and omitted them from the third, but possible that they were unavailable at one of the early revivals. The scene numbering is confused in the second and third acts; the absence of any Scene v, viii, or ix in Act II suggests the subsequent removal of episodes inserted during the early revivals. 'Scorta rea' is included, but not the amended recitative introducing it. 'Lascia ch'io pianga' is in the position it occupies in HG, with the new recitative linking it to 'Basta che sol'. The Magician's recitative 'O di bella virtù' (HG 85) is missing. The B flat March is in its later form (HG 92), not that of the autograph. The manuscript is full of errors, both in words and music, some of which have persisted ever since in all copies and HG, but shows no trace of the many additional arias and transpositions made for the revivals of 1712–17.

The *coro* presents a peculiar problem. As copied, the words ('Vinto è sol' with four lines of seven syllables) cannot be fitted to the notes or the rhythm of the music, which must have been set to a different text with the syllabic metre 7878. As we have seen, the 1711 libretto in fact has a different text, but in the metre 8787.[42] The likeliest explanation is that Handel set the text with each couplet reversed, which would not affect the sense. Other evidence supports this conjecture. It would bring the two sopranos' melisma (on 'affetti' in 'Vinto è sol') on the same word ('affetto'). There is an exact parallel in *Teseo*, where the lines in both couplets of the aria 'Tengo in pugno' are reversed in the libretto. The *coro* is missing from the autograph, but Walsh printed it in 1711 as we know it, with one significant variant: the first word of bar 23 has two crotchets as in RM 19 d 5, not a minim—clearly a survival of Handel's first version. It would seem that Linike took the music from one source and the words from another and made no attempt to reconcile them.

Handel himself effected this, altering the underlay in bars 12–13 and both the underlay and the music in the cadence of each section, to produce the *coro* as printed in HG. He also added *les Hautbois colla parte* and *NB H1* and *NB H2* against the two soprano parts. Linike had written *Tutti* against the top line: that is, both oboes to double the first violins—presumably the 1711 scoring. Handel made copious alterations and annotations in the manuscript, in ink and pencil, on two or more occasions. He corrected many, but not all, of the

[41] Deutsch, 40.

[42] The music of the *Rinaldo coro* is based on that of *Rodrigo*, 'L'amorosa dea di Gnido', but the metre there (8888) is an even worse fit.

wrong notes and faulty Italian words. The pencil amendments are discussed below. Those in ink include, besides the changes to the *coro*, the addition of the word *cembalo* below the bass in bars 15, 19, and 23 of 'Vo' far guerra' (as in HG), the bass notes in most of the B section of 'Sorge nel petto' (where Linike had left a blank), amendments to bars 7 and 10 of Argante's part in 'Al trionfo' (B flat and A in bar 7 are alternatives—the original D and F are not cancelled—but in the last note of bar 10 G cancels the original E flat both in the voice part and the bassoon, though Chrysander retains E flat in the latter), and supplementary bass notes in 'Di Sion', sometimes cancelling the originals. Chrysander prints this correctly in the 1731 score (HG 192–3), but makes an arbitrary selection in that of 1711, to which the changes do not apply.

The pencil annotations, and a few in ink, reflect Handel's use of this manuscript to prepare his revision of April 1731. It is full of instructions for making a new copy: cuts, insertions, transpositions, changes to words and music, and one or two new recitatives. Most of them agree with the eventual score, but there are a few variants and changes of mind. Handel seems first to have gone through the score making cuts before deciding which singers were to take the parts. At this stage Argante was still a bass and Goffredo an alto; much of Eustazio's part was transferred to him without any indication that he was to be a tenor. Handel was in two minds about some of the transpositions for Senesino: 'Cara sposa' was put down to D minor and restored to E minor, but sung in the lower key; 'Fermati' went from B flat down to F, then up to G. Other projected alterations were subsequently cancelled. 'Ogni indugio' was to be replaced by 'Vedrò più liete' from *Lotario* in D major (this got into Smith's new copy but was later transferred to Act III), 'Basta che sol' by Goffredo's 'Nò, nò, che quest'alma'. Goffredo was allotted an aria in the middle of the first recitative in III ii (after 'colla spada'); 'Sovra balze' and 'La gloria in nobil'alma' from *Partenope* were proposed in turn and both rejected.

Handel first cut 'Sibillar' altogether, then restored its ritornello as entrance music for Argante. On deciding to omit 'Scorta rea' he changed the note values of the next bar (HG 57) back to those of the autograph. 'Mio cor' was to be in A minor. It is impossible to be sure of Handel's intentions for the latter part of Act II, which was changed more than once. Fresh settings of the recitatives in Scenes vii and x (HG 67 and 77) were never used. Armida's accompanied recitative 'Dunque i lacci' was first marked for alteration, then transposed down a fourth (with special instructions for the adjustment of the string parts), and 'Ah! crudel' cut. There is no indication of the scene in which Argante admires Almirena's portrait (HG 180), or of 'Parolette' at the end of the act. At one point Handel seems to have intended Almirena to sing the B section of 'Ah! crudel' after Armida's 'Arma lo sguardo'. 'Di Sion' was not his first choice for Argante in the new III iii (HG 192), but the earlier note is illegible. After the cancelled B flat March Handel wrote *Tutto alterato*; there are no pencil changes to the rest of the manuscript, and no autograph for the new music.

The method by which Smith executed his task and produced the two Hamburg performing scores, MA/1046a and 1046, is explained rather confusingly in Chrysander's 1894 preface and more clearly by Clausen. After receiving further material and verbal instruction from Handel he made a complete copy of the new version, based on RM 19 d 5, with the set pieces in full score but blanks in the voice parts of many recitatives, chiefly Armida's and Goffredo's but including a few of Rinaldo's where a phrase threatened Senesino's security by going above D, and also of 'Furie terribili', Armida's one untransposed aria. He put Argante's surviving recitatives up an octave and the Magician's down an octave, and transferred most of the scene numbers and stage directions from RM 19 d 5, thus compounding confusion and leading Chrysander astray (the new libretto no doubt was still in the press). Handel then completed this copy, filling in the blanks and making a number of corrections and amendments, including a new voice part for most of 'Furie terribili'. These altered passages were recopied by Smith, who combined them with as much as possible of his first copy to form the principal performing score (MA/1046a). Since many of the altered recitatives had portions of the set pieces on the same pages or their versos, it was necessary to recopy these as well.

Some 51 leaves were removed from Smith's first copy, 28 of them containing extensive revisions by Handel. (It is not always clear why pages wholly written by Smith, sometimes in the middle of an aria, were extracted as well; one object may have been to keep gatherings or bifolios together.) Round these 51 leaves a second copyist (Hb1) built up a second score (MA/1046), supplying the remainder of the music from MA/1046a. Since this was intended as a cembalo score for the second harpsichordist, Hb1 copied only the bass and voice parts, together with a few unaltered recitatives and occasionally the first violin part of orchestral movements, leaving the other staves blank. He ensured that the two copies corresponded exactly in pagination, an obvious practical convenience, though this is obscured by the present much later foliation.[43] The division between the two copies is not entirely consistent. A few pieces are fully copied by Smith in both. MA/1046 contains new recitatives in the hand of Smith, and even of Hb1 (for example on HG 195, 198, and 208); but these nearly all belong to the latter part of Act III, which must have required (in part at least) a new autograph, now lost. Moreover both scores contain insertions, not always the same ones. Of the 87 leaves written by Hb1 in MA/1046, the following were inserted: ff. 13–14 ('Ogni indugio' restored, ejecting 'Vedrò più liete'), ff. 68–71 ('Mio cor' in B minor, replacing the same aria in A minor), ff. 135–6 ('Sì, caro' from *Admeto*, replacing 'Bel piacere'), and possibly ff. 6–7 ('Sovra balze', first intended for III ii). The B minor 'Mio cor' and 'Sì, caro' are also insertions in MA/1046a. These were late changes, made just before or even after the first performance; cancelled fragments of the originals survive in both copies.

Since MA/1046 contains most of Handel's alterations, it is best considered first. Its sudden switches between skeleton and full score present an odd aspect today; in printing it as it stands (with the parts filled up in small notes from the other copy) Chrysander perpetuated an anomaly. All that the second harpsichordist required was the bass and voice parts; the fuller passages were transferred to save labour, simply because they were available. Handel's numerous recitative changes are by no means confined to those indicated in RM 19 d 5, some of which he rejected. He sometimes changed what Smith had already copied, especially when he was simply transposing up or down an octave. In II vii (HG 175) the words *Voce di dentro (la Sirena)* and in the next

---

[43] MA/1046a has a leaf missing after p. 60, and f. 54 should follow f. 57; f. 59 in MA/1046 is blank, though included in the foliation.

line *Sirena* were amendments by Handel; Smith had written the part for Armida in the alto clef. 'Vedrò più liete' had already been copied in the first scene when Handel noted that 'Ogni indugio' was to be restored. Much of the alto voice part of 'Furie terribili' is autograph. Smith changed the words of the B section of 'Per salvarti' from the original *Lotario* text.

MA/1046a is all in full score, except the inserted B minor transposition of 'Mio cor' (voice and bass only), and all written by Smith, with a few amendments by Handel. These include the correction of the bass in bar 21 of 'Ogni indugio' (made in both scores), *Adag* twice at the B section cadence of 'Mio cor' in A minor, changes to the opening of the next recitative when the aria was transposed, and an alteration to the second violin part in bar 8 of 'Dunque i lacci'. The modified cadence in the first violin part at bars 6 and 12 of 'Il vostro maggio', mentioned in Chrysander's preface, appears to be an alteration by Smith, not Handel; it is not in the cembalo score (here complete). The viola part in bars 15–16 of 'Lascia ch'io pianga' was copied from the defective text of RM 19 d 5; it is lightly crossed out in pencil, perhaps by Chrysander,[44] who silently 'corrected' it—but again not to the true reading of the autograph. His directions for the sinfonia at the start of Act III (HG 189–90) are misleading in the text but correct in the preface. His 1731 score is otherwise accurate, apart from the stage directions and scene numbers.

The three complete manuscript copies are all closely related to RM 19 d 5, and the earliest—the Malmesbury score, written by Smith *c.* 1725–28—was probably copied from it, before most of Handel's emendations but after he had added *Cembalo* three times in the bass of 'Vo' far guerra'. The differences—chiefly dropped tempo marks, orchestral details, and stage directions—are trifling. It gives the *coro* in the inconsequent form first copied in RM 19 d 5, reproduces the errors in 'Ogni indugio' (bar 21), 'Lascia ch'io pianga' (bars 15–16), and the recitative before 'Scorta rea', and omits the Magician's recitative on HG 85, but anticipates Chrysander's emendation in bars 68–9 of 'Sibillar'; someone had evidently spotted this error. As in the Granville and Lennard copies the Christian March is in binary form with repeat signs and no trumpets or drums (but an early hand—? Elizabeth Legh—has written the word *Trombo*: and added trills or marks of emphasis on all the notes longer than a crotchet in the top line). The manuscript has two points of particular interest. The unpublished B section of 'Augelletti' appears on an inserted leaf in the hand of S2,[45] and the volume contains two appendices: five arias written by S2, and four by RM1. Since all this material is included in the original pagination, and the contents of both appendices in the index at the end, it must have been added very early, before the volume was bound with Elizabeth Legh's arms. The first appendix contains 'La *
crudele lontananza', marked *Largo* and ascribed by Elizabeth Legh to 'Almirene', and the four new arias in the 1717 libretto. 'La crudele lontananza' has a better text than in RM 19 c 9; 'Ogni tua bella stilla' and 'Pregio è sol' are both *Allegro*; the top line of 'Vieni, O caro' is for *V. unis*. The four arias in the second appendix—'Minacciami, non hò timor', 'Sà perchè pena il cor', 'Con lagrime si belle', and 'Spera chi sà', copied *c.* 1718, are ascribed to *Rinaldo* in no other source. It is possible that they were bound here in error.

---

[44] He made notes in both Hamburg scores.

[45] S2 copied it again on two blank pages at the end of the early Wiegand score of *Teseo*, where Jennens identified it.

The Granville score (S5), though copied much later (? c.1745), agrees in the main with RM 19 d 5 and Malmesbury (without the addenda), but has a different emendation in bars 68–9 of 'Sibillar': the viola doubles the second violins an octave lower. 'Di Sion' has the extra bass notes, marked for contrabasso. 'Vo' far guerra' has no oboes but includes the written out cembalo part as in Walsh's second edition (HG 117–19). Perhaps the most interesting feature is that 'Il vostro maggio' is marked *Larghetto*. An appendix, copied at the same time, contains three 1731 additions: 'Orrori menzogneri' without its stage directions, 'Fatto è Giove', and the sinfonia on HG 211.

The Lennard score (S4 with text in two others hands, those of Smith and S1) also derives from RM 19 d 5, with even heavier cuts in the stage directions. It may date from about 1740. It is a carelessly copied score with numerous errors and omissions (including the pizzicato in 'Vo' far guerra'), many of them corrected by a later hand in pencil. Eustazio is partly eliminated: 'Sulla ruota', 'Siam prossimi' (*Andante*, as in 1731), and the Magician's aria are given to Goffredo, and the duet 'Al trionfo' to Almirena and Goffredo, as in 1731. The viola part in 'Sibillar' and 'Lascia ch'io pianga' repeats the old errors, but the bass in 'Ogni indugio' is correct as in the Hamburg scores. The recitatives on HG 7 are shortened, again reflecting 1731. This copy's most original contribution is Argante's consignment of his enemies as a holocaust not to Pluto (HG 108) but to Plato.

The Flower parts (S2, late 1740s) agree in the main with RM 19 d 5, but cannot derive from it: they give 'Augelletti' as a full da capo aria, an extra bar in the ritornello after the A section of 'Venti, turbini', and the original bass line in the B section of 'Sorge nel petto' (as in Walsh). The only secco recitative included, the Magician's on HG 85 (as a cue in the cembalo part), is the only one omitted in RM 19 d 5. The overture is missing, but the other instrumental movements are present. 'Scorta rea' is *Vivace* (as nowhere else), and there is no reference to the cembalo in the ritornello after the A section of 'Vo' far guerra', though it occurs at the start.

The parts are violins 1 and 2, viola (+violin 3), cello+bassoon, oboe 1+*flauto* 1, oboe 2+*flauto* 2, tromba 1 and 2, tympano, and cembalo. The tromba 3 part belonging to this set (which does not include 'Sibillar') is in RM 18 b 5, the tromba 4 in the Folger Shakespeare Library, Washington (W b 527, ff. 5–6). Violin 1 includes the solo violin in 'Venti, turbini', oboe 1 the *flauto piccolo* in 'Augelletti', viola the third violin in 'Ah! crudel', cello the bassoon in 'Venti, turbini', 'Ah! crudel', and 'Al trionfo'; each is complete on a separate stave. Otherwise the only mention of the bassoon is in 'Il Tricerbero', where it is silenced in the A section until the ritornello. Presumably it was expected to double the cello elsewhere. The latter is silent while the voice is singing in 'Sulla ruota' and 'Andate, O forti'—an exceptional arrangement that may reflect Handel's wish or practice. The cembalo part is fully figured only in the first three arias and the A section of 'Lascia ch'io pianga'.

The oboe parts as usual are problematical. Sometimes they are manifestly wrong: they play with the violins throughout 'Venti, turbini' even when this takes them below their compass, and in 'Abbruggio' from bar 20 to the end of the A section. Generally where the manuscripts, including the autograph, have *Tutti* on the upper of two treble lines both oboes play it, for example in 'Scherzano', the sinfonia in I vii, 'Col valor', 'Abbruggio', 'Vo' far guerra', and 'È un incendio'. This was certainly Handel's usual practice (Chrysander got it right in 'Mio cor'). But there are exceptions: the oboes are divided in 'Combatti'; they play in some movements where the autograph or other sources indicate strings only ('Ogni indugio', the sinfonia in III ii), but not in 'Furie terribili' and 'Fermati' where the autograph has *Tutti* on the top line. S2's source was doubtless not always specific. As usual, except where solos are marked, the oboes are confined to ritornellos and interstices in the vocal line. The B section of 'Al trionfo' has a different distribution of parts: both violins take the top line, both oboes the second, the cello the viola part, and the bassoon the bass.

A manuscript in the Österreichische Nationalbibliothek, Vienna (Mus MS 18321), in short score except for the overture and *coro*, was evidently based on Walsh's second edition. It has the same transpositions and the full cembalo part in 'Vo' far guerra', but omits 'Augelletti'. Its variants, which include *Andante* at the start of the overture, are of no consequence. As noted above, the nine arias in the Malmesbury appendices, together with the soprano G major setting of 'Sorge nel petto', 'Splenda lieta al tuo disegno', and 'Vieni, O cara, e lieta in petto', are among the supplementary pieces in Tenbury 884, basically a score of *Amadigi* (Smith, *c.*1719), and in a Shaftesbury volume (S4, *c.*1736–40). In Tenbury 884 'Sà perchè pena il cor' (with a little figuring added in pencil) is *Andante*, 'Con lagrime si belle' *Allegro*; 'Vieni, O caro, che senza il suo core' is in an early version with differences in the vocal line and fourteen extra bars towards the end of the A section. In the Shaftesbury copy these bars are replaced by a one-bar cadenza.[46]

RM 18 c 9, an Aylesford volume in the hand of S2, contains extensive selections—three accompanied recitatives, ten arias, two duets, and three sinfonias—from the 1731 score. Most of them are transposed versions of 1711 pieces, but four are unaltered and two ('Orrori menzogneri' and the sinfonia on HG 211) are new. None of the insertions from other operas are included, presumably because Jennens already possessed them. They must have been copied about the time of the production, for 'Mio cor' is still in A minor. In a separate group at the end (ff. 57–70) are the two arias added to *Giulio Cesare* in 1730 ('Io vo' di duolo' and 'Parolette') and 'Augelletti' headed *Song in Rinaldo*, but with its long 1711 final ritornello, not that of 1731.

The Coke Collection has contemporary copies (RM4) of the four new arias in the 1717 libretto, all except 'Vieni, O caro, che senza il suo core' (without extra bars or cadenza) fully figured; 'Il Tricerbero' in an Italian hand in the same volume as the extracts from the 1713 Naples version of *Agrippina*; and two copies of 'Combatti' (1711 version), one of them (in '24 Opera Songs') figured with a few vocal ornaments. 'Vieni, O cara, e lieta in petto' occurs (in B flat) in Add MS 31993, a collection of songs from the earliest London operas also containing short scores of 'Molto voglio' and 'Abbruggio' in B flat, perhaps from Walsh. Add MS 27932 has keyboard arrangements of 'Mio cor', 'Sulla ruota', and 'È un incendio' (in A), Add MS 29386 a short-score version of 'Il Tricerbero' in E minor. Two copies survive (RM 18 b 12 and RCM 1124) of a synthetic cantata for two sopranos comprising 'Sovra balze' in A (*Non presto ma cantabile*), 'Combatti', and the duet 'Scherzano'; the RM volume, in two German hands, also contains parts for two violins and the voice parts written out for two oboes. Except where mentioned, none of the

---

[46] Differences in other pieces, notably 'Vieni, O cara, e lieta in petto', confirm that Shaftesbury was not copied from Tenbury 884.

manuscripts mentioned in this paragraph were copied by members of the Smith circle.

Harpsichord arrangements of the overture, straight transcriptions from the score except for a little ornamentation in the Largo, appear in two Malmesbury volumes (RM 1, c.1718; Smith, c.1728), the Coke Wesley MS (Smith, c. 1721), and the Coke Rivers MS (Smith junior, c.1727). The Babell transcription, printed by Walsh and Chrysander, is not found in the manuscripts. The earlier Malmesbury volume has similar arrangements of the sinfonia in III ii (RM 1, c.1718), the ritornello for 'Augelletti' (Linike, c.1718), the sinfonia in I vii, March in D, and Battaglia (H1, c.1722), and the March in B flat (Smith, c.1722). The sinfonia in III ii and the ritornello of 'Augelletti' are also in the Wesley MS, both copied by Smith; the opening bar of the former has eight notes filling up the harmony added by Handel. These notes are not present in another copy written by Smith junior in the Rivers MS.

The Marquess of Bath's library at Longleat House has a contemporary volume of excerpts from Leo's Naples pasticcio of 1718. There are fifteen pieces, but only four of them, the duets 'Scherzano' and 'Fermati' and the arias 'Cara sposa' and 'Or la tromba', belong to Handel's opera.

Walsh published many editions of *Rinaldo*. The first, *Songs in the Opera of Rinaldo*, was advertised on 24 April 1711 as 'All the Songs set to Musick . . . Together with their Symphonys and Ritournels in a Compleat Manner, as they are Performed at the Queen's Theatre. Compos'd and exactly corrected by Mr George Friderick Hendell'. It contains the overture and *coro* in full score and the vocal numbers sung in 1711 (including 'Scorta rea' but not 'Solo dal brando') in short score, but no recitatives or other instrumental movements. There are occasional indications of scoring, but few tempo marks. 'Venti, turbini' has a four-part ritornello with bassoon; those of 'Augelletti' are much shortened. 'Nò, nò, che quest'alma' and 'Lascia ch'io pianga' are followed by flute arrangements. Each aria is ascribed to the original singer, but some appear in keys outside their compass. In all, twelve arias are transposed: four of Eustazio's up a fourth, three of Goffredo's up from a third to a sixth, four of Rinaldo's up a tone or a third, the Magician's up a sixth. It is most unlikely that the four alto parts were sung by sopranos during the 1711 run; probably the transpositions were made (inconsistently) for the convenience of purchasers. Whether or not Handel corrected the proofs, the comprehensiveness of the publication suggests that Walsh had his authority. The text gives the bass of 'Ogni indugio' correctly, and 'Sibillar' (bar 2), 'Sorge nel petto' (B section bass), 'Al trionfo' (bars 7 and 10), and 'Di Sion' (bass) in their original form. The seventh and eighth bars of the A section ritornello in 'Sibillar' are repeated, a peculiarity found in none of the manuscripts.

In this edition Walsh indicated the cembalo interludes in 'Vo' far guerra' as on HG 78; two months later (Smith, *Descriptive Catalogue*, no. 3) he replaced this with the fuller version, including 'the Harpsichord Peice Perform'd by Mr Hendel' (HG 117). A fortnight earlier (5 June) he had issued *The Symphonys or Instrumental Parts in the Opera Call'd Rinaldo* (Smith, no. 13), 'which together with their Songs makes that Opera Compleat'. This curious publication, altogether exceptional in Walsh's dealings with Handel, consists of three part-books, First Treble, Second Treble, and Tenor (in the mezzo-soprano clef). Bass players were presumably expected to use the *Songs*, to which page references are given—not always to the same edition. The arrangement is scarcely practical, since one book may contain up to four parts printed one after the other. In 'Sibillar' Treble 1 has the first violin and first trumpet, Treble 2 the oboe, second violin, and second and third trumpets (the only complete source for the latter); in 'Augelletti' Treble 1 has octave flute only, Treble 2 first and second flutes (recorders) and first and second violins; in 'Or la tromba' Treble 1 has all four trumpet parts, leaving the two violins to Treble 2; in 'Ah! crudel' Treble 1 has first violin and oboe, Treble 2 second and third violins, Tenor viola, bassoon, and cello. Some solos are indicated. Keys and most tempo marks are those of the Walsh *Songs*. The pieces are not quite in the right order, and 'Il Tricerbero', 'Bel piacere', and the ritornellos of 'Andate, O forti' and 'Sorge nel petto' are omitted, though that of 'Scorta rea' is in. There are mistakes (the first four bars of the B section of 'Basta che sol' are left out), but the text confirms correct readings in several places where RM 19 d 5 (followed by Chrysander) goes wrong.

On 13 September 1711 Walsh issued *The Most Celebrated Aires and Duets . . . Curiously fitted and Contriv'd for two Flutes and a Bass*, and an edition for single flute obtained by the curiously simple method of omitting the second flute part. Early in 1723 he produced the overture in parts by a similar economy, adding a new bass to the *Symphonys* of June 1711. There were several single-sheet editions of 'Il Tricerbero' with English words, and one of 'Bel piacere' (*The Rover Song*, *c.*1714). The Gigue from the overture appears in at least two dance collections, once as *Rinaldo or the hopping Lady*. William Babell's *Suits of the most Celebrated Lessons Collected and Fitted to the Harpsichord or Spinnet* (February 1717) contains arrangements of the overture and seven arias from *Rinaldo*; Chrysander reprinted them in HG xlviii. Walsh included Babell's version in his 1730 collection of Handel's overtures for keyboard.

The *Additional Favourite Songs* issued at the time of the revival in April 1731 comprise the eight inserted arias, including 'Sì, caro' from *Admeto* and 'Parolette', which as a result has been assigned to the wrong opera ever since. It appeared again in *The Favourite Songs in ye Opera called Thessus* [sic] *& Amadis* (Walsh, 1732), a ragbag publication that also includes 'Nò, non così severe' and some pieces not by Handel. This is Smith's no. 1 under *Amadigi* and *Teseo*; a copy has since been discovered in Paris.[47]

Chrysander printed *Rinaldo* twice. His first edition (1874) gives what he took to be the 1711 score before he discovered the Fitzwilliam portions of the autograph. In 1894 he reprinted this with some (not all) of the necessary corrections, together with the 1731 version and a longer preface than he usually permitted himself. Neither volume represents the 1711 score exactly because, as already mentioned, he regarded RM 19 d 5 as an authoritative performing score and gave it precedence over the autograph, the libretto, and Walsh, reading back into 1711 changes made by Handel in subsequent revivals, including that of 1731. Among corrections that could have been supplied from the autograph are the full stage directions at the start of Act I and the top of HG 56; others omitted on HG 59, 60, 91, and 92; D, not A, for the third bass note in bar 34 of the overture (as in 1731); bass figuring in the first two bars of 'Ogni indugio' (and the correct bass in bar 21); the viola part

---

[47] Baselt, *Verzeichnis*, i. 137.

in bars 68–9 of 'Sibillar' and 15–16 of 'Lascia ch'io pianga'; and the underlay at the A section cadence of 'Andate, O forti'. Later changes are incorporated in bar 8 of 'Dunque i lacci' (from Hamburg MA/1046a), the recitative on HG 87, bar 5 of 'È un incendio', Argante's part in 'Al trionfo' (partly indicated in Chrysander's preface), and the bass of 'Di Sion'. The rising scale in bar 2 of 'Sibillar' should have nine notes in 1711 (HG 13) as well as 1731 (HG 131). In all sources the violins' third note in bar 30 of 'Basta che sol' is B flat, bar 7 of 'Vo' far guerra' has a different bass, and the bass part in bar 5 of 'Al trionfo' has the same rhythm as the oboes and bassoons (correct on HG 198). There are misprints on HG 54 (first note of sixth system) and 103 (last note). As usual the recitative cadences are wrongly printed, with the bass notes delayed.

The HHA score (1993), edited by David R. B. Kimbell, presents the opera as originally performed (except for placing 'Lascia ch'io pianga' in its later position), together with an extensive appendix (20 items) containing rejected drafts and all additional matter certainly or probably introduced in the revivals of 1712–17, most of it printed for the first time. The 1731 version will be issued in a separate volume. This is the most scrupulously edited of the five operas so far published by the HHA, and takes advantage of the new guide-lines, including a facsimile of the 1711 libretto, a German translation, and a Critical Report in the same volume.

Additional Notes

* (p. 172) In addition Rossi lifted four aria texts from Venetian librettos: 'Sulla ruota di fortuna', 'È un incendio', and 'Mio cor che mi sai dir?' from *Il trionfo della libertà* (Frigimelica-Roberti/Scarlatti, 1707), 'Vo' far guerra' from *Ciro* (Pariati/Albinoni, 1710) (Lindgren, 'Venice, Vivaldi, Vico and Opera in London . . .').

* (p. 173) Curtis Price ('English Traditions in Handel's *Rinaldo*', *Handel Tercentenary Collection*, ed. Sadie and Hicks) stresses the influence of George Granville's semiopera *The British Enchanters* (on the Amadis story), with music by John Eccles, Bartholomew Issak, and William Corbett, produced at the Queen's Theatre on 21 February 1706.

* (p. 200) A manuscript copy of 'La crudele lontananza' written by H6, inserted in an early edition of the Walsh Songs in the National Library of Scotland, describes it as 'Sung by Mrs Robinson in Rinaldo 1715'.

IL PASTOR FIDO

THE Argument in the 1712 libretto outlines the background to the story.

The People of Arcadia sacrific'd every Year to Diana, their Goddess, a Virgin of their Country, having been so forewarn'd by the Oracle, to avoid a greater Calamity: But now, consulting the Oracle about Means to put a Period to this Evil, they were answer'd *Your Miseries shall never end, till two of Heavenly Race unite in Love, and that the exalted Passion of a* Faithful Shepherd *cancels the ancient Crime of a perfidious Maid.* Titirus and Montanus, both of Divine Extraction, mov'd by this Prophecy, resolv'd upon a Match between Silvius and Amarillis, their Children; but tho' they sollicited this Affair with all their Power, they were not able to effect it.

The obstacles were two: Amarilli's love for Mirtillo, which she 'durst not discover ... because the Law wou'd have punished such a criminal Disobedience with Death', and the temperament of Silvio, neatly described by Burney as 'a gay frolicksome swain, much fonder of field-sports, than the society of females'.

Act I depicts *Shepherds Cottages, in a Grove of Arcadia*; the Italian adds *fountains, etc.*[1] Mirtillo begs fate to soften his suffering, but is resolved to remain true to Amarilli. She in turn bemoans the harshness of Diana's decree and the inhuman laws that forbid her union with Mirtillo. Mirtillo overhears her last words and *goes to Embrace her, She pushes him away* and *turns from him*. He *kneels* and asks for pity. She *looks upon him with Compassion and then speaks with some warmth*, telling him to prove his faith by leaving her for ever. Mirtillo in despair *goes to kill himself but is hindred by Eurilla*, a nymph who loves him. Dissembling, she encourages him to think he may yet win Amarilli, but plans to capture him for herself by trickery. Meanwhile Silvio ranges the woods singing the praises of the 'chaste goddess'. Dorinda, overhearing *at a Distance*, thinks he is referring to her, *comes cheerfully forward* and *presents herself to him to be embraced*. Silvio *pushes her away* and renews his vows to Diana.

In Act II (*The Country of Arcadia, with the Prospect of Hircina's [Ericina's] Cave*) Mirtillo, waiting for Eurilla to bring hopeful news, *throws himself down under a tree* and *falls asleep*. Eurilla enters with *a Garland, in which are described these Words, 'Thy Vows at last are heard, and I expect thee'*. She sings a love song over him, *put[s] the Garland on his Arm, and goes off. He waken's in a Rage and runs across the scene; then looks on the Garland, and reads*. At first *he makes to throw away the garland, then stops* as Amarilli *enters observing him at a Distance*. Thinking it may have been sent by Amarilli, he *reads the words again and kisses the garland*. She

---

[1] Many stage directions are translated incompletely or not at all in the English version of the libretto. Others appear only in Handel's incomplete autograph. Chrysander omits a large number. They are given here in the words of the 1712 English version, supplemented by translation. Minor discrepancies in the printed libretto are ignored.

concludes that he has another love and begins to feel jealous, but *checks herself* (*stà sospesa*). Eurilla tries to fan the flames by saying she has seen another beauty give Mirtillo a garland. Amarilli however cannot abjure her love for him, even if he is unfaithful. Silvio once more tries to shake off Dorinda's pursuit, and answers *without looking her in the face*. Again she misunderstands his apostrophe to Diana. *As Silvius is going she stops him* and demands an embrace. He hurries off to hunt. Eurilla tells Mirtillo that the garland came from Amarilli, who expects him in the cave. He *embraces* her and departs in hope. She then urges the jealous Amarilli to hide in the cave and watch him. Amarilli says her honour will not permit it, but *pauses a little* and presently agrees, assuring herself that the shame of a faithless person is increased by the presence of her whom he has injured. *Amarillis going towards the Cave, Mirtillo goes off*, having presumably failed to find her. *Eurilla draws his attention to her as she enters*, whereupon he *goes to the Cave, being observ'd by Eurilla*. The latter prepares to inform the High Priest, rejoicing that the lovers will be caught, Amarilli condemned to death under Arcadian law, and Mirtillo freed.

Act III (*A Wood*). Dorinda *hides her self in a Tree*[2] in order to observe Silvio hunting. He enters *accompanied by huntsmen*,[3] *looks towards the Tree where Dorinda is hid*, thinks he sees 'in yonder Covert . . . a savage Beast', and *hurls a spear in Diana's name*. He *wounds Dorinda who is brought out, supported by the Huntsmen*. Horrified, *he stands in confusion, regarding her with pity, kneels before her*, begs her pardon and *furiously* bids her strike him; she asks only for his love. As she *is carry'd off by the Huntsmen* he prays to Cupid to save her life and reproaches himself for wounding one who loved him so tenderly. Eurilla enters *in triumph* (*tutta in festa*): Mirtillo has been caught with Amarilli, who is condemned to die while he is released. *Seeing Dorinda and Silvius coming she retires into a corner*. They enter happily reconciled, *Dorinda with her arm bandaged. Eurilla comes forward weeping* and informs them of Amarilli's fate, thereby solving their problem. Amarilli's adulterous love invalidates her contract with Silvio, who goes off with Dorinda to find his father to unite them. *As she watches them go, Eurilla reverts to exultation*. The set changes to *a view of Arcadia with the Temple of Diana. Amarillis coming to be sacrificed, no longer dressed as a nymph, but wearing a long robe with a myrtle wreath on her head and escorted by priests*. She bitterly regrets her pointless cruelty to Mirtillo, who asks to die in her place. She refuses, but confesses that her indifference to him was feigned. *As the Priests are leading her off* they protest their fidelity in a duet. *Tirenius the High-Priest of Diana comes to the Holy place in sacerdotal Pomp; Silvius, Dorinda and Eurilla (in confusion) in several Parts of the Stage*. Tirenio declares Diana's anger appeased and orders the sacrifice to stop: Mirtillo is of divine race, the faithful shepherd of the oracle. Both couples are to be married. *Mirtillo runs to embrace Amarilli*. Eurilla *kneels before them* and successfully begs forgiveness. All pronounce the decrees of heaven inscrutable to men.

Giacomo Rossi's source for this libretto was Giovanni Battista Guarini's famous play of the same title (*c*.1584), which had supplied many composers

---

[2] 'Cespuglio', literally a bush.
[3] The sounding of horns is mentioned in the autograph, though there is no music for them, but not in the libretto.

with madrigal texts but inspired few if any operas.[4] It was an unpromising choice, and Rossi, working apparently without intermediary, made an indifferent job of it. The main drawback was not the pastoral convention, though this is literary rather than dramatic, with a narrow emotional range and stereotyped characters, and does not lend itself to operatic treatment except in the most stylized terms. That could be overcome, as Handel showed in *Acis and Galatea*. The difficulty lies in the nature of Guarini's play. It is renowned for the lyrical beauty of its language; but the dramatic structure is stilted and cumbersome. There are five acts and eighteen characters, including the parents and confidantes of most of the principal persons and two extra lovers for the coquette Corisca (Eurilla in the opera). The action is presented in a series of static tableaux, with the characters constantly communicating through third parties.

In reducing this to three acts and six characters, one of whom appears only in the last scene, Rossi inevitably destroyed the poetry (though he preserved a few of Guarini's lines, for example in I iii and III iii); he also obscured the motivation and covered up some links in what remained of the plot. He does not make clear that Amarilli is a nymph of divine descent and Eurilla her confidante, whose conduct is a betrayal of trust. He omits the discovery that Mirtillo is Silvio's brother and therefore a satisfactory match for Amarilli. Even the Argument does not explain the background properly. The 'perfidious maid' was one Lucrina, who scorned Aminta, a favourite priest of Diana, and gave herself to another. This infuriated the goddess, who not only visited Arcadia with the plague (requiring the annual sacrifice of a virgin to keep it in check) but insisted on the strictest observation of marriage ties and a sentence of death for every unfaithful wife—a decree that Guarini in a charming aside says is impossible to enforce. Hence the certainty, which Eurilla exploits to her advantage, that Amarilli will be condemned while Mirtillo escapes scot-free. It should be added that Handel's failure to set some lines in the libretto and Chrysander's omission of many important stage directions prevent the reader of the score from forming a just estimate of Rossi's achievement.

His decision to get rid of the confidantes (apart from Corisca–Eurilla) may be applauded, but it landed him in a difficulty. Their disappearance constantly leaves the chief characters with no one to talk to except the audience: hence a large number of monologues in awkward juxtaposition and excessive resort to the device by which one character overhears the last words of another. The two halves of the plot become unhinged; Silvio and Dorinda do not meet any of the other characters (though Silvio is betrothed to one of them) till half-way through Act III, and their scenes in the first two acts merely duplicate each other. Nor are Rossi's additions happy. Mirtillo's threat of suicide is a conventional touch, but his sleep aria at the start of Act II, when he is impatiently awaiting a message from Eurilla, is absurd, and the imported garland episode clumsy. Rossi makes a sad mess of the cave scene, the climax of the action. In Guarini Corisca (Eurilla) urges Amarilli to watch *Silvio*

---

[4] There were at least three later, by Carlo Pietragrua (Venice, 1721), Salvatore Apolloni (Venice, 1739), and Salieri (Vienna, 1789), the last with a libretto by Da Ponte. Strohm (*HJb* (1975), 110; *Essays*, 42) notes that the Elector's library at Hanover contained an Italian work with this title written for Duke Johann Friedrich (d. 1679) which Handel could have come across. Another, with words and music by Benedetto Ferrari (*c.*1603/4–1681), may have no connection with Guarini.

making love, so that she will not be obliged to marry him, and dispatches Coridon, one of her own admirers, to meet her, intending to bring along the High Priest at the strategic moment. She also presses Mirtillo to catch Amarilli in the act. In the event another of Corisca's lovers blocks the cave to prevent (as he thinks) Corisca and Coridon getting out, and calls the priests. Guarini, following the conventions of his day, does not show the cave scene on the stage. But Rossi could have done so; by refraining he missed a fine dramatic opportunity. Moreover when Amarilli enters the cave in the opera she appears to pass Mirtillo coming out, as if he had looked inside and found nothing (II ix and x). Eurilla sends him in again, a singularly flat climax to the act.

Rossi works little tension or conflict into the libretto. The first act is feeble and undramatic; the denouement in the third depends on the baldest *pontifex ex machina*. It is not clear why Diana's rage is appeased, and Eurilla's repentance is unconvincing. But two things can be said in Rossi's defence. His language, though a long way short of Guarini's, is less abstract and moralistic than in *Rinaldo* and free from the pretentiousness of Rolli. And he had, as in *Rinaldo*, to accommodate himself to Handel's demands for the inclusion of several episodes from earlier works, words as well as music. Three of the first four arias, and two more later, are so appropriated with the minimum of change. The librettist is not solely to blame for the slack temper of the opera.

It is possible that the choice of subject was Handel's, with the intention of demonstrating either his versatility after the heroics of *Rinaldo*, or, since he had plenty of suitable material from his Italian years, his command of a medium that had been repeatedly misused. Pastoral subjects with some form of musical accompaniment had long been popular on the London stage. Guarini's play was familiar in the English translation by Sir Richard Fanshawe (1647); Elkanah Settle staged an adaptation with music in 1676 and revived it later. Similar entertainments proliferated in the first decade of the century. As Duncan Chisholm remarks, 'the temptation to write bad pastoral seems to have been overwhelming'.[5] Handel perhaps saw this as a challenge, but lacked the experience to meet its full demands.

Given Rossi's libretto, it is scarcely surprising that the music has an air of mild diversion, and sometimes of irrelevance. The small scale, unpretentious scoring, and simple melodies of most of the arias, derived from the chamber cantata, suit the subject well enough. In contrast to his treatment of *Rinaldo*, Handel sets out to charm rather than astonish the ear. He cannot be said to have failed; the score is full of pretty tunes, neat rhythms, and beguiling sequences. But we know from *Acis and Galatea* and earlier from *Apollo e Dafne* that he was capable of combining an ornamental surface with a profundity that catches the breath and disturbs the memory. He seldom does so in *Il pastor fido*. The characters only momentarily grip the imagination; their arias are too generalized, the links with the context so loose that they threaten to break away—as most of them did in the event. Burney's judgement is fair: the opera 'upon the whole, is inferior in solidity and invention to almost all his other dramatic productions, yet there are in it many proofs of genius and abilities

---

[5] 'The English Origins of Handel's *Pastor Fido*', *MT* cxv (1974), 650. But 'origins' begs the question; 'antecedents' would have been a more appropriate term.

which must strike every real judge of the art, who is acquainted with the state of dramatic Music at the time it was composed'.

Eurilla is by far the most dynamic character, as befits her role in initiating the main action. Whereas Mirtillo, when his love is rejected, prepares to take his life, Eurilla in a parallel situation sets about eliminating her rival. She has more bravura arias and a higher proportion of new music than the others. 'Di goder' makes a more positive effect than anything else in Act I. Handel places it admirably after four chamber arias, employing the full orchestra for the first time since the overture, and a sharp key, the bright A major, for the first time in the opera. But it cannot be regarded as an unqualified success. It is an expansion of one of the loveliest arias of the Italian period, padded out with a couple of short Adagios and a startling efflorescence of coloratura at the words 'un gran contento'. This is dramatically motivated: she hopes to win her happiness by the practice of deceit ('Ingannata' was the first word of the aria in *Agrippina*). But the flashy continuation does not spring naturally from the melody and jars the memory of its perfect treatment elsewhere.

Eurilla's music in Act II is more consistent and original. 'Occhi belli', though no more than a brief cavatina, is masterly. The unusual scoring— violins and cellos pizzicato in octaves, *cembalo arpeggiato per tutto*—and the sustained contrast between dotted accompaniment and legato vocal line conjure up a most unusual atmosphere, not without a touch of the sinister, as if Eurilla were tiptoeing round the sleeping Mirtillo before placing the garland on his arm. This is her only aria in the minor. A telling detail is the little transition, carefully figured, that breaks the rhythm in bar 13. 'Ritorna adesso Amor' concludes the act with an outburst of vindictive anticipation: she will not be happy till Amarilli is dead. Handel sets all his engines going— double fugato, a brilliant concerto grosso layout with solo parts for violin, cello, and two oboes, varied by trio sonata texture and long stretches in which the continuo is silenced, and an exuberance of richly flowing counterpoint embracing both main sections without recourse to new material. We catch a foretaste of the superb arias that end the intermediate acts of such Royal Academy operas as *Radamisto*, *Tamerlano*, and *Admeto*. Musically and dramatically this is the finest aria in *Il pastor fido*. The polyphonic approach mirrors Eurilla's devious planning, and it reaches a grand climax in the ritornello after the A section, which substitutes a stretto for the fugal opening and brings in the full orchestra before the voice can reach its cadence. Burney acknowledged 'a very masterly composition', but thought the accompaniment too elaborate for the stage: 'in a drama where instruments are, or ought to be, the humble attendants on the voice, riot and noise should not be encouraged'. Fortunately Handel preferred to demonstrate his mastery of that Baroque intricacy in which even Bach could not surpass him.

Eurilla's two arias in Act III come in succession and in the same key. This was the result of a change of plan. Originally Handel wrote only the A section of 'D'allor trionfante' and marked it for repetition at the end of Scene vi, where 'Secondaste' now stands, producing a da capo design with secco recitative in the middle, as in Tirenio's 'Risonar mi sento' later in the act. Before performance he substituted 'Secondaste' for the repeat; later he expanded 'D'allor trionfante' into a full aria. The result is a trifle crude, but the arias make an adequate contrast. The catchy 6/8 metre of 'D'allor trionfante' incorporates a good deal of subtlety in the control of rhythm and sequence. The rising four-bar phrase at the start evades uniformity by a slight rhythmic change in bar 4; bars 5 and 6 are an echo of 3 and 4 on concertino violins; 7 and 8 repeat the rhythm of 4, *tutti*; 9–12 reverse the direction of 1–4 from the top to the lower B flat. The voice and concertino violins then take over in unison and present the material with many variants and in a different order; they have begun to deviate rhythmically and melodically before the end of a bar. This was an afterthought: in the original draft of the autograph the first two vocal bars were identical with those of the ritornello. Such modifications and extensions of germinal ideas are a constant and rewarding feature of Handel's mature style. 'Secondaste' is a little arietta in dance rhythm used in several Italian works, including *Rodrigo*[6] and the big cantata in honour of the Emperor Charles VI; though deceptively simple and full of repeats it comes off delightfully, with a fully-scored ritornello to clinch the da capo. Handel is perhaps warning us not to take Eurilla too seriously in preparation for the happy end. He drew on both these arias with great effect in the oratorio period, 'D'allor trionfante' in *Belshazzar*, 'Secondaste' in *Semele*.

Mirtillo is an anaemic hero, easily manipulated by the two women who love him. Handel's copious recourse to old material points to a lack of interest; his first five arias are all in some degree borrowed. The three in Act I are chamber cantata pieces, charming enough but weak in dramatic fibre. Each expresses an aspect of the same emotion, his hopeless longing for Amarilli. The first part of 'Fato crudo', based on a ritornello used in *Almira* and *Rodrigo* and incorporating another phrase from the latter opera,[7] is rhythmically complex; the more straightforward Allegro of the B section offers a brief contrast. 'Augelletti' had appeared in *La Resurrezione* (with 'mio Signore' for 'mio tesoro') and in the mouth of a soprano Giove in the Charles VI cantata. It is a pretty unison aria that adds nothing to Mirtillo's character and was dragged in with little regard to context, as the last phrase of the recitative ('dov'è il mio bene?') clearly indicates. 'Lontan dal mio tesoro', like Amarilli's aria before it, comes from a continuo cantata, with a final string ritornello added.

'Caro amor' in Act II was adapted from the first part of Mary Magdalene's 'Ferma l'ali' in *La Resurrezione*. One cannot feel surprise that Handel wished to keep this exquisite piece in circulation; with its long pedals (beneath a canonic ritornello), static harmony, and sensuous texture it serves very well as a sleep song. Handel modified the scoring, substituting flutes for recorders and not muting the violins; the viola parts, left defective in all the sources (as in HG 30), presumably doubled the flutes and violins at the octave throughout, though 'Ferma l'ali' has a viola da gamba that sometimes follows the voice and sometimes supplies a continuo. 'Allor che sorge' is a tired borrowing of not very distinguished music. In his last aria, 'Nel mio core', Mirtillo for the first time has a chance to be cheerful. Though again the ideas are old, going back via *Rodrigo* to Keiser, it is nicely turned and more fully developed than many pieces in the score, if scarcely first-rate Handel. Neither the character nor the singer, Pellegrini, seems to have inspired the composer; in *Teseo* too Pellegrini's music has a routine quality that contrasts unfavourably with Margherita de l'Epine's. In Act III Mirtillo at last makes a stand in resolving to die with Amarilli, but his only music other than recitative is a part in the duet, a beautiful movement in that mood of tragic resignation that never failed to draw the best from Handel.

[6] See p. 107.   [7] See p. 103.

Amarilli's start is no livelier than her lover's. The most inventive touch in 'Son come navicella' is the new final ritornello, where the original bass is elevated to the violins, two extra parts added underneath, and the material subjected to further development. 'Finte labbra' in Act II takes the principal theme of another cantata aria and coolly reverses the sense ('Dolce bocca, labbra amate'); but it is a spirited piece with the concerto grosso elaboration added and a picturesque antithesis between wind and strings. Handel makes free play with canon, suspensions, and cross-rhythms, and the B section has a fine sense of harmonic adventure, including an excursion from G minor as far as B flat minor. From jealousy Amarilli moves to a not very convincing ironic gaiety in 'No! non basta', which makes its point through rhythmic drive, the ascending figure ♪ ♫♩ ♩ forcing both the ritornello and the vocal line to a climax at the end of each phrase. In Act III Amarilli, who has hitherto lacked focus because the libretto allows her none, comes characteristically to life in her hour of crisis. Her recitative in Scenes vii and viii, both accompanied and secco, expresses a mixture of resignation and remorse (at having denied her love for Mirtillo) that lifts her into the sphere of tragedy. Handel strikes this mood unerringly in the G minor sinfonia as she is led out to die, a short but strikingly beautiful piece. The wind (oboes and bassoons) take the lead throughout, supported and finally echoed by the strings in a doleful processional lament, which leads into Amarilli's accompanied recitative. When Mirtillo decides to share her fate the duet resumes the mood of the sinfonia in the same key without exactly quoting it. Wind and strings again tend to act independently until they merge in the five-bar ritornello at the end. This is succeeded by another sinfonia, an arresting gesture in E flat as the priests come out of the sanctuary.[8] It moves abruptly in its closing bars to G, the dominant of C minor, for Tirenio's cavatina. Though conventional in itself, this gains strength from Handel's repetition of it, after the next recitative, to form an unorthodox da capo unit. The entire sequence (Scenes vii–ix), free in construction and tonally unified (the tense G minor resolves into B flat in the *coro*), is typical of the sudden spurts made by Handel's invention when his dramatic instinct was roused.

Silvio and Dorinda might have been pointed up as comic relief; their flippant reaction to the news of Amarilli's doom suggests that such was Rossi's intention. But their dialogue is too flaccid and their aria texts (especially Dorinda's) too vague to establish them as individuals. Handel could have made Silvio more bumptious (an alto Hercules) and Dorinda more kittenish; he preferred to let them take their chance with old music. Silvio's first three arias are borrowed, and two of them are gigues. That fits his profession and tastes well enough, but 'Casta dea' is unconvincing as an invocation to Diana. 'Sol nel mezzo' is better, with pleasant cross-rhythms and pedals (upper as well as lower) and a suggestion of hunting-horns in the distance. 'Non vo' legarmi', his most ambitious aria, lacks the sparkle of Eurilla's music; Handel had treated the material with more imagination in *Agrippina* and elsewhere. With 'Tu nel piagarmi' on the other hand Silvio springs to life, like Amarilli, under the impact of an emotional shock. The accidental wounding of Dorinda (who at this point in Guarini is dressed as a wild animal) sends him at last into a minor key, and he proves capable of grief, if not of passion. The long and skilfully varied ritornellos, full of interrupted cadences and remorseful

---

[8] This sinfonia was a later insertion: see pp. 224 and 226–7.

sevenths, go some way to win sympathy for this uncouth sportsman whose indifference to Dorinda is contrasted by Guarini with his love for his dog Melampo. It is a fine aria with more than a hint of tragedy. The texture is unusual for Handel, the violins adding a Bach-like intensity by accompanying the voice and bass in continuous three-part counterpoint.

The best of Dorinda's solos is the graceful 'Mi lasci', the only new music in the first act. Here again, as so often in *Il pastor fido*, Handel gilds a slight continuo aria with a four-part ritornello after the da capo, which is much abbreviated. He is only following the practice of the late seventeenth century, but he makes it sound remarkably fresh; no one knew better how to exploit slender or antiquated means. The rest of the part is borrowed with little change; 'Hò un non sò che' in III i was not in the first version.

The pattern of the borrowings is significant; seven of the eight arias in Act I and five of the first six in Act II are old matter seldom reactivated by the new context; but this applies only to two arias and the *coro* in Act III. In the last three arias of Act II, though two of them are based on earlier ideas, the style changes from pastoral cantata to the *opera seria* of intrigue, and, as Kimbell has remarked,[9] the concerto principle ousts the chamber cantata as malice pollutes the innocence of Arcadia. In Act III first Silvio's penitence and then the arrest and condemnation of Amarilli inspire a fertile crop of new material. The other scene in the opera that exhibits unusual features of design is the opening of Act II, where two cavatinas follow in succession without intervening recitative, the second leading to an exit. Here again one of them, 'Occhi belli', is new while the other is a rethought—not simply transplanted—borrowing. The secco recitative of the next scene shows Handel sensitive to dramatic nuance: witness the different inflections that Mirtillo (twice) and Amarilli give to their reading of the message on the wreath. Mirtillo reads first for information, then in rising excitement, beginning a semitone higher and running up a fifth instead of a fourth; Amarilli betrays her distress over a minor chord, with a C sharp in the vocal line at once contradicted by a C natural in the bass.

The overture, like those of several other early operas, almost certainly began as a separate composition; it may date from Handel's recent sojourn in Hanover, where the orchestra was modelled on the French pattern with strong woodwind. It is a full-scale concerto in six movements, the first almost an overture in itself, altogether out of scale with the pastoral that follows; Handel may have attached it to give substance to a slight evening's entertainment. The quality, apart from the gauche fourth movement (HG 8), which sounds earlier than the rest, is very high, especially in the slow sections. The introduction makes eloquent play with ninths, melodic and harmonic; the Lentement is brief but splendid, the F major Largo an exquisite broad melody, laid out in seven parts for full wind and strings. The Adagio is gaunt, almost tragic in mood, with much spare two-part writing for solo oboe and violin. It has an unpublished B section, seventeen bars long, the first twelve of which are scored for the remarkable and bleak combination of solo bassoon and double bass (Ex. 22, p. 214). This leads to a full da capo. The third movement, a Bourrée though not so titled, is also incomplete in HG. From bars 27 to 64 an independent second bassoon operates with the first, mostly in thirds, in the solos (bars 27–30, 35–42, 57–60, 62–4), and a second viola

9 'A Critical Study'.

Ex. 22

strengthens the bass in the *tutti*. There are thus nine parts, not seven, and the two concertino bassoons echo the oboes at a distance. The final Minuet is found in various guises in five other instrumental works and probably began as a harpsichord piece.

Apart from the overture and a few movements in concerto style, the scoring of *Il pastor fido* is very light. Many arias rely entirely on a strong bass line, with the upper strings adding a coda. But oboes and bassoons, when they are employed, enjoy more independence than in many later operas. The tonal plan is exceptionally unified—perhaps too much so. Of the 28 set pieces, including the overture but not 'Hò un non sò che', only six are in sharp keys, and D major and E major do not appear at all. This flatward tendency is particularly strong in the first and third acts. Of the ten movements in Act III, organized round G minor and B flat, all but the first are in flat keys; so is the first half of Act I. All the characters except Dorinda and all the instrumental movements lean in the same direction. Silvio's part (four arias) is confined to flat keys, beginning with two in the hunting key of F. Amarilli's is even more strictly circumscribed: it is entirely in G minor and major, including her accompanied recitative, the duet, and the sinfonia for her execution.

History and Text

Little is known about the circumstances of composition, or when Handel returned to London in the autumn of 1712. He finished the score on 24 October, but a month elapsed before production. This is surprising, since the opera shows every sign of being a hurried job. The management can hardly have hoped to repeat the success of *Rinaldo* with a work of this kind, which had no claim to novelty. There had even been an entertainment called *Pastor Fido; or, The Faithful Shepherd. Acted all by Women*, produced with songs and dancing at Dorset Garden on 30 October 1706, Drury Lane on 7 January 1707, and Greenwich on 21 May 1711. The 1712 opera season did not open till 12 November, when a pasticcio concert, *The Triumph of Love*, gave it a distinctly sober send-off. The explanation probably lies in the precarious financial status of the company, which (until the production of *Teseo* in January) required the use of old sets and costumes and a total absence of scenic spectacle. *Il pastor fido*, given outside the subscription at regular opera prices, was perhaps intended as a stopgap until *Teseo* was ready.

The first performance took place at the Queen's Theatre on 22 November 1712 with the following cast:

MIRTILLO:	Valeriano Pellegrini (soprano castrato)
SILVIO:	Valentino Urbani (alto castrato)
AMARILLI:	Pilotti (soprano)
EURILLA:	Margherita de l'Epine (soprano)
DORINDA:	Jane Barbier (contralto)
TIRENIO:	Leveridge (bass)

The staging was not impressive. The author of the Colman Opera Register commented: 'The Scene represented only ye Country of Arcadia. ye Habits were old.—ye Opera Short.' He added that neither *Il pastor fido* nor its successor (10 December), a pasticcio called *Dorinda* assembled by Haym, which had eight or ten performances and was revived in January 1714, drew full houses. The same sets and costumes were used for both; this may explain why the management followed one unsuccessful pastoral with another. The absence of a star singer since the departure of Nicolini cannot have helped the venture.

Il pastor fido had seven performances during the season, the last on 21 February 1713. A number of musical changes reflected in the sources may have been introduced during the run. They include the removal of the last two movements of the overture, the linking of the duet to the E flat sinfonia by suppression of the former's five-bar coda (Handel may never have included this), and the insertion of the B section and da capo of 'D'allor trionfante' and of 'Hò un non sò che' in III i. The latter is dramatically maladroit and higher in tessitura than the rest of Dorinda's part, but had won popular favour; Handel perhaps added it to shore up a sagging opera. The presence in an early copy of Silvio's arias in soprano transpositions suggests that Urbani may not have sung in all performances.

The 1734 Revivals

Handel's two revivals in 1734 were confused by Burney (and his modern editor, Frank Mercer) and by Chrysander,[10] whose 'second version' is a mixture of both. They can be disentangled with the aid of librettos and copies. The most important—but by no means the only—difference between them is that the November revival included dance sequences and a new prologue, *Terpsicore*, whereas its predecessor in May did not.

The first revival took place at the King's Theatre on 18 May 1734, with the following cast:

MIRTILLO:	Giovanni Carestini
SILVIO:	Carlo Scalzi
AMARILLI:	Anna Strada
EURILLA:	Durastanti
DORINDA:	Maria Caterina Negri
TIRENIO:	Gustavus Waltz

Carestini was a mezzo-soprano castrato with a wider compass than Pellegrini, Scalzi a soprano castrato; the pitch of the other parts was unchanged. The advertisements added the words 'Intermixed with Chorus's. The Scenery after a particular Manner'. There were thirteen performances, the last on 6 July. Those listed by Deutsch for 15 June (doubtfully) and 15 July are excluded from *The London Stage*, which however seems to be wrong in placing the third performance on 24 instead of 25 May—a Saturday, the regular opera night at this period. Handel had announced that the season would end on 29 June; Chrysander[11] conjectured that he extended it for the benefit of his friend and student the Princess of Orange, for whose wedding on 14 March he had put together the serenata *Parnasso in festa* and who returned to London on 2 July. She was certainly present on the 6th; the Royal Family were very assiduous in patronizing this revival.

The libretto refers to 'large Additions'; there were equally large subtrac-

---

[10] His score in turn deceived Ellen Harris into misrepresenting the version performed in May (*Handel and the Pastoral Tradition* 241–4) and drawing false conclusions from it.

[11] ii. 363.

tions. In view of the confusion in Chrysander's score, it seems best to list what was performed in tabular form, omitting only the recitatives (see Table 3). Nine of the borrowings are not identified by Chrysander.

It will be seen that of the 32 numbers in this version only eight—six arias (three transposed and one with new words for a different character), one duet (with the tempo speeded up from *Largo* to *Andante Larghetto*), and one sinfonia—survive from 1712. Fourteen arias, one duet, all five choruses, two sinfonias, and most of the overture were taken from other works, with some changes in the words but almost none in the music apart from the addition of upper parts to the ritornellos of 'Fra gelsomini' and the compression of the B section of the *Teseo* duet.[12] The only new music was the Largo of the overture and the D minor setting of 'Fato crudo', a magnificent cavatina far superior to the 1712 version. The F major overture is much more suited to a pastoral opera than its predecessor. The style is broad and mellow, with no attempt at emotional frills; the horns lend warmth to all three movements but circumscribe their range of modulation. They are also required in some of the borrowings from *Parnasso in festa*, and give the whole score a tang of the open air.

The outline of the plot is little changed. The choruses of huntsmen and priests are so much padding. A number of recitatives are shortened or cut (in I iii and viii, II vi, vii, and x, III iii and iv), and three short passages inserted. The only one of importance is a brief confrontation between Amarilli and Silvio in I vii. This is an improvement, since it illustrates their dislike of the arranged marriage from their own mouths and establishes an earlier link between the two lobes of the plot. The insertion in II x however is ludicrous: instead of entering the cave Mirtillo says he will be there in a few minutes, summons the other shepherds to share his joy, and initiates a choral finale that replaces Eurilla's air of fiendish anticipation. The almost total eclipse of Eurilla demolishes one of the few satisfactory features of the 1712 score; she is left with the slightest of her five arias and one unsuitably borrowed from Silvio with parodied words. The incongruity is all the more marked in view of the much bigger scale and elaboration of the arias inserted in 1734. It may be connected with Durastanti's failing powers; she now had a narrow mezzo compass of a ninth from middle C, though she had sung up to G in *Arianna* in January.[13] For whatever reason, Handel sacrificed his most successful character. The roles of Mirtillo and Amarilli were much expanded for the company's brightest stars, Carestini and Strada. The former had eight arias, the latter five, and they shared two duets. Handel exercised a nice economy here by giving them several arias already in their repertory: Carestini had sung three of his in *Parnasso in festa*, Strada four of hers in *Lotario* and *Ezio*. A number of them were dragged in regardless of context or character; the tautest scene of the 1712 score (III vii) was padded out with a beautiful but dramatically otiose aria for Amarilli ('Ah! non son io') after her accompanied recitative, the end of which was put down a semitone, and a chorus of priests that replaced the E flat sinfonia. Outside this scene Handel tended to cut the stronger and preserve the weaker movements of the 1712 score.[14] The best

[12] This is quite different from the second version in the Malmesbury copy of *Teseo*; in all Handel wrote three B sections for the duet.

[13] Handel at first meant her to sing 'Secondaste' in G, but put it down a further tone.

[14] He had however used five of its arias in the bilingual *Acis and Galatea*, adding three of them for its most recent revival only a few days before that of *Il pastor fido*.

TABLE 3

	Character	Source of Music	HG (1890)
Overture (F major, with horns)		'Ouverture' (unpublished, RM 20 g 13) (Allegro and Bourrée)	69–76
Act I			
i. 'Fato crudo'	Mirtillo	new setting, D minor cavatina	77–8
'Fra gelsomini'	Mirtillo	Continuo cantata no. 63 ('Son gelsomino'), transposed C to B♭	78–80
iii. 'D'amor a fier contrasti'*	Amarilli	Lotario ('Qual cor che mi donasti')	82–5
v. 'Lontan dal mio tesoro'	Mirtillo	1712, transposed C to A	(15)
vi. 'Frode sol'	Eurilla	1712 ('Casta dea')	(18)
vii. 'Finchè un zeffiro'	Amarilli	Ezio	(19–20)
'Quanto mai felice'	Dorinda	Ezio	(21–2)
viii. 'Quel gelsomino'	Silvio	Riccardo Primo, transposed F to G	93–6
'O quanto bella gloria'	chorus	Parnasso in festa	(25)
Act II			
i. Sinfonia		Ezio, Act III	(26)
'Caro amor'	Mirtillo	Teseo ('Deh! v'aprite') A section only, transposed G to E	103
iii. 'Torni pure'	Mirtillo	Parnasso in festa	(28–9)
v. 'Finte labbra'	Amarilli	1712	(30–1)
vi. 'Sol nel mezzo'	Silvio	1712, transposed E♭ to B♭	(32–3)
vii. 'Se in ombre'	Dorinda	1712	(33–4)
viii. 'Sì, rivedrò'	Mirtillo	Rodelinda (Dec. 1725), transposed F to G	(35–6)
ix. 'Scherza in mar'	Amarilli	Lotario	(37–8)
x. 'Accorrete, voi pastori'	Mirtillo	Parnasso in festa ('Non tardate')	(39–40)
'Accorriam de' vostri amori'	chorus	Parnasso in festa ('Accorriam senza dimora')	(40)

Act III

i. Sinfonia		*Partenope*, Act III	(42)
ii. 'O quanto bella gloria'	chorus	*Parnasso in festa*	(42)
iii. 'Sento nel sen'	Silvio	*Ezio* ('Finchè per te'), transposed A minor to C minor	112–13 (in D minor)
v. 'Secondaste'	Eurilla	1712, transposed B♭ to F	(45)
vi. Sinfonia		1712	(46)
'Ah! non son io'	Amarilli	*Ezio*	(46–7)
vii. 'Per te, mio dolce bene'	{Amarilli / Mirtillo}	1712 (without final ritornello)	(48–9)
viii. 'S'unisce al tuo martir'	chorus	*Parnasso in festa*	(49)
ix. 'Dell'empia frode'	Tirenio	*Riccardo Primo* (A section only)	(50)
'Caro, ti dono'	{Amarilli / Mirtillo}	*Teseo* (B section modified)	(51–3)
'Sciolga dunque'	Mirtillo	*Parnasso in festa*	(53–4)
'Replicati al ballo'	chorus	*Parnasso in festa*	(54)

*Preceded by secco recitative (HG 80–2, A).

that can be said for the revision is that it matters less in a pastoral than in a more dramatic opera. It was of course the usual procedure for an eighteenth-century pasticcio; if we experience a slight shock, it is because Handel often shows such astonishing powers of fusing *opera seria* into a unity.

The second revival of *Il pastor fido* inaugurated Handel's new season at Covent Garden on 9 November 1734 (there was a rehearsal at noon on the 8th) in the presence of the King and the Princesses. He was now in open rivalry with the Opera of the Nobility at the King's Theatre, and his agreement with Rich had brought him new allies in a ballet troop led by the French dancer Marie Sallé. This governed the form of the revival, announced as 'With several Additions, Intermix'd with Chorus's. Which will be preceded by a new Dramatic Entertainment (in Musick) call'd, Terpsichore'. There were two changes in the cast of *Il pastor fido*, Scalzi (Silvio) being replaced by the tenor Beard—his first part in a Handel opera—and Durastanti (Eurilla) by Rosa Negri, who at this stage of her career[15] was not a soprano (as stated by Deutsch and others) but a contralto like her sister. There were five performances, all in November.

The changes in the score, though less drastic than in May, were considerable. The most important was the insertion of a suite of dances in each finale: Huntsmen in Act I, Shepherds and Shepherdesses in Act II, a General Dance in Act III. Having used the first two movements of the F major overture for *Terpsicore*, Handel resurrected the first of the D minor (1712) for *Il pastor fido*, shortening the fugue by fifteen bars[16] (continuo score, HG (1890), 11). He cut the opening scene of Act I with both Mirtillo's arias; apart from this there were no verbal changes in the recitative. Amarilli now began the opera; a string accompaniment gave more weight to her recitative (HG 80–1, B). There were two substitutions in Act I, 'Sento brillar nel cor' (HG 86–90) for Mirtillo in place of 'Lontan dal mio tesoro' and 'Non vo' mai seguitar' (HG 96–100) for Silvio in place of 'Quel gelsomino'. In Act II 'Caro amor' acquired its original B section and da capo from *Teseo* (HG 104 in dotted brackets), and 'Hò un non sò che' for alto in G (HG 104–5) was given to Eurilla at the end of Scene ii, just before she places the garland on Mirtillo's arm. Beard sang 'Sol nel mezzo' presumably in the lower octave, and 'Sento nel sen' (III ii) in D minor as printed by Chrysander (HG 112–13). There was now no change of scene in the middle of Act III.

Of the two new arias, 'Non vo' mai seguitar' is feeble and flashy; Handel had lost any sympathy he felt for Silvio (whose voice is different in each of the three versions) and not yet warmed to Beard. But 'Sento brillar' is a splendid piece in the spectacular style Handel used for Carestini in *Arianna* and *Ariodante*. It tells us much about his voice, which must have been able to ride a full orchestra throughout almost two octaves. The key, D major, suggests affinities with the natural trumpet. The combination of immensely long phrases and showy' coloratura with a sonorous string texture in quaver figuration (after the manner of Vinci) and intermittent syncopation from the first violins recalls 'Dopo notte' in *Ariodante*, in the same key and composed about the same time. In both arias Handel deploys the voice's full compass within a single phrase. The ballet suites are scarcely inferior to the sterling

---

[15] Handel wrote for her in the alto clef. She sang higher parts later in Dresden.

[16] These bars were blocked out after the music had been recopied for the performing score (Hamburg MA/1041).

specimens in *Ariodante* and *Alcina*. That in Act I, unimpressive on paper, comes off brilliantly in performance thanks largely to the high horns in G. The Act II Musette has one of Handel's most captivating tunes, enhanced by the scoring for flute and first violins in unison, and the little second Minuet, which slips into the subdominant by the third bar, is delightful. The E major movement in Act III with internal pedal at the start of the B section is also most attractive, though Handel subsequently cut it. The finest stroke here is the achievement of structural unity throughout the long finale by the use of the same melody for Mirtillo's previous aria ('Sciolga dunque'), the last dance, and the *coro*. Aria and chorus come from *Parnasso in festa*, but the dance was an inspired addition. Handel was to repeat this design with equal felicity in the revival of *Arianna* and in *Ariodante* and *Alcina*.

Terpsicore

The action takes place in *the Temple of Erato, President of Musick*. Erato is surrounded by her disciples, who praise Apollo in chorus. The god enters with the other Muses, greets his 'tuneful sister', craves a blessing from Jove, and asks where Terpsicore is. A Prelude soon signifies her approach, *accompanied by her Disciples dress'd differently, agreeable to their Characters*. Apollo invites her to lead the dance, and a Chaconne follows. At the request of Apollo and Erato Terpsicore mimes various aspects of erotic passion, beginning with the heart stupefied by pleasure (Sarabande) and ending with jealousy. The dances are interspersed with recitatives, a duet, and an aria for Apollo, after which Terpsicore *imitates the Rapidity of the Wind*. During another duet she *joins with the other Dancers*. A shortened repeat of the opening chorus ends the Prologue. The singers were Strada (Erato) and Carestini (Apollo); Marie Sallé danced the part of Terpsicore.

This is nothing less than a one-act *opéra-ballet* in the French style, remembered today by such works of Rameau as *Les Indes galantes*, *Les Fêtes d'Hébé*, and *Pygmalion* but represented in the 1720s by Mouret, Destouches, and François Colin de Blamont. The model was in fact the Prologue to Colin de Blamont's *ballet héroïque Les Festes grecques et romaines* (1723), which has the same characters as Handel's Prologue (with the addition of Clio) and virtually the same plot, though Colin de Blamont treats it at greater length. When Apollo observes that Terpsicore has not come to the Muses' feast, a danced prelude announces her arrival. Colin de Blamont ends with a long 'cantata' in which Erato and Apollo sing Terpsicore's praises in a series of airs and duets, interspersed with dances as she mimes the feelings expressed in the words. The dances—Chaconne, Sarabande (with an air on the same music), two Rigaudons, Gigue, Air (Rondeau), and Menuet—are (with the exception of the Rigaudons) identical with Handel's, and in the same order. At the climax Terpsicore expresses the contrasted moods of the lover:

> Vous peignez à nos yeux les transports des Amants,
> Les tendres soins, la flatteuse espérance,
> Le désespoir jaloux, la cruelle Vengeance.
> Tous vos Pas, tous vos Pas sont des sentiments.

Even some of Handel's stage directions are taken straight from Colin de

Blamont, for example at the entry of the Muse: *Terpsicore arrive à la tête de tous ses Elèves différemment habillez & caractérisez.*

It was undoubtedly Sallé who brought Colin de Blamont's ballet to Handel's attention, although she never danced in it herself; the part of Terpsicore had been created by her teacher Françoise Prévost. Sallé was an important figure in the history of the ballet; many of her innovations anticipated the reforms of Noverre, who paid special tribute to the 'delicacy and lightness' of her 'voluptuous dancing'. She was renowned not for the virtuosity of her art but for its expressiveness, and especially for her power of miming different emotions. Among her London ballets (she had joined Rich's company, not for the first time,[17] in November 1733) were *Les Caractères de la Danse* (to music by the elder Rebel) and *Les Caractères de l'Amour*; on 14 January 1734 she won great success at Covent Garden in *Pygmalion*, which was performed 30 times in four months. This was an early example of a *ballet d'action* (that is, one that told a story), for eight dancers; the music has not been identified, but the choreography was Sallé's. Her principal aims throughout her career were to get rid of stilted and conventional costumes dating back to the old court ballet before Lully and to make dancing an integral part of the opera instead of a mere *hors d'oeuvre*.[18] Handel must have been familiar with her work in London and in sympathy with its goal. He is unlikely to have needed a musical model for the composition of *opéra-ballet*; he would have had to be very up to date to take advantage of its supreme exemplar, Rameau, whose first full stage work, *Hippolyte et Aricie*, had appeared only the previous year. Although Handel had composed dances in previous operas, he had never built a whole act round them, and he did not repeat the experiment; it would have been difficult to do so regularly with an Italian company. Nor is there another contemporary example of the French *opéra-ballet* in London.

The music of *Terpsicore*, like that of *Il pastor fido*, is largely taken from other works, but its quality is uniformly high and the variety of form, colour, and texture gives it a flavour unique in Handel's output. The choruses, the first two arias, and the Chaconne, an expanded version of a chorus with the voice parts omitted,[19] came from *Parnasso in festa*; Handel once more saved trouble by putting in the mouth of his singers what was already there. He opened with the F major *Il pastor fido* overture (May 1734) without the Bourrée. Several of the shorter dances in *Terpsicore* and the opera, and another version of the Chaconne, turn up in the Op. 5 set of trio sonatas, published in 1739. The three duets, all in minor keys, and Apollo's second aria appear to be new. All are attractive, and the first two duets, though quite short, are of exceptional beauty. 'Tuoi passi son dardi' is the finest movement and the most sumptuously scored, with a layout typical of Handel in sensuous mood: recorders (unison), muted violins and violas, pizzicato cellos, and a part on two staves marked *Les Orgues doucement, e la Teorbe*, of which the treble doubles the recorders and the bass the cellos. This is the only mention of the organ in connection with any of Handel's operas. The scoring is similar to that of *Athalia* without trumpets and drums (two horns, two recorders, one transverse

[17] She danced in London in the seasons of 1716–19 (as a child), 1725–7, 1730–1, and 1733–5. One reason for these frequent appearances was the hostility her reforms encountered in Paris.

[18] For fuller accounts of Sallé (1707–56) and her career see Emile Dacier, *Une Danseuse de l'Opéra sous Louis XV* (Paris, 1909), and Cyril W. Beaumont, *Three French Dancers of the XVIIIth Century* (London, 1934).

[19] It was originally composed as an entr'acte for the first version of *Radamisto* (1720): see p. 340.

flute, theorbo, organ) and full of delicate detail. The light-footed dance when Terpsicore imitates the wind, based on the ritornello of the aria in which Apollo bids her do so, is enchantingly scored for two recorders and *pianissimo* violins only and, like other movements, makes happy use of hemiola. Another dance based on the music of the previous vocal movement is the Sarabande. The jealousy dance in G minor—the jealousy key: compare 'Gelosia, spietata Aletto' in *Admeto* and 'È gelosia' in *Serse*—is interesting and unusual, with variations of texture and tempo (the marking *un poco più presto* occurs twice) and a *diminuendo* fade-out in the closing bars.

Terpsicore and Il pastor fido together made a long evening; Handel shortened it in some of the later performances, omitting the B section and da capo of 'Gran Tonante' and 'Di Parnasso' and a 29-bar stretch of the Chaconne in *Terpsicore*, and 'Frode sol', 'Hò un non sò che', the B section and da capo of 'Caro amor', and the E major movement in the Act III ballet in the opera. These cuts are all indicated in the Hamburg scores, and most of them in Chrysander's edition. The removal of two of Eurilla's arias suggests that Rosa Negri was no great catch.

Neither *Il pastor fido* nor *Terpsicore* was heard again during Handel's life, but dances from the opera cropped up occasionally as interludes in plays, for example *Henry IV Part 1* on 17 April 1735, *All for Love* on 22 March 1739, *Love for Love* on 23 March 1740, all at Covent Garden, and *The Merchant of Venice* at Drury Lane on 23 April 1742.[20] The 1734 overture was played at the Dublin Music Room (under 'Mr Charles the Hungarian') on 12 May 1742, the King's Theatre (for Miss Robinson's benefit) on 29 April 1745, and the Three Swans Inn, Shaftesbury, on 28 August 1752. There have been modern revivals of *Il pastor fido* at Basle (1946) and Göttingen (1948) in a German arrangement by August Wenzinger; of the 1712 version at Como (1959), Vicenza (1961), and Abingdon (1971); and of the third version, including *Terpsicore*, with choreography by Mary Skeaping, at Drottningholm (1969). This production was transferred in ruthlessly shortened form to the 1974 Edinburgh Festival. *Terpsicore* has been given separately at Göttingen (1948), Berlin (1959), Halle (1960, with *Imeneo*), and the English Bach Festival (1978).

Autograph

This is the earliest Handel opera to bear an exact date at the end; the full inscription, omitted in Squire's *Catalogue*, is *Fine dell Atto terzo G.F.H. Londres ce 24 d'Octobr. v.st. [vieux style] 1712*. Like that of *Rinaldo*, the 1712 autograph is incomplete and the surviving portions divided between the British Library (RM 20 b 12) and the Fitzwilliam Museum (Mus MS 256, pp. 17–32). They consist of I vi; II i except for the last 16 bars of 'Caro amor'; II iv–viii; and from the beginning of 'Ritorna adesso' in II xi to the end of the opera, with two omissions noted below. The eight leaves in Fitzwilliam Mus MS 256 fit in before f. 20 of RM 20 b 12; the first 51 bars of 'Tu nel piagarmi' are in the former manuscript, the rest in the latter. Of the 42 surviving leaves, only 31 (perhaps 29) belong to the autograph as first written, which did not contain

---

[20] See *The London Stage* under these dates.

'Hò un non sò che' (III i), the B section and da capo of 'D'allor trionfante' (III v), 'Secondaste al fine' (III vi), the sinfonia for the entry of the priests (III ix), or probably 'Ritorna adesso' (II xi), which is written on different paper and is not followed by the usual indication of the end of the act. Handel's curious foliation 9/10 (Fitzwilliam, p. 17) also suggests an insertion or change of plan. In addition the following leaves in RM 20 b 12 are insertions: 1–3 (new setting of recitative 'Ah! che sperar' and 'Di goder' in I vi as printed), 29–31 (Tirenio's aria 'Risonar mi sento' and recitative 'Cessate omai', HG 69–70, both on leaves with blank versos), and 34 ('Secondaste', bound at the end of the manuscript and used in the text where Handel first indicated a repeat of 'D'allor trionfante'). Handel probably composed the part of Tirenio for a tenor: he wrote the *coro* for soprano, alto, and tenor only, signed and dated the manuscript, and added the vocal bass part later on a blank stave at the bottom. He had to drop to a lower stave to avoid his signature and inscription, which he nevertheless partly covered. The presence of the stage direction for III ix at the top of f. 29 shows that when he rewrote the scene for Leveridge the sinfonia to accompany the 'pompa sacerdotale' of Tirenio's entry was not in the score. There is no autograph of it, nor of the B section of 'D'allor trionfante', which may have been added at the same time, possibly during the run (it is not in the libretto).

It is clear from what survives of Handel's foliation that the overture was never part of the manuscript; there is no room for it, since the start of Act II carries Handel's figure 5, i.e. f. 17. All that remains of the original Act I is an unpublished setting of 'Di goder' in B flat (ff. 4–5, A section only),[21] differing from the A major version in its treatment of the coloratura sections, which are even flashier and more taxing. Part of its introductory recitative survives (cancelled) in RM 19 e 4.

A curious point revealed by the autograph is Handel's indecision, paralleled in other works, about the exact metre he wanted for pieces in triple or compound time. 'D'allor trionfante' and 'Risonar mi sento' were conceived in 3/8, and 'Sol nel mezzo' and 'Nel mio core' in 6/8, before attaining their ultimate shape in 6/8, 6/8, 12/8, and 3/8. For 'Secondaste' Handel put a signature of 3/8, but changed it to 3/4 before writing the music. There is moreover an inconsistency in his corrections. Whereas in 'Sol nel mezzo' he left no doubt about the matter, even crossing out every alternate bar line, in 'D'allor trionfante' and 'Nel mio core' he altered the signature of the upper parts only, leaving the bass in 3/8 and 6/8 respectively.[22] This practice is found in other works with sufficient frequency to suggest that it is not an accident.[23] Handel may have intended a kind of double rhythm, as in those pieces (such as the first version of 'Rejoice greatly' in *Messiah*) where he runs 4/4 against 12/8. By coincidence the autograph of *Il pastor fido* includes an unidentified three-bar sketch in D minor in precisely this rhythm at the end of the B flat setting of 'Di goder'.

The Fitzwilliam section, not used by Chrysander, shows differences in the scoring of 'Ritorna adesso' (the oboe and violin entries on the last quaver of

---

[21] The paper suggests that this too may be an insertion, like all the other leaves with Ca2 and D1c watermark.

[22] In 'Nel mio core' the viola part too retains its 6/8 signature.

[23] It occurs twice for example in the autograph of *Serse* ('Nò, se tu mi sprezzi' and 'Cagion son io').

bars 44, 45, 68, and 71 are all solos) and 'Se m'ami' (the violins play the top line in the ritornello, the oboes the second) and fuller stage directions in III ii. 'Tu nel piagarmi' contains two afterthoughts. Originally the ritornello after the first part was six bars long, and that after the second repeated the opening; it was a da capo, not a dal segno aria. Both cuts improve the balance. The autograph is almost devoid of tempo marks; only 'D'allor trionfante' has one. The differences in the handwriting are surprisingly wide—so much so as to raise a suspicion that the manuscript was assembled from pages written over a long period. This however is unlikely, although some of the arias whose music is borrowed from earlier works are evidently fair copies. The recitatives are written much more hastily than the set pieces. An autograph fragment of the D minor overture arranged for keyboard (Fitzwilliam Mus MS 260, pp. 5–6) is on Italian paper used about 1724–6 and was probably intended for a pupil.

The autograph of the only new music for the May 1734 revival, the Largo of the F major overture and the D minor setting of 'Fato crudo', marked *Larghetto*, is in Fitzwilliam Mus MS 256, pp. 33–6; the loose *Ouverture* in F from which the rest of the 1734 overture was lifted is in RM 20 g 13 (ff. 33–6). Handel had already used its opening movement, transposed to G, for *Parnasso in festa*. By a slip of the pen he headed the Bourrée *Gavotte*; the keyboard arrangement in RM 18 b 6 was made before he corrected it. No autograph is known of the two arias added in November 1734 or any part of *Terpsicore*, but six of the *Pastor fido* dances—HG 102, 109, 110, 111 (C minor), 114 (Gavotte), and 115—are in Mus MS 263 (pp. 49, 59–66) together with a sketch for the Musette in a different key (p. 52), which shows this lovely tune as it first occurred to Handel.[24]

Ex. 23

He numbered the dances up to 15 (including six in *Terpsicore*); the sequence and a note that a Minuet in G was to follow the Musette shows that the C minor Minuet in Act II was an afterthought.

Librettos

1712. 'An Opera As it is Perform'd at the Queen's Theatre in the Hay-Market . . . Printed by J. Gardyner in Cary-street, near Boswell-Court, in Little Lincolns-Inn-Fields.' 45 pp. Handel is named as the composer and described as 'Maestro di Capella di S. A. E. d'Hannover'. Rossi's dedication in Italian 'All'Illustrissima Signora Anna Cartwright' is dated 22 November 1712, the

[24] These pieces are not identified in the *Catalogue*. Mann had evidently not seen Chrysander's 1890 score.

day of the first performance. Nothing is known of Anne Cartwright; Deutsch's identification of her with the mother of John and Edmund Cartwright, the political reformer and inventor of the power loom, is ruled out by the fact that they were not born till 1740 and 1743.

The libretto contains many important stage directions not in HG; most of them are in the autograph. The arias exceptionally are numbered, and briefly paraphrased rather than translated in the English text. Several passages of recitative in I ii and iii and III ix (23 lines in all) are marked with *virgole* as not set. They include dialogue essential for grasping the plot, such as Amarilli's citation of the oracle in I ii; but Handel no doubt expected the audience to read this in the Argument. The libretto does not contain 'Hò un non sò che' or the B section of 'D'allor trionfante' and there is no indication that Tirenio's cavatina is to be repeated.

1734 (May). 'The Second Edition, with large Additions. Printed for T Wood, in Little-Britain, and are to be sold at the King's Theatre in the Hay-Market.' 39 pp. The 1712 Argument is reprinted, but not the dedication. Handel is not mentioned. The dramatis personae include 'Chorus of Shepherds, Huntsmen and Priests'. The contents have been tabulated above. Act I has the pleasant heading *A Country of Arcadia, with Groves, Fountains, Cottages, Shepherds, etc.* I vii, which contains the new dialogue for Amarilli and Silvio, is headed *Silvio and Amarillis, Dorinda on one Side unseen by them*. No locations are given for Acts II and III. There is still a change of scene before the sinfonia, but the wording is different, beginning *Altare con foco acceso*. Between the duet and the new chorus of priests ('Si unisce') *it thunders*. Tirenio's cavatina 'Dell'empia frode' is marked to be repeated.

1734 (November). 'The Third Edition, with large Additions . . . and are to be Sold at the Theatre in Covent-Garden.' 47 pp. As last, with the cuts and substitutions already listed and the addition of *Terpsicore*, described as a Prologue, and the dances. Act II is headed *An open Country with a Hill, and the Cave of Ericina*, Act III (without a scene change in the middle) *A great Wood, with the Prospect of the Temple of Diana*. 'Dell'empia frode' is not marked for repetition, but this could be accidental. Chrysander printed the Italian text of this libretto in his 1890 edition.

Copies and Editions

Five copies of the 1712 version survive, three of them dating from before 1720. The earliest is RM 19 e 4, which Chrysander not unreasonably took to be Handel's performing score. Clausen denies this possibility on the supposition that the copyist is Smith, who could not have reached London before the end of 1716. But the writer is Linike,[25] and the score unquestionably dates back to 1712, since its first state gives a text that precedes some of Handel's changes in the autograph. This contains part of an otherwise lost setting of the recitative 'Ah! che sperar' (I vi) probably leading to the B flat 'Di goder' of the autograph, the A section only of 'D'allor trionfante', and no sinfonia in III ix; but 'Secondaste', the revised Tirenio scene, and the bass voice in the *coro* are integral. Very soon, still in his early hand, Linike crossed out the first nine bars of 'Ah! che sperar', removed the continuation with its cadence and the aria, and substituted four pages (ff. 11–14) with the familiar setting of the

[25] Larsen's S2 must be a slip; there is no resemblance between the hands.

recitative and 'Di goder' in A. In the same way he inserted the B section of
'D'allor trionfante' (f. 63), recopying the first bar of the recitative 'Già
Amarilli' from the previous page, and the sinfonia in III ix (f. 73); he
cancelled the five-bar ritornello at the end of the duet, which is thus
dramatically interrupted by the entry of the priests. Linike also added 'Hò un
non sò che' on two pages (ff. 79–80) now bound at the end of the manuscript,
with a cue for its insertion in III i. The ritornello after the B section, slightly
altered from its form in *La Resurrezione* and *Agrippina*, was mostly written by
Handel.[26] The omission of the two three-note violin figures in bars 12 and 13
of 'Sol nel mezzo', which are in the autograph, was presumably accidental.
The absence of the overture however suggests that it may not yet have been
attached; there is no certainty that it was played at the first performance.
Handel used this score in 1734 to prepare the second version, as noted below.

A slightly later Linike copy, Add MS 16024 (*c*.1716), is one of two complete
sources for the D minor overture, with both bassoon parts in the Bourrée (HG
5, on nine staves) and the B section and da capo of the Adagio (HG 9, here
Largo; see Ex. 22). Every movement except 'Se m'ami' and the *coro* has a tempo
mark, which in view of Linike's status must be taken as authentic. Those not
in HG are: *Largo* on the opening and the Lentement (as well as the Adagio) of
the overture, 'Mi lasci', 'Caro amor', and the duet 'Per te'; *Allegro* at bar 10 of
the overture, on its fourth and sixth movements, and on 'Augelletti', 'Son
come navicella', 'Di goder' (opening), 'Finte labbra', 'Nel mio core', 'Ritorna
adesso', 'Tu nel piagarmi', 'Secondaste', and 'Risonar mi sento'; *Andante* on
'Lontan dal mio tesoro'; *Vivace* on 'Allor che sorge'; and *Presto* on the sinfonia
in III ix. The top part beginning six bars before the end of HG 11 is for oboe
solo, and so is the treble line in bars 20–32 of 'Tu nel piagarmi' (HG 59),
though the autograph specifies only violins. This aria has some figuring in the
ritornellos. The fourth and fifth movements of the overture (HG 8, 10) and
the E flat sinfonia (HG 69) are followed by a *segue subito*. 'Hò un non sò che' is
not included; 'D'allor trionfante' is complete with B section and da capo; the
duet and E flat sinfonia appear in succession, as in HG; the repeat of 'Risonar
mi sento' is not indicated; the *coro* has no vocal bass, although Tirenio's aria
and recitative are present. This is the only copy to include the violin part in
bars 12 and 13 of 'Sol nel mezzo'. At the end of the manuscript, in a second
early hand (RM1), are Silvio's four arias in soprano transpositions, 'Casta
dea' and 'Non vo' legarmi' in B flat, 'Sol nel mezzo' in G, and 'Tu nel
piagarmi' in D minor. This can have no connection with 1734, when only 'Sol
nel mezzo' was sung by a soprano Silvio, and then in a different key.

The Malmesbury copy, 'transcribed by Mr Newman Feb[r] 1715' as Elizabeth Legh noted on the title-page, also gives the overture complete; the
Bourrée has a second bassoon part in bars 74–6 as well, a unique reading
which is probably correct. Again 'Hò un non sò che' is absent, 'D'allor
trionfante' complete, the duet and E flat sinfonia appear in succession, and
the *coro* has no vocal bass. In most other respects, including the scarcity of
tempo marks and the omission of the violins in bars 12 and 13 of 'Sol nel
mezzo', the copy follows RM 19 e 4. It is almost certainly earlier than Add MS
16024.

The Flower score (S2, 1730s), without the recitatives, is closer to RM 19 e 4,

---

[26] It is not clear why Chrysander, who used this manuscript, printed the bass of one bar in small
notes and brackets (HG 56). These notes as well as the violin part are in Handel's writing.

not only in tempo marks and 'Sol nel mezzo' but in the inclusion of 'Hò un non sò che' and the suppression of the coda of the duet; but the *coro* lacks the bass voice. The overture, without its last two movements, seems to have been assembled from parts, perhaps Walsh's; there is no second bassoon in the Bourrée, and the accidental duplication of a bar in the viola part puts the instrument a bar behind for the greater part of the movement. The Flower Collection contains a second copy of the overture in the old-fashioned hand of Dr William Turner,[27] Handel's senior by 34 years and an older contemporary of Purcell. It lacks the second, fourth, and sixth movements and contains many errors. The Bourrée has both bassoon parts, but there is no B section or da capo to the Adagio.

The Shaftesbury copy of the 1712 version (S4, one page S1) dates from 1736 or soon after and begins with the F major overture of 1734. The Bourrée is *A Tempo di Gavotta* as first written in the autograph, and both oboes double first violins; there are no oboes in the earlier movements. The rest of the score derives from RM 19 e 4, with a few tempo marks and other details (for example the omission of the 'Risonar mi sento' repeat) from Add MS 16024. 'Hò un non sò che' is present; the *coro* has all four voices. The S1 page is an insertion carrying the recitative of III iv (HG 58) and the first twenty bars of 'Tu nel piagarmi'; it replaced a page whose stub remains.

The Flower parts (S2, late 1740s), a complete set comprising violins 1 and 2, viola, cello + bassoon, oboes 1 and 2 (including flutes in 'Caro amor'), and cembalo, were evidently extracted from the Flower score, omitting the overture. Since the score seldom gives full instrumentation, S2 was thrown on his own resources in deducing the wind parts. The oboes differ considerably from HG and are often preferable to Chrysander's bracketed suggestions; but they occasionally contradict the autograph, doubling the top line in unison in the ritornello of 'Se m'ami', where the autograph has all the violins on the top line, all the oboes on the second, and 'Tu nel piagarmi',[28] where Chrysander is correct. In the movements where the autograph, generally confirmed by the early copies, has *Tutti* on the top line S2 sometimes guesses wrong, dividing the oboes in 'Finte labbra', 'Nel mio core', and 'Ritorna adesso' and omitting them altogether in 'Di goder'. In the ritornello of 'Lontan dal mio tesoro' all the oboes play the top line, all the violins the second. Both oboes double the first violins in the ritornellos of 'Augelletti', 'Casta dea', 'Mi lasci', 'Allor che sorge', 'D'allor trionfante', 'Secondaste', the sinfonia in III ix, and 'Risonar', agreeing with the autograph where it exists. The cello–bassoon part is exceptionally specific as to which instrument is to play. The viola has only one part in 'Caro amor', doubling the second violin at the octave after bar 2. There are additional details of instrumentation in 'Finte labbra' and 'Nel mio core'. 'Lontan dal mio tesoro' has some figuring in the cembalo part and the score.

As with *Rinaldo*, Handel used an old Linike copy (RM 19 e 4) to prepare the May 1734 version. He must have done this in April, for there are many references to *Parnasso in festa*, first performed in mid-March. He wrote the first words of the inserted pieces, together with their source and sometimes the new key and character's name, at the head of the numbers to be replaced, without

---

[27] Walker, *The Newman Flower Collection*, 38.

[28] But the first violin plays the top line in bars 20–32, not a solo oboe as in Add MS 16024. The latter could be a later change of Handel's.

cancelling the latter; he marked cuts in the recitatives and cues for insertions, not however adding the music; he rewrote a number of recitatives either to bring them into the right key or to alter the tessitura for a particular singer. The entire part of Eurilla was lowered for Durastanti in this way. Most of the changes are in pencil, a few in ink. The great majority of them conform to the May 1734 score as tabulated above and partly printed in Chrysander's 1890 volume, but in a few instances Handel had second thoughts. He planned some replacement for 'Fato crudo' but smudged it out so effectively that it can no longer be read. In I v he assigned the tenor aria 'Se povero il ruscello' from *Ezio* as a substitute for 'Lontan dal mio tesoro', presumably with the voice part raised an octave for Carestini. The aria is in G major; hence perhaps the alteration of the recitative cadence to B minor, though this key before the A major transposition of 'Lontan dal mio tesoro' would not be impossible. 'Nò! non basta' (II ix) was to have been replaced by something now illegible; when Handel wrote in 'Scherza in mar', he amusingly ascribed it to the wrong opera, *Ezio*. For 'Se m'ami' (III iii) he first substituted the alto aria 'Han mente eroica' from *Parnasso in festa*, presumably for Dorinda, but then wrote, partly on top of this note, *Silvio aria Ex C^{mol} finche per te mi palpita*. This aria, in A minor in *Ezio*, is printed by Chrysander (1890, p. 112) in D minor with new words as sung by the tenor Silvio (Beard) in November 1734; Scalzi sang it in C minor. 'Secondaste' was first put down a third to G, then a further tone to F, with a note over the vocal line *e li Violini all ottava*; this perhaps tells us something about Durastanti's decline, both in pitch and skill. The duet from *Teseo* in the last scene seems to have been first designed to replace the repeat of Tirenio's cavatina; Handel later moved it into the following recitative.

There are a few minor modifications to the music, not all of which appear in Chrysander's 1734 score. He does incorporate two small amendments to the vocal line of 'Frode sol' ('Casta dea'), but not the rewritten violin part in the ritornello of 'Sol nel mezzo'—Handel took the opportunity of the changed key to spread it over a wider compass—or the note about the violins doubling the voice in 'Secondaste' (in the Hamburg score they double the bass as well in the ritornellos). Although Handel did not use 'Nel mio core' in 1734, he made verbal and musical changes in it, possibly for Carestini; he adapted the coloratura in bars 35–9 so that the top note is G, not A. This could have been for one of the revivals of *Acis and Galatea* in which the aria was sung.

There is no complete score, manuscript or printed, for either 1734 version. The two Hamburg performing copies were used for both 1734 revivals. MA/1041 is in the main a full score, but the sinfonias that open Acts II and III and the choruses are represented, as in the continuo score, by the instrumental bass and sometimes the treble line of the choruses. The D minor overture has no viola part. The whole of *Terpsicore* and the Act II ballet are now missing. MA/1057[29] is an almost unfigured continuo score for the second harpsichordist.

The preparation of the material in May was evidently a rush job, involving three copyists. MA/1041, based on Handel's indications in RM 19 e 4, which must have been supplemented verbally, was written by Smith and S1 in close collaboration. Smith copied the overture and instrumental movements, most of the recitative, some arias (especially at the beginning of the opera), and nearly all the choruses. A number of the arias borrowed from other operas

[29] Accidentally omitted in Larsen's table.

were begun by Smith and continued by S1, Smith adding the words. Many pages show both hands: f. 108ᵛ illustrates them clearly, the first part of the chorus 'S'unisce al tuo martir' written by Smith, the last eight bars by S1 (see Plate 15). MA/1057, reduced from MA/1041, was divided between S1 and S3. The latter copied 'Scherza in mar' (II ix), except the first 10½ bars, and the whole of Act III, S1 the rest. In November there was less of a scramble. Smith wrote all the insertions in MA/1057 (21 leaves) and added the Act II ballet to f. 50. He also copied sixteen of the 27 new leaves in MA/1041, S1 the rest.[30] Handel added a few modifications to both scores, especially to the ballet music in November.

Although neither copy is complete (some passages performed in May were removed in November, especially from MA/1057), it is possible with the assistance of other scores, chiefly of *Terpsicore* and the Act II ballet, to reconstruct both revivals. Unfortunately Chrysander, unaware of the existence of two distinct versions, presented the material in his 1890 edition in a confusing and defective form, with a very inaccurate preface. His version of the continuo score (pp. 2–54) is reasonably close to MA/1057, but omits some directions (*Andante* on 'Gran Tonante', *Subito il Coro* before 'Cantiamo lieti' and 'O quanto bella gloria') and does not indicate all the cuts. Except 'Lontan dal mio tesoro' the movements replaced in November have been torn out of the manuscript, but vestiges remain (for example in I viii). The cuts during the November run, including the recitative before 'Frode sol', are clearly indicated, and it is possible to trace step by step the complex alterations in II i and ii and at the end of the opera. In both scores when a part was transferred from one voice to another, as happened with Eurilla and Silvio, no one bothered to regularize the clefs, especially in the recitatives.

Chrysander is no guide to the contents of MA/1041. The music printed on HG 91–2 and 108–9 (second system) belongs not to *Il pastor fido* but to the bilingual *Acis and Galatea* (1732–6) and was taken from the performing score of that work (RM 19 f 7), where the recitatives are in Handel's autograph. 'Sento nel sen' appears in C minor (for the soprano castrato Scalzi in May) as well as D minor. 'Sol nel mezzo' lacks the violin part in bars 12 and 13 but contains the rewritten ritornello of RM 19 e 4. Handel himself in May altered the underlay in bars 10–12 of 'Caro amor', incidentally supplying confirmation of the sequence of changes in this scene. The B section ritornello of 'Sciolga dunque' (HG 54) was cut in that revival, and the da capo led straight into the chorus 'Replicati al ballo'. In November the aria was complete, and the chorus followed the ballet. Handel made various adjustments to the dances. Originally the March in Act I followed the 6/4 *Pour les Chasseurs*, and both sections of each were to be repeated, with second-time bars at the end. Later the repeat signs and second-time bars were scratched out and both movements played twice *in toto*. Except that Handel noted *March Again* after *Pour les Chasseurs* in MA/1057, whereas it appears twice in MA/1041, the second time in its original position with repeats, there is no formal difference between the copies. By including the repeats in one (HG 101) but not the other (HG 24) Chrysander leaves a false impression. The E major movement in the Act III ballet is cancelled in both scores.

---

[30] The insertions are correctly identified by Clausen, but he does not distinguish the hands in ff. 47–52 and 59–61 of MA/1041; S1 wrote ff. 47 and 59.

The Library of Congress, Washington, has a not quite complete set of parts (S2) for 'Songs in Pastor Fido Revis'd', possibly extracted from RM 18 c 4 (see below); they were originally in the Aylesford Collection. The text is a mixture of the two 1734 revivals, comprising all the new music for *Terpsicore* and *Il pastor fido* (not the F major overture), together with 'Fra gelsomini' and six movements from *Parnasso in festa*. The parts are violins 1 and 2, violoncello primo, oboes 1 and 2 (incorporating flutes and recorders), bassoon (a separate part), and cembalo, but no viola. The two horn parts are in the music library of the University of Maryland (M2 1 M2). Wind parts are supplied for the dances, though by a strange error the recorders are confined to the first 8 bars of that on HG 66. The five bottom staves, including *Orgues*, appear in the cembalo part of the duet 'Tuoi passi son dardi'.

The Lennard copy (S1), misinterpreted by Chrysander, is a strange concatenation of all three versions without *Terpsicore*, dances, or choruses, 1712 predominating. Handel's amendments in RM 19 e 4 to 'Frode sol' and 'Sol nel mezzo' (in B flat) are present, but not those to 'Nel mio core'. Material taken from other London works and 'Hò un non sò che' are excluded. The duet 'Per te' leads into the E flat sinfonia without its coda. This score could serve no purpose outside a library, since Silvio appears indiscriminately as alto, tenor, and soprano. The Fitzwilliam score (Mus MS 77, dated 1767 by its first owner and probably copied at that time) and RCM 903 (1850) derive from Lennard.

Of the various 1734 miscellanies, the Aylesford volume RM 18 c 4, ff. 2–106, shared between two copyists, one of them S3 (f. 35ᵛ and 45–106), is perhaps the earliest. It gives a comprehensive selection from both revivals, omitting only secco recitatives, pieces surviving from 1712, and most of the insertions from other operas. First come ten items from the May version: the F major overture, 'Fato crudo' as reset (HG 77), 'Fra gelsomini', and the pieces borrowed from *Parnasso in festa* (except 'Replicati al ballo') and *Teseo*, but not the other operatic insertions; then (f. 45) a harpsichord arrangement of the F major overture (the Bourrée again headed *Gavotta*), all the *Terpsicore* music in the correct order except the D minor overture and the repeated chorus at the end (but 'Gran Tonante' has its *Parnasso* text); and finally the three new vocal movements and nine dances added in November, with the chorus 'Replicati al ballo' omitted earlier. The rest of the volume contains the November 1734 additions to *Arianna* (five dances and the aria 'Del labbro'), evidently copied by S3 at the same time, and an aria from *Flavio* in a different hand.

A second Shaftesbury copy (1736 or soon after) contains *Terpsicore* without title (S4) and 'Additions to Pastor Fido' (S2), both incomplete and without recitatives. *Terpsicore* has no overture and omits the opening and closing choruses and Erato's aria 'Di Parnasso' (from *Parnasso in festa*) but includes 'Gran Tonante'. The Prelude (HG 56) is *Largo*; the Chaconne has *Tutti* on the top line; the Sarabande is *pianissimo*. 'Tuoi passi son dardi' occurs twice, first as a duet with bass only, second as an instrumental dance scored as in HG. The words *Twice—2ᵈᵃ volta Violoni pizzicati e Teorbe* in the Hamburg continuo score and a direction in the libretto that Terpsicore *changing her Movements, represents those Passions* confirm that this is correct. The *Pastor fido* additions comprise most of the new music for both revivals (without the Act II ballet suite) and most of that taken from *Parnasso in festa* but not the other borrowings. 'Non vo' mai seguitar' has *Tutti* on the top line as in Hamburg.

RCM 261 (S2) gives a less complete selection from both revivals in no sort of order, including some of the *Arianna* pieces and six of the opera arias used in May, ascribed to their original contexts but with the transpositions and word changes used in *Il pastor fido*. The Lennard 'Miscellanys' volume (Fitzwilliam Mus MS 798) contains an almost complete copy of *Terpsicore* (S5, *c.*1745) introduced by the full D minor overture of 1712 (without the additions of Add MS 16024). It lacks only the two choruses, 'Di Parnasso', and the Chaconne. 'Tuoi passi' again appears twice, the dance without organ or theorbo. *Terpsicore* is followed by the November additions to the opera with the dances in a different order. The first segment of RM 19 d 11 (RM 5/6, 1750s or later) contains exactly the same material as ff. 61–114 of RM 18 c 4, beginning with the Prelude in *Terpsicore* (HG 56) and including the *Arianna* and *Flavio* items, and was taken from the same source. Someone has added an inaccurate ascription 'in Ptolemy'. This volume was used by Arnold and Chrysander, who heavily annotated it and took from it the scoring of the Act II dances and *Terpsicore* movements incomplete in Hamburg.[31]

The harpsichord arrangements of the 1712 overture are confusing. All omit the F major Largo (HG 3), and there are several detached versions of the finale, some evidently based on a keyboard piece antedating the overture. A brilliantly ornamented early arrangement, probably by Babell, embraced only the first, third, and fifth movements, the third showing signs of the second bassoon part. The 3/4 Allegro is shortened at the end (as later in Hamburg) and not repeated after the Lentement; the fifth movement has no B section or da capo. The first movement occurs alone in the earliest Malmesbury keyboard volume (Beta, *c.*1717–18) and New York Public Library Drexel MS 5856 (Smith, *c.*1721); all three are in RM 18 c 1, ff. 14–18 ('Ouverture della Pastorale', S2, *c.*1728), together with a simple treble-and-bass transcription of the fourth movement, headed *Menuet*. They were published in his fourth collection (1730) by Walsh, who supplemented them with a clumsy version of the fourth movement and finale by the old-fashioned arranger of the overtures in the first collection (1726). Handel also made his own arrangement; the first movement—but with the opening nine bars in the Babell version—and finale are in the Edwin M. Ripin MS in the Boston Museum of Fine Arts (RM1, *c.*1717), the whole in two Malmesbury volumes (RM1, *c.*1718; Smith, *c.*1728) and the Coke Wesley MS (H1, *c.*1721). About 1724–6 Handel began a second, shorter arrangement, of which fifty bars exist in autograph only, as noted above.[32]

Add MS 27932 (f. 11ᵛ) has an early keyboard arrangement of 'Se in ombre' marked *Presto*, with some ornamentation, Add MS 31504 (f. 112) a copy of 'Cara, ti dono' with the fifteen-bar B section as sung in *Il pastor fido* (*Allegro*, voice and bass only); both are in unknown hands. The Coke Collection has a very early copy of three 1712 arias, 'Mi lasci', 'Finte labbra', and 'Ritorna adesso'.

No score was printed for the 1712 production, but three isolated numbers appeared in the next few years: 'Allor che sorge' on a single sheet in 1717 (listed by Smith under *Rodrigo*),[33] 'Secondaste' in the second volume of *The*

[31] The copies of arias from the 1712 score in RM 18 c 7 (ff. 86 ff.) and RM 19 d 10 (ff. 55 ff.), written by S2 and S13, belong to revivals of the bilingual *Acis and Galatea*.

[32] Both arrangements are printed in *Twenty Overtures*, i. 1–15.

[33] Walsh included it in *The Favourite Songs in yᵉ Opera Call'd Thessus & Amadis* (1732); see p. 259.

Pocket Companion (December 1725), and the overture in parts in Walsh's third collection (*c.*1725). About November 1734 Walsh published two collections of *Favourite Songs*, shortly followed by a flute arrangement. The first group of eight songs included only one ('Se in ombre') from *Il pastor fido* proper; the others were borrowings from earlier operas, printed from old plates with the name of the new singer substituted where necessary. 'Si, rivedrò' is in F, as sung by Senesino in *Rodelinda*. The second group contained the 1734 overture, the duet 'Cara, ti dono' (from *Teseo*, marked *Allegro*) and seven songs, of which only 'Fato crudo' (the D minor setting, marked *Larghetto* as in the autograph) and 'Secondaste' (in F for Durastanti) were composed for *Il pastor fido*. With the exception of the last, which was re-engraved in a different key, none had been printed before. 'Caro amor' is in E major, complete with B section. The fact that neither collection includes any of the November additions, and that Scalzi and Durastanti but not Beard or Rosa Negri are among the singers named, suggests that both were prepared between the revivals. The two collections were later reissued together. Walsh published the 1734 overture in parts on 6 March 1737. The two Minuets on HG 111 appeared as songs in *The British Musical Miscellany* (1734-7), the first in volume iii ('Men are all traytors'), the second in volume iv ('Stay, shepherd, stay'). Later (*c.*1750) Walsh added the March with horns (HG 100) to the parts of the *Flavio* overture.[34]

Arnold (nos. 159-60, *c.*1795) put out a fragmentary score of the November 1734 version under the title *Masque*. It was evidently taken from RM 19 d 11, and contains at the end the same excerpts from *Arianna* and *Flavio*.

Chrysander based his score of the 1712 version (1876) on RM 19 e 4 and the autograph fragments in RM 20 b 12. He missed the Fitzwilliam material and Add MS 16024, and did not have the printed libretto. He printed the overture from the Walsh parts; hence the absence of the Bourrée's second bassoon and the B section of the Adagio. His publication of the 1734 material (1890), as noted above, is vitiated by his ignorance of the fact that two different versions were produced in that year. The three forms in which he presents the opera certainly do not 'supply each other's deficiencies and exhibit clearly the alterations which Handel made at the various performances'. They neither provide a practical score nor facilitate understanding of Handel's intentions and procedures. A new edition is urgently needed.

Additional Note

*   (p. 226) Clausen (*Handel Collections and their History*, ed. Best, 12-13) may be right in calling this an archive score (in which case the performing score is lost), but his assumption that Linike copied it from the autograph some time after the production when the performing score was not available and subsequently amended it is unconvincing. It would imply that Handel asked Linike to copy an obsolete text, and it conflicts with the evidence of Linike's handwriting.

[34] Smith, *Descriptive Catalogue*, 293 (no. 16).

CHAPTER 13

TESEO

THE scene is Athens in mythical times. Act I takes place in *the Temple of Minerva. The Curtain rises at the Sound of a Warlike Symphony; and behind the Scenes there is heard the Noise of Men fighting. Enter Agilea, attended by Women.* Agilea, described as 'a Princess under the Guardianship of Egeus', asks her confidante Clizia how the battle went. Clizia replies that Teseo ('a foreign Prince, known at last to be the Son of Egeus') saved her life. Agilea says she too owes her safety to Teseo and loves him. Arcane, confidant of Egeo King of Athens, reports that the issue is still undecided and Egeo is anxious about Agilea. She goes into the sanctuary after a prayer for Teseo's safety. Arcane and Clizia have a lovers' tiff. She invites him to prove his constancy by joining Teseo in the field. This makes him jealous and reluctant to leave, but he finally agrees. They go out severally after a farewell duet. Egeo enters with attendants, and Agilea returns. Now that victory is won, he proposes to marry her. She reminds him that he is pledged to Medea, but he brushes this aside. [In lines excluded from the score as performed and printed[1] she explains that, having been brought up as his ward, she loves him as a daughter, not a wife. His intention is that Medea shall marry his son in Troezen, i.e. Teseo, whom he has not recognized in the ally who is fighting for him.] *The People Shout for Joy;*[2] it is time for Egeo to lead them in thanksgiving to Minerva. He goes after a love song. Agilea resolves to keep her love for Teseo alone.

Act II. In *Egeo's Palace* Medea reflects on the happiness of the innocent; the tyrant love that impelled her to kill her brother and children has once more destroyed her peace. Egeo enters with attendants, ascribes his military success to Medea's science, and announces that his son shall marry her in his stead. Neither knows that this son is Teseo. In a duet each pours contempt on the other but rejoices in the possession of a different love. After her departure Arcane reports that the troops have proclaimed Teseo Egeo's successor. Egeo says 'We must suppress this insolence', and the scene changes to *a Square in Athens. Theseus enters in Triumph, follow'd by a Multitude of People, who Express their Joy by Singing and Dancing. The Scene opens at the Sound of a Symphony of warlike Instruments, which introduce this Chorus,* in which they hail him as King. On his command *the People retire: as Theseus is going, he is with-held by Medea.* She drops hints about Egeo's anger and jealousy, which she offers to placate in return for his (Teseo's) love. When he says he loves Agilea she replies that Egeo is his rival and volunteers to plead his cause with Agilea and Egeo. He swallows this

---

[1] Other such passages in the last three acts are summarized in brackets. Handel in fact set nearly all of them, as noted below.

[2] This and many other stage directions are omitted from Chrysander's score. The most important (HG 23, 51, 62, 63, 68, 82, 84, 89, 96, 105, 106) are included in this summary.

like a lamb and departs. She fumes with jealous rage: if Teseo refuses her, she
will avenge herself on Agilea.

Act III (*a Palazzo*[3]) begins with another love scene for Arcane and Clizia.
He apologizes for his jealousy and goes off to ask Egeo's consent to their
marriage. Agilea looks forward impatiently to Teseo's return. When he enters
she reminds him that Egeo is his rival. [He explains why he did not come
sooner—he had to disarm Egeo's jealousy. He promises to force Egeo's hand if
necessary and take Agilea abroad.] He sets out confidently to tackle the King.
Arcane tells Agilea that she is to be Egeo's Queen. Medea enters and taxes her
with loving Teseo, which she cannot deny. But she refuses to submit to threats
or abjure her love, whereupon *Medea by her Inchantments changes the Scene into a
horrid Desart full of frightful Monsters* and *goes out*. Agilea, Clizia, and Arcane cry
for help; *one of the Spirits goes against* Clizia; Arcane *draws his Sword, which the
Spirit takes from him, and flies away*. Medea returns, releases Clizia and Arcane,
and in a *Recitativo Orrido con Stromenti* invokes spirits from hell to threaten
Agilea 'and with most dismal Horror strike her Heart'. *The Spirits enter . . .* and
advance, tormenting Agilea, who runs every way to avoid them. Finally they *carry her off*
as Medea conjures up further plagues.

The location of Act IV is not specified. Arcane tells Egeo what Medea has
done; he threatens her with death and destruction. Arcane comforts himself
with the thought of Clizia's love. There must be a change of set here,
presumably to Medea's abode or the 'horrid Desart'. Agilea begs Medea to let
her die, but still refuses to deny her love. Medea *makes New Enchantments. To
them Theseus descends Sleeping, conducted by Spirits*. Agilea tries unsuccessfully to
awaken him. Medea summons the Furies, who *enter, holding in one Hand a Knife,
in the other a Torch*. She orders them to finish their work and kill Teseo, at which
Agilea offers to give him up to save his life. Medea says that is not enough: she
must tell Teseo that inclination, not *force majeure*, is her motive. Reluctantly she
agrees. At Medea's command *the Furies go off; and the Scene changes into an
Inchanted Island. Medea wakens Theseus with a Touch of her Inchanted Wand*. Agilea
tells Teseo she can no longer love him. He rages against her hard heart; she
weeps secretly and begs him to leave her and save himself. [He tells her he is
Egeo's son and will defy the powers of hell to prevent her being forced into
marriage.] *To them, Medea out of a Cloud, with Theseus's Sword*. Having
overheard their conversation, she can no longer hold out against their
happiness and Teseo's 'shining Virtues'. She *gives him back his sword*,[4] determined to prove her love by generosity. The act ends with a love duet for Agilea
and Teseo.

The libretto places Act V in *Medea's Enchanted Palace; where are shown
Magnificent Tables*. She now cannot face the prospect of the lovers' happiness.
She will die, but not before she has exacted full vengeance by exploiting the
fact that Egeo has not recognized Teseo. Egeo enters, and she gives him a cup
of poison for Teseo. He rejects it as beneath his royal dignity so to requite a
benefactor, but agrees when she points out that this stranger may deprive his
son in Troezen of his birthright. Teseo enters *leading Agilea, Arcane and Clizia
following, and afterwards great Crowds of People, to attend the Nuptials*. Teseo,
holding Agilea's hand, addresses her in a love song, then throws himself at
Egeo's feet. Egeo agrees that he shall be his successor and offers the cup as

---

[3] The early copies, followed by Arnold and Chrysander, have *Appartamenti di Agilea*.
[4] This direction is not translated in the English text.

pledge. *Theseus takes the Cup in one hand, and draws his Sword in t'other . . . The King looking attentively upon Theseus Sword, discovers it to be the same which he had left for a Token to know his Son by;*[5] *in great Fury he snatches the Cup, and throws it down.* [Teseo explains his incognito; he wished to prove himself a worthy son of Egeo.] *Medea flies away, having heard Theseus own'd by his Father.* Egeo says pursuit is vain, since 'she knows the Ways that are to others unknown'. Though he loves Agilea, he gladly gives her to Teseo, *who takes her hand and kisses it*, and grants Arcane's request for Clizia. After a duet for the secondary lovers Medea enters *in a Chariot drawn by flying Dragons*: they are not free from her rage, since hell is armed on her behalf. *Whilst Medea is going, the Palace seems on Fire* and the scene is darkened, with thunder and lightning. All pray for help; Minerva appears in glory, *descending in a Machine*, and her Priest assures them of heavenly assistance. *The Scene changes* to its former calm as all acclaim heaven's reward for constant love.

The libretto was adapted by Nicola Haym from Quinault's *Thésée*, set by Lully in 1675. This explains many of its peculiarities, including the five-act form (unique in Handel), the parallel treatment of the secondary lovers, and the casual and spasmodic use of the exit convention. Like most French grand operas of its period *Thésée* has a Prologue eulogizing Louis XIV, which Haym naturally dropped. The plot so far as it concerns Theseus, Aegeus, and Medea follows classical sources, principally Plutarch's *Life of Theseus* but also Apollodorus and Ovid. The other characters Quinault invented, taking the name Aeglé (Haym's Agilea) from one of the many nymphs who figured briefly in Theseus's past. Besides Arcas (Arcane) and Cleone (Clizia) he has a third confidante, Dorine, who loves Arcas and acts as a feed for Médée. She survives as a mute relic in Handel's libretto and Chrysander's score under the name Fedra. Originally she had recitatives in II i and V ii, and her name appeared against the soprano stave in the Act II *coro di Ateniensi* and the final *coro*.

Thésée may have been chosen because it was very successful and seemed to offer opportunities for repeating the spectacular scenic effects that proved so popular in *Rinaldo*. Here Haym hit a series of snags. Quinault's design depends as much on a prominent chorus and ballet as on scenic transformation, and the Queen's Theatre, though well equipped with machines and supers, commanded neither. In London at this period dancers were for the most part restricted to divertissements between acts; Handel used them tentatively in *Amadigi*, but not in *Teseo*.[6] A chorus seldom figured in Italian opera anywhere, and although there seems no obvious reason why such a body should not be able to memorize its part in a London as in a Paris theatre, it appears to have gone out of use with the Purcellian masque. Secondly, Quinault employed the solo air as a point of lyrical expression in the course of an unfolding scene, not in the Italian manner to discharge emotion generated in the preceding recitative, after which the singer would go out and a new scene begin. In Quinault there was no link between air and exit.

[5] It is not clear how the actor was expected to convey this; compare Sheridan's Mr Puff on the gestures of Lord Burleigh (*The Critic*, Act III).

[6] He appears to have considered them: the direction *Qui deve seguir una festa di Ballo, la quale viene interrotta dall'arrivo di Medea* (HG 104) is in the autograph, but was excluded from the libretto and all copies.

Haym made little attempt to grapple with this difficulty. He simply translated Quinault's recitative, with certain abridgements and alterations, and inserted aria texts where he thought fit. Although these were nearly all new (the cavatina 'Dolce riposo' is an exception), they were not tied in with the exits. Again and again a character sings an extended aria—on several occasions two in succession—and remains on stage to continue the conversation. Of 27 da capo arias in *Teseo*, only ten are followed by an exit, and three of these come at the end of an act. In terms of *opera seria* convention this produces a kind of aesthetic coitus interruptus: the emotion generated is not discharged, and the tension threatens to lapse into anticlimax.

Haym showed greater resource in plugging the gap left by the chorus and ballet, as indeed he had to if the libretto was to retain any sort of coherence. His task was a formidable one, nothing less than translation from one convention into another while dispensing with two of the principal props on which the original depended. The weight they supported had to be transferred to a very different pillar, the solo aria. The process might be compared to a contractor shifting the site of a house without pulling it down. Haym's solution is far from perfect, but it is judged too severely in David Kimbell's useful comparison of the two librettos.[7] It is of great interest for historians of operatic form as well as for students of Handel. Whereas French *tragédie-lyrique* could build up to spectacular finales with a packed stage, *opera seria* could not, since the curtain in early eighteenth-century London theatres was not lowered in act intervals. This alone ensured that any act except the last must end with a solo aria, or more rarely a duet.

Quinault's Act II closes with Médée alone, which suited Haym very well. But his first act culminates in a big ceremonial scene in the temple, his third in a choral ballet of shades, and his fourth in a pastoral divertissement laid on by Médée to entertain the lovers. It was to introduce this that he thought up Medea's gratuitous and hopelessly unconvincing change of front, the weakest spot in both librettos. With Agilea's final aria in Act I, Medea's in Act III, during which the spirits carry off Agilea, and the love duet in Act IV Haym achieves a perfectly adequate substitution of one type of climax for another. He tries in the dialogue to suggest the off-stage events during Act I; Handel does not back him up here, nor does Chrysander by omitting the shout of triumph that takes Egeo off towards the end. He retains the choral acclamation of Teseo and his triumphal entry in Act II, though he reduces the dramatic plausibility of the episode by severe cuts. (The abrupt change of place after the few lines of recitative for Arcane and Egeo in II iii, which looks inept on paper, must have been thrilling in the eighteenth-century theatre: a quick rotation of wings and the withdrawal of a pair of back-flats takes the audience straight into the scene described by Arcane.) The omission of the choral wedding procession in Act V is no serious loss. But in Quinault it is the chorus that appeals to Minerva when Médée threatens to incinerate the landscape, and if Haym and Handel could use a chorus in Act II (tenors and basses only—the upper parts as usual were taken by the soloists) it is difficult to see why they abjured it here. Even a few bars would have made a stronger impact than the isolated cries of the soloists. We can imagine from 'O terror and astonishment' in *Semele* how memorably the Handel of the oratorios might have dealt with the incident.

[7] 'The Libretto of Handel's *Teseo*', *M & L* xliv (1963), 371.

Haym is more open to criticism for his departures from Quinault's plot (comparatively slight as these are) and for his cuts. The scenes for Arcane and Clizia in Act III (i) and for Arcane and Egeo in Act IV (i and ii) are not in Quinault at all, and the short scene for Teseo and Agilea in III iii (their first meeting in the opera) does not occur at this point. Although the first can be defended as supplying relief between two of Medea's volcanic eruptions, they do nothing to strengthen the plot; indeed Egeo's anger when he hears about Medea's treatment of Agilea considerably weakens it, since it undermines his willingness to fall in with Medea's plan in Act V. Haym's motive was probably to throw a meaty titbit to the singers, especially the castratos. Otherwise Teseo would have had no aria in Act III, and Egeo, Arcane, and Clizia nothing at all (except Egeo's Act II duet with Medea) between the first and the fifth act. The muddle at the end of the opera, where Minerva makes a spectacular descent in a machine (as in Quinault) but a Priest sings her recitative (the bass version in Chrysander's appendix), is more apparent than real. Chrysander compounded it by implying that Minerva became a bass and advancing the eccentric theory that she could not appear in person because 'when four sopranos were employed there was no voice left to perform the part'. Handel composed the recitative for soprano but adapted it for bass, with appropriate verbal changes, before the first performance. His original intention may have been to double the parts of Fedra and Minerva.

Haym several times weakens the motivation by paring down the gradations in Quinault's recitative and substituting a crude directness more characteristic of Italian than French opera. The scenes between Agilea and Egeo in I v, Medea and Teseo in II v, and Medea and Agilea in III v are more sensitively handled by Quinault. The presence of Arcane and Clizia for part of the first torment scene is an awkward relic left by the contraction of a much longer episode in Quinault; so is Arcane's message to Agilea that Egeo means to marry her (III iv), which as it stands looks like a feeble repetition of what we already know. A few expressive details like Cléone's appeal to Arcas to intercede with Égée on Aeglé's behalf go by the board. Kimbell censures Haym for not making Medea's love for Teseo explicit in II i; but her state of mind is clear enough, and its cause soon becomes apparent. No doubt she is a more melodramatic and unsubtle figure in Haym. But an Italian opera is much further from a spoken play than a French *tragédie-lyrique* with its slow rhetoric and almost Racinian treatment of recitative; a tendency to go bull-headed for the central emotion is part of the price to be paid for its dramatic impetus. Many small flaws apparent in the study are found to vanish in the theatre.

More serious is the omission from the score of stretches of recitative printed in *virgole* in Haym's libretto. Here the blame may rest with Handel: he set nearly all of them, as well as the two Fedra scenes, but removed them before performance, fearing perhaps that the length of the opera would try the patience of the public in an unsuccessful season. In doing so he obscured the plot and sometimes made it almost incomprehensible. Everything hangs on the relationship between Egeo and Teseo, and the other characters' knowledge or ignorance of this. We cannot tell if Teseo himself is aware of it, or why he is fighting incognito, without two of the suppressed passages in Acts IV and V. Other matters concealed are Agilea's position in Egeo's household, the fact that Egeo has a son in Troezen, and Teseo's reason for not at once explaining the situation to Agilea. As the opera stands in the score the omission of these passages is a blot; but the 1713 audience could read them and the full stage directions in the libretto, and Handel no doubt relied on that.

A few points remain obscure, notably the location of Act V. The scene heading comes from Quinault, where however the palace is clearly Égée's, and the festive preparations concern his recognition of Thésée as his successor. Haym's mention of Medea's palace and magnificent tables suggests that the sorceress has invited Egeo to dinner or is giving the wedding reception for Agilea and Teseo, since the action appears to be continuous. We can either ignore Haym's act heading or assume a quick set-change before Teseo's entry, as in Act II. The advanced technique of the London theatre absolved Haym from preserving Quinault's (relative) unity of place by safeguarding that of action. It is clear from the advertisements that the visible scene transformations in the last three acts, especially the double change after Medea's entry in the last scene, were among the major attractions of the opera, and very impressive they must have been. The importance of the stage directions for any estimate of such a work requires no emphasis.

The score has two salient features, the richness and variety of the musical invention (there are far fewer borrowings than in the three previous operas) and the uncertain treatment of the drama. This springs partly from the adaptation; Handel was perhaps not yet sufficiently experienced to exert his authority over Haym in such matters as the placing of arias. Five times—twice in each of the first two acts and once in Act IV—the same character has two in succession, and the small ration of arias per act underlines the disproportion. Except in Medea's cavatina and aria at the beginning of Act II, and less explicitly in Teseo's in Act IV, Handel does not set up a structural relationship, dramatic or tonal, between the pairs. We have neither the cavatina–cabaletta design so frequently employed later nor an integrated brace of da capo arias like the hero's in Act II of *Arminio*. Agilea's at the start of the opera are both concerned with her love for Teseo, but so is everything else she sings. Egeo's later in the act and Teseo's in Act II establish neither unity nor contrast. Each scene would have been strengthened and the dramatic span extended if Handel had made the first aria a cavatina. It is interesting to discover that in all five instances Haym gave both arias a da capo. Handel overruled him twice, but this was not enough.

Equally strange, in view of later events, is Handel's failure to make dramatic use of the battle that rages off-stage during Act I. The act-heading states explicitly that the curtain rises on a battle piece. In several later operas Handel achieved a powerful and original effect in just such a situation by treating the last movement of the overture as the first of the action and raising the curtain before or in the middle of it.[8] Moreover the mention of the curtain in a libretto is so rare that one suspects a special significance. Yet the last movement of the *Teseo* overture is anything but warlike, and no 'sinfonia bellicosa' follows. It is just possible that the text is defective here, though there is a notable unanimity in the copies. More probably, as in *Il pastor fido*, Handel did not bother with a new overture but appropriated a concerto composed for the French-trained orchestra in Hanover. The French names on the second

[8] Compare the opening of *Giulio Cesare*, *Scipione*, *Riccardo Primo*, *Ezio*, *Arianna*, and *Deidamia*.

violin and viola staves (Haut Contre and Taille) in all early copies, and the use of the soprano clef for the former, are quite exceptional in his London operas.[9] The form suggests an instrumental sonata rather than an opera overture; the finale is not a dance but a lively movement in concerto style with the wind developing their own material, which the strings never manage to lay hands on. Both Largos are fine, especially the first, and alive with potent dissonance. But the music has no particular aptness to the context. It was only in later works (and not all of them) that Handel conceived the overture as an organic part of an opera or oratorio.

The male roles in *Teseo* are overshadowed by the female. Handel's tardiness in creating a satisfactory hero was not due to indifferent singers (Nicolini was an exceptional artist), but it may reflect a difficulty in reconciling himself to the castrato, less on musical than on dramatic grounds. It was not till Senesino's arrival in 1720 that he began to clear this block. As far back as *Rodrigo* he had drawn two well-contrasted heroines. In *Agrippina* he did even better, though neither of the ladies can be called a paragon. In *Rinaldo* and *Il pastor fido* the scheming woman, whether she works by sorcery or native cunning, outpaces her virtuous rival as well as the man she pursues. *Teseo* is no happier in its hero, but both Medea and Agilea are full-length portraits, and so balanced that neither runs away with the opera. This equal presentation of two opposed types of femininity was to serve Handel again and again, in *Amadigi, Radamisto, Giulio Cesare, Admeto, Orlando, Alcina, Serse,* and many other operas, as well as in oratorios.

Like all Handel's sorceresses Medea haunts the memory. She has something of Agrippina and Armida, but a fuller range than either. Every one of her solos is magnificent, and they depict the progressive disintegration of her character as much through the flexible treatment of aria form as in sheer invention. Streatfeild well described her as 'positively Aeschylean in her rugged grandeur and passionate force'. She does not appear in Act I, but completely dominates Act II, singing in every movement except the *coro* and Teseo's two arias. Quinault's imaginative idea of showing her first in repose, though a repose without tranquillity, was a gift to Handel. The whole scene is masterly. The cavatina 'Dolce riposo' with its throbbing strings, fitful oboe solo, and exquisite vocal line is a marvellous evocation of nostalgia for lost peace of mind. It is rich in irony, for no audience can come to the theatre ignorant of Medea's history. This is strengthened, fortuitously but not ineptly, by the 'Comfort ye' fingerprint, already employed as a motive of compassion in *Rodrigo*. The rhyme scheme suggests that Haym laid out the text for a da capo aria, though the libretto prints it as recitative. By setting the B section as a secco recitative[10] and following it with a foreshortened and altered version of the cavatina, which breaks off on a recitative cadence and continues in secco, Handel brilliantly reconciled musical form with dramatic continuity. The cavatina slips back without its two-bar ritornello, as if in mid-sentence; no sooner has Medea uttered the single word 'Dolce' than the oboe takes over her second phrase and extends it as she begins a series of free imitations. The sudden collapse after six bars suggests that she knows her longing to be in vain.

[9] In the earliest copy (Coke I) the bass part too is labelled in French ('Basse').

[10] The Malmesbury copy has a *subito* before and after this recitative, and uses the same word at several other points in the score to indicate that the music must not stop.

The mood is clinched by the terse and bare aria 'Quell'amor' in the relative minor; the bass scale figures move restlessly up and down as if seeking an escape from the emotional dilemma, and the reluctance of the B section to embrace a major key confirms that none is possible.

In the duet with Egeo Handel strikes a shrewd dramatic blow by using the procedure of a love scene to suggest something like its opposite, not so much a clash of wills as an agreement to differ, with strong reservations on each side. The duet 'Ich will gar von nichtes wissen' in *Almira* was perhaps its ancestor. The change of rhythm and tempo in the B section adds bite to the prevailing irony. The scoring, with two independent oboes and divided violas but the violins in unison, produces an individual texture at once open and intricate and, as Burney noted with approval, carefully designed not to cover the voices. No sooner has Teseo gone (*segue subito* again) than Medea's jealousy boils over in an accompanied recitative and an aria whose profusion of ideas suggests her teeming emotions. The contrasts of mood and texture are startling: the sudden slowing down on 'adoro' before the voice has had time to grip the material of the ritornello, the slurred thirds over a pedal, the varied treatment of the words 'la rival cadrà', ending with a unison plunge down the scale followed by silence, and the mysterious end, where the bass vanishes, leaving the upper strings poised over the chasm on a bare octave F. Disruption threatens, but the structure just holds: the dynamite is ready for the match.

The fuse is lit in the finale of Act III, one of the grandest of Handel's incantation scenes and strongly prophetic of *Alcina*. The accompanied recitative is much wilder than in Act II, with trenchant gestures as Medea summons her minions. The triple-time section, in which furious scales in both directions spanning nearly two octaves alternate with heavy crotchet unisons exploiting the lowest notes of the violins (as in Agrippina's 'Pensieri, voi mi tormentate' and 'Morirò' in Act V), is splendidly theatrical. So at the opposite extreme is the drop from C minor on to a secco chord of A flat major as the spirits enter. Agilea's cry of panic provokes the full force of the aria, in the unexpected key of B flat after a D major chord. 'Sibillando, ululando' is a spectacular showpiece for a great singer, including an invitation to two cadenzas in rapid succession. It depends not on harmony or modulation (there is scarcely an accidental in the A section, which does not venture beyond the dominant) but on the electrical charge in rhythm and texture: rolling triplets, even and slurred quavers, and hammering crotchets, variously combined. The lengthy divisions on 'atterrato' underline the *Affekt*; Medea is a fearsome creature in this mood. The B section briefly treats the same material in a different tonal area: conflict is out of place, since Medea has but a single thought.

In Act IV she exerts her power from the background. Her one aria, 'Dal cupo baratro', is remarkable for its rhythm and layout. Too angry to wait for a ritornello, she sings in unison with the violins over an empty bass line while two oboes disport themselves in a different pattern above. The effect is vivid and sinister: the 'dark abyss' yawns beneath the voice as it carries the bass of the harmony. Only in the long ritornellos that conclude each section do the instrumental basses come rumbling in. The design is that of a dance—in both sections the vocal strain is succeeded by an orchestral variation (16 + 16 bars; 16 + 8; da capo)—and the rhythm as well as the text identify the dancers. It is that of the furies in *Orlando* and Act II of Gluck's *Orfeo*:

Ex. 24

(Come, O furies, from the dark abyss to avenge my wrongs.)

Handel is careful not to weaken the portrait he has built up by allowing Medea an aria in her relaxed mood at the end of this act. Her final plunge in Act V is all the more conclusive. Having given her two scenes in which both types of recitative find issue in an aria, he chooses a new method in 'Morirò mà vendicata', combining an extraordinary range of emotion and material within the da capo form itself. Most of the ingredients—solemn unisons exploiting the resonance of the violins' G strings, frenzied semiquavers, a solo oboe forlornly echoing the voice, a change of tempo and metre (triple to quadruple) in the B section—had figured in Agrippina's 'Pensieri, voi mi tormentate', and in the same key, the 'jealousy' key of G minor. Medea's aria is even grander; the contrasts are more extreme. The A section, starting with a menacing foretaste of the 'Jealousy!' chorus in *Hercules*, alternates between Adagio and Presto both in the ritornello and after the entry of the voice. The first tempo reflects the word 'Morirò' (Handel's inspired change from the 'Vuò morir' of the libretto), the second its consequent 'mà vendicata'. The many felicities in the design illustrate Handel's growing mastery of da capo form. The A section does not exhaust Medea's passion; it overflows into an extensive twelve-bar ritornello, quite different from the opening, which continues to develop ideas introduced by the voice. The B section, in which she looks forward to seeing her rival 'lacerata, trucidata' and repeats these words over and over again with gloating relish, moves to B flat major, the key of her incantation, and a new texture punctuated by irregular fanfare figures on the strings. The startling abruptness of the return from 'm'oltraggio' to the unaccompanied 'Morirò', jumping the whole introductory ritornello, produces an effect of utter desolation (Ex. 25). The plan of this aria recurs many years later, with refinements, in Alcina's 'Ah! mio cor'.

Medea's last utterance, half-way between arioso and accompanied recitative (except that it has no accompaniment but a bass), is as remarkable for technical restraint as for its picture of emotional incoherence. The key is again G minor, approached by an unrelated secco cadence in E minor. The bass is confined to scale figures, hectic climbs answered by slow descents; the voice is too throttled by fury to pronounce its curses except in irregular gasps. The other characters invoke the aid of heaven, and a new figure, still in G minor, stalks through the bass like some thwarted tigress as Medea disappears into the shades and Minerva descends in glory. (Handel was to use the last passage again at the beginning of the mad scene in *Orlando*.) Now we see why he has

Ex. 25

(... the cruel man who outraged me. I shall die)

silenced the orchestra and limited the tonality. The radiant G major sinfonia, with its graceful arpeggiated melody over full chords, strikes in like a blaze of light, the aural equivalent of a scenic transformation that must have been truly magical (Ex. 26, p. 244).

Agilea is no unworthy antagonist for this formidable figure. Though gentle, she is never mawkish; the range and depth of her music make Almirena seem a simpering miss by comparison. Her three Act I arias reveal different aspects of her love for Teseo: admiration of his valour in 'È pur bello', anxiety for his safety in 'Deh serbate', confidence in their mutual love and eventual reunion in 'M'adora l'idol mio'. All are laid out for oboe and strings, but with a deft and varied touch: three violin parts in the first aria, a beautifully wrought texture in the second, with oboe and voice conversing in close imitation against violin arpeggios and a walking quaver bass, and a regular double concerto in the third, where the voice and the oboist share the limelight. The main theme of 'È pur bello' is related to the last movement of the overture. Handel may have meant to establish a link between the opera and material drawn from elsewhere; if it was intended as a valour motive, it is strange that he did not hit on something more warlike. The aria is well composed and has many telling details: the three contrasted ideas of different length $(4+5+6$ bars) that make up the ritornello, the Adagio bars at the entry of the voice, suggesting Agilea's wonder at her lover's prowess, the very sparing use of the bass throughout the A section, in which, whenever the voice is in action, the viola shoulders the burden and all the parts are kept close together, and the neat use of the first motive in the bass of the B section, where the upper instruments are silent. 'Deh serbate' too is closely organized, with the short

Ex. 26

second part clinging to the material of the first and eschewing contrast: the
music remains in the (dominant) minor as if to emphasize Agilea's overriding
anxiety. The predominantly descending vocal line with its chromatic intervals
works to the same end, and so does the withholding of the oboe till after the
voice enters, when its slowly lengthening phrases add an air of supplication.
The interlocking violin arpeggios recall 'Empio fato' in *Rodrigo* and are closer
to the continuous obbligato of Bach and the German school than to the more
open texture usual in Handel and the Italians.[11] 'M'adora l'idol mio', based
on a favourite rhythmic tag, is less distinctive, but it makes a conclusive end to
the act. Again the continuo is silenced for much of the A section, and the
violins are allowed to play bass to the duets of voice and oboe. The opening of
the·B section won immortality in the *Acis and Galatea* trio.[12]

[11] Compare the movement from *Florindo* quoted above, Ex. 2, p. 75.
[12] Lotti borrowed it note for note in Evandro's aria in Act II Scene xiii of *Ascanio* (Dresden,
1718). See Charlotte Spitz, *Antonio·Lotti in seiner Bedeutung als Opernkomponist* (Borna–Leipzig,
1918), 53.

In Act II Agilea yields place to Medea, but she fully holds her own in her Act III aria, 'Vieni, torna', perhaps the most perfect love song Handel had yet written. Once more a single ardent mood prevails, and Handel underlines it by drawing on the same material and the same mellow bassoon colouring in both sections and by a subtle control of phrase-lengths in the first.[13] The four-bar pattern of the opening gradually expands into phrases of seven and eight bars, with the mid-point dominant elided and the final ritornello soaring to twice the length of the introduction. The instrumental texture with four-part strings and divided bassoons, not tied to the bass, is marvellously rich. The lilting rhythm anticipates some of the great inspirations of later years, such as 'Par che mi nasca' in *Tamerlano* and 'Non fù già' in *Orlando*.

'Deh! v'aprite' in Act IV is no less remarkable for ravishing sonorities. Handel uses a pattern of slow slurred quaver arpeggios, carefully bowed, with the violin parts (muted in the earliest copy) doubled by flutes over long pedals, to suggest Agilea's approach to the sleeping Teseo. As in Rinaldo's 'Cara sposa', the voice part—for all its simplicity deemed by Burney 'fit for a great singer'—enters with delightful effect in the middle of a seemingly endless ritornello, which combines two favourite melodic patterns. The rising figure of the first bar appears many times, most strikingly perhaps in Saul's noble air 'As great Jehovah lives'; its consequent is a transformation into a different rhythm of the haunting 12/8 aria 'Felicissima quest'alma' in *Apollo e Dafne*. The nervous B section with its sudden pauses, one measured, two unmeasured, presumably reflects Agilea's hesitant efforts to awaken Teseo. But she can hardly bear to do so; the aria is a lullaby rather than an aubade, and the da capo is psychologically right. 'Amarti sì vorrei', after Medea has blackmailed Agilea into the bitter decision to reject Teseo in order to save his life, is a slow aria of very different type: deceptively simple, with no initial ritornello, little ornament, a broken continuo accompaniment, and a mood of unfathomable sadness. Scarlatti's influence is perceptible, but the combination of few notes and an overwhelming emotional impact is peculiarly Handelian.

The long duet after Medea's change of heart is decidedly verbose; Burney's verdict that it is 'equal if not superior to any one of the kind that Handel ever composed' savours of hyperbole. Yet it is well written for the voices and makes a good end to the act. And perhaps Handel is right after all: such an unpredictable shift of fortune is calculated to make any pair of lovers babble.[14] An odd point is that Handel treats Teseo as the higher voice and gives Agilea a markedly lower tessitura than in the rest of the opera[15]— perhaps a sop to the castrato. 'Sì, t'amo' is the least distinguished of Agilea's arias. It is also puzzling. The combination of gigue rhythm, minor key, and bare texture (a solo oboe doubles the voice with sparse interjections for strings and bass) suggests an almost feverish response to Teseo's kiss. Is Handel portraying her agitation? Kimbell, who finds the aria 'inscrutable', puts forward the idea that for Agilea loving might prove a richer experience than possessing. It may be so; but it is possible that the aria was a late insertion to make up the singer's complement.

Neither Pellegrini nor Valentini seems to have roused much response in

[13] And of dynamics; but these must be sought in Arnold's score, not Chrysander's (see pp. 252–3).

[14] But he drastically shortened the B section in the later adaptation for two altos.

[15] The manuscripts are so inconsistent with Italian genders ('caro', 'cara', 'solo', 'sola') that this might be taken for an error, had not Handel removed doubts by correcting one copy.

Handel, who gave them mostly routine music. *Teseo* does not appear till half-way through Act II. We are led to expect a heroic figure—he even has a choral buildup—but none of his music strikes that note. He is more like a shuttlecock propelled to and fro by forces he cannot control. His two arias in Act II, both in 12/8 dance rhythms, were perhaps intended to suggest his youth. 'Quanto ch'a me' is a simple siciliano love song with the usual Neapolitan inflections; it is a continuo aria, the counterpart of 'Amarti sì vorrei' but without the latter's poignancy or concentration. 'Non sò più che bramar', a gigue with giant leaps in the violin part, scarcely bears the weight of the words. Medea wins this round too easily. 'S'armi il fato' is more interesting, with an emphatic bass and an unexpected enrichment of the ritornello after the A section, where the oboes make a belated appearance. The B section ends in B minor and drops straight back to A major for the da capo, a progression Handel put to more memorable use in *Alcina* ('Mi restano') and *Semele* ('Where'er you walk').

The cavatina 'Chi ritorna', when Medea awakens Teseo in Act IV, is a beautiful little piece, the voice discoursing with a solo oboe against detached string chords. The angular snatched phrases suit the situation, and by keeping the movement short so as not to break the forward impetus Handel avoids his miscalculation in treating 'Quanto ch'a me' and Egeo's 'Serenatevi' as full arias. 'Qual tigre', however, despite an active accompaniment, is no very formidable discharge of indignation. The semiquaver string figure, evoked in the first place by the image of battle (cantata HWV 130) and used again in *Agrippina* ('Fà quanto vuoi'), retained an association in Handel's mind with the tiger's spring; he was to develop it fruitfully in a far finer example of *Tigermusik* in *Tamerlano*. The best of Teseo's arias is the last, 'Tengo in pugno'. It is not heroic or even virile; graceful minuets of this type with varied rhythms within the bar, Scotch snaps, coy trills, and hemiola, are more often the property of the flirtatious minx or soubrette. But there is no denying its charm. The 26-bar ritornello, designed no doubt to bring on the wedding procession, contrives a well-placed relaxation of tension just before the drama mounts to its climax.

Egeo's music is narrower in compass but more showy in coloratura. None of it shows Handel at his best; this is a conventional monarch. The florid triplet and dotted figuration of 'Serenatevi' suggests, if not insincerity, a superficial formalism in his amorous advances; nor does 'Ricordati, O bella', for all its earnest contrapuntal imitation, contradict this impression. Burney put it picturesquely in his remark that Valentini obliged Handel 'to rule Pegasus with a curb-bridle'. 'Voglio stragi', though a dramatic solecism, is a fair example of the vengeance aria. The canon between violins (later voice) and bass is no mere contrapuntal exercise; it dramatizes Egeo's determination to rescue Agilea from Medea. 'Non è da rè' contributes little except a fully-fashioned ritornello after the A section in which the oboes, as in 'S'armi il fato', make their entrance after the voice has finished.

Arcane and Clizia, though subsidiary figures in the drama, enjoy a richer musical inheritance than the castratos. Moreover by writing for them in a more intimate style Handel gives the whole opera an extra dimension that throws the main plot into relief. They are the only pair of secondary lovers in a Handel opera to enjoy two duets. Both are excellent, and particularly well integrated in their context. 'Addio, mio caro bene' flowers unobtrusively out of recitative, develops into an eloquent cavatina on a wide-ranging bass, and culminates, after a recitative cadence, in an exquisite and fully scored ritornello rich in the suspensions appropriate to the parting of lovers. The mixture of sensibility, charm, and a hint of ironic exaggeration recalls the old Venetian opera; Handel does not forget that these are minor characters. 'Unito a un puro affetto', though in da capo form, is not dissimilar in pattern: again a light opening and the full orchestra reserved for the ritornello after the da capo, beautifully elaborated with pedals taken over from the voices. The phrase-lengths throughout are pleasantly unsymmetrical. It is surprising to find Clizia and Arcane stealing the principals' limelight towards the end of the opera; this relic of Quinault's libretto was perhaps retained to throw all the more weight on Medea's unexpected return. That is certainly its effect.

Arcane has four arias, a good deal more than his ration, and three at least make their mark. 'Ah! cruda gelosia', with only a bass marked for solo cello, is plaintive and self-indulgent where we might expect an outburst of passion; but Arcane must not usurp or anticipate the prerogative of his superiors. His jealousy in any case does not run deep; there is a hint of parody in the dotted figure with trills of bar 6 and the fourfold descending 'Ah!' in bars 12 and 13. 'Le luci del mio bene' gives Act III a delicious quasi-pastoral start; if this scene is strictly superfluous, Handel makes excellent use of it as a calm plateau between major explosions from Medea. He lulls the ear with a mellow seven-part texture (two recorders, two violins, two violas, and bass) and almost motionless harmony, to which the swifter movement of the B section supplies a brief but not perfunctory contrast. 'Più non cerca libertà', on a catchy tune making neither its first nor last appearance (it recurs as late as *Susanna*), exploits hemiola to evoke a mood of uninhibited happiness. 'Benchè tuoni' too is old material,[16] and could have been dispensed with; its sole purpose seems to be to display Jane Barbier's ability to execute rapid divisions. 'Risplendete' is the better of Clizia's two arias. The sequences are interestingly developed, and the little joy motive romps gaily in the bass part, which again is marked for solo cello.

Teseo has a more varied pattern than many of Handel's operas, with four duets, five accompanied recitatives (one of them involving three characters) and a substantial ensemble in Act II as well as the usual *coro* at the end. Extra singers must have been employed, for there is a tenor as well as a bass part. Though not elaborate by oratorio standards, and abstaining from counterpoint, the Act II *coro di Ateniensi* is no mere flourish; only one or two such movements in the late operas exceed it in length. It is so effective that one wonders why Handel so seldom repeated the experiment.

There is no obvious tonal plan, though B flat and F are prominent in the first three acts, and G major and minor in the last. Except that Medea's part, including her duet with Egeo, is entirely in flat keys, this may be fortuitous. No reason is apparent for two consecutive arias in G major in Act IV, or two in G minor, shortly followed by a third, at the start of Act V. The last scene is well contrived from the tonal as well as the dramatic angle: Medea's G minor (perhaps picking up her 'Morirò', though there have been two other G minor arias in between) yields at Minerva's entry to G major, which resolves on D for the *coro* and the trumpets. The drop from E flat to D for the second of Teseo's arias in Act IV may be meant to emphasize his change of mood towards

---

[16] Part of the text as well as the music was lifted from *Aci, Galatea e Polifemo*, one of many indications that Handel played an active part in shaping his librettos.

Agilea; but he soon becomes reconciled with her, whereas the tonality remains in the region of D major till the end of the act. Rather unexpectedly the major mode is supreme in the three middle acts; Act III has nothing in the minor except Medea's accompanied recitative, and Act II nothing in a sharp key except the *coro*, where the trumpets require it.

The tonal links between recitative and aria show a growing flexibility. The mediant minor–tonic progression is now established as a favourite gambit, which it was to remain throughout Handel's career. In 'Ti credo' and 'Sibillando' we find an antecedent mediant major (D major before B flat). This is a conscious dramatic stroke: in each place the aria cuts into an incomplete cadence from another character. Both the Clizia–Arcane duets slip neatly in from the recitative. The subdominant minor chord before 'Deh serbate' is unusual. Handel is already using remoter key-shifts to mark the entry of a new character or a change of set, for example F after G minor at Egeo's first appearance ('Serenatevi') and D major after C major when the action moves from the palace to the square in Act II.

The scoring is an attractive feature of *Teseo*. Although there is nothing so spectacular as *Rinaldo*'s four trumpets or *Giulio Cesare*'s four horns, Handel uses a wide range of instruments, individually and in combination. The violins sometimes play in three groups, giving a five-part string texture, and six other instruments are used in pairs: trumpets, recorders, transverse flutes, oboes, bassoons, and violas. The division of the violas is very rare in the operas, and that of the bassoons not too common. The extra warmth in the middle register of 'Sì, ti lascio', 'Le luci del mio bene', and (most memorably) 'Vieni, torna', is all the more welcome. There are two arias in which the bass line is entrusted to a solo cello,[17] and two in which the oboes are held back till the ritornello after the A section, where they bring in new material. Handel's orchestra was evidently strong at this period. The first oboe, Galliard, had exceptional opportunities to display his prowess. There is less variety of tone colour in the voices, which apart from the Priest's recitative are all sopranos and altos. But this would not have worried the eighteenth century, and there is no reason why a modern audience should refuse to accept it. Octave transposition of any of the male parts would be disastrous.

History and Text

According to Burney Handel composed *Teseo* at Burlington House, which is likely enough. He finished the score on 19 December 1712 and conducted the first performance at the Queen's Theatre·on 10 January 1713, with the following cast:

TESEO:	Valeriano Pellegrini (soprano castrato)
AGILEA:	Margherita de l'Epine (soprano)
MEDEA:	Elisabetta Pilotti-Schiavonetti (soprano)
EGEO:	Valentino Urbani (alto castrato)
CLIZIA:	Maria Gallia (soprano)
ARCANE:	Jane Barbier (contralto)
PRIEST OF MINERVA:	(?) Richard Leveridge (bass)

---

[17] Chrysander adopted this from Arnold, but it is consistent with the style of the period; the manuscripts name no instrument.

The production was sumptuous: 'all ye Habits new & richer than ye former with 4 New Scenes, & other Decorations & Machines', as the Colman Opera Register puts it, adding that Owen Swiney, the manager, tried unsuccessfully to organize a subscription for six performances. After two nights, at which the house was very full, 'Mr Swiny Brakes & runs away & leaves ye Singers unpaid ye Scenes & Habits also unpaid for. The Singers were in Some confusion but at last concluded to go on with ye operas on their own accounts, & divide ye Gain amongst them'. Swiney (and the receipts) went to Italy, where we find him in the 1720s negotiating with the Royal Academy over singers.[18] He later returned to England and resumed his original name MacSwiney. Heidegger succeeded him as manager, beginning a long and distinguished career as an opera impresario. Swiney had in fact paid Valentini and Pilotti part of their salary.[19]

This crisis did not interrupt the run of *Teseo*, which had thirteen performances, the last on 16 May. Something went wrong on the fourth night (21 January), for the management announced that on the 24th the opera 'will be represented in its Perfection, that is to say with all the Scenes, Decorations, Flights, and Machines. The Performers are much concerned that they did not give the Nobility and Gentry all the Satisfaction they could have wished, when they represented it on Wednesday last, having been hindered by some unforseen Accidents at that time insurmountable'. The substance of this notice was repeated in connection with most of the later performances. Colman says on 31 January that *Teseo* drew a better house than *Il pastor fido* or *Dorinda*; but the performance planned for 15 April had to be postponed because few tickets were sold, and on the 18th there was 'a thin House'. The last performance, on 16 May, was for Handel's benefit and brought him the sum of £73. 10s. 11d. The *Daily Courant*[20] advertised 'an Addition of several New Songs, and particularly an Entertainment for the Harpsichord, Composed by Mr Hendel on purpose for that Day'.

These new pieces cannot be certainly identified, though the arias probably included 'Nò, non piangete' and 'La crudele lontananza'. The former (which bears no resemblance to the aria in *Floridante* beginning with the same words) is associated with 'Deh! serbate' in a publication of 1724, as is the latter in an early manuscript. This aria may also have been sung in a revival of *Amadigi*; it   * occurs in two manuscripts among excerpts from that opera. Both arias are thoroughly characteristic; the F minor 'La crudele lontananza'[21] whose compass and tessitura would fit Pellegrini, has many exquisite touches, especially in the B section (Ex. 27, p. 250). Two variant versions in the Malmesbury copy suggest that at one performance the part of Agilea was taken by an alto. A copy of 'Deh serbate' transposed down to A minor may also reflect this occasion.

Surprisingly *Teseo* appears to have contributed nothing to the concert repertory. Handel transferred 'Deh! v'aprite' in different keys to *Il pastor fido* in 1734 and *Jupiter in Argos* in 1739, and the duet 'Cara, ti dono' to the former, making a few changes. G. C. Schürmann borrowed excerpts in his *Clelia*

[18] See p. 321 ff.
[19] See Deutsch, 54 and 58–60, and p. 153 for the financial transactions of this season. Swiney resigned the lease of the theatre as from 10 May 1714 and settled his account with Vanbrugh (Downes, *Vanbrugh*, 180), though perhaps not his other debts.
[20] The first advertisement (11 May) announced that the opera would be performed 'Not in all its Perfection...' This was corrected next day by the insertion of the word 'only'.
[21] Handel used the material later in the motet 'Silete venti' (aria 'Dulcis amor').

Ex. 27

(Deprives me of the hope of returning to freedom.)

(Brunswick, 1730). Handel never revived the opera, and apart from two productions in Germany (1947 and 1977) it was not heard again until 1984.

Autograph

Only a few fragments of the last two acts survive, sixteen leaves in RM 20 c 12, one in RM 20 f 11 (f. 8). None carry Handel's foliation. The passages covered are the first two scenes of Act IV (HG 69–73), eight bars of recitative in IV vi (HG 80, from 'Mà dove è 'l brando', ending in the middle of a word), and the closing pages of the opera from the middle of bar 5 of Teseo's accompanied recitative 'Giuro' in V iv (HG 98), with the exception of Agilea's aria, 'Sì, t'amo'. The latter, cued in at the bottom of f. 7^v, may have been an insertion, as the recitative of IV i (f. 1) and the fragment of IV vi (f. 5) certainly were. Handel seems to have composed Act V piecemeal, for the last three bars of the Minerva recitative are on f. 12, with the remainder of the recto and the entire verso blank. This could hardly have been an insertion. 'Voglio stragi' was originally in 6/8. The first nineteen bars of 'Benchè tuoni' are on f. 4, the remainder on the single leaf in RM 20 f 11. The nine bars of recitative bracketed on HG 99 are not cancelled.

None of the four set pieces ('Voglio stragi', 'Benchè tuoni', 'Unito', and the *coro*) bears a tempo mark. 'Benchè tuoni' and the *coro* have *Tutti* on the first violin stave, indicating that both oboe parts were to double it; Handel may have changed his mind about the *coro*, where the parts are variously distributed in the copies. The autograph is the only source for the direction about the ballet at the bottom of HG 104. Bars 4–7 of 'Unito' were an afterthought. Medea's final arioso, first planned as secco recitative, had a four-bar ritornello (bass only) cancelled after 'l'ultimo addio'. The two forms of the Minerva recitative (*Entra*, not *Sortita* on HG 106) are superimposed. After composing it for soprano Handel wrote the bass version on top and modified the words to fit a priest rather than a goddess, but forgot to make the stage direction fit.

He used a blank page in the autograph of *Rodrigo* (f. 48^v) to jot down sketches for *Teseo* (Plate 6). Three of the four fragments, incipits for treble and bass, or bass alone ('Risplendete'), reappear in the opera with some changes in detail. 'Vieni, torna' and 'Non sò più che bramar' are identified by their first words. The ritornello of 'Risplendete' is in A major. The fourth sketch, ten bars of triple time in G minor, does not seem to have been used.

Libretto

1713. 'Printed for Sam. Buckley, at the Dolphin in Little-Britain.' 67 pp. The work is 'An Opera' in the English text, 'Dramma Tragico' in the Italian. Handel's name is spelt 'Hendel', and as in *Il pastor fido* he is described as 'Maestro di Capella di S. A. E. di Hannover'. Haym's flowery dedication to Richard Boyle, Earl of Burlington, contains fulsome praise of that nobleman's artistically enlightened family. There is no Argument, but the characters are briefly described. They include 'Minerva, in a Machine' and 'Priests of Minerva'. Clizia is spelt Clitia, and sung by 'La Sorella della Sig. Margarita'; the identification with Maria Gallia comes from Burney. She was not at this time a member of the Queen's Theatre company, and it is surprising that she and not Manina was given the part.

The arias are summarized, not translated, in the English text. Nine passages in five different scenes (I v, III iii, IV vii, V iii and iv), amounting to some 85 lines in all, are marked with *virgole* as omitted in the performance. There are a number of minor textual variants: the initial word of Egeo's second aria is 'Souvengati', not 'Ricordati'; part of the recitative for Arcane and Clizia in III i is different, but the sense is much the same; 'Chi ritorna' (IV vi) is a da capo aria with the opening repeated; Medea's aria in V i begins 'Vuò morir'; in 'Tengo in pugno' (V iv) the rhyme scheme is inverted, the second and fourth lines preceding the first and third. This explains Burney's reference to the aria as 'Hò per mano'. In each act except the second the scene numbering in the libretto differs from that of the score; neither follows a consistent principle with regard to entrances and exits.

Copies and Editions

There is no performing score in Hamburg, but manuscript copies are fairly numerous, no doubt because little of the music was printed. The earliest and most important is one of three in the Coke Collection (Coke I), which must have been copied (by Linike) at the end of December 1712 before the first performance. It has many unique features, including settings of 44 lines of recitative printed in *virgole* in the libretto. Probably all the *virgole* passages except seven lines in IV vii (HG 81) were originally in the manuscript: one or more pages have been replaced in I v, and one torn out in III iii. The manuscript also contains the two Fedra scenes, seven bars in II i and twelve in V ii, removed before publication of the libretto (see Plate 7). All these passages, including that printed in brackets on HG 99, are cancelled or covered over, with the later links supplied where applicable. 'Più non cerca libertà' was copied first as a binary arietta, followed by the direction *Arcane parte. Segue il Rittornella [sic]*. The latter follows on the next page; it is a slightly longer variant of the melody in four parts, including viola, the recorders sometimes in unison with the violins and sometimes an octave above. The whole page was cancelled and replaced by the simpler ritornello, B section, and da capo as printed. Four bars are cancelled after bar 3 of 'Ah! cruda gelosia' and another in the ritornello after the A section. The B section of 'Tengo in pugno' is crossed out, though it appears in all other copies.

In view of the loss of most of the autograph the exceptionally detailed specification of scoring and dynamics in this copy is of great interest. Almost every number, whether or not it involves the oboes, is rich in *soli–tutti* indications and expressive contrasts. The duets 'Sì, ti lascio' and 'Cara, ti dono' and the arias 'O stringerò', 'Vieni, torna', 'Sibillando', 'Morirò', and 'Tengo in pugno' are outstanding in this respect. 'Vieni, torna' (without tempo mark here) has more trills for the bassoons, written appoggiaturas, and graded dynamics, notably in bars 9–11, where the repeated figure in thirds is first *forte*, then *piano*, then *pianissimo*. 'Dolce riposo' is *forte e staccato* with many more violin trills in the first bar and a half, then changes to *pian sempre* with quavers slurred in pairs in almost every bar and *senza cembalo* at the third beat of bar 6. 'Deh! v'aprite' is *Adagio* with the violins muted, and the fourth note in bar 13 (as in every early copy) is B, not C. The treatment of the oboes differs from HG. They are clearly indicated in 'O stringerò' and 'Vieni, torna', but omitted from the final *coro* (perhaps by accident). In 'Benchè tuoni' they play *tutti* with the first violins, as in the autograph, the Wiegand score, and the Flower parts. The overture's first Allegro has three violin parts, the oboes taking the top line in unison (HG 2, fourth brace), as in all early copies and Arnold; the lower violin stave has a soprano clef throughout. 'Dal cupo baratro' has many trills for first oboe. In 'Morirò' the second violins double all the oboes at bar 55, but in the B section the oboes divide, doubling both violins, with *soli* twice indicated later. As in HG, 'Serenatevi' has a viola stave without notes—clearly an accidental omission, since there are rests where they are not to play; in the Flower parts they double the violins at the octave in ritornellos, and this is indicated in the Wiegand copy.

There are more tempo marks than in HG: *Allegro* on 'M'adora', 'Ogn'un acclami' (the names of the characters, including Fedra, appear against the soprano and alto staves), and 'Qual tigre', *Largo* on 'Quanto ch'a me' (bar 2), *Adagio e staccato* (preceded by *segue subito*) on Medea's accompanied recitative 'Ombre, sortite', *Vivace* on 'Voglio stragi', *Adagio* on 'Chi ritorna'. The Minerva recitative is already in the bass version (as in every copy) with no character specified. Linike forgot to copy the full direction at the head of V iv (HG 96), which should read *Entra con loro una gran' comitiva di popolo, che viene per adornar le nozze*, stopping at *loro*. This baffled his successors: Wiegand has *Entra con core*, Malmesbury *Entra con l'ore*; Arnold (using Coke I) not surprisingly amended to *Entra con Coro*. Bar 12 of 'Deh! v'aprite' has a mistake corrected in all but one of the later copies but reproduced by Arnold and Chrysander; the phrase on the second stave comes one beat too late, spoiling Handel's double echo, which should run:

Ex. 28

(beautiful eyes)

Another mistake, corrected by Arnold but not by Chrysander, occurs in bar 71 of 'Morirò' (HG 92), where the last beat in the voice part has the equivalent of five semiquavers. Most copies amend this to ♪ ♫ ♪ (RM 19 g 4, RM 19 d 8, Granville, Arnold) or ♪ ♬ ♪ (Wiegand, Malmesbury, Coke II, Lennard, Fitzwilliam, Flower parts); RM 19 e 6 (used by Chrysander), Shaftesbury, and Coke III follow Coke I. An interesting detail in the latter is the marking of bars 11 and 12 of 'Deh! v'aprite', almost certainly by Handel himself, with signs often used in the autographs to indicate an insertion; this was the point where he expanded the aria by six bars in the Malmesbury alto version.

Arnold based his edition on Coke I; although the manuscript was damaged by fire at Novello's some years ago, his name with the date 24 April 1787 is still legible on the inner cover. Chrysander's deep-rooted contempt for Arnold and all his works unfortunately led him to eject without ceremony the countless details of scoring, dynamics, and tempo reproduced by Arnold from this copy, and on occasion, as in *Agrippina*, to amend him when he is right and follow him when he is wrong. (Another instance of the latter is the division of the oboes in 'M'adora', where both should double the first violins.) Chrysander's bracketed suggestions for scoring are sometimes his own ('S'armi il fato' bar 42, 'Morirò' bar 67); more often they are Arnold's from Coke I ('Sì, ti lascio' bar 32, B section of 'Ogn'un acclami', tempo of 'M'adora'). In bars 47–8 of 'È pur bello' (HG 12) Chrysander had to choose between the reading of Arnold and Coke I (Ex. 29a) and that of most other manuscripts (b); liking neither, he produced his own emendation (c), even apparently pencilling it into RM 19 e 6. Wiegand, followed by the Flower parts and Coke III, comes up with a fourth, following (b) in bar 47 and (a) in bar 48.

Ex. 29

One of the BL copies, RM 19 e 6 (RM1), possibly dating from 1713, has some corrections and amendments by Handel, who altered the bass in bars 3 and 4 of the overture's second Largo to the reading of HG 4 (previously it had scales in parallel sixths[22] with the top part), added the tempo *Andante ma non troppo allegro* on 'Vieni, torna', improved the underlay in bars 58–9 of 'Sibillando' (the words 'che mi scherni' should be repeated three times), corrected the genders in the A section of 'Cara, ti dono' and the clefs in the Minerva recitative, where the copyist had written the notes and words of the bass version with a soprano clef, and removed minor errors in 'Ira, sdegni' (HG 47), 'O stringerò' (HG 50), and 'Amarti' (HG 83). Later he marked two transpositions on 'Deh! v'aprite' (*ex E♯* for *Il pastor fido* in 1734, *ex F* for *Jupiter in Argos* in 1739), on the former occasion inserting a semiquaver C before the

[22] A mistake by the copyist turned them into fifths in bar 3.

fourth note (B) in bar 13 to accommodate an extra syllable in the new text;[23] but he did not change 'Cara, ti dono' in this score. 'Serenatevi' has lost its viola part. Dynamic and instrumental details are much scarcer than in Coke I, but there are a few extra tempo marks: *Allegro* twice in the overture (HG 2 and 5) and on 'È pur bello' and 'S'armi il fato', *Andante* (over *Allegro*) on the opening bars of 'Morirò'. Several 4/4 movements have an *alla breve* signature, which appears intermittently in other copies. Chrysander, who mentioned this score in his preface, adopted most of Handel's corrections (not the underlay in 'Sibillando') but ignored the extra tempo marks[24] (except on 'Vieni, torna'), the correct text of 'Deh! v'aprite', the division of the violin parts in the overture's first Allegro, and the unison treatment of the oboes in 'M'adora'. It is conceivable that Handel used RM 19 e 6 or Coke I or both in his performances, though neither resembles the standardized Smith performing scores of later years.

A very early score owned by Armin Wiegand of Munich can be dated about 1714. Linike wrote the first page, RM1 the rest of the music; the words are probably in Linike's hand. This copy, if it does not antedate RM 19 e 6, derives from an earlier source, for it contains none of Handel's changes except a couple of obvious corrections to wrong notes. Dynamics and *soli–tutti* instructions, though fewer than in Coke I, include some that do not occur there and many more than in RM 19 e 6. As usual in library copies stage directions are sparse, but here or in the related Malmesbury copy (often in both) dramatic continuity is enjoined no fewer than nine times by the words *segue subito* or *subito*: after 'Deh serbate' (HG 16), before 'Ti credo' (HG 17), before and after Medea's recitative in 'Dolce riposo' (HG 31), before 'Ira, sdegni' (HG 47), before 'Numi, chi ci soccorre!' (bottom of HG 61), before Teseo's 'Giuro' (HG 98), at Medea's exit at the end of V vii (HG 105), and at the entry of Minerva. This is the only copy that instructs the violas in 'Serenatevi' to double the violins in octaves, marks the top line in the ritornello of the duet 'Addio' *Tutti*, and gives 'Più non cerca libertà' a tempo mark (*Allegro*). Every movement has one except 'Addio', which is so dignified in no source. They follow Coke I or RM 19 e 6, except that 'Vieni, torna' is *Largo*, 'Ombre, sortite' *Largo e staccato* and 'Morirò' *Allegro*. The movements with a tempo for the first time are: 'Ricordati', 'Quell'amor', 'Sì, ti lascio', 'Dal cupo baratro', 'Cara, ti dono', 'Non è da rè', 'Tengo in pugno', and the final *coro* (all *Allegro*), and 'Sibillando', 'Sì, t'amo', and 'Unito' (*Vivace*). The overture is headed *Sinfonia*. Its initial Largo has *Tutti* above the top line, indicating both oboes with first violins, as in Arnold. This is undoubtedly correct; the second stave as usual has the soprano clef, which would not have been used for oboes.   * This copy was formerly in the Aylesford Collection, as shown by the addition of a *Rinaldo* fragment annotated by Jennens on blank pages at the end.

The Malmesbury copy has *Elizabeth Legh her Book 1717* on the flyleaf and *Transcribed by Mr Linike June 1717* in Elizabeth Legh's hand on the title page. Except in the few details noted above it conforms closely to Wiegand, including such errors as the *Allegro* tempo on 'Morirò'. Linike corrected his mistake in bar 12 of 'Deh! v'aprite', as did RM1 in Wiegand. This manuscript, like Coke I, has unique features. It contains two alternative versions that appear nowhere else, both inserted at a very early stage before the volume was

---

[23] See the HG score of *Il pastor fido* (1734), 103, which gives bar 12 correctly.
[24] 'Le luci' has none; the *Largo* here is the only tempo Chrysander took from Arnold.

bound for Elizabeth Legh. The first (RM 1) is a setting of 'Deh! v'aprite' for alto voice in C major (*Adagio*) with a single unspecified treble line and bass. The A section is six bars longer than in the G major version, and both sections have delicate vocal ornaments in the hand of the copyist that may well derive from Handel. The extension occurs at the original bar 11:

Ex. 30

(beautiful eyes, awake to love, Ah open, awake to love)

The second insertion, in Linike's hand, is a reworking of the duet 'Cara, ti dono' for two altos in F major, accompanied by two violins and bass. The first part is essentially unchanged, except that the string parts are simplified, eliminating the viola, and the coloratura improved in detail, but the B section is quite different and much shorter, twelve bars instead of 32; nor is it identical with the version used in *Il pastor fido*.

Coke II is a composite copy. The overture, in a very early hand, lacks Handel's corrections in the second Largo (here *Lentement*); on HG 2, fourth system, while the first violins as usual have Chrysander's second oboe part, the second stave is for solo violin. The rest of Coke II, in a hand prominent in RCM MS 257 (Italian cantatas, ff. 32–200), is much later. It prolongs the Fs at the end of the A section of 'Più non cerca libertà' into the ritornello, and has certain details in common with Lennard: *Andante* on 'Quell'amor' and 'Vieni, torna', *Largo* on 'Chi ritorna', 'Tengo in pugno' as a da capo, not dal segno aria. The copyist religiously noted the number of bars at the end of each piece, counting the B sections separately.

RM 19 g 4, lacking recitatives, is an untidy copy of uncertain (perhaps early) date with the music in two hands and some of the words in a third. The neat, precise copyist of ff. 1 and 40, with very tall note-stems, contrasts sharply with the wild writing and erratic clefs of his colleague in the rest of the score (RM2), who wrote ff. 26–31 ('Ogn'un acclami') and 55–74 (from the middle of 'Cara, ti dono' to the end of the opera) on much smaller paper. Most of Handel's changes in RM 19 e 6 are incorporated, but 'Vieni, torna' has no tempo. The bass is fully figured throughout; there are hardly any dynamics. Shaftesbury (S4, 1736 or rather later) reproduces an early text close to RM 19 e 6 and incorporates some of Handel's changes, but not in the second Largo of the overture or the clefs of the Minerva recitative, where it follows the anomalous reading of RM 19 e 6. Bar 13 of 'Deh! v'aprite' however includes an appoggiatura C to the fourth note (B). Dynamic and instrumental indications as well as stage directions are scarce, and some tempo marks are dropped. Lennard (Smith), Granville (S5), RM 19 d 8 (S13), and Fitzwilliam   * (Mus MS 74, signed and dated 'R. Fitzwilliam 1767' and probably copied at that time[25]) are late copies with no independent authority or significant variants. They derive in the main from RM 19 e 6 with a few tempos from the Linike group, but differ from the latter in giving far fewer directions for scoring and dynamics.

The copyist of Coke III is something of a rogue elephant. He wrote at least four volumes,[26] each containing three operas, in a hand so minute as almost to defy reading with the naked eye. Although his copies omit recitatives and are not always complete in other respects, the amount of music he compressed into a slender volume is astonishing. He was English,[27] unconnected with the Smith circle, and cannot have worked before the 1730s (his latest known copy is of *Ariodante*), but evidently had access to good early texts and on occasion appended additional arias not in HG. He was scrupulous in supplying bass figures but not tempo marks, and had some strange habits. He gave all common-time pieces an *alla breve* signature, sometimes filled out Handel's scoring, and intermittently added in red ink an English version—not a translation—of a pastoral imbecility grotesquely at variance with the music. His *Teseo* omits the overture, the duet 'Addio', and twelve arias but includes the final *coro* in the middle of Act V. Several tempo marks ('Sibillando', 'Morirò', 'Unito', the *coro*) are found elsewhere only in Wiegand, Malmesbury, and the Flower parts. The oboe solo in the ritornello of 'M'adora' is accompanied by extraneous crotchet chords on the strong beats; this is the only copy in which the oboes are divided as in HG, and the only one apart

---

[25] The same copyist wrote the Fitzwilliam scores of *Amadigi* and *Muzio Scevola*.

[26] Two in the Coke Collection, two at the Berlin Staatsbibliothek. His hand is reproduced in the programme of a Hanover production of *Ariodante* in August 1964, where it is wrongly attributed to Handel's immediate circle, and even 'very probably' to Smith.

[27] There are later annotations in German, including the inaccurate statement that *Teseo* was 'ausgeführt 1710'.

from Coke I to give the printed scores' mistake in bar 12 of 'Deh! v'aprite'. There is an *Adagio* on the last chord in bar 15 of 'O stringerò'. The copyist marked 'Cara, ti dono' *Ex G♯* in red and appended English texts to ten pieces. He was obsessed by *Acis and Galatea*: 'È pur bello' becomes 'Once to beauty I was suing', 'Sibillando' 'Cease complaining From disdaining Whining love will never do', 'Morirò' 'Cease to grieve, see joys returning'.

The Flower Collection has a complete set of parts (S2, late 1740s), omitting the overture: violins 1 and 2 (+ violin 3 on a separate stave in 'È pur bello'), viola 1 + 2 (separate staves in 'Sì, ti lascio' and 'Le luci'), cello + bassoon (two bassoon parts but no cello in 'Vieni, torna', otherwise no provision for bassoon except an occasional *tutti*), oboes 1 and 2 incorporating flutes and recorders, trumpets 1 and 2, and cembalo. They were undoubtedly extracted from Wiegand, to which they correspond very closely in tempos and dynamics, and in mistakes (for example *Largo* on bar 1 instead of bar 2 of 'Quanto ch'a me'). This is the only source apart from Wiegand to give a viola part for 'Serenatevi', but it is omitted by oversight from 'Dal cupo baratro'. There are errors in the oboe parts where Wiegand gave no guidance: they double the violins in the B section of 'Ogn'un acclami', only the first violins in the ritornellos of 'Vieni, torna', the second violins in the B section of 'Morirò',[28] and are omitted from 'Non è da rè'. Elsewhere they are probably correct in the main: both double the first violins in the ritornellos of the duet 'Addio', 'M'adora' (solos are indicated later, including one at bar 47), most of 'O stringerò' (bars 1, 3–13, 24–5, 29, 39–46[29]), 'Benchè tuoni', and 'Sì, t'amo', but are silent in 'Cara, ti dono' and 'Unito'. In the *coro* both double the first violins at the start, but second oboe joins second violin at bar 34.

Handel arranged the overture for harpsichord, and later revised his work with further recomposition. The first version is found in two Malmesbury volumes (RM1, *c.*1717; Smith, *c.*1728) and the Coke Wesley MS (H1, *c.*1721; this has annotations in the hand of Elizabeth Legh), the second in RM 18 c 1, ff. 10–13 (S2, *c.*1728). Walsh printed the latter in his second collection (*c.*1728)[30]. RM 19 c 9 (ff. 64–9) has an S2 copy of 'La crudele lontananza' with 'Deh serbate' in A minor; this is the only place where the former is identified with *Teseo*. Jennens confirmed this in his index and added the tempo *Andante* to 'Deh serbate'; 'La crudele lontananza' has none. The latter appears with a more accurate text in Tenbury 884 (Smith, *c.*1719) and a Shaftesbury aria collection (S4). A very early volume of excerpts, mostly from *Teseo* and *Amadigi*, in the Coke Collection, in several old-fashioned hands, contains ten arias from the former, including 'La crudele lontananza' with full figuring. A slightly later volume ('24 Opera Songs') contains five, four of them the same; 'Vieni, torna' is *Largo* with the bassoons ousted by violins (an octave higher in the B section). Three of the arias have a few contemporary vocal ornaments. Add MS 29386 has short-score copies of 'Più non cerca libertà' (in G major), 'Vieni, torna', and 'Sì, t'amo' in an unknown hand. There is a copy of the Minerva recitative (bass clef, but attributed as in Arnold to Egeo) and the *coro*, with an added drum part, in RCM 1125.

[28] The sources give various readings here: probably the best is that of RM 19 e 6 and most later copies, which have second violins on the second stave and both oboes by implication on the first, except where some copies indicate solos (bars 71–4, 78–81 second beat).

[29] Coke I specifically silences them in bars 12–13, which are for *Viol. pp*, but retains them (*p. uniss.*) in the corresponding bars 45–6.

[30] Both versions are in *Twenty Overtures*, i. 16 and 34.

No score or selection was printed during Handel's life, but eight arias appeared in short score, with English translations by Carey, Leveridge, and anonymous, among the various fugitive publications of the period. 'Vieni, torna', 'Sì, t'amo', and 'Più non cerca libertà' were first issued separately (*c.* 1715–20). Volume i of Cluer and Creake's *Pocket Companion for Gentlemen and Ladies* (May 1724) reprinted the first two, volume ii (December 1725) the third, together with 'Tengo in pugno', 'S'armi il fato', and 'Amarti', in the original keys, usually with a flute arrangement. *The Monthly Masque of Vocal Music* for August 1724, a Walsh publication, added 'Nò, non piangete' (which is in no Handel copy) and 'Deh serbate'. In 1732 Walsh published *The Favourite Songs in ye Opera call'd Thessus* [sic] *& Amadis*. The recent discovery[31] of a copy of this eccentric compilation in the Schoelcher Collection at the Paris Conservatoire modifies the entry in Smith's *Descriptive Catalogue* (p. 76). Its seventeen items, not all by Handel, include six *Teseo* arias, 'Deh serbate', 'Nò, non piangete', 'Vieni, torna', 'Sì, t'amo', 'Risplendete', and 'Più non cerca libertà'. Five had been printed before, and this may also be true of 'Risplendete', which has an English version ('Damon be advis'd by me'). The first two were included in volume ii of *Apollo's Feast* (*c.*1734). Walsh published the overture in parts about 1725, and 'Deh! v'aprite' and the duet 'Cara, ti dono' in borrowed plumes among *The Favourite Songs* in *Il pastor fido* (1734). A printed copy of 'Vieni, torna' with copious ornamentation in a contemporary hand was sold by Otto Haas in 1976.

Arnold's score (1788), as already mentioned, was based on Coke I with bass figuring added throughout, and does not include Handel's emendations in RM 19 e 6. It contains a number of obvious mistakes (*flauto* for oboe on the first but not the second strain of 'Dolce riposo') and wrong conjectures (the Minerva recitative in the bass clef attributed to Egeo), but also sensible amendments. By generally following the source it gives a text much closer to Handel than Chrysander's edition (1874). Chrysander used the autograph fragments in RM 20 c 12, RM 19 e 6, and Arnold, but not the libretto (hence the many missing stage directions), and as we have seen was capricious in his treatment of all three sources. It is not clear why he reversed his usual practice in banishing the bass version of the Minerva recitative to the appendix and placing the rejected form in the text.

Additional Notes

* (p. 249) 'La crudele lontananza' was sung in *Rinaldo* in 1715; 'Nò, non piangete' occurs in a manuscript score of *Tito Manlio* (see pp. 205 and 167).
* (p. 255) In the great majority of his opera overtures Handel marks the top line of the opening movement for all oboes and first violins (or firsts and seconds when the violins are in three parts).
* (p. 257) RM 19 d 8 was probably copied from Granville about 1785.

---

[31] Baselt, *Verzeichnis*, i. 137.

CHAPTER 14

SILLA

ACT I. *A great square in Rome, in the middle of which rises a triumphal arch. Silla, mounted on a chariot drawn by six negro slaves and preceded by lictors with fasces and consular ensigns, comes forward and passes beneath the arch to the sound of all the military instruments. As he descends from the chariot he is met by* his wife Metella and his friend the tribune Lepido, who congratulates him on his victories in the east. He boasts of the captured kings who follow in chains: the proud head of Mario is his footstool; Rome will obey his laws and bow to his wishes. He goes out with his train. Metella and Lepido, shocked by his arrogance, tremble for the fate of Rome. Metella promises to do her best to moderate his ambition. Lepido's wife Flavia *enters in terror*, having dreamed that Rome is burned to ashes by a monster. Lepido tries to reassure her. At his departure and the entry of Celia ('a Roman maiden, daughter of Silla's lieutenant Catulo and secretly in love with Claudio') *a thunderbolt falls and strikes down a large part of the triumphal arch.* Flavia realizes that the gods' anger is more than a dream, prays to Jove, and goes out, having taken no notice of Celia. Claudio ('a Roman Knight, enemy of Silla and in love with Celia') *enters holding in his hands the portrait of the dead Mario, which he studies closely.* Celia, assuming it to be a picture of another woman, *angrily snatches it from his hands and throws it to the ground with contempt.*[1] He protests his love; she replies that an enemy of Silla's is unworthy of her. Alone, she admits that she loves him, but honour compels her to hide the fact and live on hope. In *a delightful garden* Claudio, *observed by Celia aside*, reproaches Silla for usurping power and trampling on the liberty of the people. He answers that this is the reward of valour. Celia, *hurriedly approaching Silla*, asks anxiously for news of her father. Silla *gives her a letter, which she reads*, but she continues to interrupt Claudio whenever he tries to speak to Silla. Eventually she tells Silla she will be his servant and daughter, and goes out with him.[2] Claudio declares that fame summons him to punish pride. (In the libretto, but not the score, the set changes and the act ends with a scene in the amphitheatre where gladiatorial shows are held. Silla pays public court to Flavia and Celia, to the indignation of Metella, Lepido, and Claudio. All sit down to watch a fight between gladiators.)

Act II. *The countryside with the temple of Berecintia at the back, where many men and women have taken refuge, seeking the protection of the goddess.* Silla makes passes at Flavia, who indignantly repels him: she is a Roman matron, her loyalty as firm as a rock. Silla invokes the god of sleep to soothe his pain and at once drops off. *The god*[3] *enters in a chariot drawn by two dragons and surrounded by furies*

---

[1] In the printed libretto (but not the score) she recognizes the portrait first.
[2] In the libretto *he goes out angrily* before her declaration, and she follows.
[3] The goddess Hecate in the libretto: see p. 263.

with lighted torches in their hands. They whirl round Silla and the sky is darkened. The god cries war and slaughter: Rome must submit to Silla's power. *He disappears with all the furies, the sky grows light again and Silla wakes up furiously repeating* 'War!' *He calls his assassins,*[4] *who arrive with drawn swords in their hands* and at his command *enter the temple and slaughter the refugees.* Lepido comes out and accuses him of profaning the sanctuary. Silla, equating his power with the gods', orders Lepido to divorce Flavia so that he can marry her; any obstacle in his path will be removed by terror. Lepido tells Flavia of these threats, and they affirm their love in a duet. Claudio finds Celia *in tears* and asks the cause. When she replies 'Silla's lasciviousness' he *turns in fury* and demands vengeance. She *restrains him* and assures him of her love; he goes with a song of joy. *Celia departing meets Silla, who detains her and takes her hand. Metella pulls her away. Silla tries to embrace Celia, but Metella prevents him; he goes out in a rage.* Metella, *addressing Celia,* expatiates on the power of love. In *a garden with Lepido's palace at the back and in the middle a statute of Silla* Flavia meets the dictator *with soldiers, whom he sends away.* He renews his importunities with a demand for 'extreme measures'. *He tries to embrace her; she kneels* in supplication; he *renews his attempted embraces,* whereupon *four spectres descend and whirl round his statue, which sinks, and a funereal cypress rises in its place.* Flavia points to the wrath of heaven, but he says his image has gone to Elysium to be crowned. His next assault causes her to cry for help; *Lepido enters with his sword drawn; Silla summons his soldiers,* orders them to throw husband and wife into 'carceri orrendi,' and goes out. *The soldiers try to snatch Lepido's sword; he prepares to defend himself, but is obstructed by Flavia,* who bids him yield and trust to heaven. They part after a brief duet. Claudio meets Celia and promises to defend her against Silla, who *with Scabro and soldiers observes them aside. He comes forward; the soldiers suddenly surround Claudio and take away his sword.* Silla orders him to death and Celia to be locked up. He tells Scabro ('favourite of Silla and confidant of Metella') to have Lepido stabbed and Claudio thrown to the wild beasts. Metella hopes for heaven's aid through Scabro, *takes him by the hand and hurries out.* The set changes to *a courtyard opposite the wild beasts' den, where the lions are seen walking about. Claudio at the window of a tower in the act of being thrown into the den* asks why the gods do not interfere. Scabro *throws at Silla's feet a torn and bloody robe 'creduta di Lepido'.* Silla thanks him and orders him to complete the dispatch of Claudio. *Scabro is about to leave when Metella enters hurriedly and detains him. Scabro runs towards Silla, who hastily confronts Metella.* She brings news that the Marian party have risen against him. He again orders Scabro to kill Claudius and *storms out* to 'cut off the head of the arrogant hydra'. Metella tells Scabro to fetch the two innocent prisoners and implores the gods for succour. At the end of her aria *Scabro quickly brings in Lepido and Claudio; she takes them by the hand and hurries them away.*

Act III. In *a corridor leading to Metella's apartments* Lepido thanks Metella for saving his life and proposes to deliver Rome by killing Silla. She silences him— Silla is her husband—but assures him of Flavia's safety. *Scabro brings Metella a letter, which she reads,* announcing Silla's departure. She arranges for Scabro to release Flavia as soon as Silla leaves the city, but thinks it cruel that her husband should go without saying goodbye. Lepido thanks Scabro for saving his life and looks forward to reunion with Flavia. Silla, finding the cares of empire heavy, wishes he could console himself with Celia and/or Flavia before setting out for Sicily. He weighs the demands of love and duty, decides to

---

[4] *Sicarii* in the score, *satelliti* in the libretto.

quench some of his ardour, *pauses to take thought*, and *resolutely* sends for Celia. She defies him: she loves only Claudio. Silla says he is dead, and leaves her *in a rage. She runs after him*, bemoans Claudio's fate, and resolves to follow. As she soliloquizes Claudio (*aside*) echoes the last word of each phrase. She *turns in terror without seeing him* and, *when he comforts her*, takes him for a ghost and *runs in terror*; he tells her how Metella saved him and, as *she approaches very quietly*, addresses her in a happy love song. Flavia *in prison* finds the prospect of life without Lepido more than she can bear. *Silla enters with a soldier carrying a covered urn and Lepido's torn and bloodstained robe*, makes the usual advances, and is repulsed with the usual contempt. *He has the robe thrown at Flavia's feet and departs in a fury. Scabro brings Lepido to the prison*: Flavia *mistakes him for a ghost*, but *nevertheless runs to embrace him.* (The libretto has a short duet here.) The set changes to *a moonlight night; the sea coast with a rock in the middle, a small vessel and a boat on the beach.* Silla, about to embark, is astonished to meet Metella and her conjugal reproaches. He begs her pardon; both declare that love is stronger after a quarrel. (In the libretto they sing a duet.) *Silla embarks, and the vessel makes for the open sea.* Metella asks heaven's blessing on him. *As she looks out to sea, the ship is shaken by a violent storm, the moon is darkened, and a large comet appears accompanied by thunder and lightning; eventually the ship is wrecked, and Silla is seen to save himself by swimming to the rock. Metella rushes about the stage calling on the gods for assistance. Then she resolutely enters the boat, rows it to the rock, snatches Silla, and conveys him away.* (A scene of hope for Claudio and Celia in the libretto is not in the score.) The last set is *a square in Rome, with the Capitol at the back at the top of a large flight of steps.* Lepido and Claudio, surrounded by the senate and people, proclaim the overthrow of tyranny and the rule of liberty. *A cloud descends and covers the Capitol, opening gradually to reveal Mars in glory; all kneel to worship him. At this point Metella enters with Silla, who kneels, then rises and surrenders his sword, renounces all the honours of the republic, and begs the pardon of Mars and the country for all his sins.* He will retire into private life. *All rise; Silla descends, embraces Metella*, and agrees to Celia marrying Claudio. All rejoice.

If Giacomo Rossi cut down the text from some Italian original, it has not been identified. It was neither Andrea Rossini's libretto, set by Giovanni Domenico Freschi (*Silla*, Venice 1683) and Francesco Mancini (*Lucio Silla*, Naples 1703), nor Vincenzo Cassani's, set by Albinoni (*Il tiranno eroe*, Venice 1711). Act III Scene vi, in which Celia takes Claudio for a ghost, was evidently suggested by the echo scene (IV viii) in Guarini's *Il pastor fido*. The Argument is for the most part a summary of the plot, with certain deviations. Silla 'was instigated, he said, by a goddess, who appeared to him while he was sleeping and put thunderbolts in his hand, encouraging him to slaughter. He repudiated several wives without reason and compelled other married men to do the same. Metella herself, though loved by him, suffered in the end a similar fate . . . [His retirement into private life] will serve as a terminal point for the present drama, so that it will have a happy end, omitting Silla's miserable death (he was eaten alive by lice).' Although Rossi put Plutarch's name to this, and the incidents are related in his life of the Roman dictator Lucius Cornelius Sulla (138–78 BC), it is not a quotation. Rossi adds: 'In addition to the true history related above several likely characters (*quei verisimili*) have been introduced into the drama.' Besides Sulla and Metella, his fourth wife, Plutarch mentions Catulus and Lepidus; but the latter was not a partisan of Sulla, whereas Appius Claudius Pulcher was.

This repulsive subject seems an odd choice for the entertainment of a newly arrived ambassador,[5] unless more lurks behind than meets the eye. It is the worst libretto Handel ever set, with scarcely a redeeming feature. The construction is clumsy, the characterization incredible. Silla's villainy is as difficult to swallow as Metella's devotion to him and his final repentance. His frenzied pursuit of Flavia and Celia leads him to commit no fewer than seven indecent assaults on stage, all singularly fruitless and most of them followed by an indignant and undignified exit. No doubt propriety and the *opera seria* convention enjoined frustration, but a more competent librettist would have managed it without portraying Silla as such an inept practitioner. Contemporaries may have found a certain titillation in this constant harping on sex and violence, a conjunction worthy of the cinema or television screen; in a modern opera-house it would be ludicrous.

All the evidence suggests the hasty and careless cutting down of an old libretto to ensure a brief entertainment (with the possible exception of *Il pastor fido* and *Imeneo, Silla* is the shortest of Handel's operas). The original would appear to have been one of those complex interlocking intrigues much favoured in seventeenth-century Venice (compare the source of the *Admeto* libretto or Cavalli's *Erismena*), the last thing Rossi ought to have chosen if his aim was conciseness. In his text, stripped to the minimum of recitative, the incidents remain, grotesquely foreshortened; the motives that occasioned them are suppressed or simplified to the point of banality. Scabro, well named as the favourite of so lecherous a tyrant, plays a vital part in the plot but has not a note to sing, doubtless because no singer was available. The entrances and exits in Act I are clumsily contrived; the last scene of the act is obscure (the episode omitted by Handel makes things no clearer); the motivation of several arias, especially Claudio's 'Mi brilla' in II vii, Metella's 'Hai due vaghe' in II viii, and 'Io non ti chiedo' in III ii, is inadequate or worse; and the later part of Act III from the middle of the prison scene to the *coro*, where enough happens to occupy a composer for a whole act, disintegrates into a few insignificant scraps of recitative. It is true that the printed libretto is less perfunctory here than the score. III ix ends with a two-line duet for Flavia and Lepido, x with a more substantial duet for Metella and Silla; Metella's words 'Assistete . . . i voti miei' in xi are printed as an aria or arioso, and a scene for Celia and Claudio follows, ending with an aria for the latter. It is possible that Handel set one or more of these (the duets in particular seem indispensable); the autograph of this part of the opera is missing. Even so the arrangement is jerky and casual. Silla, who has no solo in the whole act, should surely have been allowed an aria of renunciation before the Capitol. The odd treatment of the supernatural has another explanation. The god ('Il Dio') of II iii is clearly not the god of sleep to whom Silla prays. The printed libretto shows that he was originally not a god at all but Hecate, goddess of the underworld; her visitation followed the story in Plutarch. The change was undoubtedly due, like the similar late appearance of Leveridge in *Il pastor fido* and *Teseo*, to the restricted range of voices available in the company. The fact that the *coro* uses only sopranos and altos tends to confirm that the bass was a late substitute. Handel may have been unhappy about the nomenclature, for

[5] See below, p.269.

'Il Dio' is crossed out in the autograph and 'Astagorre' substituted in a strange hand. It is not clear who this personage is.

Handel emerges from the enterprise with scarcely more credit than Rossi. Either the score is very incomplete, or he took little trouble, or both. Many episodes that peremptorily demand music—Silla's triumphal entry, the dance of the spectres in II ix, the spectacular naval and meteorological events in III x and xi—receive none. The perfunctoriness of the closing scenes has no parallel elsewhere in his work. His lack of commitment to the libretto and failure to identify himself with the characters are not surprising. The individual arias bear the stamp of his personal artistry, but they are seldom fully developed and there is little attempt to express character or dramatic conflict. The few exceptions, chiefly in Act II, occur (as we might expect) when Claudio, Lepido, or Flavia suffer under Silla's lash. Too many arias are both dramatically and musically unsuitable; it is no surprise to discover that at least six were adapted or lifted from cantatas. Two others use motives from Keiser's *Octavia*; but the fact of borrowing is of course no indication that the material will not be assimilated.

None of the characters is fully realized, and some are not even consistent. Silla comes to life only in his last aria, 'La vendetta è un cibo', where the bare octaves of the accompaniment and the kicking rhythm admirably suggest the sinister cruelty of the man. His sleep scene ('Dolce nume') with its cooing double thirds for recorders and violins is as sensuously beautiful as one expects from Handel on such an occasion, but totally out of character. The siciliano 'È tempo, O luci belle' is equally inappropriate when he is pressing Lepido to divorce Flavia. The B section with its change of rhythm and (implied) tempo and its reinforced scoring (double bass independent of cellos and bassoons) makes a good contrast after the simple continuo accompaniment at the start, but Handel wrote finer arias of this type. It is scarcely conceivable that he would have left his central character without a set piece in the last act, and we may guess that the music of his duet with Metella in III x has been lost.

Metella's 'Fuggon l'aure' is another aria whose B section employs fuller scoring to some purpose; the music also fits the mood of the words better than that of the first part, which uses material common to many works of the Italian period. Her remaining arias all found a more suitable context later, 'Hai due vaghe' in *Radamisto*, the other two in *Amadigi*. The best moment in 'Hai due vaghe' is the placing of the top B flat in the nicely extended ritornello after the A section, but it is absurd that Silla's unbridled lust for another woman should stimulate his wife to a tender meditation on the power of love. 'Io non ti chiedo', though its hesitant double-dotted rhythm is a happy invention, strikes an equally incongruous note when Metella has just rescued Lepido and Flavia from Silla's depravity. Handel seems to have despaired of making sense of her character. 'Secondate, O giusti dei' raises no problems and brings Act II to a satisfactory conclusion.

Flavia and Lepido, the second married couple, have the only concerted music in the score. Both their duets, sung in the tyrant's shadow, are in minor keys, and both are excellent. 'Sol per te', like a number of the great duets in the Royal Academy operas, is a love scene *triste*; they renew their pledges in the face of danger. The music has a touching eloquence; the scoring is richer and the development of ideas more extended than in most of *Silla*. 'Ti lascio' on the other hand is very short, but of superb quality. In nine *Adagio* bars, mostly in canon, husband and wife utter their last farewells. There is no opening ritornello; the upper instruments, first the viola, then the violins in succession, enter at the vocal cadence and provide a five-bar threnody of haunting contrapuntal eloquence as the guards separate the pair and lead them to prison (Ex. 31). As in 'Cara! ti dono' in *Teseo*, probably composed for the same singers, Handel treats the man as the higher voice.

Neither of Lepido's arias has much distinction; they suffer from a curious similarity in their instrumental accompaniment and a burden of otiose coloratura. 'Già respira' almost redeems itself with an extended four-part ritornello after the da capo; in such details, even in his least successful operas, Handel's artistic refinement seldom fails. Flavia's solos are altogether superior. 'Un sol raggio' uses hemiola not with the usual connotation of exuberance but sadly, as if reflecting a catch in the throat. The 3/8 melody is charming, and

Ex. 31

Ex. 31 (cont.)

(I am leaving you, my idol, but my heart stays with you.)

the scoring with a light bass and oboe solos in each section (no upper strings in the second part) very delicate. 'Qual scoglio' has another attractive tune, perhaps too smooth for Flavia's protestations of rock-like fidelity, though the start, on a first inversion of the dominant of F after an A minor cadence, is resolute enough. In 'Stelle rubelle', as always when he has an innocent victim in prison, Handel is supreme. His distribution of the text, which suggests recitative rather than aria, is interesting. The A section, in which Flavia faces the prospect of an unjust death, spreads five words over 43 slow G minor bars in triple time. The second part has eighteen words but only seven bars of music, contrasted in time and tonality. The change to E flat and then D minor, over a steady procession of quaver chords, as she briefly contemplates the thought of life without her husband, has an extraordinary concentration and poignancy.

Ex. 32

(But living would be wretched if, with his death, my beloved husband
  pointed my way to Elysium)

Still more moving is the unexpected repeat of the B section when Lepido's torn and bloodstained robe is thrown at Flavia's feet. This marvellous stroke has no exact parallel in Handel's operas, though he more than once brings back earlier material for a dramatic or ironical purpose.[6] Unfortunately, apart from the *coro*, it is the last set piece in the score.

  Claudio alone is permitted five arias, including the longest and most brilliant, 'Con tromba guerriera', which makes a rousing climax to Act I. As usual when Handel deploys a trumpet obbligato there is little harmonic interest but enough colour and rhythmic vitality for this not to be missed. In the B section, exceptionally, it is not the trumpet but the oboes and violins that

  [6] For example in *Agrippina, Alessandro, Riccardo Primo,* and *Serse.*

are silenced. Ideas from this aria and Silla's 'Alza il volo' (I i) were later combined in Tiridate's 'Alzo al volo di mia speranza' in Act III of *Radamisto*, which echoes the first line of Silla's text. Claudio has two love songs in which the violins are doubled by recorders at the unison or octave, but neither ranks with Handel's best efforts in this line. Far finer is the short arioso 'Se'l mio mal da voi dipende' with its characteristic suspensions when Claudio in his turn faces death. Celia's music was written for a singer of very limited capacity. Her two arias are doubled throughout in the orchestra, but the second, 'Sei già morto', is a beautiful piece in the broken sarabande rhythm from which Handel could wring such peculiar pathos. It was to find a perfect resting-place in *Amadigi*. The *coro*, though very slight, plays prettily with 3/8 cross-rhythms in the manner of a Purcell act-tune. No doubt the singer of the god's aria doubled the bass line with suitable minor modifications.

Apart from Flavia's prison scene, the one episode in which Handel builds up dramatic tension is Silla's vision of the god and the furies in II ii–iv. The exquisite texture of his arioso is prolonged in a lingering fifteen-bar coda as he lies asleep. Suddenly a brisk fanfare with a canonic opening and a scuttering of oboes in thirds introduces the god. The material of his aria, 'Guerra, stragi', in breezy B flat mood, is not remarkable, but the structure is. The second part, containing the god's injunction, is an accompanied recitative launched from an unexpected chord of D major, after which the ritornello leading to the da capo is shortened from seven to two bars. When the god and his entourage vanish Silla wakes with a start, echoes the opening of the aria (without the orchestra), and gives orders for the massacre to begin. Though not long, the scene bears all the marks of the assured dramatic composer.

The absence of music at so many critical points is unlike the mature Handel, but has precedents in his early work, for example the battle in *Teseo* and some of the magic scenes in *Rinaldo*. The stage directions strongly suggest that the machines and other props constructed for *Rinaldo* were used again, among them Argante's car drawn by moors at Silla's first entry, Armida's dragon chariot for the god, the Siren's boat for Metella's embarcation, and the descending cloud when Almirena is kidnapped for that which covers the Capitol in the last scene. Mars in glory may have borrowed Minerva's machine from *Teseo*. It is possible that Handel brought in previously composed music at these points, as he seems to have done once more for the overture, which remains unpublished. It is a six-movement concerto in B flat for oboes and strings, and like the overtures to *Rodrigo*, *Il pastor fido*, and *Teseo* was almost certainly a separate composition. It does not at all suggest a triumphal entry; the last movement, a short minuet in binary form, is gentle and inconclusive. The stately initial Largo is the best part, but the music nowhere represents Handel at his peak. The fifth movement consists merely of four *Adagio* chords, and like similar things in the organ concertos and Bach's third Brandenburg was presumably a framework for keyboard improvisation. Most of the material was extensively reworked soon afterwards: the initial ideas of the first two movements (in the minor) in the *Amadigi* overture, and the last three movements in the concerto grosso Op. 3 no. 4. The whole French overture section of the latter also found its way into *Amadigi* (as 'the Second Overture'), confirming the close links with that opera.

Silla employs a light orchestra (possibly not the complete theatre band): solo trumpet in one aria and recorders in three, besides oboes, bassoons, and strings. There are no elaborate flights, but the layout in 'Sol per te' shows how much variety was possible with limited resources. 'Hai due vaghe' is unusual in that the oboes accompany the voice in both parts while the violins are confined to the *tutti*, the reverse of the normal procedure. As in *Teseo*, the oboe parts are unusually full, no doubt because Handel had good players; the solos were perhaps intended for Galliard. A small point worth noting is that where the violins double the recorders in 'Mi brilla' Handel avoids taking them above c''', keeping them in the lower octave. The distribution of keys seems haphazard, with a strong leaning towards B flat, F, and G minor, unrelated to design or character. The twelve set pieces in Act II are all in flat keys except one duet in A minor; but this achieves no purpose, and pairs of consecutive arias in F major and G minor have a leaden effect. There are only five movements in sharp keys, all major, and several of the commoner keys (C, E flat, E, D minor, E minor) do not appear at all. Handel manages the change of set after II xiii in the same way as that in Act II of *Teseo*: a recitative cadence in A minor as Metella leads Scabro off is succeeded by Claudio's cavatina in the unrelated key of G minor as the back-flats open to reveal him about to be thrown to the lions.

History and Text

Until very recently *Silla* had no history. Chrysander[7] conjectured that it was intended for the Earl of Burlington's private residence in Piccadilly in 1714. The discovery of a printed libretto[8] modifies the date to 1713 but confirms that the production (if it took place[9]) was private; the unusual format and the absence of both an English translation and a named cast are enough to indicate this. Rossi dated his dedication 2 June 1713, and this was almost certainly the day of performance; he had followed the same procedure in *Il pastor fido*. Burlington House is not mentioned; the scenic effects seem to demand the machinery available at the Queen's Theatre, and it is probable that the building was hired for the occasion. The libretto offers a clue to what this was. Rossi's long, windy, and obsequious dedication to the French Ambassador Extraordinary in London, Louis-Marie, Duc d'Aumont de Rochebaron, is reprinted in full in Knapp's article.[10] D'Aumont (1667–1723) had come to London the previous year in connection with the negotiations that culminated in the Treaty of Utrecht in the spring of 1713. Duncan Chisholm[11] has suggested that the libretto was an attack on Marlborough, satirized as Silla, and that the opera was staged as a political manifesto, either to gratify d'Aumont or at his expense. He had musical tastes (a concert was given for his entertainment at Stationers' Hall on 15 May) and an exceptional gift for ostentation. He gave some of the earliest London masquerades at Somerset House in the same year.[12] According to Saint-Simon he caused the stately

[7] i. 415–16.

[8] In the Huntington Library, California. See J. M. Knapp, 'The Libretto of Handel's *Silla*', *M & L* l (1969), 68.

[9] No contemporary reference to it is known.

[10] Op. cit. 70–1.

[11] 'Handel's *Lucio Cornelio Silla*, its problems and context', *Early Music*, xiv (1986), 64–70.

[12] T. Castle, 'Eros and Liberty at the English Masquerade, 1710–1790', *Eighteenth Century Studies*, xvii (1983–4), 156–76.

residence he had rented in Great Ormond Street to be destroyed by fire in order to collect double compensation from the French and English governments.

There is little doubt that *Silla* was composed for the Queen's Theatre company, whose season had closed on 30 May. Chrysander and Deutsch cannot be right in postulating an amateur cast; voices trained in the Italian style are essential, and the compass and tessitura of the parts exactly fit the *Teseo* cast. Silla and Lepido were almost certainly intended for the two castratos Valentini and Pellegrini, and Claudio for Jane Barbier, who was experienced in male roles: she had sung Arcane in *Teseo* and both Eustazio and Rinaldo in revivals of *Rinaldo*. Margherita de l'Epine and Pilotti had the compass for either Metella or Flavia; in view of the transfer of 'Secondate, O giusti dei' to Pilotti's part in *Amadigi* and her success in fiery rather than tender music it is likely that she was cast for Metella and l'Epine for Flavia. Leveridge was probably the god. Celia, an easy part, could have been taken by Maria Gallia, Manina, or Vittoria Albergotti (who had joined the company for the pasticcio *Ernelinda* in February), or even the young Anastasia Robinson, who sang in two concerts at the Queen's Theatre later in June.

Silla has had a single stage revival, in Paris in 1990, and a concert performance in Cologne in 1991.

Autograph

The autograph (RM 20 c 8) is incomplete; including one fragment in the Fitzwilliam Museum, 32 leaves out of approximately 58 survive, covering four sections of the opera: from bar 35 of 'Fuggon l'aure' to bar 60 of 'Con tromba guerriera' (HG 4–17), from the beginning of II ii to the words 'ardita tenti' in bar 7 of the recitative of II viii (HG 22–34), from the beginning of II ix to the words 'di mia gloria' in bar 4 of the recitative of II xv (HG 36–40), and from bar 17 of 'Io non ti chiedo' to the end of III iv (HG 45–48). The overture, *coro*, seven arias, and part of three more are missing. It is clear from Handel's foliation that the overture was not an original part of the score. Changes of scene numbering and irregular foliation in Act II point to considerable rearrangement during and after composition. Scenes vii and viii were originally iv and vi; others received numbers subsequently in different ink or none at all. Most exceptionally Handel foliated the manuscript after reordering it: f. 15, an insertion on different paper with the last 8¼ bars of the recitative on HG 26, followed by *Segue l'aria e tempo O luci*, carries his 7. It seems possible that the scene of Silla's dream replaced something else, possibly an earlier draft before Hecate changed sex. 'Se la speranza' has no tempo mark, and the top line is *Tutti unis.* (not *Violini* as in HG) in the autograph and all copies except Shaftesbury; in Tenbury 884 violins and oboes have separate staves, and both carry the same music in the ritornellos.

Two leaves from the autograph are in the Fitzwilliam Museum (Mus MS 256, pp. 37–40; *Catalogue*, 171); they begin at bar 34 of 'Dolce nume' (HG 23) and end with the B section of 'Guerra, stragi' (HG 25) linking two passages in RM 20 c 8. At bar 17 of 'Guerra, stragi' Handel marked the top stave for violins alone. The Fitzwilliam also contains (Mus MS 252, pp. 1–3; *Catalogue*, 163) earlier versions of 'Già respira' and 'È tempo'; they are probably part of a cantata (without recitatives) which continues on the next leaf. The music is autograph, the clefs and words written by a copyist. 'Già respira' is for alto voice in E flat, and slightly shorter than in the opera; 'È tempo' has a different B section.

Libretto

'L. C. Silla, Drama per Musica... A Londra 1713.' 32 pp. There is no publisher's imprint, no cast, and no English translation. The format is larger than that of the regular theatre librettos. Handel appears as Hendel, with his title as Kapellmeister to the Elector of Hanover. Brief descriptions of the characters and the Argument make the plot rather easier to grasp than it is in the score. Two entire scenes—I viii in the amphitheatre, which was designed to end with a trio for Silla, Flavia, and Celia ('Son fenice a doppio rogo') and a gladiatorial combat (possibly a ballet), and III xii in Celia's room ending with an aria for Claudio, 'E vicin quel dì sereno'—are marked with *virgole* as not performed. In addition III ix ends with a duet for Flavia and Lepido ('Brilla il cor') and III x with a duet for Metella and Silla ('Non s'estingue mai la fiamma'), for which no music survives. 'La Dea Ecate' appears in place of 'Il Dio' in II iii. There are minor differences in the text, and the stage directions are longer and more explicit; the lions in the 'serraglio' (II xiv) are not mentioned in the scores. A copy of the libretto (*L. C. Sylla*) is listed in the sale catalogue of Haym's library in March 1730.

Copies and Editions

No performing score survives. None of the five manuscript copies is of early date, and all may derive from a common source, itself perhaps defective. All give exceptionally detailed stage directions. Add MS 5334, from the library of Sir John Hawkins, spells the title *Sylla* and ascribes the opera to Giovanni Bononcini (hence its omission by Larsen). The scribe, who signed himself W. T. in a note on f. 26^v, is unidentified. This is the only copy to include the overture. It supplies tempo marks for 'Se la speranza' (*Allegro*) and 'È tempo' (*Largo*); 'Dolce nume' (*Adagio* in the autograph) is *Largo*, 'Io non ti chiedo' *Adagio e staccato*. The top stave of 'Qual scoglio' is for *Tutti*, implying oboes, and so is that of 'Guerra, stragi' and 'Hai due vaghe', though the oboes play as indicated in HG during the arias. In these respects all five copies agree, except that Lennard has no tempo mark on 'Dolce nume'. Flower (S2, *c.* 1738–41), Shaftesbury (S2), RM 19 d 7 (RM6),[13] and Lennard (bound with *Rodrigo* and written by the same late hand, Lenn 2) were not copies from Add MS 5334, but do not materially differ from it except in the omission of the overture. Other divergences from the autograph are trifling; the copies have all the oboes entering at bar 17 of 'Con tromba guerriera' and no viola doubling the second violins in 'Sol per te'. Rophino Lacy in the nineteenth century made a copy of the overture and Act I, stopping a few bars before the end (Add MS 31555, ff. 69–98). He took Act I from Add MS 5334, but apparently scored the overture from parts (he made a rough copy first); it differs in several minor respects, including bass figuring, from the Hawkins copy.

---

[13] RM6 was also responsible for a score of *La Resurrezione* (RM 19 d 4) and is identical with RM5, who copied the *Foundling Hospital Anthem* (RM 19 e 8) and some opera extracts in RM 19 d 11.

The Flower parts (S2, late 1740s), a complete set—cembalo, violins 1 and 2, viola, cello + bassoon, oboes 1 and 2 incorporating recorders, trumpet—were evidently taken from the Flower score. Oboes or recorders are included in all but five movements (among them 'Se'l mio mal'), though apart from solos they are generally confined to ritornellos and *tutti* and are mostly excluded from B sections. Both oboes double first violins in 'Se ben tuona', 'Se la speranza', 'Guerra, stragi', and 'Hai due vaghe'. They play throughout 'Qual scoglio' and 'Stelle rubelle', but are silent in the first ritornello of 'Con tromba guerriera' though joining in the later *tutti* (not all indicated in HG). In 'Un sol raggio' they are inconsistent, doubling first violins in the opening ritornello but seconds later. The recorders do not double the voice in 'Luci belle'. The bassoons are silenced in 'Senti', 'Ti lascio', and 'Già respira' until the final ritornellos, and in 'È tempo' till the ritornello before the B section; they enjoy a little independence only in 'Sol per te'. 'Fuggon l'aure' has no strings at all till the ritornello after the A section (reinforced by oboes), the accompaniment being left to the harpsichord.

Tenbury 884 (*Opera of Amadis & Other Songs*) contains early Smith copies of 'Hai due vaghe', 'Se la speranza', and 'Mi brilla', dating from about 1719. They recur in a Shaftesbury volume of miscellaneous early arias (S4, 1736 or soon after). 'Mi brilla', evidently the favourite, appears (in G major, short score) in an early volume of songs, mostly from *Amadigi* and *Teseo*, in the Coke Collection. Luke Pippard copied it for Drury Lane about 1716.[14] It was the only item from *Silla* published during Handel's life, in yet another key (B flat), as a separate issue (short score with an English version and flute arrangement) and in *The Monthly Mask of Vocal Musick* for July 1717. From this Walsh took it into his 1732 hotchpotch *The Favourite Songs in y*ᵉ *Opera call'd Thessus & Amadis.*[15]

Chrysander's (1875) is the only printed score. He based it on the autograph (without the Fitzwilliam fragment) and RM 19 d 7, which he called 'a very faulty copy made about 1780 by an incompetent person'. Chrysander added to the faults by omitting several tempo marks, giving that of 'Io non ti chiedo' as *Allegro* instead of *Adagio*, and misunderstanding Handel's scoring where the top stave has *Tutti*. The oboes in bars 4 and 5 of 'Guerra, stragi' are not solos in the autograph or any other source. What is more surprising, although in his biography[16] he refers to the Hawkins copy, he does not appear to have noticed that it contains the overture. He neither mentions nor prints this in his score.

---

[14] His bill is in BL Egerton MS 2159, f. 31.
[15] See p. 259.
[16] i. 415, published in 1858.

CHAPTER 15

AMADIGI DI GAULA

Act I. Amadigi, 'a famous Heroe', and Dardano, Prince of Thrace, are each (unknown to the other) in love with Oriana, 'Daughter of the King of the Fortunate Islands'. But Melissa, a sorceress, is infatuated with Amadigi and has detained him by means of her magic powers. The opera begins in *Melissa's Garden*[1] at *Night*. Amadigi suggests to Dardano that they escape under cover of darkness, and when Dardano reproaches him for not returning Melissa's love *shews him the Picture of Oriana*. Dardano recognizes the woman he himself loves, but decides to dissemble; under pretext of searching for a secret exit he goes off to warn Melissa. Amadigi invokes night to comfort his troubled heart, but *stops abruptly. The Scene grows Light on a sudden, and there arises confusedly from the Ground Vasas [vasi], Fountains, and Statues. And a Troop of infernal Spirits (sent by Melissa) on both sides of the Scene, prevent Amadis's going off the Stage. . . . Whilst he lays his Hand on his Sword, Melissa comes suddenly to him.* She taunts him with ingratitude: before he can approach Oriana's enchanted tower he will be destroyed by harpies, Cerberus, furies, and flames. He departs undaunted. Melissa shrinks from killing the man she loves. The set changes to *a Porch in Flames, which hinder the entring into Oriana's Tower.* Amadigi has defeated the monsters. Dardano reads an inscription to the effect that only the most valiant hero can conquer the obstacle. Amadigi at once *makes as if he would pass the Flames.* Dardano confesses himself Amadigi's rival and offers to put their worthiness to the test. Amadigi replies contemptuously and *passes through the Flames.* Dardano, baffled in his attempt to follow, goes to rouse Melissa to further vengeance. *The Enchanted Porch splits asunder and falls at the Sound of a loud boisterous Simphony; the Scene darkens, and it thunders and lightens, but clears up again at the appearing of Oriana, who comes surrounded with enchanted Knights and Ladies; and the Scene changes into most beautiful Rows of Pillars. Oriana descends from the throne.*[2] Amadigi tells her she is free from Melissa's enchantments. After a joyful aria apiece *they sit down; and there follows a Dance of inchanted Knights and Ladies.* Oriana begs Amadigi not to be too long over his preparations for their flight. Melissa *comes in suddenly*, with *Dardanus at a Distance* looking forward to his revenge. On her order *the Devils go and bring in Oriana*,[3] while others detain Amadigi. Melissa exults over Amadigi's grief. Left alone, he implores fate to restore Oriana or let him die.

Act II. *A Garden with a Magnificent Palace at a Distance; in the midst of it is the Fountain of True Love.* Amadigi after wandering in a forest invokes the

---

[1] Three copies of the score add further details that can only derive from Handel's lost autograph; the most explicit states that Oriana's tower—that is, the tower in which she is imprisoned—can be seen in the distance.
[2] This sentence is not in the libretto, but appears in three of the earliest scores.
[3] In fact they carry her off, apparently accompanied by Dardano.

fountain, 'whose waters faithful Lovers undeceive', and *stands viewing himself in* [it]. *Horrified by a vision of Oriana caressing Dardano, he falls in a Swoon upon a Rock*. Melissa *makes her charms*, and furies bring in Oriana, who *draws near to Amadis*. Believing him dead, *she goes to take* [his] *Sword*, intending to stab herself. *Amadis recovers his Senses, rises*, and denounces her for faithlessness. She departs angrily and he *offers to kill himself, but is hinder'd by Melissa, who comes suddenly to him*. She finds him impervious to threats and blandishments; whereupon *the Scene changes into a horrible Cave*. . . . *Monsters ascend from the Bowels of the Earth; and Thunder is heard in the Air*. She promises still greater torments (*the Furies surround him*); he shall witness Oriana making love to his rival. The scene ends with a duet of defiance. In *the Palace of Melissa* Dardano, slighted by Oriana, can find no redress for his grief. *As he is departing, he is detain'd by Melissa*, who promises him Oriana's love: she has changed his appearance by magic so that he resembles Amadigi. Dardano resolves to kill Amadigi if the stratagem miscarries. Oriana, mistaking him for Amadigi, begs his pardon for her earlier anger. He rejoices at the success of his hopes. *At the End of this Air, Amadis crosses the Stage, without seeing Dardanus, tho' Dardanus perceives him and follows him in a Passion*. . . . *Clashing of Swords is heard*. Melissa *comes in a Fury*, reveals the deception to Oriana, and says that Dardano has been killed by the real Amadigi. She accuses Oriana of stealing her lover and *threatens her* with the power of hell. *She is going off, but is detain'd by Oriana*, who declares that neither torture nor magic will make her renounce Amadigi. Melissa calls up furies and spectres from their dungeons.

Act III. In *the Palace of Melissa* Oriana, *brought in by Devils*, is resigned to dying for her beloved. The set changes to *a Cave appointed for the Enchantments of Melissa*. The sorceress, whose passion increases the more it is spurned, tries to banish love from her breast. At her orders *the Devils bring in Amadis and Oriana, both in Chains*. Each asks to be the only one punished. Melissa *is going to wound Amadis*, but cannot. She *offers to stab Oriana*, but feels that the pain caused to Amadigi will be too brief; she must prolong his agony. The lovers beg for pity in a duet. Melissa's reply is to conjure up the Ghost of Dardano. Instead of contributing to her revenge the Ghost announces that the gods protect these faithful lovers, whose torments are nearly at an end, and *disappears*. Melissa *offers to kill Oriana, but finds her self detain'd*. Rejected by heaven and hell, *she wounds her self with a Ponyard, falls down and dies*, telling Amadigi that she would still be happy 'if one kind Sigh of yours would but bemoan my Fate'. *The Cave -changes into a beautiful Palace; and after a short, but pleasant* [allegra] *Simphony, a Chariot descends covered with Clouds, in which appears the Enchanter Orgando, Uncle to Oriana*. He brings the lovers the blessing of heaven and, *descended from the Chariot*, joins their hands in matrimony. The opera ends with *a Dance of Shepherds and Shepherdesses* in honour of the event.

The fact that Heidegger, the impresario of the King's Theatre, signed the dedication of the libretto led Burney and others to assume that he was its author. It is far more likely that one of the Italian 'poets', either Rossi or (more probably) Haym, Heidegger's collaborator in a number of operatic ventures at this period, was responsible. Like *Teseo* it is an adaptation of a five-act French *tragédie-lyrique*, Antoine Houdar de La Motte's *Amadis de Grèce*, set by André Destouches in 1699 and several times revived at the Paris Opéra in the next half-century.[4] La Motte was clearly familiar with Quinault's libretto on the same subject, *Amadis de Gaule*, set by Lully in 1684. Their common source was the medieval Spanish epic (of which Southey was to publish an English translation in 1805), in which Amadis, an illegitimate son of the King of Gaul educated in Scotland, falls in love with and eventually marries Oriana, daughter of the King of England. Among his many doughty deeds are the dispatch of a rival prince Dardan and the rescue from a magic spell of the princess Niquée, whom however he does not love. Amadis of Greece is his great-grandson, whose exploits are related in a sequel.

Quinault's libretto features two pairs of faithful lovers beset by two magicians, Arcalaus and Arcabonne, brother and sister; another brother, Ardan, is killed by Amadis and returns later as a ghost. Eventually the good magician Urgande disperses the powers of evil, rescues the lovers, and offers to reconcile Oriana with the King of England, who disapproves of the match with Amadis. La Motte confusingly gives the elder Amadis the title of the younger. He cuts out the second pair of lovers and one magician (Arcalaus), renames Arcabonne Mélisse after a sorceress in Ariosto's *Orlando furioso*, and conflates Dardan and Ardan as an unnamed Prince of Thrace, retaining Quinault's ghost episode. Amadis's beloved however becomes Niquée, daughter of the Sultan of Thebes, and Urgande is replaced by the enchantress Zirphée, Niquée's aunt.

Both French operas have the usual allegorical prologue in honour of Louis XIV and make copious use of chorus and ballet. The London librettist followed much the same procedure as in *Teseo*, except that he reduced the number of acts to three (combining La Motte's first two acts in Act I, his third and fourth in Act II), and did not have to deal with secondary lovers. He removed the prologue and choruses and left only residual traces of the ballet, but preserved many of the spectacular episodes which had proved so popular in *Rinaldo* and *Teseo* (and perhaps were responsible for the choice of subject), especially those concerned with devils and furies.[5] La Motte commanded neither the literary skill nor the structural tension of Quinault; his divertissements are awkwardly placed, and his dialogue too often abandons sentiment for rhetoric and logic-chopping. Handel's librettist got rid of much dross, but seldom put anything better in its place. While restoring the names of Oriana, Dardano, and Orgando from earlier sources, he kept much of the original recitative and two or three of the airs, which he translated as they stood. These passages, including Amadigi's invocation to night in Act I and to the fountain in Act II, the Ghost's arioso, and Melissa's death scene, are among the best in the libretto. Elsewhere his work is casual and clumsy, and gives the impression of having been executed in a hurry.

One obvious absurdity is the appearance of Orgando as a gratuitous *deus ex machina* after Melissa's death, when he can do nothing but raise the question why, being a relative and a magician by trade, he has not offered his services when they were needed. Urgande is very active in Quinault's last two acts,

---

[4] A reproduction of the third edition of the score (Paris, 1712) was issued by Gregg Press in 1967. This differs somewhat from the 1699 version, which was evidently the source of Handel's libretto.

[5] Kimbell ('The *Amadis* Operas of Destouches and Handel', *ML* xlix (1968), 329–46) plausibly suggests that Heidegger found these easier to dress from stock than Destouches's sailors (of both sexes), ethnological types, and famous beauties of the past.

and La Motte's Zirphée controls the prologue and plays a part in the opera. It is she, not Mélisse, who has established Niquée in the flame-girt tower which only the bravest hero (i.e. Amadis) can penetrate. Handel's audience must have been puzzled by the Fountain of True Love or taken it for one of Melissa's more diabolical devices, since it tells a lie. This is not so in the original; La Motte makes it clear that Mélisse has already transformed the appearance of the Prince of Thrace, so that Niquée is genuinely deceived. The postponement of this leads to a string of absurdities in Handel's second act.

The Prince is a much more interesting character than Dardano. At the start he is bound to Amadis by ties of loyalty and friendship, even though they are rivals in love. Amadis's production of the portrait adds to his depression by confirming what he already knows. In Handel's libretto it presents Dardano with a new fact and therefore provokes an aria in the most unsuitable place: he has to challenge fate and plan revenge while Amadigi is still on stage. In Act IV (corresponding to the second half of Handel's Act II) he is painfully aware that Niquée only responds to him because she thinks he is someone else. He addresses the sea in an important air: a fearful storm rages in his heart, he has betrayed his friend Amadis for a shadow, and his innocence and honesty are shipwrecked. After a long scene (in his disguise) with Niquée, who of course cannot understand his agitation after Mélisse has consented to the marriage, he challenges Amadis out of desperation and remorse. In Handel's libretto this decision, coming immediately after the successful deception of Oriana and an aria of hope and triumph, appears wholly inconsequent.

Melissa's function is similar in both librettos, though she is more vindictive and less sympathetic in La Motte's, and the other characters are not essentially changed; but the interpolation of extra arias confuses the motivation and makes the action jerky and capricious. Oriana, deprived of her long duologue with Dardano (perhaps because it would have extended his role at the expense of the *primo uomo*, sung by Nicolini[6]), has to be compensated elsewhere; hence her appearance in the fountain scene, a contrived episode of conventional misunderstanding which breaks across the conflict between Amadigi and Melissa (and forces Amadigi to abandon every vestige of dignity) and the superfluous if touching aria at the beginning of Act III, which involves a change of set. On the other hand the scene in which Oriana defies Melissa at the end of Act II is an improvement on La Motte, whose fourth act fizzles out in recitative with Niquée passively enduring Melissa's threats. There was no good reason for weakening the final confrontation between Melissa and the lovers. The duet for the latter is much better placed by La Motte; it occurs when they offer to die for each other, after which Niquée faints and Amadis alone begs for mercy on her behalf. He remains consistent instead of relapsing once more into a posture the reverse of heroic. It is possible that Handel was pressed for time and asked his collaborator to modify the plot so that he could use music already in existence: the first two arias in Act III, the A section of the duet, and Melissa's 'Io già sento' were lifted almost unchanged from *Silla*. The latter part of Act III however remains closer to La Motte than the rest of the libretto.

The London librettist made no more attempt than in *Teseo* to adapt his model to the balanced pattern of arias and exits customary in *opera seria*, and so forfeited the advantages of both conventions, the formal symmetry of the

---

[6] In Destouches's opera Amadis is a bass, the Prince a high tenor (*haute-contre*).

Italian and the more flexible design of the French. Ten arias (three in succession in I vii) and the Act III duet are not followed by exits, with the result that dramatic points are not clinched and the action grows sluggish. The singers are left hanging about with nothing to do. Dardano's 'Pugnerò' in the first scene has to be sung aside—unless Amadigi obliges by walking off at the start and returning at the end. Towards the end of this act Amadigi tells Oriana to go into the next room while he prepares for their flight, but neither of them apparently makes a move; she sings a long aria, and both are still there when Melissa enters. In Act II the librettist has to slither round the fact that Dardano cannot possibly know what Oriana is apologizing for. His aria ('Tu mia speranza') is then separated from his exit by two perfunctory bars of recitative when he sees Amadigi coming and goes off to challenge him. Nor is it easy to see why the librettist deprived Handel of the effective conjuration scene in which Melissa calls up the Ghost. It is to his credit that the aria texts are straightforward expressions of feeling, free from moralizing and contrived metaphors. Otherwise whatever dramatic potency the opera possesses—and despite handicaps it is a surprising amount—must be credited to the composer, who in later years would surely have exercised a firmer control over his collaborator.

Burney pronounced a notable encomium on *Amadigi*, which had not been published in any form when he wrote his *History* (he consulted 'his Majesty's complete score', presumably RM 19 c 5): 'a production in which there is more invention, variety, and good composition, than in any one of the musical dramas of Handel which I have yet carefully and critically examined'. If we remember that Burney reckoned an opera as the sum of its individual beauties and paid little regard to characterization or dramatic unity, this judgement is scarcely an exaggeration. The quality of invention throughout the score is exceptionally high, and perhaps only the absence of any voice lower than an alto in the small cast has restricted modern revivals.

Although the whole libretto is built round the magic episodes and transformation scenes, executed of course with the curtain up, Handel seems to have been little stirred by this aspect; at any rate he composed music for only three of them—the first appearance of the spirits that interrupts Amadigi's invocation to night and the scenes in Acts I and III where a symphony is specified in the libretto—and it is not particularly appropriate. Burney remarks that for the 'boisterous Simphony' before I vii 'Handel has given us a regular overture . . . good enough for the opening of any serious opera . . . but nothing picturesque or imitative is here attempted; perhaps the orchestras of these early times were not so powerful or able to execute new and dramatic ideas, as at present.' That was certainly not the reason. Handel had been equally reluctant to write descriptive music in *Rinaldo* and *Teseo*. Several dramatic episodes in *Amadigi*, notably Melissa's attempts to intimidate the hero by subverting the landscape and producing monsters in II iv and her conjuration of Dardano's ghost in III iii, have no music beyond secco recitative. There was to be a striking change in Handel's approach to *Admeto* and *Orlando*.

What did interest him was the emotions and the sufferings of the characters. While all four of them suffer, and can therefore inspire profound music, only Melissa acts consistently and carries conviction throughout. She is the strongest element in the libretto, and Handel makes the most of her. She has a good deal in common with Armida and Medea, but is a more subtle creation than either because she is so much more human. Her impulsive alternations of hatred and love, tenderness and violence, expressed in arias of great imaginative penetration, make up an imposing protrait of a woman scorned. Her closest affinity is not so much with the two earlier sorceresses as with Alcina; like her she ends by capturing the sympathy of the audience, and evidently of the composer as well. *Amadigi* is the first of nine works—six operas, two oratorios, and a masque—in which Handel, responding to the tone of the drama, tempers the final jubilations by ending in a minor key.

Melissa's first aria establishes her as a woman in love rather than a sorceress (Handel had made the same shrewd move with Medea in *Teseo*, and was to repeat it with Alcina). The introductory recitative,[7] after Amadigi's scornful departure, dramatizes the struggle in her heart. Her sense of outrage at first finds vent on the flat side of the tonal spectrum (F minor, C minor). Then, as pain and longing overwhelm her, the tonality veers towards B minor and E minor, the key of the aria. The intensity of her emotion is reflected in the suppression of the opening ritornello and a characteristic clash in the first bar. It is a superb Largo in 3/2, the voice's drooping phrases echoed and elaborated by a solo oboe against a quiet accompaniment of repeated string chords with the harpsichord silenced (Ex. 33). In the B section (*Allegro* 4/4 G major) her spirit recovers and she turns from complaint to denunciation. But not for long: after sixteen fiery bars—just enough to make a telling contrast—the da capo sounds more desolate than ever. The general plan and mood of this aria, though not its ritornello design, look forward to Alcina's 'Ah! mio cor'.

The rest of Melissa's music until her death scene (four arias and a duet) is quick in tempo (*Allegro* or *Presto*), and all except one aria in major keys. Her derision of Amadigi in 'Io godo, scherzo e rido' is not wholly successful; the gigue-like rhythm suggests that Handel was reflecting the literal meaning of the three words rather than the gloating behind them. It is too jovial for Melissa, which may account for Handel resetting it, though the second version is not an improvement. He recalled the original for 'Mirth, admit me of thy crew' in *L'Allegro*, where it is more in place. Melissa's music in the later acts lacks nothing in variety. We encounter her in turn denouncing Amadigi's cruelty in a hate duet, encouraging Dardano ('Se tu brami', full of lively cross-rhythms and exuberant guffaws from the violins), in a towering rage (a brilliant *aria di bravura* with trumpet and oboe obbligato to conclude Act II), resolute in putting love behind her ('Vanne lungi', with the violins in unison but the oboes divided), and finally pathetic. After the earlier displays of energy her sudden collapse is profoundly moving: the Ghost's words strip her of her last defences and reveal her love not as something that can be cured by incantations but as a tragic affliction that demands the ultimate sacrifice. The accompanied recitative has a touching pathos (for example the E flat chord after a G minor cadence when her steps begin to falter). The arioso, in broken sarabande rhythm with rests between each phrase as her life ebbs away and no ritornello until the nine-bar coda,[8] is very simple but so hauntingly beautiful that the trumpetings of Orgando's arrival and Amadigi's last aria seem a

---

[7] This would seem to be the classic context for a string accompaniment, but Handel set it secco.

[8] This and Melissa's first aria are the only pieces in the opera (apart from the *coro*) without an introductory ritornello.

Ex. 33

(Ah! merciless one! does not such a constant affection, which makes me pine away for you, move you?)

braggart intrusion. It is quoted here in its original form, with Melissa dying in the middle of a sentence; her final G was a later addition (Ex. 34, p. 280).

The other characters are less convincing in the round, but each has some magnificent music, especially Oriana, whose two love songs in Act I are both exquisite. Burney considered that Anastasia Robinson 'never had so good a

Ex. 34

(I already feel the soul in my breast leaving me . . .)

part assigned to her', and that 'Gioje, venite in sen' was the best aria he had seen in any of her parts. A siciliano whose serene melody is constantly extended by the voice into paragraphs of irregular length and beautifully interwoven with the string parts, it belongs to a familiar type. 'O caro mio tesor' is more unusual. The jerky double-dotted rhythm of the orchestra may be meant to convey Oriana's anxiety lest Amadigi should return too late. The use of the same material, rhythm, and scoring throughout both sections gives the music great spaciousness. The aria as printed suggests that Handel is playing a smoother single-dotted rhythm in the vocal line against that of the accompaniment; but probably the voice should conform to the instrumental rhythm, though without the semiquaver pauses, which would produce a breathless effect in a love song. An autograph copy of the aria in the Fitzwilliam Museum, in which all parts have single dots, tends to confirm this interpretation.

Finer still is Oriana's F minor lament 'S'estinto è l'idol mio' in Act II, when she finds Amadigi apparently dead. This is one of Handel's greatest tragic arias, rich in texture (the phrases constantly overlap), intricate in contrapuntal organization, and most expressive in harmony, especially in the B section, which explores the more recondite flat minor keys in the manner of 'Voi che udite' in Agrippina and 'Già lo stringo' in Act III of Orlando, likewise in their B sections. The long ritornello (eighteen Largo bars), spun from the opening phrase of 'Liebliche Wälder' in Almira, is characteristic of this score; that of Melissa's 'Desterò' at the end of Act II breaks records by running to 41 bars. Oriana's retort to Amadigi's unjust reproaches, 'Ti pentirai, crudel', is an effective spitfire piece with strong rhythms and irregular phrase-lengths, but it gives the impression of having been dragged in for the sake of variety instead of springing from the character, to which it contributes a shrewish element. The whole scene in which the lovers bicker in a manner scarcely becoming their station reflects all too clearly the weakening of the libretto.

After this Oriana rather fades out, though less completely than Chrysander's score, which gives her next aria, 'Ch'io lasci mai d'amare', to Melissa, would have us believe. It is far too light and bouncy for the situation, but was probably intended as a stopgap. Originally Oriana had a different aria here, 'Affannami, tormentami' in B flat, which makes a better connection after Melissa's cadence in D minor. Though scarcely vintage Handel, it is memorable for the sharply contrasted Adagio B section, the voice accompanied only by a light bass and a solo oboe, which has the rare luxury of a written-out cadenza. Handel probably wrote 'Ch'io lasci mai' for a new singer when Anastasia Robinson was taken ill after the first performance. Its catchy rhythm won immediate popularity, attested by the existence of two early sheet publications and two English versions,[9] which he was not then prepared to sacrifice. It makes no sense at all in Melissa's mouth; Chrysander assigned it to her because the copyist of the Hamburg score forgot to write in Oriana's name and omitted a stage direction.

Dardano's 'Pugnerò' has a stark appearance, since the accompaniment is in octaves throughout, but the irregular spacing of the paired demisemiquavers in a basic semiquaver pattern gives it tremendous rhythmic energy. Handel

[9] 'Love grows fiercer by denials' (two editions dated c.1720 by Smith, but P. A. Motteux, author of the English text, died in 1718) and 'Be kind bewitching creature' (MS copy in RM 18 b 16).

took the figure from a ritornello in Keiser's *Octavia*, and the whole piece bears the imprint of the Hamburg style. Dardano's second aria, 'Agitato il cor', though effective enough, makes an indifferent contrast with the first. It is in the same key and metre (G minor 3/8) and another rapid tempo, and employs similar rhythmic figures in the orchestra, though there is less octave doubling. Perhaps for those reasons Handel reset 'Pugnerò' in E major and common time; this version also looks back to Hamburg, bearing a distinct resemblance to 'Proverai' in *Almira*.

Both Dardano's Act II arias would be outstanding in any company. 'Pena tiranna', an agonized expression of the pains of thwarted love with a sarabande melody rather like 'Lascia ch'io pianga' in a minor key (both arias in fact derive from instrumental sarabandes in *Almira*), has an instrumental texture of unusual richness, with the strings in five parts (three violins), the harpsichord silent throughout the A section, and a single oboe and bassoon[10] operating independently in rhythms different both from the strings and from each other. The mournful suspensions of the bassoon in the ritornello, transferred to the oboe when the voice enters, give the music deep poignancy. In the closing ritornello and the B section the same material is neatly redistributed, the bassoon's running quavers passing to the basses and later to the oboe. 'Tu mia speranza', Dardano's one incursion into a major key, is also fascinating in texture. Violins and violas in octaves play a delicious melody in catchy dancing rhythm over a drone bass (at one point with an upper pedal as well), and the voice enters in a kind of free heterophony. The strange flavour of this aria—Burney with reason described it as 'more original and different, not only from other composers, but from Handel himself, than any of his airs that I have seen'—may be intended to suggest the dramatic irony in Dardano's situation. He sees happiness at last within his grasp, yet is about to die.[11] In Act III he appears only as a ghost; the string accompaniment, *Adagio e staccato*, of his brief arioso conveys the cold breath of the underworld with rare economy.

Amadigi is hardly the most attractive of Handel's heroes. He has the largest share of the music—eight arias, an accompanied recitative, and a duet with each of the prima donnas—but it is uneven in quality and he does not emerge as a strongly drawn character. One reason no doubt is that, like Rinaldo, he is impervious to seduction and so withheld from the extremes of spiritual conflict. His quick arias are somewhat anonymous. But he has only to suffer the pains of frustrated love to evoke wonderful inspirations from his creator, and they illustrate Handel's growing theatrical powers more vividly than anything else in the opera. His appeal to night in the first scene, like Elmira's 'Notte cara' in *Floridante*, is at once an exquisite nocturne and an example of how expectation set up by *opera seria*'s closed forms can be made to further the

[10] The earliest copies are specific that, except in the ritornello after the A section, both are solo obbligato parts.

[11] The material of Dardano's Act II arias haunted Handel's imagination: both are echoed or anticipated in the *Brockes Passion*, 'Pena tiranna' in 'Heul', du Schaum' (HG 61), 'Tu mia speranza' in 'Sprichst du denn auf dies Verklagen' (HG 82). A comparison of the contexts, while not conclusive, suggests that the German settings may precede the richer and more developed Italian. Mattheson in *Critica Musica* (Feb. 1723) says that Brockes's text was set first by Keiser (1712), then by Handel, Telemann (1716), and himself (1718). If his order is chronological, Handel's setting may have been earlier than the accepted but conjectural date of 1716–17, perhaps as far back as 1714 (see note, p. 297). The autograph is lost.

Ex. 35

(Alas! assist me, friendly night of repose, and comfort my sorrowing breast)

drama. After an accompanied recitative that creates a mood of romantic expectation largely by toying with the chord of the diminished seventh Amadigi addresses night in a beautiful G minor Largo, remarkable for its freely imitative three-part texture and flexible vocal line, at first broken, then unsymmetrically expanded as his pleas gain urgency (the vocal melody was to reappear transformed in *Alcina*) (Ex. 35, p. 283). This is interrupted by an Allegro string ritornello in F major in contrasted rhythm (3/8 semiquavers), leading not to the expected B section (there is none) but back into accompanied recitative and then—after two bars in which the voice is left bewildered and alone—into secco as Amadigi's attempts to escape are baffled by Melissa's sorcery and he turns to confront her with his sword. The surprise is expertly contrived, and the music runs on without a break. The librettist's introduction of infernal spirits here was an improvement on La Motte, who makes Melissa detain Amadis with a seductive tableau of shepherds and shepherdesses beginning with a 'Marche Champestre'.

The closing aria of the act shows Handel's structural cunning deployed in a different direction. It is another G minor Largo: Amadigi, derided by Melissa and forcibly separated from Oriana, begs fate to restore her or let him die. The tension between the controlled expressiveness of the vocal line and the jagged rhythms and bare accompaniment for unison violins and bass vividly conveys his desolate plight, and the point is driven home by the placing of the aria at the end of the act after four consecutive pieces in major keys, each with a much fuller orchestration. It is strokes of this kind that make the cutting of Handel's operas an artistically perilous operation.

The first scene in Act II is no less masterly. Amadigi addresses the fountain in a long cavatina of the utmost sensuous beauty, echoing the lilt of the Italian text ('Sussurrate, onde vezzose limpidette') and aptly graced by two recorders, which appear nowhere else in the opera. His disillusionment follows in a remarkable secco recitative; the music veers wildly into remote keys, and he faints in the middle of a word, leaving the harpsichord to conclude the episode with a seven-bar coda (Ex. 36). This is not the only point in the opera where the secco recitative is unusually bold: the first scene of all passes through a bewildering series of key centres, touching rapidly on C minor, G minor, E flat major, B flat major, F major, D minor, A minor, E major, F sharp minor, F sharp major, G sharp major, F sharp minor, D major, B flat major, G minor, and reaching a cadence in D minor before the aria in G minor.

Amadigi's next aria, 'T'amai quant'il mio cor', expresses his ambivalent feelings for Oriana in a first part that alternates abruptly between *Adagio* and *Presto*, as if he cannot make up his mind. The design is original and eccentric. The B section develops the *Presto* strain, and the opening of the da capo is so compressed as to blur the impression of a repeat. Neither of the duets is the conventional love scene, and both are highly effective. That with Melissa in Act II looks forward to a more famous duet of antagonism, 'Traitor to love' in *Samson*. The improvisatory working of Handel's invention may be glimpsed in the treatment of a triplet figure, first heard towards the end of the first part, as a primary element in the closing ritornello and B section. The imploring duet with Oriana has something of the atmosphere of a Bach church cantata. Amadigi's one aria in the last act bears a striking resemblance to a movement in the Water Music, with another long ritornello and a second trumpet

Ex. 36

(Ye gods! What do I see? Oriana caressing my rival and scorning me! Cruel,
perfidious, ungrateful one! Never again will I listen to the laments of a woman.
But already my heart is overcome by intense grief at her cruelty. I faint,
I die . . .)

obbligato. It is a splendid piece of bravura writing in hornpipe rhythm, but
like the gavotte aria 'È si dolce' in Act I, which is mostly scored for voice and
solo violin without bass, seems a little too obviously tailored to the demands of
the singer (Nicolini) rather than the character.

While the quality of the score, especially the first two acts, is remarkably high, it shows less careful organization than most of the later operas. The tonal design in particular seems off balance. On four occasions—twice running in Act II—we find two consecutive arias in the same key, a practice Handel avoided in his maturity except for a clear dramatic reason. As in *Teseo*, the choice of keys is limited; for nearly two-thirds of the opera the sharp keys are all but ignored. A very high proportion of the music is in B flat or G minor, including eight of the eleven arias in Act I, and most of these are in triple time. Amadigi's first two complete arias, 'Non sà temere' and 'Vado, corro', are extraordinarily alike. Both are B flat Allegros in 3/8 with unison violin accompaniments, the same material throughout each part, rapid divisions for the voice within the same narrow compass, and even a fermata on a silent bar towards the end of the A section. The second—based on the soprano aria 'Sorga pure dal orrido Averno' in the 1707 sacred cantata 'Donna che in ciel' and in the same key—can add little or nothing to what the first has said. It is a parallel situation to Dardano's two arias in Act I. If all four were not in the libretto, one might suppose two of them to be alternatives. It is just possible that this was the result of a conscious experiment in dramatic unity, but haste seems a more likely explanation. It would seem that the conception of an opera as a coherent structural organism was slow to capture Handel's imagination.

Despite Chrysander's statement in the preface to his edition, the music may not be complete. The single ballet movement is the pastoral dance at the end, which differs from the music of the *coro* only in the scoring. There must surely have been more to justify the 'variety of Dancing' mentioned in the advertisements; even if this was confined to entr'actes, Handel may have supplied the music, as he did in *Radamisto*. And the libretto makes provision in Act I for 'a Dance of inchanted Knights and Ladies', for which no music survives.[12] These persons and the shepherds and shepherdesses required in the finale were taken over from La Motte's libretto, whose manifold diversions include 'Troupes de Matelots et de Matelottes', 'Autre Troupe d'Esprits sous la forme de divers Peuples', and 'Autre Troupe d'Esprits sous la forme des Beautez les plus fameuses'.

The most striking feature of the musical texture, as in the three previous operas, is its virtual confinement to soprano and alto voices; the only movement in which a lower voice is heard is the *coro*, and the second part of that is a duet for Oriana and Amadigi. A handful of extra singers would be required here, a reinforcement the more urgent since half the original cast are dead; but they have a bare dozen bars to memorize, and the fact that the tenor line doubles the soprano at the octave may indicate that it was not strongly manned, or even that there were no tenors at all in 1715; one of the earliest copies omits the part. The tone colour must be regarded as an intrinsic element in the texture and not an excuse for octave transposition. The scoring, though less ambitious than that of *Rinaldo* and *Teseo*, is by no means lacking in variety. Besides the solo trumpet in two arias and the sinfonia for Orgando's arrival, the recorders in Amadigi's address to the fountain, and the rich sonorities of Dardano's 'Pena tiranna', both wind and strings are treated with

---

[12] According to Burney Amadigi's previous aria, 'È si dolce', was repeated as a dance; this is a possible solution, but he gives no evidence for the statement, and it is not supported by any of the copies.

characteristic resource. In the Allegro and Gavotte of the overture, the two duets, and the final dance Handel deploys a woodwind trio (two oboes and bassoon) in alternation with the strings. This division of course was conventional, but it is highly effective. There are a number of solos for violin and oboe, the latter again perhaps for Galliard. The continuo aria has disappeared, but it remained available when required for special purposes later.

History and Text

The first performance took place at the King's Theatre on 25 May 1715, with the following cast:

AMADIGI:	Nicolini (alto castrato)
DARDANO:	Diana Vico (contralto)
ORIANA:	Anastasia Robinson (soprano)
MELISSA:	Elisabetta Pilotti-Schiavonetti (soprano)

The small soprano part of Orgando may have been sung by Galerati. The opening was first scheduled for the 21st. Although the exact dates of composition are not known,[13] the occasion was undoubtedly the return to London of the great castrato Nicolini (? April) after an absence of three years. No other Handel opera was brought out for the first time so late in the season. The advertisements make it clear that exceptional care was lavished on the production: 'All the Cloaths and Scenes entirely New. With variety of Dancing . . . And Whereas there is a great many Scenes and Machines to be mov'd in this Opera, which cannot be done if Persons should stand upon the Stage (where they could not be without Danger) it is therefore hop'd no Body, even the Subscribers, will take it Ill that they must be deny'd Entrance on the Stage.' Burney declared that 'there is more enchantment and machinery in this opera than I have ever found to be announced in any other musical drama performed in England'. There were six performances, all by subscription (another, on 18 June, was cancelled owing to intense heat). Anastasia Robinson fell ill after the first; her replacement was probably Caterina Galerati.[14] The visual side of the production was so popular that on 27 August another opera, *Idaspe*, was put on 'with the Cloaths and several Scenes belonging to Amadis; with the Fountain Scene'.

Amadigi was revived on 16 February 1716 'with all the New Scenes, Machines, and Cloaths belonging to the Opera' and the original cast, including Anastasia Robinson, and again enjoyed six performances. The third (3 March) was for Miss Robinson's benefit, the fifth (20 June) for that of 'the Instrumental Musick', i.e. the orchestra. On this occasion the advertisements mentioned the fountain scene as a special attraction, and also 'Two New Symphonies'. One of these was the first movement of the concerto grosso in F (Op. 3 no. 4), sometimes known as 'the orchestra concerto'; the other may have been the second Allegro of the overture to *Teseo*. They were probably played between acts. The sixth performance (12 July) included 'a New Symphony' by Attilio Ariosti, 'in which he performs upon a New Instrument, call'd Viola D'Amour'.

[13] An advertisement of *Arminio* on 26 March with 'several new Scenes not seen yet, (design'd for a New Opera)' can only refer to *Amadigi*.
[14] This is suggested by a document in the *Coke Papers*, 237.

There were five more performances the following season, the first on 16 February 1717. The castrato Bernacchi replaced Diana Vico as Dardano; otherwise the cast was unchanged. *The Daily Courant* of that date announced that 'Mrs Robinson will perform all the Songs which was Originally Compos'd for this Opera'. This would seem to suggest either that she omitted some of them in 1716 or that her substitute (as might be expected) had sung different music in 1715. The advertisement for 23 February added the note: 'N.B. This Opera will be performed without Scenes, the Stage being in the same Magnificent Form as it was in the Ball' (one of Heidegger's masquerades on the 21st). For the third performance (21 March), another benefit for Anastasia Robinson, the advertisement read: 'With the Addition of a New Scene, the Musick compos'd by Mr Handel, and perform'd by Signor Cavaliero Nicolino Grimaldi [Nicolini] and Mrs Robinson. And Dancing by Monsieur de Mirail's Scholar, and Mademoiselle Cerail, lately arriv'd from Paris'. The new scene cannot refer to the duet 'Cangia al fine', as Deutsch supposed, since that occurs in the 1715 libretto; nor does the wording necessarily imply a duet. It was repeated at the next performance (11 April), for Nicolini's benefit, when the advertisement mentions 'several Entertainments of Dancing, by Mr Glover, and Mademoiselle Cerail; particularly, a Spanish Dance'. The last performance (30 May) was again for the benefit of the orchestra and included 'Two Pieces of Musick between the Acts', presumably the symphonies added the previous year. A burlesque *Amadis*, a harlequinade announced as 'a new Dramatick Opera in Dancing', had thirteen performances at Lincoln's Inn Fields between January and May 1718 and was revived a year later. The libretto of another Rich pantomime, *Harlequin Hydaspes* (Lincoln's Inn Fields, 27 May 1719) contains an *Amadigi* aria, 'Torni la gioja in sen'.

At least six arias not in HG[15] were composed for *Amadigi*, but the loss of both autograph and performing score and the absence of any libretto after 1715 make it difficult to place them. As already noted, Oriana's 'Affannami, tormentami', which appears in II ix in all librettos (including the Hamburg edition), was probably replaced by 'Ch'io lasci mai d'amare' when Anastasia Robinson fell ill in 1715, and 'Torni la gioja in sen', a florid soprano aria in C major, may have ousted 'Gioje, venite in sen' on the same occasion (one copy of the music has both sets of words). It is possible that 'Ti pentirai, crudel' was transferred to Melissa, in whose mouth it would be less out of place than the rest of Oriana's part; it carries Pilotti's name in two very early copies. The second setting of 'Io godo, scherzo e rido', a dull piece in the same key as the first (B flat), cannot be dated; so far as is known, Pilotti sang Melissa at every performance. The only copy of the E major 'Pugnerò' seems to pre-date Bernacchi's assumption of the part in 1717. The G minor alto aria 'Minacciami, non hò timor', a striking piece, is something of a puzzle. The low tessitura and the text suggest that it was addressed by Amadigi to Oriana during a quarrel; it may have formed part of the new scene added on 21 March 1717. The fact that the voice part begins with the same phrase as 'Affannami, tormentami' suggests that it was composed after the latter had been abandoned; the accompaniment is related to 'Tu giurasti' in *Il trionfo del Tempo*. It is possible that Handel set 'Sussurrate' as a da capo aria, dropping the B section after the printing of the libretto, which has three extra lines here.

[15] Four of them are printed in the appendix to the HHA score.

Other changes made after the first performance are listed below in connection with the Hamburg copy.

Handel never revived *Amadigi* after 1717, but it was quickly transported to Hamburg and produced there in September 1717 under the title *Oriana*. Handel's arias and duets were sung in Italian, but the recitatives, including 'Han' penetrato' and 'Ah crudo Amadigi', were supplied with a new German text by Joachim Beccau, who added three more characters and extra scenes in all three acts. The new music—seven arias, a duet, and a ballet at the end of Act II—was composed or arranged by Keiser. There were twelve further performances at Hamburg between 6 February 1719 and 12 September 1720. After a gap of two centuries *Amadigi* was staged at Osnabrück (1929) in a new German version by Hans Dütschke, Halle (1963), Copenhagen (1967), Abingdon (1968), Warsaw (1983), Urbino (1985), and Cambridge (1991).

Autograph

According to Schoelcher's manuscript catalogue in the British Library[16] the autograph of *Amadigi* was sold by the music dealers Calkin and Budd in 1844 for five guineas. The manuscript was described as containing 72 leaves, with 26 pieces of music, including two settings of 'Gioje, venite in sen' and several arias not mentioned by Burney.[17] The purchaser was Frederick Smee 'of Arundel Villas, Balham, and The Bank of England', a minor composer of church music. His music library was sold on his death, and the *Amadigi* score appeared in Puttick and Simpson's sale catalogue for 15 December 1879 with testimonials to its authenticity by E. F. Rimbault and T. M. Mudie. Julian Marshall bought it for £35. 10s.[18] but promptly returned it as not a genuine autograph. The auctioneers put it up again on 22 March 1880, quoting the former testimonials and statements by Marshall and W. G. Cusins that it was a copy by the elder Smith. It was bought in by A. H. Smee for nine guineas (a note in the margin of the sale catalogue in the British Library adds 'Marshall 40/-', presumably a payment for the inconvenience he had suffered) and disappears from history.[19] It cannot be identified with any known copy, but was certainly not the autograph, which was probably lost during Handel's life.

The only known autograph items for *Amadigi*, apart from insertions in one copy mentioned below, are a version of the aria 'O caro mio tesor' and an embellished keyboard arrangement of the overture, reduced from 132 to 104 bars and without the Gavotte, probably made for teaching purposes about 1725.[20] Both are in the Fitzwilliam Museum (Mus MS 256, pp. 41–3, and Mus MS 260, pp. 7–9). The former, reproduced in the HHA edition of the opera (XIV–XVI), is important for the ornamentation of the vocal line.[21] It

[16] RM 18 b 2, ff. 103–4.

[17] Burney discusses every piece in the HG score, though he does not quote all the first lines.

[18] Another manuscript score of *Amadigi*, 'complete with recitatives' (possibly one of those now in the Coke Collection), was sold to W. H. Cummings for half a crown on the same occasion.

[19] All published accounts of these transactions are incomplete or inaccurate in detail, not least the note, presumably by Chrysander, in *AMZ* for 18 Feb. 1880.

[20] It is on Italian Cantoni Bergamo paper used in autographs of that period. Best printed it in *Twenty Overtures*, i. 22.

[21] For a full account see W. Dean, 'Vocal Embellishment in a Handel Aria', *Studies in Eighteenth-century Music: a Tribute to Karl Geiringer*, 151; reprinted with corrections in *Essays on Opera* (paperback edition, 1993).

is neither a sketch nor a fragment of the main autograph, but a copy prepared for a singer—presumably an English singer. The tempo is *Larghetto*, the accompaniment (except for a violin part in the ritornello after the A section) for figured bass only, and the ritornellos are either shortened or omitted. It cannot have been intended for Anastasia Robinson in 1715 since, apart from changes in rhythm and note values, it contains alterations in the bass line and harmony, some of them so radical as to require considerable rewriting of the upper instrumental parts before they could be used in performance. Nor would Handel have headed it *Aria dell'opera d'Amadigi*. He seems to have been writing out the music from memory and (characteristically) to some extent recomposing as he did so. He may have prepared the manuscript for a concert, perhaps long after the production of the opera when his memory of the original had begun to fade.[22]

Librettos

1715. 'Printed for Jacob Tonson, at Shakespear's-Head over-against Catherine-Street in the Strand.' 51 pp. The composer is not named, and there is no Argument. Heidegger's dedication to Richard Earl of Burlington and Cork, in English only, pays fulsome tribute to the youthful nobleman's 'most refin'd Taste and mature Judgment' (he was twenty in 1715), adding that 'this Opera more immediately claims Your Protection, as it was compos'd in Your own Family'—presumably at Burlington House. The text differs from the printed score in two material particulars: Amadigi's arioso 'Sussurrate' has a B section of three lines for which no music survives, and 'Affannami, tormentami' appears in place of 'Ch'io lasci mai' in II ix. In the English version the arias are summarized, not translated. No libretto is known for the revivals of 1716 and 1717.

1717 Hamburg. 'Oriana . . . vorgestellet in Monath September 1717 . . . gedruckt mit sel. Friederich Conrad Greflingers Schrifften.' The recitatives, secco and accompanied, and the arioso 'Han' penetrato' are in German, the arias set by Handel in Italian with a German translation alongside. The text contains an extra pair of lovers, Dorinde and Ergastus, a foreign prince and princess, together with Dorinde's 'lustiger Diener' Diego, whose chief function is to conclude Act II with a drinking song followed by a comic dance of harlequins pursued by magicians. There are six inserted scenes, and an extra rage aria apiece for Melissa and Amadigi in Act I. Ergastus has three arias, Dorinde and Diego one each, and there is a duet for Dorinde and Ergastus immediately after that for Oriana and Amadigi in the middle of the *coro*. With the exception of one Italian aria for Ergastus, whose text comes from *Antonino e Pompeiano* (Bussani–Pollarolo, Brescia 1689, revived at Brunswick in 1709),[23] all the additions are in German. The libretto, which contains many extra stage directions but (as usual in Hamburg) names neither author nor singers, was evidently based on that of 1715. It has 'Affannami, tormentami' instead of 'Ch'io lasci mai' and the longer form of 'Sussurrate'.

A second issue (copy in Weimar Zentralbibliothek) has the final scene extensively reworked: Orgando's recitative is expanded, Calypso appears in Melissa's interest and delivers a vengeance aria, 'Eilt, ihr Furien, helft mir zu Rache', before retiring discomfited, Minerva in a recitative summons the

[22] The paper, type Cb, appears as late as 1731 and is of little help for dating.
[23] R. D. Lynch, 'Opera in Hamburg, 1718–1738', 482.

lovers to bliss in Ithaca, and the opera ends with a different chorus, 'So überwindet beständige Liebe'. Presumably this was all set by Keiser.

Copies and Editions

More manuscript copies survive of *Amadigi* than of any other Handel opera; one reason no doubt is that no score was printed. At least eleven of them date from before 1720,[24] a fortunate circumstance in view of the loss of both autograph and 1715 performing score, since they supply the only clues to the earliest text of the opera. The Linike copy in Hamburg (MA/1003), identified by Chrysander as the performing score and taken as the basis for both the HG and HHA editions, contains important modifications in the composer's hand, but cannot have been used for the 1715 performances; it does not contain 'Affannami, tormentami' or any of the additional arias, and shows no sign of their insertion or subtraction. Clausen calls it an archive score (that is, one for preservation in Handel's library) and dates it *c*.1717, which may well be correct. Nor is it the earliest surviving copy. That honour could belong to one of several manuscripts, all of which give the text before the Hamburg alterations. This group comprises, in addition to the Hamburg score as first copied: Coke I (Linike's early hand, the most accurate and almost certainly the oldest, ? 1715); Malmesbury (Newman, dated 1716); Flower (RM1, words ? Linike *c*.1716); Washington Littleton (RM1, words ? Linike *c*.1716–17); RM 19 g 2 (RM2, without recitatives); Add MS 47848 (RM4, *c*.1717–18); Washington Landon (Linike and Smith, incomplete aria collection); Coke II (overture RM1, remainder in an unidentified hand); and RCM 902 (twelve arias, copyist unknown).   *

Apart from Handel's amendments Hamburg MA/1003 is not among the most valuable sources. By the time it was copied Handel had already modified the text of the other copies at one point, simplifying the second violin part of 'Ch'io lasci mai d'amare' in bars 14 and 15. Moreover many details of scoring and dynamics and some stage directions had dropped out and various errors crept in (their gradual accumulation offers a clue to the date order of the copies). Handel corrected a number of wrong notes (as did later hands, including Chrysander's), but understandably did not bother with the rest. There can be no doubt that, like the first Coke *Teseo*, the best of these early copies—all except RCM 902 and perhaps Coke II written by scribes closely associated with Handel's pre-Smith circle—give the most authentic text, nearest to the lost autograph. The most informative are the near-related Coke I, Malmesbury, and Flower, especially the first two. Chrysander did not see them; unfortunately the HHA editor gave them low priority. A few of the extra details are cited here: the overture has many *solo–tutti* contrasts, especially in the cello part; the viola part in the A section of 'Ah spietato' is for bassoons as well (hence the tenor clef[25]); the bass of 'O caro mio tesor' is *senza cembalo* when the voice enters; the violins double the oboes in bars 55–6 of the duet 'Crudel, tu non farai'; there are several oboe solos in 'Se tu brami' and 'Dolce vita'; the final ritornello of 'Io già sento' is *pianissimo* (*piano* in some

---

[24] The Duke of Chandos owned a manuscript score of *Amadigi*, listed in Pepusch's catalogue dated 23 Aug. 1720.

[25] Bassoons are specified in Malmesbury and Flower; in Littleton a later hand has written *Violoncello*, presumably a conjecture based on the clef.

copies); in 'Sento la gioja' the voice has a long trill beginning at bar 54. Nearly every aria has unpublished dynamics, trills, or other directions. Important details of scoring, especially for the oboes, are discussed below in connection with the Flower parts, which also give the pre-Hamburg version.

The full heading of the first scene was evidently *Giardino di Melissa, di dove in lontano si vede la torre di Oriana. Notte.* It appears thus in Coke II, which though not one of the earliest copies reflects a very early source, containing several stage directions found in no other score and others in a unique form. Coke I and Malmesbury omit *la torre di Oriana*, producing nonsense. In Coke I, Malmesbury, and Flower the heading of I vii ends with the sentence *Oriana discende dal Trono.* These directions must derive from Handel's autograph. Only Coke I, Malmesbury, Flower, and Littleton have *riguarda nella fontana* after 'Sussurrate' (HG 45). This is not just an academic matter. The omission in Hamburg MA/1003 (and elsewhere) of *[Melissa] vuol partire ma Oriana la ritiene* immediately before 'Ch'io lasci mai' (HG 69) could account for Chrysander ascribing the aria to the wrong character.

The Malmesbury copy, signed and dated 1716 by Elizabeth Legh, is of exceptional interest: though not quite as free from error as Coke I, it contains three of the arias not in HG. The second setting of 'Io godo, scherzo e rido' is pasted in on two unnumbered leaves containing 'Affannami, tormentami' (a unique complete copy) and 'Torni la gioja'. All three are in Newman's hand and must have been inserted almost at once, the first a little later than the other two. 'S'estinto è l'idol mio' has vocal ornaments in a hand at first glance not unlike Handel's, probably that of Elizabeth Legh. They are mostly simple but include a short cadenza at the fermata (bar 60). The same hand added an independent bass to all the passages in 'Ch'io lasci mai' where the voice is accompanied or doubled by upper strings, that is to the whole aria apart from ritornellos. This copy alone has no tenor part in the *coro*. A later hand has written the names Oriana, Amadigi, and Orgando against the other parts, but there is no evidence that Orgando was ever sung by a bass.

Another copy of great interest is Washington Landon. In its present form it is a composite manuscript in three sections: (i) fourteen leaves in Smith's early hand (*c.* 1719) containing the sinfonia before I vii, the duet 'Cangia al fine', and four arias; (ii) 24 leaves written by Linike (*c.* 1716) containing the alto aria 'Nò, non così severe' (an insertion by Handel in the 1716 revival of Alessandro Scarlatti's *Pirro e Demetrio*)[26], eight arias from the pasticcio *Ernelinda*, only two of which are in the 1713 libretto (it was revived in the two following seasons with 'above half the songs new'), one aria, 'Occhi belli, occhi vezzosi', from the pasticcio *Lucio Vero* (in the 1715 libretto), which may also be Handel's, and fourteen arias from *Amadigi* in haphazard order; (iii) in a later unrecognized hand an aria from *Dario*, probably Ariosti's opera of 1725. The Linike section of the manuscript, which appears to be self-contained and earlier than the rest, has an alphabetical index of contents, damaged by cropping (as are several other pages). It includes two settings of 'Pugnerò', the second in E major otherwise unknown, and two of 'Gioje, venite in sen', the second the C major aria published as 'Torni la giojà in sen' in the appendix to the HHA score, 176–81. Linike wrote both sets of words at the same time. Many movements, especially

---

[26] See p. 184.

in the Linike group, have no tempo mark, but 'Vanne lungi' is *Allego* (not *Presto*), as in RM 19 g 2, Coke II, and RCM 902. The E flat 'Gioje, venite in sen', 'S'estinto', and 'Ti pentirai' are fully figured. A solo violin accompanies the voice in both parts of 'Tu mia speranza'. The first two *Ernelinda* arias, 'Volerà la mia vendetta' and 'Fier destin', are in Handel's manner and could well be his; the others seem anonymous or clumsy.[27] None of them has been identified elsewhere. The *Dario* aria has only an accidental connection with the rest of the manuscript, but the Smith section may have been copied as a supplement to the Linike; there is no duplication.

Of the other early copies, Littleton and Add MS 47848 show a decline in instrumental and dynamic detail and an increase in mistakes. RM 19 g 2, an untidy copy with many bass figures (in Act I only), omits the sinfonia in III vi as well as all recitatives. It is closely related to the aria collection RCM 902 and to Coke II. All three generally name the original singers, and the last two are full of errors in the Italian as well as the music. RM 19 g 2 and RCM 902 attribute 'Ti pentirai' to Pilotti instead of Robinson, contain only the A section of 'Notte amica', and mark 'O rendetemi' *Largo* without *Staccato*. RM 19 g 2 and Coke II mark 'Pugnerò' *Allegro* (with Malmesbury), 'È si dolce' *Allegro e staccato assai* (with Flower and RCM 902), and the first Presto in 'T'amai' *Allegro*. The naming of the opera before several arias in RCM 902 suggests that it was copied from diverse sources, and the fact that it never mentions Anastasia Robinson (her single aria being ascribed to Pilotti) may indicate a date when she was out of the cast. Pilotti is spelt in several ways, all of them wrong; 'Sussurrate' has oboes instead of recorders and a da capo at the end, possibly a relic of a lost B section. Coke II cannot be earlier than 1717, for it ascribes 'Pena tiranna' to Bernacchi (but 'Tu mia speranza' to Diana Vico). The quick part of 'Notte amica' is *Presto*. A note on the inner cover referring to the 1879 sale of the supposed autograph suggests that this copy, formerly in the collections of Bartleman and E. Goddard, may have been that sold for half a crown on the same occasion.

Malmesbury, Coke II, and the Flower parts, as well as the aria collections, omit the final Ballo. Where it occurs it has parallel octaves between viola and bass in bar 8, bowdlerized by Chrysander. The da capo is never written out, but was doubtless played by the complete orchestra. All early manuscripts have very erratic dotting in the duet 'Crudel, tu non farai'; it is regularized (as it was undoubtedly played) in later copies, followed by HG and HHA. Tempo marks vary in the overture: the second Largo is *Lentement* in Flower, *Lent* in RM 19 g 2, *Lente* in Coke II, the Gavotte *Allegro* in Coke I, Littleton, and Add MS 47848, *Presto* in RM 19 g 2. Another subject of constant variation is the time signature of the quick 4/4 movements, most of which vary between C and ₵. There appears to be no consistency here, and it is possible that no distinction was intended; even 'O caro mio tesor' is ₵ in Landon. Chrysander retains the *alla breve* signature only in the finale, HHA in the overture's Gavotte as well. More significant is the *segue subito* found from time to time, notably before and after 'Han' penetrato' and before 'Addio, crudo Amadigi'. This probably reflects theatrical practice, but is excluded from both printed editions.

Handel's revisions in Hamburg MA/1003 (? 1716 or 1717) affect eight

[27] One contains what appears to be an echo of 'Molto voglio' in *Rinaldo*.

movements. In the score as first copied and all the manuscripts hitherto mentioned bars 72–97 of 'Vado, corro' have a different verbal underlay, the first line of text being repeated several times instead of the second; the first two bars of the following recitative are a semitone higher in G sharp minor; the B section cadence of 'Agitato il cor' is one bar shorter, differing in the last six bars of the violin and bass parts and in Malmesbury in the voice as well (there is some evidence of corruption here; the copies offer different solutions); the tempo of 'Gioje, venite in sen' is *Largo*; 'O rendetemi' has two extra bars between bars 22 and 23; the two top instrumental parts in bar 28 of 'Sussurrate' repeat the notes of the second beat in the third; the tempo of the duet 'Cangia al fine' is *Vivace*;[28] and the voice falls silent in bar 18 of 'Io già sento' as in Ex. 34. The change from *Vivace* to *Larghetto* in 'Cangia al fine' confirms the evidence of 'Il vostro maggio' in *Rinaldo* that *Vivace* for Handel was an indication of mood rather than speed.[29]

Tenbury 884, *Opera of Amadis & Other Songs by Mr Handel* (Smith, *c.*1719), stands apart. Although apparently all written at the same time, it is an anthology evidently assembled from several sources. It contains no recitatives and no instrumental movements except the Ballo; gives most of the remaining pieces in the wrong order; omits 'S'estinto', 'Vanne lungi', 'Cangia al fine', 'Han' penetrato', and 'Io già sento'; and follows the bulk of *Amadigi* with a miscellaneous group of twenty arias from several early operas before ending with the *coro* and Ballo. Among the twenty are three additions to *Amadigi*—the second (4/4) setting of 'Io godo', 'Torni la gioja in sen' (C major), and 'Minacciami, non hò timor'—one aria from *Agrippina*, and three from *Silla*. Ten of the others have recently been published in the appendix to the HHA score of *Rinaldo* (1993). Most have been described in the chapters on *Rinaldo* and *Teseo*. The scoring of 'Torni la gioja in sen' in HHA is incorrect: in the ritornellos the top stave is for unison violins, the second for unison oboes; whenever the voice is singing the oboe part is a solo. A curious feature of Tenbury 884 is the inclusion of some Hamburg revisions (the underlay of 'Vado, corro', the omission of the two extra bars in 'O rendetemi') but not others (the changed tempo of 'Gioje, venite in sen', the modified bar 28 of 'Sussurrate'). For the B section cadence of 'Agitato il cor' it produces a unique variant of its own. The other three revisions are in movements not present. Bars 14–15 of 'Ch'io lasci mai' follow the Hamburg version. In 'Crudel, tu non farai' the oboes and violins have separate staves, confirming that all should play in bars 55–6.

The Shaftesbury score (S4, *c.*1736 or soon after) incorporates all but the most striking of Handel's changes in Hamburg: it includes the two extra bars in 'O rendetemi'. Otherwise it resembles that copy so closely as to suggest that it was taken from it. The note *Segue l'aria* between Melissa's line of recitative on HG 69 and 'Ch'io lasci mai' may indicate that S4 anticipated Chrysander's mistake. The remaining copies—Granville (S5), Lennard (S1 and S5), RM 19 c 5 (S13), and Fitzwilliam (copyist unknown)—are much later and of no consequence. Fitzwilliam (signed 'R. Fitzwilliam 1767') was copied from Lennard; both omit the bass in the last three bars of the B section of 'Tu mia speranza'. All four copies have the same text, apart from mistakes and an occasional dropped tempo mark, and derive from Hamburg, incorporating

---

[28] A few copies have no tempo here, doubtless an oversight.
[29] See p. 179 and n. 23.

the revisions. Lennard has many notes and indications for ornaments in a late eighteenth-century hand; 'Tu mia speranza' is marked *In C.*

The Flower parts, a complete set—violins 1 and 2 (+ 3 on a separate stave in 'Pena tiranna'), viola, cello + bassoon, oboes 1 and 2 (incorporating recorders), trumpet, and cembalo—were extracted by S2 in the mid-1740s from an unidentified early manuscript (not the Flower score) before the Hamburg changes. They do not include the overture, Act III sinfonia, or Ballo. The cello part contains a separate stave for obbligato bassoon in 'Crudel, tu non farai' and 'Pena tiranna', and the bassoon passages in the ritornello of 'Cangia al fine' are indicated; otherwise the instrument is not mentioned. Dynamics are scarce and there is a smattering of mistakes; the text is close to Add MS 47848. The source manuscript evidently lacked full instrumentation on the top line, for in five arias where nearly all copies specify unison violins—'Non sà temere', 'Agitato il cor', 'Io godo', 'Ti pentirai', and 'Ch'io lasci mai'[30]—S2 supplies oboe parts in the ritornellos (including the intermediate *tutti*). HG omits them, probably rightly; HHA includes them in four of the arias but oddly not in the last. A more important point arises in four-stave movements where all sources, early and late, that give any instrumentation at all have *Tutti* on the top line: the B section of 'Ah spietato', the sinfonia in I vii, 'È si dolce', 'O caro mio tesor', 'S'estinto', 'Dolce vita', and the *coro*. Here, except as usual in the *coro*, both oboe parts double the first violins, and that is unquestionably correct; the printed editions go astray. Both oboes play in 'Sento la gioja' and in bars 43–50 of 'Se tu brami'; a solo doubles the voice throughout this aria and accompanies it in 'Dolce vita'. Again the parts carry conviction, except that in bars 5–8 of the B section of 'Dolce vita' all the oboes and the first violins hold the D, a palpable error. HG is correct here but omits the oboe solo (in every pre-Hamburg source) at bar 38; HHA omits all oboe solos in this aria and 'Se tu brami', as well as in 'Torni la gioja' and the B section of 'Affannami, tormentami'. This may be the result of a faulty guide-line for the entire HHA edition, that when the first oboe plays alone it is automatically a solo. That of course is a *non sequitur*.

A very early volume of arias in the Coke Collection, already mentioned in connection with earlier operas, contains fourteen items from *Amadigi* (both duets, eleven arias, and the accompanied recitative 'Ah crudo Amadigi') in two old-fashioned hands working in collaboration, supplemented once or twice by a third. 'Non sà temere' is in D major. Bars 14 and 15 of 'Ch'io lasci mai' have the original second violin part; 'Io già sento' takes its amended form, but this is a later addition by the third hand. The presence of the second Allegro of the *Teseo* overture (figured, with the second violin part in the soprano clef) on the same pages as 'Ch'io lasci mai' is the only evidence that it may have been used in *Amadigi*; but excerpts from both operas are intermingled throughout the manuscript. The later '24 Opera Songs' include 'S'estinto' (in G minor), 'Gioje, venite in sen', 'Ch'io lasci mai', and 'Io godo', all with string accompaniment and a few simple vocal ornaments. Also in the Coke Collection are a copy of 'Minacciami, non hò timor' (*aditional to Amadis*) in the miniature hand of the third Coke score of *Teseo*, and a decorated harpsichord arrangement of 'Ah spietato' (A section only).

'S'estinto' occurs again in G minor in Durham Cathedral Library (Bam-

---

[30] 'Io godo' has *Tutti* in Coke I and Littleton, 'Ch'io lasci mai' *Unisoni* in Malmesbury. RM 19 g 2 has a casual *Unisoni* almost everywhere, but was not S2's source.

burgh MS 70, pp. 18–21) in the hand of the Hon. Edward Finch, brother of the second Earl of Nottingham and Prebendary of York (1664–1738), and— in the usual F minor—in RM 18 c 1, ff. 6–9 (S2) and RM 19 d 12, ff. 28–31 (H9). These three copies have the bass figured. The duet 'Cangia il fine', with the original *Vivace* tempo but ascribed in error to *Il pastor fido*, appears in Add MS 31571, ff. 1–10 (early Smith, *c*.1719) and with slightly altered text ('Cangia il fatto', no words in B section) in RM 19 d 12, ff. 58–61 (? RM2). The Shaftesbury volume of miscellaneous arias mentioned in connection with *Rinaldo*, *Teseo*, and *Silla* (S4) contains three of the extra pieces in the HHA appendix, the second setting of 'Io godo', 'Torni la gioja in sen' (both *Allegro*), and 'Minacciami' (no tempo). Keyboard arrangements of the overture and other instrumental movements are numerous and confusing, since the sinfonia in I vii and the first movement (or the whole) of Op. 3 no. 4, both in F major, appear indiscriminately under the label Overture, Second Overture, Third Overture, or Symphony. They can be tabulated as follows:

Overture in straight transcription, probably from Malmesbury score: two copies in the Malmesbury Collection (RM1, *c*.1717; Smith, *c*.1728), Drexel MS 5856 in New York Public Library (Smith, *c*.1721).

Overture in Handel's shortened arrangement, *c*.1725: Rivers MS in Coke Collection (Smith junior, *c*.1727), RM 18 c 1, ff. 2–3 (S2, *c*.1728; the Gavotte on f. 38ᵛ). These copies have a few further changes, which may possess Handel's authority.

Sinfonias in I vii and III vi in straight transcription: two Malmesbury copies (RM1, *c*.1717; Smith, *c*.1728), Wesley MS in Coke Collection (Smith, *c*.1721), RM 19 a 4, ff. 7–9 (S2), Add MS 31577 ('Gulielmus Bogdani', ? owner, copyist, or both).

Op. 3 no. 4 in straight transcription: complete in two Malmesbury copies (Linike, *c*.1717; Smith, *c*.1728), Coke Wesley MS (Smith, *c*.1721, with octaves added by Handel to the bass in bar 11 of the opening Lentement), Add MS 31577 ('Gulielmus Bogdani'); first movement only in RM 18 c 1, ff. 3ᵛ–5 (S2, *c*.1728).

An S1 copy of the concerto in score in the Fitzwilliam volume of 'Miscellanys' (Mus MS 798) is described as *2ᵈ Overture in Amadis, called The Orchestra Concerto*. The two violin parts of an altered and much contracted version of this concerto in an unknown hand in Add MS 34074/5, headed *Overture Orchestre*, are not specifically linked with the opera.

A manuscript 'cantata' for soprano and strings in the Leipzig City Library,[31] consisting of 'Gioje, venite in sen' and 'È si dolce' with linking recitative, like the similar cantata formed from two arias in *Rinaldo*, is unlikely to have Handel's authority.

No score of *Amadigi* was published during Handel's life or for long after. A few arias appeared with English versions in fugitive publications, mostly in short score: 'È si dolce' (in C major) and 'Tu mia speranza' (*A Song in Imitation of the Bagpipes*) in *The Monthly Mask of Vocal Music* for May 1718 and February 1720 respectively, 'Ch'io lasci mai' (in F major) in two single-sheet editions, and 'Non sà temere' in volume ii of *The Pocket Companion* (December 1725). Walsh's 1732 miscellany *The Favourite Songs in yᵉ Opera Call'd Thessus & Amadis* reprinted 'È si dolce' and 'Ch'io lasci mai' in the same keys from old plates.

31 Baselt, *Verzeichnis*, i. 155 n. 5.

1. Stage of Teatro San Giovanni Grisostomo, Venice, 1709.

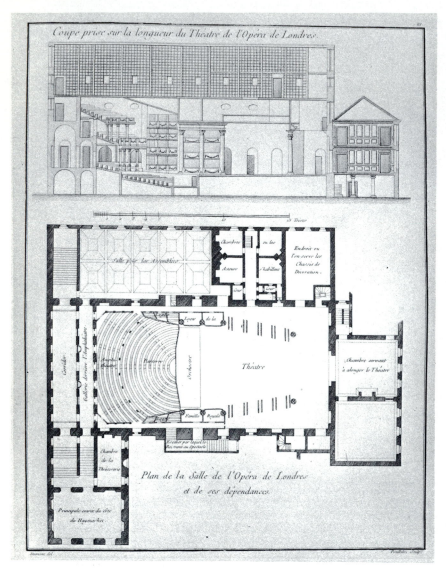

2. Elevation and plan of the King's Theatre in the Haymarket
after the alterations of 1707–8.

Vue laterale du grand Theatre roial, avec les Loges
et le Parterre.

3. Interior of Neues Opernhaus on the Zwinger, Dresden, during performance of
Lotti's *Teofane*, September 1719.

Elevation du grand Theatre roial , pris de façe ⁓

4. Stage scene in Lotti's *Teofane*, Dresden, September 1719.

5. Autograph of original opening of 'Ah! crudel' in *Rinaldo*, Act II.

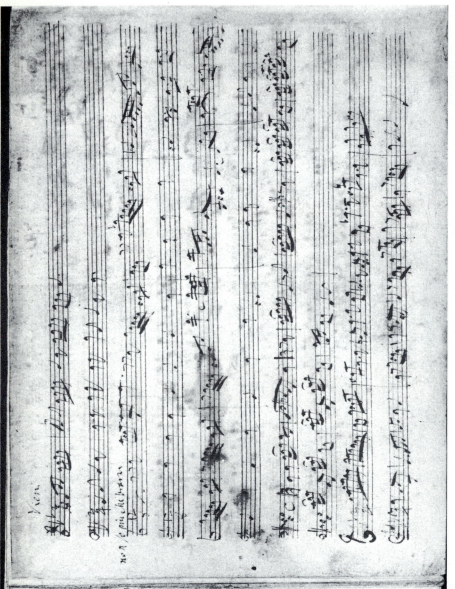

6. Autograph sketches for *Teseo* (1712) on blank page in autograph of *Rodrigo* (1707).

7. *Teseo*, Linike copy (December 1712), showing recitative for Fedra in Act V, suppressed before performance.

8A. Stage set for *Rinaldo*, Act III, Hamburg Theater am Gänsemarkt, November 1715.

8B. Stage set for final scene of *Giulio Cesare*, Hamburg Theater am Gänsemarkt, November 1725.

9. Paolo Rolli, portrait by Giovanni Battista Bellucci.

Tutta l'ira del ciel ful' crin mi piova.
   Pol. *Per te vedrai morirmi*
Quand' il mio fpofo infulti alla tua vita.
Ma fe tu porti offefa a i giormi fui
Voglio ancora fpirar morir per lui.
   Rad. *Morir per un Tiranno*
Per chi offende egualmente
La Natura, e l'amore ?
Per chi tien Farafmane *in fra catene ?*
Per chi infulta il mio onore ?
Per chi vuol la mia morte ?
Temer per lui ? tu amare
Un barbaro ? un infame ?
   Pol. *Così vuol la mia fede*
Così la gloria mia da me rtchiede.

   Rad. Vanne forella ingrata
Vanne, e rapifci a morte
Quel barbaro conforte
Che te tradifce ancor ;
Tu mi vedrai morire
E ne faprà gioire
Quel tuo fpietato cor.
     Vanne forella, &c. [Parte.

SCENA X.

POLISSENA fola.

Tra il German, tra lo fpofo
Che rifolver degg' io? " *mi fa crudele*
" *Tutta la mia pietade. Ah giufti numi*
" *foccorretemi voi, reggete il core,*
" *Rifchiarate la mente.* [Sta penfofa alquanto.
Sì: operò quel che deggio, e il mio configlio,
Sarà quello falvar, ch è più in periglio.

10. Libretto of *Radamisto*, April 1720, prepared for use as prompt copy.

11. Performing score of *Radamisto* (Act II), December 1720; signatures, voice part, and bass written by Smith, upper parts, dynamics, and amended scoring by Handel.

12. Autograph of *Tamerlano*: discarded and alternative versions in final scene of Act II.

13. Stage of the King's Theatre in the Haymarket, *c*.1725.

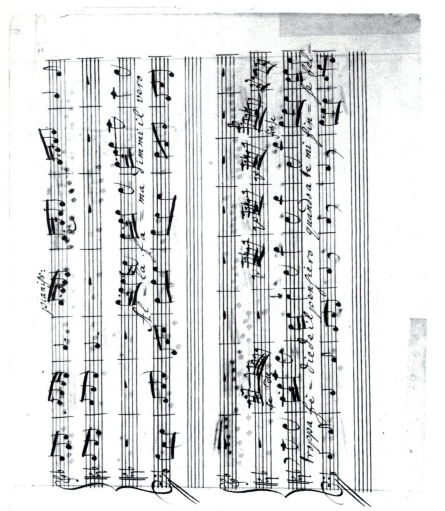

14. Smith copy of 'Alla fama' in *Ottone* (transposed), with vocal ornaments added by Handel, mostly on viola stave, ?1727.

15. Performing score of 1734 revival of *Il pastor fido* (Act III), showing hands of Smith (three top systems) and S1.

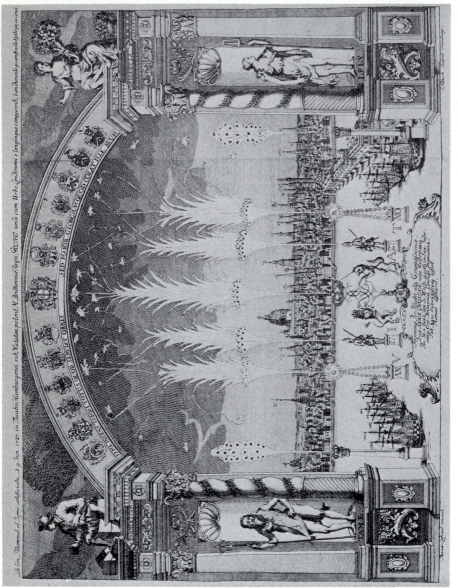

16. Thomas Lediard's design for fireworks in epilogue of Hamburg production of *Giulio Cesare*, 9 June 1727.

Walsh issued the overture in parts (the second Largo *Lentement*) about 1725, a clumsy harpsichord arrangement (not that of the MSS) in 1726, a straight keyboard transcription of the 'Second Overture' (first movement of Op. 3 no. 4) in 1728, and the duet 'Cangia al fine' among *The Favourite Songs* in the pasticcio *Solimano* in 1758.

Chrysander's score (1874) is based on the Hamburg copy as amended, with minor changes for the worse. There are two issues bearing the same date, the first almost devoid of scene headings and stage directions (as in the Hamburg copy), the second containing those of the printed libretto, which Chrysander must meanwhile have discovered. Unfortunately the Gregg Press reprint (1965) used a copy of the first. The HHA score (1971), also based on Hamburg, was published too soon to benefit from recent scholarship, though it includes four of the additional arias in an appendix.

Additional Notes

* (p. 291) Since this chapter was written a remarkable new source* has been discovered, an incomplete set of six instrumental parts in the Fürstenberg Library, held on film at the Deutsches Musikgeschichtliches Archiv, Kassel. They were evidently prepared, from a collection of detached movements, for a purely orchestral performance, since they incorporate the vocal line (generally given to the first oboe), omit two accompanied recitatives, the *coro*, and five arias, including Dardano's entire quota, and present the movements in a chaotic order. They include two arias not in HG, 'Affannami, tormentami' and 'Torni la gioja in sen', and one entirely unknown aria whose material appears, differently treated each time, in two earlier and one later work (see Appendix D under *Flavio*). Two familiar arias, 'Notte amica' and 'Non sà temere', appear in considerably longer form found in no other source, the former with a slightly higher tessitura. Five arias have a number of stylish ornaments squeezed in by a second hand; though intended for instruments, they would be equally suitable for the voice.

These parts, which must reflect a very early state of the score, perhaps while Handel was still working on it, suggest that (as with *Ottone*, *Giulio Cesare*, and *Tamerlano*) he revised the opera extensively before performance, and that he may have conceived the part of Amadigi for a different singer. If the 'New Scenes design'd for a New Opera', advertised with *Ernelinda* on 4 December 1714, as well as those advertised on 26 March 1715 (see p. 161), refer to *Amadigi*—no new scenery was advertised for *Lucio Vero* in February—Handel must have composed the opera at least six months before its production.

* (p. 294) RM 19 c 5 was probably copied from Granville about 1785.

* For a full account, see W. Dean, 'A New Source for Handel's *Amadigi*', *M&L* lxxii (1991), 27–37.

CHAPTER 16

THE ROYAL ACADEMY TO THE ARRIVAL OF FAUSTINA BORDONI, 1719–1726

A misunderstood enterprise (p. 298)—foundation of Academy (p. 299)—singers' proposed salaries (p. 302)—plans for orchestra (p. 303)—seat prices (p. 303)—first season delayed (p. 304)—arrival of Bononcini and Senesino (p. 306)—Bononcini in ascendant (p. 306)— faction and discord (p. 306)—Astarto (p. 310)—Bononcini's Vienna operas (p. 311)— Heidegger's masquerades (p. 312)—Griselda (p. 313)—Italians in trouble (p. 314)— arrival of Cuzzoni (p. 315)—Coriolano (p. 315)—renewed faction (p. 318)—Handel's first pasticcio (p. 321)—Swiney as agent (p. 322)—Faustina expected (p. 323).

FEW musical enterprises of the past have been more misunderstood than the Royal Academy of Music. Published accounts for the most part are incomplete, draw false conclusions from the known facts (even when, as is not always the case, these are stated correctly), and confuse artistic, social, and financial values. The Royal Academy was the most comprehensive attempt in the eighteenth century to establish high-quality opera in London, and arguably the most ambitious scheme of its kind before the foundation of the Arts Council in the present century. Not only did it import the greatest performing artists of the age—that has often been done since; it commissioned large numbers of new operas from three of the leading composers in Europe. Although it lasted for nine seasons instead of the twenty-one originally projected (soon reduced to fourteen) and succumbed to the notorious financial instability of opera, especially on the international level, it conferred a lasting benefit on English musical life—London has seldom since been without opera—and on posterity, which is still enjoying the fruits. Contemporary journalists drew satirical comparisons with the South Sea Bubble, and modern commentators have been unable to resist pursuing the parallel. Judith Milhous and Robert D. Hume, to whom we owe the discovery and elucidation of much valuable documentation on the period, recently called the plans of the Academy 'naive' and referred to 'the sheer folly of the undertaking'.[1]

It was neither naïve nor foolish, nor was it even extravagant. That legend arose in the eighteenth century as the result of inaccurate statements about the amount of capital raised. Mainwaring quoted a figure of £40,000; Burney and Hawkins, followed by Chrysander, Streatfeild, and others, raised it to £50,000. Burney declared 'that a sum amounting to £15,000 had been sunk in a little more than a year'—without including the product of the 4 per cent call in July 1721 to clear the deficit. It is now accepted that these figures are a gross exaggeration, but many writers, taking their cue from Burney's word 'sunk', use emotive terms like 'squandered' and repeat the false conclusion that the

---

[1] 'New Light on Handel and the Royal Academy of Music in 1720', *Theatre Journal*, xxxv (1983), 149–67.

Academy was recklessly mismanaged. Under close examination the evidence shows that, while the prospectus was too sanguine (prospectuses frequently are), it was a perfectly reasonable business proposition into which the organizers entered with their eyes open and which they carried on for a not inconsiderable time. Vanbrugh, who may have played a leading part, in a letter of 18 February 1720 to Jacob Tonson, said that the opera 'will be a very good one this year, and a better the next. They having engag'd the best Singers in Italy, at a great Price. Such as I believe will bring the Expenses to about twice as much as the Receipts. But the fund Subscribed being about £20000, may probably Support it, till Musick takes such root, as to Subsist with less aid.' A number of rich opera-lovers ventured £200 each, which they could well afford to lose; in return London enjoyed nine of the most glorious seasons in its history and some of the finest operas of the eighteenth century. The South Sea Bubble was floated on air; the Royal Academy, born coincidentally at the same time, was inspired by love of a great art form. While such matters are not susceptible to judgement in mechanistic terms, the benefits on any computation were prodigious.

In Mainwaring's words, 'during the last year of [Handel's] residence at Cannons, a project was formed by the Nobility for erecting an academy at the Haymarket. The intention of this musical Society, was to secure to themselves a constant supply of Operas to be composed by Handel, and performed under his direction.' The implication is that the idea originated with Handel's patrons, including presumably Chandos and Burlington, with his cognizance, and that he was to be in sole charge. Many writers, misled perhaps by some sentences of Mainwaring's two pages later, have assumed that Bononcini and Ariosti were involved from the start. This was not so. Bononcini was approached as the result of a minute of a directors' meeting on 30 November 1719, and arrived nearly a year later for the Academy's second season. Ariosti, though already in London (the directors consulted him about singers on the same occasion), did not compose for the Academy till the fourth season (1722/3). Two letters which he wrote from Paris to Giuseppe Riva, the Modenese envoy in London (1 February and 3 March 1720, NS), seem to imply that he had been the Academy's first choice for setting *Numitore*: 'I did not want to be the first, when I had the honour to be sent for by the gentlemen of the Academy, which I do not merit and consequently do not expect' (3 March).[2] Like most of the correspondence of Riva's circle the letters are obscure and full of malicious gossip. The Academy commissioned Giovanni Porta's *Numitore* on 2 December 1719.

The plans must have been laid well back in 1718; a letter of 15 September that year from Senesino to Riva mentions plans on foot for a London opera season.[3] On 20 February 1719 Handel wrote apologetically to his brother-in-law M. D. Michaelsen, whose wife (Handel's sister) had died the previous July, that he must postpone a visit to his mother in Halle because 'I find myself kept here by affairs of the greatest moment, on which (I venture to say) all my fortunes depend; but they have continued much longer than I had antici-pated'. On the following day the *Original Weekly Journal* jumped the gun by

[2] Lindgren, *M & L* (1977), 7–8.
[3] Lindgren, 'La carriera di Gaetano Berenstadt'.

announcing that 'Mr Hendel, a famous Master of Musick, is gone beyond
Sea, by Order of his Majesty, to Collect a Company of the choicest Singers in
Europe, for the Opera in the Hay-Market'. The documents in the Public Record
Office[4] and others recently discovered by Milhous and Hume among the Duke
of Portland's papers in Nottingham University Library[5] confirm that the
project was well in train. It proposed the floating of a Joint Stock Company
financed by capital of £10,000 divided into fifty shares of £200 each.

By February the Attorney General had confirmed the legality of the
scheme, and the King had not only reacted favourably—hence the title Royal
Academy of Musick, suggested perhaps by the Académie Royale de Musique,
the official title of the Paris Opéra—but signalized his willingness to provide a
subsidy of £1,000 for seven years. He formally granted this in early May and
ordered the incorporation of the Company. Meanwhile, probably in April,
the organizers issued a detailed 'Proposall for carrying on Operas by a
company and a Joynt Stock'.[6] This prospectus begins with an eloquent
defence of opera, perhaps from the pen of Vanbrugh, one of the original
directors.

Opera's are the most harmless of all publick Diversions. They are an Encouragement
and Support to an Art that has been cherished by all Polite Nations. They carry along
with them some Marks of Publick Magnificence and are the great Entertainment
which Strangers share in. Therefore it seems very strange that this great and opulent
City hath not been able to support Publick Spectacles of this sort for any considerable
time. The reason of which seems to be cheifly that they have been hitherto carried on
upon a narrow Bottom of Temporary Contributions Extreamly Burthensome to the
People of Quality[7] and entirely unproportioned to the Beauty Regularity and
Duration of any great Designe . . . As the Operas themselves will be in greater
Perfection that [sic] what have hitherto appeared (Joyning what is excellent both in
the French and Italian Theatre) so they will undoubtedly procure better Audiences
And by the Constancy and Regularity of the Performance the Taste rendered more
universall.

The Duke of Newcastle as Lord Chamberlain was to be 'perpetuall
Governour of the said Company' and a board of directors elected, who would
lease a theatre, offer a 'yearly Sallary and Pensions' to singers, orchestral
players, and dancers, and purchase 'the Utensills that are requisite for
carrying on their Designe'. To this end they would make periodical calls on
the subscribers. They expected that these would amount to no more than 20
per cent of the capital, and hoped to declare dividends and offer a profit of
25 per cent. The issue was rapidly over-subscribed. Deutsch prints a list of 63[8]
subscribers apparently dating from the summer of 1719, but several of them,
including Newcastle, Chandos, Burlington, and Portland, took more than one
share; and a later list owned by Burney carried 73 names. The extra ten were
perhaps those admitted at the directors' meetings on 30 November and 2
December, mentioned below. This would give a total capital of £17,600, not

---

[4] Excerpts printed by Deutsch and by J. M. Knapp, 'Handel, the Royal Academy of Music,
and its First Opera Season in London (1720)', *MQ* xlv (1959), 145–67. Deutsch contains many
errors, not least about the voices of singers.

[5] 'New Light on Handel'.

[6] Printed in full by Milhous and Hume, ibid. 165–7.

[7] This suggests that the nobility had been called in to rescue earlier ventures.

[8] Not 62 as he states on p. 91.

far short of the £20,000 mentioned in Vanbrugh's letter. A few more persons may have subscribed between December and February.

The Academy's charter, dated 27 July 1719 (when the subscribers numbered 58) and printed in full by Milhous and Hume,[9] clarifies a few particulars. The Deputy Governor and 15–20 directors were to be elected annually on or soon after 22 November. A 'General Court' of shareholders was to be held every three months, a directors' meeting once a month; either could be summoned more frequently if the Governor wished. Holders of £200 stock had one vote, those of £600 or more two. The Governor enjoyed an absolute power of veto, and the Company would forfeit the royal bounty if it disobeyed him. Anyone who refused to pay a call would forfeit his stock; this clause was constantly invoked as a threat in the next few years, but there is no evidence that it was ever enforced. It is clear from the minutes that all prospective shareholders had to be personally recommended, and approved by the directors.

On 14 May 1719 Newcastle issued a warrant to 'Mr Hendel Master of Musick . . . forthwith to repair to Italy Germany or such other Place or Places as you shall think proper, there to make Contracts with such Singer or Singers as you shall judge fit to perform on the English Stage'. He was empowered to sign contracts for one year only, except with Senesino, who was to be engaged 'as soon as possible to Serve the said Company and for as many Years as may be', and report to the directors on his proceedings and the terms on which 'an excellent Voice of the first rate' was to be had. After visiting the Elector Palatine's court at Düsseldorf and his family in Halle he reached Dresden by early July. Here the Elector of Saxony had, since 1717, maintained the finest opera company in Europe under the composer Lotti, including the sopranos Durastanti and Salvai, the castratos Senesino and Berselli, Guicciardi (the tenor who had sung in *Rodrigo*), and Boschi (bass). On 15 July Handel reported to Burlington that he was on the point of engaging Senesino, Berselli, and Guicciardi. The negotiations then stalled; Senesino and Berselli accepted another year's contract at Dresden, and Guicciardi never came to London. In the event the Elector dismissed all his Italian singers early in 1720 after a quarrel between Senesino and Heinichen at a rehearsal of the latter's *Flavio Crispo*. By that time it was too late to engage any of them for the Academy's first season.

In the autumn Newcastle called a number of meetings of the subscribers. The board of directors chosen on 18 November, twenty in number, included Portland, Burlington, Vanbrugh, and Arbuthnot; a week later the Duke of Manchester was appointed Deputy Governor. The minutes of three directors' meetings held on 27 and 30 November and 2 December are informative.[10] Handel was told to offer Durastanti £500 for the short first season of three months from 1 March 1720 and £1,600 if she stayed for the second as well (if not, she was to receive £100 for her journey home), and to return to London with the bass Grunswald (?Gottfried Grünewald) on the terms agreed and with 'the proposalls of all the Singers he has treated with'. Heidegger, the lessee and manager of the King's Theatre, was deputed to treat with Baldassari and Galerati, and Arbuthnot to approach Anastasia Robinson.

[9] 'The Charter of the Royal Academy of Music', *M & L* lxvii (1986), 50–8.
[10] Deutsch prints only extracts; Milhous and Hume give the complete texts, 'New Light on Handel', 151–3.

Baldassari and Galerati's husband were present at the second meeting. At the third the directors resolved to offer Anastasia Robinson £300, Galerati £250, and Baldassari £200 for the first season, and Galerati £400 for the second. Several other important decisions were taken at the second meeting: that Heidegger be asked to approach Senesino through Riva 'to engage him to be here in October next, to Stay till the End of May on the most reasonable terms he can get him . . . & to make his Offer for two years in case he finds him more reasonable, proportionably for two Years, than One'; 'That Mr Hendel be Master of the Orchester with a Sallary'; and that Bononcini 'be writ to, To know his Terms for composing & performing in the Orchester'.

The directors' eagerness to obtain Senesino, who had eluded Handel, was rewarded: early in 1720 he sent Riva a power of attorney to accept an offer of 3,000 guineas, evidently for two full seasons. He also wrote to Riva on 3 March recommending Salvai: 'She has a most beautiful voice, a good figure and enough talent for the purpose, on which you could obtain more exact advice from Mr Handel'.[11] Handel's salary is never mentioned again; we do not know its amount or how it was paid. Nor do we know Bononcini's terms. The invitation to him may have been proposed by Burlington, who had attended rehearsals of his *Astarto* in Rome in 1715,[12] and had just returned from another visit to Italy. Bononcini had other supporters among the subscribers, including Manchester and Henry Boyle, Lord Carleton, who had been concerned in the earlier attempt to engage him in 1707, and he counted Paolo Rolli, the newly appointed Secretary of the Academy, and Riva among his friends. Rolli, according to his biographer Giambatista Tondini, had been invited to London 'to encourage the Tuscan tongue' by 'Mylord Steers Sembuck'. This composite nobleman seems to have been a conflation of the eighth Earl of Pembroke and the second Earl of Stair.[13] Rolli spent 29 years (1715–44) in London and became a Fellow of the Royal Society. He was a prolific author in many fields, like Haym, but not a musician.

The Portland documents throw some oblique light on these negotiations, and on the general preoccupations of the directors. The surviving estimates of expenses—one (PwB 93a) for the short spring season, two (PwB 92 and 93b) for the full season to begin in the autumn—are not dated, but were clearly prepared some time in advance. Milhous and Hume assign PwB 93a to early December 1719; but it is by no means certain that the higher fees there set down for Anastasia Robinson (£500, her projected full fee for 1720/21) and Baldassari (£250) reflect salary inflation—they may well represent a precautionary estimate before the offers were agreed on 2 December—or that the singers' salaries 'cannot have totalled much less than £2,100'. The offers amounted to £1,250, to which must be added the fees for three local singers, Ann Turner Robinson, Alexander Gordon, and the minor bass Lagarde, who are unlikely to have been expensive.[14] The estimates for 1720/21, tentatively dated December 1719 and March 1720, introduce the names of Cuzzoni, La Romanina (Marianna Benti Bulgarelli), and Faustina (possibly a confusion

[11] G. Bertoni, 'Giuseppe Riva e l'opera italiana a Londra', *Giornale storico della letteratura italiana*, lxxxix (1927), 317–24.

[12] According to Rolli's dedication of the London libretto (1720) to Burlington. Rolli directed the Rome production.

[13] G. E. Dorris, *Paolo Rolli and the Italian Circle in London 1715–1744* (The Hague, 1967), 132 ff.

[14] Mrs Dennis, a very obscure singer, appeared in *Numitore*, which has no bass role; she was probably paid by the night.

with Cuzzoni). There is no concrete evidence of negotiation with them, though La Romanina was still in the running when Ariosti wrote his letter to Riva on 3 March. PwB 93b proposed the exorbitant number of nine singers at £6,400. Not surprisingly the directors decided to 'deduct one woman & a man', in order to save £900. In fact the woman deducted was 'Faustina', the most expensive at £1,500, and Anastasia Robinson only joined towards the end of the season. The figures for scenery, dancers, and incidentals are all up on the first estimate, which was certainly too low, and some items, such as the salaries of Handel, Rolli, and the Deputy Treasurer,[15] are not mentioned at all. They may have been paid from a separate account. It would be risky to place much reliance on these very rough memoranda.

The three documents dealing with the composition of the orchestra, for which the directors set up a committee, are more informative. All date from mid-February 1720. The earliest, PwB 94, written by Portland (who may have chaired the committee), lists 31 players and estimates an outlay of £473 for the first season and £946 for the second, plus about £100 for a lute (theorbo) and a trumpet. PwB 98, dated 15 February, specifies 34 players with their instruments; PwB 97 modifies this slightly, since three musicians proved to be out of town, and proposes one or more replacements. The orchestra listed in PwB 98 consists of seventeen violins (in three 'ranks', 8 + 5 + 4), two violas, four cellos, two double basses, four oboes, three bassoons, a theorbo, and a trumpet. This is rather larger than the orchestra of ten years earlier,[16] with greater strength in the violins and oboes and the addition of the theorbo. One of the cellists probably doubled at the second harpsichord, the first being played by Handel. It is a substantial orchestra for the period, and includes nearly all the top performers in London, many of whom had played in earlier operas. Haym, Loeillet, Kytch, Chaboud, and Linike are still on the roll. Among the new names are the Castrucci brothers, the cellist Filippo Amadei, formerly with Ottoboni (all three brought over by Burlington in 1715), John Festing (oboe), and the Swedish composer and violinist J. H. Roman.

The Portland papers include an estimate of box-office receipts based on three price ranges and a capacity below stairs (pit and boxes) of 413 persons (PwB 95). The galleries could accommodate perhaps another 350,[17] though the directors did not expect to fill them; by this time the second gallery was never advertised, perhaps because it was kept for liveried footmen who were admitted free after keeping places for their employers below stairs.[18] For the first season, except the first two nights of each opera (six performances in all), the directors settled for the middle range. The prices on the six expensive nights were 10s. 6d. for pit and boxes, 5s. for the gallery. Tickets other than for the gallery had to be bought in advance; no money was taken at the door. Later performances were cheaper: pit 5s., boxes 8s., gallery 2s. 6d., stage boxes 7s. 6d.—raised to 10s. 6d. on 14 May, when admission to the stage itself was offered at one guinea. This practice had been abolished earlier (see p. 152). It continued for the rest of the season, but seems then to have been dropped except on benefit nights. Milhous and Hume call these prices steep. Though

---

[15] Appointed by a resolution recorded in the minute of 27 November.

[16] See p. 154.

[17] J. Milhous, 'The Capacity of Vanbrugh's Theatre in the Haymarket'.

[18] A notice in the *Daily Advertiser* of 30 Dec. 1734 reads: 'Whereas an Abuse has been discover'd in admitting Persons into the Footmens Gallery; Notice is hereby given, that for the future no Persons out of Livery will be admitted into that Gallery' (cited by Milhous, ibid.).

higher than those charged at the playhouse and by the French comedians when they played at the King's, they were the same as in Heidegger's earlier seasons and, in view of the inevitable expense of opera, seem by no means exorbitant. However with the arrival of the foreign star singers in the autumn the cheaper prices were found to be uneconomic and abandoned. On all opera nights pit and boxes were then put together at 10s. 6d., with admission to the gallery at 5s. These prices remained unchanged until the Academy closed in 1728, though the number of tickets sold for pit and boxes was variously restricted, first to 400, later to between 340 and 360. The lower figures were to allow room for seasonal subscribers, who from November 1721 paid 20 guineas for a guaranteed 50 nights.[19] The directors were evidently in two minds as to whether shareholders should be admitted free. This was expressly ruled out in the minute of 30 November 1719, but a deduction for 53 subscribers was allowed for in PwB 95. The Governor, Deputy Governor, and directors certainly had free passes;[20] on special occasions such as benefit nights the press regularly announced that the directors 'resolve not to make use of their Tickets for the Liberty of the House for this Night'.

Milhous and Hume make various hypothetical estimates of nightly takings in relation to projected expenses. Their statement that 'the company would * have done very well indeed to average £120 a night' takes a far too gloomy view, especially after the price rise in the second season, and leaves out of account several possible sources of income: the sale of printed librettos, the charge of one guinea for admission to rehearsals (not always advertised), the proceeds from masquerades and concerts,[21] and payments from other members of the Royal Family for use of the King's box, which we know were substantial in 1732/3.[22] Moreover the contracts with singers (other than Durastanti and later Cuzzoni) ruled out the benefits that had earlier been so frequent. No figures for box-office receipts have yet come to light.

The Academy was forced to postpone the opening of its first season, which Vanbrugh in his letter of 18 February expected to be about 10 March 1720. The theatre had been let to a company of French comedians who performed harlequinades from 5 March and continued during the run of the operas, even causing the postponement of the first night of *Radamisto* 'at the particular desire of several Ladies of Quality'. Their quality is open to question. The season eventually opened on 2 April, not with *Radamisto* as might have been expected but with *Numitore*, the only opera Porta wrote for London. The scenic designer, named in the libretto, was Roberto Clerici. Durastanti was the sole imported singer. The third and last opera was Domenico Scarlatti's *Narciso* (30 May), first produced as *Amor d'un'ombra e gelosia d'un'aura* at the Queen of Poland's private theatre in Rome in 1714. The score had been brought from Italy by Thomas Roseingrave, who composed four extra pieces (two arias and two duets) in Act II and according to Burney conducted it. Although 30 performances had been planned, there was time only for 22

---

[19] This arrangement lasted until the 1727/8 season, when it was dropped as too easily abused.

[20] So had the surviving subscribers (1703) to the building of the theatre, as Vanbrugh confirmed in a letter of 13 Oct. 1720 to his brother Charles. (Gibson, *The Royal Academy*, 126).

[21] See below, p. 312.

[22] See Milhous and Hume, 'Handel's Opera Finances in 1732–3', *MT* cxxv (1984), 86–9.

before the season closed on 25 June.[23] On the last night of all three operas (during the final week) Margherita de l'Epine came out of retirement to sing Ann Turner Robinson's part, a remarkable feat if she included all the music.

Rolli dedicated the libretto of *Numitore* to the directors of the Academy, naming all 22 including the Governor and Deputy Governor. He based it on the Romulus and Remus story in the first book of Livy's *History*, adding a sub-plot, a prison scene with the administration of a sleeping draught in the guise of poison, and the inevitable disguises and misapprehensions, as a result of which Romulus narrowly escapes marriage to his mother Rhea Silvia. Rolli was likewise responsible for the *Narciso* libretto, but apart from suppressing one character and adding texts for Roseingrave's pieces he made few changes to C. S. Capeci's original. This was inevitable if Scarlatti's music was to be retained, though Rolli's dedication to the Princess of Wales characteristically claims responsibility for about half and fails to name Capeci. The plot combines two well-known episodes from Ovid's *Metamorphoses*, the legends of Echo and Narcissus and Cephalus and Procris, but undermines the first by making Narcissus fall in love with Echo's reflection, not his own, and the second by allowing Cephalus to give Procris a slight wound instead of a death blow. It is a feeble libretto; Narcissus and Echo (three times) attempt suicide, always providentially interrupted, and a love dart goes the rounds introducing fresh complications.

Walsh and Hare published most of the set pieces from both operas. Handel was later to find *Numitore* useful as a quarry for ideas in *Samson* and *Solomon*.[24] A full score of *Narciso* in its London version, without one of Roseingrave's duets, turned up recently in Chrysander's library in Hamburg.[25] Burney thought *Numitore* 'superior to that of any preceding opera which we had had from Italy'—he was unaware that Porta was already in England as virtuoso of the Duke of Wharton (1698–1731), a notorious young rake—but was less enthusiastic about *Narciso*, contrasting 'the sobriety and almost dulness' of the songs with 'the original and happy freaks' of Scarlatti's harpsichord music. However neither opera is negligible. Porta wrote well for singers, giving Gordon (Numitore) agile arias with a high tessitura and Anastasia Robinson (Lidia, an Alban patrician whose lover has been killed by the villain) mostly simple dance-like songs, but also, when she is about to take poison, an interesting arioso–recitative with changes of mood and tempo. A graceful siciliano for Durastanti (Romulus) was admired by Burney. *Narciso* contains five siciliano arias and a final *coro* in the same rhythm, but is more remarkable for occasional strokes of unconventionality: a love song for Narcissus, the A section Andante with solo violin and four-part pizzicato strings, the cello in the tenor register detached from the bass line, the B section a 3/8 Allegro; an aria for Cephalus interrupted in both sections by recitative for Procris and ending in the dominant; a jealousy aria for Aristeo in which the strings end the A section in C major after leaving the voice on B♮ ('freddo gel'); and a very effective C minor aria for Eco contemplating suicide, the A section ₵, the B section a siciliano.

Only in its second season did the Academy get fully under way. In

[23] See Table 4, pp. 308–9.
[24] See W. Dean, *Handel's Dramatic Oratorios and Masques*, 334–6, 523.
[25] See A. D. McCredie, 'Domenico Scarlatti and his Opera *Narcisso* [sic]', *Acta musicologica*, xxxiii (1961), 19–29.

September, just after the bursting of the South Sea Bubble, a powerful posse of Italians arrived in London: Senesino, Berselli, Salvai, Boschi, and not least Bononcini. A fresh board of directors was elected, with ten new names. Lord Bingley succeeded Manchester as Deputy Governor; Vanbrugh and Burlington remained, but not Arbuthnot. The season opened on 19 November with Bononcini's *Astarto*, an old opera adapted by Rolli from a libretto by Zeno based on two plays by Quinault (originally set by Albinoni for Venice in 1708) and dedicated to Burlington. It was first staged at Rome in January 1715; 25 of the 33 arias were retained in London.[26] The Academy made special arrangements. 'Neither Directors nor Subscribers will be admitted on the Stage.' There was 'Misbehaviour' in the upper gallery, and the directors threatened to close it on the second night 'unless they behave themselves more quietly and decently'. Despite the presence of 'a proper officer . . . at each Door' some people at later performances obtained unauthorized admission. On the day of the eighth (14 November) the directors announced that although only the usual number of tickets were delivered 'several Ladies who had Tickets have been disappointed of seeing the Opera for want of Room, and others were obliged to stand during the whole Performance'. They threatened to 'discharge any of the Boxkeepers who shall be detected in letting in any Person whatsoever without a Ticket'.

This was a measure of the success of Bononcini and Senesino. The Colman Opera Register noted that *Astarto* and its successor *Arsace* 'took much, very fine' and added an interesting detail about Senesino: 'his Singing [like Durastanti's] much admired, he supplyed Sig[r] Nicolino's absence & is in person & action very like him'.[27] *Astarto* received 23 performances, the highest total in one season of any opera produced by the Academy, and for two years Bononcini's operas dominated the King's Theatre stage, outnumbering Handel's by 71 performances to 26.[28] Although there was a revival of *Radamisto* in December, this was the only Academy season for which Handel did not compose an opera, apart from his contribution to *Muzio Scevola*. Mainwaring talks of 'musical disorder' during the winter, but it is clear that more than musical differences divided the parties during the next three or four years. Most of the surviving correspondence comes from the Italian side. Rolli's letters are full of scandal and snide insinuations, and often obscure to the point of incomprehensibility. Deutsch introduced further confusion by identifying the Alpine Faun or Alpine Proteus so often mentioned by Rolli with Handel; he was certainly Heidegger, who came from Switzerland. The Italian party—Bononcini, Riva, Senesino, the Florentine merchant and diplomat Giovanni Giacomo Zamboni, later Berenstadt, Cuzzoni, and other singers—formed a close-knit group, some of whom at least were not above making trouble. They had supporters among the nobility, including the Earl of Peterborough, lover and later husband of Anastasia Robinson, who was a Catholic and much more sympathetic to Bononcini than to Handel. During the summer of 1721 Bononcini, Riva, Peterborough, Anastasia, Pope, and Lady Mary Wortley Montagu were living in close proximity at Twickenham.

[26] Most of the factual information about Bononcini in this chapter is taken from L. Lindgren, *A Bibliographic Scrutiny*.

[27] K. Sasse, *HJb* (1959), 213; not in Deutsch.

[28] The performance totals in Table 4 differ slightly from those given in *The London Stage*, which does not always allow for cancellations.

Most of them were Catholics, as was the Duchess of Buckingham, to whom Pope wrote (? January 1722) of 'the ill treatment he [Bononcini] has met with here'. This cannot refer to the reception of his operas. The discovery in the spring of 1722 of a Jacobite–Catholic plot to overthrow the King and restore the Stuarts inevitably drew the Italians and their supporters closer together,[29] while Handel's association with the Royal Family ranged him with Walpole's government in the eyes of a society prone to intertwine artistic and political conflicts.

We have little positive evidence of Handel's attitude to anybody at this time, and none at all of personal antagonism between him and Bononcini. Since Bononcini was a cellist, he and Handel presumably accompanied the recitatives in all the operas. The faction was instigated by third parties, whose fanaticism eventually approached that of a modern football crowd. Mainwaring's reference to 'the perfect authority which Handel maintained over the singers and the band, or rather the total subjection in which he held them' confirms what we know from other sources—that he was a strict disciplinarian—and must be counted a virtue. It may have irked the singers; his rebukes to Gordon and Cuzzoni are the subject of well-known anecdotes, and Senesino was notoriously vain and touchy.

There was a plan to put on Steffani's *Tassilone* with recitative adjusted by Bononcini during the 1720/1 season.[30] Unfortunately it came to nothing, perhaps because it required too many singers (there are nine characters), and the second new production was *Arsace* (1 February 1721), an adaptation by Rolli of Salvi's *Amore e maestà*, set by Orlandini for Florence in 1715, with fourteen additional arias by Amadei. This had been proposed by Senesino and Durastanti, who sang the leading roles in Florence; in the previous September the directors had instructed Rolli to 'examine and shorten it' and supply additional arias for Senesino. According to Rolli, Heidegger's suggestion that the score should be arranged by Girolamo Polani, a Venetian composer who had come over with Salvai, provoked a major row with Senesino. Another of Rolli's reports, that Durastanti had annoyed the directors, and apparently her husband Casimiro Avelloni, by becoming pregnant and would return to Italy regardless of her salary, proved wide of the mark. She sang throughout the season, and on 2 March the King stood godfather to her daughter. After the triple *Muzio Scevola*, an operatic Cerberus, to which Amadei, Bononcini, and Handel each contributed an act with its own overture, the Academy produced a second Bononcini opera, *L'odio e l'amore*, under the title *Ciro* on 20 May. Rolli prepared the librettos for both, as he did for nine of the ten operas during the first three seasons; the exception was *Radamisto*. The Academy reached its target by giving 57 opera performances and three concerts (at full opera prices), for which 'the Stage will be illuminated, and put in the same Form as it was in the Balls'. The programmes consisted of Alessandro Scarlatti's serenata *La gloria della primavera*[31] (28 March) and 'above 30 Songs, chosen out of former Operas' (14 June), sung by the principal members of the company.

[29] The manuscript diary of Antonio Cocchi, a Florentine doctor resident in London from March 1723 to July 1726, throws some light on the activities of the Italian circle; excerpts are quoted in Lindgren, *A Bibliographic Scrutiny*, 330–8.

[30] According to a letter from Riva to Steffani, cited by Gerhard Croll in his preface to the full score (Düsseldorf, 1958).

[31] Identified by E. Gibson from a copy of the libretto in the Folger Library, Washington. Durastanti had sung in it at Naples in 1716.

TABLE 4. *Opera Productions by the Royal Academy*

	1720	1720/1	1721/2	1722/3	1723/4	1724/5	1725/6	1726/7	1727/8	Total
Numitore (Porta)	7									7
Radamisto	10	7	4						[some]	21+
Nariso (D. Scarlatti/Roseingrave)	5									5
Astarto (Bononcini)		23	6							29
Arsace (Orlandini/Amadei)		9	3							12
Muzio Scevola (composite)		10		3						13
Ciro (*L'odio e l'amore*) (Bononcini)		8		5						13
Floridante			15	7				2		24
Crispo (Bononcini)			18	4						22
Griselda (Bononcini)			16							16
Ottone				14	6		9	2		31
Coriolano (Ariosti)				13	2					15
Erminia (Bononcini)				8						8
Flavio				8						8
Farnace (Bononcini)					6					6
Vespasiano (Ariosti)					9					9
Giulio Cesare					13	10				23
Calfurnia (Bononcini)					11					11
Aquilio consolo (Ariosti)					4					4
Tamerlano						12				12

TABLE 4. *Opera Productions by the Royal Academy*

	1720	1720/1	1721/2	1722/3	1723/4	1724/5	1725/6	1726/7	1727/8	Total
Artaserse (Ariosti)						10				10
Rodelinda						14	8			22
Dario (Ariosti)						6				6
Elpidia (pasticcio/Handel)						10	5			15
Elisa (pasticcio/? Ariosti)							6			6
Scipione							13			13
Alessandro							13		4+	17+
Lucio Vero (Ariosti)								7		7
Admeto								19	9	28
Astianatte (Bononcini)								9		9
Teuzzone (Ariosti)									3	3
Riccardo Primo									11	11
Siroe									18	18
Tolomeo									7	7
Total	22	57	62	62	51	62	54	39	52	461
									?+11	?+11

Note. Newspapers are missing for part of January and February 1728. There were probably 11 performances of *Alessandro* and *Radamisto* during this period.

HANDEL: 235 (probably 246) performances of 13 operas, +28 of *Muzio Scevola* and *Elpidia*.

BONONCINI: 114 performances of 8 operas, +13 of *Muzio Scevola*.

ARIOSTI: 54 performances of 7 operas.

OTHERS: 30 performances of 4 operas.

The third concert, which ended the season (5 July), was a benefit for Durastanti, who sang new cantatas by Sandoni and Handel (probably 'Crudel tiranno amor,' HWV 97) and, with Senesino, four arias and six duets by Steffani. On 9 July the directors made a sixth call on subscribers, amounting to 29 per cent in all, to clear the season's deficit. This reflects not extravagance but the inevitable expense of launching the Academy. The final total of 21 calls[32] came to 99½ per cent, so that the subscribers paid an average of 10 per cent (£20) over the remaining seven seasons, one of which brought them a dividend. Not for the last time the directors made threatening noises at defaulters, and on 31 October proposed to publish their names and prosecute them 'with the utmost Rigour of the Law'. There is no evidence that they did so, or that an action would have succeeded: the defaulters would merely have forfeited their deposits. No doubt the South Sea Bubble had interfered with their cash flow.

All the arias and the instrumental movements in *Astarto* were published by Walsh. Burney submitted the score to the detailed scrutiny he usually reserved for Handel, and tried hard to be fair. While bestowing faint praise on some pieces, he comprehensively damned the whole, and the public as well. 'The spirit of party, ignorance of good Music, and an unformed and trivial taste, must have enhanced its value with the public; but, for my own part, I am not only unable to point out a single air in which there is dignity, originality of design, or a fanciful melody, but to discover that tenderness and pathos, for which Bononcini has been so celebrated, even by those who denied his invention and science.' A revival in London in April 1976, with the lost recitatives unidiomatically supplied, offered an opportunity to test this judgement. The plot, involving a forged letter, another letter without an address, and a pretended murder, is devious, stilted, and clumsy. It is easy to see why *Astarto* was more successful than *Radamisto*, which as Streatfeild remarked probably went over the heads of the audience, and why it has since been forgotten. The basic idiom is close to Handel's, but the music lacks his energy, inventive power, unpredictability, and feeling for character. The arias are mostly short and slight, with initial ideas that tickle the ear but never tax it; they are almost never developed, falling instead into sequences which, as Burney said of one of them, become 'more and more tiresome at each repetition'. There are a couple of agreeable duets, a plaintively melodious siciliano in Act II for Senesino, making his London début as an admiral (at this point under arrest), and several pieces just saved from monotony by a change of mood and tempo in the B section. As a rule Bononcini's B sections, like those of most composers at this period, repeat the A sections' motives in a different key without adding to their force. The arias for Boschi are similar to Handel's, but generate less energy. Even the best movements, thanks to their shortwindedness, suggest nothing so much as Handel on an off day.

A few externals apart, Bononcini's powers had advanced little in the quarter century since *Xerse* (1694)[33] and *Camilla*. Twelve *Arias from the Vienna Operas* of 1706–10 edited by Anthony Ford,[34] presumably chosen to represent

[32] All can be dated from contemporary newspapers. Deutsch's citations are incomplete and sometimes inaccurate; Burney mentions the majority, including several not in Deutsch. Vanbrugh's accounts (Downes, *Vanbrugh*, op. cit.) show that he paid all fifteen due during his life, the last two eleven days before his death on 26 March 1726.

[33] Full score in Add MS 22102; facsimile in Roberts, *Handel Sources*, viii.

[34] London (1971).

him at his best, permit a glance at his work during the interim. They show an occasional willingness to experiment in scoring, inspired no doubt by facilities available in Vienna, and the treatment of ritornellos. 'Ebbi di lui pietà' in *Abdolomino* (1709) has an initial ritornello for chalumeau, transverse flute, and bassoon *senza cembalo*; in *Muzio Scevola* (1710) 'Come quando alle mie pene' employs solo violin and theorbo, and 'Vado inventando' a fairly rich texture with elaborate violin and cello solos. The A section of the latter, an Andante, ends with a sudden Presto ritornello followed by a Largo cadence, and the storm aria 'Combattuta' from the same opera drops from Allegro 3/8 to Largo 3/4 in the middle of the B section. But these excursions carry little conviction. The occasional elaborate obbligatos—there is one for archlute in Act II of *Xerse* ('Il core spera')—are flashy rather than expressive. Bononcini is happiest in contrapuntal textures, where the absence of long-breathed phrases is no disadvantage. The flavourless treatment of the Neapolitan sixth in the siciliano 'Innamorato core' (*Endimione*, 1706) offers a revealing contrast with the use of the same chord by Alessandro Scarlatti and Handel; the violin suspensions in the (new) ritornello after the A section of 'Come quando alle mie pene' are softened by arpeggiation just where Scarlatti or Handel would have emphasized them. Hawkins, who like Burney strove hard for impartiality, may be allowed the last word. 'The style of Bononcini was tender, elegant, and pathetic; Handel's possessed all these qualities, and numberless others, and his invention was inexhaustible.'[35]

Little can be said about the music of the other two operas. Of *Arsace* only three arias were published, and one of them is by Lotti; of *L'odio e l'amore* two, though fifteen survive in manuscript in Dublin. *Arsace* however has a remarkable libretto. Salvi based his *Amore e maestà* on Thomas Corneille's *Le Comte d'Essex* and acknowledged this while transferring the location to Persepolis as more suited to Italian opera. It is one of the very few librettos of the period (Salvi claims it as the first) with a genuine tragic end, and it remains true to the spirit, if not the facts, of history. Arsace (Essex) is undermined by foolhardiness and pride, Statira (Elizabeth) torn by love, jealousy, and political expediency; in the last scene, after Arsace's execution, she calls down the furies on her head. We might be in the world of Donizetti. Rolli's dedication to the Duke of Montague drew attention to the English source. *L'odio e l'amore* on the other hand has a preposterous libretto, which Rolli in his dedication to Newcastle claimed to have altered and completely recomposed from Matteo Noris's original. The Persian King Cyrus has a general of the same name. Act II begins with a scene in which Queen Thomyris, the victim of the emotions indicated in the title, orders all the male characters to dip their swords in *a Vessel full of Blood*, supposed to be that of the king but in fact that of his namesake, an action that provokes supernatural intervention and the sudden onset of darkness. Senesino had sung in Orlandini's setting of this text at Genoa in 1709 and no doubt proposed it to the Academy.

The 1721/2 season began with revivals of *Arsace* (1 November), *Astarto*, and *Radamisto*. New productions were delayed because Durastanti was compelled to cancel through illness, thus promoting Anastasia Robinson to the position of prima donna. Galerati was not re-engaged, and Baldassari replaced Berselli. Vanbrugh wrote to the Earl of Carlisle on 16 November: 'We are a little Cripled in our Opera, by a Letter from Durstanta; that She is not well,

[35] *History*, ii. 861.

and can't be here this Winter, they go on however and two New Operas are preparing [presumably *Floridante* and *Crispo*], but Heydegger is much in fear the Bishops won't let his masquerades appear, till the Plague's over. I am told however, the King thinks that no very Stanch reason.' Heidegger's masquerades had been a popular social event for some years:[36] Vanbrugh told Tonson in the letter of 18 February 1720 quoted above that they 'go on with their wonted Success, they are limited to Six in a year'. It is not clear to what extent they contributed to the Academy's budget; the Prussian envoy reported in July 1717 that each brought Heidegger 300 or 400 guineas net. They were presented under various titles in an attempt to confuse the aim of the bishops. Twice during this season, on 15 February and 6 March 1722, Heidegger combined them with special concerts and advertised them as ridottos. At the first the 'Entertainment of Musick' consisted of '24 Songs chosen out of the late Operas', performed by the leading singers; on 6 March 'some new Cantatos' by Bononcini were added, and the price of seats was raised to a guinea.

On the eighth night (25 November) the directors announced the annual subscription scheme already mentioned, subscribers to pay their 20 guineas in three instalments, and guaranteed 50 performances (in fact there were 62). To accommodate them the usual number of 400 tickets for pit and boxes was reduced to 350 for the first night of *Floridante* on 9 December. The other new operas were both by Bononcini, *Crispo* on 10 January and *Griselda* on 22 February. All three were popular, Bononcini's more than Handel's. Vanbrugh wrote cheerfully to Carlisle on 6 April: 'The Publick Divertions here have flourished as if nobody had left the Towne; the opera in particular, which confirms me still more that Musick has taken deep root with us.' As a consequence the Academy during the following winter declared its first and only dividend, of 7 per cent. According to the *London Journal* of 16 February 1723 'it is thought, that if this Company goes on with the same Success as they have done for some Time past, of which there is no doubt, it will become considerable enough to be engrafted on some of our Corporations in the City, the Taste of the Publick for Musick being so much improv'd lately'.

Handel was still in charge, but much of the success was due to Bononcini. In addition to his two new operas and a revival of *Astarto*, he scored another bull's-eye with the publication of his *Cantate e duetti*, dedicated to the King. There were 238 subscribers for 442 copies (at two guineas each), more than Handel ever enjoyed—a fact that led Chrysander to suspect foul play. Pope (who was tone-deaf) had canvassed assiduously for Bononcini, and some of his aristocratic supporters subscribed for between 30 and 55 copies. The popularity of *Griselda* no doubt owed something to its sentimental flavour and to the fact that the story, as Burney remarked, seemed to reflect the personal circumstances of Anastasia Robinson, who played the low-born heroine, a shepherdess first cast out into the wilderness but finally restored to the dignity of a queen. According to Hawkins Bononcini had improved her method of singing and wrote particularly well for her in *Crispo* and *Griselda*.

Rolli dedicated *Crispo* to Lord Carleton and *Griselda* to the Duke of

---

[36] For a description of one in February 1718 see Deutsch, 80–1. The facilities included two orchestras playing 'at due Distance from each other', exotic costumes, a variety of wines, gambling, 'a noble cold Entertainment' for supper, and 'absolute Freedom of Speech, without the least Offence given thereby'. The proceedings began at 9 p.m. and ended at 7 a.m.

Rutland, who was later to be honoured with Handel's *Tamerlano*. Bononcini had composed *Crispo*, on a libretto by Gaetano Lemer, before his journey to London, and it was produced at Rome in his absence in January 1721. The Earl of Bristol, according to his diary entry of 5 June 1721, paid the Castrucci brothers and the lutenist Francisco Weiber two guineas each 'for playing to Bononcini & Senezini & Mrs Robinson, when Crispo was performed at my house'—some months before the London production.[37] Rolli's changes included a number of new aria texts. The plot is a variant of the Hippolytus story, with a happy end. Fausta, wife of the Emperor Constantine the Great, conceives a passion for her stepson Crispo, but after the usual ramifications involving Constantine's other son, a second woman loved by both, and some gesticulation with a cup of poison, all is resolved. Rolli claimed in the Argument that 'the altering of the true History [Fausta's execution] may be permitted by the Licence already granted to Dramatick Poetry'. Donizetti used the same story in his *Fausta*, keeping the tragic end. Twenty arias survive in manuscript and in the Meares and Walsh collections of favourite songs. There are hints of dramatic response in some of the arias for Fausta, played by Anastasia Robinson, for example 'Lo voglio' in I ii and 'Ingrato figlio' in III ii, but the outstanding piece is Crispo's 'Se voi abbandonate' in Act I, a siciliano with four-part strings, an attractive melody, and some variation of ritornellos.

The unedifying story of *Griselda*, whose husband persistently humiliates her out of political cowardice and nearly marries his own daughter, based on Boccaccio's tale, was a particular favourite of the early eighteenth century (and of the Romantic period): there were settings by Pollarolo, Orlandini, Sarri, Albinoni, Alessandro Scarlatti, Vivaldi, Latilla, both Bononcini brothers, and others, all derived from Zeno's libretto of 1701. Rolli says he was ordered to follow an old drama from which he took the character of the villain Rambaldo, sung by Boschi. Walsh printed the overture and all the arias; two-thirds of them were recorded in a somewhat disorderly arrangement under Richard Bonynge in 1968. Burney, who owned a manuscript full score, says that *Griselda* was considered the best of Bononcini's London operas, and detected the influence of Handel. 'It is manifest that Handel's bold and varied style, rich harmony, and ingenious contrivance, had made such an impression on the public as to render it necessary for Bononcini, in setting this opera, to quit *his ambling nag*, and to mount his great horse, accoutred in all his trappings, and endeavour to move with unusual pomp and stateliness.' If so, he did not gather much speed. Burney was right to concede grace and elegance of melody and 'a cleverness and facility of style', but there is nothing here that Handel did not do much better. Bononcini catered well for his singers, giving Senesino chances to exercise his *messa di voce* and command of rapid low-pitched divisions. As before, he strikes the mood of a piece in the first phrase,

---

[37] Bononcini, whose business sense was nothing if not shrewd, offered *Crispo* as an inducement to sell his cantatas. The *Daily Post* of 23 June 1721 carried this announcement: 'Any Lady or Gentleman may have the Opera of CRISPO rehears'd at their apartments, by all the best Performers, who will engage 20 Persons or more to subscribe to Signior Bononcini's Cantata's; but it is humbly desired no one will be invited who is not already a Subscriber, or does not promise to subscribe to the said Cantata's: N.B. Crispo is the best Composition of Bononcini, and is never to be perform'd but in this Manner, for his own Benefit; and where ever 30 Subscriptions are procured, Bononcini will play on the Violoncelli, which he never does but where he proposes a particular Advantage to himself'. (Gibson, *The Royal Academy*, 150.)

ignores its undercurrents, and falls back on formulae. He presents two types of simple melody, slow and plaintive in the minor ('Al mio nativo prato', 'Non deggio', 'Caro addio', 'Troppo è il dolore') and brisk and perky in the major ('Che giova fuggire', 'Se, vaga pastorella', 'Per te, mio solo bene'). The first is preferable, but neither has much substance, and there is little feeling for character or drama and, as Burney put it, 'little ingenuity of design in the accompaniments, or science in the harmony and modulation'. Two arias contain palpable echoes of Handel, the Water Music in 'Le fere a risvegliar', 'O ruddier than the cherry' in 'Eterni dei'. The minuet aria 'Per la gloria' was the occasion of a devastating rebuke from Tovey to Fuller Maitland, who praised it at the expense of 'Sweet rose and lily' in *Theodora*.[38]

At the end of the season Bononcini was invited to compose an anthem for the Duke of Marlborough's funeral; but in the autumn his fortunes took an abrupt turn for the worse. On 5 October Lady Bristol wrote to her husband: 'Bononcini is dismissed the theatre for operas . . . the reason they give for it is his most extravagant demands'. According to Rolli his salary (for playing in the orchestra) was cut by a quarter; Anastasia Robinson told Riva that his demands included a benefit.[39] The true reason may have been political. The discovery of a Jacobite plot, which deposited the Bishop of Rochester in the Tower and moved Parliament to suspend the Habeas Corpus Act for a year, rendered all Catholics suspect. Bononcini may have given cause; his dismissal let in Ariosti, who was not only a Catholic but a monk. Nor does Bononcini seem to have been personally attractive; Hawkins says 'he was haughty and capricious, and was for ever telling such stories of himself as were incredible'.[40] Nevertheless his friends among the directors gained him an invitation to compose operas towards the end of this season and in the next. Rolli was dismissed at the same time and replaced as Secretary by Haym. This was pure gain for Handel: the next three seasons, especially those of 1723/4 and 1724/5, saw the production of some of his finest operas, all in collaboration with Haym.

The opening of the 1722/3 season was enlivened by rumours of the approach of Cuzzoni, who arrived at the end of December (having reputedly married Sandoni on the way[41]), and disorganized by the illness of Senesino, which caused the cancellation of the first three performances. It opened with four revivals, *Muzio Scevola* (7 November), *L'odio e l'amore*, *Floridante*, and *Crispo*. Durastanti had returned, with Berenstadt as second castrato and occasional assistance from Gordon. On 12 November the Academy offered a new series of cheap weekly concerts or 'Assemblies' 'at the Long-Room at the Opera-House in the Hay-Market'. Admission cost 2s. 6d. Only three took place, but they were followed by two 'Entertainments' under the title 'Un Passo Tempo' (at 5s.) and three ridottos. On 12 February the Grand Jury of the County of Middlesex presented a pompous petition to the House of Commons against Heidegger's six proposed ridottos, recommending that they be 'prosecuted and suppressed as common Nuisances to the Publick, as Nurseries of Lewdness, Extravagance, and Immorality, and also a Reproach

[38] *Essays in Musical Analysis*, v (London, 1937), 84.
[39] Lindgren, *A Bibliographic Scrutiny*, 297–8.
[40] *History*, ii. 862.
[41] Lindgren, 'La carriera di Gaetano Berenstadt', says the marriage did not take place till 12 January 1725.

and Scandal to Civil Government'. The last three were cancelled, but they soon rose again. On 6 January 1724 the newly appointed Bishop of London, Edmund Gibson, began to throw his Puritanical weight about by denouncing them in 'the annual Sermon before the Society for the Reformation of Manners at Bow-Church'. It is by no means clear what harm they did. Vanbrugh told Carlisle on 18 February 1724 that the masquerades were flourishing more than ever and supported by the King, despite the mutterings of bishops—an obvious reference to Gibson, who in 1732 was to prevent Handel staging *Esther* in the opera-house.

Cuzzoni's sensational début in *Ottone* (12 January 1723) led to renewed faction, between her partisans and Senesino's and between Handel's and Bononcini's. According to Fabrice (15 January) 'they are as much at loggerheads as the Whigs and Tories, and even on occasion sow dissension among the Directors'. Gay's well-known letter of 3 February to Swift[42] says much the same, adding Ariosti's name, although his first Academy opera, *Coriolano*, was not produced till the 19th. It 'pleased much',[43] and received an addition of four new songs on 20 March. Durastanti (12 March in *Coriolano*) and Cuzzoni[44] (25 March in *Ottone*) each enjoyed a contractual benefit, at which 'particular Care will be taken to place Benches on the Stage for the Accommodation of the Company' and the directors undertook not to use their free tickets. They made a similar promise for the performance of *Ottone* on 4 June, which may also have been a benefit; the season's total amounted to 62. Touts were evidently reaping an illicit profit from the sale of tickets: the *London Journal* (2 March) remarked that 'they are traded in at the other End of the Town, as much as Lottery Tickets are in Exchange-Alley'. The directors, noting that very few annual subscribers were behind with their calls, assumed that they were out of town or had missed the advertisement and gave them extra time to pay, after which 'the tickets of those that have not paid their calls will be absolutely refused, other subscribers taken in their room and proper measures taken to oblige them to pay what is due'.[45] On 23 March the Academy advertised admission to rehearsals at a guinea 'to prevent the Crowd and Disorders at the Practices of the New Opera'. This was Bononcini's *Erminia*, produced on the 30th. Handel's *Flavio* followed on 14 May. The librettos of these two operas were the only ones throughout the Academy period to be printed without casts. Lindgren suggests that they were designed for the abortive visit of the Academy to Paris, which was much discussed during the early summer.[46] Bononcini spent most of the summer and autumn in France, giving concerts with Anastasia Robinson, who may have married Peterborough at this time.

Coriolano was the most successful of Ariosti's seven Academy operas. Pariati's libretto, written for Caldara in 1717, was shortened by Haym, who

---

[42] Quoted on p. 436.

[43] Colman Opera Register, *HJb* (1959), 214.

[44] According to Deutsch her salary was £2,000. This is almost certainly an exaggeration. Berenstadt (letter of 19 May 1724 to Pistocchi) says it was 1,500 guineas (Lindgren, *M & L* (1977), 20). Lord Hervey in a letter of 13 June 1727 (Earl of Ilchester, *Lord Hervey and his Friends, 1726–1738*, London, 1950, 18–19) said Cuzzoni and Faustina each received 1,500 guineas, and a year later Fougeroux quoted £1,600 for both sopranos and Senesino (W. Dean, 'A French Traveller's View of Handel's Operas', 174). Cuzzoni is unlikely to have received more on her first visit.

[45] Burney, ii. 723; not in Deutsch.

[46] See p. 437.

dedicated it to the Duchess of Newcastle, adding fulsome flattery of the female sex. This was linked with the plot, in which the women act as a peace party between warring factions. The libretto, following Livy, deals with Coriolanus's desertion to the Volscians and his siege of Rome, which he spares on the pleas of his mother Veturia. The usual ramifications are attached. Volumnia is not married to Coriolanus but only promised; the tribune Sicinio is his rival in love as well as his political enemy. Coriolanus has a sister, Claudia, who is promised to the Volscian leader. Boschi played Furio, Volumnia's father, but for once was not required to live up to his name. The Meares print, in less skeleton form than usual, contains virtually the whole score except secco recitatives. It reveals Ariosti as a much more impressive composer than Bononcini. His part-writing is ingeniously contrapuntal, his sequences less mechanical, his harmony more varied; above all, he shows a much stronger feeling for dramatic expression. In all these respects he is closer to Handel in style and stature. Hawkins singled out the prison scene in Act III as 'wrought up to the highest degree of perfection that music is capable of, and [it] is said to have drawn tears from the audience at every represen-tation'.[47] This is scarcely an exaggeration. It begins with a long accompanied recitative introduced by a ritornello in the unlikely key of D flat; the layout of the five parts, three of them in the bass clef with cellos and bassoons each taking an independent line, evokes an exceptionally sombre atmosphere (Ex. 37). The recitative is marked by violent mood-changes, enharmonic modulations, many diminished chords, wide vocal intervals, and occasional angular string phrases—Rameau praised it as an admirable example of the 'enharmonic genre'[48]—and is followed by an F minor aria (*Largo e piano sempre*) with flexible phrase-lengths and a furious Presto B section ending in C minor. Veturia (Durastanti) is well characterized with several fine arias, notably 'Sacri Numi' in Act I, a big C minor Largo with four-part strings, wide-ranging dynamics and a fair sprinkling of chromaticism. Ariosti merits closer examination than Lindgren's excellent article can find room for. It is hard to obtain a clear picture of his personality; Rolli called him 'a stupid animal' with no brain and an impostor, and defiled his memory with a vicious epitaph;[49] but that probably reflects more on Rolli than on Ariosti.

The libretto of *Erminia* was much altered by Rolli from an anonymous five-act version produced at Rome in 1719, and dedicated by Bononcini 'alle Gentilissime Dame della Gran Britannia, Amatrici della Musica'. He doubt-less knew where his principal support lay. It is a pastoral (*favola boschereccia*) based on Tasso. The heroine disguises herself as a man and writes history on the bark of trees. Two nymphs fall in love with her, and Tancredi fights and wounds her. Boschi this time played Silvio, a shepherd addicted to hunting like his namesake in *Il pastor fido*. Walsh published five arias, and others are extant in manuscript, many of them borrowed from the Rome score and other earlier works. The tunes, including a favourite minuet for Cuzzoni, are pleasant, with the usual limitations.

During the autumn the King's Theatre was redecorated 'by some of the best Masters' at a reputed cost of £1,000, which hardly suggests financial stringency. Perhaps for that reason the 1723/4 season began later than usual,

[47] *History*, ii. 867.
[48] Lindgren, *M & L* (1981), 341.
[49] Streatfeild, *Handel* (London, 1909), 9 n.

Ex. 37

with Bononcini's *Farnace* on 27 November. It was coolly received, and Bononcini, indisposed as well as annoyed, asked Ariosti to take his place at the third performance on 4 December.[50] He had been composing it in early October, when Anastasia told Riva that it had been 'chose by very good judges', perhaps including Peterborough. The only new singer this year was the minor castrato Bigonzi, who proved a poor substitute for Gordon. After a revival of *Ottone* Ariosti's *Vespasiano* appeared on 14 January 1724. Zamboni, who heard a private rehearsal at Ariosti's house and praised it highly, told Riva on 26 October that Ariosti had played his cards astutely, foreseeing that Peterborough would succeed Lord Stair as ambassador in Paris, and treated Anastasia 'very well, indeed extremely well'.[51] He certainly had, giving her more arias than Durastanti. But the Colman Opera Register noted that it 'did not please much'.[52] In fact it achieved a certain notoriety. On the 18th Mist's

[50] Lindgren, *M & L* (1981), 342.
[51] Ibid. 343.
[52] Sasse, *HJb* (1959), 215.

Weekly Journal reported 'strange Commotions in the State of Musick in the Opera-House' and 'a civil Broil . . . among the Subscribers at the Practice of the new Opera of *Vespasian*, which turn'd all the Harmony into Discord'. Lady Mary Wortley Montagu, who described Anastasia as both a prude and a kept mistress, said that she took offence at 'the too near approach of Senesino in the Opera', 'for which', Burney was told by Horace Walpole, 'Lord Peterborough publicly and violently caned him behind the scenes'.[53]

The episode inspired two scurrilous pamphlets, and press warfare continued after the first night of Handel's *Giulio Cesare* (20 February). On 7 March an anonymous poem in praise of Handel attacked his opponents as 'a spurious Breed, / Who suck bad Airs, and on thin Diet feed . . . / Supine in downy Indolence they doze . . . / And soothing whispers lull 'em to repose'. Bononcini was famous for such soothing arias as 'Amante e sposa' in *Astarto* and 'Dolce sogno' in *Griselda*, and associated with 'sighing Shepherds, bleating Flocks, chirping Birds, and purling Streams.'[54] Fabrice wrote on 10 March that 'the squabbles between the Directors and the sides that everyone is taking between the singers and the composers, often provide the public with the most diverting scenes'. Nevertheless, the standard of performance remained high. A Mr Lecoq in a letter of 31 March praised the music, the singing, and the orchestra, and said that Durastanti's benefit on the 17th (again in *Coriolano*) had brought her more than £1,000, nearly as much as the year before. He gave her salary as £1,200. She improved the occasion 'with an Addition of an English Cantata in Praise of this Nation', the words ('Gen'rous, gay, and gallant nation') written by Pope at the request of Peterborough. The line 'Let old charmers yield to new' has been taken as evidence that she felt herself defeated by Cuzzoni; a letter of 11 May 1725 from Owen Swiney to the Duke of Richmond (see p. 322, note 60, below) suggests that she hoped to return, as indeed she did nearly ten years later. The only other performance of *Coriolano* this season, on 16 April, was probably also a benefit, as Burney says—no doubt for Cuzzoni. Two new operas then appeared, Bononcini's *Calfurnia* on 18 April and Ariosti's *Aquilio consolo* on 21 May. The latter was a failure, playing for only four nights. The Academy, which gave 51 performances this season, evidently planned to serve the three composers with even-handed justice: each supplied three operas in the two seasons 1722/3 and 1723/4. Excluding revivals, Handel's received 35 performances, Ariosti's 26, and Bononcini's 25. The tide was beginning to turn.

Bononcini dedicated the libretto of *Farnace* to Peterborough, thanking him for his support, which may have included a recommendation for the commission. The text, a conventional jumble of dynastic intrigue, disguises, and forged letters, was extensively altered by an unknown hand from Lorenzo Morari's libretto for Caldara (Venice, 1703). It is the only one of Bononcini's London operas for which a full score survives, in the Schönborn Library at Wiesentheid; Walsh published ten arias. The music is skilful and fluent, with the same aura of sweetness and facile charm and the same weaknesses as before. Several arias have a solo cello part independent of the bass, played perhaps by Bononcini himself. *Calfurnia*, slightly altered by Haym from a libretto by Grazio Braccioli first set by Heinichen (Venice, 1713), was dedicated to the Duke of Queensbury and Dover. The story, from Plutarch,

[53] Burney, ii. 729 n.
[54] James Ralph, *The Touch-Stone* (1728), quoted by Deutsch, 231–2.

turns on a contrived conflict between patriotism and paternal affection. The Roman consul Marius is told by an oracle that he will only defeat the Cimbri if he sacrifices his daughter Calfurnia instead of allowing her to marry her betrothed, Trebonius; ranking glory above family ties, father and daughter 'readily consent'. The oracle turns out to have been faked by Marius's nephew Lucius, himself in love with Calfurnia. Further deceit is introduced by Alvida, daughter of the Numidian king Jugurtha (conquered by Marius), who loves Trebonius, pretends to be a prophetess of Osiris, and delivers a parallel bogus utterance. Lucius insults Trebonius and is duly dispatched, but not before he has confessed his sins. Walsh published eleven arias, of which the most interesting is 'Render voglio ogn'uno amante' for Alvida (Anastasia Robinson), on a partial ground bass with a B section more harmonically adventurous than usual.

Vespasiano was shortened by Haym from a very old libretto by G. C. Corradi for Pallavicino (Venice, 1678) and dedicated to the second Duke of Manchester, the Academy's new Deputy Governor. Its blood-and-thunder climate, suggestive of a seventeenth-century Edgar Wallace, is indicated by the first scene heading. *A Court with a Balcony, out of which Vitellius is thrown headlong by the Soldiers. Domitian treads upon the Head of Vitellius, whose Body is dragged out by Soldiers, and thrown into the Tyber.* Vitellius, the Emperor, has been caught trying to rape Titus's wife Arricida (Cuzzoni). The new Emperor Vespasian (Boschi) has two sons, Titus (Senesino), who spends most of the opera trying to evade his wife and seduce a beautiful slave, Gesilla (Anastasia Robinson), and Domitian (Durastanti), who commits or attempts every crime in the calendar in his efforts to usurp the throne. He makes advances to his sister-in-law over dinner, kicks to the ground a captain who intervenes and orders him to be thrown into the Tiber, kills two guards after Vespasian has quixotically released him, and seizes his father and brother by force, whereupon 'the Earth opens and swallows him up with his Attendants'. This has apparently been engineered by Titus, who has already tried to stab Domitian; he now brings him back wounded, whereupon Vespasian, not for the first time, lets everyone off with a caution. It is a peculiarly fatuous libretto, the characters inconsistent and unsympathetic, the Emperor a half-wit—perhaps the wettest part ever played by Boschi. As with *Coriolano* Ariosti published the complete score apart from recitatives. Burney allowed it 'considerable merit' and called Ariosti 'a perfect good harmonist . . . but [he] had little invention'. He printed a very ornate aria for Senesino; this however is not characteristic. Languishing dance tunes, inappropriate to the situations and characters, especially Domitian, outnumber the spirited pieces. Domitian ends Act I by falling asleep during a soothing aria, though this is dramatically justifiable by the fact that he has been drugged to control his sexual urge. Such was the staple diet offered by Bononcini and, for a time at least, preferred by singers and audiences; Ariosti seems to have tacked to catch the wind of popular favour, and evidently miscalculated. The anonymous poet quoted above lumped the two together as 'this lethargic Tribe'. Even so, Ariosti's music is less limp than Bononcini's, with bolder modulations in the B sections, a dramatically organized seduction duet for Domitian and Arricida in I viii, switching between major and minor and ending in the wrong key, and an expressive E flat Largo for Durastanti, 'Or che il sonno' (the concluding aria of Act I mentioned above), whose B section moves to A flat, D flat, and G minor.

Aquilio consolo, based on Silvani's *Arrenione* (Venice, 1708), has no dedication, and the Argument is not signed. The plot, from Diodorus Siculus, is laid in Syracuse in the second century BC, and deals with the deposition of the tyrant Arrenion (*recte* Athenion), formerly a slave, who loves a Carthaginian and a Roman lady. The Roman lady's brother Aquilius, a Roman consul in the unlikely disguise of a shepherd–gardener, finds himself in a complex series of amorous entanglements, from which he eventually breaks free. Walsh published six arias; one of them, 'Lascio il solco', sung by Arrenione's sister Linceste (Durastanti), is a catchy little arietta fit for a soubrette.

At the end of the 1723/4 season most of the company left for Paris.[55] Bononcini, finally dismissed by the Academy, had been induced to stay in England by the young Duchess of Marlborough's offer of a post in her private service at a stipend of £500 a year, provided (in the words of Mrs Pendarves) that 'he will *not* compose any more for the ungrateful Academy, who do not deserve he should entertain them, since they don't know how to value his works as they ought'.[56] He did produce one more opera, *Astianatte* in 1727, but otherwise confined himself for several years to directing the Duchess's twice-weekly private concerts. Durastanti and Berenstadt were likewise not re-engaged, and Anastasia Robinson retired into private life. Berenstadt was replaced by Pacini, Robinson by Anna Dotti. For the first time the Academy engaged a leading tenor in Francesco Borosini. Benedetta Sorosina, a low soprano or mezzo, sang from February 1725 till the end of the season.

The last four Academy seasons were progressively dominated by Handel. Even so, Ariosti· seems to have had substantial support among the nobility. Late in 1724 he published a volume of cantatas and lessons for the viola d'amore, dedicated to George I, with a phenomenal list of 764 subscribers, including virtually the entire peerage and diplomatic corps: 42 dukes and duchesses, 105 earls and countesses, and 146 other lords and ladies. He claimed 133 of them as subscribers to the Academy, an impossible total for any one year. Hawkins was rightly sceptical; he suspected that Ariosti had put down everyone he solicited, whether they subscribed or not. The season opened on 31 October with *Tamerlano*, followed by Ariosti's *Artaserse* on 1 December, *Giulio Cesare* (the only revival), *Rodelinda* (13 February), Ariosti's *Dario* (10 April), and *Elpidia*, a pasticcio arranged by Handel (11 May). There were 62 performances, in all but sixteen of which Handel was principally concerned. Two were perhaps benefits, but none has been identified. Peter Tillemans and Joseph Goupy may have been employed as scene-painters during this year.

Artaserse was altered by Haym from a libretto by Zeno and Pariati for Antonio Zanettini (Venice, 1705), and dedicated in flattering terms to the young Duke of Richmond, who towards the end of 1725 was to succeed Manchester as Deputy Governor of the Academy. Although Haym removed two minor characters, the residue is long, prolix, and repetitious, concerned with the amorous entanglements of the Persian monarch's children, from both sides of the blanket. No doubt Ariosti was unable to exercise the same control over Haym as Handel. When two of the legitimate sons make parallel advances to Aspasia, the Greek widow of the slain Median King Cyrus, she charmingly promises to love the one who kills the other, and attaches a dagger

---

[55] For what they did there see pp. 437–8.
[56] Lindgren, *M & L* (1977), 25.

to the throne for the purpose. Later Artaxerxes orders the execution of both his sons, but they claim that Aspasia pressed them to assassinate their father; he tries to induce one of them to dispose of Aspasia. Seven favourite songs were published, including an effective simile aria for Cuzzoni (Aspasia), 'Son come navicella in mar turbato,' with a fine ritornello, succinct word-painting, and a full contrapuntal B section. *Dario*, based on Silvani's *L'inganno scoperto per vendetta*, written for Perti (Venice, 1691), has an even more uncouth libretto, likewise set in Susa. Persians were almost by definition considered capable of anything. Haym arranged it, but there is no dedication. In this dynastic cauldron, seething with disguises, impostors, nocturnal misunderstandings, and sudden switches of affection, almost everyone makes love to everyone else—generally not the person intended—and most of the characters are at some point thrown into chains. Sidermes, posing as Cyrus's son, usurps the throne and seems to get away with it; but in the middle of Act II there is an *Earthquake . . . The Statue of Cyrus tumbles headlong down, and Sidermes endeavours to shun the Crush of its Fall, the Crown drops from his Head at the Feet of Darius, who takes it up.* In Act III Sidermes goes to sleep, and *there rises from under-ground the Ghost of Cyrus with a Torch, who, as he passes by, makes menacing motions to Sidermes.* The most unexpected detail comes at the very end, when Delia, a Scythian betrayed by Sidermes, offers herself to him after he has been banished, and he replies: 'Not so fast. I want to think more about it.' The twelve favourite songs include two duets; one of them, 'Caro, O Dio almen potessi', a reconciliation for Cuzzoni and Senesino in prison (III iv), is particularly fine, with an accompaniment of five real parts interwoven in expressive counterpoint.

Elpidia was Handel's first pasticcio. He arranged the whole and composed the recitatives.[57] Haym took the libretto from Zeno's *I rivali generosi* (for M. A. Ziani, Venice, 1697), retaining some of the recitative and two duets. Most of the aria texts were lifted with their music from Vinci's *Ifigenia in Tauride* and *Rosmira fedele* and Orlandini's *Berenice*, the three newest operas produced at the San Giovanni Gristostomo theatre in Venice only a few weeks earlier. Boschi repeated two of his arias from Lotti's *Teofane* with new words; others came from Sarri's *Merope* (1716) and Capelli's *Venceslao* (1724).[58] Cuzzoni sang five arias composed for Faustina Bordoni; this would have been inconceivable two years later. For the first time London audiences were confronted with the pre-classical style based on harmonic rather than contrapuntal bass lines and florid voice parts that go their own way rather than developing ritornello material. Handel's quickness in seizing the latest fashion, which he was soon to digest and make his own, is remarkable.[59] Burney says that the songs 'were but little noticed, and soon forgotten', and that none were published. Both statements are untrue. *Elpidia* had ten performances and a revival in the following season, and ten favourite songs were printed, mostly Vinci's with one each by Orlandini and Sarri. One has a B section with an Alberti bass throughout.

The Academy had obtained the libretto and songs of *Elpidia* through that old reprobate Owen Swiney, who had presumably purged his earlier contempt and was living in Venice; he claimed that the copying of the score and a

---

[57] The performing score is Add MS 31606; see Clausen, 136–9.
[58] Strohm, 'Händels Pasticci', 212–14, 241–3; *Essays*, 167–9, 200–1.
[59] Another example of his alertness at this period is his employment of clarinets in *Tamerlano* and *Riccardo Primo*. See p. 552.

sweetener to Vinci cost him £40. In April 1724 the Academy through Haym had invited him to act as its agent, reporting on the latest operas and recommending singers suitable for London. His correspondence with the Duke of Richmond[60] throws light both on Swiney's character—crusty, cantankerous, self-important, with a touch of Irish blarney and a chip on both shoulders—and on the Academy's method of obtaining singers. Swiney nourished grudges against Haym and Heidegger, and complained, perhaps with reason, that the Italian clique in London, among whom he numbered Bononcini, Riva, Avelloni (Durastanti's husband), and Berenstadt, were constantly interfering in an attempt to keep the plum jobs for their friends. In May 1725 he was negotiating with the castrato Giovanni Battista Minelli and the tenor Pinacci, presumably as replacements for Pacini and Borosini. The Academy, guided by reports from travellers, rejected Minelli, and Swiney recommended Baldi, 'neither a *good*, nor a *bad singer* . . . a tollerable Actor', adding that he asked 600 guineas and would not stir for under 500. Baldi was duly engaged, together with Luigi Antinori; when the latter was on his way to London Swiney asked the Duke of Richmond to give him his protection since he was coming with the worst possible recommendation, a tenor voice; he added his opinion of most Italian tenors as boisterous and bellowing Stentors. The Academy had enquired about the castratos Gizzi and Carestini; Swiney described them as 'prodigious bad Singers, with very good voices'.

The two artists who roused Swiney's passionate enthusiasm were Faustina Bordoni and Nicolini. From November 1725 he urged the claims of the latter, evidently as a substitute for the increasingly troublesome Senesino; but although the Academy was anxious to replace him, Senesino's popularity with the public, or skilful lobbying by his London supporters, won the day. Swiney was instructed to treat with Faustina in the spring of 1725. He went to hear her in Parma, and at the end of June forwarded a signed copy of her agreement. London press announcements in August and September, exaggerated as usual, mentioned a salary of £2,500; Swiney quoted the equivalent of 1,500–2,000 guineas covering two seasons, with an annual increase of £100 after the first at the discretion of the directors. Since she was engaged for the carnival season at Vienna, there was no question of her reaching London before March 1726.

Swiney was constantly pressing on the Academy singers, scene-painters, and operas that they did not want. Early in 1726 Richmond forbade him to discuss theatrical matters (he also corresponded about paintings, especially those of Canaletto), but he continued to do so, becoming more and more querulous. After the acceptance of *Elpidia* he seems to have thought that the Academy was only interested in pasticcios. He sent over a whole series, selecting the arias himself to suit what he knew about the capacity of the principal singers, and adding that Haym or Ariosti could supply the recitatives and secondary parts in ten days. From the end of 1725 he was particularly keen on *Venceslao*[61], in which he hoped Faustina would make her London début. He was disgusted when he heard about Handel's *Alessandro*, whose libretto and music he pronounced far inferior before he had any acquaintance with either, and

---

[60] In the West Sussex Record Office, Chichester (Goodwood MS 105); see Elizabeth Gibson, 'Owen Swiney and the Italian Opera in London', *MT* cxxv (1984), 82–6, and *The Royal Academy*, Appendix C.

[61] Presumably Zeno's well-known libretto. Faustina had sung in Capelli's setting at Parma in 1724 and Caldara's at Vienna in September 1725.

indeed before Handel had finished the score. He was convinced that it had been chosen by enemies to deny Faustina a fair hearing. Swiney was clearly out of touch with opera in London, and still living in the world of fifteen years earlier. He continued to correspond with Richmond (and with Haym, though this went very much against the grain) until 1729, when he met Handel in Bologna on his way to Rome; but he says disappointingly little about him.

The possibility that the Academy wanted Faustina to replace rather than supplement Cuzzoni seems to be ruled out by Riva's letter of 7 September 1725 to Muratori, which states that 'for this year and for the two following there must be two equal parts in the operas for Cuzzoni and Faustina'. This might mean that they had been offered three-year contracts. On the other hand Riva's letter is so inaccurate in other respects[62] that one cannot be sure. It indicates that Bononcini hoped to gain the Duchess of Marlborough's permission to set a libretto 'which is almost a translation of Racine's [*Andromaque*] but without the death of Pyrrhus. It is excellently adapted as an opera'. This was to be *Astianatte*, modified by Haym from Salvi's Pratolino libretto of 1701; the last sentence must refer to Salvi, not Haym, who is dismissed with profound contempt in the same letter.

The 1725/6 season, again late, opened on 30 November with a revival of *Elpidia*. There were three cast changes, Borosini, Pacini, and Sorosina being replaced by Antinori, Baldi, and Dotti (who had not sung in May), and at least seven substituted or inserted arias from operas by Sarri, Giacomelli (two each), Orlandini, Vinci, and Capelli.[63] After a revival of *Rodelinda* another pasticcio, *Elisa*, appeared on 15 January.[64] Haym arranged the text, but this was the season's one production in which Handel was not involved; he was about to set a different Scipio libretto by Rolli. Chrysander wrongly attributed two bass arias in *Elisa* to him. Most of the arias, six of which Walsh published, were assembled from at least eight operas by Porpora.[65] It is possible that this was one of the pasticcios sent by Swiney from Venice; they included *Annibale*, the name of a character in *Elisa*, and Swiney thought highly of Porpora, as his letter of 28 December 1725 makes clear. *Elisa* was a complete failure; the *Universal Mercury* (February) said that audiences grew so thin that the Academy 'for fear of making another Call, was oblig'd to drop it'. They recouped with a successful revival of *Ottone*, in which a new soprano, Livia Costantini, made the first of her few London appearances. She sang in Handel's *Scipione* (12 March), but was clearly a stopgap pending the arrival of Faustina. That event was announced in *The British Journal* of 19 March. On 5 May Faustina made her long awaited début in *Alessandro*, and the Academy moved into a new and final phase.

Additional Notes

* (p. 303) G. F. Barlow (see Appendix H) estimates 482 in pit and boxes, 309 in the gallery. See also p. 152.
* (p. 304) Barlow's estimate is about £330 for a full house.

[62] For example on the subject-matter of London operas and their treatment of duets; nor is it true that Bononcini had sent for his librettos from Rome (Lindgren, *A Bibliographic Scrutiny*, 311 ff.).   [63] Strohm, 'Händels Pasticci'.

[64] Unless we count *Muzio Scevola* and *Arsace*, *Elpidia* and *Elisa* were the only pasticcios produced by the Academy, a remarkably low incidence compared with earlier and later practice in London, or with continental practice at any time during the period.

[65] Strohm, 'Händels Pasticci', 215; *Essays*, 169.

CHAPTER 17

RADAMISTO

THE action takes place near Mount Ararat in the wild country west of the Caspian Sea (on the present borders of Turkey, Iran, and Azerbaijan) about AD 51. Farasmane, King of Thrace, has two children, Radamisto, married to Zenobia ('a Princess of Noble Blood, and Nobler Virtue'), and Polissena, married to Tiridate King of Armenia. The latter 'a little while after, coming to his Father-in-Law's Court, at a time when Radamistus was absent, saw there his Sister-in-Law, and fell in love with her. Being returned to his own Kingdom, and finding no other way to satisfy his unjust Amours, he on a sudden made War against Farasmanes, and took from him his whole Dominions, the Capital City only excepted, into which Radamistus and Zenobia were retired, in order to defend it; having before this in a Battle made Farasmanes a Prisoner. He carries his Wife with him into the Army, lest some Insurrection should happen in his Absence.'

Act I. *A royal tent with a seat and table. Polissena alone, sitting at the table.*[1] She calls on the gods for protection. Tigrane, Prince of Pontus and Tiridate's ally, tells her that the motive for the war is Tiridate's love for Zenobia. He offers Polissena his own love, urging her to leave her tyrannical and faithless husband. She sternly rebukes him, refusing to believe that Tiridate can be so described. Tiridate enters with guards, condemns Radamisto to death and the city to destruction,[2] and orders Farasmane to be brought in. When Polissena intercedes, he tells her to be off. She meekly obeys; her only wish is to please him. Farasmane, *in Chains amongst Guards*, asks permission to see and advise Radamisto. Tiridate agrees that his brother Fraarte shall conduct Farasmane to the city walls; but if Radamisto continues to resist, Farasmane must die and all the inhabitants be put to the sword. The back-flats open to reveal *Tiridate's camp; a view of the city; a small plain beneath its walls, separated from the camp by a wide moat through which runs the neighbouring river Araxes; the city gate opens, and Radamisto comes out, preceded by guards and accompanied by Zenobia.*[3] Radamisto intends to escape alone, but she refuses to leave him. He tries to comfort her: heaven will not always be hostile. *Part of Tiridate's army comes out of its quarters; shortly afterwards Farasmane in chains is seen emerging from a large tent; his chains are upheld by two soldiers, accompanied by Fraarte; they come to a halt on the near side of the moat; Radamisto and Zenobia are on the far side.*[4] Fraarte delivers Tiridate's terms:

---

[1] This (in Italian), taken over from the source libretto, is the heading in the autograph and copies. All three London librettos have: *A Camp with Tents, and a Vista of the City, before which runs the River Araxes over which there is a Bridge. Polissena alone, sitting at a Table before the Door of her Tent.* This may represent a late production change.

[2] According to the autograph he addresses these words to Fraarte without noticing Polissena's presence. This detail may have been dropped when Fraarte was cut from the scene.

[3] So (in Italian) the autograph and copies; the librettos have only *Zenobia and Radamisto come out of the City.*

[4] The reading of the librettos is slightly different and less explicit.

if the town yields, Radamisto shall go free; if not, Farasmane's execution precedes the assault. Farasmane urges Radamisto to resist: honour is more important than his own life. *A Soldier puts himself in a Posture to cast a Lance, to kill Farasmanes.*[5] Zenobia hopes to save the situation by her own death: she will wait in the palace for Radamisto to kill her. Farasmane repeats his order to resist, and Radamisto departs with a prayer to the gods to overthrow the tyrant. Farasmane bids Fraarte strike. *A Soldier goes to kill him, having receiv'd the Signal from Fraartes,*[6] but Tigrane enters and forbids such an unjust act. Farasmane, still defiant, is led off to Tigrane's tent. Tigrane and Fraarte give orders for the attack. *Whilst the Symphony is playing, the Assault on the City is begun, at which time the Scene changes*[7] to *a Court before Radamistus's Palace.* Tiridate and his army are victorious. Fraarte, to Tiridate's annoyance, reports that Farasmane has been spared on Tigrane's orders. The latter enters *with Slaves and Spoils*[8] and intercedes for Farasmane's life. Tiridate agrees on condition that Radamisto and Zenobia are brought to him. If they resist, Radamisto alone must be killed. The mention of Zenobia awakens old love in Fraarte's heart; when Tiridate orders him to fetch the couple, he goes in the hope of possessing her, but not by force. Polissena, *taking hold of Tiridate,* pleads for her brother, but is curtly repulsed. *He unloosens himself from Polissena . . . She holds him again . . . He again breaks loose from Polissena, and Exit.*[9] She thanks Tigrane for saving her father and asks him now to save her brother. He promises to help. Convinced of her husband's impure designs, Polissena resolves 'to dissemble the Affront, and suffer the Pains'.

Act II. *A Plain, through which runs the River Araxes; on one side [whereof ruins of ancient buildings, one of which]*[10] *is a subterranean Cave. Radamistus and Zenobia coming out of it,* having escaped from the city. She sinks down exhausted. Radamistus sees soldiers approaching; she urges him to kill her. *She takes his Sword from his Side, and presents it to him; Radamistus takes it trembling.*[11] He cannot bring himself to strike till she asks if she is to become the tyrant's prey. Then *he wounds her slightly, letting the weapon fall from his hand.* She says her spirit is stronger than his, bids him avenge her death if he really loves her, and *casts her self into the River.* Radamisto, *running to the River where Zenobia had thrown herself,* resolves to sell his life dearly. *He takes up his Sword from the Ground, turning himself to the Soldiers,*[12] *who encounter him . . . They all retire, at the Command of Tigranes.* Radamisto admits his identity and surrenders to Tigrane; aside, he resolves to kill Tiridate, who does not know him by sight. He bids Zenobia's shade rest in peace. Fraarte and soldiers arrive on the empty stage with Zenobia, *her clothing in disarray.* He offers to fight for her if she will return his love; it was for this that he rescued her from the river. She bitterly reproaches him for not letting

[5] In the first version of the autograph Fraarte drew his sword for this purpose. Chrysander includes the direction only in the December 1720 version (HG 131), though it belongs to the first production and is in all three librettos.

[6] Chrysander omits this direction in both his versions (HG 25, 126). It is in the autograph (barely legible), performing score, and libretto.

[7] This interesting detail is in the libretto and performing score, though the autograph and some copies have *la quale vien presa* as HG.

[8] Libretto and performing score have *con schiavi, spogliere e bandiere* (presumably in the sense of banners rather than whores) as HG 136, the autograph *con schiavi* only.

[9] All four directions are in the libretto, the first three in the autograph; Chrysander omits the last two.

[10] The bracketed words are not in the libretto.

[11] These directions, omitted by Chrysander, are in the autograph and the libretto.

[12] As note 11.

her die. *Exit Fraartes, but the Soldiers remain.* Unable to die, she invokes the furies to torment the tyrant and is led out under guard. The set changes to *the royal garden with a closet; verdant terrain.*[13] Tiridate will not be happy till he gets Zenobia. Fraarte reports her capture, and that Radamisto wounded her slightly in the arm. Expressing horror at this inhumanity Tiridate orders his soldiers to fetch her. Fraarte looks forward to discovering her feelings. She is led in, and soon *Fraartes enters without being observed* (he has gone out after his aria). He learns that Tiridate is his rival. Tiridate tells Zenobia that she has not lost her kingdom; she has won the vast Armenian empire as well. Despite her coldness he decides not to exasperate her: she will yield when she realizes the extent of his devotion and generosity. Fraarte tells her he has overheard her rejection of Tiridate and offers himself in his place. She scorns him; she loves only her husband, and begs heaven to restore him or end her life. Fraarte *stands a while pensive*, hoping his services will win her round. Tigrane brings in Radamisto disguised *in Soldiers Apparel*[14] and presents him to Polissena. Radamisto asks his sister to conduct him secretly to Tiridate. She replies that she will die for her husband or her brother if the life of either is threatened by the other. Radamisto is horrified that she can defend a man so deaf to love and nature that he keeps their father in chains and seeks to kill her brother. She says honour demands it; he leaves with a bitterly ironical and reproachful aria. Torn between loyalties, Polissena *stands a while pensive* and resolves 'to save his Life that is in greatest Danger' and to die rather than prove unfaithful. In *a Royal Room* Tiridate orders attendants to 'bring a couple of Chairs' and prepares to resume his siege of Zenobia. *Whilst they are going to sit down, Tigranes approaches them with attendants and Radamisto's garments, carried by a soldier.* He says that Radamisto is dead. Zenobia recognizes his robe, helmet, and sword and *casts herself on a Couch, putting her Handkerchief to her Eyes.* Tigrane says one of Radamisto's servants who heard his last words will tell them what happened, and Tiridate orders him to be brought in. It is Radamisto himself, under the name of Ismeno; Zenobia at once recognizes him. Tiridate orders Ismeno to speak. He reports Radamisto's last message to Zenobia: a plea to forgive him for not having the courage to die with her in the river, and a request to remember his love and despise the tyrant who planned his murder. Tiridate angrily interrupts, but is appeased when Ismeno mentions Radamisto's death. *Leaning her Head,* [Zenobia] *seems to weep.* In a cavatina addressed to each in turn she defies Tiridate and tenderly affirms her constancy to her 'dear and faithful' Ismeno. Tiridate, convinced that Radamisto is dead, enlists Ismeno to plead his cause with Zenobia, offers a reward if he succeeds, and goes out remarking that his love, though extreme, was never impure. Husband and wife embrace and sing a duet pledging eternal fidelity.

Act III. In *a Court round the Royal Palace* Tigrane and Fraarte, weary of Tiridate's misdeeds, plan a revolution, but not against his life or crown; he must recognize his errors and lose the power to be unjust. Fraarte aside confesses another motive—love.[15] Tigrane knows his hopes of winning Polissena are vain, but finds it a pleasure to serve her. In *a Royal Room with a Closet* Zenobia begs Radamisto not to let Tiridate see him too much in her

---

[13] The librettos have *Part of the Garden, with a Prospect of the Royal Palace.*
[14] *Semplice soldato* in some copies. The autograph is illegible.
[15] Handel omitted this line: see below, p. 350.

company; she fears the violence of his love. Radamisto leaves with an assurance that he will never forsake her. Tiridate enters *with Followers* and salutes Zenobia as Queen of Thrace, Armenia, and his heart. *A Page brings a Crown and Sceptre on a Golden Salver.* She throws the gifts on the ground and denounces him as a tyrant. 'Let the tyrant triumph' he replies, and *goes to take hold of her.*[16] She cries out. *Radamistus with Sword in hand; enter Polissena on one side, and Farasmanes on the other, both at the same time.* Radamisto advances on Tiridate *but is withheld by Polissena*, who interposes her body between sword and victim. Farasmane unwittingly reveals Radamisto's identity. Tiridate, *repulsing Farasmane*,[17] orders Radamisto's execution, and Farasmane's as well if he interferes. *Polissena kneels at Tiridate's feet*: having saved his life, she appeals to him to save her father's and brother's. He agrees to spare Farasmane only and orders her to be gone. Warning him that if he does not repent of his cruelty her love will change to anger, she departs. Zenobia asks to die with the others. Tiridate agrees to pardon Radamisto in return for Zenobia's hand, and tells her to make her choice in the temple. Zenobia and Radamisto say farewell and look forward to meeting in the Elysian fields. The set changes to *a Temple.* Zenobia again rejects Tiridate: if Radamisto dies, she will die with him. Polissena brings news that Tiridate's army is in revolt and, led by Tigrane and Fraarte, has surrounded the temple. Tiridate orders his supporters to his defence, but *Soldiers and Guards forsake him*, and *as he is going out, he is detained.* Tigrane and Fraarte enter with soldiers and people. Tiridate bitterly *flings his Sword on the Ground.* Tigrane offers the throne to Farasmane, who calls on Radamisto to avenge his wrongs. Radamisto asks Polissena to pardon Tiridate, who admits himself confounded and embraces her. Radamisto bids them reign in Armenia as before; since he has regained Zenobia all his sorrows have vanished. Fraarte repents of his impure love. The opera ends with a substantial *coro*, including three duets (marked 'Part of the Chorus' in the libretto) and a ballet.

This plot has a faint basis in history, derived from Book xii of Tacitus's *Annals.* Pharasmanes, Tiridates, Radamistus, and Zenobia were real persons involved in the internecine warfare that ravaged Asia Minor in the first century AD. Tigranes and Phraates were common names among the kings of Armenia and Parthia. Pharasmanes's dominion was not Thrace, which lies much further to the north-west, but the small kingdom of Iberia in the Caucasus.[18] He and his son were quite as brutal and unscrupulous as the Tiridate of the opera; Pharasmanes eventually executed Radamistus as a traitor. Tiridate is a conflation of the historical Tiridates (brother of the King of Parthia) and Mithridates of Armenia (brother and son-in-law of Pharasmanes), who was murdered by Radamistus. The opera's one historical incident is Zenobia's plunge into the Araxes (*Annals* xii 51); she was rescued by shepherds and

---

[16] This direction, omitted in both HG versions, is in the autograph, performing score, and libretto.

[17] See n. 16 for this and the preceding direction.

[18] For the historical background from a Georgian angle, see W. Gwacharija, 'Ein Oper von Georg Friedrich Händel mit einem grusinischen historischen Sujet', *HJb* (1960), 163, and 'Die historischen Grundlagen von G. F. Händels Oper "Radamisto"', in *G. F. Händel und seine italienischen Zeitgenossen*, ed. W. Siegmund-Schultze (Halle, 1979), 59.

conveyed to Tiridates, who received her kindly, an episode included in other *Radamisto* operas.

Like many stories from ancient history this was a popular operatic subject in the late seventeenth and early eighteenth centuries,[19] though most operas entitled *Zenobia* dealt with the better-known third-century Queen of Palmyra.[20] Legrenzi produced a *Tiridate* in 1668. Three of Albinoni's operas in the years 1694–8 were entitled *Zenobia*, *Tigrane*, and *Radamisto*. Handel may have seen Nicola Fago's *Radamisto* (Naples, 1707) at its Florence revival in November 1709.[21] The source of his libretto however was none of these, but Domenico Lalli's *L'amor tirannico*, set by Gasparini for Venice in autumn 1710 and adapted, apparently by the composer himself, for the Cocomero theatre in Florence in the carnival season of 1712.[22] The part of Radamisto was sung by Pacini in Fago's opera and Berenstadt in Gasparini's—both later members of Handel's London company.

*   Lalli's libretto, originally in five acts, had been reduced to three for Florence. Handel and his assistant Haym followed the Florence version fairly closely, with the usual abbreviation of recitatives and substitution of aria texts. They cut seven scenes (one of them after Handel had set it) and on three occasions ran two into one. The most important plot change concerned the character of Fraarte, who in Lalli is Tiridate's general and confidant, a conventional soldier without an emotional stake in the story. Handel and Haym made him Tiridate's brother and the assiduous but unsuccessful lover of Zenobia, paralleling Tigrane's love for Polissena; this idea was introduced after Handel had composed the first two acts and probably most of the third, and involved many changes in the autograph, including the suppression of the original I iii. Fraarte's threat to cut down Farasmane in person in I v (Lalli's I viii) was transferred to an anonymous guard when Handel decided to treat Fraarte as a lover rather than a soldier. Fraarte's deeper involvement slows up the action in the first two acts, but not to a damaging extent.

The other significant change was one of emphasis, reflected in the altered title. Gasparini's opera concentrated more on Tiridate and Polissena, less on Radamisto and Zenobia, and gave a disproportionately large part to Tigrane. Tiridate is painted in less uniformly black colours, and is therefore more interesting and perhaps more credible. He begins II iv with a reflectively amorous cavatina and ends II xiii (Handel's II xi) with an aria of hope. His behaviour in the closing scenes is a good deal more convincing. The location is not a temple but his throne-room (*Luogo magnifico con Trono Reale*). After the *coup d'état* Farasmane occupies the throne and condemns Tiridate to death. All accept the justice of the sentence, even Polissena, who asks to die with her husband. This moves Tiridate to a full confession of his sins, and he submits willingly to his fate. Farasmane in turn is moved to mercy. Handel's heavy cuts botched the motivation here, though he attempted some amends in the

---

[19] It was also the theme of a French tragedy, Crébillon's *Rhadamiste et Zénobie* (1711). Metastasio's *Zenobia* (1740) made Radamisto the villain for pushing Zenobia into the river.

[20] Marchi and Zeno wrote librettos on this theme.

[21] See p. 80.

[22] *HJb* (1975), 112; *Essays*, 44. Strohm suggests that Handel was still in touch with the Tuscan court and obtained the librettos for *Radamisto* and *Rodelinda* from that source. There were many later settings of Lalli's text, by Orlandini, Feo, Chelleri and Porta (together), Schürmann, and Ciampi among others.

December 1720 revival. Elsewhere his characteristic concentration on the sufferings of Radamisto and Zenobia, a feature of course present in Lalli, paid rich dividends. There is a curious point about the opera's most spectacular incident, Zenobia's plunge into the Araxes. According to Tacitus (where she is pregnant) and the Argument in the 1710, 1712, and 1720 librettos Radamisto, after wounding her, thinks her dead and throws her into the river. None of the librettists or composers adopted this. Handel shortened the recitative in which the couple express their devotion, but the action is the same in all three versions.

The changed emphasis is clearly illustrated by the distribution of arias. That of Handel's two principal revisions, together with the vocal pitches, is included in Table 5. Handel retained ten aria texts from the 1712 libretto, some with minor modifications: four in Act I ('Sommi Dei' with a new third line, 'Deh! fuggi un traditore', 'Tu vuoi ch'io parta', and 'Cara sposa'), and six in Act II ('Ombra cara', 'Già che morir non posso' with altered B section, 'Sì che ti renderai', 'La sorte, il ciel' in an earlier scene than in Lalli, 'Vanne, sorella ingrata' and 'Empio perverso cor'). Nothing of Lalli remained in Act III, though Radamisto's suppressed 'Senza luce' drew on his corresponding aria in 1712. Six arias are insertions where Lalli had none: 'Stragi, morti', 'Ferite, uccidete', 'Son lievi le catene' (Lalli gave Farasmane an aria earlier in Act I), 'Spero placare' (a late addition when Fraarte's role was expanded), 'Alzo al volo' (also an afterthought), and 'O scemami il diletto'. The remaining thirteen arias, duet, and *coro* replaced different texts in 1712. Of the six insertions three at least are not by Haym and must have been supplied by Handel: 'Stragi, morti' comes from the libretto of *Rodrigo*,[23] 'Alzo al volo' from *Silla*, and 'O scemami il diletto' from Salvi's *Ginevra, principessa di Scozia* (Pratolino, 1708), which years later was to furnish the source libretto for *Ariodante*. This is of particular interest, indicating not only Handel's dominant role in the preparation of his London librettos but that he had probably collected likely texts in Italy, a point confirmed by later evidence.

As usual, nearly all the substitute arias reflect a preference for direct emotional utterance over abstract and platitudinous generalization. A number of Lalli's texts fall into this category; on the other hand he deserves credit for inspiring several fine arias, including the greatest of all, 'Ombra cara'. Three times ('Troppo sofferse', 'Dolce bene', 'Deggio dunque') Handel substituted an expression of tenderness for one of violence. Zenobia's defiant 'Son contenta di morire' ousted a confident pronouncement that her injuries will placate a cruel heaven. 'Mirerò quel vago', 'Dopo torbide procelle', and, most conspicuously, 'Quando mai spietata sorte' displaced more conventional texts: Fraarte promising to carry out Tiridate's orders, Polissena reflecting that a faithful heart suffers and hopes but often triumphs in the end, Zenobia telling the winds and birds to be quiet in face of her misfortunes. For 'Vaga e bella' Lalli had an obscure quatrain about the duties of kingship, for 'Non sarà quest'alma' a cool resolve to hold a fair balance between brother and husband. In Lalli's duet the lovers merely say how delightful it is to meet again. The only texts that are not clear improvements are 'Sposo ingrato', perhaps because Handel decided to use an old aria from his Italian years, and

[23] The words as first set were identical. Handel later modified them in the autograph, but at one point (bars 16–17) forgot to do so, with the result that an anomaly survives in every subsequent copy and in HG.

TABLE 5

	Florence 1712*	London Apr. 1720	London Dec. 1720	London 1728
Radamisto	5 + duet	(S) 6 + duet	(A) 7 + 2 duets	(A) 7
Zenobia	6 (2 cavatinas) + duet	(A) 7 (2 cavatinas) + duet	(S) 7 (2 cavatinas) + 2 duets	(S) 8 (2 cavatinas)
Polissena	7 (1 cavatina)	(S) 5 (1 cavatina)	(S) 5 (1 cavatina)	(S) 8 (1 cavatina)
Tiridate	6 (3 cavatinas)	(T) 3	(B) 3	(B) 3
Tigrane	6	(S) 3	(S) 5	(A) 3
Fraarte	4	(S) 4	(S) 3	[cut]
Farasmane	1	(B) 1	(B) 1	(B) 0
Total	35 + duet	29 + duet	31 + 2 duets and a quartet	29 (no duet or quartet)

* In Gasparini's opera Tigrane and Fraarte were both women's parts.

'Qual nave smarrita', a simile piece about a storm-tossed sailor in both operas, and one which Handel originally set to different words.[24]

For more than two acts the Handel–Haym libretto is by any standards a powerful piece of work. The central conflicts are convincing, with a strong emotional motivation, the characters consistent and clearly drawn, especially Radamisto and the two heroines. Polissena's fidelity to her savage husband may strike us as quixotic; but the concept of honour was central to the *opera seria* convention in dynastic operas. Tiridate's villainy, though grotesque to the point of exaggeration in the absence of Lalli's fuller dialogue, serves as a measuring-rod for the virtues and courage of the others. The language is clear, straightforward, and free from conceit. Act III shows a decline in dramatic interest. Handel tried to remedy this by cutting two scenes at the outset in which Fraarte and Tigrane seek vainly to detach Polissena from Tiridate, promising in return to rescue Radamisto and Farasmane. But the action hangs fire, the situations become wearisome by repetition, and the arias—apart from Polissena's denunciation of Tiridate when her patience is exhausted—add nothing to the characterization. Hitherto there have been no major improbabilities or coincidences; but it is not clear how Farasmane comes to be at large in Tiridate's palace when Zenobia is assaulted (III v) or in the temple a little later (III vii). The denouement, until Handel improved it for a revival, is an anticlimax.

Burney remarked justly that 'the composition of this opera is more solid, ingenious, and full of fire than any drama which Handel had yet produced in this country'. The obvious care expended on it, the dedication to the King, and certain ambitious features of the design suggest that Handel planned it for the opening of the Royal Academy. In *Radamisto* he essayed and conquered the grandest, most elevated type of *opera seria*, in which the characters are larger than life and there is no place for the supernatural or the ironical light and shade of which he had proved himself a master. If something is sacrificed here, much is gained. As the unusually elaborate stage directions indicate (Handel wrote them scrupulously into the autograph, sometimes with significant changes), the spectacular element was strongly emphasized, especially in Act I: not the magic machines of *Rinaldo* and *Amadigi* but the pomp of pageantry, the manoeuvring of armies, and an assault on a fortified city. As befits such a theme, the overture lacks the customary dance movement. However for the first version of the opera Handel composed three ballet suites, the first two as entr'actes, the third an integral part of the finale. Dancing between acts was common in the London theatres, but this is the only opera (outside the Sallé season of 1734–5) for which Handel is known to have supplied extensive ballet music. The unusually massive *coro*, amounting to 314 bars in the first version, was undoubtedly planned to celebrate an extraordinary occasion.

Like all Handel's greatest operas, *Radamisto* has a simple theme of universal validity round which the action develops, the heroism of a married couple assailed by mortal dangers—the theme of *Rodelinda* and *Fidelio* but few other operas of the highest rank. The mutual love of Zenobia and Radamisto shines all the brighter by contrast with the very different relationship of the other

---

[24] This is also true of 'Mirerò quel vago': see p. 350.

married couple, Polissena and Tiridate. All four are drawn in depth. Despite the gallantry of Radamisto and the bluster of Tiridate, the two women dominate the opera. The first and last scenes of Act I belong to Polissena, but Zenobia is the true heroine, a character never swerving from devotion to her husband and prepared to meet death for his sake, even at his hands. It is a measure of Handel's insight that she retains her gentleness however desperate her situation. He wrote the part for Anastasia Robinson, now a contralto, a singer with a sympathetic personality, more renowned for sweetness of tone than technical accomplishment; he supported her with discreet violin doubling almost throughout three arias. It is notable that only three of her seven solos are in regular da capo form; two are cavatinas, one a binary movement without opening ritornello, and one, though a da capo aria on paper, so idiosyncratic that it suggests something quite different to the ear.

Of her first four utterances, two are fiery arias in C minor and two slow movements in the relative major E flat, a conjunction that must be deliberate. Anastasia Robinson disliked playing the termagant, but Handel gave her two explosive pieces of the highest quality. Zenobia's first action in the opera is an offer to sacrifice her life for her husband, privately if necessary in order not to humiliate him. 'Son contenta di morire', her single aria in Act I, establishes her strength of character. Burney thought it old-fashioned because of the thin accompaniment, but it goes very fast (*Presto* is not a common direction in Handel's operas), and the wide-ranging unison violin part in the ritornellos, angular rhythms, heavy accents on weak beats, and emphasis on the flattened sixth and second of the minor scale present a powerful expression of defiance mingled with anguish. This restlessness is accentuated by the ritornello's avoidance of a cadence and the unsymmetrical vocal phrases. The tender serenity at the heart of her character comes over irresistibly in the wonderful cavatina 'Quando mai spietata sorte'. The solo oboe's ten-bar melody anticipates 'Ombra mai fù', but the earlier piece is the finer. The instrumental texture, the wind solo soaring over a warm four-part string accompaniment, has something of the rapt poetry of the Larghetto of Mozart's Clarinet Quintet. When the voice enters it does not imitate the oboe but goes its own way, initiating a dialogue where the parts occasionally allude to each other's material, especially towards the end (from bar 42), but never converge. Even when a phrase is repeated each asserts its independence by moving in a different direction, so that the ear is constantly surprised and refreshed. The placing of the cavatina immediately before the most dramatic incident in the opera is a superb stroke. Radamisto cannot kill her; after his half-hearted attempt she throws herself into the river.

Like Zenobia's first C minor aria, 'Già che morir non posso' is spare in texture with many unisons, but no less potent for that. The violins double the voice almost throughout the A section, and at its first entry the bass drops out for eleven bars. For the last five of them, and again later, the violins divide in a poignant chromatic pattern ('nel mio dolor'), and the viola takes over the bass. The aria is an address to the furies, who make themselves felt in the rushing upward and downward scales. Burney admired the bass, presumably because it contains snatches of the subject (bars 26–8 and 33–5). The last phrase of the ritornello, a series of arpeggiated leaps covering two octaves and a fifth from the violins' bottom G, plays no part in the A section but supplies all the orchestral material of the B section. In 'Troppo sofferse' C minor passion again yields to a gentle E flat. Surprisingly this follows Zenobia's rejection of the unwelcome advances of both Tiridate and Fraarte; but like many Handel sarabandes—for example 'Lascia ch'io pianga' in *Rinaldo* and 'Pena tiranna' in *Amadigi*—it expresses two emotions at once, desolation and the firmness of character to overcome or transcend it. All share the same rhythm, the voice singing even notes on the first two beats followed by a rest, as if for a sigh. Both the melody[25] and the texture have great beauty; the latter, with the flute filling the interstices of the vocal line in a different rhythm, one rising as the other falls, sounds as rich as it is euphonious, although after the first two bars there are only four parts; the first violins double the voice, the seconds the flute. One doubling may be a tactful move to support Anastasia Robinson; the other, as in 'Piangerò' in *Giulio Cesare*, another pathetic lament in a major key, contributes an individual colour. The only ritornello forms an epilogue, with the melody slightly varied and the flute silent.

Zenobia's next solo again breaks the da capo pattern. 'Empio perverso cor', once more without initial ritornello, is unusual in form, addressed alternately to the lecherous Tiridate and her disguised husband, the former in stern octaves *Ardito e forte*, the latter over steady quaver chords *Adagio e piano*. There are nine changes of tempo in a piece of only nineteen bars, and the sections are cunningly shaped. Tiridate receives cursory treatment, five beats of common time at the start, then always three. Radamisto at first has the same allowance, but this is extended to seven and eight beats before monopolizing the last seven bars; the harmony grows more meltingly chromatic as she yearns for the husband she dare not acknowledge in Tiridate's presence. The duet that follows in the tonic major after Tiridate's exit is singularly happy, both in its mood of reconciliation and in subtlety of detail, especially in the orchestra. Variety within the standard layout of oboes and strings is beautifully controlled: chamber duet texture at the vocal entry; violins contrasted with *tutti*; divided oboes and continuo with an exquisite high entry for unison violins (bar 15); trio for violins, viola, and bass; then oboes and violins together but independent, the violins entering even more memorably on a high E in bar 24. Rich counterpoint in the inner parts and suspensions on 'm'abbandoni' give the duet a solidity sometimes lacking in movements of this type, though the brief B section without upper parts is a mere point of contrast.

'Deggio dunque' in Act III is Zenobia's most memorable aria, and one of great originality. The design, with the A section in two halves, Adagio and Allegro, and the B section more restless in tonality but related to the Adagio in mood, texture, and melodic shape as well as tempo, not only offers sharp contrasts but deceives the ear about the form, which sounds like ABA'AB rather than ABA. Handel underlines the extremes by accompanying the Adagios with cello obbligato and bass only, the Allegro with full orchestra including independent oboes, by a sudden plunge into G major for the Allegro after the Adagio has moved from E minor to the dominant, and by a substantial ritornello after the Allegro, the only one in the aria. Zenobia's last

---

[25] The striking first phrase was surely suggested by that of the lovely aria 'Vedi spietato nelle mie pupille' in Vivaldi's *Orlando finto pazzo* (1714), which is in the same key and rhythm, begins without ritornello, and likewise moves to the subdominant in the second bar after a D flat in the first.

aria, 'O scemami il diletto', is something of a disappointment, as if she has suffered too much to rejoice with conviction. It is effective enough, with two ideas in the ritornello, one of them in Handel's favourite syncopated rhythm, and both extensively developed in the aria, but conventional. While Anastasia Robinson receives more divisions than usual, Handel is careful to retain the violin support, again over a silent bass at her first entry.

All Polissena's best music comes in Act I, where her three solos are among the jewels of the score. The cavatina 'Sommi Dei' runs straight on from the overture, in the same key of E minor, without the relaxation of a dance movement. It establishes the tragic mood and lays down the theme of emotional and conjugal conflict in one of the grandest openings in any of the operas. The piece is a prayer to the gods; after a stark ritornello in octaves the striking intervals of the first unaccompanied phrase for the voice, a rising minor sixth followed by a falling tritone (which should not be obscured by decoration), present an epitome of Polissena's anguish. The phrase never returns. The texture, especially at the start and between the exclamations of the voice, is uncompromisingly bleak. The change to full harmony at the third line of text, 'Proteggete un mesto cor' (substituted for Lalli's 'Di chi più mi lagnerò' after composition), is masterly. Every time these words occur the dynamics change from *forte* to *piano* (Chrysander's *forte* at bar 38 should come a bar earlier). Handel ran this cavatina into the following secco without a full resolution; the final bar is not in the original score. 'Tu vuoi ch'io parta', Polissena's reply to Tiridate's brusque dismissal, is even more impressive. The key, E major after Tigrane's intervening aria in G, preserves the tonal design of this part of the opera; not till Zenobia's 'Son contenta di morire' do we encounter a flat key. Again the texture is spare, with a ritornello only after the A section. As in 'Troppo sofferse' and 'Piangerò' Handel doubles the violin line with the flute, and for most of the A section the voice as well. But there is a wealth of artful detail: the frequent rests, for the orchestra as well as the voice, suggest that Polissena can hardly bring her wounded feelings to utterance. Handel leaves no doubt that she loves the odious Tiridate. Particularly touching is the lengthened off-beat 'mà' in bar 8, followed by two silent beats before she can finish the sentence with 'senza core'. At each repetition of this text (bars 20–2 and 28–31) she sticks at the same point, but Handel varies the continuation, on the last occasion interposing a whole silent bar with a fermata. The uneasy turns toward different keys in the B section, accompanied by continuo alone, suggest her vain search for a solution. This aria, another idealized sarabande, is one of Handel's profoundest expressions of the pathetic *Affekt*.

Polissena ends Act I with a very different but equally outstanding aria. Burney called 'Dopo torbide procelle'[26] 'one of the most agreeable *arie fugate* that I know', referring to the imitations between treble and bass which, with the sumptuous inner parts, place it in the same category as 'Vedrò frà poco' in *Admeto*. It is an extraordinary fact that these four opening bars, and their two later appearances, were superimposed after the aria had been fully composed; its original first phrase was later used for 'Se in fiorito ameno prato' in Act II of *Giulio Cesare*. Yet the marvellous ten-bar melody sounds perfectly of a piece. Although the verbal simile seems a little forced in its context, the aria makes a splendid act conclusion, gaining impetus from the lilting rhythm, buoyant

26 The words in HG belong to a later version.

syncopations, and frequent five-bar phrases. The violin entries with sustained notes high above the voice in bars 20, 34, and 43 (for some unfathomable reason Chrysander crossed out the *Viol* of the Hamburg score and all the sources here) add a delightful airiness to the texture. The top B flats in bars 32 and 49—and a high A and B flat on the two semiquavers of bar 32—were written for Ann Turner Robinson and sung at the first performance.

Polissena is restricted to a single aria in each of the later acts, which (until her final volte-face) leave her little to do except cling to her husband whatever the provocation and offer Tigrane a fairly gentle cold shoulder. 'Non sarà quest'alma', an undigested and almost literal borrowing from the *Brockes Passion*, falls flat after her refusal to support her brother against Tiridate. She sits on the fence in the appeasing attitude of a Chamberlain rather than a Churchill, and Handel cannot make the posture interesting. Despite some variation of accent within the bar this is a mediocre piece; the obsessive triplets, which threaten to convert it into 9/8 time, grow tiresome before the end. 'Sposo ingrato' is even more of an anticlimax. For some reason Handel decided to resuscitate an old lag of an aria that had served three terms in its youth[27] (in the February 1707 cantata *Delirio amoroso* (HWV 99), *Rodrigo*, and *Agrippina*), presumably as a display piece for Ann Turner Robinson, who must have been a considerable singer to master its difficulties, and the soloists of his orchestra, notably the leader Castrucci. The concerto grosso accompaniment is highly ornate; quite apart from the solo violin's tiresome efflorescence of triplets, the piece strikes a dramatically false note, suggesting not so much an estranged and indignant wife as an amorous nightingale. Handel, generally so successful in reconciling the demands of character and singer, saw his mistake and made ample amends in the December 1720 revival.

It is important to recall that the part of Radamisto was composed for a woman soprano, the reliable Margherita Durastanti. Handel may have known or hoped that Senesino would sing it eventually and written music capable of transposition for him, but he always kept his eye on immediate requirements. In any event this is a young and vulnerable hero. Both his Act I arias are in A major, another sign of a tonal plan, though Handel did not stick to it. 'Cara sposa' is the only continuo aria in the opera, in the old seventeenth-century form with the single fully-scored ritornello (a mere two bars) reserved to the end after the da capo. Handel liked to introduce important characters in this way. He was to use it for Cuzzoni (to her fury) with 'Falsa imagine' in *Ottone*, and for Senesino with 'Alma mia' in *Floridante* and 'Bella Asteria' in *Tamerlano*. In each case he presents the character in the intimate role of a lover, though Radamisto has his back to the wall in a besieged city. The tempo is slow (*Larghetto* in 'Alma mia', *Largo* in the others), and the bass begins by anticipating the vocal line, which however does not follow it exactly. In 'Cara sposa' the interplay of the two parts and the varied but related responses of one to the other are a model of craftsmanship; this is art that conceals art. The music has variety, vitality, and great lyrical charm. The B section widens the scope by veering towards F sharp minor and B minor before settling in C sharp minor. 'Ferite, uccidete' paints both Radamisto's resolution and his sense of being at the end of his tether. The long ritornello (36 bars) suddenly loses its bass in the middle, and the unison violins plunge wildly into A minor.

---

[27] Burney derives it from an early Hamburg cantata, 'Casti amori', on what evidence is not known.

At the corresponding point in the aria (bar 55), at the words 'che forza a penar il misero cor', Handel cancels the signature of three sharps; but although the violin part follows that of the ritornello for six bars the added harmony of bass and voice indicates C major, a strangely emotional and romantic effect. The passage is prolonged by development of the angular rhythmic figure first heard in bars 15 and 16. Handel again changed the key signature in the ritornello after the A section (bars 120–7); Chrysander needlessly tidied this up.

Of 'Ombra cara' it is difficult to write in measured terms. It is beyond question one of the greatest arias composed by Handel or anyone else in the eighteenth century. Burney mentions the admiration of Geminiani and other contemporary masters, and recalled Reginelli singing it in 1747 'among some light Italian songs of that period, and it seemed the language of philosophy and science, and the rest the frivolous jargon of fops and triflers'. Its virtue resides in the use of that 'science' to express a mood of profound personal tragedy. The exquisite, almost rhapsodic, vocal line of Radamisto's lament for his lost wife winds its way through a complex polyphonic texture in five independent freely-moving parts. At no time is the voice doubled in the orchestra. The chromatic scale figure covering a fourth, a traditional emblem of grief, is treated with rare skill, moving in both directions, taken up by each instrumental part at unpredictable intervals, and carried by the first violins into the B section. Scarcely less memorable are the imitation between second violins and bass in the opening bars, the trio-sonata structure reinforced by high bassoons in bars 5–8 and (with an inner pedal on the voice) 21–3, the violin figure in bar 10 stepping upwards in fourths, the contrast of stationary harmonic rhythm over a pedal with imitation between the three upper strings at the start of the B section (bars 76–8), and the same thing in bars 89–91 darkened by a touch of A flat minor before the cadence in the major (relative of the tonic F minor). Handel's first tempo was *Largo*; at some time after the first performance he added *mà non troppo* to warn against dragging.

'Vanne, sorella ingrata' is Radamisto's indignant answer to Polissena's refusal to come off the fence. Naturally it starts without ritornello; the irregular phrase-lengths (2 + 1 + 2 bars) betray his agitation and shortness of breath. After this homophonic outburst and a two-bar ritornello the texture suddenly changes to a dialogue in which violins, oboes, and voice converse, each according to its nature, over a simple bass. The violins' emphasis on the G string, punctuated by huge leaps, underlines Radamisto's simmering anger. The concluding ritornello binds together the two strands, and the B section introduces a third, subdued string chords as Radamisto imagines Polissena rejoicing at his death.

His two Act III arias, in G minor and major, are in their different styles equally fine. 'Dolce bene', in which he assures Zenobia of his undying devotion, has a masterly ritornello: oboes and violins begin in unison and end in thirds, but diverge fascinatingly in between, the former mounting to long high notes while the latter busily deploy one of Handel's favourite 12/8 rhythms, destined to permeate such inspired choruses as 'The gods who chosen blessings shed' in *Athalia* and 'For ever thus stands fixed the doom' in *Theodora*. The bassoons introduce a mellow warmth in the middle register; Handel at first had them doubling the violas, but struck out the latter before the December 1720 revival. All the ideas of this ritornello, and others, are widely canvassed in the beautifully scored aria, which has more work for the bassoons and a solo oboe. It might seem strange for Radamisto to offer Zenobia a love song in gigue rhythm; but the light touch, delicate colouring, and minor tonality dispel any hint of the frivolous. 'Qual nave smarrita', the opera's third sarabande aria, has another exquisite melody, though the simile about a storm-tossed ship has little force or relationship to the music. Handel's original aria here, 'Senza luce, senza guida', based on a familiar hemiola formula first used in *Almira* ('Move i passi'), was also a simile piece, a plaintive G minor lament; its text is linked both with Lalli's 'Qual nocchiero' at this point and with 'Qual nave'. But the latter was conceived as an expression of hope ('Speranza gradita') in the last scene just before the *coro*. In transplanting it and changing the words Handel was false to the *Affekt*; yet we can hardly deplore his desire to preserve such a beautiful piece.

The character of Tiridate suffers from the truncation of Lalli's libretto. If he remains credible, it is thanks to the energy and vitality of the music. He is a complete extrovert, without a hint of self-doubt, a tyrant confident of his ability to conquer in war or love. All three of his arias are in sharp major keys (two in D, one in A); two of them are based on pieces in earlier operas, in text as well as music, expanded, reinforced by brass, and signally improved. 'Stragi, morti' was a tenor aria in Act I of *Rodrigo*; Handel now furnished it with a trumpet obbligato and a fuller texture throughout, added the menacing dotted figures, and extended both sections. The flourishes and sustained notes of the trumpet, and the consequent raising of the pitch from C to D, add force to Tiridate's battle piece, which makes a brilliant effect in the theatre; Giuliano in *Rodrigo* had to be content with an oboe. The B section has more variety of figuration; the headlong downward scales for violins and bass expand a hint in bar 15. The elaborate divisions and taxing tessitura leave no doubt that the Scottish adventurer Alexander Gordon, despite his collision with Handel during the rehearsals of *Flavio*, must have been a high tenor of no mean accomplishment.

'Sì che ti renderai' is the subtlest of his three arias. Its most distinctive feature, bringing a shock of surprise whenever it appears, is the unexpected dip into the minor, led by *pianissimo* violins, towards the end of the ritornello, which adds a veneer at once sinister and insinuating to Tiridate's braggart self-confidence. The B section closes in B minor; the return to A major for the da capo is characteristically brusque. 'Alzo al volo' has two forerunners, the first air in *Silla* and the similarly placed 'Pende il ben' in the cantata *Apollo e Dafne*. Both are sung by despots, one alto, the other bass. Tiridate's is much longer than either (Silla's with a single upper part is the least developed) and has the welcome reinforcement of two horns. They colour the whole aria, opening the way for pedal and echo effects (horns and *tutti* in bars 9–15, horns, violins, and voice in bars 88–93) and giving the music an irresistible bounce, very appropriate at a point when Tiridate believes he has won. There is a strong foretaste of 'Sound an alarm' at bars 35–40. This was the first appearance of horns in a London opera.[28] The B section is distinguished by vocal cross-rhythms, seventh leaps, arpeggio violin figures (much admired by Burney), and the strong cadence in the dominant: Tiridate is in no mood for dawdling in relative or other minor keys.

---

[28] Alessandro Scarlatti had introduced them in *Tigrane* (1715), a copy of which, now in the Music Library at the Barber Institute of Fine Arts, Birmingham University (MS 5004), had been brought to England by Gordon. The tenor may have been indirectly responsible for their appearance in his aria, though Handel was familiar with Keiser's use of them in *Octavia* (1705).

Fraarte and Tigrane, both sopranos, have a parallel status as confederates of Tiridate and suitors of Zenobia and Polissena respectively, in which role neither receives the slightest encouragement. They share seven arias, all lively in pace and all except one ('Spero placare') in major keys; Handel took almost as much trouble over them as over the principals, writing interesting and sometimes quite elaborate accompaniments with wind as well as strings. Again there are glimpses of a tonal plan: Fraarte's first and last arias are in F, his second in B flat, his third in D minor; Tigrane's first and last are in G. The expansion of Fraarte's role seems to have been a gesture of accommodation towards the castrato Benedetto Baldassari, a singer of some reputation well known in London.[29] He apparently thought the character beneath him: according to an anonymous letter in *The Theatre* of 12 March 1720 he complained 'that he had never acted any thing, in any other Opera, below the Character of a Sovereign; or, at least, a Prince of the Blood; and that now he was appointed to be a Captain of the Guard, and a Pimp... he found Friends, and was made a Prince'.[30] Perhaps that explains Fraarte's promotion to Tiridate's brother. The finest of his arias is the first, 'Mirerò quel vago volto', an outstandingly lovely piece as happily scored as anything in the opera. The opening is unusual not only for the exclusion of the strings but for its initial dominant chord—C major after a C major cadence (it was planned to follow Tiridate's A minor cadence at 'Ah! quasi dissi amore'). Subsequent changes of colour are kaleidoscopic, oboes and bassoons variously contrasted and combined with strings; long sections have a solo cello on the bass line, and sometimes a solo oboe doubling the voice, as in the whole B section.[31] The scoring counteracts the harmonic placidity of the A section, where the flattened seventh of the vocal melody, not anticipated in the ritornello, is all the more effective. The pastoral trills and delightful hemiola rhythms are at variance with the words, Fraarte's confident hope of overcoming Zenobia's resistance. They are no more apt for the original text, 'Umiliata a piedi tuoi', in which he promises to procure her for Tiridate. The music is a much-enriched expansion of 'Chiudi i vaghi rai' in *Il trionfo del Tempo*.

'Vaga e bella' too is dramatically adrift. Fraarte sings of the happiness Tiridate will enjoy with Zenobia, with whom he himself is in love. There is no sign of irony, because Fraarte's love was introduced after the aria had been composed, and Handel did not bother to change it. It is an attractive gigue saved from monotony by cross-rhythms and misplaced accents. 'Spero placare' on the other hand was inserted after Fraarte's role had been determined. It has some lively counterpoint in the A section and no lack of rhythmic interest; Handel lightens the texture by accompanying much of it with the three upper strings only, the violas providing the bass. 'S'adopri il braccio armato' is a carefree piece in which the violas, doubled by bassoons, again

[29] He sang there in 1712 and from March 1719. He is the only castrato known to have played a female role in London (see p. 157); and he created the role of Charlemagne's daughter Teodata in Steffani's *Tassilone* at Düsseldorf in January 1709. He was involved in an attempt by his patron the Elector Palatine and Steffani to convert the King and Queen of Prussia to Catholicism.

[30] Deutsch (101) prints only part of the letter. The full text (in Gibson, *The Royal Academy*, 408–9) is more explicit. 'We directed, that he should make love to ZENOBIA, with proper limitations. The Chairman signified to him, that the Board had made him a Lover; but he must be contented to be an unfortunate one, and be rejected by his mistress. He expressed himself very easy under this.'

[31] Chrysander does not make this clear; at bar 71 he changed *solo* to *soli* against the authority of all copies (the autograph has *sol. violonc.*). Bar 82 is parallel, and marked *solo* in the only complete copy of the first version.

have their niche. It adds little to the drama; Fraarte is not here concerned with his love for Zenobia. The figure introduced in bars 5 and 6, which several times punctuates the A section and takes the lead in the ritornello after it, occurs in many other works, including *Rinaldo*, *Tamerlano*, *Semele*, and *Theodora*.

Just as Handel brought up the violins to support Anastasia Robinson, he gave Galerati much oboe doubling in all three of Tigrane's arias. It is skilfully done; when released from guard duty the oboes play their full part in the ritornellos. 'Deh! fuggi un traditore' is a spirited bravura piece designed to set off Polissena's two slow arias in the first scene. 'La sorte, il ciel' is less interesting, but 'Con vana speranza', based with improvements on 'Del cielo dolente' in *La Resurrezione*, brings Tigrane very much to life. The melody's initial falling seventh, the dominant minor colouring in bars 7–8 of the ritornello, later associated with the word 'pena', and the long phrases with their undulating rhythmic repetitions deftly light up his rueful admission that Polissena is not for him. His love contrasts favourably with Tiridate's lust for Zenobia and invests him with unexpected sympathy. Farasmane's single aria, composed for a secondary bass and inserted as an afterthought, is not the equal of Handel's music for Boschi; the full accompaniment compensates in some degree for the shortness of the vocal phrases.

Radamisto is a very formal work. The first version is almost unique among Handel's operas in having no accompanied recitatives.[32] The great majority of the arias are in the strictest da capo form; apart from three cavatinas and one binary piece only four of them, including the irregular 'Deggio dunque', have a shortened dal segno ritornello. The *coro* is a huge rondo in minuet rhythm, its three episodes symmetrical duets for the six principal characters in pairs in the dominant, relative minor, and mediant minor. Even the dance suite into which it runs—a Passepied and Rigaudon, with the Passepied repeated—has close thematic connections. Indeed the Passepied, a separate piece probably dating from about 1712, seems to have been the germ from   *
which the whole *coro* sprang. It occurs in autograph[33] in the following form:

Ex. 38

<hr>

[32] *Silla* and *Deidamia*, two of the weakest, are the only other instances of this.
[33] Fitzwilliam Museum, Mus MS 263, p. 3. A. Mann (*HJb* (1964/5), 37–8) relates it to the music composed for the education of Princess Anne. B. Baselt, 'Händels Skizzenbücher: die Menuette',

In *Radamisto* Handel based the Rigaudon on the same material in common time and the minor mode:

Ex. 39

The entr'acte ballets can scarcely be regarded as integral parts of the opera, though their keys are those of the concluding movements of the first two acts, B flat and A major. The first consists of a jolly March, two Rigaudons[34] (the second in G minor), and an Air (or third Rigaudon). The second is more substantial, especially the splendid Passacaille used later (with superimposed choral parts) in *Parnasso in festa* and *Terpsicore*. It was published, transposed to G major and with the scoring simplified, in the trio sonata Op. 5 no. 4, but seems to have been composed for *Radamisto*, where it is followed by a lively Gigue.

The other orchestral movement (apart from the stately and solid French overture), the sinfonia for the assault on the city in I viii, is a conventional D major battle piece. Its most interesting feature is that it accompanied a scene-change (*nel qual tempo si cangia la Scena*). As we have seen, Handel associated certain keys with particular scenes and characters, but although the sharp major and flat minor keys predominate—the former in the first and third acts, the latter in the second—there is no overall tonal plan.

The orchestration is on a big scale. *Radamisto* lacks *Rinaldo*'s choir of recorders and battery of trumpets and drums, but the aria accompaniments are fuller and more carefully worked. Scarcely any have fewer than four instrumental parts, and many have more. Besides the horns there are obbligatos for violin, cello, oboe, and trumpet. Horns and trumpets combine in the *coro*, their colour sometimes contrasted; the second trumpet plays only here. The bassoons leave their mark on several movements and are divided momentarily in 'Sposo ingrato' and the Passacaille. Handel uses both oboes and violas more freely than usual. The former are twice replaced by flutes (played by

---

Der Komponist und sein Adressat, ed. S. Bimberg (Halle, 1976), 64, cites two more variants from the Aylesford copies, a Passepied in C and a Minuet in D.

[34] The first is a reworking of an Allemande in G from the Hamburg opera *Florindo/Daphne*; see p. 76.

the same artists); elsewhere they are silent in only six of the 33 numbers, and seldom confined to the menial role of doubling violins in the ritornellos. Their frequent solos are not always indicated by Chrysander, who, perhaps in the belief that Handel had only two oboes, several times changed *Hautb: s* or *solo* to *Ob 1* or *Oboe senza Viol*. Another misleading feature is his automatic interpretation of Handel's *Tutti* above the top line in movements with two treble instrumental staves as indicating divided oboes, whereas the presumption is that it means both oboes should take the top line. There are a number of arias in *Radamisto* where Handel, after beginning with *Tutti*, later switches violins and oboes between staves, modifying the original direction. Occasionally the result is ambiguous; but in at least six arias in the original score, and several in the December 1720 version, both oboes, *pace* Chrysander, should take the top line. This interpretation is confirmed in almost every instance by the extractor of the Flower parts, a member of the Smith circle (S2).

Radamisto is perhaps the only Handel opera of which a later version has a strong claim to rank with or even above the original. Before considering this it is necessary to tabulate the versions:

   i April 1720, that of the autograph, now defective at the end and later modified by Handel. This has never been published or properly distinguished; apart from the ballet suites its differences from HG, though not radical, are significant. Some have already been mentioned; they are listed below, p. 345.
   ii Chrysander's first version, taken from a copy (*c*.1721) incorporating changes during the original run and excluding the ballet suites.
   iii December 1720.
   iv November 1721.
   v January 1728.

Chrysander's *Seconda e Terza Versione* is a jumble of the last three, none of them indicated in full and containing many inaccuracies.

In December 1720 Handel, with a new company, including the castratos Senesino and Berselli, carried out a very extensive revision involving the transposition of three important parts, major changes in the plot, and the composition of much new music. He changed Radamisto from soprano to alto, Zenobia from alto to soprano, and Tiridate from tenor to bass. He did not confine himself to his usual practice of patching and substitution; in certain scenes he went some way towards recomposing the opera. The changes are best listed under each character; Farasmane's part, except for minor adjustments in recitative, remained untouched.

ZENOBIA. Her solo music for December 1720 has been lost through disturbance of the performing score for later revivals. What Chrysander attributes to her belongs entirely to 1728, except for 'Fatemi, O cieli' in E minor (HG 170, A version), which she sang not in III i but in II vi at the point where Chrysander (HG 158) indicates 'Ferite, uccidete'. Her new duet with Radamisto, 'Non hò più affanni', replaced 'O scemami il diletto'. For the rest, she retained 'Son contenta di morire' (probably in D minor), 'Quando mai spietata sorte', 'Già che morir non posso', 'Troppo sofferse' transferred to the beginning of II x (perhaps with an opening ritornello), 'Empio perverso cor', and 'Deggio dunque' (not as printed in HG 191). She probably sang the original versions transposed up between a tone and a third, though the narrow compass of 'Troppo sofferse' may have enabled Durastanti to keep it in E flat. 'Fatemi, O cieli' is a beautiful siciliano with strong Neapolitan inflections and frequent seventh intervals expressing Zenobia's anguish over Radamisto's fate. The sense of heart-break is accentuated by the relative major cadence in the middle of the A section. She is alone on the stage; the removal of Fraarte waiting to sing his aria is a dramatic improvement. 'Non hò più affanni', in a favourite Handel rhythm, has the tunefulness and light touch of a popular song. It is repetitive and sequential, but the absence of an initial ritornello (compensated by an enriched one with separate bassoon part at the end) and the avoidance of da capo form supply welcome variety.

POLISSENA. Handel strengthened the role dramatically and made musical changes for Salvai, a soprano with a lower compass than Ann Turner Robinson. He added vocal alternatives in bars 14, 23, and 24 of 'Sommi Dei';[35] the substitution of E for G in bar 14 takes the sap out of the opening phrase. 'Tu vuoi ch'io parta' was put down from E to D and the flute omitted. In 'Dopo l'orride procelle' (now with the Chrysander text) Salvai avoided the high B flats. 'Non sarà quest'alma' received a new and stronger text ('Che farà quest'alma', HG 162): Polissena will die before she can resolve the struggle in her heart. Handel gave Salvai continuo support in the long initial solo and changed the unison instrument from oboe to violin. Her one new aria, 'Barbaro, partirò' (in A, not B flat as HG 187), is an enormous improvement on 'Sposo ingrato'. The explosive first phrase, delivered without ritornello or bass immediately after Tiridate's order for Radamisto's death, is a brilliant stroke, and the whole aria with its angry divisions, rushing scales, and electric syncopations in the violin parts (bars 21–3) gives vivid expression to Polissena's fury, all the more potent after her meekness hitherto. Her entire character gains in depth.

RADAMISTO. In adapting the part for Senesino Handel transposed five arias down a third or fourth, with some consequent adjustments in the orchestra (HG 143, 159, 176, 193). A few details were improved, notably in the ritornello after the A section of 'Vanne, sorella ingrata', which Handel shortened by a bar, extending the semiquaver scale figure to the bass. The duet 'Se teco vive' was modified verbally but not musically, Radamisto and Zenobia simply exchanging parts. Chrysander's supposition of a lost setting derives from the accidental omission of a line in the printed libretto. Senesino received two new arias and an accompanied recitative. 'Perfido' replaced 'Ferite, uccidete' (Handel originally intended Senesino to sing the latter in E flat), and 'Vile! se mi dai vita' with its accompanied recitative 'Vieni d'empietà' was inserted in III iv. Both new arias are fiery 3/8 pieces in which Radamisto rounds on his enemies. In each he ejaculates the first word unaccompanied, with a strong gesture of a falling fourth. Both exploit Senesino's skill in executing long divisions, narrow in compass but requiring uncommon agility and breath-control. 'Perfido' in particular is a magnificent aria. The silent second bar (with a fermata), omitted in the compressed ritornello after the A section, greatly strengthens the impact. Its rhythm,

---

[35] These changes, the only ones in the autograph in red ink, could have been made for Margherita de l'Epine in the last performance of the original run (22 June 1720), but this is less likely.

generally with the octave drop of the voice's second statement, punctuates the orchestra at frequent but irregular intervals as if to renew its propulsive force—usually *forte* but with one very effective *piano*—and even invades the B section. 'Vile' with its urgent dotted figure in the accompaniment is scarcely less energetic. Both arias enlarge Radamisto's stature as a heroic figure.

TIRIDATE. The new bass aria 'Con la strage' sacrifices the trumpet of 'Stragi, morti' and has less striking material. Handel wrote many arias of this type for Boschi, but the vocal leaps and scale figures over a wide compass, the contrast between octaves and full inner parts in different rhythms, and the varied length of the ritornellos give the music a virile character apt for a tyrant. Tiridate retained his other two arias in transposed and enriched versions, 'Sì che ti renderai' in F with a written out bassoon part (HG 155), 'Alzo al volo' not in C as stated by Chrysander but also in F. Handel added two high trumpets in F (*trombini*) to the horns, which they do not merely double, and made a number of other significant changes besides entirely rethinking the vocal line, especially the coloratura, in terms of Boschi's voice.[36] The string chords in bars 60 and 62 are omitted; the dialogue in bars 89–93 is shared between horns and trumpets while the voice sustains a dominant pedal; the B section is four bars shorter, and the horns are held back till the equivalent of bar 142. Handel gave Tiridate four extra lines of recitative in the last scene in a not very successful attempt to make his repentance more convincing.

FRAARTE. His function in the plot was radically altered by the excision of his love for Zenobia, and he was demoted from his princely rank as Tiridate's brother to that of minister, reverting to his status in Lalli's libretto and the first version of Handel's autograph. His recitatives were cut altogether from five scenes (I ix and x, II v, vi, and vii) and shortened in two others (II iii and III i); but he now appeared in I i, taking over some lines from Tigrane, including three that Handel had not set in the first version.[37] Fraarte lost his three arias concerned with love for Zenobia ('Mirerò quel vago volto', 'Vaga e bella', and 'Spero placare') but retained 'S'adopri' (with simplified coloratura in bars 21, 27–9, 40, and 42) and took over 'Deh! fuggi un traditore' in I i from Tigrane, no doubt because Galerati, who had sung it in the latter role, was now cast as Fraarte.[38] It comes in very awkwardly at this point. Fraarte's one new aria, 'Lascia pur amica spene', interpolated in II iii, is a pleasant enough piece, but his attempt to console Zenobia holds up the action without contributing anything essential.

TIGRANE. Handel enlarged the part for Berselli, to the disadvantage of the opera. In I i, after 'Deh! fuggi un traditore', he has a new scene with Polissena (culminating in 'L'ingrato non amar') in which he threatens that if she cannot trust his love or Fraarte's friendship they will proceed with their cruel design. In II ii, between Zenobia's plunge into the river and 'Ombra cara', Tigrane persuades Radamisto to come to the aid of the slighted Polissena and sings an

---

[36] This version, not in HG, has been published in a facsimile of the autograph, now in Berlin, edited by W. Siegmund-Schultze (1959). If, as is just possible but unlikely, it dates from the 1728 revival, the *trombini* may have been 'the two new instruments called the Chamber Horns, never before heard in public', played in concerts at Hickford's and Lincoln's Inn Fields in March 1728, sometimes with French horns (see *The London Stage* under 15, 20, and 27 March).

[37] Chrysander, who thought that Fraarte was cut out in December, does not print them.

[38] Chrysander (HG 121), following a confusion in the libretto, allots it to Tigrane.

extended aria, 'Vuol ch'io serva',[39] gravely weakening one of the opera's finest scenes. Tigrane retained 'La sorte, il ciel', his only aria not concerned with love for Polissena, and received four new ones; the two not hitherto mentioned were 'Segni di crudeltà' at his exit in I xii and 'Sò ch'è vana la speranza' (in D major, not F as HG 174) in place of 'Con vana speranza'. All four are of good quality and similarly scored, with a delicately handled four-part orchestra. In 'L'ingrato non amar', an emotional C minor appeal to Polissena's pity, the voice is accompanied almost throughout both sections by two solo violins and a solo cello. 'Segni di crudeltà' has oboe and cello solos and an attractive springy melody striding across the bar lines. 'Vuol ch'io serva' with its pedals and triplets is also pretty, but the aria is too long and the triplets carried to excess. In 'Sò ch'è vana', based on an aria in *La Resurrezione* and other early works, Handel silences the harpsichord while the voice is singing. The form is unusual, with three vocal sections, the first two repeated, sandwiched between identical ritornellos, and no da capo.

The most striking addition for this revival, which goes far to outweigh all disadvantages, is the magnificent quartet at the climax of the action in III x. Handel deploys the full concerted style of later opera, years ahead of its time, each character clearly differentiated and the drama carried forward in the music. The three upper voices, Polissena, Zenobia, and Radamisto, appeal to Tiridate sometimes in turn, sometimes overlapping with imitative or con-trasted phrases, sometimes—notably at the end of each section—all together. He remains obdurate, preferring death to surrender. The instrumental parts are equally deft; occasionally a solo violin or oboe moves in thirds or unison with one of the voices, while the bassoons double Tiridate or the string basses (or both). One is astonished that Handel, having mastered this technique, used it so seldom. We find it occasionally in the English works (the trios in *Acis and Galatea*, *Susanna*, and *The Choice of Hercules*, the quartets in *Semele* and *Jephtha*); it is sadly rare in the operas (the trios in *Tamerlano*, *Orlando*, and *Alcina* are exceptional), owing no doubt to the almost exclusive attraction of the solo voice for both singers and audiences.

Handel composed ten new arias, a duet, and the quartet for the December 1720 revival. Its merit resides above all in the reinforcement of Act III, which instead of tapering off rises to a splendid climax. The accompanied recitative, Radamisto's heroic aria, the substitution of 'Barbaro, partirò' for 'Sposo ingrato', the quartet, and the second duet without da capo not only tighten the drama; they give the design a flexibility uncommon at this period. The formalism has sprouted wings. The weak point is the increased prominence of Fraarte and Tigrane, who together have eight arias instead of seven, and less justification for them. This however can be remedied by cutting. It is also possible to some extent to combine the versions; while some exquisite music in the first has gone, there is no falling off in the quality of the replacements. Nor is the status of the leading characters abridged. Only the removal of Fraarte's love for Zenobia, which quickens the middle of Act II, leaves him as a spare limb, ripe for lopping a year later.

---

[39] Chrysander prints it and the words of the two linking recitatives in the wrong place; they should follow HG 142.

History and Text

The exact date of composition is unknown, since the last pages of the autograph carrying most of the ballet music are lost. The nature of the opera, the dedication to the King, and Handel's position as the company's musical director support the conjecture that he expected the Royal Academy to open with *Radamisto*. For whatever reason,[40] that honour fell to Giovanni Porta's *Numitore* on 2 April 1720. *Radamisto* followed on the 27th, with the following cast:

RADAMISTO:	Margherita Durastanti (soprano)
ZENOBIA:	Anastasia Robinson (contralto)
POLISSENA:	Ann Turner Robinson (soprano)
FRAARTE:	Benedetto Baldassari (soprano castrato)
TIGRANE:	Caterina Galerati (soprano)
TIRIDATE:	Alexander Gordon (tenor)
FARASMANE:	Lagarde (bass)

This was not an outstanding cast by the standards of later seasons, but—apart from the absence of a castrato of Nicolini's reputation—it compares well with earlier London companies, and the technical demands of the music show that Handel had confidence in both the British and Italian singers.

The version performed can be reconstructed from several early copies, the libretto, and the Meares printed score, and by comparing these with different layers of the autograph, which Handel, contrary to his usual practice, modified after the opera had been produced. Apart from the three ballet suites, the fusion of 'Sommi Dei' with the following recitative, and the slower tempo (*Largo*) for 'Ombra cara', 'Son contenta di morire' (B section) and 'Dopo torbide procelle' had different texts, and the latter more high notes than indicated by Chrysander. Radamisto's part in the opening recitative of Act II had a higher tessitura. Bars 13–16 of 'Deggio dunque' took a different form, Zenobia interjecting the word 'pietà!' thrice more in a rhythm subsequently transferred to the upper instruments. Tigrane sang the upper, Fraarte the lower part in the third duet section of the *coro*. There were minor differences in several arias, notably 'Troppo sofferse', 'Non sarà quest'alma', and 'Dolce bene'.

The opera was received with enthusiasm. Lady Cowper mentions a 'Great Crowd' on the first night, including the King and the Prince of Wales, and Mainwaring says the applause 'was almost as extravagant as . . . *Agrippina* had excited', adding: 'Many [ladies], who had forc'd their way into the house with an impetuosity ill suited to their rank and sex, actually fainted through the excessive heat and closeness of it. Several gentlemen were turned back, who had offered forty shillings for a seat in the gallery, after having despaired of getting any in the pit or boxes.' There were ten performances, the last on 22 June. At the fifth (11 May) 'His Majesty, the Prince and Princess, and a prodigious Number of the Nobility were at the Opera'. On the last night

*

---

[40] The reason may be connected with the impending reconciliation of the King and the Prince of Wales after a prolonged quarrel. Since December 1717 they had not been on speaking terms and had maintained separate courts. The estrangement ended on 23 Apr. 1720; four days later they appeared in public together at the première of *Radamisto*.

Margherita de l'Epine sang Polissena, presumably because Ann Turner Robinson was ill.

Handel revived *Radamisto* on 28 December 1720 in the middle of the very successful run of Bononcini's *Astarto*. Only Durastanti, Galerati, and Lagarde remained of the original company, and the first two sang different parts. The cast was:

RADAMISTO:	Senesino (alto castrato)
ZENOBIA:	Durastanti (soprano)
POLISSENA:	Maddalena Salvai (soprano)
FRAARTE:	Galerati (soprano)
TIGRANE:	Matteo Berselli (soprano castrato)
TIRIDATE:	Giuseppe Boschi (bass)
FARASMANE:	Lagarde (bass)

This was Senesino's first Handel part, though London had heard him in *Astarto*. The changes in the score have already been described. There were seven performances, the last two in March 1721 after an interval of two months. This may have been due to the birth of a daughter to Durastanti (christened on 2 March), though there is no mention of her dropping out of Amadei's *Arsace*, which ran throughout February.

Little is known about the second revival, on 25 November 1721. Durastanti, Galerati, and Berselli had left the company, but Baldassari and Anastasia Robinson returned. The one certain fact is that Fraarte was cut out, some of his recitative (but none of his arias) being transferred to Tigrane. Senesino, Salvai, Boschi, and Lagarde probably retained their roles, with Baldassari replacing Berselli as Tigrane and Anastasia Robinson taking her old part of Zenobia. There were four performances, the last on 6 December, not six as stated by Deutsch. No libretto has been found. In December 1721 and the following month a company of French actors played a *Rhadamyste et Zénobie* at the New Haymarket Theatre, opposite the King's. This was probably Crébillon's tragedy of 1711.

Handel's fourth and final production in January 1728 has been obscured by the loss of a number of issues of the *Daily Courant*, which at this period carried the King's Theatre announcements. There is however conclusive evidence that Deutsch is wrong in doubting that it took place. Burney, who may have had information no longer accessible, says that *Alessandro* and *Radamisto* were revived and played alternately between late December 1727 and the first night of *Siroe* on 17 February 1728, and James Ralph's pamphlet *The Touch-Stone*[41] (1728), rebuking London audiences for preferring French dancers and *The Beggar's Opera* to serious plays and Italian opera, is equally specific. 'Such Judges would again drop the *Provok'd Husband* for the miserable low scenes in the B——r's O——a, and swallow greedily the wretched Dregs of MUSICK, which have occasion'd this incredible Run: while *Rhadamistus* and *Siroe* are perform'd to almost Empty Benches.' There were performances of *Alessandro* on 26 and 30 December, 2 and 6 January, after which we have no information covering eleven opera nights until 17 February. Some of these were certainly

* devoted to *Radamisto*; a new libretto was published, and Walsh presently issued two extra songs. The cast was:

---

[41] Cited by Irving Lowens in *MQ* xlv (1959), 339. Deutsch (231–2) omits the relevant passage.

RADAMISTO:	Senesino (alto castrato)
ZENOBIA:	Faustina Bordoni (soprano)
POLISSENA:	Francesca Cuzzoni (soprano)
TIRIDANE:	Boschi (bass)
TIGRANE	Antonio Baldi (alto castrato)
FARASMANE:	Giovanni Battista Palmerini (bass)

Handel made extensive changes, chiefly to accommodate Faustina and Cuzzoni, who had to enjoy parity—eight arias each on this occasion. He wrecked the opera in the process, but rewrote more of the music than has hitherto been recognized. The quartet together with the three previous recitative scenes (III viii–x), both duets, and Farasmane's single aria were cut, and Fraarte remained among the shades. The parts of Radamisto and Tiridate were otherwise unchanged, except that Tiridate's four extra lines in the last scene disappeared. Tigrane, now an alto, lost two of his arias but retained the other three transposed down a fifth or sixth: 'Segni di crudeltà' in F, 'La sorte, il ciel' in D, 'Sò ch'è vana' in F. Handel reset five sections of his recitative (in I i and ix, II iv and vii, and III ii; the first two, though in the performing score, were ignored by Chrysander) and gave him a new one in III i (HG 169–70) in which he tells Polissena that Tiridate has repudiated her and puts his forces and the last drop of his blood at her service. For the words Handel returned to Lalli's 1712 libretto, where however they are spoken by Fraarte. Tigrane's other recitatives—in I i (first part), v–ix (latter part) and xi, II ii and x, and III ult.—remained in the soprano clef in the performing score and may have existed only in the singer's part. The notes could have been changed without disturbing the bass.

All Zenobia's arias and some of her recitative (for example in I xii) as printed in Chrysander's second score date from 1728. Nearly all were transposed, and three were further modified: a solo flute replaced the oboe in 'Quando mai spietata sorte' (now in G), 'Deggio dunque' was recast in G minor with oboe obbligato replacing the cello (HG 191), and 'O scemami il diletto', returning to oust the second duet, was transposed to A and shortened by the removal of the last part of the A section (HG 204). Her other five arias were 'Deh! fuggi un traditore' (previously sung by Tigrane and Fraarte) in F with the text changed, replacing 'Son contenta di morire' in I v and making little sense; 'Già che morir' in D minor; 'Ferite, uccidete' (acquired from Radamisto), still in A but shifted to II vi in place of 'Fatemi, O cieli'; 'Empio perverso cor' in C minor; and 'Parmi che giunta in porto' from *Floridante*, a favourite with Faustina, in place of the duet at the end of Act II.

For Cuzzoni as Polissena Handel restored the original voice part of 'Sommi Dei' and the higher key (E major) of 'Tu vuoi ch'io parta', left 'Dopo l'orride procelle' and 'Che farà quest'alma' unchanged, and put 'Barbaro, partirò' up to B flat (HG 187) to exploit the top note that Faustina could not reach. Her three extra arias were lifted from other characters: Fraarte's 'Lascia pur' (now 'Vieni pur'), preceded by a new recitative, 'Misero Radamisto', which Chrysander ignored, in an extra scene after I viii, and two beautiful pieces hitherto sung by Zenobia in Act II, 'Troppo sofferse' and 'Fatemi, O cieli' (with altered text and transposition to G minor), in the reconstructed opening of Act III (HG 168–73). This was a new version of 'Troppo sofferse' with ritornello at the beginning only and a revised and shortened second part repeating the first couplet of the text, presumably because the second is less appropriate to Polissena than to Zenobia. The consistency of both characters was destroyed. Zenobia lost three of her most personal arias, receiving alien currency in exchange. Polissena came off little better. 'Vieni pur', begging Tigrane to save Radamisto and Zenobia, is ludicrous in her mouth, and the recitative before 'Fatemi', in which she asks Tigrane's permission to see Tiridate again, is even more out of character.

Not many excerpts appeared in concert programmes. The overture was played at York Buildings on 27 March 1724 for the benefit of the violinist Johnson, 'lately from Ireland'; probably at a King's Theatre Assembly on 7 April 1729 (the first item was 'the Instrumental Opera of Radamisto'); and at a Manchester Subscription Concert on 11 December 1744. Jane Barbier sang 'Ombra cara' ('a New Italian Song') at her Lincoln's Inn Fields benefit on 28 March 1726, and Kytch, 'First Hautboy to the Opera', played it at his own benefit at Hickford's on 16 April 1729. Montagnana sang 'Con la strage' as an insertion in the November 1731 revival of _Poro_. Various arias were included in three pasticcios arranged by Handel himself: 'Già che morir', 'Stragi morti', and 'Dopo l'orride procelle' in _Hermann von Balcke_ (Elbing, autumn 1737),[42] 'Vile, se mi dai vita' in _Oreste_ (Covent Garden, 18 December 1734), and 'Non hò più affanni' in _Alessandro Severo_ (King's Theatre, 25 February 1738). Others appeared in _Lucio Vero_ ('Cara sposa' and 'Ombra cara', 14 November 1747) and _Solimano_ ('Ombra cara', 31 January 1758), both at the King's Theatre.

Radamisto was produced at Hamburg on 28 January 1722 (NS) under the title _Zenobia, oder Das Muster rechtschaffener ehelichen Liebe_. This was an ungainly compound of Handel's first and third versions (April and December 1720), for which Mattheson, who arranged it, is not wholly to blame.[43] The total subversion of the vocal layout is a revealing indication of the fate of Handel's operas in Germany. Radamisto was a high baritone, Zenobia and Polissena both sopranos, Tiridate a bass, and Fraarte, Tigrane, and Farasmane all tenors, though Fraarte seems to have been first intended for a soprano. The quartet was included but its balance distorted (SSBB instead of SSAB). Unlike Telemann, who introduced comic sub-plots and extra spectacle into _Ottone_ and _Riccardo Primo_, Mattheson did maintain the heroic climate of the opera. The scenery was painted by Querfeld (Tobias Querfurt senior) and [Johann Jürgen] Rabe, and the ballet master was one Thiboust. The dances must have been entr'acte music; there are none in the surviving score. The opera enjoyed a fair success, with 27 performances up to 1726,[44] most of them in the first season, and three more in a revival of January 1736. Signora Stradiotti, who had sung in London though not under Handel, was in the 1724 cast, and a new male alto named Hebert appeared on 2 January 1725.[45]

The next production took place at Göttingen in 1927 in an arrangement by Josef Wenz. Other German versions followed, at Düsseldorf in 1937

[42] J. Müller-Blattau, 'Händels Festkantate zur Fünfhundertjahrfeier der Stadt Elbing 1737', _50 Jahre Göttinger Händel-Festspiele_, ed. W. Meyerhoff (Kassel, etc., 1970).

[43] See below, p. 363, and W. Dean, 'Mattheson's Arrangement of Handel's _Radamisto_ for the Hamburg Opera', _New Mattheson Studies_, ed. G. J. Buelow and H. J. Marx (Cambridge, 1983), 169–78.

[44] Stompor, _HJb_ (1978), 76, gives the number as 30 and says that Telemann borrowed the battle sinfonia in his _Sieg der Schönheit_ (1722).

[45] Zelm, _Hamburger Jahrbuch für Musikwissenschaft_, iii (1978), 53.

(H. Buths), Hagen in 1943, Halle in 1955 (Heinz Rückert), Leipzig in 1960 (Rückert, revised), and elsewhere. There was a concert performance at Tiflis in 1959 in a Georgian translation by Washa Gwacharija, and staged productions in English (Charles Farncombe) in London in 1960 and 1984. Other countries have still to sample the glories of *Radamisto*.

Autograph

The autograph (RM 20 c 1) has been damaged and stained by damp at the top, especially towards the end, so that words written in the upper margin and Handel's folio numbers are sometimes difficult or impossible to decipher. He foliated the manuscript twice at different stages, on every eighth side at the upper right corner in his usual manner, and in smaller figures towards the lower left of the recto of each leaf. This second foliation was hurriedly done; the ink has often left an impression on the opposite verso. Both foliations are occasionally lost through damage to the paper, including number 1 of each series; its position is difficult to determine from the present state of the manuscript, whether or not the overture was composed first as part of the opera. The small foliation begins with ?2 on modern f. 6 (the opening of Act I after the overture), the large with 2 on f. 9.[46] After that the arrangement of Acts I and III can be clearly traced, but Act II has been confused by changes during composition and by misbinding. Fortunately the double foliation enables most doubts to be resolved.

The arias 'Son lievi le catene' (ff. 26–8), 'Quando mai' (43–4), and 'Spero placare' with its introductory recitative (66–7)[47] were inserted after the large foliation but before the small. So were most if not all of the pasted-in slips (ff. 31, 32, 38, 39, 42, 58, 61, 62), which Handel naturally did not foliate; they all concern the expansion of Fraarte's part or the alterations to the main theme of 'Dopo torbide procelle'. The revised recitatives of II iii (HG 46, f. 51), which also concern Fraarte's love for Zenobia, were inserted after both foliations. The original order of folios in Act II was: 47, 64, ?two missing leaves, 65, 45, 49, 50, 52–7, 59, 60, 63 (bound back to front), 68–80. Folios 46 and 48 are blanks with inaccurate statements about missing music, added when the manuscript was bound in the late eighteenth century; 81–4 date from 1728 and are wrongly bound at the beginning of the original Act III; 116–48 are additions of December 1720.

The autograph contains many interesting revisions. The most radical, the transmogrification of Fraarte from Tiridate's general and confidant into the lover of Zenobia, was carried out when Handel had nearly finished the composition but before he reached the last scene: Fraarte's apologetic aside 'Dell'impuro mio amor anch'io mi pento' belongs to the main draft. He made numerous alterations and additions to what he had already written, cutting Fraarte out of I ii and iii (originally iv),[48] suppressing his original I iii, in which Fraarte raised political objections to Tiridate's unjust war and was put firmly in his place, modifying his actions in I v,[49] and inserting his two

---

[46] References henceforth are to the modern foliation, unless otherwise stated.

[47] Handel's small foliation is on the verso of these two leaves.

[48] A relic of the first version survives at the bottom of HG 13, where Chrysander gives Fraarte an exit before his first entry.

[49] See pp. 328 and 338.

sentences of recitative in I x (HG 30). The recitative of II iii was wholly rewritten, turning Fraarte's polite sympathy for Zenobia into ardent love. In the first draft, as in Lalli, he had not appeared at all in II v and vi. Now he returns to eavesdrop (his two jealous asides on HG 53 were added on pasted slips), and after Tiridate's exit is given several amorous remarks and an aria ('Spero placare'), though he has to wait till Zenobia has cleared the stage with 'Troppo sofferse' before he can sing it. 'Vaga e bella' in II iv was allowed to stand, despite its incongruous expression of confidence in the outcome of Tiridate's pursuit of Zenobia, but his first aria received a new text. The words of 'Mirerò quel vago volto' were originally 'Umiliata a piedi tuoi / Quella bella io porterò. / Mà vedrai ne gl'occhi suoi / Quanti amore impriggionò.' Handel had simplified the coloratura of this aria and cut seven bars at the ritornello cadence after the A section before changing the words. He altered its harmonic context by interposing two extra lines of recitative for Fraarte before it, but ignored two similar asides newly provided by Haym: 'A mio favor per che risorga il fato' in place of the line before 'Vaga e bella' (HG 50) and 'Amor mi chiama a denudare il brando' in III i after Tigrane's 'tu l'Armene' (HG 78).

Some of the changes in 'Dopo torbide procelle' have been mentioned. The unamended text in the autograph is 'Dopo torbide procelle / Par più bello un dì seren. / Son più lucide le stelle / Alla notte oscura in sen.' Handel made the remarkable change in the opening bars of the melody by pasting the new passage over the old in three places. He rewrote bars 67 and 68 in the B section, adding the voice's triplet figure. Both vocal alternatives in bars 32 and 49 are in the autograph, which also contains a third, a high A and B flat for the two semiquavers in bar 32. Handel did not cancel them; he subsequently wrote f and e [♮], but not before the higher version had been sung, copied, and printed.

The opening of Act II gave considerable trouble. 'Quando mai' (whose second line as first set was 'finirai il mio penar') was the second or third cavatina in this place. The first was an early version of 'Troppo sofferse', already in E flat and binary form with final ritornello (ff. 47ᵛ and 64, heavily cancelled in ink). There is a slightly different distribution of instrumental material, an independent bassoon part, and a different second couplet: 'Altro non bramo ch'il dolce diletto / Tu mi preservi, O nume d'amor.' The last six bars of the voice part have no underlay, which suggests that Handel may have been copying; if so, it was from a lost source, for there is no doubt that this version belongs to the first draft. It begins on the verso of the act's opening recitative, and its final bass E flat has a tie linking it with that of Radamisto's next recitative (HG 40). Handel had already rejected it when he reached Scene vi and used the music again. At the foot of f. 47ᵛ he wrote *l'aria della carta volante di Zenobia*, referring to 'Quando mai', which occupies the verso of one leaf and the recto of another, the other sides being blank. A gap in the large foliation suggests that two leaves have been lost here; they may have carried an intermediate cavatina between 'Troppo sofferse' and 'Quando mai'.

There was some rearrangement towards the end of Act III, which passed through three successive stages. The first draft had Radamisto's unpublished aria 'Senza luce, senza guida' where 'Qual nave' now stands. The music continued as HG 104–8, with the word *Chorus* after the recitative. Handel then cancelled that word[50] and wrote below it another short recitative for Radamisto, 'Non v'è più contento / Che tornar a goder doppo il tormento' with a cadence in D. This was clearly meant to introduce the aria that eventually become 'Qual nave' (f. 104), which at this stage had different words, about hope conquering pain and fulfilling itself in love: 'Speranza gradita / Di questo mio seno / Già torni a dar vita / A questo [Al fido] mio cor. / Finiscon le pene / Finiscon gl'affanni / Più dolci catene / Or dona ci amor.' This in turn was followed (f. 105ᵛ foot) by a recitative for Zenobia and Radamisto:

> *Zen.* Ogn'un godi e festeggi in questo giorno.
> *Rad.* E il piè muova alla danza il cor.
> *Zen.* Mio sposo, tu sei del questo petto.
> *Rad.* E tu del alma mia (*a 2*) dolce ricetto.

It ends with a cadence in A and the word *Coro*. The words are interesting for their reference to the ballet that ended the opera. But Handel soon decided to allow Radamisto only one aria, to omit 'Senza luce', and to replace it with 'Speranza gradita'. He cancelled the recitatives that preceded and followed it and gave the aria a new text based partly on 'Senza luce' (itself derived from Lalli's aria at this point). The new words ('Qual nave' etc.) were inserted by Smith, and ff. 104–5 shifted to their present position in the autograph.

Handel did not write out the *coro* in full, indicating the substantial repeats of the rondo theme with *NB* and *Vide Segno* in half a dozen places, for the benefit of the copyist. He added the names of the characters to the voice parts as in HG, except that in the third duet section Tigrane has the upper part, Fraarte the lower (for later changes see below). The music runs straight into the Passepied on the same theme, of which the first thirteen bars remain; the rest has been torn out, and with it the date of completion. The two entr'acte ballets were probably never part of the main autograph.

A number of smaller points are worth mentioning. (The changes to 'Sommi Dei' and 'Stragi, morti' have already been indicated.) In I i Handel cancelled two substantial passages of recitative unconnected with Fraarte; they are among those printed in *virgole* in the libretto. Part of the B section of 'Son contenta di morire' has two sets of words, neither of them in HG: its last two lines are 'Dian'a me perpetui affanni [changed to 'colmino d'affanni'] / Che la morte darà fine al lor rigor'. The cadence before 'Son lievi le catene' (HG 25) was at first imperfect, a first inversion of D major (at Farasmane's exit) leading into the recitative of I xii. Handel may have considered giving Tigrane an aria at the end of I xii, as he did later; the cadence was originally in D major. In at least three recitatives—II ii, bar 18 (HG 42), the original I iii (f. 14), and II vi (f. 60), the last two unpublished—he chose to write out a cadential appoggiatura. The autograph has both vocal alternatives in bars 80–1 of 'Ombra cara', and upper alternatives in bars 5, 6, 9, and 10 of Radamisto's recitative at the start of Act II, as in the only complete copy of the April version. 'La sorte, il ciel' was originally in 3/8. Both voice parts of the duet 'Se teco vive' are in the soprano clef; the text as first set began 'Se volge

---

[50] He may have intended to cancel the recitative 'Festeggi omai' as well; if so, the change of plan made him think again.

altrove il piè, / Se vive in te mio cor.' In the last bar of III iv (HG 88) Handel gave Zenobia an alternative high C♯ on the first syllable of 'sposo'; this is not in the copies. The recitative of III vi (HG 95) was designed to lead into that of vii, for which Handel wrote out the words; but he soon decided to insert 'Alzo al volo', altered the three preceding bars, and repeated the words, this time with music, after the aria. The tempo marks on 'Stragi, morti', 'Ferite, uccidete', 'Mirerò', 'La sorte, il ciel', 'Non sarà quest'alma', and 'Se teco vive', and Polissena's name on 'Sposo ingrato', were added by Smith; but 'Deh! fuggi un traditore' is clearly marked *Allegro* by Handel. 'Qual nave' has no tempo here or in the earliest copies.

The autograph of *Radamisto* is one of the very few that Handel modified after the work had been performed. This is proved by the existence in several copies and the Meares print of readings cancelled or amended in the autograph. The most conspicuous is the rewriting of the voice, violin, and oboe parts in bars 13–16 of 'Deggio dunque'; others occur in 'Troppo sofferse' (HG 57, viola in bar 18), 'Non sarà quest'alma' (bar 65, second violin), 'S'adopri' (changes to coloratura), and 'Dolce bene', where the viola part in bars 4, 14, and 18 was *con* or *coll Bassons*; Handel cancelled the first word—but restored it later in Hamburg II. These changes, and others (chiefly verbal) not entered in the autograph, must have been made during or soon after the original run, perhaps when Handel was preparing the December revival. It was certainly for the latter that he wrote a new distribution of characters against the voice parts of the *coro*: Zenobia, Polissena, Tigrane, and Fraarte on the soprano line, Radamisto on the alto, and Tiridate added below Farasmane on the bass, leaving the tenor blank. At the same time he switched the names of Radamisto and Zenobia in the first duet, and Fraarte and Tigrane in the third.

December 1720. Most of the new pieces for this revival are bound at the end of the main autograph. 'L'ingrato non amar' survives in three versions. The first, which breaks off after 33 bars, is on f. 127, the second (complete) in RM 20 d 2, ff. 26–8. Both are in B flat, 6/8 time, based on material that had served in the *Birthday Ode for Queen Anne* and other early works and was to find its ultimate niche in Cleopatra's 'Tu la mia stella' in *Giulio Cesare*, where it was further refined.[51] Having abandoned this idea, Handel wrote the C minor setting (ff. 116–18, HG 122), which also underwent revision; five bars were scrapped and rewritten after bar 47. Tempo marks, if any, are illegible owing to damage to the autograph.[52] Handel shortened and rewrote the cadence at the end of the B section of 'Con la strage'; made many changes in the upper parts of 'Segni di crudeltà', marking them *NB* as if Smith had already copied the aria; rewrote the triplets in bars 14–20 of 'Vuol ch'io serva' in a more flexible rhythm and marked the bass of bar 69 *e cembalo*, implying its suppression at bar 59; and wrote only the upper notes in bars 69–70 and 110–11 of 'Lascia pur'. The instrumental bass in bars 20–4 of this aria is in the autograph. 'Fatemi, O cieli', for Zenobia in E minor (text as HG 170, version A), the only new composition for Durastanti, has a B section three bars longer than the published version. 'Barbaro, partirò' is in A major, with higher vocal alternatives (apparently never used) in bars 13 and 14 and extensive revision

---

[51] See p. 511.
[52] The duet 'Non hò più' and the quartet, like 'Con vana speranza' and the *coro* in the first version, have no tempo indicated in any source.

of the voice's last five bars in the B section. 'Sò ch'è vana' is in D major for soprano without opening ritornello (like 'Augelletti' in *La Resurrezione* on which it is based); the violins originally had a triplet rhythm in the two penultimate bars.

The autograph of 'Vile! se mi dai vita' and its accompanied recitative is lost; that of the duet 'Non hò più affanni' is in the Fitzwilliam Museum (Mus MS 256, 45 ff.). Bars 33–41 were a later insertion (before performance). The same manuscript (p. 51) has a sketch for bars 10–12 of 'Sò ch'è vana' without inner parts; the bass (*Violoncelli pian senza cembalo*) is different and enters with the voice. Handel jotted this down after composing 'Non hò più affanni' but before lengthening it.

Handel composed the new recitatives for the December revival in the performing score (Hamburg II) after Smith had prepared the clefs and written the words, a procedure he adopted on other occasions. Most of them survive; a few were lost when the manuscript was overhauled in 1728. The whole of 'Dolce bene' and the upper instrumental parts of 'Sì che ti renderai' and 'Vanne, sorella ingrata' in their transposed versions were also written by Handel (Plate 11). The autograph of the F major revision of 'Alzo al volo' for bass, now in the Deutsche Staatsbibliothek, Berlin, probably once formed part of the performance score. It is more liberal with dynamics than the tenor aria, but omits most of the trills.

1728. The new material for this revival is in RM 20 c 1 (the main autograph), ff. 81–4. It comprises III i, ii, and vii (HG 170–5, 191–2). 'Fatemi, O cieli' is cued in without music (*ex g moll*), and 'Sò ch'è vana' represented by the first four and last $1\frac{1}{2}$ bars of the ritornello (in F major) with *NB etc* in between and *la seconda volta, ancora cosi* at the end: i.e. the final ritornello is to be the same as the first. 'Troppo sofferse' in G major is marked *Larghetto*. Tigrane's recitatives are in the alto clef. 'Deggio dunque', in G minor with oboe, is followed by two shots at Radamisto's next recitative, heavily cancelled. Possibly Handel considered interposing its first phrase before the da capo of 'Deggio dunque'. The fact that this aria begins on the verso of a page with Tigrane as an alto is conclusive proof that it was written for Faustina in 1728, not for Durastanti in December 1720. Some of the new recitative for Tigrane in Hamburg II has the notes written by Handel, the words by Smith.

Librettos

1720 (April). 'An Opera As it is Perform'd at the King's Theatre in the Hay-Market, for the Royal Academy of Musick. London: Printed for Tho. Wood in Little Britain' (in Italian and English). 71 pp. Handel's dedication to George I is exceptional; this was generally the province of the librettist or the manager, but Haym is nowhere mentioned. Handel cites 'the Protection which Your Majesty has been graciously pleased to allow both to the Art of *Musick* in general, and to one of the lowest, tho' not the least dutiful of Your Majesty's Servants', and says he was 'the more encouraged to this [the dedication], by the particular Approbation Your Majesty has been pleased to give to the Musick of this Drama', which suggests that he had played it to the King.[53]

The Argument is taken verbatim from Lalli's 1710 and 1712 librettos; it summarizes Tacitus's account of the Araxes incident, not that of the opera, and dates it in the twelfth year of Claudius, AD 53. The English version paraphrases the arias in reported speech, not verse translation. Many short passages in all three acts, some 75 lines in all, are printed in *virgole*; except two lines for Radamisto in the last scene, all come from the 1712 libretto, with minor variants. Handel set a few of them, subsequently cancelled, in the autograph of I i and v and copied the words of others without adding music. Three or four lines in III i and vii, though not set, have no *virgole*. 'Sommi Dei' is printed as recitative in this and subsequent librettos. Fraarte's solo scene in Act II (HG 58–60) is numbered vii, throwing out the count till the end of the act. The ballet is specifically mentioned before the last return of the rondo theme in the *coro* (*Qui si fa il Ballo*).

The many verbal variants from HG are due to several causes. Sometimes Handel altered a word or two during composition (he omitted the second line of 'Spero placare'). In places, as noted above (p. 349), the libretto introduces references to Fraarte's love for Zenobia, but Handel, who had already set the scenes, did not avail himself of them. In III i this resulted in the accidental omission of a line he did set, Fraarte's 'Con felonia si può mostrar virtude'. Chrysander altered a number of passages where the autograph agrees with the libretto. Some are simple errors: 'tutto' for 'lutto' at the bottom of HG 13, 'il cieco Marte' for 'il cieco amante' on HG 78. Some may be attempts to improve the Italian: 'parrà' for 'vorrà' in the B section of 'Sì che ti renderai', 'Sì mi vedrai morire' in the B section of 'Vanne, sorella ingrata', where the autograph and copies have 'Se', the libretto 'Tu'. Others are the result of Chrysander reading back into the first version changes that Handel adopted later: 'ministro' for 'germano' on HG 46 (end of fifth brace) and the different texts of 'Son contenta di morire' (B section) and 'Dopo torbide procelle'. As noted in the synopsis, Chrysander omitted some detailed stage directions.

A copy of this libretto prepared as a draft prompt-book for the first performance was sold at Sotheby's on 9 May 1985 and acquired by the Theatre Museum of London. It can scarcely have been used in the theatre, for the annotations, though sometimes detailed, are entered spasmodically and do not cover every scene. But they are of great interest and importance, since no other prompt copy for an opera of this period is known. They are in two hands, one confined to marking 'R. hand' and 'L. hand' for exits and entrances. The other gives advance cues for changing the scenery ('ready to change'), props ('two chairs ready'), the entry of characters, and the number of supernumeraries accompanying them. For example, during I v 'Mr Benedetti Mr Le Gard one Gent with Colours, one gent with a Spear' (for Scene vi); during I vii 'Soldiers on ye Bridge with Pikes' (for the battle sinfonia) and a little later 'Mrs Galerati slaves guards with Colours & Cloaths Mr Benedetti ready'; during II i 'Mrs Gallerati 6 guards drawn sword one Gent' (for Tigrane's entry in Scene ii); for II x 'a Gent with Mantle Sword & Cap of Durastanti' and 'Mr Gordon 6 gent 6 guards' (see Plate 10). At the beginning of the opera and in III x Polissena was attended by ten women,

---

[53] Deutsch (103) quotes the dedication from the second (December) libretto, which has slight changes, chiefly in capitalization.

Tiridate in III v by 'one Gent 10 guards'. It is clear that the set in Act I included a practicable bridge, that a minimum of nearly 30 supernumeraries was envisaged, and that the libretto must have been printed well in advance.[54]

1720 (December). Title and prefatory matter virtually unchanged, but the entire libretto reset (79 pp.) from a carelessly amended copy of the first edition. This produces confusion, notably in the opening scene, where Tigrane appears to have two consecutive arias and exits; the first ('Deh! fuggi un traditore') is certainly meant for Fraarte, who is given recitative but no entrance or exit. Still listed as Tiridate's brother, he is addressed as 'ministro'. Some prominent stage directions are omitted, though they still apply. Fifty of the lines in *virgole* remain thus, twenty are cut, and five (in I i) lose their *virgole*, since Handel now set them to music. With that exception, the treatment of these passages seems arbitrary. Some but not all of the new pieces are indicated by an asterisk.

Apart from the major plot changes there are many verbal modifications, most of them unrecognized by Chrysander, who confused the text of this revival with those of 1721 and 1728, especially in the parts of Tigrane and Fraarte. Among the passages omitted in HG are two sections of recitative in II ii and iv (if Handel altered the music, it is lost owing to subsequent disturbance to the performing score), all the recitatives of III i and ii and 'S'adopri' (the music is in Hamburg II), and four bars for Fraarte after Tigrane's 'Ah mia Reina' in I i (HG 121, fifth brace). The recitative for which Chrysander prints only the words on HG 136–7 is also in Hamburg II, though misplaced. The fourth line of the altered text for the duet 'Se teco vive' (HG 167), 'Non hò più affanni al sen' (almost duplicating the new Act III duet), was accidentally omitted from the libretto but inserted in a contemporary hand in one of the BL copies (163 g 57). Other pieces that received new texts were 'Son contenta di morire' (B section now as HG, but 'empia sorte' for 'crude stelle' in line 2), 'Dopo torbide procelle' (as HG), 'Quando mai spietata sorte' ('Fine avrà tanto penar' in line 2), 'Troppo sofferse' ('O mi rendete il dolce diletto' in line 3), and 'La sorte, il ciel' ('Raffrena i tuoi sospir' at the start of the B section). 'Qual nave' begins 'A nave', but this was clearly an error; Handel corrected it in Hamburg II. There are also a few changes that he did not adopt.

1722 Hamburg. 'Zenobia, oder das Muster rechtschaffener Ehelichen Liebe... Gedruckt bei Caspar Jakhel'. No author, composer, or singers are named. Mattheson translated the Argument into German, adding quotations from Tacitus. The recitatives, including Radamisto's accompanied 'Vieni, d'empietà' in III v, appear in German only, the arias in Italian with German paraphrases alongside. The text follows Handel's December 1720 version and was based on a copy of the London libretto, not a score. 'Deh! fuggi un traditore' is correctly ascribed to Fraarte.

1726 Hamburg. Title as last except for date and 'Gedruckt mit Stromerschen Schrifften'. Fraarte's arias 'Deh! fuggi un traditore' and 'Lascia pur' are omitted; otherwise the text is essentially unchanged.

1728. 'Sold at the King's Theatre in the Hay-Market.' 71 pp. The dedication and Argument are included, with a new note: 'The Scene is supposed in Artanissa, the Metropolis of Thrace'. The city had not been named in earlier librettos; it is mentioned in Polissena's new recitative in I ix

---

[54] See J. Milhous and R. D. Hume, 'A Prompt Copy of Handel's *Radamisto*', *MT* cxxvii (1986), 316–21. This copy is reproduced in facsimile in Harris, *Librettos*.

(not in HG), where Handel set it as Artasserte. This recitative introduced Fraarte's old aria 'Lascia pur', with the third line altered to 'Lieti i giorni che verranno'. The text of 'Deh! fuggi un traditore', now sung by Zenobia (though the English version still gives it to Tigrane), was changed to 'Lascia, mio caro sposo . . . È un tiranno' in the A section and 'fida' for 'fido' in the B section. I i is left without an aria (apart from 'Sommi Dei'); Tigrane has his last speech on HG 121 (reset) and goes out. All the remaining passages in *virgole* are omitted, together with the entire part of Fraarte except a few lines transferred to Tigrane. A tiny detail showing the care bestowed on the libretto is the addition of the words 'i miei soldati' to Tigrane's recitative in II iv (HG 154). They are not in either of the 1720 librettos and would have been inappropriate in the second, where the speaker is Fraarte; being a 'ministro' he has no soldiers. The rearranged text entailed changes in scene numbering. There are new stage directions in II iii (*Zenobia condotta dalle guardie*, etc as HG 154, everything on HG 146–53 being cut) and II xii (xi), where after 'furore del tiranno' (HG 167) *Zenobia vuol far sortir di Scena Rad.*, and five bars later, at the end of the recitative, *Si abbracciano e poi ella lo spinge nella Scena*. This cleared the stage for Faustina to end the act with 'Parmi che giunta in porto'.

Copies and Editions

The Hamburg score MA/1044 (Hamburg I), commonly regarded as the April 1720 performing score and used by Chrysander as his principal text, is (apart from ff. 1–8 of Act III, which belong to MA/1043) not a performing score at all, nor a copy of the first version; nor (*pace* Larsen) was it written by Smith, but by H1. Moreover it is defective, with a number of errors. The first performing score is lost, a fact that has turned the text of *Radamisto* into a veritable quicksand. Hamburg I was probably in Handel's possession, for he changed the names in the duet 'Se teco vive', switching Zenobia from the upper to the lower stave, one of several indications that the score was copied after December 1720. It contains no trace of the ballets. One page of 'Troppo sofferse' has the voice part in the soprano clef, although this was an alto aria until December. In the first duet of the *coro* Zenobia has a soprano clef, Radamisto an alto, as in December, and Tigrane and Fraarte are likewise reversed in the third. Against the bass part the same copyist added Tiridate's name below Farasmane's, although it already appears against the tenor. Conclusive proof that this was never a performing score is furnished by the shorthand contraction of the *coro*, with three long repeat sections represented by the words *vide Signum*, as in the autograph—an arrangement quite impracticable for performance. Handel always had such movements copied in full, as in MA/1043. The most likely explanation of Hamburg I is that he wished to preserve a record of the pre-December version—not however as he performed it in April but as he had modified it since, for it differs from the undoubted early copies and from the Meares print in the features listed above.[55]

Chrysander used Hamburg I as engraver's copy for his edition, writing all over it and sometimes obscuring the original text. He also made marginal notes on variant readings and apparently used the score for performance. Many passages, including some in the misbound pages from Hamburg II,

[55] See p. 345.

have a German translation written in, others are bracketed as cut, and 'Ombra cara' has added vocal ornaments, subsequently cancelled. Chrysander regularized the verbal and musical text, and sometimes amended both; expanded abbreviations; altered spelling and capitalization; removed superfluous accidentals (and also—gratuitously—Handel's change of key signature at bar 120 of 'Ferite, uccidete', which is found in all copies); and supplied instrumental specifications and stage directions. Much of this represented good editorial practice and the correction of mistakes. But some errors were allowed to stand, and others introduced.[56] The autograph and nearly all the other copies (except Add MS 39180, which was almost certainly copied from Hamburg I) have the second violins in thirds with the firsts in bar 6 of 'Vaga e bella', and an upbeat C for viola on the last quaver of bar 19 of 'La sorte, il ciel'. The anomalous crotchet rest for second violins in bar 16 of 'Scemami il diletto' derives from confusion in the autograph; Handel's ultimate intention was probably for the first violins to double the voice without the seconds in bars 9–16 (first beat), 28–30, 38–9, and 45–8, as in Malmesbury, Fitzwilliam, RCM 905, Add MS 31562 (the four April 1720 copies), Flower, and Coke.

Hamburg II (MA/1043) is a genuine performing score prepared by Smith in December 1720 and used again for the 1721 and 1728 revivals. Its present state is incoherent owing to the removal of many pages and their replacement by others in 1728, and also to misbinding; Clausen's analysis is very accurate. (Abandoned versions were not always removed: 'Deh! fuggi un traditore' in G, 'Son lievi le catene', 'Segni di crudeltà' in F, 'S'adopri', the quartet, and the duet 'Non hò più' are still present, as well as the last page of 'La sorte, il ciel' in B flat and the opening of 'Barbaro, partirò' in A.) The manuscript contains much autograph material for all three revivals, especially the first and third,[57] and six sections of recitative omitted by Chrysander; Handel performed five of them, two in 1720, three in 1728. As in Hamburg I, each act has a separate foliation.

From the score as copied for December 1720 the following set pieces (as well as many recitatives) are missing: 'Son contenta di morire' in Act I, 'Quando mai', 'Vuol ch'io serva', 'Già che morir', 'Fatemi, O cieli' (E minor), 'Troppo sofferse', 'Empio perverso cor', and the duet 'Se teco vive' in Act II, 'Sò ch'è vana' in D, 'Barbaro, partirò' in A (except the first $2\frac{1}{2}$ bars), 'Alzo al volo', and 'Deggio dunque' in Act III—a list that embraces Zenobia's entire part. Act II has lost more than 30 leaves, including the whole of the opening and closing scenes; only 24 (ff. 7–14, 23–6, 35–46) remain from the original copy. 'Sommi Dei' has the autograph's lower alternatives in the voice part (for Salvai, if not for L'Epine in June 1720); the final bar is now present. Four new bars of recitative for Fraarte and Polissena follow 'Ah, mia Reina' in I i (HG 121); they were suppressed in 1721 and omitted by Chrysander. 'Tu vuoi ch'io parta' is in D major without flute, after an F sharp (minor) cadence; strangely the B section has 'rimirarti' for 'rivederti', the only place where the reading of all three librettos (and Lalli) occurs with the music. In I vi, after Farasmane's 'Parti!' (HG 132), Radamisto has three bars of recitative with cadence in G minor, designed to introduce 'Ferite, uccidete' in E flat; they were cancelled, and 'Numi, e' l soffrite voi?' etc. substituted, when Handel changed the aria to 'Perfido' before performance.

The music for the text of I ix and x printed in HG 136–7 is in the

---

[56] See below, p.366.   [57] See p. 353 and Plate 11.

manuscript, but misplaced (Act II, f. 50). Bars 20–4 of 'Lascia pur' were copied with the instrumental bass, but this was subsequently cancelled and marked *Senza Basso* by Smith. Later, presumably in 1728, for the aria was cut in 1721, Handel crossed out Smith's words and substituted *coll Basso piano*. The lower voice part in bars 69–70 and 110–11 was written in by Handel,[58] probably for Galerati in December 1720; it would scarcely have been required for Cuzzoni, who as Polissena sang the aria in 1728 (when the words of the B section were not changed to agree with the libretto). The first word was changed to 'Vieni' in 1728 (traces of the erased word are just perceptible), and 'a' inserted before 'consolar' to correct the grammar. Chrysander wrote 'Lascia' into the manuscript.

The first two scenes of Act III are identical with those of the April score; Chrysander in his second version printed only the 1728 text. 'Vile! se mi dai vita' has four additional bars, two after bar 27 and two after bar 68, cancelled before performance; they are found only here. Both vocal alternatives are present in bars 85–6; the higher would have taken Senesino above his usual compass. Folios 45 and 46 of Act III are an early insertion (before performance) expanding the latter part of the duet 'Non hò più', exactly as in the Fitzwilliam autograph. The repeats in the *coro* are written in full, and the duet sections marked for the characters who sang them in December; Zenobia has the upper part in the first, Fraarte in the third, and Tiridate a bass clef in the second.

The 1721 revival involved no insertions, but many cuts and alterations resulting from the suppression of Fraarte and the transference of much of his recitative to Tigrane. All of them—words, notes, and scene headings—were written by Handel. The omission of Fraarte's new recitative in I i required adjustment to Polissena's part, which Handel noted in the margin. In II iii he cut the first ten bars of the recitative 'Mitiga il grave affanno' and marked Fraarte's later speeches for Tigrane; in 1728 a new recitative, 'Misero Radamisto', was pasted over the amended text, so that three versions are superimposed. Bar 3 of Tiridate's recitative at the start of the last scene (HG 201) also shows three versions. The December libretto reads 'empio Fraarte'; Smith copied the second word as 'germano', a survival from April; Handel changed it to 'ministro', and in 1721 to 'Tigrane'. Tiridate's recitative 'Con l'opre tue' on the same page (an insertion of December 1720) was probably pasted out in 1721 because it contains a reference to Fraarte.

For the 1728 revival fifteen arias were copied afresh: all eight of Zenobia's ('Parmi che giunta' may have been lifted from the performing score of *Floridante*, just as it was transferred later to that of *Tolomeo*), the three adapted for Tigrane as an alto, and four of Polissena's: 'Troppo sofferse' in a new version, 'Tu vuoi ch'io parta', 'Fatemi, O cieli', and 'Barbaro, partirò' in upward transpositions for Cuzzoni. 'Alzo al volo', though certainly sung, is missing from the manuscript. Among changes of detail were the restoration of the original voice part of 'Sommi Dei' for Cuzzoni and some modified recitatives, including Polissena's first four bars in I xii (as HG 140) following the transposition of Tigrane's previous aria to B flat. The leaves inserted in 1728 are:

---

[58] These alternatives appear nowhere else.

Act I

10 (a pasted slip with an alto resetting of Tigrane's recitative 'Vedrai dunque', not in HG; the words as set in December 1720 are at the bottom of HG 121);

20–1 ('Tu vuoi ch'io parta' restored to E major with the previous cadence altered to B);

34–7 ('Deh! fuggi un traditore' for Zenobia in F with modified text);

12–16 and 51–4 of Act II, bound in the wrong order and the wrong act. The correct order, after the sinfonia (I. 48), is:

II. 16 (Polissena's new recitative 'Misero Radamisto', not in HG);

12–14 ('Lascia [Vieni] pur' lifted from Act II for Polissena in I ix);

15 (opening recitative of I x—originally ix—reset for alto Tigrane, not in HG);

50 (retained from the original copy);

51–4 (recitative of xi recopied and 'Segni di crudeltà' for Tigrane in B flat).

Act II

1–6 (HG 141–2, but 'Quando mai' in G has solo flute, not oboe, and its altered second line of text);

17–22 (HG 154 to the middle of bar 8 of II v, with 'Già che morir' in D minor);

27–34 (vi and vii as HG 158 with 'Ferite, uccidete' in A for Zenobia and 'La sorte, il ciel' in D for Tigrane; this aria has the new B section text of December 1720, and Handel gave the voice an optional top D on the syllable 'con' in the A section cadence);

47–9 ('Empio perverso cor' in C minor with previous cadence altered from E to G, and the recitatives in HG 167 with a cue for 'Parmi che giunta', but no aria or duet).

Act III

1–8 of Act III in Hamburg I with III i and ii as HG 168–75 ('Troppo sofferse' in G, marked *Larghetto* as in the autograph, 'Fatemi, O cieli' for Polissena in G minor);

21–4 ('Barbaro, partirò' in B flat, the previous cadence changed from D major to D minor);

26–8 (HG 191–2, 'Deggio dunque' in G minor with oboe, and the first five bars of 'Qual nave' recopied);

46–50 (shortened version of 'O scemami il diletto' in A as HG 204–7).

Four copies, Malmesbury, Fitzwilliam Mus MS 72, Add MS 31562, and RCM 905, give the version of April 1720 and demonstrably date from that year;[59] but only the first is complete. The last two lack recitatives, and Add MS 31562 omits the *coro*. The copying of all four was a collaborative effort, with Smith taking the lead. He must have been under great pressure at this period, for very few copies dating from 1720–4 are in a single hand. Malmesbury is the work of two copyists, Smith and Gamma. The first page of

[59] The decisive factor is the form of Smith's treble clef: see W. Dean, 'Handel's Early London Copyists', 95–7.

the overture (ten leaves, not included in the pagination), pp. 1–41 (part), 46, 131–40 ('Ombra cara', on different paper), and some of the clefs on 243 were written by Smith, the rest by Gamma, who was evidently learning his job, a situation paralleled in other early copies. Elizabeth Legh signed and dated the volume 1720; she gave the day and month as well, but they have been scratched out. This is the only copy of the April version with all three ballet suites. The first appears in score nowhere else; the second is in Flower (score and parts), Lennard, and a separate set of parts in the Flower Collection, the third in RCM 905 and Coke. Two short repeats, eight bars in the Act II Passacaille and seven in the Act III Rigaudon, are not in Malmesbury, which accidentally omits the instruction to repeat the Passepied.

Fitzwilliam, in small oblong format not unlike Add MS 16108 (*Muzio Scevola*), is the work of three copyists working closely together, sometimes all in the same piece: Smith, RM1, and Delta. It is an exceedingly untidy manuscript without foliation, and was damaged at an early stage, especially at the beginning and end. Seven missing leaves in three groups were supplied later by S2, and the final page of the *coro* in yet another (later) hand. Lord Fitzwilliam signed and dated it 1767, but it is quite unlike the other operas in his collection, which were copied to his order shortly before the date of signature. It was used, along with Hamburg I, by the copyists of the Flower and Lennard scores.

Add MS 31562, a presentation or library copy in an elegantly tooled binding, and RCM 905 were both begun by Smith and carried on by others. In the former RM1, on his best behaviour, supplied the clefs for Act II (except the first page) and the conclusion of Act III (44^v–81 and 107^v–112). A neat unidentified copyist wrote the opening pages of Act III (82^r–96^r), clefs and music, except the clefs and time signatures on 82^r (Smith) and, on the same page, the first five bars of the bass of 'S'adopri', which are in Handel's autograph on top of the copyist's rests. Smith wrote the whole of Act I, the initial page of Act II (44^r), the remainder of Act III (96^v–107^r), the music of the sections prepared by RM1, and the entire verbal text.

In RCM 905 Smith again set the pace with f. 1^r, and resumed at the start of Act III (100–18^r); the rest of the main text is by Gamma. At the end, written by H2 in a hand very similar to Gamma's,[60] are the additional pieces of December 1720, all in their original keys and half of them figured. 'Fatemi, O cieli' has an interesting orchestral variant that may have some authority: the top stave is for first violin and flute,[61] and the latter is directed to play an octave higher at bar 7. 'Lascia pur' has no instrumental bass in bars 20–4. There are tempo marks for 'Con la strage', 'Segni di crudeltà', 'Vuol ch'io serva' (all *Allegro*), and 'Perfido' (*Presto*).

RCM 905, like Fitzwilliam and the Meares print (also Coke and Lennard), has *Largo* at the start of the overture; the autograph is illegible here. Apart from the ballet suites, dropped tempo marks (especially in Fitzwilliam), the supplement to RCM 905, and minor mistakes, all four early copies give the same text, with the final bar of 'Sommi Dei' either omitted or squeezed in later, the upper vocal alternatives in 'Dopo torbide procelle', the recitatives of II i (where present), and 'Ombra cara' (*Largo*), Zenobia in the alto clef in the duets, and the original version of 'Deggio dunque'. Malmesbury and RCM 905 have later (but early) annotations in different hands. Both indicate a

---

[60] It is just possible that they were the same man.
[61] No instruments are named here in the autograph; but bar 5 is marked *Viol.*

transposition to D for 'Tu vuoi ch'io parta', as sung in December 1720. In Malmesbury 'Cara sposa' too is marked *un tuono più Basso*; it appears in G in *The Pocket Companion*.[62] RCM 905 contains performance markings. An eighteenth-century hand has supplied full figuring and, where an upper part has the bass of the harmony (for example at bar 12 of 'Deh! fuggi un traditore'), repeated it with figuring on the bass line. There are a few corrections and amendments: 'Son contenta di morire' is marked *in D♮* (i.e. D minor, probably Durastanti's key in December 1720), 'Qual nave' *Adagio*. The top three parts of the quartet have an added English text of fatuous ineptitude, beginning 'O haste thee gentle swain'.

Add MS 39180 (BM1, another inelegant writer) seems to have been copied from Hamburg I, with which it corresponds with unusual exactitude down to minor errors and the same confusion of clefs at bar 14 of 'Troppo sofferse' (subsequently corrected). It gives the second version, copied after the composition of the third; Radamisto has the lower part in the duets, and an alto clef in the *coro*. Many movements are figured, and someone has adorned 'Stragi, morti' with another grotesque English version beginning 'Hail Holy God of Love', with 'Cadenza for singer and trumpet' at the end of the A section. Shaftesbury (S4) is very similar and was probably copied from the same source.

Flower (S2, *c.* 1738–40), Lennard (S5), and Coke give composite versions with many revised readings but a few (not always the same), including one or other of the ballet suites, going back to April 1720. Each has an appendix with the December additions in the same hand as the main text, but Lennard and Coke lack the quartet. All three give 'Ombra cara' its original *Largo* tempo with the upper F in bar 80, 'Fatemi, O cieli' in E minor, and 'Barbaro, partirò' in A; Flower, unlike the other two, has 'Sò ch'è vana' in the later key of F. They differ in many other respects. Flower and Coke lack recitatives; only Flower has the repeats in the *coro* written out. The Flower and Lennard texts of the Passacaille are a little more explicit than Malmesbury in instrumental detail; the wind are held back till the A minor section (bar 105), and there is an independent bassoon part in bars 134–42.

Flower has the original autograph version of 'Deggio dunque' (bars 13–16), 'Troppo sofferse' (bar 18), and 'Non sarà' (bar 65). 'Vaga e bella' is in 3/8 and defectively copied, with several sections misplaced in an order that makes nonsense. The words of 'Fatemi, O cieli' are a conflation of 1720 and 1728; the heading *3ᵈ Act* confirms that the copy is later than 1728, though the key is that of 1720. No characters or singers are named in the *coro*. As usual the hand of Jennens has been busy, supplying missing tempo marks in the fugue of the overture, 'Alzo al volo', and 'O scemami il diletto', and bass figuring (there is little in the manuscript as copied) in 'Cara sposa', 'Quando mai', 'Qual nave' (*Larghetto* in this copy alone), 'L'ingrato non amar', and part of 'Fatemi, O cieli'. The Flower parts (cembalo, violins 1 and 2, viola, cello + bassoon, oboes 1 and 2 + flutes, trumpets 1 and 2) were copied by S2 in the late 1740s from the Flower score; this accounts for the omission of the oboes from 'Qual nave' and 'O scemami il diletto', and a few other anomalies. The horn parts of this set are in the music library of the University of Maryland. The overture and additional pieces are omitted, but the Passacaille and Gigue included. The Flower Collection also contains an independent set of four string parts for these two

62 Cluer and Creake, *Pocket Companion for Gentlemen and Ladies*, vol. i (May 1724).

movements (copyist unknown, *c.* 1738–40), with a few minor variants. Although full of errors, the parts indicate many solos which are in other copies and sometimes the autograph but not in HG. The oboes play in bars 23–7 (third beat) of 'Dopo l'orride procelle', bars 28–9 (first three beats) of 'Spero placare', bars 14–18 and 24–6 (first beat) of 'S'adopri', and the ritornello after the A section of 'Con vana speranza'. In almost every movement where Handel wrote *Tutti* on the top line both oboes double the first violins.[63] The cello part gives the bassoons a separate stave where necessary (Mirerò', 'Ombra cara', Passacaille, 'S'adopri', 'Dolce bene', 'Sposo ingrato'); they are silenced in 'Cara sposa' and the B sections of 'Mirerò' and 'Dolce bene'. In the *coro* the part oscillates between *Bassons soli* and *tutti*. The bassoon part is complete, and includes a *Basson 2do* doubling the cellos in bars 134–42 of the Passacaille; but in 'Deggio dunque', apart from the ritornello after the A section, the cello solo ousts the true bass.

Lennard, though a late copy (*c.* 1740), retains some early discarded readings: it lacks the final bar of 'Sommi Dei', has the original text of 'Son contenta di morire' (but not of 'Dopo torbide procelle'), and the upper notes of Radamisto's recitative in II i, found elsewhere only in the autograph, Malmesbury, and Fitzwilliam. Like the autograph and first libretto, but no other copy except Fitzwilliam, it includes the stage direction *ritorna a fermarlo* during Polissena's last recitative in I xi. The bass part of the overture is marked *Organo;*[64] this certainly does not represent Handel's practice in the operas. 'Ombra cara' has some pencilled vocal ornaments from the mid-eighteenth century or later; they are quoted by J. Merrill Knapp in *The Musical Quarterly*, xlv (1959), 166, but the slurs are not in the manuscript. The December pieces appear to have been copied from the Meares *Arie Aggiunte* with their incomplete orchestration; tempo marks have been added to 'Vuol ch'io serva', 'Sò ch'è vana', 'Barbaro, partirò' (all *Allegro*), and 'Fatemi, O cieli' (*Larghetto*).

The Coke copy (*c.* 1734–5) is in the same miniaturist's hand as the third Coke copy of *Teseo* (see p. 257), and displays the same idiosyncrasies. Many tempo marks and other indications are missing, and a number of arias have pastoral English texts of characteristic vapidity (not translations) added by the same hand in red ink. The bass is figured throughout. The oddest feature is that someone evidently found Handel's accompaniments too thin: several arias, notably 'Son contenta di morire', 'Ferite, uccidete', 'Mirerò' (B section, where first violins and unison oboes double the voice), and 'Già che morir', are given supplementary second violin and viola parts to bring them up to full four-part standard. Some bars in the duet 'Se teco vive' likewise have a supernumerary viola. These are not additions to the manuscript, but belong to the original copy. The text is closer to April 1720 than Flower or Lennard, with the first versions of 'Son contenta di morire', 'Dopo torbide procelle', and 'Deggio dunque' (but not 'Sommi Dei') and the Act III ballet (*Paspied e Rigadoon alternativement*). 'Tu vuoi ch'io parta' is marked *non troppo forte per tutto*. The sinfonia in I viii has a unique tempo mark (*Allegro*), 'La sorte, il ciel' is *Allegro ma non presto*, 'Qual nave' *Adagio*. The additional pieces have the same tempo marks as RCM 905, plus *Allegro* for 'Lascia pur' and 'Vile!' which have no indication in any other source. The final ritornello of 'Sò ch'è vana' (in D) is

---

[63] The exceptions are 'La sorte, il ciel' and 'Vanne, sorella ingrata' (where both oboes double the second violins, an obvious error).

[64] This is also in Fitzwilliam, but on one of the late supplementary pages.

replaced by a da capo. In 'Fatemi, O cieli' (E minor) the flute doubles the first violins, as elsewhere in English copies only in RCM 905.

The score of Mattheson's Hamburg arrangement (Berlin Mus MS 9051), written by a copyist with the bass figured throughout, derives from three sources, a copy of Handel's first (April) version, the December libretto, and the new pieces composed for the latter revival, which Mattheson must have obtained in manuscript (perhaps from Handel himself), since the Meares print is defective. He knew nothing of the arias rewritten or transposed in Handel's performing score. This frustrated his attempt to bring out an up-to-date text, and resulted in several parts having an inconsistent tessitura. The eight arias suppressed by Handel in December were excluded, and 'S'adopri' replaced by a very similar aria in the same key from Bononcini's *Etearco*[65] (since it is in the soprano clef and has no words, it was probably never sung). 'S'adopri' is in both the 1722 and 1726 Hamburg librettos, and may have been restored; but the music is not in the manuscript. The rest of the material was copied in the existing keys with only the clefs altered: Radamisto bass, Zenobia soprano, Fraarte,[66] Tigrane, and Farasmane tenor. The duet 'Se teco vive' looks odd with the upper part (Radamisto) in the bass clef, the lower in the soprano; a later hand exchanged the names of the characters without altering the clefs. Thus either the intervals were inverted or a yawning gap of up to two octaves appeared between the vocal lines. Radamisto has the two new arias composed for Senesino, but his other set pieces are in the April keys, leaving them (after octave transposition) uncomfortably high. Some were then modified in detail, but 'Dolce bene' remains among the leger lines. Zenobia's music, apart from the new aria 'Fatemi, O cieli', was put unchanged into the soprano clef; here too there were later adjustments, this time to raise the tessitura. Farasmane's aria was similarly modified for tenor. Tiridate has his new Act I aria, but the other two (which Handel had rewritten) are at tenor pitch, with adjustments in 'Sì che ti renderai'; 'Alzo al volo' even retains the tenor clef. In 'Che farà' Mattheson fitted the new words of the December libretto to the April music, including the second violins' low B flat in bar 65 (altered in the autograph), unaware that Handel had recomposed the aria. Other unpublished April readings survive (though not the ballet music): 'Sommi Dei' without its final bar, 'Son contenta di morire' with the original words, 'Deggio dunque' with the suppressed version of bars 12–16. 'Dopo l'orride procelle' has the December words, but the high notes in bars 32 and 49. Among interesting details are the presence of the flute in 'Fatemi, O cieli' (as in RCM 905 and Coke), the autograph words of 'Lascia pur',[67] and the pencilled note *presto* at the end of several recitatives introducing fiery arias, evidently equivalent to the *attacca* or *segue subito* occasionally specified by Handel.

Mattheson's recitatives are much longer than Handel's, both in words and music, slower in harmonic movement, and less bold in their progressions. They must have taken still longer in performance, since (apart from the heavier gait of the German language) their high tessitura, especially in the bass parts of Radamisto and Tiridate, would enjoin a more declamatory delivery. This and

[65] Identified by R. Strohm.

[66] The opening of his first aria, 'Deh! fuggi un traditore', was first copied with soprano clef; the rest of the part, except the aria in place of 'S'adopri', is for tenor.

[67] This suggests that Mattheson obtained a very early copy of the December pieces.

the octave transpositions must have turned *Zenobia* into a very different opera.

The score was used for all Hamburg revivals up to 1736; rubrics for the insertion of several arias from Zeno's *Cajo Fabrizio*, first set by Caldara for Venice in 1729, cannot be earlier. Apart from tessitura changes, numerous cuts and transpositions are indicated. Farasmane's aria was omitted at some time, and two of Fraarte's in 1726. The part of Tigrane was especially subject to changes in pitch, besides losing two arias; three others were transposed for alto or bass. Two upward transpositions for Zenobia correspond to Handel's in 1728, but this may be chance. 'Barbaro, partirò' seems to have been replaced on one occasion by its predecessor, 'Sposo ingrato'.

Detached excerpts from *Radamisto* are widely scattered. Among the earliest (*c*.1721–2) is a group of three arias, 'Deh! fuggi un traditore', 'Cara sposa', and 'Qual nave', in short score and original keys in Fitzwilliam Mus MS 54, associated with arias from *Muzio Scevola* and Bononcini's *Astarto*. The copyist (Epsilon), distinguished by a G clef of striking exuberance, had links with Smith; their hands are found on opposite sides of the same leaf. Two arias exist in modified and ornamented keyboard arrangements, with the words written or cued between the staves: 'Ombra cara' in G minor (Coke Wesley MS, *c*.1721, H2, and a Malmesbury keyboard volume, 1722, H3) and 'Cara sposa' without final ritornello (RM 19 c 9, ff. 106ᵛ–107, *c*.1730, S2). The latter, probably made by Handel himself, closely resembles his autograph arrangement of 'Sventurato, godi' from *Floridante* (see p. 407). The ornaments are tasteful and expressive, and equally apt for voice or keyboard; the layout with separate flags to the notes suggests that they are vocal.

RM 18 c 9, ff. 71–122, gives a large and curious selection (S2). At least six of the sixteen pieces date from 1728: 'Quando mai' in G with flute and altered text, 'La sorte, il ciel' in D with 'Raffrena i tuoi sospir' in the B section, 'Empio perverso cor' in C minor, 'Troppo sofferse' in G (*Larghetta*), 'Fatemi, O cieli' in G minor, and 'Barbaro, partirò' in B flat. 'Dopo l'orride procelle' with altered text and lower vocal alternatives, 'Che farà quest'alma' (HG 162), 'Sò ch'è vana' in D, 'Vieni d'empietà', and the quartet belong to December 1720, 'Tu vuoi ch'io parta' in E and the sinfonia to April 1720. 'Troppo sofferse' in E flat, as HG 56 but with the ritornello at the beginning as well as the end, may reflect Durastanti's performance in December 1720. It is less easy to account for 'Qual nave' in A and the shortened form of 'O scemami il diletto' (without bars 40–8, as in 1728) in the 1720 key of F. 'Tu vuoi ch'io parta' and 'Dopo l'orride procelle' are figured by Jennens, who performed the like service for 'Parmi che giunta' (attributed to *Radamisto*) in RM 18 c 1, ff. 23–8 (H4). A Smith copy of 'Ombra cara' as sung by Senesino in December 1720 (D minor, *Largo ma non troppo*) in Manchester (v. 313, *Catalogue* p. 51) also belonged to Jennens.

Other fragments are a late copy of 'La sorte, il ciel' in its original key but with string accompaniment up to the vocal entry in RM 19 d 12, ff. 55–7 (S9); short-score copies in original keys of 'Alzo al volo', 'Ombra cara' (*Andante*), 'Stragi, morti' ('Song with Tromba') and 'Cara sposa' without final ritornello in Add MS 31504 (scribe unknown); 'Deh! fuggi un traditore' and 'Vanne sorella' (C minor) with reduced accompaniment in RCM 822 (scribe unknown); and a harpsichord arrangement of 'Sommi Dei' with words, many additional trills and marks of emphasis in the Coke Collection. The latter's '24 Opera Songs' has 'Deh! fuggi un traditore', lacking the viola part, with a few added ornaments, especially in the B section, in which the first violin doubles the voice *piano sempre*. Also in the Coke Collection is a set of four string parts for nine arias in the keys and versions of April 1720 (H 6/9, *c.* 1724–5); 'Ombra cara' (*Largo*) has the bassoon part, not the true bass, where the two diverge.

There are two manuscript keyboard versions of the overture: (i) A transcription by Smith (*c.*1721) in the Coke Wesley MS, where eight notes in the left hand of the first two bars are written by Handel, who seems to be showing Smith how to set about it. This version is copied in a Malmesbury keyboard volume (Gamma, 1722). (ii) A partly recomposed arrangement by Handel[68] in a second Malmesbury volume (Smith) and RM 18 c 1, ff. 19–20 (S2), both dating from about 1728. Walsh had published a clumsy arrangement in his first collection (1726). The first Malmesbury volume also contains a transcription of the sinfonia in I viii and all three ballet suites (Smith, 1722).

The printing of the score was heralded by a publicity campaign. A press announcement on 12 July 1720 stated that it 'is now Engraving finely upon Copper Plates by Richard Meares, Musical Instrument-Maker and Musick-Printer ... NB To make this Work the more acceptable, the Author has been prevailed with to correct the whole'. On 3 December 'the Printer presumes to assert that there hath not been in Europe a Piece of Musick so well printed, and upon so good Paper', adding that it 'consists of 124 large Folio Copper-Plates, all corrected by the Author' (the number of plates was later corrected to 123 and the paper described as Dutch). It appeared on 15 December, fortified by a Privilege of Copyright granted to Handel on 14 June (hitherto used only for the first set of Harpsichord Suites) and described as 'Publisht by the Author'. With Meares on the title-page was associated 'Christopher Smith at yᵉ Hand & Musick-Book in Coventry-Street near yᵉ Hay-Market. NB. Not to be sold any-where else in England'. The name of the engraver, Thomas Cross, appears on the last page of the score, which is indeed a handsome volume. Smith's name confirms that Handel was concerned in the publication; he probably corrected the plates but did not supply the bass figuring.

The score as usual omits the recitatives but includes all the set pieces except the Act I sinfonia and the ballet suites; the *coro* is reduced to its first 51 bars. Almost none of them however have their full instrumentation, the viola part usually falling by the wayside. Exceptions are the overture, 'Deggio dunque', and what remains of the *coro*. The characters are named, not the singers. Tempo marks are scarce, but the opening of the overture is *Largo*. The arias are all in their first form: 'Sommi Dei' without its final bar (the resolution is indicated by an E after the double bar), 'Son contenta di morire' and 'Dopo torbide procelle' with their original texts (the latter has the higher voice part in bars 32 and 49), 'Deggio dunque' with bars 13–16 as first composed. Dal segno indications are correct, except for 'Ombra cara', which has the high F in bar 80 but no tempo. 'Vaga e bella' has a 3/8 signature; a line after every fourth bar converts it to 12/8, as in the four April copies.

On 14 March 1721 Meares advertised 'several Additional Songs ... the Edition containing 41 Copper Plates, engraven by the same Hand, which renders this Work cheaper than any Thing of this Nature yet publish'd; which

---

[68] Printed in *Twenty Overtures*, ii.1.

will be sold at the same Price as before, and such Gentlemen and Ladies as have already purchased it, may have the Additions Gratis'. These *Arie Aggiunte di Radamisto*, comprising the ten new arias and duet composed for the December 1720 revival, but not the quartet or accompanied recitative, were published a week later on 21 March, and the two collections subsequently sold together. Again tempo marks are scarce and instrumentation incomplete. 'Fatemi, O cieli' is in E minor, 'Sò ch'è vana' in D, 'Barbaro, partirò' in A. 'Lascia pur', without instrumental bass in bars 20–4, and 'Vile!' have the upper alternatives for voice.

About 1730–1 Walsh advertised *Radamistus an Opera*. No copy is known; a reissue (*c*.1738) is obviously copied from Meares without the *Arie Aggiunte*, but includes two arias from 1728, 'Fatemi, O cieli' (misprinted 'Fate mio Ciel') in G minor with all four string parts and 'Parmi che giunta'. 'La sorte, il ciel' is *Allegro*,[69] 'Qual nave' *Adagio*. 'Deh! fuggi un traditore' has an added English text; 'Già che morir' is erroneously ascribed to Senesino. 'Tu vuoi ch'io parta', 'Cara sposa' (in G), and 'Qual nave' had appeared in short score in volume i of *The Pocket Companion* (May 1724). In 1722 Meares and Walsh each issued a flute arrangement (including the additional songs), the former made by one Bolton. The overture in parts was published by Walsh about 1725 and by Meares and Cluer independently in January 1727. Walsh's keyboard arrangement (1726) is noted above.

The only full score is Chrysander's (1875), which badly needs replacement. Both his versions are confused, and the second is seriously incomplete. His 'original form of the opera', as we have seen, is basically Handel's second version, with insertions from the first (some but not all of the high notes in 'Dopo torbide procelle') and the third or even later. His amendments to Hamburg I often put wrong what was correct. The altered scoring of 'Vanne sorella ingrata' (*Violin senza Hautb.* on both top parts in bar 1) was added by Handel in Hamburg II (Plate 11). By changing 'germano' to 'ministro' in II iii (HG 46) Chrysander gave Fraarte in April a rank he did not hold till December. The regular displacement of cadential chords in the recitative, here as elsewhere, has led countless performers astray, and on occasion inspires a superfluous editorial bass crotchet and a five-beat bar. The incorrect expansion of Handel's *Tutti* on the top line has already been mentioned; in 'Qual nave' Chrysander gets it right in his first version (HG 102) but wrong in the second (HG 193).

His treatment of scoring and dynamics is often arbitrary. In bar 14 of 'Son lievi le catene' he crossed out a *forte*, in bar 43 of 'Dopo torbide procelle' a *Viol* on the top line, in each case contradicting the autograph as well as the copy. He altered singular to plural, solo to soli, and vice versa, for example in bar 71 of 'Mirerò' and bar 1 of the *coro*. At bar 32 of 'Alzo al volo' he changed *Hautb. solo*, the reading of the autograph and all manuscripts, to *Oboe senza Viol.* In 'L'ingrato non amar' he allowed some of the many string solos to stand, but amended others to *Viol. I* or *II, Viol.* or *Violonc.*, although the autograph and Hamburg II make no such distinction. *Violoncello* on the bass line of 'Cara sposa', though doubtless correct, is Chrysander, not Handel (Hamburg I in fact has *Bassi*, the other manuscripts nothing); but the square-bracketed *Violini primi* at bar 10 of 'Che farà' (HG 162) was written by Handel in

---

[69] This was the original tempo in Hamburg I, amended by the copyist. It appears also in Lennard and RM 19 d 12.

Hamburg II. The treatment of the duet 'Non hò più' is peculiar. The bracketed directions in bars 17 (bass) and 19 (oboe) are in Handel's writing, and *Tutti* in bar 25 is in Hamburg II as copied. Handel also wrote *Cemb 1* on the bass of bar 9 and *Hautb.* in bar 19, cancelling the first C sharp. In an article, 'Zwei Claviere bei Händel. Cembalo-Partituren',[70] Chrysander defended the omission of the direction in bar 9 on the ground that he only printed what Handel wrote first—a principle he constantly set at nought, not least in this opera and this duet. Besides stage directions, he omitted a substantial number of dynamic and instrumental indications, and some bass figures, present in the autograph.

Heinz Rückert's arrangement, made for the 1955 Halle production and published in vocal score by Deutscher Verlag für Musik as recently as 1973, reduces the opera to a travesty, musically and dramatically. Its innumerable defects need not be detailed here.[71] The octave transposition of Radamisto's and Tigrane's parts for bass and tenor and the wholesale removal of arias not only from scene to scene but from act to act undermine the characterization and the entire dramatic structure, robbing some of the greatest movements (including 'Ombra cara' and 'Barbaro, partirò') of their contexts and therefore their impact. The text is in German only, and there is no prefatory explanation.

Additional Notes

* (p. 328) Haym is not named in the libretto. Burney first ascribed it to him, and is almost certainly correct: the arrangement is typical of his methods and quite unlike Rolli's.
* (p. 339) Recent paper study has shown that the Fitzwilliam autograph of the Passepied (Ex. 38) dates from *c.* 1722. It was therefore not the germ from which the *coro* sprang, but probably an exercise written for a pupil.
* (p. 345) After the second performance a Mr Southwell wrote to the future Countess of Burlington on 3 May: 'Handle's new opera pleases very much & has many good songs in it' (Chatsworth papers, quoted by Gibson, *The Royal Academy*, 133).
* (p. 346) Queen Caroline bought 'two tickets of Radamistus' on 10 February according to her expense account for 23 January to 16 March, acquired by the Coke Collection in 1987.

---

[70] *AMZ* xii (1877), 177–9 and 193–8.
[71] See review in *M & L* lv (1974), 367–9.

CHAPTER 18

MUZIO SCEVOLA

THE Argument to Rolli's libretto reads:

In the vain Attempt of Porsena, King of Etruria, to Re-enthrone the expell'd Lucius Tarquin, last King of the Romans; three valorous Actions, which following each other, signaliz'd the Roman Bravery: The Risistance which Horatio made at the Sublician Bridge; The Undauntedness of Mutius in the burning of his own Right-Hand: And the Flight of Clelia and her Companions, (when Hostages to King Porsena,) by swimming over the Tyber, to return to their own Country. These Accidents, and their Circumstances, related by Titus Livius, in the second Book of his first Decad, with the intermix'd Amours, compose the Texture of the present Drama.

The date of the action is 508 BC. The amours, of which Livy is innocent, are Muzio's and Porsena's love for Clelia, a veritable Roman Amazon, and the mutual attraction between Orazio (Horatius Cocles) and Porsena's daughter Irene. One of the 'valorous Actions' (narrated by Livy in II x, xii, and xiii respectively) forms the centre-piece of each act, but since Handel set only the third the other two need not be summarized in detail. At first Porsena intends Irene to marry the restored Tarquinio, whom she loathes; she therefore encourages Orazio to resist her father. Porsena fights in single combat with Clelia (in male armour); when her helmet falls off he spares her and begins to have second thoughts about restoring Tarquinio. Orazio, having covered the Roman retreat while the bridge is destroyed behind him, dives off a pilaster into the Tiber. In Act II Clelia catches Muzio setting out for Porsena's camp disguised in Tuscan armour, but honour forbids her to interfere. Not knowing Porsena by sight, Muzio wounds a magnificently dressed minister in error and is arrested. He incinerates his hand in the altar flame as punishment for his mistake.[1] Porsena pardons him and gives him an escort of guards, who are attacked by Clelia and her women. Porsena again shrinks from his enterprise and agrees to a truce, with Orazio, Clelia, and her companions as hostages.

Act III opens in *a Pavilion*.[2] Porsena asks for Clelia's hand in return for sparing her life and promising freedom to Rome. She replies that her love can be given only once and is already promised. He asks Muzio if he can rely on his friendship and good faith, and when he gladly agrees asks for assistance in winning Clelia. Muzio is thunderstruck, but refuses to believe that a Roman can be outdone in generosity; he tells Clelia that honour requires her to marry Porsena. She gives a bitter consent, finding honour, virtue, and reason weak obstacles to the power of love. Muzio reports his success to Porsena. *A Page* enters *with a Letter* from Clelia inviting Porsena to meet her at Irene's tent,

---

[1] This scene is said to have inspired an etching by Goupy in 1726 (Deutsch, 201).

[2] Chrysander omits nearly all scene headings and stage directions. Many are common to the printed libretto, autograph, and performing score as well as most copies; a few appear only in the libretto. All are included in this summary.

with Muzio as a witness 'to see the Action of one that injoys a Roman Heart'.
Porsena tells Muzio to send Orazio back to Rome with news of peace and
looks forward to his marriage. Muzio resolves to comply with the laws of
Roman honour and then find relief in death. Irene compares Orazio to Mars
coming to Venus's embrace, but her confidante Fidalma warns her not to be
too cocksure. Orazio and Irene indulge in a prolonged leave-taking. The set
changes to *the Bank of the Tyber*, where *Clelia with her Companions* awaits Porsena
and Muzio. When they arrive, she says she will go either to Rome or to death
and *flings herself into the Tyber, where her Companions swim after her*. Muzio offers
his blood in atonement for this breach of faith, but Porsena refuses. Muzio
invites him to the Capitol to witness the gratitude of the Romans for his gift of
liberty and to claim Clelia as his reward. Irene and Fidalma are awaiting
Orazio's return, when Tarquinio enters with soldiers, dispatches Fidalma to
the camp under guard, and orders Irene to follow him: Porsena cannot help
her since he is in Rome pursuing the hostages.[3] Moreover he has broken his
word: she was promised to him (Tarquinio), and he means to have her. But
when he sees a Roman squadron approaching he orders his men to give them a
fierce reception, leaving a few to guard Irene, and strolls off. Irene invokes her
absent father's help. *Tarquin's Soldiers retreating, are pursued by Horatio and his
Men* (battle symphony). Orazio and Irene fall into each other's arms. (Here
Handel omitted a scene in which Tarquinio, abandoned by his followers,
resolves to fight on.) The action moves to *the Capitol*, where Clelia on the orders
of the senate returns herself and the other hostages into Porsena's power.
When Muzio begs her aside not to reveal their love, she declares aloud that
Porsena is far worthier of it than Muzio; she 'fled only that a Roman Heart
might not be said to follow the infamous Example of betray'd Faith'. This
makes Porsena blush and shames him into giving her back to Muzio: if the
glory of arms is Muzio's, let at least the victory of generosity be his own. In a
duet Clelia asks Muzio how she can trust him now; he replies that only fidelity
made him false to his faith. Orazio enters with Irene and reports Tarquinio's
flight. Porsena vows by the altar 'implacable Hatred to Tarquin, and to all his
vile Generation', and peace and liberty to Roman valour. He would like a
Roman son-in-law to inherit his throne and leaves the choice to Irene, his only
child. She takes Orazio amid general agreement that 'a free Soul and joyful
Heart' are the greatest blessings heaven can bestow.

This absurd gallimaufry might have been designed as a parody of all that is
windy and inconsequent in the convention of heroic *opera seria*. The quixotic
standards of honour, whether Roman or Tuscan, involve a continual cutting
off of noses to spite faces, quite apart from the immolation of Muzio's hand.
No one pauses to explain his motives. Clelia's escape, so far from being
'valorous', seems an act of dishonourable bravado, especially in view of her
captor's liberal share in the milk-white generosity of Metastasio's Titus. But
the deadliest defect is the treatment of Tarquinio, whose villainous machinations are the fulcrum of the plot. It is pointless to demand how so noble a
figure as Porsena came to ally himself with this man of straw. Throughout all
three acts Tarquinio has no arias, merely patches of impotent recitative. One
might suppose that the part had been ruthlessly cut because no adequate

[3] Only a fragment of this scene is in print: see p. 375.

singer was available; but Galerati had been judged worthy of three arias in *Radamisto*, and if retrenchment was necessary there is the superfluous figure of Fidalma, who has several arias and no dramatic excuse for her presence.

Attempts to discover Rolli's source, other than Livy, have been largely negative. The subject had been popular since the Minato–Cavalli *Il Mutio Scevola* (Venice 1665, revived in Bologna the same year and in 1667), and it is perhaps worth summarizing its operatic history.[4] All librettos derive ultimately from Minato, but changes were introduced with every production, and the links grow increasingly tenuous as the number of scenes, characters, and arias declined and their treatment was modified by the development of taste.

?–Stradella (*Le gare dell'amore heroico* or *L'Oratio Cocle*): Genoa 1679, Genoa 1688 (*Muzio Scevola*), Milan 1690.

?–? (*Muzio Scevola*): Wolfenbüttel 1692.

F. C. Bressand–Keiser (*Clelia*): Hamburg 1695; reset by Mattheson (*Der edelmüthige Porsenna*), Hamburg 1702, and Schürmann, Brunswick 1718.

Stampiglia–G. Bononcini (*Muzio Scevola*, aria texts all new): Rome 1695, Florence 1696, Naples 1698, Genoa n.d., Turin 1700 (additions by another composer), Vienna 1710 (revised, but over half the arias from 1695).

Piovene–Lotti (*Porsenna*): Venice 1712, Naples 1713 (additions by Alessandro Scarlatti).

Minato has nearly twenty characters, reduced to twelve or thirteen in the operas of Stradella, Bononcini, and Lotti. They include the usual comic servants. Most of them have no counterpart in Rolli, who retains only Muzio, Orazio, Porsena, and Tarquinio, and the earlier Italian librettos show major differences in the plot. Muzio and Orazio both have wives, and Orazio a grown daughter; Porsena's daughter and Clelia do not appear; on the other hand Tarquinio has no aria in Cavalli's opera and only one in Stradella's. Very little remains in Rolli of Minato's complex design. He may have derived the Clelia plot from Madeleine de Scudéry's novel *Clélie*, of which an English translation was published in vast folio in 1678. It seems unlikely that he knew Bressand's *Clelia*, though they may have used a common intermediate source. The incompetence of the libretto, as woolly in language as in dramaturgy, suggests that it was largely Rolli's unaided work, though Muzio's 'Pupille sdegnose' may owe something to an aria for Porsena in Stampiglia's III iv ('Pupille amate, Vezzose stelle, Più mi sdegnate Più siete belle'); the phrases however are libretto commonplaces. Strohm considers that the text carried political implications dictated by Bononcini's noble patrons, with whom Rolli was closely associated, and that they identified themselves with the Roman patriots, Porsena with George I, and Tarquinio with Walpole. Bononcini used none of his earlier music in the new Act II, but borrowed his overture from *Thomyris*; it had served previously in his Vienna serenata *Il fiore delle eroine* (1704).

Handel's score shows that, whether or not he regarded the division of the libretto between three composers[5] as (in Burney's words) 'a premeditated plan, to try their several abilities, and determine pre-eminence', he was very

---

[4] For fuller details see H. S. Powers, 'Il Mutio tramutato', *Venezia e il melodramma nel Seicento* (Florence, 1976), 227–58, Strohm, *HJb* (1975), 113–14 (*Essays*, 45), and for the Bononcini versions Lindgren, *A Bibliographic Scrutiny*.

[5] See Chapter 16, p. 307, and p. 375 below.

much on his mettle and aware that comparisons would be made. He took a great deal of trouble, not only over the details of each number but to achieve as much variety as possible within the arias and between the different sections of the work. Each composer was allowed an overture; Handel included four accompanied recitatives (two in succession in the last scene), two duets, a battle symphony, and a jubilant and richly scored *coro*. The eleven arias[6] are nearly all long and packed with invention and resource. The workmanship is solid, in the grand manner of *Radamisto*, as the overture at once makes clear. This is a two-movement French 'Ouverture'[7] (the customary dance was probably omitted because of the length of the opera) with a noble introduction, enriched at the start by a canon between top line and bass, and a particularly splendid and compact fugue. The subject, nicely divided between a rhythmic gesture and an equable flow of quavers, lends itself to dramatic entries in stretto. The irregular answer, in which a semitone replaces a minor third, provoked a celebrated comment from Geminiani when the licence was pointed out to him: 'È vero. Mà quel semitono vale un mondo.' The interludes for oboes and bassoon vary the texture while retaining a link with the quavers of the subject.

The circumstances allowed little opportunity for the development of character, even if Handel were able to animate Rolli's puppets. He supplies suitable music for every situation, and sometimes brings the character's predicament home with startling force. Muzio was the first part he wrote for Senesino, and it is interesting to see how he exploits the peculiarities of his voice, the narrow tessitura, strong *messa di voce*, and flexible control of melisma. 'Pupille sdegnose' with its smooth sequential progressions is typical of the music with which Senesino charmed and held his public. 'Il confine della vita', preceded by a fine recitative in which 'onore', 'patria', 'pace', and 'libertà'— the mainsprings of Muzio's existence—receive a strong harmonic emphasis, is a superb Adagio, not a common tempo for a whole aria in Handel. He dramatizes Muzio's struggle with his fate in the tension between the graceful vocal line and the jagged wide-leaping violin figures over an inexorable bass. This is carried through both parts of the aria, and is all the more telling for being waged in a major key. The pull to sharp keys throughout the scene has many parallels in similar episodes. 'Spera, che trà le care gioje' is less memorable, despite the rich part-writing and five-bar phrases of the ritornellos; but the duet with Clelia, 'Mà come amar?', is a masterly example of Handel's dramatic psychology. This is no common love scene; Muzio has given great offence, and must win back Clelia's estranged affections. A subtle manipulation of design is required if the reconciliation is to convince us, and Handel manages it beautifully. The duet is long, the ritornello contrapuntal, and the voices almost wholly independent; the honeyed thirds and sixths of congruence are avoided except for occasional cadences, of which only that at the end of the first part is dwelt on. The style is carefully wrought, almost in the manner of a trio sonata or its vocal equivalent, a chamber duet. Muzio's last solo utterance, the accompanied recitative 'Per Roma giuro', is as striking as anything in his part. It follows Porsena's sonorous oath, firmly rooted in B flat, with a sudden shift (*più adagio*) to F minor and an astonishing progression five bars later, from G minor to a dominant seventh on E with all the parts marked *piano*:

[6] Chrysander omits one: see p. 375.

[7] Bononcini's overture is also in the French form, though the second section is not fugal. Amadei's is an Italian sinfonia.

Ex. 40

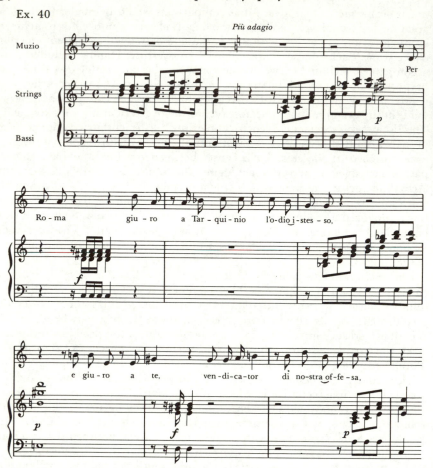

(For the sake of Rome I swear the same hate for Tarquinio, and I swear to you,
as the avenger of our injury . . .)

Clelia's set pieces, apart from the duet, come early in the act. All her music
is fiery and forthright; Durastanti's ability to play male roles (in *Radamisto*,
and later in *Flavio*, *Giulio Cesare*. and *Arianna*, not to mention Ariosti's
Vespasiano) made her a natural choice for an Amazon. 'Lungo pensar' is
propelled by the dotted accompaniment figure that was to see service for frogs
in *Israel in Egypt* and the Angel in *Jephtha* and by rising scale figures in triplets.
Her reaction to Muzio's proposal that she marry Porsena finds apt expression
in the sarcastic setting of the words 'onor', 'virtù', and 'ragione' to rising thirds
in the secco (HG 16), in the whirling scales and leaps of the accompagnato, and
with more finesse in the aria 'Dimmi, crudele amore'. Here again scales are
prominent, with a tendency to land with a thump on the second beat of the
bar, but the broken vocal line and agitated buzzing of the strings are set off by
yearning figures with a persistent falling sixth and sudden pauses of more than
a bar. The ritornello and both parts of the aria (bars 18–20, 101–4, 134–6)
bring a foretaste of the *Matthew Passion* fingerprint that Handel was to develop

with sublime effect in 'A tuoi piedi' in *Tamerlano*. This Amazon has a heart. The B section ends strikingly with an *Adagio* hemiola bar.

Of Irene's two arias the second is by far the better. Despite well-wrought string parts 'Con lui volate' is inclined to trundle. 'Ah dolce nome!' on the other hand is a haunting piece in sarabande rhythm and a mood of thoughtful introspection, commoner in Bach than Handel, that was to be immortalized in 'Cease, ruler of the day' (*Hercules*) and the finale of *Theodora*. The first three words, uttered before the ritornello, form a touching link (Adagio 4/4) between the recitative and the triple-time Larghetto of the aria. There is some expressive writing for violins, including a solo,[8] while the oboes and violas over falling fifths in the bass constantly repeat the rhythm associated with the words 'In van ti chiamo'. Chrysander emasculates the B section, which as performed in 1721 was nearly twice as long, moving from F sharp minor into the major; the return to the da capo is far more striking from the relative major than from the dominant. This aria is a model of the art with which Handel lightens a rich texture to let the voice through. The uninhibited gaiety of Irene's duet with Orazio, 'Vivo senza alma', makes a clever contrast with the weightier duet for the first pair of lovers. Irene has long made up her mind about Orazio, so that no problems arise. But Handel's control of form is again masterly. After a ritornello based on the gigue-like instrumental material, Orazio, the higher voice, has a long solo in the tonic; Irene replies at equal length, beginning in the relative minor; both voices concur happily in the tonic; and after an *Adagio* cadence the vocal melody appears for the first time in the orchestra, deliciously expanded from two to four parts. Da capo form is quite transcended.

Orazio's single aria, 'Come, se ti vedrò' (the words 'come' and 'càra' are interchanged in the libretto), is simple and sequential but touchingly beautiful. Burney calls it 'to my present feelings the most pleasing and agreeable of all Handel's charming Sicilianas' and remarks that Berselli 'must have been high in the composer's favour for taste, as he is left to himself in no less than six *ad libitum*s and adagios, which he had to embellish'. Most of these are on the words 'parto' and 'addio'; one of them, exceptionally, opens the B section of the aria.[9] Porsena's aria too is very fine. Boschi, usually type-cast as a blustering tyrant, for once found himself playing a magnanimous father-figure. But there is plenty of bluster in 'Volate più dei venti'', in which, over a striding bass, first the violas, cellos, and bassoons and later the unison violins suggest the raging of the wind. The separate part for cellos and bassoons, generally doubling the violas at the octave and swirling in semiquavers round the vocal line, produces a peculiar and powerfully sonorous effect. The B section, in which Porsena's thoughts move from impatience to the anticipation of bliss, makes a marvellous contrast: major key, triple time, slow tempo (*Larghetto*), smooth repeated chords, and scoring of sensuous sweetness (solo oboe and four-part strings, pitched for the most part close together on the treble stave). Handel begins with the melody from Keiser's *Octavia* he had put to such good use in *Il trionfo del Tempo* ('Crede l'uom') and *Agrippina* ('Vaghe fonti'), but characteristically develops it in a different direction and never brings it back.

[8] This was an afterthought; in the autograph bar 26 (not 25) is marked *Concertin*.

[9] Handel four times wrote *Adagio* over the voice part; Chrysander omits it twice and confines it once to the orchestra.

Fidalma's 'Non ti fidar', which Burney attributes to the wrong singer and comprehensively damns, is a charming song with fascinatingly unpredictable phrase-lengths in the same mixed metres (3/8, 3/4, 2/4) as 'Bel piacere' in *Agrippina*. The kittenish confidante makes a refreshing contrast with the heroic posture of the two heroines. This is the only aria Chrysander allows Fidalma; but she has another, 'A chi vive di speranza', which Handel set twice in the same key (G major) but in quite different styles. Both settings are based on earlier material, the first in 12/8 on the exquisite 'Felicissima quest'alma' in *Apollo e Dafne*, the second in 3/8 on the second setting of 'Sotto il lauro' in *Agrippina*.[10] Each, especially the latter, diverges a good deal from its prototype, and the 12/8 version has some interesting changes in scoring; in place of solo oboe and pizzicato strings the three upper parts are allotted respectively to flute and first violins, second violins with violas at the octave, and third violins with ripieno cellos at the octave. This is such a beautiful piece that it is difficult to see why Handel discarded it, unless the singer (Salvai) found it unsuited to her voice or preferred something more skittish; the 3/8 version was sung in 1721 and published the following year.

The composition of the orchestra was presumably ordained for all three acts. The instrumentation of Amadei's is incomplete in the copies; he used trumpets in two battle scenes and his overture. Bononcini ignored the brass, but employed a transverse flute in two arias. Handel has trumpets and horns in the battle symphony and the *coro* (based on a catchy and ubiquitous melody) and writes for all the instruments with care and resource. His music for Act III is of such outstanding quality that it is a pity it should be condemned to silence. It is a magnificent torso, but still a torso. A performance of the whole opera, though instructive, could never be more than a historical curiosity; there is too little doubt who would be the winner. Amadei's act is correct but colourless, full of vain repetitions and aimless progressions; the music has no life of its own and gives none to the characters. Bononcini's is considerably better. His style is not unlike Handel's—the frequent similarity in the cut of phrases might provoke long and learned arguments in a stylistic paternity suit—but he lacks Handel's melodic span and variety of phrase-lengths, and above all his gift for the unexpected detail that distinguishes period cliché from true originality. Burney's judgement on the printed selection of favourite songs, though severe, is difficult to refute. 'Bononcini's airs are easy and natural, but no vigour of genius is discoverable in the subject, design, or texture of the parts . . . compared with the three airs by Handel, which are by no means the best in his act, they seem to be rather the productions of a timid and superficial dilettante, than a professor of great original genius.'

History and Text

Handel completed his act on 23 March 1721, and the opera was produced at the King's Theatre on 15 April with the following cast:

---

[10] Mattheson in *Critica Musica* (July 1722) accused Handel of lifting the principal idea (very differently treated in the two operas) from his *Porsenna* of 1702. He also said that 'Lungo pensar' used material from an aria by Lotti, 'Bramo aver, per più goder'. There is no sign of this in Add MS 31530, conjecturally—and perhaps inaccurately—identified in the Hughes-Hughes *Catalogue* as Lotti's *Porsenna*. The text however comes from Act II of Lotti's *Giove in Argo* (Dresden, 1717 and 1719).

MUZIO SCEVOLA:	Senesino (alto castrato)
ORAZIO:	Berselli (soprano castrato)
PORSENA:	Boschi (bass)
CLELIA:	Durastanti (soprano)
IRENE:	Anastasia Robinson (contralto)
FIDALMA:	Salvai (soprano)
TARQUINIO:	Galerati (soprano)

Mainwaring appears to have started the story that the assignment of the three acts to different composers was intended as a sort of judgement of Paris: 'And he, who by the general suffrage, should be allowed to have given the best proofs of his abilities, was to be put into possession of the house'. Burney rightly scouted this, pointing out that collaborations and pasticcios were then common, but he and Hawkins accepted Mainwaring's statement that the first act was by Ariosti, who was probably then in Paris[11] and did not join the Royal Academy until the winter of 1722–3. Amadei, also known as Pippo and Mattei,[12] was a cellist in the orchestra and had composed additional music for *Arsace*, produced two months earlier.[13] Nevertheless it was inevitable that the public should treat the affair as a competition, and there was no doubt about its verdict: Fabrice reported to Count Flemming on 21 April that Handel 'easily triumphed over the others'. Elizabeth Legh recorded her predictably partial opinion to the same effect in the Malmesbury copy. In the same letter Fabrice mentioned that during the first performance the King, who was in the theatre, received news that the Princess of Wales had given birth to a son; the large audience 'celebrated the event with loud applause and huzzas'. This was the future Duke of Cumberland, whose destiny was to be linked once more with Handel's in *Judas Maccabaeus*. There were ten performances during the season, the last on 7 June.

The score performed in 1721 differed from HG in important respects. Scene viii began with Fidalma's 'A chi vive' (3/8) and continued with recitative for her and Irene. Tarquinio (soprano) entered (ix) and ordered Fidalma's arrest and removal by his troops. The whole episode was longer and different in words and music up to Tarquinio's exit. Squire (*Catalogue*, 53) prints some of the extra text but does not note two further passages for Tarquinio, two lines after 'Vano è lo sforzo' (HG 47) and one line after 'egli fù il primo' (HG 48). This version, including 'A chi vive', appears in every complete copy. Chrysander's omission of the aria is particularly odd, since it was one of the opera's popular hits, attested by its survival in single copies and among the few pieces printed at the time.

The only revival, for three nights, opened a new season on 7 November 1722;[14] three earlier performances, on 27 and 31 October and 3 November, had been postponed owing to the illness of Senesino, who again sang Muzio. Durastanti, Robinson, and Boschi probably retained their parts, but Fidalma was cut out and Tarquinio's music reset in shortened form for bass (perhaps

[11] Lindgren, *M & L* (1981), 338–40.
[12] This seems to have been a corruption introduced by Mattheson in *Critica Musica*.
[13] See Chapter 16, p. 307.
[14] Deutsch (129) gives the correct dates but attributes them to the wrong year, thus postulating a revival that never took place. His references to the opera on pp. 126 and 136–7 contain many errors. Berselli and Galerati were both sopranos, Robinson's voice changed from soprano to contralto before 1720, the part of Tarquinio is in Handel's autograph, and the date 1720 for the tenth performance is a misprint for 1721.

* Lagarde). It is not known who sang Orazio, but the part may have been reduced to recitative. Chrysander's compression of Scenes viii and ix and the reduction of the B section of 'Ah dolce nome!' from 32 bars to 19 reflect this revival but not the extent of the changes. Additional cuts were Muzio's 'Il confine della vita', the following recitative for Irene and Fidalma, the latter's 'Non ti fidar', Orazio's 'Come, se ti vedrò,' and probably his duet with Irene, 'Vivo senza alma'. According to Clausen Clelia's 'Lungo pensar' and Muzio's 'Spera' were omitted at some time, though they are not cancelled in the Hamburg score; this was perhaps a temporary measure for some individual performance. The higher notes for the voice in 'Dimmi crudele', printed incorrectly in HG, present something of a puzzle: they take the part uncomfortably high for Durastanti and may have been intended for Cuzzoni, whose delayed arrival had been expected since early autumn. Or they could apply to the aria's use in another opera—though not *Scipione*, where the tenor Fabri sang the original line in A minor. *Muzio Scevola* was never revived in London after 1722, and Handel cannibalized the score, transferring at least seven pieces to other works, some with altered words: 'Lungo pensar', 'Dimmi crudele', 'Con lui volate', and the *coro* to *Scipione* in 1730, 'Volate più dei venti' to *Admeto* in 1731, and 'Pupille sdegnose' and 'Come, se ti vedrò' to *Ottone* in 1733. The overture was played at a Manchester Subscription Concert on 5 February 1745.

There was a production in Hamburg on 7 January 1723 (NS) with an allegorical prologue in German by Keiser. The opera itself, exceptionally for Hamburg, was sung wholly in Italian. Mattheson mentions the occasion, with some obscure comments, in *Critica Musica*. The cast was:

MUZIO:	Campioli (alto castrato)
ORAZIO:	Möhring (tenor)
PORSENA:	Johann Gottfried Riemschneider (bass)
CLELIA:	Puchon (soprano)
IRENE:	Monjo senior (contralto)
FIDALMA:	Monjo junior (soprano)
TARQUINIO:	Gebhard Julius Riemschneider (bass)[15]

There were six performances. Keiser subsequently appropriated 'Pupille sdegnose', 'Dimmi crudele', and 'Con lui volate' for his *Mistevojus* (Hamburg 1726).[16] Handel's act was staged at Essen in 1928 (with Bach's *Phoebus and Pan*) and at Sulmona in 1985. Denis Arnold conducted a shortened concert version of all three acts at Oxford in 1977, and Handel's act was given at a Halle concert in 1982.

Autograph

The autograph (RM 20 b 7) has been damaged by damp, but recent treatment has restored its legibility. Handel's foliation on every fourth leaf

[15] For further information on these singers see Zelm, 'Die Sänger der Hamburger Gänsemarkt-Oper', 35–73. Campioli and J. G. Riemschneider later sang under Handel in London (see *The New Grove*). The Monjo sisters came from Cöthen; Mattheson spoke very highly of the younger in *Critica Musica*. They were of an independent spirit; in January 1728 one refused to sing until she was paid, forcing the management to give the pair a yearly contract of 1,700 Reichsthaler in March, and both were in trouble with the police in January 1736. Christel Monjo died in Hamburg on 9 February 1737.

[16] Lynch, 'Opera in Hamburg', 1718–1738', Appendix II.

excludes the overture, but makes it clear that the only subsequent insertions were the 3/8 setting of 'A chi vive' (ff. 37–8) and an extension to the B section of 'Il confine della vita' (f. 22). Three leaves may have been removed after this aria. Scenes viii and ix of course are complete as performed in 1721 (the direction for Fidalma's arrest, *Due soldati la portan via*, is in the autograph but not the libretto); HG ix is numbered x, and x is xii as in the libretto, whose xi (Tarquinio's monologue) was never set. The second setting of 'A chi vive' is inserted before the first. The B section of 'Ah dolce nome!' contains two full statements of the text with a central ritornello in F sharp minor; Handel noted the voice part of the last three bars in the later shortened version, without the bass, before the double bar. 'Come, se ti vedrò' has four additional bars before the ritornello at the end of the A section and important extra dynamics; the last beat of bar 4 is *pianissimo*, indicating a *diminuendo*, the fifth note for the voice in bar 11 is C sharp, not E (all copies follow the autograph in these two respects), the vocal cadence at the end of each part is *Adagio*.

None of the above passages is cancelled, though Handel made many cuts and changes during the process of composition. 'Il confine della vita' was shortened in the first part and extended in the second, and the duet 'Vivo senza alma' likewise underwent expansion and compression at different points. 'Non ti fidar' was originally 50 bars longer; of five substantial cuts, affecting the initial ritornello and both parts of the aria, Chrysander incomprehensibly printed the shortest in brackets, although it has exactly the same status as the others and like them was never performed. In both parts the voice is doubled by oboe. 'Pupille sdegnose' and the two duets, like the overture and *coro*, have no tempo mark. The headings *Padiglione* (HG 5) and *Campidoglio* (58) and the direction *Clelia se getta a nuoto* (41, bottom system, after 'Voi v'ingannate') are in every complete copy as well as the autograph, which contains a great many dynamics, trills, and other performance details omitted from HG, affecting almost every piece; most of them are in the copies, including the performing score. Handel marked the opening of Muzio's accompanied recitative 'Soavi affetti' (HG 11) *Sostenuto* with a wavy line under the bass B,[17] which elsewhere indicates slurred repeated quavers, and the string introduction to Porsena's 'Sù quell'ara' (HG 66) *Largo e staccato*. Chrysander relegates this and other instructions to the keyboard arrangement, where they are likely to be taken for editorial glosses. The horns in the battle sinfonia were an afterthought. In the autograph and all copies the last instrumental triplet in bar 34 of 'Lungo pensar' is a tone higher than printed, the cello and bassoons double the bass in bar 23 of 'Volate più', the top line of 'Spera' is for *Tutti* (i.e. all oboes double the first violins), and the voice note in bar 17 of 'Ma come amar?' is c″, not f″. The voice's third note in bar 27 of 'Vivo senza alma' is c″ in the autograph and HG, d″ in all copies.

'Dimmi crudele' has the lower alternatives for the voice, except in bars 69 and 133, where the first note is d″ falling a seventh to e′, as in every copy. Chrysander seems to have recomposed these two cadences, besides printing the alternatives sometimes in small and sometimes in large notes and adding further confusion with a wrong clef (tenor for alto on the bass line of bars 55–70). The original voice part in bar 68 is unclear, but the cadence may have been that of the early copy RM 19 c 8:

---

[17] Several copies—Add MS 16108, Malmesbury, and Coke—reproduce this.

Ex. 41

Handel altered the voice and bass in bars 68–9 to:

Ex. 42

Bars 131–4 read in all sources:

Ex. 43

di gio – ir, nò non vien ma – i

(to enjoy, never comes)

The small notes in these two examples are alternatives added in the performing score (Hamburg I). The HG text of bars 69 and 133–4 does not appear in any source; nor, strangely, is Handel's altered bass in bars 68–9 in any copy.

Librettos

1721. 'Drama . . . Printed by Tho. Wood in Little Britain'. 103 pp. The title page has a motto from Addison's *Cato*:

> Do thou, great Liberty, inspire our Souls
> And make our Lives in thy Possession happy
> Or our Deaths glorious in thy just Defence.

Rolli is described as 'Segretario Italiano della Medesima' (that is, the Royal Academy), but none of the composers is named. His dedication to George I is accompanied by a flowery tribute to England as an asylum for the oppressed, with the inevitable comparison between Roman and British liberty, and a fulsome eulogy of the monarch. A note states that *virgole* indicate 'an exact verbal Translation of the Speeches taken from the true History', and marginal lines 'denote that those Verses may (for brevity sake) be omitted in the Singing'. Both categories affect the first two acts much more than Handel's, which includes only one passage ascribed to 'the true History', four lines for Porsena in Scene vii beginning 'Del tuo fiero attentato' (top of HG 42), and two cuts—neither in fact set—a short recitative for Clelia in the first scene ($4\frac{1}{2}$ lines before Porsena's 'All'impensato', HG 6) and Tarquinio's monologue (Scene xi). The text of the libretto is very close to Handel's autograph, but differs from HG. Handel slightly modified the B section of 'Il confine della vita'. One line set by him (Fidalma's 'Quanto è bel quel che piace' in Scene v, HG 28) is not in the libretto. A copy containing on the last blank leaf a laundry list apparently written by a member of Handel's domestic staff (Deutsch, 125) is now at Princeton. The first item should read '12 shifts', not '12 shirts'. For a copy of this libretto modified for 1722 see note, p. 384.

1723 Hamburg ('gedruckt bei Caspar Jakhel'). Exceptionally the title-page, Argument and entire libretto, except Keiser's Prologue, are given in Italian and German. All the singers are named, but none of the seven authors involved—four composers, two librettists, and the translator. The text seems to have been compiled from the London score as well as the libretto; it contains Fidalma's missing line in Scene v and the recitative on HG 53 as set, not with the minor variants as printed, and omits Tarquinio's monologue. The one significant change is the replacement of 'Vivo senza alma' by a different duet, 'Non sento tutto il giubilo' from Caldara's *Lucio Papirio dittatore* (Vienna 1719, Brunswick 1721). In Keiser's Prologue 'Mordsucht' with a mob of furies threatens to destroy proud Rome, but is banished by Jupiter, who promises to protect his heavenly realm and the city from the legions of hell.

Copies and Editions

Of the thirteen known copies, some containing only Handel's act and others without the recitatives, seven date almost certainly from 1721. The pressure on London's copyists seems to have been so great that several scores required collaboration between three, four, or even five, one taking over when another for whatever purpose left the room. The earliest, in the Nanki Library in Tokyo (formerly owned by the Bath organists Thomas Chilcot and Thomas Field, and from 1868 by W. H. Cummings, who mentioned it briefly in print[18]), antedates not only the first performance but both Hamburg scores, and can be assigned with certainty to late March or very early April. It omits nearly all recitatives and contains music by all three composers; Amadei is represented only by his overture and four arias. H1 copied Bononcini's overture, H2 the rest of his act and all Handel's, though Smith and H1 may have written some of the words. The last two movements of Amadei's overture were copied by RM1, the rest of his work by an unidentified, primitive, and untidy hand. Handel's act contains the recitatives on HG 16–17 (including the secco) and 66–8 (from the string entry), the overture, sinfonia, and all arias

[18] 'Muzio Scevola', *MT* lii (1911), 18.

and duets, but not in the correct order; the copyist may have worked before Handel had finished with the autograph. 'Il confine della vita' comes after the duet 'Vivo senza alma', 'Ah dolce nome!' before 'Spera che trà le care gioje'. 'Come, se ti vedrò' and 'Ah dolce nome!' of course are in the full original versions; the first violin part in bar 45 of the latter seems to have been written as a correction by Handel. Several pieces have additional bass figuring. The most remarkable features of this manuscript are that it gives the 12/8 setting of 'A chi vive', which was removed from the performing score before the words were entered,[19] and includes all five additional passages in 'Non ti fidar', crossed out by Handel in the autograph and found in no other copy. Two bars in this aria (24–5) were omitted by mistake.

The performing score, Hamburg I (MA/1032), is the unaided work of H1. As first copied it contained the full versions listed in the first paragraph above under *Autograph*, but none of the cuts in 'Non ti fidar'. Since writing the autograph Handel had evidently changed his mind on two points of scoring: the top part of 'A chi vive' (3/8), originally *Tutti* (as in three early copies, Hamburg II, Malmesbury, and RM 19 c 8), is now for first violins only, and bar 25 of 'Ah dolce nome!' has a violin solo. 'Lungo pensar' and 'A chi vive', as well as the five pieces listed above, have no tempo mark. Handel modified the score more than once. Either before performance or during the original run (certainly by June 1721) he cancelled the four extra bars in the A section of 'Come, se ti vedrò' and the penultimate bar of the B section (Chrysander restored the latter but not the former). He added a fermata at the third beat of bar 9 and *Larghetto* at bar 24 (these or their equivalent reappear only in late copies) and *parte* after 'Pupille sdegnose', to indicate that Muzio must be absent during Clelia's big recitative and aria though he is back immediately after it, another instance of Rolli's poor dramaturgy.

The manuscript shows many changes made for the 1722 revival. Muzio's recitative 'Mio cor' (HG 25), the whole of Scene v, the first page of 'Come, se ti vedrò,' and 'Ah chi vive' were cancelled, and 'Il confine della vita' and 'Vivo senza alma' folded over. Most of the recitatives of viii and ix were also cancelled, and replaced by the shorter HG version with bass Tarquinio; this is on f. 61, an insertion written by Smith. The last sixteen bars of the B section of 'Ah dolce nome!' were pasted out or concealed by a slip with the shorter HG end (H3). The recitative before 'Come, se ti vedrò' was altered to end in C, perhaps leading to a substitute aria, as Clausen suggests. Unfortunately his analysis of the manuscript is vitiated by his belief in Deutsch's supposititious revival in autumn 1721 and wrong identification of the voices. There was never a tenor in the cast. Nor is there any evidence that the part of Clelia was transferred from Durastanti to Salvai, who left London before the 1722 revival, though transpositions (subsequently cancelled) were indicated on both Clelia's arias. That on 'Lungo pensar' is difficult to decipher; a small *NB* on bars 18 and 29 and two alternative notes in bars 18 and 19 may be linked with consequent changes to the violin part. 'Dimmi crudele' was marked up a tone to A minor, possibly for *Scipione* in 1730, when the voice part was put down a seventh. Besides the upper alternatives for the voice Handel wrote *in Bass* and a bass clef below bars 36, 55, and 80; but all copies retain the alto clef. Verbal changes in both parts of 'Volate più' and pencilled musical adjustments in bars 31 and 33 refer to the 1731 revival of *Admeto*.

[19] There is no reason to doubt Clausen's conclusion that RM 19 d 12, ff. 32–4, originally formed part of the performing score.

Hamburg II (MA/190) is a composite effort by H3, Smith, H2, and H1. Smith copied the first three scenes to the end of the recitative before 'Dimmi crudele', H2 'Volate più' and 'Vivo senza alma', H1 'Non ti fidar', from 'Spera' to the end of the recitative before 'Ah dolce nome!', the battle symphony and following recitative (HG 52–3), and the recitative before 'Mà come amar?' (HG 58–60); the rest—six sections including the overture—is the work of H3. The text differs little from the first state of Hamburg I (though it was not copied from it), except that it gives the shortened form of 'Come, se ti vedrò', with a sign indicating an (? unintentional) omission in bar 17. There are a few tempo variants ('Pupille sdegnose' is *Andante*); in 'Mà come amar?' both violins are doubled by oboes, as nowhere else.

This manuscript has become a confusing palimpsest through its use by Chrysander to prepare his edition. It cannot have been the printer's copy, since it differs in various particulars from HG; but it has puzzling features, besides revealing Chrysander's editorial methods in an odd light. He added a number of corrections, dynamics, scoring indications, tempo marks, and stage directions from the autograph, Hamburg I, and the libretto, as well as the German translation printed in HG (but including 'A chi vive') and numerous annotations. Many of these amendments do not appear in HG, which does however reproduce the results of Chrysander's interference with a basically sound text. In this manuscript he inserted the penultimate bar of the B section of 'Come, se ti vedrò' (but not the parallel longer cut at bar 17), crossed out many stress marks on the first note of the generative instrumental figure in 'Con lui volate' (a few are printed incorrectly with a staccato dot), cancelled the full recitatives of viii and ix, and replaced the longer B section of 'Ah dolce nome!' with the shorter. There is no clue here to his subsequent omission of 'A chi vive' or alteration of the cadences in 'Dimmi crudele'.

Two early composite copies of all three acts, Add MS 16108 and RM 19 c 8, are in the British Library. The former must have been mutilated early in its life, for several sections—ff. 1–2 (with the corrupted title *Mazio Coephola*), 37, 84–7 (Handel's overture), 95–100, 102–4, and 135–46 (the end of the manuscript)—are in a hand dating from about the middle of the century, probably copying from the Lennard score; it bears some resemblance to BM 3. The main body features H3 (ff. 3–14 and part of 19ᵛ–33, the end of Amadei's act), H2 (68–75ʳ, 108ᵛ–110ʳ, 123ᵛ–134), and Smith (the rest). The manuscript bears signs of hasty copying and contains notes by Smith in German about the placing of the recitative after 'Lungo pensar'. It shows the loop on the stem of Smith's treble clef in an embryonic stage and once or twice the older form of his C clef, and must date from the spring or summer of 1721. Handel may have used this score in the theatre, for at one point he corrected Amadei's act; H3 had erroneously copied Irene's aria 'Degno d'amor' (f. 12ᵛ) in the soprano clef and without the character's name; Handel inserted this and two alto clefs. Cummings is wrong in stating that he wrote some entire pages. The text is virtually identical with Hamburg I after Handel had shortened 'Come, se ti vedrò', which (like 'A chi vive') is specifically for strings. Smith originally marked both upper staves of 'Spera' for violins and oboes; he then corrected this by writing *Tutti* over the instrumental abbreviation on the top part but forgot to change the second.

In RM 19 c 8 Amadei's act was copied by RM4 (ff. 1–9), an unknown hand (10–42 and 47ᵛ–63), and RM1 (43–7ʳ), Bononcini's and Handel's (135–225) entirely by H2. The manuscript may be a little earlier than Add MS 16108, for it has the unique cadence quoted above in bars 68–70 of 'Dimmi crudele' and 'A chi vive' has the original scoring, *Tutti* on the top line. This also appears in the Malmesbury score (H2 again), which shows no major variants. The horns are omitted from the battle symphony as in the first draft of the autograph. Several arias—'Lungo pensar', 'A chi vive', and especially 'Pupille sdegnose'—have some bass figuring. The accompanied recitative 'Sù quell' ara' (HG 66) is *Largo e stacc: piano*. Elizabeth Legh supplied one or two tempo marks (but *Andante* on 'Pupille sdegnose', perhaps taken from Hamburg II, appears to be written by H3 in different ink). She twice recorded her relative opinion of the three composers in no uncertain terms: at the start the first two acts are 'both very bad Musick: but this 3$^{d.}$ Act is so very fine that the Musick speaks its own Praise'. This is varied at the end to: 'both excessive bad musick: but this 3^{d}: Act was composed by Mr Handel, & is incomparable, as all his works are'.

Berlin Amalienbibliothek 439b is an interesting copy, possibly prepared for the Prussian court. It shows Linike's hand in its later form,[20] and most unusually it has a precise date at the end: *London Jun: ye 6 1721*—the day before the last performance of the original run. It lacks all recitatives of both types and the sinfonia but includes the overture. It confirms the evidence of the other early copies that Handel had already shortened 'Come, se ti vedrò'; but not 'Ah dolce nome!' or Scenes viii and ix. Dynamics are fuller than in any other copy, and there are many extra trills and other performance instructions; all the instrumental triplets in 'Lungo pensar' are slurred. Several movements have unique tempo marks and variants in scoring which deserve note since Linike was almost certainly still a member of Handel's orchestra, though some of them are surprising. The overture is *Largo* leading to *Allegro*, 'Pupille sdegnose' *Allegro*, 'Non ti fidar' and 'A chi vive' *Vivace*, 'Vivo senza alma' *Largo* [*sic*], 'Mà come amar?' and the *coro Allegro*. The top part in 'Lungo pensar', 'Pupille sdegnose', 'Non ti fidar', and 'Con lui volate' is for violins only; in the B section of 'Lungo pensar' it is marked *soli*. Some variants in 'Ah dolce nome!' are certainly errors: the second violins have the oboe part in bars 35–8 and both violins in bars 42 and 43 are *forte*; the confinement of the violin part in the B section from bar 58 to firsts could be authentic.

RM 19 c 9, ff. 1–63 (early S2), complete except for secco recitatives, is a little later in date but follows the bulk of the 1721 copies, with most of the dynamics in the autograph. 'Dimmi crudele' is marked *viola col basso* at the start. Annotations by Jennens include Handel's date of completion copied from the autograph. The Coke copy is another composite, but constructed on a different principle. As first written it contained set pieces only, in an unfamiliar hand dating perhaps from the 1720s.[21] Some time later a second scribe (who wrote the score of *Teseo*—except the overture—bound in the same volume) inserted the recitatives, recopying the initial and final bars of arias to create a continuous score; but he never finished the job, stopping in the middle of Scene v (HG 28) and after that working spasmodically. The recitatives of the last scene are present, but those on HG 41–2, 53, and 58–60 are incomplete

---

[20] Illustrated in W. Dean, 'Handel's Early London Copyists', Plate C. The latest known Linike copies, identified since the publication of this article, are Add MSS 29416–26, the Chandos *Te Deum* and ten Chandos Anthems (*c*. 1725).

[21] He copied ff. 28–31 in RCM MS 257, a substantial volume of Italian cantatas also containing the hands of S1 and the copyist of the second Coke *Teseo*.

and the rest are represented by blank pages. A third hand recopied the opening bars of 'Mà come amar?'. There are no variants of moment; 'Dimmi crudele' is *Allegro assai*, 'A chi vive' *Andante*. The copying is careless with many mistakes in the Italian.

Shaftesbury (S2) and Lennard (Smith, *c.* 1736) cannot have been taken from any surviving copy, for they give the longer version of 'Come, se ti vedrò' but the shortened 1722 version of 'Ah dolce nome!'—the exact reverse of all 1721 copies except Tokyo and Hamburg I. They presumably derive from an early copy of the autograph on which the cut in 'Ah dolce nome!' was entered later. Shaftesbury has the altered end to the recitative on HG 32 (added in Hamburg I), though the aria is in A as usual. Dynamics are fuller than in most Shaftesbury copies (which date from the late 1730s), but tempos and instrumental indications are deficient. Lennard is more generous with tempos. Whereas neither duet has one in any 1721 copy except Amalienbibliothek 439b, 'Vivo senza alma' is here *Allegro* and 'Mà come amar?' *Andante*.[22] 'Lungo pensar' is *Allegro e staccato*. A later hand has noted differences from the autograph in 'Non ti fidar'. Fitzwilliam Mus MS 76, signed *R. Fitzwilliam 1768* and written by the same late hand as the scores of *Teseo* and *Amadigi* in that collection, was undoubtedly copied from Lennard, and Amalienbibliothek 439a from 439b (down to the date at the end). It is in a German hand, probably that of Berlin Mus MS 9056 (arias from *Tamerlano*, *Siroe*, and operas produced in Italy in the early 1730s).

The Flower parts (S2), complete in Manchester except for the horns, which are in the music library of the University of Maryland, include the accompanied recitatives and *coro* but not the overture or sinfonia. They derive from the same source as Lennard, though three arias and both duets follow Hamburg I in lacking a tempo mark. The oboes play in the ritornellos of *Tutti* movements, including intermediate passages where they are not indicated in HG, and in the A section of 'Volate più'. They are silent in 'A chi vive' and the B section of 'Con lui volate'; both take the top line in 'Spera'. The cello part mentions the bassoons only in 'Dimmi crudele', where they are silenced when the bass is confined to violas and cellos at bars 36, 55, and 80, and 'Volate più', where they continue playing in bar 23 and are not silenced in the B section. The viola doubles the bass or the voice (at the octave where necessary) throughout 'Dimmi crudele'. This source too has many dynamics not in HG.

RM 19 d 12 (ff. 32–4) has an H1 copy of the 12/8 'A chi vive', which Clausen plausibly assigns to the first state of Hamburg I; Add MS 31571 (ff. 11–14) an H2 copy of the 3/8 setting without tempo or instrumentation; Add MS 33238 (f. 43) 'Il confine della vita' in an unrecognized late hand; Durham Cathedral Library (Mus M 70) a copy of 'Lungo pensar' without text written by the Hon. Edward Finch, Prebendary of York (1664–1738). Fitzwilliam Mus MS 54, an early collection of arias, many from King's Theatre operas of 1720–2, contains six *Muzio Scevola* items, including one each by Amadei and Bononcini. The Handel arias are 'Con lui volate' (f. 54), 'Pupille sdegnose' (f. 71ᵛ), both copied by the master of the exuberant C clef (Epsilon), 'Ah dolce nome!' in its longer form (f. 79, H2), and the 3/8 'A chi vive' (f. 83, Smith). Only 'Ah dolce nome!' has a tempo mark. The Bononcini and Amadei arias were copied at the same time by Epsilon and H3. Two

---

[22] Chrysander presumably took this from Add MS 16108, but this part of the manuscript is one of the later insertions.

detached arias belong to later operas: 'Volate più' in Add MS 31572 (f. 156ᵛ, copyist associated with S2 *c.*1738–40) to *Admeto* in 1731 (but only the A section is adapted to the new context), 'Come, se ti vedrò' with modified text, 'Sino che ti vedrò', in RM 18 c 6 (ff. 9–11ʳ, S2) to *Ottone* in 1733.

Handel arranged two pieces for harpsichord, involving a degree of recomposition, very soon after the production. His version of the overture[23] exists in four copies: the Coke Wesley MS (Smith, *c.*1721), two volumes in the Malmesbury Collection (H3, *c.*1721; Smith, *c.*1728), and RM 18 c 1, ff. 34–5, with the spelling *Muzio Caepholo* (S2, *c.*1728). His transcription of the aria 'Come, se ti vedrò' (in G major) is elaborately ornamented. There are copies of this, and a similar but less sensitive arrangement of 'Pupille sdegnose', both with the words cued in between the staves, in the Coke Wesley MS (Smith, *c.*1721) and one of the Malmesbury volumes (H3, *c.*1721).

In August 1722 Richard Meares published *The Most Favourite Songs in the Opera of Muzio Scaevola Compos'd by Three Famous Masters*, whom he did not name. They comprised one aria from Amadei's act, the overture and four arias from Bononcini's, and three arias from Handel's, 'Lungo pensar', 'Pupille sdegnose', and the 3/8 'A chi vive' (without the second violin and viola parts). A pirated edition by Walsh and the two Hares containing the same items in a slightly different order appeared soon afterwards, as well as separate issues of 'Lungo pensar' and 'Pupille sdegnose'. The latter was included, with a flute part, in volume ii of *The Pocket Companion* (December 1725), attributed to *Muzio Coephola*. Walsh issued the overture in parts about 1725 and in a clumsy keyboard arrangement (not Handel's) the following year. Burney in his account of the opera mentions the likelihood of Arnold publishing Clelia's accompanied recitative (HG 16), presumably in his collected edition; he never did so.

Chrysander's score (1874), as already indicated, is unsatisfactory in many respects. Although he had access to all essential sources, he printed a mixture of three versions, restoring one of several rejected passages in 'Non ti fidar' from the autograph and one of two early cuts in 'Come, se ti vedrò', and confusing the 1721 and 1722 scores by retaining Fidalma in Scene v but removing her from viii and ix. He gives no indication that Tarquinio was composed for and sung by a soprano. A modern edition, if possible of the whole opera, would be a service to scholarship.

Additional Notes

* (p. 376) Lagarde is confirmed by MS notes in a copy of the 1721 libretto prepared for George I, offered for sale by an American dealer (J. and J. Lubrano of Great Barrington, Mass.) in April 1992. They state that Orazio was sung by the elderly castrato Valentini, who is not known to have been in London after 1715, though he sang in Hamburg in 1722. Evidently no fresh edition of the libretto was published for the revival.

* (p. 382) The opening recitative (pp. 19–22) was copied by Smith.

---

[23] Printed in *Twenty Overtures*, ii. 5.

CHAPTER 19

FLORIDANTE

THE Argument in the printed libretto sets the scene.

Orontes, a Persian General, rais'd an Army, and having kill'd Ninus the King, made himself King of Persia. The Day of the Victory he found a Female Infant, the only remainder of the Royal Family, all the rest being now extinct, and because a Daughter of his, of the same Age, died that very Day, to compensate his Loss, and out of Compassion, he brought it up instead of his own, and gave it the same Name with Elmira. Floridant, Prince of Thrace,[1] afterwards fell in Love with Elmira, and obtain'd from Orontes a Promise of Marriage, when he returned victorious from the Naval War, waged by him against the King of Tyre; there had been formerly a treaty of Marriage between Timante, the Prince Royal of Tyre, and Rossane, the only daughter of Orontes; but these Difficulties had put a Stop to it. Orontes in the mean time fell in love with Elmira, and breaks his Word to Floridant, which gives occasion to this Drama.

Act I begins in *a Wood*, where Elmira and Rossane enter *in hunting Attire* in order to be near Floridante, who has just won a naval victory over Tyre. Rossane recognizes Floridante at the head of his army, turning Elmira's hopes to fulfilled happiness. Rossane envies her friend: she loves the defeated Timante, though she has never seen him. Something tells her that one day she will be happy. In *a Country near Tyre,*[2] *with the Persian Army*, Floridante is welcomed home by Elmira and Rossane. *Among the Prisoners* is Timante *under the feigned name of Glicone.* Coralbo, a satrap, brings Floridante a letter from Oronte ordering him to hand over his command to Coralbo and leave the country, without giving a reason. Rossane goes off to protest to her father, confident of dispelling any baseless slander, accompanied by *Timante, Coralbo and the Army.*[3] Floridante and Elmira, distressed at the prospect of separation, proclaim their undying constancy. In *a Royal Apartment* Rossane pleads with Oronte for Floridante, who has not only won a victory but been promised Elmira's hand. Oronte agrees to receive him, but says he has changed his mind about the marriage for reasons of state. Rossane asks 'Glicone' if Timante was in the battle, receiving the reply that he escaped but expressed his ardent love for her and bitter resentment that their fathers' quarrel hindered the children's marriage. She departs with a sad aria; he expresses his delight that capture has brought such unexpected happiness and likens himself to a mariner in calm weather after a storm. In *a Royal Hall with a Chair* Floridante reports to Oronte (*sitting*) that he has laid down his command, but asks what

---

[1] The Italian version adds 'Suo Generale' here.

[2] The libretto has Persepolis, which is in the middle of modern Iran and would mean that Floridante's army had marched hundreds of miles since the first scene. Handel's geography was evidently stronger than Rolli's.

[3] Chrysander omits this direction, which is in all sources (top of HG 22).

he has done wrong. Oronte refuses to tell him. Elmira adds her pleas, and both point out that he is breaking his royal word. Oronte merely says that a ship is waiting to deport Floridante and goes out. The act ends with a duet in which the lovers say they will die of grief if separated.

Act II. In *an Apartment of Rossane's* she tells 'Glicone' that Timante must have perished, as he was not in the ships that escaped. He replies that on the contrary he is in Persia in hiding and has sent his portrait as a token. He gives it to her and leaves; she is delighted to recognize the likeness of the prisoner. The set changes to an unspecified place. Floridante, disguised as a Moorish slave captured with Timante, plans to escape with Elmira and the other pair of lovers. Timante identifies himself. Floridante welcomes him and suggests they wait for nightfall. As he sings a love song, *Timante is called by a Damsel*, with a message that Oronte wishes to speak to Elmira. *He goes out from the Scene at this Time, and after returns again at the End of the Air*. Elmira prepares to dissemble as the other couple leave. Oronte tells her she has a more worthy lover than Floridante in himself. To her exclamation of horror he replies that she is not his daughter but the only survivor of Nino's royal house. She rejects him as a usurper and a monster and bids him kill her. He is content to wait for her anger to cool. Rossane tells Timante to go with Floridante and meet her later at a secret passage, where the guards are bribed. In a duet they look forward to living like doves rescued from a predator's talons. The set changes to 'Bipartita oscura', translated as *The Scene darken'd on both Sides*. Elmira, waiting for Floridante, thinks she hears footsteps and imagines him cautiously approaching, but the footsteps die away. Presently he does enter, soon followed by Oronte bent on indecent assault. Floridante springs to Elmira's defence. *The Guards come with Torches and part them*. Floridante is arrested, still in disguise; he claims to be a slave sent by Floridante to escort his bride. Oronte promises him chains and a cruel death, and after his defiant departure orders Elmira to choose between death and a throne. She is convinced that fate has beaten her and she can only die.

Act III. No location is given. Hearing from Timante of Floridante's arrest, Rossane sends him in search of Elmira, but he feels nothing can be done when men and gods are both averse. Elmira enters *guarded by Coralbo* and explains bitterly that she is Elisa, 'the only Remains of the Noble, but Extinct Race of Ninus'. Rossane says that makes no difference to her love. Coralbo, hitherto unaware of Elmira's true identity, assures her that she may still be Queen, since Persians loved her dynasty. He *retires on one Side* when Oronte comes in and tells Elmira he has just seen the Moor die. *She swoons away in a Chair*. He orders Floridante to be fetched *in Chains*, and tells him that if he can persuade Elmira to accept him (Oronte) he shall return in freedom to Thrace; if not, both must die a painful death. Oronte *retires* to listen. Elmira, recovering, is astonished to see Floridante alive, and still more to hear him plead Oronte's cause. He does this to save her life, but she refuses such a price; let them both die. The set changes (again the location is unspecified). Rossane, learning from Timante that he has many armed supporters in the city, tells him to release Floridante while she looks after Elmira; her hand shall be the reward of his valour. In *a Prison* Floridante is chained to a pillar, tortured more by love than by his fetters. Elmira comes in *guarded, with a Cup of Poison in her Hand*. Oronte has ordered her to give it to Floridante, but she prepares to drink it herself; he cannot reach her on account of his chains. Enter Oronte, *who takes the Cup from her* and orders her to be confined separately while Floridante drinks it. Coralbo and Timante break in *with Armed Men*, snatch the cup from Floridante,[4] arrest Oronte, and proclaim Elmira Queen as Elisa. She looks forward to crowning Floridante at her side. Oronte, left alone, curses first Coralbo, then himself; refusing comfort, he remains a prey to impotent fury. The set changes to *a Royal Hall with a Throne. Elmira and Floridante upon the Throne.* She thanks everyone for restoring her to the seat of her ancestors; he promises fidelity to her and just government for the people. *They descend the Throne, Elmira meets Rossane, and Floridante, Timante.* At Rossane's request Floridante pardons Oronte. Rossane and Timante shall marry and reign in Tyre. Floridante declares himself happier as lover than as king, and Elmira orders the day to be kept as a national festival.

Paolo Rolli added a note to the printed libretto: 'N.B. The Invention is owing in a great Part to the Plot of an ancient Drama, Intituled, *Constancy in Triumph.*' *La costanza in trionfo* by Francesco Silvani was first staged, with music by P. A. Ziani, at Venice in 1696, revived there and at Ferrara in the following year, and performed at Livorno in 1706.[5] It is difficult to know which version was Rolli's source, for he retained little except the bare bones of the plot, and not all of them. He used none of Silvani's aria texts and no recitative beyond a word or two here and there. Unlike Haym, whom he despised as a mere carpenter of other men's work, Rolli for all his self-satisfaction was a careless and incompetent librettist, as his treatment of Silvani all too patently demonstrates.

The action of *La costanza in trionfo* takes place in Norway. The characters, with their equivalents in *Floridante*, are: Gustavo, tyrant of Norway (Oronte), Sveno, Prince of Sarmatia, in command of the Norwegian forces (Floridante), Lotario, Prince of France (Timante), Leonilde (Elmira), Marianne (Rossane), and Flavio, Gustavo's favourite and captain of the guard (Coralbo). Leonilde's father, killed by Gustavo, is Adolfo (Nino). Silvani has an extra character, Riccardo, a court servant; the Livorno libretto adds an old woman, Anfrisa, with whom Riccardo enjoys a long comic scene of traditional cut in each act. Silvani does not claim that his characters are historical, though he makes the usual statement that the love affairs are fictitious; since kings of Sweden were liable to be called both Gustavus and Adolphus, he probably invented the whole thing. His libretto is an average specimen of the period, simple in language but slow-moving and not particularly inspired. Too many arias are of the simile type, the singers likening themselves to butterflies, nightingales, or turtle-doves; they are often introduced at the beginning or in the middle of scenes; and several, especially in Act III, are so placed that they present an impediment to the action just when it should move forward. The worst example occurs in the equivalent of Handel's II viii, where Sveno, intent on escaping with Leonilde, pauses to sing a love song, apparently for no better purpose than to allow Gustavo time to summon the guard.

---

[4] The words *getta la coppa di mano a Floridante* are in the autograph but not the libretto.

[5] G. C. Schürmann produced a German version, *Leonilde, oder Der siegende Beständigkeit*, at Brunswick in 1704. Another, much modified, with a dedication to the Old Pretender, was staged at Fano in 1718. See Strohm, *HJb* (1975), 114–15 (*Essays*, 45–6). The alto castrato Campioli, later a member of Handel's London company, sang the part of Lotario in the 1722 revival of Schürmann's opera.

Silvani's libretto has however the sovereign merits of clear design, consistent characters, and credible motivation, all of which Rolli threw away. Gustavo has spared Adolfo's child because he interprets the death of his own pregnant wife as a judgement of the gods for his usurpation of the throne. When he falls in love with Leonilde, he has qualms of conscience and uses his preservation of her life as an argument for sympathy—not a very strong one, but less grotesque than Oronte's crude approach. Instead of sending the brutal order to Floridante via Coralbo as a bolt from the blue (*Floridante* I iv) Gustavo discusses it first with Flavio, who warns him of the likely reaction of his and Sveno's subjects. Flavio has been privy to Gustavo's actions from the start, and is himself in love with Gustavo's daughter Marianne; he does not discover Leonilde's parentage by chance (*Floridante* III ii), and Gustavo's refusal to give him Marianne helps to motivate his change of sides. Above all, Lotario is no lily-livered weakling like Timante, whom Rossane tries to bully into rescuing Floridante, but the exact opposite: a gallant and mettlesome prince, who when he hears of Gustavo's unjust treatment of his captor identifies himself as the son of the King of France, arranges the Moorish disguise to aid Sveno's escape (before there is any question of his own), and later rouses the Norwegian people against their tyrannical ruler. Moreover he and Marianne recognize each other at once; they are already in love, though he does not know till Act II that she returns his feelings. The absurd business of Rossane falling in love with a man she has never seen, and failing to recognize him until he hands her his portrait, was imported gratuitously by Rolli from older librettos of the seventeenth century. There is no equivalent in Silvani for Rolli's I vi or II i.

The obscurities and inconsistencies of the *Floridante* libretto and the abrupt jerks in the action are all due to Rolli, who seems to have worked in a great hurry. He does not bother to specify some of the sets, and several times throws two or three arias and exits into a single scene, so that the numbering is casual and erratic;[6] I v ends with a single line of recitative. His treatment of Timante's disguise as Glicone and Floridante's as a Moor is unconvincing, and so is the reconciliation of the two former enemies in II iv. To bring the action to a climax he gives Timante armed supporters without explaining how he came to acquire them while a prisoner in a foreign land. The dramaturgy of the first half of Act III is particularly slipshod; twice (in i and iv) Timante pops off-stage and back to allow first Rossane and then Floridante to sing an aria. Oronte must be presumed to have penetrated Floridante's disguise before Scene iii, but we are not told so; he sends Elmira into a swoon by saying he has killed the Moor, and then steps aside to hear Floridante pleading his (Oronte's) cause with her. None of this is in Silvani, who has a much stronger scene in which Gustavo offers to spare Sveno if Leonilde will yield to him. Rolli unwisely shifted the foiled escape, which begins Silvani's Act III, back to the middle of Act II, leaving too little plot for his last act. The scenes in which he adheres more or less closely to Silvani—I iv, v (Rossane pleading with Oronte for Floridante's life), vii, and viii (Oronte's harsh interview with Floridante and the latter's agonized parting from Elmira), II v (Elmira's confrontation with Oronte), vii–ix (the frustrated escape of the lovers and Elmira's despair), III vi–vii (the prison scene up to Oronte's entry), ix (the

---

[6] This seems to have been characteristic of Rolli's librettos; we meet it again in *Scipione*.

rescue of the lovers and Oronte's bitter outburst), and *ult.*—include all the most dramatically effective episodes, and the best music.

One modification, the unusual da capo design of the first scene (more complex in the autograph than in the published score), was probably Handel's; but it is clumsily integrated with the plot. The two girls go hunting in order to be near Floridante; why do they hope to find the victor of a naval engagement in a wood? Rolli, who cut Silvani's five introductory scenes, may have been prompted to the hunting idea (and a change of quarry) by Silvani's second set (I vi), a seascape with the victorious Norwegian fleet approaching the harbour, in which Marianne makes her first appearance fishing from a small boat. Other details possibly due to Handel are the conclusion of Act I with a duet for the parting lovers instead of two consecutive arias, and Elmira imagining she hears footsteps as she waits in the dark for Floridante to rescue her. It seems quixotic of Oronte to entrust Elmira of all people with the poison for Floridante. Silvani manages this more skilfully. When Leonilde contemptuously refuses to buy Sveno's life at Gustavo's price and says she would rather poison her lover, Gustavo takes her at her word. In Silvani's prison scene Leonilde is prevented from drinking the poison by off-stage cries of 'Viva Leonilde!' and the arrival of Flavio to salute her as Queen. The snatching of the cup by Oronte and later by Coralbo was added by Rolli.

Some of Rolli's aria texts, notably those for Rossane and Timante before they recognize each other, and Oronte's 'Mà non s'aspetti' in II iv are vague, inept, or obscure; but Silvani's are scarcely a model of dramatic cogency. Rolli's propensity for moral and political platitude, descending at times to bathos, emerges in Rossane's remark at the end of I v when Oronte announces his change of mind about Elmira's betrothal to Floridante: 'A new Aspect of Things always disturbs a Monarch.' Another line of recitative, this time Silvani's, is interesting for a different reason. When (III xv) Marianne interposes her body between Lotario's sword and her father and forces him to lower his weapon, she exclaims 'Chi vide mai più fortunato amore?' This is surely the source of one of the most striking insertions in *Tamerlano*, Andronico's accompanied recitative at the end of Act I, which begins and ends with the line 'Chi vide mai più sventurato amante?' Silvani's line must have lodged in Handel's memory; Rolli had no connection with *Tamerlano*.

Konrad Sasse[7] detected references to contemporary political events in the libretto of *Floridante*, identifying the hero with the Duke of Marlborough, whose family had close links with Bononcini, and seeing in his reconciliation with Timante (a French prince in *La costanza in trionfo*) a hint of Marlborough's approach to France in opposition to the Hanoverian 'usurper' George I. According to a letter of 19 December 1721 from Dr William Stratford, Canon of Christ Church, Oxford, to Edward Harley (afterwards second Earl of Oxford), 'some things have happened [in *Floridante*] which have given great offence . . . There happens to be a right heir in it, that is imprisoned. At last the right heir is delivered and the chains put upon the oppressor. At this last circumstance, there happened to be a very great and unreasonable clapping, in the presence of great ones'.[8] This sounds like a Jacobite demonstration

---

[7] 'Die Texte der Londoner Opern Händels in ihren gesellschaftlichen Beziehungen', *Wissenschaftliche Zeitschrift der Martin-Luther-Universität Halle–Wittenberg*, iv (1955), 632.

[8] HMC Portland vii (Harley MSS v, 1701–1729), 311; quoted by J. R. Clemens in *The Sackbut* (1931) and misinterpreted by Deutsch, 130.

rather than a protest against the opera. Although Rolli, an arch-schemer and a supporter of Bononcini against Handel (he dedicated the libretto to the Prince of Wales, a political opponent of his father), was capable of using the libretto as a political tract, it is unlikely that Handel would have consented to set what could be construed as an attack on his patron and employer, even with the names and nationalities changed.

Handel's failure to rectify at least some of these faults suggests a lack of commitment to the subject. It must also be connected with a marked change of emphasis in his approach. The great success of the previous season had been *Astarto*, in which Bononcini demonstrated his knack of catching and tickling the public ear,[9] and Handel no doubt felt obliged to meet the challenge, if only for his own security. He abandoned the grand heroic style of *Radamisto* and Act III of *Muzio Scevola*, which he was to resume only with *Giulio Cesare* after Rolli's demotion, for something more modest, distinguished by graceful tunes, light accompaniments, and a less learned approach. We may feel that he beat Bononcini at his own game. Burney was in no doubt. 'I mention the slow songs in this opera [*Floridante*] particularly, as superior in every respect to those of Bononcini, who has frequently been extolled by his admirers for unrivalled excellence in airs of tenderness.' 'The partizans for Bononcini seem to have had little foundation for their praise of his plaintive and pathetic songs; as there are generally more airs of that kind in a single act of an opera set by Handel, than in any one of Bononcini's whole dramas.' Nevertheless, though *Floridante* was no failure, the Italian continued to draw the crowds throughout the 1721–2 season.

If Handel courted his public, he did not debase his standards. The score of *Floridante* contains much excellent music; what it lacks is characters with the stature and individuality of so many predecessors and successors. They come momentarily to life, but do not consistently grip attention or build up from scene to scene with that momentum that makes Handel supreme among the masters of *opera seria*. For this the libretto must bear much of the blame. Where Rolli gives Handel an opening, for example when Elmira waits at her nocturnal rendezvous or Floridante languishes in prison, he rises to the expected heights. But there are many numb patches in the drama. None of Handel's operas on Rolli librettos can be accounted an artistic success. It is clear from Rolli's correspondence, quoted extensively by Deutsch, that there was a mutual want of sympathy, if not a clash of personalities.

Floridante is a passive hero of a type admittedly suited to Senesino's gift for pathetic expression; Handel was to give him similar roles in *Ottone*, *Tamerlano*, and *Rodelinda*, but fortunately not in *Giulio Cesare*. His arias are either love songs or reactions to banishment, separation from Elmira, or the prospect of violent death. Five of his eight set pieces, including the duet 'Ah mia cara', are slow, and only one, 'Questi ceppi', is in common time. Even the 2/4 'Tacerò', which has no tempo in the autograph or performing score but is Allegro in the Malmesbury copy, is full of triplet figuration. The predominance of triple time, simple or compound, and the tendency of several arias to break into further triplets point to a lack of force in a man who has just won a naval

[9] See Chapter 16, pp. 306 and 310.

battle. Handel may have become aware of this, for in one revival, as with
Ottone and *Rodelinda*, he supplied some counterbalance.

Three of Floridante's slow arias are outstanding. 'Alma mia', with which he
greets Elmira on his return from battle, is a siciliano of deceptive simplicity.
The A section never ventures beyond the dominant, and the only accompaniment, apart from the short four-part ritornello after it, is a bass in the
most elementary crotchet–quaver rhythm. Handel often returned to this old
seventeenth-century plan, especially to introduce his hero or heroine,[10] and
always with consummate effect. The mastery here lies entirely in the control of
the melody with its variations of rhythm and phrase-length. Each phrase is
related to, but subtly different from, its predecessor, so that the ear is
constantly surprised till the exquisite paragraph is complete. The initial
Adagio is lightly decorated in the autograph (Ex. 44, p. 392). 'Sventurato' is
almost equally spare, the upper instruments alternating with rather than
accompanying the voice almost throughout. Neither of the two
motives—the drooping quavers with silent first and last beats (♩ ♪ ♪ | ♪ ♪ ♩)
framed for the first word and echoed later by strings *senza cembalo*, and the
more animated figure at bar 7 rising and falling in sequence—suggests serious
unhappiness; Floridante seems to enjoy his misfortune. He may have lost his
command, but he is confident of Elmira's love, an idea reiterated throughout
the opera. The sequential divisions on 'fedel', narrow in compass, are a typical
tribute to the flexibility and expressiveness of Senesino's technique. The
ritornello design is particularly subtle; the same two motives reappear after
the A section, but linked in a single strain and raised in pitch, the first entering
an octave higher and the second extended from a sequence of four to seven
statements of the rhythmic unit. The B section employs this same figure at
irregular intervals, avoiding the relative minor and moving from the subdominant (A flat) to F minor and G minor, after which the voice begins the da
capo, skipping the whole initial ritornello. The aria leaves an impression of
continuous development.

'Ah mia cara' at the end of Act I, 'an exquisite duet in the grand style of
pathetic' (Burney), is one of the opera's great moments. Elizabeth Legh's
exclamation in the Malmesbury copy, 'oh imortall', is true in sentiment if
irregular in orthography. The agony of parting lovers never failed to inspire
Handel. This is one of the earliest of many such pieces, similar in mood and
key (generally E minor or F sharp minor) but never falling into stale
repetition. 'Ah mia cara' was composed (and first printed) in F minor and
underwent half a dozen revisions, three of them before the first night, when it
was sung in E minor.[11] The slurred quavers and heavy repeated crotchets of
the string parts, a little reminiscent of Radamisto's 'Ombra cara', and the
short sighing vocal phrases, often in thirds, paint a picture of unrelieved
tragedy; the B section, ending in B minor, brings little relief. The quasi-
ostinato bass, tramping inexorably up and down the scale, is almost a ground,
the E minor tonality returning at intervals of eight to twelve bars; the music
seems to go round the circle of fifths the same way each time, as if to
emphasize the hopeless plight of the lovers.

Floridante loses potency in Act II; his two arias are livelier but impersonal.

[10] For example Radamisto, Teofane in *Ottone*, and Andronico in *Tamerlano*.
[11] See pp. 405 and 410.

Ex. 44

Ex. 44 (cont.)

(My beloved, yes, you alone are my glory, my delight)

Each breaks repeatedly into triplets, so that the first approximates to 9/8 and the second to 6/8, and the effect is facile. 'Bramo te sola' has exceptionally long ritornellos (eighteen bars at the start), but the staccato thrust soon breaks down. Floridante asserts his preference for Elmira over a kingdom in falling fourths and fifths; the significance of the copious divisions is less evident. 'Tacerò' is a strangely mild and submissive response to Oronte's threats, even though Floridante dispenses with a ritornello. Rolli did not help by giving him an important solo proclaiming silence; and the repeated E—B—E of Handel's principal motive, together with a compass narrow even for Senesino, allows little scope for imagination. Rhythmic contrasts and syncopation scarcely redeem the piece from dullness.

In Act III Floridante rises far higher, especially in 'S'è dolce m'era', his acceptance of death after Oronte's ultimatum. Such a situation was often the cue for a minor-key siciliano with accompaniment for four-part strings, and seldom found Handel below his peak. The start is striking, the voice leading first and second violins in imitative entries over a pedal, without ritornello (Ex. 45, p. 394). The independent five-part texture persists almost throughout, with little doubling of the vocal line. As in many such pieces, the characteristic rhythm is most eloquently combined with a Neapolitan harmonic flavour and the harpsichord is silenced throughout the A section, entering at the enriched and extended ritornello after it. From time to time the violins sigh sympathetically in thirds; the stepwise downward bass, especially when it moves chromatically (bars 15–17) and the plaintive figure 𝅘𝅥𝅭 𝅘𝅥𝅮 𝅘𝅥, generally in descent, create a mood of anguished resignation; but the abrupt dynamic contrasts of the ritornello and the flattened second in the B section, which has difficulty in reaching the relative major, hint that Floridante's spirit is not extinct. The F minor opening of the prison scene, which promises an accompanied recitative or perhaps a sinfonia like those in Act II of *Theodora* but in fact serves as ritornello to 'Questi ceppi', is of similar quality. The dynamic and rhythmic structure, with the first violins breaking free in the middle, sets the scene with characteristic economy: the hero languishing in darkness chained to a pillar. The aria, accompanied by bass alone, is apt but less memorable; the B section was added before performance. Floridante's last aria, 'Mia bella', once more exerting his preference for Elmira over a kingdom (he now has both), is positively jaunty, the dotted and triplet figures carried through both sections. A neat touch here is the postponement of the da capo ritornello, reduced to three bars, to follow rather than precede the *Adagio* 'Mia bella!'

The two female parts underwent numerous changes before performance. This was due to Durastanti's late cancellation, reported by Vanbrugh on 16

Ex. 45

(If it was already sweet, my love, to live with you, it will also be sweet to die for you)

November.[12] Handel by then was more than half way through Act II. Elmira, the heroine, who has the larger part and pairs with the *primo uomo*, was obviously designed for Durastanti, and Rossane for Anastasia Robinson. The news of the former's illness promoted Robinson to the rank of prima donna and induced Handel to switch the voices, casting her for Elmira and the soprano Maddalena Salvai for Rossane. The new plan involved much rewriting, transposition, and other adjustments, and the substitution of one new aria for Rossane.[13] Apart from the rejected 'Mà pria vedrò le stelle' in the appendix, Chrysander printed Elmira's part in the keys of the first performance, though there are differences in detail.

Elmira emerges as a more positive and fully-rounded personality than Floridante; she is the opera's most successful character and has much of the

[12] See pp. 311-12.   [13] See p. 398.

finest music. Of her seven arias—the same number as Floridante, with whom she shares 'Ah mia cara'—four are Allegro, and all but the first (which has no tempo in any source) are in common time. She launches the opera with an original stroke: the cavatina 'Dimmi, O spene', hoping for Floridante's safe return, is followed by a recitative in which Rossane reports his victorious approach, whereupon Elmira repeats the cavatina with new words reflecting the fulfilment of her hopes. Musically the plan is a dal segno aria with a secco recitative B section; dramatically the new words advance the action while formal expectation is satisfied, a typical Handelian procedure. The version of the autograph is still more original, for 'Dimmi, O spene' itself has a B section and da capo, and its A section is repeated after the recitative, producing a free rondo design with two episodes; presumably this was abandoned because it held up the action. The first nine bars are a literal borrowing, with minor rhythmic changes and a 3/4 instead of a 6/4 signature, from Ormoena's aria 'Caro amante' in Act II of Keiser's *Octavia*,[14] and Handel's autograph has it in Keiser's key of A major. The bare texture, unison violins always in octaves with the bass, establishes Elmira as a personality to be reckoned with; the voice part shows her gentler side, the long independent melody underpinned on occasion by fragments of the ritornello. Keiser too introduces these strong phrases into his aria, mostly in the B section. His A section gives more prominence to the rising sequence of Handel's bars 7 and 8, but allows it to drift into aimless triplets; Handel uses his more rhythmically incisive version of these bars in both sections. Elmira naturally jumps the ritornello in her reprise, 'Gode, O spene'.

She protests her devotion to Floridante in the high-spirited 'Mà pria vedrò le stelle', a fiery piece with brilliant string parts, clashing appoggiaturas and suspensions, and rushing downward scales for 'precipitarsi in mar'. The earlier soprano version in G minor (HG 125) differs in more than key; it includes oboes, but gives less independence to the violins, and the compass is a third wider. The stars have further to fall to reach the sea; a straight transposition of bar 16 would have taken Anastasia Robinson out of her depth. Her part had to be modified in the duet, and 'Barbaro!' too went down a minor third; but this makes less difference. The scales (in both directions) and the ejaculation of the first word between the recitative cadence and the ritornello give pungent expression to Elmira's fury and contempt for Oronte. In the B section the violence of her emotion tears the vocal line into fragments, while the violin scales continue to buzz like angry bees. The first word evoked a borrowing from the cantata 'Cor fedele' ('Barbaro, tu non credi'); Handel was to use the idea again in *Alcina* ('Barbaro, io ben lo sò').

'Notte cara' could scarcely offer a sharper contrast. This scene, unusual in conception and superbly executed, stands out even among the Royal Academy operas for its vivid descriptive power and psychological penetration: the music expresses hope, fear, anxiety, disappointment, and resignation, all wrapped in a veil of mystery. Again Handel evolves a da capo outline with a recitative, this time accompanied, as B section. The five-bar ritornello for strings without harpsichord, which never returns, suggests the darkened scene as Elmira waits for her lover; the tempo mark *Lento* (*Largo* in the first sketch) is rare in Handel:

[14] HG supplementary volume, 90. According to John Roberts (see p. 44, n. 18), the overture and five other arias in *Floridante* contain borrowings from Keiser. See Appendix D.

Ex. 46

The B flat minor tonality (with touches of D flat and G flat), following the unclouded F major of the duet for the other pair of lovers, and the harmonic friction of the overlapping and crossing string parts evoke a mood at once sombre, brooding, and profound. Among noteworthy details are the upward yearning through the triad in bars 3 and 4, repeated several times at the words 'riportami 'l mio ben', the rhythmic displacement of the second 'notte cara', and the stress on the Neapolitan second (C♭) and flattened sixth. The B section, as she thinks she hears footsteps and follows Floridante's approach in her imagination, brings a chord change on almost every exclamation; the unexpected move into recitative (compare 'Dall'ondoso periglio' in *Giulio Cesare*) itself makes a dramatic point. The door opens slightly, and she hears a noise; her breath comes in gasps, echoed by the orchestra, an idea used again for Bajazet's death in *Tamerlano*. But she is deceived; Floridante is not there. An emphatic diminished seventh dying at once to *piano* as the chord is held ('ah no! m'inganna amore') reflects her bitter disappointment, and the arioso returns bleakly without ritornello. The material of this piece too occurs earlier ('Piangete' in *La Resurrezione*) and later ('Mourn, ye afflicted children' in *Judas Maccabaeus*). The autograph shows two interesting changes, both in the direction of simplicity. The first draft of the opening, on the same material but in C minor, lacks the violin figures in bar 2, where the voice makes an earlier entry, but uses a fuller orchestra containing three violin parts and two bassoons. The anomalous notation is as Handel left it (Ex. 47). Equally striking are the changes in the accompaniment of the recitative B section, which at first consisted largely of impressionistic gestures for unison violins unsupported.[15] It is an original idea; but Handel opted for a less external means of suggesting suspense, and rewrote the entire passage in sustained chords without altering the vocal line.

When Floridante at last appears, Handel avoids anticlimax or undramatic delay (as in Silvani's libretto) by hurrying on the action; Oronte enters before the lovers have time to react to each other. The recitatives in this scene (II ix) are among the most effective in the opera, especially when Oronte twice calls

---

[15] This is not an incomplete sketch; the lower parts had rests. See p. 406.

Ex. 47

Elmira (bottom of HG 74) and is confronted by both lovers; it is always a mistake to dismiss Handel's secco recitative as routine. When at the end of the act Oronte offers Elmira his throne or death, Handel dramatizes her despair by setting the words 'Sorte nemica, hai vinto' with string accompaniment and the rest of her speech as secco, and then—another stroke of inspired simplicity—repeating the accompanied bars exactly. Elmira is the only character in the opera to be allowed accompanied recitative. 'Mà che vuoi più' is an austere aria for the end of an act, but has considerable character.

Handel makes much of her rhetorical question ('why does not death come?'), underpinning the upward inflection of 'dov'è?' with a diminished seventh or dominant chord that is not immediately resolved and so heightens her despair. The vocal line is rhythmically varied at vital points, with the unison violins frequently below it; since she is an alto, the colour is exceptionally sombre.

In 'Vivere per penare', similarly scored and like her two previous arias and accompanied recitative in a flat minor key, Elmira takes a more resigned, reflective view of death. The little rhythmic turn at the start, which punctuates the texture of both sections over a harmonic bass moving in steady quavers, occurs both on and off the strong beats, so that it can act as echo as well as rhythmic reinforcement. The similarity to a figure in Rossane's 'O dolce mia speranza' in Act I (ritornello after the A section) can have no significance in the context of the opera; that aria comes from a cantata and was introduced into *Floridante* at a revival. The Andante tempo is important for the long division on 'vola', which is not decorative but represents perhaps a lingering farewell to life. Elmira's last aria 'Sì, coronar' is no more than adequate; the flowing main theme has little to back it up, and the music tends to trundle. As elsewhere in Anastasia Robinson's parts, Handel doubles the voice with the first violins at the octave throughout the A section; there seems to be no authority for the solo at bar 19.

Rossane's part as sung by Salvai in 1721 cannot be deduced from Chrysander's score. It did not include 'O dolce mia speranza', 'Dopo l'ombre', 'O quanto è caro amor', or 'O cara spene'. 'Sospiro, è vero', a replacement for the rejected 'È un sospir' (HG 128), was in A minor, not G minor. The rest of the part, except for the two arias in Act III, was adapted from alto originals. It is clear that Salvai, a high and agile soprano, was not a singer of the first rank. In three of her five arias Handel doubled much of the vocal line with oboes, violins, or both. Rossane stands in the shadow of her foster-sister; her music has youthful charm but little depth of feeling, even in her love for Timante. They remain a subsidiary couple; Rolli's treatment of them virtually ensured this, and Handel did not try to amend it. The light texture of the whole part, voice and accompaniment (of her arias only 'Sospiro, è vero' employs more than one upper instrumental line), suggests a half-formed immature personality. In 'Mà un dolce' she reacts timorously to the prospect of meeting Timante; the music is sequential and not very interesting. 'Sospiro, è vero' adds a coquettish element. She sighs, but is not sure why; and the sighs, though repeatedly emphasized, especially in the ritornellos after each section (there is none at the start), do not ask to be taken too seriously. The frequent oscillations between neighbouring notes and chords (bars 18–19, 25–6, 32–3, 38–9, 42–3) distil a flavour almost of operetta. 'Gode l'alma', when she knows her love is returned, has a charming youthful bounce, conveyed by the upward thrust of a favourite syncopated rhythm. The chain of sequences escapes monotony thanks to Handel's skill in changing the rhythm or melodic contour just when it threatens to become tiresome, and to the delightful two-part texture pervading both sections. The voice and violins play ducks and drakes, acting as bass in turn, while the orchestral basses pause to listen.

'Fuor di periglio', Rossane's love duet with Timante, is the most richly scored piece in the opera, with eight instrumental parts, though its basis is simple enough. There is some doubt about the scoring: in nearly all the sources where they are named, including the autograph and the S2 parts, the top two staves are for horns; but they are omitted in three early copies and the Walsh score, and Handel may have suppressed them; he crossed out their opening bars in the autograph, and the duet was never sung after 1721. There is no evidence for Chrysander's recorders. The instruments operate for the most part in thirds, sometimes double thirds, but the question and answer in the long ritornellos adds variety, and the full orchestra periodically breaks into the interstices of the voice parts. The music is not particularly inventive, less so than many of Handel's bird songs; the melodic phrases tend to fall into eight-bar sections, though the first vocal entry is extended to ten. The charm of the piece lies in the orchestral texture, and it makes a perfect foil for Elmira's 'Notte cara'. 'Se risolvi' despite its Bach-like instrumental figuration does not strike deep; Rossane's response to the prospect of losing Elmira is to compare herself with a touch of self-pity to a solitary turtle-dove. 'Vanne, segui' is even slighter, a little binary arietta in minuet rhythm with each half repeated and a regular concluding ritornello. It is as stylized and formal as a dance; indeed its source is the minuet aria from Keiser's *Claudius* that was to reappear in the overture to *Samson*.

In Rossane's music, and perhaps still more in Timante's, Handel—whether consciously or not—came close to aping Bononcini. The melodies appeal to the ear but soon exhaust their charm. Baldassari in 1721 sang Chrysander's A version of Timante's first three arias, but the B version of 'Amor commanda' (the G minor setting was scrapped before performance). This confined him to major keys. Only the A major 12/8 'Lascioti, O bella' is worthy of Handel, an exquisite little siciliano with a touch of Acis's 'Love in her eyes', which brings Timante to momentary life as a tender lover. There is no elaboration. Handel works with very few notes, excluding oboes and violas till the ritornello after the A section, but lights up the music with some neat detail: the deceptive opening on a first inversion without ritornello (after an unemphatic cadence in E omitted by Chrysander), deft changes of rhythm in the recurrent three-note call (♩ ♪♪, ♫ ♪, ♪♫ ♪, ♫ ♩). When he writes even quavers, they should on no account be 'regularized' by dotting, a besetting sin in many Handel revivals. There are nice rhythmic variants in 'Amor commanda' too, especially in the B section; the A section is a complete binary movement in itself. 'Dopo il nembo' is a routine simile aria of the beefier sort, 'Nò, non piangete' a later insertion that contributes nothing.

As so often, Boschi as Oronte was confined to minor keys, which allowed him to rage satisfactorily. The part has little light and shade; that seems to have been beyond Boschi. 'Finchè lo strale' is typical in its staccato emphasis, octave leaps, scales, and frequent doublings; except in the asseverations of 'nò, nò' the voice is tied to the instrumental basses and violas, and often to the top line as well. 'Mà non s'aspetti' is similar in mood, with more noisy negatives and a faint aroma of Polyphemus ('O ruddier than the cherry'),[16] but *sui generis* in form, a modified da capo, suggested perhaps by the repeat of the first line at the end. The words are obscure, and seem to contradict Oronte's declaration in the recitative that he will let Elmira simmer down before renewing his assault. 'Che veggio?' is much more interesting. The full da capo setting came first, with Largo and Allegro alternating throughout the A section, and the second part holding the grim mood by remaining solidly in D minor. Handel reduced it to the cavatina AB (slow–quick) before perfor-

[16] Both arias derive from an aria in Keiser's *Janus* (1698).

mance, perhaps when he followed the opposite procedure with 'Questi ceppi',[17] presumably in order not to delay the resolution of the plot. Boschi was seldom allowed the luxury of a slow tempo, but the piece is a distinct musical gain and adds something to the character as well. The impressive opening, instrumental unisons separated by long rests and the voice hurling fragmentary exclamations into the void, recalls an earlier baffled autocrat, Agrippina in 'Pensieri, voi mi tormentate'. Coralbo's single aria, though sequential, has more fire than Handel sometimes allowed to such minor figures.

The overture, unexpectedly in an opera of light specific gravity, has no dance movement and a severe A minor fugue. Burney blamed the latter for the overture's lack of popularity, finding it monotonous on account of its 'convulsive and unpleasant theme, which has given birth to no counter-subject of a different cast, or variety of style or passage, even in the solo parts for the hautbois'. But it has vitality and an individual flavour, and the interposition of the eight-bar Lentement before the repeat is an effective stroke; Handel may have improvised harpsichord cadenzas at the long fermata (HG 4). The overture was probably in existence before the opera (the fugue is a reworking of a movement from an early harpsichord suite in G minor), which may be connected with an oddity of scoring. The solo oboe parts mentioned by Burney are not in HG, the autograph, or Hamburg, where divided bassoons play them an octave lower in bars 19–22 and 42–5; but they appear in Walsh and two very early copies, and must have been authorized by Handel. The alternative Marches (the second was played in 1721) and the sinfonia introducing the last scene are conventional D major excursions. The *coro* in the same key receives a certain thrust from the use of full brass and the bounding triplets of the violins. Handel reworked the B section, with rhythmic improvements, for the penultimate chorus ('Dall'orrore di cieca notte') in *Alcina*.

There are signs that Handel planned the orchestration on a more substantial scale than he ultimately employed. Apart from the doubt about the horns in 'Fuor di periglio' and the bassoons in the overture, the abortive C minor 'Notte cara' had three violin and two bassoon parts. The rejected 'È un sospir' included two recorders, but Handel does not appear to have used them or flutes in 1721. This lightening of the texture did not affect the simultaneous use of horns and trumpets, but they play only in the ceremonial instrumental pieces and the *coro*, and horns may on occasion have been omitted: their eight-bar flourish in the Act III sinfonia is crossed out in Hamburg. The first draft of the autograph suggests a loose A minor/major—D major tonal scheme; this was inevitably subverted when the two female parts were rewritten. The abrupt and uncharacteristic switch from the A minor of the overture to the G major of 'Dimmi, O spene' sprang from the same cause; the aria was composed in A major.

History and Text

Handel completed the opera on 28 November 1721[18] and produced it at the King's Theatre on 9 December, with the following cast:

---

[17] The B section of 'Sì, coronar' too was an afterthought. It is curious that three consecutive arias should have wavered between the longer and shorter forms.

[18] The *coro* is no longer in the autograph, but Jennens added the date to the Flower copy.

FLORIDANTE:	Senesino (alto castrato)
TIMANTE:	Benedetto Baldassari (soprano castrato)
ORONTE:	Boschi (bass)
ELMIRA:	Anastasia Robinson (contralto)
ROSSANE:	Maddalena Salvai (soprano)

The singer of the small role of Coralbo is not recorded for any of Handel's productions; Lagarde may have sung it in the first two seasons. There were fifteen performances, the last on 26 May 1722. Handel revived *Floridante* in the following season 'with several Additions and Alterations' and performed it seven times in succession between 4 and 26 December 1722. The cast showed two changes, Durastanti replacing Salvai as Rossane and the alto castrato Berenstadt succeeding the soprano Baldassari as Timante. Each involved Handel in much rearrangement. For Durastanti, a dramatic rather than lyric soprano with a lower tessitura than Salvai, he recast the role of Rossane, giving it much more prominence and radically disturbing the balance of the opera. She had four new arias: 'O dolce mia speranza', 'O quanto è caro amor', and 'O cara spene' replaced 'Mà un dolce', 'Gode l'alma', and 'Vanne, segui' in I i, II i, and III v respectively, and 'Dopo l'ombre' was inserted in the middle of I iv. 'Sospiro, è vero' and probably 'Se risolvi' were transposed down a tone to G minor, and the duet 'Fuor di periglio' almost certainly cut. Of Durastanti's new arias, all but 'Dopo l'ombre' were lifted from the cantata 'Crudel tiranno amor' with the music and in two instances the text as well unchanged; the words of the cantata's eponymous aria were altered to the exactly opposite sense, 'O quanto è caro amor'. It seems probable, as suggested by Anthony Hicks,[19] that this was the new cantata introduced by Durastanti at her King's Theatre benefit on 5 July 1721. For Berenstadt Handel transposed 'Dopo il nembo' and 'Nò, non piangete' down to C and D respectively, with a few changes (HG 37, 85), and wrote a new setting of 'Lascioti, O bella' (HG 130). 'Amor commanda' was probably cut. Berenstadt apparently thought little of his part; he told Pistocchi in a letter of 8 May 1724 that in London revivals the secondary singers served as candlesticks.[20] *Floridante* was the only revival in which he sang in 1722–4.

Timante's stature was not much affected; while he lost the best of his arias, the new setting, again Larghetto without ritornello, is similar in mood and little inferior in quality, with some delightful harmonic detail towards the end of the A section. But the new music for Rossane is so sharply at variance with the character drawn in the libretto as to make dramatic nonsense. 'O dolce mia speranza' is inconceivable in the mouth of a young girl who has never seen her lover. It is a magnificent aria, another minor-key siciliano with the characteristic blend of lilting rhythm and pungently emotional harmony; Burney thought it 'the most pathetic and beautiful' he had ever heard. This is the utterance of a mature woman acquainted with love and pain; it has a clear foretaste of Rodelinda. Both ritornellos hover between minor and relative major, and the introduction of new material after the A section intensifies the emotion, as do the adventurous modulations of the B section. The other two cantata arias are on the same enlarged scale. Their inclusion shows Handel consulting his own and Durastanti's convenience, not the requirements of the opera, an impression confirmed by the reversed sense of 'O quanto è caro amor'. It should be put down not to cynicism but to Handel's usual relaxed

[19] *MT* cxii (1971), 867.   [20] Lindgren, *M & L* (1977), 21.

attitude to revivals. 'O quanto è caro amor', which has a certain resemblance to Alcina's 'Mà quando tornerai', and 'O cara spene', where unison violins double the voice except at cadences, are generalized pieces of good quality, but they have little to do with Rossane. 'Dopo l'ombre' is rather more suitable, though it too suggests a cantata origin. Pedals and rhythmic cross-currents give the music a delightful freshness. All four are full da capo arias without the dal segno abridgements one might expect in a dramatic context, and three have long formal ritornellos.

In 1727 *Floridante* was hastily revived for two performances only, on 29 April and 2 May. Burney says it was a stopgap when Bononcini's *Astianatte* (first given on 6 May) was several times postponed owing to Cuzzoni's indisposition.[21] Senesino and Boschi retained their parts; Faustina Bordoni succeeded Durastanti as Rossane; Elmira was probably sung by Anna Dotti, Timante by Antonio Baldi, Coralbo by Palmerini. Since Faustina was the prima donna of this cast, the part of Rossane was expanded to seven arias and that of Elmira abridged to five, and the dramatic balance became more lopsided than ever. Faustina sang all four Durastanti arias and a new one, 'Parmi che giunta in porto' (in the place occupied by 'Fuor di periglio'), which may have been composed for the occasion but is quite out of character with the score. It is a showy verbose piece that later found its way into *Radamisto* and *Tolomeo*, where Chrysander printed it. Dotti lost the two liveliest of her arias, 'Mà pria vedrò le stelle' and 'Barbaro!'—both essential if Elmira is to be more than a cipher—and her duet with Floridante at the end of Act I. In place of this Handel gave Senesino the splendidly vigorous B minor aria 'Amor ed empietà', composed for *Admeto* a few weeks earlier and still unpublished; it makes Floridante a more decisive character but scarcely compensates for the loss of 'Ah mia cara'. Like *Radamisto* in the following year, the opera lost both its duets. Timante was deprived of 'Lascioti, O bella' and possibly 'Amor commanda' as well; no alto version of this aria survives, though it is not cancelled in the libretto.

Handel's third and last revival took place on 3 March 1733, with four consecutive performances in that month and three more in May after an interval of eight weeks. There is considerable uncertainty about the cast, which is not named in the libretto, but little doubt that Senesino and Montagnana sang Floridante and Oronte. *Floridante* seems once more to have served as a stopgap. The *Daily Advertiser* announced on 5 March that 'Signora Strada, on Account of whose Indisposition the Run of the new Opera of Orlando was interrupted, continues very ill'. *Orlando* had last been given on 20 February, but Strada sang in *Deborah* (six performances from 17 March) and probably *Esther* (14 and 17 April), and presumably when *Orlando* came back on 21 April. However it was again deferred in favour of *Floridante* by the indisposition of a singer on 8 May. If this was Strada once more, she may never have sung in *Floridante*, which was succeeded on 22 May by a revival of Bononcini's *Griselda*, chosen perhaps because the heroine is a contralto. This was the last production before the schism that gave birth to the Opera of the Nobility. The most likely candidates for Rossane are Ann Turner Robinson, who had sung in Handel's oratorios the previous year, or Cecilia Young, who according to the *Daily Advertiser* of 20 March was in *Deborah*. Timante may have been sung by Francesca Bertolli, who often played male roles, Elmira by Celeste Gismondi, a soprano with a compass extending down to B flat, and Coralbo by Waltz, who was also in *Deborah*. Handel's transposition of 'Ah mia cara' up to G minor probably relates to this revival.

Rossane retained 'O dolce mia speranza' and 'O cara spene', but not the other two Durastanti arias or 'Parmi che giunta in porto'; 'Dopo l'ombre' was cut, and 'Gode l'alma' restored in place of 'O quanto è caro amor'. Floridante's 'Questi ceppi' reverted to the cavatina form of the autograph. In Elmira's part 'Barbaro!' and the duet 'Ah mia cara' (ousting Senesino's 1727 aria) were restored, but not 'Mà pria vedrò le stelle'. Timante, further reduced, was left only with 'Dopo il nembo' and possibly 'Amor commanda'; the whole of II vi and III i were cut, as were Oronte's last recitative and 'Che veggio?', perhaps because it lay too high for Montagnana. A number of recitatives were shortened or omitted, leaving the opera a torso, though less unbalanced than in 1727; Elmira now had six arias and a duet to Rossane's five. The box-office figures for the last performance (19 May) are known,[22] and show that the house was barely a quarter full. Receipts, at £54.7s.0d, fell considerably below expenses (£89.1s.2d, which presumably did not include the singers' salaries). The two final performances of the season, *Griselda* on 5 and 7 June, fared little better.

Floridante contributed few pieces to the concert repertory. Mrs Hill sang 'Dopo l'ombre' at the Little Haymarket Theatre on 9 August 1728, Jane Barbier 'Alma mia' at her Lincoln's Inn Fields benefit on 5 March 1729. She may also at some time have sung 'Vanne, segui'.[23] 'Se risolvi' enjoyed a certain popularity outside England; it was included in the ballad opera *The Beggar's Wedding* in Dublin (24 March 1729) and in a similar French piece, *Les Amans trompés*, at The Hague in 1758, by which time it had twice been published in Paris. Another ballad opera, *The Wedding* (Lincoln's Inn Fields, 6 May 1729), contained 'O cara spene' and the second March (HG 15) set to English words; the tunes are printed at the end of Essex Hawker's libretto. Handel incorporated 'Finchè lo strale' (with a new text) and 'Ah mia cara' in his pasticcio *Oreste* (Covent Garden, 18 December 1734).

Floridante was produced at Hamburg, as *Der thrazische Printz Floridantes*, on 28 April 1723 (NS) with the recitative translated by Joachim Beccau, and given eleven times in the season. The arias as usual were sung in Italian. This was Handel's 1721 version. The only modern revivals have been at Abingdon in 1962 (with reduced orchestration), Bad Lauchstädt in 1984, and Cambridge (1989).

Autograph

The pre-performance history of the opera is complicated and the autograph (RM 20 b 2) confusing, owing in the main to Handel's decision, after he had composed the whole of Act I and the set pieces (but not the recitatives) of Act II as far as the opening bars of 'Notte cara' (II vii, HG 71), to exchange the voice ranges of the two female roles. All the music hitherto written for them, and most of the recitatives for the other characters in Act I, had to be revised,

[22] J. Milhous and R. D. Hume, 'Box Office Reports for Five Operas Mounted by Handel in London, 1732–1734', *Harvard Library Bulletin*, xxvi (1978), 245–66.

[23] See p. 416.

transposed, replaced, or otherwise adjusted. Handel entered some of these changes in the autograph and some in the performing score, but a certain amount of autograph material is lost. The revisions were not confined to these adjustments (he rewrote one of Floridante's recitatives at a late stage, added a new scene for Timante, and reset another of his arias), nor were they all made at the same time; some pieces passed through several versions. For no obvious reason either Handel or Rolli could not make up his mind about Rossane's name, which was changed first to Rosaura, then to Rossalba, before reverting to its original form. Both Squire's *Catalogue* and Chrysander's score are unreliable guides to the autograph, which—with one possible exception noted below—contains nothing that dates from after the first performance.

Handel foliated the manuscript in his usual manner on each bifolio gathering (every eighth side), including the overture, which may have been taken from another source. He began each act with a new series. The manuscript as first written comprised the following leaves in the modern foliation. Act I: 5–11, 17–25, 28–33. Act II: 34–5, 38–46, 49–56, 59–70. Act III: 74–86, 89–96, and the leaves containing the *coro*, which were early separated from the rest and sold at Sotheby's on 16 March 1937.[24] They reached the British Library with the Zweig Collection in 1986. Apart from the 1722 and later additions, the autograph does not contain either of the Marches in I ii, the B section of 'Questi ceppi', or the sinfonia in the last scene.

All the recitatives in Act I except those on HG 16 and 34 differ from the published text. Rossane's are in the alto clef, Elmira's in the soprano. Not every phrase sung by the male characters had to be altered, but Handel later rewrote Floridante's 'Fammi bersaglio' (HG 25), probably because Senesino found the tessitura inconveniently high. In Scene vi Timante has five extra bars (three lines of verse) after 'per te s'accese' (HG 31, third system), which Chrysander omitted for no good reason; they are in every musical source, and were certainly sung in 1721. Occasionally—for a few bars in Scene iv (HG 18)—Handel added the later lower part for Elmira in small notes; but he made most of the changes in the performing score.

'Dimmi, O spene' is a full aria in A major with a B section of sixteen bars ('Quanto grata a nobil core / È l'amor chi co'l valore / Stanca l'ali della fama'), a return of the first vocal phrase, and a da capo dal segno from bar 15; then, after the recitative with Rossane, a second repeat of the A section with new words ('Godi, O spene', HG 8), Handel left this unusual design undisturbed except for the transposition *ex G*; but apart from the extra music many details differ from HG. The voice has a higher tessitura in bars 22 (where the violins double the bass in octaves), 26–8, 38–9, 48, and 53, and the closing ritornello of the A section is different and three bars shorter. Later Handel added the extra bars of this ritornello, with a cue for its completion from that at the start of the aria, without clefs or signature on the blank stave at the bottom of f. 5ʳ. The change may have been connected with his decision to omit the B section, but the latter is not cancelled.

The cadence at the bottom of HG 9 is in A major, leading to 'Mà un dolce' for alto in D minor. At the head of Scene ii Handel added a later note *NB La Marche* but no music. The ornamentation of the first phrase of 'Alma mia' (see Ex. 44, p. 392) is not reproduced in any copy. 'Mà pria vedrò le stelle' is in G

---

[24] W. C. Smith, 'Recently Discovered Handel Manuscripts', *MT* lxxviii (1937), 312–15. Apparently the manuscript came from an Aylesford sale, and therefore ultimately from Jennens.

Ex. 44, p. 392) is not reproduced in any copy. 'Mà pria vedrò le stelle' is in G minor (HG 125), marked *ex E*. Bars 47–50 of 'Finchè lo strale' were an afterthought; in the B section Handel three times altered the word 'troverà' to 'troncherà', a reading that reappears only in the Flower copy. The recitative cadence after the five unpublished bars on HG 31 is in C major, followed by 'È un sospir' in F (HG 128). The recitative on HG 41 also cadences in C major, and the duet follows in F minor with many differences from HG. Naturally the change of voices caused trouble in the opera's two duets, each of which involves one of the female roles, and it is arguable that the vocal lines are more satisfactory as first composed. The autograph of 'Ah mia cara' has fuller parts for the upper instruments in bars 43–6 and 58–63 and a four-bar ritornello after the B section (these were afterthoughts, subsequently removed) as well as many vocal variants, chiefly for a soprano Elmira, in bars 40–8, 55–63, and the whole B section. Handel noted the transposition *ex E*, but partly rewrote the piece several times before performance and again later.

The insertions in Act I are the overture (ff. 1–4), whose paper and rastration differ from the continuation of the manuscript (and the name of the opera is obviously an addition); the recitative 'Avventurosa Elmira' and aria 'Mà un dolce' in G minor for Rosaura (*sic*) in the soprano clef, now with Chrysander's A cadence (ff. 12–13, HG 9–11); 'Mà pria vedrò le stelle' in E minor without tempo mark (ff. 14–16, HG 22–4); and 'Sospiro, è vero' (replacing 'È un sospir') in A minor, not G minor (ff. 26–7, HG 31–3). The G minor 'Mà un dolce' is not a literal transposition of the D minor, which Chrysander does not print; here, as with 'Gode l'alma' and 'Barbaro!' in Act II, Handel made characteristic improvements while writing out the music in the new key, for example slightly contracting the B section cadence. In the transposed 'Mà pria vedrò le stelle', as elsewhere in the score, he retained the soprano clef for Anastasia Robinson, who had begun her career as a soprano; once or twice he wrote the alto by mistake, and generally (not quite always) amended it.

In Act II he wrote an alto clef for Rossane in all the recitatives but changed it to soprano before adding the music; in the set pieces she has alto versions, including the lower part in the duet 'Fuor di periglio'. The cadence at the bottom of HG 45 has a minim E major chord leading straight into the aria; it is in all copies, but has been pasted over in Hamburg. There are differences from HG in bars 9–10 and 25–6 of 'Lascioti', including an extra bar in the B section. 'Gode l'alma' is in D major and the alto clef; while the ritornello is the same as in the soprano version, the initial vocal melody and the whole B section, which is four bars longer and has a running quaver bass throughout and no two-part writing for voice and violins, diverges so markedly that it is astonishing Chrysander ignored it. 'Bramo te sola' has no tempo, and the second oboe originally doubled the second violins at the start; the voice's last note in bar 51 (HG 56) is B flat, not D, here and in all copies, including Hamburg. Handel accidentally omitted the third and fourth bars of Oronte's recitative at the start of Scene v (HG 59), no doubt because Elmira's reply begins with the same word. 'Barbaro!' is in B flat; the preceding cadence is in B minor because Handel transposed the aria to G before composing the recitative. He did not bother to write out the final ritornello of 'Mà non s'aspetti'.

'Fuor di periglio' is in an unpublished version, though on the same material. The voice parts are differently distributed with Rossane the lower in the alto clef.

The two main ritornellos appear to have three bass parts,[25] but the bottom line, marked simply *B*, is Handel's conflation of the horn and bassoon parts, to be played by bassoons only, and suggests that he did away with the horns altogether. The two top staves are not named on the first page of the duet (bars 1–10), where their music, and that of the original bassoon parts, is crossed out; but on the verso each is clearly marked *C[orno]*. The bass line differs from HG in bars 22–3 and 31–2 and in most of the B section, which is four bars shorter; both voices sing together from the start (bar 82), beginning in sixths. Like the overture's introduction, 'Dimmi, O spene', 'Se risolvi', 'Vanne segui', 'Amor commanda', and the *coro*, this duet has no tempo mark in any source.

On f. 59 Handel began a setting of 'Notte cara' in C minor, marked *Largo* and headed *Scena 8* (instead of 7). The material is similar to the B flat minor version, but the scoring is much richer and Elmira enters in the second bar (see Ex. 47). This seems to be the point at which Handel decided to make her the lower voice. He abandoned the sketch and started the published setting on f. 60; the ink smudges transferred to the blank verso of f. 59 as well as the foliation prove that this was part of the original manuscript. In the central recitative section the accompaniment of bars 22–35 was at first very different, scored almost entirely for unison violins, which punctuated the pauses in the vocal line with descending quaver scales (each note with a mark of emphasis), flurries of demisemiquavers (after 'il guardo solo'), and upward-leaping arpeggios in jerky rhythm (from 'solitario si vede' to 'la porta è sol socchiusa'). Elmira's recitative 'Fatto hai l'estremo' (HG 80), between the two accompanied sections, exists in three versions, the first two superimposed on f. 68[r].

The insertions in Act II are 'Gode l'alma' in B flat (ff. 36–7, HG 48–9); 'Barbaro!' in G without tempo mark (ff. 47–8, HG 61–2); the revised voice parts and bass (no upper instruments) of 'Fuor di periglio', with Rossane now the higher of two sopranos (ff. 57–8, HG 65–70); and the third and final setting of 'Fatto hai l'estremo' (f. 71[v], HG 80; the recto is blank and the leaf may be part of the previous gathering).

Rossane's music in Act III has the soprano clef throughout. The act originally began with Scene ii (HG 87); Handel must have inserted Scene i before composing the prison scene, for he had to renumber ii–v but not vi. 'Se risolvi' at first was a full da capo aria; the dal segno bars were added later. Floridante's music at 'ad ambo morte, se tu rifiuti' (middle of HG 93) was heavily rewritten; the first version was copied into the Hamburg score and subsequently altered, though not quite in the same way as the autograph.[26] At the start of 'Vivere per penare' Handel gave Elmira an alto clef by mistake. The viola part in the ritornello of 'Vanne, segui' was an afterthought. The tempo mark of 'Questi ceppi', at the start and at the voice entry, was originally *Adagio*; the B section (HG 107–8, bottom) is not present. The heading for Scene viii has *nappo* for *coppo* in all sources, including the libretto and performing score; *coppo* is a piece of tidying up by Chrysander. The B section of 'Sì, coronar' was squeezed into the bottom of two pages; Handel again inadvertently gave Elmira an alto clef, and marked the part *in Discant*.

---

[25] S2 in the Flower score, copied from the autograph, retains the three bass parts at the start, marking the second *ContraB* and the third *Bassi*, implying divided cellos doubling the bassoons. That is how he interprets them in the later parts.

[26] The Malmesbury and Lennard copies have yet another variant.

that the cavatina was substituted at an early stage, and it appears thus in every copy except the first Hamburg draft. Although the 1721 libretto has the longer form, it was probably never sung. No space is left for the missing sinfonia. In the last scene Handel forgot Elmira's name before her recitative 'Che sempre nel cor' (HG 117, sixth system); it was added, with a clef, by Smith. The F sharp minor recitative cadence on HG 118 was probably designed to lead straight to the *coro*.

The insertions in Act III are the opening scene with 'Nò, non piangete' in A major (ff. 71–3, HG 83–5); 'Amor commanda' in B flat, replacing the G minor setting (ff. 87–8, HG 105–6; the notes bracketed by Chrysander in bars 7–8 are present, and the voice has the upper part in bar 16); 'Mia bella' (ff. 97–9, HG 118–20); and Elmira's following recitative (f. 100, HG 120). This originally cadenced in E major; Handel perhaps thought of giving Elmira an aria in A before the *coro*, but then decided to compensate Senesino with 'Mia bella'. There are signs of hurry in this scene as it stands. The E major 'Mia bella' comes in oddly after an F sharp minor cadence.

One curious feature of the autograph remains for comment. Apart from the transpositions noted for the first performance, Handel indicated a number of others: *ex E moll* on 'Sospiro, è vero' (A minor), *ex D♯* on 'Dopo il nembo' (G), *ex E♯* on 'Lascioti' (A), *ex F* on 'Gode l'alma' (B flat soprano setting), *ex F* on 'Nò, non piangete' (A), *ex E* on 'Se risolvi' (A minor), and *ex C* on 'Vanne, segui' (F). These are all soprano arias for Rossane or Timante, put down a fourth (in one case a third) for alto. Rossane was never sung by an alto, and the 1722 Timante (Berenstadt) used different transpositions. The new keys do however correspond to those in the early copy RM 19 f 4, which has all four upper voices in the alto clef and was undoubtedly a special commission. It seems that Handel noted the new keys as a guide to the copyist on this occasion; the other arias already existed in alto keys, except 'Amor commanda', which Handel did not mark for transposition, and which significantly is the only vocal movement missing in RM 19 f 4. One other detail in the autograph may be connected with this transaction. In bars 24 and 27 of 'Nò, non piangete' Handel added alternatives in the lower octave for the two highest-lying phrases of the voice, which when transposed would have taken an alto up to F. These alternatives do not appear in the performing score, but they are chosen in RM 19 f 4.[27]

The Aylesford volume RM 18 c 2 contains two autographs unrecognized in Squire's *Catalogue* (p. 112), one of them, on ff. 28–9, an arrangement for harpsichord of 'Sventurato' with the words occasionally cued in between the staves. This is partly a recomposition; there are many minor variants from the aria as published, and some delicate embellishments of the melody, probably intended for keyboard but equally apt to the voice.[28] It throws valuable light on Handel's attitude to ornamentation.

Librettos

1721. 'Drama ... Printed by Tho. Wood in Little Britain.' 61 pp. Rolli, described on the title-page as Secretary of the Royal Academy, dedicated the

[27] They also appear in the Flower score, which was copied from the autograph later.
[28] See T. Best, 'An Example of Handel Embellishment', *MT* cx (1969), 933.

libretto in Italian to the Prince of Wales in the usual flowery terms, 'because in it those two most noble qualities, so difficult to express—the heroic lover and the loving hero—have been, I make bold to say, most vividly and feelingly celebrated in excellent music'. The Argument, which appears in both languages, is quoted above. Five passages of dialogue in I i and v and II i and v, some 28 lines in all, are bracketed as omitted in the performance. They are mostly concerned with the political background, and include the first seven lines in Act II. Handel set none of them. The three lines omitted by Chrysander in I vi are not bracketed. 'Questi ceppi' has its A section only, but 'Che veggio?' is a full aria.

1723 Hamburg. 'Der Thrazische Printz Floridantes . . . gedruckt bei Caspar Jakhel.' The recitatives, including the B section of 'Notte cara', are in German, the arias in Italian with a German translation at the side. Neither the singers nor the translator (Joachim Beccau) are named. The text is that of 1721, with 'Questi ceppi' a full aria. The prefatory matter includes a translation of the Argument and mentions dances.

1727. No new libretto was printed (and none is known for the 1722 revival), but a copy of the 1721 edition in the British Library (163 g 14) with four neatly written manuscript pages of *Alterazioni nell'Opera di Floridante* bound in at the end can only refer to 1727. The ten alterations are meticulously supplied with contexts and page references. In Act I 'O dolce mia speranza' replaces 'Mà un dolce', 'Dopo l'ombre' is inserted in Scene iv, 'Mà pria vedrò le stelle' is cut, and Floridante's aria 'Amor ed empietà' replaces the duet 'Ah mia cara'. In Act II 'Lascioti' and 'Barbaro!' are cut, 'O quanto è caro amor' replaces 'Gode l'alma', and 'Parmi che giunta in porto' (for Rossane) replaces the duet 'Fuor di periglio'. In Act III 'O cara spene' replaces 'Vanne, segui', and the three lines of the B section of 'Questi ceppi' are inserted. At least five of these changes had been introduced in 1722, and the last of them in 1721 after the libretto had been printed. Only the replacement of the two duets and the omission of 'Lascioti' (which had a new setting in 1722) date certainly from 1727; Anastasia Robinson had probably sung 'Mà pria vedrò le stelle' and 'Barbaro!' in 1722.

1733. 'Printed for T. Wood in Little-Britain, and are to be sold at the King's Theatre in the Hay-Market.' 45 pp. The pagination of the only known copy, BL 639 d 21(2), is defective, pages 25–32 being numbered 41–8. The dedication is omitted, the Argument in English only, and the cast not named, possibly on account of the haste and confusion attending this revival. Four of the 1727 alterations are retained; but 'Dopo l'ombre' and the B section of 'Questi ceppi' are cut, 'Ah mia cara', 'Gode l'alma' (ousting their 1727 substitutes), and 'Barbaro!' are restored, and II vi disappears entirely, the recitative as well as the duet. There are many further cuts, mostly in Act III: the opening lines of Timante's recitative before 'Dopo il nembo' up to 'prigionia' (HG 34 or 37), the whole of III i, almost all of Elmira's recitative before 'Vivere per penare' (the first and last phrases were retained; they appear in the English version as 'Yes, let us die; Yes, yes, let us die', but were accidentally omitted from the Italian), the last six lines of the recitative on HG 99 (which ends at 'amor non pera'), all but the first two lines of the recitative before 'Amor commanda' (which ends at 'impegno', HG 102), and the whole of Oronte's scene after 'Sì, coronar' including 'Che veggio?' (HG 112–15). Of the passages bracketed in the 1721 libretto only the three lines in

I i after Rossane's 'di quel soglio' (HG 9) remain—without brackets, though Handel does not appear ever to have set them. The three lines omitted by Chrysander on HG 31 are now cut.

Copies and Editions

According to Clausen RM 19 c 10, an incomplete Smith copy of Act I, was intended to form part of the original performing score. There is certainly some   *
truth in this, but the relationship between the manuscript and Hamburg MA/1018, the copy used for all Handel's performances, is complex. Both must have been prepared within a very short space of time, and there may have been interchange of material between them. The fact that f. 33 of RM 19 c 10 and f. 51 of MA/1018 (Act I) begin at the same point, in the middle of a word three bars before the end of I vii (HG 40), suggests that both may have been designed for use in the theatre, one by each continuo player (not of course at the same time). This synchronization occurs in other operas where two performing scores survive. But RM 19 c 10 comprises two quite separate segments copied at different times (A, ff. 1–32; B, ff. 33–6). Segment A, which ends with Rossane's suppressed aria 'È un sospir' in Scene vi, has the recitatives (except as noted below) in the text of the autograph, with Elmira a soprano and Rossane an alto and 'Mà un dolce' and 'Mà pria vedrò le stelle' in the original keys and versions. 'Dimmi, O spene' is still in A major, with the higher tessitura of the autograph and the ritornello as lengthened there, but Handel has removed the B section and the first repeat. After 'Mà un dolce' Smith later squeezed in the bass, but not the upper parts, of Marche B. The manuscript has three other peculiar features. Floridante's recitative 'Fammi bersaglio' (HG 25) is not in its autograph form but revised as printed, although Handel himself wrote the notes of the latter in MA/1018. This strengthens the suspicion that RM 19 c 10, at least in part, was prepared for the second harpsichordist. Secondly, whereas Timante's recitatives in Scene iii (HG 17) are complete in the soprano clef, in Scene vi (HG 30–1) they have an alto clef with the words but no music. Unless Smith made a mistake over the clef, Handel at this stage considered an alto Timante; but he must have changed his mind almost at once, for no alto music for him survives from this period. Segment A stops short of Timante's recitative and aria 'Dopo il nembo' (HG 34). Clausen's suggestion that ff. 47–50 of MA/1018 originally formed part of RM 19 c 10 is untenable: 'Dopo il nembo' (with its recitative) was composed for soprano in G in the original autograph and not transposed till 1722, when Handel noted instructions for this on the Hamburg copy of the soprano version.[29] Thirdly Handel had rewritten 'È un sospir', still for alto, before Smith made his copy, which is *Larghetto* (not *Largo*) and quite different from the autograph in bars 17–20. Throughout Segment A Smith repeatedly changed Rossane's name to Rosaura or Rossalba and back to Rossane; but he was inconsistent in his corrections, and left all three forms at different places in the text.

Segment B (ff. 33–6), which contains the close of the act from three bars before the end of Scene vii, beginning in the middle of the word 'inganni', was copied when Handel had rewritten the recitative in its final form, with an alto tessitura for Elmira, and considerably revised the duet. The key is now E

[29] Clausen's listing of Timante as a tenor stems from a mistake in Deutsch.

minor; the scoring of bars 43–7 and 58–63 is as published, and there is no ritornello after the B section. But Handel had not yet made the tricky adjustments for Anastasia Robinson. Smith copied the instrumental parts and the words in full, leaving gaps for the voices: there is no music for Elmira in bars 40–63, for Floridante in bars 46–52, for either from the third beat of bar 77 to bar 93. Smith left similar but not identical gaps in the Hamburg copy. Again the evidence points to a second performing score.

MA/1018 was assembled piecemeal, evidently in a hurry; the process involved Handel himself, Smith, and two other copyists, sometimes working in tandem. Smith, who did most of the work, copied Act II before Act I (as the manuscript now stands). In Act II he prepared alto clefs for Rossane (Rosaura at this stage) and wrote out the D major alto version of 'Gode l'alma'. Presumably he was copying as Handel composed, the set pieces before the recitative; for he subsequently altered Rossane's clefs in the latter and 'Fuor di periglio' before adding the music. In Act I up to the middle of Scene iv Rosaura (*sic*)[30] has soprano clefs, but Elmira's were originally alto. In the remainder of this act and the whole of Act III both have soprano clefs.

The first form of the existing manuscript contained, in place of either March, a sinfonia in F major for horns, oboes, and strings thematically akin to Marche A, the three extra bars of recitative for Timante in I vi (HG 31), 'Sospiro, è vero' in A minor, almost certainly the E major cadence before 'Lascioti', the longer autograph version of the latter aria, 'Gode l'alma' in D for alto, a shorter form of Oronte's first recitative in II vi (HG 59), and the first autograph setting of Floridante's words 'ad ambo morte, se tu rifiuti' in III iv (HG 93). None of these appears in HG, though some were certainly performed. The first three bars of the F major sinfonia and the first $9\frac{1}{2}$ bars of the alto 'Gode l'alma' remain cancelled in the manuscript, the rest being torn out. The recitatives were altered or amended by pasted slips. 'Che veggio?' was in its longer form with a verso left blank for the D major sinfonia. In most of the Act I recitatives Smith wrote the clefs and words and Handel added the music. The only recitatives in this act written entirely by Smith are those on HG 9 (which Handel added to the autograph with the G minor version of 'Mà un dolce'), 16, and 34. The last two, like Oronte's three bars before 'Finchè lo strale' (HG 28) and much of the recitative on HG 40, needed no adjustment of pitch. Handel filled the gaps left by Smith in 'Ah mia cara', supplying Elmira's part in bars 40–8 and 55–63, Floridante's in most of bars 45–8 (and his words in bars 43–5), and the words and music of both in the entire B section from bar 78. Elmira's tessitura of course is for alto, and sometimes differs considerably from the autograph (and from HG). Handel made further changes on at least two occasions, adding lower and higher alternatives and sometimes (but not always) crossing out what he had written before. The higher alternatives often return to the autograph version, and may date from 1733. There are differences in almost every source for this duet. Chrysander, regardless of what Handel crossed out, includes some alternatives but ignores others; he prints only the higher version in bars 42 and 58 (last quaver)–59, only the lower in bars 44, 80, and 92–3, a mixture of the two in bars 85–7. In several places (bars 40, 80, 88, 92–3) Handel raised Floridante's part when he transposed the duet down, but later reverted to the low tessitura

---

[30] She is so named on ff. 7ᵛ, 10, 18, and 32 of Act I and ff. 1 and 28 of Act II, sometimes altered later to Rossane. Each act of MA/1018 has a separate foliation.

of the autograph. Chrysander gives this last version only; the earlier is in Hamburg and RM 19 f 4.

The inserted leaves in the manuscript date from two periods, before the first performance and for the 1722 revival. The first group consists of: Act I, f. 15 (Marche B, apparently stuck over f. 12ᵛ, the opening of the F major sinfonia); Act II, ff. 5–8 ('Gode l'alma' in B flat and the recitatives of II ii–iv nearly to the bottom of HG 53, with Rossane in the soprano clef): Act III, ff. 26–7 (B flat setting of 'Amor commanda' with the bracketed bars and higher vocal cadence), 31 (B section of 'Questi ceppi', written by H3, who began it in the alto clef but reverted to soprano in the middle), and 41–2 (sinfonia, written by H1). The revision of 'Lascioti' and the omission of the bracketed bars in 'Amor commanda' probably pre-dated the first performance, since Walsh printed the later texts.

The 1722 insertions are: Act I, ff. 21–4 ('Dopo l'ombre'), 38–40 ('Sospiro, è vero' in G minor; Timante's three extra lines were removed when the cadence was altered), and 47–50 ('Dopo il nembo' in C major with rewritten recitative; Handel marked the first violin part of the G major setting *alto* or *basso* as a guide to Smith); Act II, ff. 9–10 ('Lascioti' in F major) and 11–14 ('O quanto è caro amor', the words written by Handel); Act III, ff. 2a–3 ('Nò, non piangete' in D major) and 21–4 ('O cara spene'). Introductory cadences were suitably adjusted, and Smith recopied the recitatives on HG 22 and in I vii (HG 40). Durastanti's first aria, 'O dolce mia speranza', is no longer in the manuscript, but traces of its insertion remain. There are also signs of disturbance to the cadence before 'Se risolvi', which Durastanti probably sang in G minor; it seems later to have reverted to A minor. The only insertion of doubtful date is Act I, ff. 13–14 (Marche A); it was apparently later than Marche B and may belong to 1722. Clausen lists three further insertions, 'Barbaro!' in G major, the first page of 'Notte cara', and Act III Scene i; although these were additions to the autograph, they appear to be original in Hamburg.

From the 1727 revival date the cancellation of 'Mà pria vedrò' and 'Lascioti' (F major), and the F sharp minor cadence at the bottom of HG 45 (leading straight to Scene ii). The slip carrying this has not been removed; it probably conceals the original E major cadence amended (? to C major) for the F major aria of 1722. For 1733 'Dopo l'ombre' was cancelled, and the recitatives before 'Vivere per penare' and 'Amor commanda' ruthlessly compressed, the latter altered in detail and cadencing in G minor at 'impegno'. The cut of the first six bars of the recitative before 'Dopo il nembo' was made on the 1721 soprano copy; later the whole recitative was crossed out. None of these cuts is indicated in HG. Others may have been made by stitching the leaves. The most interesting change, which can only date from 1733, is Handel's pencilled note for the transposition of 'Ah mia cara' up to G minor; this, with the higher alternative notes, suggests that Elmira was sung by a soprano (? Gismondi). The key would still have been feasible for Senesino.

A few modifications, three of them autograph, cannot be certainly dated. Handel inserted an alternative G[31] for the voice's C sharp in bar 48 of 'Mà pria vedrò le stelle' (HG 24), a quaver A (not C as in HG) in the B section cadence of 'O quanto è caro amor' (HG 52), and a lower alternative in the A section cadence of the B flat 'Amor commanda' (HG 105), on this last

[31] This appears in the Lennard score; all the other sources have C sharp.

occasion cancelling the upper part (which however remains in all other sources). What is known about cuts and the compass of the singers suggests a date of 1722 in all these instances. At one stage the B section of 'Amor commanda', if not the whole aria, was cut, and the eight bars for horns alone at the beginning of the Act III sinfonia crossed out.

Chrysander wrote the tempo mark *Largo* (from the autograph) at bar 8 of 'Questi ceppi' and a number of dynamic and instrumental directions, including *Tutti* on the top line at bars 16 and 33 of 'Sì, coronar'. This does not appear in the autograph or any other source; nor does *Solo* at bar 19.

The Malmesbury copy (pp. 1–251 H3, 252–304 Smith) is important for placing insertions and variants, since Elizabeth Legh signed and dated it 14 December 1721, the day after the second performance. The overture has solo oboe parts an octave higher in place of the bassoons' thirds. I ii begins with Marche B; Timante has his extra lines on HG 31, and the cadence on HG 45 is the E major of the autograph. 'Tacerò' is *Allegro*; no other source gives a tempo for this aria. The B section of 'Questo ceppi' is on an unnumbered page with blank verso inserted after p. 261; writing and paper are so similar to the adjacent pages that it was probably copied at the same time, and it is included in the original binding. 'Che veggio?' is the shortened B version, the top line *Tutti unis.* as in Hamburg. In the sinfonia of the last scene the oboes double the violin parts; this occurs in no other source. The bass has been figured throughout, perhaps by Elizabeth Legh.

Since the score was dated so soon after the first night (and must have been begun earlier), it is not surprising that there is some confusion, especially over the women's parts. Rossane has the original (alto D minor) setting of 'Mà un dolce' and its recitative with A major cadence, but the soprano versions elsewhere. 'Sospiro, è vero' is in A minor; a later hand has added the tempo *Allegro ma non troppo*, taken perhaps from Walsh. In 'Fuor di periglio' the two top instrumental parts are missing; bars 7–8 and 71–5 have the original bassoon parts, but the rest of the duet is in the revised form. 'Lascioti' also is a mixture; the revised bars 9 and 10 but the longer B section. Elmira has an alto clef in 'Dimmi, O spene' (G major without B section, lengthened ritornello) and the recitative on HG 16, but not elsewhere; the aria however has the higher vocal line of the autograph. Her part in 'Ah mia cara' (E minor) has the original notes of the Hamburg score, generally the lower version in HG; but both she and Floridante have many unpublished variants, for example in bars 42, 44, 59, 80, 85–6, 88, and 92–3. In bars 85–7, where Handel made numerous alterations, Elmira's part (also in RM 19 f 4, and presumably as first sung) is:

Ex. 48

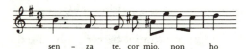

sen - za   te, cor mio,   non   ho

RM 19 f 4 is an eccentric early copy in which Smith collaborated closely with H3. Folios 1–43ʳ, 65–8, 78–81, and 83ᵛ–90 (the end of the manuscript) were written by Smith, the remainder by H3. The secco recitatives, both

Marches, and the Act III sinfonia are missing, and all four upper voices are in the alto clef throughout except in 'Alma mia' and the soprano line of the *coro*. The music must have been copied partly from the autograph, making the seven transpositions noted there by Handel. 'Dimmi, O spene' too is a transposition to G major of the autograph text with B section, longer ritornello, and original voice part, and 'Fuor di periglio' (with the two top instrumental staves omitted) is the original setting, the soprano voice parts merely notated in the alto clef. 'Ah mia cara' however is in E minor with the revised instrumental parts and the vocal lines as first written in the Hamburg score. 'Mà un dolce' is in its first D minor state, but 'Gode l'alma' is the soprano version transposed, perhaps because it had been more drastically rewritten. 'Questi ceppi' (without the seven-bar ritornello) and 'Che veggio?' are in their shorter form. Apart from the abandoned 'È un sospir', 'Amor commanda' is the only vocal movement missing. The overture has oboes, not bassoons, for the thirds. 'Vanne, segui' is headed *Menuet*. All the music antedates the first production ('Lascioti' is unrevised), and it may have been copied about that time. It cannot reflect any of Handel's performances. The manuscript, in a smart red and gold contemporary binding with the bookplate of Sir Edward Stephenson of Farley Hall, was evidently commissioned by a patron with an alto voice or voices in the family. In this and other respects it has an exact parallel in the Durham copy of *Ottone*, Handel's next opera. Both could have been executed for the same person.[32]

In the Lennard copy (S1, 1736–40) both women are in the soprano clef and 'Mà un dolce' is in G minor. Although the score was copied later, it agrees with Malmesbury in omitting all 1722 additions and including Marche B. The chief differences are that the thirds in the overture are for bassoons, not oboes, 'Dimmi, O spene' (in G) has the revised voice part, as in HG, and lacks its repeat with changed words, 'Fuor di periglio' has the two top parts for horns, and Elmira in 'Ah mia cara' has the later soprano alternatives, except those in bars 28 and 32–3, which appear nowhere outside the Hamburg score. 'Lascioti' and 'Fuor di periglio' are in their final form, but 'Amor commanda' contains the bracketed bars before the first repeat. The B section of 'Questi ceppi' is incorporated in the text. There are a few performance markings, probably from after Handel's time, including occasional bass figures and the removal of some of the more taxing coloratura in 'Bramo te sola'.

The Flower score (S2, *c.* 1740) was copied directly from the autograph, and the Flower parts by the same hand from the Flower score. It omits all secco recitatives, both Marches and the Act III sinfonia, but includes every one of the unperformed pieces ('Mà un dolce' in D minor, 'Mà pria vedrò le stelle' in G minor, 'È un sospir', 'Gode l'alma' in D, 'Barbaro!' in B flat, 'Amor commanda' in G minor). Sometimes, but not always, it follows them with their replacements: 'Sospiro, è vero' (A minor), 'Gode l'alma' in B flat, 'Amor commanda' in B flat. 'Fuor di periglio' appears in its original form, with horns on the top staves but no oboes, followed at once by the revised voice parts and bass, as in the autograph. 'Dimmi, O spene' of course is in A major with B section, 'Ah mia cara' in F minor with all the autograph's unpublished variants; oboes are not only included but have independent staves. In 'Mà non s'aspetti' the copyist made two mistakes, writing 'sapesti' for the third and

---

[32] For similar aria collections from *Giulio Cesare* and *Admeto* transposed in the opposite direction, alto to soprano, see pp. 520–1.

fourth words (but not when they return in the last line) and indicating a da capo of the whole aria instead of the ritornello. 'Questi ceppi' has the A section only, with a note in Jennens's hand that the B section (not in the autograph) is to be found in 'Fragm. p. 89'. This can be identified as the Aylesford volume RM 18 c 10, the earliest of whose three foliations has the B section on p. 89. It suggests that Jennens may sometimes have owned volumes of excerpts before he ordered scores and parts, which would account for the frequent duplication of material. Jennens also supplied the tempo mark on 'Mà non s'aspetti' (which is in the parts) and the date and place ('à Londres') at the end of the *coro*. The only material not from the autograph is the full bass figuring of 'Alma mia', perhaps added by Jennens, who liked to perform, or hear performed, continuo arias of this type.

Apart from the omission of the overture and the revised 'Fuor di periglio', the parts (cembalo, violins 1 and 2, viola, cello + bassoon, oboes + *flauti* 1 and 2, trumpets 1 and 2, late 1740s) give the same version, with the usual sprinkling of errors. The horn parts of this set are in the music library of the University of Maryland. In 'Fuor di periglio' they are marked *ex F* but agree exactly with the two top staves in HG, suggesting that they are F horns written for some reason an octave above sounding pitch.[33] The cembalo part of 'Questi ceppi' has another note (by the copyist) *2^d part wanted See fragm: p. 89* and a blank page for its insertion, but it was not copied. Since the autograph often fails to specify scoring, S2 had to exercise his judgement over oboe parts. He omitted them from 'Dopo il nembo', 'Fuor di periglio', and 'Che veggio?' where they are added or implied in Hamburg, but included them in the ritornellos of 'Nò, non piangete', 'Vivere per penare' (despite *V. unis* in the autograph, which he omitted by accident in the Flower score), and 'Mia bella'. As usual they play in intermediate as well as main ritornellos, for example in 'Gode l'alma'. In the G minor 'Mà pria vedrò le stelle' (HG 125) they have five notes in bars 20–1 and rejoin the violins in bars 22–6 and 36–41 with the variants noted in the first ritornello in HG. They double the first violins, marked down to *pp*, in bars 16–17 of 'Sventurato' and have a few notes in bars 45–6 and 48–50 of 'Finchè lo strale'. In 'Ah mia cara' they double the violins but are independent in bars 43–6 and 59–63; this of course is the rejected autograph version. Both oboes double the top line in the ritornellos of 'Lascioti'. In 'Bramo te sola' the first oboe doubles the first violin in bars 4–7 and 82–5, only the second taking the lower part; both (erroneously) are given the solo beginning at bar 65. The cello part mentions bassoons in three numbers: 'Alma mia', where they are silenced until the full ritornello, 'Mà pria vedrò le stelle' (G minor) where bars 9–12 and 16–[21] are marked *Senza Basson*, and 'Fuor di periglio', where the part (except in the B section, which is *senza Bassoni*) is unusually explicit. It amplifies the autograph, supplying two staves and sometimes three parts, and distinguishing between bassoons (unison or divided), cellos, and double bass. (But see pp. 405–6.)

Berlin Mus MS 9055 is a late German copy of the 1721 version, apparently taken from the lost score of the Hamburg 1723 production. It contains the overture, 27 arias, and the accompanied recitative 'Sorte nemica', but not the secco recitatives, duets, March, or Act III sinfonia.

There are many copies of extracts from *Floridante*, mostly dating from the 1720s. Among the earliest is Fitzwilliam Mus MS 54, mentioned in connection

---

[33] The horn parts of the fragmentary sinfonia (I ii) in the performing score are similar.

with *Radamisto* and *Muzio Scevola*. It contains six arias written by the master of the exuberant C clef (Epsilon, *c.*1722), who was working with Smith; the latter's hand appears on the other side of f. 86. The arias are 'Vivere per penare', 'Se dolce m'era' (without viola part), 'Dimmi, O spene' without recitative but with the new words for the repeat, 'Godi, O spene', written below the bass line, 'Se risolvi', 'Sì, coronar', and 'Vanne, segui' without its closing ritornello. The keys are as in HG, except that 'Vanne, segui' is in E flat. Add MS 31571, ff. 62–7, has 'Dopo l'ombre' (Smith, *Allegro*) and the F major 'Lascioti' (H1); RM 18 b 4, ff. 26–40, *The New Songs of Floridante* with the singers' names, the last two again from 1722 (H1) and 'Amor ed empietà' and 'Parmi che giunta' from 1727 (S2); RM 18 c 3, ff. 2–4, another S2 copy of 'Amor ed empietà'[34] (*Additional Song in Floridante*); Manchester v. 313 (*Catalogue*, p. 51) a Smith copy of 'Notte cara'; Add MS 29386 a copy of 'Se risolvi' in G minor in an unrecognized hand; Bodleian MS Don c 69 an S2 copy of 'Dopo l'ombre' transposed down a fifth to B flat in association with five arias from Teofane's part in *Ottone*, also in alto keys. Handel may have intended to use it in the planned *Ottone* revival for which he wrote vocal ornaments in this manuscript.[35] One of a large collection of keyboard Minuets in RM 18 b 8 (f. 82) is a much simplified arrangement of 'O cara spene' (Smith junior, *c.*1728).

A substantial group in RM 18 c 10, ff. 27–82 (S2, *c.*1730), contains, in no particular order, both Marches, the Act III sinfonia (without oboes), the accompanied recitative 'Sorte nemica', the duet 'Fuor di periglio', and thirteen arias. Three of Durastanti's are present (not 'O cara spene'), and both settings of 'Amor commanda', the second unrevised as in the autograph. 'Dopo il nembo' and 'Lascioti' (as amended in Hamburg but marked *Largo*) are in the soprano versions of 1721, but 'Nò, non piangete' is missing, as are all Rossane's 1721 arias and all Elmira's. The others present are five of Floridante's ('Alma mia' and 'Mia bella' are the exceptions; 'Questi ceppi' has its B section) and Oronte's 'Che veggio?' in the shorter form. 'Fuor di periglio' is as published except for a new instrumental disposition, the top pair of staves allotted to violins and the second pair to oboes. In the B section cadence of 'O quanto è caro amor' the voice's two semiquavers on 'per' are an octave lower than in HG.

The *Floridante* overture was one of the few from the Royal Academy period that Handel did not arrange for harpsichord. A straight transcription appears in two Malmesbury volumes (H3, 1722; Smith, *c.*1728) and a copy of Walsh's hack arrangement (published in 1726) in RM 18 c 1,[36] ff. 21–2 (S2). The first Malmesbury volume also has keyboard transcriptions (Smith 1722) of Marche B and the opening of the Act III sinfonia, which after six bars diverges inconsequently into the *Rinaldo* Battaglia. The Coke Collection contains various excerpts and arrangements, including Marche B, the first 21 bars of 'Vanne, segui' as an instrumental minuet, ornamented versions of 'O cara spene' and 'Sì, coronar', and in '24 Opera Songs' 'Se risolvi' with many added trills and a few appoggiaturas.

---

[34] Yet another copy (S5), marked *Allegro*, is in the Fitzwilliam volume of 'Miscellanys', ascribed to *Admeto*, the opera for which it was written.

[35] See pp. 439 and 437.

[36] This volume contains a copy of 'Parmi che giunta' ascribed to *Radamisto*: see p. 347.

Walsh and the Hares issued the score, described as 'Publish'd by the Author' and including Handel's privilege, on 28 March 1722. According to Walsh's cash book, Handel received £72. As usual the recitatives (apart from the B section of 'Notte cara') are omitted, as well as the Marches and Act III sinfonia and (exceptionally) the singers' names. All the other movements performed in 1721 are included, but nearly all lack the second violin and viola parts. The only pieces with complete inner parts are the overture (with solo oboes for the bassoon thirds and slight variants from HG), 'Notte cara', and the *coro*. 'Fuor di periglio' lacks the two top staves and the viola part but includes the bassoons. 'Vanne, segui', described as *Menuet*, and 'Che veggio?' are followed by flute arrangements of the voice part in C and D minor respectively. 'Questi ceppi', lacking its seven introductory bars, and 'Che veggio?' are in the shorter form. 'Sospiro, è vero' (in A minor) is *Allegro ma non troppo*. Walsh must have obtained his copy in batches: although 'Lascioti' and 'Amor commanda' are in their final form as amended in Hamburg, and the score was not published till nearly four months after the production, 'Dimmi, O spene', a cavatina in G without the second set of words, has the high voice part of the autograph (with the longer final ritornello as in HG), and 'Ah mia cara' is still in F minor with a text much closer to the autograph than to the first (December 1721) version in the Hamburg score. The voice parts differ from the former only slightly in bars 89–91, and there are traces of the original upper instruments in 43–6, though the variants in 58–63 and the ritornello after the B section have gone. The bass is figured throughout the score.

Richard Meares published *All the Aditional* [sic] *Celebrated Aires*, engraved by T. Cross, on 26 January 1723. These were the five new arias for the December 1722 revival, with the singers named. Only 'O quanto è caro amor' (with the upper notes in the B section cadence) has its parts complete. 'Dopo l'ombre' is *Allegro*, as in RM 18 b 4 but nowhere else. Walsh issued a similar edition about the same time. He and Meares had each published a collection of favourite or celebrated songs in 1722, and Walsh advertised a flute arrangement on 19 May that year. Walsh's edition of the overture in parts (*c.*1725), like his score, has oboes for bassoons. Volume i of *The Pocket Companion* (May 1724) includes 'Alma mia', 'O cara spene', 'Se risolvi', and 'Finchè lo strale' in their original keys. There were various single-sheet publications of the last three with English words added, and also 'Vanne, segui'. One issue described the latter as 'A Favourit Song sung by Mrs Barbier in the Opera of Floridante', but it is unlikely that she ever sang in the opera, least of all in the soprano role of Rossane. 'Se risolvi' achieved two Paris publications with French words, in collections by J. C. B. Ballard ('Daphnis, profitons du temps', 1730) and Jean Dubreuil ('Lorsque deux cœurs d'un tendre feu', 1758).

Chrysander's score (1876) is a confusing mixture, not least in his choice of what to put in the body of the text and what in the appendix. For convenience of reference the salient facts are repeated here. The G minor 'Amor commanda' (in the main score), 'Mà pria vedrò le stelle' in G minor, and 'È un sospir' (in the appendix) were scrapped before performance, as were three unprinted arias of parallel status. Of the score performed in 1721, the cadences before 'È un sospir' (with five extra bars of recitative) and 'Lascioti' are replaced by later versions, and 'Sospiro, è vero' is in a later key. Four of the five new 1722 arias are in the body of the score ('Dopo l'ombre' without indication that it is an insertion), as are two transpositions for Timante, but his 'Lascioti' is relegated to the appendix. 'Questi ceppi' and 'Che veggio?' both existed in their longer form by the first night, though 'Che veggio?' seems always to have been sung as shortened. The two arias added in 1727 are not present.

Additional Notes

* (p. 408) There is a second copy in the Bodleian Library, Oxford.

* (p. 409) Clausen (*Göttinger Händel-Beiträge* IV, 1991, 108–33) now considers that RM 19 c 10 was always a continuo score, that the original full performing score of Act I has been lost (this may well be true), and that the G major transposition of 'Dopo il nembo' (MA/1018, ff. 47–9) was made for an unidentified alto Timante before the first performance and formed part of RM 19 c 10. There seems to be no solid support for this, or for the conjecture that the part was originally intended for Berselli, who is not known to have been in London after June 1721.

CHAPTER 20

OTTONE RÈ DI GERMANIA

THE Argument in the libretto is essential to an understanding of the plot.

Otho, Son to the Emperor Otho the Great, being sent by his Father into Italy, got there several Victories, not only over the Grecians, who, at that time, contended with the Germans for the Possession of it; but likewise over the Saracens, who continually infested the Sea Coasts. The former being forced into a Peace, he obtained Theophane, Daughter to Romano, Emperor of the East, who long before had been promised him for his Bride. Basilio was Brother to Theophane, who being drove out of Constantinople, by the Tyrant Nicephoro, liv'd so long in Exile, till he was call'd in by Zemisces, to have a part in the Empire. It is supposed, that this Prince, during his Exile, should turn Pirate, taking the Name of Emireno; and being ignorant of what past in Constantinople, should chace the Ships which brought Theophane to Rome, and should be overcome by those of Otho as he went to meet his Bride. It is likewise supposed, that Adelberto, Son to Berengario, a Tyrant in Italy, by the instigation of his Mother, here called Gismonda, should cause Rome to rebel against the Germans, who were not long e'er they retook it: This Action here attributed to the Second Otho, in History, is reckoned among those of Otho the Great. It is also a Fiction, that Theophane should fall in the Power of Adelberto, and that he should see her and fall in Love with her at the Time he was incognito at Constantinople. This occasions the greatest part of the Accidents which are seen in this Drama.

The action takes place in Rome and the neighbouring countryside, and begins just after Gismonda's *coup d'état*. In *a Gallery adorn'd with Statues* she persuades Adelberto, when he meets Teofane (who has never seen her future husband), to pose as Ottone while the latter is engaged with Emireno's Saracens. As Adelberto *goes to meet Theophane* Gismonda congratulates herself that her final hope is achieved. Adelberto *with Attendants* welcomes Teofane effusively as his bride. She, *looking on the Picture of Otho, which she has in her Bosom*, is shocked and puzzled by the discrepancy, for she has fallen in love with the Ottone of the portrait: she was sent to establish peace between Greece and Germany, 'not to raise an eternal War, between my Duty and Inclination'. The set changes to *Tents near the Sea, and Ships*. Emireno *with a Train of Soldiers and Slaves* has been captured by Ottone, but proudly refuses to disclose his identity and departs, *follow'd by Guards*. Ottone learns of Gismonda's seizure of Rome from his cousin Matilda, who is betrothed to Adelberto. Ottone's thoughts turn to love rather than action; when Matilda, disappointed in her hopes of bringing peace between the factions, asks for troops with which to punish Adelberto he hails her as 'brave German Amazon' and gladly agrees. She proposes to treat Adelberto with the fury of a woman scorned. In *a Royal Court, with a Throne on one Side*, Teofane fences with Gismonda (posing as Ottone's mother Adelaide) and is baffled by her praise for the heroism of the Berengario party; ironical asides make the position clear to the audience.

Adelberto *with Attendants* is about to lead Teofane to the altar when Gismonda enters suddenly, *takes hold on his Sword*, and tells him that Ottone and his Germans have broken into Rome with the support of the fickle populace. *Adelberto takes his Sword from Gismonda, and departs with her.* Teofane, aware that Adelberto is not Ottone but not of his true identity, is tormented by doubts and fears. The next scene brings another battle. *Part of Otho's Army drive back the Soldiers of Adelberto, who is disarm'd by Otho in a single Combat.* Ottone orders him to be imprisoned with Emireno and tortured to make him speak. Adelberto goes defiantly, wishing he had had one night in which to enjoy Teofane. Ottone, *alone*, proclaims peace and goodwill to guilty and innocent alike, and looks forward to the harbour of marriage after the storms of war.

Act II. *A Royal Court.* Matilda, meeting Adelberto *with Guards* on his way to prison, reproaches him for wooing her when he secretly loved Teofane; but her heart at once begins to soften at his fate, and she takes counsel with Gismonda. The latter dismisses with contempt the suggestion that they should beg Ottone for mercy; she prefers death for Adelberto and herself, but when Matilda has gone she reveals a mother's heart. Ottone and Teofane, meeting for the first time, approach each other cautiously *from different sides*, but are interrupted by Matilda, who throws herself at Ottone's feet. He refuses her plea for Adelberto's life, but pities and *embraces* her, watched by Teofane, who of course draws the wrong conclusion. Matilda goes out with a curse. Teofane now receives Ottone coldly and tells him to go to his other love. He in turn taxes her with looking favourably on Adelberto but finds her more attractive for her jealousy. *A Garden and Prospect of the Tiber, with Fountains and Grotto's; to one of which, leads a Subterranean Passage, clos'd up with a Stone. Night.* Teofane in her unhappiness welcomes darkness and prays to the god of love for pity. *Emireno and Adelberto coming out of a subterraneous Way* explain that they have been guided by written instructions, according to which a boat should be near at hand with some of Emireno's men. Looking forward to becoming once more the terror of the seas, Emireno goes in search of it. Matilda and Ottone enter *separately*, Matilda looking for the entrance to the secret passage, Ottone for Teofane, who reappears but draws back on seeing first Adelberto and then the others. She *goes towards the Grotto, and Adelberto hides.* Presently *she approaches nearer* to listen as Matilda tries to lure Ottone away from the grotto. The ruse succeeds after he has sung an aria proclaiming that he is not the sort of effeminate lover who talks to trees and birds. Emireno returns *with some of his Men*. Adelberto, *taking Theophane by her Arm*, carries her fainting to the boat. Emireno tells them to row for their lives. Gismonda meets the returning Matilda; they rejoice that their stratagem has worked and sing a duet in praise of night.

Act III. Ottone in *an Appartment* laments the loss of Teofane. Gismonda tells him gleefully that Adelberto and Emireno have escaped: even if Ottone kills her, as she expects, he will never be free from anxiety while Adelberto lives. Ottone assumes they have taken Teofane with them and laments his betrayal; he will not survive without her. *A Wood with a Prospect of the Tiber.* A storm has forced the escaping party to land. Emireno sends Adelberto to find a fisherman's hut as refuge, while Adelberto looks forward to Teofane's disdain changing to compassion. Emireno learns Teofane's identity but does not disclose his own. When she says that Ottone or her brother Basilio will avenge her, and explains that her guardian Cimisco (Zemisces) has ousted the usurper in Constantinople, *he goes to embrace her*. Both she and Adelberto, who returns at that moment, put the worst interpretation on this. Emireno places Adelberto under arrest, sends him away *with Guards*, assures Teofane that she has nothing to fear, and goes out, still offering no explanation. She invites Emireno's guards to kill her: though Ottone may be now in her rival's arms, she will never be unfaithful to him. In *a Royal Court*[1] Matilda tells Ottone that Adelberto has carried off Teofane. Gismonda exultantly explains that the escape was planned by Matilda. The latter however is now penitent, and promises to make amends by taking Adelberto's life. *As she is going away*, [she] *is suddenly stopt by Emireno*, who enters *with Adelberto in Chains*. Ottone orders Emireno's Moors to put him to death. Matilda demands this right, and *is going to stab him* when his confession causes her to drop the dagger. Gismonda upbraids her for weakness, seizes the dagger, and *attempts to kill herself*, but is prevented by the entry of Teofane. The lovers are happily united. Teofane explains that Emireno is her exiled brother Basilio. Gismonda and Adelberto abjure their nature and eat humble pie, swearing loyalty to Ottone. Matilda sets Adelberto free for the second time and accepts him as her husband.

As we might guess, this confused plot, which like that of *Muzio Scevola* could pass for a parody of *opera seria*, results from the clumsy compression of an earlier libretto. The source was *Teofane* by the Dresden court poet S. B. Pallavicino, written for the wedding of the Electoral Prince Frederick Augustus of Saxony to Maria Josepha, Archduchess of Austria, and produced at Dresden on 13 September 1719 in a setting by Antonio Lotti.[2] Handel was in Dresden for several months that summer and must have seen the opera;[3] he probably took a copy of the libretto back to London. (See Plates 3 and 4.)

As indicated in the Argument, which is identical for both librettos, the core of the story is historical. Otho II, Emperor of the West from 973 to 983, married Theophano the year before his accession, at the age of seventeen; he waged war on Greeks and Saracens with little success. It was his father Otho the Great, King of Germany from 936, who overthrew the tyrant Berengarius II (d. 966);[4] the two are compressed in the title as well as the plot of Handel's libretto. Basilio is the future Byzantine Emperor Basil II, a great soldier who reigned from 976 to 1025 and was known as the Slayer of the Bulgarians. Pallavicino seems to have exchanged the roles of the Emperor Nicephorus II Phocas, assassinated in 969, and the usurper Johannes Zimisces.

Pallavicino's libretto is a more substantial and coherent piece of work than Haym's abridgement for Handel. The dramatic motivation and the political and dynastic background are alike much clearer. An extra character helps here, the Greek prince Isauro, Teofane's escort from the Byzantine court. He too is in love with her; he tries to turn her dislike of Adelberto to his own advantage and deliberately inflames her jealousy of Ottone. His chief

---

[1] The heading is omitted from the English translation in the libretto.

[2] The printed libretto is a resplendent affair, as befits the occasion, with the text in Italian and French. It gives special credits to the scenic designer, choreographer, and composer of the ballet music.

[3] See p. 301. He could have seen two other operas by Lotti, *Giove in Argo* and *Ascanio*. For the festivities attending the opening of the new opera-house and the background to Handel's visit, see J. Gress, 'Händel in Dresden (1719)', *HJb* (1963), 135–49.

[4] Handel's *Lotario* deals with this part of the story.

importance however is that his presence allows much that remains obscure in Handel's plot to be satisfactorily explained. Pallavicino's Ottone is a heroic figure, generous in victory and obdurate in misfortune. In Act I he looks forward to pardoning Emireno for his gallantry in defeat. At the start of Act III, instead of meekly asking where Teofane is and lapsing into plaintive resignation, he has a big aria, torn between grief and anger; later he threatens Isauro, whom he suspects of treachery. He initiates action instead of sitting down under it. Teofane's agony between duty and inclination is more sharply drawn, and her dialogue with Emireno in III iv less absurd; she asks him to rescue her from Adelberto and put her in Cimisco's hands, if not Ottone's. Matilda is less of a weathercock, especially in Act III, where her change of heart has a stronger motive: she bitterly regrets helping to rescue Adelberto when she learns that he has abducted Teofane. Gismonda however is delighted, and it is to her that Matilda addresses 'Nel suo sangue', in a different context and with altered text;[5] she means to bathe herself in Adelberto's blood not to wash off her guilt but to satisfy her resentment. Gismonda is a veritable tigress: instead of the light-hearted 'La speranza' she has a vengeance aria, instead of 'Vieni, O figlio' a proud and contemptuous one. In the final scene it is Isauro who recognizes Emireno as Basilio from his likeness to his father Romano; Teofane confesses her jealousy of Matilda and asks Ottone to forgive his enemies; the duet 'A' teneri affetti' comes after all the loose ends have been tidied up.

Each act concludes with a spectacular allegorical finale featuring super-natural persons and elaborate ballet: La Felicità descending to bring back the golden age in Act I, Naiads and river gods in Act II, the Temple of Hymen in Act III, with La Germania inviting the shades of Ottone and Teofane to envy the royal lovers of 1719. Haym was of course right to abolish all this, but the skill with which Pallavicino integrated it into the plot is worth passing notice. The first *festa* is planned by Adelberto to celebrate his expected victory; when Ottone wins he orders it to proceed in honour of his own. The second, by the banks of the Tiber, is his official welcome to Teofane and Isauro; Gismonda and Matilda exploit it as a cover for the escape of the fugitives.

Lotti's immensely long score compares favourably with the operas of Bononcini, but suffers like them from excessive repetition and regularity of rhythm and phrase-length, two aspects in which Handel constantly outdis-tanced his contemporaries. It eschews the variety offered by cavatina, arioso, and accompanied recitative, but there are interesting points about the scoring. Corni di caccia play in the Italian overture and elsewhere; recorders are used quite extensively; Adelberto's 'Lascia che nel suo viso' is an extended virtuoso piece with obbligato for archlute or mandoline. This part, sung by Berselli, is more prominent than in Handel's opera and has some of the most difficult music; Lotti makes him a weaker, softer figure and even less of a warrior. Isauro, endowed with attractive music in a lighter style for which Lotti had a flair, was sung by the tenor Francesco Guicciardi, who had played Giuliano in *Rodrigo* at Florence and whom Handel tried to engage for the first season of the Royal Academy.[6] Senesino (Ottone), Durastanti (Gismonda), and Boschi

---

[5] Pallavicino's is identical with that of an aria in Keiser's Hamburg opera *Jodelet* (1726), where however the music is for a different voice.
[6] See his letter of 15 July 1719 to Lord Burlington from Dresden (Deutsch, 93).

(Emireno) sang the same parts in both operas,[7] and the vocal writing is very similar in style. The resemblance extends to the flat minor keys favoured by Boschi; the two settings of 'Le profonde vie' are identical in conception and key, though the music is different. Charlotte Spitz[8] not unreasonably found more psychological insight in Lotti's 'Alla fama' than in Handel's undistinguished aria.

The primary concern of Haym and Handel (who exercised final control and must share responsibility) was to compress. As usual in London, the treatment of the recitative was drastic; whereas Pallavicino's libretto runs to nearly 1,100 lines, Haym's has fewer than 700. But although the process was carried too far, not all changes were for the worse. Some had an artistic motive, and recur constantly in Handel's operas of the Royal Academy period and later: for example the provision of a cavatina at the beginning of the first and third acts (Pallavicino began Act I with recitative and Act III with a full-scale aria), and the removal of numerous mid-scene solos in favour of exit arias that bring the emotional content of a scene to a more powerful climax. *Teofane* contains nine mid-scene pieces (eight arias, and a duet for Ottone and Teofane when they first meet in the scene corresponding to Handel's II v); Haym and Handel removed eight of them and placed the other, 'Falsa imagine', at the end of a scene. In *Teofane* the duet ''A' teneri affetti' ends the opera proper, the final chorus crowning the allegorical section; Haym and Handel continued the scene after the duet and added the *coro*. They cut a couple of vacuous nature pieces, Teofane comparing herself with a swallow confronted by a snake in Pallavicino's I iv and Gismonda requesting assistance from the breezes in II xiii (neither scene occurs in Handel's opera). 'Tu puoi straziarmi' (I xi) and 'Nò, non temere' (III v) replace (in modified contexts) much less effective arias after which the singer remains on stage. Four important scenes, all soliloquies, have no counterpart in Pallavicino: I x (Teofane with 'Affanni del pensier'), II iv (Gismonda with 'Vieni, O figlio'), II vii (Ottone with 'Dopo l'orrore'), and II viii (Teofane's accompanied recitative and aria at the start of the garden scene). To these we may add the reshaping of II iii to admit a pathetic aria ('Ah! tu non sai') for Matilda, who has none at this point in *Teofane*. As Eisenschmidt was the first to point out, the insertion of highly charged emotional texts not in the sources is characteristic of Handel's London librettos, and was undoubtedly prompted by the composer.

Apart from the suppression of Isauro, almost certainly due to the absence of a suitable singer, Haym and Handel did not greatly alter the relative prominence of the characters. They reduced Ottone's and Adelberto's parts by two solos each and Emireno's by one, but increased Matilda's ration from three to four for the benefit of Anastasia Robinson. Of the 34 arias and three duets (excluding the allegorical finales) in Pallavicino's libretto, Handel set eighteen arias and two duets, three of the arias twice and several with modified words. Not all of these were sung in January 1723: 'Io sperai trovar riposo', 'Non tardate a festeggiar', 'Non a tempre', 'Dir li potessi', and possibly 'Cervo altier'[9] were rejected, though some of these texts reappeared later. The

---

[7] Boschi was to repeat two of his *Teofane* arias in London in Handel's pasticcio *Elpidia*: see p. 321.

[8] 'Die Opern "Ottone" von G. F. Händel (London 1722) und "Teofane" von A. Lotti (Dresden 1719); ein Stilvergleich', *Festschrift zum 50. Geburtstag Adolf Sandberger* (Munich, 1918), 265–71.

[9] This aria, of uncertain date, was sung in 1726; 'Non tardate a festeggiar' was not heard till 1733, but survives in more than one copy of about ten years earlier.

Pallavicino pieces sung at the first performance (the asterisks indicate text modifications) were the arias *'Bel labbro', 'Falsa imagine', 'Del minacciar del vento', 'Diresti poi così?', 'Pensa ad amare', 'Dall'onda', 'Lascia che nel suo viso', 'All'orror', 'Alla fama', *'Le profonde vie', 'Deh! non dir', *'Trema, tiranno', 'D'inalzar i flutti', and *'Nel suo sangue', and the duet 'A' teneri affetti'. The relationship between the two librettos is confused by the numerous changes made by Handel between composition and performance,[10] and by Chrysander's misleading score, a mixture of at least five versions. Handel's revisions, due partly to cast changes and singers' preferences, were not entirely happy. He undermined Ottone's heroic status in I v and III ii by substituting a simple love song ('Ritorna, O dolce') for the more complex aria of disappointment ('Io sperai trovar'), and the plaintive 'Tanti affanni' for the bitterly defiant 'Non a tempre',[11] in both cases after setting the original texts. Like Verdi, Handel sometimes jumped a step in motivation in order to express a simple heartfelt emotion where the context demands something less clear-cut. It is interesting to note that in both these scenes he became aware of the weakness and remedied it by writing new arias in 1726, although the singer (Senesino) was the same.

As it stands Haym's libretto ranks low in his work for Handel, far beneath *Radamisto*, *Flavio*, *Tamerlano*, *Giulio Cesare*, and *Rodelinda*. Everything happens far too quickly and without sufficient explanation; by obscuring the characters' motives he makes their behaviour seem inconsequent and the plot ridiculous, especially in Act III, where his attempt to save time left a series of jerky *non sequiturs* and one of the most perfunctory of happy ends. He bungled Matilda's important change of heart in III vii by conflating two scenes in Pallavicino (ix and x), the first of them between Matilda and Gismonda before Ottone's arrival, and reduced the recognition scenes (III iv and *ult.*) to absurdity. Instead of a dashing leader Ottone becomes a static mouthpiece for amorous yearning. Against this must be set the surer dramatic handling of the arias, the well-placed initial cavatinas in Acts I and III, and a few strokes of real imagination such as the substitution of the romantic duet 'Notte cara' for 'Non tardate a festeggiar' and the repetition of Teofane's 'Ma! tal'è Otton? tale il mio sposo?' in the recitative of I iii. Several of Haym's new aria texts inspired some of the finest music in the opera; but a considerable price had to be paid.

In Handel's greatest operas the structural stresses between the articulation of the plot and the development of the characters are perfectly reconciled. This is not the case with *Ottone*, which despite much eloquent music gives the impression of being designed on no larger principle than to ring the emotional changes until it is time for the curtain to fall. Though all the characters have splendid moments, none carries total conviction; they are like puppets obeying a jerk of the string. Performance in the theatre yields none of those startling revelations common in operas like *Tamerlano* and *Alcina* but seldom predictable from the score. Handel can do little except illuminate single episodes and

[10] Shown in Table 6, p. 433.
[11] Chrysander's theory (ii. 94) that Cuzzoni's success with 'Affanni del pensier' induced Handel, later in the run, to write a similar aria in the same key and mood for Senesino is ruled out by the fact that 'Tanti affanni' was sung at the first performance. But some such episode could have occurred during rehearsals.

reactions; he often does this with marvellous penetration, especially in the tragic scenes. But this is a patchy score whose parts scarcely add up to a whole. It has more pedestrian arias than usual at this period, and a surprising number of them are placed in the mouth of hero and heroine. Even so there is a rich largesse of melody. Burney, who was not concerned with character or dramatic unity, praises almost every item. 'The number of songs in this opera that became national favourites, is perhaps greater than in any other that was ever performed in England . . . Indeed, there is scarce a song in the opera, that did not become a general favourite, either vocally or instrumentally. And the passages in this and the other operas which Handel composed about this time, became the musical language of the nation, and in a manner proverbial, like the *bons mots* of a man of wit in society.' This catchiness led Streatfeild to accuse Handel of writing down to his audience in imitation of the simple tunes of Bononcini (he excepts 'Affanni del pensier', 'Vieni, O figlio', and 'Tanti affanni'). If Bononcini had been able to invent tunes of such calibre he would be more remembered today.

Ottone is among the more insipid of Handel's castrato heroes, thanks to the authors' wilful abandonment of the character drawn by Pallavicino. In the January 1723 score they used the Dresden libretto for two of his weaker arias only. When he hears that Gismonda has seized his capital and his bride (I v) he sings a pathetic love song and tells Matilda to get on with the fighting. In the garden scene (II x) he allows her to lead him away after an aria denying that he is an unmanly lover, a sentiment that his behaviour emphatically contradicts. In III ii, confronted with the news of the prisoners' escape and Teofane's disappearance, so far from reaching for his sword and pulverizing his enemies he assumes the worst and says he cannot survive without her. He has no part in her recovery and scarcely deserves to benefit from it. Senesino was at his best in scenes of pathos, but he could play the hero too; there is nothing effeminate or self-indulgent about Giulio Cesare.

Neither of Ottone's bravura arias attains Handel's usual standard. 'Dell'onda' is a mechanical simile aria with an excess of rhythmic repetition and vacuous note-spinning. It is rare indeed to find Handel in his maturity ending an act as feebly as this. 'Dopo l'orrore' (II vii) is better but still routine. The contrast between angular main theme and flowing coloratura is ably treated, and so is the extension of the same material in the B section; but despite the euphonious string writing the music is faceless. There are indications, in the even string chords against syncopated vocal melody, of the new 'Neapolitan' style that Handel was to employ with much greater assurance in *Ariodante* and *Atalanta*. 'Ritorna, O dolce' is a lightly accompanied siciliano love song of great charm and no little subtlety, especially in melodic extensions and rhythmic variants within the phrase. The touch of the tonic minor towards the end of the first part is exquisite. The ritornello was to supply material for the symphony in Act II of *Jephtha*. 'Deh! non dir' is purely decorative; the music, as elsewhere in Handel, depicts not the emotion of the character but what his tongue denies. It is a bird song of conventional cut that makes excessive use of the two chirpy accompaniment figures, marked *forte* and *piano*.

The greatest music in Ottone's part comes early in Act III. 'Dove sei?' is a glorious outburst of lyrical melody, half agitated and half serene, as distinguished in its way as the famous aria beginning with the same words in

Rodelinda. The long richly scored ritornello, and indeed the whole piece, is dominated by the dotted figure introduced in bar 6 in the top line (first violins and all oboes) with its dying fall, generally of a sixth but sometimes more or less, especially when it returns in the B section. The singer never has it, though his rhythm, as befits an anxious lover, is sometimes dotted and sometimes smooth (the lower notes are the original). The suggestion of longing in the drooping vocal line is reinforced by suspensions and appoggiaturas in the orchestra. Handel in 1723 performed 'Dove sei?' as a cavatina, but he composed a second part in two successive versions. Chrysander incomprehensibly prints only the first, although the second, which deviates at bar 53, is not only much the finer but is in the performing score and most copies. It contains one of the boldest of Handel's enharmonic modulations:

Ex. 49

(. . . you alone can give me help; you alone can grant me joy)

The F minor scena 'Io son tradito'–'Tanti affanni' ranks with such a superb evocation of tragic despair as Radamisto's 'Ombra cara'. Both the long accompanied recitative and the aria (*Largo* and *Larghetto* respectively) have an intensity of emotional expression beyond the reach of Handel's contemporaries except Bach. The quiet opening of the recitative with an abrupt drop of a tone from the fiery G minor of Gismonda's aria is a pointer to Ottone's despair. Striking features are the crossing parts, especially the second violin's top G in bar 3 after following the first in canon, and the collapse from the resolute dotted rhythm and major key of bars 10–14 to further doubts, diminished chords, and a woeful B flat minor cadence. The anguished chromaticism and intricate part-writing of the aria is not far removed from the Bach of the Passions, but the technique is personal to Handel, dependent not on the interweaving of obbligato lines but on an empirical texture in which first one part, then another, and sometimes more than one (the cello operating in high positions with the viola while the harpsichord is silenced) takes up the mournful slurred-quaver figuration. The string parts are carefully bowed and full of subtle detail in harmony and imitation; the sequences have a relentless urgency that probes the depths of grief. One phrase from the ritornello returns divided between first violin and voice. The two parts of the aria are united by similarity and contrast: the material is related, but the string texture of the B section is closer and more concentrated, without a rest anywhere. Whereas the first part remains in the minor throughout, the second raises momentary hope by beginning in the relative major, only to sink into the despair of A flat minor and E flat minor, further darkened by suspensions and chromatic alterations. Perhaps the most memorable stroke of all is the unexpected stab of A flat minor when the major seems to have been regained three bars from the end. After this great outburst Ottone is mute until the love duet in the last scene, a light piece with attractive syncopation in the favourite rhythm of the nightingale chorus in *Solomon*. The whole act declines after 'Tanti affanni', as if Handel despaired of holding the libretto together.

Teofane has little to do but suffer the slings and arrows appointed for a princess who is never in control of her destiny. Her jealousy of Ottone is unconvincing, and in any case not expressed in an aria. She is one of the least interesting of Handel's Royal Academy heroines, perhaps because the part was not conceived for a single singer. Although sung by Cuzzoni, most of it was not written for her; the five original arias[12] show no sign of the sensuous warbling and trilling for which she was renowned, and very little bravura of any kind. The two Act I arias are the best. 'Falsa imagine', which Cuzzoni only consented to sing under threat of summary defenestration by the enraged composer,[13] according to Burney 'fixed her reputation as an expressive and pathetic singer'. Except for the little string ritornello after the da capo, at once a return to seventeenth-century practice and a stroke of genius, it is a continuo aria of the utmost simplicity but rare artfulness. The eloquent bass line throws into relief the words and the melody, which perfectly enshrines the hesitant mood, compounded of longing and disappointment, in which the girl contemplates the portrait that has deceived her. Notable once more is the mixture of dotted and smooth rhythms, and the exquisite interrupted cadence just before

[12] For the involved history of the part, see below, pp. 432 ff.

[13] Mainwaring tells the story in a footnote. Handel said he knew she was a veritable devil; she must learn to recognize him as Beelzebub, prince of devils. Evidently she did; she was to sing 'Falsa imagine' at her last London concerts nearly 30 years later.

the end of the first part. Handel was a master of these straightforward utterances which in another composer are so often nugatory. 'Affanni del pensier' is far more intense: threatened with forced marriage to a stranger she does not love, she breaks into a passionate lament, all the more heart-rending for its slow tempo and lilting 12/8 rhythm. Like 'Tanti affanni' it is in F minor, full of dissonance and closely woven counterpoint, which persists (scaled down in dynamics) while the voice sings and creates a genuine five-part texture. The chromaticism of the fourth bar, varied in the ritornello after the A section and never returning in identical form, and the nervy suspensions, most exposed at the first vocal entry, are signals of acute suffering. The main theme with its mixture of stepwise motion and wide leaps, treated first in canon, yields many surprises in both parts of the aria.

After Act I Teofane fades from the picture. Her two quick arias, like Ottone's, are substandard. 'Alla fama' does not live up to its charming ritornello; the music strikes a note of flippancy that belies the character etched in 'Affanni del pensier'. For once Handel seems to have mistaken the *Affekt*. 'Benchè mi sia', Teofane's only aria in Act III as first performed, is an uninspired rewriting from an early cantata.[14] It is not surprising that Handel later gave Cuzzoni more to do here. The nocturnal *scena* in the garden (II viii) is a different matter. The accompanied recitative 'O grati orrori', incomplete in HG (the viola part is available in the Fitzwilliam autograph and many copies), is very fine, though an expression of mood rather than a dramatic gesture. The divided bassoons, perhaps intended to suggest the dark banks of the Tiber, add a touch of romantic mystery welcome in this plainly scored opera. The music is very carefully composed, with searching progressions, a splendid first phrase for the voice that halts on the major seventh over a tonic pedal ('orrori!') and a cyclic form, the first eight bars returning (compare 'Chi vide mai' in *Tamerlano* and 'O sventurati affetti' in *Scipione*) to introduce the aria. There is some doubt as to which aria was sung here at the first performance (Handel tried no fewer than four within a year); it was either the unpublished C minor setting of 'S'or mi dai pene' (in the libretto) or 'S'io dir potessi' (printed by Walsh). The presence of the former in the Malmesbury score, its placing in the Flower copy, and the fact that it seems tailored to Cuzzoni's voice suggest that it had the preference. One cannot easily imagine Handel abandoning it for the less showy 'S'io dir potessi', which exists in fewer copies and never in its context. Probably Handel composed 'S'io dir potessi' between the two settings of 'S'or mi dai pene', but he may have performed both arias on different occasions. Both are worthy of him. 'S'or mi dai pene' is a fluent piece full of cross-rhythms with a rapid exchange of fire between voice and violins and a particularly good B section, in which the ritornello of the first part intrudes unexpectedly in G minor and is imitated by the voice in canon. 'S'io dir potessi' is a plaintive Largo based on a discarded aria in Act III. The spare accompaniment does not forbid expressive counterpoint for first violin and voice. The latter's initial phrase, not anticipated in the ritornello, begins with the same four notes as Theodora's 'Fond flattering world, adieu!' and the mighty pronouncement 'Whatever is, is right' in *Jephtha*. According to Burney this scene 'had a great effect in the performance, as I have often been assured by persons who heard the opera performed'. Nevertheless Handel always omitted it after 1723.

Gismonda has as much solo music as Teofane, and its range is wider. She

---

[14] 'Benchè tradita io sia' in 'Manca pur quanto sai' (HWV 129, summer 1708).

launches the opera with a characteristic cavatina–cabaletta design, an anxious Larghetto in G minor followed by an exuberant aria in F major,[15] linked by the appearance of the words 'più bramar non sò' in both. 'Pur che regni' is unusual in rhythm, colour, and mood. Handel's introductory cavatinas are seldom in 12/8 time. It is not a siciliano; the shape of the phrases suggests a gigue, except that the tempo is *Larghetto*. The strangely jerky ritornello is almost entirely in unison or octaves, yet the instrumental colour constantly changes, and violins and bass are both adorned with mordents and trills. The voice part is doubled irregularly by the oboe, which picks out a phrase here and there while the violins alternate between the gangling rhythm of the first bar and comments of their own that sometimes conform to the voice and sometimes imitate it. The music conveys a vivid picture of the ambitious but uneasy Queen. The gaiety of 'La speranza' is arguably not in character. It suggests rather the excitement of a young girl attending her first dance; but Handel may have intended to convey a touch of hectic self-assurance after her hesitation in the recitative about carrying through her plot. The melody is delightful and justly famous, the ritornello cleverly articulated from phrases of $2 + 4 + 4$ bars; the regular rhythms of the voice part are softened by a little deft counterpoint from the violins. If the first phrase has a faint flavour of the *Messiah* 'Hallelujah', that of her next aria, 'Pensa ad amare', might be a remote ancestor of 'Let the bright Seraphims'. The melody with its dancing violin trills,[16] very lightly turned, serves admirably for Gismonda's dissembling approach to Teofane; Handel hints at a certain imperiousness in the short choppy phrases and repetitions, which have a not inappropriate flavour of the Second Harlot in *Solomon*.

Gismonda scarcely emerges as a consistent character, least of all as the domineering matriarch postulated by the text. In Act II Handel almost overbalances the opera by giving her one of the most ravishing arias he ever wrote. Like 'Pensa ad amare', 'Vieni, O figlio' is in E major, not a tyrant's key, and it captures all our sympathy for this unscrupulous woman's love of her weak and equally unscrupulous son. Handel soars beyond the context to give immortal expression to a basic human emotion. The resemblance to 'I know that my redeemer liveth' (compare the dotted accompaniment figure in bars 27–9 and later) and 'My breast with tender pity swells' in *Hercules* is too strong to be missed. The dotted figure echoes another sublime inspiration, 'Heart, the seat of soft delight' in *Acis and Galatea*. Here it suggests the son cradled on his mother's breast; Gismonda instinctively looks back to Adelberto's childhood. The design of 'Vieni, O figlio' is all its own. The single ritornello, at the end of the A section, is a lingering twelve-bar extension of what has gone before, as if Gismonda remains wrapped in her feelings long after the voice is silent. It is not a repetition but a development; the dotted figure, hitherto confined to two appearances on second violins and bass, begins to spread over the whole orchestra, reaching the first violins six bars before the end. It continues, still drooping downwards by semitones, to dominate the B section, which begins exceptionally in the tonic to ensure a seamless continuity before rising to an

---

[15] The original G major aria gave greater tonal unity, but is musically less striking. Its hour was to come in *Belshazzar*, where Handel attached the ritornello to words of very different import ('Let the deep bowl').

[16] They may have been intended for the voice as well in unison passages, and appear thus in at least one copy.

impassioned climax as it passes through a chromatic C sharp minor to end in
G sharp minor. The aria is rich in detail: the deliciously unexpected rise of a
seventh in the fifth bar, the voice's varied phrase-lengths (three and five bars
at the beginning, twelve at the end of the first part), and the chromatic touch
on the word 'mori' at bar 31, echoed with sublime effect towards the end of the
ritornello but unspoiled by anticipation.

This does not exhaust Gismonda's part. She and Matilda conclude Act II
with a most original duet addressed to seeling night. Nearly all Handel's duets
at the end of acts are for lovers parting in adversity after swearing eternal
faith. Here two scheming women indulge in romantic fantasy, the voices
beautifully intertwined, sometimes in canon, against a light accompaniment,
half dreamy, half ironical, that chips in at irregular intervals in both sections.
There is a resemblance to the duet for Admeto and Antigona towards the end
of *Admeto*, where the dramatic situation again holds an ironic potential, and at
bars 18 and 19 a foretaste of 'For unto us a child is born'. Only in Gismonda's
last aria, 'Trema, tiranno', does Handel suggest the character drawn by
Pallavicino. The music, though lively, lacks the incisiveness of the rest of her
part and seems a dim echo of the fiery style of *Radamisto*.

Over Matilda too Handel seems at odds with his librettist; he certainly
endeavours to mask the impression of capricious inconsistency left by Haym.
'Diresti poi così?' is one of his finest arias depicting a character at the mercy of
conflicting moods. She denounces Adelberto's treachery in the recitative, but
the love she cannot dispel makes her hesitate, and the aria begins without
ritornello with a timid question moving from a first inversion to the dominant,
echoed very quietly by the upper strings. It is some time before the tonic
receives any emphasis, as if she dare not face the truth. The contrast between
the repeated question and the violins' creeping slurred-quaver figure underlines her indecision. Suddenly her anger breaks loose in the B section, with a
sharp change of rhythm, pace, and tonality, a rapid 3/8 in solid G major
against a sprinkling of resolute chords from the orchestra. This tonal firmness
reverses the normal procedure of the aria, since for the moment the struggle is
resolved. But not for long: the return to the da capo is imaginatively contrived,
with the initial question poised a third higher, ending not on the dominant but
on the chord of the leading note (D major), and the next four bars omitted, as
in the middle of the first part. The question seems more urgent and the tonic
more remote. The aria is a subtle portrait of a woman in love against her will
with a man she despises.

With Adelberto in prison Matilda's love is rekindled. 'Ah! tu non sai',
addressed to her enemy Gismonda, is an aria of touching pathos. Again
Handel's artistry shines in the treatment of the ritornellos. The introduction
for unison violins and bass stresses the slurred semiquaver figure with its
forlorn open fourths and fifths that governs the whole aria; the coda to the A
section combines this with material derived from the entirely different rhythm
of the voice and gives it expanded treatment for strings in four parts.
'All' orror' again fuses two moods, anger at her cousin's refusal to pardon
Adelberto and the sympathy she hoped to find in him, but in a manner
different from 'Diresti poi così?'. The first eight bars present three sharply
divergent ideas: a resolute arpeggio phrase for voice and violins in unison,[17] a

---

[17] Chrysander prints the autograph version, which Handel altered before performance,
removing the octaves and adding an independent bass, as in bars 9 and 10. He also rewrote bars
15–17.

brief *Adagio pianissimo* of three bars supported by four-part strings without harpsichord, and an angular ritornello with seething semiquavers for violins. The main body of the aria is based on the first and third of these, but scarcely lives up to the promise of the opening. Like that of the other characters except Ottone, Matilda's music declines in Act III. The second (3/8) setting of 'Nel suo sangue' was sung in 1723. Handel reset the words to please the singer; while neither version is exceptional, the first has a livelier pulse. The two have nothing in common except a chromatic passage over a descending bass which appears in both parts of the earlier but only in the B section of the later setting, and then at a different point in the text ('Se l'infido io svenerò').

Handel could not withhold sympathy from the despicable Adelberto, whose two slow arias in the minor, 'Bel labbro' and 'Lascia che nel suo viso', are both admirable. They are alike in having no initial ritornello, but a richly scored one for full orchestra after a first section sparely supported by unison violins. In 'Bel labbro' the ritornello has an inner part for viola and bassoon in longer notes. This is a beautiful aria in sarabande rhythm with eloquent harmonic touches; the violins, entering late, imitate the voice at a distance and are so impressed with its first paragraph that they repeat it a third higher before hovering protectively above on a dominant and then a subdominant pedal. The final cadence of the B section is cleverly designed so that the voice begins the da capo by overlapping and imitating it. Handel makes a neat point at the start of 'Lascia che nel suo viso', where the recitative leads us to expect an aria from Matilda, not Adelberto. The violins simply double the voice *pianissimo* at the octave and are silent in the B section, but this enhances the impact of the ten-bar ritornello, which is more than half the length of the first part and collects the full emotional weight of the aria. This is considerable, thanks to the harmony that takes a Neapolitan direction but defies the expectation of the ear; its further development in the ritornello emphasizes the mood of pleading. Adelberto's other arias are less interesting. 'Tu puoi straziarmi' is a conventional and rather short-breathed statement of defiance, 'D'inalzar i flutti' with its prancing triplets a simile aria that strikes a note of irrelevance when the action is approaching its climax. It uses a violin figure from Ottone's discarded 'Non a tempre'.

Emireno's three arias are very alike in style, rapid and rumbustious, with voice and instrumental bass nearly always in unison and the upper parts usually conforming at the octave; only the ritornellos vary the texture. This jolly pirate is more consistent than the other characters, but he is confined to a single facet, a reflection no doubt of the good heart but limited intelligence his behaviour indicates. Boschi, it seems, unlike his successor Montagnana, could seldom be trusted with slow music; Handel restricted him to extrovert rumblings, whether of anger or a more genial bluster. The first two arias, especially 'Del minacciar del vento' with its image of an ancient oak bent in all directions by the wind but remaining firmly rooted, have a flavour of some nautical Polyphemus. 'Le profonde vie', like 'Il Tricerbero umiliato' in *Rinaldo*, would have made a lusty drinking song for the taverns. 'Nò, non temere', an exuberant dance, draws sustenance from occasional variety in rhythm.

The overture was almost certainly not composed for the opera, and never preceded it in the form printed in HG 1–11. It seems to have been an independent piece, adapted for *Ottone* as described in Chrysander's preface:

the introduction, in the form printed on HG 144, led to the second fugal Allegro (7–11) followed by the Gavotte (6–7). The whole overture is first-rate Handel. The introduction in eight parts (three violins, three woodwind) is splendidly rich and massive, the fugue scarcely less so; the concertino episodes for oboes over a pedal are particularly attractive. The catchy Gavotte became immensely popular; Burney says it 'was the delight of all who could play, or hear it played, on every kind of instrument, from the organ to the salt-box'. The energetic Vivace[18] used as a battle piece in I iv, published later by Walsh as the first movement of the inchoate concerto Op. 3 no. 6, may also have originated in an independent overture, the work in D major (HWV 337) first published in volume 15 of the HHA Instrumental Music (1979). The autographs are in the same volume (RM 20 g 13, ff. 1–4 and 29–32). The editor of HWV 337, Terence Best, notes the irregularity of its form, in which a typical French Overture Largo ending on the dominant leads to an Adagio in B minor, and suggests that the *Ottone* Vivace, not the Largo, was the first movement. It seems even more likely that it followed the Largo as the second. In any event there is a good deal of thematic interconnection between HWV 337, both forms of the *Ottone* overture, and that of *Giulio Cesare*. The first movement of the latter is related to the Largo of HWV 337; the second, in a different key, was originally part of the ur-*Ottone* overture (HG 2–5); the finale of HWV 337 was recomposed as its other fugal Allegro (HG 7–11).

Op. 3 no. 6, or at least the Vivace, seems to have become known as 'the Concerto in Otho'. Three string parts (the second marked *Viola, Viol: 3rd*) of a Minuet in D major with this title, which may have been the finale (missing in the printed scores), are in the Fitzwilliam Museum in the hand of the younger Smith (Mus MS 265, 91–3). It is a substantial movement in four sixteen-bar paragraphs, each marked for repetition. The rests in the third and fourth paragraphs show that parts for wind or keyboard are missing. The music is related to the last movement of the organ concerto Op. 4 no. 1, and more remotely to that of the trio sonata Op. 5 no. 6. There is no evidence that it was ever used in *Ottone*. The Fitzwilliam also contains the autograph of a brief but very effective sinfonia in II xi (HG 77), before Emireno's words 'Movete, O fidi'. It accompanied the embarcation of the escape party in Emireno's ship, and appears (sometimes the bass only) in most copies, though its absence from the Malmesbury score implies that it was added after the first performance.

Ex. 50

<hr>

[18] This word is in the RM 20 g 13 autograph, but not in Chrysander's score of the concerto.

The scoring, like that of *Floridante*, is less ambitious than in most of the Royal Academy operas. Handel confined it to oboes, bassoons (divided once for a few bars), strings, and continuo. There are no trumpets, horns, or transverse flutes; the recorders in 'Deh! non dir' are in Walsh but not the autograph. Only the overture is conceived on a grander scale, though Handel's treatment of the strings is as resourceful as ever throughout the opera. The tonal scheme is worked out with some care.[19] The opera begins and ends (with a rather perfunctory *coro*) in B flat; Act I begins in the relative G minor and ends in B flat; Act II has a first aria in G minor and ends in F; Act III begins in D minor. All the more accessible flat minor keys are prominent; including accompanied recitatives no fewer than fifteen movements are in D, G, C, and F minor. Each act makes occasional excursions into a sharp key for contrast, but they amount to only eight movements out of 35 and are very rare after Act I. The progressions from recitative to aria are regular. The A minor cadence on HG 15 led to 'La speranza'; it was changed to G minor when the aria was put down to E flat. The F sharp minor cadence on HG 52 led to 'Pensa, spietata madre' (D major, HG 136); when 'Ah! tu non sai' followed, the last three bars were rewritten to end in E minor or major.

History and Text

The date of completion at the end of the main autograph (RM 20 b 9) is 10 August 1722; but Handel heavily revised the score at least twice before the public heard it. It is likely that, as with *Floridante* in 1721 and *Giulio Cesare* in 1723, he began it before his company for the following season was finally settled. But this cannot be the sole explanation, for the revisions affected all six characters (without altering the pitch of the voices). Senesino, Boschi, and Anastasia Robinson remained of the old company; Durastanti and Berenstadt, who had sung in earlier London seasons, returned in the autumn; Cuzzoni did not arrive till the last days of December, a bare fortnight before the production. The *London Journal* had mentioned her engagement as early as 27 October, when it announced that 'there is a new Opera now in Rehearsal at the Theatre in the Hay-Market, a Part of which is reserv'd for one Mrs Cotsona, an extraordinary Italian Lady, who is expected daily from Italy'. If this refers to *Ottone*, Handel must have delayed the production to await the arrival of the new prima donna; that could account for the confusion in the press about the dates of the *Muzio Scevola* revival in the autumn. The part of Teofane was perhaps intended for Maddalena Salvai, the principal soprano of the 1721–2 season; of its original five arias only the first three were sung by Cuzzoni.

The diabolical complexity of *Ottone*'s textual history, more daunting than that of any other Handel opera, is compounded by the disappearance of the first two acts of the performing score and Chrysander's failure to use (or discover) much of the autograph material, quite apart from Handel's repeated revisions before and after the first production. Since Chrysander's score gives a confusing idea of what was performed in 1723—he printed much music that was never sung, omitted some that was included (as well as several more rejected pieces), and printed later additions in the main text (the B

---

[19] The original scheme of the autograph was slightly different, but several pieces were in the same key as their replacements.

setting of 'Io son tradito', 'Un disprezzato affetto', 'Gode l'alma')—it seems best to disentangle the main threads here. Eleven complete arias and one duet were removed before performance and several others revised, some of them extensively. The suppressed pieces and their replacements are shown in Table 6.

*

TABLE 6

		Arias	Replaced by
I	i.	'Giunt' in porto'	'La speranza'
	v.	'Io sperai trovar' (version A, D major, HG 130)	'Ritorna, O dolce'
II	iii.	'Pensa, spietata madre' (HG 136)	'Ah! tu non sai'
	viii.	'S'or mi dai pene' (G minor, 3/4, unpublished) 'S'io dir potessi'	'S'or mi dai pene' (C minor, 4/4, unpublished)
	ix.	'Le profonde vie' (C major, unpublished)	'Le profonde vie' (C minor)
	xii.	'Non tardate a festeggiar' (duet, unpublished)	'Notte cara' (composed first, ousted and restored)
III	ii.	'Non a tempre'	'Tanti affanni'
	iii.	'A te lascio'	'D'inalzar i flutti'
	v.	'Qual cervetta'	'Nò, non temere' (in v, not vii)
	vi.	'Dir li potessi'	'Benchè mi sia'
	vii.	'Nel suo sangue' (version A^a, 4/4)	'Nel suo sangue' (version A^b, 3/8)

Handel used material from five of the suppressed pieces to a greater or lesser degree in later compositions for the same opera: 'Non a tempre' in 'D'inalzar i flutti', 'Qual cervetta' in the C minor 'Le profonde vie', 'Dir li potessi' in 'S'io dir potessi', the first 'Nel suo sangue' in the second, and 'Pensa, spietata madre' in 'Cara, tu nel mio petto' (added in March 1723).

There were important revisions to 'Diresti poi così?' (B section, in 4/4 time, first shortened by six bars, then wholly rewritten in 3/8 rhythm), 'Dell'onda' (substantial cuts, as noted in HG), 'D'inalzar i flutti' (earlier version unpublished), 'Dove sei?' (B section added to the cavatina but removed just before production), and 'Tanti affanni' (contracted from a da capo to a dal segno aria; the first vocal phrase lost its accompaniment and was followed by a fermata and the segno; the A section suffered cuts of eight and six bars towards the end, the second in the closing ritornello); and smaller but not insignificant changes in 'Falsa imagine' (string coda contracted to two bars), 'Affanni del pensier' (bar 12 in the orchestra, bar 24 in the voice part), 'All' orror' (bars 1–4 and 15–17), 'Alla fama' (improvements to bars 6 and 8 of the ritornello), and 'Deh! non dir' (suppression of the opening ritornello). The C major sinfonia in I xi (HG 42) was moved to the start of Act II and replaced by a similar movement in E flat. With the exception of the last, which is not in the earliest copy, and possibly the changes in 'Alla fama', these all

pre-dated the première. They were undoubtedly made in the lost portions of
the performing score; most of them are in Walsh, and all are confirmed by
reliable copies. Except in 'Diresti poi così?', 'Dell'onda', and 'Dove sei?'
(which was altered again later) Chrysander does not indicate them. He does adopt
one change, the omission of the original bar 22 of the duet 'A' teneri affetti'
(crossed out in the performing score). Although it is present in nearly all early
copies, its absence from the Barnby manuscript (see note, p. 459) indicates that it
too was cut before performance. Chrysander's version of the longer string coda
of 'Falsa imagine' is inaccurate; it is clear from Handel's asterisks and re-barring
of the bass in the autograph that the da capo ended as follows:

Ex. 51

Handel's motives for the major changes, so far as they can be discovered,
were mixed. Some—'La speranza', 'Ah! tu non sai', 'Notte cara', 'Ritorna, O
dolce', and 'Tanti affanni'—are musical improvements, though the last two
weaken the drama. The D major 'Io sperai trovar', based on the ritornello of a
cantata aria subsequently used in the *Tamerlano* trio, has some merit, especially
the beautiful two-bar *Adagio e pianissimo* at the vocal entry after a lively
ritornello. 'A te lascio', a very slight binary minuet with repeats, may have
been thought inadequate as the single Act III solo for the second castrato.
'Qual cervetta', another simile aria, was an irrelevance so late in the action. It
is less easy to see why Handel discarded the first setting of 'Le profonde vie', a
lively affair full of octave leaps and bounding triplets that would have allowed
Boschi to shine in the major mode. The changes in Teofane's part were
connected with Cuzzoni. The G minor 'S'or mi dai pene' is a beautiful little
sarabande accompanied by strings without harpsichord but, like 'A te lascio',
a simple binary piece with repeats and a final ritornello (subtly varied).
Unlike the much longer and startlingly different C minor setting it offered no
opening for virtuosity; Handel may have surrendered it as some compensation
to the singer for retaining 'Falsa imagine'. 'Dir li potessi' is far superior to the

flashy 'Benchè mi sia' that replaced it—no doubt another concession to
Cuzzoni. In revising the former for 'S'io dir potessi' Handel improved the
voice part, especially its opening bars, but a beautiful extension to the
ritornello after the A section disappeared, as did the recorders. Both arias have
a viola part. Chrysander, dependent on the Walsh score, omitted it in 'S'io dir
potessi'. It survives in one copy.

On the revisions in Matilda's part we have unexpectedly explicit testimony
in two letters from Anastasia Robinson to Giuseppe Riva, undated but clearly
belonging to the autumn of 1722. They throw a vivid shaft of light both on
her character and on the awe inspired by Handel. Not daring to approach
him, she proposed to ask Lady Darlington, George I's half-sister, to intercede
for her.

Now I want your advice for my self, you have hear'd my new Part, and the more I look
at it, the more I find it is impossible for me to sing it; I dare not ask Mr Hendell to
change the Songs for fear he should suspect (as is very likely) every other reason but the
true one. Do you believe if I was to wait on Lady Darlinton to beg her to use that
power over him (which to be sure she must have) to get it done, that she would give her
self that trouble, would she have so much compassion on a distracted Damsell that they
are endeavouring to make an abomminable Scold of (in spite of her Vertuous
inclinations to the contrary) as to hinder the wrong they would do her; you might be
my friend and represent, that the greatest part of my Life has shew'd me to be a
Patient Grisell[20] by Nature, how then can I ever pretend to act the Termagant, but to
speak seriously I desire you will tell me whether it would be wrong to beg my Lady
Darlinton to do me this very great favour, and if you think she would do it.[21]

Not knowing how to ask you to give your self the trouble of coming here, and
necessity obliging me to beg a favour of you, I must do it by writing. I am very sensible
the Musick of my Part is exstreamly fine, but am as sure the Caracter causes it to be of
that kind, which no way suits my Capacity: those songs that require fury and passion to
express them, can never be performed by me acording to the intention of the
Composer, and consequently must loose their Beauty. Nature design'd me a peaceable
Creature, and it is as true as strange, that I am a Woman and cannot scold. My request
is, that if it be possible (as sure it is) the words of my second Song *Pensa spietata Madre*
should be changed, and instead of reviling Gismonda with her cruelty, to keep on the
thought of the Recitativo and perswade her to beg her Sons life of Ottone. I have read
the Drama and tho I do not pretend to be a judge, yet I fancy doing this would not be
an impropriety, but even suposing it one, of two evills it is best to chuse the least; in this
manner you might do me the greatest favour immaginable, because then a Short
Melancholly Song would be proper. I have some dificultys allso in the last I sing, but
for fear that by asking too much I might be refus'd all, I dare not mention them. And
now I beg of you to believe no other motive induces me to give you this trouble, but the
just fear I have that it would be impossible for me to perform my Part tollerably.[22]

Whether with the aid of Riva, Lady Darlington, or her own manifest
charm, Anastasia got her way: 'Pensa, spietata madre' was replaced by 'Ah! tu
non sai' and 'Nel suo sangue' rewritten. Handel may not have been such an
ogre after all.

---

[20] Anastasia had sung this part in Bononcini's *Griselda*, produced earlier the same year; see
p. 312.
[21] Partly printed by Lindgren, *M & L* (1977), 14 n. 26; original in the Campori Collection,
Biblioteca Estense, Modena.
[22] Printed by G. Bertoni, 'Giuseppe Riva e l'opera italiana in Londra', *Giornale storico della
letteratura italiana*, lxxxix (1927), 320, also from the Campori Collection.

The first performance took place at the King's Theatre on 12 January 1723 with the following cast:

OTTONE:	Senesino (alto castrato)
TEOFANE:	Cuzzoni (soprano)
GISMONDA:	Durastanti (soprano)
MATILDA:	Anastasia Robinson (contralto)
ADELBERTO:	Berenstadt (alto castrato)
EMIRENO:	Boschi (bass)

Both the opera and the new prima donna scored a sensational success. The *Daily Journal* of 14 January emphasized 'the Surprize and Admiration of the Audience, which was very numerous'. The Colman Opera Register confirmed this: Cuzzoni 'was extreamly admired', and Durastanti, Senesino, and Robinson also 'pleased much'. Monsieur de Fabrice wrote on the 15th that 'the house was full to overflowing. Today is the second performance and there is such a run on it that tickets are already being sold at 2 and 3 guineas which are ordinarily half a guinea, so that it is like another Mississippi or South Sea Bubble.' On the 19th the *London Journal* reported that the price had risen to four guineas, adding that Cuzzoni 'is already jump'd into a handsome Chariot, and an Equipage accordingly. The Gentry seem to have so high a Taste of her fine Parts, that she is likely to be a great Gainer by them.' The scramble spread to the Footmen's Gallery, where the disorders caused so much disturbance that it was threatened with closure; and at the ninth performance (9 February) a duel between 'a Scotch Nobleman and an English Baronet' was narrowly averted by a general placing both under arrest.[23] 'Everybody is grown now as great a judge of music, as they were in your time of poetry', Gay wrote to Swift on 3 February. 'People have now forgot Homer, and Virgil, and Caesar, or at least, they have lost their ranks; for, in London and Westminster, in all polite conversations, Senesino is daily voted to be the greatest man that ever lived.'

The opera had fourteen performances during the season. The twelfth on 26 March, after an interval of more than five weeks, was a benefit for Cuzzoni, and Handel took the opportunity to add 'Three new Songs, and an entire new Scene'. The new songs were 'Cara, tu nel mio petto' (in place of 'Bel labbro' in I ii), 'Spera sì, mi dice' at the start of II v (HG 57), 'Tra queste care' (after the accompanied recitative 'O grati orrori' in II viii, the fourth aria to occupy this place), and 'Gode l'alma'. The last formed part of the new scene, the first of the two numbered III vii in HG (106–12), to which 'Nò, non temere' was shifted from its original context in III v (HG 99). This did something to clarify the plot. Of the new pieces, the first was sung by Berenstadt, the other three by Cuzzoni. It was natural that Handel should augment her part, but none of the new music shows him at his most penetrating. 'Gode l'alma', with a chirpy violin figure that makes frequent if intermittent appearances in both parts, is the first of many similar arias designed to exploit the agility of Cuzzoni's voice. Perhaps the happiest moment, an afterthought, is the unexpected rising tenth at bar 42. 'Spera sì, mi dice' has some pleasant touches, notably the use of a figure from the first ritornello in the bass of the B section. Berenstadt's new aria gave him a better opportunity for display. Another aria possibly sung on this occasion, and certainly written for it, is

[23] *Daily Post*, 11 Feb. 1723 (*London Stage*; not in Deutsch).

'L'empio sleale', now to be found (a good deal shortened) in Act I of *Giulio Cesare*. It was composed, along with some additional recitative, for Ottone addressing Adelberto in III viii (HG 117, fifth system, after 'il temerario'); for its strange subsequent adventures in *Flavio* and *Giulio Cesare* see pp. 475 and 510. The longer (unpublished) B section of 'Dove sei?' probably dates from this performance. It appears in the Malmesbury copy, and both the Brunswick 1723 and Paris 1724 librettos give the complete aria. Handel might be expected to strengthen Senesino's part as well as Cuzzoni's. Cuzzoni must have reaped a considerable harvest from her benefit if it is true, as the *London Journal* announced on 30 March, that 'some of the Nobility gave her 50 Guineas a Ticket'. According to the *British Journal* and the *Weekly Journal* of the same date she received about £700. The March additions were repeated at the two subsequent performances on 4 and 8 June, and two of them, 'Spera sì, mi dice' and 'Gode l'alma', became permanent fixtures.

John Lockman in his long introduction to the libretto of J. C. Smith's *Rosalinda* (1740) tells a pleasant story about 'Spera sì, mi dice', illustrating 'the Effect which Harmony had upon some of the Brute Creation . . . It relates to a Pigeon in the Dove-house of Mr *Lee* in *Cheshire*. That Gentleman had a Daughter who was extremely fond of Music, and a very fine performer on the Harpsichord. The Dove-house was built not far from the Parlour, where the musical Instrument stood. The Pigeon, whenever the young Lady play'd any Air, except *Spera si* in *Otho*, never stirred; but as soon as that Air was touched, it would fly from the Dove-house to the Window; there discover the most pleasing Emotions; and the Instant the Air was over, fly back again. The young Lady was so delighted with the Fancy, that she ever after called *Spera si* the *Pigeon's Air*, and wrote it under that Title in her Music-book'. Smith vouched for this anecdote, which Hawkins applied to 'Spera, sì, mio caro' in *Admeto*. Lockman and Smith were right: Elizabeth Legh's 'music-book', a manuscript full score of *Ottone*, now belongs to Lord Malmesbury, and 'Spera sì, mi dice' bears the inscription 'The Pidgeon Song' in her hand. This must have been well known in Handel's circle, for Charles Jennens added the same words to his copy.

The next development was surprising. In April 1723 the Paris paper *Le Mercure* announced that 'several Italian members of the London Opera are due to come to Paris and give twelve performances during the month of July next, for which they will receive a considerable proportion of the receipts'. Any surplus would go to the Academy (i.e. the Paris Opéra), which would 'provide everything required for the Italians' performances—dresses, sets, choruses, ballets, orchestra, etc. Those who are to share the promised sum number five persons, viz. two women, two altos, and one bass'. *Read's Weekly Journal* of 6 April in a parallel announcement adds that the two altos were 'Eunuchs', and that the King of France intended to give the company 'a Gratuity of 35,000 Livres' and 'the old [Paris] Opera 23,000 Livres to make amends for the loss which they may suffer by the new one'. This interesting visit was postponed until the following summer (July to September 1724), when it took place under rather different circumstances. There were no stage productions, but *Ottone* and *Giulio Cesare* received concert performances in the household of the retired financier and patron of the arts Pierre Crozat.[24] The 1723 plan had been to take the original London cast without Anastasia

---

[24] Lindgren, *M & L* (1977), 22.

Robinson, who was shortly to retire after her secret marriage to the Earl of Peterborough. In the event Senesino fell out, and his place in 1724 was taken by a certain Madame Palerme,[25] who sang Matilda while Durastanti doubled Gismonda and Ottone, presumably with some transposition. Cuzzoni, Berenstadt, and Boschi sang their original parts. The version given was that of 26 March 1723, with the four new arias and 'Nò, non temere' postponed to III vii; but all recitatives were omitted except short passages introducing each aria and set piece. 'Dove sei?' was a full aria, presumably with the longer B section. In the same year 'Le profonde vie' was included in a booklet of aria texts, as sung at Crozat's Academy, with literal translations in French prose by Fontenelle. There is no evidence that Handel accompanied the party to Paris.

He had meanwhile revived the opera in London on 11 December 1723. There were six performances, probably with the original cast and the score as expanded on 26 March. In August 1725 Cuzzoni gave birth to a daughter. 'The minute she was brought to bed', Mrs Pendarves wrote to her sister on the 22nd, 'she sang "La Speranza", a song in Otho'. It must have held a particular appeal for her, for it was not in her part.

At his next revival (8 February 1726) Handel made many changes. Deutsch gives the first night as 5 February, but this performance was postponed owing to Cuzzoni's indisposition; there were nine in all. Cuzzoni, Senesino, and Boschi sang their original parts. Baldi succeeded Berenstadt as Adelberto, and Gismonda and Matilda exchanged voices; the former was taken by Anna Dotti, a contralto, the latter by Livia Costantini, a soprano. The success was almost as great as in 1723; according to the *Universal Mercury* for February 'Mr Handel had the Satisfaction of seeing an old Opera of his not only fill the House, which had not been done for a considerable time before, but People crowding so fast to it, that above 300 were turn'd away for want of room'.[26]

The exchange of voices, for which the personality of the new singers must have been responsible, involved Handel in a good deal of work. There was considerable rearrangement of libretto and music in all three acts, and substantial cuts in the recitatives of I i, iii, and v, and II v and vii. By eliminating all reference to Adelberto having seen Teofane in Byzantium and his decision to impersonate Ottone they make the plot obscurer than ever. Matilda lost her duet with Gismonda and all her arias except 'Ah! tu non sai', which must have been transposed up. 'Diresti poi così?' and 'Nel suo sangue' were cut, 'All'orror' (with the words modified) transferred to Gismonda in III i, where it replaced 'Trema, tiranno'. Costantini was compensated with two new arias, 'Vinto è l'amor' in I v (bottom of HG 28) and 'Di far le sue vendette', introduced by a new recitative, in place of the duet at the end of Act II. Gismonda's surviving arias must have been transposed for Dotti; she may have sung 'La speranza' in E flat, in which key it appears in several copies, but this would take her higher than in any part Handel wrote for her.[27] Handel cut the whole of Teofane's II viii ('Tra queste care' was the

---

[25] Either Anna Dotti, whose husband was one Michele Palermo, or Gerolima Moreni, detta la Palermina, in the service of the Mantuan court, who sang at Venice in Boniventi's *Armida al campo* in 1707 and A. Cortona's *Amor indovino* in 1726. On the latter occasion her name is spelt Morenni and she is described as a servant of the Prince of Modena. According to *Le Mercure* of October 1724 Bigonzi was with the company; he seems to have been as inactive as in London.

[26] *London Stage*; not in Deutsch.

[27] The aria had been published in E flat in 1724.

only one of the March 1723 additions to disappear) and added three arias for Ottone: 'Cervo altier' in I v (bottom of HG 27), the second (E major) setting of 'Io sperai trovar' in place of 'Ritorna, O dolce', and 'Un disprezzato affetto' for 'Tanti affanni'.

Most of this did not benefit the opera. Matilda's new arias are pleasant enough. In 'Vinto è l'amor' the martellato downward scale figure of the A section[28] (trilled by the violins) is nicely combined with cross-rhythms in a phrase that the violins extend for five bars. 'Di far le sue vendette' is a gigue with resemblances to 'Happy we' in *Acis and Galatea*; the bounding theme of the first ritornello slips neatly into the middle of the B section, where for the first and only time it accompanies the voice. But they scarcely compensate for the loss of 'Diresti poi così?' and the duet, not to mention Teofane's *scena* in the garden. Two of the new arias for Ottone ('Cervo altier' is negligible) are a different matter: although they replace the superb sicilianos of the 1723 score, they reflect an undoubted attempt on Handel's part to strengthen the dramatic fibre of the character. Both the E major 'Io sperai trovar' and 'Un disprezzato affetto' are more complex than their predecessors; they bring conflict into the foreground instead of lapsing into self-indulgent inactivity. The former, which reverts to Pallavicino's text, is a striking piece whose wide upward leaps in the violin part—especially the ninth at the start—give a flavour unusual in this key without entirely contradicting its associations with serenity. The same may be said of the numerous trills in the violin and bass parts.[29] 'Un disprezzato affetto' follows the 1723 accompanied recitative and retains the key of F minor. Though less profound than 'Tanti affanni' it is much stronger dramatically, introducing a note of angry resolution. The tempo mark *Ardito, mà non presto*, the carefully indicated contrasts (*agitato forte–tenero piano*), and the unusually explicit dynamics for the voice (not all in HG) point to the effect Handel had in mind. The *pianissimo* Neapolitan sixth on 'moro' (bars 69–70) is no less potent for being a traditional gambit.

The brief revival in 1727 is something of a mystery. There were only two performances, on 11 and 13 April, and they interrupted the very successful run of *Admeto*, undoubtedly as a stopgap. The performance of *Admeto* planned for the 8th was cancelled, 'Signora Faustina being taken very ill' (Colman); the *Daily Journal* of the 15th identifies her disease—'the Measles, attended with a high Fever'.[30] Burney implies that Cuzzoni followed her into the sickroom; if so, Handel was without a soprano, for Costantini had left the company. A revival of *Ottone* would require only one soprano if Matilda and Gismonda were both sung in the alto versions; and there is evidence that Handel at some period envisaged Teofane too as an alto. A volume in the Bodleian contains five of her six arias (as the part stood after 1723) transposed into the alto clef by Smith and others with the vocal line partially decorated by Handel.[31] It is tempting to connect this with the 1727 revival and to suppose that Handel at short notice engaged an English singer who required assistance with the Italian style of decoration. He left the work unfinished; perhaps Cuzzoni's illness was diplomatic and she returned to her part with Faustina safely out of

---

[28] Many of the markings of the autograph are not in HG.
[29] Many are not in HG.
[30] *London Stage*; not in Deutsch.
[31] See below, p. 447.

the way.[32] We know that she was sometimes reluctant to appear at this period through fear of a hostile reception.[33]

The 1733 revival also ran into trouble. It is clear from the first of the two casts in the libretto that it was planned for the spring. There is no way of determining the exact date; but the inclusion of all five singers then in the company suggests that it was not connected with the two interruptions to the run of *Orlando* caused by illness.[34] It is more likely that Handel intended *Ottone* to end the season in late May or June, when he surprisingly revived Bononcini's *Griselda* for the last six performances. The cancellation of *Ottone*, if not due to Strada's illness, was perhaps connected with the preliminary rumbles of the eruption that threw up the Opera of the Nobility in the early summer. When the revival did take place (13 November, four performances) Handel had a very different company. It seems again to have been an improvisation, caused by the postponement of the Princess Royal's marriage to the Prince of Orange from November till March 1734.[35] The libretto enables both the planned and eventual versions to be reconstructed. In the former Matilda (Bertolli) and Gismonda (Celeste Gismondi) reverted to their original pitch but were given the discarded duet 'Non tardate a festeggiar' at the end of Act II. It is a brisk 3/8 piece in F major, much more conventional than 'Notte cara', though the sense is the same. Gismonda recovered 'Trema, tiranno'; Matilda naturally lost the two soprano arias of 1726 but regained 'Diresti poi così?' with its recitative and 'All'orror'—in a new context (its third) in III vii. Adelberto was allotted to the minor tenor Thomas Mountier and stripped of his arias; all were cut except 'D'inalzar i flutti', which went to Emireno (Montagnana), though he never sang it. There were a few extra recitative cuts in I v and xi and II iv. Senesino was to have sung Ottone, Strada Teofane.

All the changes in November concerned the part of Adelberto, sung for the first time by a soprano, the castrato Carlo Scalzi, who was an artist of considerable stature and received five arias. In Act I 'Bel labbro' (not heard since 1723) and 'Tu puoi straziarmi' were restored and presumably transposed up. In Act II he sang 'Come se ti vedrò' from *Muzio Scevola*, with modified words beginning 'Sino che ti vedrò', in place of 'Lascia che nel suo viso', and 'D'instabile fortuna' from *Lotario* in II ix, two lines before the end of the recitative on HG 72. This was a tenor aria, and no doubt went up an octave. In Act III 'D'inalzar i flutti' was replaced by 'Pupille sdegnose' from *Muzio Scevola*, transposed up a minor third from D to F. The part of Ottone passed from Senesino to Carestini, who had a higher tessitura and a wider compass. For him Handel wrote the B version of the accompanied recitative 'Io son tradito' (HG 90, leading to 'Un disprezzato affetto' in G minor) and put up the duet 'A' teneri affetti' from F to G. He added higher alternatives to the voice part in 'Dove sei?' and in many recitatives (for example HG 83, 113, 118, 121; Chrysander does not print all of them). There were undoubtedly

---

[32] It is just possible that the ornaments were connected with the abortive revival in the spring of 1733 and intended for the young Susanna Arne (later Mrs Cibber), who had been singing in Handel's oratorios. But her voice was then reported to be a soprano, and Handel had other sopranos available.

[33] See the letter from Lady Pembroke to Mrs Clayton in Deutsch, 207–8. It should be dated *c.* 8 Apr.

[34] See Chapter 19, p. 402.

[35] See Deutsch, 336.

further modifications and transpositions in the first two acts. 'Qual cervetta' may have been sung in place of 'Nò, non temere'.[36] Handel made one odd change in this revival. Hitherto he had consistently accentuated Teofane's name in the rhythm ∪∪——∪; he now altered it, wherever it occurs in the torso of the Hamburg score,[37] to the less euphonious ∪——∪∪. The remaining parts were sung by Strada (Teofane), Durastanti (her old role of Gismonda), Maria Caterina Negri (Matilda), and Waltz (Emireno). This was the first opera (apart from the pasticcio *Semiramide*) in which Scalzi, Carestini, Negri, and Waltz sang under Handel.

It was his last revival of *Ottone*; but this work had the doubly unique distinction of being the only Handel opera produced by the Opera of the Nobility and the only one in which the most famous of the castratos, Farinelli, ever appeared. This was on 10 December 1734 at the King's Theatre; there were five performances. Farinelli sang not Ottone but Adelberto, and although he had seven arias not one belonged to the part. Five were from other Handel operas: 'Quel gelsomino' and 'Tutta brillante i rai' from *Riccardo Primo* (in place of 'Bel labbro' and the duet 'Notte cara'), 'Rammentati cor mio' and 'D'instabile fortuna' from *Lotario* (in place of Gismonda's 'Pensa ad amare' and 'Tu puoi straziarmi'), and 'Ch'io parta?' from *Partenope* (in place of 'D'inalzar i flutti'). The other two arias, 'Se mi lasci e m'abbandoni' (in place of 'Lascia che nel suo viso') and 'La costanza all'alma mia' (between the Act III duet and the *coro*), have not been identified. One more extraneous aria, 'Da un fato traditore', was sung by Maria Segatti as Gismonda after 'Rammentati cor mio' in I ix. The rest of the cast, Senesino (Ottone), Cuzzoni (Teofane), Bertolli (Matilda), and Montagnana (Emireno), were old members of Handel's company who had either sung the same parts under him or been cast for them in the abortive 1733 revival. The Opera of the Nobility's performance coincided with Handel's production of the pasticcio *Oreste* (Covent Garden, 18 December 1734), in which he incorporated three *Ottone* arias, 'Dopo l'orrore', 'S'io dir potessi', and 'Un disprezzato affetto', the last two with changed texts. He also drew on *Ottone* for the pasticcio opera *Hermann von Balcke*, stitched together at Elbing in the autumn of 1737; 'Del minacciar' and possibly the duet 'A' teneri affetti' appeared here with German words.[38]

The great popularity of the music is attested by the frequency with which excerpts appeared at concerts or between the acts of plays. The earliest known occasion was in Dublin, where Signora Stradiotti sang 'Dove sei?', 'Alla fama', and 'Benchè mi sia' at the Smock Alley Theatre on 8 December 1725.[39] Mrs Hill sang 'Alla fama' at the Little Haymarket Theatre (9 August 1728) and Mrs Turner Robinson at her Drury Lane benefit (26 March 1729), on which occasion Clarke contributed 'Nò, non temere' and the pair combined in 'A' teneri affetti'. This duet was sung by Mrs Cibber and Mrs Barbier at Drury Lane (13 May 1734) and by Miss Jones and Master Arne at the Little Haymarket (28 June 1734) and Lincoln's Inn Fields (20 August 1734). The Gavotte from the overture featured in the quaintly titled ballad opera *The Female Parson, or The Beau in the Sudds* (Little Haymarket, 27 April 1730); the

---

[36] See below, p. 451.
[37] He overlooked it once: see p. 452.
[38] J. Müller-Blattau, 'Händels Festkantate...', in *50 Jahre Göttinger Händel-Festspiele*, ed. W. Meyerhoff (Kassel, etc. 1970), 120 ff.
[39] T. J. Walsh, *Opera in Dublin 1705–1797*, 23.

whole overture at Manchester Subscription Concerts (2 November 1744, 25 June 1745), the Little Haymarket for Waltz's benefit (9 December 1748), and again for the benefit of the boy Benjamin Hallet (6 February 1752). 'The instrumental Opera of Otho', performed at a King's Theatre masquerade on 27 March 1729, was presumably the overture. Cecilia Young sang 'Falsa imagine' and 'Affanni del pensier' at Hickford's (10 August 1734); Reinhold 'Del minacciar' in the same hall (24 April 1741), at Covent Garden in a Musicians Fund benefit (10 April 1745), and at the King's Theatre for the benefit of Miss Robinson (29 April 1745). The ageing Cuzzoni on her final visit to England returned to her first Handel part with 'Falsa imagine' and 'Benchè mi sia' at a Musicians Fund benefit (King's Theatre, 16 April 1751) and 'Falsa imagine' and 'Affanni del pensier' at Hickford's for her own benefit on 23 May the same year, her last concert in England. Casarini presumably sang 'Vieni, O figlio' in public about this period, for her name appears on the aria in a Walsh score of *Ottone*.[40]

There were three productions of *Ottone* in Germany during the 1720s. The first, at Brunswick in Italian in August 1723, was combined with the intermezzo *Barlafuso e Pipa*, the two scenes of which were given after the first two acts. The basic score was that of Handel's first performance in January, with interesting differences. Teofane's aria in II viii is 'S'or mi dai pene,' but 'Dove sei?' is a full da capo aria. The recitatives, including both accompanied sections, were severely cut. Although the music was attributed to Handel it is clear from the libretto that several arias from Lotti's *Teofane* were grafted in. The first scene includes 'Pur che regni', but 'La speranza' is replaced by Pallavicino's 'Faccia in volto'. 'Bel labbro' must be Lotti's setting, since the words will not fit Handel's, and the same is almost certainly true of 'Io sperai trovar'. Pallavicino's 'Di lago o fonte' replaces 'Dopo l'orrore' (II vii), and a recitative and aria ('Pensando alla beltà') for Adelberto after II viii, not set by Handel, is included. Some of the arias left unchanged by Haym may of course have been sung in Lotti's settings, for the score has not survived. There is no sign of Handel's March 1723 additions. The only aria omitted from the January score, apart from those already mentioned, was 'Vieni, O figlio', which reflects little credit on the Brunswick conductor.

A second Brunswick production in February 1725 brought in at least three more pieces by Lotti (who was now named): Teofane's aria 'Dall'altezza di quel soglio' in I viii, the duet 'Al guardo se chiedo' for Ottone and Teofane at the beginning of II v, and Ottone's 'Discordi pensieri', which replaced 'Dove sei?' in III i. 'Vieni, O figlio' was restored. Otherwise the text followed that of August 1723, except that there was no intermezzo. The cast was:

OTTONE:	Schneider
TEOFANE:	Madame Simonetti
GISMONDA:	Christina Louisa Koulhaas[41]
MATILDA:	Mademoiselle Jacobi
ADELBERTO:	Graue
EMIRENO:	Braun[42]

According to Chrysander Graue was the composer Carl Heinrich Graun, who

[40] Smith, *Descriptive Catalogue*, 45.

[41] She sang frequently in Brunswick between 1721 and 1735 and in three operas at Hamburg in 1722 (K. Zelm, 'Die Sänger der Hamburger Gänsemarkt-Oper', 58–9).

[42] Another Brunswick singer (1725–35) who also sang in Hamburg in 1722 (ibid. 47).

was employed as a tenor at the ducal court of Brunswick–Wolfenbüttel from 1725 to 1735 and must have sung in transposed keys.

On 4 May 1726 (OS) a version arranged by Telemann, with the arias in Italian and the recitatives in a German translation by Johann Georg Glauche, was produced at Hamburg; there were four performances in that year, one in 1727, and one in 1729. The score (Berlin MS Mus 9052) as well as the libretto survives. It is clear from internal evidence that the authors had access neither to Handel's score nor to Haym's London libretto. They grafted the music in Walsh's printed edition on to Pallavicino's 1719 libretto (omitting the allegorical finales), and not surprisingly ran into difficulties where Handel had changed the order or inserted new scenes. Unable to recognize soliloquies as such, they pushed them in where Pallavicino had given the same character an aria, often in mid-scene and always in the unsuitable presence of other characters. Gismonda sang 'Vieni, O figlio' to Adelberto and Matilda in the middle of II ii (hence Matilda had two arias in succession), and Ottone 'Tanti affanni' to Matilda and Gismonda in the equivalent of III viii. Telemann first substituted 'Affanni del pensier' for Teofane's swallow aria in the scene after 'Falsa imagine', then shifted it awkwardly to the equivalent of I ix, where Gismonda, Adelberto, and Isauro are all on stage. 'Ritorna, O dolce amore' became a mid-scene aria before Emireno's 'Del minacciar', leaving a gap in the next scene, where Telemann gave Ottone a new aria but crossed it out. Having placed 'Pur che regni' at the end of the first scene, he could find no room for 'La speranza' and omitted it. This was the only piece cut. Teofane's aria in the garden scene of course was 'S'io potessi', but Telemann spoiled the whole episode by bringing her in after Emireno's 'Le profonde vie'.

He could not have known that Handel had removed Isauro altogether, and his manipulations left other gaps. So he turned the opera into a pasticcio by composing six new arias on Italian texts (not from *Teofane*) and adding one each from Chelleri's *La caccia in Etolia* (1715) and Vinci's recent *Siroe* (1726). By an odd chance Handel was to set both these arias later, 'Non saria poco' in *Atalanta* and 'Non vi piacque' in his own *Siroe*. After he had composed the recitatives and had the score copied (sometimes with a blank viola stave, which however was not filled in), Telemann decided to reset four of Handel's texts, Teofane's 'Falsa imagine' and Adelberto's 'Tu puoi straziarmi', 'Lascia che nel suo viso', and 'D'inalzar i flutti'. He may have been influenced here by the octave transposition to which he subjected the two castrato parts (including the duet 'A' teneri affetti'), but that cannot apply to 'Falsa imagine'. Telemann's setting of this is a historical curiosity. The only thing it shares with Handel's is the key, A major. It is enormously long and verbose, *Vivace assai*, with an elaborate accompaniment for two oboes, five-part strings, and continuo, all (except the continuo) muted. There are striking details, such as the vocal entry on a bare G♮ (to suggest falseness) and the very unexpected B minor cadence at the end of the B section; but as an entrance aria for Handel's Teofane it is grotesque.

Telemann made no attempt to match Handel's style. His new music, while aping some of Vinci's mannerisms, is much less Italianate in melody, with correspondingly greater reliance on the orchestra: some of the arias are miniature concertos, Gismonda's 'Vago augelletto' (towards the end of Act II) having two concertante violas, recorders, oboes, and a four-part string band alternating between pizzicato and arco. The recitatives are more angular, less flowing, and considerably longer than Handel's. Telemann inserted short sinfonias at the start of the garden scene and the first set change in Act III, and an *Entrée* at the end of Act I, though no music for this survives. His most interesting idea was to use 'Deh! non dir' twice in the equivalent of II x, for Ottone's entrance (without the da capo) and for his exit at the end. His whole contribution has a Teutonic stolidity foreign to Handel's operatic style, and the three bass voices (with a tenor Isauro) set a ponderous precedent for modern German revivals.[43]

The first of these was at Göttingen in 1921 under the title *Otto und Theophano* with libretto and music heavily rearranged by Oskar Hagen. This version had some success, enjoying 64 performances in a dozen German and Austrian cities up to 1928 and many others since. The Handel Opera Society's London revival in 1971 was the first outside Germany, and the first since 1734 in which the voice parts were sung at the correct pitch.

Autograph

The autograph material for *Ottone* survives in five volumes, two in the British Library (RM 20 b 9 and RM 20 b 10), three in the Fitzwilliam Museum (Mus MS 256, pp. 53–63, Mus MS 262, p. 17, and Mus MS 263, p. 67). Chrysander used only the first and so presented a confused and incomplete text.[44] Virtually all the *Ottone* music survives in autograph except the arias 'Nel suo sangue' (3/8 version), 'Tra queste care', 'Di far le sue vendette', and 'Un disprezzato affetto' and the duet 'Non tardate a festeggiar'; one or two pieces are incomplete, and others have been separated from their context and bound out of sequence. RM 20 b 9 and Mus MS 256, taken together, represent the first version of the opera, with many (but not all) of the pre-performance revisions inserted. Others are found in RM 20 b 10, which also contains two preliminary drafts and a number of later additions. The collections are best considered in turn.

RM 20 b 9. Handel began a new foliation, by gatherings as usual, for each act. From this it is clear that the following folios are not original:

1–13 (*Ouverture*, without date or title, as printed in HG 1–11);

20–1 ('La speranza');

35 (B section of 'Diresti poi così?' in 3/8 as HG);

48 (bars 22 and 23 of 'Dell'onda', which replace the original at the bottom of HG 47);

55 ('Ah! tu non sai');

77–8 (two versions of the B section of 'Dove sei?', of which HG gives only the first from f. 78; the second—see Ex. 49 (p. 425)—cued in at bar 8, is three bars longer);

86–90 ('Tanti affanni' and 'D'inalzar i flutti' as HG 96–8 without preceding B recitative);

94–5 ('Nò, non temere' without tempo mark; the violin stave, but not the others, originally had a 3/8 signature).

---

[43] There is a brief comparison between Telemann's *Ottone* and Handel's in H. C. Wolff, *Die Barockoper in Hamburg*, i. 338–40 (musical examples ii. 206–10). R. D. Lynch's 'Händels "Ottone": Telemanns Hamburger Bearbeitung', *HJb* (1981), 117–27, is vitiated by his failure to recognize that Telemann was working only with Pallavicino's libretto, not Haym's.

[44] The items in RM 20 b 10 may not have been bound together in Chrysander's time.

Handel inserted all this material after composing the first draft. The following unperformed pieces belong to that draft: 'Giunt' in porto' (*Allegro*), 'Io sperai trovar' (D major), original setting (*Allegro* 4/4) of the B section of 'Diresti poi così?', 'Pensa, spietata madre', 'Non a tempre', 'A te lascio', 'Dir li potessi', and the 4/4 setting of 'Nel suo sangue'. Two more rejected arias are in the Mus MS 256 fragment, which should follow f. 67 but very soon became detached from the rest.

On some blank staves in the overture (f. 8ᵛ) is a ten-bar sketch, treble and bass in 3/4, A major, for the opening ritornello of 'Tutto può donna' in Act I of *Giulio Cesare*; it will be remembered that Handel used the overture's first fugal Allegro in that opera. The cadence at the end of the recitative in I i is in A minor, as HG 15, although 'Giunt' in porto' in G major follows on the verso. This makes no sense; the only feasible explanation is that Handel substituted the F major aria 'La speranza' very early, before setting the recitative. 'Pur che regni' is clearly marked *Larghetto* (originally the violas were included with the violins on the second stave); 'Falsa imagine' is *Largo* and has additional figuring (not in HG) in bars 10 and 19–21. Handel simply wrote the word *Concerto* (as in HG) at the beginning of I iv, but the music is in all the copies. He cut six bars from the 4/4 B section of 'Diresti poi così?' before scrapping it, and made two cuts (five bars) in the opening ritornello of 'Pensa ad amare' after filling up the inner parts. Scene x (bottom of HG 38) is indicated only in the libretto, not in the autograph or copies, which have eleven scenes in Act I. The first two bars of the sinfonia on HG 42 were an afterthought, which confused S2 when he made the Flower copy for Jennens. The third note of the voice in bar 14 of 'Dell'onda' should be G, not B flat; Handel's change is perfectly clear, and is adopted in all the copies. The passages printed at the bottom of HG 47 and 49 were part of the first draft; Handel replaced the former with an insertion and marked the latter *NB . . . 7* for alteration; the bracketed passage in the cadence of the B section (HG 49) is uncancelled.[45] The substitution of 2 bars for 3½ on HG 47 left an odd half-bar which Handel exorcized by re-barring the rest of the aria, including the B section. The original barring agreed with that of the first ritornello.

In the B section of 'Vieni, O figlio' the words 'il crudo fato' come from the 1723 libretto; the autograph and all copies have 'amica stella'. By a slip of the pen Handel numbered Scene v as iv; Chrysander's Scene xi (HG 60) should of course be vi. The second part of 'Alla fama' is squeezed into the bottom of f. 63ᵛ and may be an afterthought. Bar 27 of 'Dopo l'orrore' replaced a three-bar *Adagio* cadence in 4/4 *senza cembalo*, fully scored. After the scene-heading for II viii Handel wrote *Emireno ed Adelberto*; Teofane's appearance here was a happy afterthought. There are two cuts in her accompanied recitative; the ritornello was one bar longer, and there were 2½ bars for strings alone after 'al core amante!' In the duet 'Notte cara' (top line *Tutti unis.*) the words of the second line are 'di due cor' in the autograph and copies, 'del mio cor' in the libretto; those of the B section originally began 'Sei propizia! sei amica!'. The last three vocal bars in the first part are contracted from seven as first written. 'Notte cara' is part of the original autograph; 'Non tardate a festeggiar' must have been composed as an alternative and then (temporarily) discarded.

'Trema, tiranno' is *Allegro*. The A setting of 'Io son tradito' led originally (via a B flat major cadence) to 'Non a tempre', in which Handel heavily

---

[45] Chrysander presumably took the cut from Walsh.

revised the violin part and made two cuts before abandoning it. Scene iii (HG 95) began with a *Presto* sinfonia of 6½ bars in C minor representing the storm; Handel crossed it out before filling in the viola part. Version A of the recitative on HG 96 led to 'A te lascio', whose top line at first had recorders with the first violins, and the recitatives of iv, v, and vi followed. The original cadence at the bottom of HG 99 was version B (C major; Emireno left without an aria); Handel altered this to E flat, as printed on p. 57 of Squire's *Catalogue*, and added *NB Aria* (this was almost certainly 'Qual cervetta'). Both versions are clearly legible; why Chrysander left a blank and the statement 'the conclusion of the recitative at A is not given' is a mystery. 'Dir li potessi' was the original aria in vi, followed by the recitatives of vii in Version A on HG 113, the 4/4 'Nel suo sangue', the stage direction *Mentre vuol partire*, etc. (HG 116), and Scene viii. The autograph has the A version of the recitative before the *coro*. On the verso of the last page of the latter are the words only of three bars of recitative in I v (HG 28).

Fitzwilliam Mus MS 256. Handel's folio number ·5 on p. 53 proves that the first four leaves were a segment of the original autograph. They contain the remainder of the accompanied recitative 'O grati orrori' from bar 13 (HG 68) with of course the complete viola part (the many revisions in the placing of cadences and movement of the harmony show very careful composition), the G minor 3/4 setting of 'S'or mi dai pene', the complete recitative of ix (words only in HG), and an unpublished setting of 'Le profonde vie', 4/4 in C major. Although this is a da capo aria Handel used only the five lines of text in Pallavicino's libretto; Haym supplied three more for the B section of the C minor setting. This follows on the next leaf (pp. 61–2), an insertion, hurriedly written, with a viola part in the three ritornellos. There is no tempo mark, and the time signature is unbarred C. The next leaf (p. 63, verso blank) has the four-bar sinfonia for the embarcation in II xi, quoted above (Ex. 50), with recitative cues.

Fitzwilliam Mus MS 262, p. 17, contains the opening of an earlier version of the second (C minor) setting of 'S'or mi dai pene', twelve bars corresponding to the first 15½ bars of the autograph in RM 20 b 10. The vocal and instrumental material, like the key and the scoring, is the same but less expansively treated: the ritornello has six bars instead of eight, the first vocal phrase four bars instead of six. Handel evidently broke off here, for the verso is blank. The autograph of the little E flat sinfonia added to I xi is in Mus MS 263, p. 67 (not identified in Mann's *Catalogue*), that of the concerto in I iv, as mentioned above (p. 431), in RM 20 g 13.

RM 20 b 10. This manuscript contains fourteen detached items, all composed subsequent to the body of RM 20 b 9. Of the six pieces that antedate the first performance, 'Ritorna, O dolce' (f. 5, without bass figuring; all three staves originally had a common-time signature) and 'Benchè mi sia' (ff. 20–3 with a fragmentary sketch on f. 24; Handel first wrote an alto clef for the voice) were certainly performed then. So probably was the C minor 'S'or mi dai pene' (ff. 12–15, no tempo); Handel marked bar 30 for alteration and replaced it with three new bars, which are in the copies. These last two arias were probably composed at the same time shortly before the performance; the paper type occurs nowhere else in the *Ottone* material. 'D'inalzar i flutti' (ff. 17–18, no tempo) is here in an earlier version than that of RM 20 b 9. The material differs in detail; some of the dotted figures in the ritornello appear as triplets. This was evidently Handel's first attempt; he broke off after the first part. There is also a preliminary shot (21 bars) at 'S'io dir potessi' (f. 16, again without tempo). It has a viola part, the last beats of bars 16 and 18 have violin figures in thirds echoing the last three notes of the ritornello, and bars 19–21 move in a different direction. 'Qual cervetta' (f. 19) is headed by a cue to III v taking up the note in RM 20 b 9 *e me con lui seguite N. B. Aria*. Handel seems to have planned a B section, for the viola stave (which shares with the voice) has a bass clef at the end, and a blank page follows.

The other eight items are additions of March 1723 and 1726. The former are: 'Cara, tu nel mio petto' (ff. 1–2, the top part *Tutti unis*), 'Spera sì, mi dice' (ff. 10–11, *Andante*), the recitatives on HG 106 headed *Scene 7* with *Segue l'aria No non temere O bella* at the end (f. 24), the recitative at the bottom of HG 109 with *Segue l'aria, Gode l'alma* at the end (f. 25^r, verso blank), and 'Gode l'alma' (ff. 26–8, no tempo, with many small cuts and corrections). Folios 26 and 27 are bound in the wrong order. (The autograph of 'L'empio sleale' as composed for *Ottone* in March 1723 is bound with that of *Giulio Cesare*, and is discussed under that opera, p. 510. The 1726 additions are 'Cervo altier' (ff. 3–4)[46] with the first leaf (28 bars) missing, 'Vinto è l'amor' (ff. 6–7), and the E major setting of 'Io sperai trovar' (ff. 8–9) with a passage of nine bars cut in the A section. All three arias have many dynamic and expression marks not in HG; for example the *piano* in the B section of 'Cervo altier' occurs not at the beginning but three bars later where the violins divide. In bars 63–6 of 'Benchè mi sia' Handel added an extra part on the violin stave in later ink. It appears in none of the copies, but is very similar to the vocal ornamentation he supplied at this point in the Bodleian copy. The voice part of 'Spera sì, mi dice' originally began with the same phrase as the ritornello; the long roulade at the bottom of HG 138 was added in the margin.

The Bodleian manuscript MS Don c 69[47] contains, between the autographs of two Italian cantatas, copies by Smith, H3(?) and S2 of 'Spera sì, mi dice', 'Benchè mi sia', 'Falsa imagine', 'Affanni del pensier', and 'Alla fama' from *Ottone* and 'Dopo l'ombre' from *Floridante*. All are soprano arias transposed down a fourth or fifth into the alto clef. Handel added ornaments to the voice parts of four of them: in both sections of 'Benchè mi sia'[48] and 'Affanni del pensier', the A section of 'Alla fama' (Plate 14), and the first bar only of 'Falsa imagine'. These ornaments, recently published,[49] are of the highest importance for the light they throw on Handel's attitude to this notorious problem. Though often florid and elaborate, especially in 'Affanni del pensier', the one slow aria, they never mask the melody; where they occur in the B section—a practice that

---

[46] This could have been composed in 1722–3 and rejected.

[47] This manuscript was first described in print by J. S. and M. V. Hall, 'Handel's Graces', *HJb* (1957), 25–43. Their suggestion that the ornaments were composed for Guadagni in 1751 is untenable, apart from the fact that no Italian singer would require them. The presence of 'Dopo l'ombre' tends to strengthen the link with 1727, for *Floridante* like *Ottone* was revived as a stopgap in April of that year. Leopold Kalckreuth's portrait of Chrysander (1901) in the Hamburger Künsthalle (reproduced in *Exhibition Catalogue* opposite p. 233) shows him holding this manuscript, although it was in private hands until 1947.

[48] J. M. Coopersmith twice reproduced the first page of this aria in *Papers of the American Musicological Society* (1937, p. 21; 1939, opposite p. 25) and performed it at the Juilliard Graduate School, New York, on 14 September 1939, but was evidently unaware of the others. He identified the copyist wrongly and seems to have assumed that the decorations were to be sung first time in the A section.

[49] G. F. Handel, *Three Ornamented Arias*, ed. W. Dean (London, 1976).

Tosi approved—the music is not new but a development of the first part. The absence of ornament at main cadences may indicate that the singer knew how to deal with these. It does not mean that cadenzas were taboo; there is only one point in these arias that imperatively demands a cadenza, the end of the B section of 'Benchè mi sia', and there Handel does supply some decoration. No doubt the process of adding ornaments stimulated the creative improviser in Handel: it is clear that he was not averse to dissonance, as in the closing bars of the B section of 'Affanni del pensier'.

Ex. 52

([But alas! I already feel you in my sorrowful heart] obstinately disturbing my peace of mind)

Some of the harmonic collisions in 'Benchè mi sia' are however so eccentric as to suggest that Handel, had he finished the ornaments, would have modified the string parts.

Librettos

1723 Handel. 'Ottone, Re di Germania.' Drama...Printed by Tho. Wood in Little Britain.' 67pp. An Italian dedication to the Earl of Halifax is signed 'N. Haym'. The Argument (verbatim from Pallavicino) and cast are in Italian and English as usual. Two passages of recitative, four lines beginning 'E cadevi al mio piè' in I iv and three in II vi are printed in *virgole* as not set, but Handel did include the former. On the other hand he omitted two lines for Emireno in III iv after 'in preda siete' (bottom of HG 98) and a few words elsewhere. In II iv the libretto has a different recitative from the autograph and HG; it is a good deal shorter, consisting of six lines beginning 'Ah Matilda' (Handel set the first three in 1733). The scene headings of I i and vii, II viii and xi, and III iii and vii (HG 113) differ in various particulars from HG, which follows the autograph. After 'Del minacciar' (HG 27) the libretto has *Parte Emireno seguito da guardie*; the omission of these words from the autograph was doubtless accidental. 'S'or mi dai pene' comes at the end of Teofane's recitative (HG 69), not in the middle. 'Dove sei?' is a two-line cavatina followed by a semicolon, a sign that the B section was taken out at the last minute after the type was set up. The text of course does not include the additions of March 1723.

1723 Brunswick. 'Drama per Musica da rappresentarsi sul Famosissimo Teatro di Brunswiga Nella fiera d'Estate l'anno 1723...Wolfenbüttel druckts Christian Bartsch' (followed by a German translation). Argument (from Pallavicino), cast (including numerous 'Comparse', knights, pages, guards, maidens, soldiers, Moors, and pirates), list of scenes, and text are in Italian and German. The two characters and two scenes of the intermezzo *Barlafuso e Pipa* are placed below those of *Ottone*. The music is 'del famoso Sign. HENDEL'. The scene headings, many of them taken from Pallavicino's libretto, suggest that the staging was more elaborate than in London. There are differences in the scene numbering in Act II. As noted above, many recitatives are drastically shortened but the text includes several of Lotti's arias.

1724 Paris. 'Tragédie Mise en Musique par M. Hendel. A Paris.' 51 pp. Cast list and stage directions in French, also a brief synopsis of the action before each scene, sometimes including background material. Text in Italian only. The use of *virgole* is the reverse of that in Italian and London librettos: they indicate the passages performed, not those cut. The text is Handel's version of March 1723, with the four new arias and the new III vii, after which the scene numbering is regularized to the end of the act. As in the 1723 Brunswick libretto 'Dove sei?' is a full da capo aria.

1725 Brunswick. Title as 1723 above, except for 'Nella fiera d'Inverno l'anno 1725'. There is no intermezzo, and the music is now ascribed to Handel and Lotti. Act I ends with a ballet of knights and ladies. The libretto names the cast.

1726 Handel. 'Printed, and Sold at the King's Theatre in the Hay-Market.' v + 67 pp. Dedication and Argument are included, followed by a note: 'N.B.

The Alterations in the following Drama not being tanslated [*sic*] into *English*, as usual; it is hoped this Omission will be favourably excus'd, the Time being scarce sufficient for the Printing of it in the present Form.' All the March 1723 additions except 'Tra queste care' are present. Most of the other major changes have been listed above. Seventeen lines of recitative are cut in I i (from 'Oggi l'idea' to 'fiero incontro'), and the first ten lines of I iii (to 'e 'l dover mio'). In I v the four lines beginning 'La nave sua' are replaced by two new lines introducing 'Cervo altier'; 'Vinto è l'amor' follows 'rivedrammi il fellon' (bottom of HG 28), and the next twelve lines to 'all'armi move' are cut; at this point a new Scene vi begins, the original vi (Matilda's recitative and 'Diresti poi cosi?') having disappeared. In II v the five lines from 'Ah! la mia gelosia' to 'il cor fellone' and the nine lines from 'Quì risuona' to 'di me gelosa' are cut, together with 'All'orror'. So is the whole of II viii, causing the later scenes of the act to be renumbered. In II xii Gismonda goes out at 'salvezza il merto', and Matilda has a new four-line recitative to introduce 'Di far le sue vendette'. The music for this recitative and that before 'Cervo altier' does not seem to have survived. 'Dove sei?' is printed as a two-line recitative, but was probably sung as a cavatina.

The blank last page of the copy in the National Library of Scotland has manuscript notes in an eighteenth-century hand, possibly Burney's, comparing the autograph with the Walsh score and the 1723 libretto. They mention several unperformed and at least two still unpublished pieces, 'S'or mi dai pene' and 'Symph del mare tempestoso'. It is clear that the Fitzwilliam section of the autograph had already become detached.

1726 Hamburg. 'Otto in einem Sing-Spiele Auf den Hamburgischen Schau-Platze Vorgestellet Im Jahr 1726. Gedruckt mit Stromerschen Schrifften.' All the prefatory matter, including the Argument, and the secco recitatives are in German, the arias and set pieces in Italian. The music is 'von Herrn Capell-Meister Hendel'; Telemann is nowhere mentioned. The text corresponds to his score, already described, but the scene-headings, translated from *Teofane*, are more detailed. The new arias are 'Non saria poco' (Isauro) in Act I, 'Vorrei poterli (Gismonda), 'Quando più non languirà' (Isauro), and 'Vago augelletto' (Gismonda) in Act II, 'Come l'orso che smariti' (Ottone), 'Sospira questo cor' (Isauro), 'Non vi piacque' (Teofane), and 'Le minaccie della morte' (Gismonda) in Act III.

1733 Handel. 'Printed for T. Wood in Little-Britain, and are to be sold at the King's Theatre in the Hay-Market.' 55 pp. No dedication. The Argument (English only) is followed by the altered cast and three pages of amendments for the November performance; the spring cast and the main text follow. The recitatives are in the shortened form of 1726, but the seven lines in I v from 'Temerario Adelberto!' to 'rivedrammi il fellon' disappear with 'Vinto è l'amor', and Adelberto's five-line recitative before 'Tu puoi straziarmi' goes out with the aria. The whole of I vi is however restored. The recitative 'Ah Matilda' in II iv consists of the first three lines of the text in the 1723 and 1726 librettos. In II xii (now xi) the 1726 recitative leads to the duet 'Non tardate a festeggiar'. The inserted amendments restore the cuts so far as they concern Adelberto and give him an extra aria in II ix. 'D'inalzar i flutti', allotted to Emireno in the main text, disappears in favour of 'Pupille sdegnose' from *Muzio Scevola*.

The annotator of the 1726 libretto has been at work again in the Edinburgh copy, this time comparing the 1733 text with that of the 1723 libretto, noting which arias were published by Walsh and sometimes the source of borrowings. In Act III he supplies a new piece of information, writing against 'Nò, non temere': 'Emireno sang here a *new* song—Qual cervetta (Parte)'. If this is correct—and the performing score seems to confirm it—Handel may have restored the C major 'Le profonde vie' (which is not shown as cut), for the C minor setting is almost identical with 'Qual cervetta'.

1734 Nobility. 'As perform'd at the Royal Theatre in the Hay-Market ...Printed by Charles Bennet.' The refashioning of Adelberto's part for Farinelli involved many changes, especially in the recitative, and pulled the opera more out of shape than ever. The extra recitative and aria for Segatti (Gismonda) are printed on additional pages at the end of the libretto and cued into I ix; it is not quite clear if they precede or supersede 'Affanni del pensier' and its recitative—probably the former. The text includes two of Handel's 1726 replacements for Senesino, 'Io sperai trovar' and 'Un disprezzato affetto', and omits 'Ah! tu non sai' and Teofane's *scena* in the garden (II viii).

Copies and Editions

Of the Hamburg performing score (MA/1037) only Act III survives, in damaged condition, with part of II v incorrectly bound in the middle (ff. 41–4). It is a palimpsest of Handel's different versions; many pages have been modified on two or more occasions. All were written by Smith on paper with the same watermark (though there are differences of rastrum) except the 1733 insertions (S1). Clausen in an ingenious analysis concludes that Smith first copied the August 1722 autograph, and that only ff. 1, 4, 14, 46, and 50–9 (the end of the opera) survive from his original manuscript. This is probably correct; it implies that 'Non a tempre', 'A te lascio', 'Dir li potessi', and 'Qual cervetta' were copied and then ejected. But, *pace* Clausen, 'L'empio sleale' was not in this group; there are traces of its insertion on f. 51ʳ. A few of Clausen's conclusions need revision in the light of the Malmesbury copy and other evidence.

The changes in the manuscript are best listed by date:

(i) *Late 1722*: insertion of ff. 2 (shorter B section of 'Dove sei?', cancelled before performance), 15 and 19 (beginning and end of 'Tanti affanni'; both leaves show signs of the reduction to dal segno form, but the two major cuts in the A section, made before the printing of the Walsh score, would be on the missing intermediate leaves), 24–7 ('D'inalzar i flutti'), 29–31 and 45 ('Benchè mi sia'), 34–6 ('Nò, non temere'), and 47–9 (3/8 setting of 'Nel suo sangue'). These sections include recomposed recitatives.

(ii) *March 1723*: insertion of ff. 28 and 32–3 (new III vii for Teofane and Emireno, HG 106, shifting of his aria 'Nò, non temere', and alteration of cadence on HG 99 from A to B version), 37–9 ('Gode l'alma' and previous recitative), 40–4 ('Spera sì, mi dice' at start of II v, followed by first twelve bars of next scene, renumbered and recopied), 'L'empio sleale' (now in autograph of *Giulio Cesare*, RM 20 b 3, ff. 37–40), and probably 3 (longer B section of 'Dove sei?').

(iii) *February 1726*: cancellation of longer B section of 'Dove sei?'; insertion of ff. 16–18 ('Un disprezzato affetto' in F minor); cancellation of 'Nel suo sangue' and alteration of previous recitative to version B, HG 116; insertion of 'Nell'orror' for Gismonda (= Matilda's 'All'orror' in II vi) in place of 'Trema, tiranno' in III i (no longer in manuscript, but recitative cadence shows traces of change). This refutes Clausen's statement that there is no evidence for Gismonda and Matilda exchanging pitch in this revival.

(iv) *c. May 1733*: insertion of ff. 5–7 ('Trema, tiranno' restored in place of 'Nell'orror' with cadence change reversed; first $4\frac{1}{2}$ bars of 'Io son tradito' recopied); 'Nell'orror' for Matilda inserted at end of III vi, HG 116 (no longer in manuscript). Handel marked Adelberto's 'D'inalzar i flutti' for Emireno but changed his mind in November.

(v) *November 1733*: insertion of ff. 8–13 (B version of 'Io son tradito' from middle of unchanged fifth bar, 'Un disprezzato affetto' in G minor) and 20–3 ('Pupille sdegnose' from *Muzio Scevola* for Adelberto copied in F, transposed to E flat, then returned to F—but the G minor cadence of the recopied recitative remained). In this revival Handel added many higher alternatives and transpositions to Ottone's part for Carestini, sometimes superimposed and sometimes written afresh by S1 ('Io son tradito' illustrates both). Chrysander includes the alternatives in 'Dove sei?' and most of the recitatives, but omits others on HG 57, 83, and 118. Handel put 'Dopo l'orrore' in II vii up a minor third from D to F (the copy is now in the performing score of *Oreste*, Hamburg MA/1034[50]) and the duet 'A' teneri affetti' up a tone from F to G. The previous recitative (HG 117–18) seems to have been heavily cut, though it is complete in the libretto; the last two pages (51^v, 52^r, some 31 bars) are crossed out. The same fate befell the final recitative (HG 121); the cut in HG is found only in the Hamburg score. On this occasion Handel altered the accentuation of Teofane's name throughout the manuscript (overlooking it once, on f. 32^v, HG 106); Chrysander sometimes prints both versions, sometimes only the second, retaining the original stress on the third syllable throughout the first two acts. The omission of the B section of 'Spera sì, mi dice' may also date from 1733. This aria seems to have been cut altogether on one occasion, perhaps the mysterious revival of 1727.

According to the note in the Edinburgh copy of the 1733 libretto mentioned above, 'Qual cervetta' was sung (for the first time) in Act III, presumably by Waltz. There is unexpected confirmation of this in the Hamburg score, which on f. 34^r shows traces of a pasted insertion, now missing, over the recitative cadence at the end of III v (HG 99, version A). This can only have been version C (HG 100), with the aria following; it survives nowhere except in the RM 20 b 10 autograph, which Chrysander did not see. The insertion must have fallen out since his time. As noted above, one consequence of the fragmentary state of the manuscript is that many changes and improvements are found in early copies and Walsh but not in the autograph or HG. Many transpositions for revivals have likewise been lost. Chrysander adopted the cut of a bar in 'A' teneri affetti' after bar 21, but ignored the evidence of the contraction of 'Tanti affanni' to a dal segno aria.

The Malmesbury score, signed and dated 'Eliza Legh 1724', is the only complete early copy—indeed the only complete manuscript of any version— and a crucial source for the text. It was written by Smith (pp. 1–64) and H3 (pp. 65–304, taking over in the middle of 'Del minacciar'). An appendix (pp. 305–26), in the hand of a scribe who copied the same music in Add MS

---

[50] Clausen, 190 n. 2.

31571 (Zeta), contains the four arias added for Cuzzoni's benefit on 26 March 1723. The main text probably reflects what Handel conducted at the first performance, except that 'Dove sei?' is a full aria with the longer B section. Teofane's aria in II viii is the C minor 'S'or mi dai pene', marked *A tempo giusto*. The C major sinfonia from I xi opens Act II and has repeats, but is not yet replaced by the E flat movement. 'Tanti affanni' is in shortened form with dal segno. The cadence before 'Ah! tu non sai' is in E minor; the recitative before 'D'inalzar i flutti' is version A (top of HG 96). The ritornello of 'Alla fama' (HG 61) has the revised bar 6, but bar 8 appears in a unique intermediate form. As in nearly all copies (but not HG) the tempo of 'La speranza', the B section of 'Diresti poi così?' (3/8), and 'Pensa ad amare' is *Allegro*; that of 'Benchè mi sia' is *Allegro ma non troppo*, as in Flower and the early Add MS 31571, but Handel may have changed it later (it is *Andante allegro* in Lennard and Add MS 33238). There are a number of additional trills, slurs, dynamics, and details of orchestration. The oboe part in 'Pur che regni' is a solo from the start. The top instrumental part in 'La speranza', 'Del minacciar', 'Tu puoi straziarmi', the C major sinfonia, 'Dopo l'orrore', both duets, and the *coro* is for *Tutti* or *Tutti unis*, indicating that both oboes double the first violins. This agrees with the Flower parts and other copies; it is often misinterpreted by Chrysander. 'Nò, non temere' is ambiguous, with *Tutti* on the top line but each part marked for strings. Hamburg has the same, but (*Violini*) seems to have been added by Chrysander; no instruments are named in the autograph.

The Durham Cathedral copy (Mus D 16), written by Smith, is very early (?January 1723) but corresponds to no performance. It was evidently prepared to the order of a patron with an alto voice.[51] Apart from Emireno's part all the arias but one are transposed down by intervals from a tone to a fifth and written in the alto clef.[52] (The exception, 'Trema, tiranno', could only be transposed if the violin parts were rewritten.) This copy contains no secco recitatives and nothing later than January 1723, and may have been taken partly from the autograph. Of the pieces rejected before performance it includes the D major 'Io sperai trovar' (with 'Ritorna, O dolce'), 'Pensa, spietata madre' (with 'Ah! tu non sai'), 'Dir li potessi' (not 'Benchè mi sia'), and the 4/4 (not the 3/8) setting of 'Nel suo sangue'. 'O grati orrori' introduces the first (*Larghetto* 3/4) setting of 'S'or mi dai pene', confusingly transposed to C minor; neither the later setting nor 'S'io dir potessi' is present. The overture (as performed), concerto (first movement of Op. 3 no. 6), both duets, and the *coro* are included, but not 'Io son tradito'. Some of Handel's revisions have been incorporated, for example in bar 24 (but not bar 12) of 'Affanni del pensier', 'All'orror', 'Deh! non dir', and 'Tanti affanni', but not in 'Alla fama' or 'A' teneri affetti'. The C major sinfonia (with repeats) has already been moved to Act II, and 'Diresti poi così?' has the later 3/8 B section. 'Falsa imagine' has no string coda. 'Dove sei?' is a full aria with the longer B section.

The Flower copy (S2 late 1730s), likewise lacking secco recitatives and everything composed after March 1723, was certainly copied to a large extent from the autograph; it contains many readings and whole pieces that occur nowhere else and were never performed, among them 'Giunt'in porto', the shorter B

---

[51] Compare the similar copies of *Floridante* (RM 19 f 4) for alto, and *Giulio Cesare* (RM 19 b 3) and *Admeto* (Add MS 38002) for soprano voices.

[52] The transpositions in Teofane's part are not always the same as in the Bodleian copy.

section of 'Dove sei?', 'Non a tempre', 'A te lascio', and the incomplete C minor storm sinfonia in III iii. 'Pensa, spietata madre' and 'Dir li potessi' are found elsewhere only in the Durham copy. The copyist had another source for II viii and ix (the Fitzwilliam segment, evidently already detached), for he did not include the G minor 'S'or mi dai pene' or the C major 'Le profonde vie'; they are almost the only pieces composed by January 1723 that he omits.[53] The alternative B sections of 'Diresti poi così?' and 'Dove sei?', and the two settings of 'Nel suo sangue' appear consecutively; the 4/4 B section of 'Diresti poi così?' includes the six bars crossed out in the autograph. Other traces of a second source are a number of tempo marks not in the autograph; they are in the Malmesbury score but not all in HG. The pieces subsequently modified by Handel ('Falsa imagine', 'Affanni del pensier', 'Dell'onda', 'All'orror', 'Alla fama', 'Deh! non dir', 'Tanti affanni', 'A' teneri affetti') are all in their original form. The string coda of 'Falsa imagine' is correctly barred, as Ex. 51. This is the only copy to place the C major sinfonia (HG 42) in Act I.

It is clear that, as with other copies made for Jennens, S2 had authority to transcribe whatever he could find, even rejected and unfinished pieces. There are signs that he sometimes misread the autograph. He was puzzled by the C major sinfonia, of which Handel wrote the first two bars last and later required a repeat; the copyist's version consists of bars 3–6 followed by 1–7. His eccentric text of the overture seems to derive from a collation of the autograph with the score as performed: it agrees with Chrysander to the end of the Gavotte (HG 7), then repeats the introduction with the conclusion given on HG 144 and follows this with the second Allegro (HG 7–11). A detached copy of the overture in the same collection (v. 226, also S2) has the same arrangement. The order is confused in the middle of Act III: 'A te lascio' comes after 'D'inalzar i flutti', and 'Dir li potessi' is followed by 'S'io dir potessi'. No doubt S2 inserted the latter here because it employs the same material. This supports the conjecture that it had been discarded in favour of the C minor 'S'or mi dai pene', which follows 'O grati orrori' in the main text.

At the end of the score (*Arie adgiunte*), in the same hand, are Cuzzoni's three arias added in March 1723, but not Adelberto's 'Cara, tu nel mio petto'. There are numerous annotations by Jennens, who also had access to the autograph. He added the names of the instruments to the Gavotte in the overture, some omitted words in 'Giunt'in porto', the *Allegro* tempo mark in the 3/8 B section of 'Diresti poi così?' (with a note about the da capo) and in the 3/8 'Nel suo sangue', the date and place of completion at the end of the score (copied exactly from the autograph with its mixture of four languages[54]), and the note 'The pidgeon Song' on 'Spera sì, mi dice' in the appendix. In 'Dell'onda' he even produced a variorum text by adding Handel's shortened versions either above the stave or at the end of the aria, marking each alternative 'as perform'd' and 'left out in the performance'.

S2 extracted the Flower parts (late 1740s) from this score, with which they agree in all material respects except that the overture and the three arias in the appendix are omitted. The parts are violin 2, viola, cello + bassoon, oboe + recorder 2, and cembalo; violin 1 and oboe 1 are missing. The recorder appears only in 'Dir li potessi'; the top line of 'Deh! non dir' is *V. uniss.* as in the Flower

---

[53] Also missing are 'Qual cervetta' (in no copy), 'Cervo altier' (date uncertain), and the duet 'Non tardate a festeggiar'.

[54] As printed in Squire's *Catalogue*, 57.

and Malmesbury scores, but no instruments are named in the autograph (Chry-sander added the recorders from Walsh; they are also in Lennard and may be authentic). The cello has a *solo* mark throughout the B sections of 'Affanni del pensier' and 'Vieni, O figlio'. The bassoon is silenced in 'Falsa imagine', 'Bel labbro' (except the ritornello), and 'Tanti affanni'; it has separate staves in the 'Bel labbro' ritornello and (both parts) in 'O grati orrori', and a *soli* passage in the bass of the concerto movement. In 'Dell'onda' the viola has a separate stave for violin 3. As in other early copies the viola part of 'Trema, tiranno' is fuller than in HG and the second violin differently distributed. S2 supplied a viola part for the storm sinfonia in III iii, working in octaves with violins or bass, although its stave is blank in the Flower score as in the autograph. It is clear from the oboe 2 part that both oboes double the first violins in the ritornello of the pieces so indicated in the Malmesbury score (except that they are silent in the little C major sinfonia and in 'Nò, non temere'); here they do the same in 'Affanni del pensier' and 'Pensa, spietata madre'. S2 slipped up in 'Bel labbro', omitting oboes and viola from the ritornello and marking the cello part of the B section *senza Basson*.

The three remaining copies with recitatives, Granville, Lennard, and Add MS 33238, are late composite scores combining versions from several produc-tions with material rejected before performance. Granville (BL Egerton 2918, S5) diverges from Malmesbury in the following principal respects: 'La speranza' is in E flat with the recitative modified to end in G minor (probably 1726); the unperformed D major 'Io sperai trovar'[55] replaces 'Ritorna, O figlio'; II viii is in its March 1723 form with 'Tra queste care' (not sung after that year), and so is III vii (HG 106–12), the recitative at the bottom of HG 99 reverting to its original C major cadence (version B); 'Un disprezzato affetto' in F minor replaces 'Tanti affanni' in III ii (1726). The recitative before 'Ah! tu non sai' ends in E major. Two of the March 1723 additions, 'Cara, tu nel mio petto' and 'Spera sì, mi dice' are missing. The 3/8 'Nel suo sangue', not sung after 1723, is present, preceded by the B (1726) form of the recitative on HG 116, ending in C minor. This makes nonsense; so does the recitative before 'D'inalzar i flutti', a mixture of the A and B versions on HG 96. The little embarcation sinfonia in II xi is confined to its bass, marked *Adagio e piano*. This is the only copy with the E flat sinfonia in I xi.

Lennard (Smith, c. 1736–40) is still more of a *mélange*. The material rejected before performance, besides the D major 'Io sperai trovar', comprises the 4/4 B section of 'Diresti poi cosi?', the 4/4 'Nel suo sangue', and the full autograph text of 'Tanti affanni' preceded by the B version of 'Io son tradito' ending in B flat major. I xi has no sinfonia; 'Spera sì, mi dice' is in, but not 'Cara, tu nel mio petto'; as in Walsh (but nowhere else except Add MS 33238) recorders double the violins in 'Deh! non dir'; 'Dove sei?' has A section only. The 1726 recitative cuts are made in some scenes (I i and iii, II v) but not others, and there are differences of pitch on HG 58, 74, and 116. The recitative of II iv is reduced to the first three lines of the shorter text (1733), ending in B major. Those on HG 96 and 113 are version A. There is a fresh crop of tempo marks: 'Spera sì, mi dice' (*Andante* in the autograph), 'Dopo l'orrore', 'Deh! non dir', 'Gode l'alma' (*Andante* in Hamburg and Granville), and 'Nel suo sangue' (4/4) are all *Allegro*; 'D'inalzar i flutti' is *Allegro e staccato*, 'Benchè mi sia' *Andante*

---

[55] Its appearance in several scores might suggest that Handel at some time resuscitated it, but he had used the material in *Tamerlano*.

allegro. Teofane's name is generally accented as in the autograph, but three out of twenty-one contexts (HG 14, 50, 57) adopt the 1733 change. In other respects the text agrees with Granville. Both have the revised form of the arias except where mentioned and in 'All'orror', where they follow the autograph and HG. Add MS 33238, a late copy in an unknown hand with very small clefs, is almost identical with Lennard and was probably copied from it. It has no independent authority.

Many eighteenth-century manuscripts contain selections from *Ottone*. Some are very early, and help to date unpublished variants. Apart from the Bodleian copy the most interesting is Add MS 31571, a compilation by many hands (wrongly identified in the Hughes-Hughes *Catalogue*) of opera arias dating from *c.*1719–26. Folios 15–61 carry three groups of *Ottone* excerpts in four different hands:

(i) (a) Second setting of 'S'or mi dai pene' (C minor, *A tempo giusto*), 'Benchè mi sia' (*Allegro mà non troppo*), and second setting of 'Nel suo sangue' (HG 115, *Allegro*), written by H1 on 15–22^r; (b) 'S'io dir potessi' and the duets 'Non tardate a festeggiar' and 'A' teneri affetti' with the extra bar, written by H3 on 22^v–33. These pieces, nearly all pre-performance insertions in the August 1722 score, were clearly copied at the same time, probably in 1723 or very soon after, when both copyists were most active. This manuscript establishes the early date of 'Non tardate a festeggiar' (since confirmed by the Barnby copy); H3 had disappeared long before 1733, when Handel first performed the duet. 'S'io dir potessi' has a viola part, present in no other source.

(ii) The four arias added in March 1723, copied on 34–44 by Zeta, who wrote the same pieces in the appendix to the Malmesbury score.

(iii) Five 1726 insertions headed 'Additional Songs in Otho'—'Cervo altier', 'Vinto è l'amor', E major 3/4 setting of 'Io sperai trovar' (*Larghetta staccato* as in the autograph), 'Di far le sue vendette', and 'Un disprezzato affetto'— copied by S2 on 45–61.

Other excerpts attributable to the 1720s are Add MS 24307, ff. 10–13 ('Gode l'alma' in F major, H5); 'S'io dir potessi' in RM 18 b 4, ff. 41–2, 'Sig^{ra} Cuzzoni in Otho', without viola part (Smith); and seven fragments, mostly alterations or insertions and nearly all unpublished, in RM 18 c 10, ff. 3–10 (S2). These are the short sinfonia in C (HG 42, with repeat signs at beginning and end) and its replacement in E flat, the first setting of 'S'or mi dai pene' (*Larghetto*, G minor) without concluding ritornello, the reduced two-bar coda of 'Falsa imagine', the longer B section of 'Dove sei?', 'All'orror' with Handel's revisions, and 'Io son tradito' (version A, HG 86). Slightly later (1730s) are 'Sino che ti vedrò', adapted from 'Come se ti vedrò' in *Muzio Scevola*, and the duet 'Non tardate a festeggiar' in RM 18 c 6, ff. 9–14 (S2); 'Affanni del pensier' (in its original form), 'Io son tradito' (version A, but with a final major chord[56]), and 'Un disprezzato affetto' (HG 91) in Manchester MS 130 Hd4, v. 313, pp. 84–100 (Smith); arrangements of 'Alla fama' and 'Dell'onda' for Charles Clay's 'surprising musical clock' which so impressed the Royal Family in May 1736,[57] in RM 19 a 1, ff. 166^v and 168^v (S2); and flute arrangements of parts in six arias in RM 19 a 8 (Jennens). Most of the S2

[56] This is found in several other copies, mostly late; Handel may have changed the chord when he wrote the new aria.

[57] See W. Barclay Squire, 'Handel's Clock Music', *MQ* v (1919), 538 ff., where the tunes are printed.

Aylesford copies were supplements to the Flower score already supplied to Jennens. Immediately before the two extracts in RM 18 c 6 is a variant (ff. 5–8, S3) of the second movement of Op. 3 no. 6, the concerto that contributed its Vivace to *Ottone*; the presence of an organ part led Squire to attribute it wrongly to Op. 7 no. 4. There are slight differences from Op. 3 as printed in bars 50 and 51. It is possible, though unlikely, that the movement was connected with the 1733 revival of *Ottone*.

Add MS 31572 contains a large collection of excerpts from *Ottone*, mixed with 23 pieces from *Flavio* and an aria from Ariosti's *Coriolano*, in the hand of a scribe who wrote parts for *Alexander's Feast* in the Coke Collection (in association with S2 and others) and for *Esther* in Durham Cathedral Library, perhaps about 1740. The *Ottone* pieces, two duets and 24 arias in no sort of order, include three additions of March 1723 and five of 1726 (in a group later in the manuscript). Most are in Handel's revised versions, but 'A' teneri affetti' has the extra bar. 'La speranza' is in E flat.

Handel's harpsichord arrangement of the overture,[58] considerably recomposed except in the Gavotte, appears in two Malmesbury volumes (H5, *c*.1724; Smith, *c*.1728), RM 18 c 1, ff. 29–31 (S2, *c*.1728), an addendum to the Ripin MS in the Boston Museum of Fine Arts (S1), RM 18 c 2, ff. 1–3 (Kappa, *c*.1729), and New York Public Library Mus Res MN* (copyist unidentified).

The Coke Collection contains copies of the overture (the introduction *Largo*, the Gavotte *Allegro*) and 'Concerto in Otho' (the Vivace only) in a volume dated 1736; 'Spera sì, mi dice' with a few ornaments, the only manuscript bearing the *Andante* tempo mark of the autograph; the overture and 'Del minacciar' arranged for keyboard with octave passages harmonized; 'Alla fama' in G (revised ritornello) and 'Benchè mi sia' in G minor, both with the vocal line copiously ornamented with trills, mordents, and turns, perhaps for harpsichord. 'Benchè mi sia' has a cadenza at the end of the B section. There are two such copies of 'Alla fama', almost identical, in different volumes, both apparently from the 1720s or a little later; one also contains 'Nò, non temere' without text or decoration. The ornaments bear little resemblance to Handel's in the Bodleian copy.

A set of seven parts for the 'Concerto in Otho' (the Vivace in D) in Durham Cathedral Library (MS E34 (ii)) was formerly in the possession of Richard Fawcett, active in Oxford 1730–54; the copyist's hand is found in other Durham manuscripts and instrumental movements from *Tamerlano*, *Rodelinda*, and *Ariodante* in Add MS 29386. The latter volume contains a late copy of 'Pensa ad amare' (short score, A section only), Manchester v. 314 a keyboard version of 'La speranza' in F, Add MS 31577 ('Gulielmus Bogdani') another keyboard arrangement of the overture, a straight transcription of the score. The same copyist was probably responsible for a set of five parts for 'Pur che regni' and 'La speranza' (*Allegro*, G major) in Hamburg MA/180, the vocal line marked alternatively for *flautino traverso*.

Walsh and the Hares issued a score (*Otho an opera as it was Perform'd at the King's Theatre for the Royal Academy . . . Publish'd by the Author*) about 19 March 1723, with the Privilege dated 14 June 1720. It contains all the arias of the January

[58] Printed in *Twenty Overtures*, ii. 8.

1723 score (but 'S'io dir potessi', not 'S'or mi dai pene') together with the overture in three movements as performed, concerto Vivace, both duets, and one accompanied recitative ('O grati orrori'), but not the sinfonia on HG 42. The bass is copiously figured; tempo marks and orchestration are deficient. The viola part is frequently omitted, and sometimes the second violin as well; the instruments are seldom named. 'Falsa imagine' lacks its string coda. 'Diresti poi così?' has the 3/8 B section (*Allegro*); 'Dove sei?' is a cavatina; 'Nel suo sangue' is the 3/8 version. 'Affanni del pensier', 'Dell'onda', 'All'orror', 'Deh! non dir', and 'Tanti affanni' are in revised form, but not 'Alla fama' or 'A' teneri affetti'. 'Deh! non dir' (*Allegro*) has recorders with violins on the top line. 'Tanti affanni', though shortened, is given a da capo, as in Add MS 31572.

Walsh (3 April) and Richard Meares (about the same time) each published a selection of favourite songs, containing the same nine arias and one duet ('A' teneri affetti'). Walsh's, printed on one side of the paper, is simply extracted from his score; that of Meares, printed on both sides, differs little except in tempo marks. Walsh issued the four songs added in March 1723 in *The Monthly Mask of Vocal Musick. . .for Aprill* the same year ('Gode l'alma' is *Allegro ma non troppo*) and the five added in 1726 in *The Quarterly Collection of Vocal Musick, Containing the Choicest Songs for the last Three Months, namely January, February & March, being the 'Additional Songs' in Otho*. He also published a flute arrangement (24 April 1723) and the overture in parts (by 1727). The harpsichord version of the overture in his first collection (1726) is not Handel's but the work of a clumsy hack. The first volume of Cluer and Creake's *Pocket Companion* (May 1724) included seven songs from *Ottone* in short score, most of them with a flute arrangement: 'La speranza' in E flat, 'Nò, non temere' in E minor, 'Alla fama' with revised ritornello (but mistakes in bar 8). There were single-sheet issues of the Gavotte as *A Bacchanal* for one or two voices and of 'Nò, non temere' and 'La speranza'. The first two had English words by Leveridge. A fragment of 'S'io dir potessi' appeared with English words in *The Monthly Mask of Vocal Musick* for August 1724. Walsh paid Handel £42 for the right to publish *Ottone*: the date 1722 in his account book is presumably Old Style, the year ending in March 1723.

Chrysander (1881) used one autograph volume (RM 20 b 9), the incomplete Hamburg copy, Walsh, and the 1723 libretto. His score is a mixture of all the versions analysed above, and is most confusing in Act III, where by treating the scene added in March 1723 as part of the original he produced various anomalies, including two scenes numbered vii. This could have been clarified from the libretto. His contempt for Walsh was so great that he ignored him when he was right as well as when he was wrong; the statement that the arias in Walsh correspond with the original (except in errors) is not true. It is not clear why Chrysander bracketed the tempo marks on 'Pur che regni' and 'Trema, tiranno'; both are in the autograph and Walsh (and all copies), and the second in the performing score (twice).

Hagen's vocal score (Bergedorf, 1925) treats the text in his usual cavalier manner. The story is simplified, the recitative recomposed, the order of arias changed, most of them shortened, and extraneous instrumental movements inserted. The omission of eight arias (among them 'Diresti poi così?') and the preference for two never performed by Handel ('Giunt'in porto' and 'A te lascio') are minor blemishes in comparison with the mutilations and falsifications inflicted on the music. There are numerous rallentandos, ritenutos, and crescendos, including a 'grosses crescendo' in 'Vieni, O figlio' (marked by Handel *piano sempre*); 'Falsa imagine' incredibly is *Agitato non presto*, 'Notte cara' *Andante quasi Allegro*. 'All'orror' is given a bogus initial ritornello, whereas the balance of aria after aria is destroyed by the emasculation of Handel's own ritornellos. The *coro* is rewritten to bring in a modern chorus as well as the ensemble of soloists. Adelberto becomes a tenor, requiring transpositions and rewriting, Ottone a baritone. The transfer of 'Del minacciar del vento' to Act III, where it is very soon followed by 'Nò, non temere', is insensitive. It is symptomatic that the high G at the end of 'Pur che regni', which Handel set to the word 'Nò!', is sung here to 'Ja!'.

Additional Notes

* (p. 430) A slightly varied text of this aria is in the printed libretto of Alessandro Scarlatti's serenata *La gloria della primavera*, as performed at the King's Theatre on 28 March 1721 (see p. 307). It is not in Scarlatti's original (Naples, 1714) and was probably introduced by Boschi from Lotti's *Teofane*. He sang virtually the same text in all three works.

* (p. 433) See also W. Dean, 'The Genesis and Early History of *Ottone*', *Göttinger Händel-Beiträge* II (1986), 129–40.

* (p. 449) This libretto was evidently set up from a score, probably Handel's performing score (see Harris, *Librettos* vol. 13, xvii).

* (p. 452) A hitherto unreported score owned by Canon B. L. Barnby could be even earlier; paper and contents suggest a date of 1723. It was probably copied (by an unrecognised hand) for the Duchess of Newcastle, whose signature is on the flyleaf. It lacks all recitatives and orchestral movements except the overture and contains nothing later than January 1723, but omits three arias sung at the first performance, 'Ah! tu non sai', 'Alla fama', and 'Nò, non temere'. The aria in II viii is the C minor 'S'or mi dai pene', the duet at the end of the act 'Non tardate a festeggiar'. 'La speranza' is in E flat; 'False imagine' has no coda; 'A' teneri affetti' lacks its extra bar. While Handel's pre-performance changes are incorporated, the text differs from Malmesbury and all other sources in a number of respects. 'Non tardate a festeggiar' is dal segno with an eight-bar lead-back to the repeat (the other two isolated copies are da capo). 'Nel suo sangue' (3/8) is accompanied only by a bass and has a six-bar cut (56–61) in the A section. 'Benchè mi sia' is *Allegro ma non presto*.

CHAPTER 21

FLAVIO RE DE' LONGOBARDI

THE plot is complicated on paper (much less so in the theatre), with seven important characters and several changes of scene in each act. Flavio, King of the Lombards, has two elderly counsellors, Ugone and Lotario; he also has a queen, Ernelinda, but she never appears and has perhaps retired hurt under the impact of Flavio's infidelities. Lotario's daughter Emilia is betrothed to Ugone's son Guido. The latter's sister Teodata is in love with Vitige, a courtier, and it is clear from the start that their relationship is that of Romeo and Juliet, secret and passionate.[1] The action takes place at some period in the Dark Ages when Britain was subject to Lombard rule.

Haym's Argument in the printed libretto, though not quite accurate, deserves to be quoted in full.

This present Drama is form'd of two Actions: One is taken partly from the History of the Kings of Lombardy; the other, from the famous Tragi-Comedy call'd Cid, by P. Corneille. The first is, that Flavius, the XIIIth King of Lombardy, hearing from Ernelinda his Queen great Commendations of the Beauty of Theodata a Roman Lady falls deeply in love with her: but then reflecting on his Error, generously yields her to Vitige, to whom she had secretly promised her Faith in Marriage.

The second is, the Nuptials being fixed between Guido and Emilia, are disturb'd by a strange Accident; viz, Lotarius, the Father of Emilia, having given Hugo, the Father of Guido, a blow on the Face, his Son, to repair the Honour of his Family, challenges Lotarius and kills him. But so powerful was Love in Emilia and the sincere Demonstrations of Guido, that both renew'd their promise to accomplish the Nuptials, when Time might in Part have mitigated the Grief for the Death of her Father.

These Episods [sic] do not want connection, as may be seen in the present Drama.

Act I begins at *Night. Garden to Hugo's Palace. Vitige leading Theodata out of her Apartment.*[2] She asks him to meet her later at her brother Guido's betrothal; he refuses, since duty calls him to court. They part after a loving duet. The set changes to *a hall in Lotario's house illuminated for the wedding of Emilia and Guido. After a short symphony Lotario enters from one side and crosses to receive Ugone who comes in with Guido and Teodata and a suite of knights and ladies.* Lotario *tells a page* to summon Emilia, who *enters with attendants.* The parents join the hands of the engaged couple, and *all go out,* leaving them to sing in turn of their happiness. In Flavio's *audience chamber* Ugone presents Teodata to the king, who is much taken with her and proposes to introduce her to the queen. After father and daughter have gone Lotario brings an invitation to Emilia's wedding, which

---

[1] This is quite explicit in the libretto as first set, which refers to 'notturno amor'; it was toned down before the text was printed, and modified in the autograph and performing score (see below, p. 477).

[2] This is almost the only direction in the English version of the libretto. The others in this summary are translated from the Italian text or from the fuller version in Handel's autograph.

Flavio accepts. *A soldier enters with a dispatch* from Narsete, the Lombard governor of Britain, asking to be relieved of his post because of illness. Flavio thinks of appointing Lotario, but changes his mind and sends for 'l'antico Ugone'. *A guard goes out, and Flavio rests his hand on Lotario's shoulder.* When Ugone arrives Flavio *gives him the dispatch* and orders him to govern Britain, presumably to get him out of the way while he pays court to Teodata. Lotario is furious and, though professing loyalty, resolves on vengeance 'rather than be a Slave to a perverse Mind'. Flavio asks Vitige if he knows Teodata and if she is beautiful. The embarrassed Vitige says he does not find her so, whereupon Flavio proclaims his love for her, leaving Vitige not a little alarmed. In *a hall of the palace* Ugone *shows Guido his cheek where he has been struck by Lotario*, and asks him to avenge this insult from a base hand. Guido *remains thoughtful*, torn between love for Emilia and anger at her father's slight to the family honour. *As he makes to leave, he is held back by the entry of Emilia and stands motionless.* When she addresses him *he tries once more to leave, but she detains him.* He makes her swear to keep faith even against the king, public opinion, and her father. His extravagant behaviour leaves her puzzled and anxious.

Act II. In *a stately room in Flavio's palace* Teodata appears at his summons and *kneels* before him. He is overcome by her beauty, but before he can declare his feelings Ugone enters *crying out* in confusion. *He hides his face,* but Flavio *removes the veil* and again orders him to Britain. Teodata is embarrassed at being found alone with the king. He tells her to find out the cause of her father's trouble and goes out. When Ugone mentions an insult to his honour, Teodata concludes that he has discovered her clandestine affair, again *goes on her knees* and *cries out* for Vitige, saying he has promised to marry her. This additional affront is too much for Ugone: he denounces his daughter as a traitress and declares himself 'the Mock of Fate, and Jest of the World'. In *a garden* Lotario curtly orders Emilia to forget her proposed marriage to Guido. When Guido enters she asks why he conceals the cause of his agitation: Lotario's new command, she assures him, will not affect her love. At his request she leaves him alone with his anxiety. Guido now has a double motive for revenge on Lotario, but wonders how he can face life without Emilia. Meanwhile[3] Flavio horrifies Vitige with a request to procure Teodata for him. Teodata tells Vitige that Ugone knows their secret. Vitige gives her Flavio's message and urges her to dissemble: she will be his by sunset, or Ugone, Guido, the king, Vitige, and the world will perish by his sword. She accepts the plan, but warns him against jealousy; he refuses to doubt her faith. In *a courtyard of Lotario's house* Guido meets the still smouldering Lotario and demands satisfaction for the insult to his father. Lotario *tries to escape,* but Guido *puts his hand on his sword. They fight, Lotario falls,* and *Guido departs.* Emilia enters to find *Lotario on the ground. He rises staggering to his feet,* identifies his assailant, and *collapses on the stage.* She invokes the fury of Nemesis against her unworthy lover, but cannot face the prospect and decides to die herself.

Act III. In *a room in the palace* Emilia and Ugone approach Flavio, the one demanding justice, the other pleading justification for Guido's act in killing Lotario. They have scarcely begun to explain when Flavio, after *watching Ugone,* says he has no time to discuss such an important matter at the moment and asks them to withdraw. Vitige enters with Teodata. Flavio orders Vitige to plead his cause with the lady, but soon takes the lead himself (while Vitige

[3] Presumably there is a set change here, but none is specified.

shows signs of distress): she shall be his queen this very day. She replies: 'Since it is thus, Vitige, farewell', and Flavio goes out with a happy love song. Teodata tells Vitige to stop complaining and 'blame thy own foolish Counsel': how can she help it 'if Love will have it so'? Vitige cannot make up his mind if she is still dissembling and sings a violent aria. In the next scene[4] Emilia, *dressed in mourning*, denounces Guido as a traitor; he admits the charge, gives her the sword with which he killed her father, and begs her to use it on him. *She takes it and goes to strike him.* When he asks why she hesitates, she approaches *without looking at him* and again *goes to kill him, but on catching sight of his face drops the weapon and runs away.* Back in the palace Vitige addresses Teodata ironically as 'my Queen'; it is now her turn to be uncertain whether her leg is being pulled. After a little bickering they embrace, and are caught in the act by Flavio, who has been watching and now *comes in between them.* Shamefacedly they confess the truth. Guido enters and asks for death if his crime still makes him odious to Emilia. When that lady arrives Flavio *makes a signal to Guido unseen by Emilia* and tells her that Guido is dead: let her 'behold the proud Head of the offending Youth'. She refuses to look, demanding death for herself. When at last she turns, she *sees Guido and embraces him.* Flavio concludes the action by saying to Vitige 'For Punishment, give thy unwilling Hand to her, that does not please thee', and to Ugone 'Embrace Vitige . . . he is worthy of thy Daughter, and go thou to the Command of Britain'.

The source of this remarkable libretto was Matteo Noris's *Flavio Cuniberto*, first set by G. D. Partenio for Venice in 1682.[5] Noris connected the two 'Episods' through the person of the king, Cuniberto (Flavio was a generic name for the Lombard kings). According to the eighth-century historian Paul the Deacon's *History of the Langobards*,

King Cunincpert indeed took to wife Hermelinda, of the race of the Anglo-Saxons. She had seen in the bath Theodata, a girl sprung from a very noble stock of Romans, of graceful body and adorned with flaxen hair almost to the feet, and she praised the girl's beauty to the King Cunincpert, her husband. And although he concealed from his wife that he had heard this with pleasure, he was inflamed, nevertheless, with great love for the girl, and without delay he set forth to hunt in the wood they call 'The City' and directed his wife Hermelinda to come with him. And he stole out from there by night and came to Ticinum, and making the girl Theodata come to him he lay with her. Yet he sent her afterwards into a monastery in Ticinum which was called by her name.

Noris took over the queen's part in this affair (her nationality may have suggested the governorship of Britain as the occasion of the dispute) and her absence of credible motive in throwing Teodata into the king's arms. She goes to great lengths in describing Teodata's beauty in Act I, and does not introduce her to Cuniberto till Act II. Ernelinda's subsequent jealousy is a strong element in the plot. Noris weakened the dramatic cogency—not to

---

[4] Two more set changes must be presumed (III iv and v). Both are in the 1696 source libretto, which has *Emilia's Mourning Chamber* and *a Gallery.*

[5] Different articles in *The New Grove* ascribe the 1682 setting and that of 1688 both to Partenio and to Domenico Gabrielli. Sonneck, Loewenberg, Deutsch, Smith, and others give Haym's source as *Flavio Bertarido, rè de' Longobardi* (1706) by Stefano Ghigi. This has no relation to Handel's *Flavio*, but treats the same subject as his *Rodelinda.*

mention the poetry—of the Corneille element. In *Le Cid* Diègue (Ugone) is an elder statesman, full of years and honour, Gomès (Lotario) a man in the prime of life with a hot temper and intense pride. The cause of the quarrel is not the governorship of Britain but the king's choice of Diègue instead of Gomès as his son's tutor. Gomès is very much the aggressor; he assaults, disarms, and knocks down an older man, despite the latter's conciliatory words. The dilemma of Rodrigue (Guido) and Chimène (Emilia) after Rodrigue has killed Gomès is genuinely moving. The king is a strong statesmanlike figure; when Chimène demands vengeance for her father's death, his position is rendered doubly difficult by the fact (not mentioned in the libretto) that Rodrigue (Le Cid) has saved the kingdom from the Moors and by his bravery and resolution taken the place of the man he has killed. The climax is brought on by another duel, between Rodrigue and a courtier, Don Sanche, for the hand of Chimène; thinking that Rodrigue has been killed, she publicly reveals her love for him and refuses to obey the king's wish that she should marry the victor. To these serious strains Noris added the inevitable comic servant, Bleso, who comments satirically on his social superiors, and Teodata's lover Vitige.

This libretto enjoyed considerable success and was repeatedly revived in the next twenty years, both in Partenio's setting and in those of other composers. There were productions in Venice 1687, Modena 1688, Venice 1692, Naples 1693, Rome 1696, Florence 1697, Genoa 1702, Pratolino 1702, and the preface to the 1696 libretto mentions others at Milan, Genoa, and Livorno. Among the composers were Domenico Gabrielli (1688), Alessandro Scarlatti (1693 and Pratolino 1702), and Luigi Mancia (1696). The 1697 production seems to have been a pasticcio containing arias from Bononcini's *Il trionfo di Camilla*.[6] During the course of these revivals Noris's plot and his recitatives underwent comparatively little change, but the aria texts were constantly replaced, cut, shifted from scene to scene, and sometimes restored. This affected the musical balance of the roles. In Partenio's opera the eponymous monarch had the largest share of the arias. Scarlatti in 1693 greatly expanded Bleso's part, and Mancia gave further weight to the comic element by introducing a second servant, Emilia's nurse Zelta, and appending substantial improvised intermezzos at the end of the first two acts. He increased the prominence of Teodata and Vitige at the expense of Ernelinda and Cuniberto, and magnified Lotario, no doubt for a particular singer. Ugone seems always to have been the least important character. Table 7 gives the distribution of arias.

Haym's immediate source was the Rome libretto of 1696.[7] As usual the changes made by him and Handel are illuminating. Apart from the adjustment of arias to exits (still very casual in 1696) and the inevitable abridgement of recitative and reduction in the number of set pieces, they cut out the servants (predictably) and Ernelinda. The suppression of the latter, except as

[6] Information about the early *Flavio Cuniberto* operas, sometimes conflicting, can be found in Strohm, *HJb* (1975), 117 (*Essays*, 48), E. Dahnk-Baroffio, 'Zum Textbuch von Händels *Flavio*', *Göttinger Händel Festspiele* (Göttingen, 1967), 37–40, *The New Grove*, and the various printed librettos. Important further details have been supplied by Lowell Lindgren. Dahnk-Baroffio gives a table of scenes comparing Haym, Noris, and Corneille, but was not aware of the 1696 libretto.

[7] Strohm (ibid.) suggests that it may have been adapted by Silvio Stampiglia, and that Haym played in the orchestra at the Capranica Theatre production of Mancia's opera and brought a copy of the libretto to London. The ten singers on this occasion were all male, the four female parts being taken by castratos owing to the papal ban on women in the Roman theatres.

TABLE 7

	Partenio 1682	Scarlatti 1693	Mancia 1696	Handel 1723
Flavio (Cuniberto)	9	9	5	3
Ernelinda	4	7	3	—
Guido	4 + 1 duet	7 + 1 duet 1 arioso	4 + 2 duets 2 ariosos	4 + 1 duet
Emilia	7 + 1 duet	5 + 2 duets 2 ariosos	5 + 3 duets 2 ariosos	5 + 1 duet
Vitige	3 + 2 duets	4	6 + 1 duet 1 arioso	3 + 1 duet 1 arioso
Teodata	4 + 2 duets	7 + 1 duet	6 + 2 duets	3 + 1 duet
Lotario	1	0 + 1 duet 1 arioso	5	2
Ugone	0	0	1	1
Bleso	2	9 + 1 duet	2 + 4 duets	—
Zelta	—	—	2 + 4 duets	—
Total	34 + 3 duets	48 + 3 duets 4 ariosos	39 + 8 duets 5 ariosos	21 + 2 duets 1 arioso (+ *coro*)

a shadowy figure in the background, may have been due to the absence of a singer for her (it is difficult to see who else could have been omitted), but it was an undoubted improvement; while further reducing Flavio's status, it got rid of the tiresome convention, beloved of the seventeenth century, whereby he fell in love with a hearsay description. Ugone's introduction of his daughter does however make us wonder why Flavio has apparently not met her before. There was also a subtle change in dramatic emphasis. As if to compensate for the elimination of the servants, Haym and Handel accentuated the element of mockery and exaggeration elsewhere. In the scene corresponding to III ii, where Teodata teases Vitige with the flirtatious 'Che colpa', the 1696 libretto gives her a straight aria urging Vitige to be patient. 'Che colpa' comes later and is addressed to Flavio after the secret is out. In the earlier librettos, as in Corneille, the face-slapping incident happens on stage and is a more serious assault; Ugone draws his sword in retaliation, but Lotario knocks it from his hand and pushes him to the ground. By banishing this episode and making Ugone come on, furtive and furious, with a red face, Haym and Handel not only strengthen the impact of the duel in Act II but make the disproportion between the injury and the reactions of Ugone and Guido a matter for ridicule.

Of the 25 vocal movements other than recitative in Handel's opera, twelve (some with modifications) use texts from 1696, two of them, 'Che colpa' and Guido's 'Rompo i lacci', shifted to different contexts. Handel set another 1696 aria, 'Dille ch'il core', twice in the autograph, and two ariosos for Guido in Act III as accompanied recitatives (HG 74). Three arias, 'Benchè povera donzella', 'Chi può mirare', and 'Da te parto', adapt phrases in the old libretto. The new pieces are the two duets, the *coro*, and the arias 'Bel contento', 'Se a te vissi', 'L'armellin vita', 'Fato tiranno', 'S'egli ti chiede',

'Parto, sì' (except the first two words,[8] transferred from a different scene), and 'Mà chi punir desio?' Of these 'Bel contento' and 'Parto, sì' occur in the two scenes added by Haym, clearly to provide an extra aria apiece for Senesino and Cuzzoni. As always the new texts strongly reinforce the expression of immediate feeling. This is most evident in the two very different love duets (the second of which has no earlier counterpart), both Lotario's arias, Ugone's 'Fato tiranno', and above all Emilia's 'Mà chi punir desio?', which supplies a far more moving end to Act II than the straightforward vengeance aria in the original.

The libretto of *Flavio* has had a bad press, and it is true that it will not bear literary inspection. It is also true that Haym's habit of compressing the dialogue and sacrificing the explanation of the characters' behaviour more than once carries the action to the brink of absurdity. Flavio's exit in II ii and his dismissal of Emilia and Ugone in III i seem inconsequent for this reason. Nevertheless, when taken in conjunction with the music (and it is unfair to judge it otherwise), it emerges as a very entertaining piece of work, an anti-heroic comedy with tragic undertones. Leichtentritt pointed out the obvious resemblance to *Don Giovanni* in the killing of Lotario; there is a more revealing Mozartian parallel in the ironical flavour of the scenes for Teodata and Vitige in Act III. Among the targets for satire are some of the most sacred conventions of *opera seria*: the fidelity of lovers, family pride and honour, and the excessively 'heroic' indignation of Ugone, Guido, and Vitige in Act II. None of the characters has much dignity, least of all Flavio, an amorous and easy-principled monarch with the rare gift of a sense of humour, which softens any resemblance to the Duke in *Rigoletto*. He can laugh at himself as well as other people, as his speeches in the last scene make clear (they come straight from Noris). It would be pointless to contrast Ugone and Lotario, a pair of cantankerous old politicians with little to choose between them except that one is a tenor and the other a bass, with their prototypes in *Le Cid*. Teodata, whose role is almost that of a soubrette, is conspicuously well drawn. The design is neatly framed between the opening and closing duets for the two pairs of lovers, and if some of the later action is rather cramped the first act (except perhaps for the betrothal scene, more fully developed by Noris) deploys the various facets of the plot with ease and skill.

Handel's score has been even more underrated, because its genre has not been recognized. Again the nearest parallel is Mozart, with whom Handel shared two rare gifts: an almost limitless insight into human character, and the ability to move with ease between comic and tragic situations and to express both in the same synoptic vision. Burney, without discussing the music in detail, notes that 'there are innumerable fine and masterly strokes in it, that would have set up an inferior composer, who had his reputation to make'; Streatfeild, apart from one aria ('Amor, nel mio penar'), dismisses it altogether. Though far removed from the conventional idea of *opera seria*, which no doubt accounts

---

[8] They alone, from the set pieces, occur in all four librettos. Scarlatti retained eleven of Partenio's aria and duet texts, paraphrasing three others; Mancia retained fifteen of Scarlatti's (including ariosos), also paraphrasing three others, but only five of Noris's survived in 1696, and three of these had been excluded from Scarlatti's opera. Curiously they include the only two used by Handel, 'Di quel bel' and 'Starvi a canto'.

for the incomprehension of those who look for a heroic successor to *Radamisto*, it is in its modest way a little masterpiece. The prevailing temper is one of sly amusement at the follies and absurdities of the human species, not excluding the more convulsive passions. These flickering emotional cross-currents between tragedy and farce, irony and pathos, are held beautifully in balance. Handel was reverting, for the first time in London, to the Venetian tradition he had adorned in *Agrippina*. But, while treating some of the characters more seriously than others, he does not split them into two groups like the masters and servants of Venetian opera. The humour permeates the whole work, though its broader aspects are confined to the situations and the recitative; the arias, many of them light and based on dance rhythms, never cross into the *buffo* style. *Flavio* is unique among the Royal Academy operas—Handel's patrons of that period preferred something loftier—but he was to return to this vein of ironical detachment in *Partenope* and again in *Serse* and *Imeneo*.

Only twice, in Emilia's aria at the end of Act II and the scene for Guido and Emilia in III iv, does Handel strike the note of high tragedy. This avoidance of the grand manner was clearly deliberate. Once or twice the music seems almost to underplay the emotional content of the words, for example in the Act I arias 'Che bel contento' and 'Amante stravagante', where in other circumstances Handel might have given Vitige's jealousy and Emilia's anxiety much more violent expression. As it is, both arias make their point discreetly within the emotional framework of an opera where extreme reactions, as in Ugone's one aria, are held up to ridicule. Needless to say this policy does not exclude a wealth of subtle detail, especially in harmony and variation of rhythm and phrase-length; and the melodic invention is conspicuously fresh and resourceful.

The two pairs of lovers are skilfully contrasted. While neither couple lacks character or vitality, Emilia and Guido are much closer than Teodata and Vitige to the norm of heroic opera. They are indeed the only predominantly serious characters (Handel liked on occasion to turn his castratos into figures of fun, but he never wrote a part of that kind for Senesino). Emilia's music is outstandingly beautiful. Two of her arias, 'Quanto dolci' and 'Parto, sì', one happy, one sad, are enriched by a flute, and in both Handel uses the instrument not to add an independent line but to shade one or other of the violin parts, doubled at the unison. This is the sort of device that looks casual on paper but can sound breath-taking in performance.[9] In 'Quanto dolci' Handel makes graceful play with dancing triplet figures; 'Parto, sì', an exquisite dialogue between voice and upper instruments, begins without ritornello with the memorable phrase later attached to 'Comfort ye' in *Messiah* but previously employed with haunting effect in 'Egli è tuo' in *Rodrigo*. The mood of serene resignation makes an overwhelming impact in this context.

Emilia has the privilege of ending both the first two acts. The melody of 'Amante stravagante' is delightfully carefree—surprisingly so for the situation—but Handel is careful to touch in the shadows by invoking the relative and the tonic minor within the first six bars of the ritornello, and the unexpected unison at the voice entry, rare in Cuzzoni arias, perhaps suggests Emilia's uncertainty about her lover's next move. The siciliano lament 'Mà chi punir desio?' at the end of Act II is the crowning glory of the opera. The

[9] 'Tu vuoi ch'io parta' in *Radamisto* and 'Piangerò' in *Giulio Cesare* are outstanding examples; both, like 'Parto, sì', are arias of farewell or lamentation. Significantly all three are in E major.

secco recitative in which Emilia reacts to her father's death at the hands of her lover, with its broken declamatory phrases and sudden shifts of tonality (always within the sharp keys), gives a vivid picture of her distress. The F sharp minor aria has a second part in C sharp minor and scarcely touches a major key except at the midway cadence of the A section; the clashes and double suspensions of the ritornello recur like a throbbing pain:

Ex. 53

After this Emilia sings the first line without accompaniment, and the strings enter *pianissimo* without the harpsichord, forming a marvellously delicate five-part texture with the voice. Her last aria, 'Da te parto', is less striking in material; but the *Adagio* entry of the voice, again unaccompanied, and the unexpected five-part ritornello after the A section (scored for unison melody instruments and bass) are happy touches, and the B section has a bold range of modulation, moving from E minor to D minor, C major, and C minor, and only just regaining E minor in time.

Guido has four arias, a modest ration for Senesino; though he is less strikingly characterized than Emilia, the music is never dull. His first aria, 'Bel contento', in the main a shop-window for Senesino's *messa di voce* and agility with dotted notes and triplets, has a Purcellian jauntiness of rhythm and a memorable coda to the first part launched from a string of sevenths over a marching crotchet bass. 'L'armellin vita', in which Guido compares himself to an ermine that dislikes getting its fur dirty, is one of those simile arias that look tiresome on paper but often succeed in performance. It is a beautiful piece with an individual melody, long flowing lines—the voice's first two phrases run to ten and nine bars respectively—and an unexpected rising ninth (almost Senesino's entire compass) at the cadence. In 'Rompo i lacci' Guido rejects the ties of love for vengeance, but suddenly wonders how he can live without Emilia. The music presents a dramatic contrast between the rapid scale figures and octaves of the first part (*tutti unisoni, Allegro* 4/4 G minor) and the tenderness of the second (*Largo* 3/8 E flat), where voice and solo oboe exquisitely intertwine over quiet chords for string quartet without continuo.

Guido's finest hour is the scene in which he invites Emilia to kill him (III iv). The early part is a flexible compound of accompanied and secco recitative. Before his entry she is bent on vengeance; her F minor accompanied recitative, following at once on the G minor cadence of the previous aria, illustrates Handel's method of breaking the tonal continuity at a change of set (the curtain of course did not fall). When Guido proclaims his love the strings drop out, but they are back as soon as the tension rises. He gives her his sword (rapid broken chords) and in the next breath (*Adagio*, smooth descending progressions) longs to expire at her feet. She hesitates (secco); he renews the appeal, its urgency stressed by the change to dotted rhythm and an expressive sequence of harmonies (A flat, F, B flat minor); she looks at him, drops the sword, and runs away. It is a searing moment (Ex. 54).

Left alone, he is almost too drained of emotion to sing. The B flat minor aria 'Amor, nel mio penar' is remarkable in several respects. The voice part, narrow in compass and devoid of all coloratura, lingers over the phrase 'Deggio sperar?' ('Ought I to hope?'), especially the first word, against a unique instrumental accompaniment, the violins at first so low that they seem scarcely able to climb the stave and a solo oboe or recorder[10] high above. The ritornellos are beautifully varied, and the imploring imitations between voice and orchestra, introduced towards the end of the first part, are expanded with haunting eloquence in the second. After this it is not surprising that the lovers' final duet should be tinged with wonder, as if they cannot quite believe in the truth of their happiness.

Teodata and Vitige are more lightly treated. Handel always paid great attention to the first scene of his operas; by beginning with a happy duet for a pair of clandestine lovers he gave *Flavio* a romantic tinge that accords nicely with its unheroic tone. It is notable that only in magic and anti-heroic operas

Ex. 54

* [10] The instrument is in some doubt; it is not named in the autograph. See p. 479 and note on p. 482.

Ex. 54 (cont.)

s'io lo mi-ro in vol-to, gia-mai l'uc-ci-de-rò.) Via sù! che tar-di?

sve-na-mi, uc-ci-di-mi, sbra-na-mi!

Emilia *(senza guardarlo)* Guido

Sì, ven-go ar-ma-ta, cor-ro. Il cor del fal-lo su-o è già com-mos-so: deh!

Emilia *(va per ucciderlo, mà vedutolo in viso si lascia cadere il ferro, e parte.)*

vi-bri il col-po, E-mi-lia. Oh ciel! non pos-so.

(*Guido* Tear my breast. Kill me! My faith will live with you. I surrender
happily if I can die at your feet.
Emilia (aside) Ah! if I look at his face I will never kill him.
Guido Come on! What are you waiting for? Shed my blood, kill me, tear me
apart.
Emilia Yes, I come armed, in haste.
Guido The heart is already moved by its crime. Alas! Strike the blow, Emilia.
Emilia Oh heaven! I cannot.)

do we find lovers living in sin;[11] heroic characters are either married (and usually separated by force) or suffer agonies from being single. The duet 'Ricordati' makes charming play with rhythmic variations of its rocking motive, both on instruments and voices. The melody was an old favourite, used in *Agrippina* and elsewhere, and close in spirit to *Acis and Galatea*. The *Allegro* tempo mark should perhaps be taken as referring to mood rather than pace. As in several other Handel operas the male part (sung here by a woman) is the higher of the two, setting a deadly trap for practitioners of octave transposition.

Teodata's music is demure, teasing, and perfectly in place; one does not expect Susanna to sing in the manner of the Countess. 'Con un' vezzo' is not far from the comic vein of Handel's Neapolitan contemporaries and the accents of Pergolesi's Serpina, except that Teodata is a contralto. She is a knowing miss, a type congenial to Handel's muse (witness Atalanta in *Serse*). Two of her arias are sublimated minuets. So are two of Vitige's, but his music strikes deeper. In 'Che bel contento', which follows Flavio's declaration of love for Teodata, Handel suggests the ache in Vitige's heart, as he proclaims his freedom from jealousy, by some delicious harmonic detail derived from suspensions. It is a little gem of dramatic irony. The B section all but quotes Teodata's 'Benchè povera donzella' earlier in the scene, though this may be accidental. 'Non credo instabile' in Act II has a ritornello based on three distinct ideas, happily varied and interchanged during the aria. Economy of notes is combined with a touching eloquence in the little F sharp minor arioso 'Corrispondi' early in Act III, a ten-bar flowering out of the recitative. Only in 'Sirti, scogli' does Vitige give vent to his jealousy. There is a touch of comic exaggeration in this explosion, whose chromatic scale figures on the strings have a distinct foretaste of the wrathful Storgè in *Jephtha*. Handel is careful not to undercut the genuine tragic emotion of the next scene.

Flavio's three arias are all genial love songs, as befits this relaxed and unpolitical monarch, and include a gavotte and a gigue. Lotario, though disposed of in Act II,[12] is the better musically endowed of the two old counsellors, whose arias, like 'Sorge nell'alma mia' in *Imeneo* and 'Smanie implacabili' and 'Come scoglio' in *Così fan tutte*, are at once parodies of the serious style and brilliant expostulations within it. Both of Lotario's are admirable examples of bass bluster, as regularly purveyed to Boschi. 'Se a te vissi' recalls Farasmane's aria in *Radamisto*. The ritornellos of 'S'egli ti chiede' are enlivened by long canons between treble and bass, and the theme is neatly inverted in the B section. The bassoons add weight to the thunder by doubling much of the voice part. Burney applauded this aria, '*fugato*, and in the church style . . . extremely artificial and masterly', without perhaps suspecting the humorous intention behind it. Ugone's one aria, also composed originally in the bass clef for Boschi, is even more of a parody; the frantic semiquaver scale figures are an exuberant comment on a sore cheek and a sorer sense of dignity.

The tonality of the opera is well balanced. The sharp keys are more prominent than usual; there are four arias in E major,[13] three in A major, and

---

[11] For example *Agrippina*, *Alcina*, and *Deidamia*. In *Rodrigo* there is an illegitimate child, but the liaison has long been broken off.

[12] But Handel brings him back for the *coro*. Presumably, like the deceased Altomaro in *Sosarme*, he sang from the wings.

[13] One of them however, 'L'armellin vita', was composed and probably sung in E flat.

two in F sharp minor. To counteract this the opening duet and the *coro* are in B
flat, with a two-movement overture in the relative minor (of sterling quality,
and thematically unified by the prominent falling fifth in each main theme),
and the second half of Act III is confined to flat keys. The two weightiest arias
are posed in the rare keys of F sharp minor and B flat minor. One
characteristic feature of Handel's style is prominent in *Flavio*, his habit of
introducing an important motive late in the first part of an aria—for example
the trills on the word 'nò' (later 'sì') in 'Benchè povera donzella' and the
dotted figure tossed between voice and orchestra in 'Amor, nel mio penar'—
and proceeding to develop it in the closing ritornello and B section. Whether
or not the new idea came as a sudden inspiration at the point where he first
wrote it down, the resulting design is most effective in varying the internal
balance of the aria and avoiding a too regular symmetry. In 'Amor, nel mio
penar' this was an afterthought. The first part as originally composed does not
contain the dotted figure until the final ritornello, where it appears once in
passing. From this germ Handel spun the greater part of the B section. Later,
after the music was complete, he went back and rewrote the fifteen bars up to
and including the vocal cadence at the end of the first part. Against the
structural gain must be set the loss of some striking chromatic detail in the first
version (Ex. 55, p. 472).

The scoring, congruous as usual with the temper of the opera, is spare and
delicate. There is no brass. Apart from the standard orchestra of oboes,
bassoons, and strings the only instruments used are a flute in two arias and the
recorder in 'Amor, nel mio penar'. Several movements show a characteristic
care for balance and variety of texture. In Flavio's 'Di quel bel', quite a short
aria, Handel contrasts a concertino group of solo violin, oboe, and cello with
the full *tutti*. In the five-part ritornello after the first part of 'Da te parto' he
gives the top line to concertino first violins and oboes with two ripieno violin
parts in support.

History and Text

Handel finished the score on 7 May 1723. The original title was *Emilia*, which
remains uncancelled on the first page of the autograph of Act I. The change
may have been made to avoid confusion with Bononcini's *Erminia*, produced
on 30 March. Lowell Lindgren has suggested that Handel planned the opera
for the abortive visit of the Haymarket company to Paris in the summer,
which might account for the appearance of the libretto without the singers'
names, and perhaps for its brevity, though hardly for its atypical temper.
Moreover Pierre Crozat, the moving spirit behind that enterprise, in a letter to
Giuseppe Riva of 16 April (OS),[14] was stressing that the Academy operas
would need to be adapted to French taste by the addition of a prologue,
choruses, and dances, all of them singularly unsuited to *Flavio*. In any event
the project was soon abandoned, and *Flavio* had its first performance at the
King's Theatre a week after the score was completed, on 14 May. The *Daily
Courant* announced: 'By reason of the shortness of the Opera, to begin exactly
at Eight-a-Clock'. Although *Flavio* is shorter than *Ottone* and *Giulio Cesare*,
which preceded and followed it and both began at 6 p.m., the difference is

[14] Lindgren, *M & L* (1977), 10–12.

Ex. 55

(In my pain, should I hope to be happy one day?)

nothing like two hours. With warmer weather and longer daylight operas were regularly put forward to 7 p.m. in May and June, and occasionally in April. The singers were:

FLAVIO:	Berenstadt (alto castrato)
GUIDO:	Senesino (alto castrato)
EMILIA:	Cuzzoni (soprano)
VITIGE:	Durastanti (soprano)
TEODATA:	Anastasia Robinson (contralto)
UGONE:	Gordon (tenor)
LOTARIO:	Boschi (bass)

They are named in the autograph (against the parts in the *coro*) and in Walsh's edition of the songs.

Flavio had a run of eight performances, the last on 15 June, the closing night of the season. Although this scarcely denotes a failure, the opera made little mark. It did not reappear in any of the later Academy seasons, nor was it produced at Hamburg. Handel's only revival was in 1732, when he gave four performances between 18 and 29 April. There was a dress rehearsal on the 17th, 'at which were present a great Number of the Nobility', including Viscount Percival and his children. Senesino took his original part. Flavio was sung by the alto castrato Campioli, Emilia by Strada, Teodata by Bertolli. The other three parts were altered in pitch: Ugone, now a bass, was sung by Antonio Montagnana, Lotario, now a tenor, by Giovanni Battista Pinacci, and Vitige, now a contralto, by Anna Bagnolesi.[15] Box-office returns for the third performance on 25 April, the 41st night of the season, indicate a thin house. The takings of £65.9s.6d. from 142 persons were meagre, but they exclude subscribers and stage boxes.[16]

It is not clear why Handel, for a revival undertaken in a hurry, went to the trouble of switching the tenor and bass parts and reverting to his original conception.[17] The explanation does not lie in the different quality of the voices of Boschi and Montagnana (a baritone and a true bass), for Handel gave both Boschi's arias to Montagnana as Ugone, altering only the words and the position. He sang 'Se spegni il scelerato', a straightforward vengeance aria, to the music of 'Se a te vissi' at his exit in I x (HG 27) and 'Vado; sorte crudele' (originally 'S'egli ti chiede')[18] in place of 'Fato tiranno'. Pinacci as Lotario had two arias, Vitige's 'Sirti, scogli' (with the words slightly altered and the voice part down an octave) in place of 'Se a te vissi' in Act I, and Ugone's 'Fato tiranno' in place of 'S'egli ti chiede' in Act II. Bagnolesi as Vitige sang two of Flavio's arias, 'Di quel bel' (with new words to the B section) in place of 'Che bel contento' (omitted) and 'Chi può mirare' (with modified text beginning 'Chi può lasciare') as a substitute for 'Sirti, scogli' in Act III. The initial duet was cut and the recitative rewritten, ending in A minor (Chrysander's B version); Vitige's other two solos were transposed down, 'Non credo instabile' from E to B flat, 'Corrispondi' from F sharp minor to C sharp minor.

[15] Deutsch's conjectural cast (288) is wide of the mark. He is also wrong about two voices in the 1723 cast (153).

[16] J. Milhous and R. D. Hume, 'Box Office Reports for Five Operas Mounted by Handel in London, 1732–1734', *Harvard Library Bulletin*, xxvi (1978), 245–66.

[17] See below, under *Autograph*.

[18] Chrysander prints both sets of words for this aria, but not for the others so modified in 1732.

Flavio, sung by the inferior castrato Campioli, received no compensation for his two transferred arias, and probably lost the third as well during the run. There was some necessary rearrangement of recitatives; Flavio was given an extra line ('Ah del mio cor disturbo la pace') to get him off stage in I viii.

The artistic results of this general post can be briefly summarized. Two good numbers were lost, and no new music composed. Some of the transferred pieces suit their new contexts well enough, notably 'Sirti, scogli' and 'Se spegni il scelerato', but none can be called an improvement and several weaken both the dramatic design and the characterization. 'Di quel bel', a simple love song, is an inept substitute for the subtle 'Che bel contento'; the aria in which Lotario tells Emilia to forget Guido is totally unsuited to Ugone's denunciation of Teodata as a traitress; worst of all, the replacement of 'Sirti, scogli' by 'Chi può mirare' reduces Vitige in Act III to a cipher. Handel spoiled the opera, as he often did in revivals.

The only aria to win some popularity was 'Quanto dolci', sung by Susanna Arne at the New Haymarket Theatre on 20, 22, and 25 October 1733, at Drury Lane on 4 April 1734 and, under her married name of Mrs Cibber, a month later on 3 May 1734. The overture was the rather odd choice for 'a new *Grand Ballet* by Denoyer and others' at Drury Lane on 24 April 1739. This was revived several times, with Mlle Châteauneuf among the dancers, in November 1739 and again on 22 March 1740. The overture also featured at a Manchester Subscription Concert on 16 April 1745. Between 1732 and 1985 *Flavio* had only two revivals, at Göttingen in 1967 and Abingdon in 1969.

Autograph

The first two acts in the autograph (RM 20 b 1) show that Handel began Lotario's part for tenor and Ugone's for bass; indeed Lotario's part is complete in the tenor version, since he is dead before Act III. One can only guess at the reason for the change; it may be connected with the personalities of the singers, of whom Boschi was Handel's favourite for blustering parts whereas he is known to have been on shaky terms with Gordon. The well-known story of Handel's telling Gordon, when he grew obstreperous about the way he was accompanied in rehearsal and threatened to jump on the harpsichord, that more people would come to see him jump than to hear him sing, may refer to his performance in *Flavio*, the last Handel opera in which he appeared. But he came quite well out of the exchange of parts. In the original plan Lotario went out after his recitative in I vii (HG 20), and 'Se a te vissi' was allotted to Ugone with different words in the B section (he will do his duty and is not afraid of death). In II iii Ugone received the bass setting of 'Fato tiranno' (HG 38A), and in the next scene Lotario (tenor) had an aria, 'Dille ch'il core', in which he tells Emilia how to reject Guido. This and its introductory recitative come from the 1696 libretto. Handel set the aria twice before deciding to switch the parts. He transferred 'Se a te vissi' to Lotario, rewrote 'Fato tiranno' for Gordon as Ugone (HG 38B; the double-bass part is not in the autograph), and composed 'S'egli ti chiede' for Lotario with a new recitative in III iv, discarding 'Dille ch'il core'. Many changes to the recitative were required in these two acts. Handel began to write them out afresh (f. 9 = HG 9 as far as 'Vedrò Vitige'), but then added the new voice parts on the same staves as the old, which he generally cancelled.

This was not the full extent of the pre-performance reorganization. Act I underwent several revisions, at least one before the foliation of the autograph, which is a sure guide only to the later insertions. The fact that the first arias of Guido and Teodata, 'Bel contento' and 'Benchè povera donzella', were originally set to words that make no sense in their context (Handel added the definitive text above the voice staves; Chrysander printed them the other way round) is proof that they were conceived for another opera (? *Ottone*) or for another scene. It is possible that 'Già la fama'/'Bel contento' was Handel's first choice for Guido's aria in I xi, where the words would have taken up the reference to 'fama' in the recitative. Moreover the music fills a four-leaf gathering, which the manuscript requires. Handel was evidently in great doubt what aria to give Senesino in this scene, for at least three others, widely divergent in temper, appeared here in succession, the last of them in two keys. One was the E flat 'L'empio sleale', which had been composed for *Ottone*, probably for Cuzzoni's benefit on 26 March, and was to come to rest, after heavy revision, in Act I of *Giulio Cesare*. The autograph, bound with the latter opera (ff. 41–3), carries not only recitative for *Ottone* but a note by Handel *for the Opera Emilia* with the stage direction on p. 31 of the HG score of *Flavio* (*Mentre vuol partire* etc.) in a slightly different wording. Smith then copied the aria (*Giulio Cesare*, ff. 37–40), clearly for *Flavio*, for he repeated the stage direction but omitted the *Ottone* recitative. This however did not satisfy Handel (or perhaps Senesino), who may have preferred a lyrical to an indignant pronouncement. He made another attempt with a long F minor aria, 'Il suol che preme', which remains in the *Flavio* autograph (ff. 34–6) and is clearly an insertion, since the verso of the last leaf is blank. It is not certain whether this preceded or followed 'L'empio sleale', for the autographs of both carry Handel's number 8; he seems to have foliated the gatherings at this time and transferred the number from one aria to the other.

Both were ultimately rejected in favour of 'L'armellin vita' in E flat (ff. 31–3). Guido's previous recitative (HG 27) lacks its first two bars (possibly an oversight; the words are in the libretto, and the music was added in the performing score) and stands in the autograph a semitone lower than in HG, beginning on an F minor chord. Its cadence was originally in G (major or minor), altered to C, which would suit any of the last three arias mentioned. The cadence in G could have introduced 'Già la fama'/'Bel contento' (in D), though transition from subdominant to tonic is uncommon, or either E flat aria. (Handel seldom if ever filled in the recitative until he had composed the arias.) The raised pitch of both the recitative and 'L'armellin vita' in HG comes from the performing score. One of the oddest features of this transaction is that 'L'empio sleale', though it neither began nor ended in *Flavio*, bequeathed its principal vocal melody to Ugone's 'Fato tiranno', with a very different accompaniment.

None of the three discarded arias is any loss. Both settings of 'Dille ch'il core' are brisk Allegro movements whose perfunctory quality perhaps reflects Handel's failure to respond to a vicarious dramatic situation. The first, a sequential short-phrased cavatina in G minor, was rejected at once and used in C minor with improvements, including a B section on the same material, for Flavio's 'Chi può mirare' later in the act. The second, a da capo aria in E minor, is even weaker. 'Il suol che preme' is a recomposition and expansion of a C minor aria beginning with the same words in the early continuo cantata

Lucrezia. Handel, who must have chosen the text, slightly altered the words in each section and added three upper instrumental parts. He employed some of the old ideas, especially in the A section, but dropped the most characteristic feature of the cantata aria, the angular bass of the opening bars. The fact that he never filled up the string parts towards the end of the B section, even with rests, suggests that the music was barely finished.

Handel foliated the autograph by gatherings in his usual manner after he had reshaped Act I but before interchanging the parts of Lotario and Ugone. His beginning a new enumeration with smaller figures in Act III suggests the lapse of time, a supposition strengthened by the appearance of Ugone in the tenor clef throughout this act. Subsequent insertions, apart from f. 9, were 12 (the flute part of 'Quanto dolci', an afterthought written on the back of a sketch for 'Amante stravagante'), 31–3 ('L'armellin vita'), 89 (replacement of 43 with second setting of 'Dille ch'il core'), 44–7 ('S'egli ti chiede' with three previous bars of recitative; at the same time Handel amended the earlier part of this recitative on 42ᵛ), 68–9 ('Starvi a canto' and the short recitative after it; originally Teodata's 'Che colpa' followed the C sharp (minor) cadence on HG 66), and 78 (the rewritten bars 44–58 of 'Amor, nel mio penar', pasted over the original on 79ʳ).

The overture, on different paper from the opening of Act I (with its title *Emilia*), was probably composed on a separate occasion. The short sinfonia in I ii was originally for strings alone; Handel's *tutti unis* above the top line is an addition. The solos in bar 9 of 'Di quel bel' each begin with a trill on the first note. In bar 11 and parallel passages later the dotted figure exactly repeats that of the previous bar; the raised pitch on the first and third beats is a Smith change in the performing score. In I vi Vitige has four bars, uncancelled, introducing the soldier after Flavio's 'Ne ricevo l'invito'; they are in two late copies but not in the libretto or HG, are pasted out in the performing score, and were probably never sung. In the B section of 'Chi può mirare' the twelve bars before the ritornello have a repeat mark with a note (in German) instructing Smith to write them out; he did so in the performing score, but they were removed before performance. Handel cut more than twenty bars from the A section of 'Che colpa' during the filling-out stage. He drafted a four-bar string ritornello in 3/4 time on the theme of 'Amor, nel mio penar' before Emilia's accompanied recitative 'O Guido!' in III iv, but abandoned it without adding inner parts. In bar 47 of this recitative (HG 74) the autograph has 'corro', not 'ardo'; 'corro' is written over another word in the performing score, possibly 'avrò', the reading of RM 18 c 10. 'Corro' is in all other copies and undoubtedly correct.

Handel was very sparing of tempo marks and scoring indications. He added many of the former in the performing score, but was seldom specific about what instruments were to play the upper parts. Most of Chrysander's deductions can be defended; he was however wrong to exclude the oboes from 'Che colpa' (*Uniss.* in the autograph and performing score) and to divide them in 'Di quel bel' (*Tutti* on the top line in all reliable sources). If the oboes play in 'Che bel contento' and 'Amante stravagante', both should take the top line, as in the Flower parts

At a late stage, after the score had been copied, Handel made a number of verbal changes in the recitative; the object was clearly to modify the licentious tone, especially of Flavio's advances to Teodata. His first three asides in II i were originally set to the words 'O labro!', 'O guancia!', 'O seno!'. In II iii

Teodata said to Ugone, speaking of Vitige: 'D'amor in ricompensa *notturno amor* mi diede, ed *egli di marito a me dono* la fede'. In II vii Flavio's request to Vitige ran: 'Bramo che a *le mie voglie tu procuri* costei'. Two passages in III ii (HG 66), in which Flavio invites Teodata straight to bed ('O mio tesoro intanto ai Talami Regi'), were cut altogether. The cancelled words are all in the 1696 libretto but not that of 1723. It seems unlikely that the change was due to simple prudery (such outspokenness was common in other operas, for example *Giulio Cesare*) or to fear of provoking comparisons with the domestic life of George I. The explanation may lie in the circumstances of Anastasia Robinson, who was known to be fastidious and under the leonine protection of the Earl of Peterborough. There is no evidence that Handel touched the autograph at the time of the 1732 revival.

The Flower Collection (MS 130 Hd 4, v. 128) contains the autograph of a keyboard arrangement of the overture, which characteristically is not a mere transcription of the score. It was the source of all manuscript copies and the Walsh printed text.

Librettos

1723. 'Flavio Re de' Longobardi, Drama . . . Printed by Tho. Wood in Little Britain.' 63 pp. Haym's dedication to the directors of the Royal Academy of Music, in Italian only, refers to Italian opera as 'this noble and innocent diversion' and, not without reason, claims credit for its introduction to England. The Argument is in both languages. Handel is not named, nor (exceptionally) are the cast.

1732. 'The Second Edition . . . Printed for T. Wood in Little-Britain, and are to be sold at the King's Theatre in the Hay-Market.' 47 pp. The text is amended as described above, but no translation is given for the new passages. The dedication is omitted, and the Argument is in English only. There are slight verbal changes in the B section of 'Mà chi punir desio?' The last page of the copy in the National Library of Scotland has some early manuscript notes, probably written by Burney, comparing the orchestration of the autograph with that of the Walsh score. The list of arias is incomplete, but it includes 'Il suol che preme' and 'Dille ch'il core' (both marked 'entire'), which occur only in the autograph and the Flower material derived from it.

Copies and Editions

The performing score (Hamburg MA/1017) is a complex document; it contains the hands of three copyists as well as the composer, and was subjected to major upheaval on at least three occasions, two of them before performance. As Clausen notes, Act I was copied before Boschi and Gordon exchanged parts, and therefore while Handel was still working on the opera. 28 leaves remain of its first draft, all written by Smith: ff. 1–4, 6–10, 12–13, 23–4, 27–36, and 48–52. A relic of the original vocal distribution survives on the verso of 36, later pasted over, because the recto carries the end of 'Che bel contento'. 'Se a te vissi' at first bore another name, undoubtedly Ugone's; it was scratched out and *Lota.* written on top. The exchange of parts put a strain on the scriptorium, and Smith enlisted the help of H3; several times both worked on the same page. Of the inserted leaves (aside from two 1732 additions), H3 wrote part of 14ʳ–21, part of 25ʳ, part of 38ᵛ–42, and 47ʳ, Smith the remainder. Not all these insertions were made at the same time. Folio 22 is probably the last leaf of a segment largely replaced by 14–21, including much of 'Quanti dolci' and the whole of 'Bel contento'/'Già la fama'. The recitative of xi was copied in the lower key, ending in C, with the first two bars inserted by Smith (38–9); Handel himself altered this to the HG version, ending in C sharp; it was then recopied at its earlier pitch (46). 'L'armellin vita' presents an odd aspect with the key signature on the first page altered from three flats to four sharps (then marked E♭♮ at the top, probably by H3) and the remainder from four sharps to three flats. Clausen attributes this retro-transposition to 1732, but the aria is in E flat in the Walsh print and all primary sources, and there is no evidence that it was ever sung in E. The note *Un Tuono più Basso ex C* on 'Bel contento' probably also dates from 1723 (though Walsh and all sources give it in D); it appears to be in the hand of H3, who was no longer operational in 1732. 'Benchè povera donzella' was at some time marked up a tone to F sharp minor, but the instruction was later cancelled.

After Act I had been copied Handel seems to have called a halt until things were straightened out. Although he set Act II with the original vocal pitches, there is no evidence that it entered the performing score in that form. In consequence Acts II and III are easier to disentangle, since with the exception of 'Starvi a canto' and the following recitative (100–1), composed shortly before the first performance, all insertions date from 1732. Smith and H3 continued to share the work, the latter taking an increasing part: he copied much of Act II (59ᵛ–62, 64–6, 76–80, 85–92) and all that survives of the original Act III (93–7, 102–4, 109–12, 117–34).

In 1732 Smith had the assistance of S1, who copied two arias, 'Si spegni il scelerato' (43–5) and 'Sirti, scogli' for tenor (113–16). The other insertions (5, probably 58,[19] 63, 81–4, 98–9, 105–8) were written by Smith. Not all the altered arias were copied afresh; apart from S1's contribution Smith wrote out only 'Non credo instabile' in B flat (with extra dynamics, not in HG, and the violin part in bar 50 lowered an octave by Handel), 'Corrispondi' in C sharp minor, and 'Chi può lasciare'. The other adjustments to the arias, including word changes, are indicated on the old pages. The treatment of the recitatives, as in other revivals, is inconsistent. Handel himself wrote most of the notes for Vitige's new alto recitative in III iii (HG 70), and Smith recopied a number of others, some in their original form, some with modifications or altered cadences. Vitige's part, even as changed, alternates erratically between soprano and alto clefs. Some passages consequent on the changes of pitch were probably noted only in the singers' parts; Handel may on occasion have reverted to the original versions in the autograph, but there is no conclusive evidence on the point. His first plan was evidently to omit 'Starvi a canto', for the previous recitative was rewritten with an exit for Flavio. The decision was then reversed and the recitative recopied; but Campioli seems to have lost his only aria, for there are signs that it was pasted out.

The flute part of 'Quanto dolci' was never copied into the performing score. The manuscript has the definitive texts of 'Bel contento' and 'Benchè povera

[19] If Smith copied this in 1732, which seems certain, he used the wrong clef for Ugone's recitative; but that has many parallels.

donzella', but the first form of the recitatives in II i, iii, and vii; like Handel in the autograph, Smith substituted the bowdlerized versions. No doubt he crossed out Flavio's extra lines in III ii (HG 66); but the 1723 version of this recitative is missing. The repeat in the B section of 'Chi può mirare' was copied but pasted out. Vitige's four bars near the beginning of I vi and his two remarks at the bottom of HG 19 were cancelled rather later (they are in two secondary copies); it seems likely that he never appeared in this scene, of which Chrysander prints a mixed version. The recitative before 'Con un' vezzo' (II viii) ends with both a fermata and the words *Segue subito l'aria*. *Hautb*. on the top line of 'Amor, nel mio penar' replaced a word scratched out and illegible, possibly the *Flauto* of the Flower parts. The tempo marks on 'Ricordati', 'Quanto dolci', 'Benchè povera donzella', 'Amante stravagante', 'Fato tiranno', 'S'egli ti chiede', 'Rompo i lacci', 'Chi può mirare', 'Con un' vezzo', and 'Non credo instabile' were added by Handel in 1723. They are missing in the autograph, except the *Allegro* on 'Rompo i lacci', which Smith omitted by accident.

The Malmesbury score (not dated, but certainly 1723) is the work of three hands, H1 (Act I), H3 (Act II), and Smith (Act III). It was copied from Hamburg after Handel had added the tempo marks, removed Vitige from I vi, bowdlerized the text in II i, iii, and vi, and shortened the B section of 'Chi può mirare' but not inserted the two extra bars at the start of I xi. This recitative is at the original pitch, introducing 'L'armellin vita' in E flat. Three tempo marks are unique to this manuscript, *Allegro ma non troppo* on 'Benchè povera donzella', *Andante* on 'Da te parto', and *Adagio* on 'Amor, nel mio penar'. The controversial top stave is omitted from this aria.

The Flower Collection contains two scores of *Flavio*, MS 130 Hd 4, volumes 129 and 130. The first (S2, *c*. 1740) lacks all recitatives except that in III iv, which is complete, but includes the three unperformed arias and the bass as well as the tenor setting of 'Fato tiranno', the latter without its double-bass part. It was obviously copied direct from the autograph, and includes Handel's terminal date. It is the only copy to give the original words of 'Bel contento' and 'Benchè povera donzella' (the *Flavio* texts are added above), the flute part of 'Quanto dolci', and the extra bars in 'Chi può mirare'. No instrument is specified for the top line of 'Amor, nel mio penar'. The sinfonia in I ii is for strings only. Of the tempo marks added by Handel to the performing score, Jennens supplied six plus *Allegro* on 'Sirti, scogli'.

The second Flower score (volume 130), complete with recitatives, bears the names of two former owners, the Hon. Anne Rushout and R. Bowles, and did not come from Jennens. It was written by S5, probably *c*. 1745, but reflects the 1723 version; the only hint of post-1732 date (apart from the copyist) is that Vitige sings 'Di quel bel', but with the 1723 text in the B section. The source seems to have been a copy taken from Hamburg after most of the pre-performance changes but before Vitige was removed from I vi. Like Lennard and Coke it reproduces a verbal error in Hamburg, the first word of 'Chi può mirare' appearing as 'Si'. Handel's added tempos are present, 'L'armellin vita' is in E flat, 'Fato tiranno' has its double-bass part, and the recitative of I xi its first two bars; 'Amor, nel mio penar' is exactly as in HG. 'Da te parto' and 'Sirti, scogli' are both *Allegro*. 'Il suol che preme' is included in an appendix as an *Additional Song*.

The Lennard score (S1, *c*. 1736–40) comes from the same stable, giving virtually the same text without 'Il suol che preme'. Some movements have *da capo* in place of *dal segno* and many stage directions are omitted, both defects common in late copies. 'Con un' vezzo' is *Allegro ma non troppo*, 'Non credo instabile' *Allegro* (neither occurs elsewhere); most pieces in Act III have no tempo. The voice entry in 'Di quel bel' is doubled at the octave by an oboe; no other source specifies the instrument. The Coke copy, in the miniaturist's hand (1730s or later),[20] also gives the 1723 text, without recitatives, but with variants indicating a different descent. The most interesting is that 'L'armellin vita' is in E major. 'Ricordati', 'Che bel contento', and 'Amante stravagante' are for strings only. 'Amor, nel mio penar', without its top stave, is marked *Ex D ♮*. A few tempos are dropped, but others are unique: the opening of the overture and 'Amor, nel mio penar' are *Largo*, the sinfonia in I ii *Allegro*. Some pieces again have *da capo* for *dal segno*. The whole score is fully figured. Five arias— 'Quanti dolci', 'Se a te vissi', 'Che bel contento', 'L'armellin vita', and 'Amor, nel mio penar'—have an English version of pastoral or amorous irrelevance written by the same copyist. William Hayes (1708–77) seems to have used this copy in compiling three synthetic English cantatas, of which there is a score in his hand in the Bodleian (MS Mus d 60) and incomplete performance material in the Library of Congress, Washington, and the Santa Cecilia Library in Rome.[21] The five arias appear with the same English text (four of them transposed), together with one accompanied recitative and excerpts from *Ottone* and *Giulio Cesare* with similarly emollient words. 'Amor, nel mio penar' is in D minor, as indicated in Coke.

Add MS 31572, a volume in the hand of a late (?1740s) copyist who wrote parts for *Esther* in Durham Cathedral Library and for *Alexander's Feast* (with S2 and others) in the Coke Collection, contains all the arias and duets of the 1723 score, numbered but in no sort of order. Besides recitatives, the overture, sinfonia in I ii, the arioso 'Corrispondi', and the *coro* are missing. The copyist perhaps supplied the scoring, almost confined to strings; the oboe appears only in the B section of 'Rompo i lacci', and then not as a solo. There are few tempo marks ('Parto, sì' is *Larghetto*), but more dynamics than in other sources and a little figuring. 'L'armellin vita' is in E major, as in the Coke score.

The Flower parts (S2, late 1740s), lacking the first violin and first oboe, were extracted from Flower I (Volume 129) before Jennens added Handel's tempos. They omit the overture and the secco sections of the recitative in III iv, but include the suppressed arias. In the cembalo part 'Bel contento' and 'Benchè povera donzella' have only their original words. Since Flower I, following the autograph, often failed to specify the scoring, S2 had to exercise his judgement with regard to the oboes. He included them, where Chrysander does not, in the ritornellos of 'Bel contento', 'Benchè povera', 'L'armellin vita', 'Non credo instabile', 'Da te parto' (the opening as well as closing ritornello), 'Che colpa', and the duet 'Deh perdona'; also in 'Il suol che preme', but in neither setting of 'Dille ch'il core' and 'Fato tiranno' nor in the A section of 'Rompo i lacci' (presumably the B section solo was in the missing first oboe part). As usual the second oboe regularly doubles the first violin in the arias and the second in the *coro*. S2 evidently did not regard the wind parts in 'Quanto dolci', 'Parto, sì', and 'Amor, nel mio penar' as solos; all these are

[20] See pp. 257 and 362.
[21] Emilia Zanetti, 'A proposito di tre sconosciute cantate inglesi', *Rassegna musicale*, xxix (1959), 129–42.

included in the second oboe part, the first two for *traversa*, the last (transposing as in HG) for *flauto*. The cello + bassoon part mentions the latter instrument only twice; it doubles the voice as indicated in HG in 'S'egli ti chiede' and is silenced in 'Parto, sì'.

Four copies of the overture for keyboard reproduce Handel's autograph arrangement[22]: Smith in Fitzwilliam Mus MS 265 (*c*.1725), H5 (*c*.1724) and Smith (*c*.1728) in two Malmesbury volumes, and S2 in RM 18 c 1, ff. 32–3 (*c*.1728). 'Amor, nel mio penar', with the oboe part in four flats an octave above the first violin, was copied by an unknown hand in RM 18 c 4, ff. 112–15, and by RM5 (?1750s) in RM 19 d 11, ff. 53–7. This aria appears in its eccentric HG form among a group of pieces copied much earlier (? from Hamburg) in RM 18 c 10, ff. 11–26 (S2). The others are the sinfonia in I ii, 'Bel contento', the B section of 'Rompo i lacci', 'Mà chi punir desio?', and the accompanied recitatives in III iv with the variant in bar 47 ('avrò' for 'corro') noted above. There is an arrangement of 'Benchè povera donzella' as a binary instrumental minuet in RM 18 b 8, f. 81 (Smith junior, *c*.1728) and a second and third flute (= the two violin parts) for 'Parto, sì' in D in RM 19 a 8, f. 4 (Jennens). The Coke volume of '24 Opera Songs' contains a copy of 'Quanto dolci' without the flute part, with a few simple vocal and instrumental ornaments. A group of arias in Berlin Staatsbibliothek Mus MS 9062 contains 'Bel contento', 'Benchè povera doncella' [*sic*], 'L'armellin vita' in E flat, 'Rompo i lacci', 'Chi può mirare', 'Con un' vezzo', and 'Che colpa'. This is a late copy with incomplete scoring.

Walsh and the Hares issued the score (*Flavius an Opera . . . Publish'd by the Author*, i.e. with his authority) about 20 June 1723. It contains every item except recitatives and the sinfonia in I ii, but only the overture, *coro*, 'S'egli ti chiede', and the arias with a single melody instrument are complete. Elsewhere the viola and generally the second violin are omitted; 'Quanto dolci' and 'Parto, sì' alone have the latter, but they lack the flute. Few scoring details are given other than the oboe, violin, and cello solos in 'Di quel bel' and the oboe in the B section of 'Rompo i lacci'. 'Bel contento' is in D, 'L'armellin vita' in E flat. 'Fato tiranno' is for tenor without double bass. 'Chi può mirare' lacks the B section repeat. 'Non credo instabile' has some additional trills for the upper instrument. Tempo marks agree with HG, except that 'Con un' vezzo', 'Che colpa', and 'Sirti, scogli' are *Allegro* and 'Deh perdona' has none. No light is thrown on 'Amor, nel mio penar', which has one upper (first violin) part only. The 1723 singers are named. According to Walsh's account book he paid Handel 25 guineas for the score.

There were two editions of favourite songs, by Meares (*c*.1723) and Walsh (*c*.1725). The former was apparently copied from the Walsh score, the latter used its plates. Both include the overture, 'Quanto dolci', 'Bel contento', 'Benchè povera donzella', 'Di quel bel', 'L'armellin vita', 'Amante stravagante', 'Parto, sì', and 'Con un' vezzo'. The Walsh edition adds the duet 'Ricordati', and the Coke copy also contains two arias from *Floridante*. Walsh published a flute arrangement in July 1725, the overture in parts during the same year, and Handel's keyboard version about 1728. Six arias were printed in *The Pocket Companion*: 'Quanto dolci', 'Benchè povera donzella' (in D

---

[22] Printed in *Twenty Overtures*, ii. 13.

minor), and 'Parto, sì' in volume i (May 1724), 'Amante stravagante', 'Con un' vezzo', and 'Mà chi punir desio?' in volume ii (December 1725).

Chrysander's edition (1875) prints the 1723 version with a fair degree of accuracy, adding a random selection of alternatives: two sets of words (13, 18) and one aria (38A) suppressed before the performing score was copied, and one abbreviation (4B) and one set of words (42) substituted in 1732. He ignored several other variants, both in the autograph and the performing score, that have at least an equal claim. The final chord on HG 65 should have a sharp third in the figuring, and the tempo of 'Che colpa' should be *Allegro ma non presto*: both are in the autograph and the best copies. 'Figlio' in two directions on HG 19 should of course be 'foglio'.

The HHA edition (1993) gives a reliable text and includes previously unpublished material in the appendices. The Critical Report is confused and inaccurate in a number of particulars. There is no attempt to date copies by watermark.

Additional Notes

* (p. 468) Donald Burrows has suggested that in the 1720s Kytch had available a special oboe for use at sharp pitch in the Chapel Royal, which Handel could have employed as a transposing instrument in the normally impracticable key of B flat minor.

* (p. 480) Cardiff Central Library (M.C.I. 34(b)) has early copies from the 1720s of 'Quanto dolci', 'Benchè povera donzella', 'Da te parto', 'Non credo instabile', and 'Che colpa', the first four written by H6, the fifth by H3.

CHAPTER 22

GIULIO CESARE IN EGITTO

THE action takes place between September 48 and March 47 BC, and covers the period of the Alexandrine War, though the librettist rearranges history to suit his convenience. Caesar, having defeated Pompey at Pharsalia in Greece, has followed him to Egypt. The curtain rises on *a Plain in Egypt with an old Bridge over a Branch of the Nile. Caesar and Curius*[1] *passing over the Bridge with Attendants* are enthusiastically acclaimed by a chorus of Egyptians. Caesar applies the familiar words 'Veni, vidi, vici' to his victory over Pompey (in fact he uttered them a year later after defeating Pharnaces of Pontus at Zela). Pompey's wife Cornelia, whom Curio once vainly loved, and her son Sesto[2] come to sue for peace. Caesar agrees to embrace Pompey; but at this moment Achilla, the general and counsellor of Tolomeo (Ptolemy XII), joint ruler of Egypt with his sister Cleopatra, arrives *with a Train of Egyptians* carrying golden vessels as gifts to win Caesar's favour. *One of the Egyptians uncovers a Salver, upon which is the Head of Pompey. Cornelia faints*; Caesar is moved to tears; Achilla is captivated by Cornelia's beauty. Caesar sends Achilla back to his master with a message of contemptuous disgust. Cornelia, reviving, *endeavours to snatch from Sestus his Sword, in order to kill herself, but is prevented by Curius*, who appals her by offering to take Pompey's place as her husband. She longs only for death. Sesto, a young boy (he was 27, but is represented as little more than half that age in the opera), swears to avenge his father. The set changes to *a Cabinet*, where Cleopatra, attended by her maidens, is horrified to learn of Pompey's fate from her eunuch Nireno. She decides to exploit the situation by visiting Caesar and winning his support against Tolomeo. When the latter enters *with Guards* and brusque words she taunts him as fit only for the effeminate dominion of love. Achilla describes to Tolomeo Caesar's reception of his gift and offers to serve Caesar as he served Pompey if he can have Cornelia as reward. Tolomeo, dismissing him, looks forward to strengthening his kingdom by putting Caesar to death. *Caesar's Camp, with an Urn in the middle, wherein the Ashes of Pompey's Head are inclos'd upon an eminent Pile of Trophies.* Caesar ponders on the mutability of human greatness: a breath creates life, and a breath destroys it. Cleopatra enters with Nireno; she says she is Lidia, a noble maiden attending on Cleopatra, whose fortune has been stolen by Tolomeo. She *kneels before Caesar and weeps*, begging for justice. Caesar, captivated by her beauty (as is the susceptible Curio), *raises* her to her feet and promises redress. She congratulates herself on her wiles; everything is

---

[1] This is a false transliteration. He was C. Scribonius Curio, Caesar's legate in Sicily and later in Africa; but he does not appear to have taken part in the Alexandrine War. All the characters in the opera are historical except Nireno (unless he is to be identified with the eunuch Pothinus); all except Cornelia came to a violent end.

[2] He was really her stepson; his mother was Pompey's third wife Mucia.

possible for a beautiful woman. *Cleopatra going to withdraw is hinder'd by Nirenus . . . They retire*, but remain in the background. Cornelia enters, pays her last respects to the urn and *snatches a Sword from the Trophy*, intending to wreak vengeance on Tolomeo, *upon which Sestus enters*. He *takes the sword from Cornelia* and the task to himself, delighting his mother by his precocious courage. Cleopatra (still as Lidia) *enters unexpectedly* and, *pointing to Nirenus*, offers him as a guide; her heart fills with hope at the increasing prospect of outwitting her brother. In *a Court in Ptolomey's Palace* Tolomeo and Caesar, each with an escort of his countrymen, indulge in a bout of diplomatic fencing. Tolomeo invites Caesar to the royal apartments; the latter moves with the wariness of a big-game hunter. Achilla introduces Cornelia and Sesto, who challenges Tolomeo to a duel. Tolomeo has him arrested and orders Cornelia to work in the seraglio garden, ostensibly for the gratification of Achilla but in fact for his own. Achilla offers to let her and Sesto escape if she will marry him. She rejects the idea with contempt. *The Guards leading away Sestus, Cornelia stops him.*[3] They sing a poignant duet of lamentation before being escorted off in opposite directions.

Act II opens in *a Garden of Cedars, with a Prospect of Mount Parnassus, on which is seated the Palace of Virtue.* Cleopatra gives Nireno final instructions for leading Caesar to the place of enchantment; he is to say that Lidia will meet him at sundown to report how she fared with Tolomeo. Caesar enters as she disappears and is captivated by *a Symphony of various Instruments*, after which *Parnassus opens, Virtue appears setting on a Throne, attended by the Nine Muses* while a second symphony plays. 'Lidia', posing as Virtue, woos him in a love song, but *while Caesar runs towards Cleopatra, Parnassus shuts, and the Scene is as before.* Nireno assures Caesar that Lidia awaits him in her apartments and will introduce him to Cleopatra. In *a Garden belonging to the Seraglio, to which corresponds that of the wild Beasts*, Cornelia continues to lament her fate while plying the hoe of her new profession.[4] She is the target of ardent amorous advances, first from Achilla and then from Tolomeo. *As Cornelia goes away, Ptolomey meets her, and takes her by the Hand. He draws Achilla aside*, promises his reward, and gets rid of him by ordering him to kill Caesar at once. Tolomeo *reaches his Hand to Cornelia's Bosom, upon which she retires with Disdain.* He resolves to try force. Cornelia attempts suicide by throwing herself off a wall into the wild beasts' den, but is prevented by Sesto. Nireno brings orders from Tolomeo that Cornelia is to be taken to his harem; he protests his own sympathy and suggests that if Sesto follows he may catch the king unarmed and off his guard. Cleopatra waits for Caesar in *a Garden* ('Luogo di delizie'), *sits down* and after a prayer to Venus to make her irresistible *feigns to sleep*. Caesar, wooing her as Lidia, is shocked by her boldness. Since he seems to find her more attractive asleep, *she goes to her Place.* At once Curio enters *with Sword in Hand* and tells Caesar he is betrayed: murderers are after him. Caesar *draws his Sword*, remarks that 'this Climate proves unfortunate to me', and is about to leave when Cleopatra reveals that she is not Lidia but the queen herself: her royal presence will quell the tumult. She leaves, but soon *returns in haste*, bidding him fly. He refuses and sings a martial aria. As he goes out *Voices from within* are heard clamouring for his death. Cleopatra prays for his safety, on which her

---

[3] In the Italian direction she runs and holds him by the arm.
[4] The sentence *Cornelia con picciola zappa nelle mane che vien coltivando fiori* (HG 64) is in the Italian text only.

whole happiness now depends. *A Room in the Seraglio. Ptolomey with his Favourites, and Cornelia among them.* He *lays his Sword on the Table* and *throws* Cornelia *a Handkerchief* as a token that she is his choice for the night. *Cornelia flings away the Handkerchief with Disdain.* Sesto appears; as he *goes to catch Ptolomey's Sword* from the table, *enters Achilla in haste, and takes it from him.* Achilla summons Tolomeo to war: his men surrounded Curio and Caesar, who dived into the harbour from a high balcony and were drowned; but Cleopatra fled to the Romans, and they are mustering for vengeance. When Achilla asks for Cornelia as his reward, he finds himself abruptly dismissed as a traitor. Tolomeo, looking for a quick victory, departs with his favourites. Sesto, all hope of vengeance gone, *endeavours to stab himself.* Cornelia restrains him: they still have an ally in Nireno. Sesto once more breathes fire and slaughter against Tolomeo.

Act III. In a wood near the city of Alexandria[5] Achilla, disgusted at Tolomeo's treachery, marches with *a Train of Soldiers* to join Cleopatra. *To the Sound of a Warlike Symphony, follows a Battle between the Soldiers of Cleopatra, and those of Ptolomey, who gain the Victory: The Symphony ended, enters Ptolomey with Cleopatra made Prisoner. One of the Guards puts Cleopatra in Chains,* and her brother gloats over her humiliation. Alone, with Caesar reported dead and no one to help her, she bewails her fate; her ghost will haunt Tolomeo. She is led off, and Caesar enters *on one Side,* having escaped by swimming the harbour but lost contact with his troops and his beloved. Sesto and Nireno, *on the other* side of the stage, come upon *Achilla wounded, lying on a Bank of the Harbour.* Confessing his misdeeds, he produces a seal, tells them where they can find a hundred armed warriors pledged to recognize it and 'a subterraneous Passage' to the palace, *gives the Seal to Sestus, and dies.* Sesto has his body thrown into the harbour. *Caesar takes the Seal from Sestus* (who is astonished to find him alive) and hurries off into action. Sesto rejoices that justice is beginning to work. *Cleopatra's Apartment. Cleopatra (with Guards) among her Women that weep.* She says farewell to her friends, who are to be taken from her. When she hears *a Clashing of Arms within* she prepares to die. Caesar enters *with his Sword drawn at the Head of his Soldiers* and *drives* [out] *the Guards of Ptolomey.*[6] Cleopatra *runs to embrace him.* He tells her to collect her scattered troops and meet him at the harbour. In the *Royal Hall* Tolomeo tries once more to rape Cornelia. She breaks free, and when he *attempts again to approach her* she *draws a Dagger. As Cornelia runs towards Ptolomey, enters Sestus with his naked Sword* and demands the right to kill the tyrant. Tolomeo *draws his Sword ... They fight, Ptolomey is wounded, and drops dead.* Cornelia can relax at last. *The Port of Alexandria. Caesar and Cleopatra, with a Train of Egyptians, with Trumpets and Tymbals; after the Symphony, enter Curius, Nirenus, and then Sestus and Cornelia. A Page bearing the Crown and Scepter of Ptolomey.* Nireno hails Caesar as 'Lord of the World and Emperor of Rome'. *Cornelia and Sestus kneel* before Caesar,[7] who welcomes them as friends. Cornelia *gives to Caesar the crown and scepter of Ptolomey.* He bestows them on Cleopatra, who declares herself 'a tributary Queen to Rome's great Emperor'. They proclaim their undying love, and all welcome the return of peace.

[5] This is the heading in the manuscripts, including Handel's autograph. The libretto has *The Port of Alexandria*, which may well be correct, since the battle evidently takes place there; Achilla is found wounded 'sul margine del porto' (HG 102, 108).

[6] These two directions are omitted in HG.

[7] So the libretto; in Handel's autograph only Sesto kneels.

The source of this libretto was a work with the same title by Giacomo Francesco Bussani, set by Antonio Sartorio for Venice in 1677.[8] The subject was popular, but for some reason seldom attracted major composers. Operas based in part on Bussani appeared in Naples (1680), Messina (1681, Domenico Scorpione), Milan (1685), Bergamo (1689), Naples (1699, Aldovrandini, libretto by F. M. Paglia as *Cesare in Alessandria*), Rome (1713, C. F. Pollarolo, libretto by Antonio Ottoboni, partly based on Corneille's *Pompée*, as *Giulio Cesare nell'Egitto*), and probably Bologna in 1716 (Novi, *Cesare e Tolomeo in Egitto*) and 1722.[9] Both the libretto and the score of Pollarolo's opera survive in manuscript, the former in a private collection in Venice with eight striking designs by the scene-painter Filippo Juvarra,[10] the latter in the Library of Congress, Washington. It was probably given a private production by Cardinal Ottoboni. Juvarra had links with England, which he visited twice, but Haym does not seem to have used this source.

He did use the 1685 Milan text as well as Bussani's 1677 libretto, and possibly another intermediate version not yet identified; the amount of material untraced to some earlier source is exceptionally high for a Haym libretto. Most of his dialogue comes from Bussani, together with the words of the accompanied recitatives 'Alma del gran Pompeo'[11] and 'Che sento?' (as far as 'cor di Marte', the original extent of Handel's movement), the first part of 'V'adoro, pupille' (with a new fourth line), Cornelia's 'Nel tuo seno' (the first couplet of a six-line aria in Bussani), some rearranged lines in the duet 'Son nata a lagrimar', and 'Belle dee'. So do two arias in Handel's original Act I, Caesar's 'Questo core incatenato' (almost unchanged) and Cleopatra's 'Speranza mi dice' (adapted from an aria for Sesto in the same scene).[12] The off-stage conspirators crying death to Caesar are in Bussani. On the other hand much of the dialogue in the Parnassus scene, the *vaga Sinfonia di varij Stromenti* heard off-stage, the opening of the back-flats to reveal Cleopatra as Virtue sitting among the nine Muses, and their closure when Caesar runs to embrace her first appear in the Milan libretto. That also contains three of the four lines of Achilla's 'Tu sei il cor', but in a very different context; they form part of a love duet for Caesar and Cleopatra in Act II.[13] The great majority of Haym's aria texts have no known antecedents.

Until half-way through Act III Haym followed the outline of Bussani's plot closely, apart from conflating Cleopatra's two confidantes, her nurse Rodisbe

[8] Bussani dedicated his libretto to one Gras Iggons, who proves to have been Grace Higgons, daughter of the British Ambassador to Venice.

[9] Bussani inspired later operas by L. A. Predieri (Rome, 1728), Geminiano Giacomelli (Venice, 1735), Jommelli (Rome, 1751), Sarti (Copenhagen, 1763), and Piccinni (Milan, 1770) among others. C. H. Graun's *Cesare e Cleopatra* (Berlin, 1742) derives from a different source. F. C. Bressand's *Cleopatra*, set by Kusser (Brunswick, 1691), is not, as claimed by H. C. Wolff, *Die venezianische Oper in der zweiten Hölfte des 17. Jahrhunderts* (Berlin, 1937), 53, a translation of Bussani.

[10] Reproduced by M. Viale Ferrero, 'Antonio e Pietro Ottoboni e alcuni melodrammi da loro ideati o promossi a Roma', *Venezia e il melodramma nel Settecento*, ed. M. T. Muraro (Florence, 1978), 271–94.

[11] To judge from *virgole* in the 1677 libretto, Sartorio set only the first five lines, a reflection on his literary as well as his dramatic judgement. Nevertheless his setting, on a chromatic ground, is impressive.

[12] By an odd coincidence these are the only two suppressed Act I arias that Handel did not reuse in some form in the final score.

[13] The Milan libretto was discovered by Craig Monson, who also suggested the possibility that Handel was indebted to Sartorio's score. See his '"Giulio Cesare in Egitto": from Sartorio (1677) to Handel (1724)', *M & L* lxvi (1985), 313–43.

and the page Nireno, into one person (Cleopatra's cousin Berenice in the original version, eventually her eunuch Nireno). He cut about a dozen scenes, most of them for minor characters and extraneous to the action (one was an angry confrontation between Tolomeo and Cornelia disguised as a warrior), and completely rewrote the second half of Act III, after Scene iv. In Bussani this is largely concerned with Curio, who after a further rejection by Cornelia decides to seek love elsewhere, saves Sesto from death at Tolomeo's hands, puts the latter in chains, and ends the opera with an aria proclaiming Caesar's victory over the traitor. Both Bussani's earlier acts had ended, like many operas of the period, with an aria for a minor character (Rodisbe) and a ballet.

The strengthening of the dramatic fibre in Haym's libretto requires no emphasis. Discarding the less important issues (Curio's love for Cornelia is mentioned in a single scene, I iv), it builds up the two central themes—Caesar's love for Cleopatra and Sesto's vengeance on his father's murderer, which is very loosely handled by Bussani—to a simultaneous climax at the end of the opera. Two important scenes in Act III, Achilla's change of sides (i) and Cleopatra's lament in chains (iii), were (so far as we know) added by Haym or Handel, who tightened the characterization and converted a haphazard chronicle into a closely organized drama. By the same token the distribution of arias was radically changed. Bussani gave Curio, Rodisbe, and Nireno no fewer than thirteen between them; they have none in the Haym version, which reduced Achilla's ration from five to three and increased Sesto's by a like amount. While compressing the number of solo movements from more than 50 to 33, it expanded Caesar's part from six arias to eight, the same number as Cleopatra's. Both these changes were predictable; by 1724 the aria had grown into a far more substantial structure than it had been in 1677, and Senesino required as much scope as possible for his talents. They also improved the balance of the opera by distributing the solo music in accordance with the importance of the characters. Sartorio had no choruses; Handel's as usual were sung by the soloists.

Handel's original Act I differed very considerably, in words and music, from the published versions; moreover there were important intermediate revisions. All the set pieces are complete; with minor exceptions only the words of the recitatives were written. The music is discussed below under *Autograph*. The principal variants in the libretto are:

(i) Cleopatra's confidante is neither Rodisbe nor Nireno but her cousin Berenice, who being a person of consequence has two arias ('Tutto può donna' and 'Va tacito e soletto'), both of which were subsequently modified and transferred to other characters.[14]

(ii) The duet 'Son nata a lagrimar' occurs not at the end of the act but (in a different key) in Scene iv, where Bussani has a corresponding episode.

(iii) Tolomeo has no aria.

(iv) The recitatives in three scenes (v, vii, and viii, in this version numbered v, viii, and ix) are different. In v Cleopatra shows no reaction whatever to the news of Pompey's murder; she merely asks Berenice to dress her hair and proposes to visit Caesar. In vii she introduces Berenice as Dorisbe and tells Caesar they have both been robbed by Tolomeo. It is 'Dorisbe', not 'Lidia', to

---

[14] At a later stage Handel wrote two further arias for her.

whom Curio proposes to transfer his affections if Cornelia continues to scorn him. In viii (HG 36) Berenice offers to guide Cornelia and Sesto in their quest for vengeance.

(v) There are two extra scenes at the end of the act after the removal of Sesto and Cornelia. In the first, taken from Bussani, Cleopatra confesses to Berenice that instead of captivating Caesar she has herself fallen in love with him; this, surprisingly, is the context for Berenice's 'Va tacito': she urges her cousin to proceed like a crafty hunter. In the second Cleopatra consecrates herself to the god of love, whom she implores to help her win Caesar's heart and, by this means, the undisputed throne of Egypt.

Two separate reasons can be traced for the abandonment of this plan. First, the act was designed for a different cast of singers from that of the 1724 première. It was probably composed in the early summer of 1723, certainly before the start of the new season in the autumn. The odd fact that the opening chorus, not only in the autograph but in the copies and HG, has a part in the tenor clef, whereas there was no tenor in the 1724 cast, is one pointer. Against this part in the autograph Handel wrote the letter 'G', which undoubtedly represents the tenor Alexander Gordon, who had sung in *Flavio* in May and June 1723. He was probably cast for Tolomeo; but by August he seems to have abandoned the stage for the life of an antiquary,[15] and when Handel reached I vii (vi in 1724) he supplied Tolomeo's unset recitative with an alto clef. In this original Act I Cornelia is a soprano (presumably Durastanti), Sesto an alto (Berenstadt); Haym may have invented Berenice for Anastasia Robinson, who was otherwise unprovided.[16] Handel evidently intended to replace Gordon with a new alto castrato and gave him no aria until he could assess his talents; this was Giuseppe Bigonzi, who proved unequal to singing more than recitative.[17] Immediately after Achilla's exit in vii (vi in 1724) Handel added the words of a recitative followed by *Aria di Tolomeo*, but crossed them out.

The second motive for revision is more revealing. The reallotment of parts demoted Berenice into Nireno—a reversion to Bussani—and necessitated new recitatives in vii and viii (there is a certain loss here: it is a trifle excessive that Caesar and Curio should make simultaneous passes at Cleopatra, more acceptable that each should choose one cousin). It may have affected the end of the act, since Cleopatra cannot so easily confide in a servant. In the second stage of this draft the act ended with 'Tutto può donna', rewritten and transferred to Cleopatra. The shifting of the duet was a brilliant stroke, clearly motivated by dramatic and structural demands. The same consideration caused the other significant change, the restoration in v of Cleopatra's horror at her brother's murder of Pompey; for at this point Haym returned to Bussani's powerful dialogue of 1677, which he had watered down in his first draft. These improvements may well have been suggested by Handel.

The libretto in its final form is one of the best Handel ever received. Streatfeild's strange judgement—'an almost inextricable muddle of plots and

[15] See *The New Grove* and C. Morey, 'Alexander Gordon, Scholar and Singer', *M & L* xlvi (1965), 332.

[16] The initials of all these singers, as well as Cuzzoni, Senesino, Boschi, and Lagarde, are written against the staves of the chorus in the autograph.

[17] According to a letter from Anastasia Robinson to Giuseppe Riva in the Biblioteca Estense, Modena, Bigonzi arrived on 7 October 1723 as a replacement for Gordon.

counterplots, which positively defies analysis'—is contradicted in the theatre. It is true that Haym left one or two loose ends (in II x Sesto seizes Tolomeo's sword and is deprived of it by Achilla, but evidently retains his own, with which he tries to commit suicide a little later), and that some survivals of seventeenth-century convention—Cornelia's employment as a lady gardener (compare Antigona in *Admeto*) and Cleopatra's feigned sleep in II vii—are a little out of place. A modern audience may find the threats of rape, murder, and suicide too close-packed to carry conviction; Cornelia is assaulted almost as frequently as the unfortunate leading ladies in *Silla*. But this defect, which arises from compression, is less noticeable in performance than a reading of the score might suggest, since most of the incidents are separated by substantial arias. Haym could have omitted Curio altogether, except that this would force Caesar into soliloquy at inconvenient moments.

The action is varied, exciting, and spectacular, the characterization strong, the motives clear. It is important to realize that the characters, with the possible exception of Nireno and the two basses, are all young, some of them very young indeed. Caesar, who was 54 when he met Cleopatra, is not the middle-aged man of Shaw's play, nor is he true to history. He is a brave soldier, but a still more ardent lover, as his music makes abundantly clear and the castrato voice (especially that of Senesino) implies. Sesto is a mere boy (Cornelia is delighted that he should think of bearing arms); Cleopatra was twenty in history and is certainly no more in the opera; Tolomeo is younger. The Argument describes him as 'the young ambitious and licentious King ... naturally cruel and void of Honour'. Cornelia herself is sufficiently attractive to provoke violent and instantaneous desire in every man she meets except Caesar.[18]

Handel's score too is preoccupied with the passions of youth, a point fatally obscured when the high male parts are transposed down an octave. The Caesar–Cleopatra half of the plot, though well balanced against the theme of Sesto's vengeance on Tolomeo, far outsoars it in the intensity of the music as well as in sheer length. Caesar and Cleopatra each have eight arias and two substantial accompanied recitatives, as well as two duets together if the second part of the finale is included; a full half of the set pieces in the opera. This is an exceptionally large proportion, but it accurately reflects the temper of the score. Handel never tired of depicting the agonies, hesitations, and exaltations of love. This was of course conventional in *opera seria*, but the flaming intensity with which he carries out his task leaves no doubt that it was done *con amore*. In no other work except *Semele* does he approach the expressiveness and variety of the love music in *Giulio Cesare*. It is a glorification of sexual passion uninhibited by the shadow of matrimony: not an immoral but an amoral work, infused with a delicate irony. It is as Virtue that Cleopatra disguises herself in order to seduce Caesar. Handel could portray the indissoluble union of married love as powerfully as Beethoven, as he showed in *Radamisto*, *Rodelinda*, and elsewhere; the virginity of Theodora and Iphis was equally within his compass. There is a singular aptness in the fact that, like Shakespeare, whose range of characterization he rivals perhaps more than any other composer, he was confronted at the meridian of his career by the immortal harlot Cleopatra.

---

[18] The historical Cornelia had been married to Pompey for only four years.

Handel's Cleopatra is the equal of Shakespeare's, and one of the most subtly drawn characters in opera. Every one of her eight arias contributes to the portrait; three at least are among the supreme creations of their epoch. It is some indication of Handel's care that no fewer than seven of them are replacements or refashionings of complete earlier settings,[19] which incidentally show no sign of the tonal unity in the eventual part. Cleopatra begins in her 'tonic' E major with a flippant aria teasing her brother about the amorous dalliance that becomes him more than the royal sceptre. 'Non disperar' is not thematically exceptional, but the contrasted ideas of the ritornello, variously adorned with mordents, slurs (violins, bar 3 etc., not in HG), staccato marks, and trills, cleverly suggest the mood of bantering irony, and there is a fine opportunity for a derisive cadenza at the fermata on 'Chi sà?'. 'Tutto può donna' is still light in tone; it expresses her creed of frivolous sensuality before she has encountered any obstacle. There is an impish wit in the contrast between the repetitions of the detached 'tutto' and the long phrases of nine and ten bars, with delicately pointed cross-rhythms and hemiola, in which she exults in her power over men. Syncopation and melodic extensions, allied with a most expressive coloratura, play a further part in 'Tu la mia stella', multiplying the charms of an irresistible melody that had been in Handel's mind for years. It proves the perfect vehicle for the mixture of confidence and mischief with which she looks forward to her triumph; she addresses hope, but is in no doubt over the outcome.

Act II brings a great change: before she is certain that she has bewitched Caesar, the flirt is caught in her own toils. Cleopatra is no longer acting on policy; the emotional intensity of the music leaves no doubt that she is in love. The Parnassus scene, three movements on the same material linked by excited fragments of recitative, is an epitome of seductiveness seldom equalled in opera of any period. Handel deploys all his wizardry, using two orchestras, one in the pit, the other and richer (representing the concert of the Muses) on stage, and an assembly of continuo instruments recalling the panoply of the Mantuan court in Monteverdi's time: independent parts for harp, viola da gamba (with multiple stopping), and theorbo as well as oboes, bassoons, and strings. They are variously treated and combined in the three movements, two sinfonias of nine and seventeen bars and the aria 'V'adoro, pupille', in such a way that the climax is first delayed and then overwhelming. In the first sinfonia the pit orchestra is silent; Caesar hears the concert behind closed back-flats and takes it for the music of the spheres. In the second sinfonia the material is extended, the gamba thrums full chords, and the harp breaks into arpeggio and scale figures half-way through as the pit orchestra enters; this is probably the point at which 'Parnassus opens', the back-flats being withdrawn to reveal 'Lidia' seated among the Muses.[20] No doubt they were supers miming while the players remained concealed; but it is surely significant that Handel specifies nine instruments. Caesar exclaims in wonder at what he sees

[19] 'Da tempeste' is the exception. For the rejected versions see below, under *Autograph*.
[20] The manuscripts differ in where they place the stage direction. Hamburg, RM 19 c 7, Lennard, and Granville have it before the first sinfonia, RM 19 c 6 after the second. Chrysander compromises by putting it between the two. The libretto is not decisive, since only one sinfonia is mentioned (before the direction). The music points to the entry of the pit orchestra as the correct moment, and this is confirmed by the autograph of the A version (that of the B version does not survive), which has the direction below the closing bars of the second sinfonia. This is also its position in the Malmesbury copy. Chrysander (HG 52) prints it in the wrong place.

as well as hears, and Cleopatra begins the aria, whose theme has so far only been adumbrated, with the divided violins of both orchestras muted.[21] The mastery here lies not merely in the tune itself, one of the most haunting ever written, and the magical scoring, but in Handel's treatment of the vocal line as a vehicle for characterization. The entire first part of the aria, 35 Largo bars, is one continuous melodic chain, constantly prolonged beyond the expectation of the ear by interrupted cadences and melismas and, when the voice pauses for breath, by echoes and interjections from the pit orchestra, while the stage group supplies the main accompaniment. Seldom has the process of seduction been so vividly expressed by musical means, and in a da capo aria of the utmost regularity; the plaintive B section, with the pit orchestra again silent, hints at the same material in the minor mode until the ear craves a repeat. Before it can begin Caesar again cries out in amazement (as well he might) at the beauty of the song, a brilliant detail not in the original conception and one that further enhances the da capo.[22] In the theatre of course Handel and his stage machinist set out to captivate the eyes as well as the ears of the audience with as much craft and elaboration as Cleopatra bestows on Caesar's.

Aware that she has won the first round, Cleopatra solicits the aid of Venus for the second. The kittenish 'Venere bella' returns to the confident mood of Act I; the rising sixths of the melody, varied later by fourths and fifths, suggest invocation but not anxiety, the postponement of the tonic cadence towards the end of the A section is positively playful, and the tell-tale little violin figure

Ex. 56

anticipates another self-indulgent mortal's dealing with the gods, Semele's mirror air 'Myself I shall adore'. But Caesar, distanced once by her coyness, is now the target of conspiracy and violence, and Cleopatra is plunged in despair. The accompanied recitative and aria 'Che sento?'—'Se pietà' reveal unsuspected depths of suffering, and it is a measure of Handel's art that they do not seem out of place. The recitative opens dramatically with a diminished seventh rooted on F sharp after the clamour of the conspirators in B flat, and modulates with superb strength as Cleopatra registers fear, martial ardour, love for Caesar, and anxiety over his fate. The aria in F sharp minor, appropriately the relative minor of the key of 'Venere bella', strikes a mood of profound tragedy; Leichtentritt ranked it among the finest creations of any age, and likened it to the E flat minor and B flat minor preludes of Bach's first book. It is a prayer from the anguish of her soul, Bach-like in its harmonic probing of emotion and scored in rich dark colours. While two-thirds of the violins (a division favoured by Handel to secure a strong obbligato line) repeat

---

[21] Handel changed his mind more than once over this. In the original version of the second sinfonia he had the violins and violas of the pit orchestra muted and the basses pizzicato at their first entry (HG 53), but cancelled these directions. In some very early copies (RM 19 c 6, Bodleian) the stage violins are not muted in 'V'adoro, pupille'.

[22] Compare Eduige's exclamation at the corresponding point of Bertarido's 'Con rauco mormorio' in *Rodelinda* and (in a very different context) the Second Elder's impatient interruption of Susanna's 'If guiltless blood be your intent'. These are the only three occasions on which Handel used the device.

their drooping four-note figure, sometimes extended or turned plaintively upwards, over the steady quavers of third violins, violas, and basses, the bassoons colour the ritornellos with a mournful counterpoint in longer notes.[23] When the voice enters it takes up the dialogue with the violins, initially in fragments, but towards the end of the first part and throughout the second, as her appeals grow more urgent, in phrases of longer span. There is a masterly use of interrupted cadence when the thought of death, which she foresees if the gods prove obdurate, moves her to a sudden leap of a seventh as the music threatens to settle in the relative major and diverts it towards B minor instead, with the cadence postponed for a further eight bars (Ex. 57).

At the nadir of her fortunes, her troops defeated, herself captured and thrown into chains by the gloating Tolomeo, her lover reported dead, Cleopatra laments in still more moving terms. The choice of a major key—her own E major—and a melody and accompaniment of the utmost simplicity was another stroke of genius.[24] 'Piangerò' has no initial ritornello and very few notes, but they are disposed with rare artistry, from the varied rising intervals

Ex. 57

---

[23] Compare their similar employment in another aria of heart-break, Ariodante's 'Scherza infida'.

[24] This was the third, and characteristically the simplest, of the three fine arias Handel composed for this place before the first performance.

Ex. 57 (cont.)

(If you do not feel pity for me, just heaven, I shall die.)

of the opening bars, shared between voice and accompaniment—a third, a fourth, a fifth, an octave (Ex. 58, p. 494)—to the lovely little cadence at the end of the A section. As Leichtentritt remarks, the design is a free passacaglia on a bass descending by steps over a fourth. The interplay of voice and instruments is beautifully managed, and the scoring, with a flute doubling the first violin but not the second, adds a remote wistfulness typical of Handel's sensitivity to the emotional quality of sound. Right in the middle of the aria (bars 26–9) he incorporates an eloquent sequence from an early cantata, used again in three other works, including *Rodrigo* and *Il pastor fido*, associated each time with the idea of cruel fate and separation; it sounds the most natural thing in the world.[25] The tempo of the first part, omitted from HG, is *Largo*; the second, in which Cleopatra promises to haunt Tolomeo beyond the grave, brings a change of time (4/4) and texture (no flute, independent cello) as well as tempo (*Allegro*) and key (C sharp minor). Its brave coloratura makes more poignant the return to the pathos of the da capo.

Cleopatra's troubles are not yet over. The ten-bar F minor introduction to the accompanied recitative 'Voi, che mie fide ancelle', in which she says farewell to the maidens whom Tolomeo has ordered to leave her, is an expansion of the ritornello of the first (soprano) setting of Cornelia's 'Nel tuo seno'. Its drooping oboe solo over quiet string chords was a favourite and always memorable texture in Handel's early and middle-period operas: witness 'Dolce riposo' in *Teseo* and 'Quando mai spietata' in *Radamisto*. The

[25] See Ex. 8, p.103.

Ex. 58

(I shall bewail my fate)

recitative, interrupted by the clash of arms announcing the approach of Caesar but taken by Cleopatra as the signal for her own death, is as varied and powerful in its progressions as all such pieces in the opera. After her rescue 'Da tempeste' reverts, it seems inevitably, to E major. It has the buoyant gaiety one expects from Cleopatra's basically optimistic nature when the storms have passed. The springy tune, compounded of arpeggios, scales, and wide leaps, is as expressive as the coloratura that reflects the relief in her heart—not without another anticipation (at bar 43) of Semele's 'Myself I shall adore'.[26] Her duet with Caesar, less exuberant but equally relaxed, has another delightful tune, borrowed from an early cantata, in lilting 12/8 rhythm nicely varied by a couple of *Adagio* 4/4 bars at the vocal entry. Exceptionally, but with singular aptness in this opera, the lovers are allowed a second duet in the central section of the *coro*. They toy amorously in the tonic minor, in turn and together, doubled by the oboes and accompanied *piano*[27] by a bass line no doubt intended for bassoon. This makes the happiest contrast with the main theme in stately bourrée rhythm, replete with four horns.

Caesar's music is less consistently individual; there is often something generic about Handel's castrato heroes. But it is by no means the pedestrian stuff implied in Dent's sweeping denunciation ('on the whole the music is very conventional'). By common consent his finest scenes are the two that incorporate accompanied recitative; Burney called *Giulio Cesare* 'an opera abounding with beauties of various kinds, but in which both the composer and performers seem to have acquired even more reputation from the recitatives than the arias'. Much of the secco recitative, especially in I iii and II viii, can be included in this eulogy. 'Alma del gran Pompeo' deserves the universal praise bestowed on it; Burney in his 1785 volume called it 'the finest piece of accompanied Recitative, without intervening symphonies, with which I am acquainted. The modulation is learned, and so uncommon, that there is hardly a chord which the ear expects'. So might Shakespeare, had he been a musician, have soliloquized on the fragile thread from which the most heroic life depends. It was a favourite theme with Handel: we meet it again in *Rodelinda* ('Pompe vane di morte'), *Arminio* ('Fier teatro di morte!'), and several times in the late oratorios, especially *Theodora* and *Jephtha*. The key, G sharp minor, changing signature in the middle of a bar and ending enharmo-

---

[26] The two echoes of Cleopatra come consecutively in Semele's aria, bars 45 and 46.

[27] This is in the autograph, but not HG.

nically in A flat minor,[28] is almost unique for the period, and it falls impressively at the change of scene after the E flat major of Tolomeo's 'L'empio sleale'. The brooding modulations evoke the cold shadow of departed glory, and give the episode an extraordinary sombre power.

'Dall'ondoso periglio' is more than an accompanied recitative; it is a dramatic *scena* of most original design. Again the first chord is a surprise. Cleopatra's lament over Caesar's death ends in E major; the quiet entry of F major, the last key we expect, tells us that he is alive. The long 22-bar string ritornello suggests the rustling breezes on the bank of the Nile after the tumult of battle has passed (shades of *Aida*!), Caesar's wonder at his escape, and, at the romantic shift to B flat minor for two bars near the end, the stab of pain as he thinks of his lost Cleopatra. This is not fancy; after describing his escape and his helplessness without his legions he addresses the breezes in an Adagio unaccompanied bar ('Aure!'), and the introductory figure of the recitative turns out to be the accompaniment, exquisitely varied, of the aria as well. The link is as imaginative as that which introduces 'Dove sei?' in *Rodelinda*. The B flat minor passage proves to be associated with Caesar's sense of loss ('al mio dolor'), but is marvellously altered and developed at both its reappearances by suspensions in the voice and a different resolution. The romantic flavour, a feature of *Giulio Cesare* and other Handel operas of this period, is nowhere more explicit. The second part of the aria, introduced by the same figure, this time on violins in thirds only, plunges abruptly back into recitative as the sight of bodies slain in the battle recalls Caesar to reality. The appeal to the breezes is resumed, but with the Adagio bar and the two that follow dropped, blurring the impression of a regular da capo. The whole scene is a masterly synthesis of dramatic action and musical form.

Four of Caesar's arias show him as a man of action. His first scene is a loose cavatina–cabaletta design. Unlike many it has no close tonal unity, but it emphatically conveys a feeling for tonal progression. The D major arioso 'Presti omai' is an extension of the overture. The Egyptians, interrupting the Minuet, have welcomed Caesar in A major; he makes a soldierly reply in a related key, claiming the honours of victory. The gift of Pompey's severed head, after a long recitative introducing three of the principal characters, provokes him to denounce Tolomeo's barbarity in a powerful C minor aria, full of angry scales and bursts of that prolonged coloratura, narrow in compass, low in pitch, and intensely energetic, of which Senesino was a master. We meet it again in 'Al lampo dell'armi' and 'Quel torrente', where the context calls for more rushing string scales. It must have made a brilliant effect; it is difficult though not impossible for a modern mezzo-soprano, but grotesque in the mouth of a baritone, who can do little but suggest a man gargling to exorcize a sore throat or a bumble-bee trapped in a jam jar. 'Quel torrente' gains in impulse from the dashing rhythmic design of the main theme (4 + 2 bars) and overlapping imitations between voice and violins. 'Al lampo dell'armi', with a bustle of violin repeated notes, has a strong foretaste of 'Vorrei vendicarmi' in *Alcina* (a woman's aria); its most effective stroke, because entirely unexpected, is the extended ritornello after the B section with the off-stage voices of conspirators clamouring for Caesar's blood. These bars

---

[28] The enharmonic continuation in E major was planned from the start; this is one of the very few secco bars set to music in the original Act I.

were sung by the entire cast of soloists (except Cleopatra), including Caesar and Curio, who have barely left the stage.[29]

Caesar's two love songs are more immediately attractive. 'Non è si vago e bello', his first reaction to the sight of Cleopatra, is a light relaxed piece dependent entirely on the melody, doubled by the violins at the octave. There is no passion (Caesar does not hint at this till 'Dall'ondoso periglio'), but the delicious little tune is instinct with the pleasure of first sensations. The phrases are almost symmetrical; Handel keeps the act of uniformity at bay by varying the ritornello after the A section, which is not a restatement but a development enriched by a warm inner part for the viola,[30] and returning without pause from the brief B section to the first phrase of the voice. 'Se in fiorito', after the Parnassus scene, is more extended but still not deeply committed. Enchanted by Cleopatra's voice, he compares her to a bird that gives all the greater pleasure for singing unseen. This is the cue for a bird song with obbligato for solo violin, which teases the voice with imitations and carefree carolling. What gives the aria its distinction (if it is not destroyed by a baritone producing a cavernous gap of anything up to three octaves) is the warm colour of the ritornellos, in which divided bassoons add mellowness to the string texture. Unlike many simile arias the famous 'Va tacito e nascosto' contributes nothing to the characterization—it could scarcely do so, having been composed for Berenice[31]—but it is a splendid piece, and unique in Handel's operas in having an obbligato for solo horn.[32] The canonic opening and stealthy quaver movement, varied by bursts of semiquavers in one or other of the parts but never all at the same time, admirably suggest the hunter stalking his prey, with the horn to indicate his profession; the long divisions it is required to execute, especially in the ritornellos, are a test of stamina that makes a most exhilarating impact when successfully surmounted. If the tempo is rushed, however, it degenerates into a jogtrot. Exceptionally in a Handel obbligato aria, the voice and all the instruments are simultaneously employed almost throughout; the strings have scarcely a rest except at the cadenza points.

Cornelia is the one tragic figure in the opera. Her first four utterances, including the duet with Sesto, are all *Largo*, the fifth *Andante*, only the last *Allegro*. In Act I the poignancy of her grief acts as a counterpoise to the extrovert reactions of Caesar, the frivolity of Cleopatra, and the crafty machinations of Tolomeo and Achilla; Handel showed a sure sense of what was appropriate in transferring the duet to the end. 'Priva son d'ogni conforto' is a lament of piercing beauty, all the more effective for the placing of its major key (D) between two furious outbursts of C minor, the second of which seems to show Sesto drawn under the influence of Caesar. The simple opening without ritornello, after an imperfect cadence on F sharp major for a different voice, is very moving; it suggests, behind her grief, a character of sterling courage and potential serenity,[33] a point confirmed in her later music.

[29] Senesino's name, though not in HG, is in the autograph and the performing score.

[30] In the autograph the viola plays in the first ritornello as well; Handel may have removed it to emphasize the later entry.

[31] See p. 509.

[32] The only other instance in Handel's work is 'Mirth, admit me of thy crew' in *L'Allegro ed il Penseroso*.

[33] Significantly the first version was in E major. Handel may have made the change when he decided to associate this key with Cleopatra.

The flute, the instrument of mourning, is traditional, but its treatment is not. It plays almost continuously throughout both parts, sometimes doubling the first violin, sometimes mounting to the higher octave, but also adding its own comments, most eloquently in bars 5-8 and in the aria's single ritornello after the first part, an exquisite inspiration ending with a trill on a weak beat. Other distinctive features are the flexible rhythms, which introduce an exceptional variety into the basic 3/8 metre, the very simple but unexpected cadence at the end of the A section, and the growing intensity of the second part at the repeated phrase 'e morir si niega a me' as the desolate prospect of life without her husband forces itself to the front of her mind.

Cornelia's two cavatinas, 'Nel tuo seno' in Act I and 'Deh piangete' in Act II, are bleaker and both in minor keys; she has begun to experience the grim reality. Both are very fine, especially 'Nel tuo seno' with its hollow string octaves and prominent use of the G string. The descending dotted figure of the ritornello had served Handel before, in *Agrippina* ('Qual piacer') and at least two cantatas, but attains its utmost intensity here. For the most part it contrasts with the voice, which takes up the second, more lyrical and syncopated, element of the ritornello, except when it joins the violins in a plaintive descending scale whose dotted rhythm becomes a lingering sigh. The shorter 'Deh piangete' could also be a cantata borrowing, though it has not been identified. It gains weight from its context, the bare D minor continuo accompaniment following immediately on the sumptuous G major of Caesar's 'Se in fiorito'. The duet 'Son nata a lagrimar' is one of the score's supreme moments. These valedictory duets, here between mother and son but more often between lovers or husband and wife, always found Handel at the height of his powers. The siciliano rhythm lends itself to such sentiments; the operas are full of examples, nearly all of outstanding quality and generally scored, as here, for four-part strings with the harpsichord silenced when the voice enters.[34] The drooping theme, sung by each voice in turn, conveys an impression of overwhelming pathos. Handel adds concentration by omitting the first two bars of the ritornello after the first part and further contracting it after the second: a da capo with a difference. Needless to say the octave transposition of Sesto's part ruins the balance.

Handel did not set 'Cessa omai di sospirare' as a vengeance aria (of which the score has more than enough) but more subtly as a tentative revival of hope, not in personal happiness but in the justice of providence. The broken three-bar phrases and contrasted dynamics (seven changes in each of the main ritornellos) suggest Cornelia's hesitant response to this possibility, as if she dare not quite believe it. The material is not memorable; but the deliberate shortwindedness (sighs?) is rendered more acceptable, and the dramatic purpose confirmed, by several deft details: the opening on a first inversion, the soft water-colour of the recorders, which mostly double the voice at the octave, sometimes in alternation with the strings, the trills on weak beats, and the nicely varied ritornello after the A section with a singularly happy and unexpected dominant seventh five bars from the end. In 'Non hà più che temere' Cornelia at last has something to applaud: Sesto has proved his manhood by avenging his father. While the general tone of the aria is cheerful, Handel does not forget what she has been through; he returns to the

---

[34] Compare 'Mà chi punir desio?' in *Flavio*, in F sharp minor, the original key of the *Giulio Cesare* duet; and see p. 87 ff.

key of her first aria, D major, modulates unpredictably to F sharp minor, and fits in a chromatic descending figure, slurred across the beat, with the short trills that have become a personal feature of Cornelia's music. This figure, secondary at the start and confined to the violins, takes the lead in the ritornello after the first part and is prominently developed and extended in the second, with seven trills in place of the original four. Next to Cleopatra, Cornelia is the most fully realized character in the opera.

Sesto is less successful, if only because his range of mood is circumscribed by the plot. Apart from the duet with Cornelia and the brief 'Cara speme', a last-minute insertion, his part consists of four vengeance arias, similar in mood and all in minor keys. The first two, both in C minor, are the best. 'Svegliatevi' is saved from conventionality by the beautiful second part, in which the boy invokes the shade of his father. After the quick 4/4 Allegro[35] with rapid passage-work in Vivaldi's manner the change to Largo 3/8, with low-pitched violins picked out from time to time by recorders in double thirds, is a most imaginative stroke. The slow march of the modulations from E flat through B flat, A flat, F minor, and C minor to G minor as Sesto interprets Pompey's exhortation to be ruthless is very impressive. 'L'angue offeso' is a magnificent aria by any standard. The ritornellos in particular, in which (*pace* Chrysander) all the oboes double the first violins,[36] have a splendid breadth and power, and it is surely not fanciful to see in the contours of the main theme the coil and spring of the angry serpent to which Sesto compares himself. Of the three contrasted ideas of the main ritornello, the third (bars 13–15) was an afterthought. 'L'aura che spira', while vigorous and effective, with much crossing of the upper parts, is rather too much after the same manner. Although it makes a satisfactory end to Act II, it is not surprising that many modern revivals have brought down the curtain on 'Se pietà. 'La giustizia' is the one weak aria in the opera; it adds no new facet to the character and holds up the action. Handel never performed it after 1724. His inclusion of 'Cara speme' (this too disappeared later, but for a different reason) was a wise move. Instead of threatening the absent Tolomeo Sesto allows himself to hope. This is a continuo aria (the only one in the opera apart from Cornelia's Act II cavatina), with the violins joining in a delicious two-bar extended cadence after the da capo—a reversion to a primitive plan common in Handel's early years but still perfectly fresh. Both the bass and the vocal line, with characteristic melismatic extensions, are singularly expressive. There is something youthful and vulnerable in the intimate tone of this little aria.

Handel draws Tolomeo's character in terms of wide vocal intervals and cat-like leaps. Even in his one slow piece, where he addresses the women of his seraglio in the cavatina 'Belle dee', the bass fidgets in a dotted rhythm that carries a hint of menace; and the sudden drop into secco only two bars after launching a second part in the relative minor—a favourite device from *Rodrigo* to *Saul*—suggests capriciousness by the mere fact that it seems unmotivated. There is something feline about the whole conception of this crafty and treacherous autocrat, a petulant adolescent of criminal propensities. His three full arias are all outbursts of indignation, the first two in major keys, the third, when he crows over his conquered sister ('Domerò la tua fierezza'), in E minor. The angular vocal line here has an almost sadistic quality, thrown into

---

[35] Tempo mark in the autograph, omitted in HG.
[36] In bar 50 they play the last four notes an octave higher.

relief by the oilier second half. In 'L'empio sleale' the strings, and later the voice, leap about over a bass busy with repeated notes and scales; in each section voice and orchestra together plunge into a distinctive unison figure based on rising arpeggios as Tolomeo seems to shake his fist at Caesar in impotent rage for disturbing his kingdom and peace of mind. 'Sì, spietata' (II iv) is harder to bring off, since the triplet rhythm can suggest jauntiness, a legacy no doubt of its origin in an aria with very different sentiments ('Nobil cor non può mirare') composed for Berenice in Act I;[37] the onus is upon the singer to supply the required venom. All Tolomeo's solos were in fact written for other characters, though two of them were much altered; with Handel the expected consequences do not necessarily follow.

Achilla is not a subtle character; but this braggart Egyptian traitor, equally disposed to do his master's dirty work and feather his own soiled nest, cuts a much firmer figure when the other parts are sung at the correct pitch. If we cannot agree with Burney that 'Tu sei il cor' is 'very original, and unlike all other base songs', it makes its point: such a rough D minor wooing is as near as Achilla can come to ingratiating himself with Cornelia, and he cannot conceal the cloven hoof. Handel emphasizes the approach by making the bassoons double the voice, except at one point where they produce an appropriately hollow effect by accompanying the violins in tenths. In 'Se a me' Achilla resumes the pursuit, with a hint of a threat; the music cleverly suggests a mixture of the sinister and the awkwardly wheedling. 'Dal fulgor'[38] is the finest of Achilla's three arias. The wide vocal leaps, characteristic of many Boschi parts (and of other Handelian villains from Polifemo onwards), alternate with rousing divisions based on scales. The best moment occurs in the B section (on the same material), where the loud guffaw of the violins (bars 9 and 10) makes a sudden entry on a top D (bar 87), the highest note in the aria.

The score of *Giulio Cesare* has many points of structural interest. Handel seems to have striven even more than usual for continuity. The opening is brilliantly original: after a spacious introduction and a lively fugue composed for an overture mainly employed in *Ottone*, the expected dance movement develops without warning into a chorus, enriched by the unprecedented panoply of four horns. Their entry, two bars before the voices, was perhaps the signal for the rise of the curtain. The later acts also begin with a musical design larger than the aria and a good deal of spectacle. Something has been said about the playing of the Parnassus scene; the back-flats showed the outer prospect, and when they were withdrawn Cleopatra appeared enthroned among the Muses against another no doubt spectacular background. In Act III it seems likely that the back-flats were opened for the battle (during the sinfonia), closed after it, and opened again when Achilla is discovered mortally wounded (HG 108), or perhaps when Caesar sees the bodies during the central recitative of 'Dall'ondoso periglio'. There was of course no interruption in the music. An unusual feature of *Giulio Cesare* is the number of persons, including two of the principals,[39] killed on stage; more often wounded characters staggered into the wings to die.

[37] It also recalls the jolly hermit's 'Andate, O forti' in *Rinaldo*.
[38] Its first four bars reappear, rather surprisingly, in Iris's air 'There from mortal cares retiring' in *Semele*.
[39] They presumably sang in the final *coro* from the wings.

There are many lesser *coups de théâtre*: the off-stage chorus at the end of 'Al lampo dell'armi', which remains startling even when we expect it, the drop from 'Belle dee' into secco recitative in the seraglio scene, the compound of sinfonia and both types of recitative when Caesar's soldiers break into Cleopatra's apartment and expel Tolomeo's guards,[40] and the gorgeous pageantry of the final scene, the back-flats being withdrawn to reveal the port of Alexandria to the full depth of the stage. In the twelve-part sinfonia Handel for the first time uses his two pairs of horns of different pitch antiphonally (they play together in the Act I chorus and again in the finale). The effect must have been thrilling. It was something quite new, which he never repeated in the opera-house; nor for many decades did anyone else, so far as is known. The horns represent the 'Trumpets and Tymbals' of the libretto; there were no trumpets in the 1724 score. Otherwise the orchestra is full and varied, and must have been large to accommodate the division in the Parnassus scene. This too was a rare occurrence in Handel's operas, though we find it on a smaller scale in *Ariodante*, and there are other scenes, such as the coronations in *Almira* and *Giustino*, where the directions in the libretto place instruments on the stage. Handel uses both recorders and transverse flutes, and more than once divides the bassoons. It would be interesting to know to what extent he gave the extra continuo instruments of the Parnassus scene employment elsewhere in the opera. Chrysander suggested that the elaborate scoring was intended to characterize the oriental splendours of Egypt.

The key scheme of the 1724 score reveals a definite plan, especially in Cleopatra's music: of her eight arias, six are in keys with three or four sharps, the first and the last two being in E major. The use of the relative minor of 'Venere bella' for 'Se pietà' can scarcely have been an accident. Only in 'Tu la mia stella' and 'V'adoro, pupille' does Cleopatra move to the flat side.[41] Caesar inclines towards the more robust major keys; the flatward tendency was stronger with 'Non è si vago' in its original key of F. Cornelia's keys are closely related, beginning and ending in D major, which the absence of trumpets for once allows to assume non-military associations. Sesto alone is tied to the minor mode, which rules in five of his six pieces, including two each in C minor and E minor. Otherwise this is overwhelmingly a major-key opera (thirty numbers, as opposed to eleven in the minor), with a bias towards the sharp side. After an A major overture the first two acts both end in E minor, the third in its relative major. Very little of this reflects the original plan, in which no tonal scheme is discernible.

History and Text

Handel probably began the composition in the early summer of 1723. He forgot to date it exactly; the words *anno 1723* in pencil seem to have been added later. It was extensively revised several times before the first performance at the King's Theatre on 20 February 1724. The cast was:

CAESAR:　　Senesino (alto castrato)
CLEOPATRA:　Cuzzoni (soprano)
CORNELIA:　Anastasia Robinson (contralto)

[40] The stage directions in HG 116 are deceptive; see synopsis.
[41] The original scheme was quite different: see below, under *Autograph*.

SESTO:	Durastanti (soprano)
TOLOMEO:	Berenstadt (alto castrato)
ACHILLA:	Boschi (bass)
NIRENO:	Giuseppe Bigonzi (alto castrato)
CURIO:	Lagarde (bass)

Castrucci led the orchestra. The score was essentially that of Chrysander's main text, with the B version of the Parnassus sinfonias and the G major sinfonia on HG 122, not the March. Handel seems to have had doubts about 'Belle dee' and probably omitted it; it is not in the libretto, several early copies, or Cluer's edition, though it appears (cancelled) in the performing score.

The opera was well received, and ran continuously for thirteen nights[42] until 11 April apart from one performance of Ariosti's *Coriolano*. Friedrich Ernst von Fabrice wrote on 10 March that Senesino and Cuzzoni 'shine beyond all criticism ... The house was just as full at the seventh performance as at the first.' Burney says that in 'Dall'ondoso periglio' 'Senesino gained so much reputation as an actor, as well as singer'. It may be some indication of the success of the opera that Colley Cibber produced his *Caesar in Aegypt*, dealing with the same episode, at Drury Lane on 9 December; it was a failure, enjoying only six performances. In March one Lecoq reported that 'the passion for the opera here is getting beyond all belief'. The poetaster John Byrom, however, who saw the performance of 29 February, was not amused: 'it was the first entertainment of this nature that I ever saw, and will I hope be the last, for of all the diversions of the town I least of all enter into this'. Such a confession sets his notorious jingle about Handel and Bononcini in perspective.

In the summer of 1724 *Giulio Cesare*, like *Ottone*,[43] was given at one of Pierre Crozat's private concerts in Paris. A libretto was printed,[44] but no copy is known to survive. In March the *Mercure de France* had reported from London that even the Italians considered the opera a masterpiece.[45] Handel revived it 'with Alterations' on 2 January 1725 for a further ten performances.[46] He made many changes and considerably shortened the recitatives, omitting Curio altogether and reducing Nireno to a mute. The cuts sometimes involved the transference of words to other characters and weakened the plot in several scenes. Caesar has to answer his own questions at the start of Act I; we lose Cleopatra's reaction to the news of Pompey's murder and her excited preparation for the reception of Caesar in Act II, which now begins with a two-bar recitative for Caesar and the first Parnassus sinfonia; Sesto has to stand in for Curio in II viii. On the other hand the elimination of Curio's advances to Cornelia is welcome. There were three changes of cast: Cornelia was sung by Anna Dotti, Tolomeo by Andrea Pacini, and Sesto by the tenor Francesco Borosini. This last was the only change of voice; Deutsch (p. 177) makes two errors.

Handel's recasting of Sesto's part is interesting and important, since it shows

---

[42] Deutsch lists a performance on 27 February. This was not advertised, but may have taken place if Fabrice's count is accurate.

[43] See p. 437.

[44] It was twice listed in the catalogue of the Floncel library (Paris, 1774). Deutsch's note on this (153) contains three mistakes: the references should be vol. i. p. 206, and vol. ii, p. 215 (no. 7826).

[45] Lindgren, *M & L* (1977), 23.

[46] Deutsch omits the fourth (12 January) but includes one on 23 January, which was advertised but cancelled owing to the illness of a singer.

something of his attitude to octave transposition. He tolerated this in recitative, but seldom in arias, and never when the original was an alto or mezzo. Sesto retained his two C minor vengeance arias, with modifications in 'L'angue offeso', but lost his other four pieces, including the duet with Cornelia, where octave transposition would have inverted the voice parts. Handel compensated him with three new arias, 'S'armi a miei danni' in place of the duet, 'Scorta siate' in place of 'L'aura che spira', and 'Sperai ne m'ingannai' in place of 'La giustizia'. The first and third of these are in Chrysander's appendix; the second is unpublished. All three are extended, forceful pieces with a virile coloratura, and they transform the character of Sesto from an excitable boy into a mature and confident man of action—so much so that his slowness to act becomes a dramatic flaw. Apart from the B section of 'Svegliatevi' he has no slow music at all, since 'Cara speme' was not replaced. While 'Sperai ne m'ingannai', with an accompaniment based on a dotted figure reminiscent of the violin sonata in D major and the angel's symphony in *Jephtha*, is an improvement on 'La giustizia', by far the best of the arias is the unpublished 'Scorta siate', another demand for vengeance, this time in A minor. The angular syncopated theme of the ritornello (Ex. 59) never appears on the voice, which enters with a slight rhythmic variant of the viola part; but it returns in D minor during the first section and again in the same key in the middle of the second, where it has something of the effect of a false recapitulation in a sonata movement. It is difficult to find a parallel for this in Handel, who seldom wrote an intermediate ritornello of any kind in the B section of an aria. Here it introduces a further series of leisurely modulations that confirm the pull between D minor and C major characteristic of the A section, before settling in E minor for the return. The whole piece is very striking.

Ex. 59

II x (HG 88), after the favourites have left the stage. Chrysander prints it (HG 148), but with the words as altered when it was shifted to Act III in 1730. It has no particular merit. 'Belle dee', if not cut before the 1724 performances, disappeared now. The only other change of consequence was the substitution of the March with trumpet (HG 126) for the G major sinfonia, possibly owing to the inadequacy of the horns. This is not indicated in the libretto, but found with the other 1725 additions in the appendix to RM 19 c 7.

At some point during the 1725 run, probably for the last three nights on 2, 6, and 9 February (which followed a single performance of Ariosti's *Artaserse* on 28 January), Handel brought back Nireno, renamed Nerina, as a lady-in-waiting to Cleopatra sung by a new soprano, Benedetta Sorosina. There is no mention of this in the libretto or the newspapers, but the appendix to RM 19 c 7 contains two arias attributed to 'Signora Sorrossina', 'La speranza all'alma mia' (in G major) and 'Chi perde un momento', and both were published in the second volume of Cluer and Creake's *Pocket Companion* on 22 December 1725. They were inserted in I v and II i respectively; Chrysander prints them with their recitatives in his appendix, wrongly attributing 'La speranza' to Cleopatra. Each is a reworking in the same key of material used in one of the *Neun deutsche Arien*;[47] 'Chi perde un momento' derives from no. 2 ('Das zitternde Glänzen'), 'La speranza'—composed in A major—from no. 9 ('Flammende Rose'). Neither adds anything to the dramatic or musical potency of the opera, and 'Chi perde un momento' is feebly sequential. Handel's object was presumably to try out a new singer; Sorosina appeared a few weeks later in Ariosti's *Dario* and the pasticcio *Elpidia*[48]—there was no opening for her in *Rodelinda*, which followed the *Giulio Cesare* revival—but never sang again in London.

Handel's next revival was on 17 January 1730; Rolli told Riva in December that *Giulio Cesare* had been chosen 'because the audiences are falling away fast'. The libretto does not list the cast, but it can be reconstructed with confidence:

CAESAR:	Antonio Bernacchi
CLEOPATRA:	Anna Strada
CORNELIA:	Antonia Merighi
SESTO (tenor version):	Annibale Pio Fabri
TOLOMEO:	Francesca Bertolli
ACHILLA:	Johann Gottfried Riemschneider

The only possible doubt concerns the two contraltos, but since Bertolli regularly sang breeches parts, in which she specialized, whereas Merighi scarcely ever did,[49] we need not hesitate. There were no changes in pitch. Curio and Nireno were again cut. Handel omitted and switched round a number of arias, in every instance weakening the fabric. Caesar's 'Empio, dirò', the central recitative and repeat of 'Aure, deh, per pietà', and Achilla's 'Se a me' were cut, probably to ease the task of the singers; Bernacchi was

---

[47] Although their date is uncertain—it is clear from the autograph that they were written at different times—the texts indicate that the German settings are the earlier. The unpublished 'Questo core incatenato', part of the 1723 score of *Giulio Cesare*, is related to the first aria ('Künft' ger Zeiten'), and there are several links between the arias and *Tamerlano* and *Rodelinda*.

[48] See p. 321.

[49] Gernando in *Faramondo* is the single instance in her ten Handel parts; but she played male parts earlier in Italy.

ageing and not in good voice, Riemschneider a secondary bass. Cornelia gained two arias, which extended the narrow compass suitable for Robinson at both ends, by a minor third at the top: Nerina's 'La speranza' (transposed down to F) in the place originally occupied by 'Cara speme' in I viii and Sesto's 'L'aura che spira' (also transposed down a tone, to D minor) at the end of Act II, where it ousted 'Scorta siate'. Both arias, printed in their new keys in Chrysander's appendix, are totally out of character in Cornelia's mouth, and 'La speranza' holds up the action. Tolomeo's 'Dal mio brando' (1725), with altered words (as in HG) and a new recitative (not in HG), was transferred to III ii, replacing the much finer 'Domerò', which may have been too difficult for Bertolli.

There were eleven performances, the ninth (21 February) followed by a gap of a month. The tenth (21 March) was for Strada's benefit, and 'some New Songs' were announced; they were repeated on the 31st.[50] They and their contexts are identified in two pages of contemporary manuscript in the British Library (King's MS 442), intended for insertion in a libretto, almost certainly for the use of the Royal Family. They were 'Parolette vezzi e sguardi', which replaced 'Tutto può donna' in I vii, and 'Io vò di duolo in duolo', which replaced 'Piangerò' in III iii. Chrysander prints them in the operas to which they were transferred (with verbal changes) a few weeks later, 'Parolette' in *Rinaldo* (with the *Giulio Cesare* text below the notes in the B section), 'Io vò' in the appendix to *Tolomeo* with Cleopatra's reset recitative and the *Giulio Cesare* words uppermost in the B section. In *Giulio Cesare* 'Parolette' was a da capo aria; Handel added the dal segno bars for *Rinaldo*. Although both arias belong by prior right to *Giulio Cesare*, they do not strengthen it. The frivolous 'Parolette' is of course much more suited to Cleopatra than to the virtuous Almirena; 'Io vò', while not without merit, is a sorry substitute for 'Piangerò'. Both no doubt helped Strada to shine at her benefit.

A recently discovered libretto (facsimile in Harris, *Librettos*, xiii) clarifies Handel's last revival on 1 February 1732. There were only four performances. The cast was:

CAESAR:	Senesino
CLEOPATRA:	Strada
CORNELIA:	Anna Bagnolesi
SESTO (tenor version):	Giovanni Battista Pinacci
TOLOMEO:	Bertolli
ACHILLA:	Antonio Montagnana

One would expect Handel to give Achilla something specifically suited to Montagnana's talents, which were very different from Boschi's, but the part was unchanged. The text was a shortened version of 1730: 'Tutto può donna', 'Deh piangete', and (astonishingly) 'Piangerò' were cut, and 'Priva son', 'Svegliatevi', and 'Venere bella' reduced to their A sections. Strada did not retain her two benefit arias, which had already been removed from the performing score. This revival was the occasion of a well-known incident concerning Senesino, first mentioned in *Fog's Weekly Journal* of 10 February 1733. The singer had just uttered the boast 'Cesare non seppe mai, che sia timore' (II viii) when 'a Piece of the Machinery tumbled down from the Roof

[50] *The London Stage* mentions the new songs only under this date.

of the Theatre upon the Stage', and 'the poor Hero was so frightened, that he trembled, lost his Voice, and fell a-crying'.

Considering the popularity of the opera, few excerpts seem to have been sung at concerts. As early as 8 May 1724, at the New Haymarket Theatre, the oboist Kytch, who liked to play the vocal parts of arias as instrumental solos,[51] included 'a Solo Song out of the Opera of Julius Caesar, the Song Part by Mr Kitch, the Violin by the Youth [John Clegg, the beneficiary], as done by Sig. Castrucci in the Opera'. This must have been 'Se in fiorito', the only aria with violin obbligato. Kytch repeated the exploit at York Buildings on 27 March, when he played three unnamed songs from the opera. On 8 December 1725 Signora Stradiotti sang 'Da tempeste' and 'Venere bella' at the Smock Alley Theatre, Dublin.[52] Jane Barbier sang 'Non è si vago' at Lincoln's Inn Fields on 28 March 1726, Mrs (?Turner) Robinson 'Se pietà' at Drury Lane exactly a month later. The overture was played at a Manchester Subscription Concert on 28 May 1745, and the elderly Cuzzoni sang the duet 'Caro! Bella!' with Guadagni (who was not born when the opera was first produced) at a King's Theatre Musicians Fund benefit on 16 April 1751. A masquerade at the Opera House on 13 May 1729 began with 'the Opera of Julius Caesar', presumably the overture.

Giulio Cesare was the most successful of Handel's operas in Germany. Brunswick produced it first, in Italian as *Giulio Cesare e Cleopatra*, in August 1725. The text was based on Handel's 1724 score. Cornelia sang two substitute arias of unknown origin, 'Stelle, tiranne stelle' in place of 'Deh piangete' in II iii and 'Se tra l'erbe e i fior copito' in place of 'Belle dee' in II ix. The first two acts ended with ballets, male and female Egyptians in Act I, eunuchs and 'favorite del Seraglio' in Act II. The cast was:

CAESAR:	Schneider
CLEOPATRA:	Signora Simonetti
CORNELIA:	Signora Hess
SESTO:	Christina Louisa Koulhaas (soprano)
TOLOMEO:	Krist
ACHILLA:	Braun (bass)
NIRENO:	Johann Ferdinand Koulhaas (bass)
CURIO:	Arnoldi

Little is known of these singers, apart from Christina Koulhaas;[53] Johann Ferdinand was her husband. There were revivals at Brunswick in 1727 and August 1733; on the latter occasion Cornelia retained the first of her substituted arias but not the second.

In the Hamburg production (10 November 1725) the arias as usual were sung in Italian and the recitatives in German, translated by Thomas Lediard, who also designed the scenery.[54] The score was arranged by the former leader

[51] See the report in *The London Stage* of his benefit at Hickford's Room on 16 April 1729, when the programme contained several Handel items.

[52] Walsh, *Opera in Dublin 1705–1797*, 23.

[53] See p. 442.

[54] Lediard (1685–1743), erroneously described by Chrysander as French, came from a Cirencester family. He was a man of multifarious talents. Trained as an architect, he lived from about 1720 to 1732 at Hamburg, where he was employed as secretary first to the Danish ambassador Benedict von Alefeld and then to the British envoy Sir Cyril Wych. He soon became

of the Weissenfels court orchestra J. G. Linike, who supplied the recitatives and extra music. He allowed most of Handel's accompanied recitatives to stand, but rewrote 'Che sento?' and added the orchestra to some of Caesar's recitative in the Parnassus scene and Cleopatra's before 'Piangerò'. The production was enlivened by no fewer than six ballets: Egyptian warriors at Caesar's first entry, Moors of both sexes on his arrival at Tolomeo's palace (I ix), 'Plaisirs' before 'V'adoro pupille' in the Parnassus scene, concubines and eunuchs in the seraglio (II ix), peasants male and female at the start of Act III, and a Grand Ballet before the final *coro*. The concubines and eunuchs entertained Tolomeo with a *Freuden-Fest*, including a chorus in German in place of 'Belle dee'. Curio sang an inserted aria, 'Impallidite son le rose', in I iv, and the dialogue for Caesar and Nireno in II ii was converted into a duet, 'Cieli! è qual dalle sfere', Caesar singing the A section and da capo, Nireno the B section. After Handel's II x there was a scene for Sesto, Cornelia, and Nireno, in which Nireno sang 'Sperai ne m'ingannai' with slightly modified text. The cast was:

CAESAR:	Campioli (alto castrato)
CLEOPATRA:	Margaretta Susanna Keyser (soprano)
CORNELIA:	Monjo the elder (contralto)
SESTO:	Dominichina Pollone (soprano)
TOLOMEO:	Johann Gottfried Riemschneider (bass)
ACHILLA:	Bahn (bass)
NIRENO:	Möhring (tenor)
CURIO:	Westenholz (bass)

Unusually for Hamburg two of the male parts were not transposed down; it may be significant that Linike had recently been in London.

The career of this production, which remained in the repertory almost till the collapse of the Hamburg Opera, was not uneventful. Lediard's translation inspired a violent exchange of polemical pamphlets with one Sivers.[55] On at least one occasion Telemann's intermezzo *Pimpinone* was given between the acts.[56] Willers lists nearly 40 performances between 1725 and 1737; at least two more were cancelled, one (25 August 1735) because 'no one came', and on 3 December 1726 there were '3 people present'. It is a wonder the Hamburg Opera lasted as long as it did. On 29 May/9 June 1727 there was a special performance in honour of George I's birthday (the previous day) with

---

involved in the affairs of the opera, serving—'by the express Command of Sir Cyril Wich, and some other Persons of Distinction', according to his own account in the preface to *The German Spy*—as scenic designer and machinist (1722–8) and from 1727 until at least 1730 as sole director. Two of his published Hamburg designs illustrate the prologue and epilogue to *Giulio Cesare*. Among his other publications were a naval history of England, a life of Marlborough (with whom he claimed personal acquaintance), a history of the reigns of William and Mary and Anne, and contributions to a dictionary of etymology. In 1738 he put forward a plan for building Westminster Bridge, and was appointed surveyor of it. He was elected FRS the year before his death. See H. C. Wolff, 'Ein Engländer als Direktor der alten Hamburger Oper', *Hamburger Jahrbuch für Musikwissenschaft*, iii (1978), 75–83, and a series of essays in *Theatre Notebook*, ii (1948), 42–57.

[55] Chrysander, ii. 109.

[56] The anonymous author of *The German Spy Written by a Gentleman on his Travels . . .* (London, 1738) says in Letter XII that he saw the opera 'with a whimsical Intermezzo, set to Music, between the Acts, representing the Adventures of an Old Man who married his Chamber-maid'. Telemann was Kapellmeister at Hamburg 1722–38.

elaborate illuminations, fireworks, and additions. The versatile Lediard planned the fireworks and supplied a Prologue and Epilogue under the title *The Joy and Happiness of the British Nation*. Telemann set them to music, with the aid of 'two Choirs of Trumpets, *French* Horns and Kettle-Drums' seated in balconies at either end of the orchestra, who played 'a Pompous Martial Symphony' at the start; this was followed when the curtain rose by 'a softer Symphony of Flutes and Violins'. Mars and Minerva were the chief characters in the Prologue, with a chorus of ten nymphs on thrones signifying the British 'Blessings' of 'Moderation Tranquillity Liberty Concord Justice Toleration Plenty Security Content Joy'. At the foot of a statue of George I, 'as large as Life', sat a singer personifying Great Britain and 'on each Side of her, four others representing France, Ireland, Hannover and America, in proper Habits'. The Epilogue, featuring Neptune, Aeolus, Thames, Isis, Trade, and Wealth, was set in Oxford with a silhouette of the city's skyline on the backcloth. After choruses and dances the prospect changed to the City of London by moonlight, with ships drawn up in crescent formation in the river. A fine Marshal Symphony', followed by the discharge of '45 Cannon from the Ships and Shoar', introduced the fireworks; Neptune set fire to the Royal Cypher with his trident, and 'a great Number of Rockets, and Fire-balls, proceeded from the Top of the Grenadiers' Caps' (Plate 16). At the fall of the curtain all doors, windows, and 'Twilights' were at once thrown open to get rid of the smoke. The performance was repeated on four successive nights.[57] Despite all this the king was dead within a fortnight.

The more spectacular of Linike's insertions were gradually dropped in revivals. The comic peasants in Act III had gone by 1733, the Plaisirs, the chorus of concubines and eunuchs, and even Handel's opening chorus by 1736, when the extra scene after II x was reduced to three lines of German recitative. On 24 October 1729 Dominichina Pollone sang the role of Caesar, presumably in higher keys, and Christina Maria Avoglio that of Cleopatra. The 1735 Cleopatra was Maria Monza. These last two singers, as well as Campioli and Riemschneider of the 1725 cast, were to join Handel's company in London. In 1734 Keiser introduced Strada's two 1730 benefit arias into his Hamburg pasticcio *Circe*. The *Giulio Cesare in Egitto* produced at the Kärntnertor Theatre, Vienna, in 1731 (Deutsch, p. 280), was almost certainly Predieri's opera, not Handel's.

The so-called London revival on 1 March 1787 was a pasticcio from various Handel operas put together by Samuel Arnold. A sentence in the preface to his libretto—'The original, however, offering a great number of incongruities, both in the language and the conduct, several material alterations have been thought absolutely necessary, to give the piece a dramatic consistency, and to suit it to the refinement of a modern audience'—precisely defines the spirit behind the first twentieth-century revival, at Göttingen on 5 July 1922. Oskar Hagen's version, made for this occasion, became immensely popular in Germany and was staged in no fewer than 38 cities, including Copenhagen, Zürich, Basle, Berne, and Vienna, within five years—a total of more than 220 performances. Stage productions later reached the United States (1927), Great Britain (1930), Holland (1933), France (Strasbourg, 1935), Poland (1936), Belgium (1948), Italy (1950), Spain (1964), Czechoslovakia (1966),

[57] These particulars are taken from an eye- and ear-witness account in Letter XXXI of *The German Spy*.

Yugoslavia (1966), Hungary (1966), Japan (1967), Argentina (1968), Australia (1969/70), Russia (1979), Finland (1981), Greece (1984), Sweden (1985), and Canada (1987). No Handel opera has been staged in so many countries or enjoyed greater success; it has long been in the repertory of many German theatres. The Hagen version seems at last to have been superseded (Leichtentritt pointed out some of its deficiencies as early as 1924), but most modern productions still debase the opera. Not till 1977[58] was it revived in the theatre with all the voices at the correct pitch, the only form in which it can make its full effect. There are seven recorded versions, conducted by Swarowsky, Goehr, Rudel, Richter, Mackerras, Panni, and Jacobs, most of them heavily cut and/or marred by octave transposition or other solecisms. That of Jacobs is complete and the most stylish.

Autograph

The autograph of *Giulio Cesare* (RM 20 b 3) is a complex document, very revealing of Handel's methods in general and particular. It is not surprising that Burney's attempt to collate it with the Cluer score resulted in bafflement and confusion. He thought it must reflect the 1725 revival, with which it has no connection. Chrysander's statement that it betrays signs of haste is even wider of the mark; it carries conclusive evidence of great care exercised over an exceptionally long period. With the aid of Handel's foliation and a study of the arrangement of material on each page it can be demonstrated that the composition went through a number of stages, some of which may have partly overlapped. The following are the most important:

I. In the summer of 1723 Handel composed the first act, to a different text and for different singers from those of 1724. He wrote the words of the recitatives but not the music, except for an occasional chord as a tonal link to aid his memory, and stopped before the final aria.

II. He revised this act, probably more than once, still for the same singers and without recitatives.

III. After an interval, during which he settled on the 1724 cast and (with minor variants) the 1724 libretto, he reconstructed the first act, but did not set the recitatives in the autograph.

IV. He wrote the first draft of Act II, set pieces only.

V. He revised Act II and wrote the first draft of Act III.

VI. He revised Act III and made further changes in the earlier acts.

It is impossible to say when the secco recitatives were composed, for very few of them are in the autograph. There is conclusive evidence that Smith copied part of the score before Handel had completed it.[59] A very considerable amount of music was rejected at stages II, III, V, and VI, but much of it was adapted to other contexts.

Stage I. The original draft of Act I is represented by ff. 1–18, 21–2, 45–52, and 56–66. The differences in the libretto have been described above; the

[58] At the Barber Institute, Birmingham University (ed. W. Dean and S. Fuller)—the first complete stage revival of Handel's 1724 score.

[59] Bound with the autograph (ff. 85–6) is a Smith copy of 'Se a me' preceded and followed by the recitatives of its original context in I xi (HG 45, 47)—the words only, not the music; Sesto still has an alto clef, Cornelia a soprano.

music consists of the overture, composed first, and fourteen vocal movements. The act was designed to end with an aria for Cleopatra, but this was not written. The movements, all fully scored, are:

1. Overture, A major leading into
2. Chorus 'Viva il nostro Alcide', no tempo, A major. The voice parts are marked with initials, as noted by Squire; they stand for Cuzzoni and Durastanti (soprano), Anastasia Robinson and Berenstadt (alto), Gordon (tenor), Lagarde and Boschi (bass).
3. Cavatina (Caesar) 'Presti omai', no tempo 4/4 D major. A different setting, unpublished.
4. Aria (Caesar) 'Empio, dirò', C minor.
5. Duet (Sesto, Cornelia) 'Son nata a sospirar', F sharp minor. Sesto is the alto, Cornelia the soprano.
6. Aria (Berenice) 'Tutto può donna', G major. Many differences from HG 30; recorders, not oboes, in the accompaniment.
7. Aria (Cleopatra) 'Non disperar', D major. Many differences from HG 21.
8. Accomp. recit. (Caesar) 'Alma del gran Pompeo', G sharp minor–A flat minor.
9. Aria (Caesar) 'Non è si vago', F major, with a viola part in the opening ritornello.
10. Aria (Cornelia) 'Nel tuo seno', *Lento e piano* 3/8 F minor. A different setting for soprano, unpublished.
11. Aria (Cleopatra) 'Speranza mi dice', *Allegro* 3/8 B flat major. Unpublished.
12. Aria (Caesar) 'Questo core incatenato', *Larghetto* 3/4 D major. Unpublished.
13. Aria (Achilla) 'Se a me non sei', G major. Subsequently transferred to II iv (HG 65).
14. Aria (Cornelia) 'Priva son d'ogni conforto', E major. For soprano; slight differences from HG 15.
15. Aria (Berenice) 'Va tacito e soletto', F major. As HG 40 with verbal differences, chiefly in the B section.

It will be seen that Cornelia was a soprano, Sesto and Berenice altos, and that neither Sesto nor Tolomeo had an aria. Alto clefs were prepared for the latter in the recitatives, but the tenor line in the chorus indicates that Gordon was the original choice. The blank verso of f. 66 proves that the act was to end with an aria for Cleopatra, who has an unset recitative on the recto. Only four pieces, the overture, chorus, 'Empio, dirò', and 'Alma del gran Pompeo', held their place in the ultimate version.

Stage II. Handel decided to end the act with 'Tutto può donna', transferred from Berenice to Cleopatra. He rewrote it in A major, lifting considerable sections into a higher register (bars 38–56) and inserting a brilliant new coloratura passage towards the end of the first part (bars 72–80). The object was both to strengthen the characterization and to exploit the vocal prowess of Cuzzoni; Anastasia Robinson's voice was not only lower but very limited in compass, covering at this stage of her career only a tenth from b to d". At the same time Handel introduced much more character and contrast into the B section. He wrote at the end *Fine dell Atto Primo* (ff. 72–4). There is no tempo mark, and nothing to indicate that the third stave is for oboe. The absence of

Handel's foliation, which stops in the middle of 'Va tacito' and was never resumed, helps to date the transference. This left a gap for Berenice in Scene v, and Handel wrote two supplementary arias for her, 'Nobil cor non più mirare', *Allegro* 4/4 C major (ff. 70–1), and 'Di te compagna fida', *Allegro ma non presto* 6/8 F major (ff. 33–4); the blank versos prove that both were insertions. The latter fits the context better, musically and dramatically. Either Handel wrote both pieces in succession for the same scene, or 'Va tacito' had already been earmarked for Caesar and 'Nobil cor' was intended to replace it.

Stage III. With the cast and text now settled, Handel transposed 'Non è sì vago', 'Priva son', and the duet, and shifted the last two to different scenes. He moved 'Se a me' to Act II and replaced it with a new aria for Achilla, 'Tu sei il cor' (ff. 67–9). The suppression of Berenice released three arias: 'Va tacito' was given to Caesar in an earlier scene, replacing 'Questo core incatenato'; 'Nobil cor' and 'Di te compagna fida', much revised, presently became the basis for Tolomeo's 'Sì, spietata' in Act II (ff. 67–8, without the words, which were apparently dubbed on the music) and Cleopatra's 'Tu la mia stella' (ff. 53–5; see below). Handel rewrote 'Non disperar' in E major, which began to emerge as Cleopatra's key, greatly improving it in the process. He emphasized the note of mockery by repeating the opening words and transforming the square phrase-lengths of the D major version. In the latter, though the ritornello was already present, the voice began both sections with the same rather faceless theme, which disappeared altogether in the E major, and the phrase with the falling seventh in bars 5 and 6 of the ritornello was prominently treated by the voice. Handel composed new settings of 'Presti omai' (ff. 25–7) and 'Nel tuo seno' (ff. 23–4), again altered the position of 'Tutto può donna', inserted 'Svegliatevi' (ff. 28–9, marked *Allegro*; the recorders in the B section were originally transverse flutes) and 'L'empio sleale', and—though this cannot be precisely dated—made cuts and revisions in some of the music already composed, notably 'Empio, dirò' and (before transposition) 'Non è si vago'.

'L'empio sleale' has a most extraordinary history. It was composed for Senesino as an insertion in Act III Scene viii of *Ottone* and probably sung in that opera at Cuzzoni's benefit on 26 March 1723.[60] The autograph and a Smith copy of this version, which is a good deal longer and has a number of differences in the words, are both bound in the autograph of *Giulio Cesare* (ff. 37–44). The autograph, headed *for Otho*, includes the recitative link before and after the aria in that opera; but at the bottom Handel drew a line and wrote *for the Opera Emilia (mentre vuol partire vien rincontrato nella Scena di Emilia ed egli resta immobile)*. *Emilia* was the original title of *Flavio*, completed on 7 May 1723, and this stage direction occurs at the end of I xi (HG 31) just after Guido's aria 'L'armellin vita'. Handel evidently intended Senesino to sing 'L'empio sleale' in this position, occupied within a brief interval by four different arias, one of them in alternative keys.[61] He dropped the idea, but he did use its principal vocal theme, with a new accompaniment in brilliant semiquavers, for Ugone's angry aria 'Fato, tiranno' in Act II of *Flavio*, composed first for bass and rewritten for tenor before performance. After that the aria was adapted for *Giulio Cesare*: the Smith copy, which also carries the *Flavio* stage direction, was heavily revised by Handel, who wrote in the new

---

[60] See p. 437.
[61] See p. 475.

ext and shortened the music in both parts by a total of some 36 bars. The piece, though in different versions, thus appeared in four clefs and was sung by three singers in three different operas in the same theatre within eleven months.

No less intricate is the heredity of 'Tu la mia stella'[62], which descends from an early cantata aria via the air 'Let flocks and herds' in the *Ode for Queen Anne's Birthday*, an unpublished setting of 'L'ingrato non amar' in the autograph of *Radamisto*, and Berenice's likewise unpublished 'Di te compagna fida' (ff. 33–6). All three of these exist in two versions, though not all are complete. The matter is too complex to be unravelled here in detail, but some interesting conclusions emerge: Handel's constant urge to improve earlier material, especially in rhythmic impulse and the balance of phrase and key structure, the strange combination of an abhorrence of waste with a surpassing fertility of invention, and the resuscitation of apparently discarded ideas at a later stage. While the cantata supplies the principal germ motive of all the later settings, the other common ideas flit in and out of the successive compositions apparently at random but motivated no doubt by partly subconscious processes. Of nine thematic constituents used in 'Tu la mia stella', four appear in 'L'ingrato non amar' but not 'Di te compagna fida', three in 'Di te compagna fida' but not 'L' ingrato non amar', and two are common to both. Four of the nine are found in either the cantata or the *Birthday Ode*, but only one—the principal germ—in both. Nor are they necessarily used in the corresponding place in each aria. For example the eight-note violin figure in bars 69–71 of 'Tu la mia stella', which makes its single appearance in the ritornello after the first part, had occurred at the end of the opening ritornello in the *Birthday Ode*, in the middle of the ritornello and later on the voice in 'L'ingrato non amar', and not at all in 'Di te compagna fida'. On the other hand the distinctive dotted phrase in thirds (bars 5–7 and often later) occurs in the cantata and 'Di te compagna fida' but not in L'ingrato non amar'. Of the two versions of 'Di te compagna fida', that on f. 35–6 (*Allegro ma non troppo*) appears to be the earlier, differing chiefly in the treatment of the ritornellos. It has many cancellations, and breaks off in the middle of the ritornello after the A section, which was threatening to assume unwieldy proportions. Handel crossed out one passage of seven bars in the middle, restored it (*Si scrive*), and again cancelled it in the later version (ff. 33–4, *Allegro ma non presto*).

His sense of economy emerges in the fact that all the other rejected settings except 'Speranza mi dice' and 'Questo core incatenato' contributed material to the still unwritten second and third acts, generally for different characters in unrelated situations. Nor were the two exceptions wasted: 'Speranza mi dice', a characteristic and charming aria in 3/8, became a remote ancestor of 'Chi cede al furore' in *Serse*, and 'Questo core incatenato', not of great moment in itself, was the progenitor of 'In mille dolci modi' in *Sosarme*, to which it bequeathed the key, the outline of the melody, the triplet figuration, and the octave leap up to the top D. The ritornello is worth quoting both for this and for one happy feature it did *not* pass on, the rhythmically displaced leap of an eleventh in bars 9 and 11 (Ex. 60, p. 512).

The most startling transformation is that of the first setting of 'Presti omai' into Tolomeo's 'Belle dee' in II ix, which takes over the ritornello in octaves,

[62] According to John Roberts it originated in an aria from Keiser's *Claudius*; see Appendix D.

Ex. 60

dotted accompaniment figure, and even part of the vocal line; the same
material—differently treated, to be sure—serves the proud commands of a
world conqueror and the epicene chucklings of a decadent princeling in his
harem, without the slightest incongruity. Stranger still, several bars (21–5) of
the original 'Presti omai' are retained and expanded in the second setting
(31–7), at the corresponding structural point and to the same words, though
the rest of the material is new and totally different. Again the effect is so
natural and spontaneous that the manoeuvre could never have been deduced
from internal evidence.[63] Of the F minor 'Nel tuo seno', a beautiful piece in
its own right if less concentrated than its successor, only the initial ritornello
survived, improved and enlarged by three bars, as the introduction to
Cleopatra's accompanied recitative 'Voi, che mie fide ancelle' in III vii.
'Nobil cor', a rhetorical and somewhat otiose aria, was much improved by
contraction of the B section and the ritornello preceding it and the excision of
conventional sequences and cadences. This softened, without quite removing
the jaunty tone of the music when sung by Tolomeo in 'Sì, spietata'.
    The examples already cited by no means exhaust the list of borrowings in

---

[63] This procedure is by no means unique in Handel: compare the similar incorporation of
earlier material in 'With thee the unshelter'd moor' (*Solomon*) and 'Piangerò' (see p. 493 above).
Burney strangely preferred the original setting of 'Presti omai'.

Giulio Cesare, most of them from cantatas and other early works of the Italian period (see Appendix D). In nearly every instance Handel takes a melodic fragment, generally an opening phrase, and develops its potentialities in an unexpected direction. Sometimes a related idea in the words seems to have supplied the motive: tragic grief ('Nel tuo seno'), bustling action (the sinfonia in III ii), the happy reunion of lovers ('Caro! Bella!'), stealthy movement ('Va tacito'). In the last two instances the key is unchanged. Elsewhere Handel was gripped by the musical possibilities of a striking idea ('Quel torrente'), or even a rather ordinary one ('Questo core incatenato', 'Scorta siate'). Several of the borrowings, in addition to those already mentioned, have some special interest. The first phrase of 'Se in fiorito' originally began the lovely aria 'Dopo torbide procelle' in *Radamisto*,[64] where, astonishingly, it dovetailed into bar 4 of that aria as it now stands. 'Se a me' is a reworking of an unpublished alto aria in the same key, whose tessitura and narrow compass suggest that it was composed for Senesino. The context is unknown, but the autograph survives (RM 20 f 11, f. 13). The changes made by Handel in expanding the compass and adapting the coloratura for bass voice are most revealing. 'Domerò' combines features from two related arias, both based on angular chromatic motives but directed to very different expressive purposes: jealousy in *Aci, Galatea e Polifemo*, astonished delight in *Agrippina*, vindictive cruelty in *Giulio Cesare*. The last version is a notable advance on both its predecessors, especially in flexibility of rhythm. Handel returned to the idea as late as 1752; 'Freedom now once more possessing', added to *Jephtha* in that year, derives from the *Agrippina* aria.

Stage IV. The original Parnassus scene contained the A–A* version of the two sinfonias (HG 52–3), with the intervening line of recitative set to music, and a more primitive setting of 'V'adoro, pupille'. This aria gave Handel a great deal of trouble. The setting in the autograph has only a continuo group on stage (a single bass line marked *Viola da Gamba Harpa e Teorba*, not unlike the theorbo line in the final score) and strings in the pit. Nor was this the first plan; Handel wrote Cleopatra's name against three different staves and eventually placed it at the top of the page. There is no mention of oboes, bassoons, violas, cellos, or mutes in the stage orchestra. The string parts are simpler from bar 17, with more doubling, and there are minor differences in the note values of the vocal line. The B section, marked *Senza Hautb.* (were they meant to play *colla parte* in the first part?), has only a bass, identical with the theorbo part in HG. The da capo precedes Caesar's exclamation 'Non hà in cielo'.

Most of the recitative on HG 59 (not set) seems to have been an afterthought, for it is squeezed into the bottom of a page. 'Se in fiorito' has no tempo mark. 'Se a me', in Smith's hand and still carrying unset portions of recitative from its original context in Act I, was inserted as soon as Handel reached this point, as a rubric indicates. 'Cessa omai' was not yet present; Sesto and Cornelia went out at 'Si giusta impresa' (HG 69). 'Venere bella' had a different setting (no tempo 3/8 B minor). One leaf of Scene viii has been incorrectly bound in Act III (f. 131). Cleopatra's accompanied recitative 'Che sento?' ended at the E major cadence after 'cor di Marte' (HG 82) and was followed by a different aria, 'Per dar vita' (no tempo 4/4 A minor). The recitative after 'Belle dee' is fully set as far as 'il ferro depongo'. There are

[64] See p. 334.

slight differences in the words of Cornelia's last speech in xi (HG 88–9). 'L'aura che spira' has no tempo mark.

The B minor 'Venere bella' shares certain features with its successor, including the latter part of the ritornello, the rising sevenths of bars 46 and 50 (but in a different place), and much of the B section; but the main theme with its imploring sixths, which gives the A major aria most of its character, lay in the future, and so did many other felicities. 'Per dar vita' is another indifferent piece, all the more so in comparison with its successor 'Se pietà'. Handel reworked it for Sesto's 'La giustizia' in Act III, but here his improvements are minimal except for the contraction of the B section by five bars, and the best moment in 'Per dar vita', the Neapolitan sixth harmony at the word 'morte', disappeared with the verbal image that inspired it.

Stage V. Handel must have revised Act II before tackling Act III, since he again used music rejected from the former as an integral part of the latter. None of the new music in the Parnassus scene is in the autograph. The other insertions are 'Cessa omai' (ff. 90–1, not quite as printed), 'Venere bella' in A major (without tempo mark; confusingly bound in Act I, ff. 30–1), the seven additional bars of 'Che sento?', and 'Se pietà' (ff. 103–6, the recitative after the aria, which has no tempo mark). Handel changed his mind about the scoring of 'Se pietà'. He began it on four staves—unison violins, first viola and bassoon, second viola and bassoon, bass, the two middle parts in the tenor clef—and so prepared the staves for the whole aria before adopting the present arrangement. The autograph has very few figures, and some of them differ from those in Hamburg and HG. 'Cessa omai' has no tempo mark and no words (except the first four, added in a strange hand); it may have been a borrowing for which the text was supplied later. Both main sections of the A section are marked for repetition; the voice part differs towards the end of the B section. Handel heavily revised 'L'angue offeso' and 'L'aura che spira'. Folios 93–4 are an insertion in the former, incorporating much alteration of bars 12–40. The ritornello's semiquaver figure (bars 13–15) was an afterthought; it did not appear till bar 38 on the voice, though present in the later ritornellos from the start. Nor did the voice enter with the main theme. The first change was made before Handel filled up the string parts; the thought seems to have struck him when he reached bar 29. The reconstruction of 'L'aura che spira' affected the whole A section, chiefly in the working of the accompaniment (ff. 112–14 are insertions); this was originally in three parts— *tutti, viola e violin 3*, bass—but presently diverged into four with an independent viola annexing the margins and what blank staves it could find. The rhythmic countermotive tossed between the violins in bars 5–7 and the sequential figure in another new rhythm in bars 11 and 12 leading to a climax on the high C are not in the first version, which is much slacker in tension. Most of the energy of the aria as printed derives from the new ritornello material, and the approach to the central cadence of the A section (bars 46–54) is stronger in every respect, including the vocal line.

Stage VI. Act III shows only one major change in the course of composition, but it is a striking one. The place of 'Piangerò' was originally occupied by a very different aria, 'Troppo crudeli siete' (*Largo* 12/8 F minor, ff. 122–4), a beautiful piece that Burney considered 'one of the finest of all Handel's admirable Sicilianos'. Its rejection seems strange at first sight. Handel may have thought it too close in mood to 'Son nata a lagrimar' (though in *Admeto* he gave each of the prima donnas a similar siciliano in the same key); or the words, expressing hopeless grief, may have seemed too apathetic and lacking in the dynamic contrast the situation required. The music made several contributions to Asteria's 'Se non mi vuol amar' in Act I of *Tamerlano*, notably at bar 22; the rising bass that begins each part of the later aria derives from the opening of the B section of 'Troppo crudeli siete'. The E major 'Piangerò' (ff. 125–6) was not Handel's first shot at the new text. The Fitzwilliam Museum (Mus MS 256, pp. 65–6) contains an earlier[65] and unrelated setting, *Largo* 4/4 A major, which though adequate lacks the distinction of its supplanter. The economical composer used the music again, transposed to B flat, without the string accompaniment, and with the B section contracted, for 'Io ti bacio' in Act III of *Admeto*, where it found a perfect niche.

Otherwise there is little to remark in the autograph of this act, except that Handel began the *coro* in notes of half the value, abandoned it a few bars after the vocal entry, reversed the page, and started again. The short second part of the sinfonia with horns (HG 125) was an afterthought. One leaf is missing before f. 132, carrying the first 18 bars of the recitative on HG 108–9. Only in the last scene (HG 127–8, 131) are the recitatives complete with their music. 'Dal fulgor' and 'Da tempeste' have no tempo mark; 'Piangerò' is *Largo*, and the B section has *Violoncelli* in the plural. In the last scene (HG 127, line 4) the autograph, followed by Hamburg and the early manuscripts, indicates that only Sesto kneels to Caesar. This differs from the libretto and may have been deliberately altered by Handel; Cornelia after all was a patrician matron.

One of the last pieces composed was 'Cara speme' in I viii. It is an insertion in the autograph (ff. 36–7, without tempo mark) and the Hamburg score, and is cued in at the very end of the libretto. Other late modifications, not reflected in the autograph, were the excision of the viola from the opening ritornello of 'Non è si vago', some rewriting in 'Cessa omai', and the recomposition of the Parnassus scene; the A version of the two sinfonias, though not performed, got into one of the early copies (RM 19 c 6).

The autograph of *Rodelinda* (RM 20 c 4) contains five leaves (ff. 62–6), written on Italian paper with crescent watermark,[66] belonging to the 1725 revival of *Giulio Cesare*. They carry two of the new arias, Sesto's 'S'armi a miei danni' and Tolomeo's 'Dal mio brando'; neither has a tempo mark, and the former, without a single correction, may be a fair copy. In between (f. 64) are two fragments indicating cuts in 'L'angue offeso' when the aria was sung by a tenor, with cue references to the performing score. Bars 46–50 and 56–60 were each replaced by a single bar. The first cut, for no obvious reason, removed an intermediate ritornello; the second was clearly motivated by considerations of texture. This is not the only point where a tenor is forced below the written instrumental bass, which would of course be doubled at the octave; but nowhere else is there such a consistently low stretch. Another 1725 addition, 'La speranza all'alma mia', is in the Fitzwilliam Museum (Mus MS 256, pp. 67–72). This is a fair copy in A major written by Smith, who also prepared the words and clefs for the recitative. He evidently assumed that Nireno–Nerina would still be an alto (until his last speech, which has a soprano clef). Handel corrected the clefs when he added the music, but later had to change

---

[65] Burrows ('A Handlist of the Paper Characteristics of Handel's English Autographs') gives   *
the watermark as ? Da, which belongs to 1731–2. For several reasons this is most unlikely.
[66] See Burrows, ibid and p. 593.

the cadence when he put the aria down a tone. Its presence in a copy in the wrong key is a sign that it was borrowed from some other context. The autograph of 'Parolette' with *Giulio Cesare* text in the B section is bound at the end of the BL section of the *Rinaldo* autograph (RM 20 c 3, ff. 55–7); the dal segno bars, in different ink, were added for *Rinaldo* in 1731.

Librettos

1724. 'Drama . . . Per Tomaso Wood nella Piccola Bretagna.' 85 pp. No English title page. A flowery Italian dedication to the Princess of Wales is signed by Nicola Francesco Haym. The Argument is in both languages, the Italian lifted from Bussani. It is partly a summary of the plot, partly an excursion into Roman history, not all of it relevant to the opera, which has no concern with the fate of Cicero, Cato, and Scipio. Caesar's *Commentaries*, Dio Cassius, and Plutarch are cited as authorities for the facts. Fiction is admitted only in the final sentence; since the details of Tolomeo's end are uncertain, 'it was thought necessary in the present Drama to make Sestus the Instrument of Ptolomey's Death in Revenge for his Father's Murder, varying from History only in Circumstances of Action'. The libretto (like its successors of 1725 and 1730) does not include 'Belle dee' and the two following lines of recitative; II ix begins at 'Questo è luogo'. The text of 'Cara speme' is printed at the end of the opera, with a cue for its insertion in I viii. All the London librettos differ from the scores in a number of minor details, for example in the words of 'Va tacito', 'Al lampo dell'armi', 'Non hà più che temere', and the duet section of the final *coro*, and in the scene numbering of Act III from HG 110 onwards.

1725 Handel. 'The Second Edition, with Alterations. N.B. The Alterations have this " Mark before them . . . Printed and Sold at the Opera-Office in the Hay-Market.' 79 pp. The principal changes, noted above, were the suppression of 'Cara speme', the insertion of a new aria for Tolomeo in II x, the replacement of 'Son nata a lagrimar', 'L'aura che spira', and 'La giustizia' by three new arias for Sesto, and the excision of Curio and Nireno. The latter remains as a mute 'guardia' in several scenes (HG 36, 51, 102, 108), and Caesar continues to address him by name. Heavy recitative cuts were necessary in I i–iv, vii, viii, II i, ii, vi, III iv, vi, and *ult*. Sometimes lines were transferred to another character; in II viii Sesto takes Curio's part, but goes out before 'Al lampo dell'armi'. The dialogue of the original II x had to be altered, and the disappearance of the entire first scene of this act threw out the numbering. 'Sperai ne m'ingannai' begins 'Saprai'. The words of Tolomeo's inserted aria (HG 148) should run: 'Dal mio brando / Si veda umiliata / Quell'alma che ingrata / Io vado a pugnar. / Già nel petto / Si sveglia l'ardire / Ch'è meglio morire / Che vile regnar.' The new material is not translated.

1725 Brunswick. 'Giulio Cesare e Cleopatra. Drama per Musica Da rappresentarsi nel Famosissimo Teatro di Braunsviga Nella fiera d'estate L'anno 1725 . . . Wolfenbüttel Druckts Christian Bartsch.' The entire libretto is printed in Italian and German, including title page, Argument, cast (with singers' names), ballets ('dell'invenzione del Sign. E. A. Jaimen Maestro dei Balli'), and list of scene-changes (four in each act). Scene headings and stage directions are fuller than in the London librettos; Tolomeo's seraglio contains a bed as well as a table, and in Act III Cleopatra is imprisoned in the Temple of Isis. Insertions are listed above.

1725 Hamburg. 'Julius Caesar in Aegypten In einem Sing-Spiele Auf der Hamburgischen Schau-Platze Vorgestellet Im Jahr 1725 Gedruckt mit Stromerschen Schrifften.' One of Lediard's designs, for Alexandria Harbour in the last scene, appears on the title page (see Plate 8B). Lediard added a flowery dedication, dated 12 November 1725, to the Danish ambassador and a preface explaining that he has not slavishly followed either the Italian original or the English translation. The arias and Italian accompanied recitatives are ascribed to Handel, the German recitatives and the symphonies (? ballets) to the Weissenfels Concertmeister J. G. Linike. The words of the German chorus in the seraglio scene are the work of 'einer weit geschikterer Hand'. Argument translated from Haym. The cast are named, as well as the scene-painter (Jacopo Fabris) and ballet master (Baptista). The six dances and thirteen scene changes are listed in considerable detail. A veritable zoo ('allerhand wilde Thiere') seems to have been visible from the seraglio garden in II iii. Stage directions are fuller than in the London librettos, the German recitatives more than a hundred lines longer, and the scene numbering different. 'Alma del gran Pompeo' has a da capo. Other changes are listed above.

1730 Handel. 'The Third Edition ... Printed and Sold by T. Wood, in Little-Britain.' 75 pp. No cast is given. The text is that of 1725 with the following changes. 'Empio, dirò', 'Se a me non sei', and the B section and da capo of 'Aure, deh, per pietà' are cut. Cornelia sings 'La speranza all'alma mia' in I viii (where 'Nel tuo seno' stood in 1724) and 'L'aura che spira' (in place of Sesto's 'Scorta siate') at the end of Act II. In III ii Tolomeo has 'Dal mio cenno' instead of 'Domerò'. Changes in scene-headings suggest that reduced or stock scenery was used.   *

1733 Brunswick. As Brunswick 1725 (except date), but no cast named and inserted aria in II ix dropped.

1733 Hamburg. As Hamburg 1725, but 'im Jahr 1733 Gedruckt mit Spieringischen Schriften'. Largely a reprint of the 1725 libretto (including the cast, which can scarcely have been unchanged); but Lediard's design, dedication, preface, and plot summary are omitted, and the comic peasant scene at the start of Act III.

1736 Hamburg. Title (except date) and preliminary matter as Hamburg 1733, but no cast named. Omissions are listed above.

Copies and Editions

It seems certain that an intermediate score between the autograph and the Hamburg performing copy has disappeared. It must have contained nearly all the secco recitatives, many tempo marks (these are all written by Smith in Hamburg), some figuring, the Parnassus scene in its final version, and modifications to several arias, notably 'Non è si vago' and 'Cessa omai'. Hamburg (MA/1019), apart from amendments by Handel, is entirely in Smith's hand. As first copied, it contained 'Belle dee' but not 'Cara speme'. The recitatives on HG 36 and 37 were continuous, but the recopying of the last two syllables of the former at the bottom of f. 51ᵛ and their cancellation at the top of f. 52ʳ show that the aria was first inserted (just before the first performance, as we know from the libretto) and later removed. 'Belle dee' was pasted over, perhaps about the same time, as far as 'stelle accolto'; Chrysander closed his dotted brackets two bars too early. The manuscript is confused, with most (but not all) of the music added for revivals collected at the end, and three mistakes in binding. Folios 33–43 should follow f. 57, 83 should follow 79, and 146 is back to front. The second error was due to the words 'Mà se spietata' at the start of the B section of 'Se a me' catching the binder's eye and causing him to follow them with 'Sì, spietata'. Alterations after 1724 are listed chronologically.

January 1725. Nearly all recitative cuts and changes required by the elimination of Curio and Nireno are indicated, generally by pasted blank slips (since removed), sometimes by ink cancellation or modification. Sesto's old recitatives were left in the soprano clef, the new ones for Borosini copied in the tenor; occasionally both occur on the same page (e.g. f. 15). In I iii (HG 12, line 6) Curio's 'Grand' ardir!' was transferred to Caesar, and the words 'Olà, sì' added below Caesar's next remark. The entire recitative of II vi (HG 69) was cancelled and *Corn: Aria* written before it. In II viii Curio's name is sometimes but not consistently replaced by Sesto's. The following leaves, some of them mere slips of paper, were inserted:

12 (HG 11, bar 6 from 'Tu qui, Signor' to 15 replaced by $2\frac{1}{2}$ bars for Caesar);
156 (HG 15, the 28 bars before 'Priva son' reduced to 12);
48 (HG 33, recitative after 'Tutto può donna' reduced to six bars for Cleopatra alone);
157–60 (last $2\frac{1}{2}$ bars of 'Tu sei il cor' recopied, new recitative for tenor Sesto and aria 'S'armi a miei danni', HG 143–5, replacing HG 47–50);
66 (HG 51–2, all recitatives before first Parnassus sinfonia replaced by two bars for Caesar);
161–2 (HG 88, last six bars of Tolomeo's recitative in II x recopied, followed by aria 'Dal mio brando', printed with 1730 text on HG 148–9);
39 (tenor recitative for Sesto at end of II xi, HG 150, introducing aria 'Scorta siate', which is missing from the manuscript);
163–6 (tenor recitative and aria 'Sperai ne m'ingannai', HG 154–6, replacing HG 112–14);
135 (La Marche, HG 126)

'L'angue offeso' shows traces of Handel's two changes made in RM 20 c 4, but the substituted bars have been removed. The leaves with 'Cara speme' were taken out and the recitative restored to its original form.

? February 1725. The two inserted scenes for Nerina (Sorosina) are in the appendix (ff. 148–50 and 153–5). In the recitative on HG 146 Smith wrote the words, Handel the music. The name Nerina is perfectly clear; Handel spelt it in full on f. 153. 'La speranza' is marked for her, not for Cleopatra.

January 1730. Inserted leaves: 151–2 ('La speranza' in F for Cornelia, replacing 'Cara speme' in I viii, HG 36); 40–3 ('L'aura che spira' for Cornelia in D minor, replacing 'Scorta siate' after the 1725 tenor recitative,[67] HG 150–4); 106 (Tolomeo's recitative 'Costei, che per germana' in III ii, HG 97, reset with cadence in A). This was followed by the 1725 aria 'Dal mio brando' with changed text ('Dal mio cenno', HG 148–9), the new words written by Handel. The recopied recitative on f. 161^r was cancelled. 'Empio, dirò', 'Se a me', and 'Domerò' were pasted over, and the B section and repeat of 'Aure, deh, per pietà' possibly stitched together.

[67] Smith added the cue *Corn: l'aria* (f. 39), conclusive proof that Fabri sang Sesto in 1730.

March 1730. There are traces of the cancellation of 'Tutto può donna' in favour of 'Parolette'. Cleopatra's recitative on HG 99[68] was crossed out and replaced by a new recitative and the aria 'Io vò di duolo in duolo'. This insertion, written by Hb1, was later transferred bodily to the performing score of *Tolomeo* (Hamburg MA/1059, ff. 50–2).

February 1732. 'Deh piangete', the B sections of 'Priva son' and 'Venere bella', and Cleopatra's recitative before 'Tutto può donna' were pasted over, and 'Svegliatevi' marked to end with the A section.

Clausen lists 'Se pietà' as a cut; if so, it was stitched. The extra recitatives on ff. 12, 156, 48, 66, and 106 are not in HG. The opening of 'Priva son' has a *piano* mark. As in the autograph, 'Svegliatevi' is *Allegro*, 'Piangerò' *Largo*. The stave for *teorba* etc. in 'V'adoro, pupille' is marked *pianissimo* at the beginning.

Smith must have copied the Hamburg score shortly before the performance. He may already have written out RM 19 c 6, which has some earlier features, notably the A version of the sinfonias in the Parnassus scene (HG 52–3), found elsewhere only in the autograph. This suggests that Handel rewrote them after composing 'V'adoro, pupille'. The latter has no tempo and no mutes, and the bass part of the pit orchestra is for cembalo only. The G major sinfonia in the last scene lacks the short B section, as in the first version of the autograph. 'Cara speme' is present, but may be an insertion as it fills both sides of a single leaf. On the other hand, though the manuscript shows no sign of mutilation, there is evidence that 'Belle dee' had been composed and rejected. The heading for II ix is missing; the two bars of recitative that follow the cavatina ('Di quel che avete'— 'ascolto') are present, although it is clear from the libretto and other copies, and indeed from the sense, that when 'Belle dee' was cut the scene began at 'Questo è luogo'. Either a page from which Smith was copying had been torn out or he was given imprecise instructions. The oboe in the introduction to 'Voi, che mie fide' (HG 115) is marked *Solo*, as in RM 19 c 7, the Malmesbury copy, and (by implication) the Flower parts; this is certainly correct. There are no oboes in the duet section of the final *coro*. Most of the tempo marks missing from the autograph are supplied, except in 'V'adoro' and 'Cessa omai', but many stage directions are absent. Numerous pencil marks affecting the dynamics and scoring, and sometimes altering the original, are in Chrysander's hand; they bring the text into general conformity with Hamburg.

The main text of RM 19 c 7, a characteristically untidy RM1 copy containing many mistakes in words and music, gives the 1724 score, with the Parnassus sinfonias in the B version, the sinfonia in the last scene complete, and 'Belle dee' included. The stage directions are very full. As in the Flower parts, but not the autograph, performing score, or RM 19 c 6, there is a second violin part in the ritornello after the A section of 'Sì, spietata'.[69] 'Al lampo dell'armi' lacks its coda with chorus. The sinfonia on HG 96 is *Allegro*; 'Tutto può donna' has no tempo. A substantial appendix in the same hand contains all the 1725 additions except the recitatives: the three tenor arias 'Sung by Sigr. Borossini', 'La speranza' in G and 'Chi perde un momento' 'Sung by Sigra Sorrossina', 'Dal mio brando' 'Sung by Sigr Baccini' (Pacini), and the March. The whole manuscript was probably copied in 1725; Chrysander did

[68] Its first two bars are pasted over something else.

[69] It is not easy to account for this. It seems authentic, and is not the sort of thing a copyist would invent. Perhaps the most likely explanation is that Handel added it to the intermediate score and Smith omitted it from Hamburg by accident.

not use it, and so missed the chance to print 'Scorta siate'. It is the latest RM1 copy so far known. This manuscript was originally in the Aylesford Collection.

The Malmesbury copy, in the hand of a scribe very briefly associated with the Smith circle (Eta), also belongs almost certainly to 1725. The main text has points in common with RM 19 c 6, including the mutilation of 'Belle dee', no mutes in 'V'adoro', and no tempo for that aria or 'Cessa omai'; but the Parnassus sinfonias are in final form and the G major sinfonia is complete. 'Cara speme' has no string ritornello and 'Se in fiorito' no bassoons, but a flute or flutes (*Trav.*) double the oboe and first violin line in the first Parnassus sinfonia. An appendix (H5) contains the arias new in 1725 but not the March. 'La speranza' is in its original key of A major, as in Fitzwilliam Mus MS 256. Elizabeth Legh, knowing not Sorosina, ascribed it to Cleopatra and 'Chi perde un momento' to Caesar.

Bodleian MS Mus d 220 is an eccentric but very early copy involving at least four and possibly six hands. One of them is Smith, who was evidently in charge. He wrote the clefs, headings, and names of instruments on the first page of the overture and first chorus, and occasionally later. Hand A (Theta) then took over and wrote all the music of Act I (except f. 38, which is Smith). Up to the end of Scene vi he included the secco recitatives, but this plan was then abandoned, and they are omitted from the rest of the opera, apart from the Parnassus scene. All the words to the end of Act I, not only text, but tempo marks, instrumentation, etc. were then added by Smith, except in the secco recitatives, which have a blank skeletal look. Theta began the clefs on the first page of Act II, but was at once superseded by Smith and Hand B (Iota). The latter copied as far as the end of 'Deh piangete' (81ᵛ), most of the words again being added by Smith. After writing the clefs for the first system of 'Se a me' Smith retired in favour of Hand C (Eta, the scribe of the main text of the Malmesbury *Giulio Cesare*), who copied the rest of the opera, though at least one more hand added a few instrumental indications and yet another (? H1) may have copied many of the words. Eta was probably German; in making a correction he wrote h for b♮.

The manuscript gives the 1724 text of the opera, and probably dates from that year or soon after. 'Belle dee' is the only piece omitted. The early part of Act I is almost void of dynamics, slurs, etc., but they are frequent later and include some that are unique. The most interesting detail is the addition of recorders (*con flauti*) to the first violin part in bars 4 and 10 of 'Nel tuo seno'. Since the words were written by Smith, they may reflect Handel's practice in the theatre.

RM 19 f 3 (Smith) is another early, eccentric, and incomplete copy, whose principal interest lies in the fact that it was made for the Princess of Wales or one of her daughters (Handel's pupils), as the emblems on the contemporary binding attest. It makes no sense except as a collection of arias for drawing-room performance, chiefly by sopranos. Eight alto arias, for three different characters, are transposed up by amounts varying from a third to a fifth to bring them within a convenient soprano compass (e′–g″), whereas others for the same characters remain at their original pitch. The Act I duet reverts to its autograph form in F sharp minor with Sesto as the lower voice beginning 'Son nato a sospirar'. All the recitatives except 'Dall'ondoso periglio' are omitted, together with the Parnassus sinfonias, the sinfonia in the last scene, 'Belle dee', and the final ritornellos of 'Cara speme' and 'Al lampo'. The scoring is inconsistent. The overture (with the chorus as a binary dance without voices) is in Handel's keyboard arrangement (see below); 'V'adoro', the sinfonia in III ii, and the finale are reduced to treble and bass lines only, except the B section of the *coro*, which has both voices. Other movements, such as 'Sì, spietata' and 'Cessa omai', lack some of their instrumental parts. 'Se in fiorito' has its bassoons, but not 'Se pietà'. This copy, probably dating from 1724, has an almost exact parallel in an *Admeto* selection (Add MS 38002).[70]

The Lennard copy may be one of the earliest in that collection, since the writer was Hb1 (not Smith, as stated by Larsen), whose principal activity covered the years 1727–32; the hand suggests a slightly later date (? *c.* 1735–7). It gives the 1724 score, except that the March replaces the G major sinfonia in Act III and Cleopatra's accompanied recitative 'Che sento?' stops at 'cor di Marte', as first composed ('Se pietà' follows, not 'Per dar vita'). 'Belle dee' is included, but not 'Cara speme'. A few 1725 word changes appear in the recitatives. This copy has some pencilled eighteenth-century ornaments in 'Piangerò', the recitative before it, and the two Adagio bars of 'Caro! Bella!'. The Granville copy (S5, after 1740) likewise has 'Belle dee' but not 'Cara speme'; gives 'Che sento?' complete, and both March and sinfonia (in that order) in the last scene; and has much fuller stage directions. It may derive from Hamburg, but has no bass figuring. An incomplete arrangement of the 1724 score for voice and keyboard in the Coke Collection is in an early (unrecognized) hand, but has no independent authority.[71] The characters are not named, and all the voice parts except Achilla are in the G clef. The recitatives, sinfonias, first chorus, and three arias ('Belle dee', 'Domerò', and 'La giustizia') are missing, as are the final ritornellos of 'Cara speme' and 'Al lampo' and the da capo of 'V'adoro'. 'Non è si vago' is in G major. The finale is reduced as in RM 19 f 3. There are a few small vocal ornaments at cadences.

The Flower parts (S2, mid-1740s) are incomplete; only violin 2, viola, cello + bassoon, oboe 2 (+ flute and recorder), horn 3, and cembalo are present, but horns 1 and 2 are at the University of Maryland and horn 4 in the Folger Shakespeare Library, Washington. They were not copied from the autograph, perhaps because it was impenetrable, but from RM 19 c 7 or a lost copy very like it, with which they share the same mistakes, the same capricious supply of bass figures (almost none[72] before 'Venere bella', a large number in all the later arias except 'Dal fulgor', none in the sinfonias, duets, or finale), and several readings found in no other manuscript, notably the second violin part in the ritornello after the A section of 'Sì, spietata' and the tempo *Allegro* for the sinfonia on HG 96.[73] Both manuscripts note the total number of bars in every piece except those omitted from the parts: the first two movements of the overture, the Parnassus sinfonias, 'V'adoro', and 'Belle dee'. Presumably S2 omitted the Parnassus scene because it required a more substantial orchestra than Jennens was likely to command (though he received some of the music in mutilated form). None of the 1725 additions is included. The bassoons

---

[70] Some of the same tools were used in the binding of both manuscripts and a book published in 1728 and presented to Sir Robert Walpole (BL 78 i 16). The late Howard M. Nixon of the British Library confirmed the contemporary date of the bindings.

[71] This copy belonged to A. H. Mann, who supplied a commentary and some inaccurate information about its origins.

[72] Except in 'Cara speme', fully figured (by Jennens) in RM 19 c 7 but not in the parts, and 'Deh piangete', figured in both.

[73] Both are in the Arnold score.

are mentioned in six pieces; their parts are complete in 'Se in fiorito', 'Se pietà', and the G major sinfonia, and nearly so in 'Tu sei il cor' (they are not told to double the voice). S2 assumed that the oboes in 'Tutto può donna' and the flutes in 'Priva son' and 'Piangerò' were in unison, not solos, but the absence of the second oboe from the ritornello of 'Voi, che mie fide' implies a solo for the first. S2 omitted the oboes from several movements where Hamburg and most other copies have *Tutti* at the start ('Presti omai', 'Empio, dirò, 'Al lampo', 'Quel torrente', 'Non hà più') and from the duet 'Caro! Bella!', but included them in the ritornellos of 'Son nata a lagrimar' and 'Venere bella'. (Except in 'Quel torrente' and 'Venere bella' he was diverging here from RM 19 c 7, which suggests that he had access to another copy.) He was certainly correct in making the second oboe double the first violins in 'L'angue offeso'. 'Scorta siate', not in the parts, also has *Tutti* on the top line in the copies.

Handel's keyboard arrangement of the overture, which includes the chorus as a binary dance with repeats, arranged from the shortened instrumental version in the Cluer score, occurs in two forms. The first, which itself underwent some development, is found in the Smith copy RM 19 f 3 mentioned above, two keyboard arrangements in the Malmesbury Collection (both Smith, *c.* 1724 and *c.* 1728), RM 18 c 2, ff. 4-5 (Lambda, *c.*1729), and New York Public Library Mus Res MN* (without the chorus). Walsh published it in his second collection of keyboard overtures (1728). The second, with additional ornaments and improvements, is in the Coke Rivers MS (H1, *c.*1727) and RM 18 c 1, ff. 36–8 (S2, *c.* 1728–30).[74]

The assiduity with which Handel's copyists reinforced Jennens's library is reflected in many further volumes from the Aylesford Collection. Strada's March 1730 arias appear together in RM 18 c 9, ff. 57–61 (S2), and RM 18 b 4, ff. 43–9 (Hb1). Curiously only 'Io vò di duolo' in the former volume is attributed to *Giulio Cesare*, yet this alone gives the wrong text; the B section has the words sung in *Tolomeo*, whereas the other copy and the two of 'Parolette' (as a da capo aria) have the *Giulio Cesare* words. RM 18 b 4 also contains the March (begun by Smith, continued by Hb1); it appears again in RM 19 c 9, ff. 70–91 (Hb1), together with 'Sperai ne m'ingannai', 'La speranza' for alto in F (1730), the Parnassus sinfonias (B version)—from which the three upper parts of the pit orchestra are omitted, apparently because there were not enough staves for them—and Cleopatra's two accompanied recitatives and two of her arias ('Se pietà' and 'Da tempeste') from the 1724 score. RM 18 c 3, ff. 5–14 (S2), has three more of the 1725 additions ('Scorta siate', 'Dal mio brando', and 'S'armi a miei danni'), and RM 18 c 10, ff. 83–91 (S2), the sixth ('Chi perde un momento') together with both Act III sinfonias and 'Belle dee'. The latter stops abruptly in the middle of a phrase, after the two B minor bars but before the recitative continuation. All these volumes probably date from *c.* 1728–32. The last three have an index in Jennens's hand on the flyleaf. He also copied flute arrangements of various parts in four arias (RM 19 a 8).

A volume in the Shaftesbury Collection (S2, *c.*1736) was obviously designed to supplement the Cluer score. It supplies, with page cues, the seven 1724 movements other than secco recitatives omitted by Cluer (four sinfonias, two accompanied recitatives, and 'Belle dee'), the initial chorus with voice parts,

---

[74] Best prints the final version in *Twenty Overtures*, ii. 17, with earlier variants in the critical commentary.

the full scoring of the Parnassus scene, including 'V'adoro', and for good measure five of the six arias and the March added in 1725. 'Scorta siate' is missing and 'Dal mio cenno' has its 1730 text, conclusively dating the copy after that revival.

Other extracts written by copyists in Handel's circle are the six additional 1725 arias in order of their appearance in the opera ('La speranza' in G, 'Scorta siate' *Allegro*) in Add MS 31571 (ff. 92–109, H5, *c*.1725); 'Alma del gran Pompeo', 'Che sento?', and 'Se pietà' in Manchester MS 130 Hd, v. 313, pp. 80–3 and 101–10 (Smith, *c.* 1743–5); 'Tu sei il cor' without bassoons in Fitzwilliam Mus MS 145, pp. 17–20 (H6, *c.* 1725–6); and the two Strada 1730 arias in Hamburg MA/175 (HB1, *c.* 1735). Although they are attributed to *Giulio Cesare*, and 'Parolette' is in its original da capo form, both arias have the later texts as sung in *Tolomeo* and *Rinaldo*.

The Coke Collection contains several excerpts: the two March 1730 arias with *Giulio Cesare* text, attributed to 'Sig^ra Strada in her Benefit' (copied by the miniature master about 1731); two copies (in different volumes) of 'Non è si vago' and 'Venere bella', both in G major, arranged for harpsichord with vocal and keyboard ornamentation, including cadenzas in each section of 'Non è si vago'—one volume also has an ornamented version of 'Da tempeste' in D major; a copy of 'Va tacito', *Largo* in G major, without the horn and viola parts but with a few added trills and mordents; and a contemporary set of parts for the same aria (and others of the period, copyist unknown) with the horn part in the trumpet part-book.

There is another ornamented version of 'Non è si vago' (*Un poco vivace*, A major) in a very eccentric hand in RCM 1115, f. 5^v, with a B section cadenza added by someone else; 'Parolette' with *Giulio Cesare* words, ascribed to Strada but in a different hand to *Floridante*, in RCM 1124, ff. 18–21(S13); and the finale, with trumpets as alternatives to the second pair of horns, in RCM 1125, ff. 1–6 (same hand as *Teseo* excerpts in this volume). Two items in the BL Department of Manuscripts are not identified in the Hughes-Hughes *Catalogue*: the March and G major sinfonia, written by a copyist associated with William Hayes in various Bodleian manuscripts (*c.*1740), in Add MS 31576, ff. 83–8; and an inaccurate copy of 'Non è si vago' in F major (hand unknown) in Add MS 27932, ff. 16^v–17^r.

Hamburg MA/180 has a set of five parts for eight arias in an arrangement designed to make the voice part available alternatively for various types of flute or recorder; different transpositions are indicated. The arias are 'Non disperar' (*Allegro*), 'Tutto può donna' (*Vivace*), 'Venere bella' (*Allegro ma non troppo*), 'Se in fiorito' (*Allegro ma non troppo*), 'Da tempeste', 'Se pietà', and 'V'adoro, pupille' (in G). The copyist appears to be the same as in Add MS 31577,[75] but there is nothing to link him with Handel.

For the publication of *Giulio Cesare* Handel turned from Walsh to Cluer and Creake, thereby driving the former into the not uncongenial practice of piracy. Cluer and Creake's score was published (with the Privilege dated 14 June 1720) on 24 July 1724, but was announced as early as 2 May, when they claimed 'a Grant for the sole printing and Publishing the same', and again on 6 June as 'Curiously engrav'd on Copper Plates Corrected and Figur'd by Mr

[75] See pp. 296, 457 and 569.

Handel's own Hands; therefore beware of incorrect pirated Editions done on large Pewter Plates'. It is an octavo pocket edition, much smaller than most opera scores of the period, with an elegantly illustrated title page: *Julius Caesar: an Opera. Compos'd by G. Frederick Handel, of London, Gent.* If Handel corrected and figured the plates, he did not bother about other details; there are no dynamics, few trills, ornaments, or marks of expression, and a capricious selection of tempo indications. Nine pieces have none at all. On the other hand 'Non disperar' and 'Caro! Bella!' are both *Allegro* (as in RM 19 f 3), and 'Se in fiorito' *Allegro ma non troppo*. All the set pieces of the 1724 score are included (in their correct keys), except the four sinfonias, 'Belle dee', and the accompanied recitatives 'Che sento?' and 'Voi, che mie fide'; but 'Cara speme' and 'Al lampo' lack their expanded codas, the instruments are often not named, and a number of the accompaniments are reduced or partly omitted. The chorus 'Viva il nostro Alcide' appears as a binary dance concluding the overture, deprived of voices, horns, and ritornellos. 'V'adoro' has its accompaniment contracted to four unnamed parts. This perhaps was to be expected, but elsewhere the treatment of the instrumentation is haphazard. There is no viola in 'Non è si vago', 'Va tacito', 'Son nata a lagrimar', or 'Sì, spietata' (which also has no second violin). The oboes are missing in 'Tutto può donna' and the B section of the finale, the bassoons in 'Tu sei il cor' and 'Se in fiorito'. On the other hand the recorder parts in 'Cessa omai' are carefully incorporated with the violins, 'Piangerò' has every orchestral detail marked, and the finale has all four horns. The figuring is not identical with that of the Flower parts or Hamburg.

Before the appearance of Cluer's edition Walsh with his 'large Pewter Plates' had uttered three collections of *Favourite Songs . . . Printed and Sold at the Musick Shops*. The first contained ten arias and the duet 'Caro! Bella!', the second seven arias and 'Alma del gran Pompeo', the third the overture and nine arias, some of which had appeared in the second. Tempo marks and instrumental parts are often omitted; sometimes a flute arrangement is squeezed in at the end (in 'Non è si vago' this is in F, following the aria in E). In the first collection 'Non disperar' appears unexpectedly in D major; this is not the unpublished setting but the familiar one sung by Cuzzoni, though it seems unlikely that it was transposed down for her. As in Cluer, the overture ends with the chorus in reduced scoring as a binary minuet. There are several later Walsh editions variously compounded from other sources, including volume i of *Apollo's Feast* (1726), and the usual arrangements for one or two flutes (both Cluer and Walsh). Walsh published the overture in parts about 1725. Volume ii of Cluer and Creake's *Pocket Companion* (23 December 1725) contains ten arias from *Giulio Cesare* in short score, mostly with English translations by Henry Carey, among them the two Sorosina pieces, one of the Borosini arias ('Sperai ne m'ingannai'), 'Non disperar' in D major, 'Se pietà' in E minor, and 'Non è si vago' in G major. The last, a particular favourite, and 'Venere bella' also came out on single sheets. 'Dal mio brando' seems to have been first printed in a Walsh and Hare collection (*All the Favourite Songs—* in fact the overture, one duet, and seventeen arias) of about 1732. For this a number of the plates were re-engraved ('Non disperar' is now in E) and others modified. 'Parolette', attributed to *Rinaldo*, was included in *The Favourite Songs in ye Opera Call'd Thessus & Amadis* (1732) and the second Handel volume of

Apollo's Feast (about 1734), 'Io vò di duolo in duolo', attributed to *Giulio Cesare*, in the fourth volume (December 1734).

Arnold's score (1789) gives the complete 1724 version, with the 1725 March inserted before the G major sinfonia, as in Hamburg and Granville. Although the supply of stage directions is erratic and there are plenty of minor mistakes, Arnold (as in the other three operas he published) used a good source. It cannot be identified with any of the surviving copies; the closest is RM 19 c 7. The tempo marks are more correct than in HG.

Chrysander (1875), instead of following the policy he adopted with *Ottone*, *Tamerlano*, and *Scipione* and printing most of what he found in the autograph, opted for the Hamburg score, and did not include everything in that. His main text is the 1724 score with the first version of the Parnassus sinfonias and the 1725 March incorporated. In the stage directions he combines readings from the autograph, Hamburg, and the 1724 libretto, and sometimes seems to improvise. The scene heading for III iv (HG 102) has Achilla *malamente ferito* in all sources—not *mortalmente*, which comes later (HG 108) in the libretto only. Chrysander follows the libretto against the autograph and Hamburg in making Cornelia kneel to Caesar in the last scene. On the other hand he omits directions from the libretto in II ix (Tolomeo throwing the handkerchief to Cornelia), III vii (Caesar's entry with his soldiers—this is in all the sources—and expulsion of Tolomeo's guards), and III viii (Cornelia drawing a dagger). In I xi (HG 47) he rightly adopts the libretto reading, against Hamburg, Arnold, and all the copies, which follow the autograph in making the guards lead Sesto out; this was a relic of the first version, where the recitative led not to the duet but to Cornelia's 'Priva son d'ogni conforto'. In the 1725 version however (HG 143) he repeats the 1724 direction, which now makes no sense since the act ends with Sesto alone. The correct direction, from the 1725 libretto, is: *Mentre l'un l'altro vogliono avvicinarsi per abbracciarsi, le guardie gli dividono, e due di esse partendo con Cornelia, le altre restano con Sesto*. Most of the bass figuring in HG comes from Hamburg.

Hagen's vocal score (Leipzig, 1926) is a historical curiosity, as a sentence from the preface indicates: 'Every intelligent person knows that the unedited original form of Handel's operas is unacceptable on the modern stage'. Hagen rewrote the opera, words and music, supplying new recitatives (and sometimes scoring secco passages), new orchestration, and new stage directions and tempos, often flagrantly at variance with the music. He made arbitrary changes of rhythm (for instance in 'Dall'ondoso periglio'), omitted ten arias altogether, and shortened every one he retained. The only pieces given complete are the overture (with first chorus), the accompanied recitatives, the cavatinas 'Nel tuo seno' and 'Deh piangete', and the finale. The da capos, when supplied, are reduced to meaningless appendages, the whole of 'Non disperar' to a fragment of ritornello, which appears twice. Most of 'Belle dee' (converted into a dance) is transplanted to I ix; 'Deh piangete', 'Sì, spietata', and 'L'angue offeso', which ends Act II, come after 'Se pietà'. A movement from the G major concerto grosso of Op. 6 turns up in the middle of Act I. Parnassus and the Muses are abolished in favour of 'sultry atmosphere' and 'festive music ... from the terrace'. In the last scene the G major sinfonia appears in the wrong place as a mock war-dance. Caesar is a bass-baritone, Tolomeo and Nireno basses, Sesto (mostly with music exclusive to 1724) a tenor. There is no mention of the original pitch of the voices; the indications of scoring at the start of each piece seldom bear much relation to Handel's.

The vocal score linked with the new Halle edition (Bärenreiter, 1962), edited by Walter Gieseler, was prepared for a revival at Göttingen. It is an arrangement of Chrysander's main text (less the three insertions) with additional mistakes, of which the grossest is the printing of Caesar's, Tolomeo's, and Nireno's parts in the bass clef throughout. The preface by Walther Siegmund-Schultze attributes wrong voices to two of the 1724 cast, stresses Handel's alleged use of a regular chorus, and claims this as the first complete and authentic vocal score of the opera. The prize for fatuity goes to a vocal score issued by the International Music Company of New York in 1973. This is a reprint of Gieseler's arrangement with an English translation, preface, and 'Comments and Suggestions for performance' by Humphrey Procter-Gregg. It would be difficult to imagine a more lethal concentration of historical inaccuracy, wilful misrepresentation, and Philistine insensitivity than Procter-Gregg's proffered solutions, which leave Hagen in the shade (without his excuse) and reduce the opera to abject nonsense. One example only need be cited: the removal of 'Piangerò' to Cleopatra's first scene in Act I, where she is 'putting on an act'. This seems to have been the model for the travesty produced by the New York City Opera in 1966 and later recorded under Julius Rudel.

Additional Notes

* (p. 515) Subsequent work by Burrows and Martha Ronish relates this leaf probably to paper with a B-type watermark (B 70 in the Burrows-Ronish classification), used by Handel in 1720–22.

* (p. 517) Insert *1732 (Handel)* 'The Fourth Edition . . . Printed for T. Wood in Little-Britain, and are to be sold at the King's Theatre in the Hay-Market.' 55pp. No dedication; Argument in English only, but cast in both languages. Set up from a copy of 1730, of which it is a shortened version. Besides the cuts listed above, the recitatives before 'Tutto può donna' and 'Piangerò' are omitted.

* (p. 523) Two groups of excerpts—eighteen arias copied by Smith and Eta at the Royal Academy of Music (MS 140) and seven arias and the duet 'Caro! Bella!' copied by H6 and Eta in Cardiff Central Library (Mackworth Collection, M.C.I. 34(b))—probably date from 1724–5.

* (p. 524) Walsh published Handel's keyboard arrangement of the overture in his second collection of Handel's *Overtures fitted to the Harpsichord or Spinnet* (*c.* 1728).

CHAPTER 23

TAMERLANO

TAMERLANO, a man of humble birth who has risen by conquest to rule the vast Tartar Empire in Central Asia, has defeated the Turks in battle and captured their emperor Bajazet. Among his allies is the Greek prince Andronico. Tamerlano, though betrothed to Irene, Princess of Trebizond (whom he has never seen), and Andronico have each, unknown to the other, fallen in love with Bajazet's daughter Asteria. *The scene is Prusa, now call'd Bursa, the Capital of Bithinia, and the first City that Tamerlane possess'd himself of, after the Overthrow of the Turks.*

Act I opens in *the Place where Bajazet is imprisoned.* Andronico tells Bajazet that he has the liberty of the palace. Bajazet is unwilling to accept this from Tamerlano, whom he despises, and asks Andronico to lend him his sword. On Andronico's refusal he *snatches a Dagger from one of the Guards* and *tries to kill himself.* Andronico stops him: would he leave Asteria an orphan? Bajazet hesitates; he could accept death willingly but for the thought of his beloved child. Tamerlano offers to restore the throne of Byzantium to Andronico.[1] Andronico asks leave to delay his departure in order to 'read Conquest's Rules, and learn the Trade of War' with the conqueror of the world. Tamerlano readily agrees since he wants his help 'to subdue a stubborn Foe', his 'haughty Prisoner'. Andronico is delighted, not realizing Tamerlano's motive, which is to enlist his help in breaking down Bajazet's resistance to Tamerlano's marriage to Asteria. Tamerlano is confident that Andronico can do this, and proposes to give him the hand of Irene as reward. Andronico is appalled that his own act in bringing Asteria to Tamerlano to plead for her father's life has had such consequences. Alone, he begs Asteria to support his cause in her heart, though his tongue will seem to belie his love. The set changes to *Appartments appointed for Bajazet and Asteria in the Palace of Tamerlane.* Asteria, who has loved Andronico since their first meeting, thinks he means to leave her in bondage to acquire a throne for himself and reflects bitterly on this. Tamerlano tells her that Andronico is negotiating her father's freedom on condition that she marries Tamerlano, agrees to her request that she hear this from Andronico's own lips, and bids her remember that the happiness of three people depends on her response. She rails against Andronico's perjury; let him at least give her back her heart. *She just makes a Motion to go off, and stops upon seeing her Father and her Lover approach.* Bajazet rejects Andronico's proposal on her behalf as well as his own, but both men for different reasons are astonished by Asteria's calm demeanour. She tells Bajazet that Andronico has fallen in with Tamerlano's wishes in order to win Irene and a kingdom, which he denies. Bajazet says that if Andronico loves Asteria Tamerlano is 'a trivial

---

[1] The fact that Andronico is dependent on Tamerlano for the recovery of his kingdom is not sufficiently emphasized in the libretto.

Rival', and sends a harsh refusal: even if he throws 'the glitt'ring Thrones of Asia in the Balance', he cannot have Asteria. Asteria's love for Andronico has turned sour: let him carry Bajazet's message, but he has no authority to convey her refusal or consent. May the god of love cure her passion and leave her an enemy she can hate. *A Court in the Palace of Tamerlane. Andronicus on one Side, and Irene and Leone* (confidant of Andronico[2]) *on the other.* Irene is shocked by Tamerlano's refusal to receive her, his promised bride. Andronico informs her that he himself is to be her husband. She asks indignantly how she can obtain access to Tamerlano to vindicate her wrongs. Andronico suggests that, since Tamerlano has never seen her, she should pose as a companion to Irene 'come with a Message from the slighted Maid', with Leone as her secret counsellor. She agrees. She will try to break down Tamerlano's cruelty, but what if he refuses to listen? Andronico, alone, laments his predicament: to save Bajazet's life he must conceal his love and bear Asteria's anger, which only makes him love her more.

Act II. *A Gallery fronting the royal Cabinet of Tamerlane.* Tamerlano thanks Andronico for obtaining Asteria's consent to the marriage; Bajazet's is now unnecessary. Andronico can barely conceal his jealousy and unhappiness. Tamerlano tells him not to ask questions but to look forward to union with Irene. They will celebrate a double wedding with mutual gratitude. Andronico and Asteria pile reproaches on each other. He accuses her of sacrificing her love for a throne; she replies that he pointed the way. He claims that his motive was to make her shun it; now she may be the death of both father and lover. She replies that if he lacked the courage to defy Tamerlano, this releases her from the obligation to hate him. He resolves to denounce the marriage publicly and reject the Byzantine empire. *Enter Zaida (Confidant of Asteria, a silent part), and whispers Asteria.* Summoned by Tamerlano, Asteria tells Andronico to court her no longer: a girl often loses her heart to her first lover, but gives her hand to the second. Andronico is left in despair; his only hope now lies in the intervention of Bajazet. *The Royal Cabinet opens, and discovers Tamerlane sitting in the middle, and Asteria on one side.* Leone introduces Irene as a messenger from the princess of Trebizond. She reproaches Tamerlano for betraying a queen and giving his hand to a slave, and Asteria for accepting it. He admits his guilt; but Irene shall have a throne not inferior to his own. When she says she will have Tamerlano or no one, he replies, 'Make Asteria displease me and I will embrace Irene', and goes out. Asteria assures Irene that neither ambition nor love called her to Tamerlano's throne, and gives her hand as pledge that she will find means to displease him. Irene, puzzled by her words, tells Leone to watch her closely. But she feels a first ray of hope which she scarcely dares trust. Leone fears trouble, since love plays havoc with human hearts. Bajazet learns with indignation from Andronico that Asteria has agreed to share Tamerlano's throne, and reproaches him as a timid lover. Unless she rejects Tamerlano, she will see her father expire at her feet. Andronico decides, if Asteria still betrays him, to kill Tamerlano and then himself; her heart must be more savage than a tiger's. The set changes to *a*

---

[2] Chrysander, in listing him as 'confidente di Andronico e del Tamerlano', reproduces a mistake in the Italian cast list of the 1724 libretto; the English version is correct. Except in one of the source librettos, that of 1719, where he is Bajazet's general and Asteria's confidant, Leone is always attached to Andronico.

Throne Room.[3] Tamerlano summons Asteria to the throne. She consents, revealing (aside) that her object is to kill a monster. Bajazet, entering, angrily declares that his fetters cannot deprive him of the title of father. He spurns the notion that a daughter of the Ottomans could mingle her blood with that of a shepherd. Tamerlano replies that Asteria's beauty alone preserves her father's head, and orders him to prostrate himself; he shall be his footstool to the throne. *The Guards approach to bend Bajazet to the Earth, who throws himself on the Ground, of his own accord.* Let Asteria mount the throne over his body. *Tamerlane takes Asteria by the Hand, and placing one Foot on Bajazet's neck would draw her towards the Throne.* She refuses to mount in this inhuman way. Tamerlano orders Bajazet to rise as Andronico enters. He refuses. *The Guards come up to raise Bajazet, who rises in a Passion.* Asteria asks his forgiveness, hinting at her secret motive. *Here she looks at Bajazet, and passes close by Andronico*, who can find no appeal to add. Bajazet says she is no longer his daughter, *and turns his Back to the Throne.* The disguised Irene enters and claims the throne for her mistress, who will not appear in person till it and Tamerlano's bed are vacant. Tamerlano promises to marry Irene if she can make Asteria descend. Finding no one to help her, *Irene offers to go, but returns at the Request of Bajazet.* He orders Asteria to descend or he will renounce her for ever, and offers his breast and head to the sword. When she still makes no move, he resolves 'to go beg this Alms of Death elsewhere'. Asteria at last rises and bids him stay. Tamerlano contemptuously orders her to resume her chains: she who vacillates is unworthy of a throne. She declares herself again a slave; but Bajazet has 'stop'd a noble Undertaking'. *Tamerlane stands up in order to quit the Throne, Asteria stops him.* She draws a dagger and *plants* [it] *on the Steps of the Throne at Tamerlane's Foot.* That was to be her first embrace. Tamerlano furiously orders father and daughter to execution; in a trio they accept the sentence with equanimity. *Tamerlane goes off with part of the Guards.* Asteria asks Bajazet, Andronico, and Irene in turn if she is still an unworthy daughter, a faithless lover, a haughty woman. Each replies with a firm negative and goes out. Bajazet is pleased with her anger; Andronico lays all the blame on himself; Irene offers friendship in gratitude for her constancy. Asteria, left alone, feels avenged; if she has not killed her enemy, she has disposed of his hateful love.

Act III. *A Court-yard in the Seraglio, in which are kept Bajazet and Asteria.* Both are determined to cheat Tamerlano of his vengeance. Bajazet produces a poison, 'the last precious Remnant, that I can boast of all my mighty Treasures'. She gladly accepts it. He awaits the result of an enterprise that Orcamo[4] is planning, and begs her if Tamerlano assaults her to drink the poison at once; he will precede or follow her. She counts her father and lover happier than herself, for she will lose both. Tamerlano tells Andronico that his love for Asteria has conquered his desire for revenge and asks him to inform her, in his presence, that the throne is still vacant. Andronico prevaricates, and is abused by Tamerlano for ingratitude and by Asteria (who has overheard) for infidelity. He at once declares his love openly, and Asteria reciprocates it. Tamerlano orders Bajazet to be decapitated and Asteria 'married to the

---

[3] Chrysander omits the scene change (HG 71), which Handel forgot to indicate in the autograph. It was therefore not copied into the performing score, but is in the libretto and the Flower copy.

[4] For this shadowy figure see below, p. 533.

meanest Slave'. *Asteria throws herself on her Knees before Tamerlane* and begs him to spare her father, who enters at that moment and rebukes her for kneeling to the Tartar. Tamerlano, determined to punish all three, orders Asteria and Bajazet to be dragged headlong to his table, and Andronico to witness their indignities and still love Asteria if he can. Bajazet continues to abuse Asteria for demeaning herself, and Andronico for defending her. Leone reports that officers have come to seize Asteria. Andronico thinks of resorting to force and then dying with her. She says she will feel no pain except for her lover and her father. In a duet they bid each other a heartfelt farewell. The set changes to *an Imperial Hall* with a table laid for Tamerlano's supper.[5] Leone invites Irene to declare herself and occupy the vacant throne; she need no longer fear Asteria as a rival. But Irene will demand, not beg; she 'has an Empire in her Dower', and the refusal of her hand will turn her into an enemy. Leone advises her not to irritate Tamerlano, but to remind him of his promise to embrace Irene if Asteria displeases him. She says she will love him if he accepts her but hate him if he does not, and retires aside. Tamerlano orders Bajazet up from the vaults, challenges him to stand the coming test, and sends for Asteria. Andronico promises to defend her (though Bajazet says he has armed her in her own defence): if Tamerlano will not restore her to him, he can have no sense of pity. *As Andronico is going off the Stage, he meets Asteria, and returns.* Tamerlano orders her to take a cup, go down on her knees, and 'perform the Office of a Slave'. *Tamerlane goes to sit down to the Table, and Andronicus lays his Hand on his Sword . . . Asteria holds him.* Struck by an idea, she *goes to take the Cup,* and *throws the Poison, which Bajazet had given her, into the Cup, which she was to offer to Tamerlane; but is seen by Irene, who approaches the Table.* Asteria bids Tamerlano drink. He calls on Bajazet to witness 'the humble Office of thy servile Daughter', and dedicates the draught to him and Andronico. *Irene takes hold of Tamerlane as he offers to Drink,* says that Asteria has poisoned the cup, and declares her identity. Tamerlano·tells Asteria that he will drink if her lover or her father will do so first. *Asteria gets up from the Table, where she knelt, and with the Cup in her Hand, advances towards Bajazet and Andronicus.* She cannot bring herself to give it to either, and decides to drink it herself. *While Asteria offers to drink the Poison, Andronicus throws the Cup out of her Hands.* Asteria cries that he has deprived her of her last refuge and *goes out in a Rage, Andronicus follows her.* Tamerlano orders soldiers to watch her and decides to send her to the slaves' seraglio, where Bajazet shall observe her degradation. Bajazet calls on the gods to protect her honour; he has his own method of attaining freedom, threatens that his ghost will return to haunt Tamerlano, and goes out. Tamerlano promises to marry Irene, who accepts him. *On one side Andronicus, on the other Leone, Asteria, and the aforesaid.* Leone announces that Bajazet has at last made his submission and begs to be received. Bajazet enters, calm for the first time in the opera: by taking poison he has released himself from his chains and Tamerlano's spite. He says farewell to Asteria, sorry only to leave her in a sea of troubles. She asks him to kill her first. He replies that he would if he had the power, in pity for her grief, but bids her weep no more. He then turns on Tamerlano, invoking the furies to creep into his heart and bring him a living death before dragging him down to hell. *He goes tottering to retire within the Scenes, supported by Asteria and Andronicus. Speaking as out of Breath,* in broken syllables, he promises to be 'the greatest Fury in all Erebus'. Asteria follows

[5] 'Apparechiato per le mense di Tamerlano': not translated in the English libretto.

him out, and Tamerlano orders guards to watch her. Andronico *offers to kill himself*, but Tamerlano stops him: Bajazet's death has slaked his thirst for vengeance. He will marry Irene and give up 'Asteria and a Throne' to Andronico. The four characters left on stage hail the return of day after black night.

(This summary reflects the printed libretto of 1724 and, almost certainly, the first performance. Leone's recitative and aria in III vi (HG 109–10), the duet for Irene and Tamerlano (HG 123–4), and Chrysander's A version of the final scene (HG 132–41) were never performed by Handel and must be regarded as rejects. Chrysander's layout of the *coro* gives a misleading impression: the singers, clearly indicated in the autograph, are Irene, Andronico, Tamerlano, and Leone. The top vocal line is for mezzo-soprano; Asteria is not on stage.)

The story of the collision of two mighty conquerors Timur or Tamerlane (1333–1405), the Tartar from Central Asia, and Bajazet (1347–1403, Sultan from 1389), the Ottoman Turk defeated by Tamerlane in 1402 and imprisoned till his death,[6] had long been popular in the theatre. It was the subject of Marlowe's first play, *Tamburlaine the Great* (Part I, 1587), and verse dramas by Jacques[7] Pradon (*Tamerlan ou La Mort de Bajazet*,[8] 1675) in France and Nicholas Rowe (*Tamerlane*, 1702) in England. Rowe's play, which has no operatic links, was staged in London on 4 and 5 November every year for many decades, sometimes at two, three, or four theatres simultaneously. The reason was political: the dates were the anniversaries of William III's birth and his landing at Torbay in 1688, and Rowe's portrait of Tamerlane as a calm philosophical prince was intended as a symbolic image of the King. That Handel chose the same season for both his productions of *Tamerlano* was presumably a coincidence; none of his performances coincided with the two anniversaries.

This was a favourite operatic subject, from M. A. Ziani's *Il gran Tamerlano* (Venice, 1689) to Mysliveček's *Il gran Tamerlano* (Milan, 1771),[9] Sacchini's *Tamerlano* (London, 1773), Reichardt's *Tamerlan* (Berlin, 1800), and Winter's *Tamerlan* (Paris, 1802). The first half of the eighteenth century saw a spate of Tamerlane operas, all based on Pradon's play. They stem from the work of two librettists: Antonio Salvi, whose *Il gran Tamerlano* was set by Alessandro Scarlatti (Pratolino, 1706), Francesco Gasparini and two of his pupils (Rome, 1717, as *Il Trace in catena*), and Giovanni Porta (Rome, 1730); and Agostino Piovene, whose work proved even more popular. It was written for Gasparini (*Tamerlano*, Venice, 1711[10]), reset by him in altered form (*Il Bajazet*, Reggio, 1719), and subsequently used by Chelleri (Treviso, 1720), Leo (*Bajazete imperador de' Turchi*, a pasticcio including music by Porpora and Orlandini,[11]

---

[6] *Tamerlano* was the most recent in date of Handel's 'historical' operas, which of course have little connection with history.

[7] His name is generally given as Nicolas, but T. W. Bussom (*The Life and Dramatic Works of Pradon*, Paris, 1922) proved that this is an error.

[8] Racine's *Bajazet* (1672) is concerned with a different Sultan.

[9] Revived at Prague in 1978 and Reggio Emilia in March 1979.

[10] The libretto is dated 1710, but this is old style.

[11] Leo was responsible for two arias and the comic scenes (to words by Bernardo Saddumene). The singers included three associated with Handel, Nicolini, Faustina Bordoni, and the tenor

Naples, 1722), Giovanni Antonio Giay (Milan, 1727), Porpora (Turin, 1730), Vivaldi (partly a pasticcio, Verona, 1735), and Andrea Bernasconi (*Bajazet*, Venice, 1742). There were also a number of anonymous productions, most of them probably revivals of one or other of Gasparini's settings.[12]

    Handel's opera was not based, as might have been expected,[13] on Salvi's
* Pratolino libretto, but on a singular amalgam of both versions of Piovene set by Gasparini, and to some extent on Gasparini's 1719 score as well.[14] The disentangling of these sources is a fascinating task. Count Agostino Piovene was a nobleman from Vicenza who wrote librettos for Orlandini, Lotti, Carlo Pollarolo, and other Venetian composers as well as Gasparini, and a man of some talent. In his preface to the 1711 libretto he cites the history of the Byzantine Empire by the late fifteenth-century writer Michael Ducas, first published in Paris in 1649, as authority for Bajazet's suicide, Tamerlane's alliance with the Greeks, and his final appeasement, and Pradon's play for 'the Love-parts'—the relations between Andronico and Asteria and the arrival of the princess of Trebizond as Tamerlane's promised bride. Since Handel's collaborator Haym took over Piovene's preface verbatim, it can be quoted in the English translation of the 1724 libretto.

It is pretty currently believed, that, after the Imprisonment of Bajazet, Tamerlane was wont to make use of him as a Footstool to mount his Horse, that he inclosed him in an Iron Cage, and caused his Wife to wait upon him at Table, stark naked. The Authors of greatest Credit, give us not one Syllable of all this; and there are many again, who assert all these Accounts to be intensely fabulous and chimerical. But, notwithstanding all this, I, who am not undertaking to write a History, but to give a Turn to Tragedy, which may render it more pleasing in the Representation, have made free use of the abovemention'd Fables, and, after shaping and forming them consonant to the Decorum of the Theatre, and bringing them within the Rules of Probability, I use them, as proper Motives and Mediums, in carrying on that main Action, which has, for its End, the Death of Bajazet.

    Pradon was a somewhat shadowy French dramatist (1644–98) who had the misfortune to write a Phèdre drama (*Phèdre et Hippolyte*, 1677) at the same time as Racine's famous tragedy—two days separated their Paris productions— and to earn the comprehensive damnation of Boileau and other critics. His career was dogged by such unhappy conjunctions. He claimed to have softened the picture of Tamerlane as a savage and cruel Tartar without being false to history: 'J'ai fait un honnête homme de Tamerlan contre l'opinion de certaines gens qui vouloient qu'il fût tout à fait brutal . . . J'ai tâché d'apporter un tempérament à sa férocité naturelle, d'y mêler un caractère de grandeur et de générosité, qui est fondé dans l'Histoire, puisqu'il refusa

---

Annibale Pio Fabri. Another tenor, Giovanni Battista Pinacci, sang the part of Bajazet in *Il Trace in catena* (1717), Handel's 1731 revival of *Tamerlano*, and Bernasconi's opera, when Girolamo Zanetti, brother of the caricaturist Anton Maria Zanetti, described him in his diary (17 Nov. 1742) as a ranting idiot ('un furibondo bastione'). See A. Blunt and E. Croft-Murray, *Venetian Drawings at Windsor Castle* (London, 1957), 181.

  [12] Verona 1715, Udine 1716, Florence 1716/17 and 1748, Venice 1723, Vienna 1730 and 1732. See Strohm, *Italienische Opernarien des frühen Settecento (1720–30)* (Cologne, 1976).

  [13] No fewer than seven of Handel's operas are based on librettos by Salvi, all but one dating from 1703–10. Scarlatti's *Il gran Tamerlano* may have been the first opera Handel heard in Italy. See p. 80.

  [14] See below, pp. 539–40 and 544–7. Some passages were quoted by J. M. Knapp, 'Handel's *Tamerlano*: the Creation of an Opera', *MQ* lvi (1970), 405–30.

l'Empire des Grecs'.[15] Pradon did not succeed in making Tamerlan sympathetic or in bringing any of the characters to life. They indulge in a long and singularly frigid competition in nobility and self-sacrifice. The main lines of the plot survive from Pradon to Handel, but some details were suppressed or obscured by Piovene, and still more by Haym. Tamerlan has already caused the death of Bajazet's wife and son. Andronic is the son of the late Greek emperor of Byzantium, after whose death he was forced to enlist Tamerlan's aid against a usurping brother allied to Bajazet. But his love for Astérie, his promised bride, leads him to intercede for the fallen foe, and Tamerlan's decision to marry Andronic to the Princess of Trebizond and keep Astérie for himself presents the lovers with a classic conflict of love and duty: Andronic is tempted to declare his love, marry Astérie, and renounce hope of gaining a throne to which he is entitled, Astérie to save the lives of her father and lover by accepting Tamerlan. The latter does not discover their feelings till Act IV, as a result of Andronic's indifference to his promised favours. Bajazet plans to escape by inducing his fellow prisoners to dig a tunnel, but the attempt is foiled, and the enraged Tamerlan declares that if Astérie does not marry him he will put Bajazet and Andronic to death. Astérie places her fate in her father's hands; by taking poison he escapes Tamerlan's vengeance and softens his heart.

In his 1711 libretto Piovene, writing for the opera-house, reduced the element of moral conflict and self-questioning characteristic of the school of Racine and Corneille and increased the ration of intrigue and misunderstanding. He retained Pradon's minor characters, Léon, Zaide, and Tamur (changing the latter from Tamerlan's captain of the guard to chief eunuch[16]), but allowed them no arias. Resisting the temptation to add a sub-plot, he concentrated on Bajazet's imprisonment and Asteria's involvement with Andronico and Tamerlano. His most important innovations were the introduction of Irene, the Princess of Trebizond, in person (in Pradon she is called Araxide and never appears), and the throne-room[17] and supper scenes in Acts II and III. These were striking improvements, but the conventional operatic device of making Andronico tell Irene in person that he is her destined bridegroom weakens his character. So does the blurring of the reasons for his dependence on Tamerlano and consequent willingness to do his bidding. The most serious defect of Piovene's libretto is its anticlimactic finale. Bajazet's part ends with his exit after 'Empio, per farti guerra' (Handel's III viii). His suicide is described by Leone, who relates it to the failure of a rescue attempt by a certain Duke Orcamo: when Bajazet saw Orcamo in the hands of Andronico's soldiers, he uttered a loud cry, took poison, and died. This relic of

[15] According to Bussom (Pradon), Pradon's principle sources were Laonicus Chalcondyles's ten-volume History of Byzantium from 1298 to 1463, first translated into French in 1577, Jean du Bec's Histoire du Grand Tamerlan tiré des monuments antiques des Arabes (1587), and Magnon's tragedy Le Grand Tamerlan et Bajazet (1647). The comparatively civilized character of Tamerlan came from du Bec, Bajazet's pride and his attempted escape by means of a tunnel from Chalcondyles, the love of Tamerlan for Astérie and of Astérie for Andronic from Magnon. The princess of Trebizond was Pradon's invention. Andronicus was a historical character, but only Chalcondyles makes him the refugee son of the Greek Emperor; in his account Andronicus's eyes were put out by boiling vinegar. Pradon was accused of plagiarism from Corneille and Racine as well as Magnon.

[16] Curiously Gasparini gave the part not to a castrato but to a woman.

[17] In Pradon's Act IV Astérie thinks of receiving Tamerlan's embrace with a dagger, but desists as it would bring death to her father.

Pradon's escape tunnel survives in Handel's libretto (III i and viii), where it is merely confusing. It seems strange at first glance that Piovene rejected Pradon's conclusion, in which Bajazet, after taking poison, requests an interview with Tamerlan and dies in proud defiance. Piovene's last scene is all Asteria's; after Tamerlano has pardoned Andronico she has a furious recitative and aria, declaring herself the heir of Bajazet's implacable hatred, and rushes out. As in the 1719 and 1724 librettos she is not on stage when Tamerlano distributes his fine words before the *coro*. The probable explanation is that Gasparini's Asteria in 1711 was a leading prima donna, Santa Stella (Lotti's wife), who required more prominence than Bajazet.

This priority was strikingly reversed in 1719, when Bajazet was sung by the distinguished tenor Francesco Borosini. The Reggio libretto of that year, with the title changed to *Il Bajazet*, states that 'la Musica è Nuova del Sig. Francesco Gasparini', and the claim is undoubtedly true, since only six pieces (four in the throne-room scene, 'Folle sei', and the *coro* 'Coronata da gigli')[18] remain from 1711. The adapters ('Gli Interessati nel Dramma'), of whom the most important was the Modenese poet Ippolito Zanella, acknowledge in their *Protesta* that this is the same story produced in other theatres under the title *Tamerlano* (i.e. Piovene's), but they had to redistribute the parts for new singers. Although much of the recitative is retained, and occasionally improved, the differences are considerable. Tamur vanishes, but a second Greek prince appears in the person of Clearco, who loves Irene and so introduces a sub-plot (he was sung by the eminent but elderly castrato Antonio Pasi), and the roles of Leone and Zaida are considerably enlarged. The three peripheral characters, who had no arias in 1711, now share eight; most are idle simile pieces, and this, together with the expansion of Irene's role so that she has more arias than Andronico, unbalances the opera. But there is compensation in the reinforcement of Bajazet's part, both in the opening scene, where he now attempts suicide, and most conspicuously in the last. The entire death scene as we know it in Handel's libretto appears here for the first time, based on Pradon but strengthened by the addition of Bajazet's curse on Tamerlano.[19] The man responsible for this was not Zanella but Borosini, the singer who played Bajazet. In 1727 Borosini, who was in the service of the Imperial Court at Vienna, presented a copy of Gasparini's score to Duke Anton Ulrich of Saxe-Meiningen. That copy, now in the Meiningen Staatliche Museen, bears on the title page a slightly later inscription stating that the libretto is by Piovene, 'Toltone l'ultima Scena che fu Composta dal Zanella secondo l'Idea del Sig^re Borosini'.[20]

In July 1724 Handel composed a complete setting of Piovene's 1711 libretto as modified by Haym. Then the 1719 libretto and Gasparini's score[21] came into his hands. There can be little doubt that they were brought by Borosini when he reached London for the autumn season.[22] It is not surprising that Handel, no doubt with Borosini's encouragement, should have jumped at the

---

[18] All six were set by Handel.

[19] Another new detail, not adopted by Handel, is that Asteria begs Andronico to kill her after Bajazet's death.

[20] Strohm, *HJb* (1975), 119; *Essays*, 50. A second score of Gasparini's 1719 opera, in the Vienna Hofbibliothek, was copied for the Library of Congress in 1909.

[21] Strohm (ibid.) plausibly conjectures that this was the Meiningen copy.

[22] Antonio Cocchi's diary records a meeting with Borosini, 'newly arrived from Vienna', on 12 September (Lindgren, *A Bibliographic Scrutiny*, 336).

opportunity to remedy the major flaw in Piovene's libretto. He took over the words of the death scene virtually unchanged, including Bajazet's brief aria 'Figlia mia'. At the same time he rewrote the opening of the opera on the 1719 text and drew on it elsewhere, chiefly in modifying the part of Bajazet for Borosini. No fewer than nine scenes contain lines from the 1719 libretto. The very extensive revisions to which this gave rise are described below under *Autograph*.

Even so the greater part of Handel's libretto is Piovene's 1711 text abridged and supplemented by Haym, undoubtedly acting under Handel's close supervision. The whole process is so revealing that it must be considered in detail. Haym removed the superfluous Tamur and reduced Zaida to silence, giving their essential lines to Leone, omitted a few scenes (in several of them Leone offers Andronico cautious advice, which he invariably ignores), and compressed a good deal of the dialogue. Much of this was salutary: we are better without mention of Asteria's late brother Ortubule (Orcamo should have gone the same way[23]) and an insipid dialogue between Asteria and Zaida before the final aria in Act II. Earlier in the same scene Haym or Handel removed an absurd anticlimax: in 1711 Asteria asks Zaida for the dagger that is to greet Tamerlano's first embrace, and when Zaida enquires what she wants it for she has to repeat the request. No doubt one reason for Zaida's disappearance was that no singer was available, but it was a good riddance. Occasionally the cuts fogged the motivation, especially in regard to Andronico's satellite status (there is only a fleeting reference to his lost kingdom in I ii). In the climactic throne-room and death scenes, one from each libretto, Handel omitted remarkably little. The remaining recitatives are more extensive than in any of his other London operas.

Haym claimed only to have accommodated the libretto to the London stage, and this is strictly true. Apart from the insertions and replacements noted below, and a number of lines that Handel set and later rejected,[24] his contribution to the recitative amounted to a mere sixteen lines, most of them simple links. The only significant additions are the first two lines of the opera, the first five lines of Andronico's accompanied recitative in II iii, and a couple of brief but telling interjections in the throne-room scene: Andronico's two attempts to interrupt Bajazet's long recitative (HG 75–6) and Bajazet's impatient 'Lascia ch'io dica'. Another tiny but vivid change in Bajazet's last speech (1719) is the replacement of the passive 'L'aria ingombrarsi' by the more positive 'Morte, ti sento'. These were surely demanded, or even written, by Handel. Most of the stage directions come from the old librettos; those for Andronico to lay his hand on his sword in III viii, to follow Asteria out (with a new line of recitative) later in the scene, and to threaten suicide at the end were new, evidently to galvanize his somewhat limp behaviour. Several of the inserted numbers had the same purpose, as well as to supplement the role of the *primo uomo*, Senesino. The first, his accompanied recitative and aria 'Benchè mi sprezzi' at the end of Act I, makes a more positive impact than Piovene's scene, where Asteria tells Zaida of her intention to approach Tamerlano and her aria plays with words (she may seem guilty, but she has a

[23] Curiously Handel cut the reference to Orcamo in III i when first setting the 1711 text, but restored it when he adopted that of 1719.

[24] Especially in the first and last scenes, which dissatisfied the composer until he received the 1719 libretto.

purpose) instead of expressing direct emotion. Another inserted accompanied recitative and aria, Andronico's 'Più d'una tigre' in II viii, is equally emphatic, and the duet 'Vivo in te' in III v gives the lovers their one opportunity to express their feelings to each other, when they think they are to die—a favourite Handelian situation; it is indeed almost the only occasion on which they behave normally instead of dissimulating. (Piovene gave them successive arias here, Andronico's after Asteria has left the stage.) Andronico's third insertion, 'Se non mi rendi' in III vii, contributes nothing—indeed it emphasizes his inadequacy—and Leone's aria in II vi is a sop to Boschi. Here the service is to the singers rather than the drama.

Of the 30 set pieces in Handel's opera as performed (27 arias, the duet 'Vivo in te', the trio and *coro*), sixteen were taken—one with some expansion—from Piovene's 1711 libretto, and three ('Forte e lieto', 'A dispetto' with significant strengthening of the words, and 'Figlia mia') from that of 1719.[25] Apart from the five insertions mentioned above, there were six replacements. Two of them, Irene's 'Dal crudel' in I viii and Andronico's 'Cerco in vano' in II iii, expand four very short lines of verse into six longer lines without much affecting the sense. Clearly Handel wanted more room. On the same pattern the four lines of Irene's 'Par che mi nasca' in II vi were increased to six. The other four replacements illustrate Handel's constant urge to strengthen the dramatic and emotional impact by preferring the direct to the oblique, the particular to the general, the concrete to the abstract. Tamerlano's 'Vo' dar pace' (I ii) replaces an aria in which the Tartar contemplates the dispersal of Bajazet's rage in the A section and Andronico's prospective happiness with Irene in the B section. The latter is not a matter on which he can know anything; the situation demands an aria with a single *Affekt*, Tamerlano's hope of pacifying Bajazet. Irene's arietta 'Nò, che sei tanto costante' ousted an even less appropriate text, in which the disguised Irene by mentioning her own name drew attention to her equivocal position instead of the sincerity of her feelings.[26] Handel's substitution of Asteria's 'Se potessi' for 'Cor di padre' at the end of the act and the new *coro* (from Salvi) were inspired changes. 'Coronata di gigli', which ends both Gasparini's librettos, offers a conventional picture of peace crowned with flowers. 'D'atra notte' in its first phrase presents the idea of black night, which suffuses the whole movement and transcends the triviality of the conventional *lieto fine*. Handel ended all three acts with a new text; each is a striking improvement.

It is interesting to compare the distribution of arias in the three librettos (Table 8). The throne-room trio is common to all three, but neither of Gasparini's contains a duet. The scene locations—three in Acts I and II, two in Act III—remain the same throughout, though there are differences in wording. The first set-change in Act II is a clear example of how the Baroque theatre moved the scenery without interrupting the action: *S'alza la tenda del Gabinetto, e si vede a sedere nel mezzo il Tamerlano, ed Asteria da una parte sopra origlieri*. It will be seen that Asteria had by far the largest part in 1711, and the same number of arias as Irene in 1719. Handel struck the best balance, with six arias for Bajazet, Andronico, and Asteria, an extra duet for the lovers, and four arias for Tamerlano and Irene. Bajazet alone had no new texts: four of his arias

---

[25] Handel set and rejected several other arias from both librettos, as well as new texts by Haym: see below, pp. 558 ff.

[26] Piovene's arietta had already been replaced in the 1719 libretto, perhaps for the same reason.

TABLE 8

	Gasparini 1711	Gasparini 1719	Handel 1724 (as performed)
Tamerlano	5	5 (Bernacchi)	4 (Pacini)
Bajazet	6	6 (Borosini)	6 (Borosini)
Asteria	9	6	6 (Cuzzoni), 1 duet
Andronico	4 (Bernacchi)	5 (Diana Vico)	6 (Senesino), 1 duet
Irene	4	6 (Faustina Bordoni)	4 (Dotti)
Leone	0	3	1 (Boschi)
Zaida	0	1 (a castrato)	[*mute*]
Tamur	0 (a woman)		
Clearco		4	

came from 1711, two from 1719. The singers named were at some time in Handel's London company.

The libretto in its final form bears little sign of its tangled history. It is an outstandingly powerful specimen of the dynastic type, whose conventions of course must be accepted. This is a world of sharp social distinctions (Irene despises Asteria as a slave, although she is the daughter of an ex-emperor, Bajazet despises Tamerlano as the son of a shepherd) and diplomatic marriages: monarchs are accustomed to make alliances of convenience, and Tamerlano does not know his destined bride by sight. Asteria's waiting at Tamerlano's table does not seem such a crowning indignity, even for a proud Ottoman; the episode might impress us more if Piovene had followed legend and stripped her naked, or at least introduced the threat. Despite a few deviations and wilful twists to the intrigue, which as usual are less confusing in the theatre than on paper, the plot moves forward steadily and with reasonable consistency; the situations are strong and well motivated, the language free from obscurity, poetic conceit, and abstract vapour. The persons, instead of comparing themselves to steersmen or rivers, react to each other in the arias as well as the recitatives ('Cerco in vano' is the nearest approach to a simile aria, and then only in the B section). The story does not require an extensive knowledge of previous events before becoming comprehensible. Above all, the characters—especially Bajazet and Asteria, but not excluding Tamerlano, Andronico, and Irene—give abundant scope to Handel's dramatic genius. Tamerlano's change of heart in the last scene will not easily convince a modern audience; but this was a convention not to be disturbed, and Handel turned it to positive advantage by standing it on its head. If the Orcamo episode is a flaw (easily remedied by cutting), it is not so much on account of its obscurity but because the idea of outside intervention breaks the claustrophobic ring of tangled emotions that grips all the main figures. *Tamerlano* is unique among Handel's operas in that the entire action takes place within the oppressive ambience of the tyrant's palace. There are none of those open-air episodes, whether of pageantry or pastoral poetry, which are a ubiquitous and refreshing feature elsewhere. We never quite escape from the grim atmosphere of Bajazet's dungeon in the opening scene.

At least three scenes—the throne-room in Act II, the supper-table in Act III, and Bajazet's death, two of them due to Piovene, one to Borosini—are constructed with great care to reach climaxes of a tensile strength exceptional in *opera seria*. Handel raised all three to a higher degree, not only by the quality of his music but by subtle adjustments in the libretto. It is noteworthy that after the first performance he cut nothing from the recitative of these three long scenes except eight lines for Leone and Irene early in III vi (HG 106). That was in the 1731 revival, when London audiences were wearying of Italian recitative and Handel made drastic cuts in other parts of the opera. There is a lesson here for modern conductors and producers. Another noteworthy point is the relaxation of the exit convention. In Act III only two arias, 'A dispetto' and 'Empio, per farti guerra', are followed by the singer's exit; but there are no fewer than eight exits without arias, three by Bajazet, two by Leone and Asteria, one by Andronico. Admittedly some of these were caused by pre-performance cuts, but the main motive was clearly the demands of dramatic truth.[27] The exits of Tamerlano and Asteria in the recitative of II iv and v were due simply to Handel omitting Piovene's arias. At the end of this act however he made brilliantly positive use of the exit convention. After the trio Bajazet, Andronico, and Irene go out in turn, not with an aria but with a short arietta, leaving Asteria, who has turned the tables on them, to end the act alone with a full aria. It seems likely that this unusual plan, a theatrical master-stroke of the first order, was suggested to Piovene[28] by a similar device in an earlier Handel opera. Act II of *Agrippina* has an important scene that is identical in design, though the emotional situation is reversed.[29] *Agrippina*, produced in Venice around New Year 1710, was immensely successful; Piovene wrote his *Tamerlano* for the same city barely a year later. It was a rare irony that brought it to Handel's attention long afterwards in London.[30]

This subject, which so fascinated Gasparini that he set it three times, twice in Piovene's version and once in Salvi's, obsessed Handel in the summer of 1724, as the repeated revisions of the autograph bear witness. *Tamerlano* is one of the supreme masterpieces of eighteenth-century opera, and stands out even from the rest of Handel's output for its flexible treatment of the *opera seria* conventions. One of these was that tenors and basses were virtually confined to playing autocrats, old men, and fathers. Bajazet is all three; but he is also in every sense—musical and dramatic—the hero of the opera. Its central theme is of course not the love story but the relationship between Bajazet and Asteria, father and daughter, which Handel projects with as profound an insight as Verdi in *Rigoletto* or *Simon Boccanegra*. The extraordinary emotional intensity of their music, like that of Jephtha and Iphis in the last oratorio, suggests that for Handel, as for Verdi, it had a deep personal significance.

Bajazet is one of the great tragic figures of the operatic stage. His character is a compound of pride, obstinacy, tenderness, fearless courage, and contempt for weakness in any form. The struggle between his pride and his devotion to

[27] Both Gasparini's settings are much more regular, though they do contain exits without arias.

[28] This was the only important scene in Piovene's libretto that retained its structure in 1719 as well as in Handel's opera.

[29] See p. 126.

[30] There is of course a possibility that this feature was responsible for Handel preferring Piovene's libretto to Salvi's.

Asteria has immense grandeur; his insistence on looking death squarely in the face gives his end a Shakespearian sense of purgation. From the first bars after the overture he dominates the stage, and never releases his grip; it is his fate that haunts our memory in the *coro*. Leichtentritt saw the stark sinfonia on which the curtain rises, with its octave unisons, far-flung string gestures, spare texture, contrasted dynamics, and long pauses, as a representation of Bajazet's character. It could also signify the opening of his prison gates or the climate of the opera in general, or all three ideas. In any event it makes an original and striking introduction. The scene gave Handel much trouble. He produced no fewer than five versions, of which this last is (with one exception) the simplest. Neither the sinfonia, presented first in C minor, then varied in G minor, nor the three bars of intervening recitative in which Andronico summons Bajazet from his prison, formed part of the original conception, and Andronico's words are in neither of the source librettos.

'Forte e lieto', which replaced a less positive aria from the 1711 libretto in which Bajazet merely asks Andronico to look after Asteria when he is dead, states the core of his predicament, his readiness for death did it not involve separation from Asteria, in a slow C major aria whose B section is not a contrast but a continuation, extending the range with a series of bold modulations over a chromatically rising bass. The steady march of the bass quavers, propelled by an occasional dotted phrase, binds both parts into a single paragraph. A lesser composer might have established explicit contrasts; Handel so concentrates the expression that the emotional pull is felt in every bar. Many details contribute to this: the antithesis of syncopation and slurred semiquavers in bars 3 and 4 and often later (an effect achieved only after much trial and error), the poignancy and Bach-like flavour of the diminished seventh arpeggio over a pedal in bar 4, the abrupt switches between major and minor, the steep dynamic contrasts, for example between Bajazet's first word and the *pianissimo* that follows at once. If the initial octave drop, followed by a rest, and the firm trills on strong beats in the first two bars suggest Bajazet's resolution, the yearning harmony of the next two at once undermines it. The triadic rather than stepwise coloratura is characteristic of Handel's writing for natural male voices, as opposed to castratos and women, and of Bajazet's music in particular; it is taxing but never showy, a tribute to Borosini's technique and dramatic commitment. Several of these features—the pause after an emphatic first word ('Ciel e terra', 'Empio, per farti guerra'), the chromatically rising or falling bass[31] ('A suoi piedi', accompanied recitatives 'Asteria, che per figlia' and 'Sì, figlia, io moro'), the Bach-like harmony and part-writing ('A suoi piedi')—are associated with Bajazet throughout the opera and give his music a peculiar unity. It is a tribute rather than a reflection on Handel that Gasparini's 1719 setting of 'Forte e lieto', likewise in C major and making prominent use of an octave drop at the outset, clearly lay behind Handel's aria and its predecessor, the rejected 'Lacci, ferri' (HG 145), in which he developed Gasparini's persistent 3/4 dotted rhythm (Ex. 61, p. 540).

Bajazet's second aria, 'Ciel e terra', follows a particularly well-written recitative in which the asides of Andronico and Asteria are characterized by different melodic contours. In the aria Bajazet sends a contemptuous refusal of Tamerlano's offer of his life in return for Asteria's hand. Once more the

---

[31] Appropriately this is extended to Asteria's music, for example in 'Cor di padre', 'Folle sei', and 'Sì, Bajazette è morto' (rewritten as 'Mirami').

Ex. 61

(a)

Gasparini, 'Forte e lieto'

(b) Largo

staccato

Handel, 'Lacci, ferri'

(c) Largo

Handel, 'Forte e lieto'

driving rhythm, bass quavers throughout except at the main cadences, propelled by irregular bursts of semiquavers from unison violins, and an emphatic first word always followed by a rest underline his implacable temper. Since the mood is wholly defiant there are no harmonic undertones— this is a single, not a mixed *Affekt*—but the octave drop recurs ('sdegno') and there are more sinewy triadic melismas, this time built sequentially on the word 'forte'.

The news that Asteria has capitulated to Tamerlano wrings from Bajazet the most anguished of his arias, 'A suoi piedi'. This astonishing piece sounds more like Bach than Handel; indeed its content and technique so strongly anticipate the bass aria 'Gerne will ich mich bequemen' in the *St. Matthew Passion* as to suggest the unlikely (but not inconceivable) possibility that Bach had come across it.[32] The resemblance, striking throughout but almost literal towards the end of the A section, extends far beyond the 3/8 rhythm with occasional syncopation and the linear three-part texture. The accompaniment for violins (unison except for a single phrase) and bass produces a type of

[32] Bach is known to have copied some of Handel's works; and *Tamerlano* was in print.

sonority rare in Handel. Voice and violins are treated on an equal footing, almost as if they were two instruments; instead of the one filling the interstices of the other (Handel's usual method), their long contrapuntal lines coalesce and veer apart, as in a Bach obbligato aria. The angular intervals, especially the rising sevenths, and restless harmony show the same affinity. In fact the music had sacred associations for Handel, even if they were subconscious, for he borrowed ritornello material from two movements in his Italian oratorio *La Resurrezione*, the duet 'Dolci chiodi' and the aria 'Caddi, è ver'.

Ex. 62

(a)   (b)

'Dolci chiodi', bars 25-8
(cf. 'A suoi piedi', bars 48-51)

'Caddi, è ver', bars 7-10
(cf. 'A suoi piedi', bars 86-9)

The screw of Bajazet's agony is turned by the irregular phrase-lengths, constantly extended (by violins or voice or both) for longer than the ear expects, especially in the latter part of the A section. This is all the more arresting after the jerky two-bar phrases with which both ritornello and voice began. The B section eschews the major mode and exploits the same harmonic progressions, founded on a chromatically rising bass, as at the corresponding juncture in 'Forte e lieto'.

The throne-room scene in Act II is a *locus classicus* for the dramatic treatment of recitative.[33] Irene's turning to each of the three men for aid, a telling gesture in itself, brings on the first major climax, the accompanied section[34] in which Bajazet denounces his daughter. There is much art in the string outbursts punctuating each of his rhetorical questions, the orchestral echo of 'per averne poi tu', the silences after 'ecco il petto', 'ecco il capo', and 'che tardi?', the sudden drop of the bass (and with it the chord root) from C sharp to C natural at 'la morte', and the poignant switch from the first inversion of D minor to E major at his last—and real—question 'ciò non ti muove?'. Asteria's production of the dagger provokes a still greater climax, of a type very rare in *opera seria*—a fully-worked ensemble of confrontation. The trio is splendid music and dramatically far in advance of its time; we are not far from the world of Mozart. The emotions of the characters—Tamerlano's baulked fury, the resignation of father and daughter, with characteristic suspensions at 'per morire'—are skilfully differentiated, especially in rhythm, against the whiplash dotted accompaniment of unison violins. There is no da capo: the ritornello sends Tamerlano seething into the wings with his guards (Handel originally had a four-bar initial ritornello too, but cut it before performance, a characteristic stroke of dramatic compression). Bajazet greets

[33] See below, p. 552.
[34] The four bars at the bottom of HG 77 do not belong to a different version, as Chrysander implies, though their string parts were dropped later. Handel originally set the whole of Scenes ix and x up to the trio with continuo only.

Asteria's change of front in the first and most emotional of three exit ariettas, the only one in a minor key. His first phrase is repeated for emphasis and doubled by the bassoons; it returns twice more at the end, on the voice and in the orchestra, as if his relief were so great that it must be expressed again and again.[35] On the last occasion the violins, who have not yet had the tune, give it an inspired lift by starting on the B an octave higher.

In his first version of the opera Handel, following the 1711 libretto, gave Bajazet the first aria in Act III and wrote two splendid settings of it, both in B flat minor.[36] Perhaps when Borosini arrived he decided to reserve him for the closing scenes. Here his impact is tremendous. 'Empio, per farti guerra', introduced by a brief but eloquent accompanied recitative tenderly recommending Asteria to divine protection, is one of Handel's most powerful expressions of rage, scorn, and lust for vengeance. Its unity embraces a wealth of thematic material: the emphatic crotchet gesture of the first word, again followed by a rest; the hammering quavers, either repeated or outlining a triad; the octave and unison semiquavers that ignite the rhythm like petrol thrown on a flame; the contrasted treatment of voice and orchestra, the former marked by descending scales, suspensions, and wide leaps on 'ombra', especially the downward sevenths and rising tenths at bars 40 and 48; the typical Borosini divisions on 'ritornerà' and 'sveglierà'; the trumpet call to the gods at the start of the B section. The aria has a higher tessitura and compass than the rest of Bajazet's part. This is interesting, since it was written before Handel had heard Borosini; when he adjusted the whole part downwards for the new tenor he left the many high A's and A flats in 'Empio, per farti guerra' untouched, reserving Borosini's top notes for this climactic aria.

The death scene (HG 125–32), a compound of secco and accompanied recitative, arioso, and formal aria acknowledging no guide but the dictates of the drama, is justly renowned. It has no contemporary parallel, at least until Orlando's mad scene eight years later. Though composed of many units, it is an indissoluble whole. Beginning and ending in G minor, the key of 'Empio, per farti guerra', it ranges widely over the tonal field, generally on the flat side. The opening finds Bajazet's mind at peace for the only time in the opera, and its calm is profoundly impressive as a consequence. But Tamerlano's words goad him to almost incoherent fury. From that point he is accompanied by the string orchestra, at first in octaves, later in a variety of four-part textures. Only Asteria's two interjections are left with continuo, and besides setting her apart from her stricken father they provoke abrupt changes in his mood. The first evokes the anguish of a last farewell. The wonderful *Piano e lento* ('Sì, figlia, io moro'), whose enharmonic modulations over a drooping chromatic bass carry it in eleven bars from F sharp major to E minor, mostly with a signature of three flats, has an almost unbearable poignancy (Ex. 63).

Asteria's next speech makes Bajazet seek a sword or poison to take her with him. But a brief outburst leads to the even more beautiful Larghetto[37] 'Figlia mia', a miniature written-out da capo aria in siciliano rhythm which borrows one of its most haunting progressions (bars 7–8) from the dying Acis's 'Verso già l'alma' in *Aci, Galatea e Polifemo* in the same key (Ex. 64, p. 544). As in similar situations elsewhere the harpsichord is silenced.

[35] Here too there was a subtle afterthought: bars 46–53 were originally quite different, without the return of the tune on the voice.

[36] See p. 563 and HG 152–4.

[37] The tempo mark occurs in the Cluer score and the Malmesbury, Flower, and Lennard copies.

Ex. 63

(Yes, daughter, I am dying; farewell! You must stay . . . alas that I cannot say
'in peace'! You must remain amid distress, and this is my only anguish.)

Ex. 64

(Already my life is failing as a victim of evil cruelty)

Ex. 65

Ex. 66

(Do not cry, my daughter; let the tears flow only when I am dead and shall not
see them.)

Then Bajazet turns once more on Tamerlano, invoking the furies and powers
of hell in a Presto of unbridled violence that suddenly collapses to Largo as his
strength fails. The whole of this final section with its contradictory suggestions
of feebleness and near-insanity, expressed in contrasts of time, speed, and
rhythm, is a marvellously coherent picture of incoherence. The drooping
sevenths, the death rhythm ♩♩♩♩ in the orchestra, the detached chords twice
galvanized into desperate but *pianissimo* repetition, the gasps of the dying man
rendered in detached syllables in syncopated rhythm, punctuated by rests, as
his breath ebbs away—all contribute to an impression of extraordinary
realism. The whole scene has the ennobling quality of Greek tragedy, carrying
the spirit beyond earthly things into a higher dimension. It emerges as the end
to which Bajazet's entire role, which has an inner consistency found only in the
greatest dramatic creations, is seen inevitably to have been moving.[38]

[38] For this reason, quite apart from the quality of the music, it should never be cut in
performance.

Not its least remarkable feature is the fact that two of the most moving sections were inspired by Gasparini's music to the same words. Gasparini too had set 'Sì, figlia, io moro' in broken three-note phrases over a falling chromatic bass with the same vocal and instrumental rhythms (but no upper strings); for 'Figlia mia' he too chose a siciliano rhythm with four-part strings in a minor key (Ex. 65 and 66, pp. 544–5). There could be no clearer illustration of Handel's transfiguring genius. Gasparini's music is admirably expressive; by extending its most distinctive features (Gasparini's recitative has a simple continuo accompaniment; his 'Figlia mia' is only five bars long) Handel raised it to the sublime. Gasparini's setting of the final curse, though broken up into rhetorical patterns and not ineffective of its kind, is more formalized and lacks Handel's range of expression. Nevertheless it deserves to be quoted as an example of how a respectable contemporary treated such a situation; this is the first point in the scene where Gasparini uses the strings (Ex. 67).

Asteria's music is scarcely less memorable than Bajazet's. She has much of her father's spirit, courage, and inner strength, tempered by a hint of waywardness and softened by her love for Andronico. Her vitality is fired by youth, not simply by outraged honour. Where Bajazet's two Act I arias are resolute pieces in the major mode, Asteria's are slow and intensely emotional in the minor. Although the words of each express a measure of scorn for Andronico's apparent faithlessness, Handel with his instinctive response to nuances of character subordinates this to something not explicit in the text that is nevertheless, alongside her devotion to her father, the key to her actions—love for Andronico. 'Se non mi vuol amar' (which Piovene placed in an earlier scene, before Tamerlano's 'Dammi pace') establishes this from the start. Expanded and altered from a cantata aria of 1707 (HWV 159), it is one of Handel's loveliest sicilianos, a product of his rich legacy from Alessandro Scarlatti. The music, *pianissimo* or *piano* in five real parts, with the B section on the same material to emphasize the singleness of her emotion, is full of subtlety and surprise. The lilting rhythm is set off by chromaticism and an expressive alternation of appoggiaturas and chordal notes on strong beats at the ends of phrases. The ritornellos are scaled to different lengths (seven, four, and three bars), and the descending figure with trills in bar 5 skilfully varied when it returns in bars 16, 24, and 34—the last in the B section, its only appearance on the voice. Perhaps the most exquisite touch is the use of the highest notes for the words 'traditor' and 'perfido ingannator', thus setting up a counterpoint of emotions: the music expresses not indignation but the pain and longing of love.

In 'Deh! lasciatemi' Asteria asks for an enemy, but the music plays her false; she cannot think of Andronico as such. It is a lament, the ritornellos lightly touched with the colour of the flute, the instrument of grief, and very similar to Rodelinda's 'Ahi, perchè'; the main idea presents the same sad falling triplet followed by a drop of a fourth. The interval is varied later (the rising sixth at bar 4 is particularly happy), and the voice's irregular phrase-lengths— 7 + 7 + 4 + 5 bars, building up to a sustained paragraph (5 + 13) at the end of the A section—dispel any risk of monotony. 'Non è più tempo' in the bright key of A major could scarcely be more different. This is the one aria in a tense and tragic opera to admit a touch of humour: her reproach to Andronico is ironical, not bitter, and flies all the swifter to its mark. The light opening with

Ex. 67

(If you are weary, take away my rage or carry it with me down to the kingdom of eternal fury. To torment, to tear apart that monster, I shall be the greatest fury in hell.)

no ritornello and only continuo accompaniment, the immediate repetition of the melody with doubling violins, its several later appearances on violins or voice, the tripping three-note figure first heard in bar 7, and the merry division on 'stringerò' almost suggest a kitten playing with a mouse. Yet the aria never moves out of character; there is feeling as well as wit in the modulation to B minor, and a four-part ritornello extending the three-note figure into a delicious coda decorated with trills concludes the A section.

Asteria holds the centre of the stage throughout the throne-room scene, though apart from the trio and the aria that ends the act she is confined to secco recitative. Handel's late substitution of 'Se potessi' for 'Cor di padre' reflects his dramatic astuteness. The situation, after Asteria has been comprehensively vindicated, demands not a tragic aria but one expressing relief and at least modified joy. She is concerned not with her own sufferings but with the hope, however remote, that all may yet come right; above all, she has regained the respect of the others. 'Se potessi' with its long ritornellos (twenty bars at the outset), warbling melody, and leisurely but eloquent modulations in both sections makes a perfect close to the act after the drama of the trio and the three ariettas. The five-bar opening phrase is interestingly varied. The syncopated upward leaps perhaps reflect the surge of hope in her heart. Although Handel supplied no tempo mark, the music demands a lively pace (otherwise the aria seems interminable); early scores, which give *Allegro* (Cluer) and *Andante allegro* (Lennard), confirm this.

*

'Cor di padre' brings back the tragic heroine, torn between father and lover and afraid of losing both. The striking ritornello, with its jagged rhythm that pervades the whole aria, chromatically descending bass (she is Bajazet's daughter), and carefully marked crescendos (*p–più forte–f*, three times in consecutive bars), is typical of Handel's G minor mood, which is sustained without remission throughout A and B sections. The E minor love duet with Andronico, 'Vivo in te', is equally characteristic of its key, recalling the elegiac parting of Cornelia and Sesto in Act I of *Giulio Cesare*. The rich ensemble in eight parts, marked by plaintive echoes between woodwind and strings and their occasional unison, is unique in this opera, as if to single out the one moment of communion between the lovers. The rare doubling of transverse flutes and recorders was also perhaps intended to suggest the bitter-sweetness of a moment stolen from time, a fleeting glimpse of happiness before long separation; Handel never employed unusual scoring without a purpose.[39] He constantly varies the texture, allowing the voices to sing together only at cadences and towards the end of each part. The suspensions when this occurs in the A section are particularly potent after so much syllabic writing earlier in the duet.

The supper scene (III viii) finds Asteria again at the centre of the action. The failure of her attempt to poison Tamerlano and his order that she offer the cup first to Bajazet or Andronico produce a moment of intense poignancy. As in the death scene that follows Handel sets aside the convention. The accompanied recitative 'Padre, amante' is little more than a succession of simple chords, yet the effect as she names Bajazet and Andronico and her relationship to them, her voice broken by pauses, before collapsing into incoherence is overwhelming. So is the sequence of chords—C minor, D major, B flat

---

[39] Compare the unison obbligato for solo oboe and all the flutes in the Queen of Sheba's aria 'Will the sun forget to streak' in *Solomon*.

major—leading into the arioso 'Folle sei'. Although a mere fifteen bars long, this alternates abruptly between two tempos,[40] *Largo* for the first and third lines of text, *Allegro* (and *concitato*) for the repetitions of the second, 'il tiranno poi vivrà', as she makes the decision to drink the poison herself. The words 'e morran' once more evoke chromatic scale figures, first descending in the bass, later (at the third *Largo*) rising on the voice. Although this is anything but a display piece, the supreme crisis of the action takes Asteria only for the second time in the opera to her top B flat, approached by a leap of an eleventh (the first is in the B section of 'Se potessi'). After Bajazet's death Handel originally gave Asteria another accompanied recitative ('Sì, Bajazette è morto', later replaced by 'Mirami') and an elegiac aria ('Padre amato'). All three are splendid music: 'Mirami' is an impassioned demand for death, ending with two slow quiet bars as she thinks of Bajazet waiting for her, the aria an anguished F♯ minor Larghetto in triple time with a contrasted (Allegro 4/4) denunciation of Tamerlano in the B section. But Handel, like Mozart at the corresponding point in *Idomeneo*, knew when the drama must take precedence over even his greatest music. Between the death scene and the *coro* a big *scena* for Asteria must be an anticlimax. He removed the whole episode, substituting a brief recitative.

Andronico cuts rather a sorry figure, a shuttlecock between the two camps. He admires, and wants to save, Bajazet only less than he loves Asteria; but he is a powerless exile at the court of Tamerlano, who holds all the cards and alone can restore his throne. The libretto presents him as a lover rather than a soldier, an essentially timid person, the plaything of forces and characters stronger than himself. Since the first four (and most substantial) of his arias all occur in solo scenes, he delivers his feelings to the audience rather than the rest of the cast and can exercise little influence on the action. Inevitably he is overshadowed by Bajazet, Asteria, and Tamerlano, and to some extent even by Irene. But he is not uninteresting as a character, and is magnificently served by his music. Handel, besides using him as a lyrical foil to the turbulent emotions of the others, makes him an introvert who enjoys his own sufferings. In this respect he is utterly remote from the hero of *Giulio Cesare*, but has points in common with Bertarido in *Rodelinda*. Significantly all six of his arias are in major keys, and four of them (including the first three) in slow tempo.

Handel draws his lineaments in 'Bella Asteria', a love song of exquisite tenderness dependent entirely on the interplay of vocal line and bass, with a three-bar ritornello in four parts at the end of the A section, where the first violins carry the melody in magical sequence to a high D. Once more, as in *Radamisto*, *Floridante*, and *Ottone*, he uses a simple traditional gambit to establish at once the emotional nucleus of an important character. The opening phrase dates back to an early cantata (HWV 162). The big *scena* at the end of Act I, which must have been inserted at Handel's demand, is much more than a display vehicle for Senesino; it is a memorable piece of characterization. The accompanied recitative is very carefully composed. It begins with a grand C minor gesture, but falls almost at once to a gentle half-close on the dominant, emphasizing the self-pity of the words: 'Who ever saw a more unfortunate lover?'—sung by the lover himself. What follows—the change to the minor of the dominant, the dissonances between upper parts

[40] Specified in the Cluer score and the Malmesbury and Flower copies. Characteristically Handel simplified his first version: see p. 563.

and bass, the bold modulations—shows that Andronico's feelings are genuine. But presently the drooping outline of his first phrase becomes ever more insistent, until the initial 3½ bars are repeated literally to round off the emotional and musical pattern. This time, instead of proceeding to the dominant minor, Handel drops to E flat, the relative major of the recitative's opening, for the aria. It is as if Andronico were sinking back on the cushion of his grief. However weak the sentiment, this is a magnificent aria, remarkable for the euphony of the four-part accompaniment, retained throughout A and B sections, the beautiful rise and fall of the long melodic phrases, and the expressive divisions, which lack any element of the spectacular. If the palpitating figure heard first in bars 8–11 was intended to suggest Andronico's beating heart, what more appropriate than that he should be listening to it? The placing of this serene aria at the end of a stormy act is a master-stroke.

Handel repeats the dramatic and musical formula almost exactly in Andronico's next scene (II iii), clearly a deliberate decision (it was not his first plan, in which Andronico had an E major aria to be introduced by a secco recitative). Once more Andronico laments his unhappiness ('Ah, disperato Andronico!') and Asteria's unkindness in a substantial and harmonically trenchant accompanied recitative of almost identical length. The first inversion of G minor after Asteria's teasing A major aria is a marvellously telling gesture. Again the recitative drops from a G (? major) cadence to E flat for the aria; 'Cerco in vano' is another smoothly flowing Andante in triple time with mellow four-part accompaniment and long graceful divisions for the voice. Andronico sounds like a traveller who has lost his way but is not unduly concerned to recover it; the sheer beauty of the music spells a certain contentment. The semiquaver figuration of the bass has an Alberti look, but in fact serves as counterpoint to the upper parts, particularly in the B section.

In his next aria, 'Più d'una tigre', Andronico at last achieves a quick tempo: moved by Bajazet's self-abasement in 'A suoi piedi', he plans violent action and likens Asteria to a tigress. Handel combines two ideas that he used several times elsewhere: the opening phrase in *Rinaldo* ('Sulla ruota') and *Semele* ('No, no, I'll take no less'), the angry repeated semiquavers of bars 6 and 7 in an early continuo cantata (HWV 130) and *Teseo* ('Qual tigre'). Clearly the words evoked the second borrowing: in both opera arias the phrase illustrates the spring of a tiger. The music has great spirit; Andronico's abandonment of introspection for action is underlined by greater rhythmic vitality (fuelled by the recurring dotted figure in the bass) and a sparer texture, sometimes reduced to bare octaves. For his arietta at the end of the act ('Nò, che del tuo gran cor') Andronico naturally drops back into smooth euphony. The doubling of the voice by the violins may indicate his lack of independence. The context merely requires him to withdraw his unjust suspicions, but he takes all the blame on himself. There is some happy imitation between voice and bass, and a charming coda to which Handel adds the viola.

Andronico has no part to play in the denouement, which belongs to Bajazet and Asteria. Handel gives him the love duet and an aria in which he manages to confront Tamerlano; neither is in the source librettos. 'Se non mi rendi' is by far the weakest of his arias and asks to be cut (Handel did later remove the opening ritornello). It may be meant to suggest his inadequacy as a man of action; instead of defying the tyrant, he feebly asks for pity. But the music itself is feeble, dry, and mechanical with short phrases and squat rhythms, as if

Handel's heart were not in it. At first he compensated Senesino for his eclipse in a duet with Tamerlano on the words of Piovene's *coro*, full of rushing string scales and otiose warblings, but wisely cut it when he short-circuited the last scene. The piece has a quaint interest as the only duet for two castratos in Handel's entire output.

Tamerlano is not a wholly satisfactory figure, partly perhaps because Handel was not inspired by Pacini (who must nevertheless have been a capable singer to do justice to 'A dispetto'), but chiefly because his villainy, on which the drama depends, is exercised almost entirely in recitative. He is not a blustering tyrant (the part of course was conceived in terms of the castrato voice, and octave transposition damages the character as much as the music) but a specialist in mental cruelty, threats, and blackmail, with the serpentine attributes of an oriental despot. He must be credible as a powerful conqueror and the object of Irene's love. Moreover he is genuinely fond of Asteria, and begins by asking Bajazet's consent to the marriage instead of just grabbing her. Yet little of his complex character emerges from his four arias, all of them in *Allegro* tempo and none quite qualifying as vintage Handel. 'Vo' dar pace' and 'Bella gara' are positively jaunty—the jovial face of autocracy. The former combines an abundance of triplets with a hint of implacability in the emphatic bass crotchets on the first beat of each bar in the ritornello and later. In 'Bella gara' the prospect of amorous dalliance stimulates Tamerlano into a spiky gavotte, the dotted rhythms hopping assiduously from part to part. 'Dammi pace', a direct appeal to Asteria and his only aria in the minor, has more emotional commitment, though he is clearly more accustomed to command than to plead. The two equally terse main motives, that of the first bar and the rhythm ♪ | ♩♩♩, are nicely interspersed throughout A and B sections, sometimes against upper or lower pedals. 'A dispetto', a virtuoso exercise replete with brilliant scales and runs, conveys little more than conventional rage. It replaced a less spectacular but more interesting aria, 'Fiero, mi rivedrete' (HG 155–6), which has a touch of real menace, especially with its later more positive text, 'Empi, se mi sdegnate'. Tamerlano's most vivid music is his part in the trio, which does suggest the snarl of the tyrant scorned. The tame duets with Irene and Andronico, both suppressed before performance, add nothing to his stature.

Irene is a more convincing character, over whom Handel took considerable pains. Apart from Leone, she is the most straightforward person on stage; her open nature, with a strong sense of honour and duty, contrasts forcibly with the devious manoeuvres of the other principals. Her arias, like Andronico's, are confined to major keys. 'Dal crudel', with its persistent returns to the tonic (an indication of single-mindedness?), looks ordinary on paper but comes to life in the theatre. The rhythms are energetic; the independent bassoons add a spirited counterpoint to voice and bass, and colour the whole aria. The voice's second phrase, already employed in a similar position in *Rinaldo* ('Venti, turbini'), was to find its ultimate niche in *Messiah* ('For unto us a child is born'). The pearl among Irene's arias, and one of the glories of the opera, is 'Par che mi nasca'. Handel's depiction of the dawn of hope in the young princess's heart adds profile to her character and is profoundly moving in context amid the anfractuosities of Tamerlano's court. Both the voice part and the obbligato line, with its mixture of unisons, thirds, and sixths, are fascinating in melodic resource, cross-rhythms, and echoes. The unpredictable appearances of the little four-note figure in groups of from one to six units are managed with rare art. In the alto version sung at the performances, transposed from G to C, Handel was forced to twist the exquisite vocal line out of shape, but he expanded and enriched the B section. The cornetti of the autograph, replacing the flutes of the soprano setting, are a puzzle: no such instruments are known to have been available in London, nor did Handel write for them elsewhere. The performing score (followed by the Granville copy) has clarinets; and since it was copied immediately before the 1724 production there can be little doubt that clarinets were used. They were available in London in 1726 and 1727; Handel wrote for them in *Riccardo Primo* in the latter year. We know the names of the players, August Freudenfeld and Francis (? Franz) Rosenberg, who had benefit concerts at Hickford's Room on 25 March 1726 and 15 March 1727, and presumably played the 'Concerto for Two Clarinets' at York Buildings on 26 April 1727.[41] They could have been in London as early as 1724. It seems likely that in writing for 'Cornetti' Handel mistook the name of the new instrument.

Irene's arietta at the end of the act, 'Nò, che sei tanto costante', where the voice is doubled by yet another wind instrument, recorders, is very moving in the simple sincerity of her offer of friendship and in its haunting use of hemiola rhythm. 'Crudel più non son io' in Act III stands out less, though its deft wit suggests that Irene may command the female wile to control even Tamerlano. The playful way in which the latter part of the ritornello avoids a cadence for as long as possible betokens a flexibility that knows its own strength.

Leone's one surviving aria, 'Amor da guerra e pace', adds nothing to the drama. It was a necessary vehicle for Boschi and (like the suppressed 'Se ad un costante core') is typical of the music Handel wrote for him: a hearty Allegro in common time and a flat minor key with an energetic violin line, generally unison but breaking occasionally into two parts. The music displays a good deal of technical resource, for example in the sometimes exact, sometimes free imitation between violins and bass and in the degree of doubling, just enough to add emphasis without destroying the sense of three independent lines. At the entry of the voice Handel varies the accents of the first two bars of the ritornello by shifting the bar-line, though the notes are virtually the same; when the phrase is used in sequence to launch the B section, the rests give it a different flavour. If the aria is a candidate for the scissors in a modern revival restricted for time, its quality is not negligible.

Tamerlano has several unusual structural features. The climactic scenes in the throne-room (II ix and x), at Tamerlano's supper-table (III vi–viii), and Bajazet's death (III x) are exceptional in *opera seria* for dramatic tension sustained over a long period. Each makes extensive use of both types of recitative. Handel composed more accompanied recitatives for *Tamerlano* than for any other opera (though not all were used), and their expressive range is vast. Nor is the secco recitative perfunctory. The throne-room scene (HG 71–88) is an astonishing *tour de force*. It contains exactly 700 bars of music including necessary repeats, the first 235 in recitative: 152 secco, 31 (originally 34) accompanied (Bajazet's denunciation of his daughter), and another 52 secco. This is the longest stretch of recitative Handel ever wrote,[42] but not for

---

[41] See *The London Stage* under these dates.

[42] The most extended sections of recitative in *Rodrigo* and *Agrippina*, written for Italian audiences, have 160 and 200 bars respectively.

a moment does the tension sag; he keeps it taut by flexible declamation and the postponement, evasion, or interruption of cadential formulae. After it has at last snapped in the trio, Handel leads away from the outer climax to an even more satisfying inner climax dependent on a counterpoint of emotions. Asteria, vindicated by the revelation of the dagger intended for Tamerlano's first embrace, asks Bajazet, Andronico, and Irene if they still consider her a traitress to love and honour. She poses each question in two bars of secco recitative; each replies in a simple arietta with a closing but not an opening ritornello and goes out, leaving Asteria alone to end the act with a long aria expressing relief. Every set piece is in a different key—D major (trio), E minor, E major, and G major (ariettas), and B flat major (aria)—and each arietta answers a questioning chord on a different degree of the scale, dominant, mediant major, tonic (the trio follows a mediant minor cadence), so that the ear is constantly surprised. The change to the first flat key for Asteria's aria, after a mediant major chord (D major), is not the least of many happy strokes. The entire scene,[43] which has no parallel apart from its adumbration in *Agrippina*, is one of the most original in eighteenth-century opera. The impact cannot be adequately described in words; in the theatre it is overwhelming.

Another master-stroke is the treatment of the *coro*. The words, celebrating a conventional happy end, give the lie to the whole tragic drama we have witnessed. Handel therefore subverted their import by stressing not the bright dawn to come but the black night that has passed, and set them in a bleak E minor, almost eschewing the upper notes of violins and oboes and using only the low voices, three altos and a bass. Admittedly Bajazet is dead and Asteria off-stage and in no position to rejoice; but in earlier and later operas Handel asked dead characters to sing from the wings. The music is more solid and contrapuntal than usual in these often perfunctory finales, with touches of canon and imitation and a notably brief B section in the major. Again it needs to be heard in its theatrical context, where (as in the finales of *Alexander Balus*, *Theodora*, and a few other works) the playing of the sense of the music against that of the words produces an impression of dramatic truth scarcely attainable by other means.

The tonal plan of the opera was disturbed by late changes and transpositions. Handel began the part of Irene for a soprano of limited range and had to transpose her first two arias and rewrite the third in a lower key. Never having heard Borosini, he had similar rectifications to make in Bajazet's part. All the late settings of arias from the 1719 libretto were in different keys from those they replaced. The score as performed has no overall tonal scheme, though Act II begins and ends in B flat. The powerful overture and the opening of Act I have C minor as their tonic, and the first aria, 'Forte e lieto', moves naturally to C major, but this was not the original plan. The predominantly minor colouring of Act III is no surprise. All its five weightiest movements are in minor keys, two in G minor, one in F minor, and two (the duet and *coro*) in E minor. One reason for replacing Tamerlano's C minor 'Empi, se mi sdegnate' with the D major 'A dispetto' may have been to counteract this tendency; another was probably to flatter Pacini. Whereas all Andronico's and Irene's arias are in major keys, Asteria's incursions into that mode, apart from the arioso 'Folle sei', are confined to Act II, and Bajazet's to Act I, where Handel was concerned to establish his proud façade. His part

---

[43] Its perfection was achieved only after repeated alteration: see pp. 560 and 562.

originally contained only one major-key aria, 'Ciel e terra'; all five of his suppressed pieces—an astonishing number for one character, and a further testimony to Handel's involvement—are in minor keys.

Drops from the mediant major before arias—a peculiarly emotional effect, and a much rarer move in Handel than from the mediant minor—are characteristic of this opera. They occur, as we have seen, twice in the throne-room scene, before two of Andronico's biggest arias, and before 'Folle sei', and at three of the five set-changes (two of these are falls of a minor third). The shift from the subdominant minor for 'Figlia mia' also has an obvious emotional purpose. The unusual progressions introducing 'Cor di padre' (G minor after F major) and 'A dispetto' (D major after the subdominant G) are more problematic. These arias were substitutions, and while it is possible that Handel modified the cadences, the performing score, in which they were recopied, suggests that he did not.

The scoring, as befits a claustrophobic drama of tangled personal relation-ships, is predominantly sober. In this it contrasts sharply with *Giulio Cesare*. There are no trumpets or horns. The prominent use of three different wind groups (four with the replaced version of 'Par che mi nasca') in the arias of a secondary character, Irene, is exceptional; they help to distinguish her, and add variety of colour. Otherwise the only deviations from the minimum standard orchestra are the light touches of the flute in Asteria's 'Deh! lasciatemi' and the doubled flutes and recorders of the love duet. The vocal colour is more varied, thanks to the employment of all four voice types. The proportion of three altos to one soprano and above all the dominant role allotted to the tenor distinguish *Tamerlano* from all earlier Italian operas produced in London. Bajazet was not only Handel's first important tenor part, but one of the greatest, without a rival before the later oratorios.

Tamerlano contains many self-borrowings, from the operas *Rodrigo*, *Rinaldo*, *Teseo*, and *Ottone*, the oratorio *La Resurrezione*, the serenata *Aci, Galatea e Polifemo*, at least five cantatas, and four of the *Deutsche Arien* (see p. 503); but they are all reworked and improved. There is no question of mental laziness; the procedure is creative. An old idea came into Handel's head, sometimes as a result of verbal or dramatic association, and he spun new music from it, using on different occasions a fragment of melody or bass, a violin figure, two ideas from different works, or a phrase that is not the beginning but the continua-tion of a paragraph. This could have occurred below the level of conscious-ness. Perhaps the most literal borrowing is the opening of 'Dammi pace' from the eighth *Deutsche Arie*, 'In den angenehmen Büschen'; but it soon diverges into new ideas.

In view of Handel's indebtedness to Gasparini's 1719 opera a brief comparison may be of interest,[44] though the two are not strictly parallel. Gasparini's score, while very uneven, is sometimes refreshingly unexpected; it makes free use of hemiola, spare textures (very light basses), and quirky chromatic harmony. Some of the best music is for Andronico and Tamerlano, oddly as the latter is treated in his beautiful first aria. What *Il Bajazet* conspicuously lacks is a sense of continuing drama, whether in delineation of character or scenic structure. Many arias are tangential to the plot, and Irene receives more than her share, including two in succession just before the death scene. 'A dispetto' is an exuberant extrovert piece with oboes and two horns, running to more than 200 bars. Perhaps the most Handelian is Clearco's

[44] See also Strohm, *Italienische Oper* (1979), 95–111.

'Morte non è agli amanti' in III viii, a solid fugal structure with the subject inverted in the B section. The difference of approach is most marked in a climactic scene where the librettos are closest, the end of Act II. Gasparini's trio uses the same text and key as Handel's, and his treatment of the voices is not dissimilar; but Tamerlano's rapid semiquavers make only a mild impact, there is nothing comparable to Handel's suspensions when Asteria and Bajazet express their common resolve to die, and da capo form deprives the piece of its forward impetus. Asteria duly asks her three questions in two-bar recitatives, and Bajazet, Andronico, and Irene respond without ritornello, the first two using the same text as Handel. Their replies bring no tonal surprises (each follows a dominant), and the last two are da capo arias, not ariettas. The act ends with a dull C major setting of 'Cor di padre', the aria Handel first placed at this point. It releases no tension; there is indeed little to discharge, since Gasparini scarcely attempts to treat the scene as a dramatic unit. Nor does his final *coro*, a simple minuet, contribute anything.

There is some evidence, perhaps exaggerated by Strohm, that Handel knew Gasparini's 1711 setting. Only eight arias survive,[45] seven from Asteria's part. Five of them—'Se non mi vuol amar', 'Deh! lasciatemi', 'Non è più tempo', 'Cor di padre', and 'Sù la sponda' (a siciliano in E flat for tenor[46])—were set by Handel in a style that could scarcely be more contrasted. All five differ in mode, and four in time signature. Gasparini's 'Deh! lasciatemi' is a brilliant coloratura piece in D major with oboe obbligato and copious triplet figuration. The most interesting of his arias is 'Svena, uccidi', sung by Asteria in the last scene. The first part, in A major, is a passionate clamour for vengeance; the B section, in slow triple time, supplies not only much of the text for Handel's 'Padre amato' ('E tu padre in me riposa / Piano l'ombra generosa / A momenti volerò') but the rhythm and tonal area, moving through the sharp minor keys to end in C sharp minor.

History and Text

According to Handel's note at the end of the autograph, he began *Tamerlano* on 3 July 1724 and finished it on the 23rd (he first wrote 24th), but he was to do much more work on it before the first performance, at the King's Theatre on 31 October 1724. The cast was:

TAMERLANO:	Andrea Pacini (alto castrato)
ANDRONICO:	Senesino (alto castrato)
BAJAZET:	Francesco Borosini (tenor)
LEONE:	Boschi (bass)
ASTERIA:	Cuzzoni (soprano)
IRENE:	Anna Dotti (contralto)

Tamerlano opened the Royal Academy's sixth season, and saw the London début of Pacini, Borosini, and Dotti; it was also the first Handel opera in which the oboist and flautist Carl Friedrich Weidemann played in the orchestra.[47] *Mist's Weekly Journal* had announced on 17 October that the

---

[45] In Berlin Staatsbibliothek Mus MS 30330.

[46] Bajazet seems always to have been a tenor; Giovanni Paita sang the part in 1711.

[47] He noted the fact on the first oboe part of the six (spurious) trio sonatas attributed to Handel's early years: see Squire, *Catalogue*, 105.

opera was in rehearsal, remarking of Borosini (misspelt Borseni): '*NB*. It is commonly reported this Gentleman was never *cut out for a Singer*'. This was a tribute to his sexual, not a reflection on his artistic capacity. Lady Bristol wrote to her husband after the first night: 'You know my ear too well for me to pretend to give you any account of the Opera farther than that the new man takes extremely, but the woman is so great a joke that there was more laughing at her than at a farce, but her opinion of her self gets the better of that. The Royal family were all there, and a greater crowd than ever I saw'. The references are probably to Borosini and certainly to Dotti. The latter sang Chrysander's B version of 'Dal crudel' and 'Par che mi nasca', but did not need to transpose the recitative. For the pieces in Chrysander's main score never included by Handel, see p. 531.

The opera received nine performances up to 28 November and three more towards the end of the season in May 1725. It seems to have been only moderately successful.[48] According to Chrysander (ii. 125) it could have run longer but for public disappointment with the two chief male singers, but no evidence for this statement is known. The Colman Opera Register notes that Cuzzoni and Senesino were still 'much esteemed'. *Tamerlano* was the first Handel work mentioned in the letters of Mary Delany (then Pendarves); on 12 December she sent her sister Ann Granville 'a song out of Tamerlane, which is a *favourite*'. This was probably 'Bella Asteria', published in single-sheet form.

Tamerlano could not be given in later Academy seasons owing to the absence of a tenor. Handel revived it once only, on 13 November 1731, when it again opened the season and had three performances. Senesino was the sole survivor from the original cast; the other parts were sung by Campioli (Tamerlano), Giovanni Battista Pinacci (Bajazet), Antonio Montagnana (Leone), Anna Strada (Asteria), and Francesca Bertolli (Irene)—all at the original pitch. Campioli, Pinacci, and Montagnana were new to London. Only Montagnana was favoured with fresh music, a substantial recitative ('Principessa fedele') and aria ('Nel mondo e nell'abisso') at the start of III vii. The aria was not the piece beginning with the same words sung by Boschi in *Riccardo Primo*, but an extensive reworking, finer and much longer, transposed from C minor to B minor. Handel used material from both sections (with different words in the B section), sometimes not in the same order, and developed it with greater resource, broadening the main vocal entries and enriching the orchestra; the cellos are several times detached from the bass line. This was the first music he composed for Montagnana. It remains unpublished. He cut more than 250 lines of recitative—none of them from the throne-room and death scenes, and only one passage of twelve bars early in the supper scene—and (astonishingly) the trio, and probably shortened three arias.[49] The future Earl of Egmont was present at an early rehearsal on 1 November, 'where I saw the Duke of Lorain sing a part'. This was Francis, Duke of Lorraine, later Grand Duke of Tuscany and husband of the Empress Maria Theresa. He attended the first

---

[48] Opinions were divided; Lady Mary Wortley Montagu called it 'execrable', but the *Newcastle Courant* of 14 Nov. reported that the company 'continue performing Mr. Handel's new celebrated Opera ... with such great applause from the Nobility, and all the Audience, that 'tis order'd by the Royal Academy to be play'd six Weeks successively.' If so, the order was countermanded. (Gibson, *The Royal Academy*, 212, 215).

[49] See below, pp. 565–6. The B section of 'Forte e lieto' was shortened and simplified.

two public performances, accompanied on the first night by the Austrian Ambassador Count Kinsky and the British Royal Family in force.

Tamerlano furnished few concert favourites. Jane Barbier sang 'Bella Asteria' at her Lincoln's Inn Fields benefit on 28 March 1726, and Ann Turner Robinson an aria announced as 'Padre amante' at her benefit at Drury Lane on 26 March 1729. This is more likely to have been 'Cor di padre e cor d'amante' than 'Padre amato', which had not been performed or published. Handel introduced 'Figlia mia' with new words in his pasticcio *Oreste* at Covent Garden on 18 December 1734. 'Ciel e terra', 'Non è piu tempo', and 'A suoi piedi' were included in the Handel pasticcio *Lucio Vero* at the King's Theatre on 14 November 1747. The overture enjoyed several performances, at Ann Turner Robinson's Drury Lane benefit on 26 March 1729, and the New Theatre in the Haymarket on 27 November 1733, and at the Manchester Subscription Concerts on 19 February and 9 July 1745.

On 27 September 1725 (NS) *Tamerlano* was produced at Hamburg in an arrangement by Telemann, translated by Johann Philipp Praetorius, which made a sorry mess of Handel's opera, especially the throne-room scene. Bajazet's arias were replaced by seven (including an extra one in German) apparently composed by the British resident, Cyril Wych,[50] who had had lessons from the young Handel at Hamburg in 1703. Handel's remaining arias and Bajazet's recitative after 'Figlia mia' were sung in Italian. Telemann reset the other recitatives in German and contributed a prologue in honour of the wedding of Louis XV of France to the Polish princess Maria Leszczyńska, both on texts by Praetorius. He inserted ballets in all three acts and German choruses in the first two. The scene of Irene's arrival with Leone in Act I was transferred to the foot of Mount Olympus, with a dance for highlanders and their women ('Bergleute nebst ihren Weibern'), and Tamerlano's prospective wedding to Asteria in Act II celebrated by Tartars with drawn swords, round whom Love twined myrtles as they danced. An Entrée of knights and ladies preceded the final *coro*. Loewenberg's statement that Telemann's *Pimpinone* was probably performed as an intermezzo between the acts lacks confirmation in contemporary sources, though an intermezzo by him is mentioned in the libretto. Thomas Lediard included a design for the prologue in his 1730 volume of pyrotechnical engravings.[51] The balance of voices, as usual at Hamburg, was hopelessly compromised. Bajazet was sung by Campioli, an alto castrato (Handel's Tamerlano in 1731), Andronico by the elder Riemschneider, a bass, Tamerlano by another bass, Ernst Carl Ludwig Westenholz. The rest of the cast was: Leone: Bahn (bass); Asteria: Dominichina Pollone (soprano); Irene: Monjo the elder (contralto); Zaida: Madame Sellini, presumably a dancer (she has nothing to sing).

The first modern revival took place in 1924 at Karlsruhe in a German version by A. Rudolph and Herman Roth. This was revised for Leipzig in 1925 and used again, sometimes modified, in a number of other German opera houses up to 1962. One or both of the castrato parts were taken by basses. At the first British revival (Birmingham, 1962) only Tamerlano suffered this indignity; Andronico was sung by Catherine Wilson, Bajazet by Alexander Young, Irene by Janet Baker. The first modern stage performance

[50] W. Schulze, *Die Quellen der Hamburger Oper (1678–1738)* (Hamburg, 1938), 49–50.
[51] See pp. 565–6.

with the voices correctly pitched was given by students under Eric Cross, also at Birmingham, in 1975. The recording by Cambridge Records (1970) likewise kept the original pitches. Later recordings by Jean-Claude Malgoire and John Eliot Gardiner were faithful in this respect but put themselves out of court by ruining the Act II finale. The Welsh National Opera production in 1982 misconceived the entire nature of the work. An authentic staging in a major operahouse is long overdue.

Autograph

The autograph of *Tamerlano* (RM 20 c 11)[52] is of a daunting complexity— more so in some respects even than that of *Giulio Cesare*—but there is enough evidence to disentangle nearly all stages of Handel's work. Of the 128 leaves remaining in the manuscript (a few were evidently torn out by Handel himself) more than 40 are insertions introduced between the dating of the last page and the first performance three months later. The changes were made on at least six different occasions, probably more, and there were further important modifications, not shown in the autograph, before and after the copying of the performing score. As with *Giulio Cesare*, some of them must have been made on an intermediate score that has not survived.

The original draft of July 1724 can be deduced partly from Handel's foliation (on every eighth side, beginning each act with a new series), though this breaks down towards the end of Act III, and partly from his use of the 1711 libretto with additions by Haym. It did not include the overture. Act I comprised ff. 10, 13–18, 20–34, and 37–42; Act II ff. 43, 45–9, two lost leaves, 55–6, 59–61, 63–7, 70–3, ? two lost leaves, 75, and 79–81; Act III ff. 83–5, 88–97, 100–10, and probably 120–1 and 123–8. This draft contained (apart from lesser variants) a word-for-word setting of the first scene in the 1711 libretto (56 bars of recitative for Andronico and Bajazet, of which Chrysander inexplicably omitted the first 47, followed by the aria 'Conservate [originally 'Custodite'] per mia figlia', HG 147), the soprano (A) versions of Irene's arias 'Dal crudel' and 'Par che mi nasca', and subsequently rejected settings of 'Non è più tempo', 'Cerco in vano' (of which only the first page survives), the B section of 'A suoi piedi', and all three ariettas at the end of Act II. Bajazet's accompanied recitative in the throne-room (HG 75–7) had important differences and continuo accompaniment only; Andronico's recitatives 'Chi vide mai' in I ix and 'Ah nò! dove trascorri' in II iii and Asteria's 'Padre, amante' in III viii were similarly planned but not executed. There were significant variants in the trio, including a four-bar initial ritornello. Act II ended with Asteria's 'Cor di padre'; all its last five set pieces, and all four of Asteria's intervening recitatives, were subsequently altered, some of them more than once.[53] Act III had a different opening recitative (HG 150–1), the A setting of Bajazet's 'Su la sponda' (152–3), and a C minor aria for Tamerlano, 'Fiero, mi rivedrete' (155–6), at the end of Scene iii.

[52] Facsimile published in the Garland series, ed. H. M. Brown.

[53] Handel's foliation suggests that two leaves are missing after f. 73, which ends with Asteria's recitative 'Padre, dimmi' as on HG 150, followed by *Segue l'aria di Bajazet*. If so, it is impossible to guess what they contained. The G minor setting of 'Nò, nò, ch'il tuo sdegno' (HG 150), unquestionably part of the original autograph, is on f. 75 (Plate 12), the E minor setting that replaced it on the inserted f. 74.

There is some doubt about the last scene, owing to the breakdown of Handel's foliation. The duet 'Vedrò ch'un dì' (HG 124), which in the autograph—but nowhere else—has *NB Attacca il recitativo* after the da capo, was followed by an unpublished version of Scene ix (f. 110) in which Asteria is the first to announce Bajazet's death, after which Leone says that he took poison on discovering the failure of Orcamo's rescue attempt. (Haym shuffled the words of Piovene's Scenes xiii and xiv.) Handel made two attempts at a secco setting of Asteria's declaration of implacable hatred for Tamerlano, 'Sì, Bajazette è morto', then on a fresh page, probably an early insertion (ff. 111–12), reset it very impressively with string accompaniment. This version is unpublished, but some of its words and musical ideas, including another rising chromatic bass, recur in 'Mirami' (HG 133). The recitative ended with the words 'rendimi che gettò la mia vendetta' and (like its successor) a C sharp major cadence. It was almost certainly followed by the F sharp minor aria 'Padre amato', which occupies two complete leaves (ff. 120–1). Strohm[54] considers this a later insertion, since the 1719 libretto gives Asteria an aria beginning with the same two words, and suggests that in rejecting the aria before performance Handel was actuated by the same motives as Gasparini: Asteria's 'Padre amato, a te verrò', though in the Reggio libretto, is not in the Meiningen score, which jumps from Bajazet's death to the last scene ('Seguitela', as HG 136), omitting Scene xvii altogether. But, as we have seen, Handel's 'Padre amato, in me riposa' is based on Piovene's 1711 aria 'Svena, uccidi', reproducing nearly half its six-line text with the words in a different order. Another of Asteria's 1711 arias, at the end of Act I, begins 'Padre amato'; Handel or Haym conflated the two.

Next came another unpublished recitative (f. 126ᵛ) on an expanded version of Piovene's last scene, quoting three lines from it; the duet 'Coronata di gigli' (ff. 123–5) on the words of Piovene's *coro*; the recitative 'Ora invitta regina' on words supplied by Haym (HG 141; ff. 125ᵛ–126ʳ); and the new *coro* 'D'atra notte' with the date at the end. The only oddity is that Handel should have finished the last recitative on the other side of one that comes earlier. It is possible to think of several explanations. The most likely is that Haym supplied the new words of the recitative on f. 126ᵛ after Handel had composed 'Padre amato' and the duet; Handel then set them on a single side, squeezing in the music and overrunning into the bottom margin, and later, in a characteristic effort to save paper, used the upper staves on the other side for the last few bars of the recitative before the *coro*. In this draft Handel and Haym extended Piovene's last scene, presumably in an attempt to make Tamerlano's change of mind more convincing. Instead they produced an anticlimax, the more so as at this stage they did nothing to stiffen Andronico's feeble reaction to Asteria's distress. In Piovene he merely tells Zaida to look after her; in Handel's first draft he makes a half-hearted attempt to follow her into the wings, but is easily dissuaded when Tamerlano relents. The suicide attempt came in with the 1719 libretto.

Handel made many changes before Borosini's arrival. Their exact chronology cannot be precisely dated; a few—like the accompanied recitative 'Sì, Bajazette è morto'—may have been introduced while he was still working on the first draft. Probably among the earliest were cuts of six bars in 'Conservate per mia figlia' (before the first word was changed) and eight in 'Vo' dar pace',

---

[54] *HJb* (1975), 119; *Essays*, 50–1.

the rewriting of a substantial passage in the latter aria (f. 19), the lengthening of the opening recitative of Act II (f. 44: Handel may have been repairing an accidental omission, for all the words are in Piovene), the second settings of 'Non è più tempo', 'Cerco in vano', and 'Sù la sponda' (HG 153–4), and perhaps the parodying of stronger words ('Empi, se mi sdegnate') in 'Fiero, mi rivedrete' in III iii. The alto versions of Irene's first two arias were also early; the B minor cadence before 'Dal crudel' cannot have been filled in before the aria was transposed from B flat to G. It is not known when Dotti became available. Handel wrote the entire part in the soprano clef, and when he reached the *coro* he still did not know who was to sing it: he placed the initials of the singers (Senesino, Pacini, Boschi) against the three lowest parts, but Irene's name before the top line.

The overture almost certainly originated as a separate piece in two movements only. Handel added the name of the opera in a different ink, the Adagio perhaps later, and the Minuet certainly later still. Both Leone's arias were insertions. Originally he had none (as in Piovene), and Haym supplied the words. The changes at the end of Act II are more complex. They seem to have been made in at least four stages. The first was probably the cancellation of the original setting of Andronico's 'Nò, che del tuo gran cor' (f. 75), omitted by Chrysander. It is a simple piece in binary form with repeats (3/4, E major), and like the other ariettas has a brief ritornello (five bars) at the end only. As in the later setting, the top instrumental line (*Travers. senza Viol.*) doubles the voice in octaves (except at the first cadence) until the ritornello, which has a *Tutti forte* top line and a viola part. The whole piece is cancelled in ink (see Plate 12). Since the previous recitative, which would have been composed later, apparently ended on a D sharp chord[55] before Handel changed it to G sharp (as on HG 150), it seems probable that this arietta was replaced very soon by another piece in a different key which has been lost. The second setting of Irene's 'Nò, che sei tanto' in the alto clef (f. 77) was presumably composed when her first two arias were transposed for Dotti. At the same time Handel adjusted the two opening bars of Asteria's next recitative, 'Si, sì, son vendicata', which had originally begun as well as ended in D major. The subtle key scheme of this scene was a gradual evolution. Next perhaps came the final (?third) 4/4 setting of 'Nò, che del tuo gran cor' (f. 76). Three further alterations to this scene are mentioned below.

What had happened so far was as nothing compared with the upheaval caused by the arrival in September of Borosini with the 1719 libretto and Gasparini's score. This affected both words and music and was responsible for ff. 6–9, 11–12, 62, 68–9, 74, 78, 82, 113–19, and 122, as well as ff. 41–3 and 46–8 of RM 20 d 2. Handel proceeded to rewrite the opening scene no fewer than four times, making five versions in all. The first, that of the original draft, headed *Cortile nel Palazzo di Tamerlano. Bajazete, et Andronico*, is on ff. 10 and 13–15. Chrysander omitted all the recitative on f. 10, but printed the rest in HG 147–8, beginning with the word 'morte' on the second line. Scene ii (HG 10) came immediately after 'Conservate per mia figlia'. In his second version (ff. 7–9) Handel prefixed a scene for Bajazet alone in chains (*Bajazet incatenato fra guardie*) to the original opening. It consisted of a substantial arioso, 'Lacci, ferri', after which Andronico enters and sings 4½ lines of recitative, ordering the guards to release him (HG 145–7, second line). The words, in neither

[55] The heavy cancellation makes this difficult to read.

Gasparini libretto, are presumably Haym's, but the music shows acquaintance with Gasparini's setting of 'Forte e lieto'.[56] Next (ff. 11–12) Handel scrapped everything he had written so far and evolved the scene as printed in HG 5–7, but without the two Largo sinfonias and with 'passo' for 'piede' in the third bar of Andronico's recitative. This uses the 1719 text both for the recitative and for the new aria 'Forte e lieto', which is not in the main autograph.[57] In this form Smith copied the scene into the performing score. But Handel had not finished. Evidently feeling that a secco opening lacked dramatic weight, he produced the version on HG 149 (f. 78), a sinfonia derived from 'Lacci, ferri' framing Andronico's first recitative (with 'passo' changed to 'piede' in bar 3) and a recitative cued into the third version at bar 14 on HG 6. This may have seemed too long drawn out. The fifth and final version (f. 6, *doppo l'Ouverture*), essentially the same as the third plus the two shorter sinfonias and with 'piede' for 'passo', must have been written very shortly before the first night.

The Borosini revision produced major changes in the second and third acts. In Act II Handel composed a longer and finer B section for 'A suoi piedi', exploiting Borosini's bottom A (f. 62), reset Bajazet's big recitative in the throne-room with string accompaniment, including the four bars marked *Versione prima* on HG 77, and wrote the E minor setting of his 'Nò, nò, il tuo sdegno' (f. 74), though not in the form printed by Chrysander. Asteria's recitatives before and after this were altered at the same time, and so was 'Amica, son quella' (its third version, top of HG 84), for it follows the fourth version of I i on the verso of f. 78. Folios 6, 62, and 74 are a distinctive type of rough Italian paper of smaller format, found nowhere else in the autograph.

In Act III the second setting of 'Sù la sponda', which shares with the first a higher tessitura than Handel generally used for Borosini, was transferred to Asteria an octave higher and then almost certainly replaced by another aria for her, 'Quando il fato', the text of which is adapted from an aria for Bajazet at this point in the 1719 libretto. The music, a graceful Largo in B flat, survives in three copies but not in autograph. The key would equally fit the end of Act II, but Handel never placed so light-boned an aria in such a prominent position. At the end of III iii he replaced 'Empi, se mi sdegnate' with another new aria, 'A dispetto', again modifying the 1719 text. The most important change of course was the insertion of Bajazet's death scene, together with a new Scene ix (HG 125), on ff. 113–18, taken directly from the 1719 libretto. The recitatives on HG 132–3 and 136 were composed at the same time, but not before Handel had written out the words of 'Mirami' for continuo accompaniment. The dramatic novelty was Andronico's threat of suicide. This troublesome conclusion had still not reached its final form.

Two further stages of work can be traced. It is clear that when Handel wrote his first draft he had no acquaintance with Borosini's voice. He used too high a tessitura, which he had to adjust downwards throughout the opera (except in 'Empio, per farti guerra'). These numerous changes were not made in the autograph, but (with one exception) they had been incorporated when the performing score was copied. Hence our supposition of a lost intermediate copy. The scenes most affected were I vi ('Ciel e terra', composed in E major, was put down to D and the previous twenty bars of recitative rewritten), II vii

---

[56] See Ex. 61, p. 540.   [57] See below, pp. 562–3.

(Chrysander's upper notes in the A section of 'A suoi piedi' are the original, the lower those for Borosini), II ix (Chrysander prints both versions in bars 15 and 16 on HG 71, but only the later and longer, with 1719 text, on the seventh and eighth systems of HG 73), II x (Bajazet's part in the trio was lowered and otherwise adjusted in four places), III i (Chrysander prints the higher original with 1711 text on HG 150–1, the replacement with 1719 text in the main score[58]), and III viii ('E il soffrirete', HG 118; the higher first version is unpublished).

The changes made on the intermediate score were not confined to Bajazet's tessitura, or indeed to his part. They included verbal amendments in bars 4–6 of I vi (HG 22), little more than a change of pronouns, the composition of the viola part in 'Ciel e terra', which is not in the autograph but was written before the transposition (it is in the Flower copy in E major), the violin part in bars 100–3 of 'A suoi piedi', the removal of the string accompaniment from the last four bars of Bajazet's accompanied recitative in the throne-room, the elimination of the trio's opening ritornello, a new setting of bars 46–53 of the E minor 'Nò, nò, il tuo sdegno', and the insertion of bar 70, the voice's unaccompanied dotted minim G, in 'Empio, per farti guerra' (top of HG 121). Two modifications not connected with Bajazet were the short B version of the last scene (HG 141), of which there is no autograph, and the reconstruction of the Minuet in the overture, mentioned below. A number of missing tempo marks were also supplied: *Grave* at the end of the overture's Allegro (HG 3), *Largo* on 'Forte e lieto', *Larghetto* on 'Padre amato', and *Allegro* on 'Dammi pace', 'A dispetto', and 'Empio, per farti guerra'.

A last group of revisions dates from after the copying of the performing score. Some of them—the fifth version of I i, the revised opening recitative of III i, which compelled Smith to copy its first bar on the last page of Act II— have already been mentioned. Others were the insertion of the Adagio and Minuet of the overture,[59] the removal of 'Cor di padre' from the end of Act II to oust 'Quando il fato' in III i, and its replacement by 'Se potessi', of which no autograph survives. It could have been a late addition to the intermediate score. Clausen's evidence on the structure of the Hamburg copy suggests that 'A dispetto' replaced 'Empi, se mi sdegnate' at this stage, and that Leone's 'Se ad un costante core' was torn out. Finally Handel shortened Act III by cutting the Irene–Tamerlano duet and Chrysander's A version of the last scene, substituting the recitative on HG 141. The Minuet of the overture presents a puzzle. It is an insertion in the autograph, where the many cancellations prove that Handel was composing, not copying. The Hamburg version, printed by Chrysander, shows many differences including a simpler viola part, fewer grace notes, and an altered approach to the final cadence. They are scarcely improvements, and it is not clear why Handel introduced them.

A volume of autograph fragments, RM 20 d 2 (ff. 41–52), contains three late additions to the 1724 score, 'Forte e lieto', 'Amor da guerra', and 'A dispetto', and the *scena* composed for Montagnana in 1731, headed *Atto 3° Scena 7*. 'Forte e lieto' and 'A dispetto' have no tempo marks. In 'Forte e lieto' the five bars beginning with the last beat of bar 12 and ending with the third

---

[58] This change seems to have been made a little later than the others, for it is an insertion in the Hamburg copy.

[59] They were probably added after the first performance, since they are not in the Cluer score or the Malmesbury copy.

beat of bar 17 are represented by a longer passage of nine bars, all heavily cancelled in ink. The cuts were made in two stages: four bars between the third
and fourth beats of bar 14 probably during composition (they are in no other
source), the remainder after the performing score was copied but perhaps before
performance, though Cluer printed them. Originally the first-violin semiquavers
were not slurred but tied across the beat. Chrysander did not see these fragments, which contain a number of other minor variants. The top line in 'Amor
da guerra' is *Tutti unis.* at the start,[60] as in most copies. Handel's corrections in
this aria contain so many *NB* marks—more than two dozen—as to suggest that
Smith had already copied it in its earlier form. The vocal cadence in the B section of 'A dispetto' is marked *Ad[agio]*.

Including early versions with significant variants but omitting secco recitatives, no fewer than 26 pieces were transformed or rejected before the first
performance of *Tamerlano*, an even larger number than in *Giulio Cesare.*
Chrysander printed fifteen of them in his main score, in smaller type at the
foot of the page, or in the appendix. They vary widely in quality, from a dull
first setting of 'Nò, che del tuo gran cor' and the unpromising fragment of the
first setting of 'Cerco in vano'[61] (in the distinctive rhythm of 'Col valor' in the
fragmentary Charles VI cantata, HWV 119, 'Secondaste al fine' in *Il pastor
fido* and Ino's 'Above measure' in *Semele*) to some magnificent music for Asteria
and Bajazet. 'Sì, Bajazette è morto', 'Quando il fato', 'Padre amato', 'Lacci,
ferri', the sinfonia based on it, and both settings of 'Sù la sponda' are of
outstanding quality. Of the latter, both in B flat minor, the first was later
adapted for 'Col celarvi' in *Alcina*; the second, though the top line is marked
for unison violins, is followed by an oboe part in A minor (*la Hautbois transposée
in A*, not *les Hautbois* as in HG). This does not mean that Handel intended the
aria to be performed in that key; as in 'Amor, nel mio penar' in *Flavio*, also in B
flat minor, he treated the oboe as a transposing instrument (see note, p. 482).

The autograph has other points of interest. Handel composed 'Bella
Asteria' with the voice part in the alto clef, which he never used for Senesino;
was this a slip of memory, or did he toy with the idea of giving Andronico to
Pacini? At the bottom of the first page of the *coro* (f. 127) he wrote what
appears to be an alternative text: 'Chi sospira per amore sia costante e goderà'.
This does not fit the music of 'D'atra notte', and may have been considered for
another setting. Many pieces were extensively revised during the composition
of the first draft, notably 'Vo' dar pace', 'Se non mi vuol', the first version of
'Non è più tempo' (which suffered four cuts, and originally had two dal segno
bars leading from the B section to bar 5), the B section of 'Coronata di gigli',
and 'Folle sei'. This little piece shows great care for detail, moving always
towards simplification: at first Handel doubled the agitated phrase 'Il tiranno
poi vivrà' with the violins, and he cut a three-bar repeat of the opening words
after bar 9. He had trouble with the A section cadences of 'Dammi pace' and
'Deh! lasciatemi'; in the latter he first took the violins up to a held top D. The
evolution of the second version of 'Non è più tempo' out of the first is
fascinating. All the secondary ideas are present in both, including the last
three bars of the witty ritornello after the A section; only the main theme was

---

[60] So in the main autograph is that of 'Più d'una tigre'.

[61] This aria must once have been complete. It is fully written out as far as it goes, and the next
two folios are missing. The opening survives because the recto of the leaf carries part of the first
setting of 'Non è più tempo' which Handel salvaged for the second.

originally different and weaker, though it had a similar undulating motion and essentially the same rhythm, and was likewise repeated with the violins doubling the voice. The cuts in the first version removed further appearances of the three-note figure introduced in bars 7 and 8; Handel multiplied its effectiveness by reserving it for the latter part of the A section and the ritornello. The entire autograph bears witness to the profuseness of Handel's invention and the immense trouble he took over dramatic expression.

Librettos

1724. 'Drama . . . Printed and Sold at the King's Theatre in the Hay-Market.' 99 pp. In his Italian dedication to the third Duke of Rutland (1696–1779) Haym claims merely to have arranged (*accomodato*) the drama for the directors of the Royal Academy. He gives two reasons for approaching his patron: the Duke's known love of music, and his own service to the Duke's father and the Bedford and Devonshire families. Haym's first London post (*c.*1701) had been as chamber cellist to the second Duke of Bedford. Burney describes Rutland as 'a most intelligent judge both of the theory and practice of the art', and says that 'it is well known that [he] was an excellent performer on the violin; that his grace brought Carbonelli hither from Italy, when he returned from his tour through that country; and that the solos which this musician dedicated to him, were composed expressly for his use'. Burney wrongly calls him the first Duke. According to Chrysander Rutland played in court concerts under Handel.

In place of an Argument there is a less formal address 'To the Reader' in Italian and English, lifted from Piovene's libretto and quoted above. Leone's recitative and aria in III vi, the duet 'Vedrò ch'un dì', and Chrysander's A version of the last scene are not in the libretto. There are two minor textual variants: 'Bajazet, ma son figlia' for 'Bajazet è il mio padre' in Asteria's accompanied recitative 'Padre, amante' (HG 116, bars 5–7), and 'Questo pianto' instead of 'Tu spietato' immediately after 'Figlia mia' (bottom of HG 129). The former was a modification of Handel's. He first wrote out the words as in the libretto, then set them as printed in HG. 'Questo pianto' is in the Malmesbury copy and must have been considered, though autograph, performing score, and 1719 libretto all have 'Tu spietato'. Chrysander, who used the libretto (e.g. for the heading of I i), omitted a number of stage directions, of which the most important are *Parte con Leone* after Irene's 'Dal crudel' (HG 37), *Sala con trono* at the head of II ix (HG 71), and *Parte, ma restano le guardie* at Leone's exit in III v (HG 101).

1725 Hamburg. 'Tamerlan In einem SING-SPIELE auf dem Hamburgischen Schau-Platze vorgestellet . . . Gedruckt mit Stromerischen [*sic*] Schrifften.' The address to the reader by J. P. Praetorius, the German translator, paraphrases Piovene–Haym and sometimes quotes verbatim. It explains that the recitatives had to be reset to the German text, but in part of Act III (after 'Figlia mia') the Italian was kept in order not to damage the *Affekt*. The arias, except a new one for Bajazet, 'Zögre nicht mich bald zu tödten', in the middle of II x (HG 76), are in Italian with German versions alongside. Handel is named as composer of the opera, Telemann of the intermezzo, though no text for this or the prologue is included. There is an additional scene with German chorus ('Liebe, Liebe, dein Geschicke') before Irene's entry in I viii, and another ('Die Schönheit bedarf nicht') at the start of the throne-room scene

(II ix), repeated at the end before Irene's entry in II x. Both these choruses and the Act III *coro* are associated with ballet Entrées. Some recitatives, for example in III v, are much shortened. The trio is headed *Aria* and, like the three following ariettas, given a da capo. Four misprints are indicated with corrections on the final page. The basic text was evidently derived from the London libretto: the pieces cut by Handel are missing, and the recitative at the bottom of HG 129 begins 'Questo pianto'.

1726 Hamburg. Title as last except for date and correction of 'Stromer-ischen' in imprint to 'Stromerschen'. The text follows 1725 except that no cast is named and the corrigenda on the final page have been incorporated.

1731. 'Drama . . . Printed and Sold by T. Wood in Little-Britain.' 77 pp. This is not a cut down 1724 libretto, but a complete resetting in different type. The reference to the Royal Academy in the title and Haym's dedication are omitted; his address to the reader appears in English only. The text omits the trio and makes extensive cuts in the recitative of all three Acts: 25 passages in all, corresponding very nearly to those in the performing score (see below). The new recitative and aria for Leone appear as III vii, adding one to each number up to the end of the opera.

Copies and Editions

The performing score (Hamburg MA/1056) was copied by Smith and H1, who took over at III ix and continued till the end (ff. 128–43 and 145–7; 144 is a Smith insertion). The work was done at a late stage, after the engagement of Dotti and arrival of Borosini. Bajazet's part had already been adjusted to the lower tessitura (except in the inserted recitatives of III i), and Irene's first three arias in their alto versions are an integral part of the score. Her recitatives however remain in the soprano clef. As already noted, the upper instruments in 'Par che mi nasca' are clarinets. The late pre-performance changes have been listed above; the folios inserted at this stage were 7 (Adagio and Minuet of the overture, probably H5[62]), 8, 92–5, 98, 102–5, and 144 (Smith). Although a fair amount of recopying was required at the end of Act II and in the first three scenes of Act III, the recitative cadences before 'Cor di padre' and 'A dispetto' were transcribed without alteration. Leone's recitative and aria 'Se ad un costante core' are missing. The Irene–Tamerlano duet and the final scene in Chrysander's A version are cancelled on their final pages; the remainder must have been stitched or otherwise concealed. The *coro* bears no names of characters or singers. It has no tempo mark in any source.

A number of cuts were made by pasted slips, since removed. Not all can be dated. Among them are the Adagio of the overture (probably 1731), the five bars from the last beat of bar 12 of 'Forte e lieto'[63] (perhaps before performance; they are not in the Malmesbury copy), the entire opening ritornello of 'Se non mi rendi', and four passages in 'A dispetto': the third beat of bar 19 to the second beat of bar 21, bar 37, the third beat of bar 47 to the second beat of bar 49, and bars 69–75. The last two are very early cuts, made in the Malmesbury and Flower copies; the first two may have been an accommodation for Campioli, an unsuccessful singer, in 1731; the effect of all four is to reduce the load of coloratura. Cuts that certainly date from 1731 are

---

[62] Clausen says H4, but that symbol embraces more than one copyist.
[63] The segno at bar 6 was added in 1731, when the B section was shortened.

the suppression of the trio (indicated by *Parte* in a different hand after Tamerlano's recitative on HG 78) and of numerous passages in the recitative. Adjustments and transpositions to form new links were partly written by Handel. Since these cuts may be useful for modern performances, they are listed here. They amount to some 255 bars, more than half of them in Act I. The long throne-room recitatives are not cut at all.

I ii. 'E nel suo amante'—'l'amor del padre', 'Il Tamerlan non usurpa'—'a vostro grado', 'Signor, tutto il mio sangue'—'E d'onde il colpo', 'Ah! sì, che io sono'—'Ahi, fiero colpo' (the 1731 libretto also omits the short passage linking these two cuts).

I iii. 'Non sapevi'—'anco me stesso'.

I iv. 'Il fortunato Andronico'—'alle catene? ingrato!', 'Oggi, se voi bramate'—'ottenne da voi', 'Io lo dico'—'anzi lo bramo' (the libretto also cuts the next two words, 'il Greco'), 'Udite il Greco'—'pace e vita'.

I v. 'Ah! indegno!'—'ch'era rivale'.

I vi. 'Or l'ambition'—'mà per se stesso', 'Io rispondo per lei'—'Non più! ti dissi'.

I vii. 'Credete ciò'—'ah! principessa', 'Non consento'—'se lo temete'.

I viii. 'Quella sposa'—'ogni altro incontro?'

II i. 'Ecco al fine—'ancor veduta?'

II ii. 'Voi mio amante?'—'a un fido amante'.

II iv. 'Legga in volto'—'e la mia scusa', 'Non arrossite'—'e Irene io sono', 'Sappi, che il soglio'—'misurare il dono'.

II v. 'Basta; e sappi'—'o discesa'.

II vi. 'Gran cose'—'Irene insieme'.

III ii. 'Irritato ed effeso'—'i suoi trionfi', 'E chi seppe'—'non me lo chiede'.

III v. 'Asteria, allor che andate'—'mai contenta', 'Anche ciò contro me?'—'m'opprime i sensi'.

III vi. 'Ella Andronico adora'—'torni nemica'.

The new recitative and aria for Montagnana in 1731 are in the score, but wrongly bound in Act I (ff. 38–43), perhaps because the copy (Smith) is headed merely *Scena 7ª Leone Solo*. This does not explain Chrysander's failure to print them.

The Malmesbury score is the work of an erratic and unmethodical copyist (probably H5); the form of his rests is unpredictable and his bass clef changes radically after p. 93 (a recto), though it reverts once or twice to the old type. Elizabeth Legh did not date the score, but it is very early, probably 1724. The overture has no Adagio or Minuet. Bars 12–17 of 'Forte e lieto' are already cut, and so are the last two passages in 'A dispetto'. 'Par che mi nasca' (with the upper instruments not named) is *Non troppo allegro*; 'Folle sei' is *Largo* at bar 1 and the last beats of bars 5 and 11, *Allegro* for the dotted figure in bars 4 and 10; 'Figlia mia' is *Larghetto*. 'Cerco in vano' has an erroneous 3/4 signature, possibly a survival from the discarded first setting. The recorders are omitted from the duet 'Vivo in te'. An appendix, in the same hand and evidently copied at the same time, gives many pieces suppressed before performance: 'Lacci, ferri' (HG 145), 'Quando il fato' (Asteria), 'Conservate per mia figlia' (HG 147), recitative 'Or manca solo' (HG 132, bottom line) leading to 'Mirami' and 'Padre amato', 'Se ad un costante core' (*Allegro*, without recitative), 'Empi, se mi sdegnate' (= 'Fiero, mi rivedrete', HG 155), 'Sù la sponda' (version B, HG 153, for Asteria in the soprano clef, with no instruments named and no oboe part at the end but many more slurs than in HG), and the two duets 'Coronata di gigli' (*Allegro assai*) and 'Vedrò ch'un dì' (*Allegro*).

The Flower score (S2) is a most eccentric compilation, assembled (*c.* 1740) partly from the autograph and partly from the Malmesbury copy. It cannot reflect any performance. There is an appendix of twenty 'Additional Songs', of which in fact three are accompanied recitatives, two duets, and two fragments. The main score gives the autograph form of the Minuet, the alto versions of 'Dal crudel' and 'Nò, che sei tanto', but the soprano 'Par che mi nasca' with flutes (perhaps because Jennens would not be expected to command cornetti or clarinets)—preceded however by the recitative cadence as altered for alto. 'Non è più tempo' is in the discarded version; 'A suoi piedi' has its original B section. Bajazet's accompanied recitative in the throne-room and the E minor 'Nò, il tuo sdegno' are in their intermediate states. The trio is as first composed. All the new music for Borosini is in the main score, but almost none of the amendments ascribed above to the intermediate copy; the viola part in 'Forte e lieto' (in E major) and the lower tessitura in 'E il soffrirete' are exceptions. Yet the main score reflects Hamburg and the libretto in giving the final versions of I i and III i, 'Se potessi', and the substantial abridgements in Act III.

The appendix contains three pieces certainly performed in 1724 (the second version of 'Non è più tempo', the alto 'Par che mi nasca'—here with cornetti—and the definitive B section of 'A suoi piedi'), thirteen rejected pieces printed by Chrysander, and four still unpublished: the sixteen-bar fragment of 'Cerco in vano' in E major, Asteria's 'Quando il fato', her accompanied recitative 'Sì, Bajazette è morto', and the first (3/4) setting of 'Nò, che del tuo gran cor'. The trio in its usual form and the B flat soprano 'Dal crudel' appear nowhere. Much of this material can only have been copied from the autograph; we know that Handel allowed discarded and unfinished pieces, and cancelled passages, to be transcribed for Jennens. 'Conservate per mia figlia' even includes the six bars cut before the first word was changed from 'Custodite'; but 'Forte e lieto' and 'A dispetto' are shortened as in Malmesbury. The presence of an abortive viola part (two crotchets) in bar 73 of 'Vo' dar pace' is proof positive of the use of the autograph. This bar immediately precedes a ritornello with viola cancelled by Handel; he carelessly left the two crotchets, and the copyist incorporated them, though they make no sense. It is possible that Handel's *NB* at certain points in the autograph—for example the cut in 'Conservate' and the cancelled 3/4 setting of 'Nò, che del tuo gran cor'—is an instruction to the copyist to include the music for Jennens.

The manuscript omits a number of dynamics and stage directions, but includes the scene heading for II ix and supplies the Malmesbury tempo marks, not in the autograph or Hamburg, for 'Se ad un costante core', 'Vedrò ch'un dì', 'Folle sei', 'Figlia mia', and 'Coronata di gigli'. Jennens himself added the missing *Allegro* to 'Vo' dar pace', 'Dammi pace', and 'Empio, per farti guerra', bass figuring in 'Bella Asteria' (the continuo part as well as the score), 'Forte e lieto', and the opening bars of 'Se non mi vuol', and the date, copied from the autograph, at the end.

The Flower parts (S2)—violins 1 and 2, viola, cello + bassoon, oboes 1 and

2 (including flutes and recorders), and cembalo—were taken (mid-1740s) from the Flower score, but for no discoverable reason omit the overture, 'Nò, che sei tanto', and the *coro* from the main text, and nine of the twenty 'Additional Songs'. The bassoon is mentioned once in 'Dal crudel', where it ousts the cello when their parts diverge, and once in 'Se ad un costante core'. The oboe parts specify flutes in 'Deh! lasciatemi' (where both double the violins throughout, including the parts marked *senza Travers.* in HG 28 and 29, taking the higher octave where their compass requires it), 'Par che mi nasca' (soprano version), and the unpublished 3/4 'Nò, che del tuo gran cor' (with oboes as well in the closing ritornello), flutes and recorders in 'Vivo in te'. The oboe parts are peculiar, occasionally contradicting not only HG but the autograph and S2's usual practice in deriving them. They are included in 'Amor da guerra' and 'Più d'una tigre', correctly following the *Tutti* of the autograph (in both arias Chrysander's bracketed *Violini* are gratuitous), but silent in 'Se non mi vuol', where the Flower score specifies violins only against the autograph's *Tutti*. Most exceptionally the second oboe doubles the second violin in 'Benchè mi sprezzi', where the autograph has *Tutti* against the top line, and in 'Cerco in vano', where neither autograph nor performing score gives any indication of scoring. As usual the tutti passages are more specific than in HG, covering not only main ritornellos but shorter interludes where the voice is silent: for example, the oboes play in bars 50–4 and 120–3 of 'Vo' dar pace', 10, 11, 18, 19, 26, and 27 of 'Dal crudel' (alto), 36–9 of 'Benchè mi sprezzi', 46–8 of 'Bella gara', 47–50 of 'Cerco in vano', 12, 13, 21, and 22 of 'Amor da guerra', 14–16 of 'Più d'una tigre', 52–81 (first beat) and 94 to end of A section of 'Se potessi', 20 (last beat)–22 of 'Crudel più non son io'. This represents standard practice. The second violin is missing from the first 4½ bars of 'Forte e lieto' in the part and the score, an error found also in the Malmesbury copy. The second 'Sù la sponda' (for tenor) appears in the score of the 'Additional Songs' with the transposed oboe part at the end, as in the autograph, but there are no separate parts for this aria.

The Granville copy (S5) gives the 1724 performance version with the addition of the Irene–Tamerlano duet and the long A form of the last scene, but not Leone's recitative and aria in III vi. The recitatives are complete, no piece is shortened, and the Borosini tessitura appears throughout. The score was copied from Hamburg (uncut), which it follows almost exactly in its many omitted stage directions, especially in the throne-room scene (among them the heading of II ix), and in naming clarinets in 'Par che mi nasca'. Although it is a late copy from the 1740s, the sole indication of a post-1731 date is the word *parte* after Tamerlano's recitative before the trio, which may be an addition. The Lennard score on the other hand (Smith, *c.* 1735) reflects most of the 1731 changes, omitting the overture's Adagio, the recitative passages listed above as cancelled in Hamburg, and making all four cuts in 'A dispetto'. It is the only source for the shortened B section of 'Forte e lieto', but does not include the extra scene for Montagnana. The trio and the Irene–Tamerlano duet are present, and 'Se non mi rendi' is complete. Many arias are lazily copied with a da capo instead of their dal segno bars, and a few lack tempo marks; but 'Par che mi nasca' (the top instruments not named) is *Andante*, 'Se potessi' *Andante allegro*, the duet 'Vedrò ch'un dì' *Allegro andante*, and 'Figlia mia' again *Larghetto*. The opening scene is an anomalous compound of two versions: both Largo sinfonias appear in succession after the overture, followed by the recitative 'Esci, O signore' as first composed, with 'passo' in the third bar and leading directly into 'Prence lo so' (HG 6).

A volume of 'Aditions to Tamerlano' in the Shaftesbury Collection (S2, *c.* 1737–9) was intended to supplement the Cluer score. It includes, with page cues, the Adagio and Minuet of the overture, all the accompanied recitatives of the 1724 score, and several unperformed pieces: the duets 'Vedrò ch'un dì' and 'Coronata di gigli', Asteria's accompanied recitative 'Mirami', and her aria 'Padre amato', but not 'Se ad un costante core'. A copy of the Cluer score owned by the late Howard Mayer Brown has, bound in, a similar but less extensive selection (S2 again), mostly concerned with the part of Bajazet. The accompanied recitatives 'Chi vide mai', 'Ah nò! dove trascorri', 'Padre, amante', and 'E il soffrirete' and the two duets are missing. The copyist supplied two tempo marks on 'Folle sei' and cancelled and recopied two printed passages to link up with the insertions. Some pages have added bass figures and other details indicating use in performance. Both these supplements include Asteria's *scena* on HG 133–5; though not performed in the theatre, it was by no means rejected.

The rejected pieces in the Malmesbury appendix (apart from the two bars of secco recitative before 'Mirami') appear again in Add MS 31571, ff. 68–91 (H5, copied *c.* 1724–5 from the intermediate score). The two duets bear the names of the singers for whom they were intended, but the only character named is Tamerlano on 'Empi, se mi sdegnate'. 'Sù la sponda' is in the soprano clef, without the appended oboe part. Smith copied the death scene, together with other portions of Act III (HG 116 to the end of 'Empio, per farti guerra', and 132–5), in Manchester MS 130 Hd4 v. 313, pp. 1–38 (*c.* 1746). This gives the original tessitura of 'E il soffrirete' (the only known copy to do so) and 'Empio, per farti guerra' in its early form without bar 70. The death scene appears again, without characters' names, in RM 18 c 3, ff. 15–22 (S2, *c*, 1728); the overture's Adagio and Minuet (as revised) in RM 19 a 1, ff. 121ᵛ–122 (S2, *c.* 1738); and the final versions of all six accompanied recitatives up to and including 'E il soffrirete' in RM 18 c 10, ff. 92–9 (S2, *c.* 1731–2). In bar 4 of the last recitative S2 made a mistake that appears to be a confused recollection of the early tessitura. Jennens added *Doppo l'Ouverture* before the first recitative. He also wrote out a flute part (in D major) for the G major setting of 'Nò, che sei tanto' in RM 19 a 8.

Handel arranged the main section of the overture for harpsichord, and it appears with treble-and-bass transcriptions (? by copyists) of the Minuet in both its autograph and revised (Hamburg) forms: the former in two Malmesbury volumes (H5, *c.*1724; Smith, *c.*1728) and RM 18 c 1, ff. 39–40 (S2, *c.*1728), the latter in RM 18 c 2, ff. 9–10 (Lambda, *c.*1729). The Minuet alone, autograph form, is in RM 18 b 8, f. 100 (Smith junior, *c.*1728); as revised in Add MS 29386, f. 71ᵛ (same hand as the *Concerto in Otho* in Durham Cathedral MS E 34); and in an intermediate text, perhaps Handel's first attempt at revision, in RM 19 a 1, f. 120ᵛ (S2)[64].

Hamburg MA/180 contains a set of five parts for seven arias in the same hand as Add MS 31577.[65] This is an arrangement intended for vocal or instrumental performance, with *flautino* and *traversa* as alternatives to the voice. The arias are 'Par che mi nasca' in version B (*Larghetto*, C major), 'Se potessi'

---

[64] Handel's arrangement, with all three versions of the Minuet, is printed in *Twenty Overtures*, ii. 20–5, 40, 41.

[65] See pp. 296, 457 and 523.

(*Allegro*, C major), 'Se non mi vuol', 'Deh! lasciatemi', 'Crudel più non son io', 'Più d'una tigre', and 'Non è più tempo', the last three in G major. Transpositions are indicated for different types of flute and recorder. Another selection, in a neat copyist's hand, is in Berlin Staatsbibliothek Mus MS 9056. The eight arias are 'Forte e lieto' (uncut), 'Ciel e terra' (no tempo), 'Benchè mi sprezzi' (no tempo), 'Cerco in vano', 'Par che mi nasca' (B version in C major, *Larghetta*), 'Più d'una tigre', 'Se potessi' (*Allegro*), and 'A dispetto' (uncut). The accompaniments are for one melody instrument and bass, sparsely figured, the voice parts all in the treble clef. The music was not copied from Cluer, but may go back to one of the printed collections. The Coke Collection contains two copies of a binary arietta, 'T'amo tanto, O mio tesoro', described as *In Tamerlin* and very similar to the ariettas at the end of Act II. It is however a song by Ariosti popular in the theatre in 1728.

Cluer published a score on 14 November 1724, only a fortnight after the first night. The handsome title page reads: 'Tamerlane: an Opera Compos'd by Mr Handel And Corrected and Figur'd by his own Hand. Engrav'd on Copper Plates. And to render this Work more acceptable to Gentlemen & Ladies, every Song is *truly Translated* into English Verse [by Henry Carey], & the Words Engrav'd to the Musick under the Italian, which was never done before in any OPERA.'[66] Nor was it done again in any of Handel's. The bass figures, which are far more numerous than in HG, are probably authentic. Cluer printed Handel's Privilege. The text contains no recitatives of either type, but all the set pieces performed in 1724, including 'Folle sei' and 'Figlia mia' with the same tempo marks as in the Malmesbury and Flower copies. The overture lacks the Adagio and Minuet, as in the original state of the Hamburg score. The instrumentation as usual is incomplete, the viola part in particular making capricious appearances, though 'Se non mi vuol', 'Benchè mi sprezzi' and 'Empio, per farti guerra' have all four parts and 'Vivo in te' is laid out with six instrumental staves but no mention of recorders. The dynamics of 'Cor di padre' are simplified. Keys are as in HG. Irene's arias are in the alto versions, the top instruments in 'Par che mi nasca' unspecified, the bassoon part in 'Dal crudel' unnamed but sometimes worked into the viola line. Bajazet's music, including 'A suoi piedi' and the trio, has the Borosini tessitura. There are no cuts in 'Forte e lieto', 'A dispetto', or 'Se non mi rendi'. The full ritornello after the A section is present in 'Non è più tempo' and 'Bella Asteria'. The dal segno is printed correctly in only four of the fifteen pieces that require it; the rest have da capo. There is no tempo mark for 'Ciel e terra', but 'Par che mi nasca' (*Larghetta*), 'Nò, che del tuo gran cor' (*Allegro*), and 'Se potessi' (*Allegro*) supply one missing from the early manuscripts.

Cluer published a selection of *The Favourite Songs* from the same plates, and two similar collections appeared with no imprint except *Printed and Sold at the Musick Shops*. They were evidently pirated from the Cluer score by Walsh, who reused the plates later. The first collection contains nine arias, the second six; each is followed by a flute arrangement, generally in a higher key. The engraving is much coarser than Cluer's. Walsh and Cluer each issued the whole opera for flute, the latter including a tart note ('If J. Cluer's Name is

---

[66] Contrary to Deutsch's statement (175), the translation is not that of the printed libretto, which does not fit the music.

not in the Title Pages of those Works, they are spurrious Editions, and not those Corrected and Figur'd by Mr Handel'), and Benjamin Cooke and Walsh published the overture in parts (complete with the Minuet as in HG) early in 1727. Cooke also advertised a collection of *Favourite Songs* on 20 May 1727, but no copy is known. 'Bella Asteria' appeared on a single sheet (? late 1724); 'Nò, il tuo sdegno' and 'Non è più tempo' in John Browne's *Opera Miscellany* (May 1725), the last two with 'Se potessi' and 'Se non mi vuol' in volume ii of *The Pocket Companion* (23 December 1725), and 'Amor da guerra' in *The Modern Musick-Master*, i (1731), all with English translations or adaptations.

Chrysander's (1876) is the only full score. Exceptionally he prints many, but not all, of Handel's rejected drafts (31–4, 58–60, 77 bottom, 84–5 bottom, 145–56), and includes in his main text pieces that Handel never performed (109–10 bracketed, 123–4, 132–41). His most important omission is the new scene for Montagnana in 1731. Apart from the few dropped stage directions and an occasional dynamic his text is very accurate. Herman Roth's vocal score (Leipzig, 1925) is relatively enlightened for its date. Tamerlano suffers octave transposition to a bass-baritone, but not Andronico. Roth not unreasonably omitted Leone's two arias, Chrysander's A version of the last scene, and two recitatives in Act III, and substituted 'Fiero, mi rivedrete' for 'A dispetto'. But he reduced all the da capo arias and the two duets to their A sections, upsetting the balance with recitatives and ariettas.

Additional Notes

*   (p. 532) Except for the words of the *coro* ('D'atra notte'), which came from Salvi's *Il gran Tamerlano.*

*   (p. 548) A subtle detail: the melisma on 'contenta' (bars 40 ff.) echoes that on 'contento' in Bajazet's arietta 'Nò, nò, il tuo sdegno' (bars 20 ff.) applauding her rejection of the tyrant.

*   (p. 555) Two *Tamerlano* texts (? in Gasparini's 1711 settings) had been sung in London pasticcios, 'Par che mi nasca' by Jane Barbier in *Dorinda* (1712), 'Voglio stragi/Eccoti il petto' as a duet by Nicolini and Diana Vico in *Lucio Vero* (1715).

*   (p. 566) It was copied not from Hamburg but from the presumed intermediate score (? a reference copy, evidently kept up to date). It has far fewer errors than Hamburg and includes very late additions before performance.

*   (p. 570) The flute arrangement, unlike the Cluer score though published only a week later on 21 November, has shortened versions of 'Forte e lieto', 'A dispetto', and 'Se non mi rendi'.

CHAPTER 24

RODELINDA

THE plot has a complex dynastic background set out in the Argument of the printed libretto. Ariberto, King of Lombardy, on his death in 681 divided his realm between his sons, leaving Milan to Bertarido, Pavia to Gundeberto. They went to war over the inheritance, and Gundeberto summoned Grimoaldo, Duke of Benevento, to his assistance, promising the hand of his sister Eduige as reward in the event of Bertarido's defeat. But Gundeberto was killed, apparently through Grimoaldo's treachery. The latter fell in love with Bertarido's wife Rodelinda, rejecting Eduige, and seized the throne of Milan. Bertarido fled to Hungary, leaving Rodelinda and their young son Flavio (a mute part) in the usurper's power. Hoping to rescue them, he put out a report of his own death, persuading the King of Hungary to confirm it in a letter to Grimoaldo, and returned to Milan, the scene of the action, secretly and in disguise. Grimoaldo meanwhile erected a funeral monument to the supposedly dead Bertarido.

Act I.[1] In Rodelinda's apartments in the palace the queen *appears seated in a mournful Posture and weeping* over the loss of her husband, but resolves to live for the sake of their child. Grimoaldo offers to restore her to the throne if she will marry him; she *rises to her feet* and indignantly refuses. He explains to his confederate Garibaldo, Duke of Turin, that he loves the contemptuous Rodelinda and now finds Eduige distasteful. Garibaldo advises him to impress the former by publicly slighting the latter. When Eduige appears Grimoaldo says she scorned him when he wanted her; now he will choose his own consort. She asks Garibaldo why, if he loves her as he claims, he does nothing about it. He *offers to go* and kill Grimoaldo, but Eduige prefers to receive the faithless man as a suppliant and then punish him by offering herself to Garibaldo in his presence. Alone Garibaldo reveals his cynical motive: his 'love' for Eduige is only a means to gain the throne to which Eduige, as Ariberto's daughter, has a claim since Flavio is a minor. The set changes to *a Cypress-Grove in which are seen the Monuments of the Kings of Lombardy; and among them, the Urn newly erected to Bertarido*. Bertarido, *dress'd in an Hungarian Habit*, gloomily contemplates the urn and (aloud) *reads the Inscription on his Tomb*. Where now is his beloved Rodelinda? Unulfo, described as 'Counsellor to Grimoaldo, but a secret Friend of Bertarido', enters and assures him of his loyalty. Bertarido is *going to embrace him*; Unulfo *avoids the Honour of the Embrace*, but *kisses his hand*: he has not told Rodelinda that Bertarido is alive, since she might find it difficult to conceal the fact. Seeing Rodelinda approach *holding Flavio by the hand* Bertarido wants to reveal himself, but Unulfo restrains him. *They retire behind the urn*. Rodelinda *kisses the Urn, and makes Flavio do the like*; with difficulty

---

[1] A number of the Italian stage directions are omitted from the English text; they are translated here.

Unulfo restrains the watching Bertarido. Garibaldo enters *with some of the guards* and a message from Grimoaldo: Rodelinda must marry him at once or Flavio will be put to death. He *takes her Child from her.* Rodelinda *takes back her son,* but to the horror of the observers agrees to the terms; as soon as she is on the throne, however, she will demand Garibaldo's head. Grimoaldo enters and assures Garibaldo that he has nothing to fear. Bertarido, alone with Unulfo, complains that Rodelinda yielded too easily, and now forbids him to tell her that her husband is alive. He decides to wait till Rodelinda has pledged her faith to Grimoaldo and then expose her.

Act II opens in *a Great Hall* in the palace. Eduige, hearing of Grimoaldo's proposed marriage to Rodelinda, takes counsel with Garibaldo, who insists on her marrying him first. Eduige is horrified at Rodelinda's consent; her love for Grimoaldo, whom she helped to gain the throne, changes to hate, and she plans revenge. Rodelinda tells Grimoaldo she will marry him on one condition: that he kills Flavio before her eyes. She cannot be at once a tyrant's wife and the mother of a lawful king. He recoils, turning down Garibaldo's suggestion that he take her at her word; his heart enjoys its captivity. Garibaldo, rebuked by Unulfo, spurns the idea of pity: a usurper can only rule by shedding blood. Unulfo sees that Garibaldo intends to betray the unlawful as he betrayed the lawful king, and rejoices that Rodelinda has remained true to Bertarido. The set changes to *a delightful Prospect.* Bertarido finds all nature in tune with his mournful mood and wanders off. Eduige, *entering on the other side,* at first fancies she recognizes his voice, then, on his *re-entering* to finish his aria, recognizes his person. She is pleased to learn that he wishes only to rescue his wife and child, not to recover his kingdom, which she still hopes to gain for herself. Unulfo assures Bertarido that Rodelinda is true and he need no longer pretend to be dead; he likens himself to a swallow driven from its nest but consoled by a faithful mate. In *a Gallery in Rodelinda's Apartment* the queen hears from Unulfo that Bertarido is alive; she longs to welcome him back. He enters; she *runs to embrace him;* he *stops her* and, *on his knees,* begs forgiveness for doubting her constancy. As she *embraces him* Grimoaldo appears suddenly *with guards* and, not recognizing Bertarido, upbraids Rodelinda for unchastity. Against her wish Bertarido declares himself, outraged by the insult to her honour. Grimoaldo, uncertain whether to believe him, puts him under arrest and tells them to embrace for the last time: whether husband or lover, Bertarido shall die. He leaves them to sing their farewell duet in the presence of the guards.

Act III. In *a Gallery* Eduige and Unulfo plan to rescue Bertarido. She *gives him a key* to a passage leading from his prison through a subterranean vault to the gardens. Both look forward to the rescue; it will enable Eduige to atone for her crime in coveting the kingdom. Garibaldo urges Grimoaldo to kill the prisoner, whether or not he is Bertarido, if he hopes to reign. Grimoaldo hesitates, torn by conflicting emotions: if he consents, how can he hope to make his peace with Rodelinda? In *a very dark Dungeon* Bertarido bewails his fate. *A sword thrown by Eduige falls into the prison.* Bertarido *gropes on the Earth, draws the Sword,*[2] and *smites Unulfo just as he enters* (by means of Eduige's key), mistaking him in the darkness for the executioner. Bertarido *throws away the sword,* but Unulfo *makes him discard his outer garment* lest he be recognized and *puts the sword back in his hand. They go by a secret Passage out of the Prison.* Eduige

[2] Chrysander omits the direction *snuda la spada* at 'Dunque ti stringo' (top of HG 87).

enters *leading Rodelinda and Flavio by the hand.* She *goes out of the Prison* and *returns with a Light;* seeing Bertarido's cloak and fresh blood they assume the worst. Rodelinda *weeps;* she *kneels and embraces her son.*[3] She *rises* and hopes that someone will kill her and end her sufferings. In *a Royal Garden* Bertarido *supports Unulfo wounded; he takes up a Bandage, and ties up the Arm of Unulfo.* Unulfo goes to fetch Rodelinda and Flavio while Bertarido, comparing himself to a wild beast freed from its chain, hides among the trees. Grimoaldo enters, tormented by 'three furies, jealousy, anger and love' and by remorse for his sins: a shepherd sleeps contented by his flock, but he, a king, can find no peace of mind. *After the sinfonia* (of his aria) *he goes to sleep.* Garibaldo enters and *takes the Sword from Grimoaldo's Side, who, waking, speaks.* Garibaldo is about to kill him when Bertarido intervenes and *drives him off the Stage.* Grimoaldo calls for help; *the Guards come up.* Bertarido *returns,* having killed Garibaldo, and *throws the sword at Grimoaldo's Feet.* Rodelinda is astonished to find her husband alive. Unulfo and Eduige explain the rescue. Grimoaldo, *taking Bertarido by the Hand,* renounces the throne of Milan in his favour. He will reign at Pavia with Eduige as his queen.

The ultimate source of this story, as of *Flavio,* is Paul the Deacon's *Gesta Langobardorum.* The two operas have a connection in that the central figure of *Flavio* is Rodelinda's son in adult life; and both librettos are based in part on tragedies by Corneille. *Pertharite, Roi des Lombards* (1652) was not one of his successes. The public apparently objected to the undignified behaviour of the hero, who does not appear till the third of the five acts, having renounced his throne, wife, and child and fled the country, and to Grimoald's abrupt volte face at the end, where he proposes to kill Pertharite in revenge for the death of Garibalde but suddenly changes his mind. Both faults were to some extent remedied in the numerous operatic versions, which stem from Antonio Salvi's *Rodelinda, regina de' Longobardi,* set by G. A. Perti and produced at Pratolino in September 1710.[4] Although Handel had then left Italy, this was the first of the seven Salvi librettos he used for his London operas. Most of these were based on earlier Salvi texts, which Handel may have collected in Florence. Salvi was something of a specialist in French classical tragedy; he had begun his career in 1701 by adapting Racine's *Andromaque* for Perti's *Astianatte.* This was the libretto modified by Haym for Bononcini's opera, produced in London in 1727 but planned in 1725.[5]

The many changes in the Rodelinda story before it reached Handel have been exhaustively chronicled by Emilie Dahnk-Baroffio[6] and need not be repeated here. One or two however must be mentioned, since they left minor obscurities in Handel's opera. In Corneille's drama Gundebert has been killed

---

[3] The libretto omits this direction.

[4] Others are by Giovanni Antonio Canuti (Lucca, 1724), an anonymous *L'amor costante* (Florence, 1725), Giuseppe Boniventi (*Bertarido re de' Longobardi,* Venice, 1727), Bartolomeo Cordans (Venice, 1731), another anonymous composer (Macerata, 1732), and Carl Heinrich Graun (Berlin, 1741). In Canuti's opera Andrea Pacini, Handel's Unulfo a year later, sang Bertarido and Anna Strada Eduige; in *L'amor costante* Garibaldo was an alto castrato part, sung by Giuliano Albertini.

[5] See p. 323.

[6] 'Nicola Hayms Anteil an Händels Rodelinde-Libretto', *Die Musikforschung,* vii (1954) 295–300.

n battle by Pertharite's forces. According to Paul the Deacon he was murdered by Grimoaldo as a result of Garibaldo's insinuations. Salvi evidently accepted this, for although he does not specify the cause of death, he more than once shows Grimoaldo troubled by a guilty conscience and haunted by Gundeberto's shade, notably in some lines cut by Haym from the recitative Fatto inferno' (III vi). Haym's single allusion in II ii, where Eduige says that Grimoaldo betrayed Gundeberto, is incomprehensible without some knowledge of the background. Haym's references (I vi and III ii) to Bertarido's exile with the King of the Huns, whereas he is described as appearing in Hungarian disguise, may be due to confusion of sources rather than of etymology; in Paul the Deacon's account Bertarido flees on different occasions to several countries, including France and England.

Salvi translated parts of Corneille's dialogue word for word, but reduced the political motivation, rearranged the order of scenes, and felt free to alter the plot, often for the better in operatic terms. He brought Bertarido's entry forward to Act I, showed his escape from prison on the stage (in Corneille it is merely reported), and kept Garibaldo's villainy flourishing till the end; his death at Bertarido's hands while attempting to murder Grimoaldo becomes the climax of the opera. In Corneille, where he is a less monochrome figure, he disappears during the penultimate act: Pertharite kills him off-stage, in self-defence, a much tamer consummation. On the other hand Salvi added a confusing and unnecessary character in Unoldo, a follower of Bertarido, who duplicates many of the functions of Unulfo; the reason no doubt was the presence of an extra singer at Pratolino.

Haym and Handel made no major changes in Salvi's plot, but they transformed its balance by altering the distribution of arias and tying them more closely to the action. There is little doubt that Handel was the moving spirit here. The pattern, which recurs throughout his theatrical career, is particularly clear in *Rodelinda*, where the object was to condense and improve a not unsatisfactory original. Comparison between the two librettos is most revealing. Haym omitted eight of Salvi's scenes, shortened nearly all the rest, and added one (III v). Sometimes he ran several together; his II iv contains three arias, II v and III i two each, and II vii an aria and a duet. Haym cut the recitatives by more than half, removing nearly 650 lines of verse—some 63 of them were printed in *virgole* in the libretto—and roughly chopping and joining the remainder. As in most Handel operas, this radically altered the balance between aria and recitative; the total of arias was reduced only from 34 to 28. Even more striking is the change in distribution. The number allotted by Salvi to each character (with the Handel–Haym figure in brackets) is: Rodelinda 5 (8), Bertarido 4 (6), Grimoaldo 6 (6), Eduige 6 (3), Garibaldo 5 (2), Unulfo 5 (3), Unoldo 3 (0). Apart from eliminating Unoldo, Handel and Haym greatly increased the prominence of the hero and heroine—more so than these figures indicate, for they have the only duet and four of the five accompanied recitatives—while abridging that of Eduige, Garibaldo, and Unulfo. Only Grimoaldo, Salvi's most skilful portrait, retains his quota—and apart from minor verbal changes in one they are the same arias. While in Handel's opera the three central characters have twenty arias and the rest eight, in Salvi the figures are fifteen and nineteen. The latter gives Grimoaldo and Eduige more arias than Rodelinda, and Garibaldo and Unulfo as many; all five have more than Bertarido. Haym's adjustment was not a mere obeisance to Senesino and Cuzzoni; it strengthened the plot by throwing th main conflict into sharper relief. This was worth the sacrifice of som background material and a weakening in the motivation of Garibaldo an Eduige. The latter's ruthless ambition, and the unscrupulous willingness c both to use each other (and anyone else) to serve their own purposes, ar clearer in Salvi.

Of the 28 arias in Haym's libretto, 21 as well as the duet and *coro* were take from Salvi, four of them ('L'empio rigor', 'Io già t'amai', 'Scacciata' and 'U zeffiro') with verbal changes designed to strengthen the emotional impac That was also the purpose of the two substitutions, Garibaldo's 'Di Cupidc and Rodelinda's 'Spietati', where words that promote the plot replace flower or mythological metaphors. 'Se fiera belva' in Haym's added III v, wher Bertarido's solicitude for Unulfo's wound makes both characters mor sympathetic, increased Senesino's quota and gave him his one opportunity fo bravura. The other four new arias—one of them certainly, another probabl an afterthought—are among the glories of the opera. Three of them ('H perduto', 'Ritorna, O caro', and 'Mio caro bene') are in Rodelinda's part. Th fourth ('Dove sei?') was not in the score as first composed and reached i familiar form only after several versions. A constant feature of Handel collaboration with his librettists, the ejection of vague, abstract, or neutra texts in favour of primary dramatic responses, is vividly illustrated b 'Ritorna, O caro' in II vi, where Rodelinda first learns from Unulfo tha Bertarido is alive. At this point Salvi gives Unulfo an aria, 'Stringilo al sen urging Rodelinda to welcome her husband. Handel jumps this second-han approach and goes straight to the main issue: Rodelinda herself addresses th absent Bertarido.

Equally memorable, and more economical, is the substitution of Rodelin da's cavatina 'Hò perduto' (Handel cut the B section and da capo befor performance) for Salvi's entire first scene, taken straight from Corneille. It is long colloquy between Rodelinda and Unulfo, with an otiose aria for th latter, explaining the background of the plot. Handel not only achieves th same end in a fraction of the time; he renders most of it superfluous b presenting the emotional nucleus of the opera in the first five words ('I hav lost my dear husband'). Haym removed a number of verbose episode including a long speech of 46 lines in II iii, where Rodelinda enlarges on he terms for surrender to Grimoaldo, and a marital altercation—she reproachin Bertarido for revealing his identity to Grimoaldo, he justifying it on th ground that he could not bear to watch her suffering—before the duet in Ac II. Haym cut one or two details that might have been retained, for example scene in Act III in which Garibaldo considers betraying Grimoaldo and goin over to Bertarido, and he is sparing of references to Eduige's claim to th throne as Bertarido's sister; it is this that motivates her attitude to marriag with Grimoaldo and Garibaldo, and Garibaldo's attitude to her. This side c the plot is prominent in Salvi, and even more in Corneille. Among Haym lesser changes were the transference of 'Un zeffiro' in III i from Eduige t Unulfo (in Salvi Eduige begins Act III with two consecutive arias, and ha three of the first five), a more dramatic reordering of III vi so that Grimoald launches the scene with his violent outburst 'Fatto inferno' and ends it wit 'Pastorello' before falling asleep (in Salvi the aria comes first), and th inversion of the last two scenes in Act I. Salvi ends with Unulfo's 'Sono colpi'. Handel in accordance with his regular practice gave the last word to the major character—an outburst of passion in place of sententious comment—and buttressed Bertarido's aria with an accompanied recitative.

The libretto is one of the best Handel ever set. The main lines of the plot are clear, the characters for the most part credible, consistent, and firmly drawn. There are plenty of strong situations arising from the separation of husband and wife; their enemies, the vacillating Grimoaldo and cynical Garibaldo, are nicely contrasted. The weak points are venial. We may ask why in Act III Eduige brings Rodelinda and Flavio to the prison when she has already given Unulfo a key to let Bertarido out, and why she drops a sword through a grating instead of giving it to him later in the garden. The answer to both questions is that Salvi wanted to set up a pathetic situation where mother and son find what they take to be Bertarido's bloodstained cloak and assume his death; we can hardly complain when this elicited such a superb response from Handel. Grimoaldo's repentance may be a trifle facile, and he is let off lightly when allowed to keep Pavia and Eduige. But he has been drawn throughout as a sheep in wolf's clothing (Rodelinda's stipulation that if he wants her he must kill Flavio before her eyes only makes sense if she knows he will never consent); and his changed attitude after Bertarido has saved his life, ridding him of the baleful influence of Garibaldo, is much more convincing than Corneille's gratuitous solution. Only Grimoaldo's sudden return to courting Eduige rings false. Eduige's change of mind in I iv, where, after suggesting that Garibaldo should prove his love by killing Grimoaldo, she seems content to humiliate the latter if he returns as a suppliant, may be explained by Eduige's consciousness, like Rodelinda's, that she is dealing with a weak man. As in many Baroque operas, the plotting and counter-plotting, complex on paper, become perfectly clear in the theatre.

Rodelinda was the third major masterpiece produced by Handel in less than twelve months, an achievement without parallel in the history of opera. The year 1724–5 represents one of the peaks of his creative career as assuredly as the years that produced *Messiah* and *Samson*, *Hercules* and *Belshazzar*, or *Solomon* and *Susanna*. There is no sign of flagging invention; indeed all three autographs are full of discarded ideas that would make the reputation of a lesser composer. In one respect, the balance of voices, *Rodelinda* is to modern ears the most satisfying opera of the three. The cast—soprano, three altos, tenor, and bass—is the same as in *Tamerlano*, but the bass is an important cog in the action, not a spare wheel. All the best judges have given *Rodelinda* high rank. According to Burney, it 'contains such a number of capital and pleasing airs as entitles it to one of the first places among Handel's dramatic productions'. Chrysander called it 'one of his most complete and satisfying operas', Leichtentritt 'one of Handel's most remarkable works. A whole chapter would be necessary to point out the many musical details.'

Handel's finest operas, however complex their plots, possess a simple emotional centre, round which everything revolves. Where that of *Giulio Cesare* is sexual passion and that of *Tamerlano* a father's devotion to his daughter, *Rodelinda* presents a picture of married love withstanding every assault of malignity. It resumes the theme of *Radamisto* on a less spectacular, more intimate level; the music may be no more inventive, but the characterization, especially of Rodelinda and Grimoaldo, is more refined than that of their counterparts in the earlier opera. It is not surprising that many writers, especially in Germany, have discovered parallels with *Fidelio*: a faithful, heroic, and self-sacrificing wife, a climactic prison scene beginning with a superb *scena* for the ill-used husband, a rescue in which the tables are turned and the couple reunited. But all these things are commonplace in *opera seria*, and the differences are as conspicuous as the resemblance. *Rodelinda* is not a rescue opera in the French Revolution sense; the political content remains shadowy, Rodelinda and Bertarido are not symbols of emancipation or oppressed humanity, and the prison never suggests a concentration camp. Nor does Rodelinda—unlike several of Handel's other female figures[7]—disguise herself as a man.

She is among the most impressive of operatic heroines: though wholly good and resolute in the face of misfortune, she is never hard or sententious. Less frivolous than Cleopatra, as befits a wife and mother rather than a child of nature, and built on a grander scale that Asteria, she is magnificently in command of her destiny and by far the strongest character in the opera. Her spiritual stature sets at nought the petty meanness of Garibaldo and the vicious but weak and finally conscience-stricken Grimoaldo, and dominates a husband who, if courageous, has hints of softness in his make-up. One cannot imagine Bertarido calling Grimoaldo's bluff when his son's life is at stake. Rodelinda's music covers an enormous range of mood, from desolation to fury, from tenderness to exultation, expressed with a passionate conviction that is always memorable and often overwhelming. Yet she is all of a piece, and as the plot unfolds her character expands from a brave defiance of impossible odds to a radiance and warmth of sympathy that we recognize at once as its complement. Her eight arias fall into three types: three laments, in C minor, B minor, and F minor; three denunciations, of Grimoaldo in 'L'empio rigor', Garibaldo in 'Morrai, sì', and both in 'Spietati'; and two love songs, one of longing, the other of fulfilment. With these may be coupled the tragic duet at the end of Act II, when she and Bertarido are parted so soon after rediscovering each other. Every one of these movements is of outstanding quality and indispensable to the opera.

The opening scene, as noted above, was a refinement typical of Handel's dramatic economy. Besides conveying all essential information, it establishes the stature of Rodelinda, sketches that of Grimoaldo, and outlines the central motives of the plot. We are left in no doubt of the moral domination of Rodelinda, though Grimoaldo wears her husband's crown. Like the opening of *Lotario* and other scenes in Handel's operas, the design anticipates the cantabile–cabaletta form that was to serve early Romantic opera so fruitfully: a slow cavatina, a recitative that transforms the dramatic situation, and a quick aria for the same character releasing the accumulated tension. Whether or not this scheme was Handel's invention, he used it to superb effect. His reason for reducing 'Hò perduto' from a big dal segno aria to a cavatina was undoubtedly to project the drama without delay; but he had to sacrifice a significant reference to Rodelinda choosing life rather than death in order to preserve her child. After the extrovert C major overture has foreshadowed the outcome, notably in the graceful oboe phrases and relaxed pedals of the Presto, a long slow ritornello in C minor prepares us for Rodelinda's plight.

[7] For example Rosmira in *Partenope*, Bradamante in *Alcina*, and Amastre in *Serse*.

Falling and climbing figures, associated later with the ideas of black despair ('Hò perduto') and accumulating woe ('più cresce'), define the narrow bounds of her dilemma. Both are slightly but significantly modified when they appear on the voice, a characteristic of many arias in this opera. The broken phrases, frequent appoggiaturas on strong beats (bars 17, 39, 41, 43, etc.), desolate falling bass line, restless tonality with feints towards the dominant and relative major cancelled by a drop to F minor, the more settled B section in which she resolves to live for her child, the suppression of the da capo ritornello as her hopes abruptly vanish: all make this one of the strongest openings in any of the operas. 'L'empio rigor', though less intrinsically memorable, intensifies the scorn with which she rejects Grimoaldo's proffered love, and retains the minor mode. The break-off into quavers after the headlong semiquavers of the first two phrases suggests a breathlessness in her anger; as perhaps do the violins' rising thirds in the long wide-ranging third limb of the ritornello, which rushes on for thirteen bars before collapsing on the low G. It never occurs in the voice; but this is the only aria in the opera to exploit Cuzzoni's full range from low D to top B flat.

'Ombre, piante', sung as Rodelinda approaches Bertarido's tomb holding Flavio by the hand, strikes a note of poignant grief rather than despair, enhanced by an orchestral layout of great refinement, at once spare and varied in texture. A single flute echoes the four-part string orchestra and later the voice, while from time to time a solo violin adds its own lament. After the initial echoes with their grace notes and trills the voice's phrases grow longer and veer towards the relative major as if recalling past happiness. At bars 44–6 the vocal line expands to a lovely little flourish covering a major ninth, followed almost at once by a bitter minor ninth in the harmony and a passage of spare counterpoint for solo violin and bass against discordant appoggiaturas and suspensions on the voice, conveying a sense of extraordinary anguish (Ex. 68, p. 580).

Handel rewrote this aria more than once. The first version in F minor lacked the vivid touches of instrumental colour; the second was a cavatina leading into accompanied recitative at bar 64. Handel then happily added a B section followed by a shortened reprise rather than a regular da capo, retaining the recitative link.[8] At the start of the reprise (bar 79) the voice echoes the orchestra, instead of vice versa, and the two-bar phrase for flute alone (bars 85–6), though identical with bars 25–6, comes as a fresh surprise. The change first to accompanied recitative, until Rodelinda and Flavio kiss the urn, then to secco as the watchers mutter their asides, carries the action forward into the next scene.

Here, after a recitative whose sudden harmonic changes, at 'Sì, t'intendo' and the final turn to C sharp minor, reflect Rodelinda's realization of the nature of her antagonist, she unleashes her full contempt on Garibaldo. 'Morrai, sì' is her first aria in a major key; this and its intense rhythmic vitality express a commitment to vengeance calculated to make even that miscreant quail. The ritornello seethes with ideas—at least eight, each on a different rhythmic pattern—and Rodelinda hurls them one after another, often in varied form, at Garibaldo's head. The three emphatic crotchets ('Morrai, sì') have their intervals variously modified and inverted; the second phrase is altered by the voice from the start; the chopping violin figure in bars 4–6

---

[8] Later still he shortened the aria, but not by reverting to the cavatina: see p. 597.

Ex. 68

(you would be the delight of my breast)

illustrates what may be in store for Garibaldo; the close question and answer at bars 10–12 is partly inverted by voice and violins (echoed by the bass) in bars 24–6 and breaks loose in bars 37–40, before the bass scale figures of bars 8 and 9 bring back earlier ideas in a different order. At the end of the A section the voice is busy evolving new developments: Rodelinda will never run short of ammunition. The ritornellos are cunningly varied. That at the end of the A section omits the first three ideas, turns the fourth upside down, and contracts the rest; that after the B section is confined to the first two.

In 'Spietati' (II iii) Rodelinda again turns on her tormentors. The bounding dotted rhythms of the first three bars, borrowed from 'Nò! non basta' in *Il pastor fido*, are thoroughly apposite. The significance of the syncopated figure in bars 4–6 and its rocking extension on the oboes is less apparent, but they give the music great exhilaration. Both were used again in the duet 'Tu caro sei' in Act III of *Sosarme*, and the rocking figure, a favourite with Handel, was to reach a magnificent apotheosis (at the words 'They now contract their boist'rous pride') in the chorus 'When his loud voice' in *Jephtha*.

In bars 20–2 it should be played by two solo violins[9] above a pedal on the voice, and in bars 8 and 9 as well as 40–2 and 54–6 by two solo oboes. In his first draft Handel gave Rodelinda a different aria here, a simile piece about a snake in the grass; 'Spietati' is far more positive in its impact.

'Ritorna, O caro' is one of the simplest and most ravishing of Handel's love songs. The gentle siciliano rhythm with steady four-part string accompaniment is common enough, but several details raise it to the sublime. Rodelinda has only just learned that Bertarido is alive. The breathless phrases of the recitative yield to this incandescent melody as a mixture of relief and longing surges over her. The calm retention of the tonic–dominant axis and the use of the same material for the B section point the singleness of her thought; the frequent ninths, and in particular the haunting flattened seventh in the first bar, reveal the heartache that inevitably accompanies it. The vocal compass remains within an octave except at the climax of the tune (bar 17), where for a single note it rises to a ninth—an exquisite touch. Handel wrote few profounder duets than 'Io t'abbraccio'. Burney's panegyric in 1784[10] is no hyperbole: 'There is not a passage, or point of imitation . . . which breathes not grace and dignity; and so far is the whole composition from discovering its age, that it seems of a kind which must be immortal, or at least an evergreen; which, however times and seasons vary, remains fresh and blooming as long as it exists.' The situation is familiar. Husband and wife (or other close relatives) meet, as they think, for the last time and take a lingering farewell: compare the similarly placed duet in the same key and tempo ('Se il cor') in *Tolomeo*, 'Son nata a lagrimar' in *Giulio Cesare*, and 'Vivo in te' in *Tamerlano*. Handel was never found wanting here. The sensitive string ritornello (no violas), with its mixture of *martellato* repeated notes and yearning slurred semiquavers, emphatic sharpened leading notes in bars 5 and 6 (much admired by Burney, who found the effect 'then totally new to my ears'), and poignant suspensions, illustrates the predicament of the pair: no sooner reunited than doomed to be sundered by death. All these features recur in the duet itself, the suspensions with wonderful effect in bars 31–2. While the voices sing often in thirds and sometimes in sixths, their recourse to imitation (not exact) for the opening words and several times later banishes monotony without disturbing the unifying factor of mutual love. The treatment of the first three words (bars 10 and 11, 17–19) offers a series of eloquent variations on the initial motive of the violins. The steady tread of the bass quavers holds the music together, while at the same time suggesting inexorable fate, or perhaps a march to the scaffold.

The prison scene (III iii–iv) finds Rodelinda once more *in extremis*, overwhelmed by the discovery of Bertarido's bloodstained clothes. The harmonic inflections of the recitative ('È morto il tuo german' etc.) are deeply pathetic, and the aria 'Se 'l mio duol' even more heart-rending than her laments in Act I. Here the enriching instruments are unison recorders, floating independently above the jagged rhythm of the violins, and bassoons (as in Ariodante's 'Scherza infida') sustaining a melancholy cantus firmus in the middle of the harmony, while the bass droops chromatically downwards, the symbol of hopeless grief. Rodelinda's last aria, 'Mio caro bene', has much in

[9] This is indicated in the performing score as well as the 1725 Wiesentheid copy and the Flower parts.
[10] *Commemoration of Handel* (London, 1785), 66.

common in mood, position, springy rhythms, and certain thematic ideas (contrast between staccato and scalic motion, repeated-note figure in bars 25–6) with Cleopatra's 'Da tempeste', and brings the same sense of uninhibited release. If anything, the effect is even greater, for Rodelinda has endured a longer and harsher ordeal. Only a woman who has suffered much can achieve such unclouded happiness. The melody is adapted, with vast improvements, from the finale of the chamber duet 'Tanti strali'. This is the one aria in the opera for which a character returns to a key he or she has used before. Most appropriately it is the radiant G major of 'Ritorna, O caro': Bertarido has returned for life.

*

Bertarido's music is most eloquent—outstandingly so—in his slow arias. The three Allegro movements, though fully adequate, are less memorable; perhaps it was for this reason that Handel gave him a finer one in the first revival. If his music in the first half of the opera suggests a certain indecisiveness, he rises to the occasion when confronting Grimoaldo and vanquishing Garibaldo. In all three slow arias Handel seizes the opportunity to strengthen the drama by varying his musical resources, in particular the da capo plan. The cemetery scene provides Bertarido with one of the most memorable entrances in any of the operas. The G minor Largo ritornello of the recitative, unusually long and richly scored (oboes[11] as well as strings), follows immediately on Garibaldo's outburst of C minor savagery ('Di Cupido') with its mainly unison textures. Handel is always supreme when reflecting on the vanity of human wishes. 'Pompe vane di morte!' is the equal of Caesar's 'Alma del gran Pompeo', strikes a similar mood, and likewise changes its key signature in the middle of a bar. The ritornello with its mournful echoes and wailing thirds, alternately drooping and painfully climbing, sets the mood before the voice enters. The scene is in three sections, each with its own tonality: G minor moving to D minor as Bertarido contemplates his own monument, F major (unaccompanied) as he reads the inscription, then after a brief outburst of violence a serene E major as he thinks of his wife and wonders what has become of her.

The link between recitative and aria is one of Handel's master-strokes, achieved in his fourth grappling with this scene. Salvi gave Bertarido no aria here, and that is how Handel first set the scene, the recitative continuing after 'con gli affanni' (bottom of HG 21) (Ex. 69a). He then revised these bars and inserted 'Dove sei?' as a regular aria with an eight-bar string ritornello, separated from 'con gli affanni' by an emphatic cadence and rests (b). In this form it was copied into the performing score. Later—probably in December 1725—Handel forged the link with the recitative, writing the word 'Dove' over the rests in its last bar, followed by key and time signatures and 'sei' as a 3/8 bar before the ritornello (c). Finally he cancelled the first four bars of the ritornello, producing the form printed by Chrysander, where the aria slips in before we are aware that the recitative has finished and the ritornello seems to begin in the middle (d). It is a remarkable fact that (outside the Hamburg copy) the final form occurs in no contemporary source. Every printed and manuscript version, whether of the complete score, selections, or the aria alone,[12] give

---

[11] They were originally flutes; Handel made the change before performance.

[12] The autograph, Hamburg (first state), Wiesentheid, Malmesbury, Flower, Lennard, and Granville scores, Flower parts, excerpts in Manchester and Vienna (parts), RM 19 c 9 (harpsichord), RM 19 a 8 (flute), a keyboard arrangement in the Coke Collection, and at least five printed scores, some in transposed keys.

(Peace to my ashes? O tyrannous fates! So long as I live I shall fight with
difficulties and grief. Ah yes, I read my fate engraved in marble and already
I see . . . . But here comes Unulfo)

(Where art thou?)

the full eight-bar ritornello before the vocal entry, generally without the preliminary 'Dove sei?'.

The wonderful melody was spoiled for generations of listeners by association with inappropriate words, sacred and secular, dubbed by insensitive parodists beginning in Handel's day. It can only be fully appreciated in its context. The vocal line is an education in the art of melodic architecture. The falling second that begins each of the first three two-bar phrases receives a slightly different rhythmic emphasis on each occasion. Then, after generating a four-bar phrase, it is isolated in two single bars, each ending with a rest, on the key word 'vieni'. Slowly the tune gathers way, gaining momentum from a falling seventh and reaching its climax at bar 31 with the only top E in Bertarido's entire part, heightened by the fermata in the previous bar. A seven-bar ritornello brings the A section to a close. The falling second continues to haunt the B section, though the phrases, melodic structure, and of course the key are quite different and there are no rests in the vocal line.

Bertarido concludes Act I in a mood of bitterness at Rodelinda's apparent infidelity. The accompanied recitative is orthodox except perhaps in its emphasis on the sharp minor keys, and the B minor aria 'Confusa si miri' presents little unusual at first sight, though the minor mode after three arias in the major makes its mark. Yet the contrast between strong unisons and expressively varied harmony permits many subtle touches. The ritornello tails off into silence after the violins have been deserted by the bass. The phrasing when they resume in bars 9–17, with extra emphasis on the first beats, suggests a resolute effort from Bertarido, at once undermined by plaintive chromaticism and later by suspensions. Towards the end of the A section he gathers himself up to join the orchestra in the middle of a phrase, repeating his first line for the last time, only to be abandoned by the violins at the cadence. The temporary modulations of the B section confirm the hint of a man at the mercy of his emotions, perhaps at the end of his tether.

In all three acts Bertarido begins an intermediate scene with a marvellous inspiration, and on each occasion an unexpected key signals the set-change. 'Con rauco mormorio' (II v), starting on an E flat (tonic) pedal after Unulfo's aria in G, is a magical exercise in nature-painting; it also depicts the singer's state of mind, alone in a beautiful countryside without Rodelinda. The siciliano rhythm, extended pedals, and warm scoring—the bassoons sometimes joining the violas, sometimes the bass—evoke the murmur of brooks and fountains. The echoes, by no means stereotyped (violins and violas take the lead in turn), are both physical and mental: Bertarido's thoughts and mood are reflected in what he hears. The different falling intervals to which the words 'ruscelli e fonti' are set and the mournful timbre of the bassoons underline the irony of his sadness in such delightful surroundings—perhaps also, along with a plaintive tinge in the harmony, a certain self-indulgence. The scoring of the B section, one of the few contexts where Handel uses recorders and flutes independently, as well as divided violas and bassoons, is a *tour de force* in its kaleidoscope of colours. It is easy to believe in the pathetic fallacy that the caves and hills are sympathetic to Bertarido's complaints. Eduige's interruption, when she thinks she hears the voice of her dead brother, is dramatic in its unexpectedness and its advancement of the action; her surmise is confirmed by his da capo. On the rare occasions when Handel uses this device (in *Giulio Cesare*, and later in *Serse*[13] and *Susanna*) it never fails to make an effect out of proportion to its simplicity. Bertarido also has the next aria, 'Scacciata dal suo nido'. The music, adapted from Rodelinda's rejected 'Ben spesso in vago prato' in II iii, has a general chirpiness, buoyant rhythms, and some pretty ornament, but the unanimity of voice and violins allows little scope, and the bird simile marks time.

In Act III Bertarido has reason for alarm. 'Chi di voi' is his most powerful music in the opera. The highly dramatic key switch at the change of set—B flat minor after the A minor of Grimoaldo's 'Trà sospetti'—plunges us into the darkness of the prison. Handel's operas abound in prison scenes, several of them in B flat minor; this is one of the finest, in content and in plan. Formally it is the inverse of 'Pompe vane', beginning with a long cavatina of 51 Largo bars, breaking abruptly into accompanied recitative when the sword falls through the grating, and continuing in secco after Bertarido has wounded Unulfo. Both the Largo and the accompanied recitative are of superb quality. Burney called 'Chi di voi' 'one of the finest pathetic airs that can be found in all his works . . . rendered affecting by a new and curious modulation, as well

---

[13] The *Serse* example is not an exact parallel.

as by the general cast of the melody'. The long ritornello (16½ bars) is another vivid mood-portrait, the key, jagged rhythms, and frequent interrupted cadences suggesting Bertarido's anguish. This persists throughout the aria in the restless harmony, irregular phrase-lengths, and unpredictable falling intervals for voice and violins, especially the minor and major sevenths towards the end. Every turn to the major is firmly repelled. The final black question over a 4/2 chord is answered by the sword. The accompanied recitative expresses a whole range of emotions and actions: shock, groping in the dark, resolution when he finds the sword (*marcato* chords) and draws it (dotted rhythm at 'Dunque ti stringo'), determination to cut his way out of prison (repeated semiquaver chords), and the unhappy assault on Unulfo (in an unaccompanied bar). Every impulse is translated into the music, which, as in Bajazet's death scene, threatens to break the *opera seria* mould; Burney detected something quite new here. 'Se fiera belva', a simile aria, is not in the autograph and could have been lifted from elsewhere. The breezy C major makes a bright effect after the long stretch of flat minor keys, and the march of the bass quavers stepwise up and down gives a strong harmonic thrust to the athleticism and angular intervals of the violins. But the aria contributes little more than a delayed opportunity for Senesino to let off steam.

Grimoaldo, Handel's second great tenor part, scarcely falls below Rodelinda and Bertarido in the quality and range of his music. The vacillating character and troublesome conscience of the usurper are reflected in his febrile changes of mood. So long as his confidence lasts he holds to the major mode: the last three of his six arias are all in the minor. His rejection of Eduige in 'Io già t'amai' is untroubled by doubt. The double counterpoint of the first two bars with their emphatic minims in the upper parts (varied at the vocal entry) over a reiterated quick motive in the bass and the striding figures that follow bespeak security and a touch of the braggart; this is almost the manner of Harapha in *Samson*. Bassoons as well as violas repeatedly double his rising scales at 'sdegnasti esser mia sposa', and he drives the point home in bars 18–20 by constantly harping on F, the dominant of the key. In 'Se per te', addressed to Garibaldo, his joy at having won Rodelinda knows no bounds; it breaks out in so many triplets, beginning with the first bar of the ritornello, that he might be dancing a jig. There is something almost frivolous in his repetition of 'di chi? di che?', especially at the cadences. Rodelinda's conditions for acceptance in Act II throw him not into consternation (except momentarily in the recitative), but into a self-indulgent declaration of pleasure at being the prisoner of love. This is a soft-centred tyrant, incapable (as the others know) of killing the child. 'Prigioniera' is a beautiful aria with a touch of sadness as Grimoaldo, repeating the same phrases again and again, fondles his wounded heart. The main theme had been foreshadowed in two early cantatas (HWV 78 and 96). The ritornello has five distinct thematic ideas, contrasted in rhythm, and each recurs later in the voice part or the orchestra or both together. The music flows on with an effortless sweetness contrasting sharply with the black cynicism of Garibaldo's 'Tirannia' that follows.

Henceforth Grimoaldo's confidence evaporates. The discovery of Bertarido in Rodelinda's apartment drives him to bluster and threats. 'Tuo drudo è mio rivale', which uses a bass motive from the final chorus of *Dixit Dominus*, is dominated by the opening phrase played by the whole orchestra in octaves; this is later contrasted and combined with the rushing semiquavers of the scales and outlined triads associated with the words 'e morte avrà'. The short B section is addressed to Bertarido, but adds nothing: all Grimoaldo's rage is concentrated on Rodelinda. With 'Trà sospetti' in Act III his nerve has gone. Faced with Garibaldo's implacable advice, which he knows will not bring him Rodelinda's love even if he disposes of Bertarido, he finds every avenue blocked. The meandering violin line of the ritornello and the jumpy divisions on 'affanni' and (in the B section) 'inganni' outline his querulous state of mind; but the aria is hardly one of Handel's most distinguished.

Grimoaldo's last scene is musically his finest, and it has the advantage of bringing the plot to its climax; his going to sleep on stage, however hoary a device, tempts Garibaldo to violence and his death at Bertarido's hands. The accompanied recitative 'Fatto inferno', 46 bars long, beginning in E minor and ranging through the whole tonal spectrum as far as E flat major, stands with those composed for the same singer in *Tamerlano* among the greatest examples of the century. The wild violence of the first section, with its great upward dotted leaps on the strings, starting with an octave and later varying between a minor sixth and two octaves and a third, suggests at once that Grimoaldo's mind is deranged. It is a vision of the furies; the mad dog of his imagination that abuses and torments him is surely Cerberus. These are the terms in which Handel was to realize the dying agony of Hercules and Dejanira's madness and remorse. But Grimoaldo is not of their calibre. After a final harmonic wrench (bars 26-7) he droops suddenly to a quiet Larghetto arioso, as firmly anchored in the rare key of F sharp major as the first section is tonally disturbed. The effect is at once dramatically apt (exhausted by the emotional upheaval Grimoaldo's mind seeks an escapist refuge in dreams of a shepherd's life away from thrones and cares of state) and profoundly beautiful. The murmuring dotted figure of the strings, associated elsewhere (as in 'Heart the seat of soft delight' in *Acis and Galatea*) with pastoral sadness, gradually yields to sustained chords as he approaches the aria; the cadence is marked *piano* in the autograph.[14] 'Pastorello' is the third and last of the great sicilianos of this opera, and the only one in a minor key (E minor, in which the accompanied recitative began). There is no mistaking the characterization: Grimoaldo is as weak and helpless as a child whose world has collapsed, leaving him a prey to self-pity. The music flows gently on, drooping downwards, with a lovely echo-like refrain in bar 3 that recurs twice and temporarily halts the momentum. The B section brings no real contrast, and Grimoaldo sings himself to sleep. After this he is in no position to resist Bertarido, whose victory he accepts with relief.

Eduige also develops in the course of the opera. Handel does not explore her as deeply as he might have done had she retained more of her part, but the main lines are clear. In Act I she is ambitious and domineering, determined to gain the throne with Garibaldo's help or else to be revenged on him. 'Lo farò' begins splendidly, answering Garibaldo's A major question ('e lo farai?') with the two words declaimed to the notes of an F major triad before the ritornello, and repeated later at different pitches in both sections. The aria bristles with determination, emphasized by strong tonic accents, driving rhythms, and spirited divisions. 'De' miei scherni' (II ii), Eduige's reaction to Rodelinda's apparent acceptance of Grimoaldo, is less strong than might be expected, especially the B section with its reference to her eyes inflamed into thunderbolts of vengeance. The ritornello is fertile in ideas, beginning with a neat point of imitation and developing its central motive in bars 5-10. This has a

[14] Handel later added an exquisite coda, based on the dotted figure, which survives in a single copy: see below, p. 591 and Ex. 71.

continuous whiplash effect wherever it appears, reinforced by the buzzing semiquaver figure in bars 11 and 12, which breaks in constantly towards the end of the A section. The B section, with continuo alone, is remarkable only for one of many appearances (at 'dell'empio farò') of a favourite motive that Handel inherited from Keiser and was to use with sublime effect in 'With thee the unsheltered moor' in *Solomon*. Its presence here is a mystery. By Act III Eduige is fully committed to her brother's cause. 'Quanto più fiera' contributes little more than a pretty tune. Handel is content for the most part to double the voice with the violins; but the B section adds charming syncopations and a catchy rhythm, perhaps intended to suggest Eduige's lightness of heart after purging her guilty conscience. This is one of many Handel arias that gain in performance a potency they lack on paper. Together with Unulfo's 'Un zeffiro' it strikes a mood of carefree cheerfulness before the grim events that follow; that may have been Handel's aim.

Of Unulfo's three arias, 'Sono i colpi' (I x), a showpiece in which the voice challenges the violins in virtuosity, is a tribute to Pacini's technique. It serves no other purpose, and its sententious text at a point where no aria is required makes it an obvious candidate for the knife. Like other marginal pieces it was the subject of much attention. Handel reset the words in a totally different mood for the first revival, and adjusted the coloratura of the original for a mezzo-soprano in 1731. 'Frà tempeste' too is less than adequately motivated. It is not at all clear why Unulfo should feel so confident of the outcome after Garibaldo's enunciation of a Stalinist philosophy of tyranny, unless Handel simply wanted a contrast. This he obtained with a long, gently lyrical aria whose vocal line and rustling slurred violin figures offer a foretaste of 'O thou that tellest good tidings to Zion'. 'Un zeffiro' is better still. This is not a bland simile aria—the B section relates directly to Unulfo's hope of rescuing his master—but Handel builds the whole piece round the idea suggested by the opening words. The scoring—treble recorders mostly in unison or octaves with the violins, a largely independent line for bassoons and cello—has the freshness and charm of so many Handel nature pieces. The triadic triplet figure that plays such a large part looks otiose on paper; yet Handel obtains an astonishing variety by switching the registers and colours. Between the warm euphony of the main ritornellos the voice is answered by the leaping triplets with a delightful unpredictability (it is this that distinguishes Handel's pastoral pieces from those of his contemporaries), sometimes on violins and recorders (with or without bassoons), sometimes on violins or cello, for one, two, or three bars at a time. The familiar dotted figure in thirds creeps in towards the end of the A section.

Like Eduige, Garibaldo might have received more music; certainly his importance to the plot would justify it. His two arias—both Allegro in flat minor keys, Handel's usual prescription for Boschi—are much alike, but they serve their purpose in delineating a double-dyed scoundrel. Both are formidable outbursts of bass villainy, full of octave unisons, sequences, and whiplash rhythms, the vocal line alternating between triadic patterns, downward scale figures, and angular leaps. In 'Di Cupido' the scales are mostly confined to the strings, but subtleties of workmanship are not lacking. At bar 82 the bassoons suddenly join the voice, and later outline the same phrase on their own as a counterpoint to the closing ritornello; it is taken up once more by the second violins in the middle of the B section. This aria glances back at the duet 'Dolci chiodi' in *La Resurrezione*.

Like its two predecessors, *Rodelinda* has many points of structural interest, especially in the linking of recitative and aria. As already noted, Rodelinda in the cemetery and Bertarido in prison break from aria into accompanied recitative and then into secco so that the action moves forward unimpeded; Bertarido's first scene illustrates the reverse process, and the opening of 'Lo farò' is a brilliant stroke. So are the key switches at changes of set, especially for the two garden scenes and the prison. The tonal range is wider than in any other Handel opera, covering virtually the whole spectrum: no fewer than eight major keys (nine including the F sharp arioso of 'Fatto inferno') and nine minor are used for principal movements. The more unusual are reserved for the three central characters. Handel employs a different procedure from *Giulio Cesare* and *Admeto*, whose leading roles tend to be defined in terms of one tonality. Except Rodelinda in her last aria, no character returns to an earlier key. The scheme is clearly deliberate, and so is the balance between the modes. Rodelinda begins with three arias in the minor, Grimoaldo with three in the major followed by three in the minor; Unulfo, as an onlooker, is confined to the commoner major keys. The first half of Act I clings to flat keys, the second half (after Bertarido's return), with a single exception, to the sharp side. During the act the tonality drops a semitone from C major/minor to B minor; Act II (not counting the initial secco) does the same, from G minor to F sharp minor. Act III restores stability by beginning and ending in F major. The scoring falls between the adventurousness of *Giulio Cesare* and the restraint of *Tamerlano*. There is rich writing for flute, recorders, and bassoons, but no brass—until the *coro*, where Handel, having held back the horns for the resolution of the conflict, introduces them for the first and only time.

History and Text

Handel completed the opera on 20 January 1725 and produced it at the King's Theatre on 13 February, one year less a week after the première of *Giulio Cesare*. The cast was:

RODELINDA:	Cuzzoni (soprano)
BERTARIDO:	Senesino (alto castrato)
GRIMOALDO:	Borosini (tenor)
GARIBALDO:	Boschi (bass)
EDUIGE:	Dotti (contralto)
UNULFO:	Pacini (alto castrato)

Rodelinda was an immediate success,[15] receiving fourteen performances in the season (another on 23 February was cancelled owing to Senesino's indisposition). Cuzzoni and Senesino were again much admired: according to Burney, the former 'gained great reputation by the tender and plaintive manner in which she executed' 'Hò perduto', and Senesino 'pronounced ['Pompe vane di morte'], according to tradition, with uncommon energy and passion'. It was in connection with *Rodelinda* that Horace Walpole penned his famous description of Cuzzoni: 'She was short and squat, with a doughy cross face, but fine complexion; was not a good actress; dressed ill; and was silly and fantastical. And yet on her appearing in this opera, in a *brown silk gown*, trimmed with silver, with the vulgarity and indecorum of which all the old

[15] Handel's recalcitrant tenor Alexander Gordon, who attended a rehearsal, wrote on 12 Feb. to Sir John Clerk of Penicuik: 'Having the liberty of the house I went to the opera house & heard Julius Caesar which pleasd me exceedingly but the new one to be acted for ye first time next Saturday exceeds all I ever heard' (Gibson, *The Royal Academy*, 215).

ladies were much scandalised, the young adopted it as a fashion, so universally, that it seemed a national uniform for youth and beauty.'

Handel revived *Rodelinda* the following season on 18 December 1725, when it ran for eight performances. There were two changes of cast, a new tenor, Luigi Antinori, replacing Borosini as Grimoaldo and Antonio Baldi taking the part of Unulfo. This involved no change of voice, but Antinori, a less distinguished artist than Borosini, had a slightly higher compass. The transpositions of 'Io già t'amai' up to C and 'Prigioniera' up to B flat, indicated in the Hamburg score, were undoubtedly made for him. Handel composed five new pieces for this revival, an unusually liberal allowance. One of them was a resetting of 'Sono i colpi' for Baldi, whom the awkward divisions of the first version may have taxed. Its replacement, an E minor Andante (published only by Walsh, who wrongly ascribed it to Cuzzoni), is a pensive piece with no display whatever. It scarcely lives up to a beautiful ritornello.

Ex. 70

The other new music was all for Cuzzoni and Senesino—an aria for the former, two for the latter, and a duet for the pair. It is difficult to see why Handel chose to replace 'Se 'l mio duol' with another lament; yet 'Ahi perchè' (HG 89) is scarcely if at all inferior. The sobbing ritornello, each phrase separated by a fermata, the close proximity of all four parts in bars 5–8, the voice's jumps to the upper octave as if the pain were too great to bear, the violins' pathetic falling triplets at irregular intervals, and the wonderful ritornello after the A section, expanded from four to nearly ten bars and enriched by a viola part—all are intensely expressive of Rodelinda's grief. The aria resembles Cleopatra's 'Se pietà'; yet so inventive is Handel's genius that there is no question of stale repetition.

Bertarido's 'Sì, rivedrò' (printed by Chrysander in the 1734 *Il pastor fido*, to which it was transferred a tone higher) came in II vii, preceded by seven lines of recitative whose music survives only in the Malmesbury copy. Senesino sang it in F major, probably at the beginning of the scene. The libretto implies

that it followed 'Ritorna, O caro', and Malmesbury places it there; but the
performing score suggests that it may have replaced Rodelinda's aria and the
preceding fifteen lines of recitative. If so, it was a miserable exchange. Despite
a mild urgency imparted by repetition of the first word, 'Sì, rivedrò' is an
undistinguished piece, marred by mechanical sequences, and adds little to the
character. 'Vivi, tiranno' in III viii (after 'pur col mio sangue', HG 102, fifth
system) is a very different matter. Bertarido has just killed Garibaldo and
thrown Grimoaldo's sword at his feet. By giving him an explosion of angry
contempt, reflected in a scintillating discharge of rhythmic energy, Handel
strengthens the character and the plot. Bertarido gains a heroic dimension
hitherto absent, and Senesino a second, more dramatically motivated opening
for coloratura. (It is possible however that 'Se fiera belva' was cut.) Handel
had used the seething figure with upper pedal at bars 7–12 in *Il trionfo del
Tempo* ('Come nembo che fugge') and *Agrippina* ('Come nube che fugge'), but
builds it into something far stronger, one of his finest bravura arias for
Senesino or any other castrato. The snap of the oboes, the buzzing strings, the
vocal cross-rhythms at bars 58–60, and the exuberance of the whole voice part
epitomize Bertarido's indignation. The duet 'D'ogni crudel martir', published
only by Walsh, came immediately before the *coro*, with which it was linked
without intervening ritornello. Though strictly superfluous, it has charm and a
delightful interweaving of voice and violin parts.

Other changes that probably date from December 1725 (if they were not
introduced during the original run) are the link between 'Pompe vane' and
'Dove sei?', the abbreviation of 'Ombre, piante' from 111 to 95 bars by the
omission of bars 52–9 and 100–7, and the addition of a short coda to 'Fatto
inferno' as Grimoaldo, his passion spent, turns his thoughts to sleep (Salvi's
libretto at this point has a stage direction *Doppo breve Sinfonia s'addormenta*, but
'Pastorello' comes earlier at the beginning of the scene). Handel replaced the
recitative's closing bar with the following *breve Sinfonia*:

Ex. 71

This must be regarded as his final thought, a singularly happy one. Although it survives only in the Malmesbury copy, there are indications in Hamburg that something has been torn out, a fate that often befell shorter insertions in the performing scores.

Handel's only subsequent revival, again for eight performances (the last two completing the subscription for the previous season), took place on 4 May 1731 and seems to have been hurriedly prepared; no libretto is known. According to the Colman Opera Register it 'took much'. Senesino again sang Bertarido. The rest of the cast can be reconstructed with some confidence:

RODELINDA:	Strada
GRIMOALDO:	Annibale Pio Fabri
GARIBALDO:	Giovanni Giuseppe Commano
EDUIGE:	Antonia Merighi
UNULFO:	Francesca Bertolli

As in most of Handel's revivals at this period, the recitatives were heavily cut, by more than 150 bars. The two finest of the December 1725 additions, 'Ahi perchè' and 'Vivi, tiranno', were retained and at least three substitute pieces introduced, none of them new. 'Non pensi quell'altera' and 'Vi sento, sì', both from *Lotario*, replaced Grimoaldo's 'Prigioniera' and 'Trà sospetti' (not 'Pastorello', as indicated by Chrysander), presumably because they were already in Fabri's repertory. Both are quite different in mood from the arias they ousted; reflecting as they do Fabri's vigorous style of singing, they convert Grimoaldo from a weakling into a conventional tyrant, undermining the stature and balance of the opera. 'Io t'abbraccio' was ejected in favour of 'Se il cor', a similar duet in the same key sung in a parallel situation at the end of Act II of *Tolomeo*, again perhaps because Strada as well as Senesino already knew it. Commano, an indifferent artist, may have been allowed neither of Garibaldo's arias.[16]

The most popular concert arias were 'Scacciata' and 'L'empio rigor'. Signora Stradiotti sang the former at the Smock Alley Theatre in Dublin as early as 8 December 1725, and Ann Turner Robinson twice chose it for her Drury Lane benefit (28 April 1726 and 26 March 1729). At Lincoln's Inn Fields on 19 July 1735 it featured in a programme given 'for the Entertainment of Che-sazan Outsim, Hindy-Gylesangbier, Charadab-sina, Gulgula-chem-Chemaunim, and Tichucbactey Ormophan, Sacheoutzim-Sinadab Caocormin, the Chineze Mandarines, lately arrived in England, on a Tour through Europe, being the only People of that Nation, who have been in England since the Reign of King James I'. One hopes they were able to appreciate it.

Kytch, 'First Hautboy to the Opera', played the voice part of 'L'empio rigor' at his benefit at Hickford's Room on 16 April 1729; it was sung at the Little Theatre in the Haymarket by Susanna Arne on 6 and 8 October 1733, 19 November 1733, and 4 January 1734, and by Miss Jones on 21 and 22 August 1734. Jane Barbier included 'Dove sei?' at her Lincoln's Inn benefit on 28 March 1726. 'Ombre, piante' featured in Philip Rochetti's benefit at Hickford's Room on 30 May 1729. Burney records that he himself sang 'Dove sei?' as a treble at a country concert in 1740, 'when, without knowing how to construe or even pronounce the words, I had been taught to sing it by the

---

[16] See below, p. 598.

organist of Chester, at fourteen years old'. The overture was played at Manchester Subscription Concerts on 27 November 1744 and 25 June 1745, and at the Great Room, Dean Street, on 4 April 1752.

The Hamburg Opera produced *Rodelinda* on 29 November 1734 (NS) in a version arranged by Christian Gottlieb Wendt, who, with the aid of a literal version by one Fischer, supplied the recitatives and a translation; the arias were sung in Italian. Though advertised as 'an Intriguen und übriger Beschaffenheit . . . fürtreffliches Stück', the opera was a failure. According to Mattheson it received 'little applause', and only five performances are known, two in 1734, one in summer 1735, and two in autumn 1736.[17] The most unusual feature was the inclusion of the duet 'D'ogni crudel martir', presumably taken from Walsh, for it was inserted in the wrong place. It was added in the same year to the Brunswick revival of Caldara's *Demetrio*. Other *Rodelinda* items appeared in Schürmann's pasticcio *Clelia* (Brunswick, 1730) and the Conti pasticcio *Issipile* (Hamburg, 1737; 'Sono i colpi', probably the first setting[18]). Telemann's *Flavius Bertaridus, König der Longobarden* (Hamburg, 23 November 1729), also translated by Wendt, was based not on Salvi's libretto but on Stefano Ghigi's *Flavio Bertarido*, first set by Pollarolo (Venice, 1706). Christina Maria Avoglio sang Rodelinda in Telemann's opera.[19]

The next production of *Rodelinda* was the famous one at Göttingen on 26 June 1920, which inaugurated the twentieth-century revival of Handel's operas. Oskar Hagen's arrangement, made for this occasion, received 136 performances all over Germany before the end of 1926. In addition to later German revivals, the opera reached the United States (Smith College, Mass.) in 1931, Sweden (Göteborg) in 1932, London (Old Vic) in 1939, Vienna in 1941, Budapest in 1943, Switzerland in 1960, Holland in 1973, Italy and Czechoslovakia in 1985, and Finland in 1986. In recent years it has been increasingly recognised as one of the masterpieces of the Baroque stage.

Autograph

For some reason now impossible to fathom Handel composed the first two acts of the autograph (RM 20 c 4) on Italian paper, of two distinctive types: ff. 1–49, 58, and 88 have a watermark *Cantoni/Bergamo*, ff. 50–7 and 59–61 (and the *Giulio Cesare* 1725 additions on 62–6) a crescent watermark.[20] Act III is on the usual Cb paper of the period. The composition of this opera seems to have been less systematic than usual. Apart from a single figure '1' on f. 7— which may imply that it began with the recitatives on HG 8, though they have no scene heading and the verso is blank—Handel did not foliate the autograph. This raises occasional problems. It is clear however that he made extensive alterations in I i, vi, and vii and replaced the original arias in II iii and III v. The paper, and the almost immediate reuse of material from two

---

[17] But see note to Appendix C.
[18] R. D. Lynch, 'Opera in Hamburg, 1718–1738'; G. F. Schmidt, *Die frühdeutsche Oper und die musikdramatische Kunst Georg Caspar Schürmanns* (Regensburg, 1933–4), 18.
[19] K. Zelm, 'Die Sänger der Hamburger Gänsemarkt-Oper', 45.
[20] D. Burrows, 'Handlist'. Handel used the Bergamo paper for an aria added to *Alessandro* (RM 20 a 5, ff. 35–8), the first two *Deutsche Arien* (RM 20 f 13, ff. 1–4), and various instrumental works now bound with other material in Fitzwilliam MSS 260 and 261.

discarded arias, proves that all this took place during the main work of composition.

The first draft of Act I did not include the Minuet of the overture (squeezed into three blank staves below the Presto), 'Hò perduto', 'L'empio rigor', or 'Dove sei?', and 'Ombre, piante' had a different setting, rejected before the previous recitative was written; ff. 5–6, 8–9, 18–19, and 21–3 are all insertions. Moreover this part of the manuscript has been confused by misbinding: the original order of folios was 17, 25, 20, 24, 26. 'Hò perduto' is a complete dal segno aria, as in HG. 'L'empio rigor', or indeed the whole first scene, may have replaced something now lost; Rodelinda must always have had an aria here. The ritornello before 'Pompe vane di morte' (I vi) is for *Tutti V et Traversier*: and the scene at first contained no aria. Bertarido's accompanied recitative had three more bars after 'e con gli affanni' (bottom of HG 21), followed at once by 'Mà giunge Unulfo' (HG 23). Handel then heavily revised the last four bars on HG 21 and inserted 'Dove sei?' with an orthodox introductory ritornello of eight bars (see Ex. 69b above) but no indication of a da capo or dal segno and no final double bar, as if he were considering a different continuation.

Scene vii began with a simpler setting of 'Ombre, piante' as an F minor cavatina, followed by 'Ombra del mio bel sol' (HG 27) in secco recitative. The B minor 'Ombre, piante', which contains many dynamic marks not in HG, was at first much shorter, a cavatina ending at bar 63 and leading into the string-accompanied 'Ombra del mio bel sol'. The flute part may not have been conceived as a solo throughout; Handel wrote *Travers. unis.* at bar 67, though this is ambiguous. He added bars 64–88 on f. 22 (an insertion within an insertion) and indicated the remaining 23 bars with a dal segno. Both vi and vii underwent further changes later. 'Sono i colpi' has more taxing, rather instrumental coloratura (subsequently modified) in bars 16–17, 23–6, and 36–9. Handel cut ten bars from the ritornello of 'Di Cupido', where he first wrote an orthodox C minor signature at the start but for some reason cancelled the A flats, and made small but significant changes in 'Io già t'amai' (the minims in bars 1, 2, and 13 began as crotchets followed by rests), 'Lo farò', and 'Confusa si miri' (bars 8–10).

In Act II 'De' miei scherni' at first had a 3/8 signature for the top instrumental line only. In place of 'Spietati' stood a different aria, 'Ben spesso in vago prato' (*Allegro*, F sharp minor), which must have been promptly rejected, for Handel used the material two scenes later in 'Scacciata', which is not an insertion. 'Spietati' is not in the autograph, though Handel added a cue for it. The A section ritornellos of 'Tirannia' are each two bars longer than in any published version. 'Frà tempeste' (from whose A section Handel cut thirteen bars after filling up the inner parts) with Unulfo's previous recitative is probably an insertion. It makes the third aria in III iv, and there is no heading or direction for III v. If Burrows is right about the paper of f. 58, which carries 45 bars of secco recitative in the middle of II vii (HG 67–8), this section may be a later expansion on two detached leaves; it ends on f. 59ʳ, with a cue for 'Tuo drudo' and a blank verso. The duet 'Io t'abbraccio' is missing. Folios 62–6 belong to the 1725 revival of *Giulio Cesare* and have no connection with *Rodelinda*, but were in the manuscript when Burney saw it.

The first recitative in Act III is in Chrysander's longer version. The B section of 'Trà sospetti' underwent substantial cuts; five substituted bars are not in the autograph. The violins' C flats in bar 15 of 'Chi di voi' have wedge-shaped stress marks. Handel began the recitative 'Mà non che sò' (top of HG 86) in secco, but changed his mind after three bars and set it with strings as a continuation of the aria. He slightly expanded both aria and recitative after composition. In the last bar of the top brace on HG 87 he carefully interchanged the two violin parts. Three bars later ('ecco di morte il ministro crudel') the autograph has a different accompaniment with rests and repeated notes, not a sustained chord. Bars 13–21 of 'Se 'l mio duol' also differ significantly from the printed version, the dotted figure being transferred to the bass while the violins hold long notes. The entry on the third stave of bar 11 is for *Bassons pianiss* without violas. The aria in Scene v (after 'il tuo periglio', HG 93) is 'Verrete a consolarmi' (no tempo, D major), very different in mood from its replacement, 'Se fiera belva', which with the eight previous bars of recitative is missing. The key switch at 'Fatto inferno', which at first began with an upbeat, a semiquaver E in all four parts, was different but equally arresting. The first three bars of the Larghetto (HG 98), on f. 88 (a pasted slip), replaced four bars of similar material. For the *coro* Handel indicated the singers' names with initials only. He dated it at the end *Fine dell Opera li 20 di Genaro 1725*.

The autograph contains almost no bass figuring. Where Chrysander gives vocal alternatives, the manuscript has the higher in the cadences to the A sections of 'Se per te' and 'Prigioniera', the lower at bar 8 of 'Sono i colpi', and both (the upper written first) in the cadence to the B section of 'Tirannia'. A number of tempo marks are missing. As with *Giulio Cesare* and *Tamerlano*, it is certain that a manuscript intermediate between the autograph and the performing score has disappeared. This must have supplied 'Spietati', 'Se fiera belva' with its introductory recitative, the changed scoring of 'Pompe vane di morte', the shortened ritornellos of 'Tirannia', the rewritten passages in 'Chi di voi' (recitative continuation) and 'Se 'l mio duol', the tempo marks of 'Di Cupido', 'Confusa si miri', 'Frà tempeste', and 'Ritorna, O caro', and probably the reduction of 'Hò perduto' to a cavatina. All these had reached their final form before the Hamburg score was copied.

Of the three unpublished arias Handel used the material of two in the opera. The F minor 'Ombre, piante', a cavatina of 47 bars scored for four-part strings *senza cembalo*, has the same mood, rhythm, and main idea as its successor, but less finesse; it lacks the flute part, echoes, trills, and grace notes (except one at the last return of 'urne' in bar 35), and is much plainer. In the ritornello the falling thirds of the voice are filled in by the violins in the rhythm ♪♪♪. 'Ben spesso in vago prato', though weak in its context, is perhaps musically superior to 'Scacciata', which took over its main theme and some secondary ideas but treated them differently, and omitted the viola from the A section ritornellos. In the earlier aria the violins do not double the voice in octaves (this was introduced to suggest the twittering swallows), and the B section is quite different, with a pleasant divergence into the minor that Handel did not retain. 'Verrete a consolarmi', a gentle sequential love song, was presumably replaced because it gave Bertarido yet another plaintive aria, and in an inappropriate place. It is thematically related to 'Chi perde un momento' (*Giulio Cesare*, 1725), composed perhaps in the same month, and 'Das zitternde Glänzen', the second of the nine *Deutsche Arien*, which have many links with the operas of 1724–5. The main vocal melody begins like the former, but the continuation is closer to the latter (one of the two written on Bergamo paper). The B section repeats almost identically two bars from 'Non è si vago' (*Giulio Cesare*, 1723–4).

Four of the five additions for the first revival survive in autograph. The E minor 'Sono i colpi', hurriedly written with many corrections, 'Ahi perchè' with its introductory recitative, and 'Vivi, tiranno' are in RM 20 d 2 (ff. 31–8), the duet 'D'ogni crudel martir' with a cue for the *coro* to follow without a break, suppressing both ritornellos and producing a characteristic composite finale, in RM 20 f 11 (ff. 5–7). In bars 9–12 of 'Vivi, tiranno' and the corresponding passage at the end of the A section Handel carefully altered the oboe part to conform with the coloratura in bars 33–5, obscuring the resemblance to the arias in *Il trionfo del Tempo* and *Agrippina*. This was done after the aria had been copied for *Rodelinda*, perhaps for insertion in a later opera. It cannot be called an improvement. The Fitzwilliam Museum (Mus MS 256, pp. 73–6) has an autograph keyboard arrangement of the 'Ouverture in Rodelinda', with some recomposition in the Presto and Minuet (which is in two parts only) and more trills and appoggiaturas than in the orchestral score. On the next page is a second (later) arrangement of the Minuet, with further slight variants. In both autographs a da capo replaces the repeat of the second section. Another Fitzwilliam volume (Mus MS 260, p. 41) has a fragment of an earlier version of 'Spietati':[21] the last four bars of the A section, with the oboes a third higher in the first half of the first bar, the viola part slightly different in the third, and two extra bars (treble and bass only) cancelled before the last. Handel abandoned the sketch (on Italian paper) before starting the B section.

Librettos

1725 (February). 'Rodelinda Regiṅa de' Longobardi, Drama ... Printed and Sold at the *Opera-Office* in the Hay-Market.' 77 pp. Haym's dedication to the Earl of Essex pays tribute to him and other noblemen for supporting the opera. The Argument, in Italian and English translation, is taken verbatim from Salvi's 1710 libretto. A number of Salvi's lines in I i, iii, iv, and vi and II vii (some 63 in all) are marked with *virgole* as not set to music, and three passages—Unulfo's recitative in II iv before 'Frà tempeste', Eduige's exclamation 'Respira anima amante' in II v shortly before 'Scacciata', and Bertarido's recitative 'Miralo' in III viii—have no English translation; this is presumably an oversight, but a bracket against the last may reflect a plan to cut it. 'Hò perduto' has its full text with the B section. 'Trà sospetti' appears as 'Frà sospetti'. Otherwise the text agrees with HG (the first version on pp. 75 and 89–90), except for minor differences in stage directions. 'Tuo drudo' is marked with an asterisk, which usually means that the piece has been lifted from another source; but the words are in Salvi and the music in Handel's autograph.

1725 (December). For this revival the first edition was reprinted or reissued with four additional manuscript pages, headed 'Additional Songs to Rodalinda' [*sic*], inserted at the end. They give the four new texts: 'Quì rivedrò la cara' (seven lines of recitative)–'Sì, rivedrò' for Bertarido, cued to II vii (p. 50); 'Barbara ingiusta sorte'–'Ahi perchè' for Cuzzoni, 'Act III pag. 66

---

[21] Not identified in the *Catalogue* (194).

after the third verse' (i.e. after the line ending 'il mio Consorte'); 'Vivi, tiranno' for Senesino (p. 73, after 'col mio sangue'); and 'D'ogni crudel martir' for Senesino and Cuzzoni 'before the Chorus'. The last three name the singers, not the characters.

1734 Hamburg. 'Rodelinda Königin in der Lombardey ... Gedruckt mit Spieringischen Schrifften.' The arias are in Italian with a translation, the recitatives of both types in German only—a free and abbreviated rendering, some 85 lines shorter than in London. Bertarido does not read the inscription on his monument. Handel is named (as composer of the Italian arias), but not the singers or the author of the recitatives (Wendt). The Italian Argument is translated as 'Kurtzer Inhalt'. The characters are listed with German names: Bertaridus oder Aribert, Grimoald, Hedwig, Onulphus, Garibald. The text was based on the London libretto: 'Hò perduto' is a full aria, but a note states that the B section is cut, and the reading 'Frà sospetti' is preserved. The one significant difference is the insertion of 'D'ogni crudel martir' near the beginning of the last scene, before 'Mio caro bene'.

Copies and Editions

The Hamburg performing score (MA/1047, Smith) has copious bass figuring added by Handel; Chrysander thought that this was for an inexperienced continuo player, but it may have been for the Cluer score. As already noted, Handel had made significant changes in 'Hò perduto', 'Pompe vane di morte', 'Tirannia', the accompanied recitative continuation of 'Chi di voi', and 'Se 'l mio duol' before Smith copied the score. He made two later modifications, inserting the link between 'Pompe vane' and 'Dove sei?' over Smith's rests and rewriting much of the coloratura of 'Sono i colpi'. The former dates from 1725, possibly for the first revival; it is integral only in the Malmesbury score and a Smith copy of the recitative and aria in Manchester. Chrysander's suppression of the first four bars of the ritornello reflects the final state of Hamburg; the music occurs nowhere else in the form familiar today. The simplified coloratura of 'Sono i colpi' was undoubtedly written for Bertolli in 1731 (the E minor setting had been sung in December 1725). Smith copied the autograph version (found in all sources except the Flower parts and the late Granville copy); Handel indicated the new notes in bars 16–17 and 23–6 mostly by letters, but took advantage of a blank stave to write those in bars 36–9 in full. Chrysander inconsistently ignored the original in the first two passages but printed it on the main stave in the third, with the revision above it.

The Hamburg score shows many recitative cuts: $24\frac{1}{2}$ bars from I ii, viii, ix, and x, 111 bars from II i–vi (including the whole of i), and 39 bars from III i–iv. Chrysander indicates two only: one (out of two) in III i and one in III iv, made for the introduction of 'Ahi perchè' in December 1725. Apart from this and the removal of fifteen bars before 'Ritorna, O caro' (possibly also for the first revival), most if not all the cuts can be dated to 1731. The passages were generally bracketed and pasted over, sometimes with new cadences written in: but the contracted recitatives of I ix were rewritten on an inserted leaf with a watermark not found before 1728.[22] Other cuts are bars 52–9 and 100–7 of 'Ombre, piante' (probably December 1725), the B sections

[22] Clausen, 210, 250.

and da capos of 'Con rauco mormorio' and 'Pastorello', and the whole of 'Ritorna, O caro'.

The five numbers printed by Chrysander on pp. 89–90 (small type) and 109–23 are in the manuscript as insertions, but not the other additions. There are clear signs in the last bar of 'Fatto inferno' of the lost orchestral coda, and of a substitution at the recitative cadence before 'Trà sospetti'; this was 'Vi sento' (1731), misbound in the middle of 'Fatto inferno' (ff. 126–9). Presumably for that reason Chrysander marked it as a replacement for 'Pastorello' (HG 99), where the key (C minor after a B major cadence) is impossible and the sense far less appropriate. 'Vivi, tiranno' does not include the modifications in the autograph; the B section and much of the following recitative (ff. 139ᵛ–40) were written by H4, the only copyist other than Smith to work on the score. The upward transpositions of 'Io già t'amai' and 'Prigioniera' for Antinori are noted, and the cadence before the latter changed; it was later returned to the original pitch for 'Non pensi quell'altera' (Fabri, 1731). 'Se per te' has both alternatives at the vocal cadences, 'Prigioniera' the lower, 'Tirannia' the higher; all other manuscript copies except Flower follow Hamburg here. Clausen, apparently relying on stitch holes in the paper, lists 'Hò perduto', 'Se fiera belva', both Garibaldo's arias, and all six of Grimoaldo's as cut at some time. It is difficult to account for this treatment of Grimoaldo except on the supposition of a singer's temporary illness.

The Flower score (S2, mid-1740s) was taken largely if not entirely from the autograph, and reflects no performance. It is the only copy to give 'Hò perduto' as a full aria, 'Tirannia' with its longer ritornellos, and the autograph versions of bars 15 and 80–1 of 'Chi di voi' and the A section of 'Se 'l mio duol'. It follows the autograph, against all other copies, at the vocal cadences of 'Prigioniera' and 'Tirannia'; although in 'Se per te' it gives the same notes as HG and the other sources, it distributes them differently:

Ex. 72

di   che?

'Dove sei?' was copied with eight-bar ritornello and rests at the end of the recitative; Jennens inserted the linking phrase, key signature, and tempo mark over the rests, just as Handel did in Hamburg, but did not cancel the ritornello's first four bars. Jennens also modified the cello solo in bars 8–10 of 'Confusa si miri', which had been wrongly copied, supplied four arias with tempo marks (but left as many others bare), and added bass figuring to several movements in Act I (A section of 'Hò perduto', 'Pompe vane'–'Dove sei?', 'Ombre, piante', and the corrected portion of 'Confusa si miri'), apparently for his own use. His figures are fuller than Handel's in Hamburg. 'Ombre, piante' is complete and written out in full. All the oboes double the first violins in the *coro*, interpreting literally (but perhaps incorrectly) Handel's *Tutti* against the third stave in the autograph.

A very early score at Wiesentheid (H5), from the library of Count Rudolph

Franz Erwein von Schönborn (b. 1677),[23] gives the text of the first production before the forging of the link between 'Pompe vane' and 'Dove sei?' or the cuts in 'Ombre, piante', and was almost certainly copied from Hamburg in its first state before the December 1725 revival. The bass is unfigured. The Count was one of seven brothers who all played instruments and many of whom, including the Count himself (a cellist), were prominent in diplomatic missions. They were on friendly terms with Steffani and may have known Handel, who must have permitted the transmission of the Wiesentheid score. Two or three tempo marks were added by another hand. A stranger insertion is a devotional Latin text in praise of the Virgin Mary underlying the music of Garibaldo's cynical aria 'Di Cupido'.

Malmesbury (S2, c.1726) conflates the first two versions, incorporating the December 1725 additions in the text. The replacements ('Sono i colpi' in E minor, 'Ahi perchè') precede the originals, but the longer recitative leading to 'Se 'l mio duol' is omitted. 'Sì, rivedrò' with its introductory recitative (eleven bars, extant only here) comes immediately after 'Ritorna, O caro'. The *coro* has no opening ritornello, since the duet 'D'ogni crudel martir' led into it, but the autograph cut of the latter's final ritornello is not indicated. The marking *Viol: e Travers:* on the top line of 'Pompe vane' is presumably an accidental survival. The link with 'Dove sei?' is present, followed by the eight-bar ritornello. 'Ombre, piante' is now shortened (95 bars). The D major 'Sono i colpi' has its original coloratura and the low notes at the vocal entry. 'Prigioniera' is in Antinori's key of B flat. Tempo marks agree with HG except that 'Confusa si miri' and 'Ritorna, O caro' have none, the D major 'Sono i colpi', 'Quanto più fiera', and 'Vivi, tiranno' are *Allegro*, and 'Pastorello' *Larghetto*; these correspond to the first printed editions and other early sources. The most interesting feature of this manuscript is its unique preservation of the coda to 'Fatto inferno' (Ex. 71 above).

Lennard (S1, c.1740) and Granville (S5), like Malmesbury, are library copies and have few stage directions or scene headings. The bass figuring is sparse. Both give the first-performance text in most respects, with 'Hò perduto' as a cavatina, no recitative link before 'Dove sei?', and none of the added arias; but they were copied much later. Granville has 'Ombre, piante' complete but the revised coloratura for 'Sono i colpi'; Lennard has the former shortened and the latter in original form. In Lennard 'Dove sei?' has vocal ornaments added in pencil, probably in the later eighteenth century. A Shaftesbury collection (S2), designed like those from *Giulio Cesare*, *Tamerlano*, and several later operas to supplement the printed score, contains (with page cues) the five accompanied recitatives, two of the December 1725 additions ('Ahi perchè' and 'Vivi, tiranno'), and the three from 1731. The cue for 'Vi sento' confirms that it replaced 'Trà sospetti', not 'Pastorello'. If the music was copied from Hamburg, the coda of 'Fatto inferno' had already fallen out.

The Flower parts (S2, mid-1740s) give a haphazard and incomplete text. Though the pieces are numbered consecutively from 1 to 29, the overture, five arias ('Lo farò', 'Se per te', 'Tirannia', 'Ritorna, O caro', and 'Pastorello'), one accompanied recitative ('Fatto inferno'), and the *coro* of the February 1725 score are missing; but there is a supplement of 'Additions' containing three of

[23] See F. Zobeley, 'Werke Händels in der Gräfl. von Schönbornschen Musikbibliothek', *HJb* (1931), 98–116.

the December pieces ('Vivi, tiranno', 'Sì, rivedrò', and the E minor 'Sono i colpi') and two arias rejected before performance ('Ben spesso' and 'Verrete a consolarmi'). S2 must have taken these, and presumably the B section of 'Hò perduto', from the autograph or a derivative, but he did not reproduce the other pre-performance variants of the Flower score. He may have used Hamburg, to which most of the figuring of the cembalo part corresponds. 'Ombre, piante' is complete, but the D major 'Sono i colpi' has the revised coloratura. 'Dove sei?' has the link with the recitative followed by the full ritornello.

Although the parts are all present (violins 1 and 2, viola, cello + bassoon, oboes 1 and 2 + flutes and recorders, and cembalo), they would present difficulties if used for certain arias. Where the bassoons invade the cello part they behave like cuckoos and oust the nominal incumbent, with the result that the true bass does not appear (except on the cembalo). This happens almost throughout 'Con rauco mormorio' and at important points in 'Di Cupido' and 'Se 'l mio duol'. Solos are indicated in the violin, oboe, and cello parts, generally in agreement with the score; those for violin in bars 71–2 of 'Ombre, piante' (also in the Cluer print) and both oboes in bars 8 and 9 of 'Spietati', though not so marked in the autograph or performing score, are probably correct. The flute and recorder parts are complete (the former are unison, not solo, in 'Ombre, piante' and 'Con rauco mormorio'), but the oboes have little employment, appearing only in five arias and the ritornello of 'Pompe vane'. They play in bars 18 and 19 of 'Vivi, tiranno', where Chrysander is perhaps right to suppress them, and (logically) in bars 45–50.

The Schönborn Library has a set of parts extracted by a local copyist from the Wiesentheid score. Though possessing no authority, they are of some interest for performance practice at a contemporary German court. They consist of five bound books—violins 1 and 2, viola, 'Bassons e violone', and 'Contra-Basso'—and loose parts, incomplete, for oboes 1 and 2 + flutes and recorders. The accompaniment of 'L'empio rigor' was evidently treated as a solo; violin 2 stops abruptly after eleven bars. The bassoon–violone book includes the bass of all recitatives but, apart from cello solos at bars 16 and 29 of 'Spietati', does not distinguish between the instruments. It includes both parts in the coda of the A section of 'Di Cupido', and three for two phrases in the B section of 'Con rauco mormorio'. In 'Se 'l mio duol' the bassoon and double-bass parts were copied into the wrong books. The double-bass was expected to play in accompanied recitatives; its part in the first two bars of the F sharp major Larghetto in 'Fatto inferno' was copied and then cancelled. It drops out altogether after 25 bars of 'Mio caro bene' and six of the *coro*, leaving blank spaces; either the whole project was abandoned before performance (there are obvious uncorrected errors) or it was decided to dispense with a double-bass. The wind parts cover only the overture, 'Pompe vane', 'Dove sei?', 'Ombre, piante' (solo flute), 'Se 'l mio duol' (second recorder but not first), and 'Un zeffiro'. Oboe 2 doubles violin 2 in the introduction of the overture (though this takes it below its compass), but violin 1 in 'Dove sei?'. Both oboes play in this aria and throughout the previous recitative.

Handel made two harpsichord arrangements of the overture, one a revision of the other. As noted above, the autograph of the first survives complete, but only the Minuet of the second[24]. The former appears in two Malmesbury

---

[24] Both are printed in *Twenty Overtures*, ii. 26–30, 41–2.

copies (both Smith, c.1725 and c.1728) and RM 18 c 2, ff. 6–8 (Kappa, c.1729), the revised version in the Coke Rivers MS (H1 and Smith junior, c.1727, with a second copy of the Minuet by Smith junior) and RM 18 c 1, ff. 41–2 (S2, c.1728). Both differ from the clumsy arrangement published by Walsh in his first collection (1726). Further copies of the Minuet (treble and bass only) are in RM 18 b 8, f. 99 (Smith junior, c.1728), Add MS 29386, f. 70ᵛ (same copyist as the *Concerto in Otho* in Durham Cathedral MS E 24), and a volume of miscellanies in the Coke Collection.

The popularity of the opera resulted in a large number of excerpts appearing in composite volumes, no fewer than ten in the British Library, seven of them from the Aylesford Collection. Jennens was keen to have every note of Handel's music, even if it led to duplication. RM 18 c 11, ff. 76–87ʳ, has 'Hò perduto' as a full aria and the three suppressed pieces, the F minor 'Ombre, piante', 'Ben spesso', and 'Verrete a consolarmi', copied from the autograph; RM 18 c 10, ff. 100–9, the five accompanied recitatives (HG 20–21 ending at 'affanni', 27, 36, 86–7, and 96–9); RM 19 c 9, ff. 102–6ʳ, harpsichord arrangements of 'Dove sei?' with eight-bar ritornello, 'Prigioniera', 'Ritorna, O caro', and 'Mio caro bene', the first three with da capo instead of dal segno; Add MS 31571, ff. 110–29, the five 'Additional Songs in Rodelinda' of December 1725, 'Vivi, tiranno' (*Allegro*) with the original oboe line in the ritornellos. These are all S2 copies. Jennens himself wrote out flute and/or violin parts for the overture and seven arias, mostly in transposed keys, in RM 19 a 8; 'Dove sei?' in G has its eight-bar ritornello. RM 19 d 12, not an Aylesford volume, contains 'Scacciata' and 'Prigioniera' (ff. 52–4, 71–4, both H5). A collection of Smith copies in Manchester (MS 130 Hd4, v. 313, pp. 111–23) includes 'Io già t'amai', 'Pompe vane', and 'Dove sei?' in its penultimate state, with the recitative link but the full ritornello. An early copy of the E minor 'Sono i colpi' in the Fitzwilliam Museum (Mus MS 265, pp. 15–20) is unlikely to have fallen out of the Hamburg score—a possibility raised by Clausen— since the copyist (H4) at one point omitted the bass for 3½ bars; it was supplied in pencil by another hand, not always correctly. A set of string parts for arias in Vienna Österreichische Nationalbibliothek S. m. 4034 has 'Dove sei?' in G with full ritornello.

In the Coke volume of '24 Opera Songs' are 'L'empio rigor', 'Scacciata' (in G minor), and 'Mio caro bene' with some ornamentation in the voice and violin parts. The violin doubles the voice throughout the B sections and elsewhere in the last two arias. The same collection has a number of keyboard arrangements, with or without words, occasionally ornamented: 'Dove sei?' in G major with full ritornello, 'Scacciata' in D minor (two copies), two December 1725 additions ('Sono i colpi' in E minor and 'Sì, rivedrò'), and 'Mio caro bene' (two copies, one in the hand of William Boyce). A curiosity is a French manuscript of selections from the opera, dated 1809; it was evidently copied from the Cluer print, with many mistakes.

On 20 March 1725 Cluer invited subscriptions for 'the whole Opera of Rodelinda, in Score with all its Parts', and published it on 6 May. The 120 subscribers for 162 copies (a later issue raised the figures to 121 and 180) included Jennens and Newburgh Hamilton as well as a number of distinguished musicians. The score contains no recitatives, secco or accompanied, but is more liberal and accurate with details of orchestration than that of *Giulio Cesare*. The only missing instruments are the horns in the *coro*; most of the complex scoring of 'Con rauco mormorio' is indicated, and so are many instrumental solos. The bass figuring is very close to Hamburg and was probably supplied by Handel. A few tempo marks are omitted, and one (*Allegro* at the start of the overture) is wrong. As in other publications of the period, many dal segno arias appear with da capo, perhaps to avoid the expense of printing modified ritornellos. 'Hò perduto' (as in all contemporary prints) is a cavatina; 'Dove sei?' has its eight-bar ritornello, 'Sono i colpi' its original coloratura. 'Chi di voi', in the absence of the ensuing accompanied recitative, is given a concert end with a ritornello in B flat major; but the retention of the original figuring with an altered bass at the cadence (last bar of HG 85) makes nonsense. Cluer advertised and probably published a flute arrangement of the opera, but the only one known came from Walsh.

Several issues of *Favourite Songs ... Printed and Sold at the Musick Shops*, some including the overture, appeared at the same time, doubtless pirated from theatre copies by Walsh, who used the plates later, many in volume i of *Apollo's Feast* (1726). The songs, printed on one side of the paper, are a mixed lot in incorrect order, and generally lack tempo marks and inner parts, though dal segno indications are correct. Many are followed by flute arrangements in higher keys. The figuring differs from Cluer's and is more remote from Hamburg. Some arias appear in strange keys: 'Dove sei?' in C major and G major, 'L'empio rigor' and 'Scacciata' in A minor, 'Se 'l mio duol' in G minor.

In January 1726 Walsh and Hare published *The favourite Songs in the new Opera Call'd Elisa as also the Additional Songs in the Opera of Rodelinda*. These are the five new pieces of the previous month's revival, but the E minor 'Sono i colpi' is wrongly described as sung by Cuzzoni; so is the duet 'Dogni [*sic*] crudel martir', without mention of Senesino. 'Vivi, tiranno' (*Allegro*) has its original top line, but it is marked for violin only, and the viola part is missing. 'Sì, rivedrò' is in F major. Walsh reprinted this batch in volume iii of *Apollo's Feast* (*c.*1730); in later issues 'Sì, rivedrò' is ascribed to Carestini, who had sung it a tone higher in the 1734 revival of *Il pastor fido*. Walsh published the overture in parts by June 1727. A much later Walsh score (*c.*1750), *Rodelinda ... as it is Perform'd at the Theatre Royal in Covent Garden* (which it never was), is a very incomplete hotchpotch of items from an assortment of old plates, with 'Trà sospetti' as well as the E minor 'Soni i colpi' attributed to Cuzzoni.

Volume ii of Cluer's *Pocket Companion* (December 1725) includes 'Dove sei?', 'Mio caro bene', and 'Scacciata' in the original keys with a flute transposition of the vocal line but no middle parts. During the 1730s 'Scacciata' appeared in several single-sheet editions, sometimes as an English dialogue with words by Henry Carey, and 'Dove sei?' collected its first set of inane words ('God of Musick, charm the Charmer') in volume iii of *The British Musical Miscellany*. Even the Minuet in the overture came out in song form as 'Strephon, in vain thou courtest'.

The only full score is Chrysander's (1876), based as usual on Hamburg. Unaware of Walsh's 1726 publication and several manuscripts, Chrysander included only two of the 1725 additions together with three dating from 1731 which he subsequently printed in the operas to which they belong. He went to the autograph for the B section of 'Hò perduto', printed in brackets, and a few minor details, but left most of it undisturbed. Oskar Hagen's vocal score

(Leipzig, 1923), a modification of that used for the 1920 Göttingen production, is of no interest except as a period piece. It retains most of the recitative but butchers the arias only less brutally than those of *Giulio Cesare*. Eight are omitted, and all the others shortened except the cavatinas 'Hò perduto', 'Ombre, piante', and 'Chi di voi' and the duet. Yet a gratuitous repeat of the overture's Minuet appears as a Pantomime in the middle of Act II and two movements from the G minor concerto grosso of Op. 6 begin Act III. Tempo marks are altered indiscriminately, and objectionable rallentandos written in, notably in the last section of the *coro*. The stage directions introduce countless glosses that bear little relation to Handel's opera.

Additional Notes

* (p. 582) Bars 32–5 of 'Mio caro bene' appear to be a direct echo of bars 16–19 at the corresponding point in 'Ritorna, O caro'. Whether this was a deliberate or a subconscious allusion on Handel's part, it is singularly apt.

* (p. 601) Cluer's first advertisement (in the German but not the English edition of Deutsch) appeared on 22 February, claiming that the score was 'compos'd by Mr Handel and figur'd and corrected by his Hand . . . Care will be taken that not one Song in this Opera shall be printed by any other Persons than the Proprietors.' A vain hope!

CHAPTER 25

SCIPIONE

ROLLI's Argument in the printed libretto sets the scene: 'Publius Cornelius Scipio, being Proconsul in Spain, laid Siege to the City of New Carthage, at that Time possess'd by the Carthaginians, and took it by Assault. Among the rest of the Captive Ladies there was one of singular Beauty, with whom he fell deeply in Love; but when he found she had, by a former Promise, been engag'd to Luceius Prince of the Celtiberians; as a Testimony of his signal Magnanimity, he immediately quitted his Pretensions, and generously restor'd her to him, as well as all the Treasure her Father had before offer'd for her Ransom.' The scene is New Carthage, the modern Cartagena.

Act I begins in *a Piazza, with a Triumphal Arch. Scipio, on a Triumphal Car, follow'd by a victorious Army, Slaves of both Sexes, and Lelius, a Roman Commander.* Scipio proclaims his conquest of Spain, looks forward to enslaving Egypt, congratulates his officers, and bestows a gold diadem on Lelio, who offers him in return the fairest of the captives. Scipio, struck by Berenice's beauty, learns her name and that of her fellow prisoner Armira, rescued by Lelio from some marauders. Berenice begs Scipio to protect her virtue, and he reassures her. Lelio hears her sighing for Lucejo and recognizes the name, having once been captured by his father and generously spared. Lelio tries to console both ladies with a promise of comfortable quarters in a palace with 'delicious gardens'. Berenice can think only of Lucejo and prefers death to separation. Lucejo comes forward *in the Habit of a Roman Soldier*, which he has assumed on learning of the fall of New Carthage while on the way to his wedding. Having witnessed the first scene, he plans to steal into the garden and carry off Berenice, comparing himself to a snared turtle-dove. The set changes to *a Garden.* Lelio has fallen in love with Armira. Scipio promises her to him and declares the entrance of strangers within the palace precincts a capital offence. Armira laments her slavery; Lelio replies that only love can banish it, but she says she must be free first. He decides to free her when he can. Berenice enters and learns of Scipio's order, which Lelio mentions as proof of Scipio's love and urges her to return it. She indignantly asks if he has forgotten Lucejo, though she does not know if he has survived the fall of the city. Lelio urges her not to abandon hope. Alone, she laments her unlucky passion and bids the breezes find her love and bring him to her. Lucejo answers *from within the Scene* and enters, having deceived the guards with his disguise. She bids him return with her father's troops and his own to rescue her. He cannot bring himself to leave, but on her entreaty hides as Scipio approaches. Scipio asks the cause of her agitation, promising that her bondage will be easy, and begins to plead his love. This is too much for Lucejo, who calls out, is discovered, and defiantly claims Berenice as his own. Scipio asks who he is, but Berenice prevents him answering and to his astonishment denounces him as a madman who would rob the victor of his spoils. She orders him to go without a word, asks for Scipio's protection, and departs. Lelio enters, intent on saving Lucejo, whom he addresses as Erennio. He tells Scipio that 'Erennio' fought under his (Scipio's) father, but partly lost his senses as a result of harsh treatment in enemy hands; this camouflage is designed to lull Scipio's suspicions of Lucejo's Spanish accent. Scipio tells Lelio to look after him. Lucejo, left alone, cannot make out if Berenice's harsh words were feigned or not. How could a Spaniard be expected to listen to his rival's love-making? He fears Scipio may have made an impression on her, and implores jealousy not to torture him.

Act II opens in *a Sea-port, with a Ship newly arriv'd. Hernando the Father of Berenice* [and King of the Balearic Islands], *who disembarquing comes on Shore, and after him Lelius.* Ernando proposes to ransom Berenice and sends spies to discover her whereabouts. He has landed by leave of Scipio, to whom (through Lelio) he offers tribute and friendship. The set changes to *the Apartments of the two Prisoners.* Scipio tries to comfort the unhappy Berenice and asks about her parentage. She explains that she is Ernando's daughter, and Sitalce who fell in defence of New Carthage was her uncle. Scipio promises her freedom and again starts to make love. She interrupts, saying she has given her heart to the Celtiberian prince. He asks her to think again, but without much hope, and leaves. Lelio enters with Lucejo. Berenice brusquely tells the latter to go away and not come back, thereby confirming his jealous suspicions. He denounces her faithlessness and tells her angrily to enjoy her new love. She sends Lelio after him for his protection, and foresees wave after wave of disaster. A change of set must be presumed here. Armira rebukes Lelio's importunity: it will be time enough to love him when he sets her free. Alone, she justifies her playing for time by the hope that her father Indibile will hear of her capture and rescue her; moreover the most ardent wooer may turn out a tyrant. Lucejo returns, unable to leave Berenice, and tells Armira of his love but not his identity. She offers him her hand as proof of her good faith. *They join Hands.* Berenice, entering suddenly, hears his reply 'O bella, tu mi conforti', repeats the words with contempt, and denounces them both for immodesty. Armira leaves in a huff, and the lovers are beginning to quarrel when Scipio enters, annoyed that his orders have again been disobeyed. Lucejo admits his identity and his intention of abducting Berenice. Scipio places him under arrest. Lucejo is willing to submit to the Roman general but not to a rival who has not conquered him, and challenges Scipio to draw and fight. Lelio *enters with Guards that surround Luceius, with their Spears pointed against his Breast.* Scipio assures Berenice he will not be harmed. Lelio orders him to surrender his sword and escorts him off with the guards. Scipio urges Berenice to marry a more worthy suitor, a Roman. She acknowledges the power of love, not of the senate; admiring Roman valour and magnanimity, she could love a Roman if her heart were not pledged elsewhere. As it is, she will be as constant as a rock.

No set is indicated for the opening of Act III. Scipio bewails the fact that honour obstructs the path of love. He receives Ernando in audience and asks for Berenice's hand in return for her liberty. Ernando replies that it is too late: she is pledged to Lucejo, and although Scipio is welcome to Ernando's life and kingdom, he cannot make him break his promise. All human life would be brutalized without honour. Scipio, impressed, sends for Berenice and Lucejo; the latter must go as a prisoner to Rome. Scipio struggles with his conscience and decides to sacrifice his feelings.[1] Another set change is missing here. Lelio tells Lucejo (guarded and *in his own proper Habit*) that he must go to Rome the next day. Berenice swears to accompany him, if only as a naked ghost. Lucejo asks her to pardon his jealousy and preserve her life for a better fate; let her ask Scipio to impose a sentence of death rather than slavery, and remember Lucejo in the murmur of trees, rivers, and breezes. Lelio, overcome by emotion, follows him out. Berenice hopes Scipio will either restore her to Lucejo or let her die with him. Scipio enters, tells her in a single line to weep no more, and goes out, leaving her to express relief. The set changes to *a Great Hall with a Throne in it. Scipio seated, who receives Hernando attended by Negroes, who are laden with various Presents of Silver and Gold.* These are intended as tribute to Rome and ransom for Berenice. Scipio orders her to be brought in and, *stepping down from the throne,*[2] releases her; seeing her still downcast, he assures her that the god of war shall yield to love. In *an Apartment* Lelio asks Armira why she has concealed the fact that her father is Indibile, 'that mighty Friend to Rome'. She tells him to love her and hope for the best, and goes out.[3] He sings an aria in praise of valour and love. Lucejo, his sword restored, meets Berenice; both have been summoned before Scipio. She assures him of her love; he compares himself to a migrating bird seeking its native woods in her breast.[4] The set changes back to *the throne-room.*[5] Scipio, having conquered the enemy, will now conquer himself. He *ascends the Throne*, bestows Lucejo on Berenice, congratulates Lelio on aiding his friend's attempted escape, presents Ernando's gifts to Berenice and her bridegroom, and *descends from the Throne.* The others acclaim his magnanimity; Lucejo solemnly promises his allegiance and that of his subjects. After a love duet for him and Berenice all agree that Spain can be proud of such a conqueror.

The source of the story is Livy xxvi. 50. Publius Cornelius Scipio the elder, future conqueror of Hannibal (to be distinguished from his adopted grandson and namesake, who captured Carthage and the Spanish city of Numantia more than sixty years later), took New Carthage by storm in 210 BC. Livy does not name his beautiful captive or her father, but says she was betrothed to Allucius, a young Celtiberian desperately in love with her. Scipio, though impressed by her beauty, is not emotionally involved; he returns her to Allucius on condition of political friendship. Her parents and relatives insist on his accepting the gold they have brought to ransom her. Not liking to refuse, he bestows it on Allucius as a wedding present. The young man is so moved that he enlists 1,400 horsemen to serve under Scipio. Polybius (x. 19), one of Livy's sources, gives a different account without the love interest. Lelio is C. Laelius, who commanded Scipio's fleet in the attack on New Carthage and twenty years later became consul. Indibilis was a prince of the Ilergetes, a

---

[1] According to the libretto this accompanied recitative was never performed.

[2] The direction *scesa dal trono* is in the autograph, the Fitzwilliam section of the performing score, and the Flower copy, but nowhere else.

[3] Chrysander omits this scene, which is in all librettos and the Hamburg score, printing instead (HG 93) part of a recitative that was never performed.

[4] The librettos give this recitative and aria to Lelio. Rolli may have intended it for him in the previous scene, but Handel set it for Lucejo with slight verbal changes in the B section.

[5] Omitted from the libretto by mistake, but in the autograph.

former ally of the Carthagians; in the following year he made a treaty with the Romans which he subsequently broke.

Scipio's magnanimity was an obvious model not only for Romans but for librettists of a later age anxious to flatter a contemporary prince. He was the hero of more than one seventeenth-century opera; the War of the Spanish Succession rendered him more topical. At least three librettists made this Spanish episode the subject of an opera, identifying Scipio by implication with the Habsburg Archduke Charles (1685–1740), later the Emperor Charles VI, who campaigned in Spain from 1703 till he succeeded his brother in 1711. The Habsburgs had dominions in Italy, which was therefore involved in the war when Handel himself was in the country. Two of the librettos are well known and were set by many composers: Zeno's *Scipione nelle Spagne* (1710) and Agostino Piovene's *Publio Cornelio Scipione* (1712). The third, by Antonio Salvi, had the same title as Piovene's and was produced at Livorno in 1704 under the protection of Prince Ferdinando de' Medici. Handel's is the only subsequent opera based on it; he probably obtained the text through his connection with the Tuscan court.[6]

Rolli seems to have recovered lost ground at the Royal Academy. He arranged three librettos for Handel in 1726–7, but apparently none for any other composer; no explanation for this has been found. While *Scipione* was the first to reach the stage, *Alessandro* had been begun earlier, for Handel lifted the sinfonia at the start of Act II of *Scipione* from its autograph. *Alessandro* was undoubtedly planned to introduce Faustina Bordoni to the London stage, an event several times prognosticated by the press in the late summer of 1725. She was not free until March 1726, and Handel, after several revivals, brought forward *Scipione* as a stopgap. According to Rolli he composed the music in three weeks; ten days elapsed between the completion of the score and its performance. It is scarcely surprising that both libretto and music show signs of haste.

Salvi's drama, though long, verbose, repetitive in its situations, and overburdened with political argument, is more logical and coherent than the dog's dinner that Rolli made of it. The latter's note in the libretto, 'The first Hint of this *Drama*, and some Lines in it, are borrow'd; but what, otherwise, relates either to the Plot itself, or the Diction thro' the Whole, is entirely new', is (for Rolli) a modest exaggeration. He retained a few lines of recitative, but no aria texts, preferring to paraphrase, rewrite, and condense. Although some of his arias are at least the equal of Salvi's, he was casual about dramatic consistency and motivation and, as in *Floridante*, made no attempt at a balanced design. Each of Salvi's acts has five sets; Rolli does not always bother to indicate set changes (for example in II iv and III ii), fails to specify where the opening of Act III takes place, and shows little discrimination in the shaping of scenes. Many of them contain two or more arias and end with fragments of recitative, bearing no relation to exits and entrances. The numbering in Act III was further confused by Handel's revisions before and after performance (and muddled by Chrysander), so that some scenes, for example that on HG 96, are found with four different numbers. Haste was no doubt partly responsible for this, and for the reuse of the words of Scipio's aria

---

[6] See Strohm, *HJb* (1975), 120–2; *Essays*, 52–3, where the historical Scipio is wrongly identified. The composer of the Livorno score is not known. The 1726 Turin libretto, set by G. A. Giay, is based on Piovene, not Salvi.

'Gioja si spera' in a different order for his recitative before the *coro*; but such slapdash methods were characteristic of Rolli.

While the general outline of Salvi's plot remains, Rolli made significant changes in the secondary characters. Berenice's father (Annone, a Carthaginian noble) does not appear in Salvi: his place is taken by Bomilcare, the Carthaginian ambassador, who at Annone's instigation tries to arrange a peace treaty between Rome and Carthage, offering Berenice's hand to Scipio as one of the terms. Bomilcare is delighted to discover that Scipio loves her. Salvi has three extra characters. Scipio's batman Sifone and Armira's old nurse Zaida, who play traditional buffo roles, were eliminated as a matter of course. Lelio is a clumsy conflation of two Roman soliders, Marzio,[7] who has captured Armira and lusts after her, and Celso, Scipio's confidant, who owes a debt of honour to Lucejo's father and acts as a go-between for the lovers, arranging several meetings between them, concealing Lucejo from Scipio, and generally trying to smooth their stormy relationship. Armira's role and character are entirely different. It is she, not Berenice, who is of royal blood, and she acts the part, rebuking Berenice for jealous suspicions and Lucejo for conduct unbecoming his rank, and easily persuading Scipio to remove her from Marzio's rude household. On being admitted to Berenice's quarters late in Act I she finds herself in love with Scipio and enjoying her captivity. When Berenice rejects Scipio's hand during the treaty negotiations Armira offers to take her place, but is dissuaded by Bomilcare on account of the notorious Roman hostility to kings. She is not paired off at the end; indeed Marzio and Sifone are so impressed by Scipio's self-restraint that they renounce all unchaste desires. Salvi's Armira is an interesting character, with as many arias as Berenice and Lucejo.

Rolli understandably reduced the political element, but he also confused it. The artificial situation in II viii, where Lucejo submits to the senate but not to a rival lover, is not in Salvi's libretto, where he proclaims himself an enemy of both, and only submits (much more convincingly) when overcome by Scipio's generosity at the end of the opera. Salvi draws him as almost insane with love, wildly impetuous, and obsessed by a death-wish. He refuses to believe Celso's assurances that Berenice's deceptions were in his interest, and even when she proves her fidelity by trying to kill herself with Celso's sword and rejecting her father's peace conditions, he still wants to die, regarding Annone's suggestion that Berenice should be used as a pawn in the treaty as a moral outrage. While not changing the outlines of his character, Rolli weakens and conventionalizes him by omitting the light and shade of the dialogue.

Much more damaging is his treatment of Berenice and Scipio. Salvi's Berenice is no weathercock. Although in Act I she tells a lie to prevent Lucejo giving himself away when Scipio catches them together, and asks him to leave her in Act II, she makes it clear that it hurts her as much as him. Rolli spoils both scenes by making her over-react: in I vii she accuses him of trying to deprive Scipio of his lawful prey, and Rolli stresses the false situation by giving her a strong aria ('Vanne, parti'); in Act II she orders Lelio to send Lucejo away for ever, although there is no immediate danger as Scipio is not present. This is a device to give Lucejo a jealous aria and Berenice a despairing one; it makes her appear the author of her own troubles. Her moment of

---

[7] Lucius Marcius was another Roman commander in Spain. Zeno in *Scipione nelle Spagne* seems to have borrowed his relationship with Elvira (Armira) from Salvi.

weakness, when she gives way to jealousy on seeing Armira offer her hand to Lucejo, is grossly mishandled by Rolli. This is the one scene in which he retains a fair amount of Salvi's dialogue, but he omits the essential motivation: Armira and Lucejo, who have barely met before, recognize each other as of royal blood. Rolli, having demoted Armira, can only make Lucejo refuse to say who he is, and inserts the idiotic couplet:

> *Armira.* M'offendi; in pegno di fè la destra prendine.
> *Lucejo.* Oh bella, tu mi conforti. (*Si danno la mano.*)

Rolli even omits the line in which Berenice accuses Armira of giving her hand 'a Cavaliere ignoto'. The scene in Salvi (III v) where Berenice resists Scipio's pressure and says she must marry for love drives her temporarily out of her mind. Celso finds her raving, and can restore her only by offering to arrange another meeting with Lucejo, now in prison.

Rolli's Scipio has little backbone and all too much of the imperturbable clemency of Metastasio's Titus (parts of the libretto, especially in Act III, read like bad Metastasio). He acts the conventional lover, showing a most un-Roman forbearance in face of Lucejo's threats in I vii and leaving him unguarded not only then but for most of Act II. There is no hint of imperial power behind his approaches to Berenice, especially in II ii. He is a far more formidable figure in Salvi, who gives him three big soliloquies. The first, in II xi, is concerned with Lucejo, whose identity he has guessed; he cannot help admiring him, and begins to suspect his own motives in denouncing him as a political enemy. In III iv he is torn between desire for Berenice and fear of his reception in Rome if he returns with a foreign wife, especially one of Carthaginian blood. In III xviii he confronts his central conflict: Berenice will make him happy, but his reputation as a soldier and statesman will make him immortal. His decision once taken, the plot is soon wound up. Rolli reduces his struggle to a single sentence at the start of Act III and a speech in the next scene, where he resolves to sacrifice his feelings as a result of Ernando's pronouncements about honour. This decision, the hinge of the plot, comes so early that all dramatic tension is drained from the rest of the opera; the proposal to send Lucejo to Rome, not in Salvi, is a weak attempt to spin things out. The one line in III iii (iv in HG) in which Scipio tells Berenice to be happy is a dismal anticlimax, and his aria 'Gioja sì speri' in v (vi) rings false. His accompanied recitative 'Il poter' would have made more sense at the start of the last scene, before 'Dopo il nemico', but there is no evidence that Rolli or Handel thought of putting it there.

The spectacular and effective opening scenes of the first two acts are in Salvi, though Bomilcare's disembarcation with the ransom (and the negroes, 'Cavalieri Mori, che portano il bagaglio') begins his Act III. For Lucejo's undramatic first aria Rolli changed the words but kept the ornithological simile. In Salvi's garden scene it is Lucejo who hears Berenice singing off-stage, but he does not answer and she does not enter. The change here, an obvious improvement, was probably due to Handel, who has similar episodes in several other operas. Lelio's attempt to explain Lucejo's Spanish accent by addressing him as Erennio, another Rolli gloss, is gratuitous and verges on the absurd. But Rolli deserves credit for contracting the latter part of Act II and giving Berenice the climactic aria 'Scoglio d'immota fronte' (strangely it did not at first end the act), and for the creation of Ernando. In his first draft he included Berenice's mother Rosalba as well, presumably because Dotti was expected to be available. She accompanies her husband's embassy, echoes his sentiments, adds nothing to the plot, and was presently cut out, but not before Handel had given her two arias. Lelio's role is ambivalent. Salvi's Marzio has an interest in Scipio's marriage to Berenice, since he has been promised Armira's hand if and when it takes place; but there was no need for Lelio, while acting as Lucejo's friend, to urge Berenice to return Scipio's love. Lelio and Armira emerge as a conventional pair of secondary lovers. Their relationship scarcely develops; Armira is confined to playing the flirt and keeping Lelio on a string. Rolli seems to have been incapable of thinking in a long dramatic span, or of adapting the work of other men without reducing it to incoherence. In the last resort Handel must take some of the responsibility; but Rolli's insistence on making his personal mark, instead of leaving well alone in the manner of Haym, no doubt made him an intractable collaborator.

These weaknesses in the libretto and its author, together with the necessity for haste, are quite enough to account for the disappointing impact made by *Scipione* when compared with the three preceding masterpieces, and indeed with all the earlier Royal Academy operas except *Floridante*. Though the score contains much splendid music, it has neither the unity nor the cumulative power that Handel has led us to expect. Burney's coolness about Act I— 'There seems to be less of Handel's accustomed fire, originality, and contrivance in the airs of this act, than in any of those that preceded this period'—is not unfair, though one or two scenes can be excepted. Burney thought Act II 'equal in excellence to that of any of Handel's most celebrated operas'; by common consent, despite its dramatic incongruities, it contains the finest music. There is no denying the scrappiness of Act III. Working against time did not so much dam Handel's invention as prevent him from bringing music and drama into focus—and perhaps from insisting on Rolli supplying a viable framework. The autograph suggests that he received the libretto piecemeal. It is characteristic that he composed not too little music but too much, and was forced to cut, rearrange, and patch.

Chrysander's score of Act III is a very defective guide to what was performed in 1726; that text must be disentangled before the opera can be discussed. The arias 'Il fulgido seren' (HG 86), 'Son pellegrino' (HG 103), and the last three in the appendix (HG 131–5; this scene followed Scipio's 'Gioja si speri', HG 92) were removed before performance, together with their recitatives. The act began with an eight-bar sinfonia in E minor and a string-accompanied setting of Scipio's 'Miseri affetti'; his accompanied recitative 'Il poter' was almost certainly cut; 'Gioja sì speri' was followed by a ten-line recitative for Lelio and Armira, 'Tu d'Indibile figlia'. Originally this introduced an aria for Armira, 'Nell'amor nella speranza', succeeded by a recitative for Lelio and Lucejo, 'Prence, il rigor' (of which the last part appears on HG 93) and Lelio's aria 'Del debellar di gloria' with different words. Handel, still before performance, cut out 'Nell'amor nella speranza' and 'Prence, il rigor', altering the context and the words of Lelio's aria.

Handel had a soft spot for downtrodden heroines; Berenice evidently captured his sympathy and despite her equivocal behaviour emerges as the

most convincing character. Although her dramatic role lacks variety, consisting largely of laments for her unhappy fate, her music does not. She is most
sensitively drawn, especially in the first two acts—more so, we may feel, than
she deserves in view of her rough treatment of Lucejo. The first of her two
siciliano arias, 'Un caro amante', has a certain ambiguity of rhythm in that
the natural emphasis falls constantly on the second beat of the bar, the first
assuming the function of an upbeat. If this was intended to express her
confused state of mind on falling into the hands of the Romans, Handel
scarcely makes the point clear. In any event it is an attractive piece with the
characteristic siciliano lilt and a B section that moves from D minor to E major
(dominant of A) before dropping to A minor and a much shortened return to
the da capo. Handel was to echo more than one of its phrases in the 12/8
symphony in Act II of *Jephtha*. Berenice's meeting with Lucejo in the garden is
the high point of Act I, managed with a subtle control of form. Her
accompanied recitative 'O sventurati affetti' in the emotional key of B flat
minor strikes a profoundly tragic note after Lelio's cheery F major aria. The
change from triple to common time and the reprise of the opening, telescoped
from eight to five bars with the voice's last phrase (but not the cadence)
modified, produce a most satisfying design; all the weight falls on the three
passionately charged words, the intervening text relegated to secco. Their
return leads straight into the aria in which she invokes the breezes to bring
back her lover. 'Dolci aurette' is one of those simple Largo arias with short
phrases supported by continuo alone in which Cuzzoni made a great
impression; 'Falsa imagine' in *Ottone*, as Burney notes, was the prototype of the
class. Despite the plainness of the material, which dates back to the Italian
period (*La Resurrezione* and the cantata *La solitudine*[8]), there is much art in its
treatment. The bass acts as a unifier by anticipating and echoing the vocal
line, and plain and dotted rhythms are cunningly alternated; they should on
no account be regularized. Handel writes in his own ornamentation, giving
the voice extra notes in bars 4 and 5 and a rare sextuplet for 'velocissime' in
bar 16. Berenice's repeated question 'Dov'è?' prepares the way for the surprise
of Lucejo's off-stage answer: when Berenice reaches the dominant in a
seemingly regular da capo, he replies in that key with the first four bars of the
melody sung to appropriate new words, and the scene continues in secco
recitative.

'Vanne, parti', in which Berenice orders Lucejo out of the garden, is too
powerful a piece for its context. The short abrupt phrases, the first preceding
the sixteen-bar ritornello and cutting off Lucejo's recitative cadence, would
have better apostrophized a tyrant than a courageous if rash lover. But it is
highly dramatic, with its sudden silences as she pauses for breath before her
self-pitying asides, the contrapuntal repartee between violins and bass in bars
5–10, 73–8, and later, and the contrasts of mood and dynamics throughout.
The same principle extends to the B section, where Berenice abandons her
asides for appeals to Scipio's protection.

The cavatina 'Tutta raccolta ancor' in II ii is again superbly placed,
Berenice's C minor Largo with its initial heavy octave unisons following at
once on Ernando's B flat geniality. The texture is permeated by the drooping

---

[8] The revised version, dated 1718, edited by Malcolm Boyd and published by Bärenreiter
(Kassel etc., 1970). Chrysander printed an earlier fragmentary setting, without this aria, as no. 24
of the continuo cantatas.

first phrase, which recurs constantly in the bass, and the stressed quavers of her 'palpitating heart'. Her trembling may be discerned too in the quaver rests that break up both vocal and instrumental lines in bars 8 and 17. With the second and greater of Berenice's siciliano arias, 'Com'onda incalza', the emphasis changes from apprehension to despair. The music perfectly articulates the verbal simile: the rocking quaver groups return again and again as wave after wave comes in to submerge her hopes, each one acting as a starter to the next, and find a reluctant resolution in the A section's varied ritornello. The high tessitura and wide leaps call for a great singer. In the B section the upper pedals of the opening ritornello sink to the bass and, in association with bold rich harmony, paint a mood of emotional exhaustion. From E flat the tonality moves to D major (dominant of G minor), then suddenly in three bars to A flat minor and G minor ('di dolor in dolor in morte vanno'). Elsewhere too Handel associated the key of A flat minor with death. Dent calls these progressions typically Scarlattian.

Nothing could offer sharper contrast than the aria with which Berenice concludes Act II. Hitherto she has been confined to flat keys. Now her defiance blazes forth in the bright D major of 'Scoglio d'immota fronte', a key not yet heard in the opera, and with a fullness of orchestration unapproached elsewhere in this score. Burney, echoed by Chrysander, saw it as prophetic of 'the best dramatic songs of Vinci and Pergolesi', Leichtentritt of 'Ocean, thou mighty monster' in Weber's *Oberon*. Certainly it casts its spear into the future. Perhaps a closer parallel would be the spectacular arias, charged with intense rhythmic energy, composed by Mozart under the impact of the Mannheim school. The orchestra is laid out in eight parts, with two oboes, bassoons, and three violins, and the aria planned on a grand scale (it was twelve bars longer when first copied). The ritornello presents three ideas, rising semiquaver scales, rapid oscillations on neighbouring notes, and triadic leaping figures; all are shared by the whole orchestra, and the last by the voice as well. The great striding arpeggio covering a twelfth with which the voice enters (the bottom D was an afterthought, possibly for Strada in 1730) was clearly suggested by the mountain peak towering above the elements. The chordal groups, rising triadically while the harmony below remains static, stand for the firmness of the rock, the scales and oscillations for the raging sea and wind; the vocal line strives ever upwards in token of Berenice's constancy. For all its exuberance the scoring is rich in detail: the solo oboe at bar 18, the staccato repeated notes, now for violins over energetic lower strings (bars 28–31), now for violins, violas, and bassoons with the string basses silent (37–40), now a combination of the two (43 ff.). In the B section, without wind, the motion is downward (slurred first violin arpeggios) and the dynamic mark *piano* throughout, so that the da capo can strike with renewed impact. In her whole career Cuzzoni can seldom have had a more rewarding piece with which to end an act.

In Act III Berenice has little cause to complain of destiny, and both her arias bubble with cheerfulness. The accompanied recitative 'Ah! Scipion, dove sei?' in Scene ii ventures with brief eloquence into the more recondite sharp keys; but Scipio reassures her almost at once, and she gives vent to her joy in a dancing 3/8 aria ('Già cessata') with pleasantly irregular phrases of two, four, and seven bars. 'Il fulgido seren', Handel's first thought here, is similar in mood and metre but palpably inferior. 'Bella notte', again in 3/8, is even more exuberant and dance-like. Handel avoids the danger of monotony in this type of aria by a playful interchange between *piano* and *forte*, occasional *marcato* quavers for the violins, cross-rhythms (including hemiola), a varied disposition of the triplets, sometimes on the first two beats, sometimes on the second and third, sometimes on all three, and in the B section a switch to even semiquavers. This buoyant aria suggests that Handel saw Berenice as basically carefree and youthful; it does not quite accord with the more serious portrait of the first two acts. The love duet with Lucejo, 'Sì, fuggano i tormenti', is less interesting than most such pieces; the main theme's jogging rhythm, which penetrates both sections, grows monotonous with repetition, despite occasional savoury suspensions in the voice parts.

In the libretto Lucejo is a typical operatic Spaniard, impetuous, quixotic, and touchy about his honour. Handel seems to have matched the music rather to Senesino's peculiar talents than to dramatic propriety. His first aria, 'Lamentandomi', is a routine simile piece in which he likens himself to a dove searching for his mate and falling an easy victim to the hunter's snare, hardly a heroic posture for a soldier. The music does bring out the sense of searching. It is not clear if the *marcato* repeated notes represent the bird or the jaws of the waiting trap, but they give a rather pale aria what interest it possesses. 'Dimmi, cara', though no more military, is far superior and was the popular hit of the opera. The Adagio opening, punctuated by two silent fermata bars, no doubt took some ornament, though elaborate roulades would spoil what follows. The Andante melody with its irregular phrase lengths, $3+3+5+4$ bars in the first statement, $3+3+3+3+4$ in the second, is singularly attractive. The hesitant rhythm and the equally capricious iterations of 'sì' and 'nò', separated by rests, in the B section express the anxieties of the imploring lover. Handel seldom doubled Senesino at the octave; after the simple A section the entrance of the viola, while the violins play a $3+5$ contraction of the melody, adds a sheen to the ritornello. There are fine strokes in Lucejo's recitative in I viii, especially the rising chromatic scale in the bass (HG 31) as he indignantly repeats Berenice's reproaches; but his aria, 'Figlia di reo timor', is not the unbridled outburst that the situation and the text lead one to expect. The leisurely opening, hesitating between C minor and E flat, and two emphatic cadences in the latter key may have been designed to set off the angular jealousy motive in octaves (bars 7–9), which makes two sudden incursions into the A section and takes full control in the two subsequent ritornellos, where alone it is harmonized. The chromatic phrase that introduces it in the first ritornello (bar 5) has potentialities that Handel might have explored further.

'Parto, fuggo' (II iii) is so similar to Berenice's 'Vanne, parti' in I vii, to which it is in effect a reply, as to suggest deliberate allusion. Both arias are in a rapid 3/8 with the first word ejaculated before a long ritornello; both are based on a bustling semiquaver violin figure that desists in the B section. In Lucejo's this figure often has a little rhythmic flip on the third quaver of the bar, as in similar pieces in *Amadigi* (Dardano's first two arias) and elsewhere. The semitone lifts in the bass while the violins outline the same chord (bars 6, 7, 9, 10, etc.) increase the sense of urgency, while phrases of from one to five and seven bars and the pauses and breathless exclamations in the B section reflect Lucejo's excitable temperament. 'Cedo a Roma' is a fine example of an aria presenting two contrasted emotions, a device of which Handel seldom fails to make the most. Lucejo is content to yield on the political and military front—

he says so at once, *Sedato*, an unusual direction that occurs more than once in this opera—but not on the field of love: the very idea sends him into a loud *Concitato* outburst with buzzing string semiquavers that make a splendid contrast with the gentle rhythm, voice and strings in thirds and silent basses, of the Larghetto sections. The single ritornello comes at the end of the A section; the da capo, like the opening, sets off at once in E major after a G sharp minor cadence. Both moods exploit Senesino's strength: his command of lyrical legato and his agile coloratura in the octave above middle C.

'Se mormora rivo' (III iii) is Lucejo's finest aria. His jealousy of Berenice has been dispelled, but he must go to Rome as a prisoner. The music eloquently reflects his bitter-sweet mood, a mixture of regret and longing to which the rare B minor tonality, the use of two transverse flutes (the instrument of mourning), the dotted violin figure that keeps turning back on itself, and the marching bass octaves in the ritornellos each make a signal contribution. The texture is rich, the strings often in four parts; the plaintive B section with continuo only is brief but far from perfunctory. The tempo in all main sources is *Largo*. 'Come al natio' has another bird simile, the complement to Lucejo's first aria. It is a companion piece to Berenice's 'Bella notte', strongly masculine with firm downbeats and no feminine dance measures. The melody is free and happy, the harmony firmly rooted in tonic and dominant: the lovers' troubles are over. Handel's use of triadic decoration over a bouncing octave pedal point is always effective. In the accompanied recitative 'In testimon' before the duet Handel underlines the solemnity of Lucejo's oath with copious tempo indications, *Adagio, Sostenuto, più Andante,* and *più Adagio,* all within eight bars.

Scipio is the key character on whom the drama depends. Handel's failure to make him convincing as a conqueror is the principal reason for the opera's disappointing impact in the theatre. Rolli's contribution was not helpful, but the composer must shoulder most of the blame, especially as he seems to have cut the two strongest pieces in the part. The success of the opening scene is due not so much to Scipio's music as to the design, taken over from Salvi but immeasurably enlarged by Handel's manipulation of form and tonality. The curtain rises on a scene full of action as the dance-like third movement of the overture gives place to the noble and justly celebrated March. Scipio, his army, and his prisoners enter through a triumphal arch; he announces his victory in the cavatina 'Abbiam vinto' in G major, the key of the overture, then drops to secco recitative for the distribution of honours and his decisive meeting with Berenice. He comforts her fears in an E minor Andante, 'Scaccia, O bella', without ritornello or upper instruments. This turns out to be not a new aria but the B section of 'Abbiam vinto', whose da capo follows, naturally in G major. The entire scene, including the overture, is unified by tonality and an extended da capo form; it has presented most of the main strands of the plot, including the relationship of Lelio and Armira, with a characteristic economy. Neither section of Scipio's aria has exceptional merit, but it fulfils its function.

Scipio makes two appearances in the garden scene (I iii and vii–viii), but has only recitative till the end of II ii. At this point Handel gave him a substantial aria in E flat, 'Sò gli altri debellar'; he knows how to subdue the enemy without but carries in his heart one that threatens his honour. It is a strong manly piece, fully scored with oboes and bassoons and an independent cello part that breaks into coruscating semiquaver figuration; Handel borrowed the main theme, like Berenice's 'Dolci aurette', from the cantata *La solitudine*, but developed it on new lines. Although the aria is in the autograph Chrysander, while praising it in his biography, inexplicably omitted it from his edition. Handel was ill-advised to replace it with a light dance song composed for Rosalba. By altering the words to 'Pensa, O bella' he turned this into a declaration of love by Scipio, both dramatically and musically inept. This is no place or time for the conqueror to abase himself before his prisoner. The music is pleasant enough, but the two recorders, transparent texture, and tripping 3/8 rhythm give it an inappropriate daintiness. The substitution explains the inconsequent key succession, F major after a G minor recitative cadence (sure sign of a last-minute change) and the fact that the vocal compass is wider than in the rest of the part.

Scipio's next set piece, the 51-bar accompanied recitative 'Il poter' in III ii, also seems to have been suppressed—an extraordinary decision, for it is one of the opera's most striking movements and the only occasion on which Scipio confronts the central issue, love or honour. This is among Handel's longest and most powerful accompanied recitatives, anticipating in scale the great opening scene of *Belshazzar*. The words are almost a philosophical debate on the moral dilemma. The music ranges widely in mood, tonality, tempo, and harmony as Scipio wrestles with his conscience. The directions vary between *Presto* (bars 12 and 22—Chrysander omits the latter), *Adagio*, *Sedato*, *Adagio* again, *Cantabile*, and *Larghetto*. Deciding that virtue is a 'tormentosa opinion', Scipio builds up to an emphatic 'Sì, sì, voglio' but then turns back, a decision beautifully anticipated by the Adagio at bar 25 and the change from the dominant seventh on C to a diminished chord on C sharp. The struggle is not yet over; it flares up again, to be quelled by 'questo è un piacer che non avrai commune co' bruti e co' tiranni'. Scipio's attainment of inner peace when he comes down on the side of generosity is perfectly reflected in the four Larghetto bars of arioso at the end, returning to the initial key of C minor.

With 'Gioja sì speri' Scipio relapses into unseemly frivolity. For a Roman proconsul who has just renounced the woman he loves to reassure her in this kittenish aria verges on the ludicrous. In this scene and the last Scipio sits on a throne,[9] a piece of furniture more suited to a Habsburg Archduke than a Roman; but he vacates it as soon as he can. The cavatina 'Dopi il nemico oppresso' is another curious piece: he proclaims victory over himself in G minor in sharp angular phrases with the barest accompaniment, almost entirely in octaves. If Handel intended an emotional cross-current, a hint of what the victory costs Scipio, he fails to convey it. A peculiarity of Scipio's part is that, apart from the short Andante 'Scaccia, O bella', it is entirely in triple time.

Antinori was only the third tenor for whom Handel had written in his London operas. He was a minor artist who made little mark, and the same might be said of his first two arias. 'Nò, non si teme', in which Lelio tries to cheer Berenice's low spirits, is routine Handel with a certain rhythmic vigour in the different grouping of quavers and semiquavers but little else. 'Temo che lusinghiero' (II iv) is similar and adds nothing to the character, though it contrasts well with Berenice's 'Com'onda incalza' before it. Lelio is supposed

---

[9] This reflects a convention of the Baroque stage, whereby *ex cathedra* pronouncements by rulers were distinguished from more personal utterances.

to be in love with Armira, but shows few signs of commitment, for which the obscure words may be partly to blame. Handel falls back on repetition and sequence. 'Del debellar la gloria' in Act III is a different matter. In the autograph the aria is addressed to Lucejo with different words beginning 'La nobiltà del regno / E l'umiltà del cor'; Handel then cut the previous scene and made it a soliloquy, producing another inconsequent key sequence (G major after the A major cadence of 'Tu d'Indibile figlia'[10]). Both sets of words are equally sententious, and it is astonishing that they inspired Handel to such a beautiful piece, especially as they had no connection with Lelio's feelings for Armira. The A section ritornellos, which move from G major towards A minor and A major respectively, have an almost Mozartian flavour. The siciliano melody is lovely in itself; the hint of A minor in bar 4 is later associated with the words 'pregi immortali' (the same in both texts), which are built up in exquisite sequences towards the end of the section.

Handel began the part of Armira for a contralto, probably Anna Dotti, who was later transferred to Rosalba and then dropped out. The D minor alto version of 'Libera chi non è' (HG 124) is the original, with the instrumental alternatives printed in large notes. It is typical coquette music such as Handel wrote for Teodata (Anastasia Robinson) in *Flavio*, and effective in the theatre. The light phrases and repeated 'nò' show Armira in firm control of her destiny, and Lelio's as well. 'Voglio contenta allor' (II iv), composed for the soprano Costantini who sang the part, is similar. The syncopated rhythm with its offbeats (not till the vocal entry is there a strong downbeat), the delayed cadences, and repeated notes give an idea of teasing to a captivating little aria. There is a neat touch at the end when Lucejo's entry with an E flat chord after her tonic F cuts off her exit. Her rejected Act III aria 'Nell'amor nella speranza' is another light piece, a quick 3/8 minuet in D minor, the A section in binary form with repeats.

Boschi for once was not required to rant and roar. Ernando is a stately Spanish hidalgo with fixed notions of honour; for all his friendly feelings towards Scipio and the Romans he cannot allow Berenice to break her bond. Both his arias are admirable, and well above what Boschi was accustomed to receive, even from Handel. 'Braccio si valoroso' is full of exuberant counterpoint. The ritornello presents two subjects simultaneously, one in minims, the other in quavers. The voice adds a third, and all three disport themselves vigorously throughout the A section in a variety of combinations, producing new offshoots as they go. The free part-writing and bold interval-hopping of the voice give the music great drive. The B section supplies a memorable contrast with octave unisons in an odd rhythm, soon joined by the quaver motive from the ritornello. 'Tutta rea' makes more use of the octave doubling traditional in bass arias, but the underlying metre of the hornpipe and lively cross-rhythms give it an equal exhilaration. There is no doubting the bluff honesty of the King of the Balearic Islands, and Scipio is suitably impressed. As usual the bassoons support the voice in its highest phrases.

All the instrumental movements in *Scipione* borrow from earlier works, another indication of haste. The overture, though intrinsic to the autograph, derives its second and third sections from recorder sonatas: Op. 1 no. 7 in C major (HWV 365) and a work in B flat major in the Fitzwilliam Museum

[10] See pp. 610 and 622.

(HWV 377).[11] The former, a free double fugue with wind interludes, is a striking example of Handel's powers of expansion. The splendid sinfonia for Ernando's disembarcation in Act II, with its air of ceremonial expectancy, was lifted intact from the score of *Alessandro*. Its Allegro exploits the same type of muscular triple counterpoint as Ernando's following aria; indeed the two main subjects in each piece are so similar that Handel may have modelled the one on the other. The F major sinfonia in Act III, another strong Allegro, is expanded from a concerto movement for harpsichord, no. 33 of the Aylesford Pieces, and the short E minor sinfonia that opened Act III is based on the Air in the tenth keyboard suite. Even the March, as John Roberts has shown,[12] incorporates a striking phrase from Keiser's *Nebucadnezar*. It won instant popularity and was soon adopted on the parade grounds of the British Army, where it can still be heard. The *coro* is also march-like, with a hint of the bourrée, and makes a satisfying conclusion to the opera.

The orchestra employs two recorders in one aria and two transverse flutes in another, both doubtless played by oboists. Surprisingly in a military opera there are no trumpets or drums, but the high horns in G give a brilliant edge to the March and *coro*. They are linked to the tonality of G that seems to have been intended to frame the opera; besides governing the first and last scenes it was the key in which Act II originally ended, and its relative minor began Act III. Any extension of this idea was inhibited by the revisions. Although the opera contains spectacular and skilfully constructed scenes—the opening of the first two acts and the 'Dolci aurette' complex—and the accompanied recitatives maintain the usual high standard of the Royal Academy years, its impact remains fragmented. It suffers too from an excess of 3/8 arias, nearly all in quick tempo; indeed, apart from Lelio's 'Del debellar la gloria', none of the characters except Berenice and Lucejo is allowed a slow aria.

History and Text

Handel completed the score on 2 March 1726. It is not known when he began it, but there is no reason to doubt Rolli's statement that it took him only three weeks. The version performed at the King's Theatre on 12 March has been described above. The cast was:

BERENICE:	Cuzzoni (soprano)
LUCEJO:	Senesino (alto castrato)
SCIPIO:	Antonio Baldi (alto castrato)
LELIO:	Luigi Antinori (tenor)
ARMIRA:	Livia Costantini (soprano)
ERNANDO:	Boschi (bass)

Dotti, who was to have sung Rosalba, may have withdrawn through illness. This occurred at a late stage, for traces of Rosalba survive in many sources, including the performing score and Cluer's edition. Costantini, an intermezzo singer, was engaged as a substitute for Faustina in mid-season, and made her London début in *Ottone* on 8 February.

[11] Published by Schott (London, ed. Thurston Dart) in 1948; not in HG.
[12] See Roberts, *Handel Sources*, iii.

Scipione had thirteen successive performances, the last on 30 April, and was followed at once by *Alessandro*. Nothing is known about its reception, though Prévost was told by 'competent musicians' some years later that *Giulio Cesare*, *Scipione*, and *Rodelinda* were Handel's best works.[13] Handel's only revival opened the second season of the so-called Second Academy on 3 November 1730, after a public rehearsal on the morning of 31 October 'before a great Number of Ladies of the first Quality, and other Persons of Distinction'. Senesino retained his part. The rest of the cast was:

BERENICE:	Strada (soprano)
SCIPIO:	Annibale Pio Fabri (tenor)
LELIO:	Francesca Bertolli (contralto)
ARMIRA:	Antonia Merighi (contralto)
ERNANDO:	Giovanni Giuseppe Commano (bass)

The Universal Spectator of 7 November reported that on the first night 'there was 208l. in the House exclusive of the Subscribers'—a considerable sum. Lord Shaftesbury wrote later that Senesino, who had not sung in London for two years, 'was received with the greatest Applause',[14] and the Colman Opera Register agreed that the opera 'charm'd much'. Despite this and assiduous patronage by the Royal Family there were only six performances, and *Scipione* slept for two centuries.

Deutsch's statement that the 1730 version 'was slightly different from the original' is a *locus classicus* for involuntary meiosis. It was so comprehensively rehashed as to qualify for a young pasticcio. Of the 28 vocal movements (other than recitatives) in the 1726 score, fewer than half—Lucejo's seven arias and six of Berenice's—remained untouched, while thirteen fresh pieces were inserted, eleven of them from earlier operas. Handel went much further than was required by the three changes of vocal pitch, though this was responsible for the most radical alteration, affecting the plot as well as the music. Fabri was a much more eminent and accomplished tenor than Antinori (Handel wrote the substantial parts of Berengario in *Lotario* and Alessandro in *Poro* for him), and so merited a more central role than Lelio.[15] The change of pitch involved redrawing both parts, since in the *opera seria* of this period tenors were never cast as young lovers: Scipio became conspicuously older, and Lelio younger, than in 1726. Fabri received five arias instead of four, and they emphasized his maturity as soldier and statesman; he lost the two lyrical pieces appropriate to a castrato and a lover, though two of his insertions stressed the agonies of frustrated passion. The only music he retained from 1726 was his first scene, which he apparently transposed down an octave. In I iv he sang Grimoaldo's 'Trà sospetti' from *Rodelinda* with slight verbal changes ('Trà speranze', HG 121); in II ii, in place of 'Pensa, O bella', 'Dimmi crudele' from *Muzio Scevola*, a soprano aria transposed down a seventh to A minor, with the lower alternatives in the HG score but minor variants at the main cadences; in III vi, in place of 'Gioja sì speri', a newly composed aria on a text from *Alessandro*, 'Pregi son d'un alma grande'; and in the last scene a new setting of 'Dopo il nemico'. For Lelio, now a travesti contralto, Handel

---

[13] Deutsch, 334.
[14] Ibid. 845.
[15] There are signs that Handel began the 1730 revision before deciding that Scipio should be a tenor.

transposed 'Nò, non si teme' from F to A, raising the tessitura in several places (HG 128), replaced 'Temo che lusinghiero' with 'Pensa, O bella' slightly altered (Lelio was thus the third character to receive this aria), and inserted a new scene at the beginning of Act III with an aria from *Muzio Scevola*, 'Con lei volate', unchanged except for the pronouns. 'Del debellar la gloria' was dropped.

As Armira Merighi, a contralto of higher repute than Bertolli, had four arias instead of two. Handel gave her a new scene (I ii, resulting in changed numbers till the end of the act) with a soprano aria from *Alessandro*, 'Lusinghe più care', transposed down a fourth to D major and modified in words and music (HG 117). She sang 'Libera chi non è' in its original key of D minor— not however as written, but a transposition of the A minor version with the small-note alternatives (HG 124); 'Con un' vezzo' from *Flavio*, unchanged, in place of 'Voglio contenta' in II iv; and 'Se vuoi in amor' ('Lungo pensar' from *Muzio Scevola* with new words, transposed down from F to D) in the renumbered III vii, replacing Lelio's 'Del debellar'. Commano, an inferior singer, lost both Ernando's arias and had to be content with 'Non m'inganna' ('Non t'inganni' from *Lotario* with altered words, chiefly in the B section), a showy piece for high baritone with much doubling, in II i; this was probably the only scene in which he appeared. Handel's other changes seem gratuitous.[16] He replaced Berenice's 'Com'onda incalza' and 'Già cessata' with two arias from *Riccardo Primo*, 'Di notte il pellegrino' and 'Tutta brillante i rai', the love duet with the December 1725 addition to *Rodelinda*, 'D'ogni crudel', and the *coro* with that from *Muzio Scevola*, 'Sì, sarà più dolce'. This requires trumpets as well as horns and had no tenor part. Handel indicated that Fabri should double (or replace) Commano on the bass line; possibly the latter's inadequacy was the reason for the change. Many recitatives were shortened and others rewritten.

Neither the opera nor the characters, with the possible exception of Armira, gained much from this reorganization. Scipio's agitated 'Trà speranze' makes little sense, since he does not yet know that Berenice is committed to Lucejo. 'Dimmi crudele' is at least a forceful response to Berenice's rejection. Neither of her imported arias is an improvement, and 'Tutta brillante i rai' is far too long, formal, and complex to express instant relief. Act III now begins in *a Royal Hall* with the F major sinfonia on HG 88, after which Lelio's new solo scene serves no dramatic purpose; he merely yearns for the absent Armira. Scipio's interview with Ernando about honour is omitted altogether. He tersely informs Lelio that Ernando has refused his request for Berenice's hand, and he has therefore banished his passion. He orders Lucejo to Rome and goes out, without 'Il poter' or an aria. The place of the F major sinfonia is taken by the four-bar Grave in *Alessandro* II vi[17] (HG 87), transposed from D to F and slightly modified. Of Scipio's two new arias, 'Pregi son' is a bravura piece in G major that rings hollow in its context. Without his struggles of conscience Scipio is no more than a beefy soldier. The tenor setting of 'Dopo il nemico', again in G minor, is brief and inconsequential.

---

[16] None of the 1730 changes can have been due to haste (this was the first opera of the season) or a desire to save the singers the trouble of learning new music; none of them had sung any of the substituted pieces before.

[17] In the autograph of *Alessandro* this had replaced the big B flat sinfonia that Handel appropriated for Ernando's arrival in II i.

On 28 April 1726, during the original run, Ann Turner Robinson included five arias from *Scipione*, 'Scoglio d'immota fronte', 'Dimmi, cara', 'Com'onda incalza', 'Vanne, parti', and 'Bella notte' at her Drury Lane benefit.[18] 'Dimmi, cara' was sung by Mrs Warren at Lincoln's Inn Fields on 4 and 8 May 1727, and much later (22 February 1752) by Francesina at the Great Room, Dean Street. Songs from the opera were announced for a concert at 'the Theatre on St Augustin's Back', Bristol, on 22 November 1727. Handel incorporated 'Vanne, parti' and possibly the *coro* in the pasticcio *Hermann von Balcke* at Elbing in late 1737, and 'Tutta raccolta ancor' in *Jupiter in Argos* at the King's Theatre on 1 May 1739. The most popular piece in *Scipione* was the March; it appeared in several ballad operas—*The Quaker's Opera* (September 1728), *The Wedding* (6 May 1729), and *Polly* (published 1729)—and was taken into the repertory of that colourful character Charles the Hungarian, Master of the French Horn. He performed it in Dublin on 12 May and probably 2 June 1742 (at the Fishamble Street Music Hall during Handel's visit), for his own benefit at the Aungier Street Theatre on 12 May 1743, in the Assembly Room at Bury St Edmunds on 12 December 1744, and doubtless on many other occasions. The overture figured in a Manchester Subscription Concert on 19 February 1745.

There have been modern productions at Göttingen (1937), Halle (1965), and London (1967), the last in an unhappy mixture of Handel's 1726 and 1730 versions. A production at Karlsruhe in 1992 transferred the action to the Gulf War of the previous year.

Autograph

The autograph of *Scipione* (RM 20 c 6) is incomplete and faultily bound. Folio 22 is reversed; 33–5 ('Sò gli altri debellar') should follow 42 (after Scipio's cadence at 'e di furore', HG 43); 98–101 (HG 131–5) should follow 78. The fact that Handel omitted his usual foliation, no doubt another result of haste, makes it difficult to identify all insertions, especially as he revised the score more than once before performance. In Act I he prepared all Armira's recitatives with an alto clef. This was altered when he added the music, but in accordance with his usual practice he had already composed the arias: 'Libera chi non è' is in the D minor alto version (HG 124), with the instrumental parts as printed in large notes and the B section squeezed in as an afterthought. He then marked the aria *A moll* and rather confusingly added instrumental changes in that key; Chrysander's small notes are the result of the retransposition of this version to D minor in 1730. In Acts II and III the part is for soprano throughout.

The score as first completed differed radically from both the 1726 and 1730 versions. A very late and extensive revision was inspired partly by the need to suppress Rosalba, who appears in three scenes in the last two acts and has two arias; but Handel made many other changes, removing or replacing arias for all the characters except Lelio. In his first draft he seems to have lost control of both Act II and Act III. The former continued for several more scenes and ended with Berenice's 'Il fulgido seren' (HG 86). The latter began at HG 88; its second scene included not only 'Gioja sì speri' but three more arias as well, and the later scenes also had much extra music. Handel cut the Gordian knot

---

[18] This was presumably with Handel's consent, for the score was not published till a month later.

by putting back the end of Act II to 'Scoglio d'immota fronte' and ruthlessly compressing the sprawl that remained. He shortened Act III by five arias, 'Generoso chi sol brama' (Rosalba), 'T'aspetta fuor dell'onde' (Ernando), 'Mi par sognar' (Berenice), 'Nell'amor nella speranza' (Armira, unpublished and not in the autograph), and 'Son pellegrino' (Lucejo);[19] replaced 'Il fulgido seren' and (in Act II) 'Sò gli altri debellar'; and made further changes in the performing score. When we recall his shortage of time, it is little wonder that Act III is broken-winded. Either during this reorganization or later part of the autograph was lost; but except for the missing continuation of 'Mi par sognar' the music is recoverable, since it had been copied. There is no evidence that any of the rejected pieces was ever performed.

Act I presents few complications. The 4/4 section of the overture's fugue (HG 3) was originally marked *Lentement*; this is cancelled in the autograph, but survives in the very early Malmesbury copy. Handel's first thought for 'Scaccia, O bella', in 3/8 time, was quite different; after 22 bars and much correction he abandoned it and used the material for 'Lamentandomi'. He did not write out the repeat of 'Abbiam vinto'. The A section of 'Un caro amante' gave him trouble; at the filling up stage he reduced its last 16 bars to 8, written on the inserted f. 11[20] (Squire misinterpreted this in his *Catalogue*, p. 76), and took three bars out of the ritornello after the B section. Another insertion is f. 23, containing bars 7–27 of 'Dolci aurette'. Handel set this first as a short arioso of seven bars; the decision to expand it greatly strengthened the force of Lucejo's interruption. In the recitative of HG 28, third system, Scipio's speech begins 'Sotto Latine spoglie' in the autograph, librettos, and all sources except the Hamburg performing score, where Smith wrote 'catine'; this makes nonsense, as does Chrysander's emendation 'cattive'. The first bar of 'Vañne, parti' was a characteristic afterthought; the words printed in Roman type in HG were underlined by Handel. In 'Figlia di reo timor' the crotchets on the last beats of bars 33 and 34 have stress marks on the voice part ('*O* gelosia crudel') in the autograph and Hamburg.

The opening sinfonia in Act II is not in the autograph; it was copied directly into the performing score from the incomplete autograph of *Alessandro*. The following recitative has some lines composed for Rosalba, either cancelled or altered for Ernando. 'Braccio si valoroso' has a second set of words, beginning 'Core si generoso', written by Smith; they have nothing to do with *Scipione* but were added in 1733 when the aria was sung in a revival of *Tolomeo*. It is followed by a ten-bar recitative 'O Sommi Dei' and an aria 'Dolce speme lusinghiera' for Rosalba; the B section of the latter is perhaps an insertion. Handel crossed out the recitative and put new words to the aria, beginning 'Pensa, O bella', transferring it to Scipio in the next scene (HG 43). The original aria here, 'Sò gli altri debellar', was begun with only two instrumental parts. Handel rewrote it with much fuller scoring, violins 1 and 2 + oboes, violin 3 + viola, independent cello, and *Bassons Contrabass e Cemb*.

The recitative at the bottom of HG 46 is heavily over-written and may once

---

[19] Three of these arias were later used in *Partenope*: 'Generoso chi sol brama', expanded, modified, and transposed to D major as 'Nobil core', 'T'aspetta fuor dell'onde' musically unchanged as 'T'appresta forse amore', and 'Son pellegrino' adapted first for Arsace's cancelled aria 'Io son ferito' in I ix and then for the quartet 'Non è incauto' in III i.

[20] This leaf has a slightly narrower rastrum than the rest of the manuscript; it is identical with that of the Coke Rivers MS (*c*.1727), written by Smith junior and H1.

have been extended. Handel modified the first phrase of 'Com'onda incalza' in the ritornello and the voice part. The opening of 'Cedo a Roma' was at first *Larghetto*, not *Sedato*, but both words occur at bar 37. The recitative before 'Scoglio d'immota fronte' is the longer form (HG A). The aria was at first more lightly scored with four instrumental staves, though the violins soon divide. Only the first twelve bars of this ritornello survive, but they are filled up and the setting was probably complete; pages have been torn out here. The voice enters on the upper D. On the last beat of bar 48 it has a trill (also in the Flower copy), as in the two previous phrases of the sequence; Chrysander omitted it because Smith forgot it in Hamburg. After bar 55 Handel made a substantial cut of twelve fully-scored bars.

Instead of ending the act with this conclusive aria Handel went straight on (HG 73–83 and 86–7); Scene ii is numbered viii (although there had been one viii already), iii (HG 79) is ix, and iv (HG 83) is x. At the end of 'Tutta rea' Handel wrote *Si scrive l'ultimo Rittornello* [i.e. that after the A section] *in vece del Primo*, but changed his mind in favour of the full da capo. Bar 22 of 'Il poter' is marked *Presto*, written over *Adag*. The recitatives at the bottom of HG 79 are squeezed into the margin, and a different aria followed; stubs of torn out pages remain. 'Se mormora rivo' is *Largo*, as in all sources except the Flower parts. Scipio's cadence at the bottom of HG 83 leads to 'Il fulgido seren' and *Fine dell'Atto 2do*. 'Già cessata' is not in the manuscript (but see below).

Act III begins with the sinfonia on HG 88; the oboe figures in bars 7–9 were written first as triplets. Rosalba appears in the heading and recitatives on HG 90, singing the lines 'O degno cui tutto'—'conforto miglior' an octave higher and sharing 'O dolce figlia' and 'Vieni al materno/paterno affetto sũo amplesso' *à 2* with Ernando; Berenice replies 'O genitori amati'. As noted above, Scipio's 'Gioja sì speri' was followed by the sequence on HG 131–5; Rosalba's recitative and aria are crossed out. Berenice's fragmentary aria must once have been complete. It is established from other sources that the gap here also contained the recitative 'Tu d'Indibile figlia', Armira's aria 'Nell'amor nella speranza', and the first 8½ bars of a recitative for Lucejo and Lelio, 'Prence, il rigor della fortuna', of which Chrysander prints the continuation on HG 93. Lelio's 'Del debellar' follows with its original words ('La nobiltà del regno').

Next come Lucejo's recitative 'Squarciasi' and aria 'Come al natio' [*sic* in all sources] (HG 98–102), the recitative 'Dove, O prencipe' (HG 96, headed *Scena 5*), and Berenice's 'Bella notte' with an abortive ritornello that Handel at once abandoned for the printed version. He cut four bars after bar 14; bar 22 has *pp* on the bass line (as in the Flower score), and there are many small revisions. In bar 32 of 'Come al natio' the autograph has both alternatives for the voice, the upper (D) written first. Lucejo's recitative 'Quanto timor' and aria 'Son pellegrino'[21] follow (HG 103–5). The *Allegro* mark on 'Dopo il nemico' was written over *Andante*. In the following scene the words 'O magnanimo core' were first set for Lelio and Ernando *à 2* (the lower part later crossed out) and 'O virtù rara' for Rosalba with different notes. Handel wrote the names of the singers in abbreviated form four times in the *coro*; the second soprano part is

[21] There is no possibility of this aria or 'Come al natio' being insertions, though Lucejo sings both in close proximity. Handel seems at this stage to have set whatever Rolli put before him, regardless of its aptness to the drama.

for Senesino and 'Anna' (Dotti). He dated the end of the manuscript: *Fine dell Opera GFH March 2. 1726.*

A volume of autograph fragments (RM 20 d 2) contains 'Già cessata' (HG 84) and the tenor aria 'Pregi son d'un alma grande' (text from *Alessandro*) composed for Scipio in 1730. Neither has a tempo mark. The former, which Chrysander printed from Cluer's edition, has no figuring but many more slurs and some extra dynamics. The autograph of the third movement of the overture, in its original form as the first movement of a recorder sonata in B flat, is in Fitzwilliam Mus MS 260, p. 13. The paper (Italian with Cantoni/Bergamo watermark, as in the first part of the *Rodelinda* autograph) proves that this and the C major sonata (Op. 1 no. 7), also drawn on for the overture, were composed about 1725, not 1712 as hitherto believed.

Librettos

1726 (Theatre). 'Scipione, Drama ... Printed, and Sold at the King's Theatre in the Hay-Market.' 63 pp. Rolli is not named, and there is no dedication. The Argument is in Italian and English, the note about borrowing 'the first Hint' in English only. There are a number of differences from Handel's score and from HG. In II ii Berenice's cavatina 'Tutta raccolta ancor' occurs twice with twelve lines of recitative in between, and she has three more lines after 'Pensa, O bella'. These passages were not set to music, nor were three extra lines for Scipio after 'd'amicizia e fede' in the final scene (HG 107). 'Abbiam vinto', 'Scaccia, O bella', and 'Dopo il nemico' are incorrectly indicated as da capo arias. 'Libera chi non è' is in the text of I iv. The recitatives on HG 20 and 63 are in Chrysander's A version. Act III has no new scene number after Scipio's first three lines. His accompanied recitative 'Il poter' is bracketed as cut and not translated. The next five scenes are one behind Chrysander's numbering; iii ends with 'Già cessata'; the pieces on HG 86–7, 93, and 103–5 are not in the libretto. Scene vi (after 'Gioja sì speri') consists of the recitative 'Tu d'Indibile figlia', after which Armira goes out with 'Amami e spera', and Lelio's 'Del debellar la gloria'. In all three librettos 'Come al natio' has a slightly different text at the start of the B section, and the aria and its recitative 'Squarciasi' are given to Lelio.

1726 (Edlin). 'P. C. Scipione Drama, di Paolo Rolli ... Printed by Thomas Edlin, at the Prince's Arms, over-against Exeter-Exchange in the Strand.' Octavo, 45 pp. This libretto, like the similar edition of *Alessandro*, was a private venture of Rolli's and not intended for use in the theatre. The text, entirely in Italian, does not name the cast but has a dedication to the Duke of Richmond, comparing British virtues in flowery terms to those of the ancient Romans. After the Argument and note is the statement: 'Il celebre Signor Federico Handel ne compose la Musica, al sommo espressa ed armoniosa, ed il tutto fu eseguito in tre settimane.' The only other material difference from the theatre libretto is that II ii gives both 'Sò gli altri debellar' and 'Pensa, O bella' to Scipio, one after the other. 'Il poter' is present. The libretto was reprinted in Rolli's *Componimenti poetici* (Verona, 1744).

1730 (King's Theatre). 'Drama ... Printed and Sold by Tho. Wood in Little-Britain.' 51 pp. Argument as 1726, but the sentence about the source is replaced by a note that the lines in *virgole* 'are not to be performed'. These are all recitatives, and mostly correspond to the cuts in the Hamburg score: the first four lines after 'Abbiam vinto' in I i, Lelio's 'Generoso Scipione! Ecco la bella' in I iii (a mistake: it was included after the interpolated aria 'Trà speranze', HG 123), Lelio's recitative 'Indegno è in ver' (HG 19), most of Ernando's first speech and Lelio's last three lines in II i, Berenice's two unset passages in II ii (the repeat of 'Tutta raccolta amor' is omitted), her three lines 'Misera Berenice' in II iii (HG 49), the last four lines before 'Scoglio d'immota fronte' (= Chrysander's B version), and Lelio's three lines 'Esperienza e senno' in III i (HG 75). On the other hand a cut of six bars in the performing score of HG 90–1 is not indicated, and Scipio's three unset lines in the last scene remain without *virgole*. The last line before 'Libera chi non è' was altered (as HG 124). 'Il poter' is omitted altogether.

The text was set up from an amended copy of the 1726 theatre libretto, several of whose errors remain. 'Abbiam vinto' and 'Scaccia, O bella', but not 'Dopo il nemico', are still indicated as da capo arias. The numerous replacements and insertions listed above are all present, with consequent renumbering of scenes in Acts I and III. In the new I ii Handel changed Rolli's word order in the first line; 'Lusinghe più care' is clearly assigned to Armira after Lelio's exit. In III i, another new scene, Lelio's recitative 'Inquieti miei pensieri' is wrongly printed as part of his aria ('Con lei volate').

Copies and Editions

The performing score is divided between Hamburg MA/1049 and Fitzwilliam Mus MS 257 (pp. 1–52). Smith, who wrote it all except two short insertions by H6 and one partly by S1, probably began to copy while Handel was still composing; he had largely completed his task before the upheaval that removed Rosalba. He ended Act II with 'Già cessata'; there is no evidence that 'Sò gli altri debellar', 'Il fulgido seren', or 'Son pellegrino' were ever copied. The scene numbers, especially in Act III, were repeatedly altered. Most of the Fitzwilliam material can be fitted exactly into the Hamburg score, but a number of leaves were torn out or lost, both before performance (Rosalba material) and when the opera was revived in 1730. Since Chrysander did not use the Fitzwilliam material and omitted a great deal in Hamburg after Act I, both collections contain unpublished music of importance.

The Fitzwilliam fragments, which supply many dynamics, trills, slurs, and stress marks not in HG, consist with one exception of sections prepared for the 1726 production but replaced before that of 1730. They are listed in the order in which they occur in the manuscript:[22]

(i) I iii-iv to bar 13 of the soprano version of 'Libera chi non è', marked by Handel for the insertion of Scipio's aria ('Trà speranze') and the scenes renumbered for 1730.

(ii) The recitatives of II i (HG 37) containing passages set for Rosalba or referring to her but cancelled before performance; one of them is allowed to stand because Ernando sang it an octave lower. The last semibreve of the bass

---

[22] Mann's notes (*Catalogue*, 173–4) are not entirely accurate; he was unaware that the alto version of 'Libera chi non è' dates from 1726.

part is E flat, not G (as in the autograph and other sources). Two cuts for 1730 are already marked.

(iii) Part of II iii and iv (HG 51–6), beginning at bar 30 of 'Com'onda incalza' and ending with bar 36 of 'Voglio contenta allor'.

(iv) The unpublished opening of Act III. The E minor Largo for strings and accompanied setting of Scipio's recitative 'Miseri affetti miei' are an insertion before performance, written by H6. The next page (23) has the original secco version of the autograph and HG, heavily cancelled, as is the heading *Scena 8ᵃ* that follows; until the insertion this was still part of Act II. The fragment breaks off 7½ bars before the bottom of HG 73.

(v) The first 40 bars of 'Il poter' (HG 76–8; the rest is in Hamburg).

(vi) Part of III iii (iv in HG), beginning with the last 3½ bars on HG 83, followed by 'Già cessata' (one leaf, containing bars 47–106, is missing) and *Fine dell'Atto Secondo* (cancelled). Handel noted that *aria ex Riccardo* (i.e. 'Tutta brillante i rai') was to be substituted, and changed the recitative cadence to D minor. But Scipio is still an alto, and the cadence was further altered in Hamburg.

(vii) The original opening of Act III, with the sinfonia on HG 88–9, the recitatives on 90–1 (some passages set for Rosalba, others for her and Ernando *à 2*), 'Gioja sì speri', Rosalba's recitative 'Nulla temer', and the first four bars of her aria 'Generoso chi sol brama' (HG 131). On HG 90 Rosalba sings the words 'O degno cui tutto'—'il conforto miglior', but her name is crossed out. The six bars 'Vieni al paterno affetto'—'le preziose offerte' are cancelled; Handel planned to cut them in 1730 but later changed his mind (see below).

Pages 45–52 contain the new I ii of 1730 (HG 117–20) and offer an interesting example of Handel and Smith working in tandem. In the recitative Smith wrote the clefs and words, Handel the music. The first 16½ bars of the aria ('Lusinghe più care'), transposed and adapted from *Alessandro*, are entirely autograph, with the viola doubled by violin 3. Smith then took over the transposition, leaving occasional gaps in text and music subsequently filled by Handel (text in bars 22–3, music in bars 20–3, 30, and 60–1). The words of the A section end 'e scaltre *turbate* l'altrui libertà', not 'insidiate'.[23] Handel adjusted the pitch of the voice part from time to time in bars 18–19, 25, 28–31, and 68. Smith recopied the aria for Hamburg where Handel made further changes (see below). Pages 53–4, though derived from the rejected bass aria 'T'aspetta fuor dell'onda' (HG 132), have nothing to do with *Scipione*. Handel transferred the aria with new words to *Partenope* (1730), and in 1737 adapted it for the contralto Maria Caterina Negri. These autograph pages, without the violin part, belong to that occasion; Chrysander prints both bass and alto versions in *Partenope* (pp. 25–9).

Hamburg MA/1049 represents the 1730 version confusingly superimposed on the residue of 1726. The latter still shows changes made before performance. Folio 123 has the first version of III iv (later vi), 'Tu d'Indibile figlia', introducing bars 1–26 of Armira's 'Nell'amor nella speranza'; Handel crossed them out, removed the rest of the aria and most of the following recitative, and cancelled what remained (the last 8½ bars on HG 93), leaving 'Tu d'Indibile figlia' to lead into 'Del debellar la gloria', with its new text written in. (Chrysander printed the wrong recitative.) Later in Act III Handel

---

[23] The *Alessandro* text has 'e tutta involate l'altrui libertà', and its B section ends 'di vaga beltà'.

decided to reverse the order of the arias 'Come al natio' and 'Bella notte'. This involved the cancellation of the first $8\frac{1}{2}$ bars of the recitative 'Dove, O prencipe' (HG 96) at the end of 'Come al natio' and their recopying (by Smith) on a slip pasted over 'Squarciasi' (HG 98, f. 126ᵛ). The latter recitative was then recopied (by H6) on an inserted leaf, f. 130, and the pages rearranged in the new order.

The twelve extra bars in 'Scoglio d'immota fronte' were copied from the autograph but cancelled before performance. Handel himself added the low D at the voice entry, perhaps for Strada in 1730; it appears elsewhere only in the Granville copy. The Act II sinfonia (HG 50) is not an insertion as stated by Clausen; the presence of the act heading here but not on Fitzwilliam p. 5 proves it original. Nor is there any evidence that Fitzwilliam pp. 29–32 are insertions.

The 1730 revival however accounts for 67 of the 144 leaves in the Hamburg manuscript. These insertions are listed in detail because most of them are ignored by Chrysander:

16–21: last five bars of 'Un caro amante' recopied, new I ii copied from Fitzwilliam 45–52, recitative on HG 15 (renumbered Scene iii) recopied. In 'Lusinghe più care' Handel made further changes to a few notes and marked the violin part in bars 36 (third beat) to 39 (fourth quaver) *ottava bassa*. Chrysander misinterpreted this, printing most of the passage too high and raising the violins' last four notes (bars 39–40) by an octave.

25–32: I iv and v as HG 121–5. 'Trà speranze' is marked *Allegro*; 'timore' should be the plural 'timori'; Handel made a few changes in words and underlay. 'Libera chi non è' is in D minor with the small-type variants.

34–6: 'Nò, non si teme' for alto in A major (HG 128–30). Smith made the transposition; Handel filled gaps, and sometimes raised and improved the vocal line, in bars 28–9, 32–5, 38–9, and 48–9. The new introductory recitative was pasted over the original on f. 33.

52–5: new recitative in II i, much shortened with Lelio in alto clef, followed by the bass aria 'Non m'inganna' from *Lotario*. Handel altered the underlay towards the end of the A section.

60–3: last $10\frac{1}{2}$ bars of recitative on HG 42–3 with new music for Scipio in tenor clef, cadence in E, and aria 'Dimmi crudele' from *Muzio Scevola* in A minor.

69–78: new setting of recitative 'Seguilo, O duce' (HG 49) for alto Lelio (Berenice's four bars at the end omitted), cadence in C♯ major, Berenice's aria 'Di notte il pellegrino' from *Riccardo Primo*, new setting of recitative 'Importuno sei' (HG 52) for two altos, cadence in C major, 'Pensa, O bella' for Lelio (no repeats, higher voice part in bars 41 and 54–5), new setting of recitative 'Lusingarlo' (HG 55) for alto, cadence in E minor, aria 'Con un' vezzo' from *Flavio*.

95–102: sinfonia on HG 88–9 recopied, new III i for alto Lelio (recitative 'Ingiusti miei pensieri', aria 'Con lei volate' from *Muzio Scevola*), new Scene ii for tenor Scipio 'Lelio: a Ernando richiesi' (incorporating text of his speech on HG 75), cadence in B flat but no aria.

108–12: last four bars of recitative on HG 83 rewritten for tenor Scipio, cadence in D minor (differing from Handel's alteration to Fitzwilliam p. 29), aria for Berenice 'Tutta brillante i rai' from *Riccardo Primo*, Scene 5ᵃ *Sala con*

Trono, four-bar sinfonia in F transposed and slightly altered from *Alessandro* II vi (HG 87).

113–14: recitatives on HG 90–1, but the words 'O degno cui tutto'—'il conforto miglior', originally for Rosalba, remain in the alto clef, and Ernando has her notes (not those in HG) at 'O dolce figlia'; he sang both passages in the lower octave. These pages are an insertion within an insertion, replacing the shortened version of f. 115 whose cut is marked in Fitzwilliam pp. 38–9.

115–22: III vi (HG 90) from 'Libera sei', A minor cadence at 'gioja oppresso', then cut to Scipio's 'mà in tuo volto'. The whole page was crossed out when Handel decided to restore the longer text of 1726 (see above). Scipio is still in the alto clef, but the verso has his tenor aria 'Pregi son d'un alma grande'. A second setting of 'Tu d'Indibile figlia' follows (Scene vii, both voices alto), cadence in F♯ minor, and Armira's aria 'Se vuoi in amor' (parodied on 'Lungo pensar' in *Muzio Scevola*, transposed to D major).

135–44: *Scena ultima. Sala con Trono.* New tenor setting of Scipio's 'Dopo il nemico'; new setting of recitative 'Venga Lucejo' (HG 107) with 1730 voice pitches, 'O senza essempio anima grande!' given to Armira in alto clef;[24] Lucejo's accompanied recitative 'In testimon' with last two bars altered to end in C major; duet 'D'ogni crudel martir' from *Rodelinda*; new tenor setting of Scipio's 'Marte riposi', cadence in C major; *coro* 'Sì, sarà più dolce' from *Muzio Scevola*, with the short ritornello after the da capo subsequently cut. The music of the duet and *coro*, but not the intervening recitative or most of the words, is in the early hand of S1. Since this *coro* has no tenor part, Scipio is directed to take the bass line with Ernando. But Ernando seems to have been eliminated from the whole final scene in 1730. He is not listed in the heading; Scipio's six bars referring to his gifts ('Ernando, i doni tuoi', HG 107) are cancelled, as are Ernando's name and clef before his single remark, 'O virtù rara', which is given to Lelio together with 'O magnanimo core'. Handel changed the music, vocal line and bass, in the Hamburg score. This seems to have been a late decision; the libretto gives the same text as 1726.

Further cuts are indicated on the 1726 material: the first seven bars of the recitative 'A Tiberio' (HG 7), Lelio's 'Indegno è in ver' (HG 19), and the last 5½ bars of the recitative before 'Scoglio d'immota fronte' (= HG 63, Version B—the only 1730 change indicated by Chrysander after Act I). Armira's *parte* in II vi (HG 58) is crossed out.

The Malmesbury copy (Smith junior, text by his father) almost certainly represents the opera as performed in March 1726, except that 'Il poter' is present (this suggests that it was a last-minute cut). It is the only complete score of this version—or indeed of any other. It agrees almost exactly with the 1726 libretto (apart from the latter's errors), except that the scene numbering in Act III (ii on HG 79, iii on HG 83, iv at 'Tu d'Indibile figlia', v on HG 96) follows the first state of Fitzwilliam–Hamburg, a sign of very early date. Rosalba appears in the headings of II i, III iii (v in HG), and *ult.* (this word is accidentally omitted), but has no music. The only other echo of her is the retention of the autograph and Fitzwilliam plural 'O genitori amati' on HG

---

[24] This is unlikely to be a mistake by Smith; although Lucejo has the line in the libretto, his music throughout is in the soprano clef.

90 (III vi). This is the only copy to give the E minor Largo and accompanied recitative at the start of Act III. 'Libera chi non è' is in the A minor soprano version. 'Scoglio d'immota fronte' has the upper D. This score gives one reading cancelled in the autograph (*Lentement* on the 4/4 section of the overture's fugue). It may have been copied as early as the original run.

The Flower score (S2), though copied in the mid-1740s, contains nothing from the 1730 version, but is not quite faithful to 1726. The vocal pitches are those of the first performance with the exception of 'Libera chi non è', which appears inconsequently in D minor and the alto clef after a cadence in E, though the rest of Armira's part is for soprano. The fact that this is the original version (HG large type), not the 1730 transposition back from A minor, indicates that it was taken from the autograph; no other copy has this form. The absence of the E minor sinfonia and accompanied recitative in III i, the presence of *Presto* on bar 22 of 'Il poter', and other details (some already mentioned) also imply resort to the autograph, though this cannot have been the only source. There is no mention of Rosalba anywhere, and the text has been carefully adjusted to exclude all references to her, even by implication; the copy is unique in this respect, though of course it agrees with the libretto. 'Tu d'Indibile figlia' begins with a first inversion chord of G major, B in the bass; Handel changed this from root position in Hamburg but it appears in no other copy. A few numbers ('O sventurati affetti', 'Dolci aurette', 'Vanne, parti') have the bass figured, perhaps by Jennens.

Lennard (S1, *c.* 1736–40) and Granville (S5) are late copies intended for the library; they make no attempt at consistency of pitch, clef, or version in the music of Scipio, Lelio, and Armira. Though not identical, they have a great deal in common and doubtless derive from the same source, perhaps an archive copy. Some principles can be deduced behind the compilation of this: it excluded all 1730 material borrowed from other operas (the only exception is the little four-bar sinfonia from *Alessandro*), restored most but not all of the 1726 material rejected before performance, and added some but not all of the pieces new in 1730. It never included alternative versions of the same piece, preferring a composite but impractical text. Of the 1730 additions the following (only) occur in both copies: 'Libera chi non è' for alto as transposed back from A minor (the rest of Armira's part is for soprano), Version B of the recitative before 'Scoglio d'immota fronte', the sinfonia on HG 88–9 (without tempo mark) at the start of Act III, followed by the new recitatives 'Inquieti miei pensieri' (no aria) and 'Lelio: a Ernando' (taking the place of HG 73–8), the four-bar sinfonia in F to introduce the first throne-room scene (III v), the tenor 'Dopo il nemico', and the rewritten 'Venga Lucejo' after it, with Ernando omitted and Lelio taking his one phrase of recitative as modified in Hamburg. Neither copy has 'Pregi son d'un'alma grande'. Of the unperformed pieces, neither gives 'Son pellegrino' or the three on HG 131–5, but both have 'Sò gli altri debellar' in place of 'Pensa, O bella', 'Il fulgido seren' in place of 'Già cessata', and 'Nell'amor nella speranza' preceded by the first setting of 'Tu d'Indibile figlia' (with first inversion chord) and followed by 'Prence, il rigor'. They are the only complete sources for this recitative, which in both copies leads to 'Del debellar' with its original text ('La nobiltà del regno'). Other features in common are the mention of Rosalba in the Act II scene heading but nowhere else, the gibberish reading 'procoas' for 'proconsol' on HG 37,[25] the nonsensical ascription of Rosalba's lines 'O degno cui tutto'—'il conforto miglior' (HG 90) to Scipio, presumably because they were left in the alto clef, the Hamburg (not HG) setting of Ernando's 'O dolce figlia' on the same page, and only the upper voice alternative (D) in bar 32 of 'Come al natio'. In addition both copies have ten scenes in Act III (elsewhere the number varies between six and nine), turn some dal segno into da capo arias, thereby saving the labour of writing out the modified ritornellos, and omit many stage directions, dynamics, stress marks, and instrumental indications.

Their differences are slight. Granville alone has an appendix, containing two omitted arias, 'Pensa, O bella' (wrongly cued to follow 'Braccio si valoroso') and 'Tutta rea', and gives 'Nell'amor nella speranza' a tempo mark (*Allegro*). Lennard alone cuts the first seven bars of the opening recitative and Scipio's six bars 'Ernando, i doni tuoi' in the last scene. Unlike Granville it gives four dal segno arias in Act I a full da capo and has the scene number I viii twice; Granville amends the second to ix. In 'Scoglio d'immota fronte' Lennard starts the voice on the high D, Granville on the low.

The Flower parts (S2, mid-1740s)—violins 1 and 2, viola, cello + bassoon, oboes 1 and 2 (taking flutes in 'Se mormora rivo'), and cembalo, but no horns—also give a mixed version, but not that of any copy discussed above. The main sequence of 23 numbers generally follows 1726, omitting the overture, six arias ('Un caro amante', 'Nò, non si teme', 'Tutta raccolta ancor', 'Pensa O bella', 'Temo che lusinghiero', and 'Dopo il nemico'), the accompanied recitatives 'Il poter' and 'Ah! Scipion, dove sei?', and the *coro*. 'Libera chi non è' is the soprano version. The placing of the sinfonia on HG 88–9 at the beginning of Act III and the C major end of 'Il testimon' (though the 1726 duet follows in B flat) reflect 1730. At the end are three 'Additions', the two tenor arias new in 1730 and 'Nell'amor nella speranza'. Dal segno arias are again converted to da capo, and 'Dolci aurette' has its last seven bars replaced by a regular da capo. 'Scoglio d'immota fronte', with the upper D, appears in reduced scoring, confused by errors, of which there are many throughout the manuscript. This is the only piece in which the cello part mentions the bassoons (with incomplete instructions). In Act I the viola has a part only in 'O sventurati affetti', the oboes none at all. The latter are confined to the two sinfonias and four arias (including 'Pregi son'); they are silent in 'Voglio contenta allor' and 'Tutta rea', where they should certainly play. Presumably S2's source, unlike the autograph and the Flower score, was not specific. The cembalo part is fully figured except in the 1730 tenor arias; in 'Dopo il nemico' it has a mere two figures in the fifth bar, a peculiarity shared with all other copies of this aria (except as noted below). Bar 32 of 'Come al natio' has the voice's upper note only, as in Lennard and Granville, to which these parts are obviously related. Many tempo marks and dynamics are missing.

A group of 'Additions' in the Shaftesbury Collection (S2), again designed to supplement the Cluer score, contains the March, the accompanied recitatives 'O sventurati affetti' (including the secco section), 'Ah! Scipion' (HG 82–3), and 'In testimon' (with the C major ending of 1730 and the word *Duetto*), and the two new tenor arias of 1730, 'Pregi son' and 'Dopo il nemico', the latter

---

[25] This must derive from a misreading of the autograph, where Handel crossed out 'console' and wrote (not very clearly) 'procons'.

followed by the tenor version of the secco on HG 107. Transpositions for 1730 and insertions from other operas are ignored. The absence of 'Il poter' is further confirmation that this accompanied recitative was never performed.

Handel arranged the overture for harpsichord and revised it twice. The first version is in RM 18 c 2, ff. 11–12 (Lambda, c.1729 or perhaps earlier; no tempo marks, the Minuet with 3/8 signature); the second, much more elaborately ornamented, in two Malmesbury volumes (Smith, c.1726 and c.1728) and RM 18 c 1, ff. 43–4 (S2, c.1728); the third only in Walsh's second printed collection (c.1728).[26] The Minuet alone is in New York Public Library, Mus Res MN* (c.1739) and, as *Corent in Scipio*, in a volume in the Coke Collection; neither copyist is identified.

The mixed Aylesford volumes contain several further excerpts, with special emphasis on the unpublished arias. 'Nell'amor nella speranza' (S2), figured as in the Flower parts (? by Jennens), appears in RM 19 a 1, ff. 70–1, the 1730 tenor arias 'Pregi son' and 'Dopo il nemico' (Hb1) in RM 18 b 4, ff. 50–4; the copyist supplied the two figures in the first bar, Jennens adding the rest. The same three arias,[27] together with the accompanied recitatives (except 'Il poter'), the sinfonia on HG 88–9 without tempo mark, and the four-bar sinfonia in F added to III v (*Largo*) are in RM 18 c 10, ff. 110–20 (S2). These reflect the 1730 modifications, but 'Ah! Scipion' gives Scipio's first intervention for alto and the second for tenor. RM 19 a 5, ff. 38–9 (S2), has a copy of the March. A group of *Alessandro* pieces in RM 18 c 11, ff. 89–91 (S2), includes the Act II sinfonia and the four-bar sinfonia in its original form, *Grave* in D major. Add MS 24307 has a copy of 'Dimmi, cara' (H4), the Flower Collection (Manchester v. 313, pp. 73–9) one of 'Braccio si valoroso' (Smith). The Coke Collection has copies of several arias in unidentified hands, some with reduced scoring—'Lamentandomi' in E minor, 'Dimmi, cara', 'Dolci aurette' with da capo as in the Flower parts, 'Già cessata', and 'Pensa, O bella'—and a set of parts for twenty pieces (nineteen arias and the duet) comprising two violins, viola, basso (figured), and the vocal line for transverse flute. Transpositions have been made where necessary to suit the instrument. 'Scoglio d'immota fronte' has the upper D, 'Come al natio' the upper note in bar 32; 'Se mormora riva' is *Adagio*.

Cluer published the score by subscription on 27 May 1726; the 58 subscribers (for 80 copies) included three of Handel's future oratorio librettists, Hamilton, Jennens, and Miller. The text contains the overture (without the March) and Act II sinfonia, but not that in Act III, and no recitatives of any kind. The choice of arias agrees with the libretto and the Malmesbury copy; 'Libera chi non è' is in A minor. The instrumental parts are more complete than usual at this period, but the scoring of 'Scoglio d'immota fronte' is slightly reduced, 'Dimmi, cara' lacks the viola in the ritornello, and the *coro* has no horns. Some tempo marks are missing, and many dal segno arias have a da capo. 'Scoglio d'immota fronte' has the upper D; so has bar 32 of 'Come al natio'. The arias carry the singers' names, the *coro* those of the characters, several of them

[26] This final version is printed in *Twenty Overtures*, ii. 31.
[27] Only bars 1–24 of 'Nell'amor nella speranza' are present, without tempo mark or figuring, taken no doubt from the incomplete text in Hamburg. S2 left a blank verso and a whole leaf for the rest of the aria, but evidently failed to find it.

misspelt (Luejo, Tolio). The oddest feature is that 'Rossalba' shares the second soprano line; Cluer evidently obtained pre-performance copy for this movement and also for 'Scoglio d'immota fronte', where an anacrusis chord on the last quaver of bar 55 can only have been derived from a source containing the twelve suppressed bars.[28] Walsh and Cluer each published flute arrangements in autumn 1726, and there were several pirated issues of *Most Celebrated Aires* or *Songs*. Walsh advertised the overture in parts on 22 April 1727; Benjamin Cooke did the same on 20 May. The March (with words), 'Cedo a Roma', 'Dimmi, cara', and 'Dolci aurette' appeared on single sheets. In 1734 the Paris publisher Ballard issued the March with a French text, 'A toi Catin, il faut que je t'en verse'.

Chrysander's score (1877) has a disingenuous preface. He printed all the music for Act I in the main text or the appendix, then seems to have given up the struggle. Although he included much unperformed material from the autograph, including two fragments, he omitted 'Sò gli altri debellar' and ignored large sections of the Hamburg score relating to both Handel's productions, especially that of 1730. He did not discover the Fitzwilliam material or the autographs of 'Già cessata' and 'Pregi son d'un alma grande', but the latter aria and the tenor 'Dopo il nemico' were among much unpublished material available to him. The opera badly needs a new edition.

---

[28] There is another echo of this in the Flower parts, where the viola (only) has the anacrusis.

APPENDICES

STRUCTURAL ANALYSIS[1]

Title	Date of Composition	Accomp. Recits[2]	Arias		Duets[3]	Trios	Quartets	Cori	Instrumental Movements[4]	Total
			With da capo/dal segno	Without da capo/dal segno						
Almira	1704	4	29[5]	24	3	—	—	3	12	75
Vincer se stesso	1707	2	31[5]	4	1	—	—	1	1	40
Agrippina	1709	1	34	4	—	1	1	2	2	45
Rinaldo	1711	1	27 (?28)	2	3	—	—	1	6	40 (?41)
Il pastor fido	1712	1	19	3[6]	1	—	—	1	3	28
Teseo	1712	6	27	2[6]	4	—	—	2	1	42
Silla	1713	—	19	2	2 (?4)	—	—	1	1	25 (?27)
Amadigi	1715	3	21	4	2	—	—	1	4	35
Radamisto	1720	—	25	4	1	—	—	1	10	41
Muzio Scevola (Act III)	1721	4	11	—	2	—	—	1	2	20
Floridante	1721	1	23	4[6]	2	—	—	1	3	34
Ottone	1722/3	2	24	2	2	—	—	1	3	34
Flavio	1723	2	21	1	2	—	—	1	2	29
Giulio Cesare	1723/4	4	29	3 (?4)	2	—	—	3	4	45 (?46)
Tamerlano	1724	9	22	5	1	1	—	1	1	40
Rodelinda	1725	5	25	3	1	—	—	1	1	36
Scipione	1726	4	22	5[6]	1	—	—	1	4	37

[1] This table refers to the scores as first performed, not as printed or first composed.
[2] Excluding those that constitute B sections of da capo arias.
[3] Excluding those that form part of cori.
[4] Overture counted as one movement; dances elsewhere counted individually.
[5] Uncertain whether all six lost arias had da capo, since libretto is seldom specific.
[6] Excluding one repeat, sometimes varied.

INSTRUMENTATION

Note: This table, which also refers to first performance versions, indicates the number of separate parts, not the number of players required; no extra allowance is made for *ripieni*. Many of Handel's players doubled on several instruments, especially among the woodwind. Trumpets were often accompanied by timpani even when no part was written. Theorbo and possibly viola da gamba may have been regular members of the continuo group. Handel regularly used two harpsichords in his operas, but this is seldom specified in the scores.

	Recorder	Trans. Flute	Oboe	Bassoon	Clarinet	Horn	Trumpet	Timpani	Violin	Viola	Cello	Violone/Contrab.	Viola da Gamba	Theorbo	Harp	Harpsichord
Almira	2	—	2	1	—	—	3	1	3	1	1	1	—	—	—	1
Vincer se stesso	2	—	2	—	—	—	—	—	3	1	1	1	—	—	—	1
Agrippina	2	—	2	—	—	—	2	1	3	1	2	1	—	—	—	1
Rinaldo	3	—	2	1	—	—	4	1	3	1	1	1	—	—	—	1
Il pastor fido	—	2	2	2	—	—	—	—	2	2	1	1	—	—	—	1
Teseo	2	2	2	2	—	—	2	—	3	2	1	1	—	—	—	1
Silla	2	—	2	1	—	—	1	—	2	1	1	1	—	—	—	1
Amadigi	2	—	2	1	—	—	1	—	3	1	1	1	—	—	—	1
Radamisto	—	1	2	2	—	2	2	—	2	1	2	1	—	—	—	1
Muzio Scevola (Act III)	—	—	2	1	—	2	2	—	3	1	1	1	—	—	—	1
Floridante	—	—	2	2	—	2	2	—	3	1	1	1	—	—	—	1
Ottone	—	—	2	2	—	—	—	—	3	1	1	1	—	—	—	1
Flavio	—	1	2	1	—	—	—	—	3	1	1	1	—	—	—	1
Giulio Cesare	2	1	3	2	—	4	—	—	4	2	2	1	1	1	1	1
Tamerlano	2	2	2	1	2	—	—	—	2	1	1	1	—	—	—	1
Rodelinda	2	1	2	2	—	2	—	—	3	2	1	1	—	—	—	1
Scipione	2	2	2	1	—	2	—	—	3	1	1	1	—	—	—	1

PERFORMANCES DURING HANDEL'S LIFE

Note: Unless stated otherwise, Hamburg performances were at the Theater am Gänsemarkt, London performances at the Queen's (King's) Theatre in the Haymarket. The Hamburg performances are incomplete; most of them are taken from the diary of Wilhelm Willers, which has many gaps from summer 1724 on. Dates of continental performances are New Style. A superscript 2 in the last column indicates the presence of two copies. See end of this appendix for key to location of librettos.

Date	No. of Performances	Place	Remarks	Libretto	Location of Librettos
			ALMIRA		
1705, 8 Jan.–	c.20	Hamburg		(i) F. C. Greflinger (1704)	G 1, 2
				(ii) no imprint, 'im obgemelten Jahr' (1704)	G 7
				(iii) no imprint, 'im selben Jahr' (1704)	US 1; G 1
1732, 7, 11 Feb.	?2	,,	altered by Telemann	P. L. Stromer	US 1; G 1, 2
			NERO		
1705, 25, 26, 27 Feb.	3	Hamburg	music lost	no imprint	GB 10; US 1; G 1, 2, 7
			VINCER SE STESSO		
1707, c.Nov.	?	Florence (Cocomero)		V. Vangelisti	I 1, 2
			FLORINDO		
1708, Jan.	?	Hamburg	fragments survive	no imprint	GB 10; US 1, 11; G 1, 2, 3, 7

Date	No. of Performances	Place	Remarks	Libretto	Location of Librettos
			DAPHNE		
1708, Jan.	?	Hamburg	fragments survive	no imprint	US 1, 11; G 1, 2, 3, 7
			AGRIPPINA		
1709, 26 Dec.–Feb. 1710	27	Venice (S. Giovanni Grisostomo)		M. Rossetti	US 1, 10, 13, 14; C 1; G 1; F 1, 2²; I 1, 2, 3, 4, 5, 6, 7, 8, 9, 10, 11, 12, 13
1713, 15 Feb.	?	Naples (S. Bartolomeo)	additions by F. Mancini	F. Ricciardo	US 4; I 1, 3, 6
1718, 3, 7, 24 Nov.	3	Hamburg		C. Jakhel	US 1; G 1, 2, 6, 7
1718, 1 Dec.	1	Altona			
1719, 10 Jan., 16, 23 Feb., 27 Apr., 1, 4, 8, 10, 25 May, 15, 22 June, 10, 20 July, 7, 14, 23 Aug., 7, 27 Sept., 25 Oct., 1, 27 Nov., 6 Dec.	22	Hamburg			
1719	?	Vienna (Imperial Ballroom, Tummelplatz)	additions by Fiorè and Caldara		
1720, 22 Jan.	1	Hamburg			
1722, 5, 23 Nov.	2	„			
1724, 6 Sept., 5 Oct.	2 ?+	„	see Zelm, *Hamburger Jahrbuch für Musikwissenschaft*, iii.		
			RINALDO		
1711, 24, 27 Feb., 3, 6, 10, 13, 17, 20, 24 Mar., 11, 25 Apr., 5, 9,	15	London		T. Howlatt	GB 1, 7, 9, 12, 13, 16; EIR 1; US 1, 2, 3, 9, 12; I 1

Date	No. of Performances	Place	Remarks	Libretto	Location of Librettos
			SILLA		
1713, 2 June	?1	London (? privately at Queen's)		no imprint	US 7
			AMADIGI DI GAULA		
1715, 25 May, 11, 15, 28 June, 2, 9 July	6	London	'with variety of Dancing'	J. Tonson	GB 1², 6, 9², 14; EIR 1; US 2, 6, 9, 15; G 3; F 1
1716, 16, 21 Feb., 3, 6 Mar., 20 June, 12 July	6	"			
1717, 16, 23 Feb., 21 Mar., 11 Apr., 30 May	5	"			
1717, Sept.	?	Hamburg	as *Oriana*, tr. J. Beccau, additions by R. Keiser	F. C. Greflinger (2 issues)	GB 10; US 1, 11; G 1, 2, 3, 7
1719, 6 Feb., 14, 21, 29 June, 9, 17, 24 Aug., 2 Oct.	8	"	" "	"	
1720, 12, 19, 28 Aug., 12 Sept.	4	"	" "	"	
			RADAMISTO		
1720, 27, 30 Apr., 4, 7, 11, 14, 18, 21 May, 8, 22 June	10	London		T. Wood	GB 1, 3, 5, 14; US 5, 11
1720-1, 28, 31 Dec., 4, 21, 25 Jan., 21, 25 Mar.	7	"	(much altered)	T. Wood	GB 1², 2, 6, 9, 11, 12, 14; US 2, 14, 16, 17; F 1, 3
1721, 25, 29 Nov., 2, 6 Dec.	4	"			
1722, 28 Jan., 4, 9, 12, 16, 18, 20 Feb., 13, 15, 20, 27 Apr., 6, 7 May, 18 June, 8, 27 July, 1 Sept., 11 Nov.	18	Hamburg	as *Zenobia*, recits and arrangement J. Matiheson	C. Jakhel	G 1, 2, 7

Dates	No.	Place	Notes	Editor	Library sigla
May, 14 June					
1724, 25 May	1	„	„ „ „		GB 1; US 1; G 1
1726, 9 Sept.	1	„	„ „ „		GB 11, 12, 14; US 2, 3, 7, 8; C 1
1728, Jan.–Feb.	?	London	as *Zenobia* (with new additions)	P. L. Stromer King's Theatre	
1736, 20, 26 Jan., 13 June	3	Hamburg			

MUZIO SCEVOLA

Dates	No.	Place	Notes	Editor	Library sigla
1721, 15, 19, 22, 26, 29 Apr., 3, 6, 13, 17 May, 7 June	10	London		T. Wood	GB 1, 4, 5, 9, 11[2], 12, 14, 16; US 2, 5, 8, 16; F 1; I 13 see note, p. 384
1722, 7, 10, 13 Nov	3	„		T. Wood (dated 1721)	US 1; G 1, 2, 3, 7; A 1
1723, 7, 18 Jan., 3, 12 Feb., 8 Apr., 10 May	6	Hamburg	with Prologue by R. Keiser	C. Jakhel	

FLORIDANTE

Dates	No.	Place	Notes	Editor	Library sigla
1721–2, 9, 13, 16, 20, 23, 27, 30 Dec., 3, 5 Jan., 13, 20 Feb., 25, 28 Apr., 23, 26 May	15	London		T. Wood	GB 1, 2, 5, 6, 9, 11, 12[2]; US 5, 7, 8, 14; F 1
1722, 4, 8, 11, 15, 18, 22, 26 Dec.	7	„			
1723, 28 Apr., 3, 13, 26 May, 28 June, 4, 14, 28 July, 4 Aug., 11 Oct., 15 Nov.	11	Hamburg	'With several Additions and Alterations' as *Der thrazische Printz Floridantes*, tr. J. Beccau	C. Jakhel	US 1; G 1, 2, 3, 7
1727, 29 Apr., 2 May	2	London		T. Wood (dated 1721)	GB 1
1733, 3, 6, 10, 13 Mar., 8, 15, 19 May	7	„		T. Wood	GB 1, 9

OTTONE

Dates	No.	Place	Notes	Editor	Library sigla
1723, 12, 15, 19, 22, 26, 29 Jan., 2, 5, 9, 12, 16 Feb., 26 Mar., 4, 8 June	14	London		T. Wood	GB 1[2], 5, 8, 9[2], 10, 11[2], 12[2], 14; US 2, 5, 8, 14, 16; F 1
1723, Aug.	?	Brunswick	with intermezzo *Barlafuso e Pipa* and arias by A. Lotti	C. Bartsch	G 3, 5

Date	No. of Performances	Place	Remarks	Libretto	Location of Librettos
1723–4, 11, 14, 18, 21, 28 Dec., 1 Jan.	6	London			US 1, 13; G 1; F3
1724, summer	?1	Paris	private concert performance without intermezzo, but additional arias by Lotti	no imprint	G 3, 4
1725, Feb.	?	Brunswick		C. Bartsch	
1726, 8, 12, 15, 19, 22, 26, 28 Feb., 5, 8 Mar.	9	London		King's Theatre	GB 1, 9, 10, 11, 12, 14; US 2, 16; G 3
1726, 15, 20, 22 May, 23 Sept.	4?+	Hamburg	recits tr. J. G. Glauche, additions G. P. Telemann	P. L. Stromer	US 1; G 1, 2, 3, 7
1727, 11, 13 Apr.	2	London			
1727, 7 May	1	Hamburg	Glauche–Telemann version		
1729, 26 Jan.	1	Hamburg	,, ,,		
1733, 13, 17, 20, 24 Nov.	4	London		T. Wood	GB 1, 12; F1
1734, 10, 14, 17, 21, 23 Dec.	5	,,	by Opera of the Nobility	C. Bennet	GB 14; US 13, 16; G 3; F1

FLAVIO

Date	No. of Performances	Place	Remarks	Libretto	Location of Librettos
1723, 14, 18, 21, 25, 27, 30 May, 11, 15 June	8	London		T. Wood	GB 1[2], 7, 11, 12; US 2, 5, 8, 14; F1
1732, 18, 22, 25, 29 Apr.	4	,,		T. Wood (2nd edn.)	GB 11, 12; F1

GIULIO CESARE IN EGITTO

Date	No. of Performances	Place	Remarks	Libretto	Location of Librettos
1724, 20, 22, 25, 29 Feb, 3, 7, 10, 14, 21, 24, 28 Mar, 7, 11 Apr.	13	London		T. Wood	GB 1, 6[2], 11, 12, 14; US 2, 8, 11, 14, 16; G 3; F1; I 1 (defective)
1724, summer	?1	Paris	private concert performance		

Date	No.	Place		Edition	Sources
1725, 2, 5, 9, 12, 16, 19, 26 Jan., 2, 6, 9 Feb.	10	London	'With Alterations'	Opera Office (2nd edn.)	GB 1[2], 3, 12; US 1, 8, 16
1725, Aug.	?	Brunswick	as *Giulio Cesare e Cleopatra*, with ballets	C. Bartsch	G 3, 5
1725, 21, 22 Nov.	2 ?+	Hamburg	tr. T. Lediard, recits and additions J. G. Linike	J. P. Stromer	GB 10; US 1; G 1, 2, 7
1726, 29 Apr., 7 June, 30 Sept., 3 Dec.	4 ?+	,,			
1727, 28 Apr., 9, 12, 16, 19 June	5	Brunswick			
1727	?	Hamburg			
1729, 24 Oct.	1	London			
1730, 17, 24, 27, 31 Jan., 3, 7, 14, 17, 21 Feb., 21, 31 Mar.	11	London		T. Wood (3rd edn.)	US 2, 5, 7; C 1
1731, 5 Apr., 17 Oct.	2	Hamburg			US 18
1732, 1, 5, 8, 12 Feb.	4	London			
1732, 4 Feb.	1	Hamburg			
1733, Aug.	?	Brunswick	as *Giulio Cesare e Cleopatra*, with ballets	C. Bartsch	F 1
1733, 17 Aug.	1	Hamburg		G. F. Spieringk	US 1; G 1
1734, 25 Jan., 10 June, 11 Aug., 4 Nov.	4	,,			
1735, 12, 26, 31 Oct., 3, 10, 21, 29 Nov.	7	,,			
1736, 2 Jan., 13 Feb., 5, 19 July, 10 Aug., 1, 17 Oct., 14 Nov.	8	,,		G. F. Spieringk	G 3
1737, 14 Jan., 17 Oct.	2	,,			

TAMERLANO

Date	No.	Place		Edition	Sources
1724–5, 31 Oct., 3, 7, 10, 14, 17, 21, 24, 28 Nov., 1, 4, 8 May	12	London		King's Theatre	GB 1, 6, 10, 12[2], 14; US 1, 5, 8, 12, 16; F 1
1725, 27 Sept.	1 ?+	Hamburg	tr. J. P. Praetorius, additions Telemann and C. Wych	J. P. Stromer	US 1; G 1, 2, 7
1726	?	,,		J. P. Stromer	G 1
1731, 13, 16, 20 Nov.	3	London		T. Wood	GB 11, 14; US 16 (defective), 18

Date	No. of Performances	Place	Remarks	Libretto	Location of Librettos
			RODELINDA		
1725, 13, 16, 20, 25, 27 Feb., 2, 6, 9, 13, 16, 20, 30 Mar., 3, 6 Apr.	14	London		Opera Office	GB 1, 6, 10, 11, 12, 14; US 8[2], 14, 16; F 1
1725–6, 18, 21, 23, 28 Dec., 1, 4, 8, 11 Jan.	8	,,		Opera Office	GB 1
1731, 4, 8, 11, 15, 18, 22, 25, 29 May	8	,,			
1734, 29 Nov., 2 Dec.	2	Hamburg	recits and tr. C. G. Wendt	G. F. Spieringk	US 1; G 1, 2
1735, 15 June	1	,,			
1736, 29 Oct., 12 Nov.	2	,,			
			SCIPIONE		
1726, 12, 15, 19, 22, 26, 29 Mar., 2, 12, 16, 19, 23, 26, 30 Apr.	13	London		{ King's Theatre / T. Edlin	GB 1[2], 6, 12; US 1, 2, 5, 8, 16[2]; F 1 / GB 1[3], 8, 10, 14; US 1; I 2
1730, 3, 7, 10, 14, 17, 21 Nov.	6	,,		T. Wood	GB 1, 15

LOCATION OF LIBRETTOS

Great Britain (GB)

1. London, British Library
2. ,, Royal College of Music
3. ,, Victoria and Albert Museum (Theatre Museum)
4. ,, Guildhall Library
5. Cambridge, Fitzwilliam Museum
6. ,, King's College (Rowe Library)
7. ,, University Library
8. ,, Trinity College
9. Oxford, Bodleian Library
10. Manchester, Central Library (Flower)
11. Birmingham, Central Library
12. Edinburgh, National Library of Scotland
13. ,, University Library
14. Gerald Coke Collection
15. Anthony Hicks Collection
16. Mellerstain House, Berwickshire

Ireland (EIR)

1. Dublin, Trinity College

United States (US)

1. Washington, Library of Congress
2. ,, Folger Library
3. Boston Public Library
4. New York Public Library
5. Chicago, Newberry Library
6. ,, University Library
7. Huntington Library, San Marino, Calif.
8. Princeton, University Library
9. Yale University Library, New Haven, Conn.
10. Harvard University Library (Houghton), Cambridge, Mass.
11. Illinois University Library, Urbana, Ill.
12. Michigan University Library, Ann Arbor, Mich.
13. University of California, Berkeley
14. William A. Clark Library, University of California, Los Angeles
15. Wesleyan University Library, Middletown, Conn.
16. Howard Mayer Brown Collection
17. Ellen T. Harris Collection
18. John Ward Collection

Canada (C)

1 Toronto University, Edward Johnson Music Library

Germany (G)

1 Hamburg, Staats- und Universitätsbibliothek
2 Berlin, Staatsbibliothek, Preussischer Kulturbesitz
3 Hanover, Niedersächsische Landesbibliothek
4 Wolfenbüttel, Herzog-August-Bibliothek
5 Brunswick, Stadtbibliothek
6 Kiel, Universitätsbibliothek
7 Weimar, Zentralbibliothek

Austria (A)

1 Vienna, Österreichische Nationalbibliothek

France (F)

1 Paris, Bibliothèque Nationale (Conservatoire National de Musique), Fonds Schoelcher
2 Paris, Bibliothèque Nationale (Main Collection)
3 Paris, Bibliothèque de l'Arsenal

Italy (I)

1 Bologna, Biblioteca Universitaria
2   ,,   Conservatorio di Musica
3 Florence, Biblioteca Marucelliana
4 Milan, Biblioteca Nazionale Braidense
5 Modena, Biblioteca Estense
6 Naples, Conservatorio di Musica
7 Padua, Museo Civico
8 Rome, Biblioteca Casanatense
9   ,,   Conservatorio di Musica S. Cecilia
10   ,,   Biblioteca Nazionale
11 Venice, Biblioteca Casa di Goldoni
12   ,,   Fondazione Cini
13   ,,   Biblioteca Nazionale Marciana

BORROWINGS

THERE will always be differences of opinion about what constitutes a borrowing, as opposed to a chance resemblance or a parallel treatment occasioned by similar ideas in the verbal text. Many borderline cases are excluded here. Bar references are not given except where the borrowed passage is internal or otherwise difficult to find. Most concordances with instrumental works are omitted, since very few of them can be exactly dated; but it is likely that some precede the use of the same material in the operas. Concordances with later works are likewise excluded; in a few instances, chiefly in *Vincer se stesso*, there is doubt about precedence. All music is by Handel unless another composer is named.

Numbers in brackets refer to Basel's *Verzeichnis* (vol. i). HWV catalogue numbers are given for cantatas and other smaller vocal works.

This appendix owes a substantial debt to Dr John H. Roberts, who has corrected and supplemented it from his extensive knowledge of the subject.

ALMIRA

Act I	'Schönste Rosen' (9)	Keiser: *Claudius*, 'Liebste Blumen'
Act II	'Ob dein Mund' (43)	Keiser: *Claudius*, 'Le speme di vendetta'
Act III	Entrée (47)	Keiser: *Claudius*, Entrée der Geister in den Elisäischen Feldern

Since this is Handel's earliest dated work, no borrowings from his own music can be conclusively identified.

VINCER SE STESSO

Overture	1st movement	*Almira*, Overture, 1st movement
		Cantata 'Nel dolce dell'oblio' (HWV 134), 'Hà l'ingarno' (date uncertain)
		Mattheson: *Cleopatra*, 'So wird nach' (Act III *coro*)
	1st movement	{ Keiser: *Claudius*, 'La speme di vendetta'
		{ *Almira*, 'Ob dein Mund' (43)
	Bourrée	Motet 'Saeviat tellus' (HWV 240), 1st aria
	Minuet II	Keiser: *Octavia*, 'Es streiten mit reizender Blüthe'
Act I		Keiser: *Claudius*, 'Via, via, bugiardo bambino'
	'Pugneran con noi' (2)	*Almira*, 'Zürne was hin' (12)
		Cantata 'Donna che in ciel' (HWV 233), 'Vacillò'
	'Dell'Iberia' (5)	{ *Almira*, 'Quillt, ihr überhäufte Zähren' (55)
	'In mano al mio sposo' (7)	Cantata 'O lucenti' (HWV 144), 'Per voi languisco' (date uncertain)
	'Eroica fortezza' (8)	{ *Almira*, 'Almira regiere' (1)
	'Stragi, morti' (9)	Cantata 'Ah! crudel' (HWV 78), 'Per trofei', bars 32 ff.
	'Sommi Dei!' (11)	{ Cantata 'Casti amori' (lost)
	'Vanne in campo' (12)	{ Cantata 'Da quel giorno' (HWV 99), 'Un pensiero'
	'Per dar pregio' (13)	

VINCER SE STESSO (cont.)

Act II

- 'Egli è tuo' (16)
  { Cantata 'Aure soavi' (HWV 84), 'Care luci'
  Trionfo del Tempo, 'Urne voi', B section
- 'Empio fato' (20) — Trionfo del Tempo, 'Venga il tempo'
- 'La ti sfido' (21) — Cantata 'Tu fedel?' (HWV 171), 'Se Licori'
- 'Dolce amor' (23) — Cantata 'Tu fedel?' (HWV 171), 'Sì, crudel'
- 'Si che lieta' (24)
  { Motet 'Coelestis dum spirat aura' (HWV 231), 'Felix dies'
- 'Alle glorie' (26) — Cantata 'Cor fedele' (HWV 96), 'Tra le sfere'

Act III

- 'Qua rivolga' (27) — Cantata 'Cor fedele' (HWV 96), 'Come la rondinella'
- 'Perchè viva' (28)
  { Cantata 'Cuopre tal volta' (HWV 98), 'Per pietà'
  Cantata 'Parti l'idolo mio' (HWV 147), 'Tormentosa' (date uncertain)
- 'Allor che sorge' (32) — Cantata 'Arresta il passo' (HWV 83), 'Forse che un giorno'
- 'Il dolce foco' (33)
  { Cantata 'Cor fedele' (HWV 96), 'Un sospiretto'
  Cantata 'Da quel giorno' (HWV 99), 'Lascia omai'
  Cantata 'Cor fedele' (HWV 96), 'Và col canto'
- 'Prendi l'alma' (34)
  { Keiser: Nebucadnezar, 'Du bleibst mein Leben'
  Trionfo del Tempo, 'Il voler'
- 'Begl'occhi' (35) — Keiser: Claudius, 'Begl'occhi'
- 'Io son vostro, O luci belle' (36b) — Cantata 'Fra pensieri' (HWV 115), 'Fra pensieri' (date uncertain)
- 'L'amorosa dea' (37) — Trionfo del Tempo, 'È ben folle'

AGRIPPINA

Overture

- 1st movement
  { Keiser: Claudius, Entrée
  Cantata 'Da quel giorno' (HWV 99), Entrée
  Cantata 'Donna che in ciel' (HWV 233), Introduttione
- fugue
  { Keiser: Claudius, overture, fugue
  Mattheson: Cleopatra, overture (Chrysander i. 191 ff.)

Act I

- 'Sarà qual vuoi' (1a)
  { Keiser: La forza della virtù, 'Wenn schöner Jugend'
  Almira, 'Der Mund spricht' (22)
  Trionfo del Tempo, 'Se la bellezza'
  Cantata 'Stanco di più soffrire' (HWV 167), 'Se più non t'amo', also in Cantata 'Dolce pur' (HWV 109)

'La mia sorte' (2)
- Cantata 'E partirai, mia vita?' (HWV 111a), 'Vedrò teco'
- *Resurrezione*, 'Per celare'
- *Aci, Galatea e Polifemo*, 'Che non può'
- Keiser: *Psyche*, 'Lieben und geliebet werden'
- Keiser: *Claudius*, 'Via, bugiardo bambino'
- Keiser: Cantata 'L'amata del mio sen', 'Torna ò sonno'
- Cantata 'Hendel non può mia musa' (HWV 117), 'Ogn'un canti'
- Cantata 'Lungi da me' (HWV 125), 'Tirsi amato'
- Cesti: Cantata 'Cara e dolce libertà' (3 versions)

'L'alma mia' (4)
- Cantata 'Ah! crudel' (HWV 78), sinfonia
- Cantata 'Ah! crudel' (HWV 78), 'Ah! crudel'

'Qual piacer' (5)
- Cantata 'Un sospir' (HWV 174), 'Un sospir

'Il tuo figlio' (6)
- Cantata 'Qualor crudele, sì' (HWV 151), 'Nell'incanto' (date uncertain)
- Antiphon 'Te decus virgineum' (HWV 243)

'Allegrezza' (7)
- Cantata 'Qual sento io' (HWV 149), 'Preso sono'

'Tuo ben degno' (8)
- Cantata 'Ah! che pur troppo' (HWV 77), 'Da che persò'
- *Trionfo del Tempo*, 'Io sperai trovar', voice

'Lusinghiera' (9)
- *Vincer se stesso*, 'Fra le spine' (14)
- Cantata 'Clori, degli occhi' (HWV 91), 'Quel bel rio'
- Keiser: *Octavia*, 'Wallet nicht'

'Vaghe perle' (10)
- *Aci, Galatea e Polifemo*, 'S'agita in mezz'onde'
- Cantata 'Da quel giorno' (HWV 99), 'Lascia omai', bars 19–22
- Cantata 'Cor fedele' (HWV 96), 'Và col canto'
- *Vincer se stesso*, 'Il dolce foco' (33)

'È un foco' (11)
'Hò un non sò che' (12)
- Cantata 'Arresta il passo' (HWV 83), 'È un foco'
- *Resurrezione*, 'Hò un non sò che'
- Keiser: *Procris und Cephalus*, 'Ihr allein'

'Fà quanto vuoi' (13a)
- Cantata 'Mentre il tutto' (HWV 130), 'Combatti e poi ritorna'

'Pur ritorno' (14)
- Cantata 'Filli adorata' (HWV 114), 'Se non giunge'

'Vieni, O cara' (15)
- Keiser: *Octavia*, 'Torna, O sposo'
- Motet, 'Saeviat tellus' (HWV 240), 'O nox dulcis'
- Muffat: *Armonico tributo* (1682), II, aria

'Non hò cor' (17)
- Cantata 'Qual ti riveggio' (HWV 150), 'Se la morte'
- *Resurrezione*, 'Se impassabile'

[1] Error for 32b.

	Cantata 'Arresta il passo' (HWV 83), 'Fermati, non fuggi
	Vincer se stesso, 'Siet'assai superbe' (19)
	Keiser: *Octavia*, 'Costante ognor'
	Resurrezione, 'O voi dell'Erebo'
'Col raggio placido' (37)	Cantata 'Cor fedele' (HWV 96), 'Sai perchè l'onda'
	Vincer se stesso, 'Empio fato' (20), voice
'Spererò' (38)	Keiser: *Orpheus*, 'Du schöne Morgenröthe'
	Keiser: *Octavia*, 'Kehre wieder'
'Ogni vento' (40)	Cantata 'Arresta il passo' (HWV 83), 'Fiamma bella'
Act III	
'Tacerò' (41)	Motet 'O qualis de coelo sonus' (HWV 239), 'Gaude tellus', bass
	Trionfo del Tempo, 'È ben folle'
	Resurrezione, 'Naufragando'
	Almira, 'Move i passi' (41)
'Coll'ardor' (42)	Cantata 'Sarei troppo felice' (HWV 157), 'Giusto ciel'
	Trionfo del Tempo, 'Se la bellezza' (*v.* no. 1a above)
	Resurrezione, 'Risorga il mondo'
'Io di Roma' (43)	Keiser: *Claudius*, 'Halt ein erregter Geist', final ritornello
'Esci, O mia vita' (43a)	Cantata 'Amarilli vezzosa' (HWV 82), 'È vanità'
	Cantata 'Amarilli vezzosa' (HWV 82), 'Sì, lasciami'
'Pur ch'io ti stringo' (44)	Keiser: *Nebucadnezar*, 'So folget nach Stürmen'
	Trionfo del Tempo, 'Come nembo che fugge'
'Nò ch'io non apprezzo' (44a)	Cantata 'Cor fedele' (HWV 96), 'Amo Tirsi'
'Come nube che fugge' (46)	Matheson: *Cleopatra*, 'So wird nach'
'Se vuoi pace' (47)	*Vincer se stesso*, Overture, Minuet II
'Lieto il Tebro' (48)	Cantata 'Nel dolce dell'oblio' (HWV 135), 'Hà l'inganno'
'V'accendano le tede' (49)	*Vincer se stesso*, Overture, Bourrée I

RINALDO

Overture 1st movement	Cantata 'Arresta il passo' (HWV 83), Overture, 1st movement
Act I 'Sovra balze' (1)	Keiser: *Claudius*, 'Febo in cielo'
	Cantata 'Solitudini care' (HWV 163), 'Bella gloria'

Act I (cont.)	RINALDO (cont.)
'Combatti da forte' (2)	Keiser: *Claudius*, 'Leichtfertiger Amor' *Almira*, 'Leset, ihr funkelnden Augen' (7) Cantata 'Arresta il passo' (HWV 83), 'Fu scherzo'
'Ogni indugio' (3)	*Vincer se stesso*, 'Fra le spine' (14) *Agrippina*, 'Basta, che sol' (38)
'Sulla ruota' (4)	Motet 'O qualis de coelo sonus' (HWV 239), 'Ad plausus'
'Sibillar gli angui' (5)	Keiser: *Octavia*, 'Es streiten' Keiser: *Nebucadnezar*, 'Frolocket und scherzet' *Vincer se stesso*, 'Dell'Iberia' (5) *Aci, Galatea e Polifemo*, 'Sibillar gli angui' *Agrippina*, 'Di timpani' (21)
'Nò, nò, che quest'alma' (6)	*Almira*, 'Mi dà speranza' (38)
'Vieni, O cara' (7)	*Agrippina*, 'Coronato il crin' (19) Motet 'Saeviat tellus' (HWV 240), 'Stelle fide'
'Furie terribili' (8)	*Agrippina*, 'Pensieri' (35)
'Molto voglio' (10)	*Aci, Galatea e Polifemo*, 'Chi ben ama' *Agrippina*, 'L'alma mia' (4)
'Scherzano' (12)	Cantata 'Cor fedele' (HWV 96), 'Scherzano' *Resurrezione*, 'Caro figlio'
'Cara sposa' (14)	Cantata 'Tra le fiamme' (HWV 170), 'Pien di nuove'
'Col valor' (16)	Cantata 'La terra è liberata' (HWV 122), 'Mie piante correte'
'Venti, turbini' (17)	Cantata 'Cor fedele' (HWV 96), 'Quell'erbetta'
Act II	
'Siam prossimi' (18)	Cantata 'Arresta il passo' (HWV 83), 'Se vago rio' Keiser: *La forza della virtù*, 'Ein keusches Gemüth'
'Il vostro maggio' (19)	*Almira*, Saraband (4 and 52)
'Scorta rea' (appendix)	*Trionfo del Tempo*, 'Lascia la spina'
'Lascia ch'io pianga' (22)	*Agrippina*, 'Basta che sol' (39)
'Basta, che sol' (23)	Cantata 'Cor fedele' (HWV 96), 'Fermati'
'Fermati' (24)	*Almira*, 'Ob dein Mund' (43)
'Abbruggio, avvampo' (25)	Motet 'Saeviat tellus' (HWV 240), 'Saeviat tellus' *Vincer se stesso*, 'Pugneran con noi' (2) Cantata 'La terra è liberata' (HWV 122), 'Spezza l'arco'
'Ah! crudel' (27)	Cantata 'Ah! crudel' (HWV 78), 'Ah! crudel' Cantata 'Un sospir' (HWV 174), 'Un sospir'

Act III	Sinfonia (29)	Keiser: *Claudius*, Overture
		Almira, original Overture
	'Andate, O forti' (30)	Cantata 'Clori, ove sei' (HWV 93), 'Dell'idol mio'
		Cantata 'Da quel giorno' (HWV 99), 'Lascia omai'
	'È un incendio' (31)	*Vincer se stesso*, 'Il dolce foco' (33)
		Aci, Galatea e Polifemo, 'S'agita in mezzo'
	'Al trionfo' (33)	Cantata 'Cor fedele' (HWV 96), 'Và col canto'
	'Bel piacere' (34)	Cantata 'Se pari' (HWV 158a), 'Non s'afferra'
		Agrippina, 'Bel piacere' (45)
	'Di Sion' (35)	Cantata 'Clori, mia bella Clori' (HWV 92), 'Chiari lumi'
		Motet 'Saeviat tellus' (HWV 240), 'Alleluia'
	'Solo dal brando' (38a)	*Aci, Galatea e Polifemo*, 'Del mar fra l'onde'
		Trionfo del Tempo, 'È ben folle'
	'Vinto è sol' (39)	*Vincer se stesso*, 'L'amorosa dea' (37)

IL PASTOR FIDO

Act I	'Fato crudo' (1a)	*Almira*, 'Quillt, ihr überhäuften Zähren' (55)
		Cantata 'O lucenti' (HWV 144), 'Per voi languisco'
		Vincer se stesso, 'Sommi Dei' (11)
	'Augelletti' (2)	*Resurrezione*, 'Augelletti'
		Cantata fragment (HWV 119), 'Un sol angolo'
	'Son come navicella' (3)	Cantata 'Lungi dal mio bel nume' (HWV 127ab), 'Son come navicella'
	'Lontan dal mio tesoro' (4)	Cantata 'Lungi dal mio bel nume' (HWV 127abc), 'Lontano al mio tesoro'
		Vincer se stesso, 'Tu fedel?' (HWV 171), 'Se Licori'
	'Di goder' (5)	*Vincer se stesso*, 'Dolce amor' (23)
		Agrippina, 'Ingannata' (32)
	'Casta dea' (6)	Motet 'Saeviat tellus' (HWV 240), 'Alleluia'
		Vincer se stesso, 'La ti sfida' (21), voice
		Vincer se stesso, 'Nasce il sol', B section
	'Non vo' legarmi (8)	Cantata 'Cor fedele' (HWV 96) 'Come la rondinella', voice
		Agrippina, 'Coronato il crin' (19)

Act II	'Caro amor' (9)	Keiser: *La forza della virtù*, 'Entschlafft ihr Sinnen' *Resurrezione*, 'Ferma l'ali'
	'Allor che sorge' (11)	Cantata 'Cor fedele' (HWV 96), 'Un sospiretto' *Vincer se stesso*, 'Allor che sorge' (32)
	'Finte labbra' (12)	Cantata 'Languia di bocca' (HWV 123), 'Dolce bocca'
	'Sol nel mezzo' (13)	Cantata 'Mentre il tutto' (HWV 130), 'Dove, in mezzo'
	'Se in ombre' (14)	Cantata fragment (HWV 119), 'Con linfe dorate'
	'Nel mio core' (15)	Cantata 'O come chiare' (HWV 143), 'Più non spero' *Vincer se stesso*, 'Dell'Iberia' (5), voice
	'No! non basta' (16)	Early Hamburg Overture in G minor (see note, p. 68) Cantata 'Donna che in ciel' (HWV 233), 'Vacillò'
Act III	'Hò un non sò che' (18)	*Agrippina*, 'Hò un non sò che' (12) *Aci, Galatea e Polifemo*, 'Se m'ami'
	'Se m'ami' (19)	*Almira*, 'So ben che regnante' (6)
	'Tu nel piagarmi' (20)	Cantata 'Fra tante pene' (HWV 116), 'Se avvien' Cantata 'Frà pensieri' (HWV 115), 'Frà pensieri'
	'Secondaste' (22)	*Vincer se stesso*, 'Io son vostro, O luci stelle' (36b) Cantata fragment (HWV 119), 'Col valor'
	Sinfonia before 'Oh! Mirtillo' (23)	Mattheson: *Cleopatra*, sinfonia before 'Ruhe sanft'
	'Risonar mi sento' (26)	Keiser: *Claudius*, 'Selbst der Sonne'
	'Quel ch'il cielo' (27)	Cantata 'Un' alma innamorata' (HWV 173), 'Ben impari'
Nov. 1734	Ballo, Pour les chasseurs (10)	Keiser: *Claudius*, chorus 'O Evan Evoë'

TESEO

Overture	fugue	Keiser: *Claudius*, Overture, fugue
Act I	'È pur bello' (1)	Cantata 'O come chiare' (HWV 143), 'Tornami a vagheggiar'
	'Addio! mio caro bene' (5)	*Aci, Galatea e Polifemo*, 'Dolce'/'Caro' *Vincer se stesso*, 'Ti lascio' (6)
	'Ricordati, O bella' (7)	Cantata 'Alpestre monte' (HWV 81), 'Io son ben'
	'M'adora l'idol' (8)	*Agrippina*, 'Voi che udite' (27)
Act II	'Dolce riposo' (9)	Cantata 'Aure soavi' (HWV 84), 'Care luci' *Vincer se stesso*, 'Egli è tuo' (16)

	'O stringerò' (16)	Keiser: *Claudius*, 'Liebliche Sonne' Cantata 'Donna che in ciel' (HWV 233), 'Vacillò'
Act III	'Più non cerca' (19) 'Sibillando' (24)	Cantata 'Tu fedel?' (HWV 171), 'Sì, crudel' *Vincer se stesso*, 'Sì che lieta' (24) Cantata 'Dunque sarà' (HWV 110), 'Orrida, oscura'
Act IV	'Benchè tuoni' (26) 'Deh! v'aprite' (27) 'Qual tigre' (30) 'Cara, ti dono' (32)	Keiser: *Octavia*, 'Holde Strahlen' Motet 'Saeviat tellus' (HWV 240), 'Saeviat tellus' *Aci, Galatea e Polifemo*, 'Benchè tuoni' *Trionfo del Tempo*, 'Più non cura' Cantata 'La terra è liberata' (HWV 122), 'Felicissima' Keiser: *Procris und Cephalus*, 'Ihr allein' Cantata 'Mentre il tutto' (HWV 130), 'Combatti e poi ritorna' *Agrippina*, 'Fà quanto vuoi' (13a) Cantata 'Arresta il passo' (HWV 83), 'Fu scherzo'
Act V	'Morirò' (33) 'Non è da rè' (34) 'Goda ogn'alma' (40)	*Agrippina*, 'Pensieri' (35) Cantata 'Se pari è la tua fè' (HWV 158bc), 'Non s'afferra' (cf. 'Morirò' B section) *Aci, Galatea e Polifemo*, 'Non sempre, nò' *Resurrezione*, 'Se impassabile'

SILLA

Act I	'Alza il volo' (1) 'Fuggon l'aure' (2) 'Senti, bel idol' (5) 'Con tromba guerriera' (7)	Keiser: *Psyche*, 'Lieben und geliebet werden' Cantata 'Cuopre tal volta' (HWV 98), 'Per pietà' Cantata 'Parti l'idolo mio' (HWV 147), 'Tormentosa' Cantata 'Arresta il passo' (HWV 83), 'Forse che un giorno' *Vincer se stesso*, 'Perchè viva' (28), voice Cantata 'La terra è liberata' (HWV 122), 'Come in ciel', voice Cantata 'Nel dolce tempo' (HWV 135b), 'Senti di te' Keiser: *Nebucadnezar*, 'Hier liegt das stoltze Babylon' Cantata 'Alla caccia', (HWV 79), 'Foriera la tromba'

Act II   'Dolce nume' (9)
{ Keiser: *Claudius*, 'Wehet dann, sanfte Lüfte'
{ Cantata 'Cor fedele' (HWV 96), 'Son come quel nocchiero'

'È tempo' (11)
{ *Agrippina*, 'Pur ch'io ti stringa' (44)
{ Cantata 'La terra è liberata' (HWV 122), 'Come rosa'   (cf. B section of 'È tempo')
{ Cantata fragment (HWV 119), 'Se qu'il Ciel'

'Sol per te' (12)   Keiser: *Octavia*, 'Kann dich mein Arm'
'La vendetta' (16)   Keiser: *Octavia*, 'Atlas stützt', ritornello
'Secondate' (18)   Cantata fragment (HWV 119), 'Stragi, lutto'

Act III   'Già respira' (20)
{ Cantata 'Dimmi, O mio cor' (HWV 106), 'Mi piago d'amor'
{ Cantata 'Mi palpita il cor' (HWV 132a), 'Mi piago d'amor'

AMADIGI DI GAULA

Overture   first 2 movements   *Silla*, Overture, first 2 movements, opening bars

Act I   'Pugnerò' (1)
{ Keiser: *Octavia*, 'Atlas stützt' and 'Tenta di spargere'
{ *Silla*, 'La vendetta' (16)
Almira, 'Almira regiere' (1)

'Non sà temere' (4)
{ Cantata 'Ah! crudel' (HWV 78), 'Per trofei'
{ *Vincer se stesso*, 'Vanne in campo' (12)
Silla, 'Alza il volo' (1)

'Vado, corro' (6)   Cantata 'Donna che in ciel' (HWV 233), 'Sorga pure'

'Agitato il cor' (7)
{ Keiser: *Janus*, 'Sind die Stunden'
{ *Die verwandelle Daphne*, 'Amor, Amor, deine Tücke'
{ *Trionfo del Tempo*, 'Fido specchio', ritornello
{ *Trionfo del Tempo*, 'Chi già fù', B section

'O caro mio tesor' (11)
{ Cantata 'Qual sento io' (HWV 149), 'Ardo ben'
{ *Silla*, 'Io non ti chiedo' (19)

Act II   'Sussurrate' (14)
{ Cantata 'Cor fedele' (HWV 96), 'Son come quel nocchiero'
{ *Silla*, 'Dolce nume' (9), end of ritornello

'S'estinto' (15)	*Almira*, 'Liebliche Wälder' (13)
	Trionfo del Tempo, 'Urne voi', B section
	Agrippina, 'Voi che udite' (27)
'T'amai' (16)	Keiser: *Claudius*, 'Caro, son tua'
	Trionfo del Tempo, 'Voglio cangiar'
Act III	
'Dolce vita' (24)	*Silla*, 'Un sol raggio' (4)
'Vanne lungi' (25)	Cantata fragment (HWV 119), 'Se qu'il Ciel'
	Silla, 'Secondate' (18)
'Cangia al fine' (26)	Keiser: *Octavia*, 'Kann dich mein Arm'
'Han' penetrato' (27)	*Silla*, 'Sol per te' (12)
	Silla, 'Se 'l mio mal' (17)
'Io già sento' (28)	*Silla*, 'Sei già morto' (21)
Appendix	
'Minacciami'	*Trionfo del Tempo*, 'Tu giurasti'

RADAMISTO April 1720

Act I	
'Sommi Dei' (1)	Keiser: *Claudius*, 'Mächtige Hecate'
'Deh! fuggi un traditore' (2)	G Bononcini: *Etearco*, 'Già preparai l'inganni'
	Cantata 'Donna che in ciel' (HWV 233), 'Vacillò'
'Stragi, morti' (4)	*Vincer se stesso*, 'Stragi, morti' (9)
'Mirerò' (10)	Keiser: *Claudius*, 'Flüchtige Sinnen'
	Trionfo del Tempo, 'Chiudi, chiudi'
'Dopo l'orride procelle' (11)	*Agrippina*, 'Se vuoi pace' (47)
Rigaudon I (B♭)	*Florindo/Daphne*, Allemande (G)
Act II	
'Vaga e bella' (15)	*Silla*, 'Hai due vaghe' (14)
'Troppo sofferse' (17)	Vivaldi: *Orlando finto pazzo* (1714), 'Vedi spietato', opening
'Non sarà quest'alma' (21)	*Brockes Passion*, 'Wisch' ab der Tränen'
Act III	
'S'adopri' (24)	Keiser: *Octavia*, 'Holde Strahlen'
	Motet 'O qualis de coelo sonus' (HWV 239), 'Ad plausus'
	Rinaldo, 'Sulla ruota' (4)
'Con vana speranza' (25)	*Resurrezione*, 'Del cielo dolente'
'Dolce bene' (26)	Cantata 'La terra è liberata' (HWV 122), 'Come in ciel', bars 4–8
	Cantata 'Da quel giorno' (HWV 99), 'Un pensiero'
'Sposo ingrato' (27)	*Vincer se stesso*, 'Per dar pregio' (13)
	Agrippina, 'Per punir che m'ha ingannata' (13b)

	RADAMISTO April 1720 (cont.)
Act III (cont.)	
'Alzo al volo' (28)	Resurrezione, 'Risorga il mondo' Cantata 'La terra è liberata' (HWV 122), 'Pende il ben' Brockes Passion, 'Heil der Welt'
'Deggio dunque' (29)	Almira, 'Move i passi' (41) Motet 'Coelestis dum spirat aura' (HWV 231), 'Alleluia' Cantata 'Sarei troppo felice' (HWV 157), 'Giusto ciel' Agrippina, 'Io di Roma' (43)
'Senza luce' (30, appendix)	Chamber duet 'Tanti strali al sen' (HWV 197) Acis and Galatea, 'Cease to beauty'

	RADAMISTO December 1720
Act I 'L'ingrato non amar' (Appendix)	Keiser: Claudius, 'Wird nicht, O falsches Glück' Cantata 'Chi ben ama' ('Arresta il passo', HWV 83), 'Non si può dar'
'Colla strage' (5)	Birthday Ode for Queen Anne, 'Let flocks and herds'
'So ch'è vana' (27)	Teseo, 'Cara, ti dono' (32) Resurrezione, 'Augelletti' Cantata fragment (HWV 119), 'Un sol angolo' Pastor fido, 'Augelletti' (2)
'Barbaro, partirò' (31a)	Keiser: Claudius, 'Tödtliche Eifersucht' Agrippina, 'Nulla sperar da me' (23)

	MUZIO SCEVOLA
Act III 'Lungo pensar' (1)	Lotti aria, 'Bramo aver, per più goder' (Mattheson, Critica Musica, July 1722)
'Volate più' (6, B section)	Keiser: Octavia, 'Ruhig sein' Trionfo del Tempo, 'Crede l'uom' Agrippina, 'Vaghe fonti'
'Non ti fidar' (8)	Keiser: Cantata 'L'amata del mio sen', 'Torna ò sonno' (cf. 'Non ti fidar', bars 43–7)
'A chi vive' (12b)	Cantata 'Hendel non può mia musa' (HWV 117), 'Ogn'un canti' Agrippina, 'Volo pronto' (3) Cantata 'La terra è liberata' (HWV 122), 'Felicissima'

Mattheson, *Porsenu*, 'Diese Wangen will ich küssen'
Cantata 'Menzognere speranze' (HWV 131), 'Altra spene'
Agrippina, 'Sotto il lauro' (25b)
Agrippina, 'L'alma mia' (4)

'A chi vive' (12a)

'Si sarà più dolce' (18)

FLORIDANTE

		Source
Overture	opening	Keiser: *Claudius*, Overture, opening
Act I	'Dimmi, O spene' (1)	Keiser: *Octavia*, 'Caro amante'
	'Mà pria vedrò' (7)	Keiser: *Octavia*, 'Ziehet Titan'
	'Finchè lo strale' (9)	Keiser: *Octavia*, 'Das blinde Kind', end of ritornello
Act II	'Barbaro! t'odio' (16)	Cantata 'Cor fedele' (HWV 96), 'Barbaro, tu non credi'
	'Mà non s'aspetti' (17)	Keiser: *Janus*, 'Wenn ich dich noch'
	'Fuor di periglio' (18)	Keiser: *Octavia*, 'Wallet nicht zu laut' / *Aci, Galatea e Polifemo*, 'S'agita in mezzo' / *Agrippina*, 'Vaghe perle' (10)
	'Notte cara' (19)	*Resurrezione*, 'Piangete'
Act III	'Vivere per penare' (27)	Antiphon 'Te decus virgineum' (HWV 243) / *Agrippina*, 'Il tuo figlio' (6)
	'Vanne, segui' (28)	Keiser: *Claudius*, 'An den Marmor'
	'Amor commanda' (29a)	*Silla*, 'Fuggon l'aure' (2) and sources cited there
	'Che veggio?' (32)	Keiser: *Claudius*, 'Mächtige Hecate' / *Agrippina*, 'Pensieri' (35)
1722 additions	'O dolce mia speranza' (3c)	Keiser: *Claudius*, 'Halt ein erregter Geist' / Cantata 'Amarilli vezzosa' (HWV 82), 'È vanità d'un cor' / *Agrippina*, 'Pur ch'io ti stringa' (44), (cf. final ritornellos) / Cantata 'Crudel tiranno amor' (HWV 97), 'O dolce mia speranza'
	'O quanto è caro' (14c)	Cantata 'Crudel tiranno amor' (HWV 97), 'Crudel tiranno amor'
	'O cara spene' (28c)	Cantata 'Crudel tiranno amor' (HWV 97), 'O cara spene'

OTTONE

Act I	'Giunt' in porto' (2a)	Keiser: *Octavia*, 'Kehre wieder' Cantata 'Amarilli vezzosa' (HWV 82), 'Piacer che non' *Agrippina*, 'Col peso' (33)
	'Del minacciar' (6)	*Vincer se stesso*, 'Dopo i nembi' (22) *Aci, Galatea e Polifemo*, 'Precipitoso'
	'Io sperai trovar' (7a)	Cantata 'Fra le fiamme' (HWV 170), 'Pien di nuove'
	'Affanni del pensier' (10)	Cantata 'Alpestre monte' (HWV 81), 'Io so ben' *Agrippina*, 'Voi che udite' (27) *Teseo*, 'M'adora l'idol mio' (8)
Act II	'Lascia, che nel suo viso' (14)	*Almira*, 'So ben che regnante' (6)
	'Vieni, O figlio' (16)	Keiser: *Octavia*, 'Torna, O sposo' Motet 'Saeviat tellus' (HWV 240), 'O nox dulcis' *Agrippina*, 'Vieni, O cara' (15)
	'Alla fama' (18)	Keiser (Hebenstreit): *Octavia*, 'Amor reizt zum Springen' Keiser: Cantata 'Komm ihr angenehmen Stunden', 1st aria *Resurrezione*, 'Ecco il sol'
	'Dopo l'orrore' (19) 'O grati orrori' (20)	Keiser: *Octavia*, 'Vaghi lumi' *Trionfo del Tempo*, 'Folle dunque'
	'Deh! non dir' (23)	*Ode for Queen Anne's Birthday*, 'Let all the winged race'
Act III	'Benchè mi sia' (31b)	Cantata 'Manca pur quanto sai' (HWV 129), 'Benchè tradita' Keiser: *Octavia*, 'Tenta di spargere', bars 9–11 ff.
	'Gode l'alma' (33)	*Teseo*, 'Voglio stragi' (25)
	'Nel tuo sangue' (34b)	*Ottone*, 'Giunt' in porto' (2a) Keiser (Hebenstreit): *Octavia*, 'Amor reizt zum Springen', bars 9 ff. (cf. 17 ff.)
	'Faccia ritorno' (36)	

FLAVIO

Act I	'Ricordati mio ben' (1)	Cantata 'Amarilli vezzosa' (HWV 82), 'Piacer che non' *Agrippina*, 'Col peso' (33)
	'Quanto dolci' (3)	Cantata 'Deh! lasciate' (HWV 103), 'Deh! lasciate'

'Benchè povera'/'Ah non posso' (5)	*Trionfo del Tempo*, 'Chi già fu' *Pastor fido*, Overture, Minuet I
'Di quel bel' (7)	Cantata 'Qual ti riveggio' (HWV 150), 'Se la morte' *Agrippina*, 'Non hò cor' (17)
	Amadigi, unscripted aria (see p. 297)
'Che bel contento' (8)	Keiser: *Adonis*, 'Lass mich diesen Trost' Keiser: *Claudius*, 'Selbst der Sonne'
'Il suol che preme' (9, appendix)	Cantata 'O numi eterni' (HWV 145), 'Il suol che preme'
Act II	*Trionfo del Tempo*, 'Folle dunque', B section
'Fato tiranno' (11)	Cantata 'Aure soavi' (HWV 84), 'Care luci'
'Parto, sì' (13)	*Vincer se stesso*, 'Egli è tuo' (16) *Teseo*, 'Dolce riposo' (9), bar 5
'Chi può mirare' (15)	*Flavio* autograph, 'Dille ch'il core', 1st setting
Act III	Keiser: *Octavia*, 'So manchesmal'
'Che colpa è la mia' (22)	*Ottone*, 'A te lascio' (29b)
'Doni pace' (27)	

GIULIO CESARE IN EGITTO

Overture	Overture, mostly used in *Ottone*
fugue	Keiser: *Claudius*, 'Wehet dann, sanfte Lüfte'
Act I	Cantata 'Cor fedele' (HWV 96), 'Son come quel nocchiero'
	Silla, 'Dolce nume' (9)
'Svegliatevi' (5), B section	Anthem 'O come let us sing unto the Lord' (HWV 253), 'O come let us worship'
	Flavio, 'Fato tiranno' (11a), voice (Aria originally in *Ottone*)
'L'empio, sleale' (7)	Cantata 'Ah! crudel' (HWV 78), 'Ah! crudel'
	Agrippina, 'Qual piacer' (5)
'Nel tuo seno' (11a)	Cantata 'Un sospir' (HWV 174), 'Un sospir'
	Cantata 'Qualor crudele si' (HWV 151), 'Nell'incanto' Cantata 'Ah! che pur troppo' (HWV 77), 'Col partir'
'Cara speme' (12)	Cantata 'Nice che fa?' (HWV 138), 'Se pensate' *Brockes Passion*, 'Sind meiner Seele'

'La speranza' (6b,c)	German Aria no. 9, 'Flammende Rose' (HWV 210)
'Chi perde un momento' (17)	German Aria no. 2, 'Das zitternde Glänzen' (HWV 203)
'Scorta siate' (31b)	Cantata 'Occhi miei' (HWV 146), 'Ve lo dissi'
March (42b)	Keiser: *Octavia*, 'La Roma trionfante', bars 5–6 (cf. 22–6)

TAMERLANO

Overture — Allegro	Chandos Anthem 'Have mercy upon me', Overture, Allegro
Act I	
Sinfonia before 'Prence lo sò' (2)	*Teseo*, 'Morirò' (33)
'Conservate' (2a)	*Vincer se stesso*, 'Fra le spine' (14) *Agrippina*, 'Tu ben degno' (8)
'Forte e lieto' (3)	German Aria no. 7, 'Die ihr aus dunklen Grüften' (HWV 208)
'Bella Asteria' (5)	Cantata 'Siete rose' (HWV 162), 'Siete rose'
'Dammi pace' (6)	German Aria no. 8, 'In den angenehmen Büschen' (HWV 209)
'Se non mi vuol' (7)	Cantata 'Se per fatal destino' (HWV 159), 'Con voi mi lagnerò' Cantata 'Deh! lasciate' (HWV 103), 'Deh! lasciate', bars 32–5 (cf. 49–52)
'Deh! lasciatemi' (9)	*Trionfo del Tempo*, 'Io vorrei' German Aria no. 1, 'Künft'ger Zeiten' (HWV 202), B section
'Dal crudel' (10)	Cantata 'Tra le fiamme' (HWV 170), 'Pien di nuove', voice
Act II	
'Cerco in vano' (16a)	*Pastor fido*, 'Secondaste' (22) and sources cited there
'A suoi piedi' (19)	*Resurrezione*, 'Caddi è ver' and 'Dolci chiudi' (see Ex. 62, p. 541) Keiser: *Procris und Cephalus*, 'Ihr allein' Motet 'O qualis de coelo sonus' (HWV 239), 'Ad plausus'
'Più d'una tigre' (20)	Cantata 'Mentre il tutto' (HWV 130), 'Combatti' *Rinaldo*, 'Sulla ruota' (4) *Teseo*, 'Qual tigre' (30) *Radamisto*, 'S'adopri' (24)
'Voglio stragi' (22)	Cantata 'Tra le fiamme' (HWV 170), 'Pien di nuove' *Ottone*, 'Io sperai' (7a)
Act III	
'Vedrò ch'un dì' (37)	Keiser: Cantata 'Kommt ihr angenehmen Stunden', 'Entflieht ihr traurigen Gedancken'
'Padre amato' (42)	Cantata 'Sei pur bella' (HWV 160 bc), 'È certo allor'
'D'atra notte' (44)	German Aria no. 3, 'Süsser Blumen' (HWV 204), violin figures *Rinaldo*, 'Scorta rea' (appendix)

1731 addition	'Nel mondo e nell'abisso' (31a)	Cantata 'Tra le fiamme' (HWV 170), 'Voli per l'aria' / *Riccardo Primo*, 'Nel mondo e nell'abisso' (32)

RODELINDA

Overture	fugue	Keiser: *La forza della virtù*, Overture, fugue / Cantata 'Arresta il passo' (HWV 83), Overture, fugue
Act I	'Di Cupido' (5)	*Resurrezione*, 'Dolci chiodi'
	Sinfonia before 'Pompe vane' (6)	Mattheson: *Cleopatra*, sinfonia before 'Ruhe sanft' / *Pastor Fido*, sinfonia before 'Oh! Mirtillo' (23)
	'Sono i colpi' (12a)	Keiser: *Octavia*, 'Holde Strahlen' / *Teseo*, 'Benchè tuoni' (26)
Act II	'De' miei scherni' (15) B section	Keiser: *Octavia*, 'Kehre wieder' / Cantata 'Arresta il passo' (HWV 83), 'Fiamma bella' / *Agrippina*, 'Ogni vento' (40)
	'Spietati' (16)	*Pastor fido*, 'Risonar mi sento' (26) / *Pastor fido*, 'No! non basta' (8a)
	'Prigioniera' (17a)	Cantata 'Ah! crudel' (HWV 78), 'Per trofei' / Cantata 'Cor fedele' (HWV 96), 'Senza occhi'
	'Fra tempeste' (19)	*Vincer se stesso*, Overture, Minuet
	'Scacciata' (21)	*Rodelinda* autograph, 'Ben spesso in vago prato'
	'Tuo drudo' (23a)	*Dixit Dominus*, 'Gloria patri'
Act III	'Verrete a consolarmi' (31b)	*Giulio Cesare* (1725), 'Chi perde un momento' (17) / German Aria no. 2, 'Das zitternde Glänzen' (HWV 203)
		Keiser: *Claudius*, 'Liebliche Sonne'
	'Mio caro bene' (34a)	Cantata 'Donna che in ciel' (HWV 233), 'Vacillò' / *Teseo*, 'O stringerò nel sen' (16) / Anthem 'O come let us sing unto the Lord' (HWV 253), 'The Lord preserveth'

	'Vivi tiranno' (34)	{ *Trionfo del Tempo*, 'Come nembo' { *Agrippina*, 'Come nube' (46)

SCIPIONE

Overture	1st Allegro	Recorder sonata in C major (HWV 365), Allegro
	2nd Allegro	Recorder sonata in B flat major (HWV 377), 1st movement
Act I	March (1)	Keiser: *Nebucadnezar*, 'Ehret die Götter' { *Resurrezione*, 'Quando è parto'
	'Dolci aurette' (9)	Cantata 'L'aure grate' (HWV 121b), 'L'aure grate'
Act II	'Sò gli altri debellar' (16a)	Cantata 'L'aure grate' (HWV 121ab), 'Nò, che piacer'
	'Parto, fuggo' (17)	{ Keiser: *Octavia*, 'Atlas stützt' *Silla*, 'La vendetta' (16) *Amadigi*, 'Agitato il cor' (7)
Act III	Opening sinfonia, E minor	Harpsichord suite in D minor (HWV 436), Air
	'Se mormora' (25)	*Trionfo del Tempo*, 'Tu giurasti'
	'Mi par sognar' (appendix)	{ Keiser: Cantata 'Kommt ihr angenehmen Stunden', 'Entflieht ihr traurigen Gedancken'
		{ Cantata 'Sei pur bella' (HWV 160bc), 'È certo allor' *Tamerlano*, 'Vedrò ch'un dì' (37)
	Sinfonia (28)	Concerto movement for harpsichord (Aylesford no. 33)
1730 addition	'Dopo il nemico' (35)	Cantata 'Ditemi, O piante' (HWV 107), 'Il candore tolse'

HANDEL'S SINGERS

(Only information supplementary to articles in *The New Grove* is given here; singers marked with an asterisk have no entry.)

Albertini, Giuliano (alto castrato). He had a long career in Florence, singing in 24 operas at the Cocomero and Pergola theatres between 1701 and 1738, including several by Albinoni, Gasparini, and Orlandini.

Antinori, Luigi (tenor). He sang in G. Bononcini's *Etearco* at Rome in 1719, Lotti's *Il vincitor generoso* at Ferrara in 1724, an anonymous *Scipione nelle Spagne* at Genoa in 1728, an anonymous *Alessandro nell'Indie* at Venice in 1731, and Vinci's opera of the same name at Reggio the following year. Owen Swiney recommended him to the Academy after hearing him at Livorno. The authorship of the Florence operas in which he sang in 1733–4 is uncertain.

*Azzolini, Caterina (soprano) (*fl.* 1700–8). She came from Ferrara and was employed by the Duke of Mantua; Ferdinando de' Medici asked for her services at Pratolino in 1700. She appeared in ten operas there and in Florence (1700–8), including Handel's *Vincer se stesso*, in which she played Evanco. Her compass was apparently narrow (f′–a″); an aria in which Handel gave her a d′ was cut. She was a specialist in male roles, known as la Valentina. She sang in one opera at Venice, C. F. Pollarolo's *Vinceslao* in 1703.

Bagnolesi, Anna Maria Antonia (contralto). Her Florence seasons were 1725–6, 1732–3, 1739, and 1741–2. In 1731 she was in Porpora's *Poro* at Turin. She married Pinacci in 1732; later she became the mistress of the impresario Marchese Giuseppe Ridolfi (d. 1756).

Baldassari, Benedetto (soprano castrato). He sang in Caldara's *Tito e Berenice* at Rome in February 1714. He demanded changes to his part in Handel's *Radamisto*, and was raised from a captain of the guard to a princely (but unsuccessful) lover.

Baldi, Antonio (alto castrato). Swiney described him in 1725, when he sang in Fiorè's *Elena* at Milan, as neither a good nor a bad singer, a tolerable actor, his person well enough, 'his manner of singing but so-so'. He was the leading man in three operas at Florence in 1730–1.

Barbier, Jane (contralto) (*c.*1691–1757). Her long and active career embraced nearly all the English operas and masques between 1715 and 1734 and many Italian pasticcios (1711–14). She sang both Eustazio and the title role in different revivals of *Rinaldo*, Dorinda in *Il pastor fido*, Arcane in *Teseo*, and probably Claudio in *Silla* (June 1713). Her salary in 1712/13 was £300, including a benefit that brought her only £15. Hughes's description of her caprices at the time of her elopement (1717) suggests the very model of a modern prima donna. Her fondness for male roles led the Earl of Cork to say that 'she loved change so well, that she liked to change her sex'. Her concert repertory in the 1720s included many Handel arias, nearly all of them castrato pieces, many written for Senesino. Her first retirement (1720) is said to have followed a profit of £5,000 from South Sea Stock. After her second (1730) she visited Dublin and appeared at a concert with Dubourg in December 1731. She was expecting a baby in May 1719 and was always known as Mrs Barbier, but described herself as a spinster in her will, which included charitable bequests and detailed provisions for her funeral. Her compass was bb–f″, but Handel in music specifically written for her never took her above e″.

Berenstadt, Gaetano (alto castrato) (*c.*1690–1735). He was the son of Giorgio Berenstadt, timpanist to the Grand Duke of Tuscany, and probably a pupil of Pistocchi. He sang at Florence in January 1712 (and again in 1720), and probably remained at Düsseldorf till summer 1716, singing in serenatas, court concerts, and

Wilderer's *Amalasunta* (1713), and visiting Kassel early on 1714. His 1717 London benefit was not a success, but he enjoyed the visit (especially his role in *Pirro e Demetrio*), and said he would return if Heidegger paid him £250 with a free benefit. His Dresden salary was the equivalent of £600 plus travelling expenses; he sang there in Lotti's *Gl' odi delusi dal sangue* in February 1718. He appeared at Bologna in spring 1719 (and in July was elected to the Accademia Filarmonica, which held a memorial service for him on 15 February 1735), Brescia in August 1719, and Milan in 1720–1. He spent the summer of 1723 at a spa near Bristol, that of 1724 singing at concerts in Paris, including *Ottone* and *Giulio Cesare*. After his father's death (*c.*1728) he lived at Naples for two years, but returned to Florence in 1730 and sang at Livorno in 1730–1. In later life he suffered from rheumatism and quarrelled with old friends; his will is dated 22 September 1734. A portrait medallion was issued about this time. Berenstadt was a passionate collector of incunabula, manuscripts, and Old Master paintings. He also traded in them, and for some years ran a bookshop in Florence. Zeno paid tribute to his knowledge of literature. About 1731 he published an edition of Benvenuto Cellini's autobiography, dedicated to Lord Burlington, but the venture was not a success. He sang in at least 53 operas, 30 of them new works by 16 composers. His vast size made him unsuitable for young lovers; in later years he generally played tyrants and unsympathetic old men, and was most successful in angry and bellicose arias with jagged leaps. See L. Lindgren's full account, based largely on his unpublished correspondence with the merchant and diplomat G. G. Zamboni, 'La carriera di Gaetano Berenstadt, contralto evirato (*ca.* 1690–1735)', *RIM* xix (1984), 45–112. To the operas there cited can be added Chelleri's *Temistocle* at Padua in 1721. Lindgren gives his compass as g–e″, with a single f″ in Gasparini's *Faramondo* (Rome, 1720).

Bernacchi, Antonio Maria (alto castrato). He sang in G. Bononcini's *Abdolomino* (Vienna, 1709) and *Crispo* (Rome, 1721), apparently finding his part in the latter too difficult. His Florence seasons were 1712–15 and 1741–2. Swiney, who was given to Irish extravagance, described him in 1729 as the very best singer in the world.

Berselli, Matteo (soprano castrato). He sang in Bologna in 1712, Reggio in 1713 and 1719, and in two operas at Florence in summer and autumn 1715 and one at Reggio in May 1719.

Bigonzi, Giuseppe (alto castrato). He was in two operas at Florence in 1718–19, and in Paris with Bononcini and other members of the Haymarket company in summer 1724. He was a protegé of Durastanti's husband Casimiro Avelloni.

Borosini, Francesco (tenor). He sang in A. M Bononcini's *Nino* at Reggio in June 1720 and Conti's *Creso* and *Penelope* at Vienna in 1723–4. He was engaged for the Royal Academy through the Earl of Peterborough at a salary of 1,000 guineas. His wife, née Rosa d'Ambreville, appeared in Vivaldi's *Armida al campo d'Egitto* at Mantua in 1718.

Boschi, Giuseppe Maria (bass). He sang in Genoa with his wife in autumn 1706, and in A. M. Bononcini's *La presa di Tebe* at Vienna in 1708. In London 1710/11 he and his wife (who was known as la Cieca and presumably short-sighted) received a joint salary of £700. He was engaged for the choir of St. Mark's, Venice, on 9 December 1714 at the maximum salary of 100 ducats, and also acted as organist; he had to obtain special leave for visits to Turin in 1716–17 and Dresden in 1717–20, and was still receiving back pay in 1722. In summer 1724 he was in Paris with Bononcini and other members of the Haymarket company, singing in concerts and shortened versions of *Ottone* and *Giulio Cesare*. The first opera in which he is known to have sung is Albinoni's *Il più fedel tra i vassalli* at Genoa in 1705. He appeared at Ferrara in 1708, Verona in 1715, and Bologna and Genoa in 1717.

Campioli [Antonio Gualandi] (alto castrato). He first appeared at Hamburg in 1719, when he left Darmstadt after a pay dispute, and sang in nine operas at Brunswick in 1721–2 and more than twenty, including Telemann's arrangement of Handel's *Tamerlano*, at Hamburg in 1722–6. In 1728 he was sent to Venice to train young Italian singers for the Saxon court at an annual salary of 600 thalers. He was pensioned off in 1738.

Carli, Antonio Francesco (bass). He sang at Piacenza (in G. Bononcini's *Camilla*) in 1698, Genoa in 1706, and Florence in 1708 and 1718–20. In 1709 he received a special fee for singing a motet at St. Mark's, Venice, the previous Christmas. He composed an aria for his own part (Seneca) in the pasticcio *Nerone fatto Cesare* at Venice in 1715.

Cassani, Giuseppe (alto castrato). His first London visit was a disaster; he appeared only twice (in *Camilla*) and was so severely hissed that he withdrew or was withdrawn. By autumn 1708 he had cost the management nearly £500 in salary and expenses and left debts of £87. He was in two operas at Florence in 1717–18.

Cecchi, Anna Maria Torri (soprano) (*fl.* 1684–1708). First known appearance at Reggio Emilia 1684. Virtuosa of Duke of Mantua 1688–9 (and later), Duke of Parma 1691–5. Sang in Genoa, Piacenza, Venice, and Parma 1688–90, in Venice 1704, and in eleven operas at Florence in 1701–8, including Handel's *Vincer se stesso*, in which the part of Esilena may have been put down for her. She was known as la Beccarina.

Cuzzoni, Francesca (soprano). Early appearances were at Mantua in 1717, Florence in 1717–20, where she made her début in a comic opera, Bologna once more in 1720, and Padua in 1721. Her 1724 Paris repertory included concert versions of *Ottone* and *Giulio Cesare*; Louis XV rewarded her singing at Chantilly in July with his portrait set in diamonds. She may not have married Sandoni (who apparently composed her ornaments) until January 1725; she had another child in July 1728. The Academy dismissed her in June 1727 after the quarrel with Faustina and asked Swiney to find a substitute, but George I's threat to withdraw his subsidy procured her reinstatement. Her salary in 1727/8 was reported as £1,500 (or guineas). She revisited Paris early in 1750, when according to the Duc de Luynes those who had heard her 25 years earlier detected little if any change in her voice, which was 'still in tune, agreeable and quite loud—and she still trills too'. She died in Bologna 19 June 1778, aged 85.

Dotti, Anna Vincenza (contralto). Her earliest known appearances were at Livorno in 1715 (in G. Bononcini's *Camilla*), in three operas at Florence in 1715–16, and at Bologna and Reggio in 1716. On leaving London she sang in autumn 1727 at Brussels, where she was described as 'always perfectly good, and always smiling'. She married one Michele Palermo, and may have been the 'Madame Palerme' who sang in *Ottone* in Paris in the summer of 1724.

Durastanti, Margherita (soprano). She sang in two operas at Mantua in 1700–1, taking a male role in M. A. Ziani's *Il duello d'amore e di vendetta* (the source of Handel's *Vincer se stesso*). Other appearances were at Bologna and Reggio in 1710, Milan and Reggio again in 1713, and Florence in 1715. She missed the 1721–2 London season owing to illness. She was in Paris in summer 1724 and sang in concert performances of *Ottone* and *Giulio Cesare*.

Fabri, Annibale Pio (tenor). Other appearances were at Mantua in 1718 (in Vivaldi's *Armida al campo d'Egitto*), Milan in 1721 (in Vivaldi's *La Silvia*), Florence in 1725, 1732, and 1737, and Bologna in 1734. In March 1729 Swiney said that he sang in as good a taste as any man in Italy. On his way to London that autumn he sang a motet and arias at two concerts in Paris. In 1730 Viscount Percival (the future Earl of Egmont) employed him as music master for his daughters. He composed operas for Madrid, and in 1740 set Metastasio's *Alessandro nell'Indie* for Lisbon.

Frilli, Stefano (soprano castrato) (1664–1744). He received special payments for singing at St. Mark's, Venice, at Christmas in 1696 and 1697, and appeared in three operas at Florence in 1707–8, including Handel's *Vincer se stesso*, playing the central role of Rodrigo; the compass is d'–a'' ♭. He was for many years in the service of the Elector of Bavaria and died a rich man.

Galerati, Caterina (soprano). She was a Venetian, and entered the Tuscan service in 1701, singing in two operas at Pratolino and Florence in 1701–2, at Naples in 1705 and 1710, in G. Bononcini's *Abdolomino* at Vienna in 1709, at Genoa in 1712, and at Milan in 1718. She probably replaced the sick Anastasia Robinson at the second performance of *Amadigi* on 11 June 1715.

Gallia, Maria (soprano). Although she demanded 700 guineas for singing in Vanbrugh's 1708 season at the Queen's Theatre, he put her down for 200 and apparently paid her £3 a night.

Girardeau, Isabella (soprano). Her London salary in 1710–11 was £300. In spring or summer

1712 she received 40 guineas for singing at two concerts for the Duchess of Shrewsbury in Kensington.

Guicciardi, Francesco (tenor) (*fl.* 1705–24). In the service of the Duke of Modena, his native town. He sang in nine operas at Venice (1705, 1716–17, 1720–3), and five at Pratolino and Florence (1707–10), including Handel's *Vincer se stesso*, in which he played the substantial role of Giuliano. It demands a fine technique (compass d–a'). He sang in Orlandini's *L'odio e l'amore* at Genoa in 1709. In July 1719 Handel tried to engage him for the Royal Academy.

L'Epine, Francesca Margherita de (soprano). She was the first to sing Bononcini's music in London—an aria from *Camilla*, published by Walsh in December 1703. For an account of her career see D. F. Cook in *Theatre Notebook*, xxxv (1981), 58–73, 104–13. Cook gives her compass as c'–b''♭. Her earliest known appearances were in Venice in 1698 and 1699.

Marcello, Aurelia (soprano) (*fl.* 1706–20). She was a Venetian, in the service of the Duke of Mantua and later Princess Violante of Bavaria, wife of Ferdinando de' Medici. She sang in three operas in Venice in 1706–7 and ten at Florence in 1706–16, including Handel's *Vincer se stesso*, in which she played Florinda (compass d'–b''♭).

Merighi, Antonia Margherita (contralto). Early appearances in five operas at Florence in 1714–16 and Vivaldi's *Armida al campo d'Egitto* at Mantua in 1718. Her London salary in 1729–30 was £700 plus a benefit. Swiney applauded her engagement, though in 1728 he had bracketed her and Diana Vico as 'some He-she-thing or other'. She was probably a pupil of Bernacchi.

Negri, Maria Caterina (contralto). Early appearances in Bologna (1719), Florence (1721), and Milan (1723). She sang the male part of Filotete in Handel's pasticcio *Oreste* in December 1734.

Nicolini [Nicolo Grimaldi] (alto castrato). Vanbrugh promoted his London engagement in 1708, though when he arrived in October Swiney was in charge at the Haymarket. Nicolini sang at Bath in autumn 1709. His salary in 1710–11 was £860. In the following season the Duke of Shrewsbury, Lord Chamberlain, paid him £200 for singing at his wife's private concerts. He received special fees for singing in St. Mark's, Venice, at Christmas in 1695 and 1712. He appeared at Florence in 1725 and (in Porpora's *Arianna e Teseo*) in 1728. In 1725–7 Swiney repeatedly urged the Academy to bring him back to London (though George I was said not to like him), claiming that he was singing better than ever.

Pacini, Andrea (alto castrato). He made earlier appearances at Florence (1709–10, 1720), Rome (1711, 1721), Lucca (1711, 1714–15, 1724), and Ferrara (1713), several of them in A. Scarlatti's *Ciro* and G. Bononcini's *Camilla* and *Crispo*. He also sang at Livorno (1717–18), Bologna (1719–20), Milan (1720), and Genoa (1728).

Pasini, Nicola (bass) (*fl.* 1699–1721). He was a priest, engaged for St. Mark's choir, Venice, in 1705 at 70 ducats, raised to 90 in 1715 and the maximum 100 in 1721. He appeared in three operas at Venice in 1707–10, taking the small part of Lesbo (compass A–e') in *Agrippina*. He may have been the Nicolo Pasini who sang in Legrenzi's *I due Cesari* at Venice in 1683. He belonged to a church choir in Brescia 1699/1700.

Pellegrini, Valeriano (soprano castrato). He appeared in G. Bononcini's *La fede publica* at Vienna in 1699, and received a special payment for singing in St. Mark's, Venice, at Christmas 1709. He sent arias from *Agrippina* to the Elector Palatine in 1710.

Perini, Giuseppe (alto castrato). He sang in two operas at Florence in 1707, taking the small part of Fernando (compass c'–c'') in Handel's *Vincer se stesso*. A singer of this name, presumably not the same man, appeared in three operas at Venice in 1744–5.

Pilotti-Schiavonetti, Elisabetta (soprano). She and her husband, who was also a cellist and continuo harpsichordist, had a joint salary of £500 in the 1710–11 season at the Haymarket. In June 1712 they received 40 guineas for performing at two concerts for the Duchess of Shrewsbury in Kensington. George I gave her 20 guineas for each of her three benefits 1715–17.

Pinacci, Giovanni Battista (tenor) (1694/5–1750). Further appearances: Milan 1718 (in A. M. Bononcini's *Griselda*), Rome 1723, Florence 1718, 1720, 1723, 1732–3, 1739, 1748–9 (sixteen operas in all), and Livorno (1746). Swiney strongly recommended him to the Royal Academy in May 1725. He married Anna Bagnolesi in 1732, and died in Florence as the result of an accident in early summer 1750. The diarist Susier called him 'comico bravo' and said he left children by Bagnolesi.

Riemschneider, Johann Gottfried (bass). He sang the alto parts of Andronico in Telemann's arrangement of *Tamerlano* and Tolomeo in *Giulio Cesare* in octave transposition at Hamburg in 1725. He and his brother appeared there together in *Muzio Scevola* (1723), at least five operas by Keiser in 1724–7, and *Cleofida* (Handel's *Poro*) in 1732.

Robinson, Anastasia (soprano, later contralto). Her popularity and strong position in London are attested by Heidegger's agreement in October 1714 to pay her £500 and a benefit for an incomplete season, on condition that Nicolini returned. George I gave her 20 guineas for each of her three benefits in 1715–17. Lord Peterborough paid Bononcini £250 for coaching her in 1723. Her sister Margaret, also a singer, was a student of Bononcini and later of Rameau in Paris; in January 1728 she married Arbuthnot's brother George.

Robinson, Ann Turner (soprano). In 1719 she replaced Jane Barbier at a private concert for Mary Countess Cowper, and was apparently accompanied by Handel. The poet John Hughes thought that her recent improvement had 'plac'd her in the first Rank of our English Performers'.

Salvai, Maria Maddalena (soprano). She sang in Fiorè's *Elena* at Milan in 1725 and again at Florence, her native city, in three operas in 1730–1; her contract with Orlandini is reproduced by the Weavers (see Appendix H) on page 259. Salvai was her married name; Antonio Cocchi in a letter to Giuseppe Riva (24 January 1728) referred to her husband (a colonel) as 'her assiduous and bellicose guardian'. She was engaged for the carnival season of 1732–3 at the Kärntnertor Theatre, Vienna.

Scalzi, Carlo (soprano castrato). He made early appearances at Rome in three operas by A. Scarlatti, *Telemaco* (1718), *Marco Attilio Regolo* (1719, in a female role), and *Arminio* (1722), and at Florence in 1723 and 1729. A listener in 1723 ranked him with Faustina Bordoni, "for they both sing more than a violin can play, & with a perfect new taste'.

Scarabelli, Diamante Maria (soprano). She sang in an opera by G. Bononcini at Milan in 1713, and was greatly admired by Uffenbach for her Venice performances in 1714–15.

Senesino [Francesco Bernardi] (alto castrato). He sang in A. Scarlatti's *Ciro* at Ottoboni's private theatre at Rome in December 1711, at Bologna in 1712, Reggio in 1713, Brescia in 1714, and at Florence in Orlandini's *Amore e maestà* in summer 1715. In autumn 1723 he nearly married Mrs Sarah Cornish, 'a City lady'. There was talk of the Royal Academy replacing him at the end of the 1725/6 season; according to Swiney his illness in June 1726 and late return the following season were diplomatic moves. In December 1726 he gave deep offence to Princess Violante of Tuscany by refusing to sing or to wait on her. His London salary in 1727/8 was reported to be £1200. On leaving London in July 1728 he sang in Paris with Faustina Bordoni, but made little impression.

Sorosina, Benedetta (soprano). She sang at Genoa in 1727 and in Porpora's *Arianna e Teseo* at Florence in August 1728.

Strada del Pò, Anna Maria (soprano). Early appearances in Vivaldi's *La Silvia* at Milan in August 1721 and G. A. Canuti's *Rodelinda* at Lucca in 1724, when she was described as Venetian. She was on bad terms with Bononcini, who thought little of her, and refused to sing for him in London in 1732. She sang Ermione in Handel's pasticcio *Oreste* in December 1734.

Urbani, Valentino [Valentini] (alto castrato). His first London appearance in *Camilla* may have been as early as December 1706. Many details of his financial transactions with the Haymarket management are recorded in the *Coke Papers*. He and Nicolini sang with much acclaim at Bath in late summer 1709. In October 1722 he appeared in Conti's *Don Quixotte* at Hamburg, singing in Italian.

Vico, Diana (contralto). On her return journey from England in August 1716 she sang at a private concert in Paris and was well received. She played a male role in Gasparini's *Astianatte* at Milan in the carnival season of 1722. In 1726 Swiney dismissed her with Merighi as 'some He-she-thing or other'. She received 20 guineas from George I for each of her two benefits in 1715–16.

MODERN STAGE PRODUCTIONS TO END OF 1993

THIS table is necessarily incomplete. Nearly all German productions, and many in Britain and elsewhere, were considerably altered from the original text. Most early German productions used Oskar Hagen's arrangements, and many were revived in subsequent seasons. Total of performances includes revivals where known.

Cordial thanks are due to Professor Manfred Rätzer, Otto Gossmann, and many theatre managements for details of productions in Germany; and to Eugen Schüepp for those in Switzerland.

Date	Place	Company, Conductor, Producer	Editor/Translator	No. of Performances	Remarks
		ALMIRA			
1985, 23 Feb.	Leipzig (Opernhaus)	Horst Gurgel/Uwe Wand	Gurgel, Wand, and Eginhard Röhlig	12	also Oviedo and Dresden
		VINCER SE STESSO			
1984, 29 Aug.	Innsbruck (Tiroler Landestheater)	Alan Curtis/Shirley Wynne	Curtis	2	in Italian
1985, 17 July	London (Sadler's Wells)	Handel Opera Soc.: Charles Farncombe/Tom Hawkes		3	in Italian
1987, 16 June	Karlsruhe (Badisches Staatstheater)	Charles Farncombe/Friedrich Meyer-Oertel	tr. Meyer-Oertel (recits.)	5	arias in Italian; revived 1988
		AGRIPPINA			
1943, 21 Feb.	Halle (Stadttheater)	Richard Kraus/Heinz Rückert	Hellmuth Christian Wolff	9	
1944, 19 May	Göttingen (Stadttheater)	Werner Bitter/Max Bührmann	Wolff		

Date	Place	Company, Conductor, Producer	Editor/Translator	No. of Perfor-mances	Remarks
1952, 9 Feb.	Erfurt (Städtische Bühnen)	Heinrich Bergzog/Herbert Henze	Wolff	11	also Halle
1958, 12 Dec.	Leipzig (Opernhaus)	Heinz Fricke/Klaus Dreyer	Wolff	30	
1959, 14 Apr.	Heidelberg (Städtische Bühnen)	Karl Rucht/Karlheinz Streibing	Wolff	6	
1963, 27 June	Abingdon (Unicorn Theatre)	Frances and Alan Kitching	F. and A. Kitching and Giovanna Ballinger	6	arias in Italian
1965, 16 Sept.	London (Lamda Theatre)	Opera 1961: Peter Gellhorn/ Ande Anderson	Kitchings	6	also Ledlanet, Kinross
1965, 23 Dec.	Darmstadt (Staatstheater)	Hans Martin Rabenstein/Andreas Meyer-Hanno	Wolff	24	
1966, 13 Aug.	Munich (Cuvilliéstheater)	Heinrich Hollreiser/Rudolf Hartmann	Wolff and Hartmann	8	revived 1967
1966, 15 Sept.	London (Eltham Palace)	Opera 1961: Audrey Langford/ Ande Anderson	Kitchings and Gellhorn	2	
1967, 4 June	Halle (Landestheater)	Horst-Tanu Margraf/Renate Oeser	Waldtraut Lewin	12	revived 1968
1969, 19 Feb.	Edinburgh (George Square Theatre)	Edinburgh University Opera Club: David Kimbell/Roger Savage	Savage	4	
1970, 4 July	Nuremberg (Städtische Bühnen)	Wolfgang Gayler/Hans-Peter Lehmann	Wolff	9	
1970, July	Barga (T. dei Differenti)	John Eliot Gardiner/Peter Hunt			
1970, 12 Sept.	Zürich (Opernhaus)	Alberto Erede/Rudolf Hartmann	Wolff	12	
1978, 20 Oct.	Altenburg (Bachsaal des Schlosses)	Helmut Wünderlich/Friedrich Konrad Pemmann	Wolff	22	
1978, 6 Dec.	Weimar	Lothar Seyfarth/Ehrhard Warneke	Wolff	25	
1978, 25 Dec.	Erfurt	Ulrich Faust/Günther Imbiel	Wolff	16	
1980, 12 Apr.	Wittenberg	Klaus Hofmann/Hansjoachim Beygang	Wolff	11	
1980, 5 June	Halle (Landestheater)	Christian Kluttig/Martin Schneider	Wolff	19	

Date	Place	Company, Conductor, Producer	Editor/Translator	No. of Performances	Remarks
1981, 2 Oct.	Halberstadt	Hans Auenmüller/Günther Frische	Wolff	12	
1982, 11 Mar.	Tunbridge Wells	Kent Opera: Ivan Fischer/ Christopher Bruce and Norman Platt	Anne Ridler		also Brighton, London (Sadler's Wells), and elsewhere; revived 1985
1983, 4 Aug.	Berlin (Theatermanufaktur am Halleschen Ufer)	Berliner Kammeroper: Brynmor Llewelyn Jones/Henry Akina		8	
1983, 10 Sept.	Venice (Teatro Malibran)	Christopher Hogwood, Bernhard Klebe./Sonja Frisell		14	revived 1985
1984, 2 June	Kassel (Staatstheater)	Samuel Bächli/Rainer Winter	Bächli and Winter	5	
1984, 14 Sept.	Oldenburg (Staatstheater)	Gerhard Markson/Armin Tacke	Wolff and Tacke	14	revived 1985
1985, 14 Mar.	Fort Worth, Texas	Fort Worth Opera Association: George Del Gobbo/Ken Kazan		2	in Italian
1985, 1 May	Schwetzingen (Rokokotheater im Schloss)	Arnold Östman. George Fischer/ Michael Hampe	Hampe	22	also Cologne and Drottningholm
1985, 25 July	Iowa City (Hancher Auditorium)	Univ. of Iowa School of Music: Don V. Moses/Beaumont Glass	tr. Glass	5	also Eisenstadt and Urbino
1985, 4 Oct.	Boston (Northwestern Univ. Auditorium)	Boston Lyric Opera: Thomas Dunn/Anne Ewers	tr. B. Glass	2	
1990, 3 Nov.	College Park, Maryland (Tawes Recital Hall)	Nicholas McGegan/Leon Major	tr. B. Glass	3	
1991, 14 June	Göttingen (Deutsches Theater)	Nicholas McGegan cond. and prod.		2	in Italian
1992, 4 Jan.	Washington (Eisenhower Th.)	Stephen Lord/Michael Hampe and Florian-Malte Leibrecht	Hampe	12	Cologne production; in Italian
1992, 15 July	Buxton (Opera House)	Roger Vignoles/Adrian Slack	tr. Roger Savage	7	
1992, 3 Sept.	Ealing (open air)	Midsummer Opera: David Roblou/ Alan Privett		3	
1993, 19 Aug.	Budapest (Schloss Zichy. open air)	Obuda Festival: Geza Oberfrank/ Miklos Gábor-Kerényi	tr. Oberfrank	6	

RINALDO

Date	Place	Company, Conductor, Producer	Editor/Translator	No. of Performances	Remarks
1923, 18 June	Prague (Conservatorium)	Otakar Ostrčil/Ferdinand Pajman		1	in Czech
1933, 7 Feb.	London (Century Theatre)	Hammersmith Day Continuation School: Olive Daunt/May Burrell	Daunt	2	
1954, 16 June	Halle (Landestheater)	Horst-Tanu Margraf/Siegmund Skraup	Max Schneider, Herbert Koch, Skraup	3	
1961, 17 May	London (Sadler's Wells)	Handel Op. Soc.: Charles Farncombe, Peter Gellhorn/Douglas Craig	Farncombe	8	also Berlin and Halle; revived 1965
1964, 27 Mar.	Freiberg	Walter Stoschek/Werner Urberg	Herbert Koch	36	in Italian
1965, 22 Jan.	Rome (Santa Cecilia)				
1975, 16 Oct.	Houston, Texas (Jones Hall)	Lawrence Foster/Frank Corsaro	Martin Katz	4	in Italian
1978, 8 Nov.	London (Sadler's Wells)	Handel Op. Soc.: Charles Farncombe/Julian Oldfield	Farncombe	4	
1980, 10 June	Cambridge (Caius College)	Graeme Jenkins/Malcolm Hunter		4	in Italian
1981, 27 June	Karlsruhe (Badisches Staatstheater)	Charles Farncombe/Jean-Louis Martinoty		13	in Italian; revived 1982–5
1982, 23 May	Rome (Auditorio Pio)				
1982, 3 July	Ottawa (National Arts Centre)	Mario Bernardi/Frank Corsaro, David Selle	M. Katz	21+	also New York, Washington, and 6 other cities 1984
1985, 2 Feb.	Reggio Emilia (T. Municipale)	Charles Farncombe, John Fisher, Piero Bellugi/Pier Luigi Pizzi			also many other Italian cities to 1991
1985, 19 Feb.	London (Royal College of Music)	Christopher Adey/Basil Coleman	tr. Farncombe and Andrew Page	4	
1985, 8 June	Rio de Janeiro (T. Municipal)			5	

Date	Place	Company, Conductor, Producer	Editor/Translator	No. of Performances	Remarks
1985, 11 June	Paris (Châtelet)	Charles Mackerras, Nicholas Kraemer/Pier Luigi Pizzi		6	Reggio Emilia production
1985, 21 June	Ealing (open air)	Midsummer Opera: David Roblou/ Alan Privett	tr. Farncombe, Page, and A. Hicks	3	
1985, 8 Oct.	Coburg (Landestheater)	Marcel Meier/Peter Bent Wyrsch	tr. Herbert Koch	9	
1985, 25 Nov.	San Francisco (Hellman Hall)	San Francisco Conservatory of Music: Nicholas McGegan/ Lauretta Goldberg, Stephen Schultz		1	
1987, 15 Mar.	Halle (Landestheater)	Christian Kluttig/Peter Konwitschny	tr. Frank Kämpfer and Werner Hintze	41	often revived to 1993; also Dresden, Budapest, and elsewhere
1988, 9 Mar.	Washington (Kennedy Center Concert Hall)	Stephen Simon/Francis Rizzo		1	semi-staged
1991, 11 Feb.	Lisbon (T. Sao Carlos)	Nicholas Kraemer/Pier Luigi Pizzi		4	Reggio Emilia production
1991, 11 Apr.	Madrid (T. Lirico Nacional la Zarzuela)	Antoni Ros Marbá/Pier Luigi Pizzi		5	Reggio Emilia production
1993, 11 May	Trieste (T. Comunale Giuseppe Verdi)	Charles Farncombe/Ivan Stefanutti		10	

IL PASTOR FIDO

Date	Place	Company, Conductor, Producer	Editor/Translator	No. of Performances	Remarks
1946, 5 Sept.	Basel (St Albansaal)	Schola Cantorum Basiliensis: August Wenzinger/Richard Koelner	Wenzinger	6	2 in Italian, 4 in German
1948, 20 June	Göttingen (Stadttheater)	Fritz Lehmann/Curt Haug	Wenzinger	5	
1959, 4 Sept.	Como (T. di Villa Olmo)	Ennio Gerelli; Giulio Paternieri/ Filippo Crivelli	G. Gerelli	4	also Vicenza 1961

Date	Place	Company, Conductor, Producer	Editor/Translator	No. of Performances	Remarks
1969, 4 Sept.	Drottningholm	Stockholm Royal Opera: Charles Farncombe/Bengt Peterson	(Nov. 1734 version) + *Terpsicore*		often revived; also Brighton 1972, Edinburgh 1974, Versailles 1975, Oslo 1979–82
1971, 14 Sept.	Abingdon (Unicorn Theatre)	Nicholas Kraemer/Alan Kitching and Anna Sweeney	Kitching (1712 version)	9	also Edgware and London (Goldsmiths Hall) 1972
1982, 23 May	Amelia (Sociale)				
1983, 19 Aug.	Ipswich, Mass. (Castle Hill)	Concert Royal and N.Y. Baroque Dance Co.: James Richman/Patrick Swanson	(Nov. 1734 version) + *Terpsicore*	7	in Italian; also New York (Marymount Manhattan Th.)
1985, 13 Jan.	Halle (Junge Garde)	Leipzig Hochschule für Musik: Christian Kluttig/Renate Oeser	(Nov. 1734 version) + *Terpsicore*	9	in Italian; also Dresden, Berlin, and Brno
1987, 18 Mar.	New York (Marymount Manhattan Th.)	James Richman/John Haber	*Terpsicore* only	4	
1990, 11 Oct.	Toronto (Macmillan Th.)	Opera Atelier: David Fallis/Marshall Pynkoski	tr. Brad Walton	3	
1992, 25 Mar.	London (Britten Th.)	London Handel Soc.: Denys Darlow, Michael Rosewell/Ceri Sherlock		5	also Halle
		TESEO			
1947, 29 June	Göttingen (Stadttheater)	Fritz Lehmann/Hanns Niedecken-Gebhard	Lehmann and Emilie Dahnk-Baroffio	7	
1977, 14 May	Bad Lauchstädt (Goethe-Theater)	Max Pommer, Harald Knauff/Martin Schneider	Klaus Harnisch	27	revived 1978; also Szombathely
1984 26 Oct.	Berlin (Kammerspiele des Deutschen Theaters)	Hochschule für Musik 'Hanns Eisler': Gert Bahner/Martin Schneider	tr. Klaus Harnisch and Andreas Glöckner	6	also Halle

Date	Place	Company, Conductor, Producer	Editor/Translator	No. of Performances	Remarks
1985, 26 Mar.	Manchester (Royal Northern College of Music)	Stephen Cleobury/Malcolm Fraser		3	
1985, 30 May	Boston College (Theatre Arts Center)	Boston Early Music Festival: Nicholas McGegan cond. and prod.		9	in Italian; also Purchase, N.Y.
1985, 28 July	London (Covent Garden)	English Bach Festival: Jean-Claude Malgoire/Tom Hawkes			in Italian; also Athens, Siena, Versailles, Madrid
1986, 2 July	London (Sadler's Wells)	English Bach Festival: Nicholas Cleobury/Tom Hawkes		3	
1987, 25 Aug.	Zwingenberg, Baden	Schlossfestspiele: John Porter cond. and prod.		2	

SILLA

Date	Place	Company, Conductor, Producer	Editor/Translator	No. of Performances	Remarks
1990, 4 Oct.	Paris (Salle Dupré)	Devaux-Daumas Co.: Gabrielle Marcq/Christian Daumas		9	

AMADIGI

Date	Place	Company, Conductor, Producer	Editor/Translator	No. of Performances	Remarks
1929, 17 Jan.	Osnabrück (Landestheater)	Fritz Berend/Otto Liebscher	Hans Dütschke	4	
1963, 23 Mar.	Halle (Landestheater)	Horst-Tanu Margraf/Kurt Hübenthal	Waldtraut Lewin	34	revived 1964
1967, 15 Apr.	Copenhagen (Thorvaldsen Museum)	University Opera Studio: Per Enevold/Jørgen Heiner	Joakim Keramb Christensen	4	
1968, 26 Apr.	Abingdon (Abbey Hall)	Frances and Alan Kitching	Kitchings	3	also Claydon House in Italian; often revived to 1991; also Halle, Karlsruhe, Bratislava
1983, 21 Feb.	Warsaw (T. Wielki)	Janusz Przybylski; Maciej Gawin-Niesiolowski/Laco Adamik			

Date	Place	Company, Conductor, Producer	Editor/Translator	No. of Performances	Remarks
1985, 21 July	Urbino (T. Sanzio)				
1987, 24 July	Schloss Kleeberg, Niederbayern, open air	Walter Waidosch/Anette Pollner		11	in Italian; also Munich, Passau, and elsewhere
1988, 24 Nov.	Munich (Gasteig Big Bang Th.)	Walter Waidosch/Helmut Danninger			in Italian; also Bad Lauchstädt 1991
1991, 2 May	Cambridge (West Road Concert Hall)	Cambridge U. Opera Soc. and Selwyn College Music Soc.: Andrew Jones/Jean Chothia	tr. Jones	3	

RADAMISTO

Date	Place	Company, Conductor, Producer	Editor/Translator	No. of Performances	Remarks
1927, 22 June	Göttingen (Stadttheater)	Rudolf Schultz-Dornburg/Hanns Niedecken-Gebhard	Josef Wenz	4	
1937, 14 May	Düsseldorf	Eduard Martini/Hubert Franz	H. Buths, Martini, Franz	8	
1943, 3 Mar.	Hagen	Alfred Gillessen/Hermann Bender	Martini and Franz	6	
1955, 12 June	Halle (Landestheater)	Horst-Tanu Margraf/Heinz Rückert	Rückert	20	revived 1956-7
1959, 24 Sept.	Schwerin (Staatstheater)	Kurt Masur/Erwin Bugge	Rückert	12	
1960, 6 July	London (Sadler's Wells)	Handel Op. Soc.: Charles Farncombe/Douglas Craig	Farncombe	5	revived 1962
1960, 11 Oct.	Leipzig (Opernhaus)	Hans Wallat, Horst Gurgel/Rückert	Rückert	49	revived 1961-4
1961, 11 June	Cottbus (Stadttheater)	Frank Morgenstern/Joachim Beese	Rückert	16	
1963, 16 Oct.	Dresden (Landesoper)	Ernst Hermann/Reinhard Schau	Rückert	42	
1964, 2 July	Karl-Marx-Stadt	Günter Blumhagen/Harry Kupfer	Rückert	36	
1964, 25 Dec.	Annaberg	Erich Vietze/Paul Rabold	Rückert	16	
1967, 14 Mar.	Eisenach	Hans Gahlenbeck/Erwin Bugge	Rückert	15	
1970, 13 Sept.	Magdeburg	Roland Wambeck/Reinhard Schau	Rückert	17	
1970, 29 Oct.	Mannheim (Nationaltheater)	Hans Wallat/Wolfgang Blum	H.-T. Margraf, Rückert	13	revived 1979

Date	Place	Company, Conductor, Producer	Editor/Translator	No. of Performances	Remarks
1978, 12 May	Halle (T. des Friedens)	Volker Rohde/Martin Schneider	Klaus Harnisch	7	
1979, 19 Jan.	Rudolstadt	Konrad Bach/Auswalt Liwer	Rückert	8	
1981, 21 June	Altenburg	Helmut Wünderlich/Carl Heinz Erkrath	Rückert	14	
1984, 3 Nov.	London (Sadler's Wells)	Handel Op. Soc.: Charles Farncombe/Tom Hawkes	Farncombe	4	
1985, 22 Mar.	Wittenberg	Klaus Hofmann/Friedrich Radtke	Rückert	7	
1992, 10 Jan.	New York (Mannes College of Music)	Mannes College Opera Seminar: Will Crutchfield cond. and prod.		2	semi-staged
1993, 9 June	Göttingen (Deutsches Theater)	Nicholas McGegan/Drew Minter	Dec. 1720 version, ed. T. Best	3	

MUZIO SCEVOLA

Date	Place	Company, Conductor, Producer	Editor/Translator	No. of Performances	Remarks
1928, 9 June	Essen	Rudolf Schultz-Dornburg/Erich Hezel	Rudolf Steglich	3	Handel's act only
1985, 26 June	Sulmona (T. Comunale)	Studio Lirico: Francesco Vizioli/Talmage R. Fauntleroy		2	Handel's act only; also Arezzo

FLORIDANTE

Date	Place	Company, Conductor, Producer	Editor/Translator	No. of Performances	Remarks
1962, 10 May	Abingdon (Unicorn Theatre)	Frances and Alan Kitching	Kitchings and Giovanna Ballinger	6	
1984, 13 May	Bad Lauchstädt (Goethe-Theater)	Christian Kluttig/Peter Konwitschny	Werner Hintze, Konwitschny, and Karin Zauft	30	revived 1985–7; also Dresden, Berlin, Prague, and elsewhere
1989, 4 May	Cambridge (West Road Concert Hall)	Cambridge U. Opera Soc. and Selwyn College Music Soc.: Andrew Jones/Jean Chothia	Jones	3	

Date	Place	Company, Conductor, Producer	Editor/Translator	No. of Performances	Remarks
1990, 6 Mar.	Ottawa (National Arts Centre)	Alan Curtis/Shirley Wynne		2	semi-staged; also Berkeley

OTTONE

Date	Place	Company, Conductor, Producer	Editor/Translator	No. of Performances	Remarks
1921, 5 July	Göttingen (Stadttheater)	Oskar Hagen/Christine Hoyer-Masing	Hagen	5	
1922, 21 June	Gera	Ralph Meyer/Kurt Löffler	Hagen	1	
1922, 6 July	Göttingen (Stadttheater)	Oskar Hagen/Hanns Niedecken-Gebhard	Hagen	7	revived 1923
1923, 15 Sept.	Hanover	Oskar Hagen/Hanns Niedecken-Gebhard	Hagen	4	
1923, 7 Oct.	Bremerhaven	Hans Oppenheim/Gustav Burchard	Hagen	9	
1923, 19 Dec.	Graz	Heinz Berthold/Friedrich Neubauer	Hagen	4	
1924, 7 May	Tilsit (Musikverein)	Hugo Hartung/Hanns Niedecken-Gebhard	Hagen	4	
1924, 4 Nov.	Mannheim	Richard Lert/Richard Meyer-Walden	Hagen	5	
1925, 12 Apr.	Gera	Ralph Meyer/Hanns Schulz-Dornburg	Hagen	5	
1926, 1 July	Göttingen	Rudolf Schulz-Dornburg/Hanns Niedecken-Gebhard	Hagen	2	
1926, 6 Sept.	Berlin (Städtische Oper)	Fritz Zweig cond. and prod.	Hagen	4	
1927, 2 Sept.	Mainz	Heinz Berthold/Paul Weissleder	Hagen	7	
1927, 6 Oct.	Dessau	Artur Rother/Georg Hartmann	Hagen	4	
1927, 9 Dec.	Hamburg (Stadttheater)	Werner Wolff/Walter Elschner	Hagen	2	
1928, 17 Nov.	Königsberg (Stadttheater)	Univ. Institut für Musik: Joseph Müller-Blattau/Hans Schüler	Hagen	1	

Date	Place	Company, Conductor, Producer	Editor/Translator	No. of Performances	Remarks
1935, 24 Feb.	Halle (Stadttheater)	Bruno Vondenhoff/Hanns Niedecken-Gebhard	Hagen	7	
1943, 12 May	Freiburg/Breisgau	Bruno Vondenhoff/Arthur Schneider	Hagen	7	
1946, 22 Feb.	Frankfurt/Main (Börsensaal, Handwerkersaal)	Bruno Vondenhoff/Walter Jockisch	Hagen	16	
1947, 19 Dec.	Lübeck	Rudolf Schulz-Dornburg/Georg Reichardt	Hagen	18	
1949, 4 June	Plauen	Willy Haetzel/Werner Schindler	Hagen	15	
1958, 31 May	Halle (Landestheater)	Horst-Tanu Margraf/Heinz Rückert	Rückert	11	revived 1960
1959, 19 Sept.	Schwetzingen	Deutsche Gastspieloper Frankfurt: Robert Heger, Hans-Joachim Wunderlich/Adolf Rott	Hagen	c. 60	revived 1960 in 40 German cities and abroad
1961, 8 Feb.	Freiberg (Stadttheater)	Walter Stoschek/Annelies Thomas	Rückert	30	
1961, 24 Aug.	Stralsund (T. der Werftstadt)	Lothar Seyfarth/Harry Kupfer	Rückert	21	
1962, 4 Feb.	Görlitz	Alfred Schönfelder/Joachim Zschech	Rückert	16	
1962, 14 June	Gelsenkirchen (Musiktheater im Revier)	Ljubomir Romansky/Fritz Ditgen	Hagen	9	
1971, 24 Jan.	Frankfurt/Oder	Edgar Brandt/Wolfgang Gubisch	Rückert	9	also Halle 1972
1971, 19 Oct.	London (Sadler's Wells)	Handel Op. Soc.: Charles Farncombe, David Lloyd-Jones/Douglas Craig	tr. Andrew Porter	10	also Chichester; revived 1973; Drottningholm 1974
1985, 17 Jan.	Winchester College (Queen Elizabeth II Theatre)	Francis Wells/Tony Ayres		3	
1989, 13 May	Kiel	Karl Heinz Knobloch/Kathrin Prick	Rückert, Knobloch, Prick	6	

Date	Place	Company, Conductor, Producer	Editor/Translator	No. of Performances	Remarks
1992, 4 June	Göttingen (Deutsches Theater)	Nicholas McGegan cond. and prod.		3	in Italian
1992, 12 Nov.	Greenwich (Royal Naval Hospital)	Robert King/Patrick Garland	King and Anthony Hicks		also Tokyo, Osaka, and London (Queen Elizabeth Hall) 1993
1993, 11 Sept.	Hildesheim (Stadttheater)	Johannes van Slageren/Didier von Orlowsky	Rückert, Ingrid Zellner, van Slageren, Orlowsky	17	

FLAVIO

Date	Place	Company, Conductor, Producer	Editor/Translator	No. of Performances	Remarks
1967, 2 July	Göttingen (Stadttheater)	Günther Weissenborn/Heinrich Koch	tr. E. Dahnk-Baroffio	3	
1969, 26 Aug.	Abingdon (Unicorn Theatre)	Anthony le Fleming/Alan Kitching	Kitching	6	
1985, 25 Apr.	Princeton (Westminster Choir College)	Glenn Parker/David Gately	tr. Parker	2	
1985, 1 May	London (St John's, Smith Square)	Abbey Opera: Anthony Shelley/John Eaton	tr. Richard Burgess Ellis	4	
1985, 25 July	Batignano (Chiostro S. Croce)	Musica nel Chiostro: Graeme Jenkins/Keith Warner		6	also Fiesole and Florence
1987, 30 Apr.	Cambridge (West Road Concert Hall)	Cambridge U. Opera Soc. and Selwyn College Music Soc.: Andrew Jones/Jean Chothia	tr. Jones	3	
1989, 24 Aug.	Innsbruck (Tiroler Landestheater)	René Jacobs/Christian Gangneron		5	in Italian; also Monte Carlo 1990

GIULIO CESARE IN EGITTO

Date	Place	Company, Conductor, Producer	Editor/Translator	No. of Performances	Remarks
1922, 5 July	Göttingen (Stadttheater)	Oskar Hagen/Hanns Niedecken-Gebhard	Hagen	9	revived 1923

Date	Place	Company, Conductor, Producer	Editor/Translator	No. of Performances	Remarks
1922, 29 Oct.	Hanover	Richard Lert, Rudolf Schulz-Dornburg/Hanns Niedecken-Gebhard	Hagen	9	revived 1923
1923, 4 June	Berlin (Grosse Volksoper)	Franz von Hösslin/Alexander d'Arnals	Hagen	28	also Copenhagen 1924 (? concert)
1923, 28 Oct.	Munich (Nationaltheater)	Hans Knappertsbusch, Karl Böhm/Max Hofmüller	Hagen	14	revived to 1929
1923, 1 Dec.	Mannheim	Richard Lert/Eugen Gebrath	Hagen	15	revived 1924; also Landau and Worms
1923, 25 Dec.	Bamberg	Otto Lippits/Rudolf Hartmann	Hagen	7	
1924, 23 Mar.	Zürich	Max Conrad/Paul Trede	Hagen	5	
1924, 23 Mar.	Bremen	Adolf Kienzl/Charles Moor	Hagen	3	
1924, 26 June	Essen	Max Fiedler/Alexander Schum	Hagen	4	
1924, 6 July	Kassel	Robert Laugs/Ernst Legal	Hagen	4	
1924, 31 Aug.	Altenburg	Georg Göhler/Rudolf Otto Hartmann	Hagen	4	
1924, 3 Sept.	Basel	Gottfried Becker/Otto Wälterlin	Hagen	5	
1924, 20 Sept.	Rostock	Karl Reiss/Paul Weissleder	Hagen	6	also Neustrelitz
1924, 21 Sept.	Stuttgart	Carl Leonhardt/Otto Erhardt	Hagen	10	revived 1925
1924, 5 Oct.	Münster	Rudolf Schulz-Dornburg/Hanns Niedecken-Gebhard	Hagen	13	
1924, 7 Oct.	Erfurt	Franz Jung/Hans Schüler	Hagen	3	
1924, 18 Oct.	Cologne	Eugen Czenkar/Fritz Rémond	Hagen	28	revived to 1929; also Vienna
1925, 10 Jan.	Würzburg	Hans Oppenheim/Friedrich Perloff	Hagen	7	
1925, 12 Mar.	Breslau	Ernst Mehlich/Kurt Becker-Huert	Hagen	5	keyboard accompt. during orchestral strike
1925, 29 Oct.	Koblenz	Hermann Henrich/Karl Wallenda	Hagen	5	

Date	Place	Company, Conductor, Producer	Editor/Translator	No. of Performances	Remarks
1925, 30 Oct.	Remscheid	Hans Waldemar Steinhardt/Lothar Jansen	Hagen	4	
1925, 2 Dec.	Kaiserslautern	Fritz Müller-Prem/Hans Erdmann von Kutzschenbach	Hagen	4	
1925, 25 Dec.	Zwickau	Wilhelm Schmidt/Friedrich Perloff	Hagen	4	
1926, 10 Mar.	Barmen-Elberfeld	Fritz Mechlenburg/Carl Stang	Hagen	5	
1926, 26 Mar.	Berne	Viktor Wagner/Alois Hofmann	Hagen	4	
1926, 22 Apr.	Nuremberg	Karl Schmidt/Hans Siegle	Hagen	4	
1926, 29 May	Vienna (Akademietheater)	Hochschule und Akademie für Musik: Karl Alwin/Heinz Schulbaur	Hagen	3	
1926, 18 June	Duisburg	Paul Brach/Saladin Schmitt	Hagen	9	
1926, 19 Sept.	Bochum	Paul Brach/Saladin Schmitt	Hagen	5	
1926, 2 Oct.	Freiburg/Breisgau	Ewald Lindemann/Arthur Schneider	Hagen	5	
1927, 6 Mar.	Augsburg	Carl Tutein/Theodor Dörich	Hagen	5	
1927, 2 Apr.	Saarbrücken	Felix Lederer/Robert Becker	Hagen	3	
1927, 13 Apr.	Danzig	Bruno Vondenhoff/Walther Volbach	Hagen	2	
1927, 14 May	Northampton, Mass. (Smith College Academy of Music)	Werner Josten/Oliver Larkin	Hagen, tr. Bavard Quincy Morgan	1	
1927, 11 Sept.	Darmstadt	Karl Böhm/Arthur Maria Rabenalt	Hagen	4	
1928, 26 May	Kiel	Eugen Jochum/Fritz Tutenberg	Hagen	3	
1928, 5 July	Göttingen (Stadttheater)	Rudolf Schulz-Dornburg/Hanns Niedecken-Gebhard	Hagen	2	
1928, 24 Sept.	Aachen	Paul Pella/Gerd d'Haussonville	Hagen	8	also Hagen 1929
1929, 3 May	Halle	Erich Band/August Rösler	Hagen	4	
1930, 6 Jan.	London (Scala Th.)	Gervase Hughes/Norman Marshall	Hughes, tr. Robert Stuart and Marshall	3	

Date	Place	Company, Conductor, Producer	Editor/Translator	No. of Performances	Remarks
1931, 31 Jan.	New York (Juilliard School)	Albert Stoessel/Alfredo Valenti	Hagen	1	in English
1932, 19 Sept.	Düsseldorf	Wolfgang Martin/Friedrich Schramm	Hagen	8	
1933, 24 Oct.	Ulm	Herbert von Karajan/Felix Klee	Hagen	6	
1933, 1 Dec.	Amsterdam (Opera Studio in Stadsschouwberg)	Paul Pella/Abraham van der Vies		3	also Rotterdam
1934, 30 May	Dresden (Festspielhaus Hellerau)	Semper Oper: Karl Böhm/Hans Strohbach	Hagen	8	
1935, 8 Jan.	Strasbourg	E. G. Munch/Jean Mercier	Hagen, tr. Louise Mancini	4	
1935, 12 Feb.	Liegnitz	Karl Georg Buzengeiger/Hans Erdmann von Kutzschenbach	Hagen	4	
1935, 27 Apr.	Zürich (Stadttheater)	Robert F. Denzler/Heinz Rückert	Hagen	7	
1935, 12 May	Rostock	Adolf Wach/Alois-Erwin Dieterich	Hagen	3	
1935, 8 June	Berlin (Staatsoper)	Hans Swarowsky/Hanns Niedecken-Gebhard	Hagen	5	
1935, 25 June	Aachen (Kurhaus, open air)	Herbert von Karajan/Kurt Becker-Huert	Hagen	1	
1935, 4 Oct.	Hamburg	Hans Schmidt-Isserstedt/Rudolf Zindler	Hagen	22	revived 1936–8; also Vienna 1939
1935, 23 Oct.	Magdeburg	Erich Bölke/Richard Hein	Hagen	5	
1935, 6 Nov.	Detmold	Edwin Scholz/Igor Folwill	Hagen	5	
1935, 29 Nov.	Coburg (Landestheater)	Siegfried Meik/Erwin Dieterich	Hagen	6	
1935, 10 Dec.	Königsberg	Bernhard Conz/Fritz Schröder	Hagen	6	
1936, 23 Feb.	Halle	Bruno Vondenhoff/Paul Helwig	Hagen	4	
1936, 25 Apr.	Poznán (T. Wielki)	Zygmunt Latoszewski/Karol Urbanowicz	tr. Stanislaw Roy		
1937, 7 Oct.	Nuremberg	Bernhard Conz/André von Diel	Hagen	10	also Erlangen and Salzburg 1938
1937, 30 Nov.	Mainz	Karl Maria Zwissler/Hanns Kämmel	Hagen	5	

Date	Place	Company, Conductor, Producer	Editor/Translator	No. of Performances	Remarks
1938, 23 Nov.	Freiburg/Breisgau	Bruno Vondenhoff/Arthur Schneider	Hagen, Vondenhoff	3	
1939, 22 Nov.	Göttingen (Stadttheater)	Carl Mathieu Lange/Karl Bamor	Hagen	4	
1940, 20 Feb.	Koblenz	Gustav Koslick/Hanns Kämmel	Hagen	7	
1940, 25 Aug.	Ulm	Karl Hauf/Reinhold Ockel	Hagen	9	
1941, 29 Oct.	Elbing	Walter B. Tuebben/Walter Branker	Hagen	8	
1942, 30 Jan.	Essen	Heinrich Creuzburg/Heinz Müller-Eschborn	Hagen	9	
1942, 29 Mar.	Greifswald	Nikolaus von Lukacs/Claus-Dietrich Koch	Hagen	4	
1942, 20 Apr.	Düsseldorf	Wolf von der Nahmer/Fritz Landsittel	Hagen	8	
1942, 30 Apr.	Breslau	Philipp Wüst/Hans Schenk	Hagen	5	
1942, 13 Sept.	Regensburg	Rudolf Kleiber/Fritz Rothardt	Hagen, Rothardt	8	
1942, 25 Oct.	Cracow	Hans Antolitsch/Hans Schröck	Hagen	8	
1943, 17 Jan.	Würzburg	Cornelius Monske/Felix Klee	Hagen	16	
1947, 14 Feb.	Brussels (Monnaie)	Edgard Doneux/Georges Dalmen	tr. Louise Mancini	5	
1947, 9 Mar.	Copenhagen (Royal Th.)	Johan Hye-Knudsen/Poul Kanneworff	tr. Torben Krogh and Kai Aage Bruun	15	revived 1948
1947, 19 Apr.	Zürich	V. Reinshagen/	Hagen	6	
1950, 26 Mar.	Leipzig (Städtisches Theater)	Paul Schmitz/Heinz Rückert	Hagen (rev. Holger Hagen)	14	
1950, 17 June	Cologne (Oper der Stadt)	Richard Kraus/Erich Bormann	Hagen	4	
1950, 6 July	Pompeii (T. Grande)	Herbert Albert/Herbert Graf	Hagen	3	
1950, 21 Nov.	Oldenburg	Hans-Georg Ratjen/Heinrich Müller-Eschborn	Hagen	10	
1951, 5 Apr.	Brunswick (Staatstheater)	Heinz Zeebe/Friedrich Ammermann	Hagen	8	
1951, 10 Apr.	Münster (Städtische Bühnen)	Heinz Dressel/Alexander Schum	Hagen	9	

Date	Place	Company, Conductor, Producer	Editor/Translator	No. of Performances	Remarks
1951, 9 June	Bielefeld (Städtische Bühnen)	Carl Schmidt-Belden/Paul Hager	Hagen	10–15	
1952, 27 Sept.	Saarbrücken (Saarländisches Staatstheater)	Philipp Wüst/Hanns Niedecken-Gebhard	Hagen		
1953, 14 Apr.	Düsseldorf	Deutsche Oper am Rhein: Arnold Quennet/Hartmut Boebel	Hagen (rev. Holger Hagen)	10	
1953, 21 May	Freiburg/Breisgau (Städtische Bühnen)	Heinz Dressel/Reinhard Lehmann	Hagen (revised)	10	
1953, 22 May	Los Angeles (City College Auditorium)	City College Opera Workshop: Hugo Strelitzer/Vladimir Rosing	Hagen, tr. Henry Reese	2	
1954, 1 May	Wiesbaden (Hessisches Staatstheater)	Ludwig Kaufmann/Walter Pohl		13+	revived 1959
1954, 5 June	Vienna (Th. an der Wien)	Karl Böhm/Oskar Fritz Schuh	Hagen		
1955, 11 Feb.	Stralsund	Egon Bölsche/Friedrich Radtke	Hagen	14	
1955, 12 Aug.	Munich (Prinz-regententheater)	Bayerische Staatsoper: Eugen Jochum, Fritz Rieger, Joseph Keilberth/Rudolph Hartmann		38	often revived till 1966
1955, 26 Dec.	Rome (T. dell' Opera)	Gianandrea Gavazzeni/Margherita Wallmann		4+	also Milan 1956
1956, 15 Jan.	Berne	Georg Meyer/Stephan Beinl	Hagen	5	
1956, 11 Sept.	Mainz (Theater der Landeshauptstadt)	Karl Mariz Zwissler/Udo Esselun		13	
1957, 12 Mar.	Detmold (Landestheater)	Paul Sixt/Wolfram Humperdinck	Hagen	3+	
1957, 25 Aug.	Basel (Stadttheater)	Silvio Varviso/Oskar Wälterlin	Hagen	10	also Schwetzingen 1958
1957, 8 Sept.	Greiz	Joachim Dietrich Link/Karl-Heinz Viertel	Viertel	13	revived 1958
1958, 19 Jan.	Hanover (Landestheater)	Ernst Richter/Peter Ebert	Hagen	23	
1958, 21 Feb.	Ulm (Städtische Bühnen)	Harald von Goertz, Rudolf Mors/Bruno Voges	Hagen	7	

Date	Place	Company, Conductor, Producer	Editor/Translator	No. of Performances	Remarks
1958, 24 Apr.	Los Angeles (Schoenberg Hall)	UCLA Opera Workshop: Jan Popper/Lotfollah Mansouri	Hagen, tr. Henry Reese and Hugo Strelitzer	3	
1958, 23 Sept.	Aachen (Stadttheater)	Hans Walter Kämpfel/Werner Wickenberg	Hagen (rev. Holger Hagen)	23	also Düren
1958, 23 Nov.	Nuremberg (Städtische Bühnen)	Eric Riede/Rudolf Hartmann		15	
1958, 25 Dec.	Würzburg (Städtisches Theater)	Robert Edenhofer/Erich Kronen	Hagen	13	also Fulda
1959, 18 Jan.	Vienna (Staatsoper)	Heinrich Hollreiser/Oskar Fritz Schuh			
1959, 22 Feb.	Wuppertal (Wuppertaler Bühnen)	Hans Georg Ratjen/Georg Reinhardt	Ratjen, Reinhardt, Heinrich Wendel	14 (?17)	
1959, 27 Feb.	Münster (Städtische Bühnen)	Robert Wagner/Ulrich Reinhardt	Hagen	11 (?13)	
1959, 3 Mar.	Augsburg (Städtische Bühnen)	Anton Mooser/Hannes Schönfelder		7	
1959, 8 Mar.	Halle (Landestheater)	Horst-Tanu Margraf, Kurt Scharnacher/Wolfgang Gubisch	Harry Kupfer and Gubisch	15	
1959, 19 Apr.	Zittau	Ernst Wilhelm Schmitt/Heinz Vogt	Kupfer and Gubisch	26	also Liberec
1959, 24 Apr.	Buenos Aires (T. Cómico)	Washington Castro/	Hagen	2	in Italian
1959, 2 June	Seattle (Meany Hall)	Univ. of Washington Opera: Stanley Chapple/Ralph Rosinburn	Chapple	2	
1959, 4 June	Regensburg (Stadttheater)	Otto Winkler/Eberhard Kullman	Hagen	11	
1959, 15 Nov.	Wiesbaden	Ludwig Kaufmann/Walter Pohl		9	
1960, 11 Mar.	Frankfurt/Main (Städtische Bühnen)	Felix Prohaska, Johannes Pütz/Hans Hartleb	Hartleb	19	revived 1962
1960, 25 June	Hagen (Städtische Bühnen)	Walter Meyer Giesow/Hermann Werner	Hagen	14	

Date	Place	Company, Conductor, Producer	Editor/Translator	No. of Performances	Remarks
1961, 31 Oct.	Cleveland (Karamu Th.)	Helmuth Wolfes/Benno Frank	tr. Stephen Szaraz and Wolfes	25	also New York 1963
1961, 30 Nov.	Bonn (Beethovenhalle)	Peter Ronnefeld/Federik Mirdita		6	
1962, 11 Feb.	Freiburg/Breisgau (Städtische Bühnen)	Gustav Fülleborn/Manfred Hubrich		8	
1962, 28 Apr.	Warsaw (T. Wielki)	Mieczyslaw Mierzejewski/Ludwig Renč	tr. Jadwiga Szamotulska	18	
1962, 16 Sept.	Altenburg	Martin Egelkraut/Karl-Heinz Viertel	Viertel	35	
1963, 20 June	London (Sadler's Wells)	Handel Op. Soc.: Charles Farncombe/Norman Ayrton		3	in Italian
1963, 20 Nov.	Weimar (Nationaltheater)	Rudolf Bräuer/Dieter Bülter-Marell	Bülter-Marell and Viertel	26	
1963, 21 Dec.	Dessau	Heinz Röttger/Willy Bodenstein	Dessau Th. arrangement	12	
1964, 26 Jan.	Heidelberg (Theater der Stadt)	Hans Blümer/Günter Amberger	Hagen (rev. Holger Hagen)	11	
1964, 7 Apr.	Parma (T. Regio)	Arnold Gamson/Annabelle Gold, Beppe Menegatti			also Trieste, Florence, and Milan
1964, 2 May	Boulder, Colorado	Univ. of Colorado Opera Workshop: Andor Toth/Rolf Sander		1	in English
1964, 2 May	Eisleben	Ernst Wilhelm Schmit/Fritz Lucke	Bülter-Marell and Viertel	17	
1964, 27 Dec.	Barcelona (T. del Liceu)	Mladen Basic/Leo Nedomansky			in Italian; also Dallas, and Venice 1966
1965, 21 May	Kansas City	Dallas Civic Opera: Nicola Rescigno/Luciana Novaro		8	
1965, 8 Dec.	Stendal	Peter Gülke/Peter Brähmig	based on Bülter-Marell and Viertel	7	
1966, 4 June	Brno (Janáček Th.)	František Jilek/Miloš Wasserbauer	tr. Vera Štrelcová		

Date	Place	Company, Conductor, Producer	Editor/Translator	No. of Performances	Remarks
1966, 14 June	Madrid (T. la Zarzuela)	Oliviero De Fabritiis, Alberto Leone/Roberto Carpio			
1966, 27 Sept.	New York (City Opera)	Julius Rudel, Rolf Weikert/Tito Capobianco	H. Procter-Gregg		revived to 1981; also Los Angeles
1966, 30 Sept.	Graz	Berislav Klobucar/André Diehl	Hagen, rev. Munich Staatsoper	3	
1966, 3 Oct.	Ljubljana	Slovenisches Nationaltheater: Demetrij Žebre/Hinko Leskovšek	tr. Smiljan Samec	15	
1966, 25 Nov.	Pecs	Elemér Paulusz/Zoltan Horváth	tr. Gábor Devecseri and Klára Huszár	9	
1966, 11 Dec.	Belgrade (National Th.)	Dušan Miladinović/Mladen Sabljić	Hagen, tr. Konstantin Vinaver	4	
1967, spring	Tokyo (Nissai Th.)	Nikki-Kai Opera: Hiroshi Wakasugi/Keisuke Suzuki		3	
1967, 18 May	Santa Barbara (Campbell Hall)	UCSB Opera Theater: Ronald Ondrejka/Carl Zytowski, Edmund Kemprud	tr. Kemprud	3	
1968	Buenos Aires (T. Colón)	Karl Richter/Ernst Poettgen			
1968, 10 Sept.	Gelsenkirchen (Musiktheater im Revier)	Ljubomir Romansky/Günter Roth	Romansky, tr. E. Dahnk-Baroffio	10	revived 1970
1969, 13 Feb	Scheveningen	Netherlands Opera: Paul Hupperts/Rudolf Hartmann	Hagen	8	in Italian; also Amsterdam, Utrecht, Rotterdam
1969, 23 Mar.	Linz	Kurt Wöss/Federik Mirdita	Mirdita, tr. Dahnk-Baroffio		
1969, 26 Apr.	Plauen	Reinhard Kiessling/Wolfgang Küntz	tr. Dahnk-Baroffio	18	
1969, 1 June	Dresden	Hochschule für Musik: 'C. M. von Weber': Wolfgang Bothe/Dieter Bülter-Marell			

Date	Place	Company, Conductor, Producer	Editor/Translator	No. of Performances	Remarks
1969, 25 July	Hanover (Niedersächsische Staatsoper)	Siegfried Strohbach/Reinhold Rüdiger	tr. Dahnk-Baroffio	26	revived to 1979
1969, 24 Sept.	Trier	Francis Travis/Walter Pohl	Hagen	8	
1969, 9 Nov.	Hamburg (Staatsoper)	Richard Bonynge/Tito Capobianco		15	in Italian; revived 1971
1970, 9 May	Berlin (Staatsoper)	Helmut Koch, Peter Schreier/Erhard Fischer	E. Dahnk-Baroffio and Werner Otto	28	revived to 1982; also Lausanne, Hamburg, and Wiesbaden 1978; Tokyo 1980, Bologna 1981
1970, 13 Nov.	Sydney (Science Theatre)	Univ. of New South Wales Young Opera: Carl Pini, Richard Divall/Brian Donovan	Divall	3	
1971, 15 May	Bielefeld (Rudolf-Oetker-Konzerthalle)	Städtische Bühnen: Bernhard Conz cond. and prod.		4	
1972, 6 Feb.	Bremen (Bremer Theater)	Hermann Michael/Klaus Michael Gruber, Manfred Scholl		7	
1972, 27 July	Cambridge (Senate House)	Jonathan Rennert/Nicholas Reynolds		3	
1972, 26 Oct.	Berlin (Hochschule der der Künste)	Hans Hilsdorf, Ingo Ingensand/Jean Robert	Hagen	2	
1974, 21 Apr.	Berne	Ewald Körner/Walter Oberer	Oberer and Heinz Rückert	7	
1974, 3 May	Usti nad Labem	Jaroslav J. Wolf/Norbert Snitil	tr. Miroslav Homolka		
1974, 8 Aug.	Melbourne (Palais Theatre)	Victoria State Opera: Richard Divall/Brian Bell	Divall	4	
1975, 20 July	Pompeii (T. Grande)	Theodor Gushlbauer/Gaston Benhaim		5	
1976, 13 Mar.	Lyon (Opéra de Lyon)				
1977, 15 Jan.	Wittenberg (Elbe-Elster-Theater)	Klaus Hofmann/Erhard Holland-Moritz	E. Dahnk-Baroffio	16	
1977, 20 Jan.	Birmingham (Barber Institute)	Ivor Keys/Jocelyn Powell	Winton Dean and Sarah Fuller, tr. Brian Trowell	2	complete 1724 version

Date	Place	Company, Conductor, Producer	Editor/Translator	No. of Performances	Remarks
1977, 1 Apr.	Bremerhaven (Stadttheater)	Tassilo Jelde, Hans Tschäppät/Otto-Walter Flach		8	
1978, 7 Apr.	San Francisco (Curran Theater)	Richard Bradshaw/Michael Kahn	Bradshaw and Philip Brett		
1978, 30 Apr.	Frankfurt/Main (Städtische Bühnen)	Nikolaus Harnoncourt, Ivan Fischer/Horst Zankl		28	in Italian; revived to 1982
1978, 23 Sept.	Villedomer (Grange de la Besnardière)	Charles Farncombe/Bengt Peterson			
1978, 7 Oct.	Potsdam (Schlosstheater)	Hans-Dieter Baum/Peter Brähmig	Brähmig	24	revived 1980/81
1979, 2 Jan.	Moscow (Bolshoi Theatre)	V. E. Vais/V. G. Malkova	J. Avgustinova and M. Sokolova		
1979, 17 Jan.	Basel	Stuart Challender/John Dew	Challender and Dew	16	
1979, 10 Nov.	Flensburg	Schleswig-Holsteinisches Landestheater: Werner Stiefel/Hansdieter Sundermann		7	
1979, 5 Dec.	London (Coliseum)	English National Opera: Charles Mackerras, Noel Davies/John Copley	Mackerras and Davies, tr. Trowell		also Liverpool, San Francisco 1982, Geneva 1983; revived to 1985
1980, 4 Apr.	Görlitz/Zittau	Volker Erben/Friedrich Radkte	E. Dahnk-Baroffio and Radkte	22	
1981, 26 Nov.	Helsinki	Finnish Nat. Opera: Ari Angervo/Lisbeth Landefort	Pentti Saaritsa		revived 1982
1981, 18 Dec.	Dessau	Manfred Hänsel/Stephan Blüher		15	also Halle
1982, 3 Feb.	Vienna (Schlosstheater Schönbrunn)	Hochschule für Musik: Peter Lacovich/Dieter Bülter-Marell	Bülter-Marell	4	
1982, 8 June	Barcelona (T. del Liceu)	Rolf Weikert/Vittorio Patané		3	
1982, 6 Dec.	Pforzheim (Stadttheater)	Gerhard Boger/Bernd H. Reuter	E. Dahnk-Baroffio	14	
1983, 12 May	Gelsenkirchen (Musiktheater im Revier)	Manfred Mayrhofer/Peter Kupke		18	Berlin 1970 production

Date	Place	Company, Conductor, Producer	Editor/Translator	No. of Performances	Remarks
1984, 27 Jan.	New York (Harry De Jur Playhouse)	Henry Street Settlement Music School: Tali Makell/Lee Williams		4	2 in English, 2 in Italian
1984, 16 June	Karlsruhe (Badisches Staatstheater)	Charles Farncombe/Jean-Louis Martinoty	Farncombe	18	in Italian; revived to 1992; also Warsaw
1984, 22 June	Madrid (T. La Zarzuela)	George Alexander Albrecht/José Luis Alonso		5	semi-staged
1984, 25 Aug.	Adelaide (Opera Theatre)	State Opera of S. Australia: Denis Vaughan, Alexander Ingram/Tom Lingwood	Divall	7	} shared production
1984, 15 Sept.	Melbourne (State Theatre)	Victoria State Opera: Richard Divall/Tom Lingwood	Divall	8	
1984, 18 Nov.	Olomouc (Oldřich-Stibor Th.)	Paul Pokorný/Jiří Glogar	Vaclav Nosek, tr. Vera Wasserbauerova-Štrelcová		
1985, 18 Jan.	Athens (National Opera)	Dimitris Chorafas/Dino Yannopoulos			
1985, 26 Jan.	Osnabrück (Städtische Bühnen)	Peter Starke/Matthias Otto	tr. Dahnk-Baroffio	13	
1985, 26. Jan.	Albuquerque (Ki-Mo Th.)	Albuquerque Opera Theater: Kurt Frederick/Roger Brunyate	H. Procter-Gregg	3	
1985, 30 Jan.	Rome (T. dell'Opera)	Gabriele Ferro/Alberto Fassini		7	
1985, 14 Feb.	Montreal (Pollack Concert Hall)	McGill Univ. Opera Studio: Richard Lawton/Edith and Luciano Della Pergola		3	
1985, 23 Feb.	Stockholm (Royal Opera)	Jan Latham-Koenig, Thomas Schuback/Georg Malvius		20	revived 1988
1985, 7 Mar.	New Haven (Sprague Memorial Hall)	Yale School of Music: Scott Bergeson/Tito Capobianco	N.Y. City Opera	2	in Italian
1985, 11 Apr.	Karl-Marx-Stadt	Hans Peter Kirchberg/Carl Riha		27	
1985, 27 Apr.	Passau (Fürstbischöfliches Opernhaus)	Südostbayerisches Städtetheater: Herbert Morasch/Peter Ehrlich	tr. Dahnk-Baroffio	9	also Landshut, Straubing, Waldkraiburg
1985, 19 May	Vienna (T. an der Wien)	Nikolaus Harnoncourt/Federik Mirdita		16	in Italian; also Zürich

Date	Place	Company, Conductor, Producer	Editor/Translator	No. of Performances	Remarks
1985, 5 July	Purchase, N.Y.	Pepsico Summerfare Festival: Craig Smith/Peter Sellars		8	also Binghamton, N.Y.
1985, 5 July	Frankfurt/Oder	Peter Fanger/Waltraud Prinz	Dahnk-Baroffio, Peter Brähmig	12	
1985, 3 Oct.	Rostock	Gerd Puls/Matthias Pohl	Dahnk-Baroffio	16	in various cities
1985, 6 Nov.	Detmold (Landestheater)	Edwin Scholz/Igor Folwill			
1987, 13 Feb.	Boston	Opera Co. of Boston: Craig Smith/Peter Sellars		14	Purchase production modified; also Brussels 1988, Nanterre 1990
1987, 20 June	Paris (Opéra)	Jean-Claude Malgoire/Nicholas Hytner		24	revived 1988
1987, 30 Sept.	Toronto (Ontario Art Gallery)	Opera Atelier: Bill O'Meara/Marshall Pynkoski	tr. Brad Walton	5	also Ottawa 1988
1988, 25 May	New York (Brooklyn College)	Brooklyn College Opera Th.: Richard Barrett/Dona D. Vaughn		4	
1988, 23 June	London (Royal Academy of Music)	Trevor Pinnock/Norman Ayrton		4	in Italian
1988, 27 Sept.	New York (Metropolitan)	Trevor Pinnock/John Copley		8	ENO production, in Italian
1989, 8 Jan.	Cracow (T. Muzyczny)	Eva Michnik/Henryk Konwinski		12	in German; also France and Germany
1989, 11 Feb.	Düsseldorf	Michael Luig/Hansgünther Heyme	Günther Weissenborn	42	also Duisburg
1989, 19 Feb.	Darmstadt	Alexander Rumpf/Martin Schlumpf		18	
1989, 9 June	Heidelberg	Mario Venzago/Igor Folwill	Hans Stähli, E. Dahnk-Baroffio	5	expanded scoring in recits!
1989, 22 July	Martina Franca (Palazzo Ducale)	Festival della Valle d'Itria: Marcello Panni/Egisto Marcucci		2	

Date	Place	Company, Conductor, Producer	Editor/Translator	No. of Performances	Remarks
1989, 20 Oct.	Houston (Wortham Center)	Houston Grand Opera: Nicholas McGegan, Craig Smith/ Nicholas Hytner, Patrick Cappoen		6	in Italian; Paris 1987 production
1989, 25 Oct.	Koblenz	Christian Kluttig/Andreas Baumann	tr. Werner Hintze and Bettina Bartz	12	
1992, 8 June	Halle (Opernhaus)	Alan Hacker/Roland Velte		8	in Italian
1992, 26 June	Meissen (Stadttheater)	Hochschule für Musik 'C.M. von Weber': Stefan Bilz, Christoph König/Andreas Baumann	tr. Werner Hintze	5	also Dresden and Bad Lauchstädt
1992, 21 Oct.	Glasgow (Theatre Royal)	Scottish Opera: Samuel Bächli/ Willy Decker	tr. Trowell	13	also Aberdeen, Newcastle, Edinburgh, Ludwigshafen
1992, 4 Nov.	Seattle (Meany Th.)	Univ. of Washington Opera: Peter Erös/Theodore Deacon		3	in Italian
1992, 3 Dec.	Los Angeles (Bing Th.)	Univ. of Southern California School of Music: William Vendice/Frans Boerlage		4	in English
1993, 25 Apr.	Schwetzingen	Berlin Komische Oper: Richard Hickox/Harry Kupfer	tr. Eberhard Schmidt	28	also Berlin

TAMERLANO

Date	Place	Company, Conductor, Producer	Editor/Translator	No. of Performances	Remarks
1924, 7 Sept.	Karlsruhe	Fritz Cortolezis/Robert Volkner	Anton Rudolph and Herman Roth	2	
1925, 7 June	Leipzig	Gustav Brecher/Walther Brügmann	Rudolph and Roth (revised)	7	
1926, 6 Mar.	Magdeburg	Walther Beck/Alois Schultheiss	Rudolph and Roth	4	
1927, 17 Sept.	Hanover	Rudolf Krasselt/Hans Winckelmann	Roth	5	

Date	Place	Company, Conductor, Producer	Editor/Translator	No. of Performances	Remarks
1935, 13 May	Brunswick (Schlosstheater Celle)	Rudolf Moralt/Alexander Schum	Roth	8	also Hildesheim
1935, 19 May	Breslau	Richard Kotz/Siegmund Skraup	Roth	4	
1940, 30 Jan.	Weimar (Nationaltheater)	Albert Müller/Rudolf Hesse	Roth	3	
1940, 23 Feb.	Halle (Landestheater)	Richard Kraus/Siegmund Skraup	Roth	3	
1944, 17 Nov.	Trier	Josef Neher/Rudolf Hesse	Roth	12	also Luxembourg
1952, 6 July	Halle (Landestheater)	Horst-Tanu Margraf/Siegmund Skraup	Roth and Skraup	10	
1958, 22 Apr.	Halle (Landestheater)	Horst-Tanu Margraf/Wolfgang Gubisch	Roth, Gubisch, and Harry Kupfer	21	also Göttingen; revived 1959
1962, 21 Mar.	Birmingham (Barber Institute)	Anthony Lewis/Brian Trowell	tr. Nigel Fortune and Trowell	2	
1962, 28 Mar.	Nordhausen	Lothar Füldner/Günther Imbiel	Roth	12	
1967, 4 Mar.	Plzen (J. K. Tyl Th.)	Karel Vašata/Norbert Snitil	tr. M. Jirásková		
1975, 27 June	Birmingham (Elgar Concert Room)	Eric Cross/Andy Adamson	Fortune, Trowell, and Cross	3	
1976, 24 July	Batignano (Chiostro S. Croce)	Musica nel Chiostro: Jane Glover/Patrick Libby		9	also London and Manchester 1978
1982, 15 Jan.	Mold (T. Clwyd)	Welsh National Opera: Anthony Hose, Julian Smith/Philip Prowse	tr. Robert David MacDonald		also other Welsh towns, Birmingham, Edinburgh, and elsewhere
1982, 15 Apr.	London (Bloomsbury Th.)	Orpheus Opera Trust: Andrew Greenwood/Christopher Webber	Webber	3	
1985, 26 Jan.	Bloomington (Indiana Univ. Opera Theatre)	Richard Bradshaw/Andrew Porter	tr. B. Trowell, N. Fortune and Porter	5	also Purchase, N.Y.
1985, 23 Feb.	Halle (Klubhaus Buna)	Opera North: Clive Timms/Philip Prowse	tr. R. D. MacDonald		also Nottingham, Leeds, York, Manchester

Date	Place	Company, Conductor, Producer	Editor/Translator	No. of Performances	Remarks
1985, 11 Mar.	Lyon (Opéra de Lyon)	John Eliot Gardiner/Anthony Besch		7	in Italian; also Göttingen
1990, 28 Apr.	Halle (Opernhaus)	Christian Kluttig/Peter Konwitschny	tr. Frank Kämpfer and Werner Hintze	29	also Bad Kissingen, Winterthur, and elsewhere; revived to 1993
1990, 30 May	Sydney (Science Th.)	Univ. of New South Wales Opera: Roger Covell/Bernd Benthaak	tr. R. D. MacDonald and Covell	3	
1990, 24 July–9 Aug.	New York (Cooper Square Th.)	Measured Breaths Theatre Co.: Patricia Fortner/Robert Press	tr. Press	2	acts on separate nights
1992, 1 May	Tralee (Siamsa Tíre)	Opera Theatre Co.: Séamus Crimmins/Tim Coleman	tr. James Conroy	12	also Dublin, Wexford, Cork, and other Irish towns, and Brno
1993, 13 Feb.	Karlsruhe (Badisches Staatstheater)	Roy Goodman/Jean-Louis Martinoty		7	in Italian; revived 1993
1993, 2 Oct.	Leeds (Grand Th.)	Roy Goodman/Philip Prowse	tr. R. D. MacDonald	7	also Sunderland, Manchester, Nottingham
		RODELINDA			
1920, 26 June	Göttingen (Stadttheater)	Oskar Hagen/Christine Hoyer-Masing)	Hagen	7	revived 1921
1922, 27 Sept.	Stuttgart (Württembergisches Landestheater)	Erich Band, Carl Leonhardt/Otto Erhardt	Hagen	12	also Ludwigsburg, Zürich, Saarbrücken; revived to 1926
1923, 20 June	Oldenburg	Julius Kopsch/Kurt Löffler	Hagen	8	
1923, 6 July	Göttingen (Stadttheater)	Oskar Hagen/Hanns Niedecken-Gebhard	Hagen	6	revived 1924
1924, 13 Jan.	Rostock	Wilhelm Freund/Otto Krauss	Hagen	7	
1924, 29 Jan.	Berlin (Grosse Volksoper)	Fritz Zweig/Hans Strohbach	Hagen	14	
1924, 17 Feb.	Dessau	Franz von Hoesslin/Hanns Mietau	Hagen	5	

Date	Place	Company, Conductor, Producer	Editor/Translator	No. of Performances	Remarks
1924, 5 Sept.	München-Gladbach	Fritz Zaun/Johannes Heinrich Brasch	Hagen	6	also Neuss and Düren
1924, 18 Nov.	Nuremberg	Karl Schmidt/Otto Krauss	Hagen	8	
1925, 15 Feb.	Altona	Hans Wölffer/Hanns Fischer	Hagen and Wölffer	7	
1925, 24 Mar.	Halle	Erich Band/Hans Siegle	Hagen	9	
1925, 2 Apr.	Plauen	Ernst Cremer/Carl Samwald	Hagen	4	
1925, 26 Apr.	Augsburg	Joseph Bach/Otto Erhardt	Hagen	3	
1925, 23 May	Königsberg (Komische Oper)	Friedrich Werner Goebel/Hans Bachmann	Hagen	2	
1925, 1 Nov.	Freiburg/Breisgau	Ewald Lindemann/Alois Hadwiger	Hagen	5	
1925, 24 Nov.	Aachen	Karl Dommer/Alexander Spring	Hagen	6	
1925, 5 Dec.	Stettin	Gustav Grossmann/Georg Klemens	Hagen	3	
1926, 25 Apr.	Coburg	Albert Bing/Gottfried Mauling	Hagen	3	
1926, 24 June	Saarbrücken	Hans Mohn/Robert Becker	Hagen	5	
1926, 19 Sept.	Osnabrück	Fritz Berend/Bozo Miler	Hagen	6	
1926, 14 Oct.	Ulm	Hans J. Wedig/Walter Bültemann	Hagen	4	
1926, 2 Dec.	Bremerhaven	Walter Schartner/Hans Rudolf Waldburg	Hagen	4	
1927, 15 Sept.	Würzburg	Hans Oppenheim/Fritz Alexander Cohen	Hagen	4	
1928, 11 Apr.	Görlitz	Walter Hochtritt/Kurt Becker-Huert	Hagen	4	
1928, 4 Dec.	Weimar (Nationaltheater)	Ernst Nebbe/Alexander Spring	Hagen	3	
1929, 18 Jan.	Hamburg (Volksoper)	Hans Wölffer cond. and prod.	Hagen	2	with *Terpsichore*
1929, 30 Jan.	Trier	Peter Schmitz/Eugen Kolberg	Hagen	5	
1931, 9 May	Northampton, Mass. (Smith College Academy of Music)	Werner Josten/Margaret Linley	Hagen, tr. Bavard Quincy Morgan	1	
1932, Feb.	Göteborg (Stora Th.)	Matti Rubinstein/Paul Kanneworff	tr. Carl-Johann Holzhausen		

Date	Place	Company, Conductor, Producer	Editor/Translator	No. of Performances	Remarks
1932, 4 June	Berlin (Singakademie)	Deutsche Musikbühne, Reichs Wander-Oper: Hans Oppenheim/Hubert Franz	Karl Salomon	9	in different towns
1935, 10 Jan.	Danzig	Erich Orthmann/Hans Rudolf Waldburg	Hagen	3	also Zoppot
1935, 23 Feb.	Schwerin	Fritz Mechlenburg/Hans Brandt	Hagen	8	also Wismar, Parchim, Ludwigslust
1935, 11 May	Düsseldorf	Eduard Martini/Werner Jacob	Hagen	8	
1935, 1 Nov.	Ulm	Nonne Mommsen/Felix Klee	Hagen	5	
1938, 23 Feb.	Halle	Richard Kraus/Fritz Wolf-Ferrari	Hagen	7	
1939, 5 June	London (Old Vic)	Dartington Hall Opera Group: Hans Oppenheim/Kurt Jooss	Mark Raphael	4	
1939, 11 June	Coburg	Wilhelm Schönherr/Erwin Dieterich	Hagen	3	
1941, 20 Dec.	Vienna (Redoutensaal)	Leopold Ludwig/Oskar Fritz Schuh	Hagen, modified	12	also Breslau and Cologne, 1942
1942, 11 Sept.	Berlin (Volksoper)	Hans Udo Müller/Carl Möller	Hagen	13	
1943, 13 Apr.	Budapest (State Opera)	János Ferencsik/Gustav Oláh	Hagen. tr. Miklós Szabó	8	
1946, 5 Oct.	München-Gladbach (Kaiser-Friedrich-Halle)	Theo M. Kreyenberg/Peter Funk	Hagen	11	also Rheydt
1948, 10 Sept.	Gera	Karl Köhler/Hans Wenzel	Hagen	11	
1950, 26 Feb.	Rostock	Fritz Müller/Lars Larsson	Hagen	7	
1953, 28 June	Göttingen (Stadttheater)	Fritz Lehmann/Hanns Niedecken-Gebhard	Lehmann and E. Dahnk-Baroffio	5	
1955, 26 Mar.	Leipzig	Helmut Seydelmann/Friedrich Ammermann	E. Dahnk-Baroffio and Ammermann	9	
1955, 11 Apr.	Oldenburg (Schlosstheater)	Heinz Rockstroh/Walter Thomas	Hagen	7	
1955, 1 July	Graz (Schlossbergbühne)	Fritz Zaun/André Diehl	Hagen	2	
1955, 18 Sept.	Magdeburg (Städtische Bühne)	Walter Müller/Joachim Beese	tr. E. Dahnk-Baroffio	50	
1957, 27 July	Drottningholm	Lars af Malmborg/Lars Runsten	Hagen	23	revived 1959

Date	Place	Company, Conductor, Producer	Editor/Translator	No. of Performances	Remarks
1957, 31 Oct.	Cologne (Oper der Stadt Köln)	Otto Ackermann, – Fischer/Erich Bormann	Hagen	25	revived to 1964
1958, 26 Sept.	Brunswick (Staatstheater)	Arthur Grüber/Herbert Junkers	tr. E. Dahnk-Baroffio	11	
1959, 3 Mar.	Kassel (Staatstheater, Blaues Saal)	Paul Schmitz/Hermann Schaffner	tr. E. Dahnk-Baroffio	13	also Eschwege
1959, 6 Mar.	Coburg (Landestheater)	Helmut Henze/Josef Maria Schmitz	Rudolf Gerber, E. Dahnk-Baroffio	9	
1959, 14 Mar.	Saarbrücken (Saarländisches Staatstheater)	Carl Johannson/Herbert Henze	tr. E. Dahnk-Baroffio	9	
1959, 9 Apr.	San Francisco (Herbst Th.)	San Francisco Opera Center Richard Bradshaw/Albert Takazauckas		3	
1959, 13 June	Karlsruhe (Badisches Staatstheater)	Alexander Krannhals/Hartmut Boebel	tr. E. Dahnk-Baroffio	10	
1959, 24 June	London (Sadler's Wells)	Handel Op. Soc.: Charles Farncombe/Anthony Besch	tr. David Harris	2	
1959, 30 June	Frankfurt/Main (Städtische Bühne)	Staatl. Hochschule für Musik: Bruno Vondenhoff/Siegmund Skraup	tr. E. Dahnk-Baroffio		
1960, 26 Apr.	Lucerne	Max Sturzenegger/Walter Oberer	tr. E. Dahnk-Baroffio	6	
1966, 23 Nov.	New York (Carnegie Hall)	N.Y. Handel Soc.: Brian Priestman/Ralph Alswang		2	semi-staged
1969, 22 Mar.	Halle (Landestheater)	Thomas Sanderling/Wolfgang Kersten	Waldtraut Lewin and Kersten	20	revived 1970
1970, 23 Apr.	Budapest (State Opera)	János Ferencsik, Ervin Lukács, Gyula Borbely/András Békés	tr. Miklós Zzabó	67	revived to 1977
1971, 5 Dec.	Philadelphia (Annenberg Auditorium)	Curtis Institute of Music: David Effron/Dino Yannopoulos		3	
1972, 11 May	Birmingham (Barber Institute)	Ivor Keys/Jocelyn Powell	tr. Powell	2	

Date	Place	Company, Conductor, Producer	Editor/Translator	No. of Performances	Remarks
1973, 24 May	Salzburg	Alexander Paulmiller/Walter Oberer		15	
1973, 24 June	Scheveningen (Cirkus Th.)	Holland Festival: Richard Bonynge/Tito Capobianco		11+	also 5 other Dutch cities; revived 1975
1977, 11 Feb.	Pforzheim (Stadttheater)	Martin Mälzer/Jon Bric	Mälzer, Bric, tr. E. Dahnk-Baroffio and Rudolf Gerber	9	
1977, 29 May	Bexhill (De la Warr Pavilion)	Rother District Council Festival: Geoffrey Abbott/Andy Adamson	tr. Powell	1	
1981, 13 Jan.	Mold (Theatr Clwyd)	Welsh National Opera: Julian Smith/Andrei Serban			also Cardiff, London (Dominion Th.), Oxford, Cheltenham
1981, 3 July	Herrenhausen (Niedersächsische Staatstheater)	Knut Mahlke/Stephan Mettin	Gerber and Dahnk-Baroffio	10	
1983, 28 Apr.	Urbana-Champaign (Krannert Center)	Univ. of Illinois Opera Theatre: Tonu Kalam/Virginia Van Pelt		4	in Italian
1983, 23 Sept.	Amsterdam	Netherlands Opera: Diego Masson/ Tito Capobiano, Jaap Mosterd			revival of 1973 Holland Festival production; also The Hague and Rotterdam
1983, 5 Oct.	Copenhagen (Hofteatret)	Kaare Hansen/Ib Hemming Hansen		4	
1985, 9 Apr.	San Francisco (Herbst Th.)	Richard Bradshaw/Albert Takazauckas		3	
1985, 2 May	Colmar (Th. Municipal)	Atelier Lyrique du Rhin: Philippe Herreweghe/Pierre Barrat			also Thionville, Le Havre, Sanary, Aix-en-Provence
1985, 1 June	Cambridge (West Road Concert Hall)	Andrew Jones/Tertia Sefton-Green	Jones	2	
1985, 7 June	Snape (Maltings)	Stuart Bedford/Basil Coleman	tr. Powell	2	
1985, 8 June	Stockholm (Oskarsteater)	Musikdramatiska Skolan: Jan-Olov Wedin/Folke Abenius		1	

Date	Place	Company, Conductor, Producer	Editor/Translator	No. of Performances	Remarks
1985, 19 Sept.	Cagliari (Conservatorio)	T. Lirico Palestrina: Otto Gerdes/Vittorio Patané		3	
1985, 20 Sept.	Brno (Janáček Th.)	Václav Nosek/Alena Vanáková	tr. Eva Bezděková	2	revived 1986
1985, 25 Oct.	Berkhamsted (Civic Centre)	Chiltern Opera: Jean Cooper/Anna Sims			
1986, 23 Feb.	Hamburg (Hochschule für Musik und Theater)	Sebastian Gottschick/Katharina Kleinschmidt	E. Dahnk-Baroffio	4	
1986, 1 Mar.	Helsinki (Sibelius Academy Opera Studio)	Pekka Salomaa cond. and prod.	Hagen, Salomaa	2	
1987, 24 Feb.	Turku	Turku Chamber Opera: Ileri Lehtinen/Bror Österlund	Hagen, Salomaa, tr. Virpi Metsätähti	3	
1989, 10 Aug.	Batignano (Chiostro S. Croce)	Musica nel Chiostro: Ivor Bolton/Matthew Richardson		4	in Italian
1992, 28 Feb.	Pittsburgh (Antonian Th., Carlow College)	Pittsburgh Opera Center at Duquesne: Alan Nathan/William Farlow		2	in Italian
1992, 24 July	Hopetoun House, S. Queensferry	David Roblou/Kate Brown		3	semi-staged
		SCIPIONE			
1937, 20 June	Göttingen (Stadttheater)	Fritz Lehmann/Hanns Niedecken-Gebhard	Lehmann, Emilie Dahnk	4	
1965, 15 May	Halle (Landestheater)	Horst-Tanu Margraf/Heinz Rückert	Waldtraut Lewin	17	revived 1966; also Magdeburg 1967
1967, 9 Oct.	London (Queen Elizabeth Hall)	Handel Op. Soc.: Charles Farncombe/David Thompson	Farncombe	13	revived 1970–72; also Herrenhausen and Drottningholm
1979, 24 Oct.	London (Sadler's Wells)	Handel Op. Soc.: Charles Farncombe/David Thompson	Farncombe (revised)	4	
1989, 15 Nov.	London (Guildhall School of Music and Drama)	Clive Timms/Stephen Unwin	tr. Arnold Schmitt	4	
1992, 15 Feb.	Karlsruhe (Badisches	Roy Goodman/Daniel Benoin	Clifford Bartlett, Goodman	6	in Italian; revived 1993

INDEX OF ITALIAN FIRST LINES

THIS attempts a complete coverage of Handel's works, including Italian oratorios and cantatas and his three pasticcio operas, *Oreste* (1734), *Alessandro Severo* (1738), and *Jupiter in Argos* (1739). Recitatives are excluded, as are translations of English oratorio airs, for which see *Handel's Dramatic Oratorios and Masques*, Appendix F. Cantatas are listed with both HWV and HG numbers (Roman figures for instrumental, arabic for continuo).

Not in HG. (2) indicates that two settings exist, one of them not in HG.

†Music lost or unidentified.

Ah, sì, morrò, e allor potrò	*Admeto*
Ah spietato! e non ti muove	*Amadigi*
Ah! tigre infedele	*Serse*
Ah! tu non sai quant'il mio cor	*Ottone*
Ai Greci questa spada	*Deidamia*
Ai guardi tuoi son pur vaga	{ *Riccardo* *Tolomeo* 1733
A languir ed a penar	*Admeto*
†Al brillar de tue lucide stelle (duet)	*Florindo*
†Al dispetto di Cupido	*Daphne*
Al dispetto di sorte crudele	Cantata III (HWV 83)
Al fine amore	*Arianna*
Al furor che ti consiglia	*Arminio*
Al gaudio, al riso, al canto*	*Jup. in Argos*
Alla caccia, mie fide compagne (duet)*	Cantata (Berlin) (HWV 79)
Alla fama, dimmi il vero	*Ottone*
All'alma fedel amore placato	*Alcina*
All'amor mio, lo sò ben io	Cantata 30 (HWV 129)
Al lampo dell'armi	*G. Cesare*
All'armi, guerrieri	*Giustino*
Alla salma infedel	Cantata 46 (HWV 145)
Alla strage, alla morte, alla vittoria! (*coro*)	*Sosarme*
Alla sua gabbia d'oro	*Alessandro*
Alla vittoria! (*coro*)	*Riccardo*
Alle glorie, alle palmi, agli allori	*Vincer se stesso*
Allegrezza! Claudio giunge	*Agrippina*
Alle sfere della gloria	*Sosarme*
Alle voci del bronzo guerriero	Cantata XIX (HWV 143)
†All'impero	*Daphne*
Allor che sorge astro lucente	{ *Vincer se stesso* *Pastor fido*
Allor ch'io forte avrò	*Giustino*
All'orror delle procelle	*Riccardo*
All'orror d'un duolo eterno	*Ottone*
Al lume di due rai	*Arminio*
Alma mia, dolce ristoro (duet)	*Admeto*
Alma mia, sì, sol tu sei	*Floridante*
Almen doppo il fato mio*	Cantata II (HWV 81)
Al par della mia sorte	{ *Arminio* *Jup. in Argos*
Al sen ti stringo e parto (3)**	*Ariodante*
†Al sereno d'un volte ridente	*Florindo*
Al suon che destano	Cantata XIX (HWV 143)
Al tardar della vendetta	*Deidamia*
Altra legge nell'amare*	*Titus*
Altra spene or non alletta	Cantata 32 (HWV 131)
Al trionfo del nostro furore (duet) (2)	*Rinaldo*

Al varco, O pastori	*Atalanta*
Al voler, di tua fortuna	*Imeneo*
Alza al ciel pianta orgogliosa	*Lotario*
Alza il volo la mia fama	*Silla*
Alzo al volo di mia fama	*Radamisto*
Ama nell'armi, e nell'amar (duet)	*Deidamia*
Amante esser non voglio*	Cantata (Manchester) (HWV 149)
Amante stravagante	*Flavio*
Amanti voi ch'andate (= Seguaci di Cupido)	*Partenope* Dec. 1730
Amarilli? O dei, che vuoi (duet)	*Atalanta*
Amarti, sì, vorrei	*Teseo*
Ama, sospira, mà non ti offende	*Alcina*
A me sol giunga la morte	Cantata XIV (HWV 110)
Amico arrida il ciel (trio and *coro*)	*Alessandro*
A mirarvi io son intento	Chamber Duet
Amor commanda, onore invita (2)	*Floridante*
Amor dà guerra e pace	*Tamerlano*
Amore contro amor	*Berenice*
Amor ed empietà*	{ *Admeto* Mar. 1727 { *Floridante* Apr. 1727
Amor è qual vento	*Orlando*
Amor è un tiranno	*Admeto*
Amor gioje mi porge	Chamber Duet
Amor nel mio penar	*Flavio*
Amor, tiranno amor	*Serse*
Amo, spero (duet)*	*Alessandro*
Amo Tirsi, ed a Fileno	Cantata XXIV (HWV 96)
A nave smarrita	*Radamisto* Dec. 1720
Anche il ciel divien amante	Cantata IV (HWV 119)
Anch'io pugnar saprò	*Partenope*
Andate, O forti (2)	*Rinaldo*
Angelico splendor	{ *Esther* 1737 { *Israel* 1739
Anima infida, tradita io sono	*Serse*
A piangere ogn'ora (2)*	*Serse*
Applauda ogn'uno il nostro fato (*coro*)	*Tolomeo*
Applauda ogn'uno l'eroe sovrano (quartet)*	*F. Olibrio*
Apri le luci, e mira gli ascosi	*Ariodante*
Ardi, adori e preghi in vano	Cantata XVI (HWV 122)
Ardo ben mà non ardisco*	Cantata (Manchester) (HWV 149)
Arma lo sguardo	{ *Lotario* { *Rinaldo* 1731
Armati, O core, di cieco sdegno	*Admeto*
†Armo il petto di vendetta	*Florindo*
Arsace, O Dio, così	*Partenope*
A sanar le ferite d'un core	Cantata 22 (HWV 116)

A sprone, a fren leggiero	*Alessandro*
Astro clemente, astro sereno	Cantata XIX (HWV 143)
A suoi piedi il prence essangue	*Tolomeo* 1730
A suoi piedi padre essangue (2)*	*Tamerlano*
A te lascio, l'idol mio	*Ottone*
A' teneri affetti (duet)	*Ottone*
Atterrato il muro cada	*Riccardo*
Augelletti che cantate (2)*	*Rinaldo*
Augelletti garruletti	*Giustino*
Augelletti, ruscelletti	{ *Resurrezione* *Pastor fido*
Aure, deh, per pietà	*G. Cesare*
Aure dolci deh spirate*	? (RM) (HWV 211)
Aure, fonti, ombre gradite	*Alessandro*
†Aure lieve, che l'ali movete	*Florindo*
†Aure lieve, che rimbombi	*Daphne*
Aure, portate al caro bene	*Tolomeo*
Auretta vezzosa	Cantata 71 (HWV 177)
Avvertite mie pupille	*Berenice*
Bacia per me la mano	*Riccardo*
Barbara! io ben lo sò	*Alcina*
Barbaro fato, sì	*Partenope*
Barbaro! partirò	*Radamisto* Dec. 1720
Barbaro! t'odio a morte	*Floridante*
Barbaro! tu non credi	Cantata XXIV (HWV 96)
Basta che sol tu chieda	{ *Agrippina* *Rinaldo*
Basterebbe a tor di vita	Cantata 48 (HWV 148)
Beato in ver chi può	Chamber Duet
Begli occhi del mio ben	*Vincer se stesso*
Bel contento già gode quest'alma	*Flavio*
Bella Asteria, il tuo cor	*Tamerlano*
Bel labbro, formato	*Ottone*
Bella calma sento all'alma (= Siete rose, Cantata 61)	*Oreste*
Bella gara che faranno	{ *Tamerlano* *Tolomeo* 1730
Bella già il cor s'accende*	*Riccardo*
Bella gloria in campo armato	Cantata 62 (HWV 163)
Bella mà ritrosetta*	Cantata (Fitz.) (HWV 86)
Bella, non mi negar	*Lotario*
Bella, non t'adirar	*Admeto*
Bella notte senza stelle	*Scipione*
Bella pur nel mio diletto	*Agrippina*
Bella sorge la speranza (aria and *coro*)	{ *Arianna* *Oreste*
Bella, teco non hò	*Riccardo*
Belle dee di questo core	*G. Cesare*
Bello idolo amato (duet)	*Arianna*

Bel piacere e godere	{ *Agrippina* / *Rinaldo*
Bel ristoro de' mortali	*Giustino*
Benchè io non sappia ancor	*Atalanta*
Benchè io sia che m'allontani	Cantata 52 (HWV 156)
Benchè mi sia crudele	*Ottone*
Benchè mi sprezzi	*Tamerlano*
Benchè povera donzella	*Flavio*
Benchè tinta del sangue fraterno	*Siroe*
Benchè tradita io sia	Cantata 30 (HWV 129)
Benchè tuoni e l'etra avvampi	*Aci, Gal. e Polif.*
Benchè tuoni e l'etra avvampi	*Teseo*
Ben impari come s'ama	Cantata XXIII (HWV 173)
Ben io sento l'ingrata spietata	*Atalanta*
Ben spesso in vago prato*	*Rodelinda*
Bianco giglio	*Esther* 1737
Braccio si valoroso	*Scipione*
Bramo aver mille vite (duet)	*Ariodante*
Bramo di trionfar*	*Alcina*
Bramo restar, mà nò*	*Partenope* 1737
Bramo te sola	*Floridante*
†Brilla il cor (duet)	*Silla*
Brilla nell'alma un non inteso ancor	*Alessandro*
Brillava protetto da spene gustata	Cantata XV (HWV 113)
Cada lacero e svenato	Cantata XIV (HWV 110)
Caddi, è ver, mà nel cadere	*Resurrezione*
Cade il mondo soggiogato	*Agrippina*
Cagion son io del mio dolore	*Serse*
Camminando lei pian piano	Cantata 69 (HWV 175)
Cangia al fine il tuo rigore (duet)	*Amadigi*
Cangia il gioja il tuo dolor (duet)	*Parnasso*
Cangia sorte di ripente	*Ezio*
Cangiò d'aspetto il crudo fato	*Admeto*
Cantiamo a bacco in si lieto dì (chorus)	*Parnasso*
Cantiamo lieti della virtù (chorus)	*Terpsicore*
Cara, la tua beltà (duet)	*Alessandro*
Cara, nel tuo bel volto (duet)	*Atalanta*
Cara pianta co' miei pianti	Cantata XVI (HWV 122)
Cara se il cor*	Cantata (Manchester) (HWV 94)
Cara speme, questo core	*G. Cesare*
Cara sposa, amante cara	*Rinaldo*
Cara sposa, amato bene	*Radamisto*
Cara, ti dona in pegno il cor (duet) (3)*	{ *Teseo* / *Pastor fido* May 1734
Cara, tu nel mio petto	*Ottone* Mar. 1723

Care luci che l'alba rendete	Cantata 3 (HWV 84)
Care mura in si bel giorno	*Partenope*
Care mura in voi d'intorno	Cantata 1 (HWV 77)
Care selve, date al cor (chorus)*	*Jup. in Argos*
Care selve, ombre beate	*Atalanta*
Cari lacci, amate pene (2)*	Cantata 12, 34 (HWV 106, 132a)
Caro amico, a morti io vo (=Figlia mia, *Tamerlano*)	*Oreste*
Caro amico amplesso (duet)	*Poro*
Caro amor, sol per momenti (2)	*Pastor fido*
Caro autor di mia doglia (2)	Chamber Duet
Caro! bella! più amabile beltà (duet)	*G. Cesare*
Caro figlio, amato Dio	*Resurrezione*
Caro padre, a me non dei	*Ezio*
Caro Tebro, amico fiume	Cantata XIX (HWV 143)
Caro, tu mi accendi (duet)	*Faramondo*
Caro, vieni al mio seno (duet)	*Poro*
Caro, vieni a me	*Riccardo*
Caro voi siete all'alma	*Serse*
Casta dea, a te divoto	*Pastor fido*
Cedo a Roma, e cedo a te	*Scipione*
Cento belle ami Fileno	Cantata XXII (HWV 171)
Cerco in vano di placare (2)*	*Tamerlano*
Cervo altier, poichè prostrò	*Ottone* 1726
Cessa omai di sospirare	*G. Cesare*
Cessata è la procella	*Riccardo*
Che bel contento sarebbe amore	*Flavio*
Che colpa è la mia	*Flavio*
Che farà quest'alma mia	*Radamisto* Dec. 1720
Che non può la gelosia	*Aci, Gal. e Polif.*
Che non si dà qua giù pace*	Cantata (Münster) (HWV 142)
Che posso dir, O cara (=Vado a morir vi lascio, *Arminio*)	*A. Severo*
Che sarà quando amante	*Berenice*
Che se fiera poi mi nieghi	*Arianna*
Che tirannia d'amor	*Alessandro*
Che vai pensando	Chamber Duet
Che veggio? che sento? (2)	*Floridante*
Chiari lumi, voi che siete	Cantata IX (HWV 92)
Chi ben ama e sol brama (=Bel piacere)	*Agrippina*
Chi ben ama ha per oggetti (trio)	*Aci, Gal. e Polif.*
Chi ben ama non paventa	Cantata XXV [III] (HWV 83)
Chi ben ama ogn'altro affetto	*Faramondo*
Chi cede al furore	*Serse*
Chi di voi fù più infedele	*Rodelinda*
Chiedo amore, altro non bramo	Cantata 36 (HWV 136)
Chi è nato alle sventure	*Admeto*
Chi è più fedele	*Siroe*
Chi già fù del biondo crine	*Trionfo del Tempo*

Chi mi chiama or che non sono	Cantata XIX (HWV 143)
Chi m'insegna il caro padre	*Alcina*
Chi non ama il tuo sembiante*	Cantata (Manchester, Add. MS 29963) (HWV 101a)
Ch'io lasci mai d'amare	*Amadigi*
Ch'io mai vi possa	{ *Siroe* { *A. Severo*
Ch'io parta? sì, crudele	*Partenope*
Chi perde un momento di contento	*G. Cesare* 1725
Chi più mi piace io voglio	*Almira*
Chi possessore è del mio core	*Orlando*
Chi può lasciare	*Flavio* 1732
Chi può mirare	*Flavio*
Chi rapì la pace al core?	Cantata 5 (HWV 90)
Chi ritorna alla mia mente	*Teseo*
Chi sà dirti O core (= Può ben nascer, *Giustino*)	*A. Severo*
Chi sà, mia speme, chi sà?	*Almira*
Chi sà? vi rivedrò	Cantata 28 (HWV 126b)
Chi scherza colle rose	*Imeneo*
Chi si trova tra procella (*coro*)	*Silla*
Chi t'intende, O cieca instabile	*Berenice*
Chiudetevi, miei lumi	*Admeto*
Chiudi i vaghi rai	*Trionfo del Tempo*
Chi vive amante sai che delira	*Poro*
†Chi vuò far a modo mio	*Florindo*
Cieca notte, infidi sguardi	*Ariodante*
†Cieco infido	*Daphne*
Ciel e terra armi di sdegno	*Tamerlano*
Cielo ingiusto, potrai fulminarmi	*Tolomeo*
Cielo! se tu il consenti	*Orlando*
Ciò che Giove destinò (chorus)	*Serse*
Circonda in lor vite	*Parnasso*
Col ardor del tuo bel core	*Agrippina*
Col celarvi, a chi v'ama	*Alcina*
Colla strage de' nemici	{ *Radamisto* Dec. 1720 { *Poro* Nov. 1731
Col partir la bella Clori	Cantata 1 (HWV 77)
Col peso del tuo amor	*Agrippina*
Col raggio placido	*Agrippina*
Col tuo piede brilla amor (duet)	*Terpsicore*
Col tuo sangue smorzare vorrei*	*Jup. in Argos*
Col valor, colla virtù	*Rinaldo*
Col valor del vostro brando*	? *Rinaldo* (Fitz.)
Col valor d'un braccio forte	Cantata IV (HWV 119)
Combatti da forte (2)	*Rinaldo*
Combatti e poi ritorna	Cantata 31 (HWV 130)
Combattuta da due venti	{ *Faramondo* { *Jup. in Argos*

Come alla tortorella	*Atalanta*
Come all'urto aggressor d'un torrente	*Deidamia*
Come al natio boschetto	*Scipione*
Come il candore d' intatta neve	*Poro*
Come in ciel benigna stella	Cantata XVI (HWV 122)
Come la rondinella dall'Egitto	{ Cantata XXIV (HWV 96) *Acis and Galatea* 1732
Come nembo che fugge col vento (2)	*Trionfo del Tempo*
Come nube che fugge dal vento	*Agrippina*
Come, O Dio! bramo la morte	Cantata XIV (HWV 110)
Come onda incalza altr'onda	*Scipione*
Come rosa in su la spina	Cantata XVI (HWV 122)
Come, se ti vedrò	*M. Scevola*
Compagni nell'amore	*Poro*
Con doppia gloria mia*	? (RM) (HWV 212)
Confusa si miri	*Rodelinda*
Con gli strali d'amor	*Berenice*
Con lagrime si belle*	? *Rinaldo* (Tenbury, Fitz.) (HWV 213)
Con l'ali di costanza (2)	{ *Ariodante* *A. Severo*
Con la strage	*v.* Colla strage
Con linfe dorate	Cantata IV (HWV 119)
Con lui [lei] volate, dolce pensieri	{ *M. Scevola* *Scipione* 1730
Conoscerò, se brami	*Faramondo*
Conosco che mi piaci (complete in Münster)	Cantata XXIV (HWV 96)
Con quel sangue dipinta vedrai	*Arminio*
Con rauco mormorio	*Rodelinda*
Con saggio tuo consiglio	*Agrippina*
Conservate per mia figlia	*Tamerlano*
Conservate, raddoppiate	Chamber Duet
Consolami, mio bene (trio)	*Imeneo*
Consolami, se brami	*Deidamia*
Consolati, O bella (trio)	*Orlando*
Contento sol promette Amor (duet with chorus)	*Acis and Galatea* 1732
Con tromba guerriera	*Silla*
Con un' vezzo, con un' riso	{ *Flavio* *Scipione* 1730
Con un vezzo lusinghiero	*Parnasso*
Con valorosa mano (*coro*)	*Partenope*
Con vana speranza	*Radamisto*
Con verace dolce pace (*coro*)	*Berenice*
Con voce giuliva (*chorus*)	*Atalanta*
†Con voci care in petto	*Vincer se stesso*
Con voi mi lagnerò	Cantata 60 (HWV 159)
Coperta la frode di lana servile	*Ariodante*
Coralli e perle vogliamo offrir (chorus)	*Parnasso*
Cor di padre e cor d'amante	*Tamerlano*

Core si generoso (= Braccio si valoroso, *Scipione*)	*Tolomeo* 1733
Cor fedele in vano speri*	Cantata XXIV (Münster) (HWV 96)
Cor fedele spera sempre	{ *Esther* 1737 / *Israel* 1739
Cor ingrato, ti rammembri	*Rinaldo*
Coronata di gigli e di rose (duet)	*Tamerlano*
Coronato il crin d'alloro	*Agrippina*
Corre vola qui 'l piacere (chorus)*	*Jup. in Argos*
Corriamo pronto ad ubbidir (chorus)	*Parnasso*
Corrispondi a chi t'adora	*Flavio*
Corri, vola a' tuoi trofei (aria and chorus)	*Giustino*
Corro per ubbidirvi*	*Sosarme* 1734
Così giusta è questa speme	*Orlando*
Così la tortorella	*Resurrezione*
Così m'alletti, così sei cara a me	*Vincer se stesso*
Così suole a rio vicina (2)*	{ *Faramondo* / *Jup. in Argos*
Crede l'uomo ch'egli riposi	*Trionfo del Tempo*
Credete al mio dolore	*Alcina*
Cruda legge d'un alma costante	Cantata 19 (HWV 112)
Crude furie degl'orridi abissi	*Serse*
Crudele arciero*	Cantata 'Selve caverne' (Münster)
Crudel più non son io	*Tamerlano*
Crudel tiranno amor	Cantata X (HWV 97)
Crudel, tu non farai (duet)	*Amadigi*
Crude stelle! astri tiranni	Cantata 60 (HWV 159)
Cuor di madre e cuor di moglie	*Sosarme*
Custodite, O dolci sogni	*Atalanta*
Da balza in balza	Cantata XX (HWV 165)
Da che perso hò la mia Clori	Cantata I (HWV 77)
Dal crudel che m'ha tradita (2)	*Tamerlano*
Dal cupo baratro venite	*Teseo*
Dal fulgor di questa spada	*G. Cesare*
Dalla stirpe degli eroi (chorus)	*Atalanta*
Dall'occaso in oriente	*Giustino*
Dall'orror di notte cieca (chorus)	*Alcina*
D'allor trionfante	*Pastor fido*
Dal mio brando [cenno] si vede umiliata	*G. Cesare* 1725
Dammi pace, O volto amato	*Tamerlano*
D'amor a fier contrasti	*Pastor fido* May 1734
D'amor di Giove al canto (chorus)*	*Jup. in Argos*
D'amor fù consiglio	*Resurrezione*
D'amor nei primi istanti	{ *Deidamia* / *Imeneo* 1742
Da sorgente rilucente (2)	*Parnasso*
Da tanti affanni oppressa	*Admeto*
Da tempeste il legno infranto	*G. Cesare*
Da te parto, mà concedi	*Flavio*

Da te più tosto partir vogl'io	*Admeto*
D'atra notte già mirasi a scorno (*coro*)	*Tamerlano*
Da tuoi begl'occhi impara	*Giustino*
Da un breve riposo	*Alessandro*
Deggio dunque, O Dio, lasciarti (2)	*Radamisto*
Deggio morire, O stelle	*Siroe*
Degno più di tua beltà	*Deidamia*
Deh! cantate un bell'amor (aria and chorus)	*Parnasso*
Deh! fuggi un traditore	*Radamisto*
Deh! lascia addolcire (duet)	Cantata XVI (HWV 122)
Deh! lasciate e vita e volo	Cantata 10 (HWV 103)
Deh! lasciatemi il nemico	*Tamerlano*
Deh! lascia un tal desio	*Arianna*
Deh! m'ajutate, O dei (2)*	{ *Jup. in Argos* / *Imeneo*
Deh! non dir che molle amante	*Ottone*
Deh! perdona, O dolce bene (duet)	*Flavio*
Deh piangete, O mesti lumi	*G. Cesare*
Deh serbate, O giusti Dei	*Teseo*
Deh! v'aprite, O luci belle (2)*	{ *Teseo* / *Jup. in Argos*
Deh! voi mi dite, O numi	*Siroe*
Del ciel d'amore	*Serse*
Del ciel voi giusti numi*	*Arianna*
Del ciglio dolente	*Resurrezione*
Del debellar la gloria	*Scipione*
Del fasto di quell'alma (= La gloria in nobil alma, *Partenope*)	*Oreste*
Del labbro tuo l'accenti	*Arianna* Nov. 1734
Della guerra la caccia a sembianza (chorus)	*Deidamia*
Dell'aquila gli artigli (2)	{ *Aci, Gal. e Polif.* / *Acis and Galatea* 1732
Dell'empia frode il velo	{ *Riccardo* / *Pastor fido* May 1734
Dell'Iberia al soglio invitto	*Vincer se stesso*
Dell'idol mio	Cantata 7 (HWV 93)
Dell'onda a i fieri moti	*Ottone*
Dell'onda instabile*	? (Fitz.) (HWV 214)
Dell'onor di giuste imprese	*Riccardo*
Del mar frà l'onde (2)	{ *Aci, Gal. e Polif.* / *Acis and Galatea* 1732
Del minacciar del vento	*Ottone*
Del mio brando si veda*	*Rodelinda*
Del mio caro baco amabile	*Serse*
Del mio sol vezzosi rai	*Ariodante*
Del nume Lieo quel sacro liquor	*Parnasso*
De' miei scherni per far la vendetta	*Rodelinda*
Desterò dall'empia Dite	*Amadigi*
Dì ad Irene, tiranna, infedele	*Atalanta*
Dia si lode in cielo, in terra (*coro*)	*Resurrezione*
Dica il falso, dica il vero	*Alessandro*
Dice amor quel bel vermiglio	*Berenice*
Di cieca notte allor che l'ombra	*Imeneo*

Dì, cor mio, quanto t'amai	*Alcina*
Di Cupido impiego i vanni	*Rodelinda*
Diedi il core ad altra ninfa	*Atalanta*
Di far le sue vendette	*Ottone* 1726
Di gelosia il timore	Cantata IX (HWV 92)
Digli, ch'io son fedele	*Poro*
Di godere ha speranza*	? (pub. c. 1719) (HWV 228/7)
Di goder il bel ch'adoro (2)*	{ *Pastor fido* *Acis and Galatea* 1732
Dille ch'il core (2)**	*Flavio*
Dille, che nel mio seno	*Arianna*
Di lusinghe, di dolcezze (2)	*Deidamia*
D'Imeneo le belle tede (*coro*)	*Partenope*
Di me non ti lagnar*	*Riccardo*
Dimmi cara: tu dei morir	*Scipione*
Dimmi, crudele amore	{ *M. Scevola* *Scipione* 1730
Dimmi, O spene! quando riede (2)*	*Floridante*
Dimmi, pietoso ciel	*Partenope*
D'inalzar i flutti (2)*	*Ottone*
Di notte il pellegrino	{ *Riccardo* *Scipione* 1730
D'instabile Cupido*	*Arianna* Nov. 1734
D'instabile fortuna	{ *Lotario* *Rinaldo* 1731 *Ottone* 1733
†Dio d'Amor, nume fierissimo	*Daphne*
Di Parnasso i dolci accenti	*Terpsicore*
Di pur se il cor si piega*	*F. Olibrio*
Di quel bel che il ciel ti diede	Cantata I (HWV 78)
Di quel bel che m'innamora	*Flavio*
Di questa selva (coro)*	Cantata (Berlin) (HWV 79)
Dirà che amor per me	*Serse*
Di rendermi la calma	*Poro*
Di rè sdegnato l'ira tremenda	*Giustino*
Diresti poi così? (2)*	*Ottone*
Dir li potessi vedi, crudele	*Ottone*
Dirti vorrei non son crudele (= S'io dir potessi, *Ottone*)	*Oreste*
Di Sion nell'alta sede (2)	*Rinaldo*
†Dispensa il Dio d'Amor	*Daphne*
Disserratevi, O porte d'Averno	*Resurrezione*
Di tacere e di schernirmi	*Serse*
Dite, che fà, dov'è	*Tolomeo*
Di te compagna fida (2)**	*G. Cesare*
Ditele che il mio core (3)	Cantata 40, 41, 42 (HWV 139abc)
Di te mi rido, semplice stolto	*Alcina*
Dite pace, e fulminate	{ *Sosarme* *Oreste*
Dite spera, e son contento (duet)	*Ariodante*
Di timpani e trombe (*coro*)	*Agrippina*
D'ogni amator la fede	*Siroe*

D'ogni crudel martir (duet)*	{ *Rodelinda* Dec. 1725 { *Scipione* 1730
Dolce amico amplesso (trio)	*Aci, Gal. e Polif.*
Dolce amor che mi consola	*Vincer se stesso*
Dolce bene di quest'alma	*Radamisto*
Dolce bocca, labbra amate	Cantata XXVIII (HWV 123)
†Dolce foco mi tormenta	*Florindo*
Dolce mio letto (authenticity doubtful)	Cantata 14 (HWV 108)
Dolce nume de' mortali	*Silla*
Dolce pur d'amor l'affanno (2)	Cantata 15, 16 (HWV 109ab)
Dolce riposo ed innocente pace	*Teseo*
Dolce riso, dolci sguardi*	*Admeto* 1728
Dolce speme lusinghiera (= Pensa, O bella)	*Scipione*
Dolce vita del mio petto	*Amadigi*
Dolci aurette che spirate	*Scipione*
Dolci chiodi, amate spine (duet)	*Resurrezione*
Dolcissimo amore (*coro*)	{ *Siroe* { *A. Severo*
Domerò la tua fierezza	*G. Cesare*
Doni pace ad ogni core (*coro*)	{ *Flavio* { *Tolomeo* 1730
Dopo il nembo e la procella	*Floridante*
Dopo il nemico oppresso (2)*	*Scipione*
Dopo i nembi e le procelle	*Vincer se stesso*
Dopo la notte oscura (*coro*)	*Rodelinda*
Dopo l'ire si funeste (*coro*)	*Sosarme*
Dopo l'ombre d'un fiero sospetto	*Floridante* 1722
Dopo l'orride procelle (= Dopo torbide procelle)	*Radamisto* Dec. 1720
Dopo l'orrore d'un ciel turbato	{ *Ottone* { *Oreste*
Dopo notte atra e funesta	{ *Ariodante* { *Poro* 1736
Dopo tante amare pene (*coro*)	*Alcina*
Dopo tanto penare (*coro*)	*Poro*
Dopo torbide procelle (2)*	*Radamisto*
Dormi O cara, e sogna intento	Cantata 'Selve caverne' (Münster)
†Dormite, dormite	*Florindo*
Dove in mezzo alle stragi rimbomba	Cantata 31 (HWV 130)
Dover, giustizia, amor	*Ariodante*
Dov'è? s'affretti	*Poro*
Dove sei, amato bene?	*Rodelinda*
Dove sei? dolce mia vita (2)*	*Ottone*
Due bell'alme inamorate	*Deidamia*
Due parti del core	*Sosarme*
D'una torbida sorgente	*Lotario*
D'un barbaro scortese	*Poro*
D'un fiero tiranno (*coro*)	*Alessandro*
Dunque se il tanto piangere	Cantata 29 (HWV 128)
D'uom fiero nel soglio (*coro*)	*Alessandro*
Duri lacci! voi non siete	*Arminio*

È ben folle quel nocchier (2)	*Trionfo del Tempo*
Ecco alle mie catene	*Ezio*
Ecco il sol ch'esce del mare	*Resurrezione*
E certo allor sei la regina (2)	Cantata 54, 55 (HWV 160ac)
E che ci posso far	*Admeto*
Echeggiate, festeggiate	Cantata IV (HWV 119)
E come l'armellino* (incomplete)	*Imeneo*
È figlio il mio timore	*Partenope*
È gelosia, forza e d'amore	*Alcina*
È gelosia quella tiranna (2)*	*Serse*
È già stanca l'alma altera*	*F. Olibrio*
Egli è tuo! nè mi riserbo	*Vincer se stesso*
È il pensier nella mia mente	Cantata 50 (HWV 152)
Empio, dirò, tu sei	*G. Cesare*
Empio fato e fiera sorte	*Vincer se stesso*
Empio mare, onde crudeli*	Cantata (Koch) (HWV 150)
Empio, per farti guerra	*Tamerlano*
Empio, perverso cor	*Radamisto*
Empio, se mi dai vita (= Vile! se mi dai vita, *Radamisto*)	*Oreste*
Empi, se mi sdegnato* (= Fiero, mi rivedrete)	*Tamerlano*
E per monti e per piano e per selve	*Admeto*
È più bella quella fede (*coro*)	*Ezio*
È prezzo leggiero d'un suddito il sangue	*Poro*
È pur bello, in nobil core	*Teseo*
E quando mai (trio)	*Agrippina*
È questo ognor sarà (*coro*)	*Alessandro*
Era in sogno almen contento	Cantata 64 (HWV 167)
Esci, O mia vita*	*Agrippina*
È si dolce il mio contento	*Amadigi*
È si vaga del tuo bene (2)	*Imeneo*
Esser mia dovrà la bella tortorella	*Imeneo*
È tempo, O luci belle	*Silla*
È tormento troppo fiero	*Serse*
È troppo bella*	Cantata 72 (HWV 118)
È troppo bel trofeo (chorus)	*Imeneo*
È una tiranna la ninfa bella (2)	Cantata 40, 41 (HWV 139ab)
È un foco quel d'amore	Cantata III (HWV 83) / *Agrippina* / *Acis and Galatea* 1732
È un folle, è un vile affetto	*Alcina*
È un incendio frà due venti	*Rinaldo*
È un sospir che vien dal core	*Floridante*
È vanità d'un cor*	Cantata (Münster) (HWV 82)
†È vicin quel dì sereno (? not set)	*Silla*
È vil segno d'un debole amore	*Arminio*
È virtute in sin la frode	*Giustino*

E vuoi, con dure tempre (duet)	*Partenope*
Faccia ritorno l'antica pace (*coro*)	*Ottone*
Falsa imagine, m'ingannasti	*Ottone*
Fammi combattere	*Orlando*
Fà quanto vuoi, li scherni tuoi	*Agrippina*
Faranno gioja intera (*coro*)	*Scipione*
Farò così più bella	*Admeto*
Fatemi, O cieli almen	*Radamisto* Dec. 1720
Fato crudo, amor severo (3)*	*Pastor fido*
Fato tiranno e crudo (2)	*Flavio*
Fatto è Amor un dio d'inferno	*Partenope*
Fatto è Giove un dio d'inferno	*Rinaldo* 1731
Fatto scorta al sentier della gloria	{ *Arminio*
	Semele Dec. 1744
†Felice chi spera	*Florindo*
Felicissima quest'alma	Cantata XVI (HWV 122)
Ferite, uccidete, O numi del ciel	*Radamisto*
Ferma l'ali, e sù miei lumi	*Resurrezione*
Fermati! nò, crudel! (duet) (2)	{ Cantata XXIV (HWV 96)
	Rinaldo
Fermati, non fuggir	Cantata III (HWV 83)
Fiaccherò quel fiero orgoglio	*Arminio*
Fiamma bella che al ciel s'invia	Cantata III (HWV 83)
Fido specchio	*Trionfo del Tempo*
Fiero, mi rivedrete	*Tamerlano*
Figlia di reo timor	*Scipione*
Figlia mia, non pianger, nò	*Tamerlano*
Figli di rupe alpestra	Cantata 48 (HWV 148)
Finchè lo strale non giunge	*Floridante*
Finchè per te mi palpita	*Ezio*
Finchè prendi ancora il sangue (duet)	*Orlando*
Finchè un zeffiro soave	{ *Ezio*
	Pastor fido May 1734
Finte labbra! stelle ingrate!	*Pastor fido*
†Fiore voi, lingue del campo	*Florindo*
Folle dunque, tu sola presumi (2)*	*Trionfo del Tempo*
Folle sei, se lo consenti!	*Tamerlano*
Fonti amiche, dure leggiere	*Tolomeo*
Foriera la tromba*	Cantata (Vienna/Berlin) (HWV 79)
Formidabil gondoliero	Cantata II (HWV 104)
Forse che un giorno il Dio d'amore	Cantata III (HWV 83)
Forte e lieto a morte andrei	*Tamerlano*
Forte inciampo al suo furore	*Sosarme*
Fosco genio e nero dolo	*Trionfo del Tempo*
†Fosco velo a nobil'alma (*coro*)	*Rinaldo*

Frà dubbi affetti miei	*Siroe*
Frà gelsomini, frà grati fiori	*Pastor fido* May 1734
Frà le guerre e le vittorie (*coro*)	*Alessandro*
Frà le spine offre gl'allori (2)*	{ *Vincer se stesso* { *? Admeto* 1731
Frà le stragi e frà le morti	*Alessandro*
Frà l'ombre e gl'orrori	*Aci, Gal. e Polif.*
Frà l'ombre e gl'orrori	*Sosarme*
Frà l'orror della tempesta	*Siroe*
Frà pensieri quel pensiero (2)*	Cantata 21 (HWV 115)
Frà poco spero*	*Riccardo*
Frà sospetti	(*v.* Trà sospetti)
Frà tempeste funeste a quest'alma	*Rodelinda*
Fredde ceneri d'amor	*Vincer se stesso*
Frode, sol a te rivolta	*Pastor fido* May 1734
Fronda leggiera e mobile	Chamber Duet
Fuggi da questo sen	Cantata 27 (HWV 125b)
Fuggon l'aure in me di vita	*Silla*
†Fulminatemi, saettatemi	*Daphne*
Fuor di periglio (duet)	*Floridante*
Furibondo spira il vento	*Partenope*
Furie son dell'alma mia	*Partenope*
Furie terribili!	*Rinaldo*
Fù scherzo, fù gioco	Cantata III (HWV 83)
Gelido in ogni vena	{ *Siroe* { *Poro* Nov. 1731
Gelo, avvampo	*Berenice*
Gelosia, spietata Aletto	*Admeto*
Geloso tormento mi va rodendo	*Almira*
Generoso chi sol brama	*Scipione*
Giacchè il sonno a lei dipinge	Cantata XVII (HWV 134)
Giacchè sprezzata io sono*	*Tolomeo* 1730
Già cessata è la procella	*Scipione*
Già che morir non posso	*Radamisto*
Già la fama che il crine m'infiora (= Bel contento)	*Flavio*
Già la tromba che chiamò (chorus)	*Serse*
Già l'ebro mio ciglio	*Orlando*
Già le furie vedo ancor	*Parnasso*
Già lo stringo, già l'abbraccio	*Orlando*
Già mi sembra al carro avvinto (2)*	*Lotario*
Già nel seno comincia a compir	Cantata 46 (HWV 145)
Già respira in petto il core	*Silla*
Già risonar d'intorno	*Ezio*
Già sai che l'usignuol*	*Jup. in Argos* (= HWV 215)
Già superbo del mio affanno	Cantata 46 (HWV 145)
Già vien da lui il nostro ben (chorus)	*Parnasso*
Gioja sì speri, sì	*Scipione*

Gioje e serto (*coro*)	*Lotario*
Gioje, venite in sen	*Amadigi*
†Giovinette, state a l'erta	*Florindo*
Giù nei Tartarei regni	Chamber Duet
Giunge ben d'amore in porto	Cantata (Münster) (HWV 158a)
Giunt'in porto è la speranza	*Ottone*
Giusto ciel, se non hò sorte*	Cantata 53 (Granville & Münster) (HWV 157)
Gli dirai, dirò che amore (duet) (= Le dirai, dirò che amore, *Berenice*)	*A. Severo*
Goda ogn'alma in si bel giorno (*coro*)	*Teseo*
Gode l'alma consolata	*Ottone* Mar. 1723
Gode l'alma innamorata (2)*	*Floridante*
Godete, O cori amanti (*coro*)	*Amadigi*
Gran pena è gelosia (duet)	*Serse*
Gran tonante, Giove immenso	{ *Parnasso* / *Terpsicore*
Grave è 'l fasto di regnar	*Lotario*
Grecia tu offendi	*Deidamia*
Gridiam tutti; e viva (chorus)	*Atalanta*
Guarda pria se in questa fronte	*Ezio*
Guerra e pace, Egizia terra	*Berenice*
Guerra, stragi e furor	*Silla*
Habbiam vinto e Iberia doma	*Scipione*
Habbiate pazienza	*Almira*
Hai due vaghe pupillette	*Silla*
Hai tanto rapido leggiero il piè	*Terpsicore*
Ha l'inganno il suo diletto	Cantata XVII (HWV 134)
Ha nel volto un certo brio (3)	Cantata 40, 41, 42 (HWV 139abc)
Han mente eroica	*Parnasso*
Han' penetrato i detti tuoi	*Amadigi*
Heroica fortezza non teme sciagure	*Vincer se stesso*
Hò fuggito amore anch'io	Cantata 72 (HWV 118)
Hò perduto il caro sposo	*Rodelinda*
Hò perso il caro ben	*Parnasso*
Hò tanti affanni in petto (3)*	Cantata XXVII, 33 (HWV 132ab)
Hò un certo rossore	*Orlando*
Hò un non sò che nel cor	{ *Resurrezione* / *Agrippina* / *Pastor fido* 1712 (add.) & Nov. 1734
Hò veleno e ferro avanti	*Arminio*
Il bel pianto dell'aurora (duet)	*Trionfo del Tempo*
Il bosco, il prato, il rio*	Cantata (Münster) (HWV 95)
Il candore tolse al giglio	Cantata 13 (HWV 107)

Il confine della vita	*M. Scevola*
Il core spera e teme	*Serse*
Il cor mio, ch'è già per te	*Alessandro*
Il dolce foco mio	Cantata 2 (HWV 80)
Il dolce foco mio	*Vincer se stesso*
Il fuggir, cara mia vita (duet)	*Arminio*
Il fulgido seren	*Scipione*
Il mio core non apprezza	*Tolomeo*
Il mio cor già più non sà	*Giustino*
Il mio crudel martoro	*Ariodante*
Il mio valore	*Sosarme*
Il nocchier, che si figura	*Ezio*
Il nume vincitor (*coro*)	*Resurrezione*
Il piacer della vendetta	*Giustino*
Il primo ardor è così caro	*Ariodante*
Il sangue al cor favella	*Arminio*
Il suol che preme (2)*	{ Cantata 46 (HWV 145) { *Flavio*
Il Tricerbero umiliato	*Rinaldo*
Il tuo figlio merta sol scettro (quartet)	*Agrippina*
Il tuo sangue ed il tuo zelo	*Ariodante*
Il voler nel fior degl'anni (duet)	*Trionfo del Tempo*
Il volo così fido	*Riccardo*
Il vostro maggio	*Rinaldo*
Impara a non temer (2)*	*Arminio*
Impara, codardo	*Lotario*
Impara, ingrata, impara (2)	{ *Aci, Gal. e Polif.* { *Atalanta* { *A. Severo*
Impari del mio core*	Cantata (Fitz.) (HWV 216)
Impedirlo saprò (duet)	*Resurrezione*
In braccio al tuo spavento*	*Jup. in Argos*
In braccio a te la calma (chorus)	*Giustino*
†Infida, dispietata (duet)	*Daphne*
Ingannata una sol volta	*Agrippina*
In generoso onor (duet)	*Alessandro*
Ingrata mai non fui	*Imeneo*
†Ingrato, spietato	*Almira*
In mano al mio sposo	*Vincer se stesso*
In mar tempestoso	*Arianna*
In mezzo a voi dui	*Imeneo*
In mille dolci modi	{ *Sosarme* { *Oreste*
Innocente rassembra	Cantata 67 (HWV 172)
I nostri cori dobbiamo offrir (chorus)	{ *Parnasso* { *Terpsicore*
In quella sola, in quella	*Berenice*
In queste amene piaggie serene	Cantata XII (HWV 99)
Inquieti miei pensieri	*Scipione* 1730
In tanti affanni è immerso il core	Cantata 23 (HWV 120a)
In tanti affanni miei	Cantata XII (HWV 105)

Intendimi, ben mio (authenticity doubtful)	Cantata 14 (HWV 108)
Invida sorte avara misero	*Ariodante*
In voi, pupille ardenti	Cantata 45 (HWV 144)
Io di Roma il Giove sono	*Agrippina*
Io già sento l'alma in sen	*Amadigi*
Io già t'amai, ritrosa	{ *Rodelinda* / *Tolomeo* 1730
Io godo, rido e spero	Cantata XXIII (HWV 173)
Io godo, scherzo e rido (2)*	*Amadigi*
Io languisco frà le gioje	Cantata IV (HWV 119)
Io le dirò che l'amo	*Serse*
Io non ti chiedo più, O sposo amato	*Silla*
Io parto lieta fu la tua fede*	*Jup. in Argos*
Io più soffrir non sò*	*Riccardo*
Io seguo sol fiero	*Partenope*
Io sò ben ch'il vostro orrore	Cantata II (HWV 81)
Io son ferito*	*Partenope*
Io son qual fenice risorta dal foco	*Admeto* Mar. 1727
Io son quella navicella	*Imeneo*
Io son vostro, O luci belle*	*Vincer se stesso*
Io sperai di veder il tuo volto (= Io ti levo l'impero, *Partenope*)	*Oreste*
Io sperai trovar nel vero (2)	*Trionfo del Tempo*
Io sperai trovar riposo (2)	*Ottone* 1726
Io t'abbraccio; è più che morte (duet)	{ *Rodelinda* / *Tolomeo* 1730
Io ti bacio, O bella imago	*Admeto*
Io ti bacio, O mano augusta	*Ariodante*
Io ti levo l'impero dell'armi	*Partenope*
Io torno a sperare	Cantata XIX (HWV 143)
Io vedo si* (incomplete)	*Lotario* (Fitz.)
Io vò di duolo in duolo	{ *G. Cesare* 1730 / *Tolomeo* 1730
Io vorrei due cari in seno	*Trionfo del Tempo*
Itene pur tremendo	*Orlando*
La bella mano che mi piago	*Berenice*
La bella vita mia	Cantata 47 (HWV 147)
La bellezza è com'un fiore	Cantata 8 (HWV 102)
La beltà che t'innamora*	*Imeneo*
La bocca vaga: quell'occhio nero	*Alcina*
Lacci, ferri, che mi stringete	*Tamerlano*
La cervetta nei lacci avvolta	*Alessandro*
La crudele lontananza*	{ *Teseo* / *Rinaldo* 1715
Là dove gli occhi io giro	*Admeto*
La giustizia ha già sull'arco	*G. Cesare*

La gloria in nobil alma	*Partenope*
La gloria sola, che ogn'or bramai	*Admeto*
L'alma mia frà le tempeste	*Agrippina*
L'alto Giove al travaglio penoso (chorus)	*Deidamia*
La memoria dei tormenti (*coro*)	*Riccardo*
Lamentandomi corro a volo	*Scipione*
L'amerete? L'amerò (duet)	*Serse*
La mia bella perduta Rosmene	*Imeneo*
La mia costanza non si sgomenta	*Ezio*
La mia piaga, se v'appaga	Cantata 38 (HWV 133)
La mia sorte fortunata	*Agrippina*
La mia speranza diceva al core	*Siroe*
L'amor che per te sento	*Alessandro*
L'amor ed il destin	*Partenope*
L'amorosa dea di Gnido (*coro*)*	*Vincer se stesso*
Langue, geme, sospira e si lagna	Chamber Duet
L'angue offeso mai riposa	G. Cesare
Langue trema, e prigioniero	Cantata 36 (HWV 136)
La nobiltà del regno* (= Del debellar la gloria)	*Scipione*
L'aquila altera conosce i figli	{ *Riccardo* { *Admeto* 1731
L'armellin vita non cura	*Flavio*
L'armi implora dal tuo figlio	*Alessandro*
Lascia Amor e siegui Marte	*Orlando*
Lascia che nel suo viso	*Ottone*
Lascia ch'io parta solo [lieto]	{ *Atalanta* { *A. Severo*
Lascia ch'io pianga	*Rinaldo*
Lascia di più sperar	Cantata 32 (HWV 131)
Lascia, la dolce brama	Cantata 10 (HWV 103)
Lascia la pace all'alma	*Riccardo*
Lascia la spina cogli la rosa (2)	{ *Trionfo del Tempo* { *Jup. in Argos*
Lasciami. Tu sei fedele?	*Deidamia*
Lascia omai le brune vele	Cantata XII (HWV 99)
Lascia pur amica spene	*Radamisto* Dec. 1720
Lascio Gian e sieguo Marte (= Lascia Amor e siegui Marte, *Orlando*)	*A. Severo*
Lascioti, O bella, il volto (2)	*Floridante* 1722
La sorte, il ciel, amor	*Radamisto*
La sorte mia tiranna	*Siroe*
La sorte mia vacilla	*Admeto*
La speme ti consoli	*Partenope*
La speranza all'alma mia (2)	G. Cesare 1725
La speranza è giunta in porto	*Ottone*
La speranza, la costanza*	{ *Oratorio* 1738 { *Israel* 1739
Lassa ch'io t'hò perduta	*Atalanta*
La tigre arde di sdegno	*Admeto*
Là ti sfido a fiera battaglia	*Vincer se stesso*

La turba adulatrice	*Sosarme*
L'aura che spira (2)*	*G. Cesare*
L'aura non sempre spira	*Siroe*
L'aure grate, il fresco rio (2)*	Cantata 24 (HWV 121ab)
La vendetta è un cibo al cor	*Silla*
La virtute è un vero nume	Cantata V, VI (HWV 166, 89)
La virtute sol potea (chorus)	*Serse*
Le dirai (duet)	*Berenice*
Le luci del mio bene	*Teseo*
L'empio rigor del fato	*Rodelinda*
L'empio, sleale, indegno (2)*	{ *Ottone* Mar. 1723 { *G. Cesare*
Le profonde vie dell'onde (2)*	*Ottone*
Le vicende della sorte	*Berenice*
Libera chi non è	*Scipione*
Lieto esulti il cor (chorus)	{ *Acis and Galatea* 1732 { *Jup. in Argos*
Lieto il Tebro increspi l'onda (*coro*)	*Agrippina*
L'ingrato non amar (3)**	*Radamisto* Dec. 1720
L'odio si, mà poi ritrovo*	? (Fitz.) (HWV 217)
Lo farò; dirò spietato	*Rodelinda*
Lontan dal mio tesoro	*Pastor fido*
Lontan dal suo tesoro	*Acis and Galatea* ?1734
Lontano al mio tesoro (2)	Cantata 25, 26 (HWV 127ab)
Lo sdegno del mio cor (=Amore contro amor, *Berenice*)	*A. Severo*
Luci belle, serene stelle	*Silla*
Luci belle, vaghe stelle*	Cantata (Münster) (HWV 142)
Luci care, addio, posate!	*Admeto*
Lucide stelle, gemelle d'amor	*Vincer se stesso*
Lunga seria d'altri eroi (aria and chorus)	*Parnasso*
Lungi da te, mio speme	Cantata 20 (HWV 114)
Lungo pensar e dubitar	*M. Scevola*
L'uomo sempre se stesso distrugge (chorus in 1737)	*Trionfo del Tempo*
Lusinga questo cor*	? (Shaftesbury)
Lusinghe più care	{ *Alessandro* { *Scipione* 1730
Lusinghiera mia speranza (2)*	*Agrippina*
Lusinghiera nel mio seno (=Par che voglia)	*Arianna*
Mà che vuoi più da me	*Floridante*
Mà chi punir desio?	*Flavio*
Mà chi sà, se mi riama	*Deidamia*
Mà come amar? (duet)	*M. Scevola*
M'adora l'idol mio	*Teseo*
†Mai non posa un cor amante	*Florindo*
Mai più da te, mio ben	Cantata 66 (HWV 169)
M'ai resa infelice	*Deidamia*
M'allontano, sdegnose pupille	*Atalanta*
Manca, O Dei! la mia costanza	*Ariodante*

Mà non s'aspetti, nò!	*Floridante*
Mà pria vedrò le stelle (2)	*Floridante*
Mà quai note di mesti lamenti	*Partenope*
Mà quando tornerai	*Alcina*
Maria, salute e speme (solo & chorus)*	Cantata (Münster) (HWV 233)
Mà un dolce mio pensiero	*Floridante*
†Me deridi, e mi diletti	*Daphne*
Meglio in voi col mio partire	*Serse*
Men fedele e men costante	*Alessandro*
Menti eterne, che reggete	*Lotario*
Mia bella, godo che son per te	*Floridante*
Mi brilla nel seno un certo seren	*Silla*
Mi chiederesti meno	*Imeneo*
Mi credi infedele	*Siroe*
Mi dà speranza al core	*Almira*
Mie piante correte	Cantata XVI (HWV 122)
Mie pupille, se tranquille	Cantata IX (HWV 92)
Mie speranze, andate, andate*	*Florindo*
Mi lagnerò tacendo	{ *Siroe* / *Oreste*
Mi lasci, mi fuggi	{ *Pastor fido* / *Acis and Galatea* ?1734
Mi lusinga il dolce affetto	{ *Alcina* / *Semele* Dec. 1744
Minacciami, non hò timor*	{ *Amadigi* / ?*Rinaldo*
Mio bel sol, dove t'aggiri?	*Berenice*
Mio bel tesoro, caro mio bene (duet)	*Giustino*
Mio bel tesoro, fedel son io	*Alcina*
Mio ben, ricordati	*Poro*
Mio caro bene	*Rodelinda*
†Mio contento, mia speranza (duet)	*Florindo*
Mio cor, che mi sai dir?	*Rinaldo*
Mio dolce amato sposo	*Giustino*
Mi palpita il cor (5)**	{ Cantata XXVII, 33, 34 (HWV 132bac) / Oratorio 1738
Mi palpita il core nè intendo perchè	*Ariodante*
Mi par sognar di posseder	*Scipione*
Mi parto lieta sulla tua fede	*Faramondo*
Mi piagò d'amor lo strale (2)	Cantata 12, 34 (HWV 106, 132a)
Mira adesso questo seno (duet)	*Arianna*
Mira il ciel, vedrai d'Alcide	*Arminio*
Mirami, altero in volto	*Arianna*
Mirerò quel vago volto	*Radamisto*
Mi restano le lagrime	*Alcina*
Mi restano le lagrime*	*Titus*
Mi rido di veder*	Cantata (Fitz.) (HWV 86)
†Miro, vagheggio e adoro	*Florindo*
Mi volgo ad ogni fronda	*Tolomeo*

Molto voglio, molto spero	*Rinaldo*
M'opporrò da generoso	*Sosarme*
Morirò, mà vendicata	*Teseo*
Mormorando esclaman l'onde	Cantata 56, 57
	(HWV 161abc)
Morrai, sì; l'empia tua testa	*Rodelinda*
Morte, vieni, mà in van	*Riccardo*
Mostratevi serene	{ *Admeto* ?Mar. or Sept.
	1727
	{ *Oreste*
Mostrati più crudele*	*Daphne*
Move i passi alle ruine	*Almira*
Nacque al bosco, nacque al prato (2)	*Giustino*
Nacque un alto leggiadro pensiero	*Trionfo del Tempo*
Narrargli allor saprai	*Arianna*
Nasce al bosco in rozza cuna	{ *Ezio*
	{ *Oreste*
Nasce il sol e l'aura vola	*Vincer se stesso*
Nasce l'uomo mà nasce bambino	*Trionfo del Tempo*
Nascermi sento al core	Cantata 54a (HWV
	160a)
Nasconde l'usignolo	*Deidamia*
Naufragando va per l'onde	*Resurrezione*
Neghittosi or voi che fate?	*Ariodante*
Ne' gigli e nelle rose	Cantata IX (HWV
	92)
Nell'amor, nella speranza*	*Scipione*
Nella terra, in ciel, nell'onda	*Faramondo*
Nelle nubi intorno al fato	*Deidamia*
Nell'incanto del tuo canto	Cantata 49 (HWV
	151)
Nell'orror d'un duolo eterno	*Ottone* 1726
Nel mio core ritorna il contento	{ *Pastor fido*
	{ *Acis and Galatea* ?1734
Nel mondo e nell'abisso (2)*	{ *Riccardo*
	{ *Tamerlano* 1731
†Nel passer da un laccio all'altro	*Jup. in Argos*
Nel pensar che sei l'oggetto	Cantata 49 (HWV
	151)
Nel petto sento un certo ardor (chorus)	*Parnasso*
Nel pugnar col mostro infido	*Arianna*
Nel riposo e nel contento	*Deidamia*
Nel spiegar sua voce al canto	*Parnasso*
Nel suo sangue, e nel tuo pianto (2)	*Ottone*
Nel tuo seno amico sasso (2)*	*G. Cesare*
Nè men con l'ombre	*Serse*
Ne' tuoi lumi, O bella Clori	Cantata 38 (HWV
	133)
Niente spero, tutto credo	{ *Arminio*
	{ *A. Severo*
Nobil core che ben ama	*Partenope*
Nobil cor non più mirare*	*G. Cesare*
Nò, che del tuo gran cor (2)*	*Tamerlano*
Nò, che piacer non v'è (complete in Cardiff)	Cantata 24 (HWV
	121ab)

Nò, che sei tanto costante (2)	*Tamerlano*
Nò, che servire altrui	*Berenice*
Nò, di voi non vo' fidarmi (2)	Chamber Duet
Non a tempre per colpi si fieri	*Ottone*
Non brilla tanto il fior	Cantata 51 (HWV 153)
Non chiedo, O luci vaghe	*Partenope*
Non credo instabile	*Flavio*
Non deve Roman petto	*Arminio*
Non disperar, chi sà? (2)*	*G. Cesare*
Non disperi peregrino	*Lotario*
Non è amor nè gelosia (trio)	*Alcina*
Non è da rè quel cor	*Teseo*
Non è incauto il mio consiglio (quartet)	*Partenope*
Non è più bono*	Cantata *Amore uccellatore* (Fitz.)
Non è più tempo, nò (2)*	*Tamerlano*
Non è possibile, O Clori amabile*	Cantata (Münster) (HWV 95)
Non esce un guardo mai	Cantata 67 (HWV 172)
Non è si vago e bello	*G. Cesare*
Non fù già men forte Alcide	*Orlando*
Non fù già per amor	Cantata 67 (HWV 172)
Non ha diffesa, non ha consiglio	*Arianna*
Non ha forza nel mio petto	Cantata 4 (HWV 88)
Non ha più che temere	*G. Cesare*
Non hò cor che per amarti	*Agrippina*
Non hò più affanni, nò (duet)	{ *Radamisto* Dec. 1720 { *A. Severo*
Non ingannarmi, cara speranza*	*Jup. in Argos*
Non ingannarmi, nò	*Faramondo*
Non lasciar oppressa della sorte	*Floridante*
Non li scherzate intorno	Cantata 67 (HWV 172)
Non lo dirò col labbro	*Tolomeo*
Non m'inganna la speranza (= Non t'inganni, *Lotario*)	*Scipione* 1730
Nò, nò, che quest'alma	*Rinaldo*
Nò, nò, ch'io non apprezzo (duet)*	*Agrippina*
Nò, nò, il tuo sdegno (2)	*Tamerlano*
Nò, non basta un infedele	*Pastor fido*
Nò, non così severe*	*Pirro e Demetrio* 1716
Nò, nò, non voglio, nò	*Almira*
Nò, non piangete*	{ ? *Teseo* { *Tito Manlio* 1717
Nò, non piangete, pupille belle	*Floridante*
Nò, non si teme (2)	*Scipione*
Nò, non temere, O bella	*Ottone*
Nò, nò, se tu mi sprezzi	*Serse*
Non pensi quell'altera	{ *Lotario* { *Rodelinda* 1731
Non più barbaro furore (duet)	Cantata IV (HWV 119)
Non potrà dirmi ingrata	*Orlando*
Non s'afferra d'amore il porto (2)	Cantata 58, 59 (HWV 158bc)

Non sarà poco	*Atalanta*
Non sarà quest'alma mia	*Radamisto*
Non sà temere questo mio petto	*Amadigi*
Non sempre invendicata	{ *Lotario* *Oreste*
Non sempre, nò, crudele	{ *Aci, Gal. e Polif.* *Acis and Galatea* 1732
†Non s'estingue mai la fiamma (duet)	*Silla*
Non si può dar un cor	Cantata XXV [III] (HWV 83)
Non si vanti un'alma audace	{ *Giustino* *Semele* Dec. 1744
Non son sempre vane larve	*Arminio*
Non sò più che bramar	*Teseo*
Non sò se avrai mai bene*	Cantata (Fitz.) (HWV 219)
Non sò se sia la speme	*Serse*
Non sospirar, non piangere	Cantata 43 (HWV 141)
Non tardate a festeggiar (duet)*	*Ottone* 1733 (comp ?1723)
Non tardate, Fauni, ancora	*Parnasso*
Non ti credo, non mi fido	*Deidamia*
Non ti fidar, perchè il desire	*M. Scevola*
Non t'inganni la speranza	*Lotario*
Non trascurate amanti (chorus)	*Deidamia*
Non v'alletti un occhio nero	Cantata 8 (HWV 102)
Non vi piacque ingiusti Dei	*Siroe*
Non vo' legarmi il cor	*Pastor fido*
Non vo' mai seguitar	*Pastor fido* Nov. 1734
Non vuò perdere l'istante (2)	*Deidamia*
Nò, più soffrir non voglio (2)*	*Alessandro*
Nò, quella beltà non amo	*Deidamia*
Nò, soffrir non può il mio amore	*Berenice*
Notte amica dei riposi	*Amadigi*
Notte cara! a te si deve (duet)	*Ottone*
Notte cara, deh! riportami	*Floridante*
Nube, che il sole adombra	{ *Riccardo* *Sosarme* 1734
Nubiloso frà tempeste*	*Riccardo*
Nulla sperar da me	*Agrippina*
Numi eccelsi (*coro*)*	*Titus*
Numi! lasciarmi vivere	*Ariodante*
O cara spene del mio diletto	{ Cantata X (HWV 97) *Floridante* 1722
O care parolette, O dolci sguardi	{ *Orlando* *A. Severo*
O caro mio tesor	*Amadigi*
?Occhi belli, occhi vezzosi*	*Lucio Vero* 1715
Occhi belli, voi sol siete	*Pastor fido*
†Occhi neri, voi non siete	*Vincer se stesso*
O cedere, O perir (quartet)	*Radamisto* Dec. 1720
O come chiare e belle	Cantata XIX (HWV 143)

O del Ciel Maria Regina	Cantata XXVI (HWV 230)
O dolce mia speranza	{ Cantata X (HWV 97) *Floridante* 1722 }
O Eurimene hà l'idea di Rosmira	*Partenope*
†O fatte l'amore	*Daphne*
†O felice chi non ama	*Florindo*
O fiero e rio sospetto	*Giustino*
Oggi rimbombano (chorus)	*Atalanta*
†Oggi udirannosi (chorus)	*Jup. in Argos*
Ogni indugio d'un amante	*Rinaldo*
Ogni tua bella stilla*	*Rinaldo* 1717
Ogni vento ch'al porto lo spinga	*Agrippina*
Ogn'un acclami il nostro Alcide (*coro*)	*Teseo*
Ogn'un canti e all'armonia*	Cantata (Münster) (HWV 117)
Ogn'uno acclami bella virtute (chorus)	*Ariodante*
Ombra cara di mia sposa	*Radamisto*
†Ombra, che pallida	*Jup. in Argos*
Ombra mai fù	*Serse*
Ombre pallide, lo sò, mi udite	*Alcina*
Ombre, piante, urne funeste (2)*	*Rodelinda*
O morte, vendetta, tradite sembianze	*Vincer se stesso*
O placido il mare	*Siroe*
O quanto bella gloria (chorus)	{ *Parnasso* *Pastor fido* May 1734 *Jup. in Argos* }
O quanto è caro amor	*Floridante* 1722
Or che cinto hò il crin d'alloro	*Giustino*
Or che siete speranze tradite	*Serse*
Or ch'io sono accivettato	Cantata 70 (HWV 176)
O rendetemi il mio bene	*Amadigi*
Orgogliosetto và l'augelletto	{ *Lotario* *Oreste* }
Or la tromba in suon festante	*Rinaldo*
Or mi perdo di speranza	*Siroe*
Or pensate, amanti cori	*Deidamia*
Orrida a gl'occhi miei	*Ariodante*
Orrida, oscura l'etra si renda	Cantata XIV (HWV 110)
Or trionfar ti fanno*	*Atalanta*
O s'apre al riso	*Alcina*
O scemami il diletto	*Radamisto*
O stringerò nel sen quel ben ch'adoro	*Teseo*
O ti vorrei men bella*	Cantata (Manchester, Add MS 29963) (HWV 101a)
O vendicarmi	*Riccardo*
O voi che penate	*Serse*
O voi dell'Erebo	*Resurrezione*
Padre amato, in me riposa	*Tamerlano*
Padre, germano e sposo	*Sosarme*
Par che mi nasca in seno (2)	*Tamerlano*

Par che voglia il ciel sereno	*Arianna*
Parmi che giunta in porto	$\left\{\begin{array}{l}\textit{Floridante } 1727 \\ \textit{Radamisto } 1728 \\ \textit{Tolomeo } 1730\end{array}\right.$
Parolette vezzi e sguardi	$\left\{\begin{array}{l}\textit{G. Cesare } 1730 \\ \textit{Rinaldo } 1731\end{array}\right.$
Parto, crudel, sì, parto	*Vincer se stesso*
Parto, fuggo; resta, e godi	*Scipione*
Parto, sì, mà non sò poi	*Flavio*
Pastorella, i bei lumi	Cantata 35 (HWV 135)
Pastorello d'un povero armento	*Rodelinda*
Pena tiranna io sento al core	*Amadigi*
Pende il ben dell'universo	Cantata XVI (HWV 122)
Peni tu per un ingrata	*Ezio*
Pensa a chi geme d'amor piagata	*Alcina*
Pensa ad amare che dal tuo cor	*Ottone*
Pensa a serbarmi, O cara	*Ezio*
Pensa ch'io sono un rege amante (= Finchè lo strale, *Floridante*)	*Oreste*
Pensa, O bella, alla mia speme	*Scipione*
Pensa, spietata madre	*Ottone*
Pensier crudele, se vuoi ch'io creda	Cantata 27 (HWV 125)
Pensieri, voi mi tormentate	$\left\{\begin{array}{l}\textit{Agrippina} \\ \textit{Oreste}\end{array}\right.$
Penso al mio, mà penso insieme	Cantata 9 (HWV 100)
Per abbatter il rigore (duet)	Cantata III (HWV 83)
Pera, pera! l'alma fiera (*coro*)	*Faramondo*
Per celare il nuovo scorno	*Resurrezione*
Perchè viva il caro sposo	*Vincer se stesso*
Per ch'io goda il bel d'un riso* (= Ti vedrò regnar)	*Riccardo* (Fitz.)
Per dar fine alla mia pena	*Serse*
Per dar pace al mio tormento*	Cantata (Fitz.) (HWV 220)
Per dar pregio all'amor mio	*Vincer se stesso*
Per dar vita*	*G. Cesare*
Perdere il bene amato	*Deidamia*
Per due begl'occhi avvampo (= V'adoro, O luci belle)	*Riccardo*
Per far, mia diletta	*Orlando*
Perfido! di a quell'empio tiranno	*Radamisto* Dec. 1720
Per formar si vaga e bella	Cantata 13 (HWV 107)
Per involarmi al duolo (2)*	Cantata 61 (HWV 162)
Per le porte del tormento (duet)	$\left\{\begin{array}{l}\textit{Sosarme} \\ \textit{Imeneo } 1742\end{array}\right.$
Per me dunque il ciel non hà	*Giustino*
Per me già di morire	*Resurrezione*
Permettete ch'io vi baci	*Alessandro*
Per mia vendetta ancor	*Riccardo*

Per pietà de' miei martiri	Cantata XI (HWV 98)
Per punir che m'ha ingannata*	*Agrippina*
Per rendermi beato	*Serse*
Per salvarti, idolo mio	{ *Lotario* { *Rinaldo* 1731
Per si bella cagion	*Berenice*
Per te lasciai la luce	Cantata XII (HWV 99)
Per te, mio dolce bene (duet)	*Pastor fido*
Per te moro (duet)	*Partenope*
Per trofei di mia costanza	Cantata I (HWV 78)
Per tutto il timore	*Ezio*
Per un instante*	Cantata (Münster) (HWV 142)
Per voi languisco e moro	Cantata 45 (HWV 144)
Per voi soave e bella	*Giustino*
Piacer che non si dona*	Cantata (Münster) (HWV 82)
Piangerò la sorte mia (2)*	*G. Cesare*
Piangerò, mà le mie lagrime	Cantata II (HWV 104)
Piangete, sì, piangete	*Resurrezione*
Piangi pur, mà non sperare	*Tolomeo*
Piango dolente (=Bacia per me, *Riccardo*)	*Oreste*
Pien di nuove e bel diletto	Cantata XXI (HWV 170)
Pieno il core di timore (2)	*Imeneo*
Pietà, valore, gloria ed onore	Cantata XII (HWV 99)
Pietoso sguardo*	Cantata (Münster) (HWV 82)
Più che penso alle fiamme del core	*Serse*
Più contento e più felice	*Ariodante*
Più d'una tigre altera	*Tamerlano*
Più non cerca libertà	*Teseo*
Più non cura valle oscura	*Trionfo del Tempo*
Più non spero di lauro guerriero	Cantata XIX (HWV 143)
Più non vuo' trà sì e nò	*Almira*
Placa l'alma, quieta il petto (duet)	*Alessandro*
Poi che pria di morire	*Faramondo*
Pose Clori ed Amarilli	Cantata 70 (HWV 176)
Posso morir, mà vivere	{ *Arminio* { *Semele* Dec. 1744
Poterti dir vorrei	*Partenope*
Povera fedeltà	Cantata XXIV (HWV 96)
Precipitoso nel mar che freme	*Aci, Gal. e Polif.*
Pregio è sol d'un alma forte*	*Rinaldo* 1717
Pregi son d'un alma grande	*Alessandro*
Pregi son d'un alma grande	*Scipione* 1730

Prendi da questa mano (duet)	*Ariodante*
Prendi l'alma, prendi il core (duet)	*Vincer se stesso*
Presso ad occhi esperti	*Deidamia*
Presso sono, non sò che sguardo*	Cantata (Manchester) (HWV 149)
Prestami un solo dardo	*Vincer se stesso*
Presti omai l'Egizia terra (2)*	*G. Cesare*
Pria che si converta in polve (chorus)	*Trionfo del Tempo* 1737
Pria che spunti un dì si fiero (2)	Cantata 17, 18 (HWV 111ab)
Prigioniera hò l'alma in pena	{ *Rodelinda* { *Tolomeo* 1730
Priva son d'ogni conforto	*G. Cesare*
Pronti l'ali dispiegate	Cantata 21 (HWV 115)
Proverai di che fiere saette	*Almira*
Proverà lo sdegno mio (trio)	{ *Aci. Gal. e Polif.* { *Acis and Galatea* 1732
Prove sono di grandezza	*Alessandro*
Pugneran con noi le stelle	*Vincer se stesso*
Pugnerò contro del fato (2)*	*Amadigi*
Può ben nascer trà li boschi	*Giustino*
Può te, Orfeo, col dolce suono*	Cantata (Münster) (HWV 117)
Pupilla lucente	Cantata 5 (HWV 90)
Pupille amate, voi m'insegnate	*Alessandro*
Pupille sdegnose!	{ *M. Scevola* { *Ottone* 1733
Pur che regni il figlio amato	*Ottone*
Pur ch'io ti stringa al sen	*Agrippina*
Pur ritorno a rimirarvi	*Agrippina*
Pur sento, O Dio, che l'alma	*Tolomeo*
Qual cervetta che cacciata	*Ottone* 1733
Qual farfalletta	*Partenope*
Qual leon che fere irato	*Arianna*
Qual nave smarrita	*Radamisto*
Qual'onda e quest'alma*	*Alessandro*
Qual'or tu paga sei (= Non chiedo, O luci, *Partenope*)	*Oreste*
Qual piacer a un cor pietoso	*Agrippina*
Qual portento mi richiama	*Alcina*
Qual scoglio in mezzo all'onde	*Silla*
Qual tigre e qual Megera	*Teseo*
Quando accenderan quel petto	*Deidamia*
Quando contento di stragi*	*F. Olibrio*
Quando è parto dell'affetto	*Resurrezione*
Quando il fato e più spietato*	*Tamerlano*
Quando in calma ride il mare	Chamber Duet
Quando invita la donna l'amante	*Agrippina*
Quando mai spietata sorte	*Radamisto*
Quando meno lo pensai*	Cantata *Amore uccellatore* (Fitz.)
Quando non son presente	Cantata 9 (HWV 100)

Quando non vedo la cara madre	*Riccardo*
Quando pena la costanza (*coro*)	*Floridante*
Quando più minaccia il cielo (duet)	*Arminio*
Quando ritornerò	Cantata 65 (HWV 168)
Quando spieghi i tuoi tormenti	*Orlando*
Quanto breve è il godimento	*Parnasso*
† Quanto belle, quanto care	*Vincer se stesso*
Quanto ch'a me sian care	*Teseo*
Quanto dolce amor saria	*Alessandro*
Quanto dolci, quanto care	*Flavio*
Quanto è felice quell'augelletto	*Tolomeo*
Quanto goda l'alma mia (duet)*	*Riccardo*
Quanto godrà, allor che mi vedrà	*Admeto*
Quanto ingannata è quella	*Deidamia*
Quanto invidio tua fortuna*	Cantata (Fitz.) (HWV 221)
Quanto mai felice siete	{ *Ezio* { *Pastor fido* May 1734
Quanto più amara fù sorte crudele*	? (RM) (HWV 222)
Quanto più fiera	*Rodelinda*
Quanto più forte è il valor	*Lotario*
Quanto più rigida	Cantata 23 (HWV 120)
Quanto tarda il caro bene	*Riccardo*
Qua rivolga gl'orribili acciari*	*Vincer se stesso*
Quel bel labbro, quel vezzo, quel sguardo (duet)	*Berenice*
Quel bel rio, ch'a duro scoglio	Cantata 6 (HWV 91)
Quel ch'il cielo già prefisse (*coro*)	*Pastor fido*
Quel cor che adora	*Arianna*
Quel cor che mi donasti	{ *Lotario* { *Rinaldo* 1731
Quel finger affetto	*Ezio*
Quel fior che all'alba ride*	Cantata (Fitz.) (HWV 154)
Quel fior che all'alba ride	Chamber Duet & Trio
Quel gelsomino che imperla il prato	{ *Riccardo* { *Pastor fido* May 1734
Quel labbro di coral	*Almira*
Quella che miri aura scherzosa (2)	Cantata 6 (HWV 91)
Quella che tutta fè (2)*	*Serse*
Quella fiamma, ch'il petto m'accende	*Arminio*
Quell'amor, ch'è nato a forza	*Teseo*
Quell'erbetta che smalta le sponde*	Cantata XXIV (Münster) (HWV 96)
Quell'innocente afflitto core	*Riccardo*
Quell'oggetto ch'è caro [schernito]	{ *Berenice* { *A. Severo*
Quell'onda, che si frange	*Tolomeo*
Quell'orror delle procelle*	*Sosarme* 1734
Quel nocchiero che mira le sponde*	Cantata (Münster) (HWV 82)
Quel povero core	Cantata XXIII (HWV 173)
Quel superbo già si crede	*Lotario*

Quel torrente che cade dal monte	*G. Cesare*
Quel torrente che s'innalza	*Giustino*
Quel volto mi piace	*Partenope*
†Questa d'un fido amore	*Jup. in Argos*
Questa qual sia beltà	*Berenice*
Questi ceppi e quest'orrore	*Floridante*
Questi la disperata anima mia	Cantata 46 (HWV 145)
Questo core incatenato*	*G. Cesare*
Questo è il cielo di contenti (chorus) (2)	*Alcina*
Qui d'amor nel suo linguaggio	*Ariodante*
Qui l'augel da pianta in pianta (3)	{ *Aci, Gal. e Polif.* { *Acis and Galatea* 1732
Qui ti sfido, O mostro infame!	*Arianna*
Quivi Amor non può venire*	Cantata *Amore uccellatore* (Fitz.)
Rammentati, cor mio	*Lotario*
Recagli quell'acciaro	*Ezio*
Regno e grandezza	*Lotario*
Renda cenere il tiranno	Cantata XIV (HWV 110)
Rendi 'l sereno al ciglio	*Sosarme*
Rendimi il dolce sposo	*Arminio*
Replicati al ballo, al canto (chorus)	{ *Parnasso* { *Pastor fido* May 1734
Respira almen un poco	*Tolomeo*
Ricco pino, nel cammino	*Trionfo del Tempo*
Ricordati, mio ben (duet)	*Flavio*
Ricordati, O bella	*Teseo*
Ride il fiore in seno al prato	Cantata 37 (HWV 137)
†Ridi, O speme, al ben sereno (duet)	*Daphne*
Ridite a Clori	Cantata 4 (HWV 88)
Riportai gloriosa palma	*Atalanta*
Rise Eurilla, rise amore	Cantata 69 (HWV 175)
Risolvo abbandonar	*Alessandro*
Risonar mi sento al core	*Pastor fido*
Risorga il mondo	*Resurrezione*
Risplendete, amiche stelle	*Teseo*
Risveglia lo sdegno	*Poro*
Ritorna adesso amor	*Pastor fido*
Ritorna a noi la calma (chorus)	*Serse*
Ritorna nel core vezzosa brillante (duet)	*Arminio*
Ritorna, O caro e dolce mio tesoro	*Rodelinda*
Ritorna, O dolce amore	*Ottone*
Ritornava al suo bel viso (duet)	*Orlando*
Ritorni omai nel nostro core (*coro*)	*G. Cesare*
Ritorno alla ritorte	*Arminio*
Ritrosa bellezza	*Giustino*
Rival ti sono, mà son fedel	*Faramondo*
Rompo i lacci, e frango i dardi	*Flavio*
S'accenda pur di festa il cor (chorus)	*Parnasso*

S'adopri il braccio armato	*Radamisto*
S'agita in mezzo all'onde	*Aci, Gal. e Polif.*
Sai perchè l'onda del fiume*	Cantata XXIV (Münster)(HWV96)
Salda quercia in erta balza	{ *Arianna* / *A. Severo*
S'altri gode pensando al suo bene	Cantata 50 (HWV 152)
Sanerà la piaga un dì	*Almira*
Sà perchè pena il cor*	? *Rinaldo* (Tenbury)
Sappi, crudel, io t'amo	*Faramondo*
Saprà delle mie offese	*Serse*
Sarai contenta un dì	Cantata 52 (HWV 156)
Sarà qual vuoi accenni*	*Agrippina*
S'armi a miei danni	*G. Cesare* 1725
S'armi il fato, s'armi amore	*Teseo*
Sarò giusto e non tiranno	*Tolomeo*
Sarò qual vento che nell'incendio	*Alessandro*
Sà trionfar ognor (chorus)	*Ariodante*
Scaccia, O bella, dal seno il timore	*Scipione*
Scacciata dal suo nido	*Rodelinda*
Scaglian amore e sangue	*Arminio*
† Schernirò, con la costanza	*Daphne*
Scherza infida, in grembo al drudo	*Ariodante*
Scherza in mar la navicella	{ *Lotario* / *Pastor fido* May 1734
Scherzano sul tuo volto (duet) (2)	{ Cantata XXIV (HWV 96) / *Rinaldo*
Sciolga dunque al ballo, al canto	{ *Parnasso* / *Pastor fido* May 1734
Scoglio d'immota fronte	*Scipione*
Scorta siate a passi miei*	*G. Cesare* 1725
Scorta rea di cieco amore	*Rinaldo*
Sdegnata sei con me	*Arianna*
Sdegno, amore	*Arianna*
Se ad un costante core	*Tamerlano*
Se al pensier dar mai potrò	Cantata 53 (HWV 157)
Se a me non sei crudele	*G. Cesare*
Se amor a questo petto	*Poro*
Se a' piedi tuoi morrò	*Faramondo*
Se a te vissi fedele	*Flavio*
Se avvien che sia infedele	Cantata 22 (HWV 116)
Se ben mi lusinga l'infida speranza	*Faramondo*
Se ben tuona il ciel irato	*Silla*
Se bramate d'amor	*Serse*
Se cangio spoglia	*Serse*
Secondaste al fine, O stelle	*Pastor fido*
Secondate, O giusti dei	*Silla*
Se consulta il suo dover (chorus)	*Imeneo*
Se d'amore amanti siete*	*Imeneo*
S'è delitto trar da' lacci	*Lotario*

Se discordia ci [ne] disciolse	*Sosarme*
Se dolce m'era già viver	*Floridante*
Se fedele mi brama il regnante	*Ezio*
Se fedel vuoi ch'io ti creda	*Orlando*
Se fiera belva ha cinto	*Rodelinda*
Se giunge un dispetto (2)	*Agrippina*
Se gli ascolti ti diranno	Cantata 7 (HWV 93)
S'egli ti chiede affetto	*Flavio*
Segni di crudeltà	*Radamisto* Dec. 1720
Seguaci di Cupido	*Partenope* Dec. 1730
Seguir di selva in selva	*Deidamia*
Sei bugiarda, umana spene	Cantata 62 (HWV 163)
Sei cara, sei bella, virtute ognor	Cantata VI, VII (HWV 89, 87)
Sei del ciel dono perfetto	Cantata VII (HWV 87)
Sei già morto, idolo mio	*Silla*
Se il caro figlio (2)*	{ *Siroe* { *Oreste*
Se il ciel mi divide	*Poro*
Se il cor mai ti dirà	*Orlando*
Se il cor si perde, O cara (duet)	*Rodelinda* 1731
Se il cor ti perde, O caro (duet)	*Tolomeo*
Se il destin col suo poter (chorus) (=Se consulta il suo dover)	*Imeneo*
Se il labbro amor ti giura	*Siroe*
Se il mar promette calma	{ *Lotario* { *Poro* Nov. 1731
Se il mio amor fù il tuo delitto (duet)	*Berenice*
Se il mio paterno amore	*Siroe*
Se il timore il ver mi dice	*Deidamia*
Sei mia gioja, sei mio bene	*Partenope*
Se impassabile immortale	*Resurrezione*
Se infelice al mondo vissi	Cantata XIV (HWV 110)
Se in fiorito ameno prato	*G. Cesare*
Se in ombre nascosto	*Pastor fido*
Sei pur bella pur vezzosa (3)	Cantata 54, 54A, 55 (HWV 160abc)
Se la Bellezza perde vaghezza	*Trionfo del Tempo*
Se la mia pace a me vuoi togliere	*Imeneo*
Se la mia pace a me vuoi togliere (duet)	*Imeneo*
Se la mia vita dono è d'Augusto	*Ezio*
Se la morte non vorrà*	Cantata (Koch) (HWV 150)
Se l'amor tuo mi rendi	*Siroe*
Se l'arcano scoprire (=Con quel sangue, *Arminio*)	*A. Severo*
Se l'arco avessi e i strali	*Admeto*
Se la speranza nudrisce il mio cor	*Silla*
Se Licori, Filli ed io	Cantata XXII (HWV 171)
Se l'idol mio rapir	*Serse*
Se l'inganno sortisce felice	*Ariodante*
Se l'interno pur vedono	*Tolomeo*

Se 'l mio duol non è si forte	*Rodelinda*
Se 'l mio mal da voi dipende	*Silla*
Se mai più sarò geloso	*Poro*
Se mai turbo il tuo riposo (2)*	*Poro*
Se mai turbo il tuo riposo (duet)	*Poro*
Se m'ami, O caro (2)	{ *Aci, Gal. e Polif.* *Pastor fido* *Acis and Galatea* 1732
Se m'ascolti (duet)	*Sosarme*
Se m'è contrario il cielo	*Riccardo*
Se mi rivolgo al prato	*Orlando*
Se mormora rivo o fronda	*Scipione*
Semplicetta, la saetta	*Imeneo*
Semplicetto! a donna credi?	{ *Alcina* *Jup. in Argos*
Sempre aspira eccelso core	*Parnasso*
Sempre dolci ed amorose	{ *Berenice* *Jup. in Argos*
Sempre è infelice chi 'l vuo seguir*	Cantata IV (RM) (HWV 119)
Sempre fido e disprezzato	*Alessandro*
Se nasce un rivoletto	*Atalanta*
Se nel bosco resta solo	*Arianna*
Se nel punto ch'io moro	Cantata 68 (HWV 174)
Se non giunge quel momento	Cantata 20 (HWV 114)
Se non hò l'idol mio	*Berenice*
Se non mi rendi il mio tesoro	*Tamerlano*
Se non mi vuol amar	*Tamerlano*
Se non sei più ministro di pene (quartet) (2)	*Trionfo del Tempo*
Se non ti piace amarmi	Cantata XXII (HWV 171)
Se non ti sai spiegar	*Partenope*
Senti, bel idol mio	*Silla*
Senti di te, ben mio	Cantata 35 (HWV 135b)
Sento amor con novi dardi	*Partenope*
Sento brillar nel cor	*Pastor fido* Nov. 1734
Sento che il dio bambin	Cantata III (HWV 83)
Sento che un giusto sdegno	*Faramondo*
Sento il cor che lieto gode	*Sosarme*
Sento il cor per ogni lato	*Arminio*
Sento la gioia	*Amadigi*
Sento nell'alma (= Lucide stelle, *Vincer se stesso*)	*Oreste*
Sento nel sen distruggersi	*Pastor fido* May 1734
Sento prima le procelle (2)**	{ *Pirro e Demetrio* 1716 *Admeto* 1731
Sen vola lo sparvier	*Admeto*
Senza il suo bene la tortorella	*Tolomeo*
Senza luce*	*Radamisto*
Senza nudrice alcuna	*Berenice*
Senza occhi e senza accenti (duet)	Cantata XXIV (HWV 96)

Senza procelle ancora	*Poro*
Senza te sarebbe il mondo	*Berenice*
Se pari è la tua fè (2)	Cantata 58, 59 (HWV 158abc)
Se parla nel mio cor	*Giustino*
Se pensate che mi moro	Cantata 39 (HWV 138)
Se pensi amor tu solo	*Deidamia*
Se per colpa di donna infelice	*Resurrezione*
Se perì l'amato bene (2)*	*Riccardo*
Se per te giungo a godere	*Rodelinda*
Se pietà di me non senti	*G. Cesare*
Se più non t'amo (3)	Cantata 15, 16, 64 (HWV 109ab, 167)
Se possono tanto	*Poro*
Se potessero i sospir' miei (2)*	{ *Jup. in Argos* / *Imeneo*
Se potessi un dì placare	*Tamerlano*
Se povero il ruscello	*Ezio*
Se quì il ciel ha già prefisso	Cantata IV (HWV 119)
Serbati a grandi imprese	*Poro*
Serenatevi, O luci belle!	*Teseo*
Se ria procella sorge nell'onde	*Faramondo*
Se ricordar ten vuoi (3)*	*Imeneo*
Se rinasce nel mio cor (duet)	*Ariodante*
Se risolvi abbandonarmi	*Floridante*
S'è ristretto frà catene	*Tolomeo* 1733
Se si vanta il cieco dio (= Non si vanti un' alma audace, *Giustino*)	*A. Severo*
Se spegni il scelerato	*Flavio* 1732
S'estinto è l'idol mio	*Amadigi*
Se talor miri un fior (2)*	*Tolomeo*
Se tanto piace al cor (2)*	*Ariodante*
Se teco vive il cor (duet)	*Radamisto*
Se ti condanno, giusta vendetta	*Arianna*
Se troppo crede al ciglio	*Poro*
Se tu brami di godere	*Amadigi*
Se tu la reggi al volo	*Ezio*
Se tu meco*	Cantata (Berkeley)
Se tu non lasci amore	Chamber Duet & Trio
S'è tuo piacer ch'io mora [vada]	{ *Atalanta* / *A. Severo*
Se un bell'ardire	*Ezio*
Se un core è contento (*coro*)	*Admeto*
Se un dì m'adora	Cantata 33, XXVII (HWV 132cb)
Se un sol momento (2)	Cantata 56, 57 (HWV 161abc)
Se un solo è quel core	*Tolomeo*
Se vago rio frà sassi frange	Cantata III (HWV 83)
Se vedrà l'amena sponda	Cantata 65 (HWV 168)
Se vien tinta dal sangue fraterno	*Tolomeo* 1730

Se viver non poss'io	*Poro*
Se vuoi in amor aver piacer (= Lungo pensar, *M. Scevola*)	*Scipione* 1730
Se vuoi pace, O volto amato	*Agrippina*
Sfortunato è il mio valore	*Alessandro*
Sforzano a piangere	*Aci, Gal. e Polif.*
Sgombra dell'anima tutto il timor	{ *Siroe* { *Tolomeo* 1730
Sia guida sia stella	Cantata XV (HWV 113)
Siam prossimi al porto	*Rinaldo*
Sì, bel foco è quel che t'arde	Cantata 43 (HWV 141)
Sì, bel sembiante (duet)	*Lotario*
Sibillando, ululando	*Teseo*
Sibillar gli angui d'Aletto	{ *Aci, Gal. e Polif.* { *Rinaldo*
Sì, cadrò, mà sorgerà	*Arminio*
Sì, caro, sì, ti stringo	{ *Admeto* { *Rinaldo* 1731
Sì, che desio quel che tu brami (2)	*Deidamia*
Si che lieta goderò	*Vincer se stesso*
Si che ti rendirai	*Radamisto*
Sì, coronar vogl'io	*Floridante*
Sì, crudel, ti lascierò	Cantata XXII (HWV 171)
Si crudel tornerà*	? (Fitz.) (HWV 224)
Si dolce lusingar	*Alessandro*
Siet' assai superbe, O stelle	*Vincer se stesso*
Siete rose rugiadose	Cantata 61 (HWV 162)
Si, farò ch'il figlio avrà (= Si, cadrò, mà sorgerà, *Arminio*)	*A. Severo*
Sì, fuggano i tormenti (duet)	*Scipione*
Sì, già vedo il mio ben sole	*Riccardo*
Signor, lasciate far a me	*Serse*
Signor, lo credi a me (3)**	*Admeto*
Si godete al vostro amor (chorus)	*Ariodante*
Sì, lasciami ingrata (duet)*	Cantata (Münster) (HWV 82)
Sì, la voglio e la otterò (2)*	*Serse*
Sì, l'intendesti, sì	*Faramondo*
Sì, m'appaga, sì, m'alletta	*Deidamia*
Sì, m'è caro imitar	*Alessandro*
Sì, mel raccorderò	*Atalanta*
Sì, morrò; mà l'onor mio	*Ariodante*
Si muora, come son viva ancora*	Cantata (New York) (HWV 150)
Sincero affetto	*Sosarme*
Sin le Grazie nel bel volto (duet)	*Parnasso*
Sino che ti vedrò	*Ottone* 1733
Sin per le vie del sole (chorus)	*Alcina*
S'io cadrò per tuo consiglio	*Sosarme*
S'io dir potessi	*Ottone*
Si parli ancor di trionfar (chorus)	*Parnasso*
Sì, piangete, O mie pupille	Cantata 29 (HWV 128)
Si poco è forte dunque tua fede	*Berenice*

Sì, rivedrò la sola mia speranza	{ *Rodelinda* Dec. 1725 / *Pastor fido* May 1734
Sirti, scogli, tempeste, procelle	*Flavio*
Sì, sarà più dolce amore (*coro*)	{ *M. Scevola* / *Scipione* 1730
Sì, scherza, sì, sempre	*Partenope*
Sì, sì, minaccia e vinta	*Sosarme*
Sì, sì, mio ben	*Serse*
Sì, sì, s'uccida	Cantata XIV (HWV 110)
Sì: son quella	*Alcina*
Sì, spietata, il tuo rigore	*G. Cesare*
Sì, t'amo, O caro, quanto un dì t'amai	{ *Teseo* / *Rinaldo* 1717
Sì, ti bacio, O bella imago	*Admeto*
Sì, ti lascio (duet)	*Teseo*
Sì, tornerò a morir	*Faramondo*
Sì, trà i ceppi e le ritorte (2)	*Berenice*
Si unisce al tuo martir (chorus)	{ *Parnasso* / *Pastor fido* May 1734 / *Jup. in Argos*
Sò ben che regnante	*Almira*
Sò che non è più mio	*Arianna*
Sò ch'è vana la speranza	*Radamisto* Dec. 1720
Sò ch'il ciel ben spesso gode	*Sosarme*
Sò chi t'accese	*Ezio*
Soffri in pace il tuo dolore	*Atalanta*
Soggetto al mio volere	*Serse*
So gli altri debellar*	*Scipione*
Sol la brama di vendetta	*Faramondo*
Sollevar il mondo oppresso	*Giustino*
Sol nel mezzo risuona del core	*Pastor fido*
Solo al godere aspira (chorus)*	*Trionfo del Tempo* 1737
Solo dal brando	*Rinaldo*
Sol per te, bell'idol mio (duet)	*Silla*
Sol prova contenti	*Atalanta*
Sol ristoro di mortali	*Arianna*
Sommi Dei! che sorgete	*Radamisto*
Sommi Dei! se pur v'offesi	*Vincer se stesso*
†Son ben vecchia, mà son bella	*Florindo*
Son come navicella	{ Cantata 25 (HWV 127a) / *Pastor fido*
Son come quel nocchiero	Cantata XXIV (HWV 96)
Son come un arboscello*	*F. Olibrio*
Son confusa pastorella	*Poro*
Son contenta di morire	*Radamisto*
†Son fenice a doppio rogo (trio) (? not set)	*Silla*
Son gelsomino, son picciol fiore	Cantata 63 (HWV 164)
Son larve di dolor (chorus)	*Trionfo del Tempo* 1737
Son lievi le catene	*Radamisto*

Son nata a lagrimar (duet)	*G. Cesare*
Sono i colpi della sorte (2)*	*Rodelinda*
Sono liete, fortunate	Chamber Duet
Son pellegrino che d'alto vede	*Scipione*
Son pur le lagrime	Cantata 19 (HWV 112)
Son qual cerva ferita che fugge	Cantata 2 (HWV 80)
Son qual colombo amante*	*Riccardo*
Son qual rocca percossa dall'onde	*Tolomeo*
Son qual stanco pellegrino	*Arianna*
Sorga pure dal orrido Averno*	Cantata (Münster) (HWV 233)
Sorge il dì (duet)	{ *Aci, Gal. e Polif.* { *Acis and Galatea* 1732
Sorge infausta una procella	*Orlando*
Sorge nell'alma mia	*Imeneo*
Sorge nel petto (2)*	*Rinaldo*
S'or mi dai pene (2)**	*Ottone*
Sorte, amor, vuol che quest'alma*	*Rinaldo* 1717
Sospiro, è vero	*Floridante*
Sotto il lauro (2)	*Agrippina*
Sovra balze scoscesi e pungenti	*Rinaldo*
Spande ancor a mio dispetto	Cantata XX (HWV 165)
Sparite, O pensieri, se solo volate	*Admeto*
Spera allor, che in mar turbato	*Admeto*
† Spera alma mia	*Agrippina*
Spera che trà le care gioje	*M. Scevola*
Spera chi sà perchè la sorte*	? *Rinaldo* (RM, Tenbury) (HWV 225)
Spera e godi, O mio tesoro	*Partenope*
Sperai ne m'ingannai	*G. Cesare* 1725
Speranza gradita (=Qual nave smarrita)	*Radamisto*
Speranza mi dice*	*G. Cesare*
Speranze mie fermate	*Serse*
Spera sì, mi dice il core	*Ottone* Mar. 1723
Spera, sì, mio caro bene	*Admeto* Mar. 1727
Spererò, poichè mel dice	*Agrippina*
Spero per voi, sì, begli occhi	*Ariodante*
Spero placare	*Radamisto*
Spesso mi sento dir	Cantata 63 (HWV 164)
Spesso suol beltà tiranna (2)*	*Alessandro*
Spezza l'arco e getta l'armi	Cantata XVI (HWV 122)
Spietati; io vi giurai	*Rodelinda*
Spira al sen celeste ardore	*Parnasso*
Spira un'aura	*Esther* 1737
Spirti fieri dell'alme guerrieri (2)*	{ *Vincer se stesso* { *Admeto* ?1731
Spirto amato dell'idol mio	*Poro*
Splenda l'alba in oriente	Cantata V, VI (HWV 166, 89)
Splenda lieta al tuo disegno*	*Rinaldo* ?1717

† Sposa diletta, io parto	*Vincer se stesso*
Sposo ingrato, parto, sì	*Radamisto*
Squarciami pur il petto*	Cantata (Manchester) (HWV 94)
Stà nell'Ircana pietrosa tana	*Alcina*
Starvi a canto e non languire	*Flavio*
Stelle rubelle, a torto morirò	*Silla*
Stille amare, già vi sento	*Tolomeo*
Stimulato dalla gloria	*Orlando*
Stragi, morti, sangue ed armi (2)	{ *Vincer se stesso* *Radamisto*
Stragi, lutto incendi e morte*	Cantata IV (RM) (HWV 119)
Stringo al fine il mio contento	*Ezio*
Sù! all'armi grida Nemesi	*Vincer se stesso*
Su lacerate il seno	Cantata XIV (HWV 110)
Su l'arena di barbara scena	*Imeneo*
Sù la sponda del pigro Lete (2)	*Tamerlano*
Sull'altar di questo nume	{ *Giustino* *A. Severo*
Sulla ruota di fortuna	*Rinaldo*
Sulle sponde di Cocito	*Ezio*
Sù Megera, Tisifone, Aletto	*Berenice*
S'un dì m'appaga la mia crudele*	? *L'Allegro* 1741 (RM) (HWV 223)
† Su pensieri, all'armi	*Daphne*
Superbette luci amate	*Alessandro*
Superbetti occhi amorosi	Cantata 38 (HWV 133)
Su rendetemi colei	Cantata 11 (HWV 104)
Sussurrate, onde vezzose	*Amadigi*
Sù, via, furie e ministre	*Tamerlano*
Svegliatevi nel core	*G. Cesare*
Svenerò chi far guerra	*Almira*
Sventurata navicella	{ *Giustino* *A. Severo*
Sventurato, godi, O core	*Floridante*
Tacerò; mà non potrai	*Floridante*
Tacerò, pur che fedele	*Agrippina*
Tacete, ohimè, tacete	Chamber Duet
Taci e spera*	*Jup. in Argos*
Tal'or d'oscuro velo	*Arianna*
T'amai, quant'il mio cor	*Amadigi*
T'amo, sì, sarai tu quella (duet)	{ *Riccardo* *Tolomeo* 1730
Tanti affanni hò nel core	*Ottone*
Tanti strali al sen mi scocchi	Chamber Duet
T'appresta forse amore	*Partenope*
T'aspetta fuor dell'onde	*Scipione*
Temo che lusinghiero	*Scipione*
Tempesta e calma	*Alessandro*

Tengo in pugno l'idol mio	*Teseo*
Tergi il ciglio lagrimoso	Cantata 37 (HWV 137)
Tergi l'ingiuste lagrime	*Ezio*
† Ti conforta, O caro	*Vincer se stesso*
Ti credo, sì, ben mio	*Teseo*
Tiene Giove in mano il folgore	*Sosarme*
Ti lascio a la pena	*Vincer se stesso*
Ti lascio, idolo mio (duet)	*Silla*
Ti pentirai, crudel, d'avermi offesa un dì	*Amadigi*
Ti pentirai, crudel, d'aver offeso	*Tolomeo*
Ti prepara, ardito amante	*Tolomeo* 1733
Tiranna, mà bella	*Lotario*
Tiranna passion, lasciami in pace	*Alessandro*
Tirannia gli diede il regno	*Rodelinda*
Tiranni miei pensieri	*Tolomeo*
Ti rendo questo cor	*Giustino*
Tirsi amato, adorato mio nume	Cantata 27 (HWV 125)
Ti vedrò regnar sul trono	*Riccardo*
Ti vo' giusta e non pietosa	*Agrippina*
Tormento maggiore	Cantata 23 (HWV 120)
Tormentosa, crudele partita	Cantata 47 (HWV 147)
Torna il core al suo diletto	Cantata 66 (HWV 169)
	Cantata XIX (HWV 143)
Tornami a vagheggiar	Cantata XIX (HWV 143)
Tornami a vagheggiar	{ *Alcina* { *Jup. in Argos*
Torna sol per un momento	*Tolomeo*
Torna, vieni, non tardare (2)	Cantata 25, 26 (HWV 127ab)
Torni la gioja in sen*	*Amadigi* ?1717
Torni omai la pace all'alma	*Tolomeo*
Torni pure un bel splendore	{ *Parnasso* { *Pastor fido* May 1734
Torrente cresciuto per torbida piena	{ *Siroe* { *Poro* 1736
Tortorella che rimira	*Berenice*
Trà amplessi innocenti (duet)	Cantata VI (HWV 89)
Trà caligini profonde	*Orlando*
Traditore, traditore!	*Berenice*
Trà le fiamme tu scherzi per gioco	Cantata XXI (HWV 170)
Trà le sfere la fera più cruda	Cantata XXIV (HWV 96)
Trà le stragi (v. Frà le stragi)	
Trà queste care ombre gradite	*Ottone* Mar. 1723
Trà sentier di amene selve	*Parnasso*
Trà sospetti, affetti e timori	*Rodelinda*
Trà speme e timore	*Alcina*
Trà speme e timore	*Arminio*

Trà speranze, affetti e timori	*Scipione* 1730
Trema, tiranno, ancor	*Ottone*
Trionfa oggi 'l mio cor (*coro*)	*Orlando*
Troppo audace umano stuolo*	*L'Allegro* 1741
Troppo caro costa al core	Cantata 44 (HWV 146)
Troppo costa ad un'alma	Cantata XV (HWV 113)
Troppo cruda, troppo fiera	Chamber Duet
Troppo crudeli siete*	*G. Cesare*
Troppo oltraggi la mia fede (duet)	*Serse*
Troppo sofferse già questo mio petto (3)*	*Radamisto*
Trupcici Amor faceva*	Cantata *Amore uccellatore* (Fitz.)
Tua bellezza, tua dolcezza	*Esther* 1737
Tu ben degno sei dell'allor	*Agrippina*
Tu caro sei il dolce mio tesoro (duet)	*Sosarme*
Tu del ciel ministro eletto	*Trionfo del Tempo*
Tu di pietà mi spogli	{ *Siroe* / *Oreste*
Tu giurasti di mai non lasciarmi	*Trionfo del Tempo*
Tu la mia stella sei	*G. Cesare*
Tu mia speranza, tu mio conforto	*Amadigi*
Tu nel piagarmi al seno	*Pastor fido*
Tuo ben è il trono	*Agrippina*
Tuo drudo è mio rivale	*Rodelinda*
Tuoi passi son dardi (duet)	*Terpsicore*
Tuona, balena, sibila il vento	Cantata XI (HWV 98)
Tu preparati a morire	*Ariodante*
Tu puoi straziarmi	*Ottone*
Turbato il mar si vede	*Arianna*
Tu sei il cor di questo core	*G. Cesare*
Tu sei la bella*	Cantata (Münster) (HWV 233)
Tu solcasti il mare infido	*Atalanta*
Tutta brillante i rai	{ *Riccardo* / *Scipione* 1730
Tutta raccolta ancor	{ *Scipione* / *Jup. in Argos*
Tutta rea la vita umana	*Scipione*
Tutto contento or gode (duet)	*Tolomeo*
Tutto può donna vezzosa (2)*	*G. Cesare*
Tu vivi, e punito	*Ariodante*
Tu vuoi ch'io parta; io parto	*Radamisto*
Un affanno più tiranno	Cantata 28 (HWV 126)
Una guerra hò dentro il seno (duet)	Cantata XVI (HWV 122)
Un'altra volta ancor	*Partenope*
Una parte ma torna se fugge (chorus)	*Trionfo del Tempo* 1737
Una schiera di piaceri	*Trionfo del Tempo*
Un'aura flebile	Cantata 3 (HWV 84)

Un'aura placida e lusinghiera	*Faramondo*
Un caro amante	*Scipione*
Un cenno leggiadretto	*Serse*
Un cor infedele (trio)	*Partenope*
Un dì più felice (*coro*)	*Radamisto*
Un disprezzato affetto	*Ottone* 1726
Un gran cor non dà ricetto	*Ezio*
Un guardo solo, pupille amate	{ *Deidamia* { *Imeneo* 1742
Un interrotto affetto (= Un disprezzato affetto, *Ottone*)	*Oreste*
Unisca amor in noi (duet)	*Orlando*
Unito a un puro affetto	*Teseo*
Un lampo è la speranza	*Admeto*
Un leggiadro giovinetto (2)	*Trionfo del Tempo*
Un lusinghiero dolce pensiero	*Alessandro*
Un momento di contento	*Alcina*
Un pensiero nemico di pace (2)	*Trionfo del Tempo*
Un pensiero voli in ciel	Cantata XII (HWV 99)
Un sol angolo dal mondo	Cantata IV (HWV 119)
Un sol raggio di speranza	*Silla*
Un sol tuo sguardo (= Un vostro sguardo, *Giustino*)	*A. Severo*
Un sospir a chi si muore	Cantata 68 (HWV 174)
Un sospiretto, un labbro pallido	{ Cantata XXIV { (HWV 96) { *Acis and Galatea* 1732
Un tenero pensiero	*Arianna*
Un vostro sguardo, O luci arciere	*Giustino*
Un zeffiro spirò	*Rodelinda*
Urne voi	*Trionfo del Tempo*
V'accendano le tede i raggi	*Agrippina*
Vacillò per terror*	Cantata (Münster) (HWV 233)
Và col canto lusingando*	Cantata XXIV (Münster) (HWV 96)
Và, combatti ancor da forte	*Arminio*
Và, dal furor portata	*Ezio*
Vado al campo	*Sosarme*
Vado a morir, vi lascio	*Arminio*
Vado a recar la morte	*Faramondo*
Vado, corro al mio tesoro	*Amadigi*
Vado, e vivo con la speranza (duet)	{ *Faramondo* { *Jup. in Argos* { *Imeneo* 1742
Vado per obedirti	*Riccardo*
V'adoro, O luci belle	{ *Riccardo* { *Tolomeo* 1733
V'adoro, pupille (2)*	*G. Cesare*
Vado; sorte crudele	*Flavio* 1732
Vaga e bella ogn'or vedrai	*Radamisto*
Vaghe fonti, che mormorando	*Agrippina*
Vagheggiar de tuoi bei lumi*	*Agrippina*

Vaghe perle, eletti fiori	*Agrippina*
Vaghe pupille, non piangete	*Orlando*
† Vaghi lumi del sole, ch'adoro	*Florindo*
Và godendo, vezzoso e bello	*Serse*
Val più contento core	*Serse*
Vanne a colei che adori	*Lotario*
† Vanne, amor, tu sei tiranno	*Admeto* 1731
Vanne, che più ti miro (2)*	*Faramondo*
Vanne in campo, e vedrai	*Vincer se stesso*
Vanne lungi dal mio petto	*Amadigi*
Vanne, parti, audace, altiero	*Scipione*
Vanne pur, infido (= Vanne, sì, superbo, và, *Giustino*)	*A. Severo*
† Vanne pur tenero affetto	*Vincer se stesso*
Vanne, segui'l mio desio	*Floridante*
Vanne, sì, superbo và	*Giustino*
Vanne, sorella ingrata	*Radamisto*
Vano amore, lusinga, diletto (2)*	*Alessandro*
Và, perfido! quel cor mi tradirà	*Deidamia*
Và, speme infida, pur, và	Chamber Duet
Va tacito e nascosto	*G. Cesare*
Vedeste mai sul prato (2)*	*Siroe*
Vedi l'ape, che ingegnosa	{ *Berenice* { *A. Severo*
Vedo il ciel, che più sereno	*Resurrezione*
Vedrai con tuo periglio	*Poro*
Vedrai, s'a tuo dispetto	*Almira*
Vedrò ch'un dì si cangerà (duet)	*Tamerlano*
Vedrò frà poco, se l'idol mio	*Admeto*
Vedrò più liete e belle (2)*	{ *Lotario* { *Rinaldo* 1731
Vedrò teco ogni gioja (2)	Cantata 17, 18 (HWV 111ab)
Ve lo dissi e nol credeste	Cantata 44 (HWV 146)
Venere bella (2)*	*G. Cesare*
Venga il Tempo	*Trionfo del Tempo*
Venti, fermate, sì	Cantata XIII (HWV 105)
Venti, turbini, prestate	*Rinaldo*
Verginette dotte e belle	*Parnasso*
Verdi allori sempre unito	*Orlando*
Verdi lauri, cingetemi il crine	{ *Giustino* { *Semele* Dec. 1744
Verdi piante, erbette liete	*Orlando*
Verdi prati e selve amene	*Alcina*
Verrà, sì, verrà ch' adoro	Cantata 39 (HWV 138)
Verrete a consolarmi*	*Rodelinda*
Verso già l'alma col sangue (2)	{ *Aci, Gal. e Polif.* { *Acis and Galatea* 1732
V'è un infelice, che per te more	*Imeneo*
Vezzi, lusinghe, e brio	*Ariodante*
Vezzi più amabili chi puol veder? (duet)	*Terpsicore*
Vibra, cortese amor	*Alessandro*
† Vibri pur iniqua sorte	*Vincer se stesso*

Vi circondi la gloria d'allori (chorus)	*Partenope*
† Vi compatisco	*Daphne*
Vien Imeneo frà voi: sperate amanti (chorus)	*Imeneo*
Vieni, O cara, a consolarmi	*Rinaldo*
Vieni, O cara, ch'in lacci stretto	*Agrippina*
Vieni, O cara, e lìeta in petto*	*Pirro e Demetrio* 1716
Vieni, O caro, che senza il suo core*	*Rinaldo* 1717
Vieni, O de' viventi*	*Jup. in Argos*
Vieni, O figlio, e mi consola	*Ottone*
Vieni pur amica spene	*Radamisto* 1728
Vieni, torna, idolo mio	*Teseo*
Vi fida lo sposo	*Ezio*
Vile! se mi dai vita	*Radamisto* Dec. 1720
Vil trofeo d'un alma imbelle	*Poro*
Vinto è l'amor da sdegno e gelosia	*Ottone* 1726
Vinto è sol dalla virtù (*coro*)	*Rinaldo*
Virtù, che rende si forte un core (aria and *coro*)	*Faramondo*
Vi sento, sì, vi sento	{ *Lotario* { *Rodelinda* 1731
Viva Almira! (*coro*)	*Almira*
Viva Augusto, eterno impero! (*coro*)	{ *Giustino* { *A. Severo*
Viva, e regni fortunato (*coro*)	*Lotario*
Viva il nostro Alcide (*coro*)	*G. Cesare*
Viva la face (chorus)	*Atalanta*
Viva Partenope, viva (*coro*)	*Partenope*
Viva, sì, che nel mio seno	*Faramondo*
Viva un astro si bello (trio)	Cantata XIX (HWV 143)
Viver, e non amar (trio) (complete in Münster)	Cantata XXIV (HWV 96)
Viver, e non amar (chorus)	{ *Acis and Galatea* 1732 { *Jup. in Argos*
Vivere per penare	*Floridante*
Vivi alla pace tua	Cantata 54a (HWV 160a)
Vivi, tiranno! io t'hò scampato	*Rodelinda* Dec. 1725
Vivo in te, mio caro bene (duet)	*Tamerlano*
Vivo senza alma, O bella (duet)	*M. Scevola*
Vo' cercando trà fiori*	? (RM) (HWV 227)
Vo' dar pace a un alma altiera	*Tamerlano*
Vo' far guerra, e vincer voglio	*Rinaldo*
Voglio amare infin ch'io moro	*Partenope*
Voglio amore o pur vendetta	*Tolomeo*
Voglio cangiar desio	*Trionfo del Tempo*
Voglio che mora, sì	*Faramondo*
Voglio che sia l'indegno	*Faramondo*
Voglio contenta allor	*Scipione*
Voglio darti a mille	Cantata 51 (HWV 153)
Voglio dire al mio tesoro	*Partenope*
Voglio seguir lo sposo	*Arminio*
Voglio stragi. Eccoti il petto (trio)	*Tamerlano*
Voglio stragi, e voglio morte	*Teseo*

Voglio tempo per risolvere (quartet) (2)	*Trionfo del Tempo*
Voi che udite il mio lamento	*Agrippina*
Voi, dolci aurette al cor	*Tolomeo*
Voi mi dite che non l'ami	*Serse*
Vola l'augello dal caro nido	{ *Sosarme* / *Oreste*
Volate, amori	*Ariodante*
Volate più dei venti	{ *M. Scevola* / *Admeto* 1731
Volgete ogni desir	*Riccardo*
Voli colla sua tromba	*Ariodante*
Voli per l'aria chi può volare	Cantata XXI (HWV 170)
Volo pronto, e lieto il core	*Agrippina*
Vorrei, nè pur saprei	*Sosarme*
Vorrei poterti amar	*Orlando*
Vorrei vendicarmi del perfido cor	*Alcina*
Vuoi veder dov'è la calma (aria with chorus)	*Acis and Galatea* 1732
Vuol ch'io serva amor la bella	*Radamisto* Dec. 1720
Zeffiretti, deh venite*	Cantata (Münster) (HWV 142)
Zeffiretto, arresta il volo	Cantata 71 (HWV 177)
Zeffiretto, che scorre nel prato	{ *Giustino* / *A. Severo*

APPENDIX H
SHORT BIBLIOGRAPHY

Note: This consists largely of documentary and source material. Sources reprinted by Deutsch (e.g. from Mattheson) are not usually included. Articles on individual operas are omitted, since the book supersedes them. They can be found in the fuller bibliography in *The New Grove*.

Avery, E. L. (ed.): *The London Stage*, Part 2: *1700–1729* (Carbondale, 1960).

Baselt, B.: 'Zum Parodieverfahren in Händels frühen Opern', *HJb* (1975), 19–39.

—— *Thematisch-systematisches Verzeichnis: Bühnenwerke (Händel-Handbuch I)* (Leipzig, 1978).

—— 'Verzeichnis der Werke Georg Friedrich Händels (HWV)', *HJb* (1979), 10–139.

—— 'Händel auf dem Wege nach Italien', *G. F. Händel und seine italienischen Zeitgenossen*, ed. W. Siegmund-Schultze (Halle, 1979), 10–21.

—— 'Wiederentdeckung von Fragmenten aus Händels verschollenen Hamburger Opern', *HJb* (1983), 7–24.

Buelow, G. J., and Marx, H. J. (eds.): *New Mattheson Studies* (Cambridge, 1983).

Burney, C.: *A General History of Music from the Earliest Ages to the Present Period* (London, 1776–89), ed. F. Mercer (London, 1935; repr. 1957).

Burrows, D.: 'A Handlist of the Paper Characteristics of Handel's English Autographs' (typescript, 1982).

Chrysander, F.: *G. F. Händel* (Leipzig, 1858–67; repr. 1966).

Clausen, H. D.: *Händels Direktionspartituren ('Handexemplare')* (Hamburg, 1972).

Colman Opera Register: see K. Sasse.

Dean, W.: *Handel's Dramatic Oratorios and Masques* (London, 1959).

—— *Handel and the Opera Seria* (Berkeley and Los Angeles, 1969).

—— 'Vocal Embellishment in a Handel Aria', *Studies in Eighteenth-Century Music: a Tribute to Karl Geiringer*, ed. H. C. Robbins Landon (New York and London, 1970), 151–9.

—— 'A French Traveller's View of Handel's Operas', *M & L* lv (1974), 172–8.

—— (ed.) *G. F. Handel: Three Ornamented Arias* (London, 1976).

—— 'The Performance of Recitative in Late Baroque Opera', *M & L* lviii (1977), 389–402.

—— 'Die Ausführung des Rezitativs in den Opern der Händel-Zeit', *G. F. Händel und seine italienischen Zeitgenossen*, ed. W. Siegmund-Schultze (Halle, 1979), 94–105.

—— *The New Grove Handel* (work-list A. Hicks) (London, 1982).

—— 'The Musical Sources for Handel's *Teseo* and *Amadigi*', *Slavonic and Western Music: Essays for Gerald Abraham*, ed. M. H. Brown and R. J. Wiley (Ann Arbor and Oxford, 1985), 63–80.

—— 'Handel's Early London Copyists', *Bach, Handel, Scarlatti: Tercentenary Essays*, ed. P. Williams (Cambridge, 1985), 75–97.

—— and A. Hicks: 'The Handel Collection of the Earl of Shaftesbury', *Early Music* (forthcoming).

Dent, E. J.: *Alessandro Scarlatti: his Life and Work* (London, 1905; rev. edn. ed. F. Walker, 1960).

—— 'The Operas', *Handel: a Symposium*, ed. G. Abraham (London, 1954), 12–65.

Deutsch, O. E.: *Handel: a Documentary Biography* (London, 1955; repr. 1974).

—— *Händel-Handbuch IV: Dokumente zu Leben und Schaffen* (Leipzig, 1985) [revised German edition].

Eisenschmidt, J.: *Die szenische Darstellung der Opern Händels auf der Londoner Bühne seiner Zeit*, 2 vols. (Wolfenbüttel and Berlin, 1940–1).

Floros, C., Marx, H. J., and Peterson, P. (eds.): *Hamburger Jahrbuch für Musikwissenschaft*, iii: *Studien zur Barockoper* (Hamburg, 1978).

Fuller Maitland, J. A., and Mann, A. H.: *Catalogue of the Music in the Fitzwilliam Museum, Cambridge* (London, 1893).

Gibson, E.: *The Royal Academy of Music 1719–1728: the Institution and its Directors* (New York and London, 1989).

Gress, J.: 'Händel in Dresden (1719)', *HJb* (1963), 135–51.

Grout, D. J.: *Alessandro Scarlatti: an Introduction to the Operas* (Berkeley, Los Angeles, London, 1979).

Hawkins, J.: *A General History of the Science and Practice of Music* (London, 1776; repr. 1853; fac. 1963).

Hicks, A.: 'Handel's Early Musical Development', *Proceedings of the Royal Musical Association*, ciii (1976–7), 80–9.

Hogwood, C., and Luckett, R. (eds.): *Music in Eighteenth-Century England* (Cambridge, 1983).

Hughes-Hughes, A.: *Catalogue of Manuscript Music in the British Museum* (London, 1906–9; repr. 1964–6).

Kimbell, D. R. B.: 'The Libretto of Handel's *Teseo*', *M & L* xliv (1963), 371–9.

—— 'A Critical Study of Handel's Early Operas' (University of Oxford dissertation, 1968).

—— 'The *Amadis* Operas of Destouches and Handel', *M & L* xlix (1968), 329–46.

Kirkendale, U.: 'The Ruspoli Documents on Handel', *JAMS* xx (1967), 222–73, 518.

Knapp, J. M.: 'Handel, the Royal Academy of Music, and its First Opera Season in London (1720)', *MQ* xlv (1959), 145–67.

—— 'The Libretto of Handel's *Silla*', *M & L* l (1969), 68–75.

Kubik, R.: *Händels Rinaldo, Geschichte, Werk, Wirkung* (Stuttgart, 1982).

Larsen, J. P.: *Handel's Messiah, Origins, Composition, Sources* (London, 1957, rev. 2nd edn. 1972).

Leichtentritt, H.: *Händel* (Stuttgart, 1924).

Lindgren, L.: *A Bibliographic Scrutiny of Dramatic Works set by Giovanni and his Brother Antonio Maria Bononcini* (Ann Arbor, 1974).

—— 'Parisian Patronage of Performers from the Royal Academy of Musick (1719–28)', *M & L* lviii (1977), 4–28.

—— 'Ariosti's London Years, 1716–29', *M & L* lxii (1981), 331–51.

Lynch, R. D.: *Opera in Hamburg, 1718–1738* (Ann Arbor, 1979).

[Mainwaring, J.]: *Memoirs of the Life of the Late George Frederic Handel* (London, 1760; repr. 1964, 1967).

Merbach, P. A.: *Das Repertoire der Hamburger Oper von 1718 bis 1750* (Leipzig, 1924). (Contains Wilhelm Willers's diary.)

Milhous, J.: 'Opera Finances in London, 1674–1738', *JAMS* xxxvii (1984), 567–92.

—— 'The Capacity of Vanbrugh's Theatre in the Haymarket', *Theatre History Studies*, iv (1984), 38–46.

—— and Hume, R. D.: *Vice Chamberlain Coke's Theatrical Papers, 1706–1715* (Carbondale, 1982).

—— and Hume, R. D.: 'New Light on Handel and the Royal Academy of Music in 1720', *Theatre Journal*, xxxv (1983), 149–67.

—— and Hume, R. D.: 'The Charter for the Royal Academy of Music', *M & L* lxvii (1986), 50–8.

Price, C. A.: 'The Critical Decade for English Music Drama, 1700–1710', *Harvard Library Bulletin*, xxvi (1978), 38–76.

Sartori, C.: *Primo tentativo di catalogo unico dei libretti italiani a stampa fino all'anno 1800* (Milan [1981]).

Sasse, K.: 'Opera Register from 1712 to 1734 (Colman-Register)', *HJb* (1959), 199–223.

Schulze, W.: *Die Quellen der Hamburger Oper (1678–1738)* (Hamburg, 1938).

Simon, J. (ed.): *Handel, a Celebration of his Life and Times (1685–1759)*, Catalogue of Exhibition at National Portrait Gallery (London, 1985).

Smith, W. C.: *Handel: a Descriptive Catalogue of the Early Editions* (London, 1960; rev. 2nd edn. 1970).

Squire, W. B.: *Catalogue of the King's Music Library*, i: *The Handel Manuscripts* (London, 1927).

Stompor, S.: 'Die deutschen Aufführungen von Opern Händels in der ersten Hälfte des 18. Jahrhunderts', *HJb* (1978), 31–89.

Streatfeild, R. A.: *Handel* (London, 1909, rev. 2nd edn. 1910; repr. 1964).

—— 'The Granville Collection of Handel Manuscripts', *The Musical Antiquary*, ii (1910–11), 208–24.

Strohm, R.: 'Händel in Italia: nuovi contributi', *RIM* ix (1974), 152–74.

—— 'Händels Pasticci', *Analecta musicologica*, no. 14 (1974), 208–67.

—— 'Händel und seine italienischen Operntexte', *HJb* xxi/xxii (1975–6), 101–59.

—— *Italienische Opernarien des frühen Settecento (1720–1730)*, 2 vols. (*Analecta musicologica*, no. 16, 1976).

—— *Die italienische Oper im 18. Jahrhundert* (Wilhelmshaven, 1979).

—— *Essays on Handel and Italian Opera* (Cambridge, 1985).

Termini, O.: 'Singers at San Marco in Venice: the Competition between Church and Theatre (c. 1675–c. 1725)', *RMA Research Chronicle*, xvii (1981), 65–96.

Vanbrugh, J.: *Complete Works*, vol. iv (*Letters*), ed. G. Webb (London, 1928).

Walker, A. D.: *George Frideric Handel: the Newman Flower Collection in the Henry Watson Music Library* (Manchester, 1972).

Walsh, T. J.: *Opera in Dublin 1705–1797* (Dublin, 1973).

Weaver, R. L. and N. W.: *A Chronology of Music in the Florentine Theater 1590–1750* (Detroit, 1978).

Wiel, T.: *I teatri musicali veneziani del Settecento* (Venice, 1897; repr. Leipzig, 1979).

Willers diary: see P. A. Merbach.

Willetts, P. J.: *Handlist of Music Manuscripts Acquired* [by BL] *1908–67* (London, 1970).

Wolff, H. C.: *Die Barockoper in Hamburg 1678–1738*, 2 vols. (Wolfenbüttel, 1957).

Zanetti, E.: 'Handel in Italia', *Approdo musicale* (1960), no. 12, 3–46.

—— 'A proposito di tre sconosciute cantate inglesi', *Rassegna musicale*, xxix (1959), 129–42.

Zelm, K.: *Die Opern Reinhard Keisers* (Munich and Salzburg, 1975).

Zobeley, F.: 'Werke Händels in der Gräfl. von Schönbornschen Musikbibliothek', *HJb* (1931), 98–116.

ADDITIONAL BIBLIOGRAPHY

Barlow, G. F.: 'From Tennis Court to Opera House', University of Glasgow Ph.D. dissertation, 1983.

Best, T.: 'New light on the manuscript copies of *Tamerlano*', *Göttinger Händel-Beiträge* IV (1991), 134–45.

—— (ed.): *Handel Collections and their History* (Oxford, 1993).

Bianconi, L. (ed.): *I libretti italiani di Georg Friedrich Händel e le loro fonti*, vol. 1 [1707–1725] (Florence, 1992).

Braun, W.: 'Der *Almira*-Stoff in der vertonungen von Ruggiero Fedeli, Reinhard Keiser und Georg Friedrich Händel', *Hjb* (1990), 139–45.

Buelow, G. J.: 'Handel's Borrowing Techniques: Some Fundamental Questions derived from a Study of *Agrippina*', *Göttinger Händel-Beiträge* II (1986), 105–28.

Clausen, H. D.: 'Die Entstehung der Oper *Floridante*', *Göttinger Händel-Beiträge* IV (1991), 108–33.

Crawford, T.: 'Lord Danby's lute book: A new source of Handel's Hamburg Music', *Göttinger Händel-Beiträge* II (1986), 19–50.

Dean, W.: 'The Genesis and Early History of *Ottone*', *Göttinger Händel-Beiträge* II (1986), 129–40.

—— *Essays on Opera* (Oxford, 1990, paperback (corrected) 1993).

—— 'A New Source for Handel's *Amadigi*', *M&L* lxxii (1991), 27–37.

Edelmann, B.: 'Die zweite Fassung von Händels Oper *Radamisto* (HWV 12b)', *Göttinger Händel-Beiträge* III (1987), 99–123.

Harris, E. T.: *The Librettos of Handel's Operas* [in facsimile], 13 vols. (New York and London, 1989).

Lindgren, L.: 'The Staging of Handel's Operas in London', *Handel Tercentenary Collection*, ed. S. Sadie and A. Hicks (London, 1987), 93–119.

—— 'Venice, Vivaldi, Vico and Opera in London, 1705–17: Venetian Ingredients in English Pastichi', *Nuovi Studi Vivaldiani*, ed. A. Fanna and G. Morelli (Florence, 1988), 633–66.

—— 'The Accomplishments of the Learned and Ingenious Nicola Francesco Haym (1678–1729)', *Studi Musicali* xvi (1987), 246–380.

Milhous, J. and Hume, R. D.: 'The Haymarket Opera in 1711', *Early Music* xvii (1989), 523–37.

Parker-Hale, M. A. : *G. F. Handel, A Guide to Research* (New York and London, 1988).

Pirrotta, N. and Ziino, A. (eds.): *Händel e gli Scarlatti a Roma* (Florence, 1987).

Roberts, J. H.: *Handel Sources: Materials for the Study of Handel's Borrowings*, 9 vols. (New York, 1986).

—— 'Handel's Borrowings from Keiser', *Göttinger Händel-Beiträge* II (1986), 51–76.

—— 'Keiser and Handel at the Hamburg Opera', *HJb* (1990), 63–87.

Rogers, P. J.: *Continuo Realization in Handel's Vocal Music* (Ann Arbor, 1989).

Sadie, S. and Hicks, A. (eds.): *Handel Tercentenary Collection* (London, 1987).

Saunders, H. S., Jr.: 'Handel's *Agrippina*: The Venetian Perspective', *Göttinger Händel-Beiträge* III (1987), 87–98.

Schröder, D.: 'Zu Entstehung und Aufführungsgeschichte von Händels Oper *Almira*. Anmerkungen zur Edition des Werkes in der Hallischen Händel-Ausgabe', *HJb* (1990), 147–53.

INDEX OF HANDEL'S WORKS

GENERAL INDEX

Page numbers in **bold** type indicate the more important references. See also summaries at head of general chapters, and for singers Appendix E.